RELIGIONS OF ASIA IN PRACTICE

PRINCETON READINGS IN RELIGIONS

Donald S. Lopez, Jr., Editor

TITLES IN THE SERIES

Religions of India in Practice edited by Donald S. Lopez, Jr.

Buddhism in Practice edited by Donald S. Lopez, Jr.

Religions of China in Practice edited by Donald S. Lopez, Jr.

Religions of Tibet in Practice edited by Donald S. Lopez, Jr.

Religions of Japan in Practice edited by George J. Tanabe, Jr.

Asian Religions in Practice: An Introduction
edited by Donald S. Lopez, Jr.

Religions of Late Antiquity in Practice edited by Richard Valantasis

Tantra in Practice edited by David Gordon White

Judaism in Practice edited by Lawrence Fine

Religions of the United States in Practice: Volumes 1 and 2
edited by Colleen McDannell

Religions of Asia in Practice: An Anthology
edited by Donald S. Lopez, Jr.

RELIGIONS OF ASIA IN PRACTICE

AN ANTHOLOGY

Donald S. Lopez, Jr., Editor

PRINCETON READINGS IN RELIGIONS

PRINCETON UNIVERSITY PRESS

PRINCETON AND OXFORD

Published by Princeton University Press, 41 William Street,
Princeton, New Jersey 08540
In the United Kingdom: Princeton University Press, 3 Market Place,
Woodstock, Oxfordshire OX20 1SY

Library of Congress Cataloging-in-Publication Data

Religions of Asia in practice : an anthology / Donald S. Lopez Jr., editor.
p. cm. — (Princeton readings in religions)
Includes bibliographical references and index.
ISBN 0-691-09060-2 (alk. paper) — ISBN 0-691-09061-0 (pbk. : alk. paper)
1. Asia—Religion. 2. Religious life. I. Lopez, Donald S., 1952– II. Series.

BL1015.R45 2002
200′.95—dc21 2001050015

British Library Cataloging-in-Publication Data is available

This book has been composed in Berkeley

Printed on acid-free paper. ∞
www.pup.princeton.edu
Printed in the United States of America

1 3 5 7 9 10 8 6 4 2

PRINCETON READINGS IN RELIGIONS

Princeton Readings in Religions is a new series of anthologies on the religions of the world, representing the significant advances that have been made in the study of religions in the last thirty years. The sourcebooks used by previous generations of students, whether for Judaism and Christianity or for the religions of Asia and the Middle East, placed a heavy emphasis on "canonical works." Princeton Readings in Religions provides a different configuration of texts in an attempt better to represent the range of religious practices, placing particular emphasis on the ways in which texts have been used in diverse contexts. The volumes in the series therefore include translations of ritual manuals, hagiographical and autobiographical works, popular commentaries, and folktales, as well as some ethnographic material. Many works are drawn from vernacular sources. The readings in the series are new in two senses. First, very few of the works contained in the volumes have ever been made available in an anthology before; in the case of the volumes on Asia, few have even been translated into a Western language. Second, the readings are new in the sense that each volume provides new ways to read and understand the religions of the world, breaking down the sometimes misleading stereotypes inherited from the past in an effort to provide both more expansive and more focused perspectives on the richness and diversity of religious expressions. The series is designed for use by a wide range of readers, with key terms translated and technical notes omitted. Each volume also contains a substantial introduction by a distinguished scholar in which the histories of the traditions are outlined and the significance of each of the works is explored.

Religions of Asia in Practice is the eleventh volume in the series. It is an anthology of anthologies in the sense that it is composed of the introductions and selected chapters from the first five volumes in the series: *Religions of India in Practice, Buddhism in Practice, Religions of China in Practice, Religions of Tibet in Practice*, and *Religions of Japan in Practice*. The volume is organized under these five headings and, under each heading, the chapters appear in the order in which they appeared in the original volume. Forty-five expert contributors have provided translations of key works; many of these works were translated for the first time for this series. Each chapter begins with a substantial introduction in which the translator discusses the history and influence of the work, identifying points of particular difficulty or interest. *Religions of Asia in Practice* is intended to provide an overview of the range of religious practices across the continent of Asia and over a period of almost three millennia.

Volumes for the series on the religions of Latin America and medieval Christianity are in progress.

Donald S. Lopez, Jr.
Series Editor

CONTENTS

Religions of China in Practice

Religions of Tibet in Practice

Religions of Japan in Practice

CONTRIBUTORS

Catherine Bell teaches in the Department of Religious Studies at Santa Clara University.

William M. Bodiford teaches in the Department of East Asian Languages and Cultures at UCLA.

Stephen Bokenkamp teaches in the Department of East Asian Languages at Indiana University.

Daniel Boucher teaches in the Department of Asian Studies at Cornell University.

José Ignacio Cabezón teaches in the Department of Religious Studies at the University of California, Santa Barbara

Richard H. Davis teaches in the Department of Religion at Bard College.

Jean DeBernardi teaches in the Department of Anthropology at the University of Edmonton.

T. Griffith Foulk teaches in the Religion Program at Sarah Lawrence College.

Richard Gardner teaches at Sophia University in Tokyo.

Ann Grodzins Gold teaches in the Department of Religion at Syracuse University.

Luis O. Gómez teaches in the Department of Asian Languages and Cultures at the University of Michigan.

Phyllis Granoff teaches in the Department of Religious Studies at McMaster University.

Charles Hallisey teaches in the Religious Studies Program at the University of Wisconsin.

Valerie Hansen teaches in the History Department at Yale University.

Donald Harper teaches in the Department of East Asian Languages and Civilizations at the University of Chicago.

Marcia Hermansen teaches in Department of Theology at Loyola University, Chicago.

Charles Holcombe teaches in the Department of History at the University of Northern Iowa.

Toni Huber teaches in the Department of Religious Studies at Victoria University of Wellington, New Zealand.

Roger Jackson teaches in the Department of Religion at Carleton College.

Richard Jaffe teaches in the Department of Religion at Duke University.

Matthew Kapstein teaches in the Department of South Asian Languages and Civilizations at the University of Chicago.

Sallie B. King teaches in the Department of Philosophy and Religion at James Madison University.

Terry F. Kleeman teaches in the Department of Religious Studies at the University of Colorado.

Livia Kohn teaches in the Department of Theology and Religious Studies at Boston University.

Paul W. Kroll teaches in the Department of East Asian Languages and Civilizations at the University of Colorado.

Donald S. Lopez, Jr. teaches in the Department of Asian Languages and Cultures at the University of Michigan.

Rachel Fell McDermott teaches in the Department of Asian and Middle Eastern Cultures at Barnard College.

Hew McLeod teaches in the Department of History at the University of Otago, New Zealand.

Nālandā Translation Committee is based in Halifax, Nova Scotia.

Ellen Neskar teaches in the Department of Asian Studies at Sarah Lawrence College.

Patrick Olivelle teaches in the Center for Asian Studies at the University of Texas.

Charles Orzech teaches in the Department of Religious Studies at the University of North Carolina, Greensboro.

Ian Reader teaches in the Department of Religious Studies at the University of Lancaster, UK.

Robert H. Sharf teaches in the Department of Asian Languages and Cultures at the University of Michigan.

Daniel B. Stevenson teaches in the Department of Religious Studies at the University of Kansas.

Tony K. Stewart teaches in the Department of Philosophy and Religion at North Carolina State University.

Jacqueline I. Stone teaches in the Department of Religion at Princeton University.

Donald K. Swearer teaches in the Department of Religion at Swarthmore College.

George J. Tanabe, Jr. teaches in the Department of Religious Studies at the University of Hawaii.

Mark Teeuwen teaches in the Department for Religious and Theology Studies at the University of Cardiff, Wales.

Stephen F. Teiser teaches in the Department of Religion at Princeton University.

Kyoko Tokuno teaches in the Jackson School at the University of Washington.

Mary Evelyn Tucker teaches in the departments of Religion and East Asian Studies at Bucknell University.

Jan Van Bragt is retired director of the Nanzan Institute for Religion and Culture at Nanzan University in Nagoya, Japan.

Chün-fang Yü teaches in the Department of Religion at Rutgers University.

Religions of India in Practice

INTRODUCTION

A Brief History of Religions in India

Richard H. Davis

Now Vidagdha, Śakala's son, asked him, "Yājñavalkya, how many gods are there?"
Following the text of the Veda, he replied, "Three hundred and three, and three thousand and three, as are mentioned in the Vedic hymn on the Viśvadevas."
"Right," replied Vidagdha, "but how many gods are there really, Yājñavalkya?"
"Thirty-three."
"Right," he assented, "but how many gods are there really, Yājñavalkya?"
"Six."
"Right," he persisted, "but how many gods are there really, Yājñavalkya?"
"Three."
"Right," he answered, "but how many gods are there really, Yājñavalkya?"
"Two."
"Right," Vidagdha replied, "but how many gods are there really, Yājñavalkya?"
"One and a half."
"Right," he agreed, "but how many gods are there really, Yājñavalkya?"
"One."
"Right," Vidagdha said. "And who are those three hundred and three, and three thousand and three gods?"

Bṛhadāraṇyaka Upaniṣad 3.9.1

In one of the world's earliest recorded philosophical dialogues, the Indian sage Yājñavalkya pointed to the multiplicity of theological views concerning the number of gods in India. He then went on to show how, following different ways of enumerating them, each of these views could make sense.

Much the same can be said about the religions of India. Some scholars and observers focus on the tremendous diversity of distinct schools of thought and religious sects that have appeared over the course of Indian history. Others prefer to specify the three or five "great" or "world" religions that have occupied the subcontinent: Hinduism, Buddhism, Islam, plus Jainism and Sikhism. And still others, of a more syncretic persuasion, maintain there is really just one religious tradition.

In the introduction I provide a brief account of the main periods, principal schools of thought, and most significant texts in Indian religions. Over the course of this account, I focus on certain key issues or points of controversy that appear and reappear through Indian religious history. I focus also on a set of terms—Veda, brahman, yoga, dharma, bhakti, Tantra, and the like—that constitute a shared religious vocabulary in India. As we will see, such terms were often considered too important to be left uncontested, and so different authors or traditions would attempt to redefine the terms to suit their own purposes.[1]

The Question of Hinduism

The dominant feature of South Asian religious history is a broad group of interconnected traditions that we nowadays call "Hinduism." Although other distinct non-Hindu religious ideologies (notably Buddhism, Islam, and Christianity) have challenged its dominance, Hinduism is now and probably has been at all times the most prevalent religious persuasion of the subcontinent. According to the most recent census figures, 83 percent of India's population is classified as Hindu, a total of perhaps 700 million Hindus.

It is important to bear in mind, however, that Hinduism does not share many of the integrating characteristics of the other religious traditions we conventionally label the "world religions." Hinduism has no founding figure such as the Buddha Śākyamuni, Jesus of Nazareth, or Muḥammad. It has no single text that can serve as a doctrinal point of reference, such as the Bibles of the Judaic and Christian traditions, the Islamic Qur'ān, or the Ādi Granth of the Sikhs. Hinduism has no single overarching institutional or ecclesiastical hierarchy capable of deciding questions of religious boundary or formulating standards of doctrine and practice.

This is not to say that Hinduism, lacking these supposedly "essential" attributes of other religions, is therefore not a religion. Rather, the historical process by which Hindus and others have come to consider Hinduism a unitary religious formation differs markedly from other traditions. In one respect, Hinduism is one of the oldest, if not the oldest continuous recorded religion, tracing itself back to a text that was already edited and put into final shape by about 1200 B.C.E. In another respect, though, it is the youngest, for it was only in the nineteenth century that the many indigenous Indian religious formations were collectively named "Hinduism." Before this, not only did these groups not have a name for themselves as a religious unity, but for the most part they did not consider that they were members of a single religious collectivity.

Since histories of names often tell us a good deal about the realities they signify, let us look more closely at the word "Hinduism." The term derives originally from the Indo-Aryan word for sea, *sindhu*, applied also to the Indus River. Persians to the west of the Indus picked up the term, modifying it phonologically to *hind*, and used it to refer also to the land of the Indus valley. From Persian it was borrowed into Greek and Latin, where *india* became the geographical designation for all the unknown territories beyond the Indus. Meanwhile, Muslims used *hindu* to refer to the native peoples of South Asia, and more specifically to those South Asians who did not convert to Islam, lending the term for the first time a reference to religious persuasion. Non-Muslim Indians did not commonly take up the terminology, however, until much later.

Only in the nineteenth century did the colonial British begin to use the word Hinduism to refer to a supposed religious system encompassing the beliefs and practices of Indian peoples not adhering to other named religions such as Islam, Christianity, or Jainism. This coinage, based very indirectly on the indigenous term *sindhu*, followed the Enlightenment reification of the concept "religion" and the scholarly attempt to define a series of distinct individual "world religions," each with its own essence and historical unfolding. "Hindu" was then incorporated into the Indian lexicon, taken up by Indians eager to construct for themselves a counterpart to the seemingly monolithic Christianity of the colonizers. As much as anything, it may have been British census taking, with its neat categories of affiliation, that spread the usage of "Hindu" as the most common pan-Indian term of religious identity. To specify the nature of this religion, Western scholars and Indians alike projected the term retrospectively, to encompass a great historical range of religious texts and practices.

Even though anachronistic, the term "Hinduism" remains useful for describing and categorizing the various schools of thought and practice that grew up within a shared Indian society and employed a common religious vocabulary. However, applying a single term to cover a wide array of Indian religious phenomena from many different periods raises some obvious questions. Where is the system? What is the center of Hinduism? What is truly essential to Hinduism? And who determines this center, if there is any? Scholars and Indians have largely adopted two contrasting views in dealing with these questions, the "centralist" and the "pluralist" views.

Centralists identify a single, pan-Indian, more or less hegemonic, orthodox tradition, transmitted primarily in Sanskrit language, chiefly by members of the brahmanic class. The tradition centers around a Vedic lineage of texts, in which are included not only the Vedas themselves, but also the Mīmaṃsā, Dharmaśāstra, and Vedānta corpuses of texts and teachings. Vedic sacrifice is the privileged mode of ritual conduct, the template for all subsequent Indian ritualism. Various groups employing vernacular languages in preference to Sanskrit, questioning the caste order, and rejecting the authority of the Vedas, may periodically rebel against this center, but the orthodox, through an adept use of inclusion and repressive tolerance, manage to hold the high ground of religious authority.

The pluralists, by contrast, envision a decentered profusion of ideas and practices all tolerated and incorporated under the big tent of Hinduism. No more concise statement of this view can be found than that of the eminent Sanskrit scholar J. A. B. van Buitenen in the 1986 *Encyclopedia Britannica*:

> In principle, Hinduism incorporates all forms of belief and worship without necessitating the selection or elimination of any. The Hindu is inclined to revere the divinity

> in every manifestation, whatever it may be, and is doctrinally tolerant. . . . Hinduism is, then, both a civilization and a conglomeration of religions, with neither a beginning, a founder, nor a central authority, hierarchy, or organization.

Adherents of this viewpoint commonly invoke natural metaphors. Hinduism is a "sponge" for all religious practices or a "jungle" where every religious tendency may flourish freely. Within the pluralist view, the Vedic tradition figures as one form of belief and worship among many, the concern of elite brahmans somewhat out of touch with the religious multiplicity all around them.

In India, various contending religious groups have vied to present a view of the cosmos, divinity, human society, and human purposes more compelling and more authoritative than others. One finds such all-encompassing visions presented in many Hindu texts or groups of texts at different periods of history: the Vedas, the Epics, the puranic theologies of Viṣṇu and Śiva, the medieval texts of the bhakti movements, and the formulations of synthetic Hinduism by modern reformers. The religious historian may identify these as the paradigmatic formations of Hinduism of their respective times. Yet such visions have never held sway without challenge, both from within and from outside of Hinduism.

The most serious challenges to Hindu formations have come from outside, from the early "heterodoxies" of Buddhism and Jainism, from medieval Islam, and from the missionary Christianity and post-Enlightenment worldviews of the colonial British. These challenges have been linked to shifts in the political sphere, when ruling elites have favored non-Hindu ideologies with their patronage and prestige. In each case, such fundamental provocations have led to important changes within the most prevalent forms of Hinduism. This introduction will follow this pattern of historical challenge and transformation.

The Indo-Aryans and the Vedas

The textual history of Indian religions begins with the entry into the subcontinent of groups of nomadic pastoralists who called themselves "Āryas," the noble ones. Originally they came from the steppes of south-central Russia, part of a larger tribal community that, beginning around 4000 B.C.E., migrated outward from their homeland in several directions, some westward into Europe and others southward into the Middle East and South Asia. These nomads were the first to ride and harness horses; they also invented the chariot and the spoked wheel and fabricated weapons of copper and bronze. Such material innovations gained them obvious military advantages, and they were able to impose themselves on most of the indigenous peoples they encountered as they migrated. Wherever they went they took with them their language, and it was this language that formed the historical basis for Greek, Latin, the Romance languages, German, English, Persian, Sanskrit, and most of the modern languages of northern India. We now call these pastoral peoples the Indo-Europeans, and those who migrated south into the Iranian plateau and the Indian subcontinent we call the Indo-Aryans.

As early as about 2000 B.C.E., Indo-Aryan peoples began to move gradually into the Indus River Valley in small tribal groups. In 1200 B.C.E. they were still located primarily in the Punjab, the fertile area drained by the five rivers of the Indus system, but by 600 B.C.E. the Indo-Aryans had gained political and social dominance over the Gangetic plain and throughout much of northern India.

The Ṛg Veda

The religious beliefs and practices of this community are contained in a corpus of texts called the Vedas. Since the term *Veda* comes up frequently in all discussions of Indian religious history, it is helpful to consider briefly some of its meanings and usages. The term derives from the verbal root *vid*, "to know," and so the broadest meaning of *Veda* is "knowledge," more specifically knowledge of the highest sort, religious knowledge. It denotes several compendia of religious knowledge composed in an early form of Sanskrit (the "perfected" language) by the Indo-Aryan community, the four Vedic "collections" (*samhitā*): the *Ṛg Veda*, *Yajur Veda*, *Sāma Veda*, and the *Atharva Veda*. Supplementary compositions were attached to each of these four Vedic collections—namely, the Brāhmaṇas, Āraṇyakas, and Upaniṣads—and these too became part of the Veda. This entire corpus of sacred literature came to be portrayed by its proponents as revelation, something that was only "heard" and not composed by human beings. Additional texts were later added to the corpus: the Vedāṅgas or "limbs" of the Veda, auxiliary works that aimed to explain and extend the significance of the Vedas. These later texts did not have the same revelatory status as the Vedas themselves, but they did belong to the Vedic corpus in an extended sense. The Vedas constitute a huge, diverse, and fascinating corpus of texts composed over many centuries.

The earliest of the Vedic collections, and one of the world's oldest intact religious texts, is the *Ṛg Veda*. It consists of 1,028 hymns, numbering around 10,000 verses, roughly equal in size to the complete works of Homer. These hymns were composed over a period of several hundred years by different lineages or families of poet-priests, and then compiled into a single large collection sometime around 1200–1000 B.C.E. This great collection was carefully memorized and transmitted orally, virtually without alterations, for almost 3,000 years by generations of religious specialists.

The hymns of the *Ṛg Veda* reflect the religious concerns and social values of the Indo-Aryan community as it settled in the Punjab. Most often the hymns address and praise a pantheon of deities, of whom the most important is undoubtedly Indra. The hymns portray Indra as an active, powerful, unpredictable, combative god who leads the other gods in a series of antagonistic encounters with a competing group of superhuman beings, the demons. The poets honor and extol Indra for his courage and strength, and also supplicate him to be generous to his votaries. Moreover, they view him as a model chieftain: as Indra leads the gods in defeating their enemies, the poets proclaim, so may our leaders guide us to victory over our enemies.

Indra's paradigmatic status reminds us that the Indo-Aryans were not simply occupying uninhabited territory as they moved into the Indian subcontinent. They encountered other peoples there whom they regarded as posing a threat to their own well-being and expansion. These others, often referred to as *dāsas*, were described in the *Ṛg Veda* as dark-skinned, flat-featured stealers of cattle, speaking a different language and living in fortified citadels.

In fact, from around 2500 to 1700 B.C.E. a complex, urbanized, centrally organized civilization flourished in the Indus River Valley, with two capital cities and a host of other towns and smaller settlements. Although archeologists have excavated a great deal of evidence from the Indus Valley civilization, including several thousand brief inscriptions, much about its religious culture remains mysterious since no one has yet convincingly deciphered the Indus Valley script. Yet most linguists believe the language of this civilization was a member of the Dravidian family, which also includes the languages of southern India where the Indo-Aryan language did not penetrate. This suggests that the Indus Valley civilization was linked, in language and presumably in culture, with pre-Aryan peoples in other parts of the subcontinent.

Many elements of Indus Valley material culture suggest religious usage, and these have led scholars to postulate Indus Valley influence on the development of later Indian religion. For example, archeologists have interpreted the numerous terra-cotta figurines of fleshy women with accentuated breasts and hips and fabulous headpieces found in the Indus Valley cities as popular representations of a "Great Mother," whose domestic and rural cult would reappear in medieval Hindu literature. While such connections remain speculative, they do point to an important problem in Indian religious history. Much that appears as innovation in recorded Indian religious traditions may have been borrowed from nonliterate or undeciphered traditions that we do not yet know.

Although the urban civilization of the Indus Valley had largely collapsed prior to the arrival of the Indo-Aryans, the dāsas of the *Ṛg Veda* were probably the descendants of that culture, and they must have posed a significant obstacle to Indo-Aryan expansion. The *Ṛg Veda* shows us an Indo-Aryan culture primed for battle. Even the poets participated in battle, apparently, as singing charioteers, invoking Indra's strength on behalf of the warriors as they drove the horses.

If Indra was for the *Ṛg Veda* poets the divine prototype of the warrior, the second most important deity in the pantheon, Agni, can be seen as the model priest. Agni is fire, in its multiple forms: the sun, the hearth fire, the fire of the sacrifice, the digestive fire in one's belly, and the fire of poetic inspiration. But Agni's primary role in the *Ṛg Veda* pertains to sacrifice (*yajña*), the central ritual practice of Vedic society. Agni is the priest of the gods and yet is also accessible to humans, so he is most fit to serve in sacrifice as the primary intermediary, bringing gods and humans together. The poets of the *Ṛg Veda* know sacrifice to be a powerful ritual, one that enables the gods to defeat the demons and that likewise can assist the Aryans to overcome their earthly enemies. It brings a host of worldly results: wealth, cattle, victory, and ultimately order. Yet in the *Ṛg Veda* sacrifice remains rather loosely organized, inchoate, experimental; only later is it systematized and elaborated into a full-fledged worldview.

One other figure in the Ṛg Vedic pantheon deserves attention: the mysterious Soma, also closely associated with sacrifice. Soma is simultaneously a plant, a liquid made by crushing the stalks of that plant, and a god personifying the effects of ingesting this concoction. The identity of the botanical soma has proved to be a major scholarly conundrum, but the effects ascribed in the *Ṛg Veda* to drinking its juice are clear enough. It is a drink of inspiration, of vision, of revelation. At their sacrificial gatherings the poets pound and imbibe the soma juice, and through it they come to mingle with the gods. They perceive the resemblances and identities between things that we normally see as different and unrelated, weaving the world together in a fabric of connectedness. The revelations inspired by soma, moreover, are not regarded as mere hallucinations or dreams, but as more real, more true than the awareness of normal consciousness. This is the first example of a recurrent theme in Indian religions: what is ontologically most real is often not accessible through ordinary human experience but must be sought through some other means—whether it be soma, yoga, meditation, devotional fervor, or ritual.

Sacrifice and Society

If the Indo-Aryans entered India as nomads over the ruins of the urban civilization of the Indus Valley, during the period from 1200 to 600 B.C.E. they reinvented urban society on a new cultural basis. The later Vedic literature reflects the social transformations of this period, particularly the growing role of sacrifice in the religious life of the Indo-Aryans and the beginnings of criticism of sacrifice. By 600 B.C.E. the Indo-Aryan community had changed from a nomadic and pastoral tribal society into a predominantly agrarian one. The introduction of iron during this period facilitated the clearing of the heavily forested Gangetic plain and the development of plough agriculture. A more stable population and greater food resources led in turn to larger settlements, and the tribal organization of the Indo-Aryan nomads began to give way to an incipient class society based on occupational specialization and status distinction. Those outside the Indo-Aryan community, rather than being treated as threatening dāsas, were increasingly incorporated into society as laborers and social inferiors, śūdras. Larger political formations, primarily kingdoms, began to form, and with these early kingdoms came the rebirth of cities as capitals and centers of trade. By 600 B.C.E. there were a dozen substantial cities in northern India.

These changes naturally had their consequences for Vedic religion. Surplus production enabled society to support a nonproducing class of religious specialists, who could devote themselves to elaborating sacrificial ritual and articulating its significance. At the same time, the new rulers found in increasingly dramatic sacrifice a means to extend and legitimate their political authority over larger, mixed populations. The interests of nascent ruling and priestly groups thus converged in sacrifice. And with the defeat of the Indo-Aryans' primary autochthonous opponents, sacrifice came to be seen less as a way of defeating enemies than as a means of creating, maintaining, and stabilizing the order of the cosmos and of society.

One can already see this in some of the later hymns of the *Ṛg Veda*, most notably the famous Puruṣasūkta (*Ṛg Veda* 10.90), where the entire cosmos as well as human society come into being out of a primordial sacrifice. The sacrificial cosmology emerges still more clearly in the later Vedic texts devoted to prescribing sacrificial procedures (the *Yajur Veda*) and the interpretive texts known as the Brāhmaṇas. These texts outline a complex system of sacrificial practice, ranging in scale from modest domestic rites around home fires to elaborate public ceremonies sponsored by the wealthiest kings. The gods who figured so importantly in the *Ṛg Veda* seem to have been demoted; what is most important in the later Vedic period is the sacrifice itself.

As the role of sacrifice grew, so did the status of the new group of religious specialists who called themselves *brāhmaṇas* (Anglicized as "brahman" or "brahmin"). Like *Veda*, this is a crucial term in the history of Indian religions. The poets of the *Ṛg Veda* employ the term *brahman* primarily to refer to the Vedic hymns themselves, understood as powerful and efficacious speech. The notion that certain kinds of liturgical speech are inherently powerful is common to many schools of Indian religious thought. The Indian term most often used for such potent verbal formulae is *mantra*. The *Ṛg Veda* poets also used *brāhmaṇa* to refer by extension to those who fashioned and recited the hymns. At that time the brahman reciters did not constitute a hereditary or endogamous social group, but in later Vedic texts *brāhmaṇa* came to be defined, at least by the brahmans themselves, as a hereditary occupational social group, specializing in ritual matters and the teaching of the Vedas.

A crucial first step in the social institutionalization of the brahman class can be found in the Puruṣasūkta hymn. According to this hymn, four social classes emerged from the Puruṣa, the original sacrificial victim: the brahmans from his mouth, the kṣatriyas (warriors) from his arms, the vaiśyas (merchants) from his loins, and the śūdras (servants) from his feet. Thus the poem portrays the brahmans and other social classes not simply as social groups, but as an order of creation. Because the brahmans emerge from the mouth of the Puruṣa, they enjoy in this order the highest status.

The Puruṣasūkta hymn is the earliest depiction of what later became known as the fourfold *varṇa* scheme, a model of society as an organic hierarchized unity of classes or castes that was to have great persistence through Indian history. The word "caste" derives from *casta*, the Portuguese word for social class. Yet historically it was a flexible and contentious model, one that was just as often questioned and opposed as it was accepted and defended. One can get a taste of the kind of criticism and satire that was recurrently directed against brahmanic claims of privilege in Kabīr's poem, "The Sapling and the Seed", while a defense of the varṇa system appears even in such an unlikely setting as the "Dog Oracles" of the *Śarṅgadhara Paddhati*.

The Upaniṣads and the Renunciatory Model

Within the supplementary texts of the Vedic corpus composed around 900–600 B.C.E., one sees evidence both of a growing sophistication in reflection concerning the sacrifice and also the beginnings of an opposition to sacrifice. The texts called the Brāhmaṇas, arising from discussions and controversies that engaged the new class of brahman ritualists as they conducted the sacrifices, devote themselves particularly to explication of ritual action, providing a learned commentary on the myriad sacrifices of the Vedic system. The idea underlying these hermeneutical texts is that the most adept priest not only performs the actions of sacrifice, but also understands their inner meanings.

The Āraṇyakas (literally, "forest books") and especially the Upaniṣads ("sitting close to a teacher") took the sacrificial worldview in a different direction. As their names imply, these texts were intended for a more restricted audience, often recounting private discussions between teachers and students in the forest. The Upaniṣads pose themselves, and were later accepted by many Indians, as the "culmination of the Veda" (*vedānta*), its highest teachings. For example, in the *Bṛhadāraṇyaka Upaniṣad*, one of the earliest and most influential Upaniṣads, we learn of the brahman teacher Yājñavalkya, whom we have already met in his enumeration of the gods. At the conclusion of a royal sacrifice, Yājñavalkya claims that he is the most knowledgeable of all present in Vedic matters. A series of interlocutors—not only priests, but also a woman, a cart driver, and the king himself—question him, trying to rebuff his declaration and gain for themselves the thousand head of cattle he has claimed as his reward. Yet as Yājñavalkya substantiates his superior Vedic knowledge, he introduces several important ideas unknown to earlier Vedic tradition. So too the other Upaniṣads: together they introduce a set of new concepts that grow out of earlier Vedic thought while calling into question some of its central premises. These concepts, simultaneously old and new, proved to raise enduring issues for Indian religious and philosophical debate.

Yājñavalkya was the first recorded spokesman for the notion of transmigration, which holds that upon death a person is neither annihilated nor transported to some other world in perpetuity, but rather returns to worldly life, to live and die again in a new mortal form. This continuing succession of life, death, and rebirth is termed *saṃsāra* (circling, wandering) in the Upaniṣads. *Saṃsāra* comes to denote not just the individual wandering of a person from life to life, but also the entire world process seen as a perpetual flux. This cyclical worldview of the Upaniṣads grows out of an earlier Vedic concern with natural cycles of the moon, day and night, and the seasons, but projects it in a new direction.

Although transmigration answers the question of beginnings and ends, it also raises two new issues. What determines a person's subsequent form of rebirth? Is there anything other than eternal transmigration? To answer the first question, Yājñavalkya redefines the Vedic notion of *karman*. *Karman* (derived from the verb root *kṛ*, to do or to make, and usually Anglicized as "karma,") means action in a very broad sense; in the Vedas the term refers particularly to sacrificial actions, as the most efficacious kind of activity. In Vedic sacrifice, all ritual actions have consequences, leading to fruits (*phala*) that are often not apparent at the time but will inevitably ripen. Yājñavalkya accepts this extended notion of causality and gives it a moral dimension: the moral character of one's actions in this lifetime determines the status of one's rebirth in the next. Behave in this life as a god and you will become a god. But gods, in this view, are not immortal either, and may after a long period of heavenly hedonism be reborn as humans.

Yājñavalkya also suggests an alternative to this endless cycle of becoming. The release from the cycle of rebirth is most often called *mokṣa*, liberation or salvation. According to Yājñavalkya an individual may attain liberation through lack of desire, since desire is what engenders saṃsāra in the first place.

In postulating an alternative state superior to worldly life and attainable through individual conscious effort, mokṣa is perhaps the most consequential of all Upaniṣadic ideas for later Indian religious history. In contrast to the Vedic ideology of sacrifice, in which goals were as much social and collective as individual, the pursuit of mokṣa takes an individualist goal to be the highest attainment. If Vedic sacrifice was responsible for engendering and maintaining the world process, the search for mokṣa posed a direct abnegation of that process, an escape from saṃsāra into something transcendent. This division of aims forms a major point of contention throughout Indian religious history. It reappears centuries later in the life stories of two modern women renouncers, Mīrāṃ and Śrī Arcanāpuri Mā.

Although the Upaniṣads are not united in their views, the strategies they recommend to those seeking mokṣa most often include a regimen of renunciation and asceticism coupled with instruction in the higher forms of knowledge, namely, the world according to the Upaniṣads. If mokṣa is an escape from the world cycle, it makes sense that one would reach it through progressive abstention from worldly involvements. That is exactly what the renouncer (*sannyāsin*) does. He (or occasionally she) would leave home and family to live in relatively isolated and austere circumstances, sleeping on the ground, restricting the diet, practicing control of the breath, and bringing the senses under control—in short, withdrawing from all that might bind one to the world, with the ultimate goal of escaping from rebirth itself. Such psychophysical practices were not confined to adherents of the Upaniṣads, as we will see, but the logic of renunciatory practice was first articulated in Upaniṣadic texts such as the *Bṛhadāraṇyaka Upaniṣad*.

The Vedas, then, contained a large variety of religious ideas and practices, introducing a host of terms and questions that would recur throughout Indian religious history. In sacrifice, the Vedas provided a system of public and private rituals that engendered the order of cosmos and of society, and that was utilized by political powers to validate their own authority. The brahmans appeared as an endogamous class of religious and intellectual specialists claiming high social status, and through the articulation of the varṇa system they portrayed society as an organic unity of distinct ranked classes pursuing different occupational specialties. The renunciatory model presented by the Upaniṣads centered around the individual pursuit of liberation through austerity and knowledge.

In later times the Vedas became one gauge for Hindu "orthodoxy." Those who adhered most closely to the Vedic tradition claimed a superior status and judged others as either within or outside the Vedic fold, even though the actual language of the Vedic texts had become incomprehensible to most. Many new Hindu groups honoring new deities with new forms of worship claimed allegiance to the Vedas, or portrayed themselves as extensions of the Vedas. The epic *Mahābhārata*, for example, poses itself as the "fifth Veda," whereas the Vaiṣṇava devotional poetry of Nammālvār is said to constitute a "Tamil Veda." Nineteenth- and twentieth-century reformist movements like the Brāhmo Samāj and the Ārya Samāj sought to return Hinduism to what they claimed were its purer Vedic roots.

Proximity to the Vedic tradition, however, is not an altogether reliable criterion for defining Hinduism. Although non-Hindus like Buddhists and Jains define themselves by rejecting the authoritative claims of the Vedas, so too do many later religious teachers such as Kabīr and the Bengali Bāuls, whom most Hindus view as Hindu. Theistic Hindu schools often contested Vedic authority in a different manner. Rather than rejecting the Vedas outright, the Śaiva devotional poet Māṇikkavācakar, for instance, simply asserts that Śiva is "Lord over the Vedas."His strategy, typical of many, is to establish a new hierarchy of religious values, within which the Vedas are included but subsumed under the higher authority of his god, Śiva.

In the end, what is most striking about the Vedas is their longevity rather than their hegemony. In the shifting, changing, contentious discourse of Indian religious history, one hears over and over echoes of the concerns, the terms, the goals, and the practices first recorded in India in the ancient Vedas.

The New Religions of the Sixth Century B.C.E.

Upaniṣadic sages like Yājñavalkya were not the only renouncers in the seventh and sixth centuries B.C.E. From all indications, there were many peripatetic seekers wandering the fringes of Gangetic civilization during this period. The authors and teachers of the Upaniṣads allied themselves with the Vedas, recommending that renouncers continue reciting the Vedas and view their ascetic practices as "interior sacrifice." Other forest teachers of the same period, including some undoubtedly not of the Indo-Aryan community, were willing to dispense altogether with Vedic models. They developed new teachings and practices with no attempt to link them to the established ideology of sacrifice and the Vedas. A teacher named Ajita of the Hair-Blanket proclaimed a thoroughgoing materialism (later identified as the Cārvāka school), denying both ethical prescriptions and existence after death.

The Ājīvika school led by Makkhali Gosāla adhered to a doctrine of fatalism, claiming that human free will was an illusion; destiny was all.

Varied as they were, most teachers accepted a common intellectual foundation, not differing greatly from that taught by Yājñavalkya. With few exceptions, they accepted the notion of cyclical transmigration (*saṃsāra*), the causal connection between act and consequence (*karman*) as the moral determinant of one's rebirth, and the possibility of escape (*mokṣa*) from this cyclical existence. Within this broad consensus, disagreement and debate continued. What is the underlying cause of saṃsāra? What kinds of activities engender karma? What are the best means of avoiding or removing the consequences of one's actions? What is the character of mokṣa? What exactly is it that attains liberation?

The seekers also generally accepted certain kinds of psychological and physical practices as particularly conducive to the religious attainments they sought. The general Indian term for such practices is *yoga*, from the verbal root *yuj*, to bind together, as one harnesses animals to a yoke. In Indian religious discourse, *yoga* refers to all sorts of disciplined practices aimed at restraining one's unruly inclinations in order to attain a higher state of concentration or "one-pointedness." In the vivid metaphor of one Upaniṣad, the senses are wild horses hitched to the chariot of the body; the mind is the charioteer who must somehow bring them under control. Yoga is what one uses to do so.

The earliest systematic exposition of yoga is found in the *Yogasūtras*, a text composed by Patañjali in about the second century B.C.E. but systematizing a much older body of practices. Patañjali describes eight "limbs" of yoga, starting with physical restraints such as limiting one's food and practicing celibacy, proceeding through a mastery of physical postures, the control of the breath, gradual withdrawal of the senses from the outer world, and culminating in fixed meditative awareness. As the practitioner masters each limb, he or she gradually detaches from the physical world, reins in the wayward senses, and achieves a reintegration or unification of self.

Patañjali himself adhered to the dualistic metaphysics of the Sāṃkhya school, but the techniques he described and systematized were practical tools for all religious seekers, adaptable to various philosophical viewpoints. Later in Indian religious history, new groups developed new forms of yogic practice as well. Medieval devotional and tantric forms of yoga emphasize such practices as meditative visualization of deities, repetitive chanting of the name of God, and ritualized sexual intercourse, among many others. Alchemists incorporated yoga into their transformative practices, and non-Hindu religious specialists like Islamic Sufis also adapted yogic techniques to their own purposes.

Out of the questing milieu of the sixth century B.C.E. grew two new religious formations that have had a powerful and continuing impact on Indian religions—Jainism and Buddhism. Both were historically established in the Magadha region (present-day Bihar) by members of the warrior class who renounced their positions in society to find enlightenment: Vardhamāna (c. 599–527 B.C.E.) called Mahāvīra ("great hero"), and Siddhārtha Gautama (c. 566–486 B.C.E.) called the

Buddha ("awakened one"). Both advocated paths of monastic austerity as the most effective means of attaining liberation, and both were critical of the Vedic formation. Adherents of the Vedas, in turn, characterized followers of Jainism and Buddhism as "outside the Veda," and accordingly modern scholars often classify the two religions as heterodoxies in contrast to Vedic orthodoxy.

Jainism

The name Jains use to designate themselves, *jaina*, derives from the verbal root *ji*, to conquer, and points to the central religious concern of the Jain community. Jaina monks must fight an ascetic battle to conquer the senses and karma, seeking to attain a purity of soul that liberates them from all bondage. Those who have succeeded in this quest are Jinas, conquerors, and their followers are Jainas.

According to Jain tradition, Vardhamāna Mahāvīra was only the most recent in a succession of twenty-four Tīrthaṅkaras, or "path-makers." His most immediate predecessor, Pārśva, may well have founded an earlier Jain community, but Mahāvīra is the first clearly attested historical Jain leader. Born of royal parents, the traditional biographies relate, Mahāvīra left his family and home at age thirty, abandoned all possessions, stripped off his clothes, and pulled out his hair by the roots. With these dramatic renunciatory acts he began twelve years of severe austerities, until finally at the age of forty-two he attained mokṣa, and so became a Jina or Tīrthaṅkara. Gradually a large group of followers grew around him. The first disciple was Indrabhūti Gautama, a proud brahman and Vedic scholar; in fact, Vardhamāna's eleven primary disciples were all converted brahmans. According to one tradition, Indrabhūti's conversion occurred when Mahāvīra delivered a sermon on the virtues of nonviolence (*ahiṃsā*) at a Vedic animal sacrifice—pointing to a major issue on which the Jains would most pointedly criticize the Vedic order.

Mahāvīra was a human being born of human parents, but he was also, as all Jain accounts make abundantly clear, something more than human. They describe his conception and birth as surrounded by auspicious omens and marvels preordaining his spiritual career. After he was liberated, the supramundane quality of Mahāvīra became still more apparent. His body, free of all impurities, was said to shine like a crystal on all sides. According to the Jain texts, the Vedic gods themselves, far from condescending to Mahāvīra as a mere mortal, recognized that his powers, knowledge, and status were superior to their own and honored him accordingly. Later Jain reformers like Ācārya Vijay Ānandsūri argue that the Jina is God.

The Jain community, male and female, divided itself into two groups: lay followers and renouncers. For lay followers, Mahāvīra and later Jain preceptors advocated self-restraints and vows. A Jain layperson should avoid meat, wine, honey, and snacking at night. One should also give up falsehood, stealing, and especially violence. Jain texts also recommend fasting and distributing one's wealth to monks, nuns, and the poor as means of strengthening the discipline of a lay adherent.

Jains soon developed forms of devotional practice directed toward the Tīrthaṅkaras and other worthy figures. Most prominent among these rituals is devapūjā, in which followers worship the Jinas physically represented by statues depicting them in poses of deepest meditation. Worshipers approach and bow before the image, chant the Jina's names, circumambulate, bathe the image, make a series of physical offerings to it, and wave lamps before it. Considering the transcendent status of the liberated beings, strict-minded Jains do not regard the Jinas as actually present in their images, nor do they suppose that offerings have any effect on the Jina, but rather view devapūjā as a meditational discipline intended to remind worshipers of the ideal state achieved by the Jina and to inspire them to seek that state for themselves. However, Jain devotional hymns indicate that most Jains have looked to the Tīrthaṅkara for direct benefits, and have believed the Jina to inhabit the images they honored.

Jains also incorporated into their temple liturgy the worship of goddesses and other guardian deities, lesser beings who may intervene in worldly affairs on behalf of the votary. As the stories indicate, Jaina goddesses like Cakrā could grant practical rewards such as wealth and release from earthly prison, as well as helping their devotees on the way to escaping the prison of karma.

The ethical and ritual disciplines of the Jain laity were regarded as preparations for the more rigorous and more efficacious life of a Jain renouncer. Indeed, Jains organized their religion largely around the necessity of renunciation for attaining true purity of soul. This central theme emerges even in the didactic stories of medieval Jain collections, in which the narrator seeks to instill in his audience a feeling of revulsion toward the world and to nudge it toward renunciation through exaggeration and macabre humor.

When a lay person decides to relinquish worldly life, this is treated as a great event both in the prospective renouncer's own spiritual career and in the life of the Jain community. In the ceremony of renouncing social life and entering upon a new monastic life—a veritable death and rebirth—Jain initiates cast off all their former possessions, pull out their hair in large handfuls, and give up their own names. They are presented with the austere provisions of mendicants and with new monastic names. At this point the new monk or nun undertakes the five "great vows," abstaining from all violence, dishonesty, theft, sexual intercourse, and personal possessions, under the close supervision of monastic preceptors. Through self-restraint, careful conduct, physical austerities, and meditations, the anchorite gradually removes the karma that inhibits the soul's inherent powers and virtues, aiming always at the final victory. The Jain path of rigorous austerity may culminate most dramatically in sallekhanā, voluntary self-starvation, in which the Jain renunciant gradually abandons the body itself for the sake of the soul's ultimate purity.

One of the first major royal patrons of Jainism was the Mauryan emperor Candragupta I (r. 321–297 B.C.E.). According to Jain tradition, this ruler was also involved in the major schism of Jainism into two communities, named Śvetāmbara (white-clad) and Digambara (sky-clad—that is, naked) after the monks' characteristic robes or lack thereof. In the third century B.C.E., the Jain leader Bhadrabāhu apparently moved half the Jain community south to Karnataka in order to escape a famine in Candragupta's kingdom. Candragupta himself went along as Bhadrabāhu's disciple. Divided geographically, the two Jain communities began to diverge doctrinally, and eventually formalized those differences at the Council of Vallabhī in the fifth century C.E. The Śvetāmbaras were and continue to be based primarily in the western Indian regions of Rajasthan and Gujarat, whereas the Digambaras have always been most prominent in Karnataka, and were also influential for a time in Tamilnadu.

Throughout the early medieval period, Jain monks and advisers played prominent roles in the courts of many Indian rulers. During this period Jain authors produced a remarkable array of literary and scholarly works in virtually every field, and Jain patrons sponsored impressive Jain temples. In the later medieval period, with Islamic rulers powerful in northern India and the Hindu state of Vijayanagar dominating the south, Jains lost much of their public patronage and became a more self-sufficient, inward-looking community. They survived, however, and now number some four million adherents, mostly in India but with substantial groups of Jains in the United States, Canada, the United Kingdom, and other parts of the English-speaking world.

Buddhism

Buddhists are those who follow the way of the buddhas, beings who have fully "awakened" (from the root *budh*, to wake up) to the true nature of things. In our historical era, the Awakened One was a kṣatriya named Siddhārtha Gautama, born in the foothills of the Himalaya Mountains in about 566 B.C.E. According to traditional accounts, the future Buddha Siddhārtha spent the first twenty-nine years of his life ensconced in affluent family life before renouncing society to seek liberation as a wandering ascetic. After spending six years in austerities, study, and meditation, Siddhārtha sat down under a fig tree in the town of Bodh Gaya one night in 531 B.C.E. and vowed that he would not get up until he had gained enlightenment. That night he attained nirvāṇa and became a buddha. One may view the remainder of the Buddha's life, and indeed all of Buddhist religion, as an attempt to enable others to replicate for themselves what Siddhārtha accomplished that night under the Bodhi tree.

The Buddha delivered his first public discourse, the first "turning of the wheel of Buddhist doctrine (*dharma*)," to an audience of five ascetics outside Varanasi. As soon as he had gathered sixty disciples, he sent them out in all directions to spread his teachings. From its inception, Buddhism was a proselytizing religion, and within a few centuries it was successful not just in the Indo-Aryan society of northern India but throughout South Asia. Spreading the message still further afield, Buddhist missionaries soon traveled to Sri Lanka, Southeast Asia as far as Indonesia, China, Japan, Korea, and Tibet. From the second through the seventh centuries C.E., Buddhism was the major cosmopolitan religion throughout Asia and probably the predominant religious community in the world at that time.

As a pan-Asian religion, Buddhism receives a separate volume in this series. It would be redundant to attempt to outline the complex doctrines or practices of Buddhism here. But Buddhism was first a powerful religious movement in India, and it had a major impact on the development of other religions in India, so it is necessary to refer to a few of its salient features.

Like Mahāvīra and the early Jains, the Buddha considered that the most effective way for his disciples to work toward individual salvation was in small monastic groups. Although renunciation of society was necessary, it was desirable also to avoid the isolation of the hermit. Monastic cells would allow for instruction, support, and enforcement of moral precepts. Establishing mendicant orders, however, posed a challenge to the brahmanic religious specialists and the sacrificial order. After all, mendicants still depend on alms, and the surplus production available to support the various religious claimants was finite.

In this competitive situation the Buddha and his followers developed a penetrating critique of the Vedic religion, much as the Jains did. Not only did the Buddha denounce the public sacrifices advocated by brahman specialists as overly costly, violent, and uncertain in their results, but he also sought to undercut the brahmans' own claims to authority. Satirizing the creation myth of *Ṛg Veda* 10.90, in which the brahman class emerges from the mouth of the primordial male Puruṣa, he pointed out that anyone could see that brahmans in fact emerge from the same female bodily organ as everybody else. He questioned brahmanic claims that the Vedas were revealed texts, not human in origin, as well as their claims to a special inborn religious authority.

Even early followers in the Buddhist community, however, considered the Buddha Śākyamuni to be a superhuman figure. Buddhists preserved his bodily charisma in his ashes and relics, entombed in burial mounds called *stūpas.* Located within monastic settlements, stūpas became centers of Buddhist devotion, where votaries would circumambulate, present flower garlands, burn incense and lamps, serenade with music, and recite eulogies. By the first century C.E. if not earlier, Buddhists also began to use physical images of the Buddha and other important Buddhist figures as objects of devotion. These informal acts of homage toward the Buddha in the form of stūpa or image were later formalized as the ritual of pūjā. During this same period, bodhisattvas, those motivated by compassion to achieve enlightenment, became objects of veneration and emulation in a movement that came to be known as the Mahāyāna (great vehicle).

Buddhist monks and nuns often established their "retreats" on the outskirts of the largest cities of the time and actively sought the patronage of royalty and the wealthy urban merchant class. With the conversion of the great Mauryan ruler Aśoka in the third century B.C.E., Buddhism became the imperial religion of South Asia. Aśoka patronized Buddhist institutions lavishly and sent out missionaries to spread Buddhist teachings abroad. He also publicized his new policies with inscriptions carved on pillars or rock faces throughout the empire. In his epigraphs, Aśoka speaks of his pursuit of dharma, by which he means a common ethical code based on values of tolerance, harmony, generosity, and nonviolence. While proclaiming tolerance toward all religious seekers, he also emphasized nonviolence, thereby effectively ruling out the animal sacrifices that had been the heart of the Vedic system of sacrifice. Far better, he announced, to practice the nonviolent ceremony of dharma, by which he meant giving gifts to Buddhist monks and nuns and other worthies.

Though the Mauryan empire fell apart rather soon after Aśoka's death, he had established a model for Buddhist kingship. For several centuries, every successor dynasty seeking to claim imperial status in India would begin to patronize Buddhists as its primary, though never exclusive, religious recipients. By the time of Harṣavardhana, the seventh-century emperor of Kanyākubja, however, there were clear signs that the role of Buddhism in India was diminishing. It was at this time that the Chinese pilgrim Xuanzang toured South Asia, and he observed the dramatic ceremonies of Buddhist gift-giving that Harṣa held at his capital; but he also noticed many abandoned Buddhist monasteries and temples throughout the subcontinent. Patronage and support apparently were drying up, a trend that accelerated after Harṣa's demise. Only in eastern India, the Himalayan regions, and Sri Lanka did Buddhism continue to flourish in South Asia. By the time of the Turko-Afghan raids of the eleventh through thirteenth centuries, Buddhism in northern India was confined to a few rich monastic institutions and universities, which made ripe targets for plunder. Many of the monks fled to Tibet, and Buddhism was effectively exiled from its land of origin.

Since the 1950s, Buddhism has been revivified in India from unexpected sources. A reformer and leader in the struggle for Indian independence, B. R. Ambedkar, was a member of a Maharashtran untouchable community and spokesman for untouchables nationwide. After a lifetime fighting for social justice, Ambedkar decided that Hinduism as it existed would never allow full status to the lowest orders of society, and at a huge public ceremony in 1956 he converted to Buddhism. Many of his followers did also, and the latest census estimates nearly four million Buddhists in Maharashtra alone. During the same period, the Chinese takeover of Tibet forced many Tibetan monks and lay Buddhists to flee south. The Dalai Lama, spiritual head of the Tibetan people, established his new home in exile in India, where he leads a substantial and visible community of Buddhist refugees.

Hinduism Redefined

During the period of Buddhist initiative and imperial spread, those social and religious groups who remained loyal in some way to the Vedic tradition were not inactive. In fact, as one historian puts it, "in the face of this challenge Brahmanism girt itself up by a tremendous intellectual effort for a new lease on life."[2] This statement overstates the degree to which "Brahmanism" reacted as a cohesive entity; historical sources suggest rather a multiplicity of initiatives. Nevertheless, the intellectual and socio-political challenge posed by Buddhism, Jainism, and the other renunciatory groups did inspire many creative and fruitful responses, which collectively add up to a virtual transformation in "orthodox" circles, from the Vedic worldview to forms of classical "Hinduism" that explicitly maintained continuity with the Vedic tradition but effectively altered it into a new religious formation.

The literature of this period is extensive. There was continued production of texts within the Vedic corpus: new Upaniṣads, new auxiliary texts, and texts that styled themselves "appendices" to the Vedic corpus. During this period the formative texts of six major philosophical schools were first put together—the Mīmāṃsā, Vedānta, Sāṃkhya, Yoga, Nyāya, and Vaiśeṣika schools. Of these, the Mīmāṃsā school occupied itself primarily with the interpretation of the Vedic sacrificial texts and ritual, whereas the Advaita Vedānta reformulated some of the teachings of the Upaniṣads into a consistent monist metaphysics. Sāṃkhya developed an alternative dualist philosophy, and Yoga systematized the psychophysical practices of the ascetics in accord with Sāṃkhya teachings. Nyāya was most concerned with the logic and rhetoric of philosophical disputation and the nature of reality, and Vaiśeṣika sought to develop a realist ontology of substances.

Another major genre of religious literature was the Dharmaśāstra, whose central concern, as the name implies, was the definition and delineation of dharma. The term *dharma* comes from the root *dhṛ*, to uphold, to maintain, and dharma may well be defined as "that which upholds and supports order." Yet different parties could hold very different ideas of what constitutes "order." In the Vedas the term *dharma* referred to the sacrifice as that which maintains the order of the cosmos. In Buddhist texts it meant the teachings of the Buddha, and Jain sources spoke of a Jaina dharma. Aśoka employed the term to describe his own religio-political policies. In the Dharmaśāstra literature, dharma referred to an overarching order of the cosmos and society, and to a person's duties within the world so constituted. It determined specific duties for all groups belonging to Indo-Aryan society, varying according to sex, class, family, stage of life, and so on. The Dharmaśāstras addressed themselves especially to the male brahman householder, directing him to live a life of austerity, purity, Vedic learning, and ritual observance.

The Epics

If the early Dharmaśāstras represent the response of one important social group to the new situation, the immense epic poems formulated during this period constitute a still more significant corpus of texts explicitly meant for all Hindu society. There are two great epics: the *Mahābhārata* (at 100,000 verses, roughly six times the length of the Christian Bible) and the *Rāmāyaṇa* (a mere 25,000 verses), plus an "appendix" to the *Mahābhārata* (as if 100,000 verses weren't enough) called the *Harivaṃśa*. "Whatever is here may be found elsewhere," admits the *Mahābhārata* (1.56.34), "but what is not here is nowhere else." Not only do the epics claim to be comprehensive in depicting the world, but they also intend to be of continuing relevance. The *Rāmāyaṇa* (1.2.35) predicts, "As long as mountains and streams shall endure upon the earth, so long will the story of the *Rāmāyaṇa* be told among men." Together the epics illustrate with remarkable thoroughness and rich detail a Hindu world in transition.

Although the *Mahābhārata* was later claimed as a "fifth Veda," the Sanskrit epics developed outside the Vedic corpus. They originated as the oral literature of bards who told and retold stories of heroic battles of the past, primarily for audiences of kṣatriya chieftains and warriors. The *Mahābhārata* tells the story of a great war between two rival clans and their allies that may have taken place around 900 B.C.E. Unlike the Vedas, however, the bardic literature was never meant to be preserved and transmitted verbatim. Over the generations storytellers reworked their narratives of the great war, expanding and supplementing them with all sorts of other stories and teachings, until the tales assumed a more or less final form around the fourth century C.E.

The epics center around great battles and wars, reflecting their origins as oral literature of the warrior class. The narratives begin with family conflicts leading to disputes over royal succession. Developing this theme to an extreme, the *Mahābhārata* uses the rivalry between two related kṣatriya clans to characterize the entire warrior class as quarreling, contentious, and increasingly deviating from dharma. With the ruling classes in such disarray, disorder and violence threaten society itself. The dire situation is mirrored throughout the cosmos, where (in the *Rāmāyaṇa*) the demon Rāvaṇa has overcome Indra, the divine representative of the Vedic order, and new heroes and deities must intervene to reestablish dharma. The crises lead with tragic inevitability to great battles, involving all the warriors of India in the *Mahābhārata*—and not just humans but also demons, monkeys, bears, and vultures in the *Rāmāyaṇa*. Through war the ancient order is purged and the demonic forces are subdued. The epics conclude with victorious kings restoring the social order.

While focusing on human conflict, the epics also present a new theophany. As the Vedic gods appear unable to contend with the demons and threatening chaos of a new age, these texts introduce a deity who can overcome these threats: Viṣṇu.

Viṣṇu is not an entirely new deity. In fact, he appears even in the *Ṛg Veda*, which associates him with three steps that mysteriously stretch over the whole world; later Vedic texts relate a myth linking Viṣṇu's three steps to the sacrifice. The myth relates how the gods trick the demons, who foolishly agree to allow the gods only as much ground for their sacrificial enclosure as the dwarflike Viṣṇu can cover in three steps. The demons should have realized the danger from the name Viṣṇu, which means "the one who pervades." As the gods sacrifice at their altar, the dwarf grows to become as large as the entire world, and in three steps covers the three worlds of heaven, earth, and the netherworld. Likewise, by the time the epics were put into final shape, Viṣṇu's religious role had grown from its diminutive appearance in the *Ṛg Veda* to a position of superiority over all other gods.

The epics present Viṣṇu as a divinity with clearly heroic qualities, who takes over Indra's role as primary vanquisher of demons. Other gods have begun to recognize Viṣṇu as their superior and pay homage to him. He continues to associate himself with the sacrifice, and actively maintains the order of society. Most importantly, and paradoxically, the epics identify Viṣṇu both as the supreme deity and as an active, embodied, finite god who intervenes directly in human affairs. On the one hand, the epics assert that Viṣṇu is identical with the Puruṣa of *Ṛg Veda* 10.90, the *Brahman* of the Upaniṣads, and other previous formulations of a transcendent Absolute. Yet he also retains features of a more anthropomorphic divinity, particularly when he takes on human forms or incarnations (*avatāra*, literally a "crossing down" to human form) and intervenes directly in human society to kill demons and restore dharma.

In the *Harivaṃśa*, Viṣṇu incarnates himself as Kṛṣṇa in order to destroy the tyrannical demon Kaṃsa, who has usurped the throne of Mathura. Though born of royal parentage, Kṛṣṇa is raised among a tribe of cowherds, who only gradually become aware of his superhuman character. When Kṛṣṇa has grown to manhood, he returns to Mathura and puts an end to Kaṃsa and the other demons of his coterie. In the *Mahābhārata*, Viṣṇu appears again as Kṛṣṇa, ruler of Dwaraka and a loyal friend of the Pāṇḍava hero Arjuna. Here too the divinity of Kṛṣṇa is only occasionally revealed, though in many ways Kṛṣṇa acts as a hidden, inscrutable instigator and manipulator of events throughout the epic.

Viṣṇu takes on a different human embodiment in the *Rāmāyaṇa*, as Rāma, the young prince of Ayodhya, whose primary mission is to rid the world of Rāvaṇa and other demons. Rāvaṇa has gained a divine blessing making him invulnerable to other gods and demons, and this enables him to defeat Indra and to insinuate himself as sole recipient of sacrificial offerings. Yet he has arrogantly neglected to request invincibility from humans as well. Rāvaṇa's ruin comes about after he abducts Sītā, the beautiful and chaste wife of Rāma, and imprisons her in his palace in Lankā. With the aid of an army of monkeys and bears, the warrior-prince Rāma, divine and human, defeats Rāvaṇa's army, rescues Sītā, and finally returns to Ayodhya to rule as its king.

The concept of *avatāra*, one can imagine, offered important advantages to an expanding community of Viṣṇu worshipers. It enabled the Vaiṣṇavas to maintain their identification of Viṣṇu as the Absolute, yet also incorporate other local or regional deities and their cults as incarnations of an encompassing Viṣṇu. Historically speaking, Kṛṣṇa no doubt originated as a human hero, the warrior leader of a pastoral tribe in the Mathura region. Folkloric aggrandizement turned him into a legendary hero with godlike qualities, and finally in the *Harivaṃśa* he was revealed to be a divinity incarnate, the avatāra of Viṣṇu.

Of all portions of the Sanskrit epics, none is considered more significant to the development of Indian religions than the *Bhagavad Gītā*, the "Song of the Lord Kṛṣṇa," a part of the *Mahābhārata* composed around 200 C.E. Placed at the dramatic climax of the epic's narrative, the *Gītā* also provides the central ideological and theological vision of the epic. Just as the great battle is about to begin, with huge armies facing one another across the battlefield of Kurukṣetra, the most powerful warrior on the Pāṇḍava side, Arjuna, suffers from a paroxysm of doubt and anxiety. Why should he fight, particularly when his opponents include relatives and former teachers? Acting as Arjuna's charioteer, Kṛṣṇa responds to his doubts by offering a sustained discourse on the moral and religious propriety of war, the nature of human action, and the most effective means of attaining liberation. Kṛṣṇa argues that worldly action in support of dharma is not incompatible with mokṣa, as the various renunciatory orders had suggested. One should accept one's personal dharma as a guide to proper conduct, he avers, but without regard to the fruits of that conduct.

To clinch his argument, Kṛṣṇa also progressively reveals himself to Arjuna as a deity, indeed as the highest, supreme divinity. The teaching culminates with an overwhelming vision. Granted "divine eyes" by Kṛṣṇa, Arjuna is suddenly able to see Kṛṣṇa's complete form, the awesome, all-inclusive Viśvarūpa. Kṛṣṇa acknowledges that previous methods of self-transformation such as sacrifice and yoga may be efficacious, but in light of his self-revelation he also recommends a new and superior method of religious attainment, which he calls *bhakti* (devotion). The most efficient way to reach the highest state, he tells Arjuna, is to dedicate one's entire self to Kṛṣṇa, a personal god who is simultaneously the Absolute.

With Arjuna's vision of the embodied Absolute and Kṛṣṇa's advocacy of bhakti we are initiated into the world of Hindu theism.

The Purāṇas and Hindu Theism

Throughout the period loosely labeled as the "Gupta" and "post-Gupta" ages, 300–700 C.E., Buddhism remained a powerful religious force in India, but new groups devoted to Viṣṇu and Śiva gained in visibility and resources. The Gupta rulers themselves satisfied both sides by lavishly patronizing Buddhist institutions while also declaring themselves followers of Viṣṇu. Throughout history Indian rulers have usually diversified their religious patronage as a means of integrating multiple religious communities within their kingdoms. The earliest Hindu temples built in permanent materials appeared during this period. Images of Hindu gods increased in scale and quality of workmanship. Reflecting and consolidating this growth in the religious orders of Viṣṇu and Śiva, another genre of texts, the Purāṇas, articulated more fully the theistic worldview outlined in the epics.

The Purāṇas (literally, ancient traditions) constitute another huge corpus of texts, numbering eighteen "major" Purāṇas, eighteen "sub-major" ones, and countless others. The major Purāṇas alone run to something like 400,000 verses. Like the epics, the Purāṇas were composed orally over many centuries, so that earlier and later teachings are regularly juxtaposed in the same texts. Bards put the earliest Purāṇas into final shape by about the fifth century C.E., while other texts kept incorporating new materials. The *Bhaviṣya Purāṇa* (or "Future Purāṇa," an oxymoron), the most open-ended of the major Purāṇas, contains sections from the fifth century or earlier, yet also "predicts" such late medieval figures as Akbar, Kabīr, Caitanya, and Guru Nānak, and even foretells the coming of British rule to India.

Comprehensive and encyclopedic in scope, the Purāṇas discuss cosmology, royal genealogies, society and dharma, the sacred geography of pilgrimage sites, yogic practices, town planning, even grammar and poetics. For the religious history of South Asia, however, the most significant aspect of the Purāṇas is their presentation of the theology, mythology, and ritual of the two primary gods Viṣṇu and Śiva.

Already in the epics, proponents of Viṣṇu were advancing him as the highest lord of the cosmos. The Vaiṣṇava Purāṇas advocate this with greater confidence and fuller cosmological breadth. The cyclical epochs of creation and dissolution of the universe, we now learn, are none other than Viṣṇu's alternating periods of activity and rest. The Purāṇas flesh out the incipient notion of Viṣṇu's intervening incarnations and gradually systematize it into a list of ten embodiments, including not only Kṛṣṇa and Rāma, but also zoomorphic forms (fish, tortoise, boar, man-lion), anthropomorphic ones (the dwarf who took three steps, Paraśurāma), a future incarnation (Kalkin), and even the Buddha. As the *Viṣṇu Purāṇa* relates, once when the demons had become too powerful through sacrifice, Viṣṇu took form as the Buddha and also as a naked Jain mendicant to dissuade them from sacrificing, so that the gods could overcome them and restore the proper order of things. Generally, all his incarnations reinforce Viṣṇu's essential attributes: benevolence, a desire to preserve order in the world, and a paradoxical capacity to be simultaneously infinite and finite.

Like Viṣṇu, Śiva appears in a rather minor role in the *Ṛg Veda*, but gradually advances in status until the Śaiva Purāṇas single him out as the Absolute. In the *Ṛg Veda*, Rudra ("the howler") is a peripheral divinity. Dwelling outside society in the forests or mountains, he is associated with the destructive forces of nature and rules over undomesticated animals. Since Rudra is not numbered one of the auspicious gods, he is excluded from the soma sacrifice, and instead is offered tribute to avert his wrath. Although he is characteristically destructive in his actions, Rudra may also become beneficent if properly praised and propitiated. When Rudra shows this kinder, gentler nature he is called Śiva, the "auspicious" one.

Already in this early appearance, we can observe two traits central to Śiva's later personality. In contrast to the sociable Viṣṇu, Śiva is an outsider. Residing typically in the highest Himalayan Mountains, he is the lord and role model for yogis, less concerned with instituting dharma on earth than with leading souls toward mokṣa. Second, Śiva has a dual nature, conjoining what are to us antithetical attributes. Not only is he both malevolent and benevolent, he is also both ascetic and erotic, hermit and family man, an immobile meditator and an unruly dancer. In one iconographic form, Śiva appears simultaneously male and female, an integral hermaphrodite.

In the epics, Śiva's character remains ambiguous, capricious, fierce, and sometimes wrathful. He continues to live outside society, and if he intervenes at all it is usually to disrupt things. Though they are predominantly Vaiṣṇava in orientation, the epics nevertheless recognize Śiva's growing power and his increasing claim to certain ritual prerogatives. In one famous episode, King Dakṛa organizes a large public sacrifice but declines to invite Śiva since, after all, Śiva is rather unruly. Learning of this slight, Śiva sends a swarming horde of emanations to break up the sacrifice, and then appears in person to demand that from now on he be the primary recipient of all sacrificial offerings.

One early Upaniṣad, the *Śvetāśvatara*, had identified Rudra-Śiva as the transcendental Absolute, identical with Puruṣa and the Upaniṣadic Brahman. The Śaiva Purāṇas reassert this claim and link it with a fully developed mythology of Śiva's doings. Unlike Viṣṇu, Śiva does not incarnate himself as a human being for an entire lifetime; rather he occasionally manifests himself physically in a body to carry out his varied intentions. In the Purāṇas, Śiva's manifestations most often demonstrate his superiority over other contestants, defeat demons, and grant grace to his followers.

Viṣṇu and Śiva are not the only deities in the world of the Purāṇas. In fact, these texts present a complex, inclusive pantheon, populated with divine families, animal mounts for each deity, Vedic divinities (now cast exclusively in supporting roles), and hosts of lesser semi-divinities such as celestial dancers, musicians, titans, sages, magicians, and many more. Among them two deserve special note: Brahmā and the Goddess.

The god Brahmā, with roots in the late Vedic and Dharmaśāstra literature, appears in the Purāṇas as the god of creation and as the patron of Vedic and orthodox brahmans. Sometimes the texts portray him comically as a senile grandfather who causes trouble by indiscriminately rewarding even demons for their austerities; at other times he shows better judgment in recognizing the preeminence of Viṣṇu and Śiva. Some Purāṇas of a more integrationist tendency, however, stress the interdependence of the three principal male divinities in performing distinct cosmic functions: Brahmā creates the world, Viṣṇu protects and sustains it, and Śiva destroys it. In modern times this has become known as the "Hindu trinity."

The Goddess presents a more complex picture. In the literature of the fifth through seventh centuries, several important female deities gain a new importance. Three are consorts or wives of the principal male deities: Lakṣmī is the consort of Viṣṇu, Pārvatī of Śiva, and Sarasvatī of Brahmā. These goddesses often take on significant responsibilities in their own rights, as Lakṣmī becomes the goddess of prosperity and domestic good fortune. Some Puraṇic texts, most notably the *Devīmāhātmya* section (c. 600 C.E.) of the *Mārkaṇeya Purāṇa*, go further to present a single great Goddess not as a wife, but as the Supreme Lord, appropriating for her all the common epithets of the Absolute. In her most famous incarnation she appears as Durgā, a warrior goddess. A buffalo demon, having gained nearly invincible powers through austerities, is running rampant through the cosmos and none of the male gods can subdue it. Durgā is born from the collective anger and frustration of all the gods. She receives a weapon from each of them and then rides forth on her lion mount to confront and finally destroy the demon.

Like Viṣṇu and Śiva, this female Absolute has an absorbing personality. She incorporates many local and regional cults and manifests herself in a plethora of distinct guises and forms. Only occasionally in the major Purāṇas does she appear in full force, but these glimpses point to the existence during this period of a significant school of thought that identified the fundamental force of the cosmos as feminine in nature and devoted itself to her praise and worship. This religious sensibility reappears in new forms among the tantric schools of medieval India and the Kālī bhakti of eighteenth-century Bengal.

The rich and varied religious literature of the Purāṇas created a compelling portrayal of the theistic Hindu cosmos. Moreover, these narratives of divine characters and their supernatural doings became part of the cultural literacy of Indian audiences from this period on. Medieval poets composing epigraphic eulogies and devotional verses could take this knowledge for granted and use it as a basis for literary allusion, exploration, and satire in their own verse. Temple sculptors rendered the puranic stories visible in their iconographic figures and narrative reliefs. Still today, hymns of praise recited in domestic and temple worship reiterate the mythic deeds and attributes of the Hindu deities much as they were first spelled out in the Purāṇas.

Temple Hinduism

By 700 C.E., the religious transformation first envisioned in the epics was complete. A new form of Hindu theism, focusing upon the gods Viṣṇu and Śiva as supreme deities but incorporating as well a host of other lesser gods and goddesses, now dominated the public sphere. Harṣavardhana was the last emperor to follow the Aśokan model by converting to Buddhism and supporting the Buddhist establishment with ostentatious gifts. No longer did sovereigns proclaim their performance of Vedic sacrifices as the principal way of asserting their authority to rule. Instead, they increasingly chose to articulate royal claims in a more concrete and lasting form, by constructing massive stone Hindu temples. These mountainlike structures, rising up to two hundred feet high and covered with sculptural representations of the Hindu pantheon, assumed a conspicuous and commanding presence in the Indian religious and political landscape during the early medieval period. During the half millennium from 700 to 1200 C.E., temple Hinduism dominated the public religious life of India.

The inscriptions of the seventh-century south Indian king Mahendravarman exemplify this shift in royal patronage. Although his Pallava predecessors had performed sacrifices as their primary ritual means of establishing royal legitimacy, Mahendravarman switched dramatically to temple sponsorship. He viewed his lordship over rival rulers as directly linked to Śiva's own cosmic overlordship. By constructing temples for Śiva, he brought God into his own territory and also proclaimed his authority over defeated rivals and their territories. Similarly, the succeeding rulers and dynasties of early medieval India sought to outbuild one another in conspicuous devotion to their chosen deity, Viṣṇu or Śiva.

A Hindu temple is primarily a home or residence for a god. Located in the main sanctum of the temple is an image or icon, a physical form that serves as a support within which Viṣṇu, Śiva, or some other principal deity may make himself physically present and accessible, enabling worshipers to enact a direct personal relationship with that divinity. At the same time, the temple offers through its physical structure a vision of the orderly cosmos presided over by that deity, with hierarchical ranks of subordinate deities, semi-divinities, devotees, and other auspicious entities all finding their proper places. Finally, in its layout the temple provides a map of the spiritual path a worshiper must follow toward participation with the deity ensconced in the "womb-room" at the center. The temple is thus a place of crossing, in which god descends from transcendence and devotee moves inward from the mundane.

Anyone may build a temple, but its size will naturally depend on the resources available to the patron. From small home shrines meant for private devotions to village temples, and on up in scale to the imposing edifices put up by Hindu kings with imperial aspirations, all serve basically the same purposes. Temple liturgy centers around physical and spiritual transactions between the incarnate deity and worshipers, mediated in the case of public temples by priests. These transactions are called *pūjā*. "How to Worship at the Abode of Śiva", a nineteenth-century pamphlet instructing pious Śaiva worshipers in proper temple conduct, provides a concise and reliable account of south Indian pūjā based on early medieval formulations.

The historical origins of pūjā are uncertain. In Vedic texts, the term refers to the respectful treatment of brahman guests. Jains and Buddhists, as we have seen, developed forms of pūjā to images and stūpas quite early. Small but recognizable images of the Hindu divinities, probably employed in simple household pūjā ceremonies, have been found dating back to the early centuries C.E. It is likely that all these forms of pūjā among the written traditions derive from earlier informal practices of image worship by autochthonous peoples outside the Indo-Aryan society. Hindu texts of the medieval period, however, see this new form of worship as the result of the god's own direct intervention and instruction, as in the puranic episode of the "Origin of Liṅga Worship". There, Śiva guides a group of renunciatory sages from their earlier Vedic-based rites to the new practice of worshiping Śiva's liṅga. Pūjā replaces sacrifice, but at the same time it incorporates select portions of the Vedic repertoire of mantras and ritual gestures, much as Śiva advises the sages to recite Vedic texts when offering pūjā.

In the context of large-scale royal temples, pūjā developed into an elaborate, rule-bound, priestly activity. New genres of liturgical guides were composed—Vaiṣṇava saṃhitās, Śaiva āgamas, and Śākta tantras—claiming to be the direct teachings of the deities concerning the metaphysical organization of the cosmos and how humans ought best to worship them. Pan-Indian Hindu theological orders, such as the Pāñcarātra and Vaikhānasa schools directed toward Viṣṇu and the Pāśupata and Śaiva Siddhānta schools dedicated to Śiva, employed these texts to maintain the temples as centers of community worship.

While priests and their texts emphasized proper ritual performance as a means of religious attainment, others began to assert that emotional enthusiasm, or bhakti, played a more crucial role in worshiping god. The term *bhakti* is usually translated as "devotion," but its meaning is more complex than our English equivalent would suggest. *Bhakti* comes from the verb root *bhaj*. In its earliest usage, *bhaj* means to divide or share, as one divides and partakes of the sacrificial offerings. *Bhaj* can also denote experiencing something, as one enjoys food or relishes music. It signifies waiting upon someone, as an attendant serves a king. It can mean to make love in a very corporeal sense and to adore in a more disembodied, spiritual manner. As its Indian adherents define it, *bhakti* partakes of all these shades of meaning. It is a way of participating or sharing in divine being, however that is understood, of tasting and enjoying a god's presence, of serving and worshiping him, of being as intimate as possible, of being attached to him above all else.

As a religious attitude or way of relating to a being one takes as superior, bhakti is widespread throughout Indian religions. One finds hymns of devotion throughout the Purāṇas and the liturgical texts of temple Hinduism, and similar genres of eulogistic poetry are common in Buddhist and Jain literature. Historians also use the term in a more restricted sense, however, to refer to a series of regional movements in medieval India that stressed intense personal devotion to god or goddess, the leadership of exemplary poet-saints, and the importance of a community of devotees. The earliest of these bhakti movements date from the seventh through ninth centuries, in the southern region of Tamilnadu, and are represented by the poetry of Māṇikkavācakar. Later bhakti movements occurred in the Deccan and throughout northern India from the twelfth century through the seventeenth centuries; these will be discussed in the context of Hindu responses to Islam.

The groups of devotees to Śiva and to Viṣṇu of early medieval Tamilnadu were closely allied with the spread and growth of Hindu temples in the region. Itinerant poets traveled from village to village singing hymns of praise to their gods as they saw them in each new place of worship. Although they did not overtly criticize the temple priests or their ritualism, the bhakti poets of Tamilnadu proposed what they saw as a more satisfying and accessible means of reaching the divine. Whereas priests performed ritual invocations to bring Śiva or Viṣṇu into visible material supports, the bhakti saints used their poetry to evoke each deity in full and sensuous detail. Reiterating the god's activities, they often placed themselves as participants in those mythical scenes. They stressed the importance of establishing a close relationship with the god conceived in a personal and particularized manner. Using a trope that would become common among bhakti poets, Tamil devotees often spoke in the poetic voice of women infatuated with the alluring male deity, drawing on the conventions of secular love poetry and transforming the erotic into a religious allegory of soul and God. Women saints like Āṇṭāḻ did not require this metaphoric step. According to her hagiography, Āṇṭāḻ's single-minded love led her to reject all human suitors and unite with Viṣṇu himself, in the form of a temple image.

Yet at the same time, as Māṇikkavācakar's poetry shows, the poets recognized the paradox inherent in conceptualizing the divine this way. However anthropomorphically the poets might portray their god, Śiva and Viṣṇu remained ultimately beyond, and unknowable as well. The tensions between god's immanence and his transcendence (or, as Vaiṣṇava theologians phrased it, his simultaneous "easy accessibility" and his "otherness"), and between the devotee's mixed feelings of intimacy and alienation provide central themes that run throughout Indian devotional literature.

While temple Hinduism centered around Viṣṇu and Śiva held sway in the public sphere in early medieval India, many other religious formations were present, as well. As we have seen, Hindus never sought to develop a pan-Indian "church" structure nor did they establish a clear ecclesiastical hierarchy. Even the brahmans, seemingly the religious elite, formed a very diverse and permeable social group, with new priestly groups sometimes successfully claiming brahmanic status for themselves.

Vedic schools continued their intellectual activities even though sacrifice was no longer a significant public form of ritual. The Mīmāṃsā school developed elaborate means of interpreting the Vedic texts, and scholars of Dharmaśāstra applied these principles to the reading of dharma texts. Groups of brahmans loyal to the Vedic traditions often received special land grants called *agrahāras*, where they were able to maintain small-scale Vedic sacrificial programs free from economic need.

Other orthodox writers with a more philosophical bent developed and systematized the metaphysical monism implicit in some portions of the Upaniṣads, culminating in the ninth-century writings of Śaṅkara, a brilliant author and philosophical disputant of the Advaita Vedānta school. Śaṅkara's writings demoted temple image worship to the status of a useful but decidedly lower form of religious attainment, and reserved the highest place for intellectual realization of the oneness of Brahman. The other principal Vedānta school, the "qualified nondualist" system of Rāmānuja (c. 1050 C.E.) gave a more prominent role to devotion and engaged itself more directly in the doings of temple Hinduism. Rāmānuja even served as monastic superior in one of the largest south Indian Viṣṇu temples.

During this period, Buddhism was still strong in the areas of Kashmir and northeastern India, and such celebrated universities as Nālandā in Bihar served as international centers for Buddhist study. Communities of Jains were numerous in Gujarat and Karnataka, maintaining their own traditions of scholarship and asceticism, and not infrequently placing Jain ministers in the royal courts of those areas. We must assume the existence of many other forms of religious thought and practice during this period which, because they were esoteric or domestic or nonliterate, did not leave behind texts or other historical evidence.

The diversity of indigenous Indian religions was supplemented by religious and ethnic communities who migrated from elsewhere and settled in India, especially along the western coast. Jewish traders and Syrian Christians arrived in India at least as early as the fourth century, and from the seventh century Arab Muslim merchants set up a trading network around coastal India. Starting in the tenth century, the Parsees ("Persians"), who adhere to the ancient Iranian religion of Zoroastrianism, fled their homeland for the safer terrain of India. Each of these groups maintained itself as an autonomous, insular, and largely unthreatening religious minority within Hindu-dominated society.

In such a pluralistic setting, members of many religious persuasions articulated their differing positions and debated their views in public and at court. The stakes were sometimes high. Although some modern scholars and Hindus have portrayed the pre-Islamic period of Indian history as one of overriding religious tolerance, this was not entirely the case. The hymns of the south Indian poet-saints, for instance, included an often bitter polemic against Jains and Buddhists, and in the later biographies of these saints we hear of intentional destruction of Buddhist images and of a pogrom carried out against the eight thousand Jains of Madurai. Whatever the historicity of such later accounts, they clearly reflect an atmosphere in which religious concerns were taken as serious and consequential, not a matter of unobstructed personal choice.

Islam in India

Around 610 C.E. Muḥammad, a member of the Arab tribe ruling Mecca, began to receive revelations. By 622 his criticisms of Arab paganism and of the injustice of Meccan society had aroused considerable opposition. When residents of another city to the north invited him to come and act as arbiter, he led a few followers in an exodus to build in Medina a new society based on divine law. Muḥammad had embarked on his career as the Prophet of Islam. Revelations continued until his death in 632, and were later collected into the foundation text of Islam, the Qur'ān. These distant events held immense consequences for the history of Indian religions.

For the first 150 years of its existence, Islam was the most dynamic, expanding religious movement the world had ever seen. Imbued with a theological and ethical directive to transform the "house of unbelievers" into the "house of submission (*islam*)" through "righteous struggle" (*jihād*), the military forces of the early Muslim leaders conquered first the Arab peninsula, then the surrounding West Asian regions of Syria, Iraq, Iran, and Afghanistan, and the countries of North Africa. By the early part of the eighth century, Muslim armies had expanded into Spain and were pushing into the southern parts of France in the West; in the East they had reached as far as Sind, in present-day Pakistan. This success came at a price, though. The religious quest of Muḥammad's companions was stifled by disputes, and although the leaders of the Muslim community legitimated their regimes through Islamic law, they soon adopted the Roman Caesar and the Persian Shāh as their models of sovereignty, much to the disgust of Islamic religious scholars.

Over the next few centuries an Indian frontier was defined and gradually pushed back as Arab, Persian, and Turkish armies invaded and conquered Afghanistan, Kashmir, and the Punjab. Despite continued resistance by indigenous rulers, the more centralized and organized tactics of the invaders eventually proved successful. In the early eleventh century, Maḥmūd, the Turko-Afghan ruler of Ghazna (in Afghanistan), mounted eighteen campaigns into northern India. He conquered and incorporated the Punjab into the Ghaznavid empire and then enriched his state by sacking many of the Buddhist monasteries and Hindu temples of northern India, and transporting the loot back to Ghazna. Though he temporarily disrupted the existing Indian political and religious order, Maḥmūd did not seek to establish a permanent Islamic polity centered in the subcontinent. That was left to a successor dynasty also based in Afghanistan, the Ghūrids.

In 1193 Mu'izzuddīn Muḥammad of Ghūr and his general Qutb al-Dīn Aibak defeated the Cāhamāna ruler of Delhi, then the most powerful north Indian king, and in 1026 Qutb al-dīn declared himself Sultan of Delhi. The Delhi sultanate lasted some 320 years, under six different Turko-Afghan dynasties, and dominated much of north India. Other Islamic polities were established in the Deccan and southern India during this period. The sultanate was in turn supplanted by the Mughal empire, founded by the Central Asian adventurer Bābar in 1526. The Mughal empire held sway over much of India into the early part of the eighteenth century. Thus for roughly five hundred years of late medieval Indian history, from 1200 to 1700, rulers adhering to Islam prevailed in northern India. With these rulers came a conservative clerical elite who sought, with mixed success, to maintain Islamic social and legal order in the urban centers of India.

The face of the conqueror, however, was not the only visage of Islam in India, nor even the most common one. With Islamic rule in India, itinerant Muslim Sufi teachers came to till the fertile religious fields of India. *Sufism* is the generic term for Islamic mysticism. Already sharing features with some forms of Hinduism, Sufis found it relatively easy to acclimatize their messages and concerns to the Indian environment. Indeed, they came to regard themselves as a kind of spiritual government of India, responsible for the religious welfare of the people, parallel to but separate from the political government of the sultans. The Sufis taught an esoteric form of Islam aimed at an elite, and they were not consciously interested in attracting non-Muslim masses to Islam. They used their Indian mother tongues to compose mystical poetry, however, and their tombs became centers of a cult of saints that increasingly attracted both Muslims and non-Muslims.

In a history of Indian religions, it is necessary to recognize both sides of Islam in India. The conquests of the Turkic, Afghan, and Central Asian Muslim warriors and their continuing struggles for power both among themselves and with Hindu warrior elites like the Rajputs had significant repercussions not only for Indian political history but also for the development of Indian religions, continuing to the present. At the same time, the more conciliatory and assimilative activities of the Sufis played a greater role in implanting Islam as an indigenous Indian religious formation in South Asia. In this anthology most of the readings emphasize the role of Sufism in Indian Islam.

Orthodox Islam and Political Authority

Al-Bīrūnī, one of the great medieval Muslim scholars, accompanied Maḥmūd on his military forays into India in the early eleventh century, and wrote of the Indians he encountered there: "They differ from us in everything which other nations have in common. In all manners and usages they differ from us to such a degree as to frighten their children with us, our dress, and our ways and customs, and to declare us to be the devil's breed, and our doings as the very opposite of all that is good and proper." The response he observed was perhaps not surprising, considering that the Ghaznavids were plundering their way across northern India at the time. Yet al-Bīrūnī points to very real differences between the various ruling Islamic groups of late medieval India and the predominantly Hindu society they ruled.

The book of Allah's revelations to Muḥammad, the Qur'ān, specifies five basic constituents or "pillars" of the Islamic faith: the profession of faith, regular prayer, giving of alms, fasting during the month of Ramadān, and pilgrimage.

Islam is based on a simple, shared creed, in which the Muslim believer acknowledges his or her submission to a single supreme God and recognizes Muḥammad as the Prophet. Orthodox Islam is rigorously monotheistic. Allah's transcendence excludes all other claims to divinity. Medieval Hinduism, by contrast, was hierarchically pluralistic in its theological outlook, admitting a host of immanent divinities and semi-divinities who participate in every sphere of the cosmos. A Hindu might well regard one of these deities as the highest "God of gods," but this did not prevent recognition of many other divinities appropriate for other persons or purposes. To the orthodox Muslim, this divine multiplicity of the Hindus appeared as a clear case of polytheism, which would diminish the adoration due to Allah alone.

The Allah of the orthodox is all-powerful and transcendent. While acting as the creator of all things, Allah never takes on physical form in the world. Hindu deities like Viṣṇu and Śiva, we have seen, do intervene directly in the world, often in human or even animal bodies. They also enter into the physical forms of icons and images, and this makes possible the institution of temples and their liturgies of worship. For orthodox Muslims, the Qur'ān and other authoritative traditions contain strong prohibitions against any adoration of physical idols.

Relations between the Muslim faithful and Allah are best expressed in prayer, a nonreciprocal and nonmaterial communication from believer to God. All believers should pray five times daily while facing Mecca, the geographical center of the Islamic community. Early in its history, the Muslim community institutionalized public prayer as a regular collective act, and the mosque grew to accommodate this activity. The Islamic mosque provides a large, mostly open area for congregational prayer, an egalitarian space enclosed by a surrounding wall to separate believers from nonbelievers. Though there can be no central image or icon representing Allah, the mosque does provide a spatial focus in the form of a wall indicating the direction toward Mecca.

The fifth pillar, pilgrimage, indicates another important aspect of Islam. At least once in a lifetime, the Muslim believer ought to make a pilgrimage to Mecca. From its earliest decades Islam was a universalistic and international religion, spread out geographically from Spain through northern Africa, across the Middle East, and into southern Asia. In different regions Islam naturally took on various regional characters, but it always maintained the ideal of a single unified community of believers. The institution of pilgrimage brought about an annual assembly of Muslims from all over the Islamic world, and thereby strengthened this unity. Islam in India had a dual identity. While grounded in the distinctive social and cultural realities of India, it was also part of the wider world of international Islam.

As Islamic warrior elites from Turkey and Central Asia established their authority in new parts of India there was inevitably conflict. At the frontiers of contested control, the conquerors sometimes symbolized their victories through a physical metaphor: the destruction of Hindu temples (as well as Jain and Buddhist sites, equally "polytheistic"), often followed by the construction of mosques on the leveled sites. Hindu chieftains, in response, might reconsecrate these same religious sites as a way of claiming independence from Delhi's political overlordship. In this way temples sometimes became indices of political control.

Within areas of settled rule, however, Muslim authorities adopted a more lenient attitude toward their Hindu subjects. Early in Islamic history, Muslims had formulated an intermediate category for those who could not be classified as either "believers" or "heathens." Christians and Jews, sharing the Abrahamic lineage with Muslims, were labeled "people of the book," and treated as tolerated religious communities within the Islamic state. The Hindus of India were idolaters and polytheists, admittedly, but brahmans could be regarded as the equivalent of Christian monks, and so could be left largely to their own religious customs. Hindu subjects might even construct temples, so long as these structures did not pose a threat to the dominating Muslim institutions. Indeed, Turkish and Mughal rulers even gave endowments of land and granted tax exemptions for certain Hindu, Jain, and Zoroastrian religious foundations. Reciprocally, Hindu rulers sometimes facilitated the construction of mosques for the benefit of their Muslim subjects.

Sufism

Sufism stresses the personal relationship between believer and Allah. The word *Sufi* (Arabic *ṣūfī*) derives from the Arabic for wool, alluding to the coarse woolen garments favored by early Muslim mystics. As with Ajita of the Hair-Blanket and countless other Indian ascetics, early Sufis chose to represent their austerity and renunciation of worldly concerns through a conspicuous rejection of comfortable clothing.

Despite its mystical and renunciatory tendencies, Sufism should not be seen as outside the mainstream of Islam. Sufis ground their teachings firmly in Muḥammad's revelation, but they draw on different portions of the Qur'ān than do more conservative exegetes. Whereas conservative Muslims focus on passages emphasizing Allah's almighty, awesome, and ineffable character, Sufi interpreters stress the sections that speak of Allah's pervasive presence in the world and in the hearts of his believers. Significantly, Sufis speak of a "jihād of the heart" as a more important religious struggle than the "jihād of the sword." In the medieval Islamic world, far from being a peripheral movement, Sufism engendered some of the most powerful and influential theological writings, such as that of Ibn al-ʿArabī, and the most moving and popular Muslim poetry, as that of the thirteenth-century Jalāl al-Dīn Rumi. To a considerable extent Islam in medieval India took on a Sufi coloring.

Sufis arrived in India early. They were already in the Punjab during the Ghaznavid period. Once the Delhi sultanate was established, Sufis of the Chishti and Suhrawardi orders began to settle throughout northern India. Two other formal Sufi orders, the Naqshbandi and Qādiri, arrived during the Mughal period and became influential within the Mughal court. At court and in the urban centers, Sufis vied with the more orthodox Islamic scholars for status and influence, and needed to maintain a degree of respectability themselves. Even so they occasionally suffered persecution for their hubris, as when the Mughal ruler Jahāngīr imprisoned Sirhindi. Others held aloof as much as possible from the court and its secular ways. Certain Sufis became more involved with local culture, and adopted the local language and customs. In some cases they took on the deliberately unconventional character of the qalandar, the activist ascetic dropout who flouted the authority of respectable Muslim society.

The most basic relationship among Sufis is that of master and disciple. The master, known as a *shaykh* or *pīr*, is first and foremost a teacher, instructing his or her followers in proper ethical and spiritual conduct. As in the folk imagery of Sulṭān Bāhū's laudatory poem, the master is a "washerman" for the heart, endeavoring to "shine up those begrimed with dirt, leaving them spotless." Disciples often recorded the teachings of masters as a way of perpetuating and disseminating their cleansing wisdom. "Conversations of the Sufi Saints" provides examples of this popular genre of Sufi literature.

Notable masters came sometimes to be regarded as "saints," figures possessing extraordinary capacities who could act as virtual intercessors with God on behalf of their followers. The hagiographies of these saints depict them performing a variety of miracles such as levitation, mind reading, and physical transformations. As in Indian religious discourse generally, miracles serve in these stories as visible confirmations of inner states of attainment and as criteria for determining religious powers. Tombs of Sufi saints often became pilgrimage centers, much as the stūpas and miracle sites of the Buddha had earlier. They perpetuated the charisma of the saint enshrined there and served as centers for the transmission of Sufi teachings and practices.

The saints were all subordinate to the Prophet Muḥammad. Concomitant with the rise of Sufi orders in the medieval Islamic world was an increasing veneration of the Prophet and his family expressed through ritual and song. A few puritan critics, forerunners of modern fundamentalists, objected to this reverence as idolatry, but most of the Islamic community came to see Muḥammad as a figure of loving devotion and miraculous powers. In domestic ceremonies honoring Muḥammad's birth, Muslim women speak of the miracles surrounding his birth and childhood, and request his intercession in solving their everyday difficulties. In the various genres of devotional verse addressed to him, Muḥammad appears as a guide, benefactor, miracle worker, and a lover, the supremely desirable bridegroom. Adapting a convention common to Hindu bhakti poetry, and employed also in Jain and Sikh poetry of the period, Indo-Muslim poets represented themselves as young women tormented by separation from their beloved, in this case the Prophet. Such mutual borrowings and recyclings of poetic themes were common in the close encounters between Sufism and Hindu devotionalism in medieval India.

Religious practice within Sufi circles centered around "recollection" (*dhikr*) and "listening" (*sama'*). The Qur'ān instructs Muslims to remember Allah frequently, and Sufis developed various techniques to evoke and intensify the recollection. Most commonly, the practitioner would rhythmically chant the one hundred names of God, and often enhance the chanting through bodily postures and breath control. Much like indigenous Indian forms of yoga, these disciplines are meant to bring the body, senses, and mind under control so they would not obstruct union with the divine. Though willing to borrow useful techniques from yogic traditions, Indian Sufis were certainly not uncritical advocates or borrowers of all Hindu practices, as Chirāgh-i Dihlī shows in his vivid denunciation of image worship, reiterating a core Islamic tenet.

Sufi poetry such as that of the two Punjabi poets Sulṭān Bāhū and Bulleh Shāh grows out of the musical assembly. Emphasizing their rural origins, these poets employ the vernacular language in preference to religious Arabic or courtly Persian, and draw their images from the everyday world of village Punjab. Reiterating common Sufi themes, they advocate love of Allah as the supreme virtue, and they often figure themselves as brides entreating their bridegroom Allah. From the austere and utterly transcendent God of the conservatives, these poets render him personal and accessible. They stress the importance of inner purity and criticize religious formalism, particularly ritual and intellectual approaches to the divine, in favor of an intuitive, personal approach. Again one sees here striking parallels with existing Indian traditions, in this case with the thematic repertoire of medieval Hindu bhakti poetry.

Sufism unquestionably germinated within the earliest phases of Arab Islam and flourished throughout the medieval Islamic world, but it was uniquely suited to the Indian religious setting. From the monist cosmological formulations of Ibn al-'Arabī to the personalizing of Allah in Sufi poetry, from the familiar renunciatory appearance of Sufi masters to their use of yogalike meditative techniques, this form of mystical Islam could seem both familiar and yet new to India. Adapting to their surroundings, Sufi teachers were able to bring the message of Islam to an Indian audience that the more conservative scholars of the urban centers could never reach. In this sense, the Sufis of late medieval South Asia deserve the greatest credit in making Islam a truly indigenous Indian religion.

Although Islam did originate historically as an extraneous religious formation, it is important to bear in mind the counterargument offered in "India as a Sacred Islamic Land." Whether migrating from other parts of the Islamic world or adapting Islam through conversion, most Indian Muslims did not regard themselves as foreigners in India. Rather, from the very start they sought to integrate their homeland, India, into the larger sacred topography of the world of Islam. Indeed, in the view of Āzād, the first man—Adam—descended to earth in South Asia, and so South Asia figures as the site of the first revelation and the first mosque. For Indian Muslims no less than Hindus, Jains, or Buddhists, India is a religious terrain, a place where the divine, in whatever form, can indeed manifest itself to all.

Hinduism under Islam

Prior to the thirteenth century, as we have seen, temple Hinduism had offered a pan-Indian theory and legitimation of political authority, with royal claimants articulating their sovereignty through personal and ceremonial devotion to the Hindu deities Viṣṇu and Śiva. Subsequently, however, the most powerful rulers in Delhi and many other parts of South Asia grounded their dominion in a very different theo-political system. Hindu ruling elites were largely confined to southern India and peripheral regions. Not only was the political sphere transformed by this shift in rulership, but the growing presence in the subcontinent of new religious teachers with competing and often compelling messages, most notably the Sufis, also posed a serious challenge to the authority of existing forms of Hindu thought and practice.

Hindus responded to the presence and political sway of Islam in late medieval India in complex, diverse, and creative ways. As in any period of social change, there were many in medieval India who sought mainly to defend and hold on to what they had. Hindu warrior elites might signal their independence from Islamic overlordship by reconstructing or reconsecrating a desecrated temple. In the religious sphere this attitude manifested itself in efforts to collect, maintain, and reassert already existing aspects of Hindu traditions. By collecting and commenting on the older textual genres such as the Vedas and Dharmaśāstras, brahman scholars made a conscious attempt to recreate past formations in altered conditions. The scholarly work of orthodox brahmans at this time, aimed at conserving and reasserting what they saw as traditional Hindu values, also had a large and generally unrecognized effect. They were the first to assemble what later scholars of the nineteenth and twentieth centuries would reassemble as a Hindu canon of sacred books.

However, the eclipse of temple Hinduism as the prevailing ideological formation in northern India also set new and innovative directions in the development of Indian religions. What is most apparent in late medieval Hinduism is the vitality of forms of religion that are devotional, esoteric, or syncretic, and a corresponding deemphasis on the role of religion in constituting the political and social order.

Devotional Movements

Hindus sometimes personify bhakti as a beautiful woman, born in southern India, who grew to maturity in the Deccan. In twelfth-century Karnataka, a group of devotees called the Vīraśaivas coalesced around the Kalacuri minister Basavaṇṇa, and from the late thirteenth through seventeenth centuries, the Maharashtrian pilgrimage center Paṇḍarpur was the center of Marathi devotionalism toward the god Viṭhobā, a form of Kṛṣṇa. Tukārām was the last of the great Marathi poet-saints. Finally, according to the metaphor, the woman reached her finest flourishing in the north. Bhakti movements appeared in northern India by the fourteenth century, and from then on were a major force in north Indian Hindu life, from Kashmir and Gujarat to Bengal.

It is somewhat misleading, however, to speak of a single organic bhakti movement. Different groups used the various regional languages in their poetry, directed themselves toward different deities, and assumed distinct theological standpoints. Some poet-saints were profoundly inward and mystical in their lives and song, while others adopted a more outward, socially critical orientation to the world around them. Some north Indian poets and bhakti groups appeared oblivious to the presence of Islam, but for others this was a cardinal reality. Yet virtually all considered emotional "participation" with God as a core value. Whether devotees direct themselves toward Śiva, Kṛṣṇa, Rāma, or the goddess Kālī, they seek always to develop a personal relationship with that divine figure. For bhakti theologians mokṣa consists more in attaining or reattaining closeness to God than in gaining liberation.

The deities of medieval bhakti bring with them the mythical narratives of theistic Hinduism that had previously been set forth in the epics and Purāṇas. The Kṛṣṇa of the sixteenth-century Gauḍīya Vaiṣṇavas, for instance, is the same Kṛṣṇa whose story is told in the *Harivaṃśa* and *Bhāgavata Purāṇa*. But most bhakti poets shift the cosmic scope of the Purāṇas and temple Hinduism to the background. There is less concern with God as creator and ruler of the cosmos, and more with God as humanly alive and embodied on earth. So with Kṛṣṇa, devotional poets and theologians tend to play down his earlier identity as an incarnation of Viṣṇu and instead focus on the pastoral life of his youth among the cowherds of Vraja. At the same time, they emphasize the inward presence of God in the heart and his loving regard for the faithful. Even when they do acknowledge the deity's role in creating and sustaining the world, devotionalists often portray God as playful, inscrutable, and sometimes downright devious in his or her activities. How else could one explain the bad state of things?

Not all devotionalists, however, comprehend God as an anthropomorphic form. Although most, like the Gauḍīyas, orient themselves to a God "with attributes" (*saguṇa*) like the eminently embodied Kṛṣṇa, others like Kabīr prefer to conceptualize God "without attributes" (*nirguṇa*). For the nirguṇa poets, any attempt to characterize or comprehend God is doomed ultimately to fail, and all the mythical and ritual ways we humans seek to relate to God are distractions or delusions.

According to the sixteenth-century devotional theologian Rūpa Gosvāmī, it is possible to enjoy various relationships with God. Rūpa specified five predominant ones, largely based on analogies with human relationships. One may relate to God as an insignificant human relates to the supreme deity, as a respectful servant relates to his lord and master, as a mother relates to her child, as a friend relates to his friend, or as a lover relates to her beloved. Devotional groups explore all these modes of relationship, and particularly the latter three, through their poetic and ritual practices. In the south Indian devotional genre of piḷḷaittamiḻ, for example, poets address their chosen deities in the form of a child, employing a domestic idiom and redirecting parental love toward religious figures. Gauḍīya Vaiṣṇavas envision themselves as cowherd friends of Kṛṣṇa to participate in his divine sports. Of all forms of association, Rūpa claims, the erotic is the highest, and much bhakti poetry explores the passionate love between the cowherd women of Vraja, who represent all human souls, and the enchanting young Kṛṣṇa. Arguing against other more conventional Hindu ways of conceptualizing one's relationship with God, Rūpa values emotional intensity over the meditative stasis of the yogis or the intellectual comprehension of the Advaitins as the highest goal.

The bhakti movements engendered various forms of devotional yoga, techniques for evoking and focusing the devotee's participation with God. According to the Gauḍīya followers of Caitanya, the simplest technique, and therefore the one most suitable for the present age of decline, consists in repetitive chanting of God's name. Since Kṛṣṇa's name is more than just an arbitrary signifier—it is itself a portion of his reality—chanting his name as a mantra makes Kṛṣṇa himself actually present. The Gauḍīyas institutionalized chanting combined with ecstatic dancing as a collective practice, similar to the musical sessions of the Sufis. The tale of Haridāsa illustrates how these public displays of congregational revelry could provoke suspicion and suppression by civil authorities. At the same time, Haridāsa's miraculous fortitude in the face of adversity provides a metaphor for the resistant powers of inner bhakti against outward social pressure.

The practice most characteristic of medieval bhakti, though, was song and poetry. In contrast to Indian courtly traditions of poetic composition, poet-saints of north India sang in vernacular languages and drew their imagery from everyday life. They adopted highly personal poetic voices to speak of the tribulations and joys of the devotional life. The poetry of medieval bhakti in Hindi, Bengali, Marathi, and other vernacular languages of India is quite likely the richest library of devotion in world literature, distinguished not only by its religious intensity but also by the great variety of psychological states and emotional responses it explores. These medieval songs of devotion remain very much alive in contemporary

India. Few of us indeed can recite as much of any author as the average Hindi speaker can reel off from Kabīr, Sūrdās, or Mīrābāī.

For devotionalists, the poetic invocation of God often supplanted ritual invocation and physical images. Although the earliest devotional movements in south India treated temples as an important locus of religiosity, some later bhakti groups dispensed with the temple as superfluous or criticized it as a place of purely formal religious observances, where priests and the dull-witted could go through the motions of worship. Bhakti poet-saints often broadened this skeptical attitude toward temple ritualism into a critique of all aspects of what they considered conventional or orthodox Hindu practice: Vedic recitation, pilgrimage, and the social hierarchy of the caste system.

The critical perspective of medieval bhakti reached its apogee in the writings of Kabīr. Raised in a poor community of Muslim weavers, Kabīr was initiated into bhakti by a Vaiṣṇava guru, and later attracted a following among both Muslims and Hindus. Throughout his poetic utterances he drew from the many religious traditions around him—Sufis, devotionalists, tantrics, Buddhists, and others. Yet, as in his poem "Simple State," Kabīr was quite happy to dish out equal scorn for the orthodoxies of Islam and Hinduism, urging instead a spiritual path of merging with an indescribable Absolute outside, or perhaps equally within, those verbose schools of thought. The historical irony is that both Hindus and Muslims later claimed this irascible skeptic and mocker of formal religions, and his verse was also incorporated into the canon of a third religion, the *Ādi Granth* of the Sikhs

Tantra

Like devotionalism, the developments we now classify as tantra originated when temple Hinduism still dominated the public sphere. It developed from older and largely unrecorded practices of yoga, medicine, folk magic, and local goddess cults. From about the seventh century, Hindu and Buddhist tantra texts begin to appear, as do descriptions, often satirical, of recognizable tantric adepts. Beginning around the time of Maḥmūd's raids into north India, Hindu tantric groups and literature began to proliferate throughout the subcontinent. Reaching its greatest influence during the period of Islamic dominance, tantra continues in varied forms in present-day India, albeit much diminished, and has made itself known and notorious in the West through such international gurus as Bhagwan Shree Rajneesh.

The word *tantra* does not admit to a single unequivocal definition. Drawn from the vocabulary of weaving, where it may refer to the threads, the warp, or the entire loom, the term *tantra* was extended to signify texts as things spun out and threaded together, both physically (since palm-leaf manuscripts require strings) and verbally. Later the word came to refer especially to one genre of texts directed to the Goddess, the Śākta tantras, and to the adherents of its teachings.

Historians of Indian religions use the word *tantra* primarily in two ways. In a broad sense they employ *tantra* to identify a whole series of ritual and yogic practices not found in the Vedic lineage of texts, such as visualization, geometrical designs, impositions of mantra powers, and Kuṇḍalinī yoga. The word *tantra* in this sense refers more to a shared repertoire of techniques than to any religious system. Many religious groups in medieval India made use of these techniques, and so there were Buddhist tantra, Jain tantra, and many "tantric elements" incorporated in the rituals of the temple Hindu schools. In a more restricted sense, tantra is taken as a system of thought and practice, based on a few shared premises and orientations. In this anthology, we use tantra primarily in this narrower definition.

Hindu tantric groups most often recognize the female goddess Śakti ("energy"), Śiva's consort, as the fundamental creative energy of the cosmos, and therefore as the Absolute. Tantrics view the human body as a microcosm of the universe, and focus on it as the only vehicle for attaining powers and liberation. Through yogic practices and ritual activities the tantric adept seeks to inculcate knowledge physically. Rather than seeking a disembodied escape from bondage or a devotional relationship with divinity, tantrics set as their highest goal the transformation of the body itself into divinity.

Tantra is often promulgated away from society, within small circles of initiates clustered around preceptors. Tantric groups often compose their texts in "intentional" or "upside-down" language, making them deliberately unintelligible to those outside the initiated group. Some tantrics intentionally transgress social proprieties and consume forbidden meat and wine, in order to escape what they consider conventional reality and proceed directly to the ultimate. Though practiced by only a few tantric circles, this antinomian tendency, combined with the esoteric and ritualistic orientation of tantra, led to its widespread condemnation as a degenerate form of Hinduism by many Western scholars and by punctilious Indians, as well.

One of the most distinctive characteristics of tantra is the role played by the Goddess. Worship of goddesses is undoubtedly very ancient in South Asia. The *Devīmāhātmya* proclaimed a single pan-Indian Goddess as the Absolute. Medieval Śaiva theologians often bifurcated the godhead into male and female. They postulated an inactive but transcendent male Śiva who carries out all his worldly activities through an immanent energetic female Śakti. From this cosmic division of labor, tantra took the next logical step: if Śakti is doing everything anyway, why not focus upon her as the real force of the universe? Tantra thereby subverted Śiva's superior role and located Śakti—identified as Pārvatī, Durgā, Kālī, and all female divinities—at the top of the divine hierarchy, indeed as the animating energy of all.

As in bhakti, tantric groups paid close attention to the erotic, but they viewed it from a different perspective. Devotional poet-saints most often directed themselves toward male divinities, figured themselves as female lovers, and used human romance and sexuality as metaphor for the complex personal relationship between soul and God. According to tantric cosmology, the world itself comes into being through the primordial, recurrent coupling of Śiva and Śakti. Since the human body in tantra is a concentrated microcosm, an embodiment of the cosmos, it makes sense to view sexual union as a way of reenacting creation, bringing the practitioner in harmony with the forces of the cosmos. Detached from the romantic narratives of bhakti and given an impersonal cosmic significance, ritualized sexual union enabled the tantric adept to transcend all dualities. Ultimately, most devotionalists did not wish to overcome duality. For them, Rāmprasād Sen's observation rang true: "I like the taste of sugar, but I have no desire to become sugar."

Tantra, like bhakti, sometimes took a skeptical view of the social categories of merit and demerit, right and wrong, promulgated by the orthodox. Followers of bhakti might be led by their passionate attachment to God to transgress normal social boundaries, much as the cowherd women of Vraja willingly left their husbands and children to rendezvous with Kṛṣṇa in the forest. Some tantric groups prescribed a more deliberate, ritualized overturning of conventional mores. For the Kaula school, five normally forbidden offerings—the famous "Five Ms" of liquor, meat, fish, parched grain, and sexual intercourse—were regularly consumed or enjoyed as part of pūjā. Here too transgression acknowledged the superior claims of religious attainment over the everyday rules of social conduct. But by no means did all tantra groups accept this antinomian attitude. The eleventh-century tantric alchemical treatise *Rasārnava*, for instance, strongly criticized the Five-M mode of tantra. As in every other religious formation we have looked at, there was always internal debate among tantric proponents over the ultimate ends and the best means to reach it.

Guru Nānak and Sikhism

When conservative proponents of two seemingly irreconcilable religious systems were struggling to gain ideological supremacy, one religious option was to declare both equally wrong. Alternatively, one could consciously adopt whatever seemed most worthwhile from both traditions. In medieval India this unitarian strategy sought a domain of spiritual peace outside the pervasive disagreement between orthodox Muslims and orthodox Hindus. The most influential of medieval Indian syncretists, Guru Nānak (1469–1539) ended up founding a new religion, Sikhism.

Born in a Hindu merchant family in the predominantly Muslim Punjab, Nānak worked as an accountant until, at age twenty-nine, he had a transformative experience. He fell into a bathing pool and disappeared from sight. Unable to find him, friends and family finally gave him up for dead. When Nānak returned to society three days later, his first utterance was, "There is no Hindu; there is no Muslim." He spent the remainder of his life traveling, teaching, singing, and gathering a band of followers. The name "Sikh" is derived from the Sanskrit word for pupil, *śiṣya,* indicating the relationship first adopted by Nānak's followers toward their guru.

In his teachings and songs, Nānak gently but firmly repudiated the external practices of the religions he saw around him—the oblations, sacrifices, ritual baths, image worshiping, austerities, and scriptures of Hindus and Muslims. For Nānak, the all-pervasive and incomprehensible God must be sought within oneself. The nirguṇa Absolute has no gender, no form, no immanent incarnations or manifestations. Despite God's infinitude and formlessness, Nānak proposed a very simple means of connecting with the divine. One must remember and repeat the divine Name. Nānak rigorously refused to specify what that Name was, though he sometimes called it "Creator of the Truth," equating truth with godliness.

During his own lifetime Nānak began to organize his followers into a community of the faithful. He set up informal procedures for congregational worship centering around collective recitation. Most important, he chose one of his disciples, Aṅgad, to follow him as preceptor and leader of the group, its guru. By choosing a single successor, Nānak established a precedent of group leadership that would last through ten gurus and nearly two hundred years. Nānak's followers collected anecdotes of his life that illustrated his central teachings and located his songs within biographical events, whether factual or imagined. Hagiography became an important genre of early Sikh literature, as it was among Sufis and devotionalists.

Nānak most often identified himself as a Hindu by virtue of birth, but as his followers consolidated their own practices they gradually distinguished themselves from both Hindu and Muslim communities. The fifth guru, Arjan, collected the writings of the first five leaders and other like-minded poet-saints into the *Ādi Granth*, the foundation text of the Sikh religion. In Sikh ceremonial this book came to occupy the central place on the altar, where Hindus would place an image. Guru Arjan rebuilt the temple at Amritsar and set himself up as lord of the Sikhs. With the Sikh community now a formidable social group, its Gurus began to play a more active role in north Indian political conflicts. They took sides in Mughal dynastic disputes and sometimes suffered the consequences of backing the losing side.

In the late seventeenth century, the time of the tenth and last guru, Gobind Singh, many Sikhs identified themselves still more visibly and decisively as a separate religious community. A determined opponent of Mughal rule, Gobind Singh instituted the Khālsā fellowship (the "army of the pure"), a group of Sikh initiates who accepted a code of conduct that included five insignia: uncut hair, a dagger or sword, a pair of military shorts, a comb, and a steel bangle. Gobind Singh required initiates to renounce all previous religious affiliations and to repudiate all gods, goddesses, and prophets other than the one Name recognized by the Sikhs.

Under Gobind Singh, the Sikh community solidified both its socio-religious identity and its military strength. By the beginning of the nineteenth century a Sikh kingdom led by Ranjīt Singh posed the last major independent opposition to British rule in South Asia. Though finally defeated in the late 1840s, Ranjīt Singh's kingdom left a memory of a separate Sikh state, a Khalistan or "land of the pure," that would be evoked at the time of Partition, when the departing

British divided India along religious lines into Muslim Pakistan and Hindu India, and again in the 1980s. Though they form a relatively small religious community of around 13 million in India, roughly 2 percent of the population, the Sikhs today constitute the most visible and in many ways one of the most prosperous communities in South Asia. Large numbers of Sikhs have emigrated to the U.K., Canada, and other parts of the Commonwealth.

The British Period

From 1757 on, British traders with the East India Company gradually increased their role in South Asia until, by the time British armies defeated the Punjabi kingdom of Ranjīt Singh in 1849, they ruled most of India. And so, from the late eighteenth century until 1947, Indians were dominated by a foreign power whose seat of authority was halfway around the world in London. These foreigners brought with them not only a new language and philosophy of rule and a different set of religious beliefs but also a worldview grounded in the secular, modernizing ideology of the Enlightenment. The encounter of existing religious formations of India with new forms of Christianity and with post-Enlightenment modes of knowledge within this colonial milieu ushered in another period of challenge, debate, and dynamism within South Asian religions.

Christianity was not completely new to the subcontinent. Syriac Christian trading communities had inhabited the Malabar coast of southern India from as early as the fourth century, and continued as autonomous groups of high status integrated within the largely Hindu society around them. The Portuguese, who established themselves on the western coast in the sixteenth century, carried out Christian missionary work with rather mixed results. Some lower-class communities realized the advantages that could result from forming religious bonds with a colonizing power and converted en masse, gradually developing their own indigenized forms of Christianity. The Portuguese were unable, however, to make much headway with the large majority of Indians they proselytized. Unlike Islamic Sufism, the Catholicism of the Counter-Reformation did not seem particularly compatible with the Indian religious environment.

British administrators took a decidedly ambivalent attitude toward missionary activity in their colonial territories, fearing it might "stir up the natives," whom they wished mainly to pacify. Under pressure from evangelicals in England, though, they eventually allowed Protestant missionaries to pursue their work on a limited scale. The missions did not achieve the conversions of great masses that they hoped for, but their incisive and often hyperbolic critiques of indigenous religion in India did have the important effect of inspiring some spirited defenses from the indigens. The Tamil Śaivite Āṟumuga Nāvalar, for instance, studied and worked for many years in a Methodist school before setting out on a personal mission to refortify the Śaiva Siddhānta religion and defend it against Christian attacks. Religious apologetics, defending one's own religion against outside attack, often has the effect of altering precisely that which one seeks to defend, giving it a definition or fixity it did not have previously, and this occurred repeatedly among Indian religions during the colonial encounter.

More challenging to the self-esteem of educated Indians were the Western scholars who for the first time began to study the religions of India as historical entities. The Western concern with delineating the various religions of the world was given tremendous impetus in India through the inspiration and organizational work of William Jones, an exemplary man of the Enlightenment. Jones was the first to publicize the linguistic connection of Sanskrit with classical Greek and Latin, enabling scholars to reconstruct the Indo-European family of languages and laying the basis for the field of historical philology, an important intellectual discipline of the nineteenth century. In Calcutta, where he served as a judge, Jones organized a small group of British civil servants who had become enamored with India's classical literature into the Asiatick Society, the first scholarly organization devoted to comprehending the religions, history, and literatures of India from a Western perspective. These officials were responsible for the earliest attempts to translate what they considered to be the most important Indian texts—all ancient and Sanskrit—into English, making them available to the West and engendering a kind of "Oriental Renaissance" among educated Europeans in the late eighteenth and early nineteenth centuries.

These classical Indiaphiles, also called "Orientalists," felt less affectionate toward the present-day Indians among whom they were living. They judged contemporary Indian religions to be debased from their lofty origins in the classical past. The Orientalists' high valuation of classical antiquity, coupled with a condescending dismissal of modern India, led to a long-standing prejudice in the Western study of India, whereby the oldest, elite Sanskrit works were valued above all others.

An alternative position, still less sympathetic to the Indians, soon took shape in England and was then exported to India. Inspired by Jeremy Bentham's utilitarian philosophy, James Mill, an official with the East India Company based in London, wrote his *History of British India* in the 1820s without needing to set foot in India. Mill's *History*, an immense and thorough indictment of the Indian peoples, tried to justify the need for British rule among a population supposedly unable to govern itself. Mill especially condemned Hinduism, blaming it for much of what was wrong with India. Hinduism is ritualistic, superstitious, irrational, and priest-ridden, Mill charged, at each step implicitly contrasting it with the deist version of Christianity that he believed to be the highest form of religion. For several decades the East India Company provided a copy of Mill's tome to new Company officials embarking for India, to sustain them in their sense of racial and cultural superiority while in the colony.

The attitudes the British held toward India had far-reaching effects on the Indians who came in contact with them. While some were satisfied to reiterate what they saw as the traditional, time-tested, and therefore superior forms of Indian religiosity, other Indians, more deeply affected by Western forms of knowledge and British criticisms of Hinduism, became highly circumspect and self-critical. From this spirit of cultural self-reproach came the widespread religious reformism of colonial India.

The prototype of the Hindu reformer was Rammohan Roy (1774–1833), a Bengali brahman who received a wide education in Persian and Arabic (languages of the Indo-Muslim court culture), Sanskrit (language of his own religious background), and then English (the emerging language of commerce and administration in colonial India). Taking advantage of new moneymaking opportunities as the British expanded their operations, Roy was able to retire young as a wealthy landlord to pursue his intellectual and religious interests. Roy valued British "progress" and Western modernity, and believed there was an urgent need to modernize Hinduism, which he had come to see as a stagnant tradition. To do this, he urged a reappraisal and selective redefinition of Hinduism. Of course, Indian religious thinkers had been doing exactly this for centuries, but never before with such a historicist self-awareness. In many cases Roy accepted British and Christian judgments as valid. He agreed, for example, that Hindu "polytheism" and "idolatry" were primitive and debased, and he joined in British efforts to outlaw and suppress satī, the practice of widow self-immolation. Concurring with the Orientalists' notion that current Hinduism had degenerated from a more glorious past, Roy recommended that Hindus return to earlier, purer beliefs and practices, and he sought to advance the ancient Upaniṣads with their idealism and monotheism as the foundation texts for a new Hinduism. In 1828 he founded the Brāhmo Samāj, a voluntary religious organization, to help put his ideas into effect.

Rammohan Roy was the first but not the only religious reformer of colonial India. Reform movements arose in every region of South Asia under British control, and while each reflected its own local culture and religious tradition, all shared the fundamentalist attitude of the Brāhmo Samāj in criticizing contemporary forms of religiosity and in seeking to return to some presumed state of purity located in the past. The Ārya Samāj, founded in 1875 by Svāmī Dayānanda Sarasvatī in western India, likewise advocated returning to the Vedic texts. From the standpoint of the Vedas, Dayānanda argued, one should oppose not only religious corruption but also what he saw as the evils of contemporary Indian society, such as caste, untouchability, and the subjugation of women. Many Hindu reform movements saw their task as reforming both Hinduism and Indian society.

Among the Sikhs, the Nirankāri movement called for a rejection of existing Sikh practices and a return to the "formless" worship of the founder, Guru Nānak. The Śvetāmbara Jains had their own reform movement led by the mendicant Vijay Ānandsūri, and even the Syriac Christians experienced millenarian revivalist movements during the nineteenth century.

The Muslim-controlled areas of northern India were the last to come under direct British control, and the Muslim elite, nostalgic for the lost glories of Mughal imperium, initially resisted British learning and remained aloof from British administration. Nevertheless, by the late nineteenth century colonial reformism took shape among Indian Muslims as well. Syed Ahmed Khan set out to purge contemporary Indian Islam of what he considered its extraneous and unnecessary practices and to return to a pure Islam, while at the same time he attempted to harmonize Islamic ideology with modern science. In the early twentieth century, Mohamed Ali envisioned the reestablishment of a pan-Islamic polity centered in Ottoman Turkey. By this time religious reformism had begun to take on a more overt anti-colonial dimension among Muslim and Hindu elites as well, and Ali's call for a Turkish Khilafat was simultaneously an appeal for ending British rule.

Perhaps the most renowned nineteenth-century Hindu reformer was Svāmī Vivekānanda. He was a young member of the Brāhmo Samāj when he first met Rāmakṛṣṇa, a charismatic ascetic and devotee of the goddess Kālī. Eventually Vivekānanda became Rāmakṛṣṇa's disciple, and sought to integrate within a single religious outlook the experiential devotionalism of Rāmakṛṣṇa, the social agenda of the Brāhmo Samāj, and the nondualist philosophy of Śaṅkara and the Advaita Vedānta. As a spokesman for Hinduism in 1893 at the World's Parliament of Religions in Chicago, he created a sensation. Building on this success, he toured the United States for three years, attracted many Western followers, and set up the Vedanta Society. Returning to India, Vivekānanda founded the Ramakrishna Mission, an organization dedicated to education and social service much like Christian missions in India. Vivekānanda is still celebrated as a teacher of "practical Vedānta," which scholars sometimes label "neo-Vedānta," a significant version of modern Hindu ideology. He was also the prototype of a new breed of cosmopolitan Hindu gurus who would bring their teachings to Western audiences.

As the movement for Indian independence took shape in the late nineteenth and early twentieth centuries, activists drew upon and reworked elements from the Hindu tradition for explicitly political purposes. The Maharashtrian leader B. G. Tilak, for example, instituted a public festival to the elephant-headed god Gaṇeśa, celebrating Hindu popular culture as a means of regaining "self-rule," and not incidentally attracting large crowds for his political speeches. In Bengal the ferocious goddess Kālī lent her fierce energy to the independence struggle, and the new goddess Bhārat Māta ("Mother India") appeared, iconographically modeled on Lakṣmī, as a national focus for devotion and sacrifice. Literary and political figures alike rewrote and reinterpreted old texts like the *Bhagavadgītā* and the *Rāmāyaṇa*, making them speak to the colonial situation. Although reintroducing Hindu deities and rituals to make political statements was nothing new in India, and it certainly helped extend the politics of anticolonialism beyond the educated urban elite, in the colonial setting it also had the unfortunate effect of identifying the independence movement as a largely Hindu enterprise, alienating Muslims and other non-Hindu communities.

Throughout the colonial period, the British viewed India as a society made up of distinct, identifiable religious communities: Hindus, Muslims, Sikhs, Jains, "tribals," and so on. British administrators soon learned the advantages of "divide and rule," and often promoted religious divisions as a conscious strategy to weaken those who might oppose them. Even in seemingly nonpolitical administrative activities like census taking, the British use of unequivocal categories to classify a religious reality that was complex and mingled promoted a clarification and hardening of religious distinctions.

Indians themselves increasingly employed the same classifications, and many of the reform movements, with their weekly meetings, membership lists, and search for the essence of their traditions, also helped define and solidify community boundaries. By the early decades of the twentieth century, religious conflict increased in Indian society. The outcome of this "communalization" was that, when the English finally quit India in 1947, they felt it necessary to divide their colony along religious lines into two nation-states, Islamic Pakistan and Hindu India. This tragic decision led to terrible violence and suffering among Muslims, Hindus, and Sikhs alike during the Partition, and its consequences are still felt powerfully in the politics of modern South Asia.

Religions of Home and Village

One important dimension of Indian religions that is too often lost sight of in historical summaries like this one is the religion of the domestic sphere. Historians have frequently overlooked domestic religious traditions because the activities of the household are generally transmitted orally, from woman to woman over the generations, and do not receive the textual documentation accorded more public, male-dominated domains of religion. Only with the work of recent anthropologists and folklorists have these traditions begun to receive the attention they deserve. Several readings in this volume exemplify this new scholarly focus on the home as a locus of religiosity.

Transmitted orally, domestic religious traditions show marked local and regional diversity, but certain themes are common. Domestic forms of Indian religions directly address the concerns of women, but not only those of women. Successful marriage, healthy offspring, domestic accord, and prosperity of the home are values shared by all members of the household. Domestic rites seek to ward off the various calamities—disease, family dissension, poverty, death—that threaten the well-being of the family and lineage. Though one finds little interest here in the attainment of mokṣa that looms so large in other Indian religious traditions, these domestic concerns certainly are not trivial or parochial. Other forms of divine salvation, such as marriage or motherhood to a god, are recognized, and the world of the kitchen may even be identified with the cosmos itself, as in the Tamil poem addressed to the child-goddess Mīnāṭci, "Sway back and forth."

Female divinities figure strongly in domestic religion. Some are decidedly benign, like Mother Ten and the basil-shrub goddess Tulsī, worshiped for their capacities to bring sustenance and health. But there are other goddesses of a more uneven temperament, such as Mother Ten's opposite number, "Bad Ten," or the Bengali Śītalā, goddess of smallpox. Quick to take offense, Śītalā requires careful mollifying to insure that her wrath does not come down on one's own family. In

Rajasthan, women sing devotional songs also to satīs, exemplary women who overcame the inauspiciousness of their husbands' deaths through extraordinary adherence to purity, and who have become protector spirits of the lineage.

Although domestic religions often take a different perspective from the public traditions, they nevertheless share with them a single language of Indian religious discourse. The domestic goddess Tulsī, for instance, is linked with Kṛṣṇa, and her stories explore the jealous rivalry that may arise among co-wives attached to this famously promiscuous male god. The Rajasthani regional goddess Mother Ten, we find, is identified as Lakṣmī, the pan-Indian Sanskritic goddess of good fortune. Likewise, when Muslim women worship at moments of domestic crisis, they focus on the miraculous birth of Muḥammad, connecting their concerns about procreation and healing with the most public figure of the Islamic tradition. Domestic ceremonies, too, draw upon the common Indian repertoire of ascetic and ritual practices, such as fasting, bathing, purification rites, pūjā, and the maintenance of vows (*vrata*) to bring about the desired ends.

An earlier generation of anthropologists and Indianists spoke of the ongoing relationships between public, literary, pan-Indian traditions and localized, oral traditions in terms of the "great" and "little" traditions, and those terms may still be useful provided one observes some precautions. One should not imagine a single normative "great tradition," and one should not use the distinction to verify a hierarchical separation between two insular domains, such that the pan-Indian enjoys an assumed dominance over the local. Likewise, the little traditions of village and household are not unchanging. Although some of the concerns and aims of these traditions are grounded in the relatively constant struggles of rural and village populations of India, the stories, rituals, and deities may change.

In ongoing two-way cultural traffic, elements of local traditions may be selectively drawn into public, literate traditions, while other elements from those pan-Indian cultural traditions may be selectively drawn upon to enhance or reformulate religious practices at the level of village or household. We may take the Mother Ten story of the amazing cow with its magical dung as an illustration of one direction in this traffic. When the remarkable cow is brought to the royal court, the "little tradition" figure of Mother Ten receives the public recognition that incorporates her into a regional "great tradition." This kind of dynamic interchange has been going on in India for centuries.

The Contemporary Scene

A modern-day Vidagdha might ask, "What are Indian religions like now?"

In a cultural area as large and diverse as India, with its 800 million people, eighteen official languages, and strong regional traditions, it is never easy to get a fix on contemporary religion. Instead, one finds oneself returning to Yajñavālkya's Upaniṣadic perspective, from which a single question requires multiple answers.

Yes, but what do religions in India look like now?

In a trip around contemporary India, a religious sightseer will certainly encounter many characters made familiar by a study of the history of Indian religions, but they are often dressed in new clothes. One may see Buddhist monks chanting Buddha's teachings at the site of his enlightenment in Bodh Gaya, but then notice that they are political refugees dressed in the vermillion robes of Tibetan Buddhism. One will find ash-smeared yogis in their Himalayan ashrams discoursing in English to audiences of young Germans, Japanese, and Australians. In south Indian temples one can follow priests and devotees as they worship Viṣṇu and Śiva according to liturgical models set down in early medieval guidebooks, and then pause outside to purchase a brightly colored lithographic reproduction of the temple deity or to arrange an international pūjā by airmail. One may encounter street performances retelling the epic stories of Rāma, Kṛṣṇa, and the Pāṇḍavas, interspersed with Hindi film songs. Those epic narratives have also been reanimated for a nationwide television audience, the most widely followed television series ever in India. The devotional songs of Māṇikkavācakar and Tukārām are available on cassette and compact disk, and during festival seasons one cannot avoid them as they blare from loudspeakers outside seemingly every tea and coffee stall. One will read in the newspapers of "Hindutva" (Hinduness) and a new form of conservative political Hinduism, centering on a dispute over the birthplace of Rāma in Ayodhya and a mosque built by the Islamic Mughal conqueror Bābar, allegedly atop the ruins of the medieval Hindu temple.

Though historically grounded, Indian religions remain alive to their modernity—to their new political settings, the new international audiences, and the new possibilities of technology in the modern world. And in turn they are changed by them, sometimes subtly and sometimes profoundly.

Yes, but how can we best characterize the religions of India?

The collectivity of Indian voices will bring us closer to its complex reality, no doubt. It offers a sampling of perspectives rather than any authoritative collection or canon, and in this way approximates more closely the living texture of Indian religious thought and practice. It is important when attending to these voices, however, not to hear them as isolated, self-standing statements. One should place them in conversation with one another, and listen in on their discussions of mutual religious concerns. At times they share insights while at others they disagree over fundamental premises.

If we have seen debate as a central feature in the history of Indian religions, it would be wrong to imagine that somehow those controversies have ended. Indeed, over the past decade debates about the nature and role of religion in contemporary Indian society have taken on a renewed urgency. How does one define Hinduism? Or for that matter, Islam? Sikhism? Who gets to do the defining? Should Hinduism be defined at all? What are the key texts and narratives of the Indian tradition? How relevant are the normative works of the past—Vedas, epics, Dharmaśāstras, Qur'ān, *Ādi Granth*, and the like—to present-day concerns? How should Hindus relate themselves to other religious communities in India? How clear are the boundaries between them? What are the proper roles for religious groups and institutions in the modern secular state of India? Should Indians understand their national identity in terms of a dominant Hindu heritage, or view Hinduism as one among many threads in the cultural fabric of India? And looking beyond national borders, how may Hinduism, Islam, Sikhism, and Jainism best be reformulated to meet the new social settings and needs of Indian immigrants in the United States, United Kingdom, and around the world?

These are serious discussions not likely to end any time soon. They make the study of the religions of India, that land of ancient sages and age-old scriptures, a matter of great contempory significance.

Notes

1. I would like to thank all those who offered helpful suggestions and encouragement on drafts of this essay: Pravin Bhatt, Carl Ernst, Phyllis Granoff, Valerie Hansen, Lindsey Harlan, Norvin Hein, Donald Lopez, Rita McCleary, Sandhya Purohit, Paula Richman, Phil Wagoner, and Irene Winter.

2. U. N. Ghoshal, *A History of Indian Political Ideas* (London: Oxford University Press, 1959), p. 157.

—1—

Bengali Songs to Kālī

Rachel Fell McDermott

Kālī, the "Black Goddess," is a pan-Indian deity, known throughout the subcontinent. But it is in the northeastern regions of the country, Bengal in particular, that she is the center of an especially rich devotional (*bhakti*) tradition. Beginning in the mid-eighteenth century in Bengal with a poet named Rāmprasād Sen (c. 1718–1775), the bloodthirsty Kālī, known in Sanskrit literature since the time of the *Mahābhārata* as a battle heroine and champion of tribal and peripheral peoples, was brought within the sphere of bhakti. The fifteenth- to eighteenth-century Bengali maṅgala-kāvyas, lengthy poems glorifying particular gods and goddesses, had to some extent prepared the ground for the later bhakti poetry: the deities of the maṅgala-kāvyas were objects of propitiation, who involved themselves—often as protectors or saviors—in the lives of their worshipers, in order to spread their own cults. But it was not until the poetry of Rāmprasād Sen that Kālī's character gained a well-developed compassionate and maternal side, which made her a fitting receptacle for the heart's devotion.

Rāmprasād wrote over three hundred poems to Kālī, initiating a literary genre that has been called *śākta padāvalī*—a collection of poems to the goddess in one of her various forms. Though many questions still perplex the historian—such as, for instance, whether Rāmprasād really was the first to conceive of and write about Kālī—it is nevertheless taken for granted that his poems set the tone for Kālī's subsequent depiction and adoration in Bengal. By the beginning of the twentieth century, eighty to ninety other bhakti poets had followed suit, writing songs to and about Kālī. Even today the tradition carries on: new poets are still composing, and their work, as well as that of the more famous Rāmprasād and his followers, is heard on the radio, on cassettes, and in concerts. The greatest indicator, perhaps, of the influence of the devotional attitude towards Kālī, begun most prominently with Rāmprasād Sen, is that the modern Kālī is regarded by the majority of Bengalis today as Mother, first and foremost; her older, harsher characteristics have partially receded.

In Bengali scholarly works on the śākta padāvalī tradition, the name that almost always follows Rāmprasād's in importance is that of Kamalākānta Bhaṭṭācārya (c. 1769–1820). As might be expected of someone coming immediately after a famed innovator, many of Kamalākānta's poems incorporate themes and images used first by Rāmprasād. However, Kamalākānta was not merely an imitator; in a few areas his poetry is truly distinctive.

Kamalākānta lived his whole life in the district of Barddhamān, in south-central Bengal. He was of a poor, brahman background, with a traditional Sanskrit education. The only date connected with his life that is known for certain is 1809, the year in which Tejascānd, the "king" (actually, a rich *zamīndār*, landlord) of the Barddhamān lineage, discovered Kamalākānta in a nearby town and had him brought to Barddhamān city as court pandit, poet, and preceptor for Tejascānd's unruly son. Kamalākānta died in about 1820. It was not until 1857, however, that anyone thought to try to preserve his poems, and luckily it was still not too late. Wishing to memorialize the religious heritage of his royal line, King Māhtābcānd of Barddhamān ascertained that the wife of Kamalākānta's deceased brother still had in her possession four old, dilapidated poetry notebooks, in Kamalākānta's own hand. These he collected, edited, and published, ensuring that the 269 poems now attributed to Kamalākānta are fairly genuine reproductions of the poet's written words. For nearly seventy years thereafter, people knew of Kamalākānta only through this poetic corpus and through numerous legends that began to spread his fame.

The most famous of these legends depicts Kamalākānta as a fearless worshiper of Kālī, whose devotion is so powerful that it can even melt the most hardened hearts. In the story, Kamalākānta is traveling alone at night through a wilderness area near a village named Oṛ, when he is attacked by bandits who plan to murder him. Kamalākānta begs permission to sing one last song to Kālī before his death; upon hearing it, his captors are so overcome with remorse that they fall at his feet and become his disciples. The song traditionally associated with this story is among his most famous, and is included here as poem 20.

In 1925, a truly startling discovery was made. The librarian of a prestigious Calcutta library uncovered, in the home of the great-great-grandson of one of Kamalākānta's disciples, the manuscript of a tantric manual composed by Kamalākānta—which almost no one had previously known existed. He had it published, adding another dimension to the historical portrait of the poet. The manual, called *Sādhaka Rañjana* ("That Which Pleases the Religious Aspirant"), is written with obvious attention to meter and rhyme, unlike some of Kamalākānta's more free-flowing verses. In content, however, its style and imagery complement that of his Śakta poetry.

Like many religious poets, philosophers, and devotees throughout Indian history, Kamalākānta did not limit himself in his devotion to any one deity. Though he seems to have been particularly attracted to Kālī, 31 of his 269 poems are addressed to the Goddess in her form as Umā, the beneficent and beautiful spouse of Śiva, 24 are directed to Kṛṣṇa, and two are about Śiva. But since Kamalākānta is primarily remembered as a devotee of Kālī, the majority of the poems given below are drawn from the 212 he wrote about her. These fall into several categories: those depicting her on the cremation grounds; poems with tantric imagery and allusions; petitions to Kālī; rebukes; expressions of fulfillment; self-exhortations; and dismal portrayals of the present world. Six poems about Umā have also been included, as this is another area in which Kamalākānta developed themes beyond those undertaken by Rāmprasād.

A word about the musical aspect of these poems is necessary. Although they can stand alone as literary compositions, they are meant to be sung. Rāmprasād apparently created a single melody to fit his poems, and almost all of his over three hundred compositions can be sung to it. Kamalākānta's poems, however, were sung to individual melodies. Unfortunately, though we possess tunes traditionally associated with ten or so of Kamalākānta's most famous poems, the original melodies that he used are now lost. A modern musician trained in the performance style can approximate the way such poems might have sounded in the poet's day, through improvising a melody in the given key and rhythmic pattern. This is the way the poems are sung and heard today.

The first six poems translated below are representative of a class of poems composed for a Bengali religious festival that occurs once a year in the autumn: Durgā Pūjā. This is a ten-day festival centering on the Goddess in her form as Durgā, or Umā, the wife of Śiva, and is one of the biggest celebrations of the year. Its popularity derives from three factors, each of which is mirrored in the poetry.

First, Durgā Pūjā, perhaps in its most ancient layer, is a harvest festival of grains, and its arrival signifies the return of cool weather and the bounty of the earth. In the formal ritual worship of the pūjā, in addition to anthropomorphic images, the Goddess is depicted aniconically by a trussed-up bundle of nine plants, wrapped in a sari. The poetry reflects this emphasis on nature: Umā is frequently compared to an autumn lotus (poem 5), and her face, like the moon, cools with its soft light (poems 4 and 6). Second, this festival celebrates the victory of Durgā over the buffalo demon, Mahiṣa. Thousands of temporary shrines are erected in cities and villages all over Bengal; inside, images of Durgā slaying Mahiṣa, made from straw, clay, paint, and decorations, are worshiped ritually for several days, until the tenth day, when they are immersed in the river. For weeks before the pūjā, Durgā's face appears in advertisements, magazines, and store fronts, announcing the coming holiday. Schools close for long pūjā vacations, and families gather together, where possible.

This brings us to the third reason for the festival's popularity: the sense of longing for the return of the Goddess, conceived as a beloved daughter in Bengali religious imaginations. Unlike Kālī, whose many temples are a fixed aspect of Bengali life, Umā, or Durgā, has practically no permanent temples or cult in Bengal. Just like a real Bengali daughter who lives far away from her parents at the house of her in-laws, Umā comes only once a year to visit for a few brief days. On the first day of the festival, she sets out from her husband's home on Mount Kailāsa; from then until the sixth evening, when she finally arrives and the images of Durgā are installed in the temporary shrines, groups of musicians sing compositions known as āgamanī poems—poems in anticipation of Umā's coming. Near the end of the holiday, on the ninth evening and tenth day, before the images are submerged in the river, they turn instead to vijayā poems, which mourn her imminent departure. The musical keys for both types of song are somber and lugubrious, adding poignancy to the expectations.

Āgamanī and vijayā poems do not merely express longing and the pain of separation; they also tell a story, through which one can see Bengali attitudes towards the Goddess and Śiva, as well as Bengali experiences of the parent-daughter relationship. The cast of characters includes Umā, also called Gaurī, the "Fair One," and Bhavānī, the "Wife of Bhava," or Śiva, who is the daughter of Menakā and the Himālaya Mountain, her mother and father, respectively. The fact that Umā's father is actually a stationary mountain explains his wife's frustration at his inactivity (poem 1): he cannot move or feel, being a stone. Himālaya and Menakā are the rulers of the mountain city, Giripur, where all the inhabitants share their sorrows and joys (poem 4).

In a turn of events not uncommon for traditional Bengali households of Kamalākānta's era, the beloved daughter has been married off through the intervention of an unscrupulous rumor monger and matchmaker—here called Nārada (poem 1). Forced through their poverty or lack of connections to yield their daughter to a bridegroom they feel to be totally unsatisfactory, the parents worry constantly over her fate. In Umā's case, she has been married to Śiva, an elderly good-for-nothing, a drug-addicted, naked mendicant, who wanders around the cremation grounds with live snakes hanging on his neck, a trident in his hand, and matted hair (poems 1 and 2). To make matters worse, he is a Kulin, a brahman who takes more than one wife; Umā has to contend with a co-wife, Gaṅgā (the Ganges River). This "Celestial River," Suradhunī, dwells on Śiva's head, where she landed when she fell from heaven (poem 5).

Once a year, in autumn, Umā begs to go home to see her parents, particularly her mother, who is distraught with anxiety over her. Menakā, being a traditional Bengali woman, cannot travel alone, so she can do nothing except to beg her husband to go fetch Umā home, which he is reluctant to do for fear of Śiva's reaction. Eventually, the reunion is engineered, and for the three days that Umā spends at home, she tries to console her mother about her life with Śiva, with dubious results (poem 5). Too soon, she has to return to Mount Kailāsa, and Menakā weeps (poem 6). The visit—and Durgā Pūjā—are over.

Underlying these poems is an intentional ambiguity concerning Umā and Śiva. Who are they, really? Umā is the helpless daughter and the suffering daughter-in-law, but she is also the Mother of the World, with the ability to save her husband and her devotees. Likewise, Śiva may be the disastrous son-in-law, but at the same time he is also the Great Lord. Kamalākānta plays with these uncertain identities, maintaining Umā's status as the goddess, while continuing to humanize her. In general, such poems today in Bengal are to be found in a few cassette tapes and printed anthologies more than they are in popular devotional practice. More than the Kālī-centered poems, they are falling into disuse and neglect, particularly in cities. This can partially be accounted for by changing life styles and the increased commercialization of Durgā Pūjā itself: people live more apart from one another than they used to, and have neither the time nor the occasion to gather to listen to musicians singing of Umā's coming.

Poems addressed to or about Kālī, in contrast, are much more popular. Though especially prominent on the radio and in cassette tape stores at the time of the one-day Kālī Pūjā festival (which falls approximately three weeks after Durgā Pūjā), Śyāmā saṅgīt, or songs to Śyāmā, the "Black Goddess" Kālī, are listened to by Kālī devotees all year round. The Kālī of these poems, like her counterpart Umā, is humanized and softened. Although her gruesome iconographic features and fearsome actions are not changed, the poets tone them down. Kamalākānta, for instance, does not hesitate to paint Kālī in the traditional way: she is black and naked, with all manner of horrific ornaments, tangled hair, a sword in her hand, and her tongue lolling out. She stands on Śiva's torso, in the midst of the cremation grounds. The poet does not stop at mere description, however, and by what he adds he shows his discomfort with such a starkly portrayed goddess. He either scolds her for her indecency (poems 7 and 8), puts it in context by claiming that this naked Kālī is only one of her several manifestations (poems 9 and 10), manages to look past the dreadful attributes (poem 11), denies that such characteristics are real (poem 12), or beautifies the image, so that it is no longer frightening (poems 7 and 12). This last approach, in particular, is important: this genre is full of images and phrases that sweeten the overall picture of the goddess.

But Kālī is not only the mad dancer on top of Śiva's inert body. She is also a cosmic figure—Brahmamayī, or the "Embodiment of Brahman" (poems 10, 13, and 18). As Tripurā, the possessor of triadic attributes, she both assumes the qualities of creation and transcends them (poems 8 and 10). She is matter, spirit, and emptiness (poem 12). Everything is full of her and identified with her—even the other gods, such as Kṛṣṇa (poem 9) and Brahmā (poem 17).

Aside from her mythological and cosmic sides, Kamalākānta's Kālī has two other faces, or ways of appearing to the poet. One is her role as deluder and bewitcher: through her illusory power, she can take many forms, misleading and playing with her devotees. Sometimes, he says, even she gets caught in her own bonds (poem 9). The second, and in terms of numbers of poems written on this subject, the most prominent of Kamalākānta's portrayals of Kālī, is that of a savior. She is Tārā, the one who literally "Carries one Across" the ocean of the world to the other side (poems 10, 15, 21, and 22), and she is Cintāmaṇi, the wish-fulfilling gem that turns everything to gold at its touch (poem 19). Kālī, the supremely compassionate Mother, will rescue her worshipers in whatever way possible. This ubiquitous tendency to call Kālī, in her various manifestations, a mother, is what really gives this śākta padāvalī tradition its uniqueness.

One way of looking at the distinctive goddess-centered emphasis of this poetry is to watch what the Śakta poets, and Kamalākānta in particular, do to the characterization of Śiva, also called Hara, the "Destroyer," and Śaṅkara, the "Beneficent." According to the mainstream Hindu understanding, Śiva is the young, virile hero of the gods, whose acts of self-sacrifice such as drinking the poison churned from the ocean of milk or lying beneath Kālī to stop her world-crushing dance illustrate his personal victories over such perceived dangers. Kamalākānta's Śiva is different. In these poems, he is a disreputable old man, able to help the gods with various feats such as drinking the poison only because Umā gives him the necessary strength (poem 2). In the Kālī poems, the goddess is not Śiva's dutiful and subordinate wife, as she is in the traditional story of Satī (poem 8); Kālī is the supreme spiritual force in the universe, and it is Śiva who falls at her feet in the hopes of gaining her blessing (poems 8 and 11). He gazes up at her, bewitched; thus he is the model, par excellence, of a servant and devotee. Kamalākānta refers to him throughout his poems as his own rival; he wishes that he were lying beneath Kālī with her feet on his chest (poem 20).

Like Rāmprasād and generations of Vaiṣṇava poets before him, Kamalākānta always inserted his name in the last stanza of each poem. It is from these pithy concluding remarks, as well as from his self-descriptions in each poem, that one can glimpse at the range of attitudes and emotions he experienced in his relationship to Umā and Kālī.

In general, the point of these stanzas is to show Kamalākānta's closeness to the goddess, his involvement with her, and his desire to participate even more deeply in her activities. The concluding stanzas either continue the main speaker's thought, showing how much Kamalākānta identifies with the sentiments expressed (poems 1, 4, and 5), or depict Kamalākānta advising a character (poem 6), or actually insert the poet into the story line as an attendant (poems 2 and 3). In the Kālī poems, Kamalākānta fluctuates between emotional extremes. At times he focuses on his spiritual condition, and is dejected. The world is like an ocean which must be crossed (poem 15), or like a battleground in which the six passions (lust, anger, greed, sloth, pride, and envy) constantly assail him (poems 21 and 23). People desert him, taunt him, and lead him to fear that Kālī has forgotten him. At other times he addresses his mind, exhorting himself to the religious path. As in most Indian bhakti poetry, there is a certain anti-ritualistic tone in such compositions. Kamalākānta recommends against relying on external rituals—whether traditional (poem 18) or tantric (poem 23)—going on pilgrimage (poem 19), or using a rosary (poem 20); what is necessary is true devotion, based in the heart. The poems in which Kamalākānta addresses Kālī directly illustrate the intimacy between devotee and deity: Kamalākānta treats Kālī with a wide spectrum of human feelings. He petitions her for mercy (poem 16), rebukes her for her scandalous behavior (poems 13, 14, and 22), evinces astonishment at her divine nature (poems 11 and 12), and revels in the bliss of spiritual attainment (poems 18 and 23). In the tradition of Indian bhakti poets before him, Kamalākānta's literary creations both reflected, and inspired, his inner devotional life.

Historians of Bengali literature inevitably stress the beauty and significance of these Śākta poems on Kālī. Nevertheless, fieldwork in modern Bengal indicates that they are not very popular, and may in fact be on the decline in devotional contexts. The overwhelming popularity of Hindu film music, as well as the musical and philosophical difficulty of some of the Śākta songs, may account for this phenomenon. Another possible reason for their gradual decrease in public awareness may lie in their portrayal of Kālī. Could it be that the content of the poems no longer matches devotees' experience?

Rāmprasād and Kamalākānta berate Kālī for her appearance and her behavior—both of which are unseemly. But today's Kālī images are generally clothed, with beautiful hair and a smiling face; they are not nude, with tousled hair, and the Mother is not usually understood as sending suffering or misfortune. In other words, perhaps the modern Kālī has moved away, through the influence of the very bhakti whose introduction in the mid-eighteenth century gave Rāmprasād's and Kamalākānta's poetry such relevance and bite, towards a persona less characterized by ambiguity. Yet, how do we know that the Bengalis who heard these poets' compositions in the eighteenth and nineteenth centuries found them completely relevant? Do the literary creations of geniuses, whether religious or not, always mirror social attitudes and experiences? How much of a poet's language reflects personal eccentricity or literary convention? Perhaps these poems have never been very popular, because only a few extraordinary devotees have been willing or able to face the polarities in their once bloodthirsty goddess, now somewhat softened through bhakti. This is a problem of interpretation, and arises whenever one has little access to the historical context in which a text was written. In the case of the poems of Rāmprasād and Kamalākānta, it means that one has to be very cautious in assessing the genre's influence and internal development. What seems, in some instances, to be a strange misfit between the sentiments expressed by the poets and the opinions of today's goddess worshipers may provide clues to changes in Śākta devotionalism. Or it may simply indicate a continuity in reaction: Kālī's poets are saints because they dared express something rarely understood, then or now.

All of the translated lyrics below except one can be found in Kamalākānta Bhaṭṭācārya, *Śyāmā Saṅgīt*, collected by Nabīncandra Bandyopādhyāya (Calcutta: Barddhamān Mahārājādhirāj Māhtābcānd Bāhādur, 1857; reprint Barddhamān Mahārājādhirāj Bijaycānd Bāhādur, 1925). The one poem not in the volume sponsored by the Barddhamān king in 1857 is listed as an "unpublished" poem, and is found in the appendix to Atulcandra Mukhopādhyāya, *Sādhaka Kamalākānta* (Dhaka: Ripon Library, 1925).

POEMS TO UMĀ

1 *Yāo, Giribara he*

Go, my Lord of the Mountain,
Bring our daughter home.
After giving Gaurī away to the Naked One,

How can you sit at home
So unconcerned?
What a hard heart you have!
You know the behavior of our son-in-law—
Always acting like a lunatic,
Wearing a tiger's skin,
With matted locks on his head.
He not only roams the cremation ground himself,
But takes her, too!
Such is Umā's fate.
I heard Nārada say
He smears his body with funeral pyre ash.
The way he dresses is monstrous:
The garland around his neck is made of snakes!
And who would believe me—
He prefers poison to honey!
Tell me, what kind of a choice is that?

Kamalākānta says:
Listen, Jewel of the Mountains.
Śiva's behavior is incomprehensible.
If you can,
Fall at his feet and get permission to bring Umā home.
Then never send her back again.

Śyāmā Saṅgīt 215

2 *Bāre bāre kaho Rāṇi*

You ask me, Queen, time after time
To go get Gaurī.
But you know very well
The nature of our son-in-law.
Even a snake can survive for a while
Without its head-jewel.
But to the Trident Bearer
Umā is more than that.
If he doesn't see her even for a moment,
He dies.
He keeps her in his heart.
Why would he willingly send her to us?

Once
To win respect for the gods
Śiva drank a terrible poison.

But the pain was unbearable.
Only the shadows from Umā's limbs
Could cool Śaṅkara's burning body.
Since then
Śiva has not parted from his wife.

You're just a simple woman
You don't know how to proceed.
I will go,
But I won't say anything to the Naked Lord.
Ask Kamalākānta: see if he will go with me.
After all, she's his mother;
He may manage to bring her somehow.

Śyāmā Saṅgīt 222

3 *Ohe Hara Gaṅgādhara*

Hey, Hara, Gaṅgā-Holder,
Promise me I can go to my father's place.

What are you brooding about?
The worlds are contained in your fingernail—
But no one would know it,
Looking at your face.

My father, the Lord of the Mountain,
Has arrived to visit you
And to take me away.
It's been so many days since I went home
And saw my mother face to face.
Ceaselessly, night and day,
How she weeps for me!
Like a thirsty cātakī bird, the queen stares
At the road that will bring me home.
Can't I make you understand
My mental agony
At not seeing her face?
How can I go without your consent?

My husband, don't crack jokes
Just satisfy my desire.
Hara, let me say good-bye,
Your mind at ease.
And give me Kamalākānta as an attendant.

I assure you
I'll be back in three days.

Śyāmā Saṅgīt 225

4 *Āmār Umā elo*

"My Umā has come!" So saying,
The queen runs, her hair disheveled.

City women dash out in groups
To see Gaurī.
Some carry pitchers at the waist,
Others hold babies to their breast,
Their hair half-braided and half-curled.
They call to each other,
"Come on! Come on! Come on!
Run quickly!
Let's go see the Daughter of the Mountain!"
Rushing outside the city,
Their bodies thrill with passionate anticipation.
As soon as they glimpse that moon-face,
They kiss her lips
Hastily.

Then the Woman of the Mountain
Takes Gaurī on her lap,
Her body floating
In the bliss of love.
While instruments play sweetly,
Heavenly musicians decorate themselves,
Dancing gleefully
With the women of the mountain city.

Today Kamalākānta sees those two red feet,
And is utterly engrossed.

Śyāmā Saṅgīt 232

5 *Śarat-kamal-mukhe*

From her autumn-lotus mouth
She babbles half-formed words.
Sitting on her mother's lap,

A slight smile on her blessed face,
Bhavānī speaks of the comforts of Bhava's home.

"Mother, who says Hara is poor?
His house is built of jewels
More lustrous than hundreds of suns and moons!
Since our wedding,
Who has felt darkness?
Who knows when it's day or night?

"You hear that I'm afraid of my co-wife?
Suradhunī loves me more than you do!
From her perch in Śiva's matted hair
She sees how he holds me
In his heart.
Who else is so lucky to have such a co-wife?"

Kamalākānta says:
Listen, Queen of the Mountain.
Mount Kailāsa is the summit of the worlds.
If you ever saw it,
You wouldn't want to leave.
Forgetting everything,
You'd stay at Bhava's place,
Mountain Woman.

Śyāmā Saṅgīt 236

6 *Phire cāo go Umā*

Turn back, Umā,
And let me see your moon-face!
You are killing your unfortunate mother:
Where are you going?

Today my jeweled palace has become dark.
What will remain in my body
But a life of ashes?

Umā, stay here!
Just for once, stay, Mother!
Cool my burning body
Even for a moment.
My eyes are fixed on the road you travel.
How long must I wait
Until you come home again?

Fulfil Kamalākānta's desire,
Moon-faced One:
Call your mother,
And make her understand.

Śyāmā Saṅgīt 245

POEMS TO KĀLĪ

7 *Ke re pāgalīr beśe*

Who is this,
Dressed like a crazy woman,
Robed with the sky?
Whom does she belong to?
She has let down her hair,
Thrown off her clothes,
Strung human hands around her waist,
And taken a sword in her hand.
Her face sparkles
From the reflection of her teeth,
And her tongue lolls out.
The smile on that moon-face drips
Heaps and heaps of nectar.

Mother, are you going to rescue Kamalākānta
In *this* outfit?

Śyāmā Saṅgīt 122

8 *Kāli ki tor sakali bhrānta*

Kālī, is everything you do
Misleading?

Look, your beloved has thrown himself
Under your feet?
Mother, I beg you
With folded hands:
Don't dance on top of Śiva!
I know how Tripura's Enemy feels.
Beautiful Tripurā, kind woman,
Just this once, stop.
You're the murderer of your own husband;
You're killing your Lord!

The King of Living Beings
Is almost dead!

Once
Hearing people criticize Śiva
You got angry
And left your body
For love.
Mother! The man you're standing on
Is the same Three-Eyed one!
Calm down, and look at him;
It's the Naked Lord!

This is what Kamalākānta wants to understand:
You know everything,
So why all these deceptions?
This time, I think,
You've gone too far,
You whose seat is a corpse.

Śyāmā Saṅgīt 190

9 *Jāno nā re man*

You don't realize this, mind,
But Kālī, the Prime Cause,
Is not only female.
Sometimes
Taking the color of a cloud,
She transforms herself,
And emerges
Male.

She who terrifies demons
With her disheveled hair and brandished sword
Occasionally visits Vraja,
Captivating the cowherd women's hearts
With the sound of his flute.

Then again
Assuming the three qualities,
She creates, preserves, and destroys.
Thus bound in the illusion of her own making,
She endures, and nurses,
The pains of the world.

Whatever form you believe her to have,
She'll take that
And dwell in your mind.
In Kamalākānta's case,
She appears at the center of a lotus
In a lake,
His heart.

Śyāmā Saṅgīt 146

10 *Mā, kakhan ki raṅge thāko*

Mother,
You are always finding ways to amuse yourself.

Śyāmā, you stream of nectar,
Through your deluding power
You forge a horrible face
And adorn yourself with a necklace
Of human skulls.
The earth quakes under your leaps and bounds.
You are frightful
With that sword in your hand.
At other times
You take a flirtatious pose,
And then even the God of Love is outdone, Mother!

Your form is inconceivable and undecaying.
Nārāyaṇī, Tripurā, Tārā—
You are beyond the three qualities
And yet composed of them.
You are terrifying,
You are death,
You are a beautiful woman.

Thus assuming various forms,
You fulfil the wishes of your worshipers.
Sometimes you even dance,
Brahman, Eternal One,
In the lotus heart of Kamalākānta.

Śyāmā Saṅgīt 150

11 *Tumi kār gharer meye*

Kālī, what family are you from?
You're absorbed in your own fun and games.

Who really understands your incomparable beauty?
If I look at you
I can no longer distinguish between day and night.
I have to admit—
You're black, glossier than smeared mascara,
You don't wear saris, gold, or jewels,
Your hair's all tousled,
And you're always at the cremation grounds.
Nevertheless,
My mind forgets all this,
I don't know how.

Look! The Jewel of Men,
With masses of matted hair and snakes on his head,
Is *he* devoted to your feet?
Who are you to him? Who is he to you?
Who would ever guess
That the Crest-Jewel of the gods,
The Shelter of the shelterless,
The Entertainer of the universe,
Would cling to your feet
As the most cherished treasure?

Kamalākānta can't comprehend your endless virtues.
The earth and sky are lit by your beauty.

Śyāmā Saṅgīt 14

12 *Śyāmā Mā ki āmār kālo re*

Is my black Mother Śyāmā really black?
People say Kālī is black,
But my heart doesn't agree.
If she's black,
How can she light up the world?
Sometimes my Mother is white,
Sometimes yellow, blue, and red.
I cannot fathom her.
My whole life has passed

Trying.
She is matter,
Then spirit,
Then complete void.

It's easy to see
How Kamalākānta,
Thinking about these things,
Went crazy.

Śyāmā Saṅgīt 48

13 *Jāni jāni go Janani*

I know, I know, Mother:
You're a woman of stone.
You dwell inside me,
Yet you hide from me.

Displaying your illusory power,
You create many bodies,
With your three qualities
Limiting the limitless.

Kind to some,
Harmful to others,
You cover your own faults
By shifting the blame to others.

Mother, I don't hope for enlightenment,
Nor do I wish to live in heaven.
I just want to visualize your feet
Standing in my heart.

Brahmamayi,
This is Kamalākānta's humble appeal:
Why do you harass him unnecessarily?
What is your intention?

Śyāmā Saṅgīt 158

14 *Sadānandamayi Kāli*

Ever-blissful Kālī,
Bewitcher of the Destructive Lord,
Mother—

For your own amusement
You dance,
Clapping your hands.

You with the moon on your forehead,
Really
You are primordial, eternal, void.
When there was no world, Mother,
Where did you get that garland of skulls?

You alone are the operator,
We your instruments
Moving as you direct.
Where you place us, we stand,
The words you give us, we speak.

Restless Kamalākānta says, rebukingly:
You grabbed your sword, All-Destroyer,
And now you've cut down evil *and* good.

Śyāmā Saṅgīt 8

15 *Śyāmā māyer bhava-taraṅga*

Who can describe the waves of Mother Śyāmā's world?
I think I will swim upstream,
But who is pulling me back?
"I want to watch something funny," says my Mother,
And throws me in.
First I sink, then I float,
Laughing inside.
The boat isn't far away
It's near—
I can easily catch hold of it.
But this is my great dilemma:
Shall I reach for it or not?
I am divided.

Kamalākānta's mind!
Your desires are useless.
Take the boat.
If it is Tārā,
She may ferry you across
Out of kindness.

Śyāmā Saṅgīt 155

16 *Śyāmā yadi hero nayane ekbār*

Tell me, Śyāmā,
How could it hurt you to look at me
Just once?
You're a mother:
If you see so much pain,
But aren't compassionate,
What kind of justice is that?
I have heard from the scriptures
That you rescue the fallen.
Well? *I* am such a person—
Wicked and fallen!

You are famed as a deliverer of the wretched.
If it pleases you,
Take Kamalākānta across.

Śyāmā Saṅgīt 43

17 *Bhairavī bhairava jay Kālī*

Unperturbed at the battle,
Frightful ghouls dance,
Saying, "Victory to Kālī! Kālī!"
Śaṅkarī, immersed in the waves of battle,
Feels the spring breezes pleasant.

That very Brahmā, Lord of the Earth,
Whose wives smear red powder on his blessed body,
When in the form of Śyāmā
Plays with blood-red colors
In the company of her female attendants.

Sweating
With the fun of reverse sexual intercourse,
Young Śyāmā's flesh thrills
On top of young Śiva,
Her boat
Amidst the deep ocean of nectar.
Her long hair reaches down to the ground.
She is naked,
Ornamented with human heads and hands.

Kamalākānta watches their beautiful bodies
And sheds tears of bliss.

Śyāmā Saṅgīt 57

18 *Yār antare jāgilo Brahmamayī*

External rituals mean nothing
When Brahmamayī is aroused in your heart.
If you think on the Unthinkable,
Will anything else come to mind?
It's like unmarried girls
With their various amusements.
When they unite with their husbands,
Where are those games?
What will you worship her with?
Everything is full of her essence.

And look at degenerate Kamalākānta!
She has made even him
A storehouse of good qualities.

Śyāmā Saṅgīt 120

19 *Āpanāre āpani theko*

Stay within yourself, mind;
Don't go into anyone else's room.
You will get what you need right here.
Search in your own inner chamber.

Cintāmaṇī is like a philosopher's stone,
That greatest treasure
Able to bring countless riches:
Her front door is strewn about
With so many jewels.

Going on pilgrimage
Is a journey of sorrow,
Mind.
Don't be too eager.
Bathe in the three streams of bliss.
Why not be cooled
At their source,
Your bottom-most mystic center?

What are you looking at, Kamalākānta?
This world is full of false magic.
But you fail to recognize the magician—
And she's dwelling in your own body!

Śyāmā Saṅgīt 99

20 *Ār kicchui nei*

Other than your two red feet, Śyāmā,
Nothing else matters.
But Tripura's Enemy, I hear, has taken them.
My courage is broken.

Family, friends, sons, wives—
In good times they're all here.
But in bad times no one stays around,
And my house is deserted
Like the wilderness near Oṛ village.

If you wish to rescue me,
Then look at me with those compassionate eyes.
Otherwise
My prayers to you will have the brute force of a ghost,
Useless to win you.

Kamalākānta says:
I tell my sorrows to the Mother.
My beads, my bag, my mattress—
Let those stay hanging in the meditation room.

Śyāmā Saṅgīt 81

21 *Śuknā taru muñjare nā*

The withered tree doesn't blossom.
I'm afraid, Mother:
It may crack apart!
Up in the tree,
I feel it sway back and forth
In the strong wind.
My heart trembles.

I had great hopes:
"I'll get fruit from this tree."
But it doesn't bloom

And its branches are dry.
All because of the six hostile fires!

As far as Kamalākānta is concerned,
There is only one recourse:
The name of Tārā
Destroys birth, decay, and death.
Stamp out the flames with it,
And the tree will revive.

Śyāmā Saṅgīt 108

22 *Ekhan ār karo nā Tārā*

From now on,
Don't deprive me any more, Tārā.
Look, the danger of death is near.
What you've done to me was appropriate.
I endured, it endured.
But now I must think:
What is the recourse for a wretched man?
Death is not conquered,
But I am not afraid;
I only worry lest I forget your name
At my going.

Even though Kamalākānta is in pain,
He will smile.
Otherwise people will say
You haven't given me any happiness,
Śyāmā.

Śyāmā Saṅgīt 125

23 *Majilo āmār man bhramarā*

The bee of my mind
Is absorbed
In the blue lotus feet of Kālī.
The honey of worldly pleasures,
The flowers like lust,
All have become meaningless.
Black feet, black bee,
Black mixed with black.
Look! Happiness and suffering are now the same!

The ocean of my bliss
Is overflowing.

After so long
Kamalākānta's cherished hope has been fulfilled.
And see!
Those who get intoxicated by the Five Ms,
Seeing the fun,
Have beat a retreat.

Śyāmā Saṅgīt 165

—2—

Women's Celebration of Muḥammad's Birth

Marcia Hermansen

This selection incorporates material from a manual that is used by individuals, primarily women, in celebrating a ceremony in honor of the Prophet Muḥammad known as a "noble birth" (*mīlād sharīf*). Although this name refers to the birth (mīlād) of Muḥammad, these ceremonies may be performed at any time and are usually done at times of need or crisis, when it is hoped that a wish may be answered or a difficulty resolved through divine intervention. A person may also vow to sponsor such a ceremony after such a request has been granted.

It will be noted that some of the narrative material included in the ceremony recounts episodes from the sacred biography of the Prophet. Passages from the Qur'ān or the reports and sayings (*ḥadīth*) of the Prophet are cited to justify or enhance points made in the narrative. The manual is performative, in that there are instructions for conducting the ceremony and sections in the text that lend themselves to repetition by the listeners, such as short poems, refrains, and repeated exhortations to send blessings on the Prophet. This sending of peace and blessings is known as *durūd.*

This material indicates the importance of the Prophet Muḥammad in popular Muslim piety and the presence of popular religious rituals that take on regional forms, although versions of ceremonies honoring the Prophet are found in most Muslim cultures. These ceremonies, which often take place in private homes, provide the major context for women to participate in communal religious rituals.

In contemporary Pakistan, the issue of popular devotion to the saints and the Prophet is somewhat controversial. Although the vast majority of Muslims in the Indian subcontinent favor this type of pious expression, some groups promote a more strict reformist adherence to textual tradition and discourage the elevation of the Prophet to the status of a super-human being. In the context of this controversy, the author of this manual includes at the end of the text legal opinions by Arab Muslim scholars that affirm the permissibility and desirability of these ceremonies.

The manual finishes with a section of some twenty-five pages (pp. 144–69) of legal opinions solicited from religious scholars of Mecca and Medina, Saudi Arabia, concerning the legality of holding such ceremonies in honor of the Prophet. These are reproduced in the original Arabic with Urdu translations. This indicates both the sensitivity of the issue of whether these ceremonies are non-Islamic innovations and the appeal for legitimacy to the classical tradition and to the scholars of Arabia. One such opinion is translated here.

The translation is from Khwāja Muḥammad Akbar Wārithī, *Mīlād-e-Akbar* (Lahore: Shaikh Ghulām ʿAlī Publishers, n.d.)

THE PROPER CONDUCT FOR HOLDING AN ASSEMBLY OF IN HONOR OF THE BIRTH OF THE PROPHET (MĪLĀD SHARĪf)

The location must be clean and ritually pure; only money that has been earned by religiously approved means can be spent. The more perfumes, incense, fragrances and flowers, and so on, that are used, the better. Showing off must absolutely not enter into this. A high pulpit or chair on which is placed a stand or some ritually pure cloth should be used. Nice decoration should be employed for a pleasing effect—if possible also make arrangements for food. For performing the recitation of the Qurʾān over the food to bless it, use only sweets that are made by Muslims and preferably use candles for lighting because the bad odor of clay oil lamps should be avoided during this blessed gathering. The listeners and participants should be in a state of cleanliness and ritual purity, and should sit politely. The reciter of the mīlād sharīf ceremony should be someone who adheres to the Islamic Law. Persons should be exhorted again and again to recite salutations and blessings upon the Prophet (*durūd*).

THE BENEFITS OF MĪLĀD SHARĪF

"Mercy descends at the remembrance of the righteous ones."

In whichever place the remembrance of Aḥmad, the Chosen One, Muḥammad Muṣṭāfa—may the peace and blessings of God be upon him, the leader of all the righteous ones and messengers—takes place, in it this merit is found that voices are raised in praising him. Why shouldn't blessings descend on those present there, and why shouldn't the desired article be obtained by the audience? It is reported that, in whatever home this blessed gathering is held, for the next whole year showers of mercy will rain down on those who dwell there and they will live in protection and security with infinite good and blessings. In blessed Mecca and radiant Medina it is customary that when a son is born to someone, or when some other ceremony such as first hair cutting, circumcision, wedding, building of a new home, returning from a journey, or recovering from an illness is held, among all of the other functions a mīlād sharīf is sure to be included. May God also give us people such success that we will illuminate and ennoble our homes and gatherings with the mention of Muḥammad, and that we will be spared corruptions such as dancing and playing music, and so on. Amen.

Ḥadīth: Ḥaẓrat [the Prophet] said, "The person who sends salutations to me morning and night will obtain my intercession on the Day of Judgment."
Hadīth: The Prophet said, "Whoever recites salutation to me one hundred times on Fridays will find the sins of the whole year forgiven."

In short, true reports and ḥadīths have confirmed that sending blessings and salutation to the Prophet are a means to good and blessings in this world and a means to forgiveness and salvation in the afterlife. They cure illnesses and cheer up the grief-stricken. Doing these practices a lot brings blessings in material possession and advancement for one's children and, best of all, the one who does this often comes to love the Prophet more completely, and love for him is love for Allah—and this is faith and the basis of Islam.

> Recite the salutation, recite O lovers, recite the salutation,
> never be neglectful of the salutation, recite the salutation,
> send infinite salutation and blessings
> to the spirit of Muḥammad and the family of Muḥammad.

INTRODUCTION TO THE BIRTH OF THE LIGHT OF MUḤAMMAD, MAY THE PEACE AND BLESSINGS OF GOD BE UPON HIM.

> The mirror the divine essence was placed face to face,
> so that this form was duplicated,
> the reflection of the divine essence appeared in the mirror,
> the name of this reflection became Muṣṭāfa.
> If such an image had not been born
> the conclusion of beauty would come with him.
> All flames come from this one flame
> which illuminates from earth to heaven.

The explanation of this is given thus by the masters of knowledge and the possessors of inner wisdom. The first emanation of God, may his state be exalted, is the light of Muḥammad, may the peace and blessings of God be upon him. That is, the absolute Creator brought the light of Muḥammad into being 1,670,000 years before all other existent and created things. Hazrat ibn Jauzī wrote that God said to this light, "Become Muḥammad," so that it became a column of light and stood up and reached to the veil of divine greatness—then it prostrated and said, "Praise Be to God!" Then God said, "For this I have created you and I will make you the beginning of creation and the end of the Prophets."

BIRTH STORIES

It is reported that according to the lunar calculation exactly nine months had passed so that the time for his birth was near, when along with many other women, Āsia [wife of Pharaoh] and Mary, may peace be upon her, came to attend his mother from the spiritual world, and with them were many houris of Paradise. His mother said, "Right now I feel rather thirsty." At that very moment a radiant angel came to her holding in his hand a glass filled with a refreshing drink which was whiter than milk, sweeter than honey, colder than snow, and more fragrant than rose. He put it in her hand saying, "Drink this beverage which has come to you from paradise." She thus drank her fill. Then he said, "Have more," so she drank more and all thirstiness was lifted and she became calm. Then the angel made this appeal. "Come forth, O Master of messengers, come forth Master of the worlds, come forth, O Seal of the Prophets."

There is a report related from his paternal grandfather, Abd al-Muṭṭalib, that at that time [of his birth] he was inside the noble Kaʿba when all at once God's Kaʿba moved from its place and jumped for joy, then it bowed with its four walls and made a prostration at the station of Abraham. Then the walls stood up in their place and several times raised the call, "God's accepted one, Muḥammad may peace be upon him, is born."

His nurse [Ḥalīma] related that he grew at such a fast rate that in one day his size increased as much as most children's would in a month. In a month he grew as much as others would during a year! Thus in his second month his arms were so strong that he could crawl and after five months he could walk on his own legs and by the ninth month he could speak fluently and his first words were, "God is Great, God is Great, and praise be to God Lord of the Worlds. Praise be to God first and essentially." His statements were extremely wise. When he saw children playing he would stop them, and if they asked him to play he would say, "God did not create us for playing."

MIRACLES

One day a woman brought a person who had been dumb since birth, and had never uttered even one word. When the holy Prophet(s) asked him "Who am I?" the dumb person said, "I testify that there is no God but God and Muḥammad is his Prophet."

> Since even the dumb person has attested to his position as the
> Messenger,
> Why should not the two worlds utter the praises of Muḥammad?

A shepherd was tending goats in the forest. The Prophet, may the peace and blessings of God be upon him, arrived so that a she-wolf informed the shepherd saying, "The Prophet of God has come to your forest, I will tend your flock while you go to him." The shepherd immediately went to meet the Prophet and, having accepting the faith, began to perform the ritual sacrifice.

> The she-wolf protected the sheep folds in the wilderness
> While the shepherd became the sacrifice of Muḥammad.

A camel, after prostration before the Prophet, said, "My master loads me with too much baggage and gives me very little food." The Prophet called his master and requested him to load him more lightly and feed him until his stomach was full.

One day many companions and helpers were with the Prophet, and when they drew near to a goat pen the goats prostrated to the Prophet.

> Some prostrated, some recited the profession of faith,
> Even the wild animals were the Muslims of Muḥammad.

Stones turning into wax beneath his blessed feet is a well-known miracle of the Prophet. Once it occurred that by night in Mecca some of the most powerful unbelievers had gathered. The full moon shone in the sky. The unbelievers said that if the Prophet, may the peace and blessings of God be upon him, could perform the miracle of splitting the moon in the sky into two pieces then they would believe in him. At that very moment Ḥaẓrat, peace be upon him, lifted his index finger and pointed at the moon. It immediately split into two pieces.

> The stones turned into wax, the moon split into two pieces
> The heavens and earth are at the command of Muḥammad.

LEGAL OPINIONS OF THE NOBLE ARABS: FATWĀ FROM THE SCHOLARS OF MEDIAN, THE RADIANT, CONCERNING THE HOLDING OF MĪLĀD CEREMONIES

In the name of God the merciful, the compassionate.

Question: What is your opinion, may God have mercy on you, concerning the memorializing of the birth of the Prophet, may the peace and blessings of God be upon him, and standing up at the mention of the birth of the Prophet, and appointing a particular day for this and decorating the place and using scents and reciting some chapters of the Qur᾽ān and distributing food to the Muslims? Is this permissible and rewarded by God? Please give an explanation, may God reward you with the best reward!

Answer: Praise be to God who raised the heavens without a support. I ask Him for help, success, and assistance. Know that memorializing the birth of the

Prophet, may the peace and blessings of God be upon him, and all of his virtues in the presence of listeners is a tradition, since it has been reported that al-Ḥassān used to praise the Prophet, may the peace and blessings of God be upon him, in his presence while people were gathered to listen to him, and indeed the Prophet, may the peace and blessings of God be upon him, invited al-Ḥassān and let him mount the pulpit, so that he mentioned these virtues while standing on it. However, the holding of a noble birth ceremony in a communal form by specifying a day, standing up, and distributing food, and these other things which were mentioned in the question is a "sound innovation" (*bid'a ḥasana*) which is recommended and in which nothing prevents the obtaining of a reward from God so long as the intention is good, and especially if this is combined with exalting, honoring, and joy and happiness at the birthday of the noble Prophet. It is hoped that his reward from the Generous One will be to enter blessed Paradise through his grace. The people of Islam have continued to take care to celebrate the birthday of the Prophet, may the peace and blessings of God be upon him, and to make tasty food and give out various types of charity, and to be extremely joyful and have the recitation of the noble mīlād [ceremony] undertaken at this time.

—3—

Encountering the Smallpox Goddess: The Auspicious Song of Śītalā

Tony K. Stewart

Śītalā, the goddess of smallpox, is a deity who is popular throughout the Indian subcontinent, where smallpox has been endemic for centuries, but she is especially venerated in the delta regions of Bengal (today the Indian state of West Bengal and the country of Bangladesh), which suffered terrible outbreaks in the eighteenth and nineteenth centuries. Her name literally means the Cool One, an epithet that appears to be a euphemistic designation, since her speciality is accompanied by debilitating fever, but probably derives from her birth from the cooled ashes of the sacrificial fire. Her chief lieutenant and the organizer of her vast contingent of diseases is Jvara or Jvarāsura, the triple-headed Fever Demon. Śītalā herself is also known as Queen of Disease (Roga Rājā), Lord of Pestilence (Vyādhi Pati) and Master of Poxes (Basanta Rāya), especially smallpox, her most dreaded product. She is represented most frequently by a golden pot, although in wealthier temples she is depicted as a woman riding on a donkey, her preferred mount, and she will be represented occasionally in the village by a simply decorated stone.

Śītalā is one of the many Hindu mother goddesses invoked by the inhabitants of Bengal and, like other goddesses, she is worshiped by all classes, including many Muslims. The majority of these deities, mothers of the earth, are benevolent in obviously positive ways: they provide wealth, fertility, extensive families, and long life, and preside over knowledge, language, and the arts. With these patrons obvious salutary relations can be developed; but Śītalā's is a relationship of great ambivalence, for she represents one particularly frightful dimension of the Bengali physical environment: diseases. As mother she can be expected to nurture, but she is prone to anger and quick to offend, a characteristic she shares with Manasā, goddess of snakes, and Ṣaṣṭhī, goddess of children, along with the more well-known goddesses such as Kālī. When provoked, she can be expected to visit her wayward child and to remind that child that she is still their mother. To most, the logic of that causal connection is understandable, for those who defy her suffer her wrath in the form of pestilential disease; they get what they deserve. Yet many faithful and devoted worshipers of the goddess have also been touched by her heavy hand, and that is not so easily explained.

To the casual observer, the inhabitant of Śītalā's landscape is faced with a very uneasy set of alternatives, which run something like this. If you do not worship the goddess, you run the risk of being singled out for this egregious omission; Śītalā will extract her due. Yet, should you revere Śītalā and supplicate her, you risk coming to her direct attention, and that might prompt her to visit you, her devotee, in person. When she calls she leaves her mark, the pock, pointedly called "the grace of the mother" (*māyera dayā*). Should you survive, you bear her indelible print as a living reminder of her latent presence; should you die—and millions have—your death at the hands of the deity ensures an eventual salvation. Either way, the faithful and the corrupt alike directly encounter the divine as it is manifest in the natural world; some weather the enounter and others succumb, but none emerges unscathed. It is, as one scholar has aptly named it, a "theology of the repulsive."

Yet, to the inhabitants of Bengal, this threat of punishment is not so pessimistically burdensome because it is accompanied by a promise of well-being. Worship of the goddess does not require that Bengalis fatalistically resign themselves to her wrath, nor does a naturalistic explanation of the presence of the disease run counter to her veneration. Bengalis accept the modern scientific etiology of the disease and, at the same time, accept that Śītalā is responsible. Steps can be taken to avoid her pox, and the most popular is the innoculation, which has been prevalent in Bengal for several centuries (*guṭikā*). The advent of this particular goddess has long been associated with a cycle of drought, which reduces food availability, and famine, which weakens and makes vulnerable the local population—to which can be added the exacerbations of the rapacious tax-collector, who refuses to relent during these times of need. Worship of the goddess, which seems to peak during these periods—as demonstrated in the mid-eighteenth and nineteenth centuries—belays anxiety and creates a strong communal response that cuts across the traditional divisions of Bengali society. The natural world and the ills of society are inextricably bound one to the other, and the goddess must in these times intervene to remind, reward, and punish, while the local population must work together to overcome the challenge to the normal order of things. If they discipline themselves in proper conduct, the goddess will be benevolent.

During the eighteenth and nineteenth centuries, Śītalā's worship effloresced in direct correspondence to the epidemics that devastated the Bengali countryside. During the eighteenth century writing her texts, and in the nineteenth printing her texts became an industry of devotion, perhaps born of desperation. Yet even to compose or transmit her texts carries its own danger. The text that follows is the earliest known example of a Bengali *Śītalā Maṅgala*, the "Auspicious Song of the Cool One," written by one Kṛṣṇarāma Dāsa. Informed speculation places the date as early as 1690 C.E. but, based on internal evidence, it is probably a few years later. In this text the goddess is thoroughly provoked by the shameless behavior of an incorrigible toll collector named Madana Dāsa, who eventually suffers the full force of her wrath. Many of the poxes distributed by the goddess to this despicable man are descriptive of their shape and color and have been literally translated; where possible modern equivalents to other diseases have been noted. The language of the text itself conveys the ambivalence of Śītalā's position. Madana Dāsa's capitulation is really just that; the text even speaks of Śītalā simply frightening people into giving up their sinful ways. The humor, morbid though it is, and the mocking tones adopted by the goddess to bludgeon her hapless victims, suggest the oral and performative nature of the tale—although this is not quite so ribald nor riddled with the plethora of stinging double-entendres as the most popular and most frequently performed version of the cycle today, the story by Nityānanda, who wrote his tale in the 1750s. Kṛṣṇarāma, who collected and recorded no fewer than five maṅgala poems, explains that he has written it just as he heard it—a subtle caveat which hints that his fear of poetic failure could have personally disastrous results. The story of Madana Dāsa is the first and simplest of three episodes still extant from this earliest tale, and in its narrative starkness vividly captures the intensity of dramatic confrontation in these stories. Even though smallpox has been officially eradicated since 1978, the memory remains fresh and the worship of Śītalā continues, for to the Bengali follower, the manifestation of the pox is part of a much larger causal nexus that connects earth, heaven, and moral action; where there is the potential for drought and famine and taxes, the community must remain ever-vigilant for the visit of this mother-figure.

The following story is translated from "Madana Dāsa Pālā" of Kṛṣṇarāma Dāsa's *Śītalā Maṅgala* in *Kavi Kṛṣṇarāma Dāsera Granthāvalī,* edited by Satyanārāyaṇa Bhaṭṭācārya (Calcutta: Calcutta University, 1958), pp. 251–57.

Further Reading

A study by Edward C. Dimock, Jr., entitled "A Theology of the Repulsive: The Myth of the Goddess Śītalā," may be found in *The Divine Consort: Rādhā and the Goddesses of India,* edited by John Stratton Hawley and Donna Marie Wulff, Berkeley Religious Studies Series (Berkeley: Graduate Theological Union, 1982), pp. 184–203. Ralph W. Nicholas and Aditi Nath Sarkar, published "The Fever Demon and the Census Commissioner: Śītalā Mythology in Eighteenth and Nineteenth Century Bengal," in *Bengal: Studies in Literature, Society and History,* edited by Marvin Davis, South Asia Occasional Paper no. 27 (East Lansing: Asian Studies Center, Michigan State University, 1976), pp. 3–68. Nicholas has published three other relevant articles: "Śītalā and the Art of Printing: The Transmission and Propogation of the Myth of the Goddess of Smallpox in Rural West Bengal." in, *Mass Culture, Language and Arts in India,* edited by M. L. Apte (Bombay: Popular Prakashan, 1978), pp. 152–80, "The Village Mother in Bengal," in *Mother Worship: Theme and Variation,* edited by James Preston (Chapel Hill: University of North Carolina Press, 1982), 192–209; and "The Goddess Śītalā and Epidemic Smallpox in Bengal," *Journal of Asian Studies* 41: 1 (November 1981), 21–44. Also see Susan S. Wadley, "Śītalā: the Cool One," *Asian Folklore Studies* 39: 1 (1980), 32–62.

The Auspicious Song of the Cool One, Śītalā, Goddess of Smallpox

1. Let us bow down to you Śītalā, the Cool One,
whose enchanting lotus feet
   reap universal weal.
The serene beauty of your face soothes and delights
more than clusters of hand-picked flowers,
   forcing the fount of elixir, the moon, to hide in shame.

2. Bestower of calm and remover of fears,
you remain ever resolute
   with the name She Who Lays Waste the Corrupt.
You reside at all times
in the dark hollow of your golden pot,
   your comely shape cleansing and absolving.

3. Links of bells girdle your waist,
tinkling anklets ride above your feet,
   your limbs whispy like tender shoots of paddy.
Plain bands and ornamental bracelets
demurely grace your delicate wrists,
   while conch-shell bangles dance at your hand.

4. You provide the life-giving rains,
and plunder all suffering.
   Around your neck glisten strands of pure gold.
Your flowing tresses fly wild,
thicker than a yak-tail whisk—
   no fiery sun can compare.

5. Not once in eternity will be destroyed
the good fortune of all those who are
   blessed to serve under your motherly care.
Brahmā sings high your praise;
how can I, who am intellectually impaired,
   tell anything of your incomparable majesty?

6. With hands cupped in deference, the minstrel
places his meager offering into your pot—
Listen to your tale in song!
He who is devoted to you
sees his manifold faults destroyed,
destined never to endure more miseries.

7. Because you are suffused with compassion,
descend into our midst and
protect the clan of our dramatic subject.
You infuse yourself throughout the world,
the universe—but when taking form on earth,
you prefer that of a simple household ascetic.

8. When you spoke to me in dream
this truth alone entered my mind—
I could know nothing else whatsoever.
This tale is true, and it is truth—
your two feet alone provide shelter
from misfortune and disaster.

9. May you inhabit this sacred pot,
Goddess of Smallpox, possessor of all qualities,
and grant us an auspicious look.
Kṛṣṇarāma describes in detail
the education process directed at our subject
by that gracious glance.

10. In another realm situated across the wide waters there was a prosperous sea-trading community called Saptagrāma or "Seven Cities." Everyone referred to it as a meritorious land. The goddess, mounted on her donkey, traveled to every corner of the earth, and eventually reached that place. 11. Living in the environs of that fair city was one Madana Dāsa, appropriately named the Servant of the Lord of Spring Pleasures, a Kāyastha by caste, who labored as a toll collector along the highway. Always accompanied by a large contingent of local militia, and flanked on either side by menacing Rajput warriors, he was easily recognized by the paper and pen he held in his hand.

12. In order to test this man, the goddess called upon her venerable contingent, summoning untold numbers of dread diseases. Then the Goddess of Smallpox transformed herself into a vendor of assorted foods—fruits, vegetables, pulses, and sweetmeats. Her menagerie of bulging sacks failed calculation. 13. Jaundice hid in oil laced with turmeric, while ripe wood-apples harbored the dreaded goiter, both innocently under cover of a brace of palmyra fruits. A cluster of ripe, juicy coconuts was really nothing but hydrocele—dropsy of the scrotum—and dysentery invaded her tender young bunches of spinach leaves. 14. Typhoid fever wove itself into the leafy greens, and various wind

afflictions—flatulence, eructation, halitosis—assumed the form of irresistible milk sweets. Corns, warts, moles, wenns, sebaceous cysts, and other skin extrusions were disguised in the homologous shapes of sesame seeds. Jaundice likewise invaded the sugar of various milk sweets, while dropsy became the bulbous sweetmeat that resembled its own symptomatic protruding belly. Jujube seeds—which easily burst when ripe—were actually boils and abscesses. 15. Betel nuts were tiny enclosed sacks of elephantiasis; leprosy insinuated itself into sandalwood; and digestive diseases flowed through the succulent pith of ginger root. In melons and grains of various types were fixed morbidity of the spleen, hepatitis, and other disorders of the liver and internal organs—all of whose names filled the general populace with horror!

16. Her multitude of bags were carried on oxen, who in appropriate form trampled underfoot the garland offerings made along the road, and clumsily brushed aside the ritual vessels used to worship the many gods and goddesses. Yanking on the coarse rope lead, she beat those ornery beasts of burden with her wooden goad. And with the sweet words, "Move, you rotten sons-of-bitches!" she urged them gently down the road. 17. The Queen of Dread Diseases, on her donkey mount, now followed along behind the train, appearing to be but a successful trader. Magically the toll collector appeared, walking down to the end of the landing ghat, while our treasure-trove of virtues, the goddess, steadily advanced toward him. 18. She said nothing at all to that toll collector, gamely driving right on by. This infuriated Madana Dāsa, who watched in utter disbelief. He quickly ordered his armed guards to apprehend her—right then and right there on the road—so Kṛṣṇarāma writes, his own curiosity suddenly piqued.

19. "I do not understand! What is all the fuss about my carts? Why do you refer to my ox as lowly? By what right do you, a lordly man, treat everyone with contempt? I have never encountered such ill behavior anywhere else in the world! 20. Whose privileged son are you to determine whether and whither one passes? I have no fear of anyone . . ." and so it went.

With each word the officer twisted the end of his mustache a little harder, cranking his anger another notch higher. The head of the column of soldiers advanced quickly. 21. "I will wring your little neck!" the militiaman growled menacingly as he reached out to grab her. "It will certainly be a pleasure to punish you!"

"So you will slap the blackjack across my neck, then steal away everything I own. But it is curious how my anger checks itself, 22. For as soon as you attack and the first cry of distress is born, the full weight of your arrogance will come crashing down. I will not even have to resort to the evil eye! Even half that amount of hubris would be extremely unpleasant to bear. Let that give you pause, you insufferable brute! If the truth be known, my initial attraction to you had first inclined me to share some of my boundless hoard. 23. But now that you have cast aspersions on me there is no escaping the fruits of those deprecations. How can one so ostensibly full of good sense be so decidedly pig-headed? In your kind one finds neither honor nor respect. Listen, what I think is that everyone in your detachment is a double-talking sophist sprung from the most noxious of dung heaps! 24. The treachery in your minds is matched only by the lust harbored in your breast. Pay attention to me, you hard-hearted fools!"

The poet Kṛṣṇarāma can but describe the Goddess of Smallpox, whose deep, frightful eyes have been wrathfully cast.

25. The militia officer spoke, "Hey you addle-brained crone! Pull over by the śāla tree. Do exactly as I say! I want you front and center to explain yourself!"

"I have come from Tomabālapura, 'the City of Your Youth,' terribly far from this place, but then tell me, brother, where else is a trader to find goods and produce of such extraordinary and exceptional quality?"

26. Jumping at the bait, the officer queried, "Tell me, how exactly did you come to be so laden with this merchandise? Did you just break out of jail? All of these bags bear the unmistakable look of ill-gotten gains! . . . ." And so the accusations flew.

At last, the goddess feigned to acquiesce, "Sāheb, your honor, our negotiations clearly have reached an impasse. Take everything away. It is undoubtedly your good fortune." 27. And so the Goddess of Smallpox relented, with the cryptic parting comment, "I came to distribute my goods and distribute I have. Now happily and with a light heart I return to my home in Burdwan." But secretly she thought to herself, "You, my toll collector, are such an ass; you have neither shame nor intelligence!"

28. The toll collector never once feared for his safety. He never acknowledged requests or listened to solicitation, even when proffered by a holy man, 29. Because, you see, the toll collector was thoroughly and completely wicked. It was with a sinister pleasure that he confiscated items without number. 30. It was routine for the collector to rough up the poor and ignorant and, under pretext, to appropriate their possessions, which mysteriously but invariably found their way into his private house. 31. This day he was quite pleased to have hauled in such a handsome catch, for various important personages would come to his home expecting lavish entertainment—and so they did.

32. The Goddess of Pestilence watched from her perch in the heavens as the toll master and his guests ate. The sweets and other items that he had personally selected were eaten noisily and with great relish. 33. Afterwards, some bathed and then reached for the turmeric-laced oil, which really contained jaundice. 34. In their gluttony, the guests unceremoniously wolfed down the sugary pots of sweets, which distended their greedy stomachs. Then they turned to the small metal plates filled with the dreaded dropsy sweets of ascites and beriberi. 35. What they consumed as tasty grains entered their guts as pyemia, splenomegaly, and various necroses of the spleen. 36. The bodies of those who ate the palmyra fruits were wracked with clonic convulsions, which alas were only

portents to the lesions, boils, and furuncles that would soon appear on their thighs, in their intestines, and around their anuses. 37. The betel was consumed with much laughter and pleasant banter, only to be manifested as hepatitis and cirrhosis, and followed closely by either elephantiasis or blindness. 38. What first appeared on their bodies as a simple leukoderma was really leprosy in disguise. When they partook of the various leafy greens, they tasted typhoid. 39. When they glanced in the mirror they discovered through blurry eyes that their corneas had glazed over with cataracts. No one could speak clearly for the agonizing, hacking cries of pain—it was fever fueled by sin.

40. The punishment reserved for that mean toll collector was deemed especially appropriate—various forms of smallpox he contracted in their guise as pulses. 41. Ground pulse cakes coated with poppy seeds hid measles, chickenpox, and even the disfiguring pox of the "black death." 42. The "sackcloth" pox blanketed him in a rough patchwork of pustules, while the "māsakalāi pulse" pox clumped in painful, thick, oozing masses.

43. There is no one on earth who could weather this onslaught: it afflicted each and every one without exception. The poet Kṛṣṇarāma opines that the retribution for their folly was more than fitting.

44. Draped around the victim's neck was a breathtaking necklace of deep red coral—and his life breath it was, being drained by the reddish "bloody-mawed" pox. 45. Madana Dāsa, rogue of tax extortionists, was felled. So, too, his mighty Rajput warriors buckled under the strain. 46. That toll man found that he could no longer vent his wrath, for masses of putrid boils and abscesses had erupted to shrink his mouth to but the tiniest, painful pinhole. 47. The hideous "monster" pox appeared, so even the threads of his loose pajamas lacerated his flesh like razors. The deadly "ugly-maker black" pox turned his body into a disfigured pulp. 48. His guards shed their weapons and armor, down to undershirts and turbans, but even the light touch of their cotton left them howling in agony, so they shamelessly and without hesitation stripped stark naked—but to no avail.

49. Choosing her moment, the Queen of Pestilence resumed her disguise, and with deliberate intention returned to that now-devastated place to needle her offender. 50. "We just couldn't get enough, could we? And have we gotten tired after sampling all our scrumptious goodies? Now tell me, why is the big bad toll collector straining so hard without success? Are we suffering from a touch of tenesmus? Do we hurt? . . ." And so she made her point.

51. Grudgingly repentant, Madana Dāsa—the Servant of the Lord of Spring Pleasures—pressed his palms together in humility. "I have committed many gross and grave offenses toward your person. 52. You have left an indelible impression on this man of rank, and can on others at your will. I will worship your holy feet if only you will cure me! Remove these excruciating diseases! 53. Say that it will be so, O Gracious One! Heed my petition! For your worship I will never use anyone but my brahman who personally attends me, the em-

inent toll collector. 54. When that brahman goes to perform your evening rituals, everyone will know it is dedicated to Śītalā, Lord of the Śūdras.

55. And so it was that the goddess, that ocean of greatness, left her mark and become widely known. Said she, "You are now the son of Śītalā, the Cool One, for it is really I, Ruler of Pox, in disguise. 56. When you worship me in my pot, you will suffer no more. You will come to taste a wonderful variety of pleasures and joys, and they will expand immeasurably." 57. With these parting words, the goddess started for her own abode, and the toll collector was, as promised, relieved of all of his dread diseases.

58. He erected a winsome temple on the banks of the Gaṅgā River and had there installed the Queen of Smallpox, Śītalā, the Cool One. 59. He had her worship performed, offering the full gamut of appropriate sacral items. From that the wicked and base were frightened into good and honest people! 60. Goats and rams were sacrificed with satisfying production, and her worship was consumated with reverent concentration and attention.

61. The lowly among men, who struggle with death and disease in our world, are incapable of cognizing just how extraordinary this treasure-trove of qualities truly is. 62. The Mother's parental affection erodes one's faults and, one by one, the entire population will have their sins forgiven. 63. The goddess, compassionate as she alone can be, has offered her grace, and the whole world dances in that knowledge, letting fly the sounds of triumph. 64. Openly pleased, the Goddess of Smallpox triumphantly returned to her private heavenly citadel, and along the way nothing could be heard but praise of Śītalā, the Cool One. . . .

149. The poet Kṛṣṇarāma pleads, "Listen carefully, my dear Mother Śītalā, for I have composed your song exactly as it was recited."

—4—

Jain Stories Inspiring Renunciation

Phyllis Granoff

The following three stories are typical of many that appear in the Jain didactic story collections. Two are taken from the *Dharmābhyudayamahākāvya,* written by the Śvetāmbara monk Udayaprabhasūri sometime before 1271 C.E., and the other is from the Digambara *Bṛhatkathākośa,* composed by Hariṣeṇa in 931 C.E. These stories were meant to instill in their audience a deep revulsion for the world as we know it and a desire for renunciation and for ultimate release from the cycle of transmigration. They do so by deconstructing our notions of reality, particularly our normal understanding of human relationships as fixed and definable categories. Two stories show how relationships we assume to be one thing in this life were very different in the past; a third story tells us how in a single lifetime circumstances can arrange our lives for us in such a way that our assumptions about our relationships to those closest to us are totally wrong. This genre of story relies on shocking us to make its point; these are accounts of murder, incest, and cannibalism, but they are meant to show us how all our relationships can and do have this dark underside. The only way to be safe is to renounce human ties and seek salvation as a monk or nun.

The *Dharmābhyudayamahākāvya,* edited by Jina Vijaya Muni, was published in the Singhi Jain Series, vol. 4 (Bombay: Bhāratīya Vidyā Bhavan, 1949). The *Bṛhatkathākośa,* edited by A. N. Upadhye, was published as vol. 17 of the same series (Bombay: Bhāratīya Vidyā Bhavan, 1943). These stories have also been published in "Life as Ritual Process: Remembrance of Past Births in Jain Religious Narratives," in Phyllis Granoff and Koichi Shinohara, eds., *Other Selves: Autobiography and Biography in Cross-Cultural Perspective* (Oakville, Ontario: Mosaic Press, 1994).

THE STORY OF MAHEŚVARA FROM THE *DHARMĀBHYUDAYAMAHĀKĀVYA*

There was a famous city named Tamālinī, where the pillars of the lofty temples to the gods seemed to reach so high that they could support the very vault of the heavens, and the many palaces of the rich were like a garland around the city. There lived the wealthy merchant Maheśvaradatta, who was the foremost citizen of the town, and he was famed for being like an elephant that sported at will in the ocean of false belief. His wife was like the mistress of the school of wanton women. Her name was Nāgilā, and she was famous in the city for being a water channel to make bloom the garden of erotic delights. Now one day, on the occasion of the death anniversary of his father, Maheśvaradatta killed a buffalo as an offering to the dead. And he even fed his son, whom he held on his lap, with the meat of the sacrificed buffalo. Just at that moment a sage came to his house; his face was all wrinkled, and he had seen for himself the true nature of things. He recited this verse again and again:

"He feeds his own enemy, whom he holds on his lap, with the flesh of his very own father. And that he considers to be a proper sacrificial offering in honor of his father. Alas, could there be any more deluded act?"

When he heard those words Maheśvaradatta quickly rushed over to the lord of monks. He bowed to him and asked, "O Lord! What is this strange thing that you say?" And when he saw that Maheśvaradatta was determined to find out the truth, then that foremost of those who are restrained in speech, knowing through his great wisdom that he could help Maheśvaradatta, and being filled with compassion, replied: "That lover of Nāgilā whom you once killed long ago is now playing happily in your lap. He died just as he released his semen into Nāgilā, and because he was reborn in Nāgilā's womb, he became thereby your very own son. And that buffalo, with whose flesh you satisfied your deceased father, was really the soul of your father, Samudradatta. And, O wise one! There is a she-dog by the door that is eating the bones of the buffalo. Know O wise one that the dog is none other than your very own mother, named Bahulā. Knowing through my supernatural knowledge that all of these terribly strange and improper things were going on in your home, I hastened here to enlighten you."

"What proof is there that what you say is true, O lord?" When Maheśvaradatta asked the monk this question, the monk in turn replied, "When you take the dog inside the house it will remember its previous births and reveal to you where some jewels were buried long ago."

At this the monk took his leave. And the dog that he had told Maheśvaradatta about indeed showed Maheśvara the buried jewels when it was brought inside the house, just as the monk had said it would. And that merchant Maheśvaradatta, like an elephant brought under control by a good trainer by means of an elephant goad, was brought to his senses by the monk, by means of his pointed words. And he gave up his wrong religious beliefs and accepted the correct religious beliefs. Knowing that the whole net of relationships—father, son, and everything else—was all topsy-turvy, he realized that even he could not save himself, and that of course no son could help him.

THE STORY OF THE MONK SUḌṚṢTI FROM THE *BṚHATKATHĀKOŚA*

In the glorious realm of Avantī was the wonderful city Ujjain. Prajāpāla was king there, and his wife was named Suprabhā. Now this king had a jeweler named Suḍṛṣti, who was very knowledgeable about gems. The jeweler's wife was named Vimalā. The jeweler had a student named Vaṅka; Vimalā was in love with the student and her mind was filled with lustful thoughts about him. One day, just as Suḍṛṣti was making love to Vimalā, Vimalā had that deceitful Vaṅka kill Suḍṛṣti. And Suḍṛṣti, having been slain by Vaṅka, was reborn in Vimalā's womb. He had the ability to remember his past births and this made him not want to do very much at all. For this reason, the child, playing like all children his age, nonetheless came to be known as "the biggest lazybones in the whole world." One day when Queen Suprabhā was in her pleasure garden, her necklace broke and no one could find it. After much seeking it was only through a stroke of great luck that the king's men were able to find the necklace somewhere deep in the woods. No one among the many goldsmiths in the city was able to put the necklace together properly, not even the cleverest and most skilled of them all. Then it was that "Lazybones" rushed to the palace and fixed the necklace so that it made the very heavens shine with its radiance. The king beheld that necklace, so magnificently repaired, and then looked at the child who had always lived right there in the city. His mind was filled with wonder. "Where did you learn such skill, skill possessed by my former jeweler, Suḍṛṣti, and by no one else? Tell me child, for I am amazed by your deeds." When he heard these words of the king, the child replied, "I died and was reborn as my own son in my own wife. That Vimalā, who was formerly my wife, is now my mother. I died without a son and then became my own child. Isn't that something?" When he heard all of this about Suḍṛṣti, the king, along with many other kings, decided to practice austerities according to the Jain doctrine under the instruction of Abhinandana. Many other people were astonished at the tale, and wisely took refuge in the Jain doctrine, the source of true happiness. And that Lazybones, fearful of transmigratory existence, also became a Jain monk under the same teacher. After performing many austerities, his mind as firm in its religious resolve as Mount Mandara is strong and unshakable, in the course of his monastic wanderings Lazybones reached the northern region of the city of Sauri. In the end he died the pious death of a Jain monk, in meditation.

THE STORY OF KUBERADATTA AND KUBERADATTĀ FROM THE *DHARMĀBHYUDAYAMAHĀKĀVYA*

There was in the city of Mathura a courtesan named Kuberasenā. She was so beautiful that it seemed that the moon was just a poor copy of her face, made by the Creator in the same way a sculptor makes a special image of a god that can be used for the bathing ceremony, so that the more valuable image in the temple is not harmed by the eager devotees as they wash it. One day with great difficulty she bore a son and a daughter, just as the sword of a great king gives rise to glory and victory. Kuberasenā fought off the harsh words of the madame of the house, who urged her to abandon the twins, and she nursed them for a full eleven days. She made a signet ring for the boy inscribed with the name Kuberadatta, and a similar ring for the girl, marked with the name Kuberadattā. And then the cowardly mother, terrified of the madame, placed the two children in a casket studded with jewels. She set the casket afloat in the waters of the River Yamunā, as if it were the vessel containing all of her own future happiness, and she bade it farewell, washing it with the tears from her eyes, as one might send off a beloved guest with sprays of consecrated water. It so happened that a pair of merchants were delighted to discover the casket which had floated down the River Yamunā as far as the city of Sūryapura. They quickly opened the box and there they discovered the two children. Like heirs sharing their rightful inheritance, the two merchants divided up equally the contents of the box, each one taking home one of the two children. The brother and sister were raised with loving care by the merchants, and they grew more charming with every day, like the moon and the moonlight in the moon's waxing phase. Those two best of merchants then married off the boy and girl, who were known by the names that had been inscribed on the signet rings found with them, even though they seemed indeed to be twin brother and sister. Now one day Kuberadatta placed his own ring in his wife's hand, as if to give her a letter that would announce her renunciation of the world. Seeing that ring, so like her own, Kuberadattā was astonished, and she said to her husband, "How is it that these rings are so like each other, just as our names are so similar? I fear that we are in truth brother and sister, and that we are not the two children of those merchants at all. They must have found us somewhere and out of ignorance of the true state of affairs they married us to each other. We must find out the truth from our parents, no matter how much we have to ask them. We must know the circumstances of our birth." And after she said this, the two of them together went to the merchants. They asked them again and again about their birth and then, realizing that their suspicions were true and that they were indeed brother and sister, they deeply regretted their marriage. They lost all taste for worldly life, which they regarded as without value and as their enemy; filled with the desire for renunciation, they just stood there, heads bowed low, bereft of all their natural beauty, like the moon and the moon-lotus as early dawn breaks. And then Kuberadattā, being very wise, bid farewell to her brother and her parents and became a Jain nun. She then hid her jeweled signet ring, on which her name was inscribed; the ring was as radiant as the knowledge that would also come to Kuberadattā one day.

Kuberadatta, for his part, made his way to the city of Mathura as a trader, selling various toys. He became the lover of that very Kuberasenā who had given birth to him, as the moon is said to be the lover of the night. O fie on the Creator who makes us all do such things!

In time Kuberasenā bore Kuberadatta a son, created as it were by the ultimate delusion that governs transmigratory existence. Now Kuberadattā had perfected her knowledge to the extent that she now had the ability to know some things that were beyond the range of the senses. She desired to enlighten her brother, and she knew through her supernatural knowledge the terribly improper things that he was doing. She told her superior about herself and showed her the signet ring that she had kept concealed all that time, and like a boat to rescue her brother who was sinking quickly in the ocean of transmigratory existence, she hastily made her way to Mathura. She asked Kuberasenā for a place to stay and found lodgings there, in that unsuitable place; for religious people will do anything that they have to in order to help someone else.

Now one day the nun Kuberadattā saw the robust son of Kuberadatta, and knowing how monks and nuns enlighten others, she spoke these absolutely true words, "Child! You are my brother-in-law, for you are the brother of my husband. And our mother is the same woman, and so you are also my brother! My husband begot you, and so that makes you also my child. But your father is the child of my rival in love, and that would make you my grandson. You are the brother of my mother's husband, which makes you my uncle. And you are my brother's child, which makes you my nephew. Your mother is my mother, who bore us both in her womb. And that woman is also the mother of my mother's lover, which makes her my grandmother. She is the wife of the young man who was born from my co-wife, which makes her also my daughter-in-law. And she is the mother of my husband, which makes her my mother-in-law as well. She is the wife of my brother, which makes her my sister-in-law, and she is the wife of my husband, and so is my co-wife. And as for your father, who is the lover of my mother, I guess that makes him my father, too. You are my uncle, and he is your father, and an uncle's father is your grandfather, so he is my grandfather as well. My mother and his mother are the same woman, and so he is my brother. He is the husband of the woman who bore my husband, and so he is my father-in-law, too. He took my hand in marriage, and so he became my husband in addition to all of this. And he is the son of my co-wife, and so is my son as well."

Now when Kuberadatta heard these words of the nun, which seemed to contradict themselves at every step, he was amazed, and he asked her, "What does all of this mean?" And the nun then told everything to that Kubera, who kept asking her what she had meant. And she gave him the jeweled signet ring, which was like a lamp to enlighten the darkness of his delusion. By that signet ring, which was bright like the sun, Kubera became enlightened, and he gave up his deluded beliefs as a bee leaves a lotus. He was ashamed of his own behavior and he became a monk, and that wise Kuberadatta, though still a young man, renounced the householder's life and went into the forest. The forests were made radiant by that one, who was like a lion to destroy the elephant of karma, and who was like a mountain with natural rushing springs of his own glory; he was like a tree bearing as its fruits one austerity after another. He meditated on the Jain teachings and constantly recited Jain prayers to the Tīrthaṅkaras and sages of old, and he went to heaven, a lion that had killed the elephant of sexual desire. Even Kuberasenā saw how topsy-turvy the world of sense objects is, and she became disgusted with life in this world and took on herself the vows of the Jain householder.

5

Mother Ten's Stories

Ann Grodzins Gold

In Ghatiyali village, Ajmer District—as in many Rajasthani villages and cities—women worship the beneficent goddess Dasā Mātā (alternatively Daśā Mātā), here called Mother Ten, by telling her stories. A more accurate but awkward translation of this goddess's name would be "Condition Mother," for—as the stories teach—her power may transform a human's condition (*dasā; daśā*). Instantaneously, she bestows or removes well-being or ill-being. It seems likely that an initially accidental homonymy in Hindi and Rajasthani between the word for condition—*dasā*—and the auspicious number ten—*das* (alternatively *daś*)—led to the association of Dasā Mātā with ten days of worship, ten stories, a ten-pointed design, and a string with ten knots. Thus I shall call her Mother Ten.

The days of Mother Ten's worship in Rajasthan fall during a period crowded with rituals and festivals, and rich with songs and stories. Coming at the beginning of the hot season, this period coincides not incidentally with the harvest of winter grain crops. It begins with the major villagewide and nationwide festival of Holī on the full moon and last day of the lunar month called Phālgun (March-April). As the moon wanes and waxes again, during the succeeding month of Chaitra (April-May), many women in Ghatiyali participate in a series of ritual events appealing to and celebrating various aspects of female divinity. These rituals are all intended to secure for women and their families the comforts of a good life and, by the same token, to ward off the disasters of childlessness, widowhood, illness, loneliness, and poverty. Perhaps, above all, they are about the value of sustaining relationships.

The day after Holī is Brother Second, when sisters pray for their brothers' long lives and brothers give sisters gifts of clothing. The first day of Mother Ten's worship coincides with Brother Second, but Mother Ten's stories are told at a different time of day and in a different location from those dedicated to the goddess addressed only as "Mother of Brother Second." Eight days after Holī is the worship of Sītalā (alternatively, Śītalā) Mother, the Cool One, who controls both fertility and children's health—especially rashes and fevers. Rowdy groups of singing, laughing women celebrate Sītalā Mother's worship, visiting her shrine outside the village and alternately singing solemn devotional tunes and lyrics, and joking, bawdy ones. Mother Ten's worship on that day is quietly conducted at a lull in the activities dedicated to Sītalā. Sixteen days after Holī, and five after the culmination of Mother Ten's worship, is the festival of Gaṇgaur, in praise of the fair goddess who through austerities won Lord Śiva for her husband. Gaṇgaur worship is meant to secure auspicious wifehood for virgin girls and long-lived spouses for married women. Shortly after Gaṇgaur the spring celebration of the Goddess's semi-annual Nine Nights (Navarātri) caps this series of festivities honoring female divinity. Like Holī, Nine Nights is actively and publicly celebrated by men, but the worship performed for Brother Second, Sītalā Mother, Gaṇgaur, and Mother Ten is largely women's business.

It would be easy to overlook Mother Ten's worship during the vivid pageantry that characterizes many of the events with which it coincides and overlaps. On all but the tenth day, the ritual for Mother Ten probably takes less than two hours, from the drawing of the ten-pointed design through the stories and prayers. In many ways Mother Ten's rites are similar to the performance of vows (*vrat* or *vrata*) which both women and men, but more frequently women, undertake for the well-being of their families. Vrats, like Mother Ten's worship, typically involve a fast, a simple domestic worship ritual, and a story. However, Mother Ten's worship, although conducted in homes, has a collective aspect. Small groups of women, who may be neighbors and friends as well as relatives, perform it together. The tenth day sees the largest gatherings, as all married women who seek the goddess's protection for the coming year will attend the worship in order to obtain a blessed ten-knotted string to wear around their necks.

The three stories translated here I recorded on the second, fourth, and seventh days of Mother Ten's worship in March 1980.[1] The storyteller, Shobhag Kanvar, was then a woman in her mid-fifties, and a grandmother. She is of the Rājpūt caste—traditionally the ruling, landed gentry or "warrior" caste. Her own husband and one of her two sons had urban jobs as chauffeur and truck driver, respectively; another, more educated, son held a clerical position in a nearby town. Shobhag Kanvar, who had no formal schooling and can neither read nor write, is an acknowledged religious expert in Ghatiyali. I lived in her household from September 1979 to March 1981, and she was always quick to summon me and my tape recorder when what she considered a worthwhile cultural performance was about to take place in her home. Although other women in our village performed Mother Ten's worship, I attended and recorded only Shobhag Kanvar's rituals.

To participate in Mother Ten's worship and receive its benefits, women forego their morning meal and make sure to bathe, but otherwise they carry out their usual daily routines. Then, sometime in the afternoon, fasting women gather at the storyteller's home. In 1980, the regular participants who assembled in Shobhag Kanvar's courtyard for Mother Ten's worship were the female residents of this compound's household. These included Shobhag Kanvar, her daughter-in-law, her older sister (married to her husband's older brother), her sister's daughter-in-law, and me. A few neighbor women—none of them Rājpūts—attended irregularly. A couple of workmen were employed at the time doing masonry labor on Shobhag Kanvar's new house, and were thus professionally immune to the customs of gender seclusion that generally applied in a Rājpūt courtyard. I was surprised and amused to note how these men gravitated each day to within hearing distance of the storytelling session, positioning themselves just a little behind the small circle of women. Officially nonexistent at this female event, they nonetheless interjected appreciative exclamations and offered commentary on the stories. Shobhag Kanvar responded to their interest with her customary self-possession.

The atmosphere at Mother Ten's worship sessions was companionable as well as prayerful; no great solemnity prevailed. Children of all ages distracted and disrupted at their whim, including an infant who defecated on its doting grandmother's lap in the midst of one session, evoking general hilarity.

Before each worship Shobhag Kanvar prepared a special ritual space on the courtyard floor. With cowdung paste as her medium, she used her hands to paint a brown ten-pointed figure, upon which she placed a skein of white cotton yarn and a small pile of whole wheat grains. Next to this design Shobhag Kanvar set a small brass jar of pure water and a small dish of red powder, mixing water with powder to make a thick, bright red paste. On each day of Mother Ten's worship she used this paste to make auspicious dots on the ten-pointed design—one on the first day, two on the second, until a full complement of ten dots is made on the tenth day. Each day, as the worship began, every woman present took a few grains in her hand and held them while a story was told. At each story's conclusion, following Shobhag Kanvar's lead, the women tossed the grains in front of them while uttering prayers to the goddess.

On the tenth day the skein of yarn is twisted into necklaces called "Mother Ten's strings" which all participating women wear throughout the year that follows. Each string has ten knots in it. These strings are understood as forms of the goddess and respected as icons. For the tenth day women dressed in their best, attendance at least tripled, and the fast was broken with special festive foods offered to the goddess and eaten collectively.

Shobhag Kanvar told three stories at each worship session. The first (and longest) was always of the goddess herself; the second was always of the elephant-headed god Gaṇeśjī; the third was of a character called the Greedy One (Lobhyā). The chief feature of the Greedy One's stories was his futile efforts to snatch for himself the merit of women's fasts and offerings and stories. Shobhag Kanvar would conclude the Greedy One's tales by admonishing him that his story and his grains belonged to him, but nothing more.

In sum, then, during the ten days of Mother Ten's worship, Shobhag Kanvar produced thirty stories—ten for Mother Ten, ten for Gaṇeśjī and ten for the Greedy One—although only two of the Greedy One's tales had any substantial narrative content. Shobhag Kanvar told me that she had learned some of these stories from an aunt in her natal home, some from her (now deceased) mother-in-law in our village, and some from an elderly woman of a different and lower caste in our village.

Mother Ten is identified with Lakṣmī, the goddess of wealth and prosperity, while her opposite, Odasā—"Ill-Condition" or "Bad Ten" as I call her here—is identified with Kulakṣmī, the goddess of misfortune. Worshipers believe that Mother Ten brings well-being, comfort, and plenty to the families of the women who perform her rites. But if she is angered or neglected, abject poverty and every kind of bad luck will result—when Mother Ten departs and Bad Ten arrives.

A phrase that occurs in every Mother Ten story is "X had Mother Ten's niyam" and I have consistently translated this as "X followed the rules of Mother Ten." *Niyam* is variously glossed as "rule," "habit," or "regimen," but also includes, unlike those terms, a strong measure of self-restraint. To have the niyam of a particular deity means to act in accordance with that deity's traditional, prescriptive desires. These usually require acts of self-control and self-denial, such as fasting or renouncing certain foods, as well as acts of worship, such as offering grains or telling stories.

All Mother Ten's stories seem simultaneously to celebrate the absolute power of the goddess over human welfare and to demonstrate mortal women's great aptitude for exercising their pragmatic wits. An explicit connection between devotion to the goddess and human ingenuity is made in the first story when the narrator describes the heroine as knowing many things because "Mother Ten had turned her heart's key, and opened her heart, and put ideas in her brain." Each story begins with a woman in a difficult situation, but ends with the same woman having attained an ideal condition of general prosperity and security—through a combination of the goddess's blessings and her own efforts. Each story also ends with a prayer to Mother Ten to generalize that bliss: not only the story's heroine but the whole world should partake of it.

The tales reveal, in passing, forms of exploitation and abuse to which women are subject, but seem to view these more as challenges to feminine ingenuity than as intolerable burdens. The vocal, smart, well-behaved but unsubmissive women in these tales understand and experience, as do the narrator and her audience, a world strongly patterned by gender distinctions. Women perceive their disadvantages in this world, as when the bride of the first story fears a beating, or when the old woman of the third story acquiesces to the greedy king's unfair demand. But the stories express no resignation to imposed subordination. In the three tales presented here—and in all Mother Ten stories—potentially victimized females take fate into their own hands and, with help from the goddess, turn things around to their own advantage. In the process they often manipulate the men around them, and males are notably more voiceless and passive than women in these stories.

The heroines of Mother Ten's tales also manipulate other women. No ideology of female solidarity prevails in the story world. Realistically enough, solidarities and jealousies, mutual support and mutual predation, coexist. If a mother's worship establishes a secure fate for her daughter, and mother-in-law and daughter-in-law appreciatively bless one another, a stepmother may be deliberately cruel to her stepdaughter. If friendly neighbor-women lend grain and utensils to a lonely bride, a greedy neighbor-woman contrives to rob a defenseless old lady.

Each tale of Mother Ten seems to address one or more powerful cultural motifs surrounding female existence. "The Brahman's Daughter and the Five Bachelors" begins with an image of brothers dividing property. To separate cooking hearths is the paradigmatic act by which a joint family divides itself, and such divisions are strongly disapproved, although widely practiced, in Rajasthan. One of the most pervasive cultural truisms in north India has it that women's feuds and jealousies cause men to sever their brotherly ties. But here the five bachelors divide their property when they become an all-male group, and they are subsequently reunited by the clever bride. Thus as they worship the goddess of well-being, women powerfully deny the validity of a misogynous stereotype.

Another common characterization of north Indian kinship is that there is a painful antagonism between mother-in-law and daughter-in-law. This is supposed to be grounded in their presumed bitter competition for the son/husband. In "The Sword-Husband," however, the pair—mother-in-law/daughter-in-law—virtually creates a man for their mutual enjoyment, and they praise one another for this accomplishment. The story also sensibly enough reveals that a little disobedience to husband's mother is forgivable, and may be all for the best.

To be old and alone is a dreaded fate for anyone, perhaps most of all for women. But the story of "The Old Woman and The Yellow Calf," the third and last presented here, shows how devotion to the goddess and independent-mindedness may transform this fate. In the end, we see the old woman move from isolation to a familial situation, a move construed as one from misery to well-being. If her security lies in obtaining a new dependence, the old woman does not achieve this through begging or becoming an object of charity. Rather, her benefactor is forced to realize her personal worth. The goddess, Mother Ten, has many ways of taking care of her own. None of her devotees, as portrayed in Shobhag Kanvar's stories, lacks inner strength and all of them have lively tongues and their wits about them.

Further Reading

Two books provide further material on rituals and festivals in rural Rajasthan: Brij Raj Chauhan, *A Rajasthan Village.* (New Delhi: Associated Publishing House, 1967); and S. L. Srivastava, *Folk Culture and Oral Tradition* (New Delhi: Abhinav Publications, 1974). My earlier works treat related aspects of devotional storytelling, popular religious practices, and women's expressive traditions; Ann Grodzins Gold, *Village Families in Story and Song: An Approach through Women's Oral Traditions in Rajasthan* INDIAkit Series, South Asia Language and Area Center, University of Chicago, 1981; *Fruitful Journeys: The Ways of Rajasthani Pilgrims* (Berkeley and Los Angeles: University of California Press, 1988); and Gloria Goodwin Raheja and Ann Grodzins Gold, *Listen to the Heron's Words: Reimagining Gen-*

der and Kinship in North India (Berkeley and Los Angeles: University of California Press, 1994).

THE BRAHMAN'S DAUGHTER AND THE FIVE BACHELORS

A brahman had five sons. Their mother died, and what did the five sons do? They built five separate huts and five separate cooking hearths and five separate ovens for roasting grains, and even five separate manure piles. They went from village to village, begging for grain, and roasted it and ate it. The old man, their father, also went begging, made bread for himself, and ate it.

In another place there was a brahman who had one daughter. When her mother died, he married again and had another daughter. His second wife said, "Marry my daughter into a fine family, but give this one into any old place. Give her to a house with five bachelors."

Her husband went searching for such a house but could not find one anywhere. Many days passed and he kept wandering and searching. At last he heard about the brahman widower with his five bachelor sons and he arranged the match. They came for the marriage very poorly dressed. The stepdaughter was given in marriage to the middle brother. For wedding gifts, her stepmother gave her a broken tray, a broken brass pot, and a torn quilt and mattress. That woman was so unfeeling, as a real mother could never be, that she filled the huge clay jar with pieces of old plaster which she had dug up from the ruin of a broken-down wall [traditionally, this vessel would be filled with a special fried treat made of white flour]. She covered the mouth of the jar with a red cloth. This was the send-off that she gave to her stepdaughter.

The five bachelors, their old father, and the bride traveled in a borrowed ox cart. After some time, when they were approaching a river, the five bachelors felt they were dying of hunger. They began to grunt rudely to show how hungry they were. The father-in-law said, "Don't do that! What will this little one think? Look, you are five bachelors and you are grunting very rudely. Don't do that. Instead, let us go to the riverbank, relieve ourselves, wash, and then we will eat whatever is in the huge clay jar."

Now the girl knew there were pieces of plaster in the jar. She was a blooming young girl of seventeen or eighteen years, and very clever, and she knew that her stepmother had filled the jar with pieces of plaster. She thought, "Now these five bachelors will beat me." They were about to open the jar.

The girl's mother when she was alive had always faithfully followed the rules of Mother Ten, and during the ten special days for the worship of Mother Ten she always told that goddess's story first, and only afterward did she eat her food. Actually, her daughter had been born by the grace of Mother Ten. So now the girl prayed to Mother Ten: "Sustain my honor, sustain my honor! My mother always followed your rules and I was given to her by you. Therefore only you can sustain my honor, and if you don't, then right now the five bachelors will beat me." Just at that moment, as the men sat to eat, by the grace of Mother Ten the jar was filled with fried treats. Because the girl's mother had followed the rules of Mother Ten, Mother Ten fulfilled the needs of her daughter.

The father-in-law was quite pleased. He told her husband's younger brother to give the bride a snack of the fine treats. So she ate and drank. Then they tied up the mouth of the jar and put it back in the cart. And they all went on their way.

They came to the village of the five bachelors. When the clever women of the village saw the new bride they said, "Oh, look! Lakṣmī has come. [A new bride is often identified with Lakṣmī, the goddess of prosperity, who is of course identified with Mother Ten.] She has all good qualities and no bad qualities." Then five women of the village went to the huts where the five bachelors lived and took the new bride inside.

The bride got up early the next morning after the father-in-law and his sons had left to go begging for grain. She looked all around and saw all the huts, all the cooking hearths, all the roasting ovens and all the manure piles.

The bride went to her neighbors and said, "Aunties, please give me five kilos of wheat and just a little bit of dried greens too so that I can boil vegetable sauce."

The neighbor women said among themselves, "Lakṣmī has come, poor thing, let her have what she wants. Where else will she go?" And they gave her the grain and dried greens. Then she ground the wheat into flour and went back to ask the neighbor women for a sifter so she could sift the flour. They said, "Lakṣmī has come, let her have what she wants." They gave her a sifter. She boiled the greens into vegetable sauce and sifted the flour.

Then she asked the neighbor women, "Which cooking hearth is my husband's father's and which manure pile and which roasting oven?" They pointed the father-in-law's out to her. First she dug up all the five brothers' manure piles and combined them with her father-in-law's, making them all into one. Then she tore out the five brothers' cooking hearths and threw them in that manure pile. Then she broke up the five brothers' roasting ovens. After this she set to work cleaning all the huts. She swept and cleaned them thoroughly and then began to make bread. [Here Shobhag Kanvar broke out of her recitative storytelling voice to interject her own commentary, conversationally: "Lakṣmī is a woman and a house is not man's, it is woman's."]

Soon the five bachelors arrived, each bringing one or two kilos of grain which they had received while begging. They began at once to yell, "Oh no! Someone dug up my cooking hearth! Oh woe is me! Someone broke up my roasting oven."

But the bride said, "Don't make a racket. All of you bring your separate bags of grain and put them in a pile right here next to me. Then go to the tank and bathe. After you have cleaned your bodies and washed your clothes, on the way back, go to the temple and bow in front of Ṭhākurjī [a name often used for God, meaning "ruler"]. Then come home and eat bread."

When the brothers were returning from the tank it was easy to see that they had just bathed, because one had a wet ear and one had a wet back, and so on. The villagers were surprised and said to one another, "Ah, who has put a nose-ring on the bachelors today?" [That is, who has brought them under control like an ox?] But persons in the know said, "Ah, today Lakṣmī has come into their house." They went to the temple, and some bumped into the columns, and some looked at Ṭhākurjī, but soon they all came running home, just dying of hunger.

Then the bride said, "Don't make a racket, just sit down." They sat and she placed trays of food in front of them. First she served her father-in-law and then she served the two younger bothers of her husband and then she served the two elder brothers of her husband and last she served her husband. One of them ate five pieces of bread and one ate four and one ate six. But they all said, "Ah, today our brother's wife has satisfied us. It is good that our brother's wife has come. For so many days we have eaten nothing but roasted grains." The brothers decided, "Today we went to two villages but tomorrow we will go to four and we will bring a lot of grain and eat a lot of bread."

And so they did. The brahman's daughter returned to her neighbors the five kilos of wheat that she had borrowed from them, and there was more left over. So she cleaned it and ground it into flour. Every day she put all the grain that the men brought in one pile. They had plenty of food now because this girl was born by the grace of Mother Ten and wealth was in her hand. She knew many things in her heart. This was because Mother Ten had turned her heart's key, and opened her heart, and put ideas in her brain.

After a few days had passed, she said to her husband's younger brother, "The earnings of five sons are enough. Your old man's earnings are no longer needed. Now he is old. Let him collect small kindling and dry wood and bring it for the cooking fire." So the father-in-law went and gathered little sticks, brought them and threw them down by the hearth, and the bride ground grain and kneaded dough and prepared bread.

The five brothers brought huge bundles of grain tied up with cloth. Some days they brought 40 kilos, some days 80 kilos, some days 120 kilos, sometimes each of the five brought a full 40 kilos so that all together they had 200 kilos. They had so much grain it wouldn't fit in the huts.

One day in the rainy season the father-in-law found a dead snake lying on the ground and he brought it home and threw it up on the roof of his hut. Soon afterwards, the queen of that land was bathing. She had removed her necklace, which was worth millions, and set it down nearby. Just then it happened that a hawk flew by and took the necklace and flew away with it. It flew over the huts of the five bachelors and there was the dead snake lying on the roof. The hawk dropped the necklace and picked up the dead snake and flew away. The hawk took the snake because it was something to eat.

Now the bride was standing outside and saw this happen. She immediately took the necklace into the hut. Soon the king's men began to tour the kingdom, announcing in all the towns and villages that whoever found the queen's necklace and brought it to the king would have as a reward whatever he demanded. The whole kingdom was searching for the necklace. Then the bride told her husband's father to tie it up in a handkerchief and take it to the king. She said, "Tell him that you want nothing at all. Tell him only that on Divālī, Lakṣmī's day, light should burn in the five bachelors' huts and in the castle. But outside of those two places, in the whole kingdom, nothing should burn—no lamp, no electricity, nothing at all. Tell him, 'On the day of Lakṣmī worship, Divālī, there should be absolutely no light allowed anywhere except in the king's castle and in the five bachelors' huts.' " [Divālī falls on the pitch-dark new-moon night in fall. It is normally celebrated in each household by placing many clay lamps—small dishes of oil with wicks floating in them—on top of walls and roofs and on window sills.]

The father-in-law did as she said and the king agreed to his conditions. He called together all the chiefs of police and they went with their soldiers to each and every house to sit and enforce complete darkness. The entire city was completely dark, but lamps were burning in the five bachelors' huts and in the castle.

Both Mother Ten and Bad Ten came on Divālī night. Bad Ten slipped easily into each and every house, under cover of darkness. But where could Mother Ten enter? She saw no light and so she could not enter any house. She wandered all over the village, here and there, but Mother Ten could not enter anywhere because of the darkness. She thought to herself, "I'll find a place or else I'll turn back."

Then, suddenly, she saw lamps burning in the bachelors' huts, flickering and gleaming. The lamps had been filled with oil by the brahman girl. She had also lit a big torch and it was shining in the bachelors' huts like the moon. But the rest of the village was completely dark. Where the lamp was, there was Lakṣmī's dwelling.

Now Mother Ten wanted to enter right away, but the brahman's daughter would not open the door. She said, "No, you go present yourself elsewhere in the village." It got to be late, 4 A.M., and Mother Ten was very upset. She said, "You brahman girl, you open the door!" But the girl said, "Give me a promise, give me a promise."

So Mother Ten gave a promise. She swore: "If I forget my promise may I wither upon my feet, may I hang upside-down in a washerman's pool. For fourteen generations I will never leave you." This was the promise Mother Ten gave to that brahman girl.

Then the girl opened the door and Mother Ten put her foot in the hut. At once the hut flew away and in its place was a nine-story castle, made of glass, with gold and silver fittings, and many diamonds and rubies, and hundreds of thousands of rupees. How could this be? It was all given by Mother Ten, and what does she lack?

Oh, my Mother Ten, as her wishes were fulfilled, so let the world's wishes be.

THE SWORD-HUSBAND

There was once a brahman who had no sons or daughters. One day his wife said to him, "Take this sword, arrange its engagement, and get it married. Arrange the engagement and marriage of our 'son.' "

This brahman's wife always followed the rules of Mother Ten. During the days of Mother Ten's worship she would daily make a design on the ground with cowdung paste, put whole grains and the skein of yarn on it, and tell Mother Ten's stories. She was deeply devoted.

She told her husband to arrange the sword's marriage. She told him what to say to the bride's party: "My son has gone on a long business trip and I want to fix his engagement. If he is not back in time for the wedding, then, no matter. In the ceremony the sword can take the marriage rounds."

[Shobhag Kanvar here broke out of the story sequence to explain to me, a foreigner, that among brahmans, merchants, and her own Rajput caste, in not-so-distant times it truly happened that swords were used as proxy grooms in wedding ceremonies.]

Because she followed the rules of Mother Ten, the brahman's wife was acting out of faith. Her husband went at once. He found a suitable family and told them his son had gone on a long journey in order to earn a lot of money, but that meanwhile he wanted to arrange his marriage. He fixed the time, and on the appointed day the sword's wedding party set off with much pomp. The sword was ornamented with all the splendor of a bridegroom, including a turban and a garland and everything else that was necessary.

They reached the bride's village and went to her house. The wooden marriage emblem (*toraṇ*) was set over the doorway and the sword struck it. Then they took the sword into the house and performed the "knotting together" and the "joining of hands" ceremonies coupling the bride and the sword. In this fashion the sword took "marriage rounds" with the girl. [By mentioning these four important moments of the Rajasthani marriage ritual, familiar to everyone, Shobhag Kanvar provides verisimilitude to the outlandish image of a sword-bridegroom.]

Then the wedding party departed for the brahman's village, bringing the new bride. They took the bride inside the house, and for a few days young girls came and wanted to visit the bride. Her mother-in-law sat in the entranceway of the house, and the daughter-in-law sat there too, and every day girls and boys came to visit, and they passed the time in conversation. So a month or two went by. Then the girl's family came to take her back, so they took her. [A new bride's first sojourn in her marital home is normally a short one.]

But soon that old woman, the brahman's wife, said to her husband, "Time passes so pleasantly when my daughter-in-law is here. You must bring her back." So he brought her back to live with them. The neighbor girls wanted to visit with her, but her mother-in-law forbade it.

The mother-in-law ordered her "son's" bride, "Don't ever let the cooking fire go out, and don't ever let the water in the water pots run dry, and don't ever go to the houses of others because there you will receive false instruction."

However, one day by chance it happened that the cooking fire went out, and the water pots were empty. Then the daughter-in-law ran to the neighbor's house and said, "Oh Auntie, please give me at once some burning coals so I can start my cooking fire. Hurry before my mother-in-law calls me. If it weren't for her I would always be visiting at neighbors' homes."

Then the neighbor women all taunted her. "You fool, you have no groom, you have no man in your house, you married a sword. Your mother-in-law and father-in-law have no son."

Hearing this the girl became angry. "Oh ho, they have no son. They told me he had gone on a long journey to earn a lot of money, but you tell me they have no son."

"Yes, they have no son, they are childless, and are just taking advantage of you to live easily" [because a daughter-in-law does all the household chores]. Hearing all this made her so angry that she decided to trick her mother-in-law. One day she got her chance. The mother-in-law fell asleep sitting up; her head hung over and she was nodding. The daughter-in-law saw that she was wearing a bunch of keys at her waist. Stealthily, she took the keys and began to open the doors of the inner rooms of the house. She opened the locks of the doors with her mother-in-law's keys while her mother-in-law was sleeping.

In the first room she found grain in piles and boxes lying around. In the second room, there were various goods, and in the third, there was iron and wood and this and that, household things, lying around.

But in the seventh of seven inner rooms, there was a ten-pointed design on the floor, a ten-pointed design and upon it were whole grains of gold—whole grains of gold and a gold lamp. In this inner room a king's son was sleeping. He had been given by Mother Ten and lived in this room where the goddess provided him with food and drink.

As soon as she saw this miracle the daughter-in-law said to herself, "Oh ho, I have been in all the rooms and what is this that I have found here?" Then she asked him, "Who are you?" And he answered, "I am the brahman's son. I was given by Mother Ten. Because my mother always follows her rules and tells her stories, Mother Ten has given me to her." Right away the girl and the prince began to play parcheesi [a common way to refer to marital intimacy in Rajasthani folklore]. After that she prepared food for him.

Now the daughter-in-law worked hard and pleased her mother-in-law and father-in-law. But secretly she had a duplicate made of the key to the innermost room. She put the original back when her mother-in-law was sleeping. Her mother-in-law was not suspicious because she was a trusting person and she never knew that the girl had done this.

Every day the daughter-in-law finished her work of making bread and bringing water as fast as she could, and then she went at once to the inner room. And at night when her mother-in-law and father-in-law were sleeping, she went there also. Living in this way two years passed, and by the grace of God she became pregnant. One day when she was about seven months pregnant the mother-in-law noticed her daughter-in-law's big stomach. She said in surprise, "Oh, a lot has happened!" Now the brahman couple did not know about their son in the innermost room.

When the girl was eight months pregnant she asked her mother-in-law to get some special sweets for her and to inform her relatives of the coming happy event. But the mother-in-law said, "Daughter-in-law, aren't you dying of shame?" The daughter-in-law only repeated, "You must send the good news to my home." Then the mother-in-law answered, "How will I cut my nose [experience great public shame] and send the news to your home? My son has gone on a long journey to earn a lot of money and is not here and never has come here. You have certainly cut all our noses." This is the kind of thing she was saying. But the daughter-in-law insisted: "No, your son is here, right here, and you must send the good news to my parents' house."

So the mother-in-law thought, "All right, the nose is cut anyway." Then she sent a man immediately to tell the girl's family a child was going to be born, and they should come and bring sweets.

The girl's family was very happy when they received this message. They came to their daughter's husband's village with great pomp and celebration, with a band playing and a big display of money. They came in ox carts and horse carts and motor cars. They came making a great show; two hundred, four hundred, perhaps five hundred people came, and they had a great celebration. But the women of the village gossiped. "Aren't the brahman and his wife dying of shame? Look, there is no groom, no son, and who knows where she got her stomach. They ought to be ashamed." But the daughter-in-law said, "If anyone speaks like that then throw them out of here and don't listen to them."

Then the daughter-in-law said to her father-in-law and mother-in-law, "Clean everything in the house and bathe and have the band play and put on good clothes and I also will dress in finery and pearls." When all these preparations were complete, she told them to be seated together [as a couple would for a religious ritual or for their child's wedding]. Then she went and stood in front of the closed locked doors and prayed: "If Mother Ten is true, then all of these locks will open right now of their own accord and the prince will come out. If this does not happen then Mother Ten is false."

Then her mother-in-law mediated and prayed, "Mother Ten, I have fasted on your fast days for twenty-four years and told your stories with firm attention and always followed your rules. Now, because of my truthful principles, give me a son."

Then, "*khat, khat, khat*" the locks broke and the prince, a blooming youth with curling mustaches, twenty-five years old, emerged and sat down next to the brahman's daughter, his wife. Then the mother-in-law fell at her daughter-in-law's feet and the daughter-in-law fell at her mother-in-law's feet. The mother-in-law said, "Daughter-in-law, in your fortune, in your destiny, it must have been written that you would be a happily married woman, and for this reason Mother Ten gave me a son."

But the daughter-in-law said, "Dear Mother-in-law, you told the stories of Mother Ten, and if you had not done that, then where would it have been written for me to have a 'lord of the house' [husband]?"

Then the whole village gathered to see the wonder. They came to see what had happened. The boy given by Mother Ten was so handsome he was just like a king, his face shone like the moon's. Then their house became a nine-storey palace and Mother Ten dwelled with them there. Where Mother Ten dwells there is always wealth in plenty, so they never wanted for anything.

Hey, Mother Ten, give well-being to the whole world and then give it to me.

THE OLD WOMAN AND THE YELLOW CALF

There was an old woman who always followed the rules of Mother Ten. She ate bread only after telling the stories of Mother Ten. Mother Ten was pleased with her and thought to herself, "This is our old woman and we will give her a calf."

That night when she was sound asleep, the old woman dreamed that she heard a command: "Go to the yellow-dirt mine and make the sound '*pīlar pīlar pīlar pīlar pīlar pīlar*' and a yellow female calf will come to you" (*pīlā* means "yellow").

Immediately the old woman jumped up from her bed and went to the yellow-dirt mine and called "*pīlar pīlar pīlar pīlar pīlar pīlar.*" Right away a yellow female calf came to her, and the old lady took it back to her home. She took it to her home and tied it up outside her house.

Now this was no ordinary calf. When it made dung, its dung was pure gold. But the neighbor woman would come and take away the golden dung and the old woman didn't know anything about it. In this way several days passed and the old woman was still very unhappy because, although she always performed the proper worship of Mother Ten, still she had nothing. She did not know that the calf's dung was golden, but she did know that someone was taking away its dung every day. [Village women regularly collect cow dung as it has many household uses.] So she decided to bring the calf inside at night and she tied it to the leg of her bed. In the morning she discovered the calf's golden dung and she was very happy.

But the neighbor woman became jealous. She was so jealous she could not bear it. So the neighbor woman went to the king. She told the king, "There is an old woman and she has such a calf, such a calf as ought to live with kings. That female calf would look beautiful in your palace."

The king gave a command to summon the old woman to the palace. The king's messenger came to her house and said, "Old Woman, the king is calling you."

She replied, "Brother, when Rām [a name of God] calls then I must go but if the king is calling, why should I go? What has the king to do with me?"

But the messenger said, "Let's go, lady. The king told me: 'Inform the old woman that she must show me her calf. That very calf of hers would look fine in my palace.' "

Then the old woman agreed to go. She went to the king and said to him, "Lord, Mother Ten was satisfied with me. One day I went to sleep hungry and at midnight Mother Ten came to me and said, 'Friend, why do you sleep hungry? Go to the yellow-dirt mine and make the sound "*pīlar pīlar*" and you will get a female calf.' So, great King, for ten days I tied it outside and my neighbor came and stole the dung, but now for several days I have tied it inside. Because she could not stand her jealousy she came and told you. All right, if you demand it, then take it. Why do I need the female calf? O King, demand it and take it, if you want it."

The king said, "Bring the calf and tie it in the palace. It makes golden dung so it belongs in my palace."

So the old woman brought the calf and tied it in the king's palace. Then the calf began to make a great deal of dung, but it was not golden. The palace was soon filled with it. The calf made watery dung, all by the grace of Mother Ten. It shot out dung with great force, on top of the king's royal bed and all over his trunks and boxes; everything was covered with it. And the calf also kicked; it kicked the mirrors and the cupboards and broke them.

The king summoned the neighbor woman and said, "You wretch, you told me this calf made golden dung, but it has filled my castle with its excrement and it has broken the royal beds and the mirrors and the cupboards. It has broken everything and I am in great distress. You must bring someone at once who can remove it from the palace."

She answered, "Great King, I know nothing about it, that old woman knows." Again the king's messenger came to the old woman's house. "Old woman, old woman, the king summons you."

She replied, "What's all this? The king is always calling me. I went only yesterday." But she went to the palace.

The king said to her, "I can't stand it. Take the calf away." He said, "Old woman, you must know magic, you must be a magician, because when it was with you the calf made golden dung but as soon as it came to me it began to make foul excrement."

She said, "King, I only follow the rules of Mother Ten and I tell her stories. The calf was given to me by her. I have picked no one's pocket, I have stolen nothing. I have let nobody else's livestock loose. The calf was given to me by Mother Ten, but you couldn't bear to see me have it so you demanded it and took it for yourself."

Then the king decided to keep the old woman in his court for the rest of her days, to give her everything she needed to live comfortably. He said, "Mother [addressing her for the first time with appropriate respect], you sit here near me in my castle and praise God and tell my court about noble things, tell about Mother Ten, and eat your bread right here."

Hey, caretaker, Mother Ten, as the king looked after her, so you look after everyone.

Notes

1. I would like to acknowledge the thoughtful cooperation of Shobhag Kanvar and Vajendra Kumar Sharma, without whom I would not have been able to bring these tales to a Western audience.

—6—

The Life of Guru Nānak

Hew McLeod

The Sikh faith begins with Guru Nānak, born in the Punjab in 1469 and dying there in 1538 or 1539. Nānak himself was raised as a Hindu in a predominantly Muslim part of India, but adopted the same critical attitude toward the two religious systems. He believed that although it was possible for both Hindus and Muslims to win liberation, this could only be achieved by renouncing all trust in the external features of either religion. For Nānak the only true religion was within.

Nānak believed emphatically in Akāl Purakh (God), and for him liberation lay in the merging of the human spirit with the all-embracing spirit of God. For Nānak the key to liberation lay in the nām or divine Name. It was the nām that gathered into a single word the whole nature of God, the fullness of God's greatness being clearly perceived in all that was expressed by the all-pervading divine Name. God pervades all things (both those which lie around and those which dwell within), and the person who realizes this is the one who comprehends the Name. Recognize this, and you have taken the first essential step on the pathway to liberation. Practice with regularity and determination a pattern of meditation on the divine Name, and eventually you must attain to that condition of supreme bliss.

This message is variously spelled out in the numerous hymns of Guru Nānak, collected in the *Ādi Granth* (the *Guru Granth Sāhib*) with those of his four successors and some other religious poets who had the same message. In these hymns he tells us a great deal about his teachings, yet almost nothing about his actual life. His followers (the early Sikhs) could not be satisfied with this and inevitably there developed within the Panth (the Sikh community) the practice of relating hagiographic tales concerning the greatness of the guru. These in turn came to be written down and in their recorded form they are known as janam-sākhīs.

The janam-sakhīs consist of anecdotes about Nānak. In an early version these were ordered roughly according to the guru's childhood, adult life, and death. As they were told and retold they became more sophisticated, and in one of the later janam-sākhī traditions (the so-called Puratan tradition), much of Guru Nānak's adult life is arranged into four missionary journeys directed to the four cardinal points of the compass.

A janam-sākhī version of the birth and childhood of Nānak, together with the call to preach and his ultimate death, is contained in my *Textual Sources for the Study of Sikhism*. The selection of anecdotes offered here is taken from his adult life, most of them from the period of his travels. In the translation, words and occasionally phrases have been added to the original in order to impart continuity to the story, but in no case has anything else been added.

Further Reading

See my books, *Early Sikh Tradition* (Oxford: Clarendon Press, 1980); *Guru Nanak and the Sikh Religion* (Oxford: Clarendon Press, 1968); and *Textual Sources for the Study of Sikhism* (Chicago: University of Chicago Press, 1990).

The first anecdote is a humorous tale in which Nānak gently rebukes Hindus, gathered at the Gaṅgā.

Many people had come to the Gaṅgā to bathe. Bābā ("Father") Nānak also went there and, sitting down beside the river, he looked around. "Perhaps I shall see someone who is near to God," he thought. He observed that tens of thousands of people were bathing. Having taken their dip, they offered water to their forefathers, although they did not realize that none of their forefathers was cleansed. Bābā Nānak possessed divine knowledge, whereas the people whom he observed had only a mundane understanding. They believed that purity comes from bathing, and so they bathed. According to Bābā Nānak's understanding, however, it had no effect.

Bābā Nānak also entered the water to bathe. The people were worshiping facing the rising sun, but Bābā Nānak began to bathe facing the direction of the setting sun. Other people were casting water toward the rising sun. Bābā Nānak began to throw water in the direction of the sun's setting. Observing this, the people asked him, "Are you a Hindu, friend, or are you a Muslim?" [From the Gaṅgā River the direction of the setting sun is also, roughly, the direction of Mecca].

"I am a Hindu," answered Bābā Nānak. "If you are a Hindu," they said, "to whom are you casting water?"

"To whom are *you* casting water?" countered Bābā Nānak

"We are casting water to our forefathers," they replied.

"Where are your forefathers?" enquired Bābā Nānak.

"Our forefathers are in heaven," they answered.

"How far is heaven from here?" asked Bābā Nānak.

"Heaven is forty-nine and a half crores [ten millions] of miles from here," they replied. "The location of the land of departed souls is there, and that is where we are throwing water."

"Will it get there?" asked Bābā Nānak, and they answered, "Yes, it will get there."

When they said this, Bābā Nānak cast a little water forward and then began to toss large quantities of it.

"To whom are you throwing water?" they asked. "And so much water!"

"At home I have a field," replied Guru Bābā Nānak, "and the unripe grain in it is withering. I am watering that field."

"But Master," they protested, "how can the water reach your field? Why are you throwing water like this?"

"My friends," said Bābā Nānak, "if water will not reach my field then how can it reach your forefathers? Your forefathers are away in heaven. How can the water get there?" When Bābā Nānak said this, they exclaimed, "Brothers, this is no ordinary person. This is indeed a great one."

The next tale describes an encounter that Guru Nānak, while on his travels, had with a robber. In this story the janam-sākhī author is faithful to the message of Nānak that the divine Name is the sole and sufficient remedy awaiting the erring person.

There was once a villainous robber named Bhola who every day sat on an elevated lookout, wearing white clothes and terrorizing the road below. He was a fearless fellow who would tackle eight or ten men at a time, and he had committed many crimes. When he observed Bābā Nānak approaching, he descended from his lookout and, hovering near him, he threateningly announced, "Remove your clothes or I shall kill you."

"Well!" exclaimed Bābā Nānak. "So I have fallen into your clutches! Do one thing for me—I shall not run away. Return home and when you arrive there put a question to your family—to your mother, father, wife, and sons. You do evil and commit murder, and at the same time you provide for them. Now ask them this question: "When you are in trouble will there be anyone from your entire family who will stand by you in your misfortune?"

"You are deceiving me," said Bhola. "You will run away."

"Take my word for it," promised Bābā Nānak. "I shall not go."

Bhola the robber returned home, and when he arrived there he gathered his family together—mother, father, sons, wife, the entire family. "Listen," he said, "I have committed a thousand murders and crimes without number to provide your food. Tell me, when I am in trouble will any of you share my anguish? Will any of you break the god of death's net? Can any of you release me from his angel? Will any of you share my suffering, or will you not?"

"Your deeds will be your companions," they all replied, "for as you act so you appear for judgment before God. The relationship between you and us concerns only this life. Whether a man does good or whether he does evil, while at the same time caring for his family, in the court of God he must answer alone. No one can be taken as a substitute for another."

At this Bhola was most distressed, and beat upon the ground with both hands. "Have I foolishly wasted all these years with you?" he cried. "If at the end you are going to desert me then why have I spent my life committing a thousand crimes and murders, while providing for you?"

He went off wailing and coming to Bābā Nānak, fell at his feet. Then he stood up with palms joined in supplication. "I have been grossly negligent," he humbly confessed. "Forgive my evil deeds. My whole life has been spent in this manner. Accept me. Amend my life that I may be restored."

"Prostrate yourself," commanded Bābā Nānak, and then he released Bhola from the penalty of his misdeeds. Having forgiven him, Bābā Nānak sang a hymn in sūhī rāga.

> Bronze shines brightly, but rub it and it sheds an inky black.
> Though I clean it a hundred times, polishing will never remove its stain.
>
> O heedless one! They are my real friends who accompany me now and who will accompany me into the hereafter,
> Who, where accounts are demanded, will stand and give an account of good deeds done.
>
> Houses, temples, and palaces may be colorful without,
> But let them collapse and they are useless and empty.
>
> The heron wears garments of white and dwells at places of pilgrimage.
> But as it pecks and rummages it consumes and destroys life; how then can it be regarded as pure?
>
> My body is like a simmal [silk-cotton] tree which men, when they observe it, mistake as useful.
> But as its fruit is devoid of value, so is my body empty of virtue.
>
> A blind man bearing a burden and climbing a precipitous path;
> I scan the road but, finding nothing, how can I hope to pass over?
>
> Of what use is any service, virtue, or wisdom other than the divine Name?
> Cherish the Name, O Nānak, for only thus shall your bonds be broken.
>
> Bābā Nānak thus relieved Bhola the robber of his distress and proceeded on his way.

According to the janam-sākhī accounts, Bābā Nānak traveled to Mecca.

When Bābā Nānak was making his way toward Mecca, on the road he happened to encounter some fakirs (faqīr). They asked him, "What is your name?" Bābā

Nānak answered, "It is Nānak." They then asked him, "Are you a Hindu or a Muslim?" and he replied, "I am a Hindu." Hearing this they drew away from him. "Nānak!" they exclaimed, "this is no road for Hindus!"

"Very well," said Bābā Nānak. "Let us make the pilgrimage to Mecca separately and whoever God takes will go there. Proceed on your way." When Bābā Nānak said this they left him and went on their way, while he remained there. It was a year's journey to Mecca, and after a year the fakirs reached the city. When they arrived, whom should they see but Bābā Nānak already there! The fakirs were astounded. "We left him behind and yet he has arrived ahead of us!" they exclaimed. "What marvel is this?"

The fakirs then enquired from the people of Mecca concerning Bābā Nānak. "How long has this fakir been here, friends?" they asked.

"This fakir has been here for a year," answered the people of the place.

"O God, has a Hindu drawn so near to you?" cried the fakirs. "Glory to your grace whereby he has been brought near to you. You have imparted your grace to a Hindu." They then related what had happened along the way. The people of Mecca, however, assured them: "This is no Hindu. This is a great sage, one who recites the nāmāz [Muslim prayer, particularly the prescribed daily prayers]. Everyone recites the nāmāz after him. He recites the nāmāz before anyone else."

"He told us he was a Hindu," said the fakirs, "but he is really a Muslim and thus he has come near to God. We were amazed, wondering how a Hindu could draw near to God in this way."

While in Mecca, Bābā Nānak went into a mosque and dropped off to sleep with his feet toward the mosque's miḥrāb (the niche in a mosque which marks the direction of the Ka'bah in Mecca). The story is a familiar one in Sufi hagiography, telling how the very house of God moves in obedience to the presence of a great Muslim mystic. In this case it revolves for one who is not a Muslim and is greater than the greatest of Sufis.

Bābā Nānak lay down in the Mecca mosque and went to sleep with his feet toward the miḥrāb. A mulla, who was the mosque attendant, appeared and cried out, "You blasphemous fellow! Why have you gone to sleep with your feet in the direction of the house of God?"

"My friend," answered Bābā Nānak, "lay my feet in whatever direction the house of God is not be found."

When the mulla pulled Bābā Nānak's feet around in a northerly direction, the miḥrāb moved in the same direction. When he moved Bābā Nānak's feet to the east, the miḥrāb also moved in that direction, and when he dragged Bābā Nānak's feet to the south, the miḥrāb went the same way. Then from the cupola of the mosque there echoed a voice, mysterious and resonant: "Praise be to Nānak! Praise be to Nānak!" it boomed.

During the lifetime of Nānak, the Mughals under Bābar invaded from Afghanistan, and following the battle of Panipat in 1526, Mughal rule was established in north India with Bābar as the first emperor. Janam-sākhīs naturally include anecdotes concerning Bābā Nānak's encounter with Bābar. Although none of these is likely to have occurred, Guru Nānak certainly witnessed the Mughal invasions, as he has left four hymns that are clearly the work of an eyewitness. The most famous of these centers on the Mughal sack of the Punjabi town of Saidpur.

Carrying on to Saidpur, Bābā Nānak stopped outside the town and rested. Further on, a wedding was being celebrated in the house of some Pathans [Afghans], and the Pathans were dancing. With Bābā Nānak there were some fakirs who were very hungry. He remained for some time at that place, but no one paid any heed to him sitting there. The fakirs were weak with hunger, and so Bābā Nānak arose and, taking with him Mardana [the guru's faithful companion] and the fakirs, went into the town. There they asked for food, but at all the houses they visited their request was ignored. Bābā Nānak became exceedingly wrathful. "Mardana," he commanded, "play the rabāb [rebec]!" In anger he sang a hymn in tilaṅg rāga.

> I proclaim the tidings that I have received from the Lord, O Beloved.
> From Kabul he has descended with sin as his marriage-party
> and forcibly demanded a dowry, O Beloved.
> Modesty and sacred duty have gone into hiding,
> and falsehood struts around as Lord, O Beloved.
> The writ of the qāḍī and the brahman no longer runs,
> for it is Satan who reads the marriage ceremony, O Beloved.
> In their agony Muslim women read the Qur'ān
> and cry for help to God, O Beloved.
> And Hindu women, both high caste and low,
> they too suffer the same violation, O Beloved.
> It is a song of blood that is sung, O Nānak;
> and blood, O Beloved, is the saffron wherewith they are anointed.
>
> In the city of the dead Nānak praises the Lord, and to all he proclaims this belief:
> He who created the world in all its manifestations sits alone, observing all.
> When the fabric of our body is torn to shreds, then will Hindustan recall my words;
> For the Lord is true, his justice is true, and true will be his judgment.
> He will come in seventy-eight and go in ninety-seven,
> and another disciple of a warrior will arise.
> This is the truth that Nānak utters, the truth that he will proclaim,
> for now is the moment of truth!

On the third day Bābā Nānak returned to Saidpur and entered it. When he gazed around at the town he observed that all its inhabitants had been killed. "Mardana," said Bābā Nānak, "what has happened?"

"My Lord," replied Mardana, "that which pleased you has come to pass."

"Play the rabab, Mardana," said Bābā Nānak. Mardana played the āsā rāga on the rabāb and Bābā Nānak sang this hymn [omitted here].

And so all the Pathans there were slain. The female prisoners of the Pathans were carried off and the rule of Mīr Bābar prevailed. Hindustan was seized and joined to Khurasan.

Bābā Nānak then proceeded to the army encampment and entered it. Now Mīr Bābar was a Sufi. According to the janam-sakhīs, he was secretly a darvīsh or mystic. During the day he performed his royal duties, but at night he cast the fetters off from his feet, bowed his head, and worshiped God. When day dawned he would recite the nāmāz, read the thirty sections of the Qur'ān, and after this consume bhang (cannabis).

Bābā Nānak entered the army encampment and began to sing a hymn. Nearby were the prisoners, and when he looked at them he observed how dreadfully miserable they were. "Mardana," he said, "play the rabāb." He then sang a hymn in tilaṅg rāga.

> You spared Khurasan but yet spread fear in Hindustan.
> Creator, you did this, but to avoid the blame you sent the Mughal
> as the messenger of death.
> Receiving such chastisement, the people cry out in agony
> and yet no anguish touches you.

When Mīr Bābar heard this hymn, he exclaimed, "Friends, fetch that fakir." Some men went and brought Bābā Nānak into his presence. Bābar said, "Fakir, repeat what you just sang." When Bābā Nānak repeated the hymn, the portals of Bābar's understanding opened. "Friends," he declared, "this is a noble fakir!"

He then opened his bhang pouch and offered it to Bābā Nānak, saying, "Have some bhang, fakir."

"Mīrjī," replied Bābā Nānak, "I have already eaten bhang. I have taken a kind of bhang which induces a condition of permanent intoxication." Bābā Nānak continued, "Mardana, play the rabāb." He then sang a hymn in tilaṅg rāga [omitted].

Bābā Nānak then looked at the prisoners again and was much grieved by their misery. "Mardana," he said, "play the rabāb." Mardana played the rabab and Bābā Nānak sang a hymn in āsā rāga [omitted].

Having uttered this hymn, Bābā Nānak passed into a trance, fell to the ground, and lay there. Bābar came and, standing over him, asked, "What has happened to the fakir?"

"Sir, the fakir is in agony," answered the people. "Seeing the wrath of God, he has fallen into a trance."

"Pray to God that the fakir may arise, friends," commanded Bābar.

Bābā Nānak then sat up, and as he did so there blazed forth a radiance as if a thousand suns had risen. Bābar salaamed and cried, "Have mercy!"

"Mīrjī," replied Bābā Nānak, "if you desire mercy then release the prisoners."

"May I make one request?" asked Bābar.

"Speak," answered Bābā Nānak.

"Promise me one thing and I shall release them."

"Make your request," Bābā Nānak said to him.

"This I ask," said Bābar, "that my kingdom may endure from generation to generation."

"Your kingdom will endure for a time," replied Bābā Nānak.

Having clothed the prisoners, Bābar released them, and Bābā Nānak rejoiced. He took leave of Bābar and went on his way. Crossing the Ravi and Chenab rivers, he made his way through the Punjab inspecting waste lands, in search of a suitable place to stay. Traveling on, he reached a spot beside a river. Crowds of people flocked there. All who heard that he was there came to him. "A true fakir of God has been born," they declared. "His name is Nānak and he is absorbed in his God." Many people gathered there and became disciples. All who came were overjoyed. Whenever Bābā Nānak composed a hymn it was circulated. He composed hymns, and fakirs sang devotional songs. In Nānak's house the truth concerning the one divine Name was expounded. His praises resounded and enormous crowds came to him. Hindus, Muslims, [all manner of people] came and were captivated. All extolled his greatness.

While on his travels, Guru Nānak encountered a frightening creature who turned out to be Kaliyuga, an incarnate version of the fourth cosmic age. The cosmic cycle is divided into four ages and the Kaliyuga, the iron age, is the period of deepest degeneracy which precedes the restoration of absolute truth and fulfilment in the Kṛtayuga or Satyayuga. (We are at present living in the Kaliyuga.) Guru Nānak is here confronted by an incarnate form of this, the evil age, and in his discourse with it he reduces it to total subjection.

Guru Nānak and Mardana entered a great and fearsome wilderness, where no dwelling was to be seen. One day, in accordance with the divine command, there came darkness and a terrible storm. Around them flashed black, white, and red. Torrents of rain fell as awesome black clouds rolled over. Mardana was terrified. "Bābājī!" he cried. "A mighty storm has blown up! It is raining! Let us flee! Come, let us take shelter under a tree!"

"Say 'Praise to the Guru,' Mardana, and nothing will come near you," answered Bābā Nānak. "This darkness and rain with these clouds of smoke will go. Keep calm."

Gradually the darkness and the rain lifted. When they had cleared, there appeared the figure of a demon with huge fangs, the top of his head touching the heavens and its feet the ground. Enormous was its belly and terrifying its evil eyes. Fearsomely it advanced. "Bābājī!" cried Mardana. "God saved us from the storm, but this calamity we shall not escape!"

"Say 'Praise to the Guru,' Mardana," replied Bābā Nānak, "and like the storm this too will depart. Keep calm."

In accordance with the divine command, the apparition assumed the form of a man standing respectfully before them in an attitude of submission. "Who are you?" asked Bābā Nānak. It replied, "Gracious one, I am Kaliyuga. I am greatly honored by your entry into my kingdom, into this domain of mine. Accept an offering from me."

"What is there in all that you have to offer?" asked Bābā Nānak. "Tell me, may I ask whatever I please?"

"Gracious one," replied Kaliyuga, "if you command I shall erect a palace studded with pearls and annointed with musk."

Bābā Nānak, in response, sang a hymn in the measure sirī rāga. "Mardana," he said, "play the rabāb so that I may sing a hymn."

> If I should own a priceless palace, walled with pearl and tiled with jewels,
> Rooms perfumed with musk and saffron, sweet with fragrant sandalwood,
> Yet may your Name remain, O Master, in my thoughts and in my heart.
>
> Apart from God my soul must burn,
> Apart from God no place to turn,
> The guru thus declares [refrain omitted].

Kaliyuga then said, "If you so command I shall encrust the whole world with diamonds and stud a bed with pearls and rubies." In reply, Bābā Nānak sang the second stanza.

> If, in a world aglow with diamonds, rubies deck my bed;
> If, with alluring voice and gesture, maidens proffer charms;
> Yet may your Name remain, O Master, in my thoughts and in my heart.

Kaliyuga then said, "My Lord, if you so command I shall lead the whole of creation captive and lay it in obedience before you." Bābā Nānak then sang the third stanza.

> If with the yogi's mystic art I work impressive deeds,
> Present now, then presto vanished, winning vast renown;
> Yet may your Name remain, O Master, in my thoughts and in my heart.

Kaliyuga then said, "If you so command I shall give you kingship over all lands." Bābā Nānak sang the fourth stanza.

> If as the lord of powerful armies, if as a king enthroned,
> Though my commands bring prompt obedience, yet would my strength be vain.
> Grant that your Name remain, O Master, in my thoughts and in my heart.

"I have no use for the things you have been describing," continued Bābā Nānak. "What else do you have? What kind of kingdom have you? What manner of deeds do you expect from your subjects and what way of life do you impose on them?"

"My Lord, in my kingdom the way of life is of the kind that is typical of this evil age, the Kaliyuga. It consists of hunger, lethargy, thirst, abuse, avarice, sloth, drunkenness, and indolence. Highway robbery, gambling, strangling, slander, the four cardinal sins, falsehood, deceit, wrath, greed, covetousness, and pride abound. There is scarcely one in ten million who can evade my authority. No, *all* are in my power."

"I am asking you for a boon, brother," said Bābā Nānak. "Gracious one," replied Kaliyuga, "I shall do whatever you command."

"Let not any of my Sikhs who may be under your authority be harassed, brother," said Bābā Nānak, "nor any gathering of my followers that may be within your domains. Do not let your shadow fall upon them. Let not the recitation of hymns be neglected, nor the works of mercy and benevolence, holy charity, remembrance of the divine Name, and bathing at the pilgrimage center of truth."

"Merciful one, forgive me," said Kaliyuga humbly. "Of all ages the authority of mine is the greatest."

"If you are going to give a boon," replied Bābā Nānak, "then let it be this. Let the congregation of my followers live in peace, happiness, and the fear of God."

"You are omniscient, merciful one," answered Kaliyuga, "but even if one is regarded by others as a mighty seer (*sadhu*) yet to me he is a mere man."

"If you are going to give a boon then let it be this," repeated Bābā Nānak.

Kaliyuga then adopted an attitude of submission. "My Lord," he said, "my life, my soul, everything is at your disposal."

"Swear to me that this is the case, brother," answered Guru Bābā Nānak.

Kaliyuga swore it three times and fell at his feet. Bābā Nānak was filled with joy. "Go on your way," he said. "Your glory shall exceed that of all ages. In your kingdom there will be the singing of hymns and preaching of the most exalted kind. Previously people performed austerities for a hundred thousand years in order to obtain liberation, but in your age if anyone meditates on the divine Name with undivided concentration for a few short minutes, that person will be liberated."

Later in their travels, Bābā Nānak and Mardana came to a country that was ruled by women. This particular story clearly shows the janam-sākhī debt to puranic and tantric tradition, as the narrative descends from a famous Nāth legend concerning the capture of Machendranāth by the women who ruled the country of Kadali (or Kāmarūpa) and their magical transformation of him into a sheep. Machendranāth was subsequently rescued by Gorakhnāth, as here Mardana was rescued by Bābā Nānak.

Bābā Nānakjī came to a land beside the sea where no man was to be found. Women rule there, and in all villages throughout the country women receive the earnings, not the men. "Bābājī, let us see this country," suggested Mardana.

"This is a land of women," replied Bābā Nānak. "It would be unwise to proceed further into this country."

"Now that we have come so far let us see it," persisted Mardana. "Who else comes so far?"

"Go then if you so desire," said Guru Nānak, "and having seen it return here."

Mardana took his rabāb so that he might beg and, proceeding straight to a town, he entered it. When the women observed him all of them slowly closed in upon him. No man was to be found there. "Come inside," they said, but Mardana replied, "No, I cannot enter."

When they perceived that he would not go in voluntarily, they pushed him in and tied his hands with thread. Their thread was enchanted by means of a potent spell, and through the magic power of the thread they could do whatever they wished with him. When they tied his hands with the thread he changed into a ram. They threw his rabab inside and, having turned him into a ram, they tethered him in the courtyard.

Meanwhile Bābā Nānak was scanning the road, but Mardana did not return. "God be blessed!" said Guru Bābā Nānak. "He used to pluck the strings of his rabab and meditate on the divine Name of God. Wherever has he gone? He had another man with him and he has not returned, either."

Guru Bābā Nānak arose and went to the town. As he proceeded into the town he came to the place where Mardana had been ensnared, and there entered the courtyard. Seeing him enter the women all came to him. "You have my man. Return him to me," commanded Bābā Nānak.

"He is not here," they replied.

When Mardana, who had been turned into a ram, observed Bābā Nānak, he began to scratch the ground with his hoof. He was unable to speak, for when he tried to do so he only bleated. Bābā Nānak saw that it was Mardana and motioned to him to be patient, although he could not help being amused at the same time.

Bābā Nānak then said to the women, "If you would do a good deed, restore my man."

"Sir," they replied, "where is this man? Come in, take food and drink. Where else would you go now?"

As soon as they had said this, Bābā Nānak's hands were instantly tied by the magic thread. But Bābā Nānak is a perfected one. What can overcome him? When their thread was tied on him nothing happened. They called others skilled in sorcery, but those who came also failed. "Restore my man," said Bābā Nānak.

They began to whisper to each other. "This must be some great warrior, someone of mighty power upon whom our charms have no effect."

Bābā Nānak repeated, "If you would do a good deed then restore my man."

"Find your man, wherever he may be, and take him," they replied.

"But you are not giving him to me," said Bābā Nānak.

"Take him!" they answered.

Bābā Nānak released Mardana from the enchanted thread and he stood before them, a man again.

"This is no man!" cried the women [referring to Bābā Nānak]. "This is a god! He on whom our charms were ineffectual must be God!"

All the women came and fell at Bābā Nānak's feet and from their hearts they made this request: "Sir, we have suffered much from the absence of men. Free us, sir, from this suffering." Bābā Nānak, being one who understands inner thoughts and motives, heard their petition and blessed them. They found peace and began to sing the praises of God.

In the first of his lengthy poems (known as *vars*) the celebrated Sikh poet Bhai Gurdās tells, with remarkable brevity, the famous story of how Bābā Nānak approached Multan. As he drew near the city the Muslim holy men of the city brought out for him a cup brimful of milk.

> Bābā Nānak arose and journeyed from the fair to Multan.
> As he drew near, the pīrs of Multan came bringing a cup filled [to the brim] with milk.
> Bābā Nānak plucked a nearby jasmine flower and laid it on the milk,
> Just as the Gaṅgā flows into the ocean!.

In laying the jasmine petal on the milk, Bābā Nānak had not spilled any of it. The intention of the pīrs in offering milk was to indicate that Multan was already brimful of holy men and that accordingly there was no place in the city for Guru Nānak. The point of the guru's response was that as a flower petal could be laid on a brimming cup without causing it to overflow, so Multan could find room for one more holy man, and that the most sublime of them all.

This anecdote is contained in Sufi tradition of an earlier date. The Sufi pīr was ʿAbdul Qādir Jīlānī, the city was Baghdad, the cup was filled with water, and the petal was that of a rose. It is, however, essentially the same anecdote, communicating exactly the same message. The anecdote had, moreover, been transferred by the Sufis to Multan and attached to two different pīrs. The earlier was Baha' al-Dīn Zakariyya, who died in 1266. The second was the slightly later Shams al-Dīn Tabrīzi who was sent the cup by Baha' al-Dīn Zakariyya. In both instances, the cup contained milk.

Before he died in 1539, Nānak passed the leadership of his Sikhs on to the second guru, a man called Lahiṇā whom he renamed Aṅgad. The reason for Guru Nānak's trust in the absolute loyalty of Aṅgad is well illustrated by several stories from the janam-sākhīs. The following serves as an example.

One day Bābā Nānak was bathing and Aṅgad, who had already bathed, was sitting nearby. Bābā Nānak was standing in the river. It was winter and as a result of the squalls and the rain that had fallen it was exceedingly cold. Guru Aṅgad suffered greatly from the cold and the rain. The clothes he was wearing were soaked. Eventually the cold overcame Guru Aṅgad and, losing consciousness, he collapsed.

Having emerged from the river, donned his clothing, and performed his prostrations, Bābā Nānak went to Aṅgad and, reaching him, nudged him with his foot. When Bābā Nānak nudged him, Guru Aṅgad regained consciousness. He was restored. The chill departed, he became warm, and sat up.

"Aṅgad, my son, what happened to you?" asked Bābā Nānak.

"Lord," replied Aṅgad, "you know all things."

"But tell me what happened to you, my son," said Bābā Nānak.

"Sir, my clothing was soaked with rain and I lost consciousness. I was aware of nothing that had happened. I had no knowledge of it at all."

"How are you now?" asked Bābā Nānak.

"Because of you," answered Guru Aṅgad, "I now know that my spirit has been illumined by the light of ten million suns, and that because of you warmth has been restored."

"Well, my son, are you comfortable now?" asked Bābā Nānak, and he replied, "I am comfortable."

Bābā Nānak then said, "This discipline which I perform I do only for my Sikhs. I perform this service in your stead, my son, for your body cannot endure its rigor." If anyone bears the title of Nānak-panthi [a follower of Nānak's way, a disciple of Nānak, a Sikh; in practice the term is generally restricted to Sikhs of the pre-Khālsā period or to those of the later period who do not take the Khālsā vows] he will be liberated.

—7—

Ascetic Withdrawal or Social Engagement

Patrick Olivelle

The sixth century B.C.E. was a watershed in the history of Indian religions, a period that witnessed momentous social, economic, and political changes. A surplus economy, the establishment of cities and large kingdoms, the facility of travel, and the rise of a merchant class contributed to the emergence of several significant religious doctrines and institutions, including the new religious movements of Buddhism and Jainism. A major concept in the emerging new world was *saṃsāra,* a category that provided the framework for understanding and evaluating human life. According to this new understanding, life is ultimately and essentially suffering, subject as it is to repeated births and deaths. The goal of human existence, therefore, should be to transcend this bondage to the cycle of rebirth and to reach the realm of total freedom and bliss called *mokṣa.* The religions sharing this world view challenged the society-centered ritual religion of the earlier Vedic period. The result of this confluence of two opposing worlds was a deep and lasting conflict within Indian religions between the value of responsible social engagement within the context of marriage and family and the ascetic withdrawal from society that was seen as the necessary precondition for achieving liberation.

The conflict between these world views is revealed in the emerging diversity of opinion regarding dharma, that is, the proper way to act and the right doctrines to believe. In the mainstream of the Vedic tradition, dharma meant the rules for ritual and moral behavior contained in the Vedic scriptures. By the sixth century B.C.E., such a simple solution to the question, "What is dharma?" was no longer possible, especially because of the new value systems resulting from ascetic ideologies that considered society and social norms as well as the ritual religion to be part of saṃsāra, the world of suffering subject to rebirth. Good and intelligent people were asking serious questions about ultimate truth and proper conduct, all trying in their own way to define the "true" dharma. The Buddha himself, for example, called his new doctrine and way of life dharma. This spirit of inquiry and doubt is captured well in the following passage from the *Mahābhārata*

(14.48.14–17, slightly abbreviated here), which also reveals the diversity of opinions regarding the proper dharma within the brahmanical tradition itself.

Some sages question a divine being:

> Which of the different paths of proper behavior and conduct (dharma) do the scriptures advise us to follow most closely? The various paths that people take as proper, it appears to us, are diverse and contradictory.
>
> Some, for example, claim that there is life after death, while others maintain that there is not. Some express doubt about everything, while others claim certainty.
>
> Things are impermanent according to some and permanent according to others, unreal according to some and real according to others, while still others claim that they are both real and unreal.
>
> Some believe that the one reality appears as diverse. Some teach unity, others separateness, and yet others multiplicity. So do wise brahmans who know the truth opine.
>
> Some wear matted hair and deer skin, some shave their heads, while others go naked. Some say that one should not bathe, while others insist on bathing. Some favor eating, while others are given to fasting.
>
> Some praise rites and others cessation from them. Some assert the influence of both place and time [in astrology], while others deny it. Some extoll liberation and others diverse pleasures.
>
> Some desire wealth, while others strive after poverty. Some maintain the efficacy of worship, while others deny it.
>
> Some are devoted to noninjury (*ahiṃsā*) and others to injury. Some claim that we attain glory through good deeds, while others deny it.
>
> Some proclaim certainty as to the truth, while others adhere to skepticism. Suffering is the motive for some, pleasure for others.
>
> Some assert the primacy of meditation, others that of sacrifice, and still others that of giving gifts. Some assert the existence of everything, while others deny that anything exists.
>
> Some praise austerity, while others extoll Vedic study. Some assert that knowledge comes from renunciation, while nature philosophers claim that it comes from nature.
>
> With so much disagreement regarding proper belief and conduct (dharma), leading in so many directions, we are bewildered, O God Supreme, unable to reach any certainty.

"This is ultimate bliss," "No, that is ultimate bliss": so thinking, people charge on, for one always praises the dharma to which one is devoted.

Our judgment is confounded in this regard, our mind bewildered. This we want you to tell us, O Lord: what is ultimate bliss?

Centrality of the Householder: Ritual and Procreation

The ideal religious person within the Vedic theology was a married householder devoted to study and ritual activities and intent on fathering children, especially sons, to continue his line. A conversation between King Hariścandra, who had a hundred wives but still failed to obtain a son, and Nārada, recorded in the *Aitareya Brāhmaṇa* provides perhaps the clearest and boldest enunciation of the theological significance of a son and, by implication, of a wife, although, as we shall see below, it also contains hints that significant challenges to this theology were brewing.

The Brāhmaṇas translated in this chapter are printed in *The Aitareya and Kauṣītaki Brāhmaṇas of the Rigveda,* translated by A. B. Keith; Harvard Oriental Series 25 [1920; reprinted Delhi: Motilal Banarsidass, 1971], 7.13. I have benefited greatly from Keith's translation.

Hariścandra asks:

Now, since they desire a son,
Both those who are intelligent and those who aren't;
What does one gain by a son?
Tell me that, O Nārada.

Nārada replies:

A debt he pays in him,
And immortality he gains,
The father who sees the face
Of his son born and alive.

Greater than the delights
That earth, fire, and water
Bring to living beings,
Is a father's delight in his son.

By means of sons have fathers ever
Crossed over the mighty darkness;
For one is born from oneself,
A ferry laden with food.

What is the use of dirt and deer skin [of ascetics]?
What profit in beard and austerity?
Seek a son, O brahman,
He is the world free of blame.

Food is breath, clothes protect.
Gold is for beauty, cattle for marriage.
The wife is a friend, a daughter brings grief.
But a son is a light in the highest heaven.

The husband enters the wife;
Becoming an embryo he enters the mother.
Becoming in her a new man again,
He is born in the tenth month.

A wife is called "wife,"
Because in her he is born again.
He is productive, she's productive,
For the seed is placed in her.

The gods and the seers
Brought to her great luster.
The gods said to men:
"She is your mother again."

"A sonless man has no world."
All the beasts know this.
Therefore a son mounts
Even his mother and sister.

This is the broad and easy path
Along which travel men with sons, free from sorrow;
Beasts and birds see it;
So they copulate even with their mothers.

The importance of a wife for the religious welfare of the husband is a recurring theme in the Vedic texts. The wife is said to be one-half of the husband: "A full half of one's self is one's wife. As long as one does not obtain a wife, therefore, for so long one is not reborn and remains incomplete" (*Śatapatha Brāhmaṇa,* 5.2.10). The fully complete person includes the father, the mother, and the son. Being reborn in the wife as the son, therefore, the wife becomes the husband's mother. According to a popular etymology, the Sanskrit term for wife, *jāyā,* is seen as derived from the fact that the husband is born (*jāyate*) in her. Apart from her indispensable role in procreation, the wife is also essential for the husband's ritual activities, for only a married man accompanied by his wife is entitled to perform a sacrifice. The *Taittirīya Brāhmaṇa* (2.2.2.6) declares: "A man who has no wife is not entitled to sacrifice."

The religious obligation to get married, to study the Vedic scriptures, to offer sacrifices, and to beget offspring was given theological expression in the doctrine of debts. A person is born with debts to significant categories of persons inhabiting the Vedic world. Two parallel formulations are found in the Vedic literature, one enumerating three debts and the other four. The first is found in the *Taittirya Saṃhitā,* 6.3.10.5:

> A brahman, at his very birth, is born with a triple debt—of studentship to the seers, of sacrifice to the gods, of offspring to the fathers. He is, indeed, free from debt, who has a son, is a sacrificer, and who has lived as a student.

The second and more elaborate formulation is found in the *Śatapatha Brāhmaṇa,* 1.7.2.1–6:

> Now, whoever exists is born indeed as a debt at his very birth to the gods, to the seers, to the fathers, and to men. Because he has to sacrifice, he is born as a debt to the gods; and he pays it to them when he sacrifices to them and when he makes offerings to them.
>
> Because he has to study the Veda, furthermore, he is born as a debt to the seers; and he pays it to them, for they call a person who has studied the Veda "the guardian of the seers' treasure."
>
> Because he has to desire offspring, furthermore, he is born as a debt to the fathers; and he pays it to them when he has children that provide the continuity of their lineage.
>
> Because he has to provide shelter, furthermore, he is born as a debt to men; and he pays it to them when he offers them shelter and food.
>
> Whoever does all these things, has done what he has to do; he obtains everything, and he conquers everything.

Centrality of the Ascetic: Celibacy and Renunciation

In the early Upaniṣads we already find evidence of antiritual tendencies that favored celibate modes of life and advocated withdrawal from family and society. The inability of sacrifices to assure liberation from the cycle of rebirth is presented in the following satirical dialogue with a proponent of sacrificial religion recorded in the *Muṇḍaka Upaniṣad,* 1.2.6–10:

> Saying, "Come, come!" the splendid offerings carry that sacrificer on the rays of the sun, praising him and saying sweet words to him: "This is your Brahma-world of merits and good acts."

> These are indeed unsteady rafts, the eighteen sacrificial forms, which teach an inferior ritual (*karma*). The fools who hail it as superior lapse repeatedly into old age and death.
>
> Living in the midst of ignorance, self-wise, and thinking themselves to be learned, the fools go about hurting themselves, like blind men led by one who is himself blind.
>
> Living endlessly in ignorance, the fools think "We have reached our goal!" Because of their passion, those who perform rites (*karmin*) do not understand. When their worlds are exhausted, therefore, they fall down wretched.
>
> Regarding sacrifices and good works as the best, the fools know nothing better. After enjoying the highest heaven of good acts, they enter again this or even a lower world.

The *Bṛhadāraṇyaka Upaniṣad* (4.4.22) associates three central features of the ascetic mode of life—celibacy, mendicancy, and homeless wandering—with those who possess the liberating knowledge of the self as well as with those who aspire to such knowledge:

> The great unborn self, indeed, is he who among the senses consists of knowledge. In the space within the heart lies the controller of all, the lord of all, the ruler of all. He does not increase by good acts (*karman*) or decrease by evil acts. He is the lord of all, he is the ruler of beings, and he is the protector of beings. He is the causeway that separates and keeps these worlds apart. It is he that brahmans seek to know by reciting the Vedas, by sacrifices, by gifts, by penance, and by fasting. It is he, on knowing whom one becomes a silent sage (*muni*). It is he, in desiring whom as their world, wandering ascetics wander forth. When they came to know this, indeed, the men of old had no desire for offspring: "We possess this self, this world; what is the use for us of offspring?" Rising above the desire for sons, the desire for wealth, and the desire for worlds, they lead a mendicant life.

The householder is thus replaced by the celibate renouncer as the new ideal of religious living. Ascetic ideologies, moreover, even denied that it was possible for a householder to attain liberation. A frequently cited stock phrase in the Buddhist canonical texts reveals the ascetic perception of domestic life: "The household life is a dusty path full of hindrances, while the ascetic life is like the open sky. It is not easy for a man who lives at home to practice the holy life (*brahmacariya*) in all its fullness, in all its purity, in all its bright perfection" (*Dīgha Nikāya*, I.63).

The Upaniṣads express the contrast between the ideals of the new theology and those of the Vedic tradition in terms of the opposition between wilderness and village, the respective habitats of ascetics and householders. The *Chandogya Upaniṣad* (5.10.1–2) applies the doctrine of the two paths along which the dead travel—the path of the gods and path of the fathers—to the two classes of people, those who live in the wilderness and those who dwell in villages.

> Now, those who know this and those in the wilderness here who worship with the thought "Faith is our austerity," pass into the flame, and from the flame into the day, from the day into the fortnight of the waxing moon, from the fortnight of the waxing moon into the six months when the sun moves north, from these months into the year, from the year into the sun, from the sun into the moon, from the moon into lightning. There is a person there who is not a man. He leads them to Brahman. This is the path leading to the gods.
>
> But those in villages here who worship with the thought "Sacrifice and good works are our gift," pass into the smoke, and from the smoke into the night, from the night into the latter [i.e., dark] fortnight, from the latter fortnight into the six months when the sun moves south—they do not pass into the year—from these months into the world of the fathers, from the world of the fathers into space, from space into the moon. . . . They live there until [their merits] are exhausted and return by the same course along which they went.

The central activities, especially sacrifice, of those who live at home in a village are associated with return, that is with the prolongation of the rebirth process. Cessation of that process is associated with the activities of those who have left home and village and live in the wilderness.

Defense of Domesticity: Argument and Compromise

In the passage of the *Aitareya Brāhmaṇa* cited above we already see the rejection of ascetic celibacy and the strong defense of marriage and procreation. Later literature focuses especially on the suffering a person causes his forefathers when he assumes a celibate life without leaving any progeny to continue his line. Several episodes found in the *Mahābhārata* illustrate this concern. One day the sage Agastya finds his forefathers hanging upside down in a cave and discovers that they have been reduced to that miserable condition because of his decision to turn celibate without leaving any progeny to continue his line and to provide his forefathers with ritual offerings (*Mahābhārata*, 3.94.11–15). A similar story is told even more graphically in the case of the ascetic Jaratkāru (*Mahābhārata*, 1.41–42). As Jaratkāru was wandering the earth devoted to a life of celibacy and asceticism,

> he saw his forefathers hanging from their feet in a pit, suspended from a single remaining strand of a clump of grass. And a rat living in that pit was

> slowly gnawing through that strand. They lived in that pit without food, emaciated, wretched, and tormented, yearning for help.

Jaratkāru is overwhelmed with compassion and, without recognizing them as his own forefathers, asks how he may help them. His ancestors also do not recognize him and reply:

> We are seers called Yāyāvaras, faithful to our vows. We have fallen here from heaven, sir, because our lineage has been cut off. Our reservoir of austerities and merit has been destroyed, for we have lost our strand. There is, however, one strand left for us now, but that too is as good as lost. To us, luckless as we are, there remains a single unfortunate relative in our family. His name is Jaratkāru, an expert in the Vedas and the auxiliary sciences, full of self control, magnanimous, keeping to his vows, and performing great austerities. Living without a wife, son, or any relative, it is he who out of his greed for austerity has reduced us to this miserable state. So here we hang senseless in this pit without a protector. Be our protector, and when you see him tell him: "Your poor forefathers are hanging from their feet in a pit. Come on, good man, take a wife and bear children!" For a single family strand is left for us, great ascetic. And this clump of grass you see us hanging from, O brahman, it was our family tree that assured the growth of our family. The roots of this clump you see here, O brahman, they are our strands eaten away by Time. And its half-eaten root you see, O brahman, from it all of us hang, and even that one is given to austerity! The rat you see, O brahman, that is mighty Time itself. And it is striking him and slowly killing off that foolish Jaratkāru, the stupid ascetic greedy for austerity. For all that austerity of his will not save us, good man. Our roots are cut, Time torments our minds, and we have fallen. See us stuck in hell like sinners! Since we are fallen here together with our forefathers, he too in due course, when he is cut down by Time, will surely descend here into hell. Whether it is austerity, sacrifice, or other great purificatory act, nothing, dear child, equals offspring—that is the view of the good men. Tell him that, dear child, when you see the ascetic Jaratkāru. Tell him all that you have seen, and speak to him, O brahman, in such a manner that he will be persuaded to get married and beget offspring. You will thus become our protector.

Jaratkāru, torn with grief and guilt, tells his forefathers:

> I am Jaratkāru, your wicked son. This nitwit has committed a crime. Wield your rod of punishment over me!

A compromise between the values of domesticity and asceticism is found in the widely shared view that ascetic modes of life are best suited for people of advanced age who have fulfilled their domestic obligations and whose natural passions have subsided. This view finds expression in the classical āśrama system, according to which a person should live as a student during his adolescent years, get married and live as a householder during his prime and, when his domestic obligations are fulfilled, leave the world and devote himself to ascetic pursuits. This position is stated clearly in the following verses of *Manusmṛti* (4.1; 6.33):

> Having spent the first quarter of his life at his teacher's, a twice-born should get married and spend the second at home.
>
> And having thus spent the third quarter of his life in the forest, he should give up attachments and live as a wandering ascetic during the fourth.

Even in texts that follow the compromise established in the classical āśrama system, we find repeated panegyrics extolling the virtues of domesticity and the superiority of the householder. These texts especially seek to instill in their readers the sinfulness of taking to celibate asceticism without first fulfilling their domestic responsibilities.

> Through a son one wins the worlds, through a grandson one attains eternal life, and through one's son's grandson one ascends the very summit of heaven. A man saves himself by begetting a virtuous son. A man who obtains aia virtuous son saves from the fear of sin seven generations—that is, six others with himself as the seventh—both before him and after him. . . . Therefore, he should assiduously beget offspring.
>
> *Baudhāyana Dharmasūtra* 2.16.6, 8, 9, 11
>
> A householder alone offers sacrifice. A householder afflicts himself with austerities. Of the four āśramas, therefore, the householder is the best.
>
> As all rivers great and small find their rest in the ocean, so people of all āśramas find their rest in the householder.
>
> As all creatures depend on their mothers for their survival, so all mendicants depend on householders for their survival.
>
> *Vasiṣṭha Dharmasūtra,* 10.14–16
>
> As all living beings depend on air for their survival, so all the āśramas depend on the householder for their survival.
>
> The householder constitutes the most excellent āśrama, because it is the householder who daily supports everyone belonging to the other three āśramas with knowledge and food.
>
> After paying the three debts, a man may set his mind on renunciation; a man who practices renunciation without paying them, however, will fall.

A man may set his mind on renunciation only after he has studied the Vedas according to the rule, fathered sons according to precept, and offered sacrifices according to his ability.

A twice-born man falls when he seeks renunciation without first having studied the Vedas, fathered sons, and offered sacrifices.

Student, householder, hermit, and renouncer: these are four distinct āśramas arising from the householder.

Now, all these, when they are undertaken in the proper order and in accordance with the law, lead a brahman who acts properly to the highest state.

Yet, among all of them, according to the dictates of the Vedas and smṛtis [sacred texts], the householder is said to be the best, for he supports the other three.

Manusmṛti 3.77–78; 6.35–37, 87–89

Continuing Debate

Attempts to blunt the opposition between domesticity and celibate asceticism were at best only partially successful. Proponents of asceticism objected especially to the fact that the grand compromise of the āśrama system relegated asceticism to old age, equating it thereby with retirement. The urgency of personal salvation could not brook such postponement. In this final section is a selection of texts that capture the ongoing debate between the two value systems.

The first comes from a *Life of the Buddha* written in the first century C.E. by Aśvaghoṣa, a brahman who converted to Buddhism and became a Buddhist monk. Although the setting is formally Buddhist, the dialogue between the future Buddha and his father, Śuddhodana, captures the controversy both within and outside the brahmanical mainstream regarding the proper age for becoming an ascetic. When the future Buddha informs his father of his intention to leave the world, Śuddhodana tells him:

Give up this plan, dear child; the time is not right for you to devote yourself to religion (dharma). For in the first period of life, when the mind is unsteady, the practice of religion, they say, can cause great harm.

His senses easily excited by sensual pleasures, a young man is incapable of remaining steadfast when confronted with the hardships of ascetic vows. So his mind recoils from the wilderness, especially because he is unaccustomed to solitude.

But for me, lover of religion, it is the time for religion, after I hand over the kingdom to you, prosperity incarnate. If you, however, O man of unwavering

> courage, should forsake your father in violation of the proper order, your religion (dharma) will in fact be irreligion (*adharma*).
>
> So give up this resolve and devote yourself fully to the religion (dharma) of a householder. It is, indeed, a beautiful sight to see a man enter the penance grove after he has enjoyed the pleasures of youth.

The future Buddha listens to his father's plea and gives this terse reply:

> I will not enter the penance grove, O King, if you will be the surety for me in four things. My life shall not be subject to death. Sickness shall not rob me of my health. Old age shall not strike down my youth. And misfortune shall never plunder my wealth.

The father advises the son to refrain from making such extravagant wishes, but the future Buddha replies:

> If this course is not possible, then do not stop me, for it is not right to impede a man trying to escape from a burning house.
>
> Given that separation is certain in this world, is it not better to separate oneself voluntarily for the sake of religion? Or should I wait for death to separate me forcibly even before I have reached my goal and attained satisfaction?
>
> *Buddhacarita* 5.30–38, selections

The rejection of the compromise proposed in the classical āśrama system is also presented vividly in a conversation recorded in the *Mahābhārata* (12.169, selections) between a father, the guardian of the old order, and his son, representing the troubled and anguished spirit of the new religious world. This story, appearing as it does in Jain (*Uttarādhyayana,* 14) and Buddhist (*Jātaka,* 509), and later brahmanical (*Markaṇḍeya Purāṇa,* 10) texts as well, probably belonged to the generic ascetic folklore before it was incorporated into the *Mahābhārata.* This text, just like the story of the Buddha, points to the ascetic rejection of societal attempts to convert asceticism into an institution of old age. To the son's question regarding how a person should lead a virtuous life, the father replies:

> First, learn the Vedas, son, by living as a Vedic student. Then you should desire sons to purify your forefathers, establish the sacred fires, and offer sacrifices. Thereafter, you may enter the forest and seek to become an ascetic.

The son retorts:

> When the world is thus afflicted and surrounded on all sides, when spears rain down, why do you pretend to speak like a wise man?

Father:

> How is the world afflicted? And by whom is it surrounded? What are the spears that rain down? Why, you seem bent on frightening me!

Son:

> The world is afflicted by death. It is surrounded by old age. These days and nights rain down. Why can't you understand?
>
> When I know that death never rests, how can I wait, when I am caught in a net?
>
> When life is shortened with each passing night, who can enjoy pleasures, when we are like fish in a shoal?
>
> This very day do what's good. Let not this moment pass you by, for surely death may strike you even before your duties are done.
>
> Tomorrow's task perform today. Evening's work finish before noon, for death does not wait to ask whether your duties are done.
>
> For who knows whom death's legions may seize today? Practice good from your youth, for uncertain is life's erratic path.
>
> Those who do good enjoy fame in this life and happiness hereafter. Foolish indeed are those who toil for the sake of son and wife, providing for their welfare by means proper and foul.
>
> Such a man, full of desire and attached to sons and cattle, death carries away, as flood waters would a tiger sound asleep.
>
> Death will carry away a man obsessed with amassing wealth, his desires still unfulfilled, as a tiger would a domestic beast.
>
> "This I've done. This I must do. And that I have yet to complete." A man who is thus consumed by desires and pleasures, death will bring under its sway.
>
> Death carries away a man who is attached to his field, shop, or house, even before he reaps the fruits of the works he has done, fruits to which he is so attached.
>
> When death, old age, disease, and misery of all sorts cling to the body, why do you stand as if you were in great shape?
>
> Death and old age accompany an embodied soul from his very birth so as to destroy him. The two embrace all these beings, both the mobile and the immobile.

> The delight one finds in living in a village is truly the house of death, while the wilderness is the dwelling place of the gods—so the Vedas teach.
>
> The delight one finds in living in a village is the rope that binds. The virtuous cut it and depart, while evil-doers are unable to cut it.
>
> Those who do not cause injury to living beings in thought, word, or deed, are themselves not oppressed by acts that harm their life or wealth.
>
> Without truth one can never check the advancing troops of death. Never abandon truth, for immortality abides in truth.
>
> I do not injure, I seek the truth, I am free of love and hate, I remain the same in pleasure and pain, and I am safe—so I laugh at death like an immortal.
>
> In the self alone and by the self I am born, on the self I stand, and, though childless, in the self alone I shall come into being; I will not be saved by a child of mine.

The text concludes:

> Of what use is wealth to you, O brahman, you who must soon die? Of what use are even wife and relatives? Seek the self that has entered the cave. Where have your father and grandfather gone?

The final selection illustrating the debate between societal and renunciatory values is an argument between Janaka, the famous king of Mithilā, and a female ascetic named Sulabhā (*Mahābhārata* 12.308, selection). Janaka was reputed to have attained liberation (*mokṣa*) without abandoning household life and to have acquired the fruit of renunciation while he continued to rule the world. Sulabhā, hearing this news, wanted to test Janaka's claim. Using her yogic powers she entered Janaka's body. Janaka tells her how he had learned the Sāṃkhya doctrine from Pañcaśikha and how that knowledge had liberated him even though he did not abandon his kingdom. He argues that if it is knowledge that liberates, then with regard to the attainment of liberation it is immaterial whether one is an ascetic or a king.

> If knowledge is the cause of liberation even when one possesses triple staffs [of ascetics] and the like, then how can it not be so also when one possesses royal parasols and the like? For the possession of these articles can be traced to a common cause.
>
> Even a person who, noting the defects of household life, leaves it for a different order of life (*āśrama*), however, is not freed from attachment, for he gives up one thing only to grab hold of another.

> Ochre robes, shaven head, triple staff, water pot—in my opinion these are extravagant emblems having little to do with liberation.
>
> If, even when these emblems are present, knowledge alone is here the cause, all emblems are useless for getting rid of suffering in this world.
>
> There is no freedom in poverty, as there is no bondage in plenty; both in plenty and in poverty it is knowledge that liberates a person.
>
> This noose of royal power is tied with seats of passion. See, I have cut it off with the sword of renunciation sharpened on the whetstone of liberation.

Janaka goes on to admonish Sulabhā about the impropriety of her entering his body. Taking her to be a brahman, Janaka asserts that she has thus created a confusion of castes. He then inquires who she is and where she comes from. In her response, Sulabhā points to these questions as demonstrating Janaka's lack of true knowledge. A man who is liberated would not ask such questions. Sulabhā thus exposes the fallacy that a householder can acquire the liberating knowledge without abandoning home and family.

> You have asked me: "Who are you? Whose daughter are you? Where do you come from?" Listen attentively, O King, to this reply of mine.
>
> As you claim that by yourself you see the self within your self, in like manner, if you in fact consider another's self to be the same as yours, why do you fail to see in others also your own self?
>
> So, why do you ask me who and whose daughter I am? "This is mine and this is not": for a liberated man, O King of Mithilā, what is the use of such duality? And what profit is there in the queries: Who? Whose? Wherefrom?
>
> A man who makes distinctions between friends, foes, and neutrals in victory, war, and peace—how can he, O King, possess the mark of liberation?
>
> A man who fails to look equally upon one who is dear to him and one who is not, or upon one who is powerful and one who is weak—how can he possess the mark of liberation?
>
> Your friends should hold you in check, you who imagine yourself to be liberated when you are not, as doctors a deranged man.

—8—

The Exemplary Devotion of the "Servant of Hari"

Tony K. Stewart

Gauḍīya Vaiṣṇavas are named after the geographical region of Gauḍa, which is central to modern Bengal in northeastern India. Today, because the Gauḍīya Vaiṣṇavas have spread far beyond the confines of that region, some people prefer the name Caitanyaites, after the community's founder Kṛṣṇa-Caitanya (1486–1533 C.E.). Caitanya was, during his lifetime, believed to be God himself, Kṛṣṇa—not just a holy man or accomplished devotee. Born Viśvambhara ("He Who Bears the Burden of the World") to a good brahman family in the scholastic center of Navadvīpa, in Nadīya District, Caitanya lived a relatively normal childhood, according to the traditional accounts. He was destined to become a Sanskrit scholar, a pandit, following in the footsteps of his father, or so it seemed. During his youth, two events seem to have made a profound impression on him: one was his brother's renunciation into the orders of ascetics, the other was Caitanya's father's death. To commemorate that death, Viśvambhara traveled to the Vaiṣṇava holy city of Gayā, today in the state of Bihar, to perform the rituals that would ensure the sustenance of his father's lineage for the seven previous generations. While there, Viśvambhara met a famous ascetic who had such an effect on the young man that he was transformed, apparently overnight, into the greatest of Vaiṣṇava devotees. And it all started, so the tradition goes, by kīrtana—chanting and singing the name of God.

Kīrtana literally means song, especially a song of praise which glorifies its subject, in this case the god Kṛṣṇa. For the Vaiṣṇavas of Bengal, it is the simplest form of devotional activity and one of the top five of the sixty-four prescribed ritual forms, according to the scholastic analysis of devotion by Caitanya's disciple and theologian, Rūpa Gosvāmī in his *Bhaktirasāmṛtasindhu* ("Ocean of the Immortal Nectar of the Rapturous Experience of Devotion"). This devotional act, however, is much more than a mechanical ritual enjoined to discipline the devotee. Rather, the formal and proper repetition of the name of God turns that name into a mantra, a holy utterance which invokes God's very presence. The sound is a projection of aural power, for traditionally it is generally believed in India that the name of a thing is the aural dimension of its ontological reality, which is to say that the name of a thing at least partially constitutes the thing itself. By invoking Kṛṣṇa, a devotee effectively makes Kṛṣṇa present, allowing the devotee to come into contact with Kṛṣṇa and to enjoy the benefits of that direct association. The Gauḍīya Vaiṣṇavas invoke Kṛṣṇa in a variety of ways, but the great mantra is a recitation of three names sixteen times in thirty-two syllables, all in the vocative form: Kṛṣṇa, Hari, Rāma.

> Hare Kṛṣṇa Hare Kṛṣṇa
> Kṛṣṇa Kṛṣṇa Hare Hare
> Hare Rāma Hare Rāma
> Rāma Rāma Hare Hare

If someone utters this mantra prior to accepting Kṛṣṇa as God, Vaiṣṇavas believe that it has the effect of initiating devotion, bhakti, by providing the seed for its proper beginning. This ancient idea of sound possessing seedlike potency, the bīja mantra or seed syllable, goes back to the Veda, and in Bengal this was prominently found among the rituals of Tantra.

Chanting was often done with beads to keep the count, usually a string of 108 (an auspicious number that factors into $1^1 \times 2^2 \times 3^3$), marking one round of 16 names per bead. To "do the rosary" itself 108 times in the course of a day—the recommended count—means that the devotee will invoke Kṛṣṇa 186,624 times, an act bound to make one aware of Kṛṣṇa's eternal presence! The effect is to cloak oneself in the protective aural cover of the name. It is no accident that Kṛṣṇa-Caitanya's own religious name means "He Who Makes People Cognizant (*caitanya*) of Kṛṣṇa." Repeating the name has obvious benefits as an aid to meditation for the highly trained adept practitioner, but it was also meant to be done by the ordinary devotee in his or her daily life. Among the many early followers of Caitanya, a humble man named Haridāsa—the "Servant of Hari"—was renowned for his diligence in daily kīrtana and serves as a model for all devotees.

Haridāsa was a converted Muslim, a religion that in Bengal has its own long tradition of repeating the name of God in the practice of the Sufi dhikr. That Haridāsa was converted was a phenomenon of some importance in its own right. Conversion to Islam was fairly common in Bengal, but not until the Vaiṣṇavism preached by Caitanya was it possible to become a Hindu by any means other than birth. In the selection translated below, we find that the local ruling Muslims are having a difficult time knowing how to deal with their former brother who had fallen in with the local "infidels," the Vaiṣṇavas. But the piece, which comes from the most popular of the early biographies of Caitanya, the *Caitanya Bhāgavata* of Vṛndāvana Dāsa, shows that kīrtana was not always terribly palatable to local Hindus either. One of the reasons is that kīrtana, when practiced in groups (*saṃkīrtana*), involved individual and collective singing of songs of praise, which in turn often led to dancing (a style of devotional worship that is by no means unique to Bengal). When the sessions continued late into the night, as they often did, the emotions of the participants would peak in public displays of ecstasy that to the uninitiated sounded and looked like the revelry of a drunken party. The physical manifestations are, however, the signs of true devotion: sweating, trembling, fainting, roaring, crying, hair standing on end, gooseflesh, and so on. As will become clear in the reading, the trained devotional eye could distinguish between the ecstasy of devotion and other forms of possession, in spite of the similarities of their physical form. Because these possessions departed so dramatically from ordinary conduct, it is easy to see why outsiders were suspicious and how misunderstandings could ensue. Kīrtana precipitated responses both positive and negative, which suggests something of its power. Haridāsa had to suffer extreme punishment for converting to Vaiṣṇavism, and even more for his refusal to abandon the ritual action of repeating the name of Kṛṣṇa; yet it is the repetition of the name which enabled him to endure, which invoked Caitanya's comforting presence, and which dissipated the pain of the torture.

As he endured this pain, reportedly enough to kill an ordinary man, Haridāsa projected a general image of the holy man for Bengali culture, an image that resonated strongly in both Muslim and Hindu communities, cutting across those sectarian boundaries. For the Hindu, his power is that of the accomplished ascetic yogi, who sits in rapt meditation to gain control over his physical and spiritual world. The imagery is reinforced in the two stories of Haridāsa as a lord over snakes, for the serpent energy (*kuṇḍalinī*) is common to traditional and tantric yogic practice. Yet the association for Vaiṣṇavas goes further, for kīrtana is the very support of their devotion and the means for structuring God's message of love, whereas the cosmic serpent Ananta-Śeṣa is mythologically the support of Viṣṇu-Kṛṣṇa and the ontological source of Kṛṣṇa's projected environment, the emanations that create the world itself. Haridāsa, of course, projects and participates in both of these constructs. For the Muslim, however, Haridāsa's action is interpreted through the model of the pīr, a Sufi saint. That the same Haridāsa can be understood by the two communities through different and competing models of piety demonstrates that the Hindu and Muslim worlds were not, in their daily experience, as far removed from each other as is often depicted. In fact, in the throes of his trial, we shall see that Haridāsa goes so far as to argue that the Muslim's Allah and the Hindu's Kṛṣṇa were not different from each other except in name. What was different between Muslims and Hindus was simply the outward, physical garb of their practices, and that is a significant theological and sociological position that many Bengalis have continued to hold through the last five centuries.

The translation is from Vṛndāvana Dāsa, *Caitanya Bhāgavata,* edited with Bengali commentary *Nitāikaruṇākallolinī ṭīkā* by Rādhāgovinda Nātha (Calcutta: Sādhana prakāśanī, 1373 B.S. [1966 C.E.]), 1.11.

Further Reading

Two helpful discussions of Vaiṣṇava religious observance are Sushil Kumar De, *Early History of the Vaiṣṇava Faith and Movement in Bengal,* 2nd ed. (Calcutta: Firma KLM, 1961), and Edward C. Dimock, Jr., "Doctrine and Practice among the Vaiṣṇavas of Bengal," *History of Religions* 3.1 (1963), 106–27, reprinted in *Kṛṣṇa: Myths, Rites and Attitudes,* edited by Milton Singer (Hawaii: East-West Center Press, 1966), pp. 41–63. A fundamental source is the work of an early biographer of Caitanya, Kṛṣṇadāsa Kavirāja, *Caitanya caritāmṛta,* translated with an introduction and notes by Edward C. Dimock, Jr., edited with revisions and addenda by Tony K. Stewart, Harvard Oriental Series no. 52 (Cambridge: Harvard University Press, 2000). Also see Dimock, "The 'Nectar of the Acts' of Caitanya," in The *Biographical Process,* edited by Frank E. Reynolds and Donald Capps (The Hague: Mouton, 1976), pp. 109–17 and Norvein Hein, "Caitanya's Ecstasies and the Theology of the Name," in *Hinduism: New Essays in the History of Religions,* edited by Bardwell Smith (Leiden: E. J. Brill, 1976), pp. 15–32.

The Exemplary Devotion of the "Servant of Hari"

1. Glory, glory be to the revered Golden One, friend of the wretched. Glory, glory be to the Lord of All, Husband to Lakṣmī. 2. Glory, glory be to the incarnation who serves as the shelter of devotees. Glory to the essential truth of the ages, the play of kīrtana, praise [to Kṛṣṇa]. 3. Glory, glory be to the Golden-Limbed One along with his family of devotees. If one hears the story of Caitanya, devotion is the gain. 4. The story of the first part [of his life] is a stream of immortal nectar, wherein the play of the Golden-Limbed One enchants completely.

5. And so [Kṛṣṇa-Caitanya,] the chief actor of Vaikuṇṭha heaven, lived in the city of Navadvīpa. Disguised as a brahman householder, he taught. 6. This incarnation was intended to spread prema-bhakti, pure devotional love—but he did not desire to do it right then. 7. The further reaches of the cyclic world were devoid of this highest of truths, yet he was concerned that everyone experience at least a tiny portion of this love. 8. Even those who taught the [*Bhagavad*] *Gītā* and *Bhāgavata* [*Purāṇa*] failed to sing or get others to sing in saṃkīrtana. 9. But those who were devotees would assemble and spontaneously perform kīrtana, clapping their hands— 10. and this aroused joy in their hearts.

[Detractors puzzled,] "What is it that makes them shout out in a loud voice, 11. "I am Brahman; within me resides the Stainless One, Nirañjana'? On what basis do they distinguish between servant and master?" 12. People who were caught up in the cycle of life observed, "To eat they beg, then they preach to everyone to repeat loudly the name of Hari. 13. We shall batter down and desecrate the doorways to their houses"—This is what much of [the city of]

Nadīya gathered together and decided. 14. When they heard about this, the devotees were extremely anguished, but talk among themselves relieved them. 15. The devotees saw the material world as meaningless. With sighs of "O Kṛṣṇa!" they felt their misery to be without limits. 16. And so it was at the arrival of Haridāsa, who embodied pure devotion to Viṣṇu.

THE WHIPPING OF HARIDĀSA THROUGH TWENTY-TWO MARKETS

17. Now hear the story of Haridāsa Ṭhākura, the stalwart servant of Kṛṣṇa, by whose hearing one gains Kṛṣṇa in all ways. 18. In the village of Būḍhana, Haridāsa took his birth. To benefit [the villagers], he spread the praise of Kṛṣṇa, kīrtana, completely throughout that land. 19. After residing there for a while, he moved to the banks of the Gaṅgā, finally settling in Phuliyā in Śāntipura [the home of Advaitācārya]. 20. When the venerable [Advaita] Ācārya received him, he responded with a huṃkāra roar, his joy knowing no bounds. 21. Together with the saintly Advaita, Haridāsa floated on the waves of the ocean of the rapturous pleasure of Lord Govinda's love. 22. Endlessly did Haridāsa wander along the banks of the Gaṅgā, crying out rather strangely, "Kṛṣṇa." 23. He showed no interest in the pleasures of the senses. His mouth was filled with the name of Kṛṣṇa, his only sustenance. 24. Never did he experience boredom with the name of Govinda. His frame of mind shifted constantly in his devotional experience. 25. Sometimes he danced all by himself; other times he roared like a lion enraged. 26. Sometimes he wailed in a loud, mournful voice; and other times he laughed, that deep paroxysm of extreme humor. 27. Sometimes he would howl, making the full-throated huṃkāra sound; and other times he would fall down, completely insensate. 28. One moment he would call out with an inhuman voice and the very next talk in the most polished of manners. 29. He cried effusively, his flesh thrilled in waves, he laughed, he fainted, he perspired—such was the delirium of Kṛṣṇa-devotion which he experienced.

30. When the lord Haridāsa entered into solitary dance, everyone came and gathered around this holy image. 31. At such times tears of bliss would soak his entire body, a sight which evoked great pleasure, even for the exceedingly wicked. 32. Whoever witnessed this [dance] flushed with an extraordinary ripple of gooseflesh; even Brahmā and Śiva delighted to see it. 33. Everyone in the village of Phuliyā, many brahmans among them, was overwhelmed by watching him. 34. When Haridāsa lived in Phuliyā, an abiding belief was fostered in everyone there. 35. When he bathed in the Gaṅgā he ceaselessly took the name of Hari. Everywhere he went, he took the name in a strong voice.

36. One day a qāḍī went to the seat of the governor of the land and described these activities in great detail. 37. "A Muslim (*yavana*) is conducting himself as a Hindu. It would be advisable to haul him in and try him." 38. Listening to the words of this sinner, [the governor] was inclined to evil. He promptly

had [Haridāsa] arrested and dragged before him. 39. By the grace of Kṛṣṇa, the great devotee Haridāsa had no fear of death, regardless of the charges of the Muslim. 40. As he was going forward and was presented to the governor, he muttered "Kṛṣṇa, Kṛṣṇa" over and over again. 41. Hearing Haridāsa as he arrived, a number of those present were simultaneously thrilled and saddened. [The commentator, Rādhāgovinda Nātha, notes that the name of Kṛṣṇa clearly brightened the spirits of these men, while the realization of what was about to happen to Haridāsa dampened those spirits.]

42. There were a number of prominent individuals held in the jail, and inside they were, to the man, excited when they heard [of Haridāsa]. 43. "It is the great Vaiṣṇava, the eminent Haridāsa. Just to get a glimpse of him will destroy the misery of our bondage!" 44. The guards struggled to restrain the inmates who were determined to get a glimpse.

45. The stalwart Haridāsa arrived in that place and when he looked at the prisoners, his was the glance of heartfelt mercy. 46. Gazing hard at the feet of the venerable Haridāsa, the inmates were motionless, fixed in prostration. 47. [He stood] with arms hanging to his knees, lotus eyes, his moonlike face unsurpassed and completely charming. 48. With great affection and reverence they greeted him. Everyone felt transformed by Kṛṣṇa-devotion. 49. Seeing the devotion of those of the group, Haridāsa blessed all of the prisoners, 50. "Be still. Stay! May you remain as you are now." He laughed strangely as he proferred this cryptic blessing. 51. The prisoners did not fully fathom this mystifying expression and so became a bit depressed. 52. Then Haridāsa, moved by compassion for them, explained the hidden meaning of this blessing. 53. "You feel bad from not fathoming the real meaning of the benediction I pronounced over you. 54. I would never offer a prayer that was base or mean. Pay close attention and understand clearly what I meant. 55. Right now each and every heart is turned toward Kṛṣṇa—and it is just in that condition that you should always remain. 56. Now may you always join together to dance, to take the name of Kṛṣṇa, to reflect on Kṛṣṇa! 57. Now let there be no more violence, no more persecution of people. Say 'Kṛṣṇa' and dwell on this gentle advice. 58. Should you forget this when you reenter the ordinary, sensual world, you will rejoin the depraved, 59. and all of your shortcomings will reappear. Such is the nature of worldly affairs; listen carefully to the real meaning of what I said. 60. The blessing I gave did not mean, 'May you remain prisoners!' rather 'May you forget the ordinary, sensual world and say Hari day and night!' 61. My strategy for giving that blessing was that you would not consider your miseries, even for a minute. 62. My look of mercy is directed toward all living beings. May all of you develop an unfaltering devotion to Kṛṣṇa. 63. Do not worry, for within two or three days your bonds will be lifted—this I have promised. 64. Live in the ordinary, sensual world, but wherever you reside, never let any of this advice slip from your memory." 65. Imparting this advice for the welfare of the prisoners, he went to the court of the regional governor.

66. When he saw [Haridāsa's] magnificence and charm, [the governor] had him seated in the place of highest honor. 67. The regional governor cross-examined him personally. "How, O brother, am I to understand your attitude, your action? 68. Look, it was by great fortune that you had been a Muslim. How, then, can you believe and act like a Hindu? 69. Consider that we do not eat food with the Hindus, yet you have cast aside your [Muslim] religious heritage in doing so. 70. You transgress the obligations of your position and do things contrary to it. How will you be delivered in the afterworld? 71. You did not realize that you performed an abominable act. Efface this sin by uttering the kalima [the Islamic creed]."

72. When Haridāsa heard these words from a man enchanted by the phenomenal world, he laughed loudly and pronounced, "Aha! The magic (*māyā*) of Viṣṇu!" 73. Then he began to speak gently [to the governor], "Listen, father! Humanity has but one Lord! 74. Hindus and Muslims differ in name only. The Supreme is described as One in both the Qur'ān and the [*Bhāgavata*] *Purāṇa*. 75. The One is flawless, of eternal substance, indivisible, unchanging. Indwelling in all things, it lives in the hearts of all. 76. This Lord, who motivates the hearts of men, effects the action of the entire world. 77. Everyone claims throughout the world that the names and qualities of this Lord are the preserve of their particular scripture. 78. Should anyone commit an act of violence, it is an injury directed toward that God who periodically assumes the burden of this world. 79. And so, in whichever direction this God leads my heart, I follow and act accordingly. 80. Should some brahman within the Hindu community desire to become a Muslim by following the dictates of that inner self, 81. what can the Hindus do to him for that action? What kind of law can punish one who has killed himself [by converting]? 82. Good sir, now you judge! If fault be found, then punish me!"

83. The words of the eminent Haridāsa had the sure ring of truth and all of the Muslims gathered were satisfied with what they heard. 84. The sole sinner among them, the qāḍī, advised the governor, "Punish him! 85. This is evil! And he will do much more evil, for he will bring disgrace down on the Muslim community! 86. So you would be well advised to mete him a severe punishment. If not, at least force him to preach his own [Muslim] scripture!"

87. The governor addressed [Haridāsa] again, "O brother! Recite your own scripture and there will be no further consideration [of this matter]. 88. Otherwise, all of the qāḍīs will administer punishment, after which they will still wonder what other little things they can do to you."

89. Haridāsa replied, "No one is able to do anything other than that which God has him do. 90. You must fully understand that God precipitates an outcome perfectly appropriate to the offense. 91. Even if my body is torn to pieces and my breath disappears, I will never quit saying the name of Hari."

92. Listening to that statement, the governor questioned [the qāḍī], "Now what would you do to him?"

93. The qāḍī replied, "Flog him through twenty-two market places! Take his life! I make no other judgment. 94. Let him be beaten through twenty-two market places and if he survives, then I will know that this man is truly learned and has spoken the complete truth."

95. The governor called the guards and ordered with vehemence, "Thrash him so badly that no life remains! 96. He is a Muslim acting as if he were a Hindu. When his life comes to an end he will finally escape this horrible sin." 97. With those vile words he ordered this terrible misdeed—and the wicked came forward and seized Haridāsa.

98. As they moved from market to market, those malicious men beat him senseless, their hearts seething with hatred. 99. Haridāsa meditated, "Kṛṣṇa! Kṛṣṇa!" and through the ecstasy of that name, the suffering of his body failed to register. 100. As they watched the extraordinarily cruel punishment administered to Haridāsa's body, all of those who were good suffered immeasurably. 101. Some predicted, "The entire kingdom is bound to be destroyed because of their perverse treatment of this good and honest man." 102. Some in their anger cursed the wazirs, the king's ministers, while others stepped forward to add blows of their own. 103. Some begged the Muslims, clasping their feet, "Let up! Do not flog him so hard!" 104. Still, no mercy was inculcated in those malefactors and they obdurately whipped him through market after market.

105. Through the wonderful grace of Kṛṣṇa, Haridāsa's body felt not the slightest pain from those awful beatings. 106. It was precisely as the demons had beaten the body of Prahlāda, for all the scriptures attest that he felt no pain at all.[1] 108. Even though Haridāsa remembers, all of the suffering was effaced at the time—how extraordinary this story of Haridāsa! 109. All of those iniquitous men who thrashed him suddenly felt the pain throbbing in their own hearts, 110. [for Haridāsa beseeched his Lord,] "O Kṛṣṇa! Be gracious to all of these living souls! Do not hold them responsible for any wrongdoing because of my punishment!"

111. In this way did those pernicious men beat the stalwart Haridāsa through one city after another. 112. They whipped him mightily to take away his life, but the beatings never even registered on Haridāsa. 113. All of the Muslims were dumbfounded, "Can any human being live through such a thrashing? 114. People die after being beaten in two or three market places, yet we have whipped him through twenty-two markets! 115. Not only does he not die, he appears to laugh the whole time! Is this man really a pīr?" And so they wondered.

116. Then the Muslims bemoaned, "O Haridāsa! The destruction of our community is certain to ensue because of you! 117. Even after such fierce punishment, you have not given up your life. The qāḍī is certain to kill us all!"

118. Haridāsa smiled and replied, "If by my living you meet with destruction, 119. then I will die to this worldly existence." Saying that, he quickly absorbed himself in deep meditation. 120. Replete with all powers, the adept Haridāsa became insensate; no breathing could be discerned.

121. Watching this the Muslims grew even more bewildered. They dragged and dumped him before the governor. 122. The governor simply ordered, "Bury his body."

The qāḍī rejoined, "But does he deserve such good treatment? 123. That would make honorable his despicable action. Therefore match the treatment to his deed. 124. If he is buried, he will reap the benefits in the afterlife. Toss him into the Gaṅgā so that he may suffer for a very long time."[2] 125. The Muslims accepted the command of the qāḍī and they started to pick him up to cast him into the Gaṅgā. 126. When those Muslims picked up Haridāsa to take him to the Gaṅgā, he remained in a seated position, firmly fixed. 127. As the venerable Haridāsa sat absorbed in the bliss of deep meditation, the Bearer of the Burden of the Universe came and took over his body. 128. His body had become the seat of the holder of a billion worlds, Viśvambhara.[3] Who could possibly have the power to budge Haridāsa? 129. Strong men converged on him from all sides, but the master remained motionless, fixed like a great stele [as they carried him]. 130. Haridāsa was drowning in the purified ocean of the bliss of Kṛṣṇa; he was not outwardly conscious. 131. Whether in the firmament, or on hard ground, or in the Gaṅgā—Haridāsa was totally unaware of where he was. 132. Just as Prahlāda had called on his Kṛṣṇa-devotion, so too was the power of the venerable Haridāsa.

133. All of those in whose heart the Golden-Limbed One [Caitanya] dwelled found this not at all unusual for Haridāsa. 134. Just as Hanūmān had subdued the demon and then was himself taken, out of respect for Brahmā,[4] 135. So too did Haridāsa consent to be punished by the Muslims for the sake of instructing the world— 136. 'Being under severe and ceaseless adversity, even to the point of death, even then the name of Hari does not fail to come from his mouth.' 138. Even though Haridāsa remembers all of the pain, it was annulled at the time—how extraordinary this tale of Haridāsa! 139. Truly, truly Haridāsa is lord of this world, the foremost among the followers of the Moon Caitanya!

140. And so when Haridāsa was committed to the Gaṅgā, he simply floated, and a short while later he was brought to consciousness by the will of God. 141. The honorable, adept Haridāsa became conscious enough to crawl up on the riverbank; he was filled with the highest bliss. 142. In this condition he returned to Phuliyā village, crying out the name of Kṛṣṇa in a loud voice. 143. All of the Muslims witnessed this unbelievable, strange power and immediately abandoned their violent ways, goodness filling their hearts. 144. They recognized him as a pīr and paid their respects. The entire lot of those Muslims gained salvation.

145. A short while later Haridāsa regained his normal consciousness. With a smile of compassion, he met the governor [who had come]. 146. The governor placed his palms together in deference and began to speak with great humility. 147. "Truly, truly I have come to realize that you are a great pīr. You have become firmly ensconced in the knowledge of the One. 148. Empty words

[about the One] spew from the mouths of so many yogis and monists, but you have realized it, gaining power in this fabulously wondrous realm. 149. I have come here specifically to meet with you. O honorable devotee, please forgive my many shortcomings! 150. For you there is neither friend nor foe; you treat everyone the same. I recognize no one in the three worlds such as you. 151. You may go and do your good as you wish. You may go back and live in your hut on the banks of the Gaṅgā. 152. You may stay wherever you yourself desire. Do whatever suits you without any restriction."

153. When the socially elevated [Muslims] looked upon the feet of the venerable Haridāsa, they abandoned convention and forgot that he was low. 154. They had dragged and beaten him with such incredible anger and now they recognized him as pīr and reached to grasped his feet. 155. The eminent Haridāsa looked with compassion on the Muslims and then returned to Phuliyā.

156. Haridāsa returned to the community of brahmans, constantly taking the name of Hari in a loud voice. 157. The brahmans of Phuliyā were collectively overjoyed when they saw Haridāsa. 158. The brahmans began to make the sounds of Hari, and Haridāsa, the Servant of Hari, began to dance in ecstasy. 159. Haridāsa's delirium was extraordinary and endless—crying, shaking, laughing, fainting, rippling with gooseflesh, shouting. 160. Haridāsa crashed to the ground in the rapturous experience of love, and the brahmans who witnessed it floated in great bliss. 161. After a great while Haridāsa became still and sat down. The brahmans sat in rows all around him. 162. Haridāsa spoke, "Listen brahmans! Do not in any way suffer on account of me. 163. I have listened to endless slander of my Lord, but my God has punished that. 164. Good resulted, and for that I am deeply gratified. Huge faults have been forgiven with a minimum of punishment. 165. To listen to Viṣṇu being slandered portends the Kumbhīpāka hell, and plenty of that I heard through these sinful ears. 166. They have been appropriately punished by God so that such sin will occur no more."

167. In this manner did Haridāsa join the brahmans in performing kīrtana, without fear and with great public display. 168. The families of all of those Muslims who had made them miserable were destroyed within a few days, as well. 169. Haridāsa then erected a small hut on the banks of the Gaṅgā and lived in solitude, meditating on the name of Kṛṣṇa day and night.

HARIDĀSA VANQUISHES THE SERPENT

170. Haridāsa took the name [of Kṛṣṇa] three hundred thousand times per day, which transformed his hut into the citadel of Vaikuṇṭha heaven. 171. Underneath that shack a monstrous serpent took up residence, his heat so radiant that nothing else could stay alive in there. 172. No one who came to converse with the stalwart Haridāsa was able to bear it. 173. Everyone without exception felt the incredible burning of the poison, but Haridāsa never noticed it at all.

174. The brahmans all gathered around to discuss why Haridāsa's abode radiated such massive heat.

175. In Phuliyā there lived a great physician, who came and determined that the cause was a serpent. 176. The physician pronounced, "Under the floor of the hut lies a single, extraordinary snake! The heat comes from that! 177. It can be said with certainty that no one can possibly survive there. Haridāsa must move quickly to another dwelling. 178. He can not continue to live there with that serpent. Come, let us go to his place and tell him!"

179. And so they came and addressed the venerable Haridāsa, explaining why he must abandon the hut. 180. "A monstrous serpent dwells underneath your hut. No one can stay here exposed to its radiance. 181. Consequently, it is not appropriate for you to remain here. You must remove yourself to another residence elsewhere."

182. Haridāsa replied, "I have been here a great many days, yet I have never felt any burning sensation in my hut. 183. The misery in all of this is that you are not able to bear it! So because of that I will go somewhere else tomorrow. 184. If it is true that an honorable creature lives here and if by tomorrow it has not abandoned this dwelling, 185. then by all means will I leave and go elsewhere. Do not worry yourselves! Recite the stories of Kṛṣṇa!"

186. And so they did, telling the stories of Kṛṣṇa in auspicious song, kīrtana. As they were engaged, a marvelous event took place. 187. When the great serpent had heard that Haridāsa would leave that place, it left instead. 188. As they entered the evening, the snake rose up from its burrow and all who saw it ran for cover. 189. It was the most awesome of serpents, incredibly terrifying, yet strangely beautiful with its yellow, blue, and white coloration. 190. A huge gem glistened upon its head. The brahmans stared, terrified, silently calling, "Kṛṣṇa, Kṛṣṇa!" 191. The serpent simply slithered away and the heat was dissipated. The brahmans felt a relief without measure. 192. When the brahmans witnessed the tremendous power of the eminent Haridāsa, a greater devotion toward him was born among them. 193. What magnificent power is in the possession of Haridāsa, by whose mere words a serpent fled his quarters, 194. whose mere glance casts off the bonds of ignorance! Kṛṣṇa never counters Haridāsa's words.

THE FALSE POSSESSION

195. Listen now to another of his marvelous legends, which reveals more of his majesty as master of serpents. 196. One day in the fine house of an important man, a snake charmer was performing various versions of the dance of the snake bite. 197. The snake charmer circled everyone, singing in a loud voice, swaying to the rhythms of the mantra, accompanied by the double-ended mṛdaṅga drum, the cymbal, and instrumental music. 198. Just by chance, Haridāsa came by that place and he stood to one side to watch the snake charmer's dance. 199. Through the power of mantra, the King of Snakes [Ananta, upon

whom Viṣṇu sleeps] took possession of the man's body and danced in delight. 200. In a loud voice, he sang the compelling song depicting Kṛṣṇa's dance on the serpent Kāliyadaha. 201. Listening to the innate majesty of his Lord, Haridāsa fell down in a dead faint, not breathing. 202. Shortly he regained consciousness, emitted a roar, and began to dance in an ecstasy without bounds. 203. When he saw the venerable Haridāsa's possession, the snake charmer stepped aside and waited. 204. The stalwart Haridāsa rolled around on the ground and put on an amazing display of rippling gooseflesh, tears, and the trembles. 205. This great devotee, Haridāsa, cried, absorbed in listening to the qualities of his Lord. 206. Haridāsa circled the group as he sang with joy, while to one side stood the snake charmer, palms pressed together in obeisance. 207. When Haridāsa's possession subsided, the snake charmer reentered the dance. 208. When they witnessed the lordly Haridāsa's possession, the entire group experienced a strange pleasure. 209. Wherever the dust of his feet had brushed them, they smeared it around on their bodies with delight.

210. There was one particular brahman, very affected in manner, who lived in that area. He calculated cleverly, "Today I, too, shall dance! 211. I have realized that although it is only the foolish and ignorant who dance, even the most insignificant man can exhibit a supreme devotion." 212. Thinking in this vein, he suddenly crashed to the ground, falling as if he were completely insensate. 213. As soon as he fell in the snake charmer's dance arena, the snake charmer began to beat him unmercifully, thoroughly incensed. 214. From all quarters the cane pole rained blows down on his neck, for the snake charmer struck, never missing his mark—there was no escape! 215. The brahman was shattered by the cane beating. He fled, crying in terror, "Dear Father, Father!"

216. Pleased with himself, the snake charmer danced at length—while all those present felt mystified. 217. Pressing their palms together in respect, they questioned the snake charmer, "Explain to us why you beat that brahman, 218. and why you remained with your hands pressed in obeisance while Haridāsa danced! Can you explain all this?"

219. Then through the mouth of the snake charmer, that serpent who is the devoted servant of Viṣṇu [Ananta], began to speak of Haridāsa's greatness. 220. "That which you have asked is a great mystery, and although it is inexpressible, I shall try to explain. 221. When you saw the venerable Haridāsa's possession, your esteem for him grew to something special. 222. The brahman also watched this and, faking it, he fell to the ground, his mind brimming with jealousy. 223. What person has the right to break up the enjoyment of my dance by his jealousy and hypocrisy? 224. And he had the audacity to pull this sham in the presence of Haridāsa—so I punished him severely. 225. To convince me and the other people that he was a great man, he exhibited this seemingly righteous behavior before you. 226. There is no love for Kṛṣṇa in all of this personal pride. If one is honest and unaffected, then he gains Kṛṣṇa. 227. This could be seen when Haridāsa danced. Just to witness that dance was to have all of one's bonds destroyed. 228. Kṛṣṇa Himself dances in the dance of Haridāsa! The

Brahmā-egg [the universe] is sanctified by watching this dance. 229. The name of Haridāsa—the servant of Hari—is perfectly appropriate to his calling, for Kṛṣṇa is eternally captured within his heart. 230. Kind and benevolent toward all living beings, he accompanies God down to earth in each and every birth.[5] 231. So faultless is his conduct toward Vaiṣṇavas and Viṣṇu that he never strays from the path, even in his dreams! 232. That living creature who is in his company even for a second is certain to gain the shelter of the lotus feet of Kṛṣṇa. 233. Brahmā and Śiva join Haridāsa as such devotees who ceaselessly cogitate the great drama [of Kṛṣṇa]. 234. Fully realizing that one's birth and lineage are ultimately without meaning, he took birth in a lowly clan [*nīcakula,* which in this case means Muslim, according to the commentator] at the order of the Lord. 235. If devotion toward Viṣṇu can occur in the lowest of classes, how much more the possibilities among the self-consciously righteous, say all of the scriptures. 236. If one is born into the highest ranks but does not worship Kṛṣṇa, what can be done for his clan as he sinks into hell? 237. In order to bear direct witness of all of these scriptural truths did Haridāsa take birth in a lowly lineage. 238. Just as Prahlāda did for the titans (*daitya*) and Hanūmān did for the monkeys, so too did Haridāsa bring honor to a lowly community. 239. Deities crave the touch of Haridāsa; the Gaṅgā desires Haridāsa to immerse himself [in her waters]. 240. Let alone his touch, even Haridāsa's glance could shatter the beginningless bonds of karma for all living beings. 241. Whoever will seek refuge in Haridāsa will have the imprisonment of this cyclic world torn asunder by a mere look from him. 242. Should his greatness be told through a hundred mouths for a hundred years, its limit would not be reached. 243. That has made you fortunate, yet only a tiny portion of his majesty has been made public from within your community. 244. Surely he who speaks the name of Haridāsa but once will journey to the abode of Kṛṣṇa!"

245. When he had spoken thus, the Lord of Serpents became silent. The gathering of righteous and good people who heard were gratified. 246. Such was the greatness of the lordly Haridāsa which the holy Vaiṣṇava serpent [Ananta] had described since the ancient times. 247. The group was amazed when they listened to the speech of the serpent, and they felt an abiding love for Haridāsa. In this way did the venerable Haridāsa live prior to the Golden Moon, [Caitanya] manifesting his devotional love.

Notes

1. See *Bhāgavata Purāṇa* 7.5, 8. In this famous story, Prahlāda, who was a devotee of Viṣṇu-Kṛṣṇa, was ordered killed by his father, who felt that Prahlāda's devotion was a threat to his own aspirations to cosmic sovereignty. He enlisted hosts of demons to kill the boy with their celestial weapons, but to no avail, as Viṣṇu-Kṛṣṇa protected him. To avenge this attack, Kṛṣṇa descended to earth as Narasiṃha, the Man-Lion, who finally destroyed the megalomaniacal Hiraṇyakaśipu. The association seems to voice a certain yearning on the part of the current author.

2. It is perhaps worth noting that in Bengal, Hindu householders are cremated, whereas ascetics are never burned, but buried. Those who have died an unnatural death, by snakebite or some other

means, are thrown into the river unburned in the hopes that they may be revived. The qāḍī, however, clearly deems Haridāsa to be a Muslim, so throwing him into the river would lead to his continued suffering, whereas burial would lead to eternal residence in heaven or confirm Haridāsa's piety.

3. Verses 127–28 contain a typical ambiguity in designating the figure who took control of Haridāsa's body—Viśvambhara. The line can be read three ways: either Viṣṇu as Viśvambhara came, or Caitanya as Viśvambhara came, or simply his body was as heavy and rigid as the billion worlds held by Viśvambhara. Vaiṣṇavas, including the commentator, opt for all three.

4. Hanūmān, the monkey general of Rāma's army, led the forces in the overthrow of the demonic king Rāvaṇa on the isle of Laṅkā. Rāvaṇa's son, Indrajit, employed the weapons of the god Brahmā in fighting Hanūmān. So as not to insult Brahmā and the power of his weapons, Hanūmān acquiesced to capture.

5. Because Kṛṣṇa descends to earth with his entire environment, Haridāsa is part of that eternal retinue that surrounds Kṛṣṇa at each visit, and he personifies the same kind of loving service each time.

9

The Origin of Liṅga Worship

Richard H. Davis

The primary ritual act of Śaivism is the worship of the Śiva-liṅga. This reading, drawn from the *Kūrmapurāṇa,* is an exemplary tale describing how that practice was first instituted among humans.

During the early medieval period (roughly 700–1200 C.E.), devotional cults and temple worship directed toward the divinities Viṣṇu, Śiva, and the Goddess increasingly supplanted Vedic sacrifice and the Veda-based religious practices of orthodox brahmans, as well as the Buddhist and Jain monastic communities, as the dominant religious and political order of South Asia. Yet even as it introduced major innovations in Indian religious practice, temple Hinduism sought to maintain continuity with the earlier Vedic tradition, unlike Buddhism and Jainism, which had rejected Vedic authority more decisively.

The genre of texts known as Purāṇas (literally, "Old Traditions") served as the main cosmological texts of this new form of Hinduism, setting forth the structure of the cosmos, the roles and activities of the deities within that cosmos, and the proper courses of conduct for human beings to follow in such a world. The *Kūrmapurāṇa* was originally composed by the Pāñcarātra ("Five Nights") school, worshipers of Viṣṇu, some time between the sixth and eighth centuries. At the beginning of the text, the bard Sūta Romaharṣaṇa (who "Makes the Hair Stand on Edge" with his tales) relates to a group of sages gathered in Naimiṣa ("Transient") Forest how Viṣṇu in the form of a tortoise (*kūrma*) had once held up Mount Mandara while the gods and demons used it to churn the Milk Ocean. A group of sages present at the churning asked the great turtle a question, and in response Viṣṇu narrated the teachings constituting the *Kūrmapurāṇa,* while still supporting the cosmic mountain on his mighty shell.

However, sometime around the early eighth century, the text was appropriated and recast by a group of Śiva worshipers, the Pāśupatas. The most prominent early Śaiva school, the Pāśupatas were particularly devoted to Śiva in his aspect as Paśupati, the "Lord of Animals," here understanding animals in a metaphoric sense to denote all human souls in their condition of bondage, fettered like sacrificial beasts. The Pāśupatas reworked the *Kūrmapurāṇa* to reflect their own premises and concerns, adding numerous accounts of Śiva's deeds and directions for worshiping Śiva. The lengthiest and most important of the insertions was the *Īśvara Gītā* ("Song of the Lord Śiva"), evidently a Pāśupata reply to that preeminent Vaiṣṇava catechism, the *Bhagavad Gītā* ("Song of the Lord Kṛṣṇa"). Though they still allowed a substantial role in the text to Viṣṇu, his position in the Pāśupata recension has clearly been subordinated to Śiva's. In one interpolated episode, for example, the god Kṛṣṇa, an incarnation of Viṣṇu, must go to the hermitage of the sage Upamanyu (the "Zealous One") and receive initiation into the ascetic regimen called the "Pāśupata vow" to enable him to procure a son.

The well-known narrative excerpted here, "The Origin of Liṅga Worship" (which is told, with variations, in many other Purāṇas), exemplifies several of these points. The story focuses on a group of sages who have retired to the Pine Forest (*devadāruvana*) in the Himālayas to perform Vedic-style sacrifices and renunciatory austerities, the kinds of practices described in Vedic and Smārta texts as appropriate to the "forest-dweller" stage of life. Observing them from his own mountain residence, Śiva judges that these practices may be useful for worldly purposes (*pravṛtti*), but they do not lead to the highest liberations (*nivṛtti*, "cessation"). (This reflects a charge commonly leveled at Vedism by schools of temple Hinduism.) He decides to intervene, and sets out to impart to the sages a new and superior form of religious practice, worship of his own liṅga. By the end of the story the sages are diligently engaged in the religious exercises into which Śiva has initiated them.

Although the *Kūrmapurāṇa* presents liṅga worship as a new practice, instituted for the first time among humans (though, as Brahmā reveals, gods have long known of it), the text grants an important role in the Pāśupata liturgy to Vedic texts. The god Brahmā, often portrayed as the creator of the Vedas, advises the sages to employ mantras from the Vedas and to chant the "Hundred Names of Rudra" from the *Yajur Veda* in worshiping the liṅga, explaining that Śiva had initially imparted the Vedas to him in olden times. (Rudra, the "Howler," is the form in which Śiva appears in the Vedas, a capricious and frightening god associated with storms and disease.) Śiva himself cautions the sages against following any systems of knowledge outside the Veda, and claims that he himself embodies the Vedas. The Pāśupata vow that he recommends to the sages, he says, is the "essence" of the Veda.

Śiva certainly plays the leading role in this story, but the other primary deities of temple Hinduism appear as well. In a Śaiva Purāṇa, these divinities may be presented as powerful, glorious, and immensely knowledgeable in their own rights, but they are also made to recognize the ultimate preeminence of Śiva. Here we see Viṣṇu as Śiva's partner in tricking the Pine-Forest sages, and Brahmā as the wise adviser who explains to the sages the great error they have committed and what they need to do to make recompense. The goddess Pārvatī, "Mountain-Born" daughter of Himālaya, puts in an appearance at the end, and the narrator tells us that she should be considered as identical with Śiva. Elsewhere in the *Kūrmapurāṇa*, both Viṣṇu and Brahmā are also revealed to be aspects of Śiva. So it is that the Pāśupata school resolves the apparent multiplicity of Hindu deities into a single godhead, identified as Śiva.

Such realizations are precisely what is at stake here, for the episode revolves around the initial inability of the Pine-Forest sages to see beyond particular form to true reality. Deities such as Śiva and Viṣṇu have the superhuman ability to control or alter the appearances of things, termed *māyā.* (Māyā is used in the text also as an epithet for the goddess Lakṣmī, consort of Viṣṇu, and as a name for Pārvatī, Śiva's wife.) So when they show up at the forest hermitage in the form of naked beggar and lascivious companion, the hermits are fooled or deluded (*moha*) by their appearances. Later, Brahmā chastises the sages for their failure to recognize (*vijñāna*) Śiva in his true nature, and he prescribes practices that will enable them to gain the ability to see Śiva properly in the future. Sure enough, Śiva does visit the Pine Forest once again, and when the sages recognize him this time and praise him profusely, he presents his highest form to them and reveals the secret mystery of things.

If recognition of Śiva is presented in this text as the fundamental aim of religious practice, worship of the liṅga is advanced as the key to recognition. The word *liṅga* has three primary meanings, and all three are important here. *Liṅga* denotes the penis, the male generative organ. It also denotes a mark, emblem, badge—a sign that allows one to identify or recognize something, as one may identify someone as a member of the male sex by his penis. Finally, it also denotes the primary cult object of Śaivism, an upraised cylindrical shaft with rounded top, rising from a rounded base. The icon resembles, in a generally abstract manner, an erect male member, and serves at the same time as a sign of Śiva. In the Pine-Forest episode, the link between penis and icon is clear: the sages order Śiva to rip out his penis, and Brahmā orders the sages to make a copy of Śiva's sundered penis as an object of worship. This, he tells them, will enable them to perceive Śiva, for it is his mark, the easily formed emblem on earth that allows all of us to recognize the god who is at the same time transcendent Lord of the cosmos.

"The Origin of Liṅga Worship" is framed by an account of holy bathing spots or fords (*tīrtha,* literally "crossing places"). The assembled sages of Naimiṣa Forest hermitage, the primary auditors of the *Kūrmapurāṇa,* request the narrator Sūta Romaharṣaṇa to describe to them the greatest and most celebrated holy places in the world. Sūta responds with a detailed list, comprising eight chapters of text. Like a good tour guide, he not only lists the sites and praises each one as worth a visit, but also retells the past events that distinguish each spot. The Pine Forest (near Badarināth in present-day Garhwal, Uttar Pradesh) is the sacred spot where Śiva once tricked the sages, he tells them, and where Śiva's liṅga was first worshiped by humans. Yet in Sūta's generous view, one need not make a pilgrimage there to gain its benefits. Just reading or listening to the story of the sages of the Pine Forest, he says, is enough to release one from all sins.

The text of the inscription may be found in Anand Swarup Gupta, ed., *The Kūrma Purāṇa* (Varanasi: All India Kashiraj Trust, 1971), 2.36.49–2.37.164.

The Origin of Liṅga Worship

Sūta Romaharṣaṇa said:

"Adepts and celestials live in the auspicious Pine Forest, where the great god Śiva once granted a great favor. He tricked all the sages there, and when they worshiped him again, the glorious Lord Śiva was pleased and said to those devout sages:

" 'Dwell here always, in this lovely hermitage, meditating on me. In this way you will reach the highest state of attainment. To those righteous persons who offer worship to me in this world I grant the high status of "leader of my followers" permanently.

" 'I will stay here always, along with Viṣṇu. A man who gives up his life here will never again be reborn. And I destroy all the sins even of people who have gone to other regions and recollect this holy place, excellent brahmans. Funeral rites, gift-giving, austerities, fire sacrifices, ancestral offerings of rice balls, meditation, mantra repetitions, and vows—all ritual acts performed here will be free from decay.'

"For that reason, twice-born brahmans should make every effort to see the auspicious Pine Forest where the great god Śiva dwells. Wherever the Lord Śiva and the highest being Viṣṇu are, there also the Gaṅgā River, holy bathing spots, and temples are present."

The sages asked:

"How did the Lord Śiva, who carries the banner of the bull, fool those lordly sages when he went to the Pine Forest? Please tell us that now, Sūta."

Sūta narrated the story:

Once, thousands of sages along with their sons and wives were practicing austerities in that pleasant Pine Forest, where gods and adepts also dwell. Performing the kind of activities that engender continued existence (*pravṛtta*), the great seers performed various sacrifices and practiced self-restraints, as prescribed in the Vedas.

The trident-bearing god Śiva declared that those sages whose minds were intent on continued existence were committing a grave mistake, and set out for the Pine Forest. Taking Viṣṇu, the teacher of the world, at his side, the beneficent god Śiva went there to establish the doctrine of cessation (*nivṛtti*).

Śiva, Lord of the World, took on a fine form: nineteen years of age, frolicking playfully, with big arms, muscular limbs, beautiful eyes, and a golden body. His face glowed gloriously like the full moon, and he swayed like a rutting elephant, stark naked. Wearing a garland of water lilies and adorned with every jewel, he approached smiling. The eternal person Viṣṇu, imperishable womb of the worlds, assumed a female form and followed the trident-bearer. He had a full-moon face, breasts full and firm, and a gleaming smile; very gracious, with a pair of jingling anklets, nice yellow clothes, divine, dark-colored beautiful eyes. He moved like a fine swan, charming and enchanting. In this manner, the Lord Śiva went with Viṣṇu begging in the Pine Forest, fooling everyone with their power of appearance (*māyā*).

The women saw the trident-bearing Śiva, Lord of Everything, weaving this way and that, and followed him, beguiled by his appearance. These chaste wives abandoned modesty, their clothes and jewelry disheveled, excited by desire, and began sporting playfully with him. Though their minds were usually subdued, all the young sons of the sages were overcome with desire and followed Viṣṇu, Lord of the Senses.

When they saw the deceitful sole Lord Śiva, looking exceedingly attractive along with his wife, the groups of women began singing flirtatious songs and dancing, desiring and embracing him. When they saw the original god Viṣṇu, husband of Prosperity, the sons of the sages fell at his feet. They began to smile. Some sang songs, while others arched eyebrows at him. The demon-slayer Viṣṇu cunningly entered the minds of women and men. He created mental activity for their enjoyment, as if they were truly embraced by the goddess Māyā. Viṣṇu, support of all gods and living beings, shone in the midst of those women as the Lord of lords, Śiva, shines surrounded on his throne by many energies, seated with his single Śakti. Then Śiva rose up again and danced with utmost splendor. The original god Viṣṇu also rose and showed his true nature, nectar through Śiva's action.

The excellent sages saw Śiva and Viṣṇu fooling the women and sons, and were infuriated. Tricked by his appearance, they unleashed harsh words at Śiva, god with shaggy locks, and cursed him with a swarm of oaths. Yet all the ascetic heat they directed at Śiva was rebuffed, as the stars in the sky are driven off by the sun's splendor.

Confused, their ascetic powers defeated, the sages approached the bull-bannered god Śiva and asked him, "Who are you?"

The illustrious Lord Śiva replied, "I have come here today with my wife to practice austerities in this place with you, men of excellent vows."

Those eminent sages, Bhṛgu and the others, listened to his words and commanded, "Put on your clothes, get rid of your wife, then you can do austerities!"

Laughing and looking at Viṣṇu, womb of the world, standing nearby, the Lord Śiva, who carries a staff, spoke: "How can you tell me to abandon my wife, while you who know proper conduct and have calm minds are yourselves devoted to supporting your own wives?"

"It is said that a husband should shun women who are fond of wrongdoing," replied the sages. "So, we should avoid this charming lady, who is that type of woman."

The great god said, "Sages, this woman never desires another, even mentally, and so I never abandon her."

"You vile person!" the sages exclaimed. "We have seen her making mischief right here. You have told a lie. Leave here immediately!"

When they ordered him so, Śiva replied, "I have spoken the truth. She only appears like that to you." And saying this, he left. . . .

The brahmans looked at the naked, mountain-dwelling, mutilated Śiva moving, and began to beat him with sticks, clods of dirt, and fists. They yelled at him, "You foul-minded one! Pull out your liṅga!"

"I will do it," replied Śiva, the great yogi, "if you feel some aversion toward my liṅga." And so saying, Śiva, who had once plucked out Bhaga's eyes, ripped it out.

Immediately, Śiva, Viṣṇu, and the liṅga were no more to be seen. Then began strange portents, betokening danger to all the worlds. The sun with its thousand rays did not shine. The earth began to tremble. All the planets lost their splendor, and the ocean roiled.

Anusūya, chaste wife of the sage Atri, had a dream and announced to the other sages, her eyes full of fear, "The one whom we saw begging alms in our homes was certainly Śiva, whose emanating energy illuminates the whole world, accompanied by Viṣṇu."

When they heard her words, all the sages were perplexed, and they went to the great yogi Brahmā, creator of everything. There they saw him seated on a spectacular throne full of many marvels, shining with a thousand rays, and endowed with knowledge, lordliness, and the other powers. He was accompanied by his wife Sāvitrī, and surrounded by throngs of pure yogis, all knowers of the Vedic texts, and by the four Vedas themselves in bodily form. Brahmā shone, smiling, radiant-eyed, with four faces, big arms, his body composed of Vedic hymns, unborn, supreme, the Vedic Person, gentle-faced, and auspicious.

Putting their heads to the ground, the sages propitiated the Lord.

Feeling well-disposed toward them, the four-formed, four-faced god asked, "Excellent sages, what is the reason you have come?"

They placed their folded hands atop their heads and all began to narrate the whole incident to the eminent Brahmā. The sages said: "A certain person of extreme beauty came to our auspicious Pine Forest, stark naked, accompanied by his wife, beautiful in every limb. This lord beguiled our wives and daughters with his handsome figure, and his wife seduced our sons. We made various curses, but he repelled them. We beat him soundly, and his liṅga was thrown down. The lord, his wife, and the liṅga all disappeared. Then terrible portents began, frightening every creature. Who was this man? Lord, highest of beings, we are scared! We take refuge with you, firm one. You know everything that stirs in this world. Protect us with your grace, Lord of Everything."

When the band of sages had told him this, lotus-born Brahmā, the inner soul of the world, meditated on the trident-marked god Śiva, and spoke with his hands reverently folded.

Brahmā said: "What an error you have made! What has happened today ruins everything. Damn your strength! Damn your ascetic power! In this world, all your good conduct is worthless. Through your auspicious rites you have obtained the most precious treasure among treasures, and you have ignored it here, fooled by appearances. Your good conduct is in vain. Yogis and ascetics constantly exert themselves, seeking the treasure that you have obtained and foolishly neglected. Vedic experts perform myriad sacrifices to attain that great treasure that you have obtained and foolishly neglected. You have obtained and neglected the imperishable treasure through which the gods achieve their lordship over the entire world. My own universal sovereignty results from identifying myself with that treasure. But you, abandoned by fortune, have seen it and neglected it. Divine sovereignty is united in that imperishable treasure which you have obtained and foolishly rendered useless.

"This god is the great god Śiva, recognized as the greatest lord. One can attain no higher abode than this.

"This Lord Śiva becomes the god Time, and reabsorbs all embodied beings—gods, sages, ancestors, and all others—during the cosmic dissolution, at the end of a thousand aeons. And this one god emits all beings through his own emanating energy. He is Viṣṇu bearing the discus, Indra wielding the thunderbolt, and Kṛṣṇa marked with the curl of chest hair. In the first age, the god is "Yogi"; in the second age he is called "Sacrifice"; in the third he is Lord Time; and our present fourth age he is the Buddha, whose banner is righteousness. The entire world is suffused by the three embodiments of Rudra—the dark quality is Fire, the active one is Brahmā, and the virtuous one is the Lord Viṣṇu. And another form of his is also recognized: naked and eternal Śiva, where Brahmā remains, full of yoga.

"And that wife you saw following him—that was the eternal god Viṣṇu Nārāyaṇa, the highest soul. The whole world is born from him, and into him it also disappears. He deceives everyone. He alone is the highest abode. Viṣṇu is the Person of the ancient traditions, with a thousand heads, a thousand eyes, a thousand feet, a single horn, and eight syllables. The revealed texts say that the highest Viṣṇu Nārāyaṇa has four embodiments, which are the four Vedas; three embodiments, which are the three qualities of matter; and one embodiment, which is the immeasurable Soul. This blessed Lord, existing as water, a body of changeable appearance, is the womb of cosmic order. Brahmans seeking liberation through proper conduct praise him with a variety of mantras.

"When the supreme being Viṣṇu reabsorbs all of creation at the end of the aeon, drinks the nectar of yoga, and sleeps—that is Viṣṇu's highest state. Creating everything, he is not born, nor does he die, nor does he grow. Experts in the Vedas sing him as the unmanifested, unborn, originating source of all substance. Then, when the cosmic night is completed and Śiva desires to emit the whole world again, he places a seed in Viṣṇu's navel. Know that I am that seed—the eminent Brahmā, with faces in every direction, a great being, the unsurpassed watery womb of everything.

"You were fooled by his power of appearance. You did not recognize the great god Śiva, the Creator, God of Gods and Lord of all creatures. This god is the greatest god. Śiva is without beginning. Accompanied by Viṣṇu, he makes and unmakes. He has no obligation to perform, and there is none superior to him. His body made of yoga, he gave me the Vedas in former times. Possessing the goddess Māyā, he makes the world and unmakes it with his power over appearances (*māyā*).

"You should recognize him as Śiva and take refuge with him to attain liberation."

Feeling very dejected, Marīci and the other sages listened to the Lord's speech, bowed to the mighty god, and asked Brahmā, "How can we see that bow-wielding god again? Tell us, Lord of all immortals. You protect those who seek your shelter."

"You should make a copy of the god's liṅga which you saw fall on the ground," answered Brahmā, "and with your wives and sons attentively offer worship to that matchless liṅga, following Vedic rules only and observing celibacy. You should consecrate the liṅga using the mantras from the *Ṛg*, *Yajur*, and *Sāma* Vedas pertaining to Śiva. Then, following the highest ascetic regime and chanting the hundred names of Śiva, you, your sons, and your kinsmen should worship it intently. You should all approach Śiva with hands folded in reverence. Then you may see the Lord of gods, who is difficult to perceive for those who have not done this. When you see him, all your ignorance and unrighteousness will be destroyed."

They bowed to the beneficent Brahmā, unlimited in his power, and returned to the Pine Forest, their hearts rejoicing. They began to worship just as Brahmā had advised them. Still not knowing the highest god, but without desire and without jealousy, some worshiped him on multicolored ritual platforms, some in mountain caves, and some on empty, auspicious riverbanks. Some ate duckweed for food, some lay in water, and some stood on the tips of their toes, abiding amid the clouds. Others ate unground grain, or ground it with a stone. Some ate vegetable leaves, and some purified themselves by subsisting on moonbeams. Some dwelled at the foot of trees, and others made their beds upon rocks. In these ways they passed their time performing austerities and worshiping Śiva.

Then the bull-bannered Lord Śiva, who takes away the pain of those who approach him, decided to enlighten them as a form of grace. In the first age the god dwells on the auspicious peak of Mount Kailāsa. Naked, his body smeared with white ash, holding a fire brand, his eyes red and yellow, disfigured with wounds, the gracious Lord Śiva went to the Pine Forest. At times he laughed wildly, and at times he sang arrogantly. Sometimes he danced lasciviously, and at other times he howled over and over. When he approached the hermitage, he begged for alms again and again. The god entered the forest, assuming his own form through his power of appearance. Taking Pārvatī, daughter of the Himālaya mountain, at his side, the god who carries the bow came, and she came to the Pine Forest accompanying Śiva.

When they saw the knotted-haired god approaching with the goddess, they bowed their heads to the ground and pleased the Lord with a variety of Vedic mantras and auspicious hymns pertaining to Śiva. Others pleased Śiva by reciting the *Atharvaśiras Upaniṣad* and Brāhmaṇas such as the *Rudra.*

Praise to the first God among gods.
Praise to you, O Great God.
Praise to you, three-eyed one, who carries the excellent trident.
Praise to you, sky-clad one, wounded one, bearer of the bow.
Before your body all are bowed down, while you yourself are never bowed.
Praise to you, who puts an end to death, and who yourself reabsorbs everything.
Praise to the dancer, to the one with a fearsome form.
Praise to the one who is half female, to the teacher of yogis.
Praise to the restrained, tranquil, ascetic Śiva.
Praise to you, most fearful Rudra, wearing clothes of skin.
Praise to you, flickering-tongued one.
Praise to you, blue-necked one.
Praise to the ambiguous one, whose form is both dreadful and not dreadful.
Praise to the one garlanded with jimson flowers, and who gladdens the goddess.
Praise to the highest god granting happiness,
who bears the waters of the Gaṅgā in his hair.
Praise to the lord of yoga, the lord over Brahmā.
Praise to you, the life-breath of all.
Praise to the one who loves smearing ashes on his body.
Praise to you, who rides the clouds, who has fangs, whose semen is fire.
Praise to you, in the form of Time, who once severed Brahmā's head.
We do not know your comings or your goings. O great God,
you are what you are. Let there be praise of you.
Praise to the lord of the fiends, and to the giver of good fortune.
Praise to you, a skull-cup in your hand.
Praise to you, most bountiful one.
Praise to you, gold liṅga, water liṅga.
Praise to the fire liṅga.
Praise to you, liṅga of knowledge.
Praise to the one who wears snakes as garlands, and loves the pea blossom.
Praise to you, crowned one, ear-ringed one, the Destroyer of Time the destroyer.

"O ambiguous One, great Lord, God of gods, three-eyed One, forgive what we have done in our confusion, for you alone are our refuge. Śiva, your deeds are marvelous, profound, and inexplicable. You are difficult to recognize for all, from Brahmā on down. Whatever a man does, whether through ignorance or knowledge, it is the Lord who does it all through his yogic power of appearance."

They praised Śiva in this way, and thrilling within they bowed and asked the Lord of the Mountains, "Let us see you as before."

Moon-bejewelled Śiva listened to their praises, and he showed them his own highest form.

When they saw this mountain-dwelling god, bearer of the bow, along with the goddess, as previously, the sages stood and bowed, minds rejoicing. Then all the sages praised the great Śiva—Bhṛgu, Aṅgiras, Vasiṣṭha and Viśvāmitra, Gautama, Atri and Sukeśa, Pulastya, Pulaha and Kratu, Marīci and Kaśyapa, and the great ascetic Saṃvartta. Bowing to the God of gods, they asked him a question: "How may we worship you, the Lord of all gods, at all times—through the yoga of worldly action, or through knowledge, or through yoga? Or by what divine route should Your Lordship be worshiped? What should we do, and what should we not do? Tell us all this."

"I will tell you the secret, highest mystery, sages, which I once explained to Brahmā," replied Śiva. "Knowledge and yogic practice should be understood as a twofold method for man's attainment. Knowledge together with practice grants liberation to men, but the highest being is not seen through yoga alone, since only knowledge can give the fruit of final liberation. You abandoned pure knowledge and exerted yourselves practicing yoga alone to gain release. For that reason, sages, I have come to this place, showing you the confused state of men who follow proper conduct only. So now, through your own efforts, you should hear, see, and understand the pure knowledge that leads to the attainment of liberation.

"The soul is one, all-pervading, amounting to consciousness alone. It is joy, without stain, and eternal. This is the correct view, which is the highest knowledge. This is praised as liberation. It is described as pure autonomy, the status of Brahman. When eminent ascetics who are devoted to him and take him as their highest resort seek that highest Brahman, they see me, Lord over all. This is the highest knowledge, pure and unique. For I should be known as the Lord. My embodiment is auspicious (*śiva*).

"Many methods of attaining success in this world have been promulgated. This knowledge of mine surpasses all of them, excellent brahmans. I immediately put an end to the frightening ocean of fluctuating existence for all ascetics who, tranquil and intent on both knowledge and yogic practice, take refuge with me, continuously meditating on me in their hearts, their bodies smeared with ashes, their impurities removed—always the highest among my devotees.

"Calm, his mind controlled and body powdered with ash, celibate and naked, one should perform the Pāśupata vow. For liberation, I once established the supreme Pāśupata vow, secret among secrets, subtle, the very essence of the Vedas. A learned sage devoted to Vedic study should wear either a loincloth or a single cloth, and should meditate on Śiva in his form as Paśupati, lord of the animals. It is said that those seeking liberation who are without desire and are covered with ashes should observe the Pāśupata vow continuously. Many who are devoted to me and have taken refuge with me have been purified by this yogic practice, their passion, fear, and anger removed, and have reached my abode.

"But I have also declared other systems of knowledge in this world, which contradict what is said in the Vedas and lead to confusion. You should not observe the systems I have set forth outside the Veda, such as the left-handed Pāśupata, the Skull-bearer, Lākula, Bhairava systems, and others like that. I embody the Vedas, sages. Those who know the meanings of other systems cannot recognize my true form if they abandon the original Veda.

"Establish this path. Worship the great God. The true knowledge of Śiva will arise quickly. There is no doubt about it. Excellent and venerable ones, have devotion toward me, for as soon as you meditate I will grant my presence to you, most eminent sages."

When he had said this, the Lord Śiva vanished from that place. And the sages—celibate, calm, and intent on both knowledge and yogic practice—began to worship Śiva in the Pine Forest. The excellent sages, explicators of the Vedic interpretive texts, assembled and held many theological discussions.

"What is the source of the world?"

"The soul."

"And what would be our source?"

"Śiva alone is the cause of all beings."

While the sages took to the path of meditation and discussed these matters, the goddess Pārvatī, daughter of the mountain, appeared among them, shining like ten million suns, enveloped in a garland of flames, filling the sky with her immaculate radiance. They saw the boundless Pārvatī seated among a thousand flames and bowed to her, sole wife of Śiva. They recognized her as the seed of the highest. For us, Śiva's wife is the abode known as heaven and likewise the soul. These brahmans and sages then saw themselves and the whole world within her.

When Śiva's wife saw them, they saw amidst them the wise god Śiva himself, cause of everything, the great Being of the ancient traditions, highest of the gods. They saw the goddess and the Lord Śiva, bowed, and became exceedingly joyful. At that moment the knowledge of Śiva, which puts an end to the cycle of rebirth, became apparent to them through the Lord's grace. . . .

Then the Lord Śiva, first among the gods, became invisible together with the goddess, and the forest-dwelling sages once again set about worshiping the god Śiva.

"So I have told you the entire episode of what Śiva did in the Pine Forest, just as I heard it long ago. One who reads it or listens to it constantly is released from all sins, and one who recites it to peaceful twice-borns will attain the highest state."

Buddhism in Practice

INTRODUCTION

Buddhism

Donald S. Lopez, Jr.

There is a remarkable diversity and range among the practices of persons who over the course of 2,500 years have been identified, by themselves or by others, as Buddhists. In this diversity there are often contradictions, such that the practices of a Buddhist community of one time might seem strange or unfamiliar to a Buddhist community elsewhere. Indeed, one of the questions that must be raised is whether one can accurately speak of something called "Buddhism" or "the Buddhist tradition," or whether those terms are better rendered in the plural. At the same time, there is evidence of often surprising parallels among the practices of Buddhist cultures widely separated by both history and topography, parallels to be accounted for in large part by a constant retrospection to the figure of the Buddha, making Buddhism less the inevitable unfolding of a distinct and self-identical entity and more a dynamic process of borrowing, conflict, and interaction between and within traditions that have been identified as Buddhist.

This introduction is meant to serve two purposes. First, it will provide a brief historical sketch of the history of Buddhism. Second, it will provide a description of some of the Buddhist doctrines that have come to be considered fundamental by the tradition of scholars, both Buddhist and Western.

The life and teachings of the Buddha as they recorded in traditional sources are recounted in some detail below.[1] After the death of the Buddha, the community of his followers is said to have met in a series of councils, each sponsored by a different king, to settle disputes regarding what the Buddha had taught and what rules the monastic order should follow. The Buddha had preached for over forty years to a wide variety of audiences, and there was a concern that those teachings be remembered and preserved before they could be forgotten. This preservation was done orally, with different groups of monks responsible for the memorization and retention of what evolved into a variety of oral canons. None of these was committed to writing until the last decades before the common era, and not in India but in Sri Lanka, some four hundred years after the Buddha's death. Despite the sophisticated mnemonic devices that Buddhist monks employed in preserving these teachings, there can be little certainty as to which of them, if any, were actually the words of the Buddha; there remains debate even about which language the Buddha spoke. Thus, it is no longer tenable to accept the assumption shared by both early Western scholars of Buddhism and Buddhist figures in Southeast Asia (often under Western influence) that what is known as the Theravāda tradition (the tradition of the Elders) found in the Pāli language represents an original Buddhism from which all other forms of Buddhism derived (and sometimes deviated). The original teachings of the historical Buddha are extremely difficult, if not impossible, to recover or reconstruct.

The Buddhist community flourished in India during the Mauryan dynasty (324–187 B.C.E.), especially during the reign of the emperor Aśoka, whose rule extended over most of the Indian subcontinent and who, in a series of rock edicts, professed his faith in the Buddha, his teaching, and the monastic community. Although Aśoka's edicts set forth a generalized morality that allowed him to support many religious groups in his vast kingdom, he is remembered in Buddhist legends as the ideal Buddhist king, deeply devoted to the propagation of the Buddha's teaching and to the support of the monastic community. By the end of Aśoka's reign, Buddhist monks and nuns were established in monasteries throughout the Indian subcontinent, monasteries that were often located near cities and that relied on state support. From this point on, the fortunes of Buddhism in India waxed and waned largely in dependence on the policies of local rulers.

In the first centuries of the common era, a movement, or series of movements, occurred in India that came to be referred to as the *Mahāyāna,* the Great Vehicle. This seems to have begun as a disparate collection of cults centered around newly composed texts and their charismatic expositors, the dharmabhāṇaka. These texts, although composed centuries after the Buddha's death, were accepted by their devotees as sūtras (discourses attributed to the Buddha or spoken with his sanction). Some of the texts, like the *Lotus Sūtra* (discussed below), in addition to proclaiming their own unique potency as the means to salvation, would also praise the veneration of stūpas, the reliquaries in which the remains of the Buddha were enshrined. Other texts, like much of the early Perfection of Wisdom (*prajñāpāramitā*) corpus, would proclaim their superiority to stūpas, declaring themselves to be substitutes for the body and speech of the absent Buddha, equally worthy of veneration and equally efficacious.

It is perhaps best to regard the Mahāyāna as a social movement of monks, nuns, and lay people that began in reaction against the controls exercised by a powerful monastic institution. This movement was responsible for the production and dissemination of a body of literature that challenged the authority of that institution by having the Buddha proclaim a superior and more inclusive path and a more profound wisdom. In subsequent centuries, during which sūtras continued to be composed, the Mahāyāna became not merely a collection of cults of the book but a self-conscious scholastic entity. Adherents of the Mahāyāna devoted a good deal of energy to surveying what was by then a rather large corpus and then attempting, through a variety of hermeneutical machinations, to craft the myriad doctrines into a philosophical and doctrinal system. In short, it is in this later period that the sūtras, which seem at first to have been recited and worshiped, became the object also of scholastic reflection. The fact that these treatises commonly contain a defense of the Mahāyāna as the authentic word of the Buddha—even treatises composed a millennium after the composition of the first Mahāyāna sūtras—may provide evidence of the minority status of the Mahāyāna in India.

These new movements came to designate themselves by the term "Mahāyāna," the "Great Vehicle" to enlightenment, in contradistinction from the earlier Buddhist schools who did not accept their new sūtras as authoritative (that is, as the word of the Buddha). They disparagingly referred to these earlier schools with the term "Hīnayāna," often rendered euphemistically as the "Lesser Vehicle," although *hīna* means also "inferior," "base," and "vile." Members of these earlier schools, of course, never thought of or referred to themselves as passengers on the Hīnayāna. It has thus become common in Western writing about Buddhism to avoid this term by replacing it with "Theravāda." But the terms "Hīnayāna" and "Theravāda" do not designate the same groups; there is a traditional list of some eighteen Hīnayāna schools with diverse doctrines, only one of which has survived into the present, the Theravāda of Sri Lanka and Southeast Asia, whose works are preserved in the Pāli language.

The term "Mahāyāna" is less objectionable for the reason that it was used self-referentially. Most anthologies provide selections from the Pāli texts followed by a sampling from Mahāyāna sūtras, suggesting that with the rise of the Mahāyāna the earlier traditions were both superseded and eclipsed. This is, however, historically inaccurate. The reports of Chinese pilgrims to India in the seventh century indicate that followers of the Mahāyāna and the "Hīnayāna" lived together in monasteries (*vihāras*) and that they all maintained the same "Hīnayāna" monastic vows. The reports further indicate that in many monasteries adherents of the Hīnayāna outnumbered those of the Mahāyāna. Thus, as an alternative to the polemical "Hīnayāna," the term "foundational Buddhism" may be used, referring to the members of Buddhist monastic communities and their supporters who did not accept the legitimacy of the new scriptures composed by followers of the Mahāyāna. As the seventh-century Chinese pilgrim Yijing observed about India, "those who worship bodhisattvas and read Mahāyāna sūtras are called Mahāyāna, while those who do not do this are called the Hīnayāna." The foundational nature and persistence of the Hīnayāna schools in India is often forgotten because of the domination of the Mahāyāna in China, Japan, Korea, Mongolia, and Tibet.

Some five centuries after the rise of the Mahāyāna, another major movement occurred in Indian Buddhism, which was retrospectively designated as the Vajrayāna (the Thunderbolt or Diamond Vehicle). Its origins are even less clearly understood than those of the Mahāyāna. Like "Hīnayāna" and "Mahāyāna," "Vajrayāna" is a retrospective designation, in this case coined to describe a rather disparate set of practices by which the long path to buddhahood could be traversed more quickly than was possible via the Mahāyāna, a path on which various supernormal powers were gained in the process. Some of these practices, such as engaging in behaviors that broke caste taboos, appear to have been borrowed from ascetic movements current in India at the time. Others were developments of themes long present in Buddhist texts, such as the possibility of coming into the presence of the Buddha through visualization practices. Despite the efforts of generations of Buddhist thinkers, it remains exceedingly difficult to identify precisely what it is that sets the Vajrayāna apart. And this difficulty of identifying distinguishing features applies more generally to the issue of distinguishing the Buddhist vehicles, the Hīnayāna, the Mahāyāna, and the Vajrayāna. Adherents of this or that vehicle have much invested in claims to uniqueness. However, these three vehicles share more than is usually assumed.

Anthologies of Buddhist texts have often been organized according to vehicle. One difficulty with such an approach is the almost unavoidable propensity to see the Hīnayāna-Mahāyāna-Vajrayāna sequence as a value-laden development of one kind or another, in which one member of the triad is exalted above the others. According to one view (found especially among European scholars of Buddhism in the nineteenth century), the Hīnayāna (what they called "original Buddhism") was a simple ethical creed of self-reliance, free of ritual elements. In the rise of Mahāyāna, they saw a concession to the masses, in which the Buddha was deified and became an object of worship, and salvation became possible not through diligent practice but through faith in a dizzying pantheon of buddhas and bodhisattvas. The Vajrayāna was an even later development in which, they believed, debased Hindu practices polluted Buddhism until any kind of licentious behavior became accepted.

Another view (found particularly among scholars of Chinese and Japanese Buddhism) also sees the Hīnayāna as an ethical creed, which became an institution of self-satisfied and complacent monks who cared only about their own authority. The Mahāyāna, they believe, was a popular lay movement that sought to restore to the tradition the Buddha's original compassion through the ideal of the bodhisattva, the person who sacrifices his or her own welfare in order to lead all sentient beings in the universe to nirvāṇa. The bodhisattva path is a long one, and requires many millions of lifetimes of practice. According to this view, the Vajrayāna was again a late development, coming at a time when people were no longer interested in dedicating themselves to this protracted path to enlightenment for the sake of others, and imagined that the Vajrayāna provided a shortcut.

Finally, there is the view that sees the Vajrayāna as the pinnacle in the evolution of Buddhism, moving from the austere individualism of the Hīnayāna to the relatively simple compassion of the Mahāyāna, which sees salvation only in the ever-distant future, and finally to the culmination in the Vajrayāna, where buddhahood is possible in this very body and in this very lifetime, not through a suppression of desire and the sensual but through the discovery of ultimate reality even there.

The processes by which Buddhist practices developed through Asia are far more complex than any of these three models suggests. For example, the first model ignores the wealth of rituals and devotional practices found in the Theravāda. The second model ignores the important role played by monks and nuns throughout the history of the Mahāyāna. And the third model places far too much emphasis on the claim of buddhahood in this very lifetime, an important but hardly universal claim of tantric texts. Beyond these specific errors, a more general problem with such an evolutionary (or devolutionary) model is that it suggests that one vehicle ceases or dies out before the next becomes fully formed. Such a suggestion is supported in those anthologies that only provide works from the Pāli "canon," the early collection of works considered by the Theravāda to represent the authentic teachings of the Buddha and his early followers. These anthologies ignore the great mass of literature composed in subsequent centuries in both Pāli and the vernaculars of Southeast Asia, as if the Buddhism of this region essentially ceased its literary output after the fifth century of the common era.

Buddhist institutions had disappeared in India by the thirteenth century. The reasons for this demise remain much debated. The overt cause was a series of Muslim invasions, beginning in the eleventh century, during which the major monastic centers of northern India were destroyed. There had been persecutions of Buddhism by various Hindu kings in the past, but these had been localized and short-lived, often followed by an infusion of support under another dynasty. In this case, however, no such dynasty arose. It also appears that by the end of the first millennium, the locus of Buddhism in India had become the large monastery, which depended on royal rather than local patronage; the most famous of these was Nālandā, said to have housed ten thousand monks. When such centers were destroyed (as Nālandā was by Turkic troops in 1197), the power and influence of the monastic institutions quickly dissipated. Some scholars argue as well that by this time many Buddhist practices had been incorporated into Hinduism and that the local functions fulfilled by Buddhist monks in the past were being performed by Hindu priests. Historians no longer subscribe to the further claim that Buddhism was already weak during this period due to the degenerating influence of tantra. Indeed, tantric Buddhism has survived in Nepal until the present day in a tradition of Mahāyāna devotionalism officiated by a saṅgha of married priests.

Buddhism is often described as the only pan-Asian religion, the only Asian religion to spread beyond the boundaries of its native culture. This is not entirely accurate. Confucian thought has had a profound influence on Korea and Japan, for example, and Hindu epics, with their gods, demons, and social ideals have shaped the cultures of Southeast Asia. It is true, however, that Buddhism spanned both the Indian and Chinese cultural domains of Asia. But it is important to think not so much of a disembodied dharma descending on another culture from above, but rather of a more material movement—of monks, texts, relics, and icons—along trade routes and across deserts, mountains, and seas.

The Buddha is reported to have exhorted his monks to "go and travel around for the welfare of the multitudes, for the happiness of the multitudes, out of sympathy for the world, for the benefit, welfare, and happiness of gods and humans. No two should go in the same direction." Although this last admonition seems not to have been heeded, it is true that Buddhist "missions" were not large and well-organized movements, and instead often took the form of itinerant monks (or groups of monks) traveling by land and sea in the company of traders and royal emissaries. According to traditional accounts, the first foreign mission was to the island of Sri Lanka, and was led by the son of Aśoka.

In descriptions of Buddhism outside of India, one sometimes encounters the term "Southern Buddhism" to describe the Buddhism of Sri Lanka, Thailand, Cambodia, Burma, Laos, and parts of Vietnam, and the term "Northern Buddhism," used in reference to China, Japan, Korea, Tibet, and Mongolia. It is often said that Southern Buddhism is Theravāda and Northern Buddhism is Mahāyāna. This is not historically accurate. Theravāda has been the dominant school of Buddhism in most of Southeast Asia since the thirteenth century, with the establishment of the monarchies in Thailand, Burma, Cambodia, and Laos. Prior to that period, however, many other strands of Buddhism were also widely present, including other Hīnayāna sects, as well as Mahāyāna and tantric groups. The great monument at Borobudur in Java reflects Mahāyāna doctrine, and there are reports of Indian monks traveling to Sumatra to study with Mahāyāna and tantric masters there. Indeed, Buddhists texts, icons, and institutions (Hīnayāna, Mahāyāna, and Vajrayāna) were just some of the Indian cultural forms introduced into Southeast Asia by traders and travelers, beginning as early as the fourth century. Buddhist Bengal exerted a strong influence from the ninth through thirteenth centuries, and Sanskrit Mahāyāna and tantric texts were donated to Burmese monasteries as late as the fifteenth century. It was only after the demise of Buddhism in India that the Southeast Asian societies looked especially to Sri Lanka for their Buddhism, where by that time Theravāda was established as the orthodoxy. The monarchs of the kingdoms of Thailand, Burma, Cambodia, and Laos found an effective ideology in Theravāda notions of rulership, often invoking the model of Aśoka.

Just as Southeast Asian Buddhism was not always Theravāda, so "Northern Buddhism" was not always Mahāyāna. The monastic codes practiced in China, Japan, Korea, and Tibet were all derived from the Indian Hīnayāna orders. Furthermore, several of these orders flourished in Central Asia (including parts of modern Iran and Afghanistan), whence Buddhism was first introduced into China via the silk route.

Buddhist monks came to China from the northwest sometime during the first century of the common era. China was the most advanced of the civilizations to encounter Buddhism, as measured in terms of literary culture and the organization of social and political institutions. Unlike Tibet and areas of Southeast Asia, for example, China was not a place to which Buddhist monks brought Indian cultural forms, such as writing, which would powerfully shape the future history of the society. It is sometimes argued that if China had not been suffering a period of political disunity in the first centuries of the common era, Buddhism would never have taken hold. It is also argued that Buddhist institutions tended to be strongest in China when the central government was weakest and that Buddhist institutions existed in a state of atrophy after the Tang. Indeed, the first patrons of the dharma were the leaders of the foreign or "barbarian" dynasties in northern China. However, such claims can be overstated, for the influence of Buddhism on a wide range of Chinese cultural forms, such as vernacular literature, has been and remains profound. It is also often stated that Buddhism did not truly take hold in China until it had been fully "sinified," that is, made Chinese. It is important to consider the degree to which Chinese Buddhism is Chinese and the degree to which it is Buddhist, as well as to ponder the bases upon which such judgments might be made.

Contacts with China brought Buddhist monks into the Korean peninsula in the late fourth century. As elsewhere in Asia, these monks did not simply carry texts and icons, but brought with them many of the products of their own civilization, in this case, that of China. Buddhist institutions thrived especially after the unification of the Korean peninsula under the Silla Dynasty in 668. As had been the case in China and would be the case of Japan, part of the appeal of Buddhism to kings was the claim that worshiping the Buddha, promoting the dharma, and supporting the monastic community would protect the state from foreign invasion and calamity, a view set forth in apocryphal works such as the *Sūtra for Humane Kings*. During this period, a number of Korean monks became influential figures in China, Japan, and even in Tibet.

As in China, Buddhism has been both embraced and condemned in Japan as a foreign religion. In the sixth century, monks from Korea first introduced Buddhist texts and teachings into Japan, which, according to traditional accounts were received with enthusiasm at court. Just as Buddhist monks had served as carriers of Indian cultural forms to Southeast Asia, so they brought the products of Chinese civilization to Japan. The Japanese have since looked to China as the source of their Buddhism, and for centuries Japanese monks made the often perilous journey to China to retrieve texts and teachings. These monks, such as the founders of the Tendai and Shingon schools of the Heian period (794–1185), were generally rewarded with imperial support upon their return. During the Kamakura period (1185–1333), when the nation was ruled by a series of military dictators, the shoguns, new sects came to prominence with their patronage. The foremost of these were Zen, Pure Land, and Nichiren, which came to eclipse the previous schools in popular support. In contrast to the more eclectic approach of the Heian sects, each of these three claimed that their single practice offered the only effective means to salvation.

According to traditional accounts, Buddhist monks did not come to Tibet until the seventh century. As was the case with Japan, Buddhism was initially introduced to the court. Indeed, the Tibetan king is said to have been converted to Buddhism by two princesses—one from China and one from Nepal, but both Buddhists—whom he received in marriage as the result of treaties. The dissemination of Buddhist teachings and institutions in Tibet took place in two waves. The first, during the seventh and eighth centuries, saw royal support for the founding and maintenance of Buddhist monasteries, the invitation of Buddhist teachers from India, and the beginnings of a massive project to translate Buddhist texts from Sanskrit into Tibetan. The Tibetan script is said to have been invented for this purpose. Around 838, a king who was not kindly disposed to the dharma closed the monasteries. He was assassinated four years later by a Buddhist monk, thus ending the Tibetan monarchy. A revival of Buddhism took place in western Tibet almost two centuries later. One of the signal events of this second wave was the invitation of the Indian monk Atiśa. There followed a period of extensive contact with India, when Tibetans went to study at the great monasteries of northern India, often inviting their teachers to come back with them. By the end of the fourteenth century, most of the work of translation had been completed. The Tibetans were able to avoid invasion by the Mongols by serving as preceptors to a succession of Mongol khans, who were the first in a series of foreign patrons for the sects of Tibetan Buddhism. In the seventeenth century, the head of one of these sects, the fifth Dalai Lama, was able to consolidate political power over Tibet with the help of his Mongol patron. A succession of Dalai Lamas (or their regents) continued to rule Tibet until 1959, when the current Dalai Lama was forced to flee to India after the invasion and occupation of his nation by China.

In the history of Buddhism in each of these cultures, it is usually possible to discern two general periods. The first is one of assimilation in which Buddhist practices were introduced, with much attention devoted to the translation of texts, the founding of monasteries (with state support), the establishment of places of pilgrimage, often centered on a relic or icon, and close contact with the culture from which Buddhist cultural forms were being received (for example, India in the case of Tibet, Central Asia in the case of China, China in the case of Japan, Sri Lanka in the case of Thailand, and Tibet in the case of Mongolia). In most cases, the period of assimilation lasted for several centuries. This was followed by a period of adaptation, in which Buddhist forms were more fully integrated into the society and made more distinctively its own. It is during this period that schools developed that did not have precise analogs in Indian Buddhism, local deities were incorporated into the Buddhist pantheon, and Buddhist deities were incorporated into the local pantheon. Of course, the adherents of these new schools and devotees of these local cults would reject the suggestion that their practices could not be traced back directly to the Buddha. This concern with the authentic source of the teaching is evinced in the pan-Asian practice of pilgrimage to Bodhgayā, the site of the Buddha's enlightenment. The history of Buddhism in Asia continues to the present day.

Buddhism has a vast literature dealing with what we term logic, epistemology, and ontology—works that are (depending on one's perspective) as profound or as impenetrable, as rich or as arid, as anything produced in the West. However, like philosophical works in other cultures, Buddhist treatises are the products of a tiny, highly educated elite (largely composed of monks in the Buddhist case) and their works rarely touch the ground where the vast majority of Buddhists have lived their lives.

It is important to recall, however, that the Buddhist philosopher was also a Buddhist and, in most cases, a Buddhist monk. He was thus a participant in rituals and institutions that provided the setting for his work. The authors of Buddhist philosophical treatises do not, therefore, fulfill our traditional image of the philosopher engaged in a quest for knowledge "for its own sake," with an overarching concern with logic, rationality, and theoretical consistency. Although these enterprises find an important place in Buddhist traditions, it is also true that for many Buddhist scholastics the faculty of reason provides a relatively superficial awareness, insufficient to the task of directly apprehending the truth. All endeavors in the realm of what might be termed "philosophy" were theoretically subservient to the greater goal of enlightenment, and the ultimate task of the philosopher, at least in theory, was to attain that enlightenment. The Tibetan authors who are regarded as preeminent scholars, for example, devoted great efforts to the performance of tantric rituals or to various sophisticated forms of meditation, in an effort to manifest a fantastic world of benign and malevolent forces, propitiating deities and repelling demons. What we term "philosophy" was but one concern of these authors; a perusal of the titles in the collected works of any of Tibet's most erudite thinkers reveals that among the commentaries on Indian logical treatises and expositions of emptiness are myriad works devoted to tantric ceremonies and visualizations, along with instructions on techniques for drawing maṇḍalas, making rain, stopping smallpox, and manufacturing magical pills. The biographies of the most famous Buddhist philosophers are replete with the most extraordinary events. Thus, although there is a large and significant body of Buddhist literature devoted to such issues as the validity of sense experience and inference as sources of knowledge, the study of such texts must be undertaken with careful attention to their contexts, in the broadest sense of the term, so that the ideas and arguments are not regarded as denizens of a free-floating world, whether that world be the history of ideas or the dharma.

Buddhist texts speak often of the three jewels: of the Buddha, the dharma, and the saṅgha, that is, the Buddha, his teachings, and the community of his followers. In Buddhist texts, a Buddhist is defined as someone who takes refuge in these three, and the refuge ceremony is the most widely performed ritual in the Buddhist world. The Buddha, dharma, and saṅgha are called jewels because they are precious and rare. It is said that it is difficult to encounter them in the cycle of rebirth and when they are encountered they are of great value. The notion of refuge suggests two points fundamental to the Buddhist worldview. The first is that sentient beings are in need of protection, of a place of refuge where they can escape from the sufferings of saṃsāra, the cycle of rebirths. The second point is that the three jewels can provide such protection, that they themselves are free from the dangers and vicissitudes of saṃsāra, and thus can offer refuge to others. In the medical metaphor of which Buddhists are so fond, the Buddha is the doctor, the dharma is the medicine, and the saṅgha are the nurses. It is the Buddha who finds the path to liberation and shows it to others. The dharma is the path itself, and the saṅgha are one's companions who offer assistance along the way.

Before discussing the three jewels in more detail, it would be useful here to outline some of the doctrines most basic to Buddhist practices, as they have been understood by Buddhist authors and by Western scholars. Although there are significant variations among Buddhist cultures, Buddhists in Asia generally accept a view of the universe and of the afterlife that originated in India. Some elements of this cosmology seem to have been current in India at the time of the Buddha, whereas others are the results of elaborations by Buddhist thinkers, perhaps including the Buddha himself. The most standard cosmology divides the universe into three realms, called the realm of desire (*kāmadhātu*), the realm of form (*rūpadhātu*) and the formless realm (*arūpyadhātu*).

The realm of desire is the universe inhabited by humans. Its topography is symmetrical, with four islands surrounding a central mountain, Mount Meru (or Sumeru). Ours is the southern island, called Jambudvīpa (Rose-Apple Island). The other three islands are also inhabited by humans (although of different height and lifespan), but are generally regarded as inaccessible; a buddha can become enlightened only in Jambudvīpa. Mount Meru is the abode of a class of beings called *asuras,* often translated as "demigod" or "titan." They are usually depicted as mean-spirited lesser deities who can bring harm to humans. At a higher elevation on and above Mount Meru is the abode of six classes of gods (*deva*) who inhabit increasingly pleasant realms for increasingly long lifespans. The first two godly realms are on Mount Meru itself. The lower is that of the four royal lineages, ruled by the guardians of the cardinal directions. Next is the "Heaven of the Thirty-Three," on the flat summit of Mount Meru, where thirty-three gods abide. Here, as elsewhere, we see Buddhists assimilating elements from rival groups or other cultures, because thirty-three is the traditional number of gods in the *Ṛg Veda.* Although early Buddhists rejected any ultimate power for Vedic deities, such as Indra, they nonetheless incorporated them into their pantheon, acknowledging their worldly powers but placing them on the second lowest rung of their heavenly hierarchy. Indeed, throughout Buddhist cultures, the worship of local deities is not proscribed, unless that worship involves animal sacrifice. Gods are honored for the boons they can bestow. The thirty-three gods live very long lives: their lifespan is one thousand years, but each of their days is equal to one hundred human years. Yet they are not immortal; they are also subject to rebirth. The remaining four heavens of the realm of desire float in the sky above the summit of Mount Meru. It is in the fourth of the six godly realms, called Tuṣita (Joyous) that the future buddha, Maitreya, waits.

Also inhabiting the realm of desire are, of course, all manner of animal and insect life, as well as a pitiful class of beings called *pretas,* usually translated as "ghosts" or "hungry ghosts." These beings—some of whom are visible to humans, some of whom are not—are depicted iconographically with huge, distended bellies and emaciated limbs. Their throats are said to be the size of the eye of a needle, rendering them constantly hungry and thirsty and forcing them to search constantly for food and drink. The feeding of these beings was seen as a special responsibility of Buddhist monks and nuns. Located far below Jambudvīpa (usually measured from Bodhgayā, the place in India where the Buddha achieved enlightenment) in the realm of desire is an extensive system of hells, some burning hot, others freezing cold. The beings there undergo a variety of tortures, often depicted in gruesome detail in Buddhist texts and paintings.

The realm of form is situated above the realm of desire and is regarded as superior to it. The beings here are gods who experience the pleasures of sight, sound, and touch, but not taste and smell. They are distinguished from the gods of the realm of desire by their greater powers of concentration, which provide deep states of mental bliss. There are four major levels within the realm of form, categorized by the increasing power of concentration of its inhabitants. Even more sublime is the formless realm, where gods exist in states of pure consciousness, without bodies and sense organs. This is considered the most blissful of abodes, yet it does not receive a great deal of attention in Buddhist literature outside the psychological treatises.

This universe has no beginning, although its physical constituents pass through a fourfold cosmic cycle of evolution, stasis, devolution, and vacuity. Mount Meru and its surrounding islands are said to have evolved over a period of eons, during which, according to one of the Buddhist creation myths, they came to be populated. At the beginning of this process, the lifespan of humans is said to have been immeasurable. Human life had an Edenic quality about it: there was no need for food and humans illuminated the world with their own inner light. As the result of curiosity and desire (to taste the milky froth that covered the surface of the earth), humans began to eat, which required that they expel waste. Their bodies developed accordingly, leading eventually to sexual intercourse. Their natural light faded, the sun and moon appeared, and they began to hoard food for themselves, creating private property for the first time; the eventual result was human society. The human lifespan also gradually diminished until it reached an average of one hundred years, at which point the Buddha appeared in the world to teach the dharma. The quality of human life and the human life span will continue to decline until it reaches ten years of age, coinciding with a time of pestilence, poverty, and warfare. All memory of the Buddha and his teaching will have disappeared from the world. The human lifespan will then begin to increase once more, until it reaches eighty thousand years again, at which point the next buddha will appear. At the end of twenty such cycles, this universe will gradually be destroyed and will then enter into a long period of vacuity, after which a new universe will be created. As the current Dalai Lama has said, Buddhists do not believe in one Big Bang, they believe in many Big Bangs.

The realm of desire, the realm of form, and the formless realm are not only locations in the Buddhist universe, they are also places of rebirth. Buddhists conceive of a cycle of birth and death, called *saṃsāra* (wandering), in six realms of rebirth: those of the gods, demigods, humans, animals, ghosts, and hell beings (although sometimes the realm of demigods is omitted). The entire cycle of rebirth in which the creations and destructions of universes is encompassed has no ultimate beginning. The realms of animals, ghosts, and hell beings are regarded as places of great suffering, whereas the godly realms are abodes of great bliss. Human rebirth falls in between, bringing as it does both pleasure and pain. The engine of saṃsāra is driven by karma, the cause and effect of actions. Like adherents of other Indian religions, Buddhists believe that every intentional act, whether it be physical, verbal, or mental, leaves a residue. That residue, like a seed, will eventually produce an effect at some point in the future, an effect in the form of pleasure or pain for the person who performed the act. Thus Buddhists conceive of a moral universe in which virtuous deeds create experiences of pleasure and nonvirtuous deeds create experiences of pain. These latter are often delineated in a list of ten nonvirtuous deeds: killing, stealing, sexual misconduct, lying, divisive speech, harsh speech, senseless speech, covetousness, harmful intent, and wrong view. Wrong view can mean many things in Buddhist thought, but here refers especially to the belief that actions do not have effects. Buddhist texts provide extensive discussions of the specific deeds that constitute these ten nonvirtues and their respective karmic weight. The ten virtues are the opposites of this list: sustaining life, giving gifts, maintaining sexual decorum, and so on.

These deeds not only determine the quality of a given life but also determine the place of the rebirth after death. Depending on the gravity of a negative deed (killing being more serious than senseless speech and killing a human more serious than killing an insect, for example) one may be reborn as an animal, a ghost, or in one of the hot or cold hells, where the lifespan is particularly lengthy. Among the hells, some are more horrific than others; the most tortuous is reserved for those who have committed one of five heinous deeds: killing one's father, killing one's mother, killing an arhat, wounding a buddha, and causing dissent in the saṅgha.

Rebirth as a god or human in the realm of desire is the result of a virtuous deed, and is considered very rare. Rarer still is rebirth as a human who has access to the teachings of the Buddha. In a famous analogy, a single blind tortoise is said to swim in a vast ocean, surfacing for air only once every century. On the surface of the ocean floats a single golden yoke. It is rarer, said the Buddha, to be reborn as a human with the opportunity to practice the dharma than it is for the tortoise to surface for its centennial breath with its head through the hole in the golden yoke. One is said to be reborn as a god in the realm of desire as a result of an act of charity: giving gifts results in future wealth. Rebirth as a human is said to result from consciously refraining from a nonvirtuous deed, as when one takes a vow not to kill humans. The vast majority of Buddhist practice throughout Asia and throughout history has been directed toward securing rebirth as a human or (preferably) a god in the next lifetime, generally through acts of charity directed toward monks and monastic institutions. Despite repeated admonitions that birth as a god is a temporary state from which one must eventually fall, to be reborn in a lower realm—admonitions such as those made by the twentieth-century Thai monk Buddhadāsa—a happy life and an auspicious rebirth have remained goals more sought after than escape from saṃsāra into nirvāṇa. Indeed, much Buddhist literature intended for both monks and lay people has promoted a social ideal, defining the good life and explaining how to lead it.

Rebirth as a god in the realm of form or formless realm is achieved somewhat differently. Because these realms are characterized by deep states of concentration, one must achieve one of those states in this life through the practice of meditation in order to be reborn there in the next. For example, one must reach the third level of concentration in order to be reborn as a god in the third level of the realm of form. Because these states require a specialized and sustained practice, they have been little sought as places of rebirth. The formless realm in particular seems to have been more important as an abode to which non-Buddhist meditation masters could be consigned. For example, such a master may have wrongly imagined that he had achieved the ultimate state and liberation from rebirth, when in fact he was only in the realm of infinite consciousness of the formless realm, from which he would eventually be reborn into a lower abode; liberation is possible only by following the teachings of the Buddha.

In the Mahāyāna sūtras, a further cosmic wrinkle is provided by the description of buddha fields (*buddhakṣetra*) or "pure lands," worlds created by buddhas and presided over by them. Through a variety of pious acts, humans can be reborn in these blissful abodes, where the conditions are ideal for rapid progress on the path to enlightenment. The marvels of the pure lands are described in elaborate detail in certain Mahāyāna sūtras, which tell of every variety of jewel growing from trees, streams of variable temperature for bathing, and soothing breezes that carry sermons appropriate to each listener. Rebirth in one of these lands became a prominent goal of Buddhist practice in India, China, and Japan, where it seemed to serve as either a replacement or a temporary substitute for the purportedly greater goal of buddhahood. In some Mahāyāna sūtras, the notion of the buddha field was given a somewhat different twist with the claim that this benighted world in which humans now live is in reality itself a buddha field; it need only be recognized as such. This view was to be important in tantric Buddhism.

A brief description of the Buddha, the dharma, and the saṅgha follows below, organized under these three headings both to reflect this most traditional of Buddhist categories and to call these categories into question by demonstrating the myriad ways in which Buddhists have answered the questions: Who is the Buddha? What is the dharma? And who belongs to the saṅgha?

The Buddha

Scholars are increasingly reluctant to make unqualified claims about the historical facts of the Buddha's life and teachings. There is even a difference of opinion concerning the years of his birth and death. The long accepted dates of 563–483 B.C.E. have recently been called into question with the suggestion that the Buddha may have lived and died as much as a century later.

The traditional accounts of the Buddha's life are largely hagiographic and tend to include the following narrative. It tells of the miraculous birth of a prince of the warrior (*kṣatriya*) caste in a kingdom in what is today southern Nepal. Astrologers predict that the prince, named Siddhārtha ("He Who Achieves His Goal") will be either a great king or a great religious teacher. His father the king, apparently convinced that dissatisfaction with the world is what causes one's mind to turn to existential questions and the spiritual quest, is determined to protect his son from all that is unpleasant, and keeps him in a palace where he is surrounded by beauty and all forms of sport and delight. Only at the age of twenty-nine does the prince become sufficiently curious about the world beyond the palace walls to venture forth on four chariot rides. During the first he sees an old person for the first time in his life, and is informed by his charioteer that this is not the only old man in the world, but that old age eventually befalls everyone. On the next tour he sees a sick person, on the next a corpse. It is only then that he learns of the existence of sickness and death. On his final chariot ride he sees a religious mendicant, who has renounced the world in search of freedom from birth and death. He decides to follow a similar path and, against his father's orders and leaving behind his wife and infant son, goes forth from the life of a householder in search of liberation from suffering.

Over a period of six years he engages in a number of the yogic disciplines current in India at the time, including severe asceticism, and concludes that mortification of the flesh is not conducive to progress toward his goal of freedom from birth, aging, sickness, and death. He eventually sits beneath a tree and meditates all night. After repulsing an attack by the evil deity Māra and his armies, at dawn he comes to a realization that makes him the Buddha ("Awakened One"), forever free from future rebirth. Exactly what it was that he understood on that full-moon night has remained a source of both inspiration and contention throughout the history of Buddhism. Some accounts say that the content of the enlightenment was so profound that the Buddha was initially reluctant to try to teach it to others, and decided otherwise only after being beseeched by the great god Brahmā, himself subject to rebirth and hence desirous of liberation. In this volume, the life of the Buddha and the content of his enlightenment is recounted in a Thai ritual for consecrating (that is, animating) a statue of the Buddha.

The Buddha was one of an infinite series of buddhas, all of whom reached their exalted state in the same manner, at exactly the same spot in India under one or another species of bodhi tree. When the Buddha gained enlightenment (*bodhi*), he did so all at once, in an instant, and his realization of the truth was perfect. He also made his momentous discovery by himself, without the aid of a teacher. It was this fact above all that distinguished the Buddha from his enlightened disciples, called *arhats,* in the early tradition. The disciples had to rely on his teachings to realize nirvāṇa, and typically did so only in stages. The Buddha was able to reach his enlightenment on his own and in a single night of meditation because he had previously devoted himself to the practice of virtues such as generosity, patience, and effort over countless previous lifetimes. In one of his previous lives, in the presence of a previous buddha, he had made the firm resolution to become a buddha himself at a future time when the path to liberation had been lost; he had dedicated his practice of virtue over the next eons of rebirth to that goal.

Seven weeks after his enlightenment, the Buddha is said to have walked to the city of Varanasi (Banaras) and to a deer park on its outskirts, where he encountered five renunciates with whom he had previously practiced asceticism. To them he gave his first teaching, usually referred to as the "four noble truths." However, it is not the truths that are noble. The term is perhaps less euphoniously but more accurately rendered as the "four truths for nobles." The term "noble" or "superior" in Sanskrit is *āryan,* the term with which the Indo-European migrants to India had described themselves and which Buddhism appropriated to mean one who is spiritually superior, that is, who has had a vision of a state beyond birth and death. The four things that the Buddha set forth to the five ascetics are known to be true by such people, not by others. Although some Mahāyāna texts dispute that this was the Buddha's very first teaching after his enlightenment, all agree that the teaching of the four truths was of great importance. Over the centuries it has received numerous renditions, the general contours of which follow.

The first truth is that life is inherently unsatisfactory, qualified as it inevitably is by birth, aging, sickness, and death. Various forms of suffering are delineated in Buddhist texts, including the fact that beings must separate from friends and meet with enemies, that they encounter what they do not want, and do not find what they want. The fundamental problem is presented as one of a lack of control over future events; a person wanders constantly from situation to situation, from rebirth to rebirth without companions, discarding one body to take on another, with no certainty or satisfaction, sometimes exalted and sometimes debased. Briefly stated, the problem is change or, as more commonly rendered, impermanence (*anitya*). Because suffering can occur at any moment without warning, even pleasure is in a sense a form of pain, because it will eventually be replaced by pain; there is no activity in which one can engage that will not, in the short or long term, become either physically or mentally painful.

The second truth is the cause of this suffering, identified as action (*karma*), specifically nonvirtuous action, and the negative mental states that motivate such action. As described above, the experience of pleasure and pain is the direct result of actions performed in the past. These actions are motivated by states of mind called *kleśas* (often translated as "afflictions" or "defilements"), the most important of which are desire, hatred, and ignorance. The exact content of this ignorance is again the subject of extensive discussion in Buddhist literature, but it is represented as an active misconception of the nature of reality, usually described as a belief in self (*ātman*). There is, in fact, no permanent and autonomous self in the mind or the body, and to believe otherwise is the root cause of all suffering. It is this imagined self that is inflamed by desire and defended by hatred. As long as one believes in the illusion of self, one will continue to engage in deeds and accumulate karma, and will remain in the cycle of rebirth. This belief in self, in short, is not merely a philosophical problem, but is the cause of the egotism and selfishness that harm others now and oneself in the future through the negative karma they create.

The third truth is the truth of cessation, the postulation of a state beyond suffering. If suffering is caused by negative karma, and karma is caused by desire and hatred, and desire and hatred are caused by ignorance, it follows that if one could destroy ignorance then everything caused by ignorance, directly or indirectly, would also be destroyed. There would be a cessation of suffering. This state of cessation is called *nirvāṇa* ("passing away") and, again, a remarkable range of opinion has been expressed concerning the precise nature of this state beyond suffering—whether it is the cessation also of mind and body or whether the person persists in nirvāṇa.

The postulation of a state beyond suffering would be of little interest if there were not some means to achieve it. The fourth truth, then, is the path, the technique for putting an end to ignorance. One useful way to approach the topic is through the traditional triad of ethics, meditation, and wisdom. Ethics refers to the conscious restraint of nonvirtuous deeds of body and speech, usually through observing some form of vows. Meditation (*dhyāna*), in this context, refers to developing a sufficient level of concentration (through a wide variety of techniques) to make the mind a suitable tool for breaking through the illusion of self to the vision of nirvāṇa. Wisdom is insight, at a deep level of concentration, into the fact that there is no self. Such wisdom is said not only to prevent the accumulation of future karma but eventually to destroy all past karma so that upon death one is not reborn but passes into nirvāṇa. A person who has achieved that state is called an *arhat* ("worthy one"). Two paths to becoming an arhat were set forth. The first was that of the *śrāvaka* ("listener"), who hears the Buddha's teachings and then puts them into practice. The second was the *pratyekabuddha* ("privately awakened one") who becomes an arhat in solitude.

It is important to reiterate that although many Buddhists throughout history have known the teaching of the four truths in more or less detail, not very many have actively set out to destroy the ignorance of self and achieve nirvāṇa through the practice of meditation. Lay people tended to see this as the business of monks, and most monks tended to see it as the business of the relatively few among them who seriously practiced meditation. Even for such monks, the practice of meditation should be understood as a ritual act in a ritual setting, replete with devotions to the three jewels.

If the Buddha taught the four truths, he also must have taught many other things over the course of the four decades that followed his enlightenment. He is renowned for his ability to teach what was appropriate for a particular person, for adapting his message to the situation. Indeed, in the more spectacular descriptions of his pedagogical powers it was said that the Buddha could sit before an audience and simply utter the letter *a* and each person in the audience would hear a discourse designed specifically to meet his or her needs and capacities, in his or her native language. What he taught was represented as a truth that he had not invented but discovered, a truth that had been discovered by other buddhas in the past and would be discovered by buddhas in the future. Importantly, this truth, whatever it may be, was portrayed as something that could be taught, that could be passed on from one person to another, in a variety of languages. It is in this sense that we may speak of a Buddhist tradition. At the same time, the emphasis on the flexibility of the Buddha's teaching helps to account for the remarkable range of practices described as "Buddhist."

According to traditional accounts, at the age of eighty the Buddha died, or passed into nirvāṇa. He is said to have instructed his followers to cremate his body and distribute the relics that remained among various groups of his followers, who were to enshrine them in hemispherical reliquaries called stūpas. For all Buddhist schools, the stūpa became a reference point denoting the Buddha's presence in the landscape. Early texts and the archeological records link stūpa worship with the Buddha's life and especially the key sites in his career, such as the site of his birth, enlightenment, first teaching, and death. A standard list of eight shrines is recommended for pilgrimage and veneration. However, stūpas are also found at places that were sacred for other reasons, often associated with a local deity. Stūpas were constructed for past buddhas and for prominent disciples of the Buddha. Indeed, stūpas dedicated to disciples of the Buddha may have been especially popular because the monastic rules stipulate that donations to such stūpas became the property of the monastery, whereas donations to stūpas of the Buddha remained the property of the Buddha, who continued to function as a legal resident of most monasteries in what was called "the perfumed chamber."

The Mahāyāna stūpa later became a symbol of buddhahood's omnipresence, a center of text revelation, a place guaranteeing rebirth in a pure land. By the seventh century, the practice of enshrining the physical relics of the Buddha ceases to appear in the archaeological record. Instead, one finds stūpas filled with small clay tablets that have been stamped or engraved with a four-line verse that was regarded as the essence of the Buddha's teaching: "The Tathāgata has explained the cause of all things that arise from a cause. The great renunciate has also explained their cessation." Although this pithy statement is subject to wide interpretation, we can see here an intimation of the four truths: the Buddha has identified that suffering arises from the cause of ignorance and he has also identified nirvāṇa, the cessation of suffering. It is said that the wisest of the disciples, Śāriputra, decided to become the Buddha's follower upon simply hearing these words spoken by a monk, in the absence of the Buddha. But of perhaps greater importance in this context is the fact that this statement functions as a slogan, a mantra, and as a substitute for the relics of the Buddha to be enshrined in a stūpa. The teaching has become the teacher.

Stūpas were pivotal in the social history of Buddhism: these monuments became magnets attracting monastery building and votive construction, as well as local ritual traditions and regional pilgrimage. The economics of Buddhist devotionalism at these centers generated income for local monasteries, artisans, and merchants, an alliance basic to Buddhism throughout its history. At these geographical centers arrayed around the monument, diverse devotional exertions, textual studies, and devotees' mercantile pursuits could all prosper. The great stūpa complexes—monasteries with endowed lands, a pilgrimage center, a market, and support from the state—represent central points in the Buddhist polities of Central, South, and Southeast Asia.

The Buddha was also worshiped in paintings and statues. The production and worship of Buddhist icons—whether images of buddhas such as Śākyamuni and Amitābha, or bodhisattvas such as Avalokiteśvara and Maitreya—has been a central feature of Buddhist religious life throughout Asian history. The worship of Buddhist icons was promoted by sūtras, and sponsoring the production of an icon was considered an act of great merit, as was bathing an image, a practice that continues in Southeast Asia, China, and Japan. A common goal of both devotional and ascetic Buddhist practice was to recollect the good qualities of the Buddha, which sometimes led to seeing the Buddha "face to face." Images of the Buddha seem to have been important aids in such practices, in part because, far from being a "symbol" of the departed master, images of the Buddha were ritually animated in consecration ceremonies intended to transform an inanimate image into a living deity. Icons thus empowered were treated as spiritual beings possessed of magical powers, to be worshiped with regular offerings of incense, flowers, food, money, and other assorted valuables. Buddhist literature from all over Asia is replete with tales of miraculous occurrences associated with such images.

The Buddha was thus the object of elaborate ritual devotions, often accompanied by recitations of his myriad virtues and powers. These devotions were later incorporated into a larger liturgy that included the visualization of vast offerings and the confession of misdeeds. But not all buddhas were so extraordinary. Indeed, the Japanese Zen master Dōgen went to some lengths to explain why the extraordinary telepathic powers that were supposedly a standard byproduct of enlightenment were not necessarily possessed by enlightened Zen masters in China. The true Zen master is utterly beyond all such categories of Buddhist doctrine.

The question arose early as to the object of devotion in the universal practice of taking refuge in the three jewels: the Buddha, the dharma, and the saṅgha. In some formulations, the Buddha was regarded as having a physical body that was the result of past karma; it consisted of his contaminated aggregates (*skandha*), the final residue of the ignorance that had bound him in saṃsāra until his last lifetime. Because that body was the product of ignorance and subject to disintegration, it was not considered suitable as an object of veneration, as the Buddha-jewel. The Buddha was at the same time said to possess certain qualities (also called *dharma*) that are uncontaminated by ignorance, such as his pure ethics, his deep concentration, his wisdom, his knowledge that he has destroyed all afflictions, and his knowledge that the afflictions will not recur. The qualities were later categorized as the eighteen unshared qualities of a buddha's uncontaminated wisdom. This "body of [uncontaminated] qualities" was deemed the true object of the practice of refuge. Thus, the term "body" came to shift its meaning from the physical form of the Buddha, corporeal extension in space and over time, to a collection of timeless abstract virtues. In addition, the early community had to account for those fantastic elements in the Buddha's hagiography such as his visit to his mother, who had died shortly after his birth and been reborn in the Heaven of the Thirty-Three. The Buddha is said to have made use of a "mind-made body" for his celestial journey. These notions were later systematized into a three-body theory encompassing the physical body (*rūpakāya*), the body of uncontaminated qualities (*dharmakāya*), and the mind-made or emanation body (*nirmāṇakāya*).

In Mahāyāna literature also there is a doctrine of the three bodies of the Buddha. There we find references to the dharmakāya as almost a cosmic principle, an ultimate reality in which all buddhas partake through their omniscient minds. After the dharmakāya comes the enjoyment body (*saṃbhogakāya*), a fantastic form of a buddha that resides only in the highest pure lands, adorned with thirty-two major and eighty minor physical marks, eternally teaching the Mahāyāna to highly advanced bodhisattvas; the enjoyment body does not appear to ordinary beings. The third body is the emanation body (*nirmāṇakāya*). It is this body that appears in the world to teach the dharma. Thus we can discern an important change in the development of the conception of the Buddha in India: whereas in the earlier tradition, the nirmāṇakāya had been that specialized body employed by the Buddha for the performance of occasional supernormal excursions, in the Mahāyāna there is no buddha that ever appears in the world other than the nirmāṇakāya. All of the deeds of the Buddha are permutations of the emanation body—they are all magical creations, the reflexive functions of the dharmakāya. These functions are by no means random. Indeed, the biography of the Buddha is transformed from the linear narration of a unique event into a paradigm, reduplicated precisely by all the buddhas of the past, present, and future in twelve deeds: descent from the Joyous Pure Land, entry into his mother's womb, being born, becoming skilled in arts and sports as a youth, keeping a harem, taking four trips outside the city that cause him to renounce the world, practicing austerities for six years, sitting under the bodhi tree, defeating Māra and his hosts, attaining enlightenment, turning the wheel of doctrine, and passing into nirvāṇa.

The effects of this final deed have long been felt by Buddhist communities. Their sense of loss was not limited to the direct disciples of the Buddha but has been expressed by generations of future followers, often in the form of the lament that one's negative karma caused one to be reborn someplace other than northern India during the lifetime of the Buddha, that one's misdeeds prevented one from joining the audience of the Buddha's teaching. A standard part of Buddhist rituals became the request that other buddhas not pass into nirvāṇa but remain in the world for an eon, which they could do if they wished.

The absence of the Buddha has remained a powerful motif in Buddhist history, and remedies have taken a wide variety of forms. In Burma, secret societies, with possible antecedents in tantric traditions, concentrate their energies on kinds of supernormal power that the mainstream tradition regards with some suspicion. Specifically, they engage in longevity practices to allow them to live until the coming of the next buddha, Maitreya. In China and Japan, rituals constructed around the chanting of the name of the buddha Amitābha offer a means of being delivered at death into the presence of a buddha who is not present here but is present now, elsewhere, in the western paradise of Sukhāvatī.

With the absence of the historical Buddha, a variety of substitutes were conceived to take his place. One such substitute was the icon, as we already noted. Another was the written text of his teaching, the sūtra, described below. In the absence of the Buddha, the transcendent principle of his enlightenment, sometimes called the buddha nature, became the subject of a wide range of doctrinal speculation, devotion, and practice. This impersonal principle, which made possible the transformation of Prince Siddhārtha from an ignorant and suffering human being into an omniscient and blissful buddha, was most commonly referred to as the *tathāgatagarbha. Tathāgata,* "One Who Has Thus Come [or Gone]" is one of the standard epithets of the Buddha. *Garbha* has a wide range of meanings, including "essence" and "womb," which were exploited in works like the *Tathāgatagarbha Sūtra,* a popular and influential Mahāyāna work which declared that this seed or potential for buddhahood resides equally in all beings, and it needs only to be developed. A related work states that everything in the universe contains in itself the entire universe, and that, therefore, the wisdom of a buddha is fully present in each and every being. Such an impersonal principle was not only an important point of doctrine but could also be the object of devotion and praise, prompting the Japanese monk Myōe to address an island as the Buddha. In so doing, Myōe, who had desired to go to India, was able to find the Buddha in Japan.

There is a vacillation in the metaphors and similes employed in these texts as if between two models of the means of making manifest the buddha nature, of achieving enlightenment. One model regards the buddha nature as something pure that has been polluted. The process of the path, therefore, is a gradual process of purification, removing defilements through a variety of practices until the utter transformation from afflicted sentient being to perfect buddha has been effected. Other tropes in these texts, however, do not suggest a developmental model but employ instead a rhetoric of discovery: buddhahood is always already fully present in each being. It need only be recognized. It was this latter model that exercised particular influence in the Chan and Zen schools of China and Japan, which were at least rhetorically dismissive of standard doctrinal categories and traditional practices. And in Tibet, the most ancient Buddhist school spoke of a first buddha, a primordial buddha who is the fundamental embodiment of enlightenment.

One of the earliest substitutes for the Buddha was the wisdom by which he became enlightened and, by extension, the texts that contained that wisdom. This wisdom was called the "perfection of wisdom" (*prajñāpāramitā*). In part because it was this wisdom that metaphorically gave birth to the Buddha and, in part, because the word *prajñāpāramitā* is in the feminine gender in Sanskrit, this wisdom was anthropomorphized and worshiped as a goddess, referred to sometimes as Prajñāpāramitā, sometimes as "the Great Mother." But not all of the important female figures in Buddhism have been anthropomorphized principles. The eighth-century queen of Tibet is identified as a female buddha, and the tantric symbolism of her vagina as the source of enlightenment is set forth. The story is told of Gotamī, not the Buddha's metaphorical mother, but his aunt and foster-mother (his own mother died shortly after his birth). She was instrumental in convincing the Buddha to establish the order of nuns, and her life story has served as a female parallel to the life of the Buddha. The account of her passage into nirvāṇa clearly mimics the story of the Buddha's death.

Perhaps the most popular substitute for the absent Buddha, however, was the bodhisattva. The Buddha is said to have been able to remember all of his past lives, and he is said to have employed his prodigious memory to recount events from those lives. The Buddha's remarkable memory provided a scriptural justification for the appropriation of a diverse body of folklore into the canon. The Jātakas ("Birth Stories"), of which there are over five hundred, were transformed from an Indian version of Aesop's Fables into the word of the Buddha by a conclusion appended to each story, in which the Buddha represents the tale as the recollection of one of his former lives and inevitably identifies himself as the protagonist ("in that existence the otter was Ānanda, the jackal was Maudgalyāyana, the monkey was Śāriputra, and I was the wise hare"). In these tales, the Buddha is referred to as the *bodhisattva,* a term widely etymologized in later literature, but which generally means a person who is intent on the attainment of bodhi, enlightenment. If very few Buddhists felt that they could emulate the Buddha in his last life by leaving their families, living the life of an ascetic, and practicing meditation, the stories of the Buddha's previous lives provided a more accessible model. Stories of the Bodhisattva's deeds of generosity, morality, patience, and perseverance against great odds have remained among the most popular forms of Buddhist literature, both written and oral, and both in the Jātaka tales and in another genre called Avadāna.

In the early Mahāyāna sūtras, the bodhisattva's deeds were represented not merely as an inspiration but as a model to be scrupulously emulated. Earlier in the tradition, the goal had been to follow the path set forth by the Buddha and become liberated from rebirth as an arhat. But in the Mahāyāna, the goal became to do not what the Buddha said but what he did: to follow a much, much longer path to become a buddha oneself. It seems that, at least in the time of the Buddha, it had been possible to become an arhat in one lifetime. Later Mahāyāna exegetes would calculate that, from the time that one made buddhahood one's goal until buddhahood was achieved, a minimum of 384×10^{58} years was required. This amount of time was needed to accumulate the vast stores of merit and wisdom that would result in the omniscience of a buddha, who was able to teach the path to liberation more effectively than any other because of his telepathic knowledge of the capacities and interests of his disciples. It was not the case, then, that bodhisattvas were postponing their enlightenment as buddhas; instead, they would forego the lesser enlightenment of the arhat, which offered freedom from suffering for oneself alone, in favor of the greater enlightenment of a buddha, whereby others could also be liberated.

Formal ceremonies were designed for taking the vow to become a bodhisattva and then follow the long bodhisattva path to buddhahood in order to liberate others from saṃsāra. This included the promise to follow a specific code of conduct. At those ceremonies, the officiant, speaking as the Buddha, would declare that a particular disciple, at a point several eons in the future, would complete the long bodhisattva path and become a buddha of such and such a name, presiding over such and such a pure land. So, with the rise of the Mahāyāna we see the goal of enlightenment recede to a point beyond the horizon, but with the millions of intervening lives, beginning with this one, consecrated by the Buddha's prophecy that these present lives are a future buddha's former lives, part of a buddha's story and thus sacred history.

But the bodhisattva was not simply an object of emulation; the bodhisattva was also an object of devotion, for if the bodhisattva had vowed to liberate all beings in the universe from suffering, all beings were the object of the bodhisattva's compassionate deeds. The bodhisattvas mentioned in the Mahāyāna sūtras were worshiped for the varieties of mundane and supramundane succor they could bestow—bodhisattvas such as Maṇjuśrī, the bodhisattva of wisdom; Kṣitigarbha, who as Jizō in Japan rescues children, both born and unborn; Maitreya, the bodhisattva who will become the next buddha; and most of all, Avalokiteśvara, the most widely worshiped bodhisattva, who takes a female form as Guanyin in China and Kannon in Japan, and who in Tibet takes human form in the succession of Dalai Lamas.

Yet another substitute for the absent Buddha is to be found in the Vajrayāna, in which rituals (called *sādhana,* literally, "means of achievement") are set forth in which the practitioner, through a practice of visualization, petitions a buddha or bodhisattva to come into the practitioner's presence. Much of the practice described in tantric sādhanas involves the enactment of a world—the fantastic jewel-encrusted world of the Mahāyāna sūtras or the horrific world of the charnel ground. In the sūtras, these worlds appear before the audience of the sūtra at the command of the Buddha, as in the *Lotus Sūtra,* or are described by him, as in the Pure Land sūtras. In the tantric sādhana, the practitioner manifests that world through visualization, through a process of invitation, descent, and identification, evoking the world that the sūtras declare to be immanent, yet only describe. The tantric sādhana is, in this sense, the making of the world of the Mahāyāna sūtras here and now. Tantric sādhanas usually take one of two forms. In the first, the buddha or bodhisattva is requested to appear before the meditator and is then worshiped in the hope of receiving blessings. In the other type of tantric sādhana, the mediator imagines himself or herself to be a fully enlightened buddha or bodhisattva now, to have the exalted body, speech, and mind of an enlightened being. Those who become particularly skillful at this practice, it is said, gain the ability to appear in this form to others.

Dharma

Before the Buddha passed away, it is said that he was asked who would succeed him as leader of the community. He answered that his teaching should be the teacher. That teaching is most commonly referred to with the name *dharma,* a word derived from the root *dhṛ,* "to hold," a term with a wide range of meanings. Indeed, ten meanings of *dharma,* including "path," "virtue," "quality," "vow," and "nirvāṇa" were enumerated by a fifth-century scholar. Nineteenth-century translators often rendered *dharma* as "the law." But two meanings predominate. The first is the teaching of the Buddha, creatively etymologized from *dhṛ* to mean "that which holds one back from falling into suffering." The second meaning of dharma, appearing particularly in philosophical contexts, is often rendered in English as "phenomenon" or "thing," as in "all dharmas lack self."

The ambiguities encountered in translating the term are emblematic of a wide range of practices that have been regarded as the teaching of the Buddha. And because the Buddha adapted his teachings to the situation and because (at least according to the Mahāyāna), the Buddha did not actually disappear into nirvāṇa but remains forever present, works that represented themselves as his teaching (which begin with the standard formula, "Thus did I hear") have continued to be composed throughout the history of Buddhism. The term "Buddhist apocrypha" has generally been used to describe those texts composed outside of India (in China, for example) which represent themselves as being of Indian origin. Yet strictly speaking all Buddhist texts, even those composed in Indian languages, are apocryphal because none can be identified with complete certainty as a record of the teaching of the historical Buddha. This has, on the one hand, led to a certain tolerance for accepting diverse doctrines and practices as Buddhist. Sometimes new texts were written as ways of summarizing what was most important from an unwieldy and overwhelming canon. In some cases, these new texts represented themselves as the words of the historical Buddha; in other cases, essays were composed in poetry and prose with the purpose of explicating for a newly converted society the most essential teachings from a bewildering scriptural tradition.

The absence of the Buddha did not merely occasion the creation of substitutes for him. Over the course of the history of Buddhism in Asia, it also portended crisis, notably in a variety of texts that responded to the notion of the decline of the dharma. Within a century or two after the Buddha's death, there were predictions of the eventual disappearance of the dharma from the world. Various reasons were given for its demise, ranging from a general deterioration in human virtue to the fact that the Buddha had agreed to admit women into the order. These texts, like most Buddhist sūtras, are set at the time of the Buddha, and the dire circumstances that signal the demise of the dharma are expressed in terms of prophecies by the Buddha of what will happen in the future. We can assume that the authors of the sūtras were in fact describing the events of their own day, usually including the corrupt and greedy behavior of monks, the persecution of Buddhism by the state, or the threat posed by foreign invaders. Some works of this genre not only prophesied decline of the dharma but offered prescriptions so that decline could be averted. One Chinese work criticizes the traditional practice of offering gifts to monks and monasteries, and advocates acts of charity directed instead toward the poor, the orphaned, the aged, the sick, and even animals and insects. An Indian work composed at the time of the first major incursion of Muslim armies into northern India foretells an apocalyptic war in which Buddhist forces will sweep out of the Himalayas to defeat the barbarians and establish a utopian Buddhist kingdom. In another Indian text, there is no such threat. Instead, the text may be addressed to a community whose very security and complacency would allow the eventual disappearance of the dharma.

When works such as these were composed to respond to a particular historical circumstance, it was sometimes necessary to account for the fact that there had been no previous record of such a text. It was explained that a certain text had been found locked inside an iron stūpa, having been placed there long ago to be discovered at the appropriate time. The fact that the version which eventually reached China seemed little more than an outline was the result of an unfortunate circumstance: the larger and more comprehensive version of the work had inadvertently been thrown overboard on the sea journey from India to China. Likewise, the Tibetan ritual text of the Great Bliss Queen is an example of a Tibetan genre of texts known as *gter ma* (treasures). It is believed that the Indian tantric master who visited Tibet in the late eighth century, Padmasambhava, and his followers buried texts all over Tibet, knowing that they would be uncovered at an appropriate time in the future.

As one might imagine, there were those who found such claims fantastic, and the Mahāyāna was challenged by the foundational schools for fabricating new sūtras and distorting the Buddhist teaching. A sixth-century Mahāyāna author, Bhāvaviveka, summarizes the Hīnayāna argument that the Mahāyāna is not the word of the Buddha: the Mahāyāna sūtras were not included in either the original or subsequent compilations of the word of the Buddha; by teaching that the Buddha is permanent, the Mahāyāna contradicts the dictum that all conditioned phenomena are impermanent; because the Mahāyāna teaches that the buddha nature is all-pervasive, it does not relinquish the belief in self; because the Mahāyāna teaches that the Buddha did not pass into nirvāṇa, it suggests that nirvāṇa is not the final state of peace; the Mahāyāna contains prophecies that the great early disciples will become buddhas; the Mahāyāna belittles the arhats; the Mahāyāna praises bodhisattvas above the Buddha; the Mahāyāna perverts the entire teaching by claiming that the historical Buddha was an emanation; the statement in the Mahāyāna sūtras that the Buddha was constantly in meditative absorption is unfeasible; by teaching that great sins can be completely absolved, the Mahāyāna teaches that actions have no effects, contradicting the law of karma. Therefore, the opponents of the Mahāyāna claim, the Buddha did not set forth the Mahāyāna; it was created by beings who were demonic in order to deceive the obtuse and those with evil minds.

Centuries earlier we find implied responses to these criticisms in the Mahāyāna sūtras themselves, side by side with the assertions that the Hīnayāna found so heretical. The most influential defense of new sūtras as authoritative teachings of the Buddha is found in the *Lotus Sūtra,* with its doctrine of skillful means (*upāya*). In that work the validity of the Mahāyāna and the Mahāyāna vision of buddhahood is defended by the use of parables. Because the *Lotus* is the most influential of Buddhist texts in all of East Asia, it is worthwhile to consider some of these.

The *Lotus Sūtra* must somehow account for the fact that the Mahāyāna has appeared late, after the Buddha had taught a path to nirvāṇa that had already been successfully followed to its terminus by his original disciples, the great arhats such as Śāriputra, Maudgalyāyana, and Kāśyapa. If the Mahāyāna is the superior teaching why had it not been evident earlier? Several of the parables place the fault with the disciples themselves. Thus, in the parable of the hidden jewel, a man falls asleep drunk in the house of a friend who, unbeknownst to him, sews a jewel into the hem of his garment. The man awakes and goes on his way, only to suffer great poverty and hardship. He encounters his friend, who reveals the jewel, showing him that he had been endowed with great wealth all the while. In the same way, the disciples of the Buddha have constant access to the path to supreme enlightenment but are unaware of it; they are bodhisattvas unaware of their true identity. Again, the Buddha compares his teaching to the rainfall that descends without discrimination on the earth. That this rain causes some seeds to grow into flowers and some into great trees implies no differentiation in the rain but rather is due to the capacities of the seeds that it nurtures. Thus, the teaching of the Buddha is of a single flavor but benefits beings in a variety of ways according to their capacity. The Buddha knows the abilities and dispositions of his disciples and causes them to hear his dharma in a way most suitable to them.

Other parables employ a more radical strategy of authorization, suggesting that the Hīnayāna nirvāṇa is but a fiction. The oft-cited parable of the burning house tells of a father distraught as his children blithely play, unaware that the house is ablaze. Knowing of their respective predilections for playthings, he lures them from the inferno with the promise that he has a cart for each waiting outside, a deer-drawn cart for one, a goat-drawn cart for another, and so on. When they emerge from the conflagration, they find only one cart, a magnificent conveyance drawn by a great white ox, something that they had never even dreamed of. The burning house is saṃsāra, the children are ignorant sentient beings, unaware of the dangers of their abode, the father is the Buddha, who lures them out of saṃsāra with the teaching of a variety of vehicles—the vehicle of the śrāvaka, the vehicle of the pratyekabuddha, the vehicle of the bodhisattva—knowing that in fact there is but one vehicle, the buddha vehicle whereby all beings will be conveyed to unsurpassed enlightenment. And the Buddha tells the parable of the conjured city, in which a skillful guide leads a group of travelers on a long journey in search of a cache of jewels. Along the way, the travelers become exhausted and discouraged and decide to turn back. The guide magically conjures a great city in the near distance, where the travelers can rest before continuing toward their ultimate goal. The travelers enter the city where they regain their strength, at which point the guide dissolves the city and announces that the jewel cache is near. The travelers are those sentient beings who are weak and cowardly, intimidated by the thought of traversing the long Mahāyāna path to buddhahood. For their benefit, the Buddha creates the Hīnayāna nirvāṇa, more easily attained, which they mistakenly believe to be their final goal. He then announces to them that they have not reached their ultimate destination and exhorts them on to buddhahood, revealing that the nirvāṇa they had attained was but an illusion.

Thus, the claim to legitimacy of the earlier tradition is usurped by the Mahāyāna through the explanation that what the Buddha had taught before was in fact a lie, that there is no such thing as the path of the arhat, no such thing as nirvāṇa. There is only the Mahāyāna (also called the *ekayāna,* the "one vehicle"), which the Buddha intentionally misrepresents out of his compassionate understanding that there are many among his disciples who are incapable of assimilating so far-reaching a vision. But what of those disciples of the Buddha who are reported in the early sūtras to have become arhats, to have passed into nirvāṇa—what of their attainment? In an ingenious device (found also in other Mahāyāna sūtras) the great heroes of the Hīnayāna are drafted into the Mahāyāna by the Buddha's prophecies that even they will surpass the trifling goal of nirvāṇa and go on to follow the Mahāyāna path to eventual buddhahood. The first such prophecy is for the monk Śāriputra, renowned in the works of the foundational tradition as the wisest of the Buddha's disciples, who is transformed into a stock character in the Mahāyāna sūtras as one who is oblivious of the higher teaching. When his ignorance is revealed to him, he desires to learn more, coming to denounce as parochial the wisdom that he had once deemed supreme. The champion of the Hīnayāna is shown to reject it and embrace that which many adherents of the foundational tradition judged to be spurious. Thus the early history of the movement, already highly mythologized into a sacred history, was fictionalized further in the Mahāyāna sūtras, and another sacred history was eventually created. To legitimate these newly appearing texts, their authors claimed the principal figures of the earlier tradition, indeed its very codifiers, as converts to the Buddha's true teaching and central characters in its drama. The early story of Gautama Buddha and his disciples, preserved in the Pāli canon and already accepted as an historical account by the "pre-Mahāyāna" traditions, is radically rewritten in the *Lotus* in such a way as to glorify the *Lotus* itself as the record of what really happened. Such rewriting recurs throughout the history of the Buddhist traditions in the perpetual attempt to recount "what the Buddha taught."

And who is this Buddha that the *Lotus Sūtra* represents? In the fifteenth chapter, billions of bodhisattvas well up out of the earth and make offerings to the Buddha. The Buddha declares that all of these bodhisattvas who have been practicing the path for innumerable eons are in fact his own disciples, that he had set each of them on the long path to buddhahood. The bodhisattva Maitreya, who has witnessed this fantastic scene, asks the obvious question. He reckons that it had only been some forty years since the Buddha had achieved enlightenment under the tree at Bodhgayā. He finds it incredible that in that short period of time the Buddha could have trained so many bodhisattvas who had progressed so far on the path. "It is as if there were a man, his natural color fair and his hair black, twenty-five years of age, who pointed to men a hundred years of age and said, 'These are my sons!'" Maitreya, representing the self-doubt of the early Mahāyāna and reflecting the Hīnayāna critique, is deeply troubled by this inconsistency, fearing that people who hear of this after the Buddha's passing will doubt the truth of the Buddha's words and attack his teaching.

It is at this point that the Buddha reveals another lie. He explains that even though he is widely believed to have left the palace of his father in search of freedom from suffering and to have found that freedom six years later under a tree near Gayā, in fact, that is not the case. He achieved enlightenment innumerable billions of eons ago and has been preaching the dharma in this world and simultaneously in myriad other worlds ever since. Yet he recognizes the meager intelligence of many beings, and out of his wish to benefit them resorts to the use of skillful methods (*upāya*), recounting how he renounced his princely life and attained unsurpassed enlightenment. And, further recognizing that his continued presence in the world might cause those of little virtue to become complacent and not ardently seek to put his teaching into practice, he declares that he is soon to pass into nirvāṇa. But this also is a lie, because his lifespan will not be exhausted for many innumerable billions of eons.

Thus, the prince's deep anxiety at being confronted with the facts of sickness, aging, and death, his difficult decision to abandon his wife and child and go forth into the forest in search of a state beyond sorrow, his ardent practice of meditation and asceticism for six years, his triumphant attainment of the liberation and his imminent passage into the extinction of nirvāṇa—all are a pretense. He was enlightened all the time, yet feigned these deeds to inspire the world.

But we should not conclude that once the *Lotus* and other Mahāyāna sūtras declared the superiority of the bodhisattva path, the supremacy and authority of the Mahāyāna was finally and unequivocally established. Defenses of the Mahāyāna as the word of the Buddha remained the preoccupation of Mahāyāna scholastics throughout the history of Buddhism in India. Nor should we assume that teachings were ranked only as Hīnayāna and Mahāyāna. Even sects that exalted the *Lotus Sūtra* above all others, for example, could disagree about whether there was more than one true practice, one true sūtra, one true buddha. In Japan, a dispute over the meaning of "original enlightenment" in what is called the Matsumoto Debate led to a bloody conflict in 1536 that involved thousands of troops on each side. In China, the promotion and control of sacred scripture was the prerogative of the highest imperial offices. A sect that came into conflict with this authority, the "Teaching of the Three Stages," had its texts declared heretical and banned from the official collection of Buddhist texts.

Thus, the significance of Buddhist texts does not lie simply in their doctrinal or philosophical content but in the uses to which they have been put. We find, for example, that the Abhidharma (literally, "higher dharma," sometimes rendered as "phenomenology"), a class of Buddhist scriptures concerned with minute analyses of mental states, is chanted at Thai funerals. Contained in virtually every Mahāyāna sūtra was a proclamation of the marvelous benefits that would accrue to those who piously handled, recited, worshiped, copied, or circulated the text itself—again, the teaching had become the teacher. Ritual enshrinement and devotion to the sūtra as a vital embodiment of the dharma and, in a certain sense, as a substitute for the Buddha himself was instrumental to the rise of the disparate collections of cults of the book that came to be known as the Mahāyāna. In China, no text was more venerated than the *Lotus,* and tales were told of the miracles that attended its worship.

The importance of texts in Buddhism derives in part from the fact that the tradition represents the Buddha as being eventually persuaded to teach others after his enlightenment. This suggests that the dharma is something that can be passed on, something that is transmittable, transferable. The Buddha is said to have spoken not in Sanskrit, the formal language of the priests of his day, but in the vernacular, and he is said to have forbidden monks from composing his teachings in formal verses for chanting. The implication was that the content was more important than the form. This led to the notion that the dharma could be translated from one language to another, and the act of translation (and the sponsorship of translation) has been regarded throughout Asia as one of the most pious and meritorious acts that could be performed. It was therefore common for Buddhist kings and emperors to sponsor the translation of texts from one language into another: from Sanskrit into Chinese, from Sanskrit into Tibetan, from Tibetan into Manchu, from Pāli into Burmese, and so on. Adding to this notion of translatability was the fact that the primary objects of Buddhist devotion—texts, relics, icons—were all portable; stories of the transportation and enshrinement of a particularly potent image of the Buddha figure in the histories of almost all Buddhist cultures. We should not conclude, however, as Buddhists sometimes do, that the dharma is something self-identical and transcendent, that showers over the cultures of Asia, transforming and pacifying them. In a Japanese text, for example, Buddhism is portrayed as a Korean possession that can be offered in tribute to the Japanese court as a means of protecting the state. It is this universalism of the Buddhist dharma with its plastic pantheon into which any local deity could easily be enlisted, its doctrine of the Buddha's skillful methods for accommodating conflicting views, and its claims about the pervasive nature of reality that have made it a sometimes useful ideology for rulership and empire.

Buddhism has indeed transformed Asia, but it has been transformed in the process. We may consider even whether there ever was some entity called "Buddhism" to be transformed in the first place. What cannot be disputed is that if Buddhism exists, it is impossible to understand it outside the lives of Buddhists, outside the saṅgha.

Saṅgha

The last of the three jewels is the saṅgha, "the community." Technically taken to mean the assembly of enlightened disciples of the Buddha, the term more commonly connotes the community of Buddhist monks and nuns. In the rules governing the ordination ceremony, the saṅgha is said to be present when four fully ordained monks are in attendance. However, in its broadest sense the saṅgha is the whole body of Buddhist faithful. The selections in this section fall under two broad categories. The first deals with monastic life or, more specifically, life organized by vows. The second deals with the lives of Buddhists.

As mentioned earlier, Buddhist practice was traditionally subsumed under three headings: ethics (*śīla*), meditation (*dhyāna*), and wisdom (*prajñā*). Ethics, which in this context refers to refraining from nonvirtue through the conscious control of body and speech, was regarded as the essential prerequisite for progress in meditation and wisdom. It was the element of the triad most widely practiced both by lay people and monks and nuns, and this practice generally took the form of the observance of vows. Since in Buddhist ethical theory karma, both good and bad, depended not on the deed but on the intention, if one could make a promise not to kill humans, for example, and maintain that promise, the good karma accumulated by such restraint would be far greater than had one simply not had the occasion to commit murder. From the early days of the tradition, therefore, elaborate systems of rules for living one's life, called *vinaya,* were established, along with ceremonies for their conferral and maintenance. Lay people could take vows not to kill humans, not to steal, not to commit sexual misconduct, not to lie about spiritual attainments (for example, not to claim to be telepathic when one actually was not), and not to use intoxicants. Novice monks and nuns took these five vows, plus vows not to eat after the noon meal (a rule widely transgressed in some Buddhist cultures through recourse to the evening "medicinal meal"), not to handle gold or silver, not to adorn their bodies, not to sleep in high beds, and not to attend musical performances. Fully ordained monks (*bhikṣu*) and nuns (*bhikṣunī*) took many more vows, which covered the entire range of personal and public decorum, and regulated physical movements, social intercourse, and property. Monks and nuns convened twice monthly to confess their transgressions of the rules in a ceremony and reaffirm their commitment to the code, with transgressions carrying punishments of various weights. The gravest misdeeds entailed expulsion from the order, whereas others could be expiated simply by confessing them aloud. In Buddhist traditions across Asia, ritual maintenance of these monastic codes has served as the mark of orthodoxy, much more than adherence to a particular belief or doctrine. Indeed, it is said that the teaching of the Buddha will endure only as long as the vinaya endures.

The Buddha and his followers were probably originally a group of wandering ascetics. However, they adopted the practice of other ascetic groups in India of remaining in one place during the rainy season. Wealthy patrons had shelters built for their use, and these shelters evolved into monasteries that were inhabited throughout the year. It seems that early in the tradition, the saṅgha became largely sedentary, although the tradition of the wandering monk continued. Still, the saṅgha was by no means a homogeneous community. The vinaya texts describe monks from a wide variety of social backgrounds. Mention is made of monks from all four of India's social castes. There were also a wide variety of monastic specialties. The vinaya texts describe monks who are skilled in speech, those who memorize and recite the sūtras, those who memorize and recite the vinaya, and those who memorize and recite lists of technical terms. There are monks who live in the forest, who wear robes of felt, who wear robes made from discarded rags, who live only on the alms they have begged for, who live at the foot of a tree, who live in a cemetery, who live in the open air, who sleep sitting up, and so on. There were also monks who specialized in meditation, monks who served as advisors to kings, and monks responsible for the administration of the monastery and its property. One of the tasks of this administrator was to insure that the wandering monks were not given mundane work, that meditating monks not be disturbed by noise, and that monks who begged for alms received good food. Whether they wandered without a fixed abode or lived in monasteries, monks and nuns that lived in a designated region, called a *sīmā,* were to gather twice a month to confess and affirm their vows communally, a ceremony that laypeople also attended.

Throughout the Buddhist world, monks and laypeople have lived in a symbiotic relationship: the laity provide material support for monks while monks provide a locus for the layperson's accumulation of merit (by supporting monks who maintained their vows). The rules and regulations in the vinaya texts were meant to govern the lives of Buddhist monks and to structure their relations with the laity. Monks in the vinaya literature are caught in a web of social and ritual obligations, are fully and elaborately housed and permanently settled, and are preoccupied not with nirvāṇa, but with bowls and robes, bathrooms and buckets, and proper behavior in public. The saṅgha was also a community where disputes arose and had to be settled. Because it is said that the Buddha only prescribed a rule in response to a specific misdeed, the vinaya texts often provide the story of that first offense and the Buddha's pronouncement of a rule against such behavior in the future.

There were also rules for nuns, although these receive much less attention in the vinaya literature. According to several traditions, the Buddha was approached early in his career by his aunt and step-mother, Mahāpajāpatī, also called Gotamī, at the head of a delegation of women who wished him to institute a Buddhist order of nuns. The Buddha initially declined to institute such an order. But when the Buddha's cousin and personal attendant, Ānanda, asked him whether women were able to attain the fruits of the practice of the dharma, the Buddha unhesitatingly answered in the affirmative and agreed to establish an order for women. However, the same text states that if the Buddha had not agreed to establish an order for nuns, his teaching would not disappear from the world so quickly. The rules for nuns are both more numerous and stricter than those for monks, and placed nuns in a position of clear subordination to monks. For example, seniority in the order of monks and nuns is measured by the length of time one has been ordained, such that someone who has been a monk for five years must pay respect to a monk of six years, even if the first monk is chronologically older. However, the rules for nuns state that a woman who has been a nun for one hundred years must pay respect to a man who was ordained as a monk for one day. The difficulties entailed in maintaining the strict nuns' vows and a lack of institutional support led to the decline and eventual disappearance of the order of nuns in India, Sri Lanka, and Southeast Asia, and to an order of novices alone (rather than fully ordained nuns) in Tibet. The tradition of full ordination for women was maintained only in China.

Throughout the development of the Mahāyāna and the Vajrayāna, the rules for monks and nuns seem to have remained fairly uniform and the adherents of the new vehicles seem to have seen no contradiction between the monastic life and the practices of the Mahāyāna and the Vajrayāna. But if we understand the vinaya not as that which restricts individuals and their actions but as that which creates them, we will not be surprised that additional vows were formulated for the bodhisattva and the tantric practitioner, and that rituals which mimicked the monastic confession ceremony were designed for their administration. The vows of a bodhisattva included not only the vow to liberate all beings in the universe from suffering but also to act compassionately by always accepting an apology, not to praise oneself and belittle others, to give gifts and teachings upon request, and so on. Those who took the bodhisattva vows also promised never to claim that the Mahāyāna sūtras were not the word of the Buddha.

Vajrayāna practice also entailed extensive sets of vows. As mentioned above, it was common for Buddhist monks, especially in late Indian Buddhism and in Tibet, to hold bodhisattva and tantric vows in addition to their monk's vows. In the case of the more advanced tantric initiations, which involved sexual union with a consort, this presented problems, for monks were bound by the rule of celibacy. Whether or not monks were permitted to participate in such initiations became a question of some gravity when Buddhism was being established in Tibet, and a famous Indian monk and tantric master, Atiśa, composed a text that dealt with this issue.

Just as important as the vows of monks and nuns are stories of Buddhists from across Asia. Some of these accounts are ancient, like the life story of a "miraculous and strange" Chinese monk of the sixth century; some are modern, like the autobiographies of Japanese Buddhist women after the Second World War. Some are hagiographies of famous masters, and some tell of miraculous voyages; others recount the deathbed visions of devotees of Amitābha. Some of the biographies are highly stereotyped with often transparent agendas.

Because of the portability of relics, texts, and icons, sacred sites were established across the Buddhist world and pilgrimage to those sites was a popular form of Buddhist practice throughout Asia. Pilgrimage was sometimes to a stūpa associated with the life of the Buddha; Bodhgayā, the site of the Buddha's enlightenment, has drawn pilgrims from the outer reaches of the Buddhist world for centuries. Particularly powerful buddha images also attracted pilgrims; it was not uncommon for pilgrims from as far east as Manchuria and as far west as the Mongol regions of Russia to travel to Lhasa, the capital of Tibet, to visit the statue of the Buddha there. They would travel on foot or on horseback; the most pious would proceed by prostration—bowing and then stretching their bodies on the ground before rising, taking one step forward and prostrating again, along the entire route. In China, mountains believed to be the abodes of munificent bodhisattvas were (and are) popular destinations of communal pilgrimages. Women pilgrims in modern China reported a variety of reasons for making the pilgrimage: to insure a good harvest, to protect the silkworms, to promote the health of family members and domestic animals. But we should not assume that Buddhist travel was always directed from the periphery to the center. A renowned Buddhist scholar left one of the great monastic universities of India on a perilous sea voyage to Sumatra, where the preeminent teacher of the practice of compassion was said to reside. Nor was travel always so concerned with what or who was to be found at the end of the journey; the Japanese monk Ippen saw travel itself as essential to his practice of devotion to Amitābha.

Thus, the category of the three jewels is not without its own ambiguities. The reader is asked again to consider: Who is the Buddha? What is the dharma? And who belongs to the saṅgha?

Note

1. The historical survey that follows is drawn largely from Joseph M. Kitagawa and Mark D. Cummings, ed., *Buddhism and Asian History* (New York: Macmillan, 1989), a collection of the most recent scholarship on Buddhist history. Readers are referred there for more detailed histories and bibliographies of sources.

—10—

Consecrating the Buddha

Donald K. Swearer

Images of gods and other sacred persons figure prominently in various forms of popular religious practice. Although the figure of the Buddha seems not to have been depicted in the earliest Buddhist iconography, by the first century of our era images of the Blessed One occupy a prominent place in Buddhist devotional ritual. Scholarly opinion varies regarding the origin and function of the Buddha image, but it is reasonable to assume that from the beginning Buddha images represented two interconnected aspects of the person and the story of the Buddha: the knowledge of the dharma [Pāli *dhamma*] attained at his nirvāṇa [Pāli *nibbāna*], and the supermundane powers associated with the renunciant practices linked with that extraordinary attainment. Buddha images have continued to convey these meanings in culturally specific forms up to the present day.

In contemporary northern Thailand, an elaborate ceremony is held to consecrate Buddha images prior to their installation in temples or other buildings. During the ceremony various ritual acts infuse into the image the wisdom and power associated with Prince Siddhārtha's [Pāli Siddhattha] victory over Māra and his attainment of enlightenment. Monks chant in Pāli or preach in northern Thai several texts including the *Buddha Abhiṣeka (Consecrating the Buddha [Image])*. The text rehearses the life of the Buddha as the Bodhisattva (Pāli *bodhisatta*), Prince Siddhārtha. The narrative focuses, in particular, on the Buddha's enlightenment, the path leading up to this achievement, and the power of the extraordinary states of consciousness (Pāli *ñāṇa;* Sanskrit *jñāna*) associated with the Buddha's enlightenment. The translation of the term ñāṇa, poses special difficulties. It may denote "knowledge" and is often so translated. In our text, however, the term points to a state of extraordinary or transcendental consciousness, a state of awareness or knowing involving a state of being. Thus, the Buddha attains to various ñāṇas that define or characterize the power of his buddhahood.

The text discusses at some length aspects of the Buddha legend found in later Pāli canonical and commentarial texts, most of which postdate the Aśokan age, such as *Chronicle of the Buddhas (Buddhavaṃsa) Basket of Conduct (Cariyāpiṭaka),*

Birth Stories of the Buddha (*Jātaka*), and the Pāli life of the Buddha (*Nidāna Kathā*). Although legendary lives of the Buddha, such as *Nidāna Kathā, Buddhacarita,* and *Lalitavistara,* may differ in details, students familiar with them will recognize the story of the Buddha recounted in the *Buddha Abhiṣeka*. Major topics of these texts that appear in the *Buddha Abhiṣeka* include the following: the attainment of buddhahood after the achievement of eons of moral perfection, which make the Buddha of popular cult a field of meritorious power; the realization of trance states or meditative absorptions; and the extraordinary spiritual powers realized by the Buddha in these higher states of consciousness. The text also provides a summary of various seminal Theravāda teachings such as causality and interdependent co-arising, the three characteristics of existence (impermanence, not-self, suffering), the four noble truths (suffering, the cause of suffering, the cessation of suffering, and the path to the cessation of suffering), the four paths (stream-enterer, once-returner, never-returner, and arhat [Pāli *arahant*]) and their fruits, the law of moral causality and the consequences of rebirth in various Buddhist hells, and the various forms of sensory attachment leading to those states of punishment.

We should see the *Buddha Abhiṣeka* not simply as a later noncanonical, popular construction of the Buddha, but as a portrayal of the variegated meanings the Theravāda tradition has attributed to its founder. Much about this portrayal conflicts with the modern predilection to make the Buddha into a "rational renouncer" who espoused a universal message of human suffering. From a historical perspective this modern interpretation of Prince Siddhārtha's realization of buddhahood should not exclude other tales, but should take its place among the many stories the Theravāda tradition has told about the Buddha.

As an oral text preached or chanted within a ritual context, the *Buddha Abhiṣeka* serves several different functions. It provides an abbreviated summary of the life of the Buddha derived from Pāli canonical and commentarial texts; it links the life of Prince Siddhārtha with the lineage of previous buddhas recounted in the *Buddhavaṃsa* and *Cariyāpiṭaka,* and the moral perfection attained through previous bodhisattva rebirths, such as Prince Vessantara. Perhaps most importantly, the ritual infuses these elements into the Buddha image, a material object representing the story, wisdom, and power of the person of the Buddha.

This translation is based primarily on a version currently preached during the Buddha image consecration ceremony at monasteries throughout the Chiang Mai valley of northern Thailand. The text is of the vohāra genre, a vernacular (that is, a Tai Yuan or northern Thai) exposition of a text in which the Pāli progenitor appears in the omnipresence of Pāli words and phrases. Not infrequently, these texts appear to be written as a commentary, an explanation/exposition (in the vernacular) of a sūtra (Pāli *sutta*). Our text is a redaction edited by Mahābunkhit Wajarasāt, a major publisher of sermons and other types of texts purchased and then presented to the saṅgha on various auspicious, merit-making occasions. Prior to the twentieth century lay donors would commission a monk or a layperson to inscribe a text on bundles of palm leaves or to calligraph a text on heavy mulberry paper folded in accordion fashion. Today this custom has virtually disappeared. Instead, the lay donor purchases a facsimile printed on heavy brown paper folded in the rectangular shape of a bundle of palm leaves. Because Mahābunkhit and the other major publishers—most of whom were former monks—in the towns of Lampang and Chiang Rai edit or redact these texts from older palm leaf or mulberry paper copies, they function as unofficial transmitters and transformers of the Theravāda textual tradition in northern Thailand.

A second text consulted was a palm-leaf manuscript from the Duang Dī monastery in Chiang Mai. It was copied in 1576 C.E. in the town of Chiang Saen, one of the early Tai Yuan political and cultural centers. The Mahābunkhit edition abbreviated the traditional text represented by the Duang Dī monastery copy, but in other respects is remarkably similar to the content of the sixteenth-century manuscript. Pāli manuscripts of the *Buddha Abhiṣeka* are also found in northern Thai monastery collections and appear in *The Royal Book of Chants* compiled in the nineteenth century during the reign of King Mongkut. In northern Thailand the *Buddha Abhiṣeka* is always preached in the northern Thai vohāra form, but when it is chanted the Pāli version is used.

Consecrating the Buddha

The Buddha, our great teacher, the Enlightened One, out of his great compassion for all beings, practiced the thirty perfections. His resolve to realize the perfections began with his first birth and continued throughout his countless lifetimes. In his birth as Vessantara he practiced the perfection of generosity, relinquishing even his wife and children. After his death as Vessantara, the Enlightened One was reborn in Tuṣita heaven [the fourth level of the heavenly realm]. There the deities of the countless universes met and addressed him saying, "O, thou of great resolve, the appropriate time has come for you to be reborn in the realm of human beings in order to be enlightened as the Buddha." Then, the Bodhisattva departed from Tuṣita heaven and was born into the family of the king of the Śākyas, having been carried in his mother's womb for ten months. Upon his birth he faced the north, took seven steps, and gazed in all directions declaring, "I am supreme in the three worlds."

The Enlightened One lived as a layman [Prince Siddhārtha] for twenty-nine years. One day, while traveling in his pleasure gardens, he chanced upon four sights: an old person, a sick person, a corpse, and an ascetic. He was so moved by this experience that he gave away all his belongings and departed to become a hermit, residing in the forest on the bank of the Anomā River. There he practiced austerities for six years. On the full moon day of Viśākhā he received an offering from the maiden Sujātā, which he consumed while sitting on the bank of the Nerañjarā River. That day the Buddha cast his golden begging bowl in the river where it [miraculously] floated upstream. In the evening the Bodhisattva, taking eight clusters of Kuśa grass given to him by the brahman gods. Spreading the grass under the tree he seated himself and made the following vow, "I shall sit here and not move from this place until I am freed from all defilements and from all forms of evil." Then, facing eastward as the sun set, he conquered the forces of Māra. Afterwards, the Bodhisattva sat in meditation practicing breathing awareness, alternating exhaling and inhaling short and long breaths. While engaged in the mindfulness of breathing, he comprehended both physical and mental suffering, overcame bodily and mental formations, and experienced both physical and mental rapture. His mind was so concentrated that it was freed from the four kinds of feeling: mental and physical suffering, and mental and physical happiness. He perceived the impermanence of all things, the nature of nirvāṇa, and the freedom from all passion and suffering. While Prince Siddhārtha was investigating breathing meditation he experienced supreme bliss. Persevering in this practice, he concentrated his mind so intently that he was freed from all sensual pleasure and material pleasure. Free from all taint of evil, he attained the first stage of meditative absorption, a state composed of thought-conception (*vitakka*) and discursive thinking (*vicāra*), physical and mental nonattachment, and the rapture of bliss. He reached the second level of absorption, eliminating both *vitakka* and *vicāra* and attaining the rapture of supreme bliss. He experienced physical and mental joy as a result of unwavering concentration (*samādhi*), realizing a wisdom characterized by equanimity, by five kinds of rapture and without avarice. The third stage of absorption (*jhāna*) combines equanimity, unwavering mindfulness, and contentment. Prince Siddhārtha, having attained this third jhāna, contemplated the fourth, in which both mundane happiness and suffering and all feelings of joy and grief are eliminated. He was completely suffused with equanimity, freed from suffering and filled with pure mindfulness. The Bodhisattva Siddhārtha attained serenity and purity, totally eliminating the 1,500 major defilements and all the minor defilements. He took delight only in the good and was never tempted by the eight worldly elements.

Regarding the higher spiritual powers, the Lord realized the mental state in which he was able to recall his previous lives. During the first watch of the night he recalled the family of his birth, the color of his complexion, his diet, his experiences of happiness and suffering, the span of his life, his death and rebirth. He recalled the nature of each of his previous lives until his present existence. Then Siddhārtha firmly resolved to become pure and to rid himself of the least trace of defilement. With his mind pacified and pure, he was not overcome by the eight worldly elements [gain, fame, praise, happiness, and their opposites]. In the second watch he entered the absorption in which he gained the knowledge of death and rebirth of all things.

Prince Siddhārtha, seeing all beings with the divine eye, transcended all human and godly capabilities. He then spoke as follows:

"Some people harbor evil thoughts, do evil deeds, and speak evil words.

Because of their evil thoughts they condemn the saints, and they reject the four noble truths. When such human and divine beings die, they are reborn in hell, where they experience suffering in the four fearful realms. But when those of pure action and pure heart who lead a virtuous life and do not condemn the saints die, they will be reborn in heaven."

The Bodhisattva, realizing that those who die and are reborn experience the consequences of their actions, whether good or evil, with the good being rewarded with good and the evil with evil, sat in meditation, uninfluenced by the eight worldly factors. At that time the Bodhisattva came to understand the nature of all compounded things which, because of ignorance continually die and are reborn. Attachment to consciousness comes from attachment to mental formations, which in turn comes from attachment to name and form. Because of the six kinds of contact there arise the six spheres of sense consciousness and the six different kinds of feeling. Grasping for existence comes from attachment, which leads to birth, old age, lamentation and suffering. The cessation of this process is the complete cessation of dharmic formations: the cessation of consciousness leads to the cessation of mental formations; the cessation of mental formations leads to the cessation of name and form; the cessation of name and form leads to the cessation of the six sense spheres; the cessation of the six sense spheres leads to the cessation of the six modes of contact; the cessation of the six modes of contact leads to the cessation of the six kinds of feeling; the cessation of feeling leads to the cessation of grasping, old age, and rebirth.

The Bodhisattva Siddhārtha, attaining the knowledge-state of insight meditation with a wisdom like the radiance of a great diamond, perceived the three characteristics of existence—impermanence, suffering, and not-self—and the nature of the cause and effect of all things. Then the Lord reached the knowledge of the noble (*ariya*) lineage and the knowledge that conforms to reaching the state of stream-enterer. There he overcame the limitations of speculative views, doubt and perplexity, and all of the ten fetters [false view of individuality, doubt and perplexity, adherence to rules and rituals, sensual lust, irritation, attachment to the realm of form, attachment to formless realms, conceit, distraction, ignorance] which constitute the body of ignorance.

In the transcendental state of consciousness of the stream-enterer, its contemplations and its fruits, the Lord perceived the four noble truths: The existence of suffering, the cause of suffering, the cessation of suffering, and the way to the cessation of suffering. In the transcendental state of insight consciousness, he further contemplated the three characteristics of existence. He realized the state of consciousness of the final stage of insight knowledge and the purification associated with wisdom, thereby achieving the condition of the once-returner. Again he contemplated the four noble truths and the nature of suffering, which characterizes the cycle of birth and death. He realized that grasping is the cause of suffering; that the end of rebirth is the end of suffering; and, that there is a path to the end of suffering. In the transcendental state of insight consciousness, the Lord contemplated the three characteristics of existence or all compounded things.

At this point the Lord reached the state of the never-returner in which he overcame all sensual desire, lust, and ill-will. This was the transcendental state of consciousness of the fruit of the never-returner. In the transcendental state of consciousness of the contemplations, the Lord perceived the four noble truths: that rebirth (*saṃsāra*) is suffering (*dukkha*); that grasping (*taṇhā*) is the cause of suffering; that nirvāṇa is the cessation of suffering; and that there is a path to the cessation of suffering. The Lord understood these truths thoroughly. In the transcendental state of insight consciousness he understood the three characteristics of existence and thus attained to the transcendental state . . . of arhatship. Hence, the Lord realized the transcendental state of consciousness of the fully Enlightened One. His course was completed. He had achieved the transcendental state of the fruit of arhatship, the transcendental state of the contemplations, and so on.

The Bodhisattva Siddhārtha perceived the four noble truths through the transcendental states of knowing the path and the contemplations, being purified from the effects of saṃsāra. Together with all the previous buddhas he came to know the truth of suffering.

In his enlightenment the Bodhisattva Siddhārtha achieved the condition of omniscience, becoming the foremost in the world of human beings and gods, of Māra and Brahmā, and in the realm of religious practitioners. He fully realized that this was the end of rebirth (*saṃsāra*). He attained to the state of sublime bliss while seated under the bodhi tree, proclaiming, "Having realized the endlessness of saṃsāra, I have destroyed all grasping (*taṇhā*)."

"O, housebuilder (*gahakāra*) [That is, *taṇhā*, the maker of this body of ignorance]! Before I was enlightened I traveled through many cycles of birth and death, and for an infinite number of lifetimes I experienced suffering. O, housebuilder! Now I have seen you. Hereafter you will not build a house [that is, the five aggregates]. Having broken the crossbeams and destroyed the peak of the roof of that house, I have attained to nirvāṇa, and am freed from all conditions. I have attained to the transcendental state of the destruction of the intoxicants in which all grasping is destroyed."

The Tathāgata reached the supermundane state through perseverance and effort. As one in whom the passions are extinct, the Tathāgata burned up all demerit, and through his wisdom realized the dharma of cause and not-cause. During the first watch of the night all of the Tathāgata's doubts disappeared.

At that time the Buddha was able to recall his previous lives. His heart was pure. Devoid of defilements, he resisted the eight worldly factors [gain and loss, fame and obscurity, blame and praise, happiness and pain]. In the middle watch he was able to see the death and birth of all beings through the divine eye superior to all human beings and gods.

"O, brāhmaṇas, all beings who are subject to evil karma, those who speak and think in evil ways, will be reborn in hell, and will suffer in the four hells after their death. Those, on the other hand, who act and speak in beneficial ways, upon death will be reborn in the realm of bliss."

The Buddha knew the condition of the life and death of all beings: those who are stubborn, those who are superior and inferior, those who are beautiful and ugly, those who are punished in hell and who are rewarded in heaven because of their karma. Then the Buddha, having attained enlightenment, was suffused with calm and established in the good so that he was not influenced by the eight worldly factors. In the middle watch of the night he attained to this state of omniscience.

At that time he understood the nature of conditioned reality and of rebirth caused by ignorance, which in turn is caused by mental formations, which in turn depends upon consciousness, mind-body, the six senses, contact, sensation, thirst, clinging, coming-to-be, birth, old age and death. . . . [The next two paragraphs are omitted because of redundancy.]

In the transcendental state of insight awareness the Blessed One contemplated the three characteristics of existence. The following day he . . . eliminated all of the intoxicants, ignorance, the bonds, and the five hindrances. Then, attaining to the transcendental state of the fruit of arhathood, he perceived the four noble truths by means of the transcendental state of consciousness of the path and the contemplations, namely, that the cycle of birth and death is suffering. This noble truth has been realized by all of the noble ones, and in eliminating grasping they have eliminated suffering. They have also eliminated the cause of suffering, and realized the unconditioned state which is nirvāṇa. That is the cessation of suffering. The "practice leading to the cessation of suffering" is called [in Pāli] the *dukkha-nirodha-gāmini-paṭipadā*. . . . [Next two paragraphs omitted because of redundancy.]

In the last watch of the night the Buddha reflected both forward and backward on the law of interdependent coarising: that ignorance is the cause of the mental formations; that mental formations cause consciousness [and so on]; that birth is the cause of old age, death, grief, and lamentation; and that all physical and mental suffering arises accordingly. The Buddha, thereby coming to know the cause and cessation of all forms of suffering and suffused with supreme bliss exclaimed, "O, housebuilder! Having identified you as the builder of this house, no longer will you be able to construct the five aggregates. All construction materials composing the 1,500 defilements have been totally destroyed. Even the pinnacle of the house is gone. I have reached nirvāṇa which is beyond cause and effect, the cessation of all defilements and the supreme transmundane state. All demerit has been burned up. I have entered the higher meditative absorptions and am devoid of all the intoxicants. The Tathāgata, greater than all beings, has a radiance more brilliant than the sun shining in a cloudless sky."

The Tathāgata, he who is without physical blemish and is devoid of doubt, reached the further shore of enlightenment. He overcame all evil, abided in the bliss of the six kinds of seclusion and realized nirvāṇa was without anger, cared for all living beings, was free from desire, and dwelt in sublime bliss.

The Buddha, filled with boundless compassion, practiced the thirty perfections for many eons (four *asaṅkheyya* and one-hundred thousand kalpas), finally reaching enlightenment. I pay homage to that Buddha. May all his qualities (*guṇa*) be invested in this Buddha image. May the Buddha's boundless omniscience be invested in this image until the religion (*sāsana*) ceases to exist.

May all of the transcendental states of the Blessed One—analytical insight, perseverance, the four perfect confidences, the forty paths—a total of seventy-seven different properties be invested in this image. May the boundless concentration (*samādhi*) and the body-of-liberation of the Buddha be invested in this image for five thousand years during the lifetime of the religion. May the supermundane reality discovered by the Buddha during his enlightenment under the bodhi tree be invested in this image for the five thousand years of the religion. May all of the miracles performed by the Buddha after his enlightenment in order to dispel the doubts of all humans and gods be invested in this image for all time. May the powers (*guṇa*) of the reliquary mounds miraculously created by the Buddha at the places of his enlightenment in order that both humans and gods might worship him be invested in this image for five thousand rains-retreats.

May the Buddha's boundless virtue (*guṇa*) acquired during his activities immediately after his enlightenment be stored in this image forever. May the knowledge contained in the seven books of the *Abhidharma* [Pāli *Abhidhamma*] perceived by the Buddha in the seven weeks after his enlightenment be consecrated in this image for the rest of the lifetime of the religion. May the power acquired by the Buddha during the seven days under the ajapāla tree, the seven days at the Mucalinda pond, and so on, be invested in this Buddha image for five thousand rains-retreats. The Buddha then returned to Ajapālanigrodha, where he preached the eighty-four thousand teachings. May they also be stored in this Buddha image. May the Mahābrahma who requested that the Buddha preach come into this image.

The Buddha then went to Varanasi, where he preached his first discourse. May the transcendental state of knowledge embodied in this text be instilled in this Buddha image. The Buddha observed the rains-retreat in the Deer Park where he ordained Yasa. May the supernatural power of that event be stored in this image. The Buddha preached to the ascetics headed by Uruvela Kassapa and his brothers together with their retinues. May the supernatural power of that conversion be invested in this Buddha image for five thousand rains-retreats. The Buddha then entered Kapilavastu in order to teach his relatives and performed many miracles such as flying through the air and walking on a pure crystal road. May the supernatural power of that occasion be instilled in this Buddha image for the lifetime of the religion.

Mahākassapa Thera approached the Buddha and asked him about the tradition of the buddhas (*buddhacarita*). The Buddha then preached the *Cariyā-*

piṭaka to him. May the transcendental truth of this text become a part of this Buddha image for the remainder of the life of the religion. The Buddha, the conqueror of Māra, descended from the air and sat under a mango tree where he preached to the people of the Śākya clan in order for them to pay their respects to him. May the supernatural power of that event be invested in this Buddha image. The Buddha, referring to the miracle of the Pokkhara rainfall during the time of Prince Vessantara, preached the *Mahāvessantara Jātaka*. May the supernatural power of that text also be instilled in this Buddha image for five thousand rains-retreats.

Then the Buddha entered Sāvasthi and stayed at the Jetavanārāma. He received this land out of his great compassion for the lay disciple, Anāthapiṇḍika. There he preached to both human beings and gods. May the supernatural power of that occasion be invested in this Buddha image. The Buddha preached out of compassion for all living beings. May all of his teachings be instilled in this Buddha image for five thousand rains-retreats.

The Buddha performed numerous marvelous acts and taught continually, ordaining monks for the first time into the noble path. May all the gods, together with Indra, Brahmā, Māra, and all people protect this Buddha image, as well as the relics and the religion for five thousand years for the welfare of all human beings and gods.

—11—

Sūtra on the Merit of Bathing the Buddha

Daniel Boucher

This *Sūtra on the Merit of Bathing the Buddha* is a short text—a little over a page in the standard Chinese Buddhist canon—that was translated into Chinese, presumably from Sanskrit, by the famous monk and pilgrim Yijing (635–713 C.E.). Yijing was born near modern Beijing and entered the monastic order at age fourteen. Because the monastic rules of his order were incomplete in China, he set out for India from Canton by boat in 671 in search of a complete vinaya (monastic code). He arrived at Śrīvijaya (modern Sumatra) where he studied Sanskrit before continuing to Nālandā, the premier Indian monastic university. Having spent ten years studying in India, he returned to China in 689 and spent his remaining years translating the texts he had acquired. The *Sūtra on the Merit of Bathing the Buddha* was translated in 710 at the Dajian fu ("Great Sacrificial Blessings") Temple.

The authenticity of this text is far from certain. There is neither an extant Sanskrit version nor any known Tibetan translation. Furthermore, it is possible that Yijing may have himself constructed this "translation" by drawing from two related texts already known in China. In 705—just five years before Yijing's translation—the Indian monk Manicintana translated the *Sūtra on the Merit of Bathing the Image,* which parallels Yijing's text quite closely, with the addition in the latter of the four-line dharma-relic verse. This dharma-relic verse was found in a similar context—the consecration of miniature stūpas (funerary monuments)—in the *Sūtra on the Merit of Building a Stūpa* rendered into Chinese in 680 by the Indian translator Divākara. It could be argued that Yijing's *Sūtra on the Merit of Bathing the Buddha* reflects a synthesis of themes from two texts already known in China in translation.

It was not uncommon for Chinese Buddhists to produce apocryphal sūtras under the guise of translations from Sanskrit—the criterion for an "authentic" Buddhist text. Such texts could be made to argue for a particular doctrine or sectarian position in China or, as was often the case, they could attempt to legitimate the sponsoring political regime. There does not appear to be any such motive behind Yijing's text. Regardless of the history of the text underlying Yijing's translation, there is considerable evidence that the practices it describes reflect actual Indian Buddhist practice—something that can seldom be said for the vast majority of Indian Buddhist texts. A brief discussion of these practices and their implications will throw light on the developing conceptions of the Buddha in the medieval period.

The *Sūtra on the Merit of Bathing the Buddha* is primarily concerned with the appropriate methods of rendering homage to the Buddha. The sūtra begins with the Pure Wisdom Bodhisattva asking three questions: How does the Buddha acquire his glorified body? What offerings should living beings make when in the presence of the Buddha? And what merit will accrue from this homage? The Buddha responds with two sets of answers: one describing attendance upon the living Buddha, and the other describing how the Buddha is to be worshiped after his death.

In the first case, the Buddha enumerates the perfections and virtues he has cultivated that resulted in the accomplishment of his purified body. By offering incense, flowers, food, drink, and so forth to the Blessed One, and by bathing his body, one can produce unlimited merit that will eventually lead to enlightenment. Note that the text does not espouse the cultivation of particular virtues or contemplative practices for the attainment of enlightenment. Ritual attendance upon the Buddha—fulfilling his corporeal needs—is sufficient.

The majority of the text is, understandably, preoccupied with ways of worshiping the deceased Buddha—a problem all historically founded traditions face. The sūtra picks up here by explaining the nature of the Buddha's body. It is threefold; the Buddha—as all buddhas before and after him—has a dharma body (*dharmakāya*), a glorified body (*saṃbhogakāya*), and a manifestation body (*nirmāṇakāya*). The development and history of these three bodies is a long, complicated, and not entirely understood feature of Mahāyāna Buddhism. Their appearance in this text seems to be aimed at demonstrating the compatibility of the philosophical conception of the Buddha (as an historical manifestation of an eternal body of truth) with the widely held belief that the Buddha was still fully—and physically—present at his shrines and could therefore still be ritually approached.

To begin with, the text specifies that in order to worship the Buddha, one should worship his relics. The worship of the Buddha's relics (his bodily remains after cremation) enshrined in a funerary mound (*stūpa*) goes back to the early period of Buddhism—possibly although not necessarily to the Buddha's death itself. Numerous stūpas within and outside of India were believed by the faithful to contain some remnant of the Buddha's body.

By the sixth or seventh century, the practice of enshrining the corporeal relics of the Buddha ceases to appear in the archeological record. Instead we begin to find at Buddhist sites numerous clay tablets that were stamped or engraved with the four-line verse epitome of the Buddha's teaching on causality. This is the very dharma-relic verse Yijing's translation recommends as an alternative to a corporeal relic. Yijing, in fact, described this cultic practice in the account he wrote of his travels to India:

> [People in India] make [incense] paste caityas [another term in this context for stūpa] and paste images from rubbings. Some impress them on silk or paper, and venerate them wherever they go. Some amass them into a pile, and by covering them with tiles, they build buddha-stūpas. Some erect them in empty fields, allowing them to fall into ruin. Among the monks and laity of India, they all take this as their practice. Furthermore, whether they build images or make caityas, be they of gold, silver, bronze, iron, paste, lacquer, brick, or stone; or they heap up sand like snow, when they make them, they place inside two kinds of relics. One is called the bodily relic of the Great Teacher; the second is called the dharma-verse relic on causation. This verse goes as follows:
>
> All things arise from a cause.
> The Tathāgata has explained their cause
> And the cessation of the cause of these things.
> This the great ascetic has explained.
>
> If one installs these two [relics], then one's blessings will be extremely abundant. This is why the sūtras, expanded into parables, praise this merit as inconceivable. If a person builds an image the size of a bran kernel or a caitya the size of a small jujube, and places on it a parasol with a staff like a small needle, an extraordinary means [is obtained] which is as inexhaustible as the seven seas. A great reward [is obtained] which, pervading the four births, is without end. Details of this matter are all given in other sūtras.
>
> *Taisho,* 2125; vol. 54, p. 226c.

The *Sūtra on the Merit of Bathing the Buddha* would appear to be one of these "other" sūtras.

The development and history of the use of this dharma-verse is not entirely clear. The Buddhist tradition appears to have struggled since early times between two tendencies: to locate the Buddha in his physical presence, especially as left behind in his corporeal relics; and to identify the "true" Buddha as the dharma, his teachings. The former inspired the stūpa cult; the latter devalued the physical body of the Buddha in favor of his career as teacher, typified by canonical passages in which the Buddha states: "He who sees the dharma sees me; he who sees me sees the dharma." More specifically, the teachings on causality (that is, the twelve-fold chain of dependent coproduction; Sanskrit *pratītyasamutpāda*) were viewed as the very heart of the Buddha's message and remained the subject of rigorous commentary and debate. In the medieval period, the essence of the Buddha's teaching on causality—his dharma par excellence—was located in a single four-line verse from the scriptures. By depositing this "essence" in the traditional shrine of the Buddha's corporeal relics, these Buddhists were able to bring together and harmonize the two tendencies suggested above—tendencies that reflect two different conceptions of the Buddha, one concrete and physically present, the other abstract and metaphorically present.

In addition to relic worship, Yijing's translation commends the construction and ritual bathing of the Buddha image. The construction of Buddha images dates from several centuries after the earliest record of the stūpa cult and its origins remain obscure and controversial. Some look for foreign, especially Greco-Roman, influence in the first sculptured statues from the Indo-Greek regions of northwest India around the turn of the common era. Others locate the first images in India proper as continuations of indigenous artistic traditions. By the sixth or seventh century, the image cult was fully incorporated into Buddhist practice—both lay and monastic. Yijing describes a ritual treatment of the Buddha image in his travel account that has much in common with the ritual in the *Sūtra on the Merit of Bathing the Buddha:*

> In cultivating the foundation of devotion, nothing exceeds the three honored ones (the Buddha, his teachings, and the monastic community); in dedicating oneself to the pursuit of contemplation, how could anything surpass the four noble truths? Nevertheless, the principles of truth are profound and worldly affairs obstruct simple minds. Bathing the holy image is practical for the sake of universal succor. Although the Great Teacher is extinguished, his image is still present. One should venerate it with an elevated mind as if the Buddha were still here. Some may place incense and flowers [before the image] every day, enabling them to produce a pure heart. Others may constantly perform the bathing ritual, completely cleansing their tenebrous karma. Those who apply their thoughts to this practice will automatically receive their unmanifested reward. As for those who exhort others to do it, the merit they have already produced will be compounded. Those who seek blessings should set their minds on this.
>
> Moreover, all the monasteries of the Western Regions [especially India and Central Asia] bathe the noble image. Every morning the monastic director sounds the bell. He spreads a jeweled awning over the courtyard of the monastery. At the side of the [image] temple are arranged jars of incense. He takes the gold, silver, bronze, or stone image and places it inside a basin made of bronze, gold, wood, or stone. He orders the female musicians to play their music while he smears the image with ground incense and bathes it with scented water. He rubs it with a clean, white cloth, and afterwards puts it back in the temple, furnishing it with floral decorations. This then is the custom of the majority of monasteries and the task of the revered director of monastic affairs. In the same manner the monks individually bathe the noble image within their respective cells. Each day they all perform the essentials without deficiency.
>
> *Taishō* 2125; vol. 54, p. 226b

The third question asked by the Pure Wisdom Bodhisattva concerns the merit that accrues from performing these reverential acts. Attendance upon the living Buddha as well as attendance upon his shrine or image after his death are both stated to produce infinite merit and blessings. In fact this merit is efficacious enough to lead one to enlightenment and "the other shore," a typical Buddhist expression for nirvāṇa. But the text also describes a number of other benefits from these ritual performances: prosperity, protection, and comfortable old age in this life; fortunate rebirth—especially the avoidance of a female body—and perpetual encounters with buddhas in future lives.

Western students of Buddhism have generally regarded ritual attainment of enlightenment and desires for prosperity and fortunate rebirth as indicative of lay Buddhist interests and goals. This is contrasted with the presumption that monastics seek enlightenment strictly through contemplative practices and a strict moral life—the so-called "true" path expounded by the Buddha. Such a dichotomy is not supported by much of the evidence. Yijing's travel log, for example, specifically describes activities taking place in the monasteries. Although we do not want to detract from the importance of meditation and related practices for Buddhist mendicants, this is certainly only part of the picture. The vast majority of our data suggests that an array of practices were available to and taken up by monks and nuns of all periods. Not all of these practices were necessarily complementary. Many, in fact, may have been in competition with one another, reflecting competing conceptions of how the presence of the departed teacher—be it the legacy of his teachings or his bodily remains and representation—was to be maintained and, importantly, to be encountered. Such tensions inspired repeated attempts over time to harmonize these various strands of the tradition. The *Sūtra on the Merit of Bathing the Buddha* might be described as one of these attempts.

The translation has been made from *Taishō shinshū daizōkyō* (Tokyo, 1924–1934), 698; vol. 16, pp. 799c–800c.

Further Reading

For a brief discussion of Yijing's translation and its relationship to related texts, see Ryojun Mitomo, "An Aspect of Dharma-śarīra," *Indogaku bukkyōgaku kenkyū (Journal of Indian and Buddhist Studies)* 32.2 [64] (1984); (4)–(9) (in English). For a complete translation of Yijing's travel account, describing the many practices he personally witnessed, see I Tsing, *A Record of the Buddhist Religion as Practiced in India and the Malay Archipelago,* translated by J. Takakusu (London, 1886; reprint Delhi: Munshiram Manoharlal, 1966).

For a more detailed discussion of both the literary and archeological development of the dharma-verse relic, see Daniel Boucher, "The *Pratītyasamutpādagāthā* and Its Role in the Medieval Cult of the Relics," *Journal for the International Association of Buddhist Studies* 14.1 (1991), 1–27.

For some general information on the stūpa cult, see among others David L. Snellgrove, "Śākyamuni's Final Nirvāṇa," *Bulletin of the School of Oriental and African Studies* 36 (1973), 399–411. An anthology of papers of mixed quality has appeared in Anna Libera Dallapiccola and Stephanie Zingel-Avé Lallemant, eds.,

The Stūpa: Its Religious, Historical and Architectural Significance (Wiesbaden: Franz Steiner Verlag, 1980); see also Gregory Schopen, "Burial 'Ad Sanctos' and the Physical Presence of the Buddha in Early Indian Buddhism: A Study in the Archeology of Religions," *Religion* 17 (1987), 193–225.

One of the few scholarly treatments of the ritual of bathing the Buddha is Ferdinand Lessing, "Structure and Meaning of the Rite Called the Bath of Buddha According to Tibetan and Chinese Sources," in Soren Egerod and Else Glahn, eds., *Studia Serica Bernhard Karlgren dedicata* (Copenhagen, 1959), pp. 159–71.

Sūtra on the Merit of Bathing the Buddha

Thus have I heard. At one time the Blessed One was in Rājagṛha, on Vulture's Peak, together with 1,250 monks. There were also an immeasurable, unlimited multitude of bodhisattvas and the eight classes of gods, nāgas, and so forth, who were all assembled. At that time, the Pure Wisdom Bodhisattva was seated in the midst of this assembly. Because he aspired to extend compassion toward all sentient beings, he thought: "By what means do the buddhas, tathāgatas, obtain the pure body, furnished with the marks of the great person?" Again he thought: "All classes of living beings are able to meet the Tathāgata and approach him with offerings. The blessings that are obtained are without measure or limit. I do not yet know, however, what offerings living beings will make or what merit they will cultivate after the death of the Tathāgata so as to bring about those roots of good merit that quickly lead to final, supreme enlightenment." After thinking this, he then arose from his seat and bared his right shoulder; having bowed his head at the feet of the Buddha, he knelt upright, with palms in salutation, and spoke to the Buddha, saying, "World-Honored One, I wish to ask questions and hope that you deign to acknowledge them." The Buddha said, "Noble son, I will teach according to what you ask."

At that time, the Pure Wisdom Bodhisattva spoke to the Buddha, saying, "By what means do the buddhas, tathāgatas, perfectly enlightened ones obtain the pure body, furnished with the marks of the great person? Also, all living beings are able to meet the Tathāgata and approach him with offerings. The blessings that are obtained are without measure or limit. I have not yet discerned what offerings living beings will make or what merit they will cultivate after the death of the Tathāgata so as to bring about those good qualities that quickly lead to final, supreme enlightenment."

At that time, the World-Honored One said to the Pure Wisdom Bodhisattva: "Excellent, excellent, that you are able for the sake of future beings to bring forth such questions! Now listen carefully, reflect on this well, and practice as I say. I will explain for you in detail."

The Pure Wisdom Bodhisattva said, "So be it, World-Honored One. I dearly wish to listen."

The Buddha explained to the Pure Wisdom Bodhisattva: "Noble son, you should know that because giving, morality, patience, vigor, meditation, and wisdom; benevolence, compassion, delight, and should know that because giving, morality, patience, vigor, meditation, and knowledge and experience of liberation; the [ten] strengths and the [four] confidences are all the characteristics of the Buddha and are all various kinds of knowledge, virtue, and purity, they are the purity of the Tathāgata.

"If the buddhas, tathāgatas, are in this way given various offerings with a pure heart—incense, flowers, gems, garlands, banners, parasols, and cushions—displayed before the Buddha, multifariously adorning him, and the marvelously scented water is used to bathe his noble form, the dark smoke of the burning incense will carry your mind to the dharma realm. Furthermore, if you celebrate the extraordinary merit of the Tathāgata with food and drink, percussion and stringed music, you will manifest the superb vow to direct [your mind] to the supreme ocean of omniscience. The merit thereby produced will be immeasurable and without limit; it will be perpetually continued [through successive rebirths] to the point of enlightenment. Why is this? The blessed wisdom of the Tathāgata is inconceivable, infinite, and unequaled.

"Noble son, all buddhas, world-honored ones, have three bodies. They are known as the dharma body (*dharmakāya*), the glorified body (*saṃbhogakāya*), and the manifestation body (*nirmāṇakāya*). After my nirvāṇa, if you wish to do homage to these three bodies, then you should do homage to my relics. But there are two kinds: the first is the bodily relic; the second is the dharma-verse relic. I will now recite the verse:

> All things arise from a cause.
> The Tathāgata has explained their cause
> And the cessation of the cause of these things.
> This the great ascetic has explained.

"If men, women, or the five groups of mendicants would build an image of the Buddha; or if those without strength would deposit one as large as a grain of barley, or build a stūpa—its body the size of a jujube, its mast the size of a needle, its parasol equal to a flake of bran, its relic like a mustard seed—or if someone writes the dharma-verse and installs it inside the stūpa, it would be like doing homage by offering up a rare jewel. If in accordance with one's own strength and ability one can be truly sincere and respectful, it [the image or stūpa] would be like my present body, equal without difference.

"Noble son, if there are beings who are able to make such excellent offerings, they will glorify themselves by achieving the fifteen superb virtues. First, they will always be modest. Second, they will manifest a mind of pure faith. Third, their hearts will be simple and honest. Fourth, they will cleave to good friends. Fifth, they will enter a state of passionless wisdom. Sixth, they will constantly encounter buddhas. Seventh, they will always maintain the correct teaching. Eighth, they will be able to act according to my teaching. Ninth, they will be reborn in pure buddha fields according to their wishes. Tenth, if they are reborn among men, they will be noblemen of great families; being respected among men, they will produce joyous thoughts. Eleventh, being born among men, they will naturally set their minds on the Buddha. Twelfth, an army of demons will not be able to harm them. Thirteenth, they will be able in the final age to protect and maintain the true dharma. Fourteenth, they will be protected by the buddhas of the ten directions. Fifteenth, they will be able to quickly obtain the five attributes of the dharma body."

At that time, the World-Honored One uttered these verses:

> After my death
> You will be able to honor my relics
> Some will build stūpas
> Or images of the Tathāgata.
> At the place of the image or stūpa,
> One who anoints that spot of ground
> With various incenses and flowers
> Scattering them over its surface,
> Uses pure, beautifully scented water
> To pour onto the body of this image,
> Offers it various flavorful drinks and foods,
> Fully maintaining it with oblations,
> Eulogizes the virtue of the Tathāgata
> Which is endlessly difficult to conceive;
> Through the wisdom of skillful means and the supernatural power [of the Buddha],
> Such a one will quickly reach the other shore [of nirvāṇa].
> He will obtain the diamond body
> Complete with the thirty-two marks of a great person
> And the eighty minor signs of excellence.
> He will ferry the multitude of living beings [to the shore of nirvāṇa].

At that time, the Pure Wisdom Bodhisattva, having heard these verses, addressed the Buddha saying, "Future living beings will ask, 'Why bathe the image?'" The Buddha answered the Pure Wisdom Bodhisattva: "Because you will equal the Tathāgata in producing right mindfulness. You will not be attached to the two sides that deceive people with 'emptiness' and 'being.' You will long insatiably for virtuous conduct. The three emancipations, morality, and wisdom will be constantly sought to escape the endless cycle of birth and death. You will produce great compassion toward all living beings. You will aspire to obtain and quickly perfect the three kinds of bodies.

"Noble son, I have already expounded for your sake the four noble truths, the twelve conditioned co-productions, and the six perfections. And now I teach the method of bathing the image for your sake and the sake of the various kings, princes, ministers, concubines, princesses, gods, nāgas, men, and demons. Among the various types of homage, this [the bathing of the image] is the best. It excels the giving of the seven jewels equal to the sands of the Ganges.

"When you bathe the image, you should use oxhead sandalwood, white sandalwood, red sandalwood, or aloewood incenses. You should burn Mountain Top Tulip incense, 'Dragon's Brain' incense, Ling-ling [Mountain] incense, and so forth. On the surface of a clean stone, you should grind these to make paste; use [this paste] to make scented water and place it in a clean vessel. At a clean spot, make an altar with good earth, square or round, its size suited to the circumstances. On top establish the bathing platform, and place the Buddha image in the middle. Pour on the scented hot water, purifying and cleansing it, repeatedly pouring the pure water over it. The water that is used must be completely filtered so as not to cause harm to insects. Drops from two fingers of the water with which you bathed the image should be taken and placed on your own head—this is called 'good luck water.' Drain off the water onto clean ground without allowing your feet to tread upon it. With a fine, soft towel wipe the image, making it clean. Burn the above-named incenses, spreading the aroma all around, and put the image back in its original place.

"Noble son, the consequence of performing this bathing of the Buddha image is that you and the great multitude of men and gods will presently receive wealth, happiness, and long life without sickness; your every wish will be fulfilled. Your relatives, friends, and family will all be at ease. You will bid a long farewell to the eight conditions of trouble and forever escape the fount of suffering. You will never again receive the body of a woman, and will quickly achieve enlightenment.

"When you have set up the image and burned the various incenses, face the image, clasping your palms together in pious salutation, and recite these praises:

> I now bathe the Tathāgata.
> His pure wisdom and virtue adorn the assembly.
> I vow that those living beings of this period of the five impurities
> May quickly witness the pure dharma body of the Tathāgata.
> May the incense of morality, meditation, wisdom, and the knowledge and experience of liberation
> Constantly perfume every realm in the ten directions.
> I vow that the smoke of this incense will likewise
> Do the Buddha's work [of salvation] without measure or limit.
> I also vow to put a stop to the three hells and the wheel of saṃsāra,
> Completely extinguishing the fires and obtaining the coolness [of relief]
> So that all may manifest the thought of unsurpassed enlightenment
> Perpetually escaping the river of desires and advancing to the other shore [of nirvāṇa]."

The Buddha finished expounding this sūtra. At this time, there were among this assembly an immeasurable, unlimited number of bodhisattvas who obtained stainless concentration. The countless gods obtained never lapsing wisdom. The multitude of śrāvakas (lit. "hearers," a title for the early disciples of the Buddha) vowed to seek the fruits of buddhahood. The eighty-four thousand living beings all manifested the thought toward unexcelled, complete enlightenment.

At that time, the Pure Wisdom Bodhisattva said to the Buddha: "World-Honored One, being fortunate to receive the compassion and pity of the great teacher [the Buddha], we shall teach the method of bathing the image. I will now convert kings, ministers, and all those of good faith, cheer, or merit. Every day I will bathe the noble image to procure great blessings. I pledge to always receive and carry out with pleasure the *Sūtra on the Merit of Bathing the Buddha*."

—12—

The Whole Universe as a Sūtra

Luis O. Gómez

The following selection is a translation of two versions of a single passage from a Mahāyāna sūtra entitled "The Teaching Regarding the Source from which Tathāgatas Arise" (*Tathāgatotpattisaṃbhava-nirdeśa;* here *Tathāgatotpatti,* for short). This sūtra is not preserved in any complete Indian version; only short quotations occur here and there in the Sanskrit literature. Three different versions of the sūtra survive, however, as part of a monumental collection preserved in Chinese and Tibetan translations, and known as the *Buddhāvataṃsaka Sūtra.* This collection is commonly known in the West as the *Avataṃsaka Sūtra* or by its Chinese and Japanese names: *Hua-yen jing* and *Kegon kyō,* respectively.

The *Tathāgatotpatti* describes the way in which the knowledge and enlightenment of buddhas is present in all sentient beings, in fact, in all things, and is therefore accessible to all as "the source from which tathāgatas will arise." This is a common theme in the doctrine known as *tathāgatagarbha.* This is the idea that buddhahood is somehow inherent or innate to all sentient beings as a pure and enlightened core underlying the deluded mind. As part of the *Avataṃsaka Sūtra* collection, however, the *Tathāgatotpatti* may be seen also as expressing two themes common to that collection: first, that all things reflect each other perfectly, so that every thing in the universe may be said to contain in itself the whole universe, and, consequently, that the ultimate reality and the wisdom of a buddha are present in each and every being.

The short section translated below occurs as part of a description of ten intuitions or understandings that accompany the enlightenment of bodhisattvas. According to the passage, all bodhisattvas realize that truth is already present "in every particle of dust in the universe." Stated in this way, this is a common enough theme; but in the present extract the idea is developed with a metaphor that has interesting connotations for our understanding of what a religious text or image is, and what it means to interpret, render, or imagine religious truths. The whole universe is represented on a text or a canvas (depending on which version we use), but this representation is itself contained in every particle of dust in the universe. With this tantalizing image the text can lead us to reflect on the relationship between text and interpretation, or between representation and reality.

Of the two extracts translated below, the first and longer selection is a translation of Buddhabhadra's Chinese version of the whole section explaining the bodhisattva's "tenth intuition" in the *Buddhāvataṃsaka, Taishō shinshū daizōkyō* (Tokyo, 1924–1934), 278, vol. 9, pp. 623c23–624a26, 625a6–13. There are parallels in Śikṣānanda's translation, *Taishō shinshū daizōkyō* 279, vol. 10, pp. 272c5–29, 273b15–22; and in Dharmarakṣa's translation of the *Tathāgotpattisaṃbhava, Taishō shinshū daizōkyō* 291, vol. 10, pp. 607c3–608a13. In this Chinese version, the *Tathāgatotpatti* is book 32 of the *Avataṃsaka Sūtra* (corresponding to book 43 in the Tibetan translation, Peking edition).

The second, and shorter, passage included below is an English translation of a Sanskrit version of the same passage that is quoted in the commentary to the *Ratnagotravibhāga,* a treatise on the tathāgatagarbha doctrine of uncertain authorship (Sāramati?) and date (4th–5th centuries C.E.). This version includes only the central simile describing the "tenth intuition." The *Ratnagotravibhāga,* of course, uses the passage to argue for the tathāgatagarbha doctrine. Thus, the *Ratnagotravibhāga* introduces the selection translated below with the following comment: "The immaculate qualities of a buddha are forever found even in [that human state called] the stage of profane, ordinary people, which is a stage that is totally defiled and afflicted. [These immaculate qualities] are found there without qualification or distinction. This is something inconceivable." See the *Ratnagotravibhāga-uttaratantra-śāstra,* edited by E. H. Johnston (Patna: Bihar Research Society, 1950), pp. 22–24.

The Whole Universe Contained in a Sūtra

Moreover, Son of the Buddha, there is no place where the knowledge and wisdom of the Tathāgata does not abide. There is not a single sentient being, and no single body of a sentient being, that is not endowed with the knowledge and wisdom of the Tathāgata. Still, because sentient beings see things contrary to what they are, they do not know this wisdom of the Tathāgata. Only when they abandon their deluded, contrary views, will omniscience, the knowledge that needs no teacher, the unimpeded knowledge, arise [for them].

Son of the Buddha, it is as if there were a sūtra scroll, as large as this world system of three-thousandfold multi-thousand worlds. And on this [scroll] would be recorded all things without exceptions in this world system of three-thousandfold multi-thousand worlds. And the two-thousandfold multi-thousand worlds would be recorded in full detail on this [scroll], including all things in the two-thousandfold multi-thousand worlds. And the single-thousand worlds would be recorded in full detail on this [scroll], including all things in the single-thousand worlds.

And whatever is in the [realm] of the four guardian deities and below would be recorded in full detail on this [scroll], including all things in the [realm] of the four guardian deities and below.

And whatever is found on Mount Sumeru would be recorded in full detail on this [scroll], including all things on Mount Sumeru.

And whatever is in the [realm] of the earth deities would be recorded in full detail on this [scroll], including all things in the [realm] of the earth deities.

And whatever is in the [realm] of the deities of the realm of desire would be recorded in full detail on this [scroll], including all things in the [realm] of the deities of the realm of desire.

And whatever is in the [realm] of the deities of the realm of form would be recorded in full detail on this [scroll], including all things in the [realm] of the deities of the realm of form.

And whatever is in the [realm] of the deities of the formless realm would be recorded in full detail on this [scroll], including all things in the [realm] of the deities of the formless realm.

This sūtra scroll [thus containing] the world system of three-thousandfold multi-thousand worlds would be contained in a minute particle of dust. And every particle of dust [in the universe] would in the same way [contain a copy of this sūtra scroll].

Now, at one time, there would appear in the world a certain person who had clear, penetrating wisdom, and was endowed with a perfectly pure divine eye. And this person would see the sūtra scroll inside [every] particle of dust, and it would occur to this person, "How can this vast sūtra scroll be present in[every] particle of dust, yet it does not benefit sentient beings in the least? I should gather all my energy and devise a means to break open a dust particle and let out this sūtra scroll, that it may benefit all sentient beings." Thereupon this person would find the means to break open a dust particle, let out the sūtra scroll so that it could benefit all sentient beings.

Son of a Buddha, this is the way it is with the wisdom and knowledge of the Tathāgata. This wisdom is without [limiting] characteristics and without impediments, it is present in the body of every sentient being; and yet foolish living beings [persisting in their] deluded, contrary views, do not know, do not see [this wisdom], and do not put their faith and trust in it. Then the Tathāgata surveys all sentient beings with his unimpeded, pure divine eye, and having examined them, exclaims, "Isn't it strange, strange indeed, how the wisdom of the Tathāgata is present in the body [of every sentient being] and yet they do not know or see it! I will teach these [sentient beings] so that they may awaken fully in the noble path. I will free them of deluded conceptions, of contrary views, and from the fetters of [worldly] impurity; then they will see that the Tathāgata's wisdom is present in their own bodies, that they are no different from a buddha."

The Tathāgata thereupon teaches these sentient beings how to practice the eightfold noble path, and they abandon false, erroneous, and contrary views. Having abandoned contrary views, they [are able to] see the wisdom of a tathāgata, they become equal to buddhas, and [are able to] benefit sentient beings.

Son of a Buddha, this is the tenth [intuition] of bodhisattvas mahāsattvas, [by which bodhisattvas] perfectly practice, know, and perceive the mind of the perfectly awakened, who are tathāgatas and arhats.

It is as if in the heart of a minute particle of dust
Were present a vast sūtra scroll,
As large as the three-thousandfold world,
[Yet] bringing no benefit to any living being.
Then this one person
Would arise in the world,
Who would break a speck of dust, let out the scroll,
And benefit the whole world.
It is the same with the Tathāgata's wisdom.
All sentient beings possess it;
[But] contrary views and deluded thoughts hide it,
So that sentient beings cannot see it or know it.
[Then] the Tathāgata instructs sentient beings
On how to cultivate the noble eightfold path,
So that they can remove all the veils [of delusion],
And finally attain awakening.

The Universe Painted on a Canvas

[Son of the Conqueror,] there is no living being whatsoever in the mass of living beings [in the universe] who is not pervaded by the whole knowledge of the Tathāgata. Yet, because of [our] grasping at [preconceived] notions, [we are] not able to discern this knowledge of the Tathāgata. But if we abandon [our] grasping at [such] notions, the knowledge of the all-knowing, the knowledge of the self-made, is manifested unattached and unhindered.

O Son of the Conqueror, it is as if there were an immense canvas the size of the three-thousandfold, multi-thousand world system; and on this immense canvas one were to paint the three-thousandfold, multi-thousand world system in its entirety. The great earthly plane would be [painted] to the measure of the great earthly plane; the two-thousandfold world system would be [drawn] to the measure of the two-thousandfold world system; the thousandfold world system to that of the thousandfold world system; the plane of the four continents to that of the plane of the four continents; the great ocean to the measure of the great ocean; the Rose-Apple continent to the measure of the Rose-Apple continent; the Pūrva-Videha continent to that of the Pūrva-Videha continent;

the Godavarī continent to that of the Godavarī; the Uttarakuru continent to that of the Uttarakuru; the [Great Mount] Sumeru would be [drawn] to the measure of [Mount] Sumeru; the abodes of the gods on earth to the measure of the abodes of the gods on earth; the abodes of the gods of the realm of desire to the measure of the abodes of the gods of the realm of desire; the abodes of the gods of the realm of form to the measure of the abodes of the gods of the realm of form. [The text omits the formless realm.] And this immense canvas would correspond in extent, detail, and proportions to the three-thousandfold, multi-thousand world system.

Furthermore, this immense canvas would be folded into a single atomic particle of dust. And, in the same way that this immense canvas was folded into a single atomic particle of dust, similar immense canvases would be enclosed in every single atom of dust [in the universe].

Now, a certain person would appear, knowing, alert, discerning, intelligent, and endowed with the analytic faculty necessary for comprehending [the nature of this reality]. And this person would have purified his divine eye, perfectly, so that it was most lucid. With that divine eye this person would look with discernment [at a particle of dust], [and perceive] that although this immense canvas is present in its entirety here [in this] minute, atomic, particle of dust, this is of no avail to any living being. Thus it would occur to him: "If I could only break open this particle of dust, by means of the force and strength of my energy, and turn this immense canvas into a support and sustenance for the whole world!" Producing the force and strength of his energy, he would break open that particle of dust with a minute pestle (*vajra*), and would turn the immense canvas into a support and sustenance for the whole world, in accordance with his [original] intention. And as he had done with this particle of dust he would do with all the rest.

In the same way, O Son of the Jina, the knowledge of the Tathāgata, the measureless knowledge, the knowledge that supports and sustains living beings, in its entirety pervades every instant of thought in the mind of all living beings. And every single series of thoughts in the mind of [every] living being is [manifested] to the measure of the knowledge of the Tathāgata. Yet, childish beings, bound by their grasping at notions do not know this, do not discern this, do not experience this, do not perceive directly this knowledge of the Tathāgatas. Therefore, the Tathāgata, looking at the abodes of all living beings in the dharmadhātu with his unhindered and unattached Tathāgata knowledge, reflects with astonishment: "Alas, these living beings fail to discern the knowledge of the Tathāgata as it is, yet the knowledge of the Tathāgata pervades all of them. If only I could remove all of the fetters which these beings have fashioned with notions [by instructing them] with a noble instruction on the path, so that once they have undone the great knot of notions using the power that arises from the noble path, they may themselves come to recognize the knowledge of the Tathāgata, and become equals of the Tathāgata."

By means of the Tathāgata's instruction on the path, living beings undo the fetters formed by notions. And when the fetters formed by notion are cast aside, there remains this measureless knowledge of the Tathāgata, the support and sustenance of the whole world.

—13—

The Book of Resolving Doubts Concerning the Semblance Dharma

Kyoko Tokuno

The *Book of Resolving Doubts Concerning the Semblance Dharma (Xiangfa jueyi jing)* is a Buddhist apocryphon dating from the mid-sixth century. C.E. The term "apocrypha" in this context refers to Buddhist texts written in China and modeled upon translations of Indian and Central Asian scriptures. Because of their indigenous origins, these texts were traditionally called "spurious scriptures" and the majority of them were proscribed from the Buddhist canon. Consequently, they remained dispersed and uncollected for centuries. Little was known about the content of such texts until the discovery of the Dunhuang manuscript cache at the turn of this century, which included recensions of many of these proscribed materials. The burgeoning research on this corpus revealed the startling fact that many of the scriptures most important in the Chinese tradition were in fact not the translations of Indian texts at all, but instead were works of Chinese origin.

The doctrines and practices described in Chinese Buddhist apocrypha are the culmination of a protracted process of adaptation and assimilation of imported Indian Buddhist ideologies with the indigenous Chinese *Weltanschauung*. Furthermore, the overwhelmingly popular orientation of these scriptures has proven to be a treasure-trove of information for the study of Buddhism among the people at large. Most studies of Chinese Buddhist history have been concerned mainly with the theoretically oriented Buddhism of religious specialists and scholarly elites within the Buddhist ecclesia. In order to understand the full range of the Chinese manifestations of Buddhism, however, Buddhism as accepted, interpreted, and practiced at the local level cannot be ignored. When "apocryphal" or "spurious" scriptures are acknowledged to be an integral and organic part of Chinese Buddhism, it no longer seems appropriate to refer to these texts using such pejorative terms, but rather a more neutral designation such as "indigenous Chinese scriptures."

Resolving Doubts claims to be the Buddha's last sermon before entering complete quiescence (*parinirvāṇa*), using a scenario that is well known in canonical scriptures. The theme of the Buddha's discourse is the imminent demise of the Buddhist religion: the Buddha prophesies the advent of a period of semblance dharma, when monks will disregard the teachings and violate the precepts. This misconduct will induce the lay followers of the religion to lose their reverence for the three jewels of Buddhism (the Buddha, the dharma, the saṅgha). Ultimately, the conduct of all Buddhist followers and others will degenerate and the decline of the religion and society will soon follow. The text outlines strategies to cope with this socio-religious crisis.

The notion of the decline and imminent demise of Buddhism, also of Indian Buddhist origin, permeated Chinese Buddhism from the fifth century onward. This eschatological concern was one of the principal impulses behind the compilation of indigenous Chinese scriptures, which was one expression of the efforts among Chinese Buddhists to confront the religious crisis they believed to be facing them. *Resolving Doubts* is just such an example of an attempt to ensure the survival of the religion by composing a new scripture that would specifically address the severity of the times and offer measures necessary to survive them.

The apocalyptic prophecy contained in *Resolving Doubts* mainly addresses the degenerate condition of Buddhist followers, both ordained and lay. The cause of that degeneration includes transgression of specific precepts of their religion. The worst culprits are evil monks who fail to observe the precepts, cultivate the spiritual path, transmit the teachings to others, or convert others, who are greedy for fame and material gain, and who harbor hatred and jealousy toward those few noble monks who are keeping their religious vocations. Moreover, lay adherents are also called to task for showing disrespect toward the three jewels of Buddhism, inviting only a few selected monks to vegetarian feasts, failing to repair old religious edifices, selling Buddhist images for profit, and ignoring the lay precepts. Such criticisms are directed at all strata of society, from kings and high officials to merchants and other householders.

Resolving Doubts' emphasis on precepts is a common theme in indigenous Chinese scriptures. The purpose of these injunctions is twofold. First, as with all Buddhist preceptive texts, canonical and apocryphal alike, precepts are said to provide a model for ethically appropriate behavior. The injunctions against engaging in wrong livelihoods, meat eating, drinking intoxicants, and so forth, all have such an edifying role. But second, *Resolving Doubts* seems to use some of these rules as a means of conveying certain messages or criticisms regarding contemporary religious issues and social conditions. Injunctions that are not attested in other Indian Buddhist sources were most likely intended to fulfill this function. These include the usurpation of objects belonging to the monastic community by the laity, or the taxation of monastic properties or expropriation of its resources by governmental authorities. But even some of its precepts that have their antecedents in earlier preceptive materials may also be addressing conditions that Buddhism specifically faced during the sixth century. Thus the preceptive aspect of *Resolving Doubts* is a clever blend of traditional edifying precepts with critiques—disguised as injunctions—on contemporary religious and social conditions.

The only Buddhists who will be able to resist the perverse tendencies of this degenerate time will be bodhisattvas who actively strive to benefit other sentient beings out of their loving-kindness and compassion. One of the major themes of the text is to describe the single most efficacious religious practice during this corrupt age: universal giving. Unlike most Indian Buddhist texts, *Resolving Doubts* specifies that the optimal recipients of charity were not the monks but instead the impoverished, the orphaned, the aged, the sick, and even animals and insects. Such recipients are called the field of compassion, which this scripture defines as the most excellent field of merit (*puṇyakṣetra*) for Buddhists to cultivate. This attitude toward the act of giving and its ideal recipients is an innovation unique to this scripture.

The practice of giving had been advocated since the early days of Buddhism. Charity was seen as one of the essential religious activities of the laity, who were expected to supply the monks with their requisites of food, clothing, shelter, and medicine. Indeed, the viability of the Buddhist monastic institution was almost entirely dependent upon the largess of the laity. The recipients of one's charity were called a field of merit, for they were the source from which merit accrued to the donor through his or her charitable deeds. The amount of merit received by a donor was determined by the spiritual status of the recipient, and hence the Buddha and his disciples in the monastic order were considered to be the most meritorious field for giving. Such material sacrifice on the part of the laity was motivated by the goal of generating enough merit to ensure rebirth in the heavens. The earliest stratum of Indian Buddhist scriptures, in fact, explicitly instructs the laity to practice giving and to observe precepts in order to obtain heavenly rebirth.

Later in Mahāyāna scriptures, giving becomes one of the perfections (*pāramitā*, along with morality, patience, energy, concentration, and wisdom), the essential elements in the practice of the bodhisattvas, whose great compassion motivated them to seek the salvation of all sentient beings. Mahāyāna scriptures refute the conception that a donor obtains merit from his charitable deeds in direct proportion to the spiritual status of the recipient. Some texts in this branch of Buddhism say, for example, that there are no distinctions in the quality of the various fields of merit: parents and teachers, the poor and the indigent are as deserving fields of merit as are the monks. Still other scriptures claim that the merit deriving from giving depends not on the recipient but on the quality of mind of the donor himself.

Resolving Doubts adopts the Mahāyāna conception of giving, and modifies it to meet specific needs. It asserts that the underprivileged in society are the worthiest recipients of donations, surpassing even the three jewels of Buddhism. The central message of the text was intended, in effect, to repudiate the exclusiveness of the original conception of giving, which specified members of the order as the principal beneficiaries of charity. It issues a clarion call for all Buddhists, clergy and laity alike, to pay attention to neglected segments of society, rather than simply take care of their own. The significance of giving is also upgraded so that the cultivation of the other five perfections is said to be contingent upon giving; in fact, the text goes so far as to suggest that buddhahood can be attained solely through the practice of giving. Such a claim is indeed a radical departure from the traditional Buddhist conception of giving.

Resolving Doubts also includes an array of doctrinal ideas drawn from major Indian Mahāyāna scriptures then available in Chinese translation, as well as from a fifth-century apocryphon, the *Book of Brahmā's Net (Fanwang jing)*. The ideas include the apophatic characterization of the Thus Come One (*Tathāgata*) and sentient beings—in terms of what they lack or are empty of—and the insubstantiality of all phenomena. The doctrinal ideas included seem often to be afterthoughts and appear rather incongruous. Still, their presence was vital if this indigenous scripture was to be successful in passing itself off as an authentic translation of an Indian Buddhist text.

One of the more important influences *Resolving Doubts* exerted in the development of Chinese Buddhism was on the Sect of Three Stages (*Sanjie jiao*), whose teachings were based on the eschatological notion of the imminent demise of Buddhism. One of the most important scriptures written by the sect, which described this degenerate age of the dharma, was the *Yoga Dharma Mirror that Exposes Transgressors (Shi suofanzhe yuqie fajing jing)*, a text closely based on *Resolving Doubts*. This sect is perhaps best known for developing the institution of the Cloister of the Inexhaustible Treasury *(Wujinzang yuan)*, which gathered public contributions and distributed them for religious and altruistic purposes. This activity was also clearly influenced by *Resolving Doubts*, which had praised the notion of collective giving over individual donations: the most meritorious manner of giving was said to be for all persons to offer what they could regardless of their financial or social status, and the needy would receive according to their needs from those pooled resources. Other evidence of the long-term influence of *Resolving Doubts* is found in the writings of such Buddhist thinkers in China and Japan as Zhiyi (538–597), Jizang (549–623), Hōnen (1133–1212), and Dōchū (d. 1281), as well as in a scripture of religious Daoism, the *Book of the Repository of Knowledge on the Sea of Voidness of the Most High One Vehicle (Taishang yisheng haikong zhizang jing)*.

The translation here is from *Foshuo xiangfa jueyi jing, Taishō shinshū daizōkyo* (Tokyo, 1924–1934), 2870; vol. 85, pp. 1335c–1338c.

Book of Resolving Doubts Concerning the Semblance Dharma

Thus I have heard. At one time the Buddha was on the bank of the Vatī [a kind of tree] River between the twin sal (*sāla*) trees, [where] he had completed the ordination of Most Splendid (Subhadra). All the congregation—great bodhisattvas [beings intent on enlightenment], disciples, great Brahmā kings, dragons, spirits, and all the [earthly] kings—gathered together solemnly.

At that time the World-honored One announced to the congregation: "The great quiescence (*parinirvāṇa*) has already been extensively expounded; and I have already described all the buddha lands in the ten directions for the bodhisattva Universal Expanse (Puguang). If anyone in the congregation has doubts, he should ask about them promptly, for the supreme jewel of the dharma will before long be obliterated." Upon hearing these words of the Buddha, the congregation wailed, sobbed, and choked with tears, unable to control themselves. Only those who achieved deliverance through realization did not give rise to sorrowful affection.

At that time there was a bodhisattva named Constant Donor (Changshi) in the congregation. Relying on the awesome spiritual power of the Buddha, he rose from his seat, joined his palms before the Buddha, and spoke these words: "There is something I would ask, but I am afraid it might break the heart of the Sage. I only wish that the Thus Come One would not consider [me to be] at fault." The Buddha told Constant Donor: "I, the Thus Come One, have already delivered [you from] the eight worldly concerns [such as gain and loss, and so on]; what do you need to worry about?" The bodhisattva Constant Donor replied to the Buddha: "World-honored One. After the Thus Come One leaves this world, no sentient being will ever again see the form-body of the Thus Come One, or hear the true dharma. In future generations, during the period of the semblance dharma, the good dharma will gradually decline and evil activities will flourish. Instruct all the sentient beings as to what meritorious virtues are the most excellent at such a time."

At that time, the World-honored One told the bodhisattva Constant Donor: "Excellent, excellent. Future sentient beings are extremely pitiable. Why so? Although all the sentient beings will arduously practice, they will not comprehend the right principle. [Therefore] although they increasingly add to their performance of meritorious [deeds], the fruit they obtain will be infinitesimal. Son of good family! In future generations, monks, nuns, laymen, laywomen, kings, vassals, merchants, householders, and brahman priests will slight my dharma and be disrespectful toward the three jewels, and [consequently] will be devoid of truthfulness. Although they perform numerous good deeds, [since their purpose is] to seek name and gain, or to surpass others, they will not have even one thought of renouncing the world.

"Son of good family! In the future, at the time of the semblance dharma age, immeasurable disasters and calamities and loathsome events [will occur]. What are they? All the clergy and laity will not be conscious about the rules of the dharma. [For example], a donor might arrange a gathering to invite monks, but he will dispatch men to guard the gates and protect the doorways in order to screen out [uninvited] monks and not allow them to join the gathering. If impoverished beggars wish to enter seeking food, [the guards] again will bar their passage and not allow [them to enter]. This sort of gathering merely wastes food and drink, and is devoid of the slightest portion of wholesomeness.

"Furthermore, there will be sentient beings who only wish for their own goodness, and do not edify other sentient beings; seeing others carry out good [deeds], they cannot rejoice, which would augment their small allotment [of goodness]. The merit of such people will be minute and inferior.

"Moreover, there will be sentient beings who will see other ancient reliquaries, images, and scriptures that are ramshackle or ruined, but will be unwilling to repair them. Then they will say: 'These were not built by my ancestors. What is the use of fixing them? I would much rather build a new one myself.' Son of good family! It is better that sentient beings repair old ones than build new ones—the merit [of the former] is extremely great.

"Moreover, there will be sentient beings who see other people congregate and carry out meritorious activities; but, merely seeking name and fame, they will exhaust family wealth and use it for donation. But when they see the impoverished and the orphaned, they will curse them and drive them away without offering even one iota of help. Sentient beings like this are called 'those whose performance of good deeds is perverted.' They are ignorant and insane in cultivating merit, and are called 'unjust producers of merit.' Such people are extremely pitiable, [for] though their use of wealth [for donation] is abundant, the merit they obtain will be extremely minute.

"Son of good family! I once told the congregation that even if a person, over an infinite number of lives, were to make offerings to all the buddhas of the ten directions, and all the bodhisattvas and disciples, it would not be as good as a person giving a mouthful of drink and food to an animal. The merit accruing therefrom is superior to the former by one million or ten million times, immeasurably and infinitely. Son of good family! The reason that I have expounded giving everywhere in the scriptures is because I aspired to have renunciates and householders cultivate thoughts of loving-kindness and compassion and give to the impoverished, the orphaned and the aged, and even to starving dogs. But none of my disciples understand my intention, and hence they give only to the field of reverence (*jingtian*) and do not give to the field of compassion (*beitian*). The field of reverence is the jewels of the Buddha, dharma, and monks. The field of compassion is the poor, the orphaned, the aged, and even ants. Of the two fields of merit, the field of compassion is more excellent.

"Son of good family! Even if, moreover, there were a person who, with his abundant wealth, carried out giving single-mindedly from the time of his birth until old age, [his charity still would] not be as good as a multitude of people, regardless of whether they are poor or rich, noble or lowly, clergy or laity, together exhorting and influencing one another to each take a little of their resources and accumulate them at one place and, as needed, donate them to the poor, the orphaned, the aged, and those suffering from malignant diseases and serious illnesses. The merit [thus acquired] will be extremely great. Even when [such people] do not donate [personally], the merit of giving is generated every moment, limitlessly. The merit [acquired] by practice of giving alone will be extremely minute [compared to this].

"Son of good family! In future generations, all my disciples will delight in fine clothes and dine on delicacies. They will covet profit and gain, which they will avariciously accumulate. They will not cultivate thoughts of compassion, but only harbor hatred. Seeing others do good, they will criticize and envy them, saying, 'This person pursues wrong livelihood and [his purpose in doing good is] to curry favor and to seek fame and gain.' If they see someone giving alms to the poor and to beggars, they again will be enraged and think, 'Why should a renunciate give alms? He only has to cultivate the practices of meditation and wisdom. What is the use of these hurly-burly, futile affairs?' Those who produce such thoughts are the retinue of the devil and at the end of their life they will fall into the great hell, where they will pass through progressive torments. Escaping hell, they will fall into the realm of hungry ghosts, where they will suffer great afflictions. Upon emerging from the hungry ghosts, they will be reborn as dogs for [as long as] five hundred births. Upon emerging from the [realm of] dogs, they will always be reborn among the poor or the lowly for five hundred generations, constantly afflicted by hunger and other sorts of sufferings. There will not be even a moment of satisfaction. Why is this? It is because, when they see others give, they do not rejoice.

"Son of good family! My attainment of buddhahood is all due to practicing giving since time immemorial, in order to succor impoverished and distressed sentient beings. All the buddhas of the ten directions also attained their buddhahood by [practicing] giving. This is why giving is placed at the head of the six perfections whenever I have expounded them in the scriptures.

"Son of good family! Suppose there is a person whose legs are both broken: even if he wants to walk a long way, he cannot go. Monks are also like this person. Even if they spend eons as innumerable as the sands of the Ganges practicing the five perfections, if they do not practice giving, they will not be able to arrive at the other shore of quiescence (*nirvāṇa*).

"Son of good family! If [a monk] does not practice giving, then his precepts are not genuine; if his precepts are not genuine, then he will have no compassionate thoughts; if he lacks compassion, then he cannot persevere; if he lacks perseverance, he will not exert spiritual effort; if he does not exert spiritual effort, he will not practice meditation; if he does not practice meditation, he will not posses wisdom; if he does not possess wisdom, he will constantly be taken advantage of by immeasurable intruding afflictions.

"Son of good family! This teaching of giving is what all the buddhas of the three times [past, present, and future] have each revered. For this reason, of the four means of conversion [giving, kind speech, benefiting others, emulation of religious training], the means through wealth is by far the most excellent.

"Son of good family! Sometimes I preach the observance of precepts, and at other times I preach perseverance. Or again sometimes I commend meditation, while at other times I commend wisdom. Or again sometimes I commend ascetic practices. Or again sometimes I commend contentment. Or again sometimes I commend disciples. Or again sometimes I commend bodhisattvas. In such a way [my teaching] varies in accordance with the differing potential [of people]. In the future, all the evil monks will not comprehend these intentions of mine and each will adhere to his own view, attacking one another [over who is] right or wrong, and thereby destroying my teaching.

"Moreover, all the evil monks will be in the lecture seat expounding the teachings of the scriptures. [But their exposition] will not penetrate to the profundity of my intentions, [and instead] they will grasp the meaning on the basis of the phraseology and defy the truth, the supreme and true dharma. [These evil monks] will incessantly utter self-praise: 'The purport of my exposition is in accordance with the intent of the Buddha. Other masters of the dharma deceive the clergy and laity.' One who speaks thus will eternally be submerged in the ocean of suffering.

"All the evil monks, seeing others practice meditation, will furthermore say, 'This person is ignorant like a tree stump. Without understanding the scriptures and treatises, what will he practice? What is the use of cultivating himself through religious practice?' One who says this will [be afflicted by] calamities eon after eon.

"All the evil monks will vilify each other for fame and gain. Some of the evil cultivate merit without relying on scriptures and treatises. Naturally, they follow their own views and take what is not as what is, unable to discriminate what is wrong from what is right. To anyone they face, be it clergy or laity, they say, 'We are competent to know what is right, and we are competent to see what is right.' You should be aware that such persons will in no time destroy my dharma.

"All the evil monks furthermore observe the monastic discipline, but they do not understand the profound import of the discipline (*vinaya*). They would say, 'The Buddha allowed meat eating in the discipline.' Son of good family! If I had expounded the idea of meat eating, disciples and self-enlightened ones (*pratyekabuddha*) as well as bodhisattvas on the lower stages [of spiritual progress] would have been perplexed, and common people and monks would have slandered [this idea] upon hearing it. Hence it is altogether inconceivable that the discipline allows meat eating.

"Son of good family! Since my first attainment of the path up to the present day, all those cases in which my disciples, here or there, accepted meat and ate it are those which common people saw as actually eating meat. Moreover, there are sentient beings who see all the monks seeming to eat meat. Moreover, there are sentient beings who know that when monks eat meat they enter deep within the immeasurable gate of counteractive techniques (*pratipakṣa*). Innumerable monks will eradicate subtle defilements; innumerable monks will eradicate average defilements; innumerable monks will eradicate serious defilements; innumerable monks will deliver sentient beings, whom they enable to enter the path to buddhahood. The edification of the Thus Come One is inconceivable, [for] ever since I attained buddhahood, none of my disciples has yet consumed or devoured the flesh of sentient beings.

"As for the cases in the discipline where I allowed meat eating, you certainly should know that this flesh was not born from the four great [elements of earth, water, fire, and wind]; it was not born from the womb, not from the egg, nor from moisture, nor spontaneously born; it was not united with consciousness, nor united with the life force. You should know that nowhere in this world is there such flesh.

"Son of good family! In the future, all evil monks, wherever they are, will expound the scriptures and monastic rules. [However,] they will understand the meaning [of the scriptures and so on] according to the phraseology, without being aware that the Thus Come One had concealed secrets [in those phrases]. Son of good family! There were no such cases where the Buddha allowed his disciples to eat the flesh of sentient beings after his appearance into the world. If [the disciples] ate meat, then why would they be named for great compassion?

"Son of good family! Each of the infinite number of people in today's assembly sees [the Thus Come One] differently. Some see the Thus Come One entering complete quiescence (*parinirvāṇa*); others see the Thus Come One dwelling [in this world] for an immeasurable number of eons. Some see the Thus Come One as six feet tall; others see him as small-bodied; others see him as big-bodied. Some see his enjoyment body sitting in the sea of the lotus-womb worlds, where he expounds the discourse on the mind-ground for one hundred trillion Śākyamuni buddhas. Some see his dharma body as equal to the expanse of space and without distinctions, marks, or hindrances, pervading the realm of the dharma. Some see this place, the sal grove, as all earth, pebbles, grass, trees, rocks, and walls; others see this place as immaculately embellished with gold, silver, and the seven precious jewels; some see this as the place where all the buddhas of all time periods wandered; some see this place as the inconceivable buddha realm, which is the true essence of the dharma.

"Son of good family! All the buddhas appearing in this world, and all their deeds, whether wandering or cenobitic, are completely separate from worldly marks; and yet they are not separate from the worldly dharma that reveals the true marks. What the Thus Come One expounded includes myriad teachings. And every character and every phrase he explicated, and every syllable he uttered, can catalyze each and every sentient being to obtain different [teachings] according to their varying types of births and varying types of basic natures. The special teachings of the Thus Come One are inconceivable: they are not something of which the disciples and self-enlightened ones are aware. The Thus Come One, utilizing his power of autonomy, edifies sentient beings surreptitiously or explicitly, depending on the capacity [of the individual]. During the period of the semblance dharma, all evil monks will not understand my intention; they will adhere to their own views and propagate the twelve divisions of the scriptures. [These evil monks] will grasp the meaning of [the scriptures] according to the phraseology and will offer definitive explanations. You ought to know that these people are reproved by the buddhas of the three time periods for quickly destroying my dharma.

"Son of good family! All the buddhas propounded the dharma by constantly relying on two truths. When they expound the dharma of mundane truth, it does not deviate from the ultimate truth, and they allude to the familiar in order to represent the abstract [as in the example of] using images to portray the obscure. Evil monks are unable to comprehend this intent and will slander and not believe it. They will grasp at the meaning according to the [surface] features, and pass through eons, receiving afflictions. These monks will also give themselves titles, saying, 'I am a master of the dharma,' 'I am a master of the discipline,' or 'I am a master of meditation.' It is precisely these three types of people who annihilate my dharma. These three types of people talk about each others' faults and criticize each other. These three types of people will enter hell like a shot arrow."

At that time the bodhisattva Constant Donor addressed the Buddha, saying, "World-honored One. When will such monks appear?"

"Son of good family! One thousand years after my extinction the evil dharma will gradually flourish. One thousand and one hundred years after [my extinction] all the evil monks and nuns will fill all of the Rose Apple Continent (Jambudvīpa; India). Not cultivating the virtues of the path, many will seek wealth, practicing only what is not the dharma. Many of them will accumulate the eight types of impure objects [slaves, gold, silver, grain, cattle, sheep, elephants, horses]. Even without possessing ten virtues himself [which allow him to perform novice ordinations], [a monk will] keep two novices, or before his ten years [after receiving full ordination] are completed, he will ordain novices [as fully ordained monks]. Because of these causes and conditions, all the laymen will come to slight and despise the three jewels. From that time onward, every one of the clergy and laity will vie with one another in constructing reliquaries and temples, which will entirely fill the world. Reliquaries, temples, and images will be everywhere: some in mountain groves and open fields, some at roadsides, some in alleys and in stinking, filthy, despicable places. [Even if reliquaries and so on are] falling into ruin, no one will repair them. At such a time, even if the clergy and laity construct reliquaries and temples and make offerings to the three jewels, they will not have reverence toward the three jewels. They will invite monks to stay at the monasteries without providing them with drink and food, clothing, bedding, and medicine. On the contrary, they will instead go ahead and borrow and beg [from the monks they invite] and devour the food belonging to the monastic community, without fearing the suffering of the three [evil] destinies [animals, hungry ghosts, hell denizens]. At such a time, all the lay followers, whether noble or lowly, will have no desire to offer any support whatsoever to the monks and will encroach upon [the monasteries], creating disorder without desiring to protect [monks]. People such as these will fall for an eternity into the three [evil] destinies.

"Son of good family! In future generations no civil officials will believe in merit and demerit, and they will steal away the monks' possessions by taxation. Or they will tax livestock and grain, and even worthless things. Or they will order about the serfs belonging to the three jewels. Or they will ride around on the cattle and horses of the three jewels. No civil official should either strike the serfs and animals of the three jewels, or receive reverence from the serfs of the three jewels. [If the civil officials do any of the above,] they will all reap calamitous faults. How is it possible that they should drive or strike [what belongs to the monastic community]? I declare to all civil officials! If you would avoid taxation at the place of the king of death [Yama rāja], then take care not to tax monks. If you wish to tax renunciates, then you will obtain immeasurable demerits.

"Son of good family! At such a time, if all the clergy and laity would perform meritorious activities, they should give to the orphaned, the aged, the impoverished, and those stricken with malignant illness. Moreover, they should repair broken and damaged reliquaries and temples, as well as all kinds of images. Do not question whether you have been given permission yourself or whether others have been given permission. [If] everyone performs repairs in accordance with their individual capacity, then the meritorious virtue of those people will be inconceivable, because they will repair just the old without futilely constructing anything new.

"Son of good family! Why in future generations will all the lay followers slight and look down upon the three jewels? It is precisely because monks and nuns do not conform to the dharma. While their bodies may be robed in the garment of the dharma, they belittle principle and trivialize conditionality. Some, furthermore, will engage in trade in the marketplace to support themselves. Some, furthermore, will tread the roads conducting business to seek profit. Some will engage in the trades of painters and artisans. Some will tell the fortunes of men and women, and divine various types of auspicious signs and evil omens. They will consume alcohol and under its influence become disorderly, sing, dance, or play music. Some will play chess. Some monks will preach the dharma obsequiously and with distortion in order to curry favor with the people. Some will recite magical spells to cure others' illnesses. Some will, furthermore, practice meditation, but since they cannot focus their minds, they will employ heterodox methods of meditation in order to divine fortunes. Some will practice acupuncture and moxibustion (moxa cautery) and various other types of medicine as a means of getting clothing and food. These are the causes and conditions which prompt the laity not to feel reverence [toward the three jewels]. The only exception will be bodhisattvas who benefit sentient beings."

Then the World-honored One told the bodhisattva Constant Donor: "Son of good family! In future generations, among the clergy and laity, there will be various wicked people who construct images of me or of bodhisattvas and sell them for profit in order to support themselves. All the clergy and laity, not knowing [what constitutes] merit and demerit, will purchase those images and make offerings to them. Both [those who sell and purchase] images incur demerit [as a result of which] they will be constantly sold by others for as long as five hundred generations.

"Son of good family! In future generations sentient beings will construct images that will lack all the characteristics [of a buddha or bodhisattva]. Some will be only the torso, some will have incomplete hands and feet, and the ears, nose, eyes, and mouth will all be incomplete; they will have only the rough appearance [of an image]. Some will build reliquaries without installing images. Even if there are broken reliquaries and damaged images, they still will not repair them. The demerit that such people incur will be immeasurable.

"Son of good family! In future generations, every monk, and so forth, will restrict his living accommodations to himself or his group in order to keep out all the monks of the four directions. They will impose food restrictions to have one meal in one day, ten days, or five, four or three days. When the lives of these monks come to an end, they will fall into hell [or be reborn] as hungry ghosts or animals, experiencing infinite suffering. Furthermore, there will be monks and even novices who consider the things of the monastic community to be their own and appropriate them as they please, eat them at wrong hours, or give them away to their friends. These monks and novices will never hear the dharma even though one thousand buddhas appear in this world; and they will remain in the three [evil] destinies without any opportunity to repent. If one dwells or sojourns with such people, all activities of the dharma, such as the fortnightly confessional, will be incorrectly performed, and will all inevitably incur demerit.

"Son of good family! Even if someone were to commit all of the four serious sins [sexual intercourse, grand theft, murder, lying about supernatural powers] and the five heinous acts [patricide, matricide, killing an enlightened person, injuring a buddha, fomenting schism in the order], he is easily succored and [his sins] can be repented. But if someone appropriates from the monastic community even one strand of hair or one grain of millet and eats it at wrong hours, or takes it and gives it away as he pleases, then he will be eternally submerged in the ocean of suffering without any chance of escape, or he will obtain all sorts of vexation in this world. If one dwells or sojourns with people like this, he will incur sins day and night.

"Son of good family! In future generations, there will be various lay followers who are not aware of merit and demerit. Then they will sell to others the buddha images, scriptures, banners, and [artificial] flowers made by their ancestors or by themselves, and use them to support their wives and children. These also should not be bought. At such a time, all the civil officials and those who have authority will arrest these people, and should punish them severely and banish them from the kingdom.

"Son of good family! In future generations, monks, nuns, laymen and laywomen, kings, vassals, empresses, and consorts will transgress prohibitions and precepts, knowing neither shame and dread nor repentance. These causes and conditions will defile the dharma and make it impure.

"Son of good family! In future generations, all the evil monks will be attached to their dwelling places, just like laypeople. They will guard their own lodgings and be unable to move once every three months according to [the changes] of the seasons. When they see other monks keep their robes and alms bowls at hand in their lodging and move when the ninety-day sojourning period is completed, all these evil monks will say in unison, 'These monks have wavering intentions and are vexed with various duties; they have gone crazy and lost their minds. [That is why] they move around so often.' Those who speak in this manner will incur immeasurable demerits.

"Son of good family! In future generations when all types of evil have arisen, all the clergy and laity should cultivate and train themselves in great loving-kindness and great compassion. Patiently accepting the vexation of others, one should think, 'Since time immemorial, all sentient beings have been my father and mother; since time immemorial, all sentient beings have been my brother, sister, wife, children, and relatives. This being the case, I will have loving-kindness and compassion toward all sentient beings, whom I will succor according to my ability. If I see beings who are suffering, I will devise various contrivances [in order to save them], without concern for my own body and life.

"At such a time, kings, vassals, mayors, village heads, influential merchants, brahman priests, and powerful monks should admonish them so as to help save them from backsliding. With the aid of these influences, one will never allow evil people to create difficulties, or allow evil people to appropriate and snatch away one's possessions. The merit of people who aid [others] in this manner can never be fully described.

"At such a time, the merit of giving compassionately to the impoverished, the orphaned, the aged, all those in distress, and even to ants, will be most excellent. Son of good family! If I were to expound comprehensively the merit and virtue of giving to orphans, the impoverished, and those afflicted by illness, then [it would take] inexhaustible eons and still not be completed. As the time for my quiescence has arrived, I have expounded it for you in brief."

At that time, all the congregation heard the Buddha describe the various calamities [that are to occur] in future generations, at the end of the semblance-dharma period. [Upon hearing this,] their body hair stood on end and they cried and wailed, unable to control themselves. The Buddha told the congregation: "Stop! Do not lament. It is the fixed principle of the world that good necessarily contains evil and prosperity necessarily involves decline."

The Buddha, furthermore, told the bodhisattva Constant Donor: "Let us put this matter aside. By what marks do you observe the Thus Come One; by what marks do you observe a sentient being?" The bodhisattva Constant Donor addressed the Buddha: "World-honored One. I observe that the Thus Come One does not come from the past, does not arrive at the other shore [of enlightenment], and does not dwell in between. He is neither existing nor nonexisting, neither appearing nor disappearing, neither formed nor formless, neither conditioned nor unconditioned, neither permanent nor transitory, neither having outflows nor free from outflows. He is equal to empty space, and commensurate with the nature of the dharma. We do not see the Thus Come One expound a single phrase of the dharma from his first attainment of the path until his quiescence, or anytime in between. However, all sentient beings see [him] appear and disappear to expound the dharma in order to succor people. The realm of the Thus Come One is inconceivable, uncognizable through consciousness, unknowable through knowledge. He transcends the three times, and yet is not separate from the three times. It is only the Thus Come One, who has awakened himself to this dharma. I observe the Thus Come One in this manner.

"World-honored One. I now observe the [material] marks of four great elements of all sentient beings. They are like clouds in the sky, like heat waves in the hot season, like a heavenly musician's city, like a phantom, like a mirage, like a hamlet in the sky, like a reflection in a mirror, like the moon in water, like an echo in an empty valley. Feelings, perception, volition, and consciousness are all like this. World-honored One. The [mental] marks of sentient beings are inconceivable. They are not something that the disciples, the self-enlightened ones, or the bodhisattvas in the lower stages [of spiritual advancement] can know. World-honored One. The marks of sentient beings neither come nor go, are neither existent nor nonexistent, are neither internal nor external, neither come from somewhere nor go anywhere. And yet [sentient beings] are revolving in perpetual transmigration, incurring afflictions in vain.

"Since time immemorial, sentient beings have been deeply attached to the view that the self exists; and due to their attachment to the self, they compound their craving, [according to] the dharma of the twelvefold chain of dependent origination. Thus, they incur afflictions unceasingly throughout the long night [of transmigration]. The marks of sentient beings are intrinsically ethereal. On account of these causes and conditions, great compassion arises in the bodhisattvas.

"World-honored One. All the good and evil actions of all sentient beings are merely produced by the one mind; they are not residual phenomena. These are the marks of sentient beings as I observe them."

At that time, the Buddha addressed the bodhisattva Constant Donor: "Excellent, excellent. You have expounded the dharma joyfully. The explanation you have now given would be approved of by all the buddhas. The bodhisattva who practices the four means of conversion and the six perfections [giving, morality, patience, energy, meditation, and wisdom] should observe the marks of sentient beings in such a way.

"Son of good family! When a bodhisattva practices giving, he does not observe [whether the recipient is] a field of merit or not a field of merit; if he sees poor and suffering sentient beings, then he will give to all of them. When practicing giving, one should undertake the following contemplation: 'I see neither recipient, nor donor, nor the thing given. These three matters are all nonsubstantial, [and hence I am] equanimous and nonattached toward them.' Why so? [It is because] all elements of reality are devoid of either self or anything belonging to a self. When [a bodhisattva] practices giving, he neither is hopeful for present rewards nor hopeful for the future pleasures [contingent on rebirth among] humans or gods. [A bodhisattva] seeks great enlightenment only for sentient beings. Because he wishes to comfort and gladden incalculable sentient beings, he practices giving. Because he aspires to embrace all evil sentient beings and cause them to abide in wholesome phenomena, he practices giving. He furthermore makes this observation: 'The marks of the realm of enlightenment and the marks of the realm of sentient beings are both ethereal.' He relies on words and letters and consequently delivers sentient beings, and attains enlightenment. [But] in the true dharma, there is neither attainment nor realization.

"Son of good family! It is like a person who dreams about various events at night. He might dream that his own body is imprisoned by officials, undergoing all sorts of torment. He suffers great vexation, and then later obtains liberation. He again finds himself dreaming that he has become the prince of a great state, and now has power and autonomy and enjoys great pleasure. Then he thinks in his dream, 'I formerly suffered such afflictions but now I am free, enjoying great pleasure.' Having thought this, he suddenly wakes from his sleep, and does not know where the events of suffering and pleasure are. Just as the events in a dream neither exist nor do not exist, so it is for all the elements of reality. This sort of contemplation is called 'right contemplation.'"

When [the Buddha] expounded this teaching, immeasurable numbers of bodhisattvas attained the stage of buddhahood; immeasurable numbers of bodhisattvas attained the stage of imminent buddhahood; immeasurable numbers of bodhisattvas, according to what they had cultivated, each attained excellent progress; immeasurable numbers of humans and gods attained the four stages of fruition; immeasurable numbers of disciples entered the bodhisattva stage; immeasurable numbers of various species of sentient beings aroused the thought of enlightenment.

"Son of good family! If in future generations the four types of disciples are able to hear this scripture, then they will have thoughts of joy. The meritorious virtues they obtain will be immeasurable and boundless."

The Buddha told Ānanda and all the congregation: "Receive and retain well [this scripture], and be prudent that it not be lost and forgotten. This scripture is entitled *Resolving Doubts Concerning the Semblance Dharma* and is also entitled *The Salvation of the Widowed and Orphaned.* Receive and retain it."

At that time, having heard the exposition of the Buddha, the great congregation received it wholeheartedly and reverently paid respects and withdrew. All together they solemnly prepared the implements for [the Buddha's] cremation. Their grief shook heaven and earth.

—14—

Auspicious Things

Charles Hallisey

Theravāda Buddhism, like other Buddhist traditions, has an extensive body of authoritative literature and, like participants in other religious traditions with large scriptural and commentarial canons, Theravādins have frequently created functional canons within the canon. The *Maṅgalasūtraya* (Pāli *Maṅgalasutta*) or *The Scripture about Auspicious Things* is a text that is found in many of these canons within the canon. It is one of the most popular and influential texts throughout the Theravāda Buddhist world, from Sri Lanka to Southeast Asia, although it might appear, at first glance, to be a very slight text. In length, it is only twelve verses accompanied by a brief introduction, and its contents approximate a common-sense morality found in many cultures. But some indication of the significance that Theravāda Buddhists have seen in its verses can be gathered from numerous commentaries that have been written on this text over the centuries. One of the largest of these, *The Lamp on the Meanings of Auspiciousness (Maṅgalatthadīpanī)* was composed in northern Thailand in the sixteenth century and is over five hundred pages long; it continues to provide a core to monastic education in contemporary Thailand. Of more modest length is the selection presented here, a translation of a thirteenth-century commentary on the *Maṅgalasutta* found in a Sri Lankan story-collection known as *The Jewels of the Doctrine (Saddharmaratnāvaliya)*.

Before introducing the translated text, we should first look briefly at the *Maṅgalasutta* itself. It is found in two places in the Pāli canon (*Khuddaka Paṭha* 2 and *Suttanipāta* 46), but it does not seem to be among the oldest strata of Buddhist literature, and a preoccupation with it seems to be peculiar to the Theravāda; the *Maṅgalasutta* is also included in the collection of texts that are chanted as part of the protective rituals performed by Buddhist monks to ward off misfortunes. The verses are as follows:

1. Many gods and humans, desiring well-being, have thought
   about auspiciousness. Tell what is the highest auspiciousness.

2. Not to associate with fools, to associate with the wise,
to worship those worthy of worship—that is the highest auspiciousness.
3. To live in a suitable place and to have done good deeds before,
having a proper goal for oneself—that is the highest auspiciousness.
4. Learning, craftsmanship, and being well-trained in discipline,
being well-spoken—that is the highest auspiciousness.
5. Care for mother and father, supporting wife and children,
and spheres of work that bring no conflict—that is the highest auspiciousness.
6. Generosity, morality, helping of relatives, and
doing actions that are blameless—that is the highest auspiciousness.
7. Ceasing and refraining from evil, abstaining from intoxicants,
diligence in morality—that is the highest auspiciousness.
8. Respect, humility, contentment, gratitude,
listening to the truth (*dharma*) at the proper time—
that is the highest auspiciousness.
9. Patience, obedience, seeing ascetics, and
timely discussions of the truth—that is the highest auspiciousness.
10. Ascetic practice, the religious life, seeing the four noble truths,
and the realization of perfect peace (*nirvāṇa*)—that is the highest auspiciousness.
11. If someone's mind is sorrowless, stainless, secure, and does not shake
when touched by the things of the world—that is the highest auspiciousness.
12. Having acted like this, unconquered everywhere,
they go to well-being everywhere—for them, this is the highest auspiciousness.

Maṅgala is a concept found in many Indian religions, including Hinduism and Jainism, but it is a difficult word to translate into English, there being no close conceptual equivalent or even analogue. For lack of a better term and following the example of many others, I have translated it as "auspicious," or "auspiciousness," terms that in English can be traced back to the ancient Roman practice of interpreting omens provided by birds. But it is worth noting that there is a wide range of possible translations of *maṅgala:* luck, fortune, happiness, prosperity, welfare, auspiciousness, good omen, whatever conduces to an auspicious issue, blessing, and in some contexts, lucky object, amulet, solemn ceremony, festival, and especially marriage. In the passage presented here, we can see that questions about the meaning of the word *maṅgala* are not only a problem for the translator. The introduction sets the stage for the Buddha's preaching of this sūtra by explaining that it was occasioned by a long discussion among gods and humans about what exactly maṅgala is. It also connects the discussion of maṅgala to the contemporary context of the audience insofar as it mentions various types of good and bad omens, some of which are still noted by many Buddhists in Sri Lanka. This introduction thus implicitly acknowledges the diversity of religious practice among Buddhists in local contexts and gives us an example of how some practices are made to appear non-Buddhist by a Buddhist reinterpretation: just as the Buddha used the model of brahmanical practices to instruct about Buddhist ethics (the *Advice to Sigāla,* for example, reinterprets Vedic worship of the directions in terms of the ethical relations between people; see *The Dīgha Nikāya,* edited by J.E. Carpenter [London: Pali Text Society, 1960], vol. 3, pp. 180–93.), so here the *Maṅgalasutta* "applies" the assumptions and imagery of auspiciousness to ethical behavior to make broader points about Buddhist practice.

These broader points represent part of the significance of the *Maṅgalasutta.* It is best read not as a Buddhist perspective on auspiciousness, but as a comprehensive vision of the Buddhist religious life. In this, the *Maṅgalasutta* might be compared and contrasted with better known schema of Buddhist practice, such as the noble eightfold path described in the four noble truths, or the structuring of the Buddhist life according to morality, meditation, and wisdom, as the fifth-century commentator Buddhaghosa did in his *summa* of Theravādin thought, the *Path of Purification (Visuddhimagga).* It could also be compared and contrasted with the vision of the Buddhist life as a gradual path, such as is found in *The Advice to Layman Tuṇḍila.* The concept of maṅgala provides a thematic framework for organizing various Buddhist values as well as a consistent rationale for the performance of diverse Buddhist practices.

The commentaries on the *Maṅgalasutta* are a locus for Theravādin thought about what might be called social ethics, an aspect of Buddhist life that is often lost in scholarship because of an overemphasis on the individualism of a renouncer's life. We can see here an appealing vision of a model, if still imperfect, society, one in which care for others is part and parcel of everyday life: Buddhist values and practices of every sort are portrayed as omens of the good life. But we also see shadows of a harsher "real" world, since this text clearly assumes a world of agriculture and labor, of subsistence and hard work; this is a text that belongs to the largely rural peasant societies in which traditional Theravāda thrived for centuries. It is often said that early Buddhism appealed especially to city- and town-dwellers who suffered from a spiritual malaise and were disenchanted with the wealth displayed in city and town life. This hardly seems to be the audience of this commentary of the *Maṅgalasutta.* From a reference to hands that could become like wish-fulfilling creepers and fulfill every desire, for example, we might conclude that it belonged to a world that knew poverty all too well, a world where people too often had only dry cakes made from the husks of rice to eat.

This closeness to the world of its audience is connected to choice of language. Commentaries on the *Maṅgalasutta* have been composed in both Pāli, a learned international language, and in various vernaculars. The text translated here is from Sinhala, one of the vernacular languages used in Sri Lanka, although some verses remain in Pāli. As another translator of the *Saddharmaratnāvaliya* has said, this text "is written in an easy flowing, colorful prose, in the half-colloquial, half-literary language used by Buddhist monks in their sermons. The speaking voice and narrative persona of the author/translator cuts into the text constantly, revealing his humanity and humor, . . . and above all the intellectual and psychological subtlety with which he explores and illuminates abstract elements of Buddhist doctrine, relating them to the everyday needs and actions of ordinary people" (Ranjini Obeyesekere, *Jewels of the Doctrine*, xiii). We might keep in mind, then, that men and women have learned how to be Buddhists over the centuries through texts like this one, vernacular texts that present, often quite creatively, ideas found in canonical and commentarial literature written in Pāli.

The translation below is from Dharmasena, *Saddharmaratnāvaliya* (Colombo: Sri Lanka Pracina Bhasopakara Samagama, 1986), vol. 2, 795–800 and 827–33, with abridgments.

Further Reading

A portion of *Saddharmaratnāvaliya* has been translated by Ranjini Obeyesekere; see Dharmasena Thera, *Jewels of the Doctrine,* translated by Ranjini Obeyesekere (Albany: State University of New York Press, 1991). For a series of essays discussing maṅgala in Indian religions, see *Purity and Auspiciousness in Indian Society,* edited by John Carman and Frédérique Marglin (Leiden: E. J. Brill, 1985).

The Commentary of the Scripture on Auspicious Things

Furthermore, in order to show what should be done in order to be established in what is good and what should be given up to stay away from what is wrong, we will tell stories from texts like *The Commentary on the Scripture about Auspicious Things (Maṅgalasūtra Aṭuvā).*

How do they go?

In the famous cities of the Rose-Apple Island [Dambadiva or Jambudvīpa, that is, India] and in the various provinces and territories, wealthy people would gather in prosperous times and pay for the recitation of stories which actually are a hindrance to the attainment of heaven and liberation, such as the story of Rāma and Sītā [this story is probably best known from the version in the *Rāmāyaṇa*], stories that have nothing to do with the right which is conducive to the pleasant. These stories were so long that they could not be finished in even four months' time.

One day, a certain person among those coming together to hear those stories raised the question, "what is it that is called an auspicious thing (*maṅgala*)?" when he heard people say that they were going to something auspicious. This question, once raised, was taken up by the storytellers, in between their recitations, as it happened to be a very useful topic. Now one of those there was not content to say that auspicious things are those which are conducive to well-being, nor was he willing to ask someone who actually knew, but rather announced, "I know about auspicious things." He went on, and said that an auspicious thing was something that could be seen, as when someone in this world wakes up and sees a young bird, or a woodapple stalk, or a pregnant woman, or infants decorated with necklaces and bangles, or pots full of water, or a fresh sheatfish, or a thoroughbred horse, or a chariot drawn by a thoroughbred horse, or a brahman.

Those people who knew only what they heard from him agreed, but others did not. They began to argue with the one who said that an auspicious thing is something seen: "The eye sees both the good and the bad. If what is auspicious is something seen by the eye, then whatever is seen would be auspicious. It would not be correct to say that. We, however, know what is auspicious." They said that an auspicious thing is something heard by the ear, as when someone wakes up and hears a statement like, "They increase," "They should increase," "He who is filled with," "O happy one," "O prosperity," "May prosperity increase," "Today there is a good conjunction of the stars," or "The day is good." Some people agreed with what they said. Others, not knowing themselves what is auspicious, disagreed. They started arguing, saying, "The ear hears both the good and the bad. If what is auspicious is something heard, it looks as if there is no utterance in this world which is inauspicious."

When things are discussed only for the sake of argument, one's ignorance is never apparent and the only thing that is clear is one's own bungling desires. Thus others said, "We know what is auspicious. An auspicious thing is something smelled, as when someone awakes and smells the scent of sandalwood in the nose." And others said that if one were to bite a fresh toothstick, the taste that is felt on the tongue is auspicious. Still others thought touch was auspicious, as when one handles the earth, or blue paddy, or freshly reaped wheat, or a mound of sesame seed, or the flowers of the ironwood tree, or the fruits of the jackfruit tree.

Some people accepted that smell, taste, and touch were auspicious, but others said, "What is this? If the nose smelled only good fragrance, if the tongue knew only good tastes, if everything the body touched felt good, then what you say would be correct. But the nose smells both the good and the bad and it is the same with the tongue and the body. If everything that is smelled, tasted, or touched is auspicious, why do you wrinkle your nose at a bad smell or pucker your mouth on a bitter thing? Why do you die when you eat poison? Why do you say when you carry a stone or a tree trunk that your back aches and that your sides hurt?" Thus they argued with those who said that what is auspicious is something sensed, saying that there is no justification for saying this.

In the end, there was no one who could back up what she or he said with proper proof, and since each appeared to know what he or she was talking about, there was nothing that they could do but argue with each other. In due course, this discussion about what is auspicious spread throughout the Rose-Apple Island. All the people of the continent gathered in groups and began to think, "What is really auspicious?" The gods who are guardians to the people began to think about this in their own way too. Then, the tree spirits who were friendly to these deities, their friends among the celestial deities, and the gods in heavens began to ask about auspicious things, and soon the beings throughout the three worlds were talking about what is really auspicious.

In just the same way that this argument began in the Rose-Apple Island, so it continued throughout all the ten thousand world systems: there were different opinions about what is auspicious but no agreement about fact. Leaving aside those who had seen nirvāṇa, all the gods and humans divided into three factions, with one group sure that what is auspicious is something seen, another sure that it is something heard, and the third sure that it is something sensed. But they stayed divided into factions because they were not able to convince each other, and thus this brouhaha continued without resolution for twelve long years.

Then the gods, still not able to agree, said to one another, "O happy ones, just as there is a head for those in a household, and a chief for the residents of a village, and a king for the inhabitants of a country, so Śakra, king of the gods, is the leader of the deities in our divine world. It would be good to inform him about this." Putting on their finest garments and ornaments, they went before him as he was seated on his red throne and honored him. "Lord, we have something to tell you about. There has been a great furor about what is auspicious, and since we do not know if what is auspicious is something seen, heard, or otherwise sensed, it would be good if you would tell us which it is."

Since Śakra was himself intelligent, he asked where the argument had started, and when he heard that it was in the human world, he asked where the Buddha was living and whether anyone had asked him about this. "Why should we try to weigh something by hand when scales are right here? What do I know, that this question should be saved for me when no one has asked the Buddha, who is auspicious himself? He is auspicious because both worldly and transcendent prosperity are given to those who merely recollect his qualities—not to mention what happens for those who see him repeatedly, who worship him, and give offerings to him. He alone is fit to proclaim what is auspicious. All of you are like those who blow on fireflies to start a flame when there is already a burning fire nearby. If it is really necessary to know what is auspicious, then you should go to the Buddha."

Śakra then ordered a particular deity to ask the Buddha about this, because it would be impossible for all of the gods to ask together. That son of a god, bedecked with ornaments suitable to the occasion and shining like a flash of lightening, went to the Devram Monastery [the Jetavana Monastery in Śrāvastī, which was built for the Buddha by Anāthapiṇḍika] in the middle of the night, accompanied by all the gods of the ten thousand worlds who had gathered in the human world in order to hear the Buddha talk about what are auspicious things; these deities had all taken on visible forms, but there were so many that ten, twenty, thirty, forty, fifty, seventy, or eighty had to stand on the tip of a hair. This deity then said to the Buddha, "You who are a god greater than all the gods assembled here, a Brahmā greater than all Brahmās, I invite you, on their behalf. It would be good if you would tell us what is auspicious so that there might be some concurrence among humans and gods on this matter."

The noble Buddha then said, "O divine friend, those three groups gave their opinion about what is something auspicious just because they were asked, and not because they had any evidence or basis for what they said. Something is called auspicious when it is a cause for welfare in this world or the next. You have asked for one thing that is auspicious, but I will tell you thirty-eight."

So the Buddha began to speak first of what should not be done before what should be done: "Not associating with foolish, ignorant people is an auspicious thing. Friend, if someone were to do what a fool does, or say what a fool says, or think what a fool thinks, then that one will receive blame in this world, and even if they are full of regret later, they still destroy their prospects for the next world.

"But how is not associating with fools something that is auspicious? Because not associating with them is a means to welfare in this world and the next. What is the evil that results from associating with them? Just as the leaf that covers putrid meat becomes putrid, so a person possessing noble ideas of any kind eventually becomes evil by associating with fools. Moreover, as a fear of water only comes from water, not fire, and a fear of fire does not come from water, there is no fear of wise ones except for that which has ignorant people as its cause. Therefore, associating with ignorant people is evil. On account of associating with disgraceful naked ascetics like Pūraṇa Kāśyapa [a teacher who was the contemporary of the Buddha and is said to have taught a doctrine that denied karma and the fruits of actions], eighty thousand kings were born in hell. And King Ajātaśatru, who did merit and aspired to become enlightened, was deprived of seeing perfect peace (*nirvāṇa*) because of his association with Devadatta [Prince Ajātaśatru helped Devadatta in several of the latter's attempts to kill the Buddha].

"Furthermore, the future Buddha, when he was born as Akīrti, received a boon from Śakra because his fame had spread so widely: 'As there is no profit from seeing them, may there be no seeing of fools; and because there is no use in hearing about them, may I hear nothing about fools; having come together with them, may I not live with fools even for a moment; forget about actually living together with fools, may there not even be talk of seeing them.' Because he obtained that boon, he did not associate with fools, and because it was a means to prosperity in both this world and the next, it is the highest auspicious thing. [This refers to the story found at *Jātaka* IV.236. Akitti, the Pāli form of Akīrti, gave away all his wealth and retired to the forest. When gifts were brought to him as homage to his virtue, he sought obscurity and lived alone eating leaves. Because of his asceticism, Śakra's throne became hot, and Śakra gave him a number of boons, including one that Śakra should not visit him any more and disturb his asceticism.]

"Now if someone were to do just one thing, it should be just worshiping enlightened ones, silent enlightened ones, and disciples. Such beings do not do anything unless it increases merit and do not consciously do things like taking life; if they speak, they do not say lies, but only truth or something which is righteous, or an admonition; and they do not think anything that increases evil, but only things that increase merit. Associating with buddhas, silent buddhas, and disciples is the highest auspicious thing because it increases prosperity in both this world and the next. [The word for association here, *bhajana,* can also mean worshiping or serving, and it has been translated that way in the first sentence of this paragraph. It is worth noting that it is from the same verbal root as *bhakti,* a ubiquitous term in Indian religions that is commonly, if somewhat misleadingly, translated as "devotion."]

"The Buddha is supreme among those who are wise and those who have associated with him have all attained prosperity. Among those who have associated with him, there are many who have realized perfect peace (*nirvāna*), including the eighty great disciples, such as Śāriputra and Maudgalyāyana. Eighty times eighty thousand have been born in heavenly worlds. Therefore association with intelligent people is auspicious because it leads to one's own benefit.

"The homage paid to a buddha, silent buddha, or to disciples, all of whom should be worshiped [*pidi,* a Sinhala derivative of *pūjā*] is auspicious because it leads to both worldly and transcendent benefits. This can be seen in the story of the flower maker Sumana, who offered eight quarts of jasmine flowers to the Buddha in eight handfuls. As a result of that, he did not go to the four evil states but enjoyed heavenly pleasures and comforts in the human world, not for eight hours, or eight days, or eight months, or eight years, or eight centuries, or eight millennia, but for one hundred thousand eons. At the end of this he became the silent buddha Sumana. Further evidence is found in our great future buddha when he was born as the brahman Śaṅkha. On account of a slight offering to the shrine of a silent buddha, he received the homage of beings from the nāga world [nāgas are a class of deity in the traditional Buddhist cosmology] to the Brahmā world when he himself became enlightened, as is described in the text on the ascent of the Ganges. [A reference to the account of the Buddha's visit to Vaiśālī, where he preached the *Ratana* (Jewel) *Discourse* and ended a famine and plague. The commentary on this text describes the praise that the Buddha received when he returned to Rājagṛha along the Ganges.]

"Living in an appropriate place is auspicious because it is conducive to worldly and transcendent benefits. An appropriate place is some place like the Middle Country [north India] if the four-fold Buddhist community [renunciant men, renunciant women, laymen, and laywomen] is living there, and if occasions for the ten meritorious practices are found there, and if the word of the Buddha in the form of the Buddhist canon is there. Righteous universal monarchs, silent buddhas, and worthy ones are all born in the Middle Country. When they are alive, people adhere to admonitions and thus receive worldly comforts, but when buddhas are alive, they get both worldly and transcendent comforts. Therefore living in such a place at such a time is auspicious.

"The prior accumulation of merit with respect to buddhas, and so on, which brings one to the presence of buddhas again and again, is auspicious because it leads to worldly and transcendent comforts.

"If a person were to observe at least the five precepts—or perhaps more—while considering the bad results that come from not observing the five precepts for just a brief span of time, even one as brief as the time it takes for a cobweb to singe, it is auspicious because observing the precepts for even so brief a time leads to endless heavenly comforts.

"If one were to have faith, thinking that if one were to be devoid of faith one would not get a harvest of worldly and transcendent benefits from the karmic seed of the good deeds, just as rice will not grow on the surface of a rock, that would be auspicious because faith of that kind is conducive to merit, as was the case with Anāthapiṇḍika and Viśākhā. [These two lay disciples of the Buddha, one male, the other female, were unparalleled in the care which they gave to the Buddha and the monastic order.]

"It is also auspicious to be generous. The good deed of giving cannot be accomplished by being miserly, but only by being generous. Not only the good deed of giving, but other meritorious actions are accomplished by generosity. This can be understood by reflecting on the stories of Adattapūrvaka and Miserly Kauśika. [These two are famous for their miserliness; Adattapūrvaka's name means "Never Gave."]

"Being learned is auspicious, as can be seen in the case of the great elder Kautthila who, living in the time of seven different buddhas, practiced the religious life near them and effortlessly attained enlightenment in the dispensation of our Buddha.

"Learning any craft is auspicious because it is conducive to benefit in this world and the next, both for oneself and for others, provided that that craft is not harmful in this world or the next. Benign crafts include astrology for householders and the sewing of robes, which is appropriate for renouncers.

"If a layperson were to observe the five precepts, such as abstaining from taking life, and were to give alms and pay homage, or if a renouncer were to be established in the four pure moralities [the precepts for fully ordained men, fully ordained women, novices, and laypeople], it would be auspicious because it is supportive of worldly and transcendent benefit.

"Uttering words that are not false, not slanderous, not coarse, not surly, and not frivolous is auspicious because it is conducive to welfare in this world and the next. Preaching sermons to others with selfless thoughts is also auspicious, and it is conducive to the attainment of perfect peace for the people who preach the doctrine.

"Attending to parents by bathing them, washing their hair, giving them food and drink is auspicious because such actions bring benefits in this world and the next. Parents are of immense help to the children that they have brought forth, as when children return after playing outside and parents brush the sand from their bodies, kiss them on the heads, and thus shower them with love. This love can never be compensated even if one were to carry one's parents on the shoulders without putting them down for a hundred or a thousand years.

"If a man were to be respectful to his wife and children, and not run them down, and not attempt to override them, and were to give them wealth and make ornaments for them—if he were to treat them in this manner, then the wife of such a person would look after the household affairs carefully, and his children would be very attached to him. The servants in such a house would be loyal and faithful and not ignore the words of the master; they would protect whatever wealth has been earned against destruction and they would be diligent and energetic in all matters. Those who treat their wife and children well receive homage even from the king of the gods, since he said:

> O Mātali, I worship those people who make merit as householders,
> Pious lay disciples who look after their family in a righteous manner.
>
> *Saṃyutta nikāya,* edited by L. Feer
> (London: Pali Text Society, 1991), vol. 1, p. 234.

Treating one's wife and children well is thus auspicious.

"Being engaged in such pursuits as plowing or sowing is auspicious because it earns wealth and grain, but they should be pursued in a manner that avoids procrastination, or delay, or carelessness, or laziness. Knowing that one should engage in such actions at appropriate times, one should do so without being too lazy, since it has been said:

> The person who does appropriate action and bears the burden of work,
> Who does the work carefully, he enjoys wealth.
>
> *Suttanipāta,* edited by Dines Anderson and Helmer Smith
> (London: Pali Text Society, 1990), verse 187.

and

> Whoever's habit is to sleep by day and is seen to rise by night,
> And constantly gets drunk with wine is not fit to keep a house.
> "Too cold! Too hot! Too late!" they say;
> Saying these things, not concentrating
> On work, thus his prosperity is destroyed.
> If one were to do whatever a man should do
> Without considering cold or heat as more than straws,
> He is not separated from happiness.
>
> *Dīgha nikāya,* vol. 3, p. 185; cf. *Theragāthā,* edited by H. Oldenberg
> (London: Pali Text Society, 1966), Verses 231–32.

and

> To the one who collects wealth, acting like a bee,
> Wealth accumulates just as an anthill gradually grows.
>
> *Dīgha nikāya,* vol. 3, p. 188.

"Giving away alms as well as believing in karma and its fruits are auspicious because they are conducive to benefits in this world and the next, because even the daughters of a garland maker were able to achieve the rank of a queen because they gave cakes made from rice bran. Moreover, people who only plucked leaves to wash a monk's bowl were reborn as tree-dwelling deities. Then there are those who merely pointed the way to a house where alms were being given, but consequently achieved everything that they desired, their hands becoming like wish-fulfilling creepers in heaven.

"Being engaged in the ten meritorious deeds, such as giving alms, being moral and keeping the precepts, meditating, transferring merit, rejoicing in the merit of others, preaching sermons, listening to sermons—all these are auspicious because they are conducive to birth in heaven. [In addition to the seven actions mentioned here, giving service, showing respect, and right beliefs are also included in the list of ten meritorious deeds.]

"Treating relatives who have come to visit well, as far as one is capable, is auspicious because it is conducive to welfare in this world and the next. Relatives are those to whom one is related up to seven generations back on one's mother's and father's sides. One should give rice, clothes, and so forth to relatives who come because they are destitute.

"Observing the eight precepts without exception on the first day of each phase of the moon, attending upon one's teachers and the elders in one's family and, for the sake of merit, planting flower gardens, building ponds, making parks, erecting waystations [this refers to a platform or support where someone carrying a load on the back or shoulders can put it down for a rest without having to place the burden on the ground], shelters, and bridges, and so on, all this is auspicious because it is beneficial in this world and the next.

"Refraining from committing wrong acts, thinking in one's mind that this is not in keeping with our family's position, with our place in society, and consequently not doing an evil deed, saying, 'From today onward, I will not do a thing of this nature'; all this is auspicious because it has benefits in this world and the next.

"Abstention from intoxicating drinks is auspicious because it is beneficial in this life and the next. Those who drink cannot understand what is good or bad, and they do not acknowledge their own parents or elders in their family or even buddhas, silent buddhas, and worthy ones. They go about now as if they were insane, and in their next birth, they suffer in horrible conditions.

"Not being indolent when it comes to doing meritorious deeds is auspicious because it brings perfect peace without delay. Thus one should do any meritorious deed well, and one should do it consistently, with effort and mindfulness and without being lazy.

"Paying respect to those who deserve respect is auspicious. If one were to pay respect to those worthy of respect and high esteem, such as buddhas, silent buddhas, and worthy ones, or parents, aunts, uncles, elder brothers and sisters, then one will be born in a heavenly world, enjoying great comfort, and when one is born among humans, then one will be born only in a noble family. In this way, paying respect is a cause for one's own improvement.

"Always being of a humble disposition is auspicious. However high a position one might have because of good qualities and intelligence, if because of one's modest nature one were to be like a doormat used for rubbing feet, being subservient to everyone, such conduct is conducive to qualities like fame, and so on. Furthermore, if a monk were to subsist on whatever he gets by way of the four requisites—namely, robes, food, dwellings, and medicine—whether they be good or bad, he should not expect anything better. If he were ill and could not wear heavy robes, partake of rough food, lie down in a dwelling because he found it uncomfortable, or use coarse medicines, he should give all these to his companions and use whatever they give in return. If he were to get very fine robes, food, dwellings, and medicine, he should give them to aged companions in celibacy and should be content with a robe from a dust heap, food from begging, the feet of trees or open space, and, by way of medicine, cow's urine or yellow myrobalan. The twelvefold noble contentment that exists in this manner, the destruction of the inclination to want each particular thing one sees, the destruction of the desire to have many things, and the ending of the pretension of having qualities that one doesn't—this twelvefold contentment and this threefold destruction is auspicious because it is conducive to the attainment of good qualities.

"Remembering the help that others gave you, whether it be big or little, and helping them in return is auspicious because through these grateful actions, one engages in meritorious deeds. The Buddha has said that those who help others and those who bear in mind the help done to them are rare indeed.

"Listening to sermons is auspicious because it is at the root of all meritorious deeds. One should listen to sermons at those times when one's mind is filled with arrogance, and if one cannot do it everyday, then one should listen to sermons at least once in every five days.

"If one could be as patient as the ascetic Kṣāntivādin who considered as help the harm done to him by the king of Banaras called Kalāpa [in order to test Kṣāntivādin's forbearance, Kalāpa had his limbs cut off], such forbearance is auspicious because it is conducive to one's own benefit, just as that forbearance brought buddhahood to the ascetic Kṣāntivādin. The future buddha Śarabhaṅga has said the following regarding patience:

> If one were to suppress hatred, one would never come to grief.
> Even sages praise the destruction of anger.
> One should be patient toward whatever is harshly spoken.
> Those at peace said, "that forbearance is supreme."
>
> *Jātaka* v.141

Even Śakra, king of the gods, has said that one should practice forbearance toward those who do harmful things even when one is able to strike back [see *Dhammapada,* verse 399]. The Buddha has also extolled in various places the virtues of forbearance.

"It is auspicious to be obedient like the venerable Rāhula [the biological son of the Buddha], and not be displeased when advice is given about how to improve one's conduct—neither with the advice nor the advisor—and not be disrespectful, because these are conducive to benefit in this world and the next.

"Seeing virtuous people is also auspicious. 'Seeing' means approaching virtuous people, waiting on them, inquiring about how they are, and looking at them, because one who looks at a virtuous person with a delighted mind will not have eye disease for one thousand births. When the Buddha was living surrounded by monks at Vediya Mountain, an owl looked at him with a delighted mind, and that owl did not go to an evil birth for one hundred thousand eons. Instead, he came to possess an appealing face, and after enjoying heavenly comforts, he became the silent buddha Saumanasa.

"The Buddha's sermons (*sūtra*), as well as philosophical texts (*abhidharma*), stories of the Buddha's previous births (*jātaka*), and the commentaries should be discussed by those who know them in the first watch or the last watch of the night. Such informed discussion is conducive to clear understanding of the scriptures (*āgama*) and other good qualities, and thus it is auspicious.

"If a person were not to be attached to the six objects of the senses, such as physical form, and were not to be repelled by unpleasant objects of the senses, that person could be said to be restrained in the senses. That restrained person would have zeal for destroying the defilements and would be able to attain profound contemplative states, and therefore such restraint of the senses is auspicious.

"If a person were to abstain from sexual relations and engage in other observances of a monk, or, if someone, having already become enlightened, were to still engage in the study and practice of Buddha's teachings, such things are auspicious for attaining worldly and transcendent good qualities.

"Realizing the path and realizing the fruits of the path by meditation is auspicious because it leads one to escape from suffering in the cycle of existence. And becoming a worthy one by means of these two—that is, realization of the path and its fruits—is auspicious because it leads one to get rid of all suffering such as birth, and so on.

"If someone, having received wealth, fame, praise, and comfort, were not to become arrogant by thinking such things are permanent but were instead to see them as an annoyance, like a louse, or a form of censure or a kind of suffering, then that person would not be grieved by discovering their impermanence. People who possess that kind of attitude are auspicious because it is conducive to becoming a buddha.

"To be free of sorrow and to be free of such blemishes as passion, and not to be tormented by the defilements that are one's enemy is an achievement that is possible only for a worthy one. Being free from sorrow and the defilements is auspicious because even if one were a scavenger, if one were also endowed with such virtues, one would be able to receive homage from Śakra and other gods."

The Buddha thus preached about thirty-eight auspicious things with eleven verses beginning with "not associating with fools." And when he preached this *Scripture on Auspicious Things*, a million gods became worthy ones, and an incalculable number became stream-winners, once-returners, and nonreturners. [Stream-winner, once-returner, nonreturner, and worthy one are the four stages of highest attainment on the Buddhist path to moral and cognitive perfection.]

On the following day, the Buddha addressed Ānanda: "Last night a certain deity approached me and asked me what is auspicious. I told him of thirty-eight things that are auspicious. Ānanda, learn this *Scripture on Auspicious Things* and teach it to the monks." Ānanda learned it and taught it to other monks. Therefore, from that day to this day, and from this day up to the end of five thousand years, this text is beneficial. [The reference to five thousand years is to the prediction that the Buddha made about how long his teachings would survive. Note that this sentence adds the text itself to things that are auspicious in this world.]

One should make one's birth fruitful by associating with intelligent people; coming to meet them; paying homage to them; living a comfortable life in an appropriate place because of meritorious deeds done earlier; learning crafts that are not harmful; becoming learned; illuminating the Buddha's teaching by one's conduct; saying something good if one says anything at all; attending upon one's parents; and, as expounded by the future Buddha when he was born as a parrot [*Jātaka* IV.276–82], paying back one's debts by treating one's wife and children well, and giving a loan that is to be collected in the future by engaging in such faultless means of livelihood as agriculture, trade, accruing wealth and grain. One should possess the essence of living by observing the precepts; win over relatives by treating them well; win over outsiders by faultless conduct; not cause oppression to others by abstinence from harmful deeds; abstain from intoxicants and thereby avoid harm to oneself; be heedful and perform meritorious deeds; and when one has a mind inclined toward merit, relinquish household comforts and become ordained.

As a monk, one should have respect for the Buddha and the rest. As haughty conduct is not in keeping with monkhood, one should be of a submissive nature to everyone at all times; observe the monastic regimen and rites assiduously; take twelvefold delight in the four requisites, thereby getting rid of greed toward them; and become a good person by knowing the good qualities in actions that have been done. If one has lost interest in doing meritorious deeds, get rid of that state of mind by listening to sermons; get rid of all misfortunes by being patient, obedient, and ready for anything. Seek out virtuous people and listen to their advice, and so become virtuous oneself. If any doubts arise regarding merit, dispel such doubts by talking to intelligent people; attain purity for oneself by establishing oneself in the fourfold morality; and attain mental purity by practicing calming (*śamatha*) meditations. As one is not able to attain purity of knowledge without purification of beliefs, investigate the characteristics and character of mental and physical things. Thus getting various states of purity for oneself, one will then become an enlightened worthy one by proceeding in the sequence of the path. Just as a mountain as big as Mount Meru cannot be shaken by the wind, so you will not be shaken by eight ways of the world. In this manner, one should make one's birth worthwhile by becoming free of sorrow and defilements, undefeated in any situation.

—15—

Daily Life in the Assembly

T. Griffith Foulk

Modern scholars have often presented the history of Buddhism in China in terms of "sinification"—the adaptation to the Chinese cultural milieu of a set of religious beliefs, practices, and social structures that were originally imported from India and Central Asia beginning in the first centuries of the common era. Basic Indian Buddhist beliefs in karma, rebirth, and individual salvation gradually took root in Chinese soil, but only through a process of selection and adaptation in which they were tempered by native cosmologies and beliefs in ancestral spirits. The complex, competing systems of metaphysics, psychology, and soteriology that had emerged from the Indian Buddhist scholastic tradition of analysis were even more difficult for the Chinese to grasp and accept; the process of translating, interpreting, and assimilating them eventually gave rise to new and distinctively Chinese schools of Buddhist thought. It was in the sphere of social organization and mores, however, that the Indian Buddhist model—that of a community of monks and nuns who had "gone forth from the world" to seek salvation—appeared most alien to the Chinese.

The difficulties that beset the establishment of Buddhist monastic institutions in China were formidable. In the first place, there was the problem of learning just what the "orthodox" standards of behavior were for monks and nuns. No complete recensions of the Indian vinaya, or rules of discipline for individuals and monastic communities, were translated into Chinese until the beginning of the fifth century. Well before that time a number of canonical and paracanonical vinaya texts were known to Chinese, and foreign monks had served as role models for the Buddhist monastic life in China, but the leaders of Chinese monastic communities were often forced to improvise rules. Daoan (312–385 C.E.), for example, produced a set of "Standards for Monks and Nuns" to supplement those parts of the vinaya that were not known to him.

When complete recensions of the Indian vinaya did become available in Chinese, there were many problems in interpreting and applying them. For one thing, they presented a profusion of technical terminology, which was often simply transliterated. Some of the specific rules set forth in translations of the vinaya, moreover, were incomprehensible or inapplicable due to cultural and geographic differences between India and China. To make matters worse, different recensions of the vinaya sometimes disagreed on specific procedural points. In response to these difficulties, a number of schools of vinaya exegesis arose in China, and many commentaries were produced. The most long-lived and influential exegetical tradition was the so-called Nanshan school that was based on the *Guide to the Practice of the Four-Part Vinaya* and other commentaries by Daoxuan (596–667), who came to be regarded as the founder of the school.

Finally, the establishment and spread of Buddhist monastic institutions in China was constrained throughout history, to varying degrees, by opposition from the Confucian elite and from the imperial government. Certain features of Buddhist monastic life, such as the principle of celibacy or that of subsisting on alms donated by the laity, were bitterly attacked as inimical to native Chinese values. The conception of the Buddhist saṅgha as a sacred community essentially independent of secular rule, regulated by its own distinct body of regulations laid down by the Buddha, was also perceived as a threat to the authority of the emperor and the sanctity of the imperial state.

Despite all these difficulties, the Buddhist monastic institution did manage to take root and flourish in Chinese society, and to maintain its distinct identity as an establishment ostensibly founded and sanctioned by the Buddha Śākyamuni. Given the pressures to conform to Chinese cultural norms, it is remarkable that so many features of the Indian monastic model survived in China.

The late Tang and Five Dynasties (907–960) periods represent a watershed in the history of Chinese Buddhism. The harsh suppression of Buddhism that was carried out by imperial decree during the Huichang period of the Tang (841–846), followed by the social and political chaos associated with the breakup of the imperial state, dealt the monastic institution a severe blow that it only recovered from when relative peace and unity were restored under the Song. One of the salient features of the restored institution was its domination by monks who presented themselves as members and followers of an elite lineage of dharma transmission—known variously as the Chan lineage, Buddha Mind lineage, and the lineage of Bodhidharma—which they claimed was traceable back to the Buddha Śākyamuni in India. The Chan school was so successful in promulgating its ideology and mythology that many large, state supported monasteries were designated by imperial decree in the Song as Chan monasteries, that is, establishments where the abbacies were restricted to monks certified as dharma heirs in the Chan lineage. The Chan school's main competition was from the Tiantai school, which succeeded in having a lesser number of abbacies reserved for itself. One result of this situation was that most of the saṅgha regulations compiled in the Song and later were nominally rules for Chan monasteries, although there were also nearly identical rules compiled for use in Teachings (Tiantai) monasteries and vinaya monasteries.

One of the recurrent themes that one finds in modern as well as traditional writings on the history of Chan Buddhism is the idea that the Chan school developed a unique, independent system of monastic training that allowed it to exist apart from the mainstream of Chinese Buddhist monastic institutions. According to the traditional account, this development was instigated by the Chan master Baizhang Huaihai (749–814), who is credited with founding the first Chan monastery and authoring the first Chan monastic rules (known generically as *qinggui* or "rules of purity"). Modern historians of Chan have generally accepted the traditional account, although some have assumed that independent Chan monasteries must have come into existence even before Baizhang, and others have argued that Baizhang was not so much an actual founder as a symbol, projected retrospectively, of the development of independent Chan institutions that took place in his day.

In point of fact, there is very scant historical evidence to support either the traditional account of the founding of the Chan monastic institution in the Tang dynasty or any of the modern revisions of that account. The biographies and epigraphs memorializing Baizhang that were written closest to his lifetime say nothing about the founding of an independent Chan school monastery. Nor is there mention of such monasteries, whether associated with Baizhang or not, in any other sources dating from the Tang or earlier. The oldest historical source which indicates that there were independent Chan monasteries in the Tang is a brief text known as the *Regulations of the Chan School (Chanmen guishi)*, the same work that was responsible for establishing Baizhang's place in history as the putative founding father of the Chan monastic institution. It was written during the last quarter of the tenth century, more than 150 years after Baizhang's death.

The oldest extant Chan monastic rule is the *Rules of Purity for Chan Monasteries (Chanyuan qinggui)*, compiled in 1103. The text sets guidelines for many aspects of monastic life and training, including the qualifications and duties of major and minor monastic officers, ritual procedures for numerous ceremonies and religious practices, and rules concerning deportment and etiquette. The table of contents reads as follows:

> Fascicle One: Receiving the Precepts; Upholding the Precepts; A Monk's Personal Implements; Contents of a Wandering Monk's Pack; Staying Overnight in a Monastery; Procedures for Morning and Midday Meals; Procedures for Having Tea or Hot Water; Requesting a Sermon from the Abbot; Entering the Abbot's Room for Individual Instruction
>
> Fascicle Two: Large Assemblies in the Dharma Hall; Recitation of Buddha Names [in the Saṅgha hall]; Small Assemblies [in the abbot's quarters]; Opening the Summer Retreat; Closing the Summer Retreat; Winter Solstice and New Year's Salutations; Inspection of the Various Quarters [by the abbot]; Entertaining Eminent Visitors; Appointing Stewards
>
> Fascicle Three: Controller; Rector; Cook; Labor Steward; Retirement of Stewards; Appointing Prefects; Chief Seat; Scribe; Sūtra Prefect

Fascicle Four: Guest Prefect; Prior; Bath Prefect; Solicitors of Provisions; Water Chief; Charcoal Manager; Decorations Chief; Mill Chief; Garden Chief; Manager of Estate Lands; Manager of Business Cloister; Manager of Infirmary; Chief of Toilets; [Buddha] Hall Prefect; Chief of Bell Tower; Holy Monk's Attendant; Chief of Lamps; Watchman on Duty in Saṅgha Hall; Common Quarters Manager; Common Quarters Chief Seat; Abbot's Quarters Acolytes

Fascicle Five: Traveling Evangelist; Retirement of Prefects; Abbot's Tea Service; Tea Service in Saṅgha Hall; Stewards' and Prefects' Tea Service; Tea Service for Assigning Places in the Common Quarters on the Basis of Seniority; Special Tea Service Sponsored by the Great Assembly of Monks; Special Tea Service for Venerable Elders Sponsored by the Great Assembly of Monks

Fascicle Six: Special Tea Service for the Abbot Sponsored by His Disciples and Trainees; Procedure for Burning Incense in Connection with a Tea Service for the Great Assembly of Monks; Serving a Specially Sponsored Meal; Thanking the Sponsor of a Tea Service; Sūtra Reading Ceremony; Special Feasts; Going Out [for a feast at a sponsor's] and Bringing In [the sponsor of a feast held in a monastery]; Signaling Activities for the Great Assembly of Monks [with bells, drums, wooden clappers, etc.]; Formal Decrees [by the abbot]; Sending out Correspondence; Receiving Correspondence; Sick Leave and Returning to Duty

Fascicle Seven: Using the Toilet; Funeral for a Monk; Appointing Retired Officers [as advisors/assistants]; Appointing an Abbot; Installing an Abbot; The Ideal Abbot; Funeral for an Abbot; Retirement of an Abbot

Fascicle Eight: Admonition [behavior models for monastery officers]; Instructions for Sitting Meditation; Essay on Self-Discipline; 120 Questions [for testing one's spiritual progress]; Disciplining Novices

Fascicle Nine: Liturgy for Novice Ordinations; Regulating Postulants; Guiding Lay Believers; Procedure for Feasting Monks; Verse Commentary on Baizhang's Rules

Within a century of its compilation in 1103, the *Rules of Purity for Chan Monasteries* had gained a wide circulation and become the de facto standard for all major monasteries in China. It was also an important vehicle for the spread of Song-style Buddhist institutions outside of China. For example, both Eisai (1141–1215) and Dōgen (1200–1253), famous Japanese monk pilgrims to China, quoted the *Rules of Purity for Chan Monasteries* frequently in their writings and used it as a basis for establishing what became known as the Zen monastic institution in Japan. The text was also transmitted to Korea. It was reedited (with new material added) and reprinted a number of times, with the result that it survives today in several different recensions.

The second oldest set of Chan monastic rules that survives today is the *Daily Life in the Assembly (Ruzhong riyong)*, also known as the *Chan Master Wuliang Shou's Short Rules of Purity for Daily Life in the Assembly (Wuliang shou chanshi riyong qinggui)*. The text was written in 1209 by Wuliang Zongshou, who at the time held the office of chief seat in a Chan monastery. Unlike the *Rules of Purity for Chan Monasteries*, the *Daily Life in the Assembly* was not intended to regulate all aspects of monastery life. Rather, it comprised a very detailed set of rules for the so-called "great assembly" of monks who had no administrative duties and thus were free to concentrate mainly on a daily routine of meditation, study, and devotions. As chief seat, Wuliang Zongshou was the monastic officer in charge of leading the monks of the great assembly in all of their activities. He stated deferentially in his colophon that he wrote the text for the benefit of monks first joining the great assembly, not for old hands. He also explained that he did not treat a number of activities in which the great assembly participated—including "large assemblies in the [dharma] hall, entering the [abbot's] room, small assemblies, chanting sūtras, reciting buddha names, inspecting [monastery] offices, rituals for opening and closing retreats, packing the knapsacks and donning the bamboo hat [for pilgrimage], and sending off deceased monks and auctioning off their belongings"—because detailed rules for those activities were "already included in the *Rules of Purity*." The *Rules of Purity* that Zongshou referred to in the colophon was almost certainly the *Rules of Purity for Chan Monasteries,* for most of the activities mentioned are in fact the topics of sections of that text (see the table of contents above). Actually, some of the activities that the *Daily Life in the Assembly* does treat, such as procedures for taking meals on the platforms in the saṅgha hall and going to the toilet, are also covered in the *Rules of Purity for Chan Monasteries,* but they are scattered throughout that much longer text. The virtue of the *Daily Life in the Assembly* was that it brought together, in convenient handbook form, detailed procedures and admonitions for the activities that the monks of the great assembly engaged in most frequently. The activities that Zongshou explicitly left out, it should be cautioned, were not necessarily less important in the lives of the great assembly; indeed, they may well have been experienced as more significant. However, because they were on the order of special ceremonies rather than daily routine, the ritual procedures involved could be learned when the occasions arose, and need not have been mastered immediately by monks entering the great assembly.

Chan monasteries in Song China, following a pattern established long before the emergence of the Chan school, were organized in a way that allowed a group of monks (the so-called "great assembly") to engage in meditation and other religious practices for a three-month long retreat without having to concern themselves with practical affairs such as the provision of food or shelter. Basically, the monasteries were divided into two sectors: a practice wing, which housed the monks of the great assembly and the officers who led them, and an administrative wing, which provided living and working places for the monk officers and lay postulants and servants who handled meals, finances, supplies, building maintenance, guests, and numerous other tasks necessary for the operation of a large institution. In order to understand the physical setting that the *Daily Life in the Assembly* takes for granted, therefore, it is only necessary for us to consider the facilities that made up the practice wing, that is, the buildings that were home base to the great assembly.

The facility mentioned most often in the *Daily Life in the Assembly* is the saṅgha hall (sometimes translated "monks' hall"). Saṅgha halls were large buildings divided internally into an inner and outer hall. The inner hall was further divided into an upper and lower section, one being located in front and the other to the rear of a large central altar bearing an image of the "holy monk"—the bodhisattva Mañjuśrī dressed in monk's robes. Mañjuśrī was the tutelary deity who watched over the saṅgha hall, its occupants, and their spiritual endeavors, and was the object of regular devotional worship with offerings of incense and prostrations before his altar. The inner hall was outfitted with low, wide platforms arranged in several blocks in the middle of the floor and along the walls. Individual places on the platforms were assigned in order of seniority, based on time elapsed since ordination. It was on the platforms that the monks of the great assembly spent much of their time, sitting in meditation, taking the morning and midday meals, and lying down for a few hours of sleep at night. Their bowls were hung above their seats, their sleeping mattresses were kept on the platforms, and their other personal effects and monkish implements were stored in boxes at the rear of the platforms. The outer hall was outfitted with narrower platforms suitable for meditation and taking meals, but not for sleeping. They were mainly for use by officers of the administrative wing, novices, and other persons who did not belong to the great assembly.

Another facility referred to frequently in the *Daily Life in the Assembly* is the common quarters. Located near the saṅgha halls, common quarters were arranged internally in much the same way, with platforms on which the monks of the great assembly were seated in order of seniority, and a central altar with an image, usually Avalokiteśvara. The main difference was that the platforms in common quarters were equipped with tables for studying sūtras and writing, activities that were forbidden in the saṅgha hall. The common quarters were also used for drinking tea and medicinal potions, and for taking evening meals, which were referred to euphemistically as "medicine" (because the vinaya forbids eating after midday). Other facilities mentioned in the text are the washstands that were located behind the saṅgha hall, the toilet, bathhouse, laundry place, and hearth. All of these served the daily needs of the great assembly and thus were treated by Zongshou in his rules.

As he leads his readers through a typical day's activities for monks of the great assembly, Zongshou frequently backs up his own formulation of particular procedures and admonitions with what appear to be legitimizing quotations from a preexisting text. The quotations, which all begin "of old it was said," typically repeat points that Zongshou himself has just made. When this stylistic feature is coupled with the claim made by Zongshou in his preface, that he has "collected the standards produced by Baizhang, and has studied them thoroughly from beginning to end," the reader is left with the impression that Zongshou is actually quoting a work by Baizhang himself. In point of fact, as is explained above, no such work was available to Zongshou. I have not been able to trace more than a few of the quotations, but even that is enough to show that they derive from a number of different sources, none of which is attributable directly to Baizhang. When Zongshou speaks of "Baizhang's standards," therefore, what he means is the *Rules of Purity for Chan Monasteries* and perhaps other contemporary monastic rules (now lost) that likewise claimed to preserve Baizhang's heritage.

It is also worth noting that the *Daily Life in the Assembly* evinces a tremendous concern with "impurity" and "purity." It is tempting to see in this a concern for hygiene that would have made good, practical sense in any institution with communal facilities, but there is more to it than that. A number of rules speak not only of avoiding the contamination of neighbors' bowls, wash buckets, and so on, but of avoiding the communication of impurities from social juniors to their seniors. For example, one rule stipulates that the end of chopsticks and spoons that goes in one's mouth (and hence is polluted by saliva) must always point toward the right (where one's juniors sit) when the utensils are set down on the platform. In this respect, the *Daily Life in the Assembly* sounds very Indian, and even cites a passage to the effect that distinctions of senior and junior are necessary when brahmans gather (typically in a line) to take a meal together. The designation of the two smallest fingers of the left hand as "impure" because they are used in the toilet is also an Indian custom. At the time when Chan monastic rules were taking shape in the late tenth and eleventh centuries, there was in fact an upsurgence of interest in Indian Buddhism. Sanskrit studies were revived in China, delegations of monks were sent to India, and a number of Indian monks were received as honored guests and scholars in residence by Chinese rulers. Although Chan rules are often held up by modern scholars as epitomizing the sinification of Buddhist monasticism, the evidence of the *Daily Life in the Assembly* suggests that there may have been considerable Indian influence on Chan monasteries in the Song.

The *Daily Life in the Assembly* was originally composed as a handbook for monks newly entered into the "great assembly," but the text proved so useful that it was later incorporated into full-scale monastic rules such as the *Zongli jiaoding qinggui Zongyao,* compiled in 1274, the *Chanlin beiyong qinggui,* compiled in 1317, and the *Chixiu baizhang qinggui,* completed in 1343. Much later, in Tokugawa-period (1603–1868) Japan, the text was widely studied and commented on by both Rinzai and Sōtō Zen monks who were striving to revive Song-style communal monastic practice. That, and the similarity of many of the rules with ones laid down by Dōgen in his *Shōbōgenzō* and *Eihei shingi,* accounts for the remarkable congruence between the procedures explained in the *Daily Life in the Assembly* and those followed in contemporary Zen monastic training.

The translation is from *Dai Nippon zokuzōkyō,* 2-16-5. 472a–474b.

Daily Life in the Assembly

Having left the dust [of the world] and separated from the vulgar, we shaven-headed and square-robed [Buddhist monks], for the most part, spend our lives in monasteries. The first requirement [of monastic life] is to understand the rules clearly. If one has not yet memorized the regulations with regard to conduct, then one's actions will not be in accord with the ritual restraints. If even one's good friends and benevolent advisors do not have the heart to severely reprimand and harshly criticize, and if one continues on with one's bad habits, then reform is extremely difficult. In the end his [behavior] will bring desolation upon the monasteries, and induce negligence in peoples' minds. Because I frequently see such transgressions and evils, which are commonplace before my very eyes, I have collected the standards [for behavior] produced by Baizhang, and have studied them thoroughly from beginning to end. From morning to night, to avoid every particular offense, one must straightaway obey every single provision. Only after that may one presume to say that one has investigated the self, illumined the mind, understood birth, and penetrated death. Worldly dharmas are [ultimately] identical with supraworldly dharmas, but those who are on pilgrimage [monks] can nevertheless set a precedent for those who are not yet on pilgrimage [the laity]. May we not forsake the body and mind of monkhood, and may we together humbly repay the blessings of the buddhas and patriarchs.

Respectfully submitted.

RULES FOR [MONKS] IN THE ASSEMBLY

Do not go to sleep before others, or rise later than others. You should quietly get up before the bell of the fifth watch. Take your pillow and place it under your legs, but without folding it, lest the noise startle [the people at] the neighboring places [on the platform in the saṅgha hall]. Rouse your spirit, draw the blanket around your body and sit up straight, without fanning up a breeze that would cause peoples' thoughts to stir. If you feel sleepy, you may instead take the blanket and place it at your feet, turn your body, pick up your hand cloth and get down from the platform. With the cloth draped over your left hand, mentally recite the following verse:

> From the wee hours of dawn straight through to dusk,
> I will make way for all living beings.
> If any of them should lose their bodily form under my feet,
> I pray that they may immediately be born in the pure land.

Quietly push the [saṅgha hall doorway] screen aside with your hand, and exit to the wash stand. Do not drag your footwear, and do not make a noise by coughing. Of old it was said,

> When pushing aside the curtain, one's rear hand should hang at one's side;
> when exiting the hall, it is strictly forbidden to drag one's footwear.

Quietly take a basin in hand and wash your face, without using much water. When using tooth powder, take a single dab with your right hand and rub the left side [of your mouth], and take a single dab with your left hand and rub the right side. Do not allow either hand to dip [into the powder] twice, lest there be drainage from the teeth or mouth infections passed to other people. When rinsing your mouth and spitting out water, you must lower your head and use your hands to draw [the water] down. Do not stand with the waist straight and spit water, splashing it into the neighboring basins.

Do not wash the head. There are four reasons why this is harmful to self and others. First, it dirties the basin, and second, it dirties the [public] hand cloth: these are the things harmful to others. Third, it dries out the hair, and fourth, it injures the eyes: these are the things harmful to self.

Do not make sounds within one's nostrils. Do not make loud noises clearing one's throat. Of old it was said,

> The fifth-watch face washing is fundamentally for the sake of religious practice. Clearing one's throat and dragging one's bowl [sic] make the hall noisy and disturb the assembly.

Having wiped your face, return to the [saṅgha] hall. If you are in the upper section, enter with your left foot first. If you are in the lower section, enter with your right foot first. When you get back to your blanket place, take your sleeping mattress, fold it in half, and sit in meditation.

If you change your outer robe, you must take the new one and put it around your body first. Do not expose yourself, and do not fan up a breeze.

Burning incense and making prostrations are suitable in the time before the bell rings. To don the kāṣāya [formal robe symbolic of monkhood], first recite the following verse with your palms joined and the kāṣāya resting on your head:

> Wonderful indeed is the garment of liberation,
> the robe of the signless field of merit.
> I now receive it on my head;
> may I be able to wear it always, in all worlds [of rebirth].

To fold the kāṣāya, first fold the place where it hangs on your arm, and then release the ring. Do not use your mouth to hold the kāṣāya. Do not use your chin to hold up the kāṣāya. When you have finished folding it you should bow with palms joined and proceed.

Just as when making prostrations in the various halls [such as the buddha hall or dharma hall], do not take a place in the center [of the saṅgha hall] that interferes with the abbot's coming. Do not make any sound reciting the Buddha's name. Do not walk through the area around other peoples' heads [when they are making prostrations]. Walk behind them [not between them and the image they are bowing to].

When the bell signaling the fifth watch rings, and the abbot and the chief seat are sitting in the hall, do not go out or in the front entrance.

At the preliminary signal for rising, immediately fold your blanket and gather up your pillow. The method for folding the blanket is first to find the two corners, and stretch them out with your hands. Fold it in half twice, once to the front, and then back toward your body. Do not turn it horizontally, obstructing the neighboring places. Do not shake it out and make a noise, and do not create a breeze with the blanket.

[Next] you may return to the common quarters and drink medicinal tea, or walk about in the tea hall.

When proceeding in a line back to your bowl place [in the saṅgha hall], you must follow the person [who sits] above you [on the platform]. When turning, do not turn your back toward others. If using the front entrance, enter on the south side. Do not walk on the north side or the middle, out of respect for the abbot. After the wooden fish has sounded, do not enter the hall. Either have a postulant fetch your bowl [from your place on the platform] and sit in the outer hall [to eat], or return to the common quarters. Having entered the hall and returned to your bowl place, humble yourself and bow with palms joined to [the persons at] the upper, middle, and lower seats. If you are already seated first, when the [persons on] the upper, middle, and lower seats arrive, you should have palms joined. Of old it was said,

> If one does not pay one's respects to the upper, middle, and lower seats,
> then there are no distinctions in a gathering of brahmans.

When you hear the long sounding of the [signal] board, take down your bowls. When raising your body, get up straight and stand still. Only then may you turn your body, making sure to follow the person above you [on the platform]. [Gesture with] palms joined and then take your bowls. One hand holds the bowls while the other hand releases the hook: the left hand holds [the bowls]. With the left hand holding [the bowls], turn your body. Lower your body in a proper crouch, and set down the bowls. Avoid bumping into others with your hips or back.

When the bell in front of the hall sounds, get down from the platform and bow with palms joined. This is for receiving the abbot. Do not wave your hands left and right. When you have gotten off the platform, step forward and bow with palms joined. Do not allow your kāṣāya to rest on the edge of the platform. Always lower it carefully.

When getting up onto the platform, do not move abruptly. Take the bowl and place it in front of your seat. When you hear the sound of the mallet, with palms joined silently recite the following verse:

> The Buddha was born in Kapilavastu;
> He gained enlightenment in Magadha;
> He preached the dharma in Varanasi;
> And entered nirvāṇa in Kuśinagara.

RULES FOR SETTING OUT BOWLS

First silently recite the following verse with palms joined:

I am now able to set out
The Tathāgata's bowls.
May I, together with all beings,
Be equal in the threefold emptiness [of giving].

Having finished the verse, remove the [bowls'] wrapping cloth. Spread this pure cloth out to cover your lap. The cloth is folded back on itself so that three edges are tucked under. Do not allow it to extend beyond your place [on the platform]. Spread out the bowl mat. Using the left hand, take the bowls, and place them on the mat. Using both thumbs, remove the bowls and set them out in order, beginning with the smallest. Do not knock them together and make a noise. Always hold back your fourth and fifth fingers; as impure fingers, they are not to be used. When folding the bowl rag, make it small. Set it down horizontally in line with the spoon and chopsticks bag, near your body. When putting them in [the bag], the spoon goes first. When taking them out, the chopsticks are first. The place where your hand grasps [the utensils] is called the "pure place" and should be pointed toward the person on your left [above you on the platform]. The swab should be placed in the second gap between the bowls, sticking out just half an inch.

When gathering up the spirit rice [the offering to hungry ghosts], do not use your spoon or chopsticks to remove it [from your bowl]. The spirit rice should not exceed seven grains, but if it is too little, that is being stingy with food.

When joining the palms while the rector chants the buddhas' names, the fingers of the hands should not be separated. You should adjust your hands to the height of your chest. Do not let your fingers touch the area around your mouth. Of old it was said,

> Having unevenly joined palms, not aligning [the hands] with one's chest, intertwining the ten fingers, sticking them into one's nose, dragging one's sandals, lifting the [saṅgha hall] curtain, lacking courtesy, clearing one's throat, and sighing are disrespectful.

Lift the bowl with both hands to receive the food, and silently recite the following verse:

Upon receiving this food,
I pray that living beings
shall have as food the bliss of dhyāna,
and be filled to satiation with joy in the dharma.

Raise your right hand to stop [the server] when the [desired] amount of food has been received. When you hear the hammer signaling eating, look above and below you [on the platform]. Then, looking straight at it, lift your food. Do not, when you are facing forward, swing your hands to either side. Having lifted the bowl, make five reflections and silently recite:

> First, considering how much effort went into [producing] it, I reflect on where this [food] came from.
>
> Second, I consider whether my own virtue and practice are worthy of this offering [of food I am about to eat].
>
> Third, I take restraining the mind and forsaking my faults, such as greed and the rest, as the essential thing.
>
> Fourth, in principle [this food] is like good medicine, to keep my body from withering away.
>
> Fifth, I should receive this food for the sake of the work of attaining enlightenment.

Put out the spirit [rice] and chant the following verse:

> You host of spirits,
> I now give you an offering.
> May this food reach to
> all the spirits in the ten directions.

RULES FOR EATING

Bring the food to your mouth; do not bring your mouth to the food. When taking up your bowl, putting down your bowl, and the spoon and chopsticks as well, do not make any noise. Do not cough. Do not blow your nose. If you have to sneeze, you should cover your nose with the sleeve of your robe. Do not scratch your head, lest dandruff fall into your neighbor's bowl. Do not pick your teeth with your hand. Do not make noise chewing your food or slurping soup. Do not clear out rice from the center of your bowl, and do not make big balls of food. Do not extend your lips to receive food. Do not spill food. Do not use your hands to pick up scattered food. If there are inedible vegetable parts, leave them out of sight behind the bowl. Do not make a breeze that fans your neighbor's place. If you are worried about flatulence, tell the rector and sit in the outer hall. Do not rest your hands on your knees. Judge the amount when you take your food, and do not ask to throw any away. Do not fill your largest bowl with moist food. Do not use soup to clean rice out from your largest bowl. Do not wipe vegetables in your largest bowl and eat them together with the rice. During the meal, you must observe those above and below you [on the platform]. Do not be too slow, and do not swab out your bowl before seconds are offered.

Do not make any noise licking your bowl swab. When the mealtime has not yet arrived, do not give rise to greedy thoughts. Of old it was said,

> To look within grumblingly and give rise to regret and anger; to think of food and salivate; to cough; to spill gruel in one's haste [to eat]; to slurp

soup; to stuff one's mouth full; to disturb those on the neighboring seats when opening up the place mat and setting out the bowls...

To wash your bowls, take the largest bowl and fill it with water; then wash the other bowls in order [of size]. Do not wash the spoon, chopsticks, or smaller bowls in the largest bowl. Again, bend back your fourth and fifth fingers. Do not make any noise rinsing the mouth. Do not spit water back into the bowls. Do not fill the bowls with boiled water before washing them. When the [bowl-washing] water has not yet been collected, do not put away your lap covering cloth. Do not use the lap cloth to wipe sweat. Do not pour the leftover water on the ground. Silently recite the verse for pouring off the [wash] water:

I now take this bowl-washing water,
Which has a flavor like heavenly ambrosia,
and give it to you spirits.
May all achieve satiation.
An mo xin luo xi suoke!

When putting away the bowls, use the thumbs of both hands to arrange them in order, then place them in the wrapping cloth.

When finished, with palms joined silently recite the verse following the meal:

Having finished the meal, our countenance and energy are restored. We are [like] heroes whose majesty shakes the ten directions and the three times. It reverses causes and turns around effects without conscious effort, and all living beings gain supernatural powers.

When the board in front of the [common] quarters sounds, return to the quarters and bow with palms joined. Not to return is called "insulting the great assembly." The procedures for entering the door and returning to one's place are the same as in the saṅgha hall. Stand still and wait for the quarters manager to finish burning incense; then bow with palms joined to those above and below [on the platform].

If there is tea, take your seat. Do not let your robes dangle. Do not gather together and talk and laugh. Do not bow to [greet] people with one hand. Do not hoard tea leaves. Of old it was said,

When mounting the platform and sitting in rest, it is not allowed to dangle one's robe. How could it be proper to bow with one hand [instead of with palms joined]? Privately stashing powdered tea, eliciting smiles . . .

When looking on [at a text], students who are next to each other at the tables are strictly forbidden to put their heads together and chat.

When the tea is finished, if you read sūtras, do not unfold the sūtra to a great length. That is to say, only two pages [of the accordion-folded text may be open]. Do not walk about the quarters with a sūtra in your hand. Do not allow the sūtra cord [used to tie the text when folded up] to dangle. Do not make any noise. Of old it was said,

> To make a noise holding and chanting [sūtras] is to offend people around you, and to rest one's back on the board is to be disrespectful to the great assembly.

Leave the quarters beforehand; do not wait for the board signaling sitting meditation [in the saṅgha hall] to sound.

If you need to go to the toilet, then [according to] the old custom, you wear your five-section robe. Take the pure cloth [used to cover the kāṣāya] and hang it over your left hand. [In the toilet changing room] release your sash, and tie it to the bamboo pole. Take off your short kāṣāya and outer robe, arrange them neatly, and bind them with the hand cloth. Then tie the hand cloth [to the pole so that the bundle hangs down] a foot or more. Make sure you remember [which bundle is yours]. Do not talk or laugh. Do not, from outside, importune others [to hurry and make room for you in the toilet].

Take some water in your left hand and put it in the privy. When changing shoes [prior to entering the stall], do not allow a gap between them [that is, line up the ones you have removed neatly]. Set the pure bucket in front of you and snap your fingers three times to frighten off the feces-eating spirits. When you squat, your body must be upright. Do not make a noise exerting. Do not blow your nose. Do not chat with people on the other side of the partition. Of old it was said,

> When the door is shut, just lightly snap your fingers. Even if people are concealed, who would be so bold as to shamelessly make a noise?

Upon entering the [clean-up] place, use a wiping block. Keep the used and clean ones separate. When you come out, you must have water. Do not splash water all around. Do not use water to wash both sides [of the wiping block]. Wash [the block] with your left hand, holding back the thumb and the two fingers next to it. Do not use many wiping blocks. Of old it was said,

> Use but a little warm water for washing, and refrain from taking up [too many] wiping blocks.

There are those who, when they have finished using [a block] wash it with water and set it aside in some vacant place, thereby disturbing many persons in the assembly.

It is not good to linger for long [in the toilet]. The pure bucket should be put back in its original place. Using your dry hand arrange your five-section robe, and tuck it into your breeches. Use your dry hand to open the door. Use your right hand to lift the bucket, and leave. Do not use a wet hand to grasp the leaf of the door or the door frame. With the right hand, pick out [from the container] some ashes, and afterwards pick out some earth. Do not use the wet hand to pick up ashes or earth. Do not spit out saliva and mix it together with the earth. Only after washing the hands should you use "black horn" [pod soap powder] to wash. Wash up to the elbow. You should keep your mind focused at all times on the dhāraṇī [incantation] of entering the toilet. Use water to wash the hands and rinse the mouth. In the vinaya, these purifications also apply to urinating. Next, chew on a willow twig.

Return to the [saṅgha] hall for sitting meditation before the fire board [signaling the preparation of the meal] has sounded. Do not return to the [common] quarters first.

Before the midday meal, do not wash your robes. Do not open your platform box before the morning or midday meal, or after the release from practice. If there is some pressing need, tell the officer in charge. In the [common] quarters, tell the quarters manager. In the [saṅgha] hall, tell the holy monk's attendant.

When the midday meal is over in the saṅgha hall, do not put your heads together and chat. Do not read sūtras or [secular] books in the saṅgha hall. Do not make circumambulations between the upper and lower sections of the hall. Do not pass through the hall as a shortcut [to get somewhere else]. Do not string cash on your seat. Do not sit with your legs dangling off the front of the platform.

A space one foot wide along the front of the platform is called the "area of threefold purity," [because it is the place for] 1. setting out bowls, 2. resting the kāṣāya, and 3. is the direction in which the head points [when sleeping]. Do not walk on the platform. Do not kneel to open the platform box. Do not step on the platform edge when climbing down to the floor. When wearing straw sandals and the five-section robe [that is, the robe for use in the toilet, bath, and manual labor] going about the monastery, do not pass through the buddha hall or dharma hall. Of old it was said,

> When entering the halls with the folded kāṣāya on one's shoulder, and when wearing straw sandals to go about the monastery, do not set foot in the dharma hall.

Make way for venerable elders [when going about the monastery]. Do not wear monkish shoes over bare feet. Do not hold hands [with another person] when walking, or discuss worldly matters. Of old it was said,

> What was your purpose in separating from your parents, leaving your ordination teacher and seeking the instruction of a wise master? If you have not discussed and grasped the essential matters of our school, and if when your hair is white you still have no attainment, whose fault will it be?

Do not lean on the railings in front of the halls. Do not run about in wild haste. Of old it was said,

> When going about, one should walk slowly; learn from the dignified manners of Aśvajit. When speaking, one's voice should be low; learn from the standards set by Upāli.

Do not go for leisure to the buddha hall. Of old it was said,

> One should not, for no purpose, go up into the treasure hall [buddha hall]; one must not, for leisure, go into a stūpa. If one sweeps the ground or gives perfumed water without reason, then even though there be merit as numerous as the sands of the river [Ganges], it comes to naught.

When starching garments after the midday meal, do not bare your left shoulder. Do not upset the hot water jug when dipping your robes. When you are done using the bamboo poles [for drying] and the flat-iron, put them back in their original places.

When the board signaling foot-washing sounds, do not fight to snatch the foot bucket. If you have boils or itches, then you should dip and wash [your feet] after the others have finished, or take the bucket to some screened-off place and wash. Avoid disgusting others in the assembly. Do not wait for the striking of the board signaling sitting in the [saṅgha] hall, but go back into the hall as soon as you are done and sit in meditation.

When release from practice [is signaled], take the sleeping mattress and spread it out [folded] in half. When the board in front of the [common] quarters sounds, immediately turn your body and face outward.

You must attend [the meal] with the assembly when the time arrives. While the small board is sounding, do not enter the [saṅgha] hall, and do not stand in the outer hall. When the abbot and chief seat leave the hall, open up the mattress, get down from the platform, bow with palms joined, and return to the [common] quarters.

For the evening meal, when each person is at their own table place [in the common quarters], do not be the first to rise and fill [your bowl] with food. Do not make a loud noise shouting for gruel, rice, salt, vinegar, and the like. When the meal is over and you exit the quarters, do not leave the monastery grounds, and do not go into the officers' rooms. Do not return to the saṅgha hall or walk around the corridors with your kāṣāya folded and resting on your left shoulder. Do not wait for the striking of the board to leave the quarters.

When the evening bell sounds, with palms joined recite the following verse:

> Upon hearing the bell,
> Vexations are lightened;
> Wisdom is strengthened,
> Bodhi is produced;
> We escape from hell,
> Leaving the fiery pit.
> May I attain buddhahood,
> And save living beings.

You should first return to your place [in the saṅgha hall] and sit in meditation. Do not scratch your head when on the platform. Do not make a noise fingering your prayer beads on the platform. Do not talk with your neighbors on the platform. If your neighbor is remiss, you should use kind words to help him; do not give rise to a resentful, bad state of mind.

When the bell signaling time for sleep has yet to ring, do not go out or in the front entrance [of the saṅgha hall]. When the time of the sounding of the fire [watchman's] bell has passed, then the chief seat may permit the "unfolding of pillows" [that is, going to sleep].

To burn incense and make prostrations [at the saṅgha hall altar], you must wait until late at night. When the members of the assembly are not yet asleep, do not be the first to sleep; but when the members of the assembly have not yet gotten up [for additional meditation or devotions], you should get up before them. When you arise and sit, do not startle and rouse the people at neighboring places.

When sleeping, you should be on your right side. Do not sleep facing upward [that is, on your back] Facing upward is called "the sleep of a corpse," and facing downward is called "lewd sleep." [With these incorrect postures] there are many evil dreams. Use your pure cloth to wrap your kāṣāya and place it in front of your pillow. Nowadays many people place it at their feet. This is wrong.

If you have occasion to enter the bath, enter carrying your toilet articles in your right hand. When you get inside the threshold of the lower section [of the bathhouse], bow with palms joined and retire to an empty space. After you have bowed to the persons on your left and right, first take your five-section robe and hand cloth and hang them on the bamboo pole. Open up your bath cloth [used to carry bath articles], take out your [bathing] articles, and set them to one side. Open up, but do not yet completely remove, your outer robe. First, remove your undergarments. Take your leg cloth, wrap it around your body, and tie your bath wrap. Take your breeches, roll them up, and place them in your bath cloth. Next remove your outer robe and five-section robe and put them together in a bundle. Take your hand cloth and tie [the bundle] to the bamboo pole. If you do not have a hand cloth, use your sash to tie it. Of old it was said,

> When the drum signaling the bath sounds three times and you enter the [bath] hall, one must separate outer and under garments as "impure" and "pure."

Proceed to remove the remainder of your garments, make them into a bundle, and set them aside turned upside down [so the "impure" garments are not exposed].

Do not go about in the bath with bare feet: you must wear [wooden] clogs. Dip water at an empty place in the lower section [of the bathhouse]. Do not take the sitting places of officers or respected elders, that is, those in the upper section. Do not splash people's bodies with hot water. Do not take the buckets onto the floor and soak your feet. Do not urinate in the bathhouse, or wash your private parts. Do not rest your feet on the buckets. Do not talk or laugh. Do not rub your feet on the [drain] trough. Do not bail out water [from the trough]. Do not stand up, pick up a bucket, and pour water over your body, lest you splash the people to the left, right, front or back of you. You must keep your whole body covered. Do not use much bath water. Do not let the leg cloth become separated from your body.

If there are persons whose leg cloths should not get into the buckets, such as those with boils, those washing moxa blisters, or those using itch medicine, they should be the last to enter the bath. Do not use the public hand cloths that are on either side to wipe your head or face. In the bathhouse the hand cloths are there to use after donning your robes, to clean your hands before putting on your short kāṣāya.

When leaving the bath, bow left and right. First put on your undershirt and outer robe. When you are completely covered, then put on your lower underclothing and remove your bath wrap. Take your leg cloth and lay it inside your bath wrap, lest it moisten your bath cloth [used to carry bath articles]. The hand cloth should be held in your left hand. Do not take the wet leg cloth and drape it over your hand. Bow left and right and depart. Read the characters of the name of the donor who arranged for the bath, chant sūtras or dhāraṇīs of your choice, and dedicate the merit.

During the cold months when you face the fire, first sit above the hearth, then turn your body and enter the hearth. Bow with palms joined and then sit. If there is a place for removing shoes, leave them outside. Do not play with the incense spoon or fire tongs. Do not stir up the fire. Do not put your heads together and talk. Do not roast things for snacks. Do not make a bad smell by toasting your shoes. It is not permitted to dry such things as leggings or clothing over the fire. Do not grasp and lift your outer robe, exposing your breeches. Do not spit or throw balls of filth and grease into the hearth.

The rules of etiquette for daily activities in the assembly as collected above are not presumed as advice for old hands; they are intended for the edification of newcomers to the training. Minutely detailed rules that should be followed for assemblies in the [dharma] hall, entering the [abbot's] room, minor assemblies, chanting sūtras, reciting buddha names, inspecting [monastery] offices, rituals for opening and closing retreats, packing the knapsacks and donning the bamboo hat [for pilgrimage], sending off deceased monks and auctioning off their belongings, are already included in the *Rules of Purity*. Abbots each have [their own] special admonitions [for their monasteries], so I will not make any further statement.

Compiled on the Buddha's birthday [8th day of 4th month] in the second year of the Jiading era [1209]. Respectfully, the monk Zongjia of the chief seat's office at Qianguifeng (Thousand Tortoise Peak) [Monastery].

—16—

Awakening Stories of Zen Buddhist Women

Sallie B. King

The status of women in Buddhism has been problematic throughout Buddhist history. According to scripture, the Buddha was approached early in his career by his aunt, Mahāprajāpatī, at the head of a delegation of women who wished him to institute a Buddhist order of nuns. The Buddha initially declined to institute such an order. But when the Buddha's close disciple, Ānanda, asked him whether women were able to attain the fruits of spiritual practice, the Buddha unhesitatingly answered that women could attain such fruits. This affirmation on the part of the Buddha has been of the first importance to Buddhist women throughout history, while his reluctance to establish an institutional place for women has haunted them.

The ordination of the first Buddhist nuns followed shortly after this interview. In the order instituted, all nuns were formally subordinated to all monks by means of the "eight weighty rules," which forbade nuns' admonishing or teaching monks and declared the most senior nun to be subordinate to the most junior monk in the monastic seniority system. As reflected in their place in the monastic hierarchy, the social standing of nuns as a group has always been inferior to that of monks. The nuns' order died out in Theravāda countries and in Tibet, but has continued to the present in East Asia. But in East Asia as well, the nuns' order has been subjected to unequal treatment. For example, in 1913 in the Japanese Soto Zen sect, from which the translations here derive, the sect annually spent 600 Japanese yen per nun and 180,000 yen per monk or male priest. With such poor institutional support, it is obvious that the social standing of nuns was far inferior to that of monks and that provisions for their education and training were minimal. Social reform came to the Soto sect, as to much of the rest of Japan, in the Meiji era and especially after World War II. But it was not until 1970 that nuns were formally permitted to hold meditation retreats by themselves, without male supervision. The selections below give accounts of women-only meditation retreats held in the 1940s and 1950s, led by a nun ahead of her time.

These selections are excerpted from a text entitled *A Collection of Meditation*

Experiences, published in Japan in 1956. The book records the meditation experiences of laywomen and nuns practicing under the Zen master and nun, Nagasawa Sozen Roshi. (Her family name means Long Valley; her Buddhist name means Zen-ancestor.) Nagasawa Roshi was in her time perhaps the only nun directing a Japanese Zen nunnery and practice center and holding meditation retreats without the supervision of a male Zen master. She was a disciple of the famous Harada Daiun Roshi, who, though a member of the Soto Zen lineage, supplemented traditional Soto practices with Rinzai Zen koan practice. The present selections show Nagasawa Roshi at work, training nuns and laywomen in the Tokyo Nuns' Practice Center. Her nun disciples themselves had previously undertaken an extensive alms-begging tour in order to raise funds to build the meditation hall in which the retreats were held.

It is noteworthy that Nagasawa Roshi is depicted as training her disciples in the same manner as other teachers in her line. Though a number of contemporary Western feminist Buddhists have criticized aspects of Zen training as "macho," and some modern Zen masters have dropped some such practices, Nagasawa Roshi seems to employ them all. She is depicted as being quite stern and even fierce with her disciples before they make a breakthrough in their practice, shouting at them and abruptly ringing them out of the interview room with her dismissal bell; she relies heavily on a koan practice in which the disciple aggressively assaults the ego, suffering a roller-coaster ride of blissful highs and despairing lows in the process; and she uses the "encouragement stick," a flat hardwood stick with which meditators may be slapped on the shoulders during prolonged meditation sessions to help them call up energy for their practice (it functions much like cold water splashed in the face and is not a punishment). This severity is what Zen calls "grandmotherly kindness": the teacher's aid to the student working to free herself from the limitations of ego. The atmosphere of the meditation retreats is portrayed as taut and austere; Nagasawa Roshi herself is described as possessing exalted experience and, though hard and demanding before a disciple makes a breakthrough, warm and gentle when the breakthrough is achieved. It is clear that her students deeply respect her and are grateful to her. All this is classic Japanese Zen. Thus, while Nagasawa Roshi does represent for her time a female incursion into a male world, she makes no changes in behavior within that world other than the significant change of inviting other women into it.

The text from which these selections are drawn contains some sixty accounts written by laywomen and nuns studying under Nagasawa Roshi. In the Zen sect, it is believed that enlightenment comes in varying depths and is subject to ever greater deepening. In the lineage which Nagasawa Roshi represents, it is customary upon attaining kensho, the first awakening experience, to write an autobiographical account of the events that led one to practice Zen and a description of one's practice, culminating in an account of the kensho itself. Two such accounts follow.

These accounts depict students working with koans, meditation devices which give the practitioner a puzzle that cannot be resolved by rational means. It functions as both goad and carrot to the inquiring mind. The accounts translated below show one nun and one laywoman working with the well-known koan "*Mu.*" This is very frequently given as the first koan to serious practitioners; it is believed to be a good tool for helping the practitioner to make the breakthrough to a first awakening, or preliminary enlightenment, experience. The *Mu* koan reads: "A monk once asked Master Joshu, 'Has a dog the Buddha nature or not?' Joshu said, '*Mu!*' "

A koan is assigned by a Zen master with whom a student has an ongoing relationship; the teacher assesses the student's character and degree of understanding and assigns a koan which he or she believes will best work for the student at his or her current stage. The teacher may or may not give additional instructions or explanations to the student. The student then meditates on the koan for a period that may last hours or years, attempting to resolve the puzzle embedded in it. Periodically, the student returns to the private interview with the teacher, or dokusan, to demonstrate his or her progress in working with the koan. These interviews are not the time for casual discussion; they are the student's opportunity to demonstrate understanding and ask for specific instructions, and the teacher's opportunity to test the student and give further instruction. Their atmosphere is extremely formal and intense.

As the following selections demonstrate, students working with *Mu* frequently concentrate their minds entirely on the *Mu* itself, repeating the word *Mu* over and over to themselves with great energy as an aid to concentration. When the student working on the koan *Mu* returns to the private interview with the teacher, any answer spoken from dualistic thinking will be rejected; an answer that is an expression of buddha nature, in whatever form it takes, will be accepted.

In the following selections, both students work on the koan *Mu,* most importantly in the setting of sesshin. In this tradition, sesshin are severe and intensive week-long meditation retreats. In a typical day at such a retreat, all present rise well before the sun and spend the entire day in meditation. Most of the day is given to formal zazen, or sitting Zen meditation, done usually in the full- or half-lotus position, sometimes in kneeling Japanese style. The rest of the day is occupied with light meals, chanting, a work period (mostly cooking and cleaning), usually one talk per day by the teacher, and mandatory private interviews with the teacher. The student is expected to maintain a meditative state of mind throughout all of these events. Strict silence is required and eye contact is avoided at all times, except in the private interview room. Formal rules of decorum and ceremony cover all movements and interactions, contributing to the taut and intense atmosphere. The programmed part of the day ends around 9:00 or 10:00 P.M., but many students stay up later, sometimes through the whole night, to continue working on their meditation practice.

In reading the following accounts one should recall the dual heritage of Buddhism for women: the Buddha's affirmation of women's spiritual ability paired with the weighty neglect of women in Buddhist institutions. In Nagasawa Roshi and her lay and nun disciples we see three modern Japanese women encountering this heritage, embracing what helps them and transforming what could hold them back.

The translations are from Iizuka Koji, ed., *Sanzen Taiken Shu (A Collection of Meditation Experiences),* with a Foreword by Nagasawa Sozen (Tokyo: Chuo Bukkyosha, 1956), pp. 30–38 and 242–46.

Further Reading

On the *Mu* koan, see Zenkei Shibayama, *Zen Comments on the Mumonkan,* translated by Sumiko Kudo (New York: New American Library, 1974), p. 19.

Remembering My Child

In the first account, written in 1949, a laywoman named Nakayama Momoyo shares with us her life before and during Zen practice. We are given a picture of a woman who manages impressively as virtually a single mother in prewar and wartime Japan, but who finally cannot cope with her grief over her son's death. Her initial encounter with Zen is instructive in its outsider's perspective and skepticism. Her experiences in retreat, with her roller coaster of emotions, are typical. Finally, however difficult it is to understand her awakening experience, it is at least clear that her broken spirit has been healed.

My beloved son, my only son, for whom there is no replacement in heaven or earth, him I lost in the war. Just three days after graduating as a reservist from Tokyo Imperial University, he left for the front in high spirits. In a corner of a northern island his life came to an end; this young sapling of just twenty-six years died.

Our son had cultivated his parents' fields—his father's as a man of religion, mine as an educator. . . . From the time of his childhood, idealizing his good but ordinary father and mother, he had cherished the hope of inheriting the child-care center which I ran and becoming a religious educator. His smaller motives were to give joy to the children and to express his filial piety toward his mother; his greater concern was, as a true man of religion, with the people of the world and, by extension, with the religious path. Thus he revered all buddhas and patriarchs. . . .

As a consequence, his personality was easy-going and generous. I, on the other hand, who was raising and guiding children, was always being taught and purified by him. I never stopped reflecting, "Can this child have developed in my womb? Can he have been born and raised by a mother with such deep sins as I? There must have been some mistake for me to come to be his mother."

After his preschool days, and throughout his school days, many people—teachers, classmates, all who knew him—loved him for his personality. From the bottom of their hearts, they grieved over his death in battle. A wounded soldier who had miraculously returned alive and who had served under my son from beginning to end called on me after the war was over. Kneeling before the Buddha altar, he spoke to me for thirty minutes, hands palm-to-palm and tears flowing:

"He was truly a kind commander. He loved his subordinates. No matter what, he never reprimanded us. In other squads, the commander always ate first, but our commander always gave food to his subordinates first. Consequently, all his subordinates adored him and had confidence in him. In the end, when we knew there was no hope, no one spoke of giving up. There wasn't a single person who didn't want to share the fate of the commander. I myself was wounded in the chest, but when I told the commander that I absolutely must die with him, I upset him. Uncharacteristically angry, he admonished me, 'Dying is not the only way of serving your country and your parents. You're young; your wound will certainly heal. Take responsibility for the seriously wounded; take them to the rear for me.' Then he put in good order all the mementos, charms, and photographs he had from you. He threw away his saber, saying, 'This kind of thing is why we've lost,' and calmly walked, unarmed, toward the enemy camp. This is what I have to say to you, his mother."

. . . As a foreign missionary, my husband lived [away from the family] for a long time in a temple in Hawaii. During his absence, in addition to running the child-care center, I had put my whole heart into raising my son; his growing up had filled me with delight. This great objective of my beloved son's adulthood, had been the one and only shining light in my life; whatever pain, whatever sorrow I experienced were nothing. My life had been full to bursting, like an always full moon.

The day I can never forget arrived! May 7, 1945: while I still held in my hands the news of my son's death in battle, his remains were ceremoniously delivered. The agony and grief I felt as I held in my arms the small box of plain wood cannot be expressed with such phrases as "I felt like vomiting blood," or "my heart was broken." Only another mother who has experienced it can know.

I was pushed from a world of light into a world of gloom. I lost all desire to live; every bit of happiness was taken away in grief and hopelessness. A soulless puppet, I mourned day in and day out, wretched with the loss of my son. How many times did I decide to follow my beloved son in death? In my need, I could clearly hear the longed-for voice of my son come back to me: "Mother, you must not die! Please, be happy! Please, live in happiness!"

So my son would not permit me to die, suffer, or sorrow. But I . . . would cry until I was emptied. People criticized me as a foolish mother, a prisoner of my emotions. I fell to a very low place. I felt it would be best if my life would end. I cried on and on for over three years. Day and night I consoled myself at the family altar, offering scripture readings, flowers, and incense before his spirit. Thus passed the dreary days and nights. I realized that I had been a teacher to over two thousand pupils and young mothers, but now my life took on a pitiful appearance.

On June 3, 1949, I met the nun-teacher Nagasawa Sozen of the Nun's Practice Center (*dojo*) and listened to her give a talk. At first I thought, "How could she understand this pain, this suffering? She's never given birth to a child or raised a child, much less had a child be killed." My hard heart was shut tight, leaving me without a soul in the world to turn to. However, as I listened to the talk, and was touched by her character, I felt somehow that there was dragged out from me some kind of innocence free of poison which was just on the other side of my deep and relentless bitterness. My feelings toward Nagasawa Roshi changed a little, and as I was pulled along more and more by her lecture I decided, "maybe I'll give meditation (*zazen*) a try." The upshot was that I tried meditating for two days, then three, and finally completed a week's retreat (*sesshin*). As the retreats piled up, my shallowness bored deeply into me, by which I mean I realized that though it was true that Nagasawa Roshi had not borne a child, raised him, and had him die, with respect to the search for knowledge she possessed exalted experience surpassing that of the world's mothers.

I was bitter. And yet, wasn't there deep within me a great, shining compassionate heart which spontaneously wrapped itself around humankind in all their infinite variety? Yes, a compassionate heart! I made my decision: "I too will be the disciple of this teacher. I'll break through the barrier!" Henceforth, as I pressed ahead on the path, I depended upon the teacher in my literally do-or-die struggle. However, I did not escape from the saying, "It's easy to say but hard to do." During the retreats, my pain and sorrow, my melancholy and wretchedness were beyond words; those who haven't had this experience cannot know what I suffered.

As a beginner, jumping headfirst into this world without knowing the first thing about it, my first surprise was a big one. When I saw the group earnestly taking up the practice of *Mu*, I didn't know whether to think it was a joke, or some kind of stupid incompetence, or perhaps that I was in a mental hospital and they were psychotics. Meals were even more surprising. When we received two slices of pickle, we reverently joined our palms in thanks. How often we joined our palms—for the rice gruel, the water, the clearing up—from beginning to end, the whole meal seemed like it was taken with joined palms! These harmonious manners were truly graceful and beautiful, but on the other hand, I felt that the solemnity brought with it an oppressive restraint.

In the search for *Mu*, I didn't relax my meditation posture, I didn't sleep, and I lost sensation in my whole body from the pain in my legs. But despite the fact that I was struggling with the misery of a thousand deaths and ten thousand pains, just when I wished for some mercy, I was hit from behind [with the encouragement stick], making sparks fly from my eyes. It was the first time in my life that I had ever been hit by anyone. "How barbaric!" flared up my rebellious thoughts. I went furiously into the private interview with the teacher (*dokusan*).

"Don't spout logic! It's just your ego!" she thundered at me, driving me out with the ringing of her bell.

"*Mu*—, *Mu*—, *Mu*—" with all my might. I thought, "I am driving myself to death or insanity knocking up against this." But each time the teacher would crush me with, "That's emotion! That's theory! That's interpretation! What are you waiting for?" My faith, my ideas were demolished. "*Mu*—, *Mu*—, *Mu*—," while sleeping, while eating, while in the toilet room, just *Mu*.

As time passed, I lost my appetite. At night I couldn't sleep, but sat up in meditation. The fatigue of body and mind reached an extreme. I was seized, tormented by *Mu* to the extent that during walking meditation, my feet could not take a single step forward. Though *Mu* was in my tears, I could not seize *Mu*. Private interview was always, "That's an hallucination! That's just a belief! That's just an idea! That's just a blissful feeling!"—an unbearable, merciless, cutting whip of words.

Soon all means were exhausted and I had nothing left to cling to. "Oh, I'm no good. I'm an evil person totally lacking the necessary qualities to be helped." How many times I gave up, sinking to the bottom with a sorrowful "thud"! I even thought, "My son disappeared with the dew of the battlefield, but I don't think his suffering was worse than mine is now."

At one time I clung to the Roshi, overflowing with hope, believing that only she was capable of being my spiritual teacher; but after all, that was still my ignorance. Another time I decided to run away as fast as I could from this practice center. I went to my room, and as I was tearfully packing my bag, I heard a voice from deep within my heart saying: "Under the sky of a far-away foreign land, no food, nothing to drink, lying down in a field, sleeping in the mountains, how many times did he dream of his home? I'm sure he wanted to see his father and mother, his beloved younger sister. Cutting off his unsuppressable personal feelings, fully aware of the preciousness of his life, with no way to advance and, following his superiors' orders, no way to retreat, what was his distracted state of mind like?"

"I must think of my child's death in war!" I thought. "What is my hardship? It doesn't amount to a thing! If I don't open up the way here and now, when will my dead son and I be released from the world?" Instantly, all thought of fleeing vanished. Greatly stirred and with courage renewed, I picked up the practice again.

Previously I had been cramped, immobilized in my own narrow and rigid shell. As my practice progressed, I gradually got rid of my egotism, freed of my distracting thoughts, and able to emerge out into a bright and wide-open world. For a slice of pickle, a morsel of rice-gruel, even the intense "whip" of words, from deep in my heart a grateful prostration came. Heretofore, as the wife of a religious man, I had eaten Buddhist food, was taught Buddhism and read Buddhist books; I thought of myself as having understood Buddhist thought. But I had come to realize keenly that since I had never really suffered, never really tasted experience, I couldn't stand up to a real battle in a crisis. I was truly abashed and could hardly bear my shame. Now this realization soaked into the marrow of my bones.

In high spirits I went into the private interview, but once again, "You're just finding religious joy in the world of faith. . . . Hey, reluctant one, where are you? Come out! Come out! Come out and grab *Mu!* Don't be unwilling! Come out naked and exposed! Come on out and grab it! Come on! Come on!" she pressed her urgent command. She sent me staggering away, thrown back upon my own resources and writhing in pain.

"Now I have arrived here where there is only death. . . . It is death, it is *Mu,* it is death, it is *Mu,* it is *Mu,* it is *Mu.*" Soon I forgot all about the private interview. *Mu—, Mu—, Mu—,* there is only *Mu.* . . . I went out into the yard and quietly sat down. Before the temple house one great tree stood alone, reaching to the clouds. In harmony with my chant of *Mu,—, Mu—, Mu—,* the earth trembled and urged me on. Azalea leaves and small flowers spoke to me one by one. The bright moon laughed and became one with me.

Night passed. How pleasant the morning practice, how sweet the little bird's song! The crisp crunch, crunch, crunch of the kitchen master at the cutting board, the sound of the mallet as a woman out back hammered away cracking soybeans—from everywhere I could hear wonderful, indescribable music. Was this a visit to the paradise of the pure land? I didn't know, but it was the greatest of joys. No longer was there either a corrupt and troublesome world nor an honored teacher. My clinging to my beloved dead son vanished, and the painful search for *Mu* also disappeared in this ecstatic, exalted state of mind (*samādhi*).

However, later, I was again slapped in the face by the teacher's ferocious roar and returned, startled, to *Mu.* Again, *Mu—, Mu—, Mu—.* A tiny insect flew onto the paper door; it was *Mu.* An airplane flew through the sky; it was *Mu.* The whole universe was nothing but *Mu.* In the midst of this, the wooden frame of the paper door fell away and vanished. My body felt as if it were being dragged up from deep within the bowels of the earth. "Gong!" rang the temple bell, and suddenly, I cried out and returned to myself. It was attained! "Heaven and Earth are of one piece. The universe and I are one body. I am the Buddha! We're joined in one!" It was *Mu.*

This greatest of treasures, which I hold, is without a shred of falsehood, even of the size of a cormorant's down; no one could ever harm it. This treasure, which I hold, transcends death; even the teacher herself could never damage or destroy it.

"It's nothing, it's nothing, it's nothing." . . . Imperturbable, I at long last went into the private interview as my original self. Now, for the first time, the teacher herself smiled warmly and I received formal approval. Then she gave me various instructions and advice.

The joy itself passed in a moment. When I was made aware of the responsibility and difficulties of those who aspire to the way, I fully understood what the teacher meant in the private interview when she said, "That's just religious joy." I was introduced to koan practice as the way to the most exalted spheres. And while it is a path of trials, there is all the difference in the world between it and the suffering I formerly experienced within my narrow and rigid shell. These are the hardships one suffers while punting one's boat over to the territory of the buddhas and patriarchs; in reality this is the greatest of joys.

Eternal life presents me with ongoing, daily occupations. Words cannot express what it is like to live and work together with my dead son. That is buddha mind. This too is buddha mind. Apart from buddha mind, there is nothing. That is joy. This too is joy. My life is full in this vast, delightful and pure world. In one of my teacher's lectures she spoke the lines,

> My clear dew mind
> Is a ruby
> When amongst the autumn leaves.

It's because my mind is clear or colorless that it can adapt to any and all circumstances.

Because of the kindness of the buddhas and patriarchs, a life worth living, a life that requires only the slightest effort, has begun. I can never in my life forget the austerities of the retreat. For the trouble taken by my teacher I have truly deep gratitude which I can only express with hands palm to palm. I bow to you.

Seizing the True Body

The following account is the story of a nun, Nachii Keido, who manages through sheer persistence to overcome the limitations of her background. Born and raised in rural Japan, she was almost completely uneducated; the prewar educational neglect of girls and of nuns was her daily experience. She attained a somewhat minimal literacy largely through her own determined efforts; in the same way, she rebuilt a deteriorated shrine with little community support. Lacking in training herself, she soon found herself the head of her convent. Her sincere spiritual questioning led her to seek doggedly the training she was never given, culminating in her encounter with Nagasawa Roshi. Unlike the laywoman in the previous account, the now elderly nun who speaks to us in this account is not surprised by what she finds at Nagasawa Roshi's retreat, but is delighted to have found what she has sought throughout a lifetime as a nun. Note that her long-held personal devotion to the bodhisattva Kannon, the female embodiment of perfect compassion, becomes transformed through Zen practice into an experiential sense of ongoing union.

I know that our world is full of heavenly beings living in peace, but at the same time, I see that sentient beings are being endlessly consumed in a great fire. I have eaten Buddhist food for forty-eight years, hoping to escape from this burning house of the triple world. When I look back on those years, there is nothing that does not move me to deep gratitude. My motive for leaving home and becoming a nun was rooted in my horror of the burning house. In the spring of my twentieth year, I wrenched myself away from my loved ones. Crying and begging, I finally obtained my mother's consent and hurried to the village convent.

At the time that I grew up, there were no schools like today's schools. In those days only special people went to school; girls especially were thought to have no need for schooling. So in the daytime I worked for a teacher and in the evenings I went over to my elder brother's house in the neighboring village to study basic reading and writing. I still remember how happy I was when I received an inkstone case as a reward for being able to write the Japanese syllabary without looking. With this background, my struggles to learn the Buddhist scriptures were indescribable. While unflaggingly laboring at this, I grew accustomed to a nun's life, and was fortunate enough to be sent to school in Toyama for four years.

From this time on, I gradually began to scrutinize myself and ask myself: What is human life? What is the mission of one who has left home? In the midst of this, the management of the convent was turned over to me and my responsibilities piled up. If I didn't work, there wouldn't be any food even to offer the Buddha. The convent was in a state of deterioration unworthy of the enshrinement of revered Kannon, the object of everyone's faith. Somehow or other, I wanted to build a shrine for Kannon; this would be the great undertaking of my life. I vowed before the Buddha, "From now on, I dedicate my life to revered Kannon. I offer to her the greatest effort I can possibly make." From then on, I was quite literally stirred up. I begged for monthly contributions that people would not give. Evil things were said about me, and I became physically and mentally exhausted. How many times I went before revered Kannon with tears pouring down my face! When I think about it now I realize that I did a good job, and what's more I can clearly see that that hard struggle became a great shining light for me.

I breathed a sigh of relief when I accomplished the enshrinement of revered Kannon in her new shrine without going too far into debt. But as I did this, the questions from my youth that I had forgotten in the interim rose up in my mind. What is the purpose of going around begging (*takuhatsu*)? What is the point of reading scriptures? What in the world is revered Kannon? I accosted the heads of four or five neighboring temples with these questions. Once or twice a year we studied how a nun should progress on the path and I proposed setting up some kind of association for this purpose.

My elder brother who, happily, had become a monk and was chief priest in a nearby temple, shared a great deal of wisdom with me. With his assistance and that of an abbot whom he knew, a training institute for nuns was organized. This institute was made possible by the great efforts of everyone, but since I was the eldest attending, I was always made to sit in the seat of honor, raised above the rest. I didn't know anything, though, so while my body was raised in a position of status, my embarrassed mind always took a low seat. No matter how many scriptures I heard or books I read, I didn't understand anything. This worried me; I always felt uneasy because I didn't understand anything. Once while visiting a Buddhist friend's sickbed, I was deeply struck: "All his distress, all his grumbling—it's common enough in this world, but he's a monk!" I trembled as if I were the one who was sick. My uneasiness grew.

Three years ago in May, I heard that the nun teacher Nagasawa of the Tokyo Nuns' Practice Center (*dojo*) would be coming to the area for a meditation retreat. Deciding I must by all means go, I waited impatiently. Unfortunately, I had to do some temple business which made me miss the first two days of the retreat. When I, white-headed and knowing nothing, first went into the midst of them, they all seemed as young to me as my own novices. I felt embarrassed, but even more I feared that I might hinder them in their zealous practice. But as I got used to it, I felt, "How wonderful! Thank goodness! This is what I've been searching for all these years! I understand, I understand! Well, if it's a matter of sitting in meditation, I'll sit! I'll sit until I understand the true body of Kannon!" Taking courage, I embraced my faith and forgot my years. I returned home, aiming for that bright light of hard struggle I had previously discovered.

I had heard that practice in the midst of activity surpasses practice in inactivity a hundred-, a thousand-, ten thousand-fold, so when going and coming from reading scripture at parishioners' houses I purposefully took the long way around. I also chose quiet places to practice, such as while weeding, sweeping the garden, caring for the Buddha altar, and so on. I tried hard to practice in the midst of all these activities. I struggled to keep this up, but I just couldn't do it. How my mind wandered! I was thoroughly disgusted with it. Just as a monkey leaps from branch to branch, my mind grasped at the branches of desire for sense experience. It was pathetic. In the face of this unconscious and unknown bad karma which I had created in former lives, I could do nothing but press my palms together and bow my head.

I had not been able to attend all of the previous year's retreat, but had had to miss a little. At the time of the following year's retreat I had to stay in bed with an intestinal problem and was unable to attend. And so another year went by. But anyway, there was no other way than this. "If I don't cross over to liberation in this body, in this lifetime, then I'll cross over in some other lifetime," we say; all things are impermanent and ephemeral.

This year, though, I attended the retreat from the day before it began, together with a novice. I helped out as my age allowed and at long last the opening day arrived. From the three o'clock bell to the unrolling of my bedding at nine P.M., I exerted myself with enthusiasm. I sat in meditation with all the zeal I had, but I didn't make much progress. The young people were full of energy as they practiced. Whatever face or figure I looked at, all were strained, as if pulled taut. Such austere, yet noble figures! Forgetting about myself, how many times I revered them as I sat behind them, thinking, as tears welled up, "these are truly living buddhas."

One day, two, three, gradually the days were gone.

> Life and death is a great concern,
> All things are impermanent and ephemeral.
> Each of you must quickly wake up!
> Be careful, don't miss your chance!

The verse recited at bedtime echoed on and on in my ears. I couldn't sleep.

It was the middle day of the retreat. I was sitting in meditation with fresh spirits. I don't know how or why, but all of a sudden, out of the blue, a happy feeling came over me, and I cried out. I realized: "It's *Mu,* it's *Mu! Mu* is overflowing! I understand *Mu!* I understand Kannon's true body, my true body, no—the true body of all things! It's all one! No matter what anyone says, I have penetrated to my original self (*honrai no jiko*). How wonderful! How wonderful that even I could have such an exalted experience!"

At the private interview, I presented the important points. The teacher smiled. In gentle words such as she had not used before, she said this experience was a matter of paradoxical self-knowledge that was completely inexpressible.

The uncertainty I had felt before this experience has been swept away and I have become constantly one with Kannon. I pass my days in peace and gratitude. Since the joy of realizing that the triple world is composed of mind only, I clearly understand that all things, from the doors and windows and the straw floor-mats to Kannon herself, all things that strike my eyes, indeed, all invisible things too, are full of life and vigor. It's strange: the triple world has remained the same before and after I experienced myself, before and after I experienced the truth, but since I woke up and saw, the triple world seems so different.

Wanting even one more person to penetrate to the bright light of this great truth, I have forgotten my white hair and sixty-eight years, and related my foolish feelings. Please, dear readers, be my companions on the path for life after life. We will strive to advance on the path toward the realization of buddhahood and to send a refreshing breeze to the countless sentient beings. I bow to you, hands palm to palm.

—17—

Death-Bed Testimonials of the Pure Land Faithful

Daniel B. Stevenson

These three documents from Pure Land hagiographical compendia illustrate some of the paradigms and rhetoric that attend Pure Land notions of sanctity, as well as various ways in which the goal of rebirth in Sukhāvatī (the pure land) organizes the everyday expectations of Pure Land believers.

In literary and oral Buddhist lore, it is commonly claimed that the last thoughts of a dying person have a direct influence on the status of rebirth in the next life. While this may seem a fairly straightforward matter of self-control—just "think good thoughts"—it is complicated by the belief that, with the waning of one's conscious powers, the mind is overwhelmed by subliminal karmic propensities or "memories" that manifest as visions before the dying person. In this way, the habits and events of one's current and previous existences quite literally draw one toward one's future destiny. As frightful and unpredictable as it might seem, this liminal moment of transition between death and rebirth is considered a time of enormous spiritual potential. For at no other time (except, perhaps, upon attaining the knowledge of former lives that comes to accomplished meditation masters) is a person afforded such a chance to remove the veil between the conscious and unconscious dimensions of self, review directly his or her karmic stock, and refashion one's being. Shandao's rites for the dying person, as well as the diverse repertoire of funerary ceremonies that are performed for the deceased over the forty-nine days following death, devolve around a common belief in the potency of this moment.

The primary aim of Shandao's deathbed procedures is to ensure that the dying person successfully forges what is known as *jingyin* or *jingyuan,* "the connection or nexus of conditions that will bring rebirth in the pure land." The ritual process itself unfolds as a fluid symbiosis between the two complementary activities of divination and ritual response. Throughout the last days or minutes of life, a careful watch is maintained for any signs of visions that may be indicative of the dying person's spiritual disposition. On the basis of these divinatory clues, different modes of ritual procedure—confession, *nianfo* (reciting the Buddha's name), reading of sūtras, and the like—are applied accordingly, the ultimate aim being to absolve the mind of worldly attachments and karmic obstructions, and direct it toward rebirth in the pure land. The successful forging of this "connection with the pure land" is itself indicated by the appearance of the desired auspicious signs at the time of the person's death or, as the case may be, during the weeks of funerary observances that follow.

Precedents for such a concept can be found in the Pure Land sūtras themselves. The *Sūtra on the Contemplation of the Buddha of Limitless Life,* for example, distinguishes various visionary signs that will confirm for the dying person that he or she is destined for the pure land. Having set this prognostic tone, the "ten moments of recollection of Amitābha" are touted as the only effective means for turning the situation around should less desirable omens appear and salvation be in doubt. At the same time, other sources are also at work in Shandao's system, including forms of ritual penance and prognostication traditionally associated with Chinese buddhānusmṛti practice. One will notice, for example, that Shandao's procedure for dealing with manifestations of evil karma entails an orchestration of invocation or veneration of the Buddha, confession, and vow—the three basic building blocks of Chinese Buddhist liturgy and cult devotion.

It is one thing for the individual Pure Land practitioner to seek an auspicious vision or sign as confirmation of having secured a "connection with the pure land," but something quite different is at stake when Shandao insists that these "signs" (*xiang*) and the entire deathbed drama should be written down "just as they happened." For rather than the deceased, it is the generations who survive him or her that become the point of focus here. This unusual practice brings us to another important aspect of Pure Land culture and representative genre of Pure Land literature—namely, the writing of exemplary testimonials and creation of hagiographical collections for the purposes of spreading the faith.

Records of auspicious wonders and exemplary devotees are as old as Pure Land practice itself in China. As early as the Shanxi Pure Land masters Daochuo and Shandao, we find dedicated collections of rebirth testimonials attached to or circulating alongside of the more familiar treatises on Pure Land doctrine and practice. Nearly every generation since has seen the publication of some compendium or other of this sort, usually by persons bent on promoting a particular redaction or movement of Pure Land teaching. Individual records or entries may involve a diversity of religious themes. Some of these, such as the healing of illness, the averting of evil reciprocity or demonic influence, are perennial concerns of Chinese religion. Others, such as meditative visions of Amitābha and the deathbed conversion of sinners, are more peculiar to Pure Land. Throughout these narratives, however, exclusive devotion to the Pure Land path and omens verifying a successful "forging of the connection with the pure land" are bedrock elements.

Among the signs that confirm rebirth in these tales, deathbed and mortuary anomalies are certainly popular. Some involve the dying person, such as visions of Amitābha and his retinue coming to greet one with a lotus pedestal, as described in the *Sūtra on the Contemplation of the Buddha of Limitless Life*. An unusually peaceful death (often while seated erect in meditative posture) or the hearing of marvelous strains of music, the smell of rare fragrances, or the sight of unusual auroras on the part of friends and relatives are also common features. Another variety of post-mortem omen centers around the disposition of the corpse or the experience of the mourners over the weeks of mortuary observance that follow. One phenomenon that is a universal sign of sainthood or high spiritual attainment in Chinese Buddhism is the discovery of auspicious relics (*sheli* in Chinese, from the Sanskrit *śarīra*) amid the ashes of the cremated corpse, usually in the form of glassine or jadelike beads. If burial is chosen over cremation, natural mummification of individual bodily organs or the corpse itself will be taken as an indication of sanctity. Another frequent occurrence, but one which seems to be more peculiar to Pure Land devotees, is the experience of visitations from the deceased to the surviving relatives or friends. Usually these occur in dreams and take the form of either a vision of the beatified dead person or a "spirit-journey" with the dead person to the pure land. Upon occasion, however, a layperson or cleric of highly developed religious ability will have a vision of the deceased while in a state of samādhi or meditative transport.

Although death signs are an important and frequent topic of discussion among Pure Land believers, it is essential to realize that great emphasis is placed on confirmatory signs for the living practitioner as well. After all, when one has decided to devote a lifetime to Pure Land practice rather than wait until the last breath to turn to Amitābha, it is perfectly natural to expect some confirmation of spiritual progress along the way. Following the cue of such Pure Land scriptures as the *Sūtra on the Contemplation of the Buddha of Limitless Life,* together with various other buddhānusmṛti sūtras popular in China, Pure Land practitioners looked to two sorts of visionary phenomena as assurance of their future rebirth in Sukhāvatī: One was auspicious dreams of Amitābha and the pure land; the other, visitations from Amitābha and previous saints or "spirit journeys" to the pure land experienced in a state of samādhi or meditative ecstasy. Both forms of experience were considered valid proof that the "connection with the pure land" was or would soon be secured—provided, of course, that the character and behavior of the individual who claimed the experience fit the profile of a dedicated Pure Land devotee. Nevertheless, in Pure Land hagiography and doctrine, samādhi is given precedence over dreams. The biography of nearly every major Pure Land saint—especially the patriarchal figures—is marked by the watershed experience of a vision of this sort.

Here we find an important point of soteriological convergence between the Pure Land ritual and meditative manuals and the Pure Land hagiographical collections. In certain respects, it requires us to reevaluate the way in which the long-range goal of rebirth in the pure land actually functions within the lives of Pure Land believers. It is easy, but perhaps ultimately misleading, to think of Pure Land spirituality as having a morbid obsession with death and the afterlife just because its stated aim is rebirth in Sukhāvatī. This is especially so if we are to take Zunshi and Shandao seriously when they claim that sustained practice of *nianfo* will bring a vision of the Buddha in this very life. In effect, such a vision of Amitābha does more than confirm that one is destined for the pure land in the near future, for it implies that one already has access to the Buddha now. Thus it becomes a mark of sainthood that is virtually equivalent (in anticipated form) to the irreversibility on the bodhisattva path that will be formally achieved when one is reborn in the pure land itself. In this respect, it represents a kind of Pure Land "enlightenment" experience that is equally compelling and equally vital to establishing religious identity and authority as the "seeing into one's original nature" of Chan/Zen.

The three pieces below are representative of the testimonials that one finds in Pure Land miracle tale and hagiographical anthologies. The first, which is taken from the thirteenth-century *Comprehensive Record of the Buddhas and Patriarchs (Fozu tongji),* concerns the life of the late Tang-period monk, Shaokang. Shaokang is regarded variously as the fifth or sixth "patriarchal ancestor" (*zu*) of the Chinese Pure Land tradition. Hence, his story gives a sense of the paradigms associated with Pure Land monasticism and patriarchal sanctity.

The remaining two testimonials, the "Record of the Lady Yueguo," by Huang Ce, and the "Record of the Parrot of Hedong," by Wei Gao (746–805) governor of Chengdu, are taken from Zongxiao's *Topical Selections on the Land of Bliss (Lebang wenlei),* another influential thirteenth-century Pure Land anthology. Both pieces are acknowledged to have circulated as independent testimonials prior to being collected by the anthology's author. Thus, in addition to touching upon dimensions of Pure Land spirituality that extend beyond the Buddhist monastic system, they give us some insight into the process by which many such miracle tales and exemplary original biographies came into being.

The tale of the Lady of Yueguo is especially pertinent, for it deals with an exemplary woman who dedicates herself to the Pure Land faith within the cloistered environment of an aristocratic Song dynasty household (she was the wife of one of the younger brothers of Emperor Shen). The testimonial itself is written by the Buddhist layman and literatus, Huang Ce (1070–1132), which obviously shapes the Lady Yueguo to norms of female virtue representative of Chinese society and the Buddhist monastic system at large. Although we can sense various ways in which her role as a woman of upper-class birth may have contributed to a distinctive form of Pure Land spirituality, it is difficult if not impossible to obtain any immediate sense of this religious world through the materials at hand. One can, however, raise the issue of divergent or multiple cultural domains within Chinese Pure Land tradition, as well as the corollary question of just what certain documents can and cannot tell us about Chinese religion. As a backdrop to Lady Yueguo's story, one might begin with the narrative setting of the *Sūtra on the Contemplation of the Buddha of Limitless Life* itself. The sūtra devolves around the suffering figure of Queen Vaidehī. Imprisoned in the palace by her evil son Ajātaśatru, she beseeches the Buddha to grant her a teaching that will enable her to endure her torment, eliminate her sinful karma, and lead to life in a "pure" world free of all such wickedness. The Buddha Śākyamuni appears and preaches the meditation on the pure land of Amitābha specifically in response to her request. This narrative and its accompanying paradigms provide material to explore Lady Yueguo's understanding of sin, suffering, purity, and salvation.

The translations are from *Fuozo tongji* by Zhipan (*Taishō*, vol. 49.264a–b); *Jingwang yūeguo furen wangsheng ji* by Huang Ce (*Taishō*, vol. 47.189c–190a); and *Hedong yingwu sheli ta ji* by Yi Weigao (*Taishō*, vol. 47.191a–c). The latter two are found in *Lebang wenlei* by Zongxiao (*Taishō* 1969).

The Biography of Dharma Master Shaokang

The dharma master Shaokang was from the Zhou clan of Jinyun. His mother was of the Luo clan. Once she dreamed that she journeyed to Dinghu Peak, where a jade maiden gave her a blue lotus blossom, saying, "This flower is auspicious. You are destined to give birth to a precious son." When [Shaokang] was born, a radiant blue light filled the room, and there was a pervading fragrance of lotus blossoms in full bloom.

Even at seven years old, Kang still did not speak. Prognosticators thought it very strange. Once his mother took him with her to Lingshan Monastery. Directing him to the Buddha hall, she said, "When you reverence the Buddha, don't be hasty." To which he replied, "Who wouldn't be reverent toward our Lord Buddha Śākyamuni?" [After this episode,] his mother and father looked upon him with even greater respect and awe. Ultimately, they allowed him to leave home [as a novice monk].

By age fifteen he had perfectly memorized five scriptures, including the *Lotus* and *Sūraṅgama* sūtras. Later he set off for Jiaxiang Monastery in Kuaiji to study the vinaya codes. After that, he went to Longxing Monastery in Shangyuan, where he attended lectures on the *Avataṃsaka [Sūtra]* and various treatises such as the *Yogācārabhūmi*. At the beginning of the Zhenyuan reign-period of the Tang [785–805 C.E.] [he was residing] at White Horse Monastery in Luoyang. There he once saw light radiating from a text [stored] in the hall. He picked it up and found it to be the venerable Shandao's *Tract on Converting to the Way of the Western [Pure Land] (Xifang huadao wen)*. Master [Shaokang] thereupon proclaimed, "If I have a karmic connection with the pure land, may this [text] again put out radiance." No sooner did he speak these words than [the text] again blazed with light. Kang said, "Though stones may grind me for an eon, I will not deviate from my vow."

Subsequently he proceeded to Shandao's mortuary hall at Radiant Light Monastery (Guangming si) in Changan. There he set out a great array of offerings. All of a sudden he saw [Shandao's] commemorative image rise up into the air and address him, saying, "By relying on my teaching you will widely convert sentient beings. On a select day [in the future] your meritorious efforts will bear success and you will assuredly be born in the land of ease and succor."

The master heard the voice of the Buddha, which seemed to be a confirmation [of Shandao's charge]. Thereupon he set off southward for Jiangling. On the road he met a monk who told him, "If you wish to convert people you should go to Xinding [the present-day Yanzhou]." As soon as he finished speaking these words, he disappeared. When the master first entered [Xinding] commandery, no one there knew him. So, he begged money and enticed little boys saying, "The Buddha Amitābha is your teacher and guide. Recite the Buddha's [name] one time and I will give one piece of cash." Setting his sights on the money, the boy would recite along with [Shaokang].

After a little more than a month, he had gathered a considerable crowd of urchins who would come to recite the Buddha's name for cash. The master thereupon said to them, "To anyone who can do ten recitations of the Buddha's name [without interruption] I will give one coin." He continued this for a full year, [after which] there was no person—young or old, nobleborn or mean—who didn't intone "A-mi-tuo-fuo" whenever they met the master. [Thus,] the sound of reciting the Buddha's name (*nianfo*) filled the streets.

In the tenth year [of the Zhenyuan reign period], [Shaokang] built a Pure Land chapel (*jingtu daochang*) on Mount Wulong. He constructed an altar (*tan*) of three levels, where he gathered his followers to perform ritual services and circumambulation. Whenever the master ascended the high seat and chanted the Buddha's name out loud, the congregation would see a single buddha issue from his mouth. When he strung together ten such recitations, they would see ten buddhas. The master said, "Those of you who see these buddhas are certain to achieve rebirth [in the pure land]." At that time the group numbered several thousand. Those among them who failed to see [the buddhas] wailed and reprimanded themselves, [resolving] to persevere even more zealously [in their practice].

On the third day during the tenth month of the twenty-first year [of the Zhenyuan reign], [the master] called together his lay and monastic followers and charged them [saying]: "You should engender a heart that delights in the pure land and despises [this deluded world of] Jambudvīpa. [If] on this occasion you can see [my] radiant light then you are truly my disciple." Thereupon, the master put forth various unusual beams of light and passed away. The people of the local commandery built a reliquary (*stūpa*) for him at Terrace Crag. During the third year of the *qianyu* reign period of the Posterior Han [950], the state preceptor Chao of Mount Tiantai urged that his pagoda be renovated. People who came after him often point to the master as a latter-day Shandao.

The Record of the Rebirth of the Lady Yueguo, Wife of the King of Jing

I have observed that beings caught up in deluded thinking and enmeshed in the five desires ordinarily give no thought to escape and are almost never able to make a decisive resolution to seek rebirth in the land of highest bliss to the west. However, when faced with something unbearable—such as malicious intentions or an unfavorable turn of events, separation from their loved ones, signs of [oncoming] old age, sickness, and death, pressing danger, or being overcome by pain and poison—they suddenly weep and wail out loud and turn to the Buddha for refuge. Hoping to escape death's grip, they recite a few words out loud with their profane minds, professing their refuge in the Compassionate Lord and praying that he might greet and lead them to rebirth in the pure land.

The lady Yueguo from the Wang clan is the only person I know who was not like this. Her ladyship was the wife of the king of Jing [paternal uncle to Emperor Zhe of the Song dynasty]. Seeing that [her husband] was caught up in the five desires and had no interest in departing from them, she kept her thoughts to herself. [Inwardly] she took refuge in the Buddha of Infinite Life and made the vow to seek rebirth [in his pure land] to the west. When someone has suffered a host of tribulations, faced the unbearable, and begun to seek release, how can one speak with that person about commonplace things?

People say that her ladyship planted the roots of virtue in former lives and had already received prophesy [of her future] buddhahood. For eons since, she has taken birth among human beings as a preacher of the way in order to establish the teaching in the Buddha's stead. [Since we know that] she personally enjoined the noble and well-to-do, both within and outside [of her household], to practice Pure Land meditation together with her, and together take refuge in the land of the Buddha, doesn't this [claim] make sense?

In her ritual service to the western [pure land], her ladyship was tried and true, never missing [the appointed hour of worship], whether it be day or night. The people who scurried about in attendance on her had no other thought in their minds [than to serve her and her religion].

There was only one maidservant who was indolent and refused to respond [to her commands]. One day her ladyship scolded her, saying, "My entire household is diligent. Only you are lazy and will not do what you are told. If delusion is present in the group I fear that others will falter in their determination for the way. I cannot permit [such a person] to be part of my retinue."

The maidservant suddenly awoke to her errors and recanted with deep remorse. Thereafter she dedicated herself to contemplation and strove to maintain thought of the pure land at all times. After a long while she finally confided to one of her fellow servants, "I too am a [Pure Land] practitioner." One evening an unusual fragrance filled her room, and she passed away without any sign of illness. The next day her fellow servant informed the lady of the house, "Last night I had a dream of our late maidservant who just passed away. She came to me and said, 'The lady of the house once admonished me to dedicate myself to cultivation of the western [pure land]. Today I have been reborn there, thereby realizing incalculable meritorious virtues.' "

Her ladyship responded, "When I also have a dream like this, I will believe it."

That very night her ladyship dreamed that she met the dead maidservant, who spoke to her much as she had the previous woman. Her ladyship said, "Can the pure land be reached [by the living]?"

The maid said, "If your ladyship will come with me . . . "

The lady of the house set off with the maid, and in time they came to two pools of water, both of which were filled with white lotus blossoms of varying size. Some were glorious. Others were withered or drooping. However, each one was different. Her ladyship said, "Why are they like this?"

To which the maid replied, "They all represent persons of the mundane world who have made the resolution to seek rebirth in the western pure land. With the arousing of the [first] flicker of thought [of the pure land], one's wholesome [karmic] roots will have already sent forth a sprout. Eventually it will form a single blossom. However, because people's degrees of diligence are not the same, there are differences in the quality of the blossoms. For those who are unrelenting in their efforts, [the blossom] is fresh and resplendent. For those who are sporadic, it is withered. If people continue to practice for a long time without giving up, to the point where their mindfulness becomes stabilized [in samādhi] and their contemplation reaches fruition, then when their physical bodies perish and their life [in the mundane world] reaches its end they will be reborn by miraculous transformation in the center [of one of these lotus blossoms]."

In the middle of the pool there was one particular blossom, the calyx of which suddenly fell away, showing a person dressed in courtly garb seated in the midst [of its newly opened petals]. His robes were whisked away by the breeze, revealing a body bedecked with jeweled crown and intricate necklaces. Her ladyship asked, "Who is that?"

The maid replied, "It is Yang Jie [Cigong] [a famous Pure Land devotee, 980–1048]."

Another flower then opened, revealing a person in courtly dress seated in its center. However, soon thereafter the blossom withered away, leaving nothing but the sepals. Her ladyship again asked who it was, to which the maid replied, "It was Ma Gan [another famous Pure Land devotee]."

Her ladyship asked, "Where might I be reborn?" The maid led her ladyship forward another several leagues, then had her look off into the distance. She saw nothing but a single sprawling altar (*tan*) which glistened resplendently of gold and azure, with splinters [of rainbow] light intertwining in intricate patterns. The maid said, "This is the spot where your ladyship will be reborn by spontaneous transformation. It is the golden altar that represents the highest level of the highest grade of rebirth."

When [her ladyship] awoke she set out, with mixed feelings of joy and grief, to visit the homes of Yang Jie and Ma Gan. Jie had, in fact, passed away. Gan was free of misfortune.

On the day when her ladyship herself finally realized rebirth, she took her censer in hand, lit incense, gazed toward the Guanyin Pavilion, and stood up. At that moment, the grandchildren and attendants approached her ladyship to receive her ceremonial blessing [of long life]. As soon as it was done, she passed away while standing there. The birds all gave out a cry, which was very strange indeed.

As a rule, fortunate and happy people will find little time for Buddhist matters. Those who do are often lost for lack of faith. The few who are capable of belief are plagued by the inability [fully] to resolve their doubts. Those who embrace the faith when confronted with distress and suffering for the most part fail because it is just too late. How, then, could knowing true faith, manifestation of true mindfulness, and cultivation of the wholesome conditions [that lead to rebirth] be considered such an easy thing? Yang Jie Cigong had a keen understanding of the teachings of this Chan school, but people did not know that he practiced Pure Land meditation in secret. On his deathbed he revealed his mistakes and composed his verse on "going from mistake to mistake." [According to his biography, Yang experienced a vision of Amitābha coming to greet him when he died. The verse that he composed upon departing the world reads: "Although I take birth, there is yet no place to dwell. Although I die, there is nothing to relinquish. One who abides in the grand void on the basis of error goes to error—the land of highest bliss to the west."] When I heard the tale of her ladyship's experience, I weighed it and set it down in writing, primarily to help those who have already aroused faith in [the pure land]. However, nonbelievers will surely be moved to faith by this text as well, and thereby turn to pure meditation on the Buddha's land.

Recorded by Huang Ce, [also known as] the Buddhist layman Suiyuan.

Inscription for the Reliquary of the Parrot of Hedong

The primal essence gave form to the myriad species by means of the five elemental energies. Even though some creatures may have scales, and others shells, fur, or feathers, there are sure to be some whose [sentient] endowments are keen and pure. Whether resplendent like fire or an unusual pure green in color, all respond to human culture. If [the training] that they receive is timely and orderly, there will be instances where their animal nature is transformed and they learn the ability to speak. Upon coming to understand single-minded [absorption in] emptiness, they [may] leave behind genuine relics after they die.

Most likely these will not simply be manifestations produced by the primal sage [that is, a buddha such as Amitābha], but something [instigated by] the stimulus of the human heart. We are the same [in essence], but different by circumstance—transformed on the basis of a single reality.

Some years ago there was a man who had a parrot for sale, claiming that "in this parrot's call one could detect the sounds of Chinese." Mr. Pei of Hedong had a keen love for the Way of the Golden immortal. He had heard that, in the western [pure land of Sukhāvatī or highest bliss], there was a type of precious bird that would flock together with its fellows, harmonize its call, and warble forth songs of the dharma. The name of this bird is recorded in the Sanskrit sūtras.

Seeing that [this bird's] perspicacity far exceeded that of the common species, Pei figured that it was produced deliberately from the Buddha's own essence. Thus, he constantly kept it nearby [or tended it closely] and showed great reverence toward it. First he taught the bird to keep the prohibitions of the six monthly uposatha fast days, so that the bird would not even look at food from the time noon approached until the night was ended. [If an animal is capable of this,] surely it is possible to bring the wayward and vulgar populace to uprightness and the observance of brahma purity!

Pei also taught the bird to keep the Buddha's name, explaining to it, "Through mindful thought (*nian*) [of the Buddha], one reaches no-thought (*wunịan*)." In response, the bird thereupon raised its head and spread its wings, as though it were ready to listen attentively to his instructions. Thereafter, whenever Pei commanded the bird to perform recollection or recitation of the Buddha's name (*nianfo*), it would stand there silently and not respond. But when he told it to not recollect the Buddha's name, it would immediately cry out, "A-mi-tuo-fuo, A-mi-tuo-fuo." Pei tested the bird many times over, and it was always the same, never different.

I believe that, since [Pei told the bird] that having thoughts led to existence [in saṃsāra] and no-thought was absolute reality, the bird would not respond to [the command to recollect the Buddha], because to do so entailed conditions for dependent origination [in saṃsāra]. Although the bird chattered away when ultimate reality [was mentioned], [he was justified in doing so because he knew that] words are fundamentally empty.

Every morning the parrot would signal the approach of day from its empty room by calling out in harmonious song. Keeping time with his beak, he would lightly drum out the beat in the air, while at the same time he would raise and lower his voice in a continual stream of recitation. Whoever heard it never failed to feel cleansed and delight in the good.

Coming to birth, do desport [oneself in life] and proceed by the stars. But these circumstances must also come to an end. [Or: Does the sport of life proceed by the planets? Or does it come to an end by cause and condition?] During the seventh month of this year, the bird became weak and unresponsive. After several days, the keeper knew it was going to die. He struck the sounding stone and called out to the bird, "Are you getting ready to return to the western [pure land]? I will keep time on the sounding stone, and you maintain recollection [of the Buddha] accordingly."

Each time he struck the stone, the bird would recite "A-mi-tuo-fuo." When Pei had struck the stone ten times and the bird had completed ten recitations, it smoothed its feathers, tucked up its feet, and, without wavering or fidgeting, serenely ended its life.

According to the Buddhist scriptures, with the completion of ten recollections or recitations [of the Buddha's name] one may achieve rebirth in the western [pure land]. It is also said that one who has acquired the wisdom of a buddha will leave śarīra relics when he dies. One who really understands this concept certainly will not make distinctions based on species! Consequently, Pei ordered a fire to be built and immolated [the bird] according to standard cremation procedure. When the blaze finally died out, lo and behold, there were more than ten beads of śarīra relics. They glistened brightly before the eye and felt smooth to the palm, like fine jade. Those who saw them gaped in amazement. Whoever heard about them listened with alarm. Everyone agreed that if the bird was able to entice the wayward and bring benefit to the world [like this], how could it not have been the manifestation of a bodhisattva!

At that time there was a certain eminent monk named Huiguan, who had once made a pilgrimage to Mount Wutai to pay reverence to the sacred sites [connected with the bodhisattva Mañjuśrī]. Hearing people speak of this bird, he wept tears of compassionate grief and begged that he might erect a porcelain [stūpa] for the relics on the holy mountain in order to commemorate the wonder.

I say that this creature was able to keep and follow the way, and when it died, [these relics] verified it. In ancient times, beings that penetrated the level of the sages and worthies and appeared as manifestations include Nügua, who came with a serpent's body to instruct the thearch [Fuxi], and Chongyan, who had the body of a bird and came to establish the marquis [of Qin]. They are recorded in the secular annals. Who says that these tales are strange? How much the less should it be so when this bird spread the way and left such clear proof of its sagehood? How could one remain silent? Hence, there is no reason to think it strange that I set it down in words.

This record was made on the fourteenth day of the eighth month of the nineteenth year of the Zhenyuan reign period (803).

Religions of China in Practice

INTRODUCTION

The Spirits of Chinese Religion

Stephen F. Teiser

Acknowledging the wisdom of Chinese proverbs, most anthologies of Chinese religion are organized by the logic of the three teachings (*sanjiao*) of Confucianism, Daoism, and Buddhism. Historical precedent and popular parlance attest to the importance of this threefold division for understanding Chinese culture. One of the earliest references to the trinitarian idea is attributed to Li Shiqian, a prominent scholar of the sixth century, who wrote that "Buddhism is the sun, Daoism the moon, and Confucianism the five planets."[1] Li likens the three traditions to significant heavenly bodies, suggesting that although they remain separate, they also coexist as equally indispensable phenomena of the natural world. Other opinions stress the essential unity of the three religious systems. One popular proverb opens by listing the symbols that distinguish the religions from each other, but closes with the assertion that they are fundamentally the same: "The three teachings—the gold and cinnabar of Daoism, the relics of Buddhist figures, as well as the Confucian virtues of humanity and righteousness—are basically one tradition."[2] Stating the point more bluntly, some phrases have been put to use by writers in the long, complicated history of what Western authors have called "syncretism." Such mottoes include "the three teachings are one teaching"; "the three teachings return to the one"; "the three teachings share one body"; and "the three teachings merge into one."[3]

What sense does it make to subsume several thousand years of religious experience under these three (or three-in-one) categories? To answer this question, we need first to understand what the three teachings are and how they came into existence.

There is a certain risk in beginning this introduction with an archaeology of the three teachings. The danger is that rather than fixing in the reader's mind the most significant forms of Chinese religion—the practices and ideas associated with ancestors, the measures taken to protect against ghosts, or the veneration of gods—emphasis will instead be placed on precisely those terms we seek to avoid. Or, as one friendly critic stated in a review of an earlier draft of this introduction, why must "the tired old category of the three teachings be inflicted on yet another generation of students?" Indeed, why does this introduction begin on a negative note, as it were, analyzing the problems with subsuming Chinese religion under the three teachings, and insert a positive appraisal of what constitutes Chinese religion only at the end? Why not begin with "popular religion," the gods of China, and kinship and bureaucracy and then, only after those categories are established, proceed to discuss the explicit categories by which Chinese people have ordered their religious world? The answer has to do with the fact that Chinese religion does not come to us purely, or without mediation. The three teachings are a powerful and inescapable part of Chinese religion. Whether they are eventually accepted, rejected, or reformulated, the terms of the past can only be understood by examining how they came to assume their current status. And because Chinese religion has for so long been dominated by the idea of the three teachings, it is essential to understand where those traditions come from, who constructed them and how, as well as what forms of religious life are omitted or denied by constructing such a picture in the first place.

Confucianism

The myth of origins told by proponents of Confucianism (and by plenty of modern historians) begins with Confucius, whose Chinese name was Kong Qiu and who lived from 551 to 479 B.C.E. Judging from the little direct evidence that still survives, however, it appears that Kong Qiu did not view himself as the founder of a school of thought, much less as the originator of anything. What does emerge from the earliest layers of the written record is that Kong Qiu sought a revival of the ideas and institutions of a past golden age. Employed in a minor government position as a specialist in the governmental and family rituals of his native state, Kong Qiu hoped to disseminate knowledge of the rites and inspire their universal performance. That kin of broad-scale transformation could take place, he thought, only with the active encouragement of responsible rulers. The ideal ruler, as exemplified by the legendary sage-kings Yao and Shun or the adviser to the Zhou rulers, the Duke of Zhou, exercises ethical suasion, the ability to influence others by the power of his moral example. To the virtues of the ruler correspond values that each individual is supposed to cultivate: benevolence toward others, a general sense of doing what is right, and loyalty and diligence in serving one's superiors. Universal moral ideals are necessary but not sufficient conditions for the restoration of civilization. Society also needs what Kong Qiu calls *li*, roughly translated as "ritual." Although people are supposed to develop propriety or the ability to act appropriately in any given social situation (another sense of the same word, li), still the specific rituals people are supposed to perform (also li) vary considerably, depending on age, social status, gender, and context. In family ritual, for instance, rites of mourning depend on one's kinship relation to the deceased. In international affairs, degrees of pomp, as measured by ornateness of dress and opulence of gifts, depend on the rank of the foreign emissary. Offerings to the gods are also highly regulated: the sacrifices of each social class are restricted to specific classes of deities, and a clear hierarchy prevails. The few explicit statements attributed to Kong Qiu about the problem of history or tradition all portray him as one who "transmits but does not create."[4] Such a claim can, of course, serve the ends of innovation or revolution. But in this case it is clear that Kong Qiu transmitted not only specific rituals and values but also a hierarchical social structure and the weight of the past.

The portrayal of Kong Qiu as originary and the coalescence of a self-conscious identity among people tracing their heritage back to him took place long after his death. Two important scholar-teachers, both of whom aspired to serve as close advisers to a ruler whom they could convince to institute a Confucian style of government, were Meng Ke (or Mengzi, ca. 371–289 B.C.E.) and Xun Qing (or Xunzi, d. 215 B.C.E.). Mengzi viewed himself as a follower of Kong Qiu's example. His doctrines offered a program for perfecting the individual. Sageliness could be achieved through a gentle process of cultivating the innate tendencies toward the good. Xunzi professed the same goal but argued that the means to achieve it required stronger measures. To be civilized, according to Xunzi, people need to restrain their base instincts and have their behavior modified by a system of ritual built into social institutions.

It was only with the founding of the Han dynasty (202 B.C.E.–220 C.E.), however, that Confucianism became Confucianism, that the ideas associated with Kong Qiu's name received state support and were disseminated generally throughout upper-class society. The creation of Confucianism was neither simple nor sudden, as three examples will make clear. In the year 136 B.C.E. the classical writings touted by Confucian scholars were made the foundation of the official system of education and scholarship, to the exclusion of titles supported by other philosophers. The five classics (or five scriptures, *wujing*) were the *Classic of Poetry (Shijing), Classic of History (Shujing), Classic of Changes (Yijing), Record of Rites (Liji),* and *Chronicles of the Spring and Autumn Period (Chunqiu)* with the *Zuo Commentary (Zuozhuan),* most of which had existed prior to the time of Kong Qiu. (The word *jing* denotes the warp threads in a piece of cloth. Once adopted as a generic term for the authoritative texts of Han-dynasty Confucianism, it was applied by other traditions to their sacred books. It is translated variously as book, classic, scripture, and sūtra.) Although Kong Qiu was commonly believed to have written or edited some of the five classics, his own statements (collected in the *Analects* [*Lunyu*]) and the writings of his closest followers were not yet admitted into the canon. Kong Qiu's name was implicated more directly in the second example of the Confucian system, the state-sponsored cult that erected temples in his honor throughout the empire and that provided monetary support for turning his ancestral home into a national shrine. Members of the literate elite visited such temples, paying formalized respect and enacting rituals in front of spirit tablets of the master and his disciples. The third example is the corpus of writing left by the scholar Dong Zhongshu (ca. 179–104 B.C.E.), who was instrumental in promoting Confucian ideas and books in official circles. Dong was recognized by the government as the leading spokesman for the scholarly elite. His theories provided an overarching cosmological framework for Kong Qiu's ideals, sometimes adding ideas unknown to Kong Qiu's time, sometimes making more explicit or providing a particular interpretation of what was already stated in Kong Qiu's work. Dong drew heavily on concepts of earlier thinkers—few of whom were self-avowed Confucians—to explain the workings of the cosmos. He used the concepts of yin and yang to explain how change followed a knowable pattern, and he elaborated on the role of the ruler as one who connected the realms of Heaven, Earth, and humans. The social hierarchy implicit in Kong Qiu's ideal world was coterminous, thought Dong, with a division of all natural relationships into a superior and inferior member. Dong's theories proved determinative for the political culture of Confucianism during the Han and later dynasties.

What in all of this, we need to ask, was Confucian? Or, more precisely, what kind of thing is the "Confucianism" in each of these examples? In the first, that of the five classics, "Confucianism" amounts to a set of books that were mostly written before Kong Qiu lived but that later tradition associates with his name. It is a curriculum instituted by the emperor for use in the most prestigious institutions of learning. In the second example, "Confucianism" is a complex ritual apparatus, an empire-wide network of shrines patronized by government authorities. It depends upon the ability of the government to maintain religious institutions throughout the empire and upon the willingness of state officials to engage regularly in worship. In the third example, the work of Dong Zhongshu, "Confucianism" is a conceptual scheme, a fluid synthesis of some of Kong Qiu's ideals and the various cosmologies popular well after Kong Qiu lived. Rather than being an updating of something universally acknowledged as Kong Qiu's philosophy, it is a conscious systematizing, under the symbol of Kong Qiu, of ideas current in the Han dynasty.

If even during the Han dynasty the term "Confucianism" covers so many different sorts of things—books, a ritual apparatus, a conceptual scheme—one might well wonder why we persist in using one single word to cover such a broad range of phenomena. Sorting out the pieces of that puzzle is now one of the most pressing tasks in the study of Chinese history, which is already beginning to replace the wooden division of the Chinese intellectual world into the three teachings—each in turn marked by phases called "proto-," "neo-," or "revival of"—with a more critical and nuanced understanding of how traditions are made and sustained. For our more limited purposes here, it is instructive to observe how the word "Confucianism" came to be applied to all of these things and more.[5] As a word, "Confucianism" is tied to the Latin name, "Confucius," which originated not with Chinese philosophers but with European missionaries in the sixteenth century. Committed to winning over the top echelons of Chinese society, Jesuits and other Catholic orders subscribed to the version of Chinese religious history supplied to them by the educated elite. The story they told was that their teaching began with Kong Qiu, who was referred to as Kongfuzi, rendered into Latin as "Confucius." It was elaborated by Mengzi (rendered as "Mencius") and Xunzi and was given official recognition—as if it had existed as the same entity, unmodified for several hundred years—under the Han dynasty. The teaching changed to the status of an unachieved metaphysical principle during the centuries that Buddhism was believed to have been dominant and was resuscitated—still basically unchanged—only with the teachings of Zhou Dunyi (1017–1073), Zhang Zai (1020), Cheng Hao (1032–1085), and Cheng Yi (1033–1107), and the commentaries authored by Zhu Xi (1130–1200). As a genealogy crucial to the self-definition of modern Confucianism, that myth of origins is both misleading and instructive. It lumps together heterogeneous ideas, books that predate Kong Qiu, and a state-supported cult under the same heading. It denies the diversity of names by which members of a supposedly unitary tradition chose to call themselves, including *ru* (the early meaning of which remains disputed, usually translated as "scholars" or "Confucians"), *daoxue* (study of the Way), *lixue* (study of principle), and *xinxue* (study of the mind). It ignores the long history of contention over interpreting Kong Qiu and overlooks the debt owed by later thinkers like Zhu Xi and Wang Yangming (1472–1529) to Buddhist notions of the mind and practices of meditation and to Daoist ideas of change. And it passes over in silence the role played by non-Chinese regimes in making Confucianism into an orthodoxy, as in the year 1315, when the Mongol government required that the writings of Kong Qiu and his early followers, redacted and interpreted through the commentaries of Zhu Xi, become the basis for the national civil service examination. At the same time, Confucianism's story about itself reveals much. It names the figures, books, and slogans of the past that recent Confucians have found most inspiring. As a string of ideals, it illuminates what its proponents wish it to be. As a lineage, it imagines a line of descent kept pure from the traditions of Daoism and Buddhism. The construction of the latter two teachings involves a similar process. Their histories, as will be seen below, do not simply move from the past to the present; they are also projected backward from specific presents to significant pasts.

Daoism

Most Daoists have argued that the meaningful past is the period that preceded, chronologically and metaphysically, the past in which the legendary sages of Confucianism lived. In the Daoist golden age the empire had not yet been reclaimed out of chaos. Society lacked distinctions based on class, and human beings lived happily in what resembled primitive, small-scale agricultural collectives. The lines between different nation-states, between different occupations, even between humans and animals were not clearly drawn. The world knew nothing of the Confucian state, which depended on the carving up of an undifferentiated whole into social ranks, the imposition of artificially ritualized modes of behavior, and a campaign for conservative values like loyalty, obeying one's parents, and moderation. Historically speaking, this Daoist vision was first articulated shortly after the time of Kong Qiu, and we should probably regard the Daoist nostalgia for a simpler, untrammeled time as roughly contemporary with the development of a Confucian view of origins. In Daoist mythology whenever a wise man encounters a representative of Confucianism, be it Kong Qiu himself or an envoy seeking advice for an emperor, the hermit escapes to a world untainted by civilization.

For Daoists the philosophical equivalent to the pre-imperial primordium is a state of chaotic wholeness, sometimes called *hundun,* roughly translated as "chaos." In that state, imagined as an uncarved block or as the beginning of life in the womb, nothing is lacking. Everything exists, everything is possible: before a stone is carved there is no limit to the designs that may be cut, and before the fetus develops the embryo can, in an organic worldview, develop into male or female. There is not yet any division into parts, any name to distinguish one thing from another. Prior to birth there is no distinction, from the Daoist standpoint, between life and death. Once birth happens—once the stone is cut—however, the world descends into a state of imperfection. Rather than a mythological sin on the part of the first human beings or an ontological separation of God from humanity, the Daoist version of the Fall involves division into parts, the assigning of names, and the leveling of judgments injurious to life. *The Classic on the Way and Its Power (Dao de jing)* describes how the original whole, the *dao* (here meaning the "Way" above all other ways), was broken up: "The Dao gave birth to the One, the One gave birth to the Two, the Two gave birth to the Three, and the Three gave birth to the Ten Thousand Things."[6] That decline-through-differentiation also offers the model for regaining wholeness. The spirit may be restored by reversing the process of aging, by reverting from multiplicity to the One. By understanding the road or path (the same word, dao, in another sense) that the great Dao followed in its decline, one can return to the root and endure forever.

Practitioners and scholars alike have often succumbed to the beauty and power of the language of Daoism and proclaimed another version of the Daoist myth of origins. Many people seem to move from a description of the Daoist faith-stance (the Dao embraces all things) to active Daoist proselytization masquerading as historical description (Daoism embraces all forms of Chinese religion). As with the term "Confucianism," it is important to consider not just what the term "Daoism" covers, but also where it comes from, who uses it, and what words Daoists have used over the years to refer to themselves.

The most prominent early writings associated with Daoism are two texts, *The Classic on the Way and Its Power,* attributed to a mythological figure named Lao Dan or Laozi who is presumed to have lived during the sixth century B.C.E., and the *Zhuangzi,* named for its putative author, Zhuang Zhou or Zhuangzi (ca. 370–301 B.C.E.). The books are quite different in language and style. *The Classic on the Way and Its Power* is composed largely of short bits of aphoristic verse, leaving its interpretation and application radically indeterminate. Perhaps because of that openness of meaning, the book has been translated into Western languages more often than any other Chinese text. It has been read as a utopian tract advocating a primitive society as well as a compendium of advice for a fierce, engaged ruler. Its author has been described as a relativist, skeptic, or poet by some, and by others as a committed rationalist who believes in the ability of words to name a reality that exists independently of them. The *Zhuangzi* is a much longer work composed of relatively discrete chapters written largely in prose, each of which brings sustained attention to a particular set of topics. Some portions have been compared to Wittgenstein's *Philosophical Investigations.* Others develop a story at some length or invoke mythological figures from the past. The *Zhuangzi* refers to Laozi by name and quotes some passages from the *Classic on the Way and Its Power,* but the text as we know it includes contributions written over a long span of time. Textual analysis reveals at least four layers, probably more, that may be attributed to different authors and different times, with interests as varied as logic, primitivism, syncretism, and egotism. The word "Daoism" in English (corresponding to Daojia, "the School [or Philosophy] of the Dao") is often used to refer to these and other books or to a free-floating outlook on life inspired by but in no way limited to them.

"Daoism" is also invoked as the name for religious movements that began to develop in the late second century C.E.; Chinese usage typically refers to their texts as Daojiao, "Teachings of the Dao" or "Religion of the Dao." One of those movements, called the Way of the Celestial Masters (Tianshi dao), possessed mythology and rituals and established a set of social institutions that would be maintained by all later Daoist groups. The Way of the Celestial Masters claims its origin in a revelation dispensed in the year 142 by the Most High Lord Lao (Taishang Laojun), a deified form of Laozi, to a man named Zhang Daoling. Laozi explained teachings to Zhang and bestowed on him the title of "Celestial Master" (Tianshi), indicating his exalted position in a system of ranking that placed those who had achieved immortality at the top and humans who were working their way toward that goal at the bottom. Zhang was active in the part of western China now corresponding to the province of Sichuan, and his descendants continued to build a local infrastructure. The movement divided itself into a number of parishes, to which each member-household was required to pay an annual tax of five pecks of rice—hence the other common name for the movement in its early years, the Way of the Five Pecks of Rice (Wudoumi dao). The administrative structure and some of the political functions of the organization are thought to have been modeled in part on secular government administration. After the Wei dynasty was founded in 220, the government extended recognition to the Way of the Celestial Masters, giving official approval to the form of local social administration it had developed and claiming at the same time that the new emperor's right to rule was guaranteed by the authority of the current Celestial Master.

Several continuing traits are apparent in the first few centuries of the Way of the Celestial Masters. The movement represented itself as having begun with divine-human contact: a god reveals a teaching and bestows a rank on a person. Later Daoist groups received revelations from successively more exalted deities. Even before receiving official recognition, the movement was never divorced from politics. Later Daoist groups too followed that general pattern, sometimes in the form of millenarian movements promising to replace the secular government, sometimes in the form of an established church providing services complementary to those of the state. The local communities of the Way of the Celestial Masters were formed around priests who possessed secret knowledge and held rank in the divine-human bureaucracy. Knowledge and position were interdependent: knowledge of the proper ritual forms and the authority to petition the gods and spirits were guaranteed by the priest's position in the hierarchy, while his rank was confirmed to his community by his expertise in a ritual repertoire. Nearly all types of rituals performed by Daoist masters through the ages are evident in the early years of the Way of the Celestial Masters. Surviving sources describe the curing of illness, often through confession; the exorcism of malevolent spirits; rites of passage in the life of the individual; and the holding of regular communal feasts.

While earlier generations (both Chinese bibliographers and scholars of Chinese religion) have emphasized the distinction between the allegedly pristine philosophy of the "School of the Dao" and the corrupt religion of the "Teachings of the Dao," recent scholarship instead emphasizes the complex continuities between them. Many selections in this anthology focus on the beginnings of organized Daoism and the liturgical and social history of Daoist movements through the fifth century. The history of Daoism can be read, in part, as a succession of revelations, each of which includes but remains superior to the earlier ones. In South China around the year 320 the author Ge Hong wrote *He Who Embraces Simplicity (Baopuzi)*, which outlines different methods for achieving elevation to that realm of the immortals known as "Great Purity" (Taiqing). Most methods explain how, after the observance of moral codes and rules of abstinence, one needs to gather precious substances for use in complex chemical experiments. Followed properly, the experiments succeed in producing a sacred substance, "gold elixir" (*jindan*), the eating of which leads to immortality. In the second half of the fourth century new scriptures were revealed to a man named Yang Xi, who shared them with a family named Xu. Those texts give their possessors access to an even higher realm of Heaven, that of "Highest Clarity" (Shangqing). The scriptures contain legends about the level of gods residing in the Heaven of Highest Clarity. Imbued with a messianic spirit, the books foretell an apocalypse for which the wise should begin to prepare now. By gaining initiation into the textual tradition of Highest Clarity and following its program for cultivating immortality, adepts are assured of a high rank in the divine bureaucracy and can survive into the new age. The fifth century saw the canonization of a new set of texts, titled "Numinous Treasure" (Lingbao). Most of them are presented as sermons of a still higher level of deities, the Celestial Worthies (Tianzun) who are the most immediate personified manifestations of the Dao. The books instruct followers how to worship the gods supplicated in a wide variety of rituals. Called "retreats" (*zhai*, a word connoting both "fast" and "feast"), those rites are performed for the salvation of the dead, the bestowal of boons on the living, and the repentance of sins.

As noted in the discussion of the beginnings of the Way of the Celestial Masters,

Daoist and imperial interests often intersected. The founder of the Tang dynasty (618–907), Li Yuan (lived 566–635, reigned 618–626, known as Gaozu), for instance, claimed to be a descendant of Laozi's. At various points during the reign of the Li family during the Tang dynasty, prospective candidates for government service were tested for their knowledge of specific Daoist scriptures. Imperial authorities recognized and sometimes paid for ecclesiastical centers where Daoist priests were trained and ordained, and the surviving sources on Chinese history are filled with examples of state sponsorship of specific Daoist ceremonies and the activities of individual priests. Later governments continued to extend official support to the Daoist church, and vice-versa. Many accounts portray the twelfth century as a particularly innovative period: it saw the development of sects named "Supreme Unity" (Taiyi), "Perfect and Great Dao" (Zhenda dao), and "Complete Perfection" (Quanzhen). In the early part of the fifteenth century, the forty-third Celestial Master took charge of compiling and editing Daoist ritual texts, resulting in the promulgation of a Daoist canon that contemporary Daoists still consider authoritative.

Possessing a history of some two thousand years and appealing to people from all walks of life, Daoism appears to the modern student to be a complex and hardly unitary tradition. That diversity is important to keep in mind, especially in light of the claim made by different Daoist groups to maintain a form of the teaching that in its essence has remained the same over the millennia. The very notion of immortality is one way of grounding that claim. The greatest immortals, after all, are still alive. Having conquered death, they have achieved the original state of the uncarved block and are believed to reside in the heavens. The highest gods are personified forms of the Dao, the unchanging Way. They are concretized in the form of stars and other heavenly bodies and can manifest themselves to advanced Daoist practitioners following proper visualization exercises. The transcendents (*xianren,* often translated as "immortals") began life as humans and returned to the ideal embryonic condition through a variety of means. Some followed a regimen of gymnastics and observed a form of macrobiotic diet that simultaneously built up the pure elements and minimized the coarser ones. Others practiced the art of alchemy, assembling secret ingredients and using laboratory techniques to roll back time. Sometimes the elixir was prepared in real crucibles; sometimes the refining process was carried out eidetically by imagining the interior of the body to function like the test tubes and burners of the lab. Personalized rites of curing and communal feasts alike can be seen as small steps toward recovering the state of health and wholeness that obtains at the beginning (also the infinite ending) of time. Daoism has always stressed morality. Whether expressed through specific injunctions against stealing, lying, and taking life, through more abstract discussions of virtue, or through exemplary figures who transgress moral codes, ethics was an important element of Daoist practice. Nor should we forget the claim to continuity implied by the institution of priestly investiture. By possessing revealed texts and the secret registers listing the members of the divine hierarchy, the Daoist priest took his place in a structure that appeared to be unchanging.

Another way that Daoists have represented their tradition is by asserting that their activities are different from other religious practices. Daoism is constructed, in part, by projecting a non-Daoist tradition, picking out ideas and actions and assigning them a name that symbolizes "the other."[7] The most common others in the history of Daoism have been the rituals practiced by the less institutionalized, more poorly educated religious specialists at the local level and any phenomenon connected with China's other organized church, Buddhism. Whatever the very real congruences in belief and practice among Daoism, Buddhism, and popular practice, it has been essential to Daoists to assert a fundamental difference. In this perspective the Daoist gods differ in kind from the profane spirits of the popular tradition: the former partake of the pure and impersonal Dao, while the latter demand the sacrifice of meat and threaten their benighted worshippers with illness and other curses. With their hereditary office, complex rituals, and use of the classical Chinese language, modern Daoist masters view themselves as utterly distinct from exorcists and mediums, who utilize only the language of everyday speech and whose possession by spirits appears uncontrolled. Similarly, anti-Buddhist rhetoric (as well as anti-Daoist rhetoric from the Buddhist side) has been severe over the centuries, often resulting in the temporary suppression of books and statues and the purging of the priesthood. All of those attempts to enforce difference, however, must be viewed alongside the equally real overlap, sometimes identity, between Daoism and other traditions. Records compiled by the state detailing the official titles bestowed on gods prove that the gods of the popular tradition and the gods of Daoism often supported each other and coalesced or, at other times, competed in ways that the Daoist church could not control. Ethnographies about modern village life show how all the various religious personnel cooperate to allow for coexistence; in some celebrations they forge an arrangement that allows Daoist priests to officiate at the esoteric rituals performed in the interior of the temple, while mediums enter into trance among the crowds in the outer courtyard. In imperial times the highest echelons of the Daoist and Buddhist priesthoods were capable of viewing their roles as complementary to each other and as necessarily subservient to the state. The government mandated the establishment in each province of temples belonging to both religions; it exercised the right to accept or reject the definition of each religion's canon of sacred books; and it sponsored ceremonial debates between leading exponents of the two churches in which victory most often led to coexistence with, rather than the destruction of, the losing party.

Buddhism

The very name given to Buddhism offers important clues about the way that the tradition has come to be defined in China. Buddhism is often called Fojiao, literally meaning "the teaching (*jiao*) of the Buddha (Fo)." Buddhism thus appears to be a member of the same class as Confucianism and Daoism: the three teachings are Rujiao ("teaching of the scholars" or Confucianism), Daojiao ("teaching of the

Dao" or Daoism), and Fojiao ("teaching of the Buddha" or Buddhism). But there is an interesting difference here, one that requires close attention to language. As semantic units in Chinese, the words Ru and Dao work differently than does Fo. The word Ru refers to a group of people and the word Dao refers to a concept, but the word Fo does not make literal sense in Chinese. Instead it represents a sound, a word with no semantic value that in the ancient language was pronounced as "bud," like the beginning of the Sanskrit word "buddha."[8] The meaning of the Chinese term derives from the fact that it refers to a foreign sound. In Sanskrit the word "buddha" means "one who has achieved enlightenment," one who has "awakened" to the true nature of human existence. Rather than using any of the Chinese words that mean "enlightened one," Buddhists in China have chosen to use a foreign word to name their teaching, much as native speakers of English refer to the religion that began in India not as "the religion of the enlightened one," but rather as "Buddhism," often without knowing precisely what the word "Buddha" means. Referring to Buddhism in China as Fojiao involves the recognition that this teaching, unlike the other two, originated in a foreign land. Its strangeness, its non-native origin, its power are all bound up in its name.

Considered from another angle, the word buddha (*fo*) also accentuates the ways in which Buddhism in its Chinese context defines a distinctive attitude toward experience. Buddhas—enlightened ones—are unusual because they differ from other, unenlightened individuals and because of the truths to which they have awakened. Most people live in profound ignorance, which causes immense suffering. Buddhas, by contrast, see the true nature of reality. Such propositions, of course, were not advanced in a vacuum. They were articulated originally in the context of traditional Indian cosmology in the first several centuries B.C.E., and as Buddhism began to trickle haphazardly into China in the first centuries of the common era, Buddhist teachers were faced with a dilemma. To make their teachings about the Buddha understood to a non-Indian audience, they often began by explaining the understanding of human existence—the problem, as it were—to which Buddhism provided the answer. Those basic elements of the early Indian worldview are worth reviewing here. In that conception, all human beings are destined to be reborn in other forms, human and nonhuman, over vast stretches of space and time. While time in its most abstract sense does follow a pattern of decline, then renovation, followed by a new decline, and so on, still the process of reincarnation is without beginning or end. Life takes six forms: at the top are gods, demigods, and human beings, while animals, hungry ghosts, and hell beings occupy the lower rungs of the hierarchy. Like the gods of ancient Greece, the gods of Buddhism reside in the heavens and lead lives of immense worldly pleasure. Unlike their Greek counterparts, however, they are without exception mortal, and at the end of a very long life they are invariably reborn lower in the cosmic scale. Hungry ghosts wander in search of food and water yet are unable to eat or drink, and the denizens of the various hells suffer a battery of tortures, but they will all eventually die and be reborn again. The logic that determines where one will be reborn is the idea of *karma*. Strictly speaking the Sanskrit word karma means "deed" or "action." In its relevant sense here it means that every deed has a result: morally good acts lead to good consequences, and the commission of evil has a bad result. Applied to the life of the individual, the law of karma means that the circumstances an individual faces are the result of prior actions. Karma is the regulating idea of a wide range of good works and other Buddhist practices.

The wisdom to which buddhas awaken is to see that this cycle of existence (*saṃsāra* in Sanskrit, comprising birth, death, and rebirth) is marked by impermanence, unsatisfactoriness, and lack of a permanent self. It is impermanent because all things, whether physical objects, psychological states, or philosophical ideas, undergo change; they are brought into existence by preceding conditions at a particular point in time, and they eventually will become extinct. It is unsatisfactory in the sense that not only do sentient beings experience physical pain, they also face continual disappointment when the people and things they wish to maintain invariably change. The third characteristic of sentient existence, lack of a permanent self, has a long and complicated history of exegesis in Buddhism. In China the idea of "no-self" (Sanskrit: *anātman*) was often placed in creative tension with the concept of repeated rebirth. On the one hand, Buddhist teachers tried to convince their audience that human existence did not end simply with a funeral service or memorial to the ancestors, that humans were reborn in another bodily form and could thus be related not only to other human beings but to animals, ghosts, and other species among the six modes of rebirth. To support that argument for rebirth, it was helpful to draw on metaphors of continuity, like a flame passed from one candle to the next and a spirit that moves from one lifetime to the next. On the other hand, the truth of impermanence entailed the argument that no permanent ego could possibly underlie the process of rebirth. What migrated from one lifetime to the next were not eternal elements of personhood but rather temporary aspects of psychophysical life that might endure for a few lifetimes—or a few thousand—but would eventually cease to exist. The Buddha provided an analysis of the ills of human existence and a prescription for curing them. Those ills were caused by the tendency of sentient beings to grasp, to cling to evanescent things in the vain hope that they remain permanent. In this view, the very act of clinging contributes to the perpetuation of desires from one incarnation to the next. Grasping, then, is both a cause and a result of being committed to a permanent self.

The wisdom of buddhas is neither intellectual nor individualistic. It was always believed to be a soteriological knowledge that was expressed in the compassionate activity of teaching others how to achieve liberation from suffering. Traditional formulations of Buddhist practice describe a path to salvation that begins with the observance of morality. Lay followers pledged to abstain from the taking of life, stealing, lying, drinking intoxicating beverages, and engaging in sexual relations outside of marriage. Further injunctions applied to householders who could observe a more demanding life-style of purity, and the lives of monks and nuns were regulated in even greater detail. With morality as a basis, the ideal path also included the cultivation of pure states of mind through the practice of meditation and the achieving of wisdom rivaling that of a buddha.

The discussion so far has concerned the importance of the foreign component in the ideal of the buddha and the actual content to which buddhas are believed to awaken. It is also important to consider what kind of a religious figure a buddha is thought to be. We can distinguish two separate but related understandings of what a buddha is. In the first understanding the Buddha (represented in English with a capital B) was an unusual human born into a royal family in ancient India in the sixth or fifth century B.C.E. He renounced his birthright, followed established religious teachers, and then achieved enlightenment after striking out on his own. He gathered lay and monastic disciples around him and preached throughout the Indian subcontinent for almost fifty years, and he achieved final "extinction" (the root meaning of the Sanskrit word *nirvāṇa*) from the woes of existence. This unique being was called Gautama (family name) Siddhārtha (personal name) during his lifetime, and later tradition refers to him with a variety of names, including Śākyamuni (literally "Sage of the Śākya clan") and Tathāgata ("Thus-Come One"). Followers living after his death lack direct access to him because, as the word "extinction" implies, his release was permanent and complete. His influence can be felt, though, through his traces—through gods who encountered him and are still alive, through long-lived disciples, through the places he touched that can be visited by pilgrims, and through his physical remains and the shrines (*stūpa*) erected over them. In the second understanding a buddha (with a lowercase b) is a generic label for any enlightened being, of whom Śākyamuni was simply one among many. Other buddhas preceded Śākyamuni's appearance in the world, and others will follow him, notably Maitreya (Chinese: Mile), who is thought to reside now in a heavenly realm close to the surface of the Earth. Buddhas are also dispersed over space: they exist in all directions, and one in particular, Amitāyus (or Amitābha, Chinese: Amituo), presides over a land of happiness in the West. Related to this second genre of buddha is another kind of figure, a bodhisattva (literally "one who is intent on enlightenment," Chinese: *pusa*). Budhisattvas are found in most forms of Buddhism, but their role was particularly emphasized in the many traditions claiming the polemical title of Mahāyāna ("Greater Vehicle," in opposition to Hīnayāna, "Smaller Vehicle") that began to develop in the first century B.C.E. Technically speaking, bodhisattvas are not as advanced as buddhas on the path to enlightenment. Bodhisattvas particularly popular in China include Avalokiteśvara (Chinese: Guanyin, Guanshiyin, or Guanzizai), Bhaiṣajyaguru (Chinese: Yaoshiwang), Kṣitigarbha (Chinese: Dizang), Mañjuśrī (Wenshu), and Samantabhadra (Puxian). While buddhas appear to some followers as remote and all-powerful, bodhisattvas often serve as mediating figures whose compassionate involvement in the impurities of this world makes them more approachable. Like buddhas in the second sense of any enlightened being, they function both as models for followers to emulate and as saviors who intervene actively in the lives of their devotees.

In addition to the word "Buddhism" (Fojiao), Chinese Buddhists have represented the tradition by the formulation of the "three jewels" (Sanskrit: *triratna*, Chinese: *sanbao*). Coined in India, the three terms carried both a traditional sense as well as a more worldly reference that is clear in Chinese sources.[9] The first jewel is Buddha, the traditional meaning of which has been discussed above. In China the term refers not only to enlightened beings, but also to the materials through which buddhas are made present, including statues, the buildings that house statues, relics and their containers, and all the finances needed to build and sustain devotion to buddha images.

The second jewel is the dharma (Chinese: *fa*), meaning "truth" or "law." The dharma includes the doctrines taught by the Buddha and passed down in oral and written form, thought to be equivalent to the universal cosmic law. Many of the teachings are expressed in numerical form, like the three marks of existence (impermanence, unsatisfactoriness, and no-self, discussed above), the four noble truths (unsatisfactoriness, cause, cessation, path), and so on. As a literary tradition the dharma also comprises many different genres, the most important of which is called *sūtra* in Sanskrit. The Sanskrit word refers to the warp thread of a piece of cloth, the regulating or primary part of the doctrine (compare its Proto-Indo-European root, **syū*, which appears in the English words suture, sew, and seam). The earliest Chinese translators of Buddhist Sanskrit texts chose a related loaded term to render the idea in Chinese: *jing*, which denotes the warp threads in the same manner as the Sanskrit, but which also has the virtue of being the generic name given to the classics of the Confucian and Taoist traditions. Sūtras usually begin with the words "Thus have I heard. Once, when the Buddha dwelled at . . ." That phrase is attributed to the Buddha's closest disciple, Ānanda, who according to tradition was able to recite all of the Buddha's sermons from memory at the first convocation of monks held after the Buddha died. In its material sense the dharma referred to all media for the Buddha's law in China, including sermons and the platforms on which sermons were delivered, Buddhist rituals that included preaching, and the thousands of books—first handwritten scrolls, then booklets printed with wooden blocks—in which the truth was inscribed.

The third jewel is saṅgha (Chinese: *sengqie* or *zhong*), meaning "assembly." Some sources offer a broad interpretation of the term, which comprises the four sub-orders of monks, nuns, lay men, and lay women. Other sources use the term in a stricter sense to include only monks and nuns, that is, those who have left home, renounced family life, accepted vows of celibacy, and undertaken other austerities to devote themselves full-time to the practice of religion. The differences and interdependencies between householders and monastics were rarely absent in any Buddhist civilization. In China those differences found expression in both the spiritual powers popularly attributed to monks and nuns and the hostility sometimes voiced toward their way of life, which seemed to threaten the core values of the Chinese family system. The interdependent nature of the relationship between lay people and the professionally religious is seen in such phenomena as the use of kinship terminology—an attempt to re-create family—among monks and nuns and the collaboration between lay donors and monastic officiants in a wide range of rituals designed to bring comfort to the ancestors. "Saṅgha" in China also referred to all of the phenomena considered to belong to the Buddhist establishment. Everything and everyone needed to sustain monastic life, in a very concrete sense, was included: the living quarters of monks; the lands deeded to temples for occupancy and profit; the tenant families and slaves who worked on the farm land and served the saṅgha; and even the animals attached to the monastery farms.

Standard treatments of the history of Chinese Buddhism tend to emphasize the place of Buddhism in Chinese dynastic history, the translation of Buddhist texts, and the development of schools or sects within Buddhism. While these research agenda are important for our understanding of Chinese Buddhism, many of the contributors to this anthology have chosen to ask rather different questions, and it is worthwhile explaining why.

Many overviews of Chinese Buddhist history are organized by the template of Chinese dynasties. In this perspective, Buddhism began to enter China as a religion of non-Chinese merchants in the later years of the Han dynasty. It was during the following four centuries of disunion, including division between non-Chinese rulers in the north and native ("Han") governments in the south as well as warfare and social upheaval, that Buddhism allegedly took root in China. Magic and meditation ostensibly appealed to the "barbarian" rulers in the north, while the dominant style of religion pursued by the southerners was philosophical. During the period of disunion, the general consensus suggests, Buddhist translators wrestled with the problem of conveying Indian ideas in a language their Chinese audience could understand; after many false starts Chinese philosophers were finally able to comprehend common Buddhist terms as well as the complexities of the doctrine of emptiness. During the Tang dynasty Buddhism was finally "Sinicized" or made fully Chinese. Most textbooks treat the Tang dynasty as the apogee or mature period of Buddhism in China. The Tang saw unprecedented numbers of ordinations into the ranks of the Buddhist order; the flourishing of new, allegedly "Chinese" schools of thought; and lavish support from the state. After the Tang, it is thought, Buddhism entered into a thousand-year period of decline. Some monks were able to break free of tradition and write innovative commentaries on older texts or reshape received liturgies, some patrons managed to build significant temples or sponsor the printing of the Buddhist canon on a large scale, and the occasional highly placed monk found a way to purge debased monks and nuns from the ranks of the saṅgha and revive moral vigor, but on the whole the stretch of dynasties after the Tang is treated as a long slide into intellectual, ethical, and material poverty. Stated in this caricatured fashion, the shortcomings of this approach are not hard to discern. This approach accentuates those episodes in the history of Buddhism that intersect with important moments in a political chronology, the validity of which scholars in Chinese studies increasingly doubt. The problem is not so much that the older, dynastic-driven history of China is wrong as that it is limited and one-sided. While traditional history tends to have been written from the top down, more recent attempts argue from the bottom up. Historians in the past forty years have begun to discern otherwise unseen patterns in the development of Chinese economy, society, and political institutions. Their conclusions, which increasingly take Buddhism into account, suggest that cycles of rise and fall in population shifts, economy, family fortunes, and the like often have little to do with dynastic history—the implication being that the history of Buddhism and other Chinese traditions can no longer be pegged simply to a particular dynasty. Similarly, closer scrutiny of the documents and a greater appreciation of their biases and gaps have shown how little we know of what really transpired in the process of the control of Buddhism by the state. The Buddhist church was always, it seems, dependent on the support of the landowning classes in medieval China. And it appears that the condition of Buddhist institutions was tied closely to the occasional, decentralized support of the lower classes, which is even harder to document than support by the gentry. The very notion of rise and fall is a teleological, often theological, one, and it has often been linked to an obsession with one particular criterion—accurate translation of texts, or correct understanding of doctrine—to the exclusion of all others.

The translation of Buddhist texts from Sanskrit and other Indic and Central Asian languages into Chinese constitutes a large area of study. Although written largely in classical Chinese in the context of a premodern civilization in which relatively few people could read, Buddhist sūtras were known far and wide in China. The seemingly magical spell (Sanskrit; *dhāraṇī*) from the *Heart Sūtra* was known by many; stories from *Lotus Sūtra* were painted on the walls of popular temples; religious preachers, popular storytellers, and low-class dramatists alike drew on the rich trove of mythology provided by Buddhist narrative. Scholars of Buddhism have tended to focus on the chronology and accuracy of translation. Since so many texts were translated (one eighth-century count of the extant number of canonical works is 1,124),[10] and the languages of Sanskrit and literary Chinese are so distant, the results of that study are foundational to the field. To understand the history of Chinese Buddhism it is indispensable to know what texts were available when, how they were translated and by whom, how they were inscribed on paper and stone, approved or not approved, disseminated, and argued about. On the other hand, within Buddhist studies scholars have only recently begun to view the act of translation as a conflict-ridden process of negotiation, the results of which were Chinese texts whose meanings were never closed. Older studies, for instance, sometimes distinguish between three different translation styles. One emerged with the earliest known translators, a Parthian given the Chinese name An Shigao (fl. 148–170) and an Indoscythian named Lokakṣema (fl. 167–186), who themselves knew little classical Chinese but who worked with teams of Chinese assistants who peppered the resulting translations with words drawn from the spoken language. The second style was defined by the Kuchean translator Kumārajīva (350–409), who retained some elements of the vernacular in a basic framework of literary Chinese that was more polished, consistent, and acceptable to contemporary Chinese tastes. It is that style—which some have dubbed a "church" language of Buddhist Chinese, by analogy with the cultural history of medieval Latin—that proved most enduring and popular. The third style is exemplified in the work of Xuanzang (ca. 596–664), the seventh-century Chinese monk, philosopher, pilgrim, and translator. Xuanzang was one of the few translators who not only spoke Chinese and knew Sanskrit, but also knew the Chinese literary language well, and it is hardly accidental that Chinese Buddhists and modern scholars alike regard his translations as the most accurate and technically precise. At the same time, there is an irony in Xuanzang's situation that forces us to view the process of translation in a wider context. Xuanzang's is probably the most popular Buddhist image in Chinese folklore: he is the hero of the story *Journey to the West (Xiyou ji)*, known to all classes as the most prolific translator in Chinese history and as an indefatigable, sometimes overly serious and literal, pilgrim who embarked on a sacred mission to recover original texts from India. Though the mythological character is well known, the surviving writings of the seventh-century translator are not. They are, in fact, rarely read, because their grammar and style smack more of Sanskrit than of literary Chinese. What mattered to Chinese audiences—both the larger audience for the novels and dramas about the pilgrim and the much smaller one capable of reaching his translations—was that the Chinese texts were based on a valid foreign original, made even more authentic by Xuanzang's personal experiences in the Buddhist homeland.

The projection of categories derived from European, American, and modern Japanese religious experience onto the quite different world of traditional Chinese religion is perhaps most apparent in the tendency of traditional scholarship to treat Chinese Buddhism primarily as a matter of distinct schools or sects. Monks and other literati did indeed make sense of their history by classifying the overwhelming number of texts and teachings they inherited under distinctive trends, and some members of the Buddhist elite claimed allegiance to certain ideals at the expense of others. But any clear-cut criterion of belief, like the Nicene Creed, or a declaration of faith like Martin Luther's, is lacking in the history of Chinese Buddhism. It may have been only in the fourteenth century that there developed any social reality even approximating Ernst Troeltsch's definition of a sect as a voluntary religious association that people consciously choose to join and that excludes participation in other religious activities—and even then, the type of sect that developed, the Teaching of the White Lotus (Bailian jiao), was only tenuously connected to the "schools" of Chinese Buddhist thought on which scholars usually focus. Trends of thought and clearly identified philosophical issues are part of Chinese Buddhist history from the early centuries, and in the sixth through eighth centuries some figures identified themselves as concerned with one particular scripture: authors in the Tiantai school (named after Mount Tiantai) focused on the *Lotus Sūtra,* and figures of the Huayan school emphasized the comprehensive nature of the *Huayan* ("Flower Garland") *Sūtra.* But the founders of these schools—identified as such only by later generations—and their followers never stopped reading broadly in a wide range of Buddhist texts. Certain emphases also developed in Chinese Buddhist practice and Buddhology, foremost among them the invocation of the name of Amitāyus Buddha (*nianfo,* "keeping the Buddha in mind"), whose powers to assist those who chanted his name and whose resplendent paradise are described at length in scriptures affiliated with the Pure Land (Jingtu) school. In China, however—in contrast to late medieval Japan—dedication to Amitāyus Buddha was rarely viewed as a substitute for other forms of practice. Esoteric forms of Buddhism, characterized by restricting the circulation of knowledge about rituals to a small circle of initiates who perform rituals for those who lack the expertise, were also a strong force in Chinese Buddhism. But here too, even as they performed rites on behalf of individuals or to benefit the state, the monks of the Zhenyan (Sanskrit: Mantra, "True Word") school participated in other forms of Buddhist thought and practice as well. Even the school of Chan ("Meditation"), known in Japanese as Zen, which claimed to be founded on an unbroken transmission from Sākyamuni through twenty-eight Indian disciples to the first Chinese disciple in the late fifth century, was far less exclusive than its rhetoric seems to allow. Claims about transmission, the naming of founders, and the identification of crucial figures in the drama of Chan history were always executed retroactively. The tradition, which claimed its own content to be a non-content, was not so much handed down from past to present as it was imagined in the present, a willful projection into the future, against the reality of a heterogeneous past. As a "school" in the sense of an establishment for teaching and learning with monastery buildings, daily schedule, and administrative structure, Chan came into existence only in the twelfth and thirteenth centuries, and even then the social institution identified as "Chan" was nearly identical to institutions affiliated with other schools.

The Problem of Popular Religion

The brief history of the three teachings offered above provides, it is hoped, a general idea of what they are and how their proponents have come to claim for them the status of a tradition. It is also important to consider what is not named in the formulation of the three teachings. To define Chinese religion primarily in terms of the three traditions is to exclude from serious consideration the ideas and practices that do not fit easily under any of the three labels. Such common rituals as offering incense to the ancestors, conducting funerals, exorcising ghosts, and consulting fortunetellers; belief in the patterned interaction between light and dark forces or in the ruler's influence on the natural world; the tendency to construe gods as government officials; the preference for balancing tranquility and movement—all belong as much to none of the three traditions as they do to one or three.

The focus on the three teachings is another way of privileging precisely the varieties of Chinese religious life that have been maintained largely through the support of literate and often powerful representatives. The debate over the unity of the three teachings, even when it is resolved in favor of toleration or harmony—a move toward the one rather than the three—drowns out voices that talk about Chinese religion as neither one nor three. Another problem with the model of the three teachings is that it equalizes what are in fact three radically incommensurable things. Confucianism often functioned as a political ideology and a system of values; Daoism has been compared, inconsistently, to both an outlook on life and a system of gods and magic; and Buddhism offered, according to some analysts, a proper soteriology, an array of techniques and deities enabling one to achieve salvation in the other world. Calling all three traditions by the same unproblematic term, "teaching," perpetuates confusion about how the realms of life that we tend to take for granted (like politics, ethics, ritual, religion) were in fact configured differently in traditional China.

Another way of studying Chinese religion is to focus on those aspects of religious life that are shared by most people, regardless of their affiliation, or lack of affiliation with the three teachings. Such forms of popular religion as those named above (offering incense, conducting funerals, and so on) are important to address, although the category of "popular religion" entails its own set of problems.

We can begin by distinguishing two senses of the term "popular religion." The first refers to the forms of religion practiced by almost all Chinese people, regardless of social and economic standing, level of literacy, region, or explicit religious identification. Popular religion in this first sense is the religion shared by people in general, across all social boundaries. Three examples, all of which can be dated as early as the first century of the common era, help us gain some understanding of what counts as popular religion in the first sense. The first example is a typical Chinese funeral and memorial service. Following the death of a family member and the unsuccessful attempt to reclaim his or her spirit, the corpse is prepared for burial. Family members are invited for the first stage of mourning, with higher-ranking families entitled to invite more distant relatives. Rituals of wailing and the wearing of coarse, undyed cloth are practiced in the home of the deceased. After some days the coffin is carried in a procession to the grave. After burial the attention of the living shifts toward caring for the spirit of the dead. In later segments of the funerary rites the spirit is spatially fixed—installed—in a rectangular wooden tablet, kept at first in the home and perhaps later in a clan hall. The family continues to come together as a corporate group on behalf of the deceased; they say prayers and send sustenance, in the form of food, mock money, and documents addressed to the gods who oversee the realm of the dead. The second example of popular or common religion is the New Year's festival, which marks a passage not just in the life of the individual and the family, but in the yearly cycle of the cosmos. As in most civilizations, most festivals in China follow a lunar calendar, which is divided into twelve numbered months of thirty days apiece, divided in half at the full moon (fifteenth night) and new moon (thirtieth night); every several years an additional (or intercalary) month is added to synchronize the passage of time in lunar and solar cycles. Families typically begin to celebrate the New Year's festival ten or so days before the end of the twelfth month. On the twenty-third day, family members dispatch the God of the Hearth (Zaojun), who watches over all that transpires in the home from his throne in the kitchen, to report to the highest god of Heaven, the Jade Emperor (Yuhuang dadi). For the last day or two before the end of the year, the doors to the house are sealed and people worship in front of the images of the various gods kept in the house and the ancestor tablets. After a lavish meal rife with the symbolism of wholeness, longevity, and good fortune, each junior member of the family prostrates himself and herself before the head of the family and his wife. The next day, the first day of the first month, the doors are opened and the family enjoys a vacation of resting and visiting with friends. The New Year season concludes on the fifteenth night (the full moon of the first month, typically marked by a lantern celebration.

The third example of popular religion is the ritual of consulting a spirit medium in the home or in a small temple. Clients request the help of mediums (sometimes called "shamans" in Western-language scholarship; in Chinese they are known by many different terms) to solve problems like sickness in the family, nightmares, possession by a ghost or errant spirit, or some other misfortune. During the séance the medium usually enters a trance and incarnates a tutelary deity. The divinity speaks through the medium, sometimes in an altered but comprehensible voice, sometimes in sounds, through movements, or by writing characters in sand that require deciphering by the medium's manager or interpreter. The deity often identifies the problem and prescribes one among a wide range of possible cures. For an illness a particular herbal medicine or offering to a particular spirit may be recommended, while for more serious cases the deity himself, as dramatized in the person of the medium, does battle with the demon causing the difficulty. The entire drama unfolds in front of an audience composed of family members and nearby residents of the community. Mediums themselves often come from marginal groups (unmarried older women, youths prone to sickness), yet the deities who speak through them are typically part of mainstream religion, and their message tends to affirm rather than question traditional morality.

Some sense of what is at stake in defining "popular religion" in this manner can be gained by considering when, where, and by whom these three different examples are performed. Funerals and memorial services are carried out by most families, even poor ones; they take place in homes, cemeteries, and halls belonging to kinship corporations; and they follow two schedules, one linked to the death date of particular members (every seven days after death, 100 days after death, etc.) and one linked to the passage of nonindividualized calendar time (once per year). From a sociological perspective, the institutions active in the rite are the family, a complex organization stretching back many generations to a common male ancestor, and secondarily the community, which is to some extent protected from the baleful influences of death. The family too is the primary group involved in the New Year's celebration, although there is some validity in attributing a trans-social dimension to the festival in that a cosmic passage is marked by the occasion. Other social spheres are evident in the consultation of a medium; although it is cured through a social drama, sickness is also individuating; and some mediumistic rituals involve the members of a cult dedicated to the particular deity, membership being determined by personal choice.

These answers are significant for the contrast they suggest between traditional Chinese popular religion and the forms of religion characteristic of modern or secularized societies, in which religion is identified largely with doctrine, belief about god, and a large, clearly discernible church. None of the examples of Chinese popular religion is defined primarily by beliefs that necessarily exclude others. People take part in funerals without any necessary commitment to the existence of particular spirits, and belief in the reality of any particular tutelary deity does not preclude worship of other gods. Nor are these forms of religion marked by rigidly drawn lines of affiliation; in brief, there are families, temples, and shrines, but no church. Even the "community" supporting the temple dedicated to a local god is shifting, depending on those who choose to offer incense or make other offerings there on a monthly basis. There are specialists involved in these examples of Chinese popular religion, but their sacerdotal jobs are usually not full-time and seldom involve the theorizing about a higher calling typical of organized religion. Rather, their forte is considered to be knowledge or abilities of a technical sort. Local temples are administered by a standing committee, but the chairmanship of the committee usually rotates among the heads of the dominant families in the particular locale.

Like other categories, "popular religion" in the sense of shared religion obscures as much as it clarifies. Chosen for its difference from the unspoken reality of the academic interpreter (religion in modern Europe and America), popular religion as a category functions more as a contrastive notion than as a constitutive one; it tells us what much of Chinese religion is not like, rather than spelling out a positive content. It is too broad a category to be of much help to detailed understanding—which indeed is why many scholars in the field avoid the term, preferring to deal with more discrete and meaningful units like family religion, mortuary ritual, seasonal festivals, divination, curing, and mythology. "Popular religion" in the sense of common religion also hides potentially significant variation: witness the number of times words like "typical," "standard," "traditional," "often," and "usually" recur in the preceding paragraphs, without specifying particular people, times, and places, or naming particular understandings of orthodoxy. In addition to being static and timeless, the category prejudices the case against seeing popular religion as a conflict-ridden attempt to impose one particular standard on contending groups. The presence of non-Han peoples in China suggests that we view China not as a unitary Han culture peppered with "minorities," but as a complex region in which a diversity of cultures are interacting. To place all of them under the heading of "popular religion" is to obscure a fascinating conflict of cultures.

We may expect a similar mix of insight and erasure in the second sense of "popular religion," which refers to the religion of the lower classes as opposed to that of the elite. The bifurcation of society into two tiers is hardly a new idea. It began with some of the earliest Chinese theorists of religion. Xunzi, for instance, discusses the emotional, social, and cosmic benefits of carrying out memorial rites. In his opinion, mortuary ritual allows people to balance sadness and longing and to express grief, and it restores the natural order to the world. Different social classes, writes Xunzi, interpret sacrifices differently: "Among gentlemen [*junzi*], they are taken as the way of humans; among common people [*baixing*], they are taken as matters involving ghosts."[11] For Xunzi, "gentlemen" are those who have achieved nobility because of their virtue, not their birth; they consciously dedicate themselves to following and thinking about a course of action explicitly identified as moral. The common people, by contrast, are not so much amoral or immoral as they are unreflective. Without making a conscious decision, they believe that in the rites addressed to gods or the spirits of the dead, the objects of the sacrifice—the spirits themselves—actually exist. The true member of the upper class, however, adopts something like the attitude of the secular social theorist: bracketing the existence of spirits, what is important about death ritual is the effect it has on society. Both classes engage in the same activity, but they have radically different interpretations of it.

Dividing what is clearly too broad a category (Chinese religion or ritual) into two discrete classes (elite and folk) is not without advantages. It is a helpful pedagogical tool for throwing into question some of the egalitarian presuppositions frequently encountered in introductory courses on religion: that, for instance, everyone's religious options are or should be the same, or that other people's religious life can be understood (or tried out) without reference to social status. Treating Chinese religion as fundamentally affected by social position also helps scholars to focus on differences in styles of religious practice and interpretation. One way to formulate this view is to say that while all inhabitants of a certain community might take part in a religious procession, their style—both their pattern of practice and their understanding of their actions—will differ according to social position. Well-educated elites tend to view gods in abstract, impersonal terms and to demonstrate restrained respect, but the uneducated tend to view gods as concrete, personal beings before whom fear is appropriate.

In the social sciences and humanities in general there has been a clear move in the past forty years away from studies of the elite, and scholarship in Chinese religion is beginning to catch up with that trend. More and more studies focus on the religion of the lower classes and on the problems involved in studying the culture of the illiterati in a complex civilization. Much recent scholarship reflects a concern not only with the "folk" as opposed to the "elite," but with how to integrate our knowledge of those two strata and how our understanding of Chinese religion, determined unreflectively for many years by accepting an elite viewpoint, has begun to change. In all of this, questions of social class (Who participates? Who believes?) and questions of audience (Who writes or performs? For what kind of people?) are paramount.

At the same time, treating "popular religion" as the religion of the folk can easily perpetuate confusion. Some modern Chinese intellectuals, for instance, are committed to an agenda of modernizing and reviving Chinese spiritual life in a way that both accords with Western secularism, and does not reject all of traditional Chinese religion. The prominent twentieth-century Confucian and interpreter of Chinese culture Wing-tsit Chan, for instance, distinguishes between "the level of the masses" and "the level of the enlightened." The masses worship idols, objects of nature, and nearly any deity, while the enlightened confine their worship to Heaven, ancestors, moral exemplars, and historical persons. The former believe in heavens and hells and indulge in astrology and dream interpretation, but the latter "are seldom contaminated by these diseases."[12] For authors like Chan, both those who lived during the upheavals of the last century in China and those in Chinese diaspora communities, Chinese intellectuals still bear the responsibility to lead their civilization away from superstition and toward enlightenment. In that worldview there is no doubt where the religion of the masses belongs. From that position it can be a short step—one frequently taken by scholars of Chinese religion—to treating Chinese popular religion in a dismissive spirit. Modern anthologies of Chinese tradition can still be found that describe Chinese popular religion as "grosser forms of superstition," capable only of "facile syncretism" and resulting in "a rather shapeless tradition."

Kinship and Bureaucracy

It is often said that Chinese civilization has been fundamentally shaped by two enduring structures, the Chinese family system and the Chinese form of bureaucracy. Given the embeddedness of religion in Chinese social life, it would indeed be surprising if Chinese religion were devoid of such regulating concepts. The discussion below is not confined to delineating what might be considered the "hard" social structures of the family and the state, the effects of which might be seen in the "softer" realms of religion and values. The reach of kinship and bureaucracy is too great, their reproduction and representation far richer than could be conveyed by treating them as simple, given realities. Instead we will explain them also as metaphors and strategies.

Early Christian missionaries to China were fascinated with the religious aspects of the Chinese kinship system, which they dubbed "ancestor worship." Recently anthropologists have changed the wording to "the cult of the dead" because the concept of worship implies a supernatural or transcendent object of veneration, which the ancestors clearly are not. The newer term, however, is not much better, because "the dead" are hardly lifeless. As one modern observer remarks, the ancestral cult "is not primarily a matter of belief. . . . The cult of ancestors is more nearly a matter of plain everyday behavior. . . . No question of belief ever arises. The ancestors. . .literally live among their descendants, not only biologically, but also socially and psychologically."[13] The significance of the ancestors is partly explained by the structure of the traditional Chinese family: in marriages women are sent to other surname groups (exogamy); newly married couples tend to live with the husband's family (virilocality); and descent—deciding to which family one ultimately belongs—is traced back in time through the husband's male ancestors (patrilineage). A family in the normative sense includes many generations, past, present, and future, all of whom trace their ancestry through their father (if male) or their husband's father (if female) to an originating male ancestor. For young men the ideal is to grow up "under the ancestors' shadow" (in Hsu's felicitous phrase), by bringing in a wife from another family, begetting sons and growing prosperous, showering honor on the ancestors through material success, cooperating with brothers in sharing family property, and receiving respect during life and veneration after death from succeeding generations. For young women the avowed goal is to marry into a prosperous family with a kind mother-in-law, give birth to sons who will perpetuate the family line, depend upon one's children for immediate emotional support, and reap the benefits of old age as the wife of the primary man of the household.

Early philosophers assigned a specific term to the value of upholding the ideal family: they call it *xiao,* usually translated as "filial piety" or "filiality." The written character is composed of the graph for "elder" placed above the graph for "son," an apt visual reminder of the interdependence of the generations and the subordination of sons. If the system works well, then the younger generations support the senior ones, and the ancestors bestow fortune, longevity, and the birth of sons upon the living. As each son fulfills his duty, he progresses up the family scale, eventually assuming his status as revered ancestor. The attitude toward the dead (or rather the significant and, it is hoped, benevolent dead—one's ancestors) is simply a continuation of one's attitude toward one's parents while they were living. In all cases, the theory goes, one treats them with respect and veneration by fulfilling their personal wishes and acting according to the dictates of ritual tradition.

Like any significant social category, kinship in China is not without tension and self-contradiction. One already alluded to is gender: personhood as a function of the family system is different for men and women. Sons are typically born into their lineage and hope to remain under the same roof from childhood into old age and ancestorhood. By contrast, daughters are brought up by a family that is not ultimately theirs; at marriage they move into a new home; as young brides without children they are not yet inalienable members of their husband's lineage; and even after they have children they may still have serious conflicts with the de facto head of the household, their husband's mother. Women may gain more security from their living children than from the prospect of being a venerated ancestor. In the afterlife, in fact, they are punished for having polluted the natural world with the blood of parturition; the same virtue that the kinship system requires of them as producers of sons it also defines as a sin. There is also in the ideal of filiality a thinly veiled pretense to universality and equal access that also serves to rationalize the *status inaequalis.* Lavish funerals and the withdrawal from employment by the chief mourner for three years following his parents' death are the ideal. In the Confucian tradition such examples of conspicuous expenditure are interpreted as expressions of the highest devotion, rather than as a waste of resources and blatant unproductivity in which only the leisure class is free to indulge. And the ideals of respect of younger generations for older ones and cooperation among brothers often conflict with reality.

Many aspects of Chinese religion are informed by the metaphor of kinship. The kinship system is significant not only for the path of security it defines but also because of the religious discomfort attributed to all those who fall short of the ideal. It can be argued that the vagaries of life in any period of Chinese history provide as many counterexamples as fulfillments of the process of becoming an ancestor. Babies and children die young, before becoming accepted members of any family; men remain unmarried, without sons to carry on their name or memory; women are not successfully matched with a mate, thus lacking any mooring in the afterlife; individuals die in unsettling ways or come back from the dead as ghosts carrying grudges deemed fatal to the living. There are plenty of people, in other words, who are not caught by the safety net of the Chinese kinship system. They may be more prone than others to possession by spirits, or their anomalous position may not be manifest until after they die. In either case they are religiously significant because they abrogate an ideal of proper kinship relations.

Patrilineage exercises its influence as a regulating concept even in religious organizations where normal kinship—men and women marrying, having children, and tracing their lineage through the husband's father—is impossible. The Buddhist monkhood is a prime example;[14] sororities of unmarried women, adoption of children, and the creation of other "fictive" kinship ties are others. One of the defining features of being a Buddhist monk in China is called "leaving the family" (*chujia,* a translation of the Sanskrit *pravrajya*). Being homeless means not only that the boy has left the family in which he grew up and has taken up domicile in a monastery, but also that he has vowed to abstain from any sexual relations. Monks commit themselves to having no children. The defining feature of monasticism in China is its denial, its interruption of the patrilineage. At the same time, monks create for themselves a home—or a family—away from home; the Buddhist order adopts some of the important characteristics of the Chinese kinship system. One part of the ordination ceremony is the adoption of a religious name, both a new family name and a new personal name, by which one will hence forth be known. The family name for all Chinese monks, at least since the beginning of the fifth century, is the same surname attributed to the historical Buddha (Shi in Chinese, which is a shortened transliteration of the first part of Śākyamuni). For personal names, monks are usually assigned a two-character name by their teacher. Many teachers follow a practice common in the bestowal of secular personal names: the first character for all monks in a particular generation is the same, and the second character is different, bestowing individuality. "Brothers" of the same generation can be picked out because one element of their name is the same, as far as their names are concerned, their relationship to each other is the same as that between secular brothers. Not only do monks construct names and sibling relations modeled on those of Chinese kinship, they also construe themselves as Buddhist sons and descendants of Buddhist fathers and ancestors. Monks of the past are not only called "ancestors," they are also treated as secular ancestors are treated. The portraits and statues of past members are installed, in order, in special ancestral halls where they receive offerings and obeisance from current generations.

Another domain of Chinese religion that bears the imprint of Chinese kinship is hagiography, written accounts of gods and saints. Biographies of secular figures have long been part of the Chinese written tradition. Scholarly opinion usually cites the biographies contained in the first-century B.C.E. *Records of the Historian (Shiji)* as the paradigm for later biographical writing. Such accounts typically begin not with the birth of the protagonist, but rather with his or her family background. They narrate the individual's precocious abilities, posts held in government, actions deemed particularly virtuous or vile, and posthumous fate, including titles awarded by the government and the disposition of the corpse or grave. They are written in polished classical prose, and, like the writing of Chinese history, they are designed to cast their subjects as either models for emulation or unfortunate examples to be avoided. Gods who are bureaucrats, goddesses, incarnations of bodhisattvas, even immortals like Laozi and deities of the stars are all conceived through the lens of the Chinese family.

The logic of Chinese kinship can also be seen in a wide range of rituals, many of which take place outside the family and bear no overt relationship to kinship. The basic premise of many such rites is a family banquet, a feast to which members of the oldest generation of the family (the highest ancestors) are invited as honored guests. Placement of individuals and the sequence of action often follow seniority, with older generations coming before younger ones. Such principles can be observed even in Buddhist rites and the community celebrations enacted by groups defined by locale rather than kinship.

What about the other organizing force in Chinese civilization, the bureaucratic form of government used to rule the empire? It too has exerted tremendous influence on Chinese religious life. Before discussing bureaucracy proper, it is helpful to introduce some of the other defining features of Chinese government.

Chinese political culture has, at least since the later years of the Shang dynasty (ca. 1600–1028 B.C.E.), been conceived of as a dynastic system. A dynasty is defined by a founder whose virtue makes clear to all—both common people and other factions vying for control—that he and his family are fit to take over from a previous, corrupt ruler. Shortly after assuming the position of emperor, the new ruler chooses a name for the dynasty: Shang, for instance, means to increase or prosper. Other cosmically significant actions follow. The new emperor installs his family's ancestral tablets in the imperial ancestral hall; he performs the sacrifices to Heaven and Earth that are the emperor's duty; he announces new names of offices and institutes a reorganization of government; and the office of history and astronomy in the government keeps careful watch over any unusual phenomena (the appearance of freakish animals, unusual flora, comets, eclipses, etc.) that might indicate the pleasure or displeasure of Heaven at the change in rule. All activities that take place leading up to and during the reign of the first emperor in a new dynasty appear to be based on the idea that the ruler is one whose power is justified because of his virtue and abilities. When the new emperor dies and one of his sons succeeds to the throne, however, another principle of sovereignty is invoked: the second emperor is deemed fit to rule because he is the highest-ranking son in the ruling family. First emperors legitimate their rule by virtue; second and later emperors validate their rule by family connections. The latter rationale is invoked until the end of the dynasty, when another family asserts that its moral rectitude justifies a change. Thus, the dynastic system makes use of two theories of legitimation, one based on virtue and one based on birth.

Another important principle of Chinese politics, at least since the early years of the Zhou dynasty, is summarized by the slogan "the mandate of Heaven" (Tianming). In this conception, the emperor and his family carry out the commands of Heaven, the latter conceived as a divine, semi-natural, semi-personal force. Heaven demonstrates its approval of an emperor by vouchsafing plentiful harvests, social order, and portents of nature that are interpreted positively. Heaven manifests its displeasure with an emperor and hints at a change in dynasty by sending down famine, drought, widespread sickness, political turmoil, or other portents. It is important to note that the notion of the mandate of Heaven can serve to justify revolution as well as continuity. Rebellions in Chinese history, both those that have failed and those that have succeeded, usually claim that Heaven has proclaimed its displeasure with the ruling house and is transferring its mandate to a new group. The judgment of whether the mandate has indeed shifted is in principle always open to debate. It furnishes a compelling rationale for all current regimes at the same time that it holds open the possibility of revolution on divine grounds.

The dynastic system and the mandate of Heaven were joined to a third basic idea, that of bureaucracy. A bureaucratic form of government is not, of course, unique to China. What is important for our purposes is the particular shape and function of the bureaucracy and its reach into nearly all spheres of Chinese life, including religion.

Max Weber's listing of the characteristics of bureaucracy offers a helpful starting point for discussing the Chinese case. According to Weber, bureaucracy includes: (1) the principle of official jurisdictional areas, so that the duties and powers of each office are clearly stipulated; (2) the principle of hierarchy, which makes clear who ranks above and who ranks below, with all subordinates following their superiors; (3) the keeping of written records or files and a class of scribes whose duty is to make copies; (4) training of officials for their specific tasks; (5) full-time employment of the highest officials; and (6) the following of general rules.[15] Virtually all of these principles can be found in one form or another in the Chinese bureaucracy, the root of which some scholars trace to the religion of the second millennium B.C.E. The only consistent qualification that needs to be made (as Weber himself points out[16]) concerns the fourth point. Aspirants to government service were admitted to the job, in theory at least, only after passing a series of examinations, but the examination system rewarded a general course of learning in arts and letters rather than the technical skills demanded in some posts like engineering, forensic medicine, and so on.

The central government was also local; the chief government official responsible for a county was a magistrate, selected from a central pool on the basis of his performance in the examinations and assigned to a specific county where he had no prior family connections. He was responsible for employing lower-level functionaries in the county like scribes, clerks, sheriffs, and jailers; for collecting taxes; for keeping the peace; and, looking upward in the hierarchy, for reporting to his superiors and following their instructions. He performed a number of overtly religious functions. He made offerings at a variety of officially recognized temples, like those dedicated to the God of Walls and Moats (the so-called "City God," Chenghuang shen) and to local deified heroes; he gave lectures to the local residents about morality; and he kept close watch over all religious activities, especially those involving voluntary organizations of people outside of family and locality groups, whose actions might threaten the sovereignty and religious prerogative of the state. He was promoted on the basis of seniority and past performance, hoping to be named to higher posts with larger areas of jurisdiction or to a position in the central administration resident in the capital city. In his official capacity his interactions with others were highly formalized and impersonal.

One of the most obvious areas influenced by the bureaucratic metaphor is the Chinese pantheon. For many years it has been a truism that the Chinese conception of gods is based on the Chinese bureaucracy, that the social organization of the human government is the essential model that Chinese people use when imagining the gods. At the apex of the divine bureaucracy stands the Jade Emperor (Yuhuang dadi) in Heaven, corresponding to the human Son of Heaven (Tianzi, another name for emperor) who rules over Earth. The Jade Emperor is in charge of an administration divided into bureaus. Each bureaucrat-god takes responsibility for a clearly defined domain or discrete function. The local officials of the celestial administration are the Gods of Walls and Moats, and below them are the Gods of the Hearth, one per family, who generate a never-ending flow of reports on the people under their jurisdiction. They are assisted in turn by gods believed to dwell inside each person's body, who accompany people through life and into death, carrying with them the records of good and evil deeds committed by their charges. The very lowest officers are those who administer punishment to deceased spirits passing through the purgatorial chambers of the underworld. They too have reports to fill out, citizens to keep track of, and jails to manage. Recent scholarship has begun to criticize the generalization that most Chinese gods are bureaucratic, raising questions about the way in which the relation between the human realm and the divine realm should be conceptualized. Should the two realms be viewed as two essentially different orders, with one taking priority over the other? Should the two bureaucracies be seen as an expression in two spheres of a more unitary conceptualization of power? Is the attempt to separate a presumably concrete social system from an allegedly idealized project wrong in the first place? Other studies (and the discussion in the next section) suggest that some of the more significant deities of Chinese religion are not approached in bureaucratic terms at all.

An important characteristic of any developed bureaucratic system, earthly or celestial, is that it is wrapped in an aura of permanence and freedom from blame.

Office-holders are distinct from the office they fill. Individual magistrates and gods come and go, but the functions they serve and the system that assigns them their duties do not change. Government officials always seem capable of corruption, and specific individuals may be blameworthy, but in a sprawling and principled bureaucracy, the blame attaches only to the individuals currently occupying the office, and wholesale questioning of the structure as a whole is easily deferred. Graft may be everywhere—local magistrates and the jailers of the other world are equally susceptible to bribes—but the injustice of the bureaucracy in general is seldom broached. When revolutionary groups have succeeded or threatened to succeed in overthrowing the government, their alternative visions are, as often as not, couched not in utopian or apolitical terms, but as a new version of the old kingdom, the bureaucracy of which is staffed only by the pure.

Bureaucratic logic is also a striking part of Chinese iconography, temple archictecture, and ritual structure. For peasants who could not read in traditional times, the bureaucratic nature of the gods was an apodictic matter of appearance: gods were dressed as government officials. Their temples are laid out like imperial palaces, which include audience halls where one approaches the god with the proper deportment. Many rituals involving the gods follow bureaucratic procedures. Just as one communicates with a government official through his staff, utilizing proper written forms, so too common people depend on literate scribes to write out their prayers, in the correct literary form, which are often communicated to the other world by fire.

The Spirits of Chinese Religion

Up to this point the discussion has touched frequently on the subject of gods without explaining what gods are and how they are believed to be related to other kinds of beings. To understand Chinese theology (literally "discourse about gods"), we need to explore theories about human existence, and before that we need to review some of the basic concepts of Chinese cosmology.

What is the Chinese conception of the cosmos? Any simple answer to that question, of course, merely confirms the biases assumed but not articulated by the question—that there is only one such authentically Chinese view, and that the cosmos as such, present unproblematically to all people, was a coherent topic of discussion in traditional China. Nevertheless, the answer to that question offered by one scholar of China, Joseph Needham, provides a helpful starting point for the analysis. In Needham's opinion, the dominant strand of ancient Chinese thought is remarkable for the way it contrasts with European ideas. While the latter approach the world religiously as created by a transcendent deity or as a battleground between spirit and matter, or scientifically as a mechanism consisting of objects and their attributes, ancient Chinese thinkers viewed the world as a complete and complex "organism." "Things behaved in particular ways," writes Needham, "not necessarily because of prior actions or impulsions of other things, but because their position in the ever-moving cyclical universe was such that they were endowed with intrinsic natures which made that behaviour inevitable for them."[17] Rather than being created out of nothing, the world evolved into its current condition of complexity out of a prior state of simplicity and undifferentiation. The cosmos continues to change, but there is a consistent pattern to that change discernible to human beings. Observation of the seasons and celestial realms, and methods like plastromancy and scapulimancy (divination using tortoise shells and shoulder blades), dream divination, and manipulating the hexagrams of the *Classic of Changes* allow people to understand the pattern of the universe as a whole by focusing on the changes taking place in one of its meaningful parts.

The basic stuff out of which all things are made is called *qi*. Everything that ever existed, at all times, is made of qi, including inanimate matter, humans and animals, the sky, ideas and emotions, demons and ghosts, the undifferentiated state of wholeness, and the world when it is teeming with different beings. As an axiomatic concept with a wide range of meaning, the word qi has over the years been translated in numerous ways. Because it involves phenomena we would consider both psychological—connected to human thoughts and feelings—and physical, it can be translated as "psychophysical stuff." The translation "pneuma" draws on one early etymology of the word as vapor, steam, or breath. "Vital energy" accentuates the potential for life inherent to the more ethereal forms of qi. These meanings of qi hold for most schools of thought in early Chinese religion; it is only with the renaissance of Confucian traditions undertaken by Zhu Xi and others that qi is interpreted not as a single thing, part-matter and part-energy, pervading everything, but as one of two basic metaphysical building blocks. According to Zhu Xi, all things partake of both qi and *li* (homophonous to but different from the *li* meaning "ritual" or "propriety"), the latter understood as the reason a thing is what it is and its underlying "principle" or "reason."

While traditional cosmology remained monistic, in the sense that qi as the most basic constituent of the universe was a single thing rather than a duality or plurality of things, still qi was thought to move or to operate according to a pattern that did conform to two basic modes. The Chinese words for those two modalities are *yin* and *yang;* I shall attempt to explain them here but shall leave them untranslated. Yin and yang are best understood in terms of symbolism. When the sun shines on a mountain at some time other than midday, the mountain has one shady side and one sunny side. Yin is the emblem for the shady side and its characteristics; yang is the emblem for the sunny side and its qualities. Since the sun has not yet warmed the yin side, it is dark, cool, and moist; plants are contracted and dormant; and water in the form of dew moves downward. The yang side of the mountain is the opposite. It is bright, warm, and dry; plants open up and extend their stalks to catch the sun; and water in the form of fog moves upward as it evaporates. This basic symbolism was extended to include a host of other oppositions. Yin is female, yang is male. Yin occupies the lower position, yang the higher. Any situation in the human or natural world can be analyzed within this framework; yin and yang can be used to understand the modulations of qi on a mountainside as well as the relationships within the family. The social hierarchies of gender and age, for instance—the duty of the wife to honor her husband, and of younger generations to obey older ones—were interpreted as the natural subordination of yin to yang. The same reasoning can be applied to any two members of a pair. Yin-yang symbolism simultaneously places them on an equal footing and ranks them hierarchically. On the one hand, all processes are marked by change, making it inevitable that yin and yang alternate and imperative that humans seek a harmonious balance between the two. On the other hand, the system as a whole attaches greater value to the ascendant member of the pair, the yang. Such are the philosophical possibilities of the conceptual scheme. Some interpreters of yin and yang choose to emphasize the nondualistic, harmonious nature of the relationship, while others emphasize the imbalance, hierarchy, and conflict built into the idea.

How is human life analyzed in terms of the yin and yang modes of "material energy" (yet another rendering of qi)? Health for the individual consists in the harmonious balancing of yin and yang. When the two modes depart from their natural course, sickness and death result. Sleep, which is dark and therefore yin, needs to be balanced by wakefulness, which is yang. Salty tastes (yin) should be matched by bitter ones (yang); inactivity should alternate with movement and so on. Normally the material energy that constitutes a person, though constantly shifting, is unitary enough to sustain a healthy life. When the material energy is blocked, follows improper patterns, or is invaded by pathogens, then the imbalance between yin and yang threatens to pull the person apart, the coarser forms of material energy (which are yin) remaining attached to the body or near the corpse, the more ethereal forms of material energy (which are yang) tending to float up and away. Dream-states and minor sicknesses are simply gentler forms of the personal dissociation—the radical conflict between yin and yang—that comes with spirit-possession, serious illness, and death. At death the material force composing the person dissipates, and even that dissipation follows a pattern analyzable in terms of yin and yang. The yin parts of the person—collectively called "earthly souls" (*po*)—move downward, constituting the flesh of the corpse, perhaps also returning as a ghost to haunt the living. Since they are more like energy than matter, the yang parts of the person—collectively called "heavenly souls" (*hun*)—float upward. They—notice that there is more than one of each kind of "soul," making a unique soul or even a dualism of the spirit impossible in principle—are thought to be reborn in Heaven or as another being, to be resident in the ancestral tablets, to be associated more amorphously with the ancestors stretching back seven generations, or to be in all three places at once.

Above I claimed that a knowledge of Chinese cosmology and an anthropology was essential to understanding what place gods occupy in the Chinese conceptual world. That is because the complicated term "god," in the sense either of a being believed to be perfect in power, wisdom, and goodness or a superhuman figure worthy of worship, does not correspond straightforwardly to a single Chinese term with a similar range of meanings. Instead, there are genaral areas of overlap, as well as concepts that have no correspondence, between the things we would consider "gods" and specific Chinese terms. Rather than pursuing this question from the side of modern English usage, however, we will begin with the important Chinese terms and explain their range of meanings.

One of the terms crucial to understanding Chinese religion is *shen,* which in this introduction I translate with different versions of the English word "spirit." Below these three words are analyzed separately as consisting of three distinct spheres of meaning, but one should keep in mind that the three senses are all rooted in a single Chinese word. They differ only in degree or realm of application, not in kind.

The first meaning of shen is confined to the domain of the individual human being; it may be translated as "spirit" in the sense of "human spirit" or "psyche." It is the basic power or agency within humans that accounts for life. To extend life to full potential the spirit must be cultivated, resulting in ever clearer, more luminous states of being. In physiological terms "spirit" is a general term for the "heavenly souls," in contrast to the yin elements of the person.

The second meaning of shen may be rendered in English as "spirits" or "gods," the latter written in lowercase because Chinese spirits and gods need not be seen as all-powerful, transcendent, or creators of the world. They are intimately involved in the affairs of the world, generally lacking a perch or time frame completely beyond the human realm. An early Chinese dictionary explains: "Shen are the spirits of Heaven. They draw out the ten thousand things."[18] As the spirits associated with objects like stars, mountains, and streams, they exercise a direct influence on things in this world, making phenomena appear and causing things to extend themselves. In this sense of "spirits," shen are yang and opposed to the yin class of things known in Chinese as *gui,* "ghosts" or "demons." The two words put together, as in the combined form *guishen* ("ghosts and spirits"), cover all manner of spiritual beings in the largest sense, those benevolent and malevolent, lucky and unlucky. In this view, spirits are manifestations of the yang material force, and ghosts are manifestations of the yin material force. The nineteenth-century Dutch scholar Jan J. M. de Groot emphasized this aspect of the Chinese worldview, claiming that "animism" was an apt characterization of Chinese religion because all parts of the universe—rocks, trees, planets, animals, humans—could be animated by spirits, good or bad. As support for that thesis he quotes a disciple of Zhu Xi's: "Between Heaven and Earth there is no thing that does not consist of yin and yang, and there is no place where yin and yang are not found. Therefore there is no place where gods and spirits do not exist."[19]

Shen in its third meaning can be translated as "spiritual." An entity is "spiritual" in the sense of inspiring awe or wonder because it combines categories usually kept separate, or it cannot be comprehended through normal concepts. The *Classic of Changes* states, "'Spiritual' means not measured by yin and yang."[20] Things that are numinous cross categories. They cannot be fathomed as either yin or yang, and they possess the power to disrupt the entire system of yin and yang. A related synonym, one that emphasizes the power of such spiritual things, is *ling*, meaning "numinous" or possessing unusual spiritual characteristics. Examples that are considered shen in the sense of "spiritual" include albino members of a species; beings that are part-animal, part-human; women who die before marriage and turn into ghosts receiving no care; people who die in unusual ways like suicide or on battlefields far from home; and people whose bodies fail to decompose or emit strange signs after death.

The fact that these three fields of meaning ("spirit," "spirits," and "spiritual") can be traced to a single word has important implications for analyzing Chinese religion. Perhaps most importantly, it indicates that there is no unbridgeable gap separating humans from gods or, for that matter, separating good spirits from demons. All are composed of the same basic stuff, qi, and there is no ontological distinction between them. Humans are born with the capacity to transform their spirit into one of the gods of the Chinese pantheon. Hagiographies offer details about how some people succeed in becoming gods and how godlike exemplars and saints inspire people to follow their example.

The broad range of meaning for the word shen is related to the coexistence, sometimes harmonious, sometimes not, of a number of different idioms for talking about Chinese gods. An earlier section quoted Xunzi's comment that distinguishes between a naive fear of gods on the part of the uneducated and a pragmatic, agonistic attitude on the part of the literati. Although they share common practices and might use the same words to talk about them, those words mean different things. Similarly, Zhu Xi uses homonyms and etymology to abstract—to disembody—the usual meaning of spirits and ghosts. Spirits (*shen*), he says, are nothing but the "extension" (*shen,* pronounced the same but in fact a different word) of material energy, and ghosts (*gui*) amount to the "returning" (*gui,* also homophonous but a different word) of material energy.

Chinese gods have been understood—experienced, spoken to, dreamed about, written down, carved, painted—according to a number of different models. The bureaucratic model (viewing gods as office-holders, not individuals, with all the duties and rights appropriate to the specific rank) is probably the most common but by no means the only one. Spirits are also addressed as stern fathers or compassionate mothers. Some are thought to be more pure than others, because they are manifestations of astral bodies or because they willingly dirty themselves with birth and death in order to bring people salvation. Others are held up as paragons of the common values thought to define social life, like obedience to parents, loyalty to superiors, sincerity, or trustworthiness. Still others possess power, and sometimes entertainment value, because they flaunt standard mores and conventional distinctions.

Books on Chinese religion can still be found that attempt to portray the spirit—understood in the singular, in the theoretical sense of essential principle—of Chinese tradition. That kind of book treats the subject of gods, if it raises the question at all, as an interesting but ultimately illogical concern of the superstitious. We might instead attempt to move from a monolithic or abstract conception of the Chinese spirit to a picture, or an occasionally contentious series or pictures, of the many spirits of Chinese religion.

Notes

I am grateful to several kind spirits who offered helpful comments on early drafts of this essay. They include the anonymous readers of the book manuscript, Donald S. Lopez, Jr., Yang Lu, Susan Naquin, Daniel L. Overmyer, and Robert H. Sharf.

1. Li's formulation is quoted in Beishi, Li Yanshou (seventh century), Bona edition (Beijing: Zhonghua shuju, 1974), p. 1234. Unless otherwise noted, all translations from Chinese are mine.

2. The proverb, originally appearing in the sixteenth-century novel *Investiture of the Gods (Fengshen yanyi),* is quoted in Clifford H. Plopper, *Chinese Religion Seen through the Proverb* (Shanghai: China Press, 1926), p. 16.

3. The first three are quoted in Plopper, *Chinese Religion,* p. 15. The last is quoted in Judith Berling, *The Syncretic Religion of Lin Chao-en* (New York: Columbia University Press, 1980), p. 8. See also Timothy Brook, "Rethinking Syncretism: The Unity of the Three Teachings and Their Joint Worship in Late-Imperial China," *Journal of Chinese Religions* 21 (Fall 1993): 13–44.

4. The phrase is *shu er bu zuo,* quoted from the *Analects, Lunyu zhengi,* annotated by Liu Baonan (1791–1855), in *Zhuzi jicheng* (Shanghai: Shijie shuju, 1936), 2:134.

5. For further details, see Lionel M. Jensen, "The Invention of 'Confucius' and His Chinese Other, 'Kong Fuzi,'" *Positions: East Asia Cultures Critique* 1.2 (Fall 1993): 414–59; and Thomas A. Wilson, *Geneaology of the Way: The Construction and Uses of the Confucian Tradition in Late Imperial China* (Stanford: Stanford University Press, 1995).

6. *Laozi dao de jing,* ch. 42, *Zhuzi jicheng* (Shanghai: Shijie shuju, 1936), 3:26.

7. For three views on the subject, see Kristofer Schipper, "Purity and Strangers: Shifting Boundaries in Medieval Taoism," *T'oung Pao* 80 (1994): 61–81; Rolf A. Stein, "Religious Taoism and Popular Religion from the Second to Seventh Centuries," in *Facets of Taoism,* edited by Holmes Welch and Anna Siedel (New Haven: Yale University Press, 1979), pp. 53–81; and Michel Strickmann, "History, Anthropology, and Chinese Religion," *Harvard Journal of Asiatic Studies* 40.1 (June 1980): 201–48.

8. In fact the linguistic situation is more complex. Some scholars suggest that Fo is a transliteration not from Sanskrit but from Tocharian; see, for instance, Ji Xianlin, "Futu yu Fo," *Guoli zhongyang yanjiuyuan Lishi yuyan yanjisuo jikan* 20.1 (1948): 93–105.

9. On the extended meaning of the three jewels in Chinese sources, see Jacques Gernet, *Buddhism in Chinese Society: An Economic History from the Fifth to the Tenth Centuries,* translated by Franciscus Verellen (New York: Columbia University Press, 1995), p. 67.

10. *Kaiyuan shijiao lu,* Zhisheng (669–740), T 2154, 55:572b.

11. *Xunzi jijie,* edited by Wang Xianqian, in *Zhuzi jicheng* (Shanghai: Shijie shuju, 1935), 2:250.

12. Wing-tsit Chan, *Religious Trends in Modern China* (New York: Columbia University Press, 1953), pp. 141, 142.

13. Francis L. K. Hsu, *Under the Ancestors' Shadow: Kinship, Personality, and Social Mobility in China,* 2d ed. (Stanford: Stanford University Press, 1971), p. 246.

14. See John Jorgensen, "The 'Imperial' Lineage of Ch'an Buddhism: The Role of Confucian Ritual and Ancestor Worship in Ch'an's Search for Legitimation in the Mid-T'ang Dynasty," *Papers on Far Eastern History* 35 (March 1987): 89–134.

15. Max Weber, *Economy and Society: An Outline of Interpretive Sociology,* ed. Guenther Roth and Claus Wittich, translated by Ephraim Fischoff et al., 2 vols. (Berkeley: University of California Press, 1978), pp. 956–68.

16. Ibid., p. 1049.

17. Joseph Needham, with the research assistance of Wang Ling, *Science and Civilisation in China,* vol. 2: *History of Scientific Thought* (Cambridge: Cambridge University Press, 1956), p. 281.

18. *Shuowen jiezi*, Xu Shen (d. 120), in *Shuowen jiezi gulin zhengbu hebian*, edited Duan Yucai (1735–1815) and Ding Fubao, 12 vols. (Taibei: Dingwen shuju, 1977), 2:86a.

19. Jan J. M. de Groot, *The Religious System of China: Its Ancient Forms, Evolution, History and Present Aspect, Manners, Customs and Social Institutions Connected Therewith*, 6 vols. (Leiden: E.J. Brill, 1892–1910), 4:51. My translation differs slightly from de Groot's.

20. *Zhouyi yinde*, Harvard-Yenching Institute Sinological Index Series, Supplement no. 10 (reprint ed., Taibei: Ch'eng-wen Publishing Co., 1966), p. 41a.

—18—

Laozi: Ancient Philosopher, Master of Immortality, and God

Livia Kohn

Traditionally Daoism is described as having developed in two major phases: there was first the so-called philosophical Daoism, the quietistic and mystical philosophy of the ancient thinkers Laozi and Zhuangzi. This began around 500 B.C.E., was the dominant form of Daoism for several hundred years, and since then has continued, as one among many schools of Chinese thought, well into the present day. The second form of Daoism is known as religious Daoism. It began in the second century C.E. with the revelation of the Dao to Zhang Daoling, who became the first Celestial Master or representative of the Dao on Earth. This was an organized religion, with doctrines, rituals, gods, and the ultimate goal of ascension to the heavens of the immortals. It, too, has continued as one among many other forms of Daoism until today.

While this picture is basically correct, the reality is slightly more complex. Not only are there various schools in both kinds of Daoism, but the transition between the two main streams, during the Han dynasty (202 B.C.E.–220 C.E.), also contains elements of religious doctrine and practice that influence both. These are notably the doctrines of the so-called Huang-Lao school and the practices of the immortality seekers and magico-technicians (*fangshi*—fortune-tellers, astrologers, medical practitioners), who were then wandering throughout the country.

Despite their differences, all these forms of Daoism have several things in common. The most obvious among these is their reverence for Laozi, the "Old Master." In philosophical Daoism, he is venerated as the first thinker of the school, the author of the *Classic on the Way and Its Power (Dao de jing)*, a text that has been translated into English well over a hundred times. Historically speaking, no single person wrote the text, nor does it go back to 500 B.C.E., the alleged lifetime of Laozi. Rather, the work was put together on the basis of aphorisms from various sources in the Warring States period, around 250 B.C.E. It definitely existed at the beginning of the Han dynasty, as two copies of the text in the tomb at Mawangdui of 168 B.C.E. show.

Laozi, the philosopher, is similarly elusive. The account of his life in the *Records of the Historian (Shiji)* of the year 104 B.C.E. includes information on four distinct people, none of whom is properly identified as the Daoist philosopher. There is first a person called Li from the south of China; then, there is a historian by the name of Dan who served in the Zhou archives; third, there is a ritual master who met and taught Confucius; and fourth, there is a saint by the name of Laolaizi who wrote a Daoist book in fifteen sections. Any one of these people might have been the Old Master of the Daoists, yet none of them is a truly historical figure.

In religious Daoism, in its first documents of the second century C.E., Laozi is worshiped as the personification of the eternal Dao, the "Way," the ultimate power that makes the universe exist and causes beings to be alive. Known then as the god Taishang Laojun, the Most High Lord Lao, he is believed to reside in the center of Heaven and at the beginning of time. He is the origin and vital power of all-that-is. Like the universe at large, he changes and transforms in rhythmic harmony. As the original ancestor of yin and yang, he appears and disappears continually, serving in every age as the inspired divine adviser to the ruler and guiding the world to truer harmony with the Dao.

Laozi here is regarded as the savior of humanity who has appeared over and over again in the course of history, revealing the Dao to the sagely rulers of old as well as to the inspired religious leaders of the Han. Laozi is said to have made a pact with the first Celestial Master Zhang Daoling that allowed him and his descendants to represent the Dao on Earth and guaranteed the believers of this sect to survive all cosmic disasters and be saved as immortals.

The magico-technicians and Huang-Lao Daoists of the Han, finally, saw Laozi as an inspired leader of their own kinds of practices. He was a teacher of the right way to govern the country while at the same time cultivating oneself and extending one's life. He was, for them, not yet a god and yet no longer a mere thinker, reclusive official, or master of ritual. Laozi of the immortality seekers is himself a practitioner of longevity techniques, one who has lived for several hundred years, maintained his vigor, and attained the magic of the immortals. He has full control over life and death, foresees the future, and knows all about the patterns of the heavenly bodies. He can order demons about at will, and he wields talismans and spells as if he were born to it.

The text translated below contains traces of all three visions of Laozi. It is his biography from the *Biography of Spirit Immortals (Shenxian zhuan),* written by Ge Hong (283–343), an aristocrat and scholar of the early fourth century, who had a lively interest in all things Daoist and researched them with great acumen. Ge Hong lived in South China, where he wandered around the country to find ancient manuscripts and learned masters, then came home to write down his findings. In his autobiography—the first of its kind in Chinese literature—he describes how he eschewed all official positions and even avoided social interaction with his equals, because his one aim in life was to become immortal. For Ge Hong, immortality was not to be reached through religious observances such as prayers and rituals, although he certainly believed in the magical efficacy of talismans and spells; he believed that the desired state could be attained first and foremost through the practice of longevity techniques such as gymnastics, breathing exercises, special diets, meditations, and—most of all—alchemy.

Accordingly his main remaining work, *He Who Embraces Simplicity (Baopuzi)*, which he named after his pen name, is a vast compendium of the techniques and practices of the immortals. It details the protective measures one has to take to keep the demons and evil spirits at bay. It describes how to reach alignment with the yin and yang energies of the universe; how to absorb the energies of the sun and the moon; how to use various herbs and minerals to improve one's health and extend one's life; how to attain magical qualities such as being in several places at once, becoming invisible, and flying in the air; how to prepare various kinds of elixirs or "cinnabars" that will have the power of instantaneously transforming one into an immortal or at least bestow very long life on Earth and power over life and death; and many many more.

The Laozi that Ge Hong presents in his collection of immortals' biographies is a Laozi in transition. The beginnings of Daoism as an organized religion under the Celestial Masters had taken place about 150 years earlier, but in an entirely different part of the country. Ge Hong himself was not familiar with the movement and had only heard rumors that some people claimed Laozi was the Dao itself, a kind of god and spiritual being who came to Earth again and again.

For him, Laozi was first of all a historical figure, an ancient philosopher who had had profound insights—insights based on his particular intellect or, as the Chinese of the time would say, on his inherent spirit, his nature-given energy. In addition to this, Ge Hong saw Laozi as a successful practitioner of immortality, as a famous and inspiring example for all practitioners. His own desire to prove that one could learn and practice to become immortal—live very long, acquire magical powers, and eventually ascend to heaven in broad daylight—required that he cast Laozi in this role. He had no interest in stylizing him as the Dao, as the religious follower did, and explicitly counters any suggestions in this direction.

The text below is therefore a collection of notes on Laozi, interspersed with Ge Hong's comments to guide the reader in the desired direction. It refers to many different sources, sometimes mentioned by title, sometimes just introduced as "some say." The texts cited explicitly are all lost today, but we know that they were among the so-called apocrypha of the Han dynasty. The apocrypha or non-orthodox materials were a group of texts that interpreted the Classics of the Confucian elite in terms of the magico-technicians' arts: astrology, fortune-telling, numerology, and other esoteric speculations.

These texts tended to stylize the emperors of ancient Chinese history—mythical rulers—as semisupernatural beings. The great culture heroes of old, like Fu Xi, who invented the eight trigrams of the *Classic of Changes (Yijing)* and thereby made the order of the cosmos accessible to humanity, or Shennong, the Divine Agriculturist, who discovered farming and animal husbandry, in these texts were more than the powerful rulers of the historians. They had special powers and marvelous features to show their stature. Shun, for example, one of the five great Confucian rulers, had double pupils—a symbol of his extraordinary perception. Yao, another Confucian hero, was born after his mother had seen a shooting star—an indication of his Heaven-inspired rule. Many mythical rulers also had the "sun horn" and the "moon crescent," two specially shaped bones sticking out over the eyebrows. They are so named because, in Chinese body mythology, the left eye is the sun and the right eye is the moon. Some rulers also had more sense openings than ordinary people did, and others had strange signs in the lines on their hands and feet—all features that in due course were also attributed to Laozi.

In addition to Han dynasty apocrypha and "miscellaneous records," some of which are obviously influenced by the religious movement, Ge Hong relied on historical sources. He cites the Laozi biography in the *Records of the Historian* and retells many stories contained in the *Zhuangzi*. In all these, Laozi appears as a philosopher—a reclusive and withdrawn person with uncanny powers of insight, who puts the great Confucius to shame. He immediately identifies Confucius's disciple and tells him so; he stuns the master with his dragonlike mind; he advises him on the futility of his efforts to perfect benevolence and righteousness; and so on. This more historical Laozi, too, is a stylized figure. Used in polemics among the various philosophical schools, he appears as the superior contemporary and counterpart of Confucius. Expounding a philosophy of withdrawal and serenity, Laozi is depicted as the one who has all the answers but cannot teach them, since the Dao can only come to those who are ready to receive it.

The key episode of Laozi's philosophical life is at the same time the pivot of the religion: his transmission of *The Way and Its Power* in five thousand words to Yin Xi, the guardian of the pass. The story goes back to the *Records of the Historian*. It says,

> Laozi lived under the Zhou for a long time. When he saw that the dynasty was declining, he decided to leave. He reached the pass [on the western frontier]. There Yin Xi, the guardian of the pass, told him: "You are about to withdraw completely. Would you please write down your ideas for me?" Thereupon Laozi wrote a work in two sections to explain the Dao and its Power. It had more than five thousand words. Then he left. Nobody knows what became of him. (chap. 63)

This is later taken up by all biographies and hagiographies of Laozi and becomes the standard motif of Laozi pictures: the old man sitting on his ox cheerfully leaving his homeland. Still, the story ends differently in different versions. While the historical account ends the description of Laozi's life with the transmission of *The Way and Its Power,* Ge Hong implies that he pursued his goal of immortality and ascended to Mount Kunlun, both a mountain range in Central Asia and an immortals' paradise of Chinese mythology. He then emphasizes that Yin Xi, inspired by Laozi and following the instructions of *The Way and Its Power,* became an immortal himself and in the following illustrates the power and efficacy of the sacred scripture.

In later sources, on the other hand, Laozi is said to have continued his way over the pass and wandered through Central Asia until he reached India. Everywhere he went, he converted the local population, the "barbarians," to Daoism. Adapting its ways to their primitive state, he set up particularly strict rules for them and called himself the Buddha. This version is known as the "conversion of the barbarians," a theory that led to much debate with the Buddhists and caused, more than once, the prohibition and persecution of religious Daoism.

Ge Hong exploits the scene on the pass in a set different way. Describing how Laozi controlled the life and death of his servant Xu Jia with a special talisman, he shows the ancient philosopher effectively as a master of magic and the powers of the immortals. His suggestion, of course, is that by studying the words of this sagely person and following the methods he revealed—the list includes all the longevity, immortality, and demon-fighting techniques of the Dao—one can become such a master oneself. Indeed, the scripture Laozi revealed must contain some of his essence and therefore can bestow certain powers and benefits. No wonder, then, that the recluses and aspiring immortals of Ge Hong's day all had the greatest veneration for the Old Master.

From *Shenxian zhuan* (Biographies of Spirit Immortals), chap. 1, pp. 1b–3b (ed. *Daozang jinghua* 5.11). Other editions: *Taiping guangji* 1; *Han Wei congshu* 1; *Yiwen leiju* 78. For a complete translation of the entire *Shenxian zhuan,* see Gertrud Güntsch, *Das Shen-hsien-chuan und das Erscheinungsbild eines Hsien* (Frankfurt: Peter Lang, 1988).

Further Reading

Judith Boltz, "Lao-tzu," in *Encyclopedia of Religion,* edited by Mircea Eliade (New York: Macmillan, 1987), vol. 8, pp. 454–59; A. C. Graham, "The Origins of the Legend of Lao Tan," in *Studies in Chinese Philosophy and Philosophical Literature,* edited by A. C. Graham (Albany: State University of New York Press, 1981, 1990), pp. 111–24; Livia Kohn, "The Mother of the Tao," *Taoist Resources* 1.2 (1989): 37–113; Jay Sailey, *The Master Who Embraces Simplicity: A Study of the Philosophy of Ko Hung (A.D. 283–343)* (San Francisco: Chinese Materials Center, 1978); Kenneth J. DeWoskin, *Doctors, Diviners, and Magicians of Ancient China* (New York: Columbia University Press, 1983); Livia Kohn, ed., *Taoist Meditation and Longevity Techniques* (Ann Arbor: University of Michigan, Center for Chinese Studies, 1989).

Biography of Laozi

Laozi was called Chong'er (Double Ear) or Boyang (Lord of Yang). He came from Quren Village in Hu County in the state of Chu (modern Luyi District in Henan Province).

His mother had become pregnant when she was touched by a huge meteor. Although Laozi had therefore received his basic energy directly from Heaven, he yet appeared in the Li family and took Li as his surname.

Some say that Laozi has existed since before Heaven and Earth. Others say that he is the essential soul of Heaven, a spiritual and wonderful being. Then again some claim that his mother remained pregnant for seventy-two years and only then gave birth. At birth, he split open his mother's left armpit and emerged. Being just born, he already had white hair—which is why he was called Laozi, "Old Child." Others maintain that his mother had been unmarried [at the time of his birth] so that Laozi adopted her family name. Then there are those who insist that his mother had just come to stand under a plum tree when he was born. As soon as he was born, he was able to speak. He pointed to the plum tree (*li*) and said: "I shall take this [Li] to be my surname."

Other sources, moreover, state that Laozi, in the time of the ancient Three Sovereigns (mythical rulers in the early stages of the universe), was [their teacher under the name] Preceptor of the Mysterious Center. In the time of the later Three Sovereigns, he was the Imperial Lord Goldtower. Under Fu Xi [the Prostrate Sacrificer and first ruler], he was the Master of Luxuriant Florescence. Under Shennong [the Divine Farmer], he was the Old Master of Ninefold Numen. Under Zhurong [the Lord Firedrill], he was the Master of Vast Longevity. Under Huangdi [the Yellow Emperor], he was the Master of Vast Perfection. Under Emperor Zhuanxu [a mythical ruler], he was the Master of Red Essence. Under Emperor Ku, he was the Master of Registers and Sacred Charts. Under Emperor Yao, he was the Master of Perfected Duty. Under Emperor Shun, he was the Master of Ruling Longevity. Under Yu, the founder of the Xia dynasty, he was the Master of True Practice. Under Tang, the founder of the Shang dynasty, he was the Master of Granting Rules. Under King Wen, the first ruler of the Zhou dynasty, he was the Master of Culture and Towns.

However, some also maintain that Laozi was a mere archivist, while others say that he was [the statesman] Fan Li in [the southern state of] Yue and accordingly appeared under the name of Chi Yizi in [the eastern state of] Qi and as Dao Zhugong in [the southeastern state of] Wu.

All these are statements found in miscellaneous records but not in the authentic scriptures of divine immortals. Thus they cannot be considered reliable. I, Ge Hong, state: For my part, I think that if Laozi was a spiritual being of celestial origin, he should indeed have appeared in each successive generation, exchanging his honorable rank for a humble condition, sacrificing his ease and freedom in order to subject himself to toil. He should indeed have turned his back on the pure serenity [of the heavenly spheres] in order to immerse himself in the foulness and defilements [of the world], giving up his celestial position and accepting inferior rank in the world of humanity.

Most certainly, the arts of the Dao have existed ever since there were Heaven and Earth. The masters of these arts of the Dao—when would they not have been there, even for a short while? They have appeared and worked their arts from [the beginnings of culture under] Fu Xi to the time of the three dynasties [of the Xia, Shang, and Zhou]. They existed from generation to generation—yet why should they all have been only forms of [the single figure] Laozi? Adepts who pursue learning in their old age tend to love the marvelous and value the weird. Wishing to do great honor to Laozi, they produce such theories. In reality, as far as I am concerned, Laozi was a person who realized the deepest essence of the Dao. But he was not of an extraordinary or superhuman kind.

The *Records of the Historian* says: "The son of Laozi was named Zong. He served as a general in the army of the state of Wei and enfeoffed in Duan. Then came Zong's son Wang, Wang's son Yan, and Yan's great-grandson Xia, an official in Han. Xia's son Jie was grand tutor of the Prince of Jiaoxi and lived in [the eastern state of] Qi."

Thus the theory that Laozi was originally a spiritual and wonderful being goes back to the efforts of inexperienced Daoists who wished to see the strange and supernatural in him. They hoped that scholars of later generations would follow their ideas and never realized that such strange tales would only increase the disbelief people already had about the feasibility of prolonging life. Why is this? Well, if one says that Laozi was a man who realized the Dao, then people will be encouraged in their efforts to emulate his example. However, if one depicts him as a spiritual and wonderful being of a superhuman kind, then there is nothing to be learned.

In regard to his life, there is the following record: Laozi wished to emigrate to the west. The guardian of the border pass, a man named Yin Xi, knew that he was not an ordinary man. He therefore requested instruction in the Dao. Laozi was surprised and thought this strange, thus he merely stuck out his tongue. It was soft and rimless [like the Dao]. Because of this Laozi was also called Lao Dan, "Old Rimless."

This latter statement is not correct either. According to the *Scripture of [Laozi's] Nine Transformations (Jiubian jing)* and the *Scripture on [Laozi's] Original Birth and Twelve Transformations (Yuansheng shier hua jing)*, Laozi had the name Dan already before he ever approached Yin Xi's pass. In fact, Laozi changed his names and appellations several times—he was not just called Dan. The reason for this is that, as described in the [astrological texts] *Scripture of the [Constellation] Nine Palaces (Jiugong jing)*, *Scripture of the Three [Powers] and Five [Phases] (Sanwu jing)*, and the *Scripture of Primordial Planets (Yuanchen jing)*, all people must face difficult situations in their lives. When such a difficult time comes, one should change one's name or appellation to accommodate the transformation of primordial cosmic energy that is taking place. Doing so, one can extend the span of one's life and overcome the difficulty.

Even today in our generation, there are Daoists who practice this with enthusiasm. Laozi himself lived for over three hundred years under the Zhou.

Living for so many years, he was bound to encounter many difficult situations. Thus he has rather a lot of names.

To determine the exact dates of Laozi's birth and departure, it is best to rely mainly on historical works and factual records, but one should also take into consideration esoteric scriptures like the *Scripture of Lao the Immortal (Laoxian jing)*. Other materials, such as folklore and local stories, can be ignored as void and specious.

The *Central Essence of [Laozi's] Western Ascension (Xisheng zhongtai)*, the *Diagrams on the Restoration of Life (Fuming bao)*, and the *Esoteric Scripture in Chapters of Gold on the [Constellations] Pearl-Studded Bowcase and Jade Pivot (Zhutao yuji jinpian neijing)* all give some indication of Laozi's looks. He had a yellow-whitish complexion, beautiful eyebrows, and a broad forehead. He possessed long ears, big eyes, gaping teeth, a square mouth, and thick lips. On his forehead he had the signs of the three [powers] and five [phases]. He had the sun horn and the moon crescent sticking out above his eyebrows. His nose was broad and straight and had a double rim, while his ears had three openings. On the soles of his feet he had the signs of the two [forces yin and yang] and the five [phases]; his palms contained the character for the number ten.

Under King Wen of the Zhou (1150–1133 B.C.E.), he served as an archivist. Under King Wu (1133–1116), he was a historian. The common people of the time noticed that he lived very long and thus called him Laozi, "Old Master." By destiny he was endowed with a penetrating spirit and far-reaching foresight. The energy he had received at birth was unlike that of ordinary people. All this caused him to become a master of the Dao. It was because of this unusual quality that the divine powers of Heaven supported him and the host of immortals followed him.

> Thus he came to reveal various methods of going beyond the world:
> the [alchemy of the] nine cinnabars and eight minerals;
> the [dietetics of] metallic wine and the golden fluid;
> the visualization of mysterious simplicity and of guarding the One;
> the recollection of spirit and penetration of the hidden;
> the guiding of energy and refinement of the body;
> the dispelling of disasters and exorcism of evil;
> the control over demons and the nourishing of inner nature;
> the abstention from grain and the many ways of transforming the body;
> the serenity of a life in accordance with the teaching and the precepts;
> the overcoming and control of demons and malevolent specters.

These methods fill 930 scrolls of texts as well as 70 scrolls of talismans. They are all recorded in the *Essential Chapters on Laozi's Origins and Deeds (Laozi benqi zhongpian)*, as is already evident in the list of contents. But beware! Anything not contained in these was only added by later Daoists, following their personal preferences. It cannot be considered part of the perfected scriptures.

Laozi was basically a man of calm and serenity. Free from desires, he pursued only the extension of life. Thus it was that he lived under the Zhou for a long time but never strove for high rank or fame. He only wished to keep his inner light in harmony with the world of dust and grime, to realize spontaneity within, and to leave once his Dao was perfected. He was indeed a true immortal.

Confucius once went to ask Laozi about the rites. But first he sent [his disciple] Zigong to see him. Zigong had hardly arrived when Laozi told him: "Your master's name is Qiu (Confucius). After you have followed him for another three years, you can both be taught."

Confucius eventually came to see Laozi himself. Laozi told him: "A good merchant fills his storehouses but appears to have nothing. A gentleman is overflowing with virtue but acts as if he was worthless. Give up your pride and haughtiness as well as your many desires and your lasciviousness. None of these is doing you any good!"

On another occasion, Confucius was studying a text. Laozi observed this and asked what he was reading.

"The *Classic of Changes,*" Confucius replied. "The sages of old studied it, too."

"If the sages of old read it," Laozi commented, "so be it. But why are you reading it? What are its essential ideas?"

"Its essential ideas are benevolence and righteousness."

"Ah well," Laozi said, [then explained.] "See, it's like that. When mosquitoes and horseflies buzz around and bite your skin, you can't catch a wink of sleep the whole night long. Similarly, when benevolence and righteousness are around with their miserable nature, they only confuse people's minds. There is no greater disorder than this.

"Now, the swan is white even without taking a bath every day; the raven is black even without being dyed every day. Heaven is naturally high; Earth is naturally thick. The sun and the moon are naturally luminant; stars and planets are naturally arranged. Even trees and grasses are naturally varied.

"You, if you cultivate the Dao without delay, you will certainly reach it! But what use can benevolence and righteousness have in that? Using them would be as if you tied on a drum to search for a lost sheep! With benevolence and righteousness you only create confusion in your inner nature!"

[Another time] Laozi asked Confucius, "Have you attained the Dao yet?"

"I have pursued it for twenty-seven years," Confucius replied, "but so far I have not attained it."

"Small wonder," Laozi said, "If the Dao could be given to people, all would present it to their lord. If the Dao could be handed to people, all would hand it to their family. If the Dao could be told to people, all would tell it to their brothers. If the Dao could be passed down, all would pass it down to their sons. However, it cannot. And why? Because without a host on the inside, the Dao cannot come to reside."

"I have mastered the *Classic of Poetry,*" Confucius said again, "as well as the *Classic of History,* the *Record of Rites,* the *Classic of Music,* the *Classic of Changes,* and the *Spring and Autumn Annals.* I have recited the Dao of the ancient kings and explained the deeds of [the dukes of] Shao and Zhou. I have taken my teaching to over seventy rulers, but I have never been employed. How hard it is to convince people!"

"Really," Laozi countered, "the Six Classics are only the leftover traces of the ancient kings. How could they be their real teachings, the substance behind the leftovers? What you do today is merely following these old leftover traces! Still, even traces are made from actual steps—but what a big difference between them!"

Confucius returned and did not speak for three days. Zigong [his disciple] wondered at this and finally asked him.

"When I see people using their intentions like flying birds," Confucius replied slowly, "I adapt my intention to a bow and shoot them—and never once have I failed to hit and best them. When I see people using their intentions like deer, I adapt my intention to running dogs and chase them—and never once have I failed to bite and devour them. When I see people using their intentions like deep-sea fish, I adapt my intention to a hook and throw it for them—and never once have I failed to hook and control them.

"Except one. The one animal beyond me is the dragon—riding on the energy of the clouds, wandering freely through Great Clarity. I cannot follow him. When recently I saw Laozi I knew I had met my match. He is like a dragon!

"He made my mouth gape wide, leaving me unable to shut it. He made my tongue stick out, leaving me unable to pull it back. My spirit was so amazed that I no longer knew where I was."

On another occasion [the philosopher] Yangzi was received by Laozi.

"The patterns [in the fur] of leopards and tigers," Laozi told him, "and the nimbleness of apes and monkeys only cause them to be caught and killed!"

"May I dare," Yangzi hesitated, "to ask about the rule of the enlightened kings?"

"The rule of the enlightened kings," Laozi mused. "Their merit covered all under Heaven, yet they did not think of it as issuing from themselves. Their influence reached to the myriad beings, yet they took care to keep the people independent. They had virtue, yet did not boast of their fame and position. They were impossible to figure out, wandering as they were freely around nothingness."

Laozi was about to leave [his homeland]. He therefore went westward to cross the pass, from there to ascend to Mount Kunlun. Yin Xi, the guardian of the pass, divined the winds and energies [of the world] and thus knew in advance that a divine personage would soon come past. He duly had the road swept for forty miles. When he saw Laozi approach, he knew that he was the one.

Laozi for his part had never handed down his teaching while he resided in the Middle Kingdom. However, he knew that Yin Xi was destined to realize the Dao and therefore willingly stopped on the pass.

He arrived in the company of a retainer called Xu Jia, whom he had hired as a child for a wage of one hundred [copper pieces of] cash per day. By now Laozi owed him 7,200,000 cash. When Jia saw that Laozi was about to go beyond the pass in his travels, he quickly demanded his money. Laozi did not pay him.

At this time, a servant [on the Hangu pass heard the story and] instigated Jia to file a complaint against Laozi with the guardian of the pass. But this instigator did not know that Jia had been with Laozi already for over two hundred years. He only calculated that Jia would come into a lot of money and proposed to give him his daughter in marriage. When Jia saw that the woman was fair he rejoiced.

They then went to file the complaint with Yin Xi, who was disturbed and greatly alarmed. They all went to see Laozi.

Laozi spoke to Xu Jia: "You should have died long ago! When I first hired you in the old days, you were a slave and a pauper, but I did not have a valet, so I took you on and gave you long life through the Pure Life Talisman of Great Mystery. Only thus were you able to see the present day. Why do you speak against me now? Also, I have told you that I would pay you the full amount in gold once we got to Parthia. Why can't you be patient?"

Laozi then made Jia open his mouth and told them all to look at the ground: The perfected talisman of Great Mystery was sticking upright in the earth with its cinnabar characters as good as new. In the same instant Jia collapsed into a heap of withered bones.

Yin Xi knew that Laozi was a divine personage and had the ability to restore the man to life. He therefore touched his head to the ground and begged Laozi for Jia's life. He also requested permission to provide the necessary funds to satisfy the retainer's demands.

Laozi thereupon returned the Talisman of Great Mystery to the bony remains and, lo and behold, Xu Jia immediately rose alive and well. Yin Xi duly gave him two million in cash and sent him on his way.

Later on Yin Xi served Laozi with the proper pupil's formality and received Laozi's teachings of extending life. When Yin Xi further begged him to teach him formal precepts of the Dao, Laozi told him [the scripture in] five thousand words. Yin Xi withdrew to seclusion and wrote it down faithfully. It was named *Dao de jing*. Practicing its teaching of the Dao, Yin Xi also attained immortality.

Under the Han dynasty, the Empress Dou was a great believer in the words of Laozi, and through her influence Emperor Wen (179–156 B.C.E) and all the members of the Dou family could not help but read the scripture. Reading and reciting the text, they all gained tremendous benefits. Thus the whole empire was at peace under the emperors Wen and Jing, and the empresses of the Dou family preserved their power and glory for three generations.

Also, Shu Guang, the head tutor of the crown prince, and his son and colleague deeply penetrated the meaning of the scripture. Through it they understood the relative importance [and timeliness] of worldly merit and withdrawal to seclusion. One day they decided to give up their offices and return home. There they gave money to the needy and freely distributed goodwill, yet always remained noble and pure.

This attitude was continued by numerous later recluses following the arts of Laozi. They stripped off all glory and splendor on the outside and nourished their lives to high longevity within, without ever tumbling into the perilous world of human society. Instead they were with the vast spring of the Dao, which flows long and is ever creative. Being like this, how could they not be raised on the very principles of Heaven and Earth? How could they not be masters and models for ten thousand generations? Thus all those today who follow [the model of the recluse] Zhuang Zhou (Zhuangzi) honor Laozi as their original teacher.

—19—

The Lives and Teachings of the Divine Lord of Zitong

Terry F. Kleeman

The Divine Lord of Zitong is a local god from a small town in northern Sichuan who came to have a national following as Wenchang, the God of Literature and patron of the civil service examinations. The three short texts translated below are part of a corpus of scriptures, ethical tracts, liturgical manuals, and divinatory works deriving from his cult. The first, *The Esoteric Biography of Qinghe (Qinghe neizhuan),* was revealed to a medium, who transcribed the words revealed through a process called "spirit writing." This took place in the Chengdu, Sichuan, area around 1168 C.E. It is an autobiographical account of a god, from his first human incarnation at the turn of the first millenium B.C.E. to his apotheosis in the fourth century, and is the prototype for a much longer scripture about the same god, the *Book of Transformations* (HY 170). The *Esoteric Biography* was the first salvo in a fifteen-year stream of revealed documents that reshaped the god's image, claiming for him the identity of this astral deity. Qinghe, a city in Hebei Province, is the ancestral home of an important clan of the Zhang surname, a surname with which the god has been associated since the fourth century. Members of the clan controlled the temple in Zitong for at least part of the Song dynasty (960–1279), and the god at times takes on the character of a clan progenitor deity. The text tells of how even a god goes through a process of self-cultivation and merit-building before he attains his full godhood, and it suggests that gods may be abroad in the world, hidden in human form, unknown even to themselves.

The second text, *The Scripture of the Responses and Proofs of the Divine Lord of Zitong (Yuanshi tianzun shuo Zitong dijun yingyan jing),* is a good example of a Daoist scripture with strong Buddhist influences. Like a Buddhist sūtra, it begins with an audience with the supreme deity, but here the deity is not the Buddha but a Daoist god, the Primordial Heavenly Worthy. The Divine Lord of Zitong comes forward and describes the hardships he has undergone in aeon after aeon of rebirth. Having finally escaped from rebirth through his devotion to the Heavenly Worthy, he declares, like a bodhisattva, his wish to free others from the ignorance he once suffered. The Primordial Heavenly Worthy praises him for his compassionate deeds. The Divine Lord next asks how human beings can avoid disaster. In response, the Primordial Heavenly Worthy declares that people who contemplate the virtuous deeds of the Divine Lord of Zitong will be saved, especially those seeking success in the civil service examinations and an official career. Not surprisingly, the cult to the Divine Lord of Zitong was especially popular among those who sought or held positions in the government. The text is not explicitly dated, but it can probably be safely placed in the Yuan dynasty (1280–1368). In any case, it can be no earlier than 1168 and no later than 1444.

The third work, *The Tract on the Hidden Administration (Yinzhiwen),* is a text of uncertain date, perhaps as early as the Southern Song (1127–1279), certainly no later than the late Ming (1368–1643). Like the *Esoteric Biography,* it is a spirit-writing text, that is, a work said to be the words of a god transcribed by a medium. Together with the *Tract of the Most Exalted on Action and Response (Taishang ganying pian,* see chapter 29), with which it shares many characteristics, this early representative of the morality book (*shanshu*) genre is among the most widely printed, distributed, and read books in China. The "hidden administration" of the title refers to the otherworldly bureaucracy that the Chinese believed observed, noted, and reported every good and evil act. The revealing god of this text was at the apex of this bureaucracy, the cosmic guardian of the records. He speaks of exemplary actions to be emulated and evil ones to be avoided. The intended audience certainly included elite aspirants to government office but was not restricted to them; many of the moral injunctions would seem applicable to all, and some (like the warning against using inaccurate measures) are clearly directed to non-elite groups. The ethical strictures themselves range from the socially oriented (e.g., statements on the proper treatment of travelers) to the ritual centered (e.g., prohibitions on discarding paper with writing on it). Their sum can be said to reflect fairly the majority ethical views of at least the elite portion of late imperial Chinese society.

The *Esoteric Biography of Qinghe* is translated from *Qinghe neizhuan,* 1a–2b, Daozang, HY 169. *The Scripture of Responses and Proofs* is from *Yuanshi tianzun shuo Zitong dijun yingyan jing,* Daozang, HY 28. *The Tract on the Hidden Administration* is from *Yinzhiwen,* Daozang jiyao *xing* 9/36a–96a, collated by Zhu Guishi of Daxing, reedited by Jiang Yupu (Mengying) of Suiyang.

Further Reading

Cynthia Brokaw, *The Ledgers of Merit and Demerit: Social Change and Moral Order in Late Imperial China* (Princeton: Princeton University Press, 1991); R. H. van Gulik, "On the Seal Representing the God of Literature on the Title Page of Old Chinese and Japanese Popular Editions," *Monumenta Nipponica* 4 (1941): 33–52; David K. Jordan and Daniel Overmyer, *The Flying Phoenix: Aspects of Chinese Sectarianism in Taiwan* (Princeton: Princeton University Press, 1986); Terry F.

Kleeman, "Taoist Ethics," in *A Bibliographic Guide to the Comparative Study of Ethics,* edited by John Carman and Mark Juergensmayer (Cambridge: Cambridge University Press, 1991), pp. 162–95; Kleeman, "The Expansion of the Wen-ch'ang Cult," in *Religion and Society in T'ang and Sung China,* edited by Patricia Ebrey and Peter N. Gregory (Honolulu: University of Hawaii Press, 1993), pp. 45–73; Kleeman, *A God's Own Tale: The Book of Transformations of Wenchang* (Albany: State University of New York Press, 1994); Sakai Tadao, *Chūgoku zensho no kenkyū (A Study of Chinese Morality Books)* (Tokyo: Kokusho kankōkai, 1960).

Esoteric Biography of Qinghe

I was originally a man from around Wu and Gui. Born at the beginning of the Zhou dynasty (ca. 1027–256 B.C.E.), I subsequently underwent seventy-three transformations, repeatedly becoming a scholar-official. Never have I mistreated the people or abused my clerks. I am ardent by nature but circumspect in my conduct. Like the autumn frost or the bright light of day, I am not to be disobeyed.

Later, at the end of the Western Jin dynasty (265–317), I incarnated west of Yue and south of Sui, between the two commanderies. I was born in a *dingwei* year on a *xinhai* day, the third day of the second lunar month. An auspicious glow veiled my door and yellow clouds obscured the fields. The place where I lived was low and close to the sea. A man of the village said to the elder from Qinghe, "You are now sixty yet you have obtained a precious heir."

As a child, I did not enjoy playing games. I always longed for the mountains and marshes, and often my words seemed to have hidden meanings. I copied and recited all the books. At night I avoided the gangs of children, laughing contentedly to myself. My body emitted a radiant glow. When the local people prayed [to statues of gods] I scolded and rebuked them. Giving a long cry, I said, "These images are of wood and clay, yet they wear the clothing of men and eat the food of men. When you entertain them, they respond to your wishes. When you calumnate them, they visit upon you disaster. I am a human being, how can it be that I lack spiritual power?"

After this I had strange dreams at night. Sometimes I dreamed I was a dragon. Sometimes I dreamed I was a king. There was a heavenly talisman saying that I was an official of the Water Office. I thought this strange and did not really believe it was an auspicious omen. Later drought plagued the three classes of farmers and no enriching moisture revived the plants. The farmers danced the Yu raindance and invoked the spirits, all to no avail. I thought, "At night I dream that I am in charge of the Water Office. This has been going on for a long time and by now there should be some confirmation."

That night I went to the edge of the river to throw in a memorial to the Earl of the Sea on which I had written the name of the office which I held in my dreams, but my heart failed me and I was too embarrassed to do it. Suddenly clouds converged swiftly from the four directions and wind and thunder roared. A clerk bowed before me, saying, "The Judge of Fates should transfer his residence." I said, "That is not me. I am the son of old Mister Zhang, named Ya. Later, because I became prominent through the Water Office, I was given the sobriquet Peifu (Deluger)." The clerk said, "I have been commanded to speed you on your way." I said, "What about the members of my family?" The clerk said, "Let us first go to your headquarters." I was confused and had not yet made up my mind. The clerk with a bow bade me mount a white donkey and I was gone. When I looked down I saw the village gate, then in the midst of the roar of wind and rain I suddenly lost sight of my native place.

I arrived at a mountain in the Knife Ridge range which supports the asterism Triaster. It was shaped like a phoenix lying faceup. There was an ancient pool that led me into a huge cave, by the entrance to which there were several stone "bamboo shoots." The clerk said, "When the people pray, if they call using these stones there is a response. They are called 'thunder pillars.'" I had just lifted the hem of my robe to enter the cave when the clerk said, "Do you recall that you were incarnated during the Zhou and have up until now transmitted hidden merit to your family through seventy-three transformations?" Suddenly I was enlightened as if waking from a dream. The clerk said, "In the rolls of Heaven you have the rank of a god, but there are few in the human world who know this. Soon there will be portents of a revival of the Jin dynasty. You should search out a place to manifest your transformation." I said, "Thank you, heavenly clerk, for having made this resounding report."

When I entered the cave, it was like dropping down a thousand-fathom ravine. Approaching the ground, my feet made no contact and it was as if my body could soar through the sky. There was a palace fit for a king and guards ringed about it. I entered and found that my entire family was there.

Later I assumed the form of a scholar and went to Xianyang to tell the story of Yao Chang. This is the *Esoteric Biography of Qinghe*. Those who worship me with incense must remember it!

The Scripture of the Responses and Proofs of the Divine Lord of Zitong

At that time the Primordial Heavenly Worthy was in the Heavenly Palace of Occluded Brilliance. Within Jade Metropolis Mountain he had formed a canopy of five-colored clouds. Leading the corps of transcendents of the various heavens, the sun, moon, and asterisms, he glistened and glowed. The gods and spirits of the mountains and streams folded their hands and sighed in amazement, "We have been born into and reside in a filthy, muddy, dusty, temporal world. We hope to meet with Heavenly compassion that will broadly enlighten us."

At that time, the Divine Lord of Zitong stepped forward, his countenance placid. Bowing twice before the Thearch [the Primordial Heavenly Worthy], he knelt down and said, "[I], your disciple has lost his original form myriad times in aeon after aeon. I was exiled to the land of Shu [modern Sichuan]. Mindful of the commoners below, I subjected myself to the kalpic disasters. At times I was born into the body of a bird or beast; at others, I dwelt among the Man and Rong barbarians. [Among these lives] there were distinctions in wealth and status, differences in poverty and meanness. I suffered the disasters of water, fire, weapons, and soldiers, endured the sufferings of the wheel of life, of birth and death. I did not know there were heaven, earth, the sun, moon, and stars. I slandered religions and did not revere the three jewels (in a Daoist context, usually the Dao, the scriptures, and the teachers), one's teacher, or father and mother. In the end, although my life was happy, I could not escape falling into the five evil tendencies and the three [evil] paths of rebirth. For aeon after aeon I cycled in the wheel of rebirth, ignorant of enlightenment, observing the various forms of retribution that such a person experiences. Now I have encountered the Heavenly Worthy presiding over this below. I wish to preach on your behalf in order to enlighten the benighted."

At that time the Primordial Heavenly Worthy revealed a single ray of his light and it illuminated ten thousand *li*. The corps of transcendents of the various heavens and the gods and spirits of streams, waterways, and sacred peaks in Heaven above and Earth below each dwelled within the crystalline five colors in order to hear the preaching of the Law.

The Primordial Heavenly Worthy said, "How rare, godling, that you, taking pity on sentient beings, have told this tale of karmic affinity. My mind has been enlightened. The transmutations of yin and yang, the movements of the sun and moon, the motions and occlusions of the stars, the rending of the earth, all are transformations from Heaven above. Whenever a person is born between Heaven and Earth, he is endowed with the breaths of yin and yang; the five agents bring him to completion, the two breaths bind him together. He does not know how difficult it is to receive a human body, how difficult it is to be born into the Middle Land. He is jealous and greedy, does not yet know to repent. When he suffers military, pestilential, water, and fire disasters, all derive from this."

The vassal [the Divine Lord of Zitong] from the front row pressed head to floor and announced to the Heavenly Worthy, "The people have suffered disaster and calamity yet no one heeds and commiserates with them. How can they gain release and absolution?"

The Heavenly Worthy, leaning on his armrest, said, "You occupy a position as aide to august Heaven and are equal in prestige to the Supreme One. Your name is loftier than the Southern Polestar, your virtue envelops the four quarters. You control the wheel of rebirth of the Chaotic Prime, administer the Cinnamon Record of public servants. You have investigated the Six Classics and the reports or all five scared peaks. Common people who contemplate this shall be saved.

The Heavenly Worthy then made a pronouncement:

Thereupon the Primordial Worthy,
Seated within his crystalline [palace],
Lamented the evils of sentient beings
On the three evil paths following the five tendencies.
In a daze, they do not awaken [to reality]
Always they are like the occulted sun or moon.
They do not know they are endowed with the five agents, that the stars move on their behalf.
At that time the Lord of Zitong
From his seat extended compassionate love.
Dividing his body, he performed transformations,
With his pen he expressed samādhi.
Absolving and exorcizing he opened a door.
The Jade Metropolis repeatedly proclaimed his correctness.
He observed men in the world below
Suffering without elders.
They did not realize it, did not know how to become enlightened.
Now on your behalf he repents.
Sentient beings listen as he points out their delusions,
The five sacred peaks present no obstruction.
On the wheel of rebirth charged with rescuing from suffering,
In the hells he does not gallop off, abandoning them.
Fortunate or damned, he makes sure they continue on,
He knows the lucky and unlucky, present and past.
Caring about sentient beings, he serves the Great Dao,
Compassionate, he eliminates harm for them.
Opening forever the door of transcendent teachings,
He relies on these teachings, forever supreme.

He further intoned:

The Cinnamon Record of emoluments, you administer,
Documents are brought to completion by you.
If one wishes to ascend the path to governmental service,
They depend on you to act as balance.
Good and evil, these are fortune and misfortune,
Success lies in karmic affinities.
Grasping a brush you write it out for us,
How could prosperity and decay be accidental?
If there are blessings, there must be retribution.
He has no favorites, none to whom he is partial.

The Heavens proclaim this good.
How [else] can one attain promotion?

Thereupon the Primordial Heavenly Worthy concluded this scripture. He addressed the Divine Lord of Zitong, saying, "You dwell on Mount Phoenix in the western Shu region and have manifested your numinous power in the profane world, fully manifesting your accomplishments. When I examine your actions and retirements through ninety-four transformations and make manifest your metamorphoses through quadrillions of aeons, you have had charge of one office, the relief of suffering, and have administered fortune and misfortune throughout the four quarters. Hear my few words that supplement your 'inch of goodness.' I moreover grant you my reverent awe to repay your compassion."

The Tract on the Hidden Administration

The Divine Lord said: "I have assumed the identity of a scholar-official seventeen times. Never have I mistreated the people or abused my clerks. I saved people in distress, helped them through emergencies, took pity on the orphaned, and forgave humans their transgressions. Extensively have I carried out my hidden administration, extending up to the blue vault of the sky. If people can maintain a heart like mine, Heaven will certainly bestow blessings upon them."

Then he instructed the people, saying, "Long ago, when Elder Yu was in charge of the jails, he raised a gate large enough for a team of four to enter [in expectation of the reward of the hidden administration for his good deeds in administering the jails justly. Upon retirement he was given a carriage and a team of four.]. Master Dou helped others and broke five high twigs from the cinnamon tree [of fate] [as a result of which his lifespan was extended for thirty-six years and his five sons reached high office]. By [diverting a stream and] saving an ant [hill], selection for the position of valedictorian [in the civil service examinations] was won [by Song Jiao]. By [killing and] burying an [ominous two-headed] snake [when he was a young boy], a man [Shun Shu'ao of Chu] enjoyed the glory of the prime ministership.

"To expand your field of blessings, you must rely on the foundations of your heart. Respond to the needs of others again and again, creating one type after another of hidden merit. Benefit creatures and benefit man; cultivate good and cultivate blessings. Be upright and straightforward, promote moral conversion on behalf of Heaven. Be compassionate and moral; rescue people on behalf of the state. Be loyal to your ruler, filial to your parents, respectful to your elder brother, trustworthy toward your friends. At times, make offerings to the Perfected and pay court to the Dipper. Other times, bow to the Buddha and recite sūtras. Repay the Four Graces [of Heaven, Earth, lord, and parents]; broadly promulgate the Three Teachings [of Daoism, Confucianism, and Buddhism]. Help others through crises as if helping a fish in a dried wheel rut; save the imperiled as if saving a sparrow caught in a fine net. Take pity on the orphaned and sympathize with the widowed. Respect the elderly and commiserate with the poor. Prepare clothing and food to relieve the hunger and cold of travelers. Donate coffins to avoid the exposure of corpses. If your household prospers, lend a helping hand to relatives and in-laws. In years of famine, aid neighbors and friends. Weights and measures must be fair; do not underpay or overcharge. Treat slaves and servants leniently. How can you lay all blame upon them or make intemperate demands? Print copies of the scriptures; build and repair monasteries. Distribute drugs to save the afflicted; provide tea to quench thirst. On occasion, buy animals and release them alive; other times, observe a fast and renounce killing. Always look for bugs and ants when stepping. Do not burn mountain forests when fires are prohibited (i.e., spring). Light a night-lamp to illuminate the paths of men. Build riverboats to help others cross. Do not ascend mountains to net birds or beasts. Do not poison fish or shrimp in the rivers. Do not slaughter plowing oxen. Do not throw away paper with writing on it. Do not scheme to take the wealth of others. Do not envy others' abilities. Do not sexually defile the wives or daughters of others. Do not incite others to litigation. Do not destroy the reputation of others. Do not wreck others' marriages. Do not sow dissension among brothers for the sake of a private feud. Do not cause discord between father and son for the sake of a small profit. Do not, relying upon power and position, humiliate the virtuous. Do not, depending on wealth and influence, cheat those in straitened circumstances. If there is a good person, then draw near to him, thus supporting virtuous conduct within yourself. If there is an evil person, then avoid him, thus forestalling disaster at the eyebrows and eyelashes. Always you must hide evil and herald good. You must not condone with your mouth while condemning with your heart. Cut the thorns and underbrush that obstruct the roads; remove tiles and stones on the paths. Rebuild roads that will wind circuitously for hundreds of years; erect bridges that tens of millions will cross. Leave behind teachings to deter the evil actions of others; donate your wealth to facilitate their good deeds. Actions must comply with heavenly principles; words must accord with the hearts of men. Observe former sages even while they are supping or sitting on walls [as Shun observed Yao]; be circumspect even in actions known only to yourself and your quilt or shadow. If you do not practice evil, but serve good, then never will a baleful star shadow you; always auspicious spirits will protect you. When immediate retribution is exacted upon yourself and long-term retribution is visited upon your sons and grandson, or when a hundred blessings arrive together and a thousand auspicious omens gather like clouds, how could these not derive from hidden administration?"

20

A Sūtra Promoting the White-robed Guanyin as Giver of Sons

Chün-fang Yü

Ever since the fourth century C.E., a few hundred years after the introduction of Buddhism into China, Guanyin has been one of the most beloved Buddhist deities in China. By the tenth century, Guanyin began to assume feminine characteristics. The sexual transformation became complete by the sixteenth century, and the Jesuit missionaries could thus nickname her the "Goddess of Mercy." In the development of the cult of Guanyin in China, the bodhisattva appeared in several forms. Among them, the "White-robed (*baiyi*) Guanyin" is the one most familiar to her devotees.

White-robed Guanyin began to appear in sculpture, paintings, poetry, accounts of the founding of monasteries, miracle tales, and pilgrims' visions from the tenth century on. The deity is clearly feminine. She wears a long, flowing white cape, whose hood sometimes covers her head and even arms and hands. The conventional view in Buddhological scholarship traces her to tantric female deities such as White Tārā or Pāṇḍaravāsinī, the consort of Avalokiteśvara and one of the chief deities of the World of Womb Treasury Maṇḍala (*garbhakośadhātu, taicangjie*). The received wisdom in art historical circles has, on the other hand, identified this figure as a typical subject of the so-called Zen paintings, symbolizing the serenity and wisdom of Chan meditative states.

It is now time to reconsider the above interpretations. The popularity of White-robed Guanyin was not due simply to promotion by Chan monks and literati painters. Moreover, instead of being traced to tantric Buddhism, the origin of this deity may lie with a group of indigenous scriptures that portray her primarily as a fertility goddess. Although Guanyin's power of granting children is already mentioned in the *Lotus Sūtra,* these indigenous scriptures are noteworthy on two accounts: they emphasize Guanyin's power to grant sons, and they also call attention to her protection of pregnant women and assurance of safe childbirths.

These texts also provide the basis for the iconography of "Child-giving (*songzi*) Guanyin," which is indeed a variant of the White-robed Guanyin.

Indigenous scriptures celebrating Guanyin have had of course a long history in China. Since 1970, chiefly through the work of Makita Tairyō, we have known that there were a number of such scriptures composed during the Six Dynasties (420–581) and later. Although their titles remain in various catalogs, many did not survive. Of those that did, Makita extensively studied two: *Guanshiyin Samādhi Sūtra as Spoken by the Buddha (Foshuo Guanshiyin sanmeijing)* and *Guanshiyin Sūtra [Promoted by] King Gao (Gao Wang Guanshiyin jing)*. Instead of dismissing these scriptures as forged, Makita regarded them as valuable documents revealing contemporary understandings of Buddhism. His sympathetic attitude has elicited similar responses in scholars in recent years. Studying similar apocryphal scriptures in other Buddhist traditions, they also see these scriptures as creative attempts to synthesize Buddhist teachings and adapt them to native cultural milieu.

One indigenous scripture bearing the title *The Dhāraṇī Sūtra of the Five Mudrās of the Great Compassionate White-robed One (Baiyi Dabei wuyinxin tuoluoni jing)* enjoyed particular popularity among the Chinese people in late imperial China who hoped to have sons. Although the exact date of its composition cannot be established, there is clear indication that it was already being circulated by the eleventh century at the latest. A stele dated 1082 with the White-robed Guanyin holding a baby and the text of this sūtra penned by Qin Guan (1049–1100) has survived. This scripture is not included in any existing editions of the Buddhist canon, but its existence came to light as a result of happy coincidences. I first came across a handwritten copy of this text in the rare book collection of the Palace Museum in Taipei, Taiwan, in the summer of 1986. It was written by the famous Ming dynasty calligrapher Dong Qichang in 1558 and bore seals of both emperors Qianlong and Jiaqing. A few months afterward, while I was doing research in the rare book section of the Library of Chinese Buddhist Cultural Artifacts located at the Fayuan Monastery in Beijing, I found thirty-five copies of this scripture. They were all printed during the Ming, the earliest one in 1428 and the majority during the Wanli period, around the 1600s.

Literati living in the late Ming, during the sixteenth century, appeared to have given the cult of the White-robed Guanyin a new boost. Yuan Huang (1533–1606), the literatus who promoted morality books, was forty but had no son. He started to chant this scripture and became the father of a son in 1580. When he compiled a collection of texts to help people in obtaining heirs, entitled, *True Instructions for Praying for an Heir (Qisi zhenquan)*, he put this text at the very beginning. He also identified the dhāraṇī contained in the scripture as the *Dhāraṇī Conforming to the Heart's Desire (Suixin tuoluoni)*, the same dhāraṇī the great pilgrim Tripiṭaka relied on in crossing the perilous desert on his way to India. The dhāraṇī, according to Huang, was therefore a translation from Sanskrit and was contained in the Buddhist canon, even though the scripture as it now stood could not be found there. Qu Ruji (1548–1610) and his friend Yan Daoche, two scholars responsible for the compilation of an important Chan chronicle, the *Record of Pointing to the Moon (Zhiyue lu)*, were also faithful chanters of this dhāraṇī.

The copies of this scripture that I saw in Beijing were printed and distributed free of charge by donors who wanted to bear witness to White-robed Guanyin's efficacy and promote her cult. Depending on the economic ability of the donors, who ranged from members of the royal family, literati-officials, and merchants all the way down to obscure men and women, the quality and quantity of the printing varied greatly. But in all cases the donors provided accounts of miracles witnessed by others or by the donors themselves. The former, which sometimes are several pages in length, are appended immediately after the scripture, while the latter, which are usually no more than a few lines, are enclosed within a dedicatory plaque. A dedicatory plaque dated 1599, for instance, recorded the following:

> Mrs. Zhao, née Shen, prayed for a male heir a few years ago and made a vow promising the printing of the "White-robed Guanyin Sūtra." Thanks to divine protection, twin boys Fengguo and Fengjue were born to me on the twelfth day of the ninth month, 1597. Now I have finished printing one canon [*yicong*, e.g., 5,048 copies] of this scripture and donate them to fulfill my earlier vow. I pray that the two boys will continue to receive blessings without end. Donated on the New Year's Day, 1599.

A great number of miracles accumulated around this text. The chanting of the dhāraṇī of the White-robed Guanyin was believed to lead to the miraculous arrival of a long-awaited baby boy who would be born doubly wrapped in white placenta (*baiyi chongbao*), which indicated that he was a gift from White-robed Guanyin. The earliest testimony of this was traced to the Tang, and miracles attributed to this scripture were reported during the six hundred years between the twelfth and the seventeenth centuries.

In the following, a translation of the entire text of the sūtra printed in 1609 is given. Since the miracles appended at the end of the text are more numerous than in other copies, I have selected only the ones with historical dates. I have also translated the postscripts written by the Ming literati mentioned above. They provide an explanation of the origin of this scripture, the author's understanding of the correct attitude in keeping the dhāraṇī, and other interesting autobiographical details about the author's own experiences with this text.

Further Reading

Robert Buswell, *Chinese Buddhist Apocrypha* (Honolulu: University of Hawaii Press, 1990).

The Dhāraṇī Sūtra of Five Mudrās of the Great Compassionate White-Robed One

The mantra which purifies the karma of the mouth: An-xiu-li, xin-li, mo-ke-xiu-li, xiu-xiu-li, suo-po-ke [svāhā].

The mantra which pacifies the earth: Nan-wu-san-man-duo, mo-tuo-nan, an-du-lu-du-lu-di-wei, suo-po-ke.

The sūtra-opening gātha:

> The subtle and wondrous dharma of utmost profundity
> Is difficult to encounter during millions, nay, billions of kalpas.
> Now that I have heard it [with my own ears], I will take it securely to heart
> And hope I can understand the true meaning of the Tathāgata.

Invocation:

> Bowing my head to the Great Compassionate One, Po-lu-jie-di
> Practicing meditation with the sense of hearing, [the bodhisattva] entered samādhi
> Raising the sound of the tide of the ocean,
> Responding to the needs of the world.
> No matter what one wishes to obtain
> [She] will unfailingly grant its fulfillment.

Homage to the Original Teacher Śākyamuni Buddha
Homage to the Original Teacher Amitābha Buddha
Homage to the Bao-yue-zhi-yan-guang-yin-zi-zai-wang (Lord Iśvara Buddha of Precious-Moon Wisdom-Splendor-Light-Sound)
Homage to Great Compassionate Guanshiyin Bodhisattva
Homage to White-robed Guanshiyin Bodhisattva
Front mudrā, back mudrā, mudrā of subduing demons, mind mudrā, body mudrā.

Dhāraṇī. I now recite the divine mantra. I beseech the Compassionate One to descend and protect my thought. Here then is the mantra:

Nan-wu he-la-da-na, shao-la-ye-ye, nan-wu a-li-ye, po-lu-jie-ti, shao-bo-la-ye, pu-ti-sa-duo-po-ye, mo-ke-jie-lu-ni-jia-ye, an-duo-li, duo-li, du-duo-li, du-du-duo-li, suo-po-ke.

When you ask someone else to chant the dhāraṇī, the effect is the same as when you chant it yourself.

EVIDENCE ATTESTING TO THE MIRACULOUS RESPONSES OF THE WHITE-ROBED GUANSHIYIN BODHISATTVA

Formerly a scholar of Hengyang (in present Hunan Province) was already advanced in age but still had no son. He prayed everywhere for an heir. One day he met an old monk who handed him this sūtra, saying, "The Buddha preached this sūtra. If a person is capable of keeping it, he will receive responses in accordance with his wish and obtain unlimited blessing. If he desires to have a son, a boy of wisdom will be born to him. The baby will show the wonder of being wrapped in a white placenta." The man and his wife chanted this sūtra with utmost sincerity for one *canon* (5,048 times), and within several years they had three sons who were all born wrapped in white placenta. The governer saw these events with his own eyes and ordered the printing and distributing of this sūtra. He also obtained a son before the year was over.

A scholar named Wang Xin and his wife named Zhao of Jiangning (in present Jiangsu Province) had the misfortune of losing several children. In the spring of 1147 they obtained this sūtra and chanted it with faith everyday. On the second day of the fourth month in 1148 a son was born to them.

Zheng Zhili of Pujiang, Mao District (province unspecified), was forty years old and still had no heir. In 1207 he decided to print 5,048 copies of this sūtra and distribute the copies for free. On the seventh day of the eighth month in 1208 a son was born to him.

Yu Muzhai and his wife Wang of Danyang Village in Maoyuan County (province unspecified) decided to have one thousand copies of this sūtra printed and distributed free. In the eighth month of 1250 when the work of distributing was only half completed, a son arrived.

Fangyan and wife Wang of Yungfeng Village, She County (in present Anhui Province) decided to chant this sūtra 5,048 times and print one thousand copies for free distribution in the spring of 1254. They had a son in 1255 and named him Wanggu.

Wang Yinlin, who lived in the 6th ward in Chongle City, south of Hui District (in present Anhui Province), had five hundred copies of this sūtra printed and distributed. A son was born to him in the hour of *mou* on the twenty-first day of the fifth month in 1269 and was given the name Yinsun. A pious woman named Zheng who lived in the third ward of the north side of Shangbei City of the same district became seriously ill in the first month of 1274 when she was a young girl. She burned incense and promised to have one thousand copies of the sūtra printed and distributed free. At night she dreamt of two monks who came to protect her. She recovered from the illness.

Wang Yuyu lived in Daning ward in Nanjing and was forty years old but still had no son. He prayed to various gods but had no success. One day in the latter half of the tenth month in 1265 he received this sūtra from his friend Ma, who kept it enshrined in front of the Guanyin image on his family altar. Wang chanted it every day without interruption. On the night of the fourteenth day in the fourth month, 1267, his wife née Liu dreamt of a person in white who, wearing a golden crown and accompanied by a boy, said to her, "I am delivering to you a holy slave (*shengnu*)." Liu accepted the boy, and upon waking up the next morning she gave birth to a baby boy who was handsome and wrapped in white placenta. They named him Slave of Holy Monk (Shengsengnu).

Wang Mengbai, a metropolitan graduate from Qingjiang (in present Jiangxi Province) was born because his parents faithfully chanted this sūtra. When he was born, he had the manifestation of the "white robe." He himself also chanted the sūtra and in 1214 had a "white-robed son (*baiyizi*)" whom he named Further Manifestation (Gengxian).

Xie Congning, a native of Guangyang (Daxing, the capital) who served as a staffer in the Central Drafting Office, came from a family which had only one son for the past five generations. In 1579 he and his wife, née Gao, started to chant the sūtra, which they had also printed and distributed for free. In 1582 they had a son whom they named Gu, in 1585 another son whom they named Lu, and in 1586 twin boys Qu and Ying. All were born with double white placentas.

Ding Xian of Yibin, Nanyang (in present Henan Province), was fifty years old and had no son. So he decided to print this sūtra and distribute it for free. He also had a thousand catties of iron melted down in the south garden of the city to make a gilded image of Guangyin. It stood over six feet. At the same time, in order to seek for a son, Xing Jian, the grand commandant, had a shrine dedicated to the White-robed Guanyin erected in the northern part of the city. So the image was moved there to be worshiped. The local official set aside several thousand acres of good farmland to provide for the shrine's upkeep so that people could continue to offer incense in future generations. Not long after this, one night Ding dreamt of a woman who presented him with a white carp. On the next morning, a son was born wrapped in a white placenta. That was the fourth day of the twelfth month, 1583. Earlier, when the image was moved to the White-robed Guanyin Shrine, the gardener had a dream in which the bodhisattva appeared to him looking rather unhappy. When he told Ding about his dream, Ding had another image cast that looked exactly like the first one in the south garden. He invited a monk of repute to stay in the temple to take care of it. He subsequently dreamt of an old man wearing a white gown who came to visit him. The day after he had this dream, while he was relating it to his friend, a man suddenly came to the house seeking to sell the woodblocks of this sūtra. Ding bought them and printed a thousand copies for distribution. He also hired a skilled painter to paint several hundred paintings of the White-robed Guanyin to give to the faithful as gifts. In the fourth month of 1586, he had another son. By then, Xing Jian, the grand commandant, had also had a son and a daughter born to him and his wife.

Zhao Yungxian, the son of a grandee of the Tenth Order (the eleventh highest of twenty titles of honorary nobility conferred on meritorious subjects), was a native of Changshu (in Jiangsu Province). His wife née Chen chanted this sūtra with great sincerity. On the sixteenth day of the seventh month in 1586, a daughter was born. She was covered with a piece of cloth as white as snow on her face, head, chest, and back. When the midwife peeled it away, the baby's eyes and eyebrows could then be seen. The parents already had sons, but only this daughter had the miraculous evidence of the white-cloth. It was for this reason that it was written down.

Yuan Huang, the metropolitan graduate who served in the Ministry of Rites, was a native of Jiashan (in Zhejiang Province). He was forty but had no son. After he chanted this sūtra, in 1580 a son was born. He named the son Yuansheng (Born from Universal Penetration) because he believed that the boy was a gift from Guanyin, the Universally Penetrating One. The boy had a very distinguished appearance and was unusually intelligent.

A POSTSCRIPT TO THE SŪTRA WRITTEN BY QU RUJI

I began to chant this dhāraṇī in the second month of 1580 together with my friends Li Boshu and Yan Daoche. Soon afterward Li had a son, and three years later Yan also had a son. I alone failed to experience a divine response. I often blamed myself for my deep karmic obstructions, for I could not match the two gentlemen in their piety. Then one evening in the third month of 1583 I dreamt that I entered a shrine and a monk said to me, "In chanting the dhāraṇī, there is one buddha's name you have not chanted. If you chant it, you shall have a son." Upon waking up, I could not understand what he meant by the missing buddha's name, for I had always chanted the various names of Guanyin on the different festival days of her manifestation. In the winter of 1585 I traveled north and was stuck at a government post-house because the river was frozen. On the twelfth day of the twelfth month I entered a small temple and saw this sūtra by the side of the *hou* animal mount on which Guanyin sat. It was donated by Wang Qishan, a judicial clerk. When I opened it to read and saw the name of Lord Iśvara Buddha of Precious-Moon Wisdom-Splendor-Light-Sound, a name of which I had never heard up until that time, I had a sudden realization. I knelt down and kowtowed to the seat. I started to chant the name of the buddha upon returning, and after only three days a son was born. It accorded perfectly with my dream.

In 1586 I went to the capital. Xu Wenqing, Yu Zhongpu, and other friends were all chanting the dhāraṇī in order to obtain sons. Yu's wife, furthermore, became pregnant after she had a strange dream. So we discussed plans of printing this sūtra to promote its circulation. I had earlier consulted the catalogues of the Northern and Southern Tripiṭakas (two collections of Buddhist scriptures compiled in the Ming) but did not find it listed in either one. I thought this must be a true elixir of life secretly transmitted by foreign monks. Later Yuan Huang told me that this was actually the same dhāraṇī as the *Dhāraṇī Conforming to Heart's Desire,* two versions of which were included in the Tripiṭaka. When I learned about this, I rushed to Longhua Monastery to check the Tripiṭaka kept in the library. Although there were some variations in the sequence of sentences and the exact wordings of the mantra between the text found in the Tripiṭaka and the popular printed version, the efficacy of chanting the dhāraṇī was universally warranted. I could not help but feeling deeply moved by the wonder of Guanyin's universal responsiveness and divinity of the faithful chanters' sincere minds. The text in the Tripiṭaka did not just promise sons, but the fulfillment of many other desires in accordance with the wishes of sentient beings. According to the instruction given in the sūtra contained in the Tripiṭaka, this dhāraṇī should be revealed only to those who were in possession of great compassion. If given to the wrong person, disastrous results would happen, for bad karma caused by hatred might be created if the person used the dhāraṇī to subdue enemies or avenge past wrongs. Taking this warning to heart, my friend Xu and I decided that instead of reprinting the version found in the Tripiṭaka, we would print the dhāraṇī alone together with the stories about obtaining sons included in the popular versions of this text that were in circulation. After fasting and bathing, Xu wrote out the sūtra and gave it to an engraver to make the woodblocks for printing.

The term "dhāraṇī" means to keep all virtues completely. The extended meaning of the term, then, is the keeping of all virtues. For this reason, the merit of keeping the dhāraṇī is indeed limitless. With this Guanyin teaches people to do good. Therefore if the practitioners do good, when they chant the words of the dhāraṇī, blessings as numerous as the sands of the Ganges will instantly come to them. But if they do not dedicate themselves to goodness, they will lose the basis of the dhāraṇī. Even if they chant it, the benefit will be slight. I cannot claim to have realized this ideal, but I am willing to work hard toward it together with fellow practitioners. The conventional view of the world says that the ordinary people are totally different from sages and people cannot be transformed into holy persons. Because they narrow their potentiality this way, they cannot keep the dhāraṇī. On the other hand, if people fall into the other extreme of nihilism and think that in emptiness there is no law of causality, they also cannot keep the dhāraṇī because of their recklessness. When one realizes that the common man and the sage possess the same mind and there is not the slightest difference at all, one has left the conventional view. When one realizes that this one mind can manifest as either ordinary or saintly and this is due to the clear working of the law of causality, one has then left the nihilistic view. Leaving behind these two erroneous views and following the one mind in teaching the world, one can then chant the dhāraṇī. Like blowing on the bellows for wind or striking the flint for fire, the effect will be unfailingly efficacious.

A POSTSCRIPT WRITTEN BY YAN DAOCHE AFTER PRINTING THE SŪTRA

The *Dhāraṇī of the White-Robed Guanyin* was not included in the Southern and Northern Tripiṭaka collections. Its miraculous efficacy in obtaining whatever one wishes, however, and more particularly sons, has been vouchsafed in the world for a long time. Is it because Indian monks such as Subhākarasiṃha and Amoghavajra (tantric masters active in the eighth century) transmitted this sūtra to gentlewomen in China who then kept it secretly, that, although it was not introduced into the canon collection, it has come down to us because of the many miracles connected with it? Or is it because Guanyin revealed her teaching in accordance with the audience and the old monk of Hengyang was actually her transformation? I do not know. I do know that originally I did not have a son, but after my wife and I chanted this sūtra for three years, in 1582 we had two sons in quick succession. That is why I am now having the sūtra printed and distributed for free in order to fulfill my earlier vow.

The keeping of the dhāraṇī is actually not limited to the vocal chanting of the dhāraṇī. To believe in the Buddha constantly, to listen to the dharma with pleasure, to serve people, to have a straight mind and a deep mind, to be vigorous in one's practice, to give donations generously, to observe strictly the precepts, to sit in meditation with unperturbed mind, to subdue all evils and cut off all passions, to be patient and gentle in adversities, and to help bad friends but draw near to good friends—all these are meant by "keeping the dhāraṇī." I am keenly aware of my own inferior qualities and cannot attain even one iota of the true way of keeping the dhāraṇī as I outlined above. Nevertheless, I am trying my best. Since I started to chant the dhāraṇī, I have insisted on observing the precept against killing. This precept heads the list of the perfection of discipline. If you want to have a son of your own, how can you bear to take another life? When you fail to obtain any response by merely mouthing the dhāraṇī, you may begin to doubt and want to stop. This then is to commit a blasphemy against the Buddha with your body. I ask all good friends in Buddhism who want to chant this sūtra to begin by observing one precept. Gradually you can extend to all precepts. You start with one goodness and extend to all goodness. This will be the real keeping of the dhāraṇī. When this is done, not only sons but all kinds of marvelous things will be yours as you wish.

—21—

Body Gods and Inner Vision: *The Scripture of the Yellow Court*

Paul W. Kroll

The *Scripture of the Yellow Court*, or *Huangting jing*, is one of the cardinal scriptures of medieval Daoism. A text by this name is mentioned by Ge Hong (283–343), author of *He Who Embraces Simplicity (Baopuzi)* and collector of the occult traditions of South China, but that version—if it was indeed seen by Ge Hong—no longer exists. The *Scripture of the Yellow Court* that was known from the mid-fourth century on, and which became a fundamental and hugely popular text, shows clear signs of being influenced by or adapted to the new, Shangqing revelations.

There are in fact two redactions of the *Scripture of the Yellow Court*, an "inner" (*nei*) scripture and an "outer" (*wai*) one. Both are composed in verse of heptasyllabic lines—the longer inner scripture consisting of 435 verses, divided into 36 stanzas, and the shorter outer scripture made up of a single run of 99 verses. Generally speaking, the inner scripture is a more difficult and grammatically troublesome text to read, perhaps bearing out the suggestion that "inner" connotes esoteric, as opposed to the "exoteric" teachings of the "outer" scripture. However, scholars are divided over the question of which version is primary—that is, whether the inner scripture represents an intricate elaboration of the outer scripture, or whether the latter is a summary in simpler language of the former.

In any event, the focus of the *Scripture of the Yellow Court* is on the corporeal divinities believed to reside in one's physical form and on the means by which they may be cultivated, so as to ensure the production within and ultimate escape from one's mortal frame of a refined and purified embryo, an etherealized self. Central to this goal is the practice of "inner vision," by which the adept is able to turn his gaze within and fix distinctly and sensibly the gods of his body, whose appearance and attributes are closely described in the scripture. This process of visualization or, to render the Chinese term literally, "actualization" (*cun*) further reveals that the indwelling spirits of one's body are identical with their counterparts in the macrocosm; indeed the somatic landscape is a perfect, complete microcosm.

Prominent among the body spirits are the Five Viscera—liver, heart, spleen, lungs, and kidneys—which are fundamentally involved with the traditional system of the Five Phases (*wuxing*) and thus coordinated symbolically with the five directions, five colors, five flavors, five sacred peaks, and so forth. It is in fact the spleen, symbolizing the center and known by the esoteric name "Yellow Court," that invests the scripture with its title. In addition to the viscera, each with its individual powers referred to in detail in the text, there is much allusion to the three "cinnabar-fields" (*dan tian*) situated in the brain, near the heart, and below the navel, which control the three major divisions of the body, and also to the two-tiered "nine palaces" (*jiu gong*) of the brain—all of these points with their own presiding spirits and complex of connections linking the body with the universe. Conduction and circulation of the vital breath through the somatic passages, along with the swallowing of saliva and channeling of other bodily humors—the one a yang action, the other a yin—are critical practices for the nourishing and harmonizing of these inner organs and spirits.

But the *Scripture of the Yellow Court* is less a manual than an aide-mémoire. The rhythmic gait of the verses, with jingling end-rhyme on every line (instead of on every other line, as in classical poetry), betokens the oral/aural nature of the text and its basically mnemonic function. It is to be recited in order to render one's body fit for meditation and ultimate etherealization. In one of the scripture's prefaces we are given instructions for the proper method of recitation, requiring the burning of incense, the ritual purging and purifying of oneself. Ten thousand recitals, we are told, will enable one to "see one's five viscera, one's entrails and stomach, and also to see the spectres and spirits of the whole world and put them in one's own service." The therapeutic powers of the scripture are such that if one can recite it when at the point of death, one will be made whole again.

The imagery of the *Scripture of the Yellow Court* is often puzzling, and sometimes seemingly incomprehensible, when considered literally. But the adept will have learned, through private training with his teacher, the true reference and secret significance of the lines—the reality behind the words. Thus, as with Laozi's *Classic on the Way and Its Power (Dao de jing)*, that often cryptic scripture that stands at the head of the Daoist tradition, commentators occasionally differ radically in their interpretation of specific terms and lines. The *Scripture of the Yellow Court* is not, in this regard, a text for reading—it is a script pointing primarily beyond itself, to action.

The selection below features the first four stanzas of the inner scripture. The translation is as close as possible to the original and aims to suggest the metrical—sometimes mesmerizing—pulse of the verses. The prose paraphrase following each stanza then unpacks the meaning in plainer words, relying mainly on the explications offered by medieval commentators.

Further Reading

There is at present no English translation of either version of the *Scripture of the Yellow Court.* Studies in Western languages include Rolf Homann, *Die wichtigsten Korpergottheiten im Huang-t'ing ching* (Goppingen: Verlag Alfred Kūmmerle, 1971); Isabelle Robinet, "The Book of the Yellow Court," in Robinet, *Taoist Meditation: The Mao Shan Tradition of Great Purity,* translated by Julian F. Pas and Norman J. Girardot (Albany: State University of New York Press, 1993); K. M. Schipper, *Concordance du Houang-t'ing ching nei-king et wai-king* (Paris: Ecole Française d'Extrême-Orient, 1975).

First Stanza

In the purple aurora of Highest Clarity, before the Resplendent One of the Void,
The Most High, Great Dao Lord of the Jade Source of Light,
Dwelling at ease in the Stamen-Pearl Palace, composed verses of seven words,
Dispersing and transforming the five shapes of being, permutating the myriad spirits:
This is deemed the *Yellow Court,* known as the *Inner Book.*
The triple reprise of a concinnate heart will set the embryo's transcendents dancing;
Glinting and luminous, the nine vital breaths emerge amidst the empyrean;
The young lads under the Divine Canopy will bring forth a purple haze.
This is known as the *Jade Writ,* which may be sifted to its essence—
Chant it over ten thousand times, and ascend to the Three Heavens;
The thousand calamities will thereby be dispelled, the hundred ailments healed;
You will not then shrink from the fell ravagings of tiger or of wolf,
And also thereby you will hold off age, your years extended forever.

First Stanza—Paraphrase

In the light of perpetual morning, in the Shangqing heaven, in the realm of the cosmocrat who puts all of space in order,

The great deity whose seat is in the ultimate illumination of dawn,
Who resides in a palace symbolic of perigynous jewels, wrote a poem in seven-word lines,
4 Having the power to affect all entities, from fish, birds, men, mammals, and invertebrates to the multitudinous gods.
That poem was this very text, the *Inner Scripture of the Yellow Court.*
Once the three "cinnabar fields" are brought into harmony through it, the spirits of one's immortal embryo will respond with delight,
And the pneumata of the Nine Heavens, conducted through the three "cinnabar fields," will shine forth from the chambers of one's brain,
8 As the deities of one's eyes, beneath the eyebrows' arch, emit a vaporous aura of supernatural purple.
This text, also called the *Jade Writ,* deserves the closest study,
For, after ten thousand recitations of it, one may be translated to the highest heavens,
Immune to earthly misfortune, impervious to disease,
12 Proof against attacks from savage beasts,
And able to enjoy perpetual life.

Second Stanza

Above there are ethereal souls, below is the junction's origin;
Left serves as lesser yang, the right as greatest yin;
Behind there is the Secret Door, before is the Gate of Life.
4 With emergent sun and retreating moon, exhale, inhale, actualizing them.
Where the Four Breaths are well blended, the arrayed mansions will be distinct;
Let the purple haze rise and fall, with the clouds of the Three Immaculates.
Irrigate and spray the Five Flowers, and plant the Numinous Root.
8 Let the channeled course of the Seven Liquors rush into the span of the hut;
Circulate the purple, embrace the yellow, that they enter the Cinnabar Field;
Make the Shrouded Room bright within, illuminating the Gate of Yang.

Second Stanza—Paraphrase

The spirits of the liver, lungs, and spleen are above, representing Heaven, as contrasted with the navel (or, alternatively, a spot three inches below the navel), representing the underworld of matter and generation.

The left and right kidneys are yang and yin.

The Secret Door of the kidneys is at the back of one's body, while the Gate of Life, located below the navel (equivalent either to the lower cinnabar field or to the "junction's origin" where semen is stored), is in front.

4 Sun and moon, imaged in one's left and right eyes, respectively, are to be made sensibly present in concentrated visualization, so that they will shed their light on one's internal organs, while one conducts the breath carefully through the body.

Bringing together the pneumata of the four seasons in oneself will render distinct the astral lodgings and somatic dwellings of sun, moon, and Dipper.

As the purple vapor of the divinities of the eyes infuses one's body, it is joined by clouds of purple, yellow, and white, symbolic of the Primal Mistresses of the Three Immaculates—goddesses who preside over the three major divisions of the body and the twenty-four major corporeal divinities.

One should swallow the saliva that nourishes one's internal organs, especially the essential "flowers" of the five viscera, taking care to cultivate the "Numinous Root" of the tongue, which activates and gathers in the saliva.

8 The humoral juices of the the body's seven orifices are channeled throughout the body and into the bridge of the nose, the "hut" between the eyebrows.

The spreading purple vapor from the eyes and the rising yellow pneuma from the spleen are brought into the upper cinnabar field located three inches behind the sinciput,

While, below, the "Shrouded Room" of the kidneys is bathed in light, as in the Gate of Yang (the Gate of Life) in front.

Third Stanza

The mouth is the Jade Pool, the Officer of Greatest Accord.

Rinse with and gulp down the numinous liquor—calamities will not encroach;

One's body will engender a lighted florescence, breath redolent as orchid;

4 One turns back, extinguishes the hundred malignities—one's features refined in jade.

With practice and attention, cultivate this, climbing to the Palace of Ample Cold.

Not sleeping either day or night, you will achieve then full perfection;
When thunder sounds and lightning spurts, your spirits are placid, impassive.

Third Stanza—Paraphrase

The mouth is the reservoir of the jade liquor of saliva, controlling in this capacity the nourishing and harmonizing of the body's organs.
Drinking down the spiritually potent saliva and circulating it in prescribed fashion will enable you to avoid misfortune;
Your body will be lit from within like a luminous flower, and your breath will acquire a sweet fragrance;
All debilitating influences will be opposed, and your skin will become pure as snow, white as jade.
Through repeated exercises you will become expert in this practice and be able to ascend to the celestial palace where the white moon itself is bathed when at apogee, at the winter solstice.
Unstinting concentration will lead to complete spiritual realization,
Such that your corporeal spirits will remain serenely fixed when confronted by any outer startlements.

Fourth Stanza

The person within the Yellow Court wears a polychrome-damask jacket,
A volant skirt of purple flowering, in gossamer of cloudy vapors,
Vermilion and azure, with green withes, numinous boughs of halcyon-blue.
With the jade cotter of the Seven Panicles, shut tight the two door-leaves;
Let the golden bar of the layered panels keep snug the door-post and catch.
The shrouded barrier of the murky freshets will be lofty, tall and towering;
In the midst of the Three Fields, essence and breath will become more subtle.
The Delicate Girl, winsome but withdrawn, screens the empyrean's radiance;
The tiered hall, shiningly iridescent, illumines the Eight Daunters.
From the celestial court to the earthly barrier, arrayed be the axes and bills;
With the numinous terrace hardy and firm, forever one will not weaken.

Fourth Stanza—Paraphrase

The "Mother of the Dao," one of the spleen's indwelling divinities, is clothed in a rich coat with the symbolic colors of all Five Viscera;
Her buoyant skirt, made of the silky gauze of cloud-breaths, is decorated in the purple hues of the deepest heavens and the celestial pole,
With tints of red, green, and blue, in sylvan designs, embellishing her other garments.
4 One must keep one's gaze focused within, concentrating on the interior gods, oblivious of the outside world, letting nothing escape through the doors of one's eyes, turning the key of one's seven orifices.
Barring the exits at all bodily levels, keeping the portals shut fast.
Then the shrouded barrier of the kidneys, source of bodily juices, will grow in strength;
Elemental essence and vital breath will become rarefied, less carnal, within the three "cinnabar fields."
8 The shy divinity of the ears turns away from the brilliant lights of the heavens,
While the layered chamber of the throat—passageway for the saliva—now gleams with a splendor that shines out to the divinities of the eight directions.
All the inner spirits are stalwart as arrayed weapons, from the celestial hall between the eyebrows to the earthly barrier of the feet,
And the sacred estrade of the heart will prove an everlastingly impregnable structure.

—22—

Teachings of a Spirit Medium

Jean DeBernardi

In this chapter, the teachings of a Malaysian Chinese spirit medium are presented. They are unusual in a collection of this sort: while they have their roots in textual sources they are oral performances and as such are not designed as written texts. However, these oral narratives are significantly related to the written word, and through that word to a cultural past that is made present through performance.

In Southeast Asia, Hong Kong, and Taiwan, spirit mediums are visible and active religious practitioners. They are folk healers; more rarely they teach religious ideas, drawing on a deep tradition of popular literature and the textual works of the "three doctrines"—Buddhism, Daoism, and Confucianism. These together provide many of the exemplary heros and moral principles of popular religious culture. Indeed, some of these heros and heroines are embodied in trance performance, where they make use of an elevated moral vocabulary to explicate the Dao and exhort their followers to good behavior.

By contrast with the well-worked-out conceptual schemes and elegant ritual practices of Confucianism or Buddhism, local religious practice is eclectic and dynamic. For example, the temple fairs celebrating a god's birthday are ideally "hot and exciting": these events overwhelm the senses with gaudy reds and golds, clamorous drumming and gonging, eye-stinging clouds of incense. Spirit mediums are as likely as Daoist priests to be the ritual practitioners at these events, but instead of chanting texts they perform rites of self-mortification, walking on hot coals, playing with red-hot iron balls, "bathing" in hot oil or burning joss sticks. Scholars of religion politely describe these religious practices as "syncretic," but Chinese popular religious culture has also been described in the last century as "barbaric," "objectionable," and "pragmatic" (rather than spiritual). Many have emphasized the gulf between the "great traditions" of China and local practice, though anthropologists have persisted in insisting that the two are merely variations on a theme, or transformations rung on a shared conceptual order.

Here, Chinese local religious practice is explored as a practice that animates the textual and literary as lived performance. The sensually appealing practices of the "folk" are perhaps a world apart from the calm and controlled ritual practice of the elite, but many of the basic concepts of the world traditions live in popular discourse. In particular, they are given voice in a moral discourse on the art of "being human": indeed often it is the "god" (while possessing the body of the spirit medium) who makes the textual local and accessible through speech, bridging past and present, literary and lived realities.

Spirit Mediums

In everyday practice, spirit mediums perform a variety of services, ranging from the treatment of illness with magical charms or herbs to the provision of gambling advice and ambiguously written predictions of lottery numbers. Their worshippers are indeed pragmatic in their approach to the god, whom they regard as a savior who will aid them in their everyday life problems.

Mediums are possessed by a variety of Chinese deities. Often these are categorized as martial and literary gods, and the two are different in performance. Martial gods perform martial arts displays, often with sword, spear, or halberd, as well as performing the acts of self-mortification described above. Observers often note that these acts are convincing proof of the genuineness of the presence of the god. Literary gods by contrast are more restrained and demonstrate a scholarly learning. Often it is noted that the spirit medium's personality or manner changes dramatically when the god possesses him (or, more rarely, her), and a changing style of speech and movement is convincing proof to the audience that a god is truly present.

The identities of the gods who possess spirit mediums connect these gods to a literary archive. Many of the deities are drawn from popular literature: Guan Gong is one of the heroes of the *Three Kingdoms (Sanguo yanyi);* Ji Gong is from *Ji Gong's Tale (Jigong zhuan);* the Monkey God is from *Journey to the West (Xiyouji);* the Inconstant Ghost is from the hell journey books frequently distributed in temples. Many of these deities also appear in folk opera, films, even comic book renditions. In trance performance they come alive as individuals with well-defined personalities; Ji Gong, the "Mad Monk" or "Dirty Buddha," for example, is a trickster who despite his Buddhist vows eats dog meat and drinks rather than fasting and abstaining. As he possesses the god, he will call for ale, and he jokes and teases his clients. His trance performances are at times serious, though in many cases his teachings were parodies of orthodoxy rather than solemn didactic events.

It is often commented that the god speaks a literary form of the language spoken (in Malaysia, usually Southern Min), which is described as a "deep" version of that language. By contrast, contemporary Malaysian Chinese are judged to speak a form of their "dialect" (or "topolect") that is not at all deep. The god's literary Southern Min most notably excludes common borrowings from English and Malay and includes many literary terms that are not frequently encountered in spoken conversation. The god's language is often considered difficult to understand,

and a temple committee member usually stands by the god to translate his or her words into colloquial language.

"Deep" or literary Southern Min is in fact a register of Southern Min that at one time had social connotations of education and style. Before Mandarin was adopted and promoted as the national language of China, literate persons learned to read characters in the literary form of their topolect. In Southern Min, this now rarely used literary register is quite distinctive from vernacular language in both pronunciation and vocabulary. Use of the literary register continues to carry social overtones of high status and learning; in English much the same effect is carried by vocabulary (consider what is communicated by saying that you must "deliberate" on a matter instead of "think it over"). In contemporary Penang, deep Southern Min is now almost exclusively the style of the gods who possess spirit mediums.

In the practice of spirit mediumship, the use of words drawn from a literary lexicon links the present to the past and creates a unique situation of authoritative transmission. In the classical Chinese view of textual interpretation, in reading a written text one reads the written word in order to know the heart of the writer. To cite a fifth-century Chinese scholar: "None may see the actual faces of a faraway age, but by viewing their writing, one may immediately see their hearts and minds" (Stephen Owen, *Remembrances: The Experience of the Past in Classical Chinese Literature* [Cambridge: Harvard University Press, 1986], p. 59). When the "god" speaks, however, one hears the voice of that faraway age. One spirit medium—said to be an avatar of his deity—offered inspired textual exegesis of the *Classic on the Way and Its Power (Dao de jing)* to a class of students; another offered his teachings while possessed by Laozi himself. Possessed spirit mediums offer a uniquely authoritative form of textual interpretation.

Text and Performance

The transmission of tradition through the teachings of spirit mediums may be compared with the Chinese tradition of reading and interpreting texts. "Orality" and "literacy" had a special relationship in traditional Chinese education, and while China has the world's deepest literary tradition, the transmission of that tradition has emphasized the transformation of the written into the oral. In reading classical Chinese, the approach to the written word had two important dimensions. First, the text to be studied was memorized and recited and was not considered to be known until known by heart. Second, the text was condensed, and ancient texts in particular were "terse, fragmentary, and incomplete" (Owen, p. 69). Understanding the written word involved exegesis, and later scholars built frames for understanding the author's words. For example, a text such as the *Classic of Changes (Yijing)* is read together with several layers of exegetical commentary.

Chinese literary critics express the view that "by means of meditating on the words of a poem, one reaches the state of wordless communication with the spirit of the poet" (James Liu, *Language—Paradox—Poetics: A Chinese Perspective* [Princeton: Princeton University Press, 1988], p. 102). Owen has characterized the condensed style of literary Chinese as "synechdochic," and he compares the process of recovering meaning to the rite in which an article of clothing is used to recall a soul (Owen, p. 2). The reader must take the text—a fragment—and use it to recall the intention of its author. Take, for example, the problem of interpreting the following two lines of poetry:

> All day long I seek but cannot find it,
> Yet at times it comes of its own accord.

But what is "it"? Poet-critic Mei Yao Chen in his commentary remarks that the poet means that "a good line of poetry is hard to get." (He corrects another [possibly facetious] interpreter who said, "This is a poem about someone's lost cat" [Liu, p. 100].)

In the process of transmission, the past is always being reread from the perspective of the present. As Liu points out (p. 104), Chinese critics accepted interpretive indeterminacy in reading the fragments of the past. Confucius's relativistic comment on this subject was that "when a humane one sees it, he calls it humane, when a wise man sees it, he calls it wise." Reading from a Confucian perspective, both the love poems and spirit invocations of the *Songs of the South (Chuci)* were political allegories on the often entangled relationships of ministers with their lords; in a recent lecture a well-known Chinese novelist in exile retold China's history starting with the birth of the cosmos and reinterpreted the most famous poem in *Songs of the South* to demonstrate that the love of democracy was as old as China itself. Different times, different meanings, but the same conclusion: as the Chinese author put it when questioned, history is important because China's past is its present.

It was the role of Confucian scholar-gentry to transmit the past; in the trance performance, the past is also transmitted, but it meets the present in a unique way, for here the spirit of the poet, teacher, philosopher is given voice again. The oral recitation of cosmology, the invention of poetry, and exegesis of the moral concepts handed down from the past are all basic to the authority of the god, much as mastery of Confucian texts provided educational capital for the scholar-gentry of imperial China.

Reference to the literary tradition is not always explicitly made but rather resides in the use of extraordinary vocabulary—discussion of the Dao, of the Confucian virtues of filiality and loyalty, of Buddhist ideas of merit and rebirth. The presence of the past is nowhere more fully symbolized than in the use of the literary register known as deep Southern Min, and of a moral vocabulary that links the present to the transmitted values of the past. The "orality" of the trance performance, then, cannot be simply contrasted with "literacy." The trance performance is indeed a form of transmission of ideas, a lived exegesis, a giving voice to the past.

The text that follows translates the teachings of a Chinese spirit medium and is based on interviews conducted in the course of ethnographic research in Penang, Malaysia, in 1980–81. The spirit medium worked in a remote area of Penang, in a temple hidden at the end of an unpaved road. Other spirit mediums reported that this spirit medium had once been the master at a major urban temple and had been widely famous in Singapore and Malaysia. Low attendance at a temple fair celebrating his patron deity's birthday suggests to me that his influence had waned and perhaps explains his willingness to teach me. When I went to his temple the first time, Mr. Lim was in trance, and the temple committee member who brought me there urged me to ask the god to help me write my book. With some reluctance I abandoned my observation point, stepped up to the altar where a martial artist god (the Second Commander of the Eastern Quarter) possessed the medium, and asked for help. The "god" began to lecture me on the basic tenets of the three religions—Daoism, Buddhism, and Confucianism, illustrating his points allegorically. I returned to Mr. Lim's temples several times with a male research assistant, and we interviewed Mr. Lim out of trance in these visits. Though not in trance, Mr. Lim repeated parts of his initial lecture, expanding on many points.

Further Reading

Kenneth Dean, *Taoist Ritual and Popular Cults of Southeast China* (Princeton: Princeton University Press, 1993); Jean DeBernardi, "Space and Time in Chinese Religious Culture," *History of Religions* 31.3 (1992): 247–68; David K. Jordan and Daniel Overmyer, *The Flying Phoenix: Aspects of Chinese Sectarianism in Taiwan* (Princeton: Princeton University Press, 1986); Graeme Lang and Lars Ragvald, *The Rise of a Refugee God: Hong Kong's Wong Tai Sin* (Hong Kong: Oxford University Press, 1993); Steven Sangren, *History and Magical Power in a Chinese Community* (Stanford: Stanford University Press, 1987); Arthur Wolf, ed., *Religion and Ritual in Chinese Society* (Stanford: Stanford University Press, 1974).

The Great Ultimate

The Ultimate of Nonbeing produced the Great Ultimate. The Great Ultimate opened Heaven and Earth. Heaven and Earth produced creatures, then humankind. First there were animals, then there were humans. People began to worship the gods in the Early Six Kingdoms period: they passed this on to people in the Middle Six Kingdoms. [He broke from his narrative to express his uncertainty as to our motives in wanting him to teach us.]

I must influence you, and help you. I don't know your heart in doing this,

I don't know if you are good or bad. I can tell you how to behave, how to worship, things like that, and then I can influence you.

People come, and they can return. How can they return? One way is to meditate, and to follow a vegetarian diet. . . . I will discuss *dao li* for you.

The Ultimate of Nonbeing produced the Great Ultimate. The Great Ultimate opened Heaven and Earth. Heaven and Earth produced creatures, then humankind.

What is *dao*? What is *li*? All religions are persuasive words. Religion calls people to do things in a certain way. Religion persuades and advises people. This is not the same as discussing *dao li*. Religion advises us "do not do that, you must do good, you must not do bad." This is advice, it is not *dao li*. *Dao li* is very deep. The Three Religions and the Nine Streams have yet to talk of *dao li*. And no race has yet explained it.

What is a race, what are the five races? Red race, white race, black race, yellow race, brown race. And there are four types of hair. This is *dao li*. Red hair, white hair, black hair, brown hair. All are the same, but their languages are different. Where is *dao li*? It is in our bodies.

The Three Religions and Nine Streams are in our bodies. What are the Nine Streams? The Nine Streams are man. . . . There are three religions: Daoism [he touches his forehead], Buddhism [he touches his left shoulder], and Confucianism [he touches his right shoulder].

In our bodies there are eight "people": Daoism, Buddhism, Confucianism, and inside there are five elements. Gold is the heart, wood is the liver, water is the stomach, fire is the lungs, and earth is the kidneys. There are five people inside. Dogs are the same, birds are the same, pigs are the same. If you kill them and look, their organs are the same. But they only have two souls.

The organs are the same, the body structure is the same. But when people speak, their speech is not the same. She speaks English, he speaks Hindi, he speaks Bengali, she speaks Malay, he speaks German: they are all different. Within the Chinese race, the yellow race, there are also differences. Within the Chinese race there are Hoq Jiu, Teo Jiu, Hong Kong, Hainan, Shanghai, Keng Hua, all are part of the yellow race. The languages they speak are not the same.

Animals have two souls. We humans have three souls. People say that when we die, the soul does not die. What are the three souls called? The yin soul, the intelligence soul, the heart soul. The first two vanish, they break, scatter, and are no more. The heart soul does not die—it goes and travels. I don't know where it wants to go. The intelligence soul and the yin soul die. They scatter, they break, they disperse. It's like ashes scattering—inside there is absolutely nothing. This heart soul can fly.

The heart soul flies. I do not know what it wants to combine with. It must go and combine. How to combine? You must have good deeds and good morals, then you will have good rewards. Then the heart soul can combine with a human womb and be reborn.

If you are not good you will go and join with the animals of Heaven, of Earth, of water, with these animals, or with worms or grass. Grass also has one soul—without a soul, there is no life.

The heart soul is flown down by Heaven, and depending on where you want to fly, where you want to go, you are flown there to join up and be born. This is what you call reincarnation. Here is the seed of rebirth: the heart soul does not die. What is the intelligence soul? The intelligence soul accompanies our consciousness. The yin soul is matter and flesh. Everything in hell, below, of the soil is called yin. Yin is the soul of below, and I speak of matter and flesh. A person's intelligence soul is aware of the three souls. The intelligence soul comes and holds together the three souls. When this happens it is called our consciousness, and it must stay if we are to endure. You must have the intelligence soul. Do you know?

You must keep the Dao. People can come to Earth, and they must return. But today, no one wants to return. People no longer meditate and go to Heaven. Why is this? It is because people today are greedy for office, greedy for sex, greedy for money, greedy for power. People cannot return—they go instead to Hell. When you are born, you come to Earth. When you die, it is not definite that you will return to Heaven. These days, everyone goes to Hell.

What is it like to return? You meditate, and you can take soul and matter and return to Heaven. If you go to Hell, your flesh and bones are lost to you. It's not that you cannot return, but you must know how to go back. . . .

When people come to be born, they have sin, and we repay our sins. We have sin, and we have desire. This word "desire" is very deep. If there were no desire, no one would come down, no one would desire the world. Heaven gives you the choice of how to make up for your sins. You decide where you want to go, and what you want to link up with. You look and say: "Wa! The world is so pretty!" and you want to be reborn in the world. Good. So Heaven lets you link up with a womb to be reborn. Once you have been reborn, you arrive in the world and know the bitterness. This is called "taking the sins." It is the same for everyone. This is called *dao li*. *Dao li* is very deep. I will tell you about it.

It makes no difference whether you are male or female, or what color you are: red race, yellow race, white race, brown race, black race. We all are the same, it's only our languages that are different. Did you know this?

You are ten months in the womb. Is this not so? I was ten months, she was ten months, the black race, Bengalis, are also ten months. No less, no more. . . . Before 300 days, a child will not be born. After 295 days it will be born (300 days is not exact). This is desire. This is *dao li*.

Those who understand these things will discuss filiality. You can follow this or not. You can chose to be filial or unfilial to your parents: you can think and decide which is right. You are born of a mother, I am also born of a mother, she is also born of a mother, am I right or not? You are carried in the womb how long? 295 days. Your mother carries you like a burden. And when you are born, how is your mother? She risks her life for you.

When you are born, this is called "crossing the sea of blood." Below you, all is blood. Your mother is swooning, as if dead, and below is blood. You must cross the sea of blood. When you are born, your eyes are open, and your hands are also open. You see the sea of blood and are frightened: your eyes close, and you clench your fists. Your mouth is plugged by blood, "dirt" blocks the mouth, and your fist clenches. When your eyes meet the blood, they close, the eyelids close, and the hands make a fist. The blood must be removed from your mouth, then you let out three cries: "Wah, wah, wah!" After crossing the sea of blood, you must cross the sea of suffering. The three cries are the sea of suffering.

People have desire, but they do not know the sorrow. If you know the sorrow, you know how to keep the Dao, and how to "be human." If you want to suffer the sins, how can you take them on? You can return to Heaven if you follow Heaven, and follow Earth. Heaven is man's grandfather, father, mother; Earth is our elder brother, elder sister, younger brother, younger sister.

When you are one, two, three, and four years old, your parents bear eight parts of your sin. You bear only two parts. When you are five, six, seven, eight, you bear four parts, and your parents bear six parts.

What sins do you have? You do not know what food is, what rice is. When you are a child, you do not understand. . . . You do not know that you can eat some things, but others you cannot. . . . Some things are good, others are bad, but the child does not understand, and he takes food and wastes it recklessly.

For him, everything is paste, and he does not understand that you must not mix excrement with things that you eat. When you are a child, you do not know these things, so you do not sin. But if your parents do not take care of you, if they fail to tend their children, then they bear eight parts of the sin, and the child only two parts, until the child has reached the age of sixteen. Once you have reached sixteen, whatever you do—murder men, set fires, be wicked, be poisonous—it's your affair. Your parents do not bear the responsibility.

This filiality is very deep. You cannot repay your parents. If men follow them and please them, then this is good. You must do things to please them, you must "follow father follow mother." You must not oppose Heaven and Earth. To "follow" you must recognize that he is big, you are small. He is the elder, and in a certain instance he is wrong. He is the one who taught you and raised you, and now clearly he is wrong. But he is still right. You must not correct him to his face. When he has passed by, then you can speak. This is called "following." People must not oppose their elders. We are small, and he is big, and she is the mother who gave us life.

A bird understands filiality. How is a bird born? From an egg, hatched from a layer of shell. We humans are born from the womb. A bird can repay his parents love: you are human, but you do not understand how to repay the kindness of your parents.

The eggshell hatches what bird? A crow, and in three years the crow must molt. He has no feathers and cannot fly, and is in danger of starving. But when his stomach is empty he can cry "Wah, wah, wah," and his grandson will know to feed him worms until his feathers have grown back again. This is called "repaying kindness." . . . We humans do not understand how to repay the favors that our parents have done for us. Birds know how: humans are ungrateful.

Speaking of animals of the Earth, which is the most filial? Take the goat. He is born from the womb, like us. The goat's mother has tears, like us. When the kid is born, he faces Heaven and kowtows: one, two, three—then he gets to his feet. When he stands up and is hungry, he kneels on his front legs to suckle his mother's milk. The goat is born like us, and he understands filiality. . . . The kid knows how to find his mother when he is hungry, and he knows how to be a filial son. If you are human, you must know how to be a filial child.

Speaking of being bad, a tiger will attack and eat people, but you can teach tigers to be obedient. Tigers are bad and eat humans, but you can tame them. You are a human being, but no one can teach you to be good.

What is it to be faithful or grateful? People forget about gratitude and are unfaithful. They fail us in loyalty, in faithfulness, in filiality.

If you raise a dog, he cannot speak, but he is the most grateful and the most faithful creature. If today he does something wrong and the master hits him, he will not keep resentment in his heart. He does not criticize or blame the master. If you leave him and then return, he will wag his tail on seeing you. This is called "having gratitude and loyalty." A dog understands gratitude and loyalty. You must not be ungrateful and disloyal.

People don't obey. Those who are born from eggs, who are wrapped in a single membrane, can obey. You do not know how to obey. Take chickens and ducks. This house has chickens, that one has ducks. If you let them out to play, then later call for your ducks "gu gu gu," they will understand and return home to eat. Other people's chickens or ducks do not come near. A chicken or a duck will obey. You are human, and you don't obey. . . . What use are people? They're useless.

These things, *dao li,* are very deep, very long. If you want to study the Dao, it is very deep, very long. If you want to study the Dao, you must not covet money or power, status or women. You must take the world lightly and refuse money. You must seek perfection. You must go to the deep forest to study. After fifty years, you can become an immortal. These days, people are greedy for sex, for power, for money. They hurt people, kill people, set fires—they dare to do this sort of thing. We have this sort of thing.

People see what is good. Everyone says that they want to be filial, and that people ought to be honest. No one intends to do people in recklessly, or to hurt them by talking behind their backs.

Do you want to obey me or not? If not, I can repeat myself a hundred times, you know. If you don't want to obey, then think it over slowly. If you understand how to think about people, then you will hear me and know that I am right. You must study this yourselves. Good.

Now, I tell you not to hurt people, but you defy me. You say "No," you don't want to hear this. I say: "Don't go and steal." You say: "If I don't steal, I don't eat." But "Heaven will not starve people to death." You want to have your needs satisfied, you want your children to eat. "For every blade of grass a drop of dew." But you want to do things like that. You tell him not to, but he wants it like that. He definitely wants to be a success. These days people are like this: "Do it now, get it now, it's okay now." These people say that if you "do good," then your children get nothing. If you "do bad," then they will get something: "Be fierce, be poisonous, set fires, ride a horse." He rides a horse [enjoys high status], but there will be a day. The next generation will suffer.

No one takes notice of people who are good. But the future generations will be better off. These days you cannot find three consecutive generations rich. After two generations, the wealth is gone. If you are impatient to get, you are not thinking of the next generation. Have you no concern for your children and grandchildren? If you want to understand, it's like that.

I don't look at you and ask what religion you practice. Daoism is fine, Buddhism is fine, it doesn't bother me. I want to call you to do good.

In the world today, people do as they like. There is no distinction between men and women, and people are anarchic. No one know how to distinguish Heaven and Earth, no one understands principles. They lack reason.

Officials, those in the government, are the same. They do not, "follow the road" in their actions. Do you know what this is called? This is a "gold-money world." If you murder someone, you can fix it so that there's no trial. The money is given to you [by your fate], and in a "gold-money world," money buys a life. It is true. If you have money you can murder men. A gold-money world.

If you have money, you can talk. If you have no money, no matter what you say, it is not the truth. I call this a "glass" but you say "cup." I say that "glass" is more correct, but I don't have money. You have money, and you say that "cup" is more correct, so it's "glass" that's wrong. If you have money, everyone speaks your language. He says "glass" is right and I say "cup." I have no money, so even if I'm right, he will say I'm wrong. It's like that. Most people call this a "biscuit," but he calls it "cake," even though most people say "biscuit." If you have money, people will speak your language.

—23—

Spellbinding

Donald Harper

Spellbinding (Jie) is a short account of demons and uncanny phenomena written on forty-five bamboo slips. It forms one section of a sizable bamboo-slip manuscript that treats astrological, numerological, and other occult lore. This and a second similar manuscript were discovered during excavation of Tomb 11 at Shuihudi, Hubei Province, in 1975–76; the burial is dated ca. 217 B.C.E. While we know from bibliographic records that demonological literature circulated among the elite of the Warring States (403–221 B.C.E.), Qin (221–207 B.C.E.), and Han (202 B.C.E.–220 C.E.) periods, none of this literature survived the vicissitudes of transmission down to the present. Thus *Spellbinding* is a unique example of an otherwise lost genre of ancient magico-religious literature.

Spellbinding contains seventy separate entries (numbered in the translation for convenient reference). Entry 1 is a prologue that gives the following explanation of the purpose of the text:

> The Wanghang bogy who harms the people,
> Treats the people unpropitiously.
> May the way to spellbind it be declared,
> Enabling the people to avoid the baleful and disastrous.

Wanghang is one of several cognate words (including Wangliang, Fangliang, and Panghuang) that denote a much-feared telluric bogy who preyed on people. Legend relates that when the flood hero Yu founded the Xia ruling house (in the late third millennium B.C.E., according to tradition), Yu cast nine talismanic caldrons—emblazoned with the images of all the spirits and demons of the terrestrial realm—that served magically to protect the people from the evil Wangliang and all manner of demonic harassment. *Spellbinding* fulfills the promise of the legend of Yu's caldrons in the form of a text that describes how to deal with specific varieties of demonic phenomena, from talking animals (entry 15) to revenants (entry 19) and the wolf at the door (entry 52).

The sixty-nine entries that follow the prologue are remarkable evidence of everyday beliefs of the third century B.C.E.. At that time certain naturalistic ideas had already gained currency among the elite; most notably the concept of "vapor" (*qi*) as the stuff of all existence, and the cyclical theories of Yin Yang and the Five Phases (*wuxing*) that were used to describe the operation of nature. *Spellbinding* reveals the magico-religious aspects of the beliefs of the time that coexisted with naturalistic ideas and continued to thrive in their own right. Some of the entries may appear to describe unreal situations and demons who are reminiscent of the fantastic composite creatures recorded in the *Classic of Mountains and Seas (Shanhai jing)*, our chief source for knowledge of the early Chinese spirit world. However, *Spellbinding* shows that such creatures had real existence in the popular mind—not only did they exist, they often inhabited the immediate environment of the home and represented safety and health hazards. For example, entry 27 describes the Morphic Spirit (the name may refer to the ability of the demon to change shape as it pleases) that can occupy a house and paralyze its residents. By digging down "to the springs" (that is, to a depth that touches the subterranean level of the world), a "red pig with a horse tail and dog head" is obtained. Once caught, the Morphic Spirit is cooked and eaten, which should satisfy any doubts we might have concerning the substantiality of the creature in contemporary estimation (consumption of the offender is described in other entries as well). Even Yin and Yang are reified as demons whose mischief must be neutralized exorcistically (entries 12, 13, 32); and vapor (*qi*) is often the medium through which a demonic entity exerts its influence on its victims.

The religious viewpoint reflected in *Spellbinding* is basically animistic. Several tens of demons are named using a nomenclature that is most often descriptive: Demon of Abandoned Places (entry 3), Spirit Dog (entry 9), Demon Who Was Mourned as a Suckling (entry 49), and so forth. Most of the demons are not known from other written records, and it is difficult to know what larger religious significance they may have had outside their single occurrence in *Spellbinding*. Even given the difficulty of using *Spellbinding* to deduce the nature of popular animistic religion, the text gives us at least a glimpse of religion in action in the late Warring States period. The subsequent success of Buddhism in China and the indigenous formation of religious Daoism must be seen against the background of the popular traditions that produced *Spellbinding* several centuries earlier. Religious Daoism, in particular, regarded illness and the presence of demons as equivalent phenomena; and Daoism emphasized therapeutic measures to relieve the suffering of believers. A similar approach is evident in *Spellbinding*, which also includes many demonifuges that anticipate the exorcistic element of Daoist liturgy. Entry 42, which concerns the Hungry Demon (E Gui), bears witness to the Buddhist adaptation of popular religion. Previously it was thought that the name E Gui was invented as a translation of Buddhist *preta*, one of the lowest and most miserable of the ranks of rebirth. We now know that Buddhism did not introduce the Hungry Demon to China, but rather it adopted an indigenous demon to become the Buddhist *preta*.

While *Spellbinding* identifies many individual demons, a number of the entries concern uncanny or troubling phenomena that for lack of a better term I call quasi-demonic. Entries 18, 20, 37, and 38 provide techniques to alleviate harmful emotions. Sadness, sorrow, anxiety, and anger are not demons per se, but it is interesting that *Spellbinding* regards their effects as comparable to the actions of demons. Fear of bugs (*chong*) is also prevalent in *Spellbinding* (the category of *chong* includes snakes and other reptilian creatures). Some bugs are individual demons; for example, the Spirit Bug in entry 26 and the Conjunction Bug in entry 28. Entry 41 describes the mischief caused by the vapor (*qi*) of Bug-misfortune (*yang*). The word *yang* is used in Warring States, Qin, and Han texts. From a root meaning of misfortune caused by bugs, *yang* has the extended sense of misfortune in general (which is the meaning of *yang* in entry 70). The belief that all bugs were potential agents of misfortune is reflected in the several entries that concern household bug extermination (entries 10, 17, 54, and 66).

The exorcistic methods described in *Spellbinding* were intended to be employed by anyone. Beginning with the four exorcistic body postures listed in entry 1 (sitting like a winnowing basket is to sit with legs stretched out in front and spread open; the leaning stand is standing on one foot; linked movement may refer to a kind of shuffling movement), successive entries provide a catalogue of exorcistic magic. Before the discovery of *Spellbinding* we did not know that this kind of magic was part of common practice, and that it was not limited to the shamanic specialists or the officiants of state-sponsored rituals and cults. The very nature of *Spellbinding* as a text that teaches people to identify demonic phenomena and deal with them expeditiously broadens our perspective on magico-religious traditions before Buddhism and religious Daoism.

The translation of *Spellbinding* is made difficult by several factors. Some of the original bamboo slips are damaged and characters are missing. When it is possible to surmise what kind of word is missing, I supply a probable translation in brackets. Otherwise two dots mark one missing character. With a newly excavated manuscript, unattested vocabulary and unusual grammar represent another kind of difficulty. Continuing research on the text and the possible archaeological discovery of related texts will undoubtedly improve the translation. At several places in the translation it is necessary to add words to the text to make the English meaning clear; these words are also placed in brackets. Explanatory comments are placed in parentheses. Because it constitutes a unified concept in third-century B.C.E. thought, the word *qi* is regularly translated as "vapor," even though a functional translation might adopt a number of different translations; for example, "vitality" (entry 5), "breath" or "air" (entry 27), "essence" or "influence" (entry 13), and "taste" (entry 27). The following measure words are translated conventionally, but represent third-century B.C.E. measures: cup (*sheng*, 200 cc), inch (*cun*, 2.3 cm), and foot (*chi*, 23 cm). Entries 36–38 utilize calendrical numerology associated with the ten Celestial Stems (*tian gan*) and twelve Earthly Branches (*di zhi*), which are combined to form a set of day designations in a sixty-day cycle. Entry 38 specifies a day with the Celestial Stem *wu* in its designation and further specifies the time of midday—appropriate since *wu* is also associated with the center. The choice of sunrise on a *geng* day in entry 36 and sunset on a *gui* day in entry 37 is clearly significant, but the explanation is not obvious.

The text below is from *The Bamboo-slip Manuscripts from the Qin Tomb at Shuihudi (Shuihudi Qin mu zhu jian)* (Beijing, 1990), pp. 212–19.

Further Reading

Donald Harper, "A Chinese Demonography of the Third Century B.C.," *Harvard Journal of Asiatic Studies* 45 (1985): 459–98; Harper, "Warring States, Ch'in and Han Periods," in "Chinese Religions: The State of the Field," *Journal of Asian Studies* 54.1 (1995): 152–60; Mu-chou Poo, "Popular Religion in Pre-Imperial China: Observations on the Almanacs of Shui-hu-ti," *T'oung Pao* 79 (1993): 225–48.

Spellbinding

1. Spellbinding and casting odium on demons:

> The Wanghang bogy who harms the people,
> Treats the people unpropitiously.
> May the way to spellbind it be declared,
> Enabling the people to avoid the baleful and disastrous.

What demons detest are namely: reclining in a crouch, sitting like a winnowing basket, linked movement, and the leaning stand.

2. When without cause a demon attacks a person and does not desist—this is the Stabbing Demon. Make a bow from peach wood; make arrows from non-fruiting jujube wood, and feather them with chicken feathers. When it appears, shoot it. Then it will desist.

3. When without cause a demon lodges in a person's home—this is the Demon of Abandoned Places. Take earth from an old abandoned place, and make imitation people and dogs with it. Set them on the outside wall, one person and one dog every five paces, and encircle the home. When the demon comes, scatter ashes, strike a winnowing basket, and screech at it. Then it stops.

4. When without cause a demon deludes a person—this is the Enticing Demon who likes to sport with people. Make a staff from mulberry heartwood. When the demon comes, strike it. It will die of terror.

5. When without cause a demon takes hold of a person and becomes glued—this is the Sad Demon who is homeless and becomes the follower of the person. It causes the person to be pale in complexion and lack vapor (*qi*; *qi* deficiency

leads to loss of vitality); he enjoys observing the cleansing and purifying abstentions, and he does not drink or eat. Use a jujube-wood hammer that has a peach-wood handle to strike the person's heart. Then it does not come.

6. When without cause the people in a household all become diseased, and some die while others are sick—this is the Jujube Demon who is situated there, buried in an upright position. In the drought season the ground above it is damp; in the wet season it is dry. Dig it up and get rid of it. Then it will stop.

7. When without cause the people in a household all become diseased, most of whom suffer from nightmares and die—this is the Childbirth Demon who is buried there. There is not grass or matting above it. Dig it up and get rid of it. Then it will stop.

8. When without cause the people in a household all become diseased; some die while others are sick; and men and women have whiskers that shed, head hair that falls out, and yellow eyes—this is the fertilized egg. The kernel of the egg (the embryo in the fertilized egg) was born and became a demon. Pound one cup of selected kernels. In the same mortar, eat the egg kernels along with millet and meat. Then it will stop.

9. When a dog continually enters someone's house at night, seizes the men and sports with the women, and cannot be caught—this is the Spirit Dog who feigns being a demon. Use mulberry bark to make . . and . . it. Steam and eat it. Then it will stop.

10. When in summer during the period of Great Heat (late July) the house becomes cold without cause—young ants (*long;* it may also mean a dragon) are occupying it. Fumigate the inside of the house with nonfruiting jujube wood. The ants (or dragon) will depart.

11. When wild beasts or the six domestic animals encounter a person and speak—this is the vapor (*qi*) of the Whirling Wind. Strike it with a peach-wood staff, and take off a shoe and throw the shoe at it. Then it will desist.

12. When without cause the stove cannot cook food—the Yang Demon has taken its vapor (*qi*). Burn pig feces inside the house. Then it will stop.

13. When without cause a person's six domestic animals all die—the vapor (*qi*) of the Yin Demon has entered them. Then quickly crumble tiles and use them to encircle . . . . It will desist.

14. When cold wind enters a person's house, and he is alone without anyone else being there. Sprinkle sand. Then it will desist.

15. . . birds and beasts are able to speak—this is a prodigy. They should not speak more than thrice. If they do speak more than thrice, the person should increase the number of people around him. Then it will stop.

16. When his vapor (*qi*) is not circulating and yet the person can move. When it lasts for the whole day, there is a great matter; when it does not last for the whole day, there is a small matter.

17. When killing legged and legless bugs, they are able to rejoin after having been broken in two. Spew ashes on them. Then they will not rejoin.

18. When a person has thoughts that are sad and does not forget them. Take foxtails or cattails from an abandoned place, pick twice seven of their leaves, face the northeast and wad them, and lie down to sleep. Then it will stop.

19. When a person's wife and concubine or his friend dies and their ghost returns to him. Wait for it with an ignited [torch made of] nutgrass on a nonfruiting jujube-wood shaft. Then it will not come.

20. When a person's heart is sorrowful without cause. Take a stick of cinnamon one foot one inch long and break it in the middle. On the day of the full moon when the sun first rises, eat it. After doing that, then by late afternoon it will stop.

21. When the demon of an old abandoned place continually terrifies people and terrifies human habitations. Make straw arrows and shoot it. Then it will not terrify people.

22. When a demon continually summons a person saying, "You must die on such-and-such a month and day"—this is the Earth Demon who feigns being a rat and enters people's vinegar, fermented sauce, fermented gruel, or drink. Search for it and get rid of it. Then it will desist.

23. The dwelling place of a great spirit cannot be passed through. It likes to harm people. Make pellets from dog feces and carry them when passing through the place. On seeing the spirit throw them at it. It will not harm the person.

24. When a demon continually drums on a person's door at night, singing or wailing to be admitted by the person—this is the Malevolent Demon. Shoot it with straw arrows. Then it will not come.

25. When people or birds and beasts as well as the six domestic animals continually go into a person's home—these are spirits from above who are fond of those below and enjoy entering. Have men and women who have never entered the home (a euphemism for sexual intercourse) beat drums, ring clappered bells, and screech at them. Then they will not come.

26. When a demon continually follows men or women and goes away when it sees another person—this is the Spirit Bug who feigns being a person. Stab its neck with a good sword. Then it will not come.

27. When the people in a household all do not have vapor (*qi*) to breathe and cannot move—this is the Morphic Spirit who is situated in the house. Dig down to the springs. There is a red pig with a horse tail and dog head. When cooked and eaten, it has a fine vapor (*qi*).

28. When the people in a household all have contracting muscles—this is the Conjunction Bug who occupies the west wall of the house. Clear away the southwest corner to a depth of five feet below ground level. Strike it with an iron hammer. You must hit the bug's head. Dig it up and get rid of it. If you do not get rid of it, within three years everyone in the household has contracting muscles.

29. When a demon continually scolds a person and cannot be dismissed—this is the Violent Demon. [Stab] it with a nonfruiting jujube-wood sword. Then it will not come.

30. When a demon continually causes a person to have foul dreams, and after waking they cannot be divined—this is the Master of Diagrams. Make a mulberry-wood staff and prop it inside the doorway, and turn a cookpot upside down outside the doorway. Then it will not come.

31. When a demon continually follows a person as he travels and he cannot dismiss it. Jab it with a female writing-brush (*nü bi;* perhaps the name of a plant, or a name for a woman's hairpin). Then it will not come.

32. When a woman is not crazy or incoherent, yet sings in a high-pitched voice—this is the Yang Demon who takes pleasure in following her. Take twice seven seeds from a north-facing . . and incinerate them. [Put] the ashes into food and feed it to her. The demon leaves.

33. When without cause a demon treats a person's home as its sanctuary and cannot be made to leave—this is the Ancestral . . who is roving. Throw dog feces at it. It will not come.

34. When a demon continually enters a person's home naked—this is the Child Who Died Young and Is Unburied. Spew ashes on it. Then it will not come.

35. When a demon continually encounters a person and enters a person's home—this is the Roving Demon. Use broad cattails to make corded arrows and incinerate them. Then it will not come.

36. When a person continually gives birth to a child who dies before able to walk—this is the Blameless Demon who inhabits it. On a *geng* (the seventh Celestial Stem) day when the sun first rises, spew ashes on the gate, and after that offer sacrifices. On the tenth day collect the sacrifices, wrap them in woolly grass, and bury them in the wilderness. Then there will not be disaster.

37. When a person is anxious without cause. Make a peach-wood figurine and rub it. On a *gui* (the tenth Celestial Stem) day at sunset, throw it into the road and quickly say, "So-and-so will avoid anxiety."

38. When a person is angry without cause. On a *wu* (the fifth Celestial Stem) day at midday, eat millet in the road. Then suddenly it will stop.

39. When without cause the people in a household are all injured—this is the Gleaming Fang Demon who inhabits it. Take woolly grass and yellow soil, and sprinkle them in a ring around the house. Then it will leave.

40. When a demon enters a person's house, appears suddenly and vanishes, and does not desist. Get fermented gruel made from bran and wait for it to come. Pour [the gruel] on it. Then it will stop.

41. When without cause a person's head hair lifts up like bugs and chin or cheek whiskers—this is the vapor (*qi*) of Bug-misfortune that inhabits it. Boil grass shoes, and use them to paper [the hair]. Then it will stop.

42. Whenever a demon continually enters a person's house holding a basket and says, "Give me food"—this is the Hungry Demon. Throw a shoe at it. Then it will stop.

43. Whenever there is a great Whirling Wind that harms people. Take off [a shoe] and throw it at it. Then it will stop.

44. When a person continually loses a newborn infant—this is the Child Who Perished in Water who has taken it. Make an ash house to imprison it. Hang a scrub-brush inside. Then it will be captured. Slash it with the scrub-brush. Then it will die. If boiled and eaten, it will not be harmful.

45. Whenever a grove has been established in a land (the grove is sacred to spirits of the locality), and a demon there continually shouts in the night—this is the Ferocious Demon who seizes people and punishes them on its own. Enter with clothes undone and lapel-straps untied. The captives can be obtained.

46. When the people in a household suffer nightmares while sleeping and cannot occupy [the house]—this is the . . Demon who occupies it. Take peach-wood stakes and pound them into the four corners and center. Slash the outside walls of the home with a nonfruiting jujube-wood knife and shout at it saying, "Again quickly hurry out. If today you do not get out, your clothes will be stripped away with the nonfruiting [jujube-wood] knife." Then there will not be disaster.

47. When a large goblin continually enters a person's home and cannot be stopped. Strike it with a peach-wood figurine. Then it will stop.

48. When a demon continually summons a person to come out from the house—this is the Ferocious Demon who has no place to live. Do not respond to its summons. Throw white stones at it. Then it will stop.

49. When a demon baby continually calls to people saying, "Give me food"—this is the Demon Who Was Mourned as a Suckling. Some of its bones are on the outside. Spew yellow soil on them. Then it will desist.

50. When in a household someone who is sleeping sinks down together with the bedmat—this is the Earth Imp who occupies it. Pour plain boiling water over it and fill it with yellow soil. It will not be harmful.

51. When without cause there is a demon who joins with a person—this is the Elf Demon. Pour water on it. Then it will desist.

52. When a wolf continually shouts at a person's door saying, "Open. I am not a demon." Kill it, boil it, and eat it. It has a fine taste.

53. When there is the sound of a drum in the household and the drum is not to be seen—this is the Demon Drum. Respond to it with a handmade drum. Then it will desist.

54. When a horde of bugs covertly enters a person's house—this is wildfire that feigns being bugs. Respond to it with manmade fire. Then it will desist.

55. When a demon continually startles and reviles a person—this is the Blameless Demon. Stab it with a nonfruiting jujube-wood sword. Then it will stop.

56. When a demon continually steals a person's domestic animals—this is the Violent Demon. Shoot it with straw arrows. Then it will stop.

57. When a demon continually follows someone's woman and cohabitates saying, "The son of God-on-High descends to roam and wishes to leave [with her]." Bathe oneself in dog feces and strike it with reeds. Then it will die.

58. When a demon continually says to a person, "Give me your woman" and cannot be dismissed—this is a spirit from above who descends to take a wife. Strike it with reeds. Then it will die. If it is not expelled, after it comes five times the woman will die.

59. When Heaven fire burns a person's home and cannot be expelled. Halt it with white sand. Then it will stop. When a bolt of lightning ignites a person's [home] and cannot be stopped. Oppose it with man-made fire. Then it will desist.

60. When lightning attacks a person. Strike it with the same wood (the piece of wood struck first by the lightning). Then it will desist.

61. When cloud vapor (*qi*) covertly enters a person's home. Oppose it with man-made fire. Then it will stop.

62. When a person passes by an abandoned waste and a woman carrying a child chases the person. Oppose it by opening an umbrella. Then it will desist.

63. When a person is traveling and a demon stands blocking the road. Unbind the hair and rush past it. Then it will desist.

64. When birds and beasts continually make a person's house ring with noise. Burn loose head hair as well as the fur and whiskers of the six domestic animals at the places where they stop. Then it will stop.

65. When a person is sleeping and in the night a demon crouches over his head. Strike it with a bamboo whip. Then it will desist.

66. When birds, beasts, and legged or legless bugs enter a person's house in great hordes or singly. Strike them with a bamboo whip. Then it will stop.

67. When without cause the people in a household all have spreading welts—the Gibbon Mother inhabits the house. It is the size of a pestle and is red and white. In the wet season the place it occupies is dry; in the drought season it is damp. Dig to a depth of three feet inside the house and burn pig feces there. Then it will stop.

68. When the people in a household all have itching bodies—the Pestilence Demon inhabits it. Burn fresh paulownia wood inside the house. Then it will desist.

69. When the well of a household is bloody and has a putrid smell—the Earth Bug battles down below and the blood seeps upward. Dump sand in it and make a new well. Feed it mush and give it morning dew to drink. In three days it will be able to be human. If not, feed it for three months. If it is captured and is not a human, it will invariably be a dried out bone. Pick it up at dawn, enclose it in woolly grass, wrap it with hemp, and discard it at a distant spot. Then it will stop.

70. When the Whirling Wind enters a person's home and takes something from it. Throw a shoe at it. If the thing it took is recovered, place it in the center of the road. If not recovered, discard the shoe in the center of the road. Then there will be no misfortune (*yang*). Within one year there is invariably a misfortune in the family.

—24—

Record of the Feng and Shan Sacrifices

Stephen Bokenkamp

The account that follows is not a religious text, but a description of one of the most venerated and austere of the ancient imperial Confucian rituals, the Feng and Shan rites, as they were performed in 56 C.E. It was written by Ma Dibo, a minor official who participated in the rite, probably as a subordinate to the Chamberlain of State Ceremonials. Ma's specific function, as described in his account, seems to have been the inspection and readying of the stones which were to form parts of the ritual altar. Having, in his official capacity, ascended Mount Tai, where the Feng rite was to be held, ahead of the imperial party, Ma is able to describe the event from several perspectives. Through him, we learn of the setting and preparations for the rite, the performance and meaning of the ritual, the supernatural responses to the rite, and even a few comical details ignored in more sober histories. More important, Ma, by turns inspired by what he witnesses and annoyed at what he has to endure, gives us a real sense of what it must have felt like to participate in an imperial ritual.

While some early texts attempt to establish the antiquity of the Feng and Shan rites, we have verifiable accounts of only six performances in all of Chinese history. Such was the respect in which the rite was held that quite a few Chinese sovereigns, urged to perform the Feng and Shan, declined to do so on the grounds that they were unworthy or that the times were not right. In 56 C.E., Liu Xiu, posthumously known as the Thearch of Shining Martiality, deemed the times to be right. Thirty years earlier, he had reestablished the Han dynasty after a sixteen-year interregnum; now the kingdom was at peace and he could properly announce to Heaven and Earth the new beginning of the Liu-family dynasty. At the same time, through this rite he could connect in the minds of his subjects his rule with that of the most powerful of the Former Han rulers, Liu Che (posthumously styled the Martial Thearch), who had conducted the rites in 110 B.C.E., and with that of Ying Zheng, the unifier of the Central Kingdom, who called himself while living the "First Illustrious Thearch of the Qin" and who had conducted the rites in 219 B.C.E.

According to traditions established by these powerful emperors, the Feng rite to Heaven was to be conducted atop lofty Mount Tai (in modern Shandong Province), while the Shan rite to the feminine Earth spirit was held on a lesser peak, Liangfu, at the foot of Mount Tai. As this ritual program indicates, Mount Tai was regarded as an axis where the deities of Heaven and those of Earth might meet. China did not have a single *axis mundi,* however, but five—all holy mountains located roughly in the four cardinal directions and the symbolic "center" of the realm. Mount Tai was associated, in this five-phase ordered symbolic map of the kingdom, with the east, spring, and new growth. It was thus appropriate for a rite celebrating the beginning of a new dynastic line. While all of the five mountains received imperial sacrifice, Mount Tai was the sole mountain deemed suitable for the Feng and Shan.

But Mount Tai was more than the royal passage between Heaven and Earth or a symbol of cosmic beginnings. Popular belief held that the souls of the dead proceeded to an administratively organized purgatory beneath the mountain and its peaks hid caverns and springs that were the dwellings of spirits. In addition, during the Qin (221–207 B.C.E.) and Han (206 B.C.E.–220 C.E.) dynasties, Shandong was home to various schools of *fangshi* (wonderworkers and wizards), some of whom were able to win the allegiance of both Ying Zheng and Liu Che. These *fangshi* told of islands of immortality, inhabited by winged Transcendent beings, which floated just beyond sight in the eastern seas. Some held that the floating islands could sometimes be glimpsed from the summit of Mount Tai; others, arguing that specific ritual observances could cause the Transcendent beings to appear, held that the emperor could gain long life through accomplishing the Feng rite. The Feng rites of Ying Zheng and Liu Che were conducted in the strictest secrecy, in hopes of just such occurrences.

Liu Xiu's performance of the rites was somewhat different. He explicitly denied the goal of attempting to "meet with Transcendents" and organized his rites according to the instructions of his Confucian officials instead of relying on the sort of *fangshi* who had advised the previous two emperors. One token of the devout Confucian purpose of Liu Xiu's rites is recorded by Ma Dibo—the emperor visited the ancestral home of Confucius before beginning the ritual. The purpose of Liu Xiu's rite was simply to announce to Heaven and to Earth his achievements as emperor and to ask their continued blessing for his dynasty. A result of this determination was that Liu Xiu performed the Feng and Shan openly before his assembled officials, a decision that occasioned the logistical problems Ma describes so well.

Despite this, the basic elements of the rite remained the same. The term *feng* means "to seal." Liu Xiu's announcement to Heaven was to be written on stone tablets and enclosed in a stone coffer sealed with his official insignia. This coffer was further to be "sealed" within the piled earth of the ritual platform and covered with two massive stones. The earth placed around the coffer was to be of the "five colors" symbolizing the four directions and the center; that is, the entire realm. *Shan* means "to clear away" and was interpreted to mean the clearing of a ritual space on Liangfu for the rites to Earth. Ma Dibo is much less explicit concerning this lesser rite—his official duties may have prevented him from attending it—but it is likely that a stone coffer bearing an announcement to Earth was buried in the Shan rite as well.

The ultimate purpose of the Feng rite, then, was to enact the sealing of a new covenant between the emperor, one of whose titles was "child of Heaven," and Heaven, also called the "Thearch on High." The Shan rite was meant to actualize a similar covenant with the feminine divinity of Earth. Through this covenant, the position of humanity between Heaven and Earth was secured and the mediating status of a specific dynastic assured.

Acting as spirit "associates" in the conduct of the rites in 56 C.E. were the founder of the Han dynasty in the case of the Feng and his empress in the case of the Shan. This means that the spirits of these two ancestors were believed present at the rite and were charged with ensuring that the announcements were properly received in the spiritual hierarchy. The role of ancestors as intermediaries was common not only in imperial rites, but in family ritual as well. It should be noted here that what Western sources mistakenly call "ancestor worship" actually involved not "worship" of the ancestors, but the maintenance of family ties through ritual means in the hope that one's forebears might continue to aid their descendants. The imperial ancestors were, of course, believed to inhabit the summit of the celestial bureaucracy and were sometimes envisioned as dwelling in the constellations that ring the North Pole.

Imperial rites such as this were meaningful on a symbolic level, but to be regarded as truly effective they were expected to be accompanied by signs of acceptance on the part of Heaven and Earth. Ma records that the emperor Liu Xiu regarded the fine weather and lack of mishap during his performance of the rite as ample confirmation of Heaven's pleasure. The populace and presumably the history books as well required more dramatic wonders. Ma records several of these, all having to do with propitious vapors that appeared in the sky at key points during the ritual program. The Han court included officials whose job it was to scrutinize the skies for such atmospheric anomalies. Perhaps it was one of these officials who reported the white vapor that extended down to the altar at the conclusion of the rite. And why was it that all of the assembled officials failed to notice this token of Heaven's pleasure? They were inside the vapor, Ma reports, and so could not see it. Thus, despite Liu Xiu's Confucian attempts to demystify the rite, its mystery was preserved.

Further Reading

Hans Bielenstein, *The Restoration of the Han Dynasty*, vol. 4, *Bulletin of the Museum of Far Eastern Antiquities* 51 (1979): 3–300; Edouard Chavannes, *Le T'ai chan: Essai de monographie d'un culte chinois* (Paris: Annales du Musée Guimet 28, 1910); Howard J. Wechsler, *Offerings of Jade and Silk: Ritual and Symbol in the Legitimation of the T'ang Dynasty* (New Haven: Yale University Press, 1985), pp. 170–211; Arthur P. Wolf, ed., *Religion and Ritual in Chinese Society* (Stanford: Stanford University Press, 1974).

Record of the Feng and Shan Rites

In the thirty-second year of the Established Martiality reign-period (56 C.E.), the emperor went by carriage on a ritual inspection tour of the eastern lands. On the twenty-eighth of the first month (March 4, 56), he departed the palace at Luoyang, arriving in the state of Lu on the ninth day of the second month (March 14). From there he despatched the recently appointed Receptionist Guo Jianbo to lead five hundred convict laborers to repair the road to Mount Tai.

On the next day, the prince of Lu sent all of the Lius of the imperial household, together with members of the Kong clan and the Ding clan of Xiaqiu, to wish the emperor long life and to receive presents from him. Together they visited the house of Confucius (ancestral home of the Kong clan) where the emperor held for them a banquet of meats and liquors.

On the eleventh (March 16), the imperial party set out, reaching lodgings in Fenggao on the next day. On the same day, the emperor despatched the leader of the Court Gentlemen Brave as Tigers to ascend the mountain to inspect everything thoroughly. He also increased the convict labor force that was repairing the road to one thousand persons.

On the fifteenth day (March 20), purification rituals were begun. (The Confucian purification ritual [*zhai*] usually lasted for three days and was to be performed preparatory to any rite in which the spirits or ancestors were invoked. The official or emperor was to seclude himself in a special chamber for contemplation, eat only pure foods [especially highly polished rice], bathe, and in other ways prepare for the main rite to follow. For a Daoist version of this ritual, see chapter 20.) The representative of our kingdom and families went into seclusion in the residence of the Grand Protector. (The term "kingdom and families" is used metonymically throughout this text to refer to the emperor, who represents his kingdom and all of the families it contains. Hereafter, this term will be rendered simply "emperor.") The princes performed their purifications in the offices of the Grand Protectorate, while the Imperial Marquises all held theirs in the offices of the county seat. All the Chamberlains, Commandants, Generals, Grandees, Gentlemen of the Palace Gate, and other lesser officials, as well as the Duke of Song (senior heir to the Shang dynasty), the Duke of Wei (senior heir to the Zhou dynasty), the "Praising Perfection" Marquis, all of the Marquises of the eastern regions, and the Lesser Marquises of the Luoyang area conducted their purification rituals beyond the walls of Fenggao on the banks of the Wen River. The Defender-in-Chief and the Chamberlain for Ceremonials conducted their purifications at the residence of the

Supervisor for Forestry and Hunting. (These two officials are the highest rank of those mentioned here. The Defender-in-Chief was one of the "Three Dukes," the highest officials in the land, while the Chamberlain for Ceremonials was one of the "Nine Chamberlains," who reported directly to the emperor. He was not only responsible for imperial ritual, but also administered the National University. Presumably they were provided with this spot close to the mountain for their ritual seclusion so that they and their staffs could oversee preparations for the rite.)

I had earlier gone to the residence of the Supervisor for Forestry and Hunting, together with seventy others. We had inspected the altar for sacrifices to the mountain, as well as the old Hall of Light and the site where the Court Gentlemen had once carried out suburban offerings.

(The Hall of Light was a ritual building of five chambers in which the emperor was to carry out rites in accord with the seasons and the movement of the stars. The Hall of Light mentioned here was built by the Han emperor Liu Che before his performance of the Feng and Shan. It was a simple, thatched pavilion of two stories, the bottom square and the top round in shape. The suburban sacrifices were sacrifices personally conducted by the emperor on the outskirts of the capital city. Usually, at the time of the winter solstice Heaven was worshipped at an altar in the southern suburbs, and at the time of the summer solstice Earth was worshipped at an altar in the northern suburbs. Before his Feng rite, however, Liu Che had instructed his officials to carry out the suburban rite on an altar at the foot of the mountain. Presumably this is the site mentioned here.)

Entering the Supervisor's field pavilions, we inspected the stones they were preparing for the rite. Two of the stones were thin, flat, and nine feet in circumference. These were placed on the ritual platform. One of them was from a stone dating to the rites of the Martial Thearch. At that time, they had used five carts but still were unable to haul it up the mountain, so they positioned it at the foot of the mountain to form part of a building. This rock was thereafter known as the "five-cart stone."

The four massive stones for the corners of the ritual platform were twelve feet long, two feet wide, and about a foot and a half thick. The stone slats meant for the coffer were three feet long and six inches wide. [When fit together] they formed a shape like a slender box. There were ten of these. In addition, there was a stone for the stele inscription that was twelve feet tall when set upright, three feet wide, and one foot two inches thick. It had been inscribed with a text recording the meritorious activities and virtues of the emperor.

That same morning we went up the mountain on horses. Often the road became excessively steep and we were repeatedly forced to dismount and lead our horses. We spent about as much time walking as riding. When we reached Midpoint Observatory, we left our horses behind.

The Midpoint Observatory is twenty *li* from level ground. Looking to the south, one could see to the horizon and everything was plainly visible. Looking up, one could see the peak Celestial Pass. Despite the altitude, it was still like looking up to a soaring peak from the very bottom of a valley. So high was it that it was like gazing up at soaring clouds; so precipitous was it that it looked like a stone wall, steep and stark, as if no path could possibly ascend to it.

Looking up at people on the peak, I took some to be small white stones, others to be patches of snow. But when you watched long enough, these white things would pass by a tree or something and you knew them to be people.

When I really could ascend no more, I would throw myself spread-eagle on a rock. After lying still for awhile, I would revive again. I also availed myself of the liquor and dried meats that were sold at various spots along the route. At some places there was spring water, which greatly refreshed our spirits. In this way we urged one another along until we came to Celestial Pass peak.

When we arrived at this spot, I thought that we had reached the top. I asked someone along the way and he said that we still had another ten *li* to go.

From this point on, the road followed along the side of the mountain. Where it was broad, it was only eight or nine feet wide, but it sometimes narrowed to five or six feet. Looking up, I could see sheer precipices clustered darkly and pine trees a grizzled green, as if all were in the clouds. When I looked down into the stream-cut valley, there was only a roiling blue haze so dense that I could not see more than a few feet.

Then we came to a spot just below Heaven's Gate peak. This peak shadowed over us so hugely that, looking up, one felt as if one were gazing up a shaft at the sky from deep within a cave. We went straight up for a distance of seven *li*, clinging to a path that twisted and turned on itself like a sheep's entrails. This is called the "encircling path." In many places there were cables that one could grasp to ascend. My two servants supported me below the arms while the person ahead of me pulled. At such spots one saw only the heels of the one in front, while those in front could glimpse only the top of the head of the one following. It was like one of those paintings where people are depicted as if lined up one on top of the another. (Apparently Ma is referring here to the sort of Han painting [which we now know only through mortuary art] in which rows of officials are depicted without perspective so that they seem to be standing on each other's heads.) Our mode of ascent was just like what old texts call "scraping the chest along while hugging the rock"—it was harder than clawing one's way into Heaven.

When we first started out on this stretch of road, we would rest every ten steps or so. I gradually became exhausted, breathing so hard that my lips were parched. Then we rested every five or six steps—one tiny step after another before we would stop in our tracks. There was no way to avoid the mud. You might see a bit of dry ground before you, but your feet just would not go where you willed them.

We had started our ascent at breakfast time and reached Heaven's Gate after the *bu* hour (after 5:00 P.M.).

One of Guo Jianbo's men found an implement of bronze. It was shaped like an amphora with a square handle and an opening. No one recognized it. We thought that it might have been an implement used in earlier Feng and Shan rites. The person who found it was Yang Tong of Zhaoling in Runan.

We ascended to the east for another *li* or so until we came to the Mujia shrine. Mujia was a deity of the Martial Thearch's time. A little over one hundred paces to the northeast of this shrine, we reached the site where the Feng rite was to be performed. The First Illustrious Thearch of the Qin had erected a stele and a ceremonial gateway to the south; the Martial Thearch of the Han had his to the north of that. Some twenty paces beyond, to the extreme north of the area, we came to the round earthen platform to be used for our ritual. It was nine feet tall, square with rounded corners, and about thirty feet across. It had two stairways leading up to it that were forbidden to us ordinary mortals. His highness would ascend the easternmost stairway.

On top of the platform was a square altar of about twelve feet around, topped by the square stones. On the corners of the altar were the four massive stones mentioned previously, and there were four ceremonial arches on the four sides. We faced this altar and bowed repeatedly, announcing our presence.

Many people had placed offerings and money on the altar, and none of it was swept away. When the emperor eventually ascended to this altar, he encountered acrid pears and soured dates, hundreds of piles of coins, and even bolts of silk, all scattered about in disorder. When he asked the reason for this, the person in charge said: "Formerly, when the Martial Thearch was below Mount Tai preparing to ascend for the Feng and Shan rites, his officials ascended first to kneel and offer their respects. They scattered pears, dates, and money along the road, hoping to gain good fortune thereby. This is the same sort of thing."

His highness responded: "The Feng and Shan are important rites, which are to be performed only once every thousand years. Why should capped and belted officials of the kingdom act in such a fashion?" (The emperor's point is that his rite will naturally benefit all of his subjects. There is no need for anyone to seek extra blessings. Further, his officials should know better than to engage in such superstitious behavior.)

Seventy *li* up Mount Tai, we reached the summit to the southeast of Heaven's Gate, which is called "Solar Observatory." It is so named because when the cock first crows, one can see the sun just about to emerge. When the sun comes out, it seems to be about three feet across. Those looking toward the region of Qin might see as far as Chang'an; those looking toward Wu might see Mount Guiji; and those gazing toward Zhou might see as far as Qi. The Yellow River is over two hundred *li* from Mount Tai, but from the shrine it looks like a belt girdling the foot of the mountain.

To the south side of the mountain is a temple, entirely planted with one thousand cypress trees. The largest of these are fifteen or sixteen arm spans in circumference. Legend has it that these were planted by the Martial Thearch of the Han. On Lesser Heaven's Gate peak there are the "Five Grandee" pines.

When the Inaugural Illustrious Thearch of the Qin performed the Feng sacrifice on Mount Tai, he met with violent winds and rain squalls. He took shelter under these pine trees and, because they had ensured his safety, he appointed them the "Five Grandees."

To the northeast of the mountain is a stone chamber. South of the ritual platform is a jade basin with a jade tortoise inside. To the south of the mountain is the Elusive Spirits spring. Drinking of it, we found its waters to be clear and delicious. Its waters are said to be beneficial to one's health.

As the sun began to set, we descended. After we traveled down several times around the "encircling path," dusk fell and it began to drizzle. We could not see the path. We proceeded in file, sending one person out in front so that we had only to follow along by listening to his footsteps. Late in the night we reached safely the spot just below Heaven's Gate peak.

On the nineteenth (March 24), the emperor's procession reached the offices of the Supervisor of Forestry and Hunting. The emperor took up residence in a pavilion, while his officials spread themselves out in the fields. On this day, the clouds and vapors over the mountain took the form of a palace with lofty gateways. The officials all gathered to observe this.

On the evening of the twenty-first (March 26), when bullocks were sacrificed, the white, vaporous smoke, ten feet wide, rose to the southeast. It stretched as far as one could see and was extremely dense. At the time, the sky was completely clear and cloudless. According to the *Catalogue of Auspicious Signs of Heaven's Mandate (Ruiming pian),* favorable omens from Mount Tai all involve responses of the sun.

On the morning of the twenty-second, burnt offerings were presented to Heaven from the foot of Mount Tai when the sun was about twenty feet high. The smoke of these offerings went directly north.

Once these offerings were complete, all of the officials began to ascend the mountain in order. The Commandery had supplied three hundred wagons. These were to convey the most exalted officials—the Dukes, Princes, and Marquises—while the majority of the Chamberlains, Grandees, and lesser officials were to walk up the mountain. The emperor rode in the first wagon. All of the wagons were pulled up the mountain by men.

Upon reaching Midpoint Observatory, there was a brief rest before the ascent began again. It was midday when they reached the ritual site. In only a short while, all of the officials had taken up their positions. The emperor was on the ritual platform facing north. The Court Gentlemen Brave as Tigers took up positions with their halberds below the steps to the platform.

The Director of the Imperial Secretariat then presented the jade tablet and stone slats. He kneeled facing south. The Chamberlain for Ceremonials then said: "It is requested that you seal it." The Resplendent Thearch personally placed his seal on the tablet, then retreated to his original position. At this, over two thousand mounted warriors pulled open the two square stones atop the altar by pulling ropes attached to them from the spot where the Martial

Thearch's Feng rite had taken place. The Director of the Imperial Secretariat secreted the jade tablet inside and further held it in place with the stone slats. It was bound with cables of gold, sealed shut with a paste (of gold and quicksilver). Running from south to north there were two slats on each side and from east to west, three slats. Within the slats, the coffer formed by the sealing paste and the earth packed around it were green, red, white, and black—each according with the appropriate directions (east, south, west, and north, respectively).

Once this major portion of the rite had been completed, the Chamberlain for Ceremonials announced: "It is requested that you bow." At this, the Resplendent Thearch bowed repeatedly. The assembled officials all shouted "Ten thousand years!" with a sound that shook the mountain and valleys.

There was a white vapor of ten feet across that stretched from the southeast directly toward the altar. Also, from the altar, a blue vapor rose to Heaven. From a distance, the mountain peak was invisible. Those atop the peak were in the midst of this vapor and did not notice it.

A short while after the Feng ceremony was completed, the emperor ordered all the higher officials to descend in order. The emperor followed them. The several hundreds of lesser officials then began their descent, urging and pushing one another along. The ranks of officials stretched for over twenty *li.*

Since the path down had many narrow spaces, with deep valleys and cliffs of over a thousand feet high, those walking along behind would trip upon the ones in front who crawled through such dangerous spots. When those in front drew near to one of the torches [set out along the way], they would rise up. Further on, they would stop and the procession would bunch up again.

Those following along began to strike great rocks so that the rocks began to sound out noisily. But even though those making a racket with the rocks found no one to harmonize with them, they just could not control their excitement or keep silent. (Chinese court musical instruments included stone chimes, hung on racks. Ma is being sarcastic here. The music of such instruments would naturally be much more mellifluous than that produced by haphazardly striking stones, and there was certainly no court orchestra accompanying the officials' descent of the mountain.)

It was after midnight before the emperor reached the foot of the mountain. The various officials did not all arrive until the next morning. The elderly among them, when they had felt their strength give out and could no longer walk, had spent the night sleeping under the overhanging cliff faces.

Early in the morning of the following day, the Imperial Physician respectfully asked the emperor concerning his health. The emperor replied: "Yesterday we ascended and descended a mountain. When I wished to move forward, I was rushing those in front; when I wanted to rest, those behind stepped on my heels. The path was precipitous and dangerous. I was afraid that I could not pass through it, but I am unfatigued. There were those among the officials and underlings who lay exposed to the elements all night and had only water to drink, but not one of them fell, not one of them has become ill. Is this not the doing of Heaven? Mount Tai often has thunderstorms, but we have ascended and descended, offered burnt offerings, and completed the Feng rite atop the mountain, and all the while the weather has been clear and mild. Our achievements must be worthy that Heaven should respond in this fashion!"

On the next day, all the officials came to wish the emperor long life, but he ritually declined their congratulations. He curtailed the responsibilities of the hundred ranks of officials. Once this brief ceremony was concluded, he set out to spend the night at Feng gao, thirty *li* away. On the twenty-fourth (March 29), the emperor proceeded ninety *li* to Mount Liangfu, where he made offerings of cattle in the evening. On the next day, he accomplished the Shan sacrifice to Earth at the northern side of Liangfu. This is because one sacrifices to Heaven on the yang (southern side) of a mountain and to earth on the yin (northern side). In accordance with the old ritual regulations of the Inaugural Prime reign-period (86–80 B.C.E.), sacrifices were made to the High Thearch (the founder of the dynasty, Liu Bang) as an associate to Heaven; and to the High Overseer (his empress) as associate to Earth.

—25—

The Law of the Spirits

Valerie Hansen

In traditional China, as in most cultures, there was some uncertainty about what happened after death. Some Buddhist sects promised rebirth in a paradise, and Daoism, immortality to a chosen few. Still, the majority of the dead, it was thought, went to an underworld. There they retained the power to influence events on earth. If they wanted to hurt the living, they could play tricks, cause illness, provoke misfortune, or even bring death. Some of the deceased performed miracles and came to be worshiped as gods. The Chinese feared the dead, but they believed that they adhered to their own laws. The three readings below from the eleventh and twelfth centuries show how the living used the law of the spirits to protect themselves from the dangers that the dead posed.

The first document is a model tomb contract from *The New Book of Earth Patterns (Dili xinshu),* a government manual for siting graves initially published in 1071. Starting in the first century C.E., if not earlier, and continuing through to the twentieth century, some Chinese buried tomb contracts with the dead. Mimicking this-worldly contracts for the purchase of land, these contracts recorded the purchase of a grave plot from the earth gods. Tomb contracts were intended to ward off the dangers that resulted from penetrating deep into the earth to dig a grave. The practice seems to have peaked in the Song dynasty (960–1279), when the government paid for such contracts to be drawn up on behalf of dead officials. Just after the Song had fallen, Zhou Mi (1232–1298) said: "Today when people make tombs they always use a certificate to buy land, made out of catalpa wood, on which they write in red, saying: 'Using 99,999 strings of cash, we buy a certain plot, and so forth'" (Zhou Mi, *Guixin zashi* [Xuejin taoyuan edition], bieji xia 7a–b). Nine was an auspicious number, hence the figure 99,999. The money in these contracts was not real money, but spirit money (facsimiles of real money) that could be burnt. Not all contracts were written on catalpa wood. Hundreds of lead and stone tomb contracts have been excavated, and presumably more were written on cheaper materials, like paper or wood, that have since decayed.

The New Book of Earth Patterns was written at imperial order by a team of scholars, headed by Wang Zhu, who examined preexisting ritual manuals and then compiled this book. This manual was intended for official use, but commoners also consulted it, Wang Zhu tells us. In the section about tomb contracts, this book cites *The Spirit Code (Guilü)* to say that burial without using a tomb contract is tantamount to wrongful burial and very unlucky. The idea of a law code for spirits raises interesting issues: Why should spirits have a law code? Is it written down? What is its relation to human law? These questions are not easily answered, but the widespread use of tomb contracts reveals that many people believed (or hoped) that the spirits of the dead could be bound by contracts. The similarity of the contracts to this-worldly contracts also suggests that people thought the law of the spirits resembled earthly law.

Because *The New Book of Earth Patterns* spells out the many steps of an official funeral ritual, it describes the ritual context in which tomb contracts were used. The manual specifies that any official with the posthumous rank of lord or marquis and below (or any commoners paying for their own funerals) should have two iron contracts: one was to be placed in the temporary aboveground funeral structure and the other, buried in front of the coffin. Then a prayer was said. Once prayer was completed, the two copies of the contract were held together and the characters for agreement (*hetong*) were written on the seam where the two join. Borrowed from real life, this practice ensured that either the buyer or seller could check the authenticity of a contract by matching it with their copy to see if the characters met exactly. If they did, then the contract was authentic and the signatories were bound to honor it. If they did not, it was a forgery. At the end of the funeral, the participants took the iron contract in the temporary funeral structure and buried it in the ground. That was the gods' copy. The one at the foot of the coffin was for the master of the tomb, the dead official. He needed to have his copy with him in case he had a dispute in the underworld with the spirits of the dead about his ownership of his funeral plot.

The text of the model contract follows contemporary land contracts very closely. It gives the date of the transaction, here the date of the funeral, and the name of the buyer, the dead person, without naming the seller, the lord of the earth. As was true of land contracts, the dimensions of the plot are given in two ways: on a grid with the north-south and east-west axes, and by naming the neighbors, who were the animals who watched over the four directions. The price was the usual 99,999 strings of cash as well as five-colored paper offerings. The contract then specifies the consequences if the contract is violated: any spirits who return from the dead (read: to bother the deceased or his living kin) will be tied up and handed over to earl of the rivers. Like a land contract, the contract contains a clause saying it will take effect once the money and land have been exchanged, which in this case must mean when the paper money is burned at the funeral and the body interred. The contract ends with the names of the witnesses, who can serve as intermediaries should any disputes occur, and the names of the guarantors, who will make good the buyer's price should he or she fail to come up with the money. The mystical identities of the neighbors, witnesses, and guarantor mark this as a tomb contract. After the end of the contract comes an amendment specifically prohibiting the former occupants of the grave plot from approaching the dead. Only if they stay 10,000 *li* (a great distance) away can the deceased and his or her kin enjoy peace and good fortune. The contract ends by invoking the statutes and edicts of Nüqing, the emissary of the Five Emperors of the directions (north, south, east, west, and middle). These statutes and edicts are part of the spirit law code.

Of fifteen excavated contracts I have found that follow the model given in *The New Book of Earth Patterns,* eleven date to the Song. They show a surprising geographic range, which testifies to the wide circulation the manual enjoyed: to the west, from Xinjiang and Sichuan; to the north, from Shanxi and Shaanxi; in Central China, from Hebei, Henan, Hubei, and Anhui; and to the southeast, from Jiangsu, Zhejiang, Jiangxi, and Fujian. Most of these tombs contain lavish grave goods, suggesting the people who used this text were well-off.

The New Book of Earth Patterns does not explicitly mention the dangers the spirits of the dead pose to the newly dead or their living kin, but another text found in a tomb in Southeast China, in Jiangxi, does. The text is written on the eight-sided body of a cypress figure, which had a carved human head with ears, eyes, mouth, and nose. Dated 1090, the figure was found in the tomb of the eighth daughter of the Yi family, a woman from an important local family (according to her biography, which is only partially quoted in the excavation report). She was interred in a wood coffin enclosed in a stone coffin. With her were buried two pottery vases, a pottery figure, her biography carved on a stone plaque, porcelain plates, wooden combs, iron scissors, an iron knife, an iron stick, a copper mirror, a large ax, and some items of relatively high quality: a silver comb, two silver bracelets, and a pair of gold earrings. Clearly, this was an expensive burial.

This text presumes a different relationship with the spirits of the dead from that presumed in *The New Book of Earth Patterns.* Here there is no contract with the lord of the earth for the purchase of the grave. Instead a cedar figure is deputed by those who preside over the world of the dead to prevent any lawsuits against the dead woman's family. The text repeats the same phrases over and over in its list of who cannot be summoned or sued by those in the middle of the earth, that is, the spirits of the dead. It does not say what such a summons would result in, but presumably the people mentioned in the text—the dead woman's children, husband, siblings, family, and in-laws—would suffer some kind of misfortune or even death. Those in the middle of the earth also have the power to bring epidemics. And they can summon fields, silkworms, farm animals, and trees, and so cause havoc on people's farms. Because this text is designed to protect the dead and their descendants, its repetitious phrasing takes on the quality of an incantation. The cypress figure is the subterranean equivalent of a henchman whose job it is to prevent anyone from serving his mistress with a court summons.

The final text shows what happens when the underworld court issues a summons. It is an anecdote from a collection called *The Record of the Listener (Yijianzhi)*. From 1157 to 1202 an official named Hong Mai transcribed thousands of strange and unusual tales. Many of these tales, like the one translated here, are about people who visit the netherworld and come back. The Chinese word for death, *si*, means both to faint and to lose consciousness; many people had unusual visions when they fainted, which they recounted on awakening. The events and miracles Hong Mai describes may defy belief, but these were the kind of stories circulating in twelfth-century China, and Hong Mai often, as here, gives the name of the person who told him the anecdote. This source, then, can provide insight into the beliefs of common people in the Song dynasty, people who could not afford elaborate burials like those specified in *The New Book of Earth Patterns* or like that of eighth woman in the Yi family.

The anecdote begins with the facts of the case: how the debtor Mr. Lin bribed the clerks in the local court to frame the lender, Registrar Xia. The one person willing to speak out on Registrar Xia's behalf is Liu Yuan Balang. In his eloquent refusal to be bought off by Mr. Lin's underlings, he raises the possibility of a court in the underworld where wrongs can be righted. Registrar Xia then dies, after instructing his sons to bury all the relevant documents concerning Mr. Lin's unpaid debt, because he plans to sue in the underworld court. A month later Mr. Lin's eight underlings die. And Liu Yuan Balang has a premonition that he is going to be summoned to testify. Because he is convinced of his innocence, he does not fear that he personally has to stand trial, so he assures his wife that he will return after two or three days. And he loses consciousness.

The narrative resumes when he wakes up. He has indeed been summoned to the netherworld court to serve as a witness. When Liu Yuan Balang arrives, he sees that Registrar Xia has succeeded in his suit against Mr. Lin's eight underlings, whose necks are encased in a wooden frame called a cangue. Liu's account reveals much about the workings of the netherworld court, which are similar but not identical to those of a human court; in this vision, the presiding official is the king of the netherworld, not an underworld district magistrate. As on earth, he is served by clerks, who keep records and guide the prisoners from place to place. On hearing Liu's account, he awards him an extra ten years of life.

The king sits in judgment on the dead, who await their appearances before him in a kind of purgatory that Liu visits on his way out. There Liu sees people who have committed various offenses. They tell him they "borrowed" money, rent, and possessions, but in fact they stole them with no intent to return the goods. Now that they are awaiting trial, they claim to have borrowed the items. Some ask for money. Others ask their family members for merits; this reflects the Buddhist belief that merits accrued by one person for doing good deeds can be transferred to another. The king urges Liu to tell the living about his court, and then the runner who has accompanied Liu asks for a bribe. The always righteous Liu refuses, and he wakes up in this world when the clerk in the netherworld pushes him to the ground. The proof that he did indeed journey to the netherworld is twofold: his false topknot lies dislodged on his pillow, and he lives for an extra decade past eighty. The story concludes with Hong Mai's explanation of how he heard it.

The central theme in this story is justice. Registrar Xia is unable to obtain justice in human courts, but, as Liu Yuan Balang suspects, the underworld does have a court where wrongs can be righted. Many accounts of visits to the netherworld survive, and many tell of bureaucratic incompetence, of clerks who summon someone with an identical or a similar name by mistake. These people are then allowed to return to life. Strikingly, no one is ever punished in the subterranean court for a crime he or she did not commit. What about the real villain, Mr. Lin? The account does not reveal his fate, and the reader knows only that Registrar Xia is able to sue the eight underlings. Mr. Lin may be punished after he dies when he is tried before the king. Or perhaps he has already been punished, but Liu simply does not see him because he was not party to the bribery attempt.

The story about Registrar Xia and Mr. Lin illustrates exactly what the people who used tomb contracts and the cedar figure feared. Registrar Xia may be dead, but he is still able to bring charges against the living in the underworld court. He causes not only the deaths of the eight underlings but also their continued suffering in the afterlife. Other spirits had the same power to sue in underworld courts. Digging a grave is dangerous: one could unwittingly antagonize the previous owners, who could claim title to the plot. That was why people used tomb contracts. That was not the only danger. Once someone went before the underworld court, a host of charges could be brought against the deceased and their descendants based on their previous conduct. It was in order to block those charges that the eighth woman of the Yi family buried the cypress figure in her tomb.

The legalistic vision of the afterlife so evident in these three readings is striking and suggests that they are products of people thoroughly familiar with the earthly legal system. The model tomb contract in *The New Book of Earth Patterns* is like a contract to purchase land. The cedar person is like a henchman hired to prevent the issuing of summonses. And Registrar Xia encounters a court in the netherworld very much like the one in the human world—except that justice is done there.

The model tomb contract is from Wang Zhu, *Dili xinshu* (Beijing library Jin edition), 14:13a. The text written on a cedar figure is from Peng Shifan and Tang Changpu, "Jiangxi faxian jizuo BeiSong jinian mu," *Wenwu* 5 (1980): 29 (p. 35 photo). The tale from *The Record of the Listener* is from Hong Mai, *Yijian zhi* (Beijing: Zhonghua shuju, 1981), *zhiwu* 5:1086.

Further Reading

Valerie Hansen, *Changing Gods in Medieval China* (Princeton: Princeton University Press, 1990); Valerie Hansen, *Negotiating Daily Life in Traditional China: How Or-*

dinary People Used Contracts, 600–1400 (New Haven: Yale University Press, 1995), where an earlier version of the translation below appears. I would like to thank Victor Mair, Liu Xinru, and Bao Weimin for their help with these translations, and the late Anna Seidel for her many insights into the netherworld system of justice.

A MODEL TOMB CONTRACT FROM THE *NEW BOOK OF EARTH PATTERNS*

Blank year, month, and day. An official of blank title, named blank, died on blank year, month, and day. We have prognosticated and found this auspicious site, which is suitable for the grave, in this plain, in this district, in this county, and in this prefecture. We use 99,999 strings of cash as well as five-colored offerings of good faith to buy this plot of land. To the east and west, it measures so many steps, to the south and north, it measures so many steps. To the east is the green dragon's land, to the west the white tiger's, to the south the vermillion sparrow's, and to the north the dark warrior's.

The four borders are controlled by the imperial guard. The deputy of the grave mound and the earl of the tomb sealed it off by pacing the borders and the thoroughfares; the generals made orderly the paths through the fields so that for one thousand autumns and ten thousand years no spirit will return from the dead. If any dare to contravene, then the generals and neighborhood heads are ordered to tie them up and hand them to the earl of the rivers.

We have prepared meat, wine, preserved fruits, and a hundred types of sacrificial food. All these things constitute a contract of our sincerity.

When the money and land have been exchanged, the order will be given to the workers and carpenters to construct the tomb. After the deceased is peacefully buried, this will forever guarantee eternal good fortune.

The witness represents the years and months. The guarantor is the direct emissary of this day.

Bad ethers and heterodox spirits are not allowed to trespass. Those formerly living in the residence of the deceased must forever stay 10,000 *li* away. If any violate this contract, the main clerks of the earth government will be personally responsible for punishing them. The master of the tomb, and all his own kin and in-laws, whether living or dead, will enjoy peace and good fortune. Hastily, hastily, in accordance with the statutes and edicts of the emissary of the Five Directional Emperors, Nüqing.

A TEXT WRITTEN ON A CYPRESS FIGURE

On the twenty-second day of the sixth month of the fifth year of the Yuanyou reign (1090), Teacher Qiao Dongbao of the western region association of the

Five-Willow District, Pengze County, Jiang Prefecture, died and the grave of his late wife, the eighth woman of the Yi family, was relocated. The elders of the Haoli death precinct by Mount Tai, the envoy of the Celestial Emperor, and the emissary of the First Emperor's True Law, aware that the spirits disturbed by the relocation of the grave might call the living, issued an enlightened decree that one cedar person should cut off all summons and suits from the middle of the Earth.

If the eighth woman's sons and daughters are summoned, the cypress person should block the summons. If Teacher is summoned by name, the cypress person should block the summons. If her family is summoned, the cypress person should block the summons. If the siblings are summoned, the cypress person should block the summons. If the in-laws are summoned to testify, the cypress person should block the summons. If pestilence and plague are summoned, the cypress person should block the summons. If the fields or silkworms or the six domestic animals—horses, cattle, sheep, chickens, dogs, and pigs—are summoned, the cypress person should block the summons. If the first and second trees are summoned, the cypress person should block the summons. If the summoning does not end, the cypress person should block the summons. Quickly, quickly in accordance with the statutes and edicts.

A TALE FROM *THE RECORD OF THE LISTENER*

Registrar Xia of Ningbo and the wealthy Mr. Lin together bought a concession to sell wine in a government store. They sold the wine wholesale to other stores, who paid their share depending on how much wine they sold. After many years, Mr. Lin owed Register Xia two thousand strings of cash. Registrar Xia realized he would not get the money back so he sued Mr. Lin in the prefectural court. The clerks took a bribe and twisted his words to reverse the story so that Registrar Xia became the debtor. Prior to this Mr. Lin ordered eight of his underlings to change the accounts to show that he was in the right. Registrar Xia refused to change his story and was put in jail and beaten. Accordingly he fell ill.

In the prefecture lived a man named Liu Yuan Balang, who was generous and did not trouble himself over details, and who was upset by Registrar Xia's treatment. He proclaimed to the crowd, "My district has this type of wrongful injustice. Registrar Xia is telling the truth about the money from the wine but is miserable in jail. What is the point of prefectural and county officials? I wish they would call me as a witness, as I myself could tell the truth, which would definitely cause someone else to be beaten."

Lin's eight underlings secretly heard what he said and were afraid it would leak out and harm their case, so they sent two eloquent men who extended their arms to invite Liu to drink with them at a flagged pavilion, where they talked about the case and said: "Why are you concerning yourself with other people's affairs? Have some more wine." When the wine was done, they pulled out paper money with a face value of two hundred strings and gave it to Liu saying, "We know that your household is poor, so this is a little to help you."

Liu furiously replied, "The likes of you start with unrighteous intent and then bring an unrighteous case. Now you again use unrighteous wealth to try to corrupt me. I would prefer to die of hunger. I refuse even one cash of your money. This twisting of the straight and distortion of truth is definitely not going to be resolved in this world. If there is no court in the netherworld, then let the matter rest. If there is such a court, it must have a place where wrongs can be righted." Then he called the bar owner, "How much was today's bill?"

He said, "1,800 cash."

Liu said, "Three people drank together, so I owe six hundred." He suddenly took off his coat and pawned it to pay the bill.

After a while, Registrar Xia's illness worsened, and he was released from jail to die. As he was about to die, he warned his sons: "I die a wronged man. Place in my coffin all the previous leases for the wine concessions and contracts specifying each person's share so that I can vigorously sue in the underworld."

After just one month Mr. Lin's eight underlings abruptly died one by one.

After another month, Liu was at home when he suddenly felt shaky, and everything went dark. He said to his wife, "What I see is not good. It must be that Registrar Xia's case is being heard, and I'm wanted as a witness, so I must die. But since I have led a peaceful life with no other bad deeds, I probably will return to life, so don't bury my corpse for a period of three days. After that you can decide what to do." Late that night he lost consciousness.

After two nights he sat up with a start and said, "Recently, two government clerks chased me. We went about thirty miles and reached the government office. We encountered an official wearing a green robe who came out from a room in the hall. When I looked at him, I realized it was Registrar Xia. He repeatedly apologized and said, 'I am sorry to trouble you to come. All the documents are in good order, we just want you to serve as a witness briefly. It shouldn't be too taxing.' Then I saw Lin's eight underlings, all wearing one cangue that was five meters long and had eight holes for their heads.

"Suddenly we heard that the king was in his palace, and the clerks led us to the court. The king said, 'The matter of Xia's family needn't be discussed. Only tell me everything that happened when you drank wine upstairs.'

"I testified, 'These two men sent an invitation. Then we drank five cups of wine and bought three types of soup. They wanted to give me paper money with a face value of two hundred strings of cash, but I didn't dare accept it.'

"The king looked left and right, sighed, and said, 'The world still has good people like this. They really are important. We should discuss how to reward him, so let's take a look at his allotted lifespan.'

"A clerk went out and after a moment came back and said, 'A total of seventy-nine years.'

"The king said, 'A poor man doesn't accept money, how can we not reward him? Add another decade to his lifespan.'

"He then ordered the clerk who had brought me to take me to see the jail in the earth. Then I saw many types of people and prisoners in fetters. They were all from the city or the counties of my prefecture. Some bore cangues and some were tied up; some were sentenced to be beaten. When they saw me coming, one by one they cried out and sobbed. They then told me their names and addresses and asked me to return to the world to tell their families. Some said they had borrowed somebody's money, some said they had borrowed somebody's rent, some said they had borrowed somebody's possessions, and some said they had stolen people's land and harvest. They all asked their families to return their goods so as to lessen the sentences they had to serve in the underworld. Others asked for money and others for merit to be transferred by their relatives. I couldn't bear to look at them and turned away, and I still heard ceaseless sighs.

"As I went again to the palace, the king said, 'Since you have completed your tour, when you return to life, please tell each detail to the living, and teach them about the underworld court.' I bowed and took my leave.

"As I went out the gate, the clerk seeing me off wanted money, and I steadfastly refused. He berated me, 'For two or three days I have served you. How is it that you don't even say thank you? Moreover, give me 10,000 strings.' I again refused him saying, 'I myself have nothing to eat, so where am I going to get extra money for you?' The clerk then grasped and knocked off my topknot. He pushed me on the ground, and then I regained consciousness."

He rubbed his head, which was already bald, and his topknot lay between the pillows. Sheriff Wang Yi from Jinan, Shandong, lived in Ningbo at the time and himself saw that it was as told here.

Around 1180, Liu had his eightieth birthday, and he fell ill. Sheriff Wang went to see him and was very concerned. Liu said, "Sheriff, you needn't worry. I haven't died." Afterward he turned out not to be ill. He was probably counting the additional years the king of the netherworld had given him.

When he reached ninety-one, he died. Sheriff Wang is now the administrator of public order in Raozhou, Jiangxi. This story was told by Administrator Wang.

—26—

Shrines to Local Former Worthies

Ellen Neskar

A common view of Confucianism regards it not as a religion, but as a rational, ethical teaching based on fundamental human relationships. Religious elements or institutions, if at all acknowledged, are most often associated with either the family or the state and are thought to serve the interests of the bureaucratic hierarchy. Thus, for example, the family altars for ancestral worship and the state-regulated temples to Confucius promoted a stable social order and supported the prevailing state ideology. However, in the Han dynasty (202 B.C.E.–220 C.E.), Confucian scholars and local administrators living in the provinces began to build sacrificial shrines honoring exemplary men of the past. During the Song dynasty (960–1279), such "local former worthies shrines" emerged as an important religious institution among elites. Belonging to neither the family nor the state, these shrines represent a new level of communal and individual religion in Confucianism.

The worthies were "former" because they were men, not gods, who lived in historical times. Although some had lived hundreds or thousands of years earlier, most belonged to the very recent past, and some were honored only months after their deaths. They were "local" both because their shrines were built by local elites and administrators for the benefit of other local elites and, more importantly, because in life they had had some connection to the places where their shrines were founded. The most common connections were birth and official service in the region, but a visit to, or retirement in, the region might also suffice. And they were "worthy" because their lives and deeds manifested certain ideal virtues: compassion, humaneness, loyalty, erudition, and wisdom.

Few rules governed worthies' shrines: the classical Confucian ritual texts did not sanction them, and the central government was little involved or concerned with their spread. Local elites and administrators made all decisions concerning the shrines. The documents that follow all date to the Song dynasty, when worthies' shrines were becoming important. Because there was little precedent or tradition, some Song men attempted to establish conventions for shrine-building, standards or criteria for enshrinement and guidelines for the functions of and activities held in the shrines. The authors of our documents were trying to control or shape a growing phenomenon in the absence of central government regulation or clear guidance from the past.

The first document is a commemorative essay written by the famous Neo-Confucian philosopher Zhu Xi (1130–1200) to mark the founding of a shrine in honor of a certain Gao Deng (fl. 1127). Similar essays commemorated all manner of other projects: the establishment or repair of government schools and private academies, Buddhist and Daoist temples, bridges and granaries, prisons and examination halls. Such essays praised the founders of the project for their service to the community, the community for producing such diligent servants, and the subject of the essay—be it a bridge or a temple—for its value to the community. Since it was customary to inscribe the essay on a large stone stele and place it at the site of the project, the praise was designed as much to inform and inspire future generations as it was to commemorate the past.

Inscriptions written for worthies' shrines dwell on the life of the former worthy and are clearly eulogistic and hagiographic in nature. Authors tend to combine formulaic praise with detailed accounts of the worthy's life and deeds. Whether or not the material included in these essays provides a historically accurate rendering of the worthies' accomplishments and contributions to society, it can be argued that it does reflect the ideal self-image of the elites who promoted the shrines.

Zhu Xi's essay for Gao Deng's shrine is particularly important, for in it Zhu discusses the kinds of men who might be honored in shrines. Former worthies were men of widely varied roles and occupations. From the Han through the early years of the Song, most of those honored in shrines had empirewide reputations as statesmen and officials, military leaders, martyrs and imperial loyalists, or poets and prose writers. In his essay Zhu Xi argues for honoring a different kind of man.

Zhu opens by quoting Mencius on the ancient sages Bo Yi and Hui of Liuxia. Although Zhu cites only snippets, his readers would have known the whole of Mencius's argument. In several different conversations, Mencius distinguishes between the qualified sageliness of Bo Yi and Hui of Liuxia and the perfect sageliness of Confucius (see *Mencius*, 2A:2.22–28, 2A:9.1–3, 5B:1.1–7, 6B:6.2, and 7B:15.). Bo Yi was the "pure sage," willing to serve only a good ruler in times of order, but Mencius questioned his inflexibility. And although Hui of Liuxia was the "accommodating sage," willing to serve any kind of ruler in both times of order and times of disorder, Mencius worried about his lack of discrimination. Mencius did not worry about Confucius, for he was the "complete concert of sagehood," the "timely sage," whose actions were always in accord with time and circumstances. Mencius may have wished to follow the example of Confucius in his own life, but nevertheless he offers the ways of these qualified sages for others to follow.

Zhu Xi uses Mencius to provide a classical Confucian provenance for enshrining men who were not famous and were less than perfect. His central message is that there were many paths to virtue. Worth was to be judged neither by a high position in the government nor by occupation, but by success in cultivating humaneness and improving society. From the mid-twelfth century on, the repertoire of worthies grew to include men who had served at best in low-level local posts or who had lived their entire lives in retirement and relative obscurity. On occasion even Buddhist monks and Daoist priests were honored as former worthies. Gao Deng is typical of the men, of small political accomplishment and even lesser fame but of great personal virtue, who came to be enshrined in this period.

Zhu Xi's praise in fact focuses precisely on Gao Deng's outspoken criticism of government policies and his subsequent exile from court: in effect, on his political failure. Gao's unsuccessful career must be understood within the context of the factional struggles that rocked the Song state. In 1126 the foreign Jurchens had conquered the northern part of China, forcing the Song court to flee south. Court officials and elites tended to divide into two factions. Those who wished to pursue a policy of accommodation to the Jurchens supported the prime minister, Qin Gui, the antagonist of Zhu's essay. Those who wished to attack the Jurchens and retake the north followed the general Li Gang, also mentioned in the essay. Many of those who, like Zhu Xi, were later to become famous for creating the new philosophy we now know as Neo-Confucianism were affiliated, directly or by descent, with the prowar faction. Qin Gui's faction won the struggle and initiated a comprehensive purge of prowar agitators from court.

Zhu Xi notes that Gao had participated in the 1127 antigovernment demonstrations held by students at the national academy. A meeting with Qin Gui led to Gao's first demotion to a low-level position in local government office. While serving there, Gao was hounded by a superior in the prefectural government who supported Qin Gui. When the superior himself suffered persecution, Gao Deng rose to the post of examination official. True to his convictions, Gao used the opportunity to pose an exam question that, although somewhat oblique, criticized Qin Gui and the government's policies. For this he was stripped of all official rank and exiled to Rongzhou Prefecture, deep in the undeveloped and unpopulated south. Until his death, Gao lived in Rongzhou as a private teacher.

Although the traditional goal for most Confucians was to serve as adviser or minister to a ruler, the topos of the persecuted, unappreciated, or disaffected Confucian had a long and venerable tradition. Local worthies' shrines institutionalized this image. Gao Deng is representative of those who ran afoul of the government but were enshrined as local worthies. Local shrines turned victims into heroes and alienated officials into brave and staunch supporters of Confucian virtues: to have been exiled by a corrupt government was for many a true sign of worth.

During the Song the typical worthy changed from being a man of power and renown in the central government to a man whose fame did not depend on political rank or might even rest on the state's rejection of him. Local worthies, then, were not necessarily representatives of the central government, nor did they promote the prevailing state ideology. If we can use the worthies as a measure of elite self-image, we must conclude that the Song elite had swung from defining themselves in terms of their success at court to seeing themselves as the neglected talents or persecuted victims of a corrupt, faction-ridden government.

The second document is a legal judgment issued by a local magistrate, Mr. Hu, concerning a shrine honoring the famous general Zhuge Liang of the third century. The text is found in the *Pure and Clear Collection of Judgments by Famous Judges (Minggong shupan qingming ji)*, a collection of legal cases from the late thirteenth century. Magistrate Hu had at his disposal numerous sources dealing with earlier shrines, and he cites liberally from local histories and commemorative essays.

Unlike Zhu Xi's commemorative essay, Magistrate Hu's judgment is not a celebration of the virtue of a newly enshrined worthy. Rather, it addresses questions raised by a local sheriff concerning the propriety of an existing shrine. Unfortunately, the original complaint is not extant, and the exact circumstances surrounding the case remain unclear. As a result, some of the magistrate's comments on the sheriff's complaint are obscure. Yet the case is important because it raises general issues: What sort of connection must a worthy have to the place he is enshrined? Do sacrifices to former worthies comply with legal and ritual codes? How is a shrine appropriately furnished? What kind of rituals should be held in them? Who may participate in the rituals? While Magistrate Hu deals directly with these questions, he also discusses the more fundamental problem of distinguishing between licit and illicit sacrifices. And his final judgment offers a set of guidelines for establishing a proper or licit former worthy's shrine.

Magistrate Hu's definition of licit sacrifices comes from the canonical Confucian text, the *Record of Rites (Liji)*. There it is stated that sacrifices might properly be offered by emperors and nobles to natural forces, such as the wind and rain, to geographical landmarks, such as mountains and rivers, and to various worthy men who had in some way ensured the security and peace of their country. All these were to be entered in the *Sacrificial Statutes* of the state. In late imperial times, *Sacrificial Statutes,* or lists of licit sacrifices and shrines, were compiled by both the central and local governments. Shrines not included in these lists could be considered illicit and might be subject to closure by government officials.

Local worthies' shrines were not included in the *Sacrificial Statutes* compiled during the Song dynasty. Still, central government officials took no action against them, and local elites considered them licit. Those who built shrines interpreted the line from *Record of Rites* that reads "the various nobles may sacrifice to those of their own region" to mean that local administrators and elites might offer sacrifices to various natural forces and worthy men that were in some way connected to the region in which they were enshrined.

A local connection became the only quasi-objective requirement for the enshrinement of worthies. At first even Zhu Xi, one of the most prolific shrine-builders of the twelfth century, refused to commemorate a shrine honoring the three founders of his Neo-Confucian movement. Explaining his reluctance, Zhu Xi wrote:

> It is my view that the Way of the three masters is grand and marvelous. However, this county, Wuyuan, is neither their native home nor a place where they sojourned or served in office. Nor have they been given ranks in the *Sacrificial Statutes* of the prefecture. How might sacrificing to them comply with the ritual codes or be considered appropriate? (*Zhuzi daquan,* Sibu beiyao edition, 79:3a)

Magistrate Hu went to considerable lengths to verify Zhuge Liang's connection to Shaoling County, the location of the shrine at issue. According to the local histories, Shaoling had centuries ago been part of a larger territory that Zhuge had administered. Therefore, although Zhuge was not a native of the region, he had served there and might be offered sacrifices as a local worthy.

While the notion of a local connection might seem straightforward enough, it was open to various interpretations. Some even argued that especially worthy men might be honored in places to which they had no connection whatsoever. Magistrate Hu refers to one interpretation when he cites Su Shi's (1037–1101) analogy between spirits of the dead and water. Su had offered this analogy in an essay commemorating a shrine built in Chao Prefecture to honor the Tang literary figure Han Yu (768–824). Han Yu was not a native of Chao Prefecture, nor had he served in office there. He had, however, spent less than a year there in exile from the central government. The original Su Shi passage reads:

> Some say: "His excellency [Han Yu] was a thousand miles from his native country, and he was here in Chao Prefecture less than a year. If he were to have consciousness after death, he would not care about Chao Prefecture." I, Su Shi, say that is not right. His excellency's spirit is in the world as water is in the ground. There is no place it does not go. . . . It is as though one were to dig a well and find water and then say, "Here is the only place that there is water." How could that be right? (*Su Shi wenji,* Zhongguo gudian wenxue jiben congshu edition [Beijing: Zhonghua shuju, 1990], 17:509)

Despite Su Shi's claim for the universal presence and mobility of spirits, few Song men were willing to enshrine worthies in regions where they were not connected. Rather, this argument led only to a looser interpretation of the local connection and was used to strengthen claims for enshrining worthies whose local connection was somewhat tenuous.

Magistrate Hu clearly accepted Zhuge Liang as a legitimate, locally connected worthy. But he argues that, however legitimate a worthy's connection may be, any shrine or sacrifice to him that smacks of popular cults was to be considered illicit. Physical condition, the quality of sacrifices, and the manner in which they are offered are as important as the local connection is in deciding the legitimacy of a shrine. Therefore, he still considered the existing shrine and the sacrifices offered Zhuge inappropriate. A visit to the shrine horrified Magistrate Hu: it was built by a busy road; the statue of Zhuge was vulgar and sat in the midst of statues to various strange ghosts and spirits; and all manner of people freely visited the shrine to offer strange sacrifices and prayers.

The magistrate is typical of Song gentlemen who were concerned about the ease with which sacrifices to Confucian worthies, popular deities, and illicit spirits could be confused. He suggests that local devotees were treating Zhuge Liang as an efficacious popular god by offering him lively and sometimes improper prayers. Claiming that the spirit of Zhuge Liang could not be pleased by all this, the magistrate decided that something had to be done. And nothing less than a new shrine in a new location would do. The entire list of orders in his final judgment ensures that Zhuge Liang would be offered sacrifices in a location and manner befitting his stature as a former worthy.

Apparently, some prefects and local elites felt they had to be constantly vigilant to maintain physical and functional boundaries between shrines to worthies and shrines to popular deities. One problem, of course, was location. In principle, local worthies' shrines could be, and were, built almost anywhere—in government-sponsored schools and private Confucian academies, in government offices and examination halls, in pavilions on mountaintops, at town gates and crossroads, in Buddhist monasteries, in the old residences or study halls of the worthies. Often the site was chosen to commemorate a specific local connection. A man who had held an administrative post might be enshrined in his government office; another might be enshrined in the rooms where he had once studied. But elites found it difficult to control the shrines placed at city gates or along busy roads.

Like Magistrate Hu, Song men increasingly thought to solve this problem by moving shrines to the precincts of the local government schools. In late imperial China, local schools were the most important and visible institution associated with Confucianism. Since the Tang dynasty (618–907), the central court had mandated and funded the establishment of temples to Confucius in each prefectural and county school. Schools were already by design the site of state-sanctioned and legitimate sacrifices to Confucian sages and worthies. Shrines established in schools came under the jurisdiction of professors, students, and local administrators. In many cases they were perceived as extensions of the official temple to Confucius, and their worthies would share in the state-mandated sacrifices to Confucius held twice a year. Shrines built at miscellaneous sites could not share in this official and Confucian protection.

Clearly, the magistrate's judgment was an attempt to replace the existing shrine to Zhuge Liang with an appropriate and dignified local worthies' shrine. By associating Zhuge's shrine with the school and with other former worthies, he ensured that Zhuge would be revered as a former Confucian worthy. And by ordering that only the educated elite officiate at sacrifices and barring practitioners of popular religion from entering the shrine, he has reclaimed the worship of Zhuge Liang as the sole prerogative of the elite.

It seems that wherever shrines to worthies were built, dignity, restraint, and order were the guidelines. Although we have no sketches or floor plans of worthies' shrines, commemorative essays and prayers suggest that the ideal shrine was bright and spacious. Near the entrance were large stone steles inscribed with commemorative essays. Inside, the atmosphere was sober, and decorative furnishings sparse. Portraits of the worthies were drawn on silk and usually accompanied by eulogistic colophons. Worthies were represented by either spirit tablets or images molded out of clay or carved from wood.

The use of images was controversial. Some felt they were more the custom of Buddhists and Daoists than of Confucians. Others, like Magistrate Hu, complained that images would be vulgar and could be confused with those of popular deities. Still others argued that images depicted the worthies in undignified postures: they were made to sit on the bare ground, they sat cross-legged (like the Buddha), and they showed the soles of their feet beneath their skirts. During ceremonies, sacrifices of cooked foods, fruits, and wines were offered to the images or spirit tablets. Both Zhu Xi and Su Shi argued that the use of an image would give the impression that the worthies had to "creep and crawl [along the ground] to eat [the offerings]" (*Zhuzi daquan,* Sibu beiyao edition, 46:7b, 68:1b–2a). To prevent such indignities, they suggested that during each sacrificial ceremony the officiants temporarily place on the altar a plain wooden spirit tablet, inscribed with the worthies' names.

Portraits, on the other hand, were treated as a matter of course. They were to capture as true a likeness as possible and were to be drawn and mounted with dignity. A prayer offered to the famous Song literatus, Ouyang Xiu, says that "a portrait of his excellency [Ouyang] was drawn and hung in the school to celebrate his loyalty, to praise his heroism, to inspire later generations, and to move those who come here to pay obeisance to and revere him. His portrait is awesome; it is as though he were alive" (Li Geng, in *Ouyang Xiu xuan shiji,* Wenyuange siku quanshu edition, 7:13b). Whereas the spirit tablet or the image was the concrete focus of sacrificial offerings, portraits were to be contemplated as a means to understanding the essence of the worthy. For inspiration and to encourage thoughts of reverence, students were urged to "gaze upon the [worthies'] countenances" or "regard their comportment."

The religious ceremonies and sacrificial rites performed in the shrines were not codified or standardized. Varying from shrine to shrine, the offerings could include live animals, cooked meats, seasonal fruits, silk and cotton, tea, wine, incense, and the performance of music, dance, and prostrations. Generally, the sacrifices were offered by the community of elites as an act of thanksgiving and recompense: worthies were not asked to bestow favors or to act as intercessors for the benefit of individual petitioners. The first prayer in the third selection is typical of the prayers and sacrificial reports that were burnt as offerings on these public occasions. Often they expressed the hope that the spirits of the worthies would approach or descend, listen to the words of the prayer, and be satisfied with the offerings. Like this prayer, which was offered to ten worthies during a ceremony celebrating the renovation of their shrine, most were solemn. They praised the men for their exercise of virtue, which was a model for others, and thanked them for their benevolence on behalf of the local people.

The second prayer, which Zhu Xi addressed to Confucius, is more typical of those offered to the worthies by individuals during private visits to shrines. Although Zhu tells Confucius about a problem he was having with one of his students, he does not ask Confucius to solve the problem or to effect a change in the student. Rather, Zhu requests guidance in perfecting his own learning and furthering his own moral cultivation. One of the primary functions of the worthies was to act as models of moral excellence that would inspire elites to behave virtuously. Worthies were enshrined so that their virtuous example might continue to teach and inspire others in death as it had in life. When a shrine was located in a local school or private academy, obeisance or sacrifices were offered daily, bimonthly, or monthly by students and teachers. In these cases ritual obeisance to the worthies was incorporated into the regular curriculum of study and was an integral part of students' education in ritual forms of behavior. Students were exhorted to study the worthies' deeds and writings, gaze upon their portraits, and use the worthies as models. The shrines were meant to encourage local elites to emulate the virtue of the worthies and to aspire to attain the stature of a worthy in their own lives.

The translations are from Hong Hua, *Panzhou wenji (The Collected Works of Panzhou)*, Wenyuange siku quanshu edition, 71:10b–11a; *Minggong shupan qingming ji (Pure and Clear Collection of Judgments by Famous Judges)* (Beijing: Zhonghua shuju, 1987), pp. 542–43; and Zhu Xi, *Zhuzi daquan (The Complete Works of Master Zhu)*, Sibu beiyao edition, 79:22a–23b; 86:1b–2a.

Further Reading

John Shryock, *The Origin and Development of the State Cult to Confucius* (New York: Paragon, 1966); Rodney Taylor, *The Way of Heaven: An Introduction to the Confucian Religious Life* (Leiden: E. J. Brill, 1986); Thomas Wilson, *Genealogy of the Way: The Construction and Uses of Confucian Tradition in Late Imperial China* (Stanford: Stanford University Press, 1995).

Essay Commemorating the Sacrificial Hall to the Master Gao Dongxi at the Prefectural School in Zhangzhou

> Mencius said: A sage is the teacher of a hundred generations: this is true of Bo Yi and Hui of Liuxia. Therefore, when people hear of the character of Bo Yi, the corrupt become pure and the weak acquire determination. When they hear of the character of Hui of Liuxia, the mean become generous and the corrupt become honest. They distinguished themselves a hundred generations ago, and after a hundred generations, all those who hear of them are inspired.

Mencius's discussions of the two masters were detailed. He considered Bo Yi the "pure sage" and [Hui of Liuxia] the "accommodating sage." But he was still distressed by Bo Yi's narrow-mindedness and Hui's "insufficient respect." Moreover, since their ways were different from that of Confucius, Mencius did not wish to learn from them. Then one day he understood them and wrote these discussions. Afterward, people followed them as teachers of a hundred generations. Yet Confucius, in contrast, did not reach such [status]. Why?

Confucius's way was great and his virtue harmonious. Yet he left no concrete legacy. Therefore those who study to be like him try to "penetrate his doctrines" and "look up to him for their whole lives." Still it is not enough. The two masters were pure in their intentions; their conduct was eminent; and their legacy is clear. Therefore, those who admire them are suddenly moved to the point of excess. Thus, the merit of the two masters is truly not insignificant. Mencius's intentions can be understood.

In Linzhang there was a Master Dongxi, his excellency Gao. His given name was Deng and his courtesy name was Yanxian. During the Qinggang reign-period (1126) he studied at the Imperial University, where he joined his excellency Chen Shaoyang in the student demonstrations [calling for war against the invading Jurchens who had captured the north]. They sent up a memorial condemning the "six bandits" (six ministers who led the propeace government faction) and asking to retain Li Gang [leader of the prowar faction]. Those in authority did not want to mobilize the troops [against the Jurchens].

At the beginning of the Shaoxing reign-period (1131–1163), Gao was summoned to an audience in the Administrative Chambers. His discussion with the [propeace] prime minister, Qin Gui, was not suitable. So he was removed from his office and demoted to the post of vice prefect of Gu County in Qingjiang Prefecture, where he had an extraordinary administration. But the governor hoped to gain Qin Gui's favor, and he gathered a list of Gao's faults and turned the case over to the judiciary. It happened that the governor was himself slandered and died in jail. Subsequently, Gao Deng was released and summoned to examine *jinshi* degree candidates in Chaozhou. He made the students answer the policy question: Did the dreadful government policy of not listening to straightforward words cause the floods of the Min and Zhe rivers? He then gave up his commission and returned home. When Qin Gui heard of the exam question he was extremely angry. He removed Gao from office and exiled him to Rongzhou.

His excellency Gao's learning was extensive and his conduct eminent. In written essays he liberally explained [his points] and in discussions he gave illustrations. The whole day long, like a torrent, he spoke of nothing but being a filial son and loyal minister and of sacrificing one's life in favor of righteousness. Those who heard him were in awe; their souls were moved and their spirits lifted. When he was in Gu County, students were already fighting to come to him. And when he was here in Rongzhou, his disciples were indeed numerous. When he became ill, he wrote his own tomb inscription and summoned the students who had studied with him to give his parting words. He sat up straight, folded his arms, smoothed his whiskers, opened his eyes, and died. Alas! He can indeed be called a hero of his generation.

Gao's learning and conduct were not entirely in accord with that of Confucius. Still, the eminence of his purpose and actions indeed merit his being considered the "pure worthy." Those who hear of his character after one hundred generations will have the principles to purify the corrupt and make the weak determined. How can we speak of his merit as a teacher of the age in the same breath as we speak of those who styled themselves followers of Confucius's harmonious conduct but who tolerated everything and covered up for each other?

More than twenty years after Gao died, Mr. Tian Dan of Yanping became professor at the prefectural school. He sought out Gao's extant writings and had them carved on woodblocks. He also had a portrait of Gao made and performed sacrificial offerings to him in order to inspire and discipline the students. In the course of this he [sent a letter to me] via Mr. Wang Yu, a native of the prefecture. He wanted a piece of writing as a commemorative record. I was ill and before I got around to it, Mr. Tian left Rongzhou. When the present prefect, Mr. Lin Yuanzhong of Yongjia, arrived, he and Mr. Wang sent off another letter urging me not to put it aside. I felt that my base writings truly could not match his honor Gao's outstanding integrity and his venerable determination. For a long time I used my illness as an excuse. But they forcibly roused me to write it. Yet my words do not come up to my intentions. Mr. Lin has ventured to have it inscribed on stone and placed into the wall of the shrine.

May the students of Zhangzhou and all scholars from the four directions who come here on business read them and truly be deeply moved and inspired.

Written in the ninth month of autumn of the fourteenth year of the Qunxi reign-period (1187) by Zhu Xi of Xin'an.

Former Worthies Ought Not to Be Mixed with Weird Spirits and Cruel Ghosts

The abundant virtue of Zhuge Liang—is it Mr. Wang Tong alone who dares not forget it? Across a thousand years, what loyal minister or gentleman of determination can hear of his spirit and not be inspired? Whenever I read his two reports on his military campaign, I close the book and shed tears over it. If the underworld could rise, I would be happy even to hold the whip and drive his carriage. How could I grudge a room of one beam to offer him sacrifices for a hundred generations? Furthermore, on examining the records of the [ancient kingdom of Sichuan], I find that when Zhao Lie commanded Jingzhou, Zhuge Liang, as army supervisor and leader of Court Gentlemen, concurrently supervised the three commanderies of Lingling, Guiyang, and Changsha. At that time, Shaoling County was still attached to Lingling. His carriage wheels and horses' hoofs may well have passed often through this spot. Is this not sufficient reason to enshrine him and offer him sacrifices here?

However, today I have examined the shrine that has been set up alongside the road, all grimy amid the hustle and bustle. Is this adequate as a cottage for peaceful repose? The sculpted image is dirty and vulgar, utterly lacking [Zhuge's] heroic demeanor, his whistling and singing. Moreover, [images of] weird spirits and cruel ghosts are mixed in fore and aft [on the altar], while hayseeds and country bumpkins stand half-naked to the left and right. Even supposing the sacrificial animals were fat, the ritual vessels fine and pure, and the officiant of the rites rose up strong and tall to make the sacrifices, ghosts of mere horse-doctors and peasants of the summer fields can still come and spit on him. Can we say that Zhuge Liang would enjoy it? The county sheriff's report acknowledges one part of this but not the other. He is particularly wrong when, based on the precedent of offering Zhuge joint sacrifices [nationally] in the military schools, he argues that [separate local] sacrifices should not be offered in the region of Sichuan.

[According to the classical *Record of Rites,*] he who possess the realm [i.e., the emperor] sacrifices to the hundred spirits: from Heaven, Earth, the four directions, the famous mountains and great rivers, to all who virtuously benefited the people, died in diligent service, labored to stabilize the state, ably warded off great disasters, and forestalled great worries—these are all recorded in the *Sacrificial Statutes.* The various noble lords may sacrifice only to those of their region: those in Jin sacrificed to the Yellow River, in Lu to Mount Tai, in Chu to the Sui, Zhang, and Han rivers. To sacrifice to those one ought not sacrifice to is called illicit sacrifice and brings no fortune.

Today it is said, "whom the emperor sacrifices to, all in the realm may sacrifice to." The sacrificial ordinances of the Three Dynasties [the Xia, Shang, and Zhou], I fear, were not like this. Some say, "since his excellency's spirit is in the realm as water is in the earth, then there is no place it does not go"; and indeed one may find this in a discussion by Su Shi. At the time [Su Shi wrote this], the people of Chao Prefecture had built a new temple to the south of the prefectural city in honor of Han Yu. It took a full year to complete. One may imagine the [propriety] of its construction, from its ridge pole above to the walls below. Although [the spirits of] the wise and upright do not care about red columns and carved pillars, still such people "have become the stars and planets in Heaven and the rivers and mountains in Earth." Even if those below fast and purify themselves and don their richest clothing in order to offer them sacrifices, I still fear they would be unable to cause the spirits to approach. If the temple building and the fasting chamber are rained on from above and blown by the wind from the sides; if the sacrificial animals are lean and the sacrificial wine sour; if the ritual vessels are only temporarily placed; and if the libationer's rising and bowing does not fit the proper forms, then even though Han Yu be called a spirit of the South Sea (present-day Hainan), he would not be willing to enjoy the offerings.

Now when the county sheriff speaks of Zhuge's spirit, he is probably referring to this [precedent]. But I do not know how the shrine in Shaoling compares to that temple in Chao. Zhuge once had a shrine in Hengyang, on the Zheng River. During the Qiandao reign-period (1165–1173), the Ever-Normal Intendant, Mr. Fan Chengxiang, went searching for its old ruins and found an abandoned building in the midst of a wild overgrowth. He then moved it to a bright and high spot and had it entirely rebuilt. Zhang Shi wrote a piece to commemorate the affair. That being so, could they have been lax in the plans for the shrine's appearance?

Now the county sheriff wishes to preserve this [building] in order to convey his reverence, but he does not understand that its unkempt condition can not be countenanced either.

Judgment: I have undertaken to tour the inner and outer precincts of the city to determine whether or not there is another shrine to Zhuge Liang. If there is not another, then I will order artisans to seek a true likeness and draw a copy using one piece of fine silk. In the second month of spring and autumn I will offer sacrifices at the shrine to the former worthies in the prefectural school. This will ensure that all those [spirits] who dwell with [Zhuge] day and night will be the highest disciples [of Confucian learning]. The class of confused and malicious spirits will not get to wreak their havoc [upon Zhuge], those who officiate at the spring and autumn sacrifices will all be noble men who wear the officials' cap and the jade belt, and the sorcerers and exorcists of strange and malicious spirits will not get to creep into [the shrine]. If we do all this, then perhaps [Zhuge's] spirit will have no cause for shame. All existing vulgar shrines are to be destroyed. I have hung a notice on the sight.

Sacrificial Prayers and Reports

A PIECE FOR THE SACRIFICE TO THE TEN WORTHIES

In the northeast corner of the Yucheng there was a building in which several columns were arrayed with the portraits of ten prefects from the Jin and Tang dynasties. All were purely upright and were good administrators. They may act as models for those to come in the future. Generation after generation ought to sacrifice to them without shame. It happened that there was a typhoon and the roof tiles flew off and the ridge pole snapped. This was contrary to the idea [in the *Classic of Poetry*]: "Do not hew the sweet pear tree [under which Prince Shao sat]." After I rebuilt the parapet, I repaired the shrine and set up portraits. On an auspicious day I set out the sacrificial animals and wine and performed repeated prostrations to please their spirits. The spirits are regarded today as they were in the past. Eternally, they protect our people. They cause those who follow in their footsteps to be without fault in their official duties. Thus, the way we repay them is ever more reverential.

SACRIFICIAL REPORT TO THE FORMER SAGE ON DISMISSING A STUDENT

I am an unworthy and ordinary man. But the students have selected me to be an official in this county. In that capacity, I have managed the school's affairs, but my behavior and ability are so meager and my governing and teaching are not to be trusted. Among the students under my direction, there is a certain Mr. X, who was put in charge of cleaning the toilets because of his bad behavior. I believe that since I have not carried out the Way myself, I have been unable to lead and hone others and have allowed matters to come to this. Moreover, as I was not able to establish proper regulations early on, I controlled him by suppression. As a result, both virtue and regulations were lax, and ultimately disobedient gentlemen had no restrictions. Therefore, I am reporting to the former sage and former teacher [Confucius] to request that I may rectify the school's rules and shame the students by making punishments clear. By raising the two rods in teaching, one receives their awe and steadfastness. The former sage and former teacher said that the way to pass laws down to later generations was through the proper running of schools. If the former sage and former teacher approaches and resides above, dare I not clasp my hands [in prayer] and knock my head to the ground?

—27—

The Scripture in Forty-two Sections

Robert H. Sharf

The Scripture in Forty-two Sections (Sishi'er zhang jing) is a short collection of aphorisms and pithy moralistic parables traditionally regarded as the first Indian Buddhist scripture to be translated into Chinese. There are, in fact, good reasons to question the purported Indian origins of this scripture—it may well have been compiled in Central Asia or even China. Moreover, all versions of the text that have come down to us show signs of later revision at the hands of medieval Chinese editors. Nevertheless, most scholars believe that the original *Scripture in Forty-two Sections,* whatever its origins, was indeed in circulation during the earliest period of Buddhism in China.

According to tradition, the *Scripture in Forty-two Sections* was translated at the behest of Emperor Ming of the Han dynasty (r. 58–75 C.E.). The earliest surviving account of the story runs as follows: One night Emperor Ming had a dream in which he saw a spirit flying around in front of his palace. The spirit had a golden body, and the top of his head emitted rays of light. The following day the emperor asked his ministers to identify the spirit. One minister replied that he had heard of a sage in India called "Buddha" who had attained the Way and was able to fly. It seemed that the spirit observed by the emperor must have been he. Thereupon the emperor dispatched a group of envoys led by Zhang Qian who journeyed to Yuezhi (Scythia?) and returned with a copy of the *Scripture in Forty-two Sections.* The text was later deposited in a temple.

There is considerable debate among scholars concerning the date of this legend. The brief account given above is found in an early preface to the *Scripture in Forty-two Sections* that may date to the middle of the third century C.E. The story was considerably embellished in time, and at least one glaring anachronism was removed. (Zhang Qian, the leader of the envoys, was in fact a historical figure who went to Bactria in the second century B.C.E., and thus his name is omitted in later renditions.) Sources disagree as to the date of the departure (given variously as 60, 61, 64, 68 and C.E.), the return date (64 to 75 C.E.), and the destination of the envoys (some versions mention India rather than Yuezhi). While the "Preface" makes mention only of the scripture, a fifth-century source reports that the envoys managed to secure the famous Udayana image of the Buddha as well. (See chapter 19 in this volume.) In the fifth and sixth centuries we also begin to find mention of two Indian monks, Kāśyapa Mātaṅga and Dharmaratna, who return with the Chinese envoys, and by the medieval period these monks are regularly cited as cotranslators of the scripture. Finally of note is another relatively late tradition that has Emperor Ming build the first Chinese Buddhist temple—the Baimasi at Luoyang—as a residence for the two Indian translators. This temple became an important center for the translation of Buddhist texts for centuries to come.

Despite questions concerning the date and authenticity of the legend, scholars are generally agreed on two points: (1) Buddhism was introduced into China *prior* to the traditional dates given for the "dream of Emperor Ming," and (2) some form of the *Scripture in Forty-two Sections* did in fact exist in the Eastern Han dynasty (25–220 C.E.). Evidence for the first point comes from both art-historical remains and casual references in Han historical sources, while the second point can be deduced from a passage in a memorial presented to Emperor Huan by the scholar Xiang Kai in 166 C.E. In a long diatribe against the moral abuses of the court, Xiang Kai criticizes the emperor for venerating saints but failing to emulate them:

> Moreover I have heard that altars have been established for Huanglao and the Buddha within the palace. Their Way is that of purity, emptiness, and reverence for nonaction. They value life and condemn killing. . . . Since your Majesty has deviated from this teaching, how can you hope to obtain its rewards? . . . The Buddha did not pass three nights under the [same] mulberry tree; he did not wish to remain there long, for this would give rise to attachment and desire. That was the perfection of his essence. A deity sent him a beautiful maiden but the Buddha said: "This is nothing but a leather sack filled with blood," and he paid no further attention to her. His concentration was like this, and thus he was able to realize the Way.

Xiang Kai was likely referring to some early form of the *Scripture in Forty-two Sections;* compare the quote above with section 2 of the scripture: "Taking a single meal at midday, and lodging a single night under a tree, [*a śramana*] takes care not to repeat either." And the anecdote concerning the gift of the maiden to the Buddha may well have been derived from section 24: "A deity presented a woman of pleasure to the Buddha, wanting to test the Buddha's will power and examine the Buddha's Way. The Buddha said: 'Why have you come here bearing this leather sack of filth? Do you think to deceive me? . . . Begone! I have no use for her.'"

In addition to evidence provided by Xiang Kai's memorial, there are stylistic and linguistic features that mark this work as one of the earliest Buddhist texts in China (notably the archaic transliterations used throughout the work). Yet the text remains somewhat of a mystery: it bears none of the characteristics of a formal sūtra, and no Sanskrit, Tibetan, or Central Asian versions are known to exist. Indeed; it seems that it was not originally considered a sūtra in the formal sense of the word at all: early Buddhist catalogues refer to it simply as "Forty-two Sections from Buddhist Scriptures," or "The Forty-two Sections of Emperor Xiao Ming." Such titles are in fact appropriate, as the text consists largely of snippets culled from longer Buddhist sūtras scattered throughout the Buddhist canon. (Parallel sections are found in the *Dīgha, Majjhima, Saṃyutta,* and *Aṅguttara Nikāyas,* as well as the *Mahāvagga.*) But while we can identify the source of many of the forty-two sections, scholars have yet to determine whether the collection was first assembled in India, Central Asia, or China.

We also know little about the role the scripture played in the propagation of early Buddhism. At first glance the *Scripture in Forty-two Sections* appears to be a sort of handbook or introduction to basic Buddhist terms and principles for the benefit of novices. Yet this view is not without its problems; one cannot help but notice, for example, the many technical terms and allusions that go unexplained in the text, such as the "nineteen heavens," the "three honored ones," the "three poisons," and the "five hindrances." This might suggest that it was intended for Buddhist adherents rather than for neophytes, or that it was meant to be used in conjunction with oral teachings (as was often the case with Chinese Buddhist texts).

In order to appreciate the place of the *Scripture in Forty-two Sections* within the Chinese Buddhist world, it might be useful to turn for a moment to the much better known Pāli compilation, the *Dhammapada* (*Verses on the Teachings*). Although considerably longer (423 verses), the *Dhammapada* is similar insofar as it provides a general and attractive overview of the ethical teachings of Buddhism. It too consists primarily of extracts culled from the most popular Pāli literature, and like the *Scripture in Forty-two Sections* it consists largely of short aphorisms and parables. The *Dhammapada* is widely employed as a handy summary and reminder of the Buddha's teachings, to which the pious may refer for inspiration or solace. It is also commonly used to provide themes for sermonizing. And even today, despite copious references to technical Buddhist doctrines, the *Dhammapada* is widely used as a vehicle for the dissemination of Buddhism into non-Buddhist cultures.

It is quite possible that the *Scripture in Forty-two Sections* was compiled in the early days of Chinese Buddhism with a similar range of functions in mind. In fact, it has been put to such use in this century. Shaku Sōen (1859–1919), the first Japanese Zen master to visit and teach in the West, used this scripture as the basis of a series of talks given during a tour of America in 1905–1906. And John Blofeld, a Western convert to the religion who devoted his energies to the transmission of Buddhism to the West, chose this scripture as the first to be translated in a series begun in 1947. Although the tenets of the scripture are not presented in any systematic way, the simplicity and brevity of the work make it suitable for use as an introductory text.

Whether initially compiled in India, Central Asia, or China, the version of the *Scripture in Forty-two Sections* disseminated in East Asia bears certain unmistakably

Chinese stylistic features. The most obvious Sinitic touch is the phrase "The Buddha said," which is used to introduce most sections. This peculiarity, along with the decidedly moralistic tone of the work, is strongly reminiscent of certain Confucian classics, such as the *Classic of Filial Piety* (*Xiaojing*) and the *Analects* (*Lunyu*). Both texts are similarly comprised of short moralistic maxims and illustrative anecdotes, many of which are prefaced with the phrase "the Master said."

Beyond this rather obvious stylistic adaptation there are a few passages that are most certainly interpolations by a Chinese editor. One obvious example is found in the earliest extant edition of the text, namely, that now found in the Korean Canon. The key passage is found at the end of section 9:

> Feeding one billion saints is not as good as feeding one solitary buddha (*pratyekabuddha*). Feeding ten billion solitary buddhas is not as good as liberating one's parents in this life by means of the teaching of the three honored ones. To teach one hundred billion parents is not as good as feeding one buddha, studying with the desire to attain buddhahood, and aspiring to liberate all beings. But the merit of feeding a good man is [still] very great. It is better for a common man to be filial to his parents than for him to serve the spirits of Heaven and Earth, for one's parents are the supreme spirits.

Recent work on Indian Buddhist inscriptions has shown that filial piety was not an exclusively East Asian concern, but played an important role in Indian Buddhism as well. But the phrasing and context of the references to filial piety in this passage marks it as a Chinese insertion.

Another interesting example of the "sinification" of the work is the regular use of the word *dao* ("way" or "path") as a translation equivalent not only for *mārga*, for which it is a standard and appropriate semantic equivalent, but also for what one suspects would be *nirvāṇa* ("extinction") or *dharma* ("teachings" or "truth") in an Indic original. This is characteristic of early translations influenced by Daoist and "dark learning" (*xuanxue*) ideas, and it lends a distinctly Chinese "mystical" tone to what is otherwise a moralistic Hīnayānist work. I have translated *dao* as "Way" whenever possible to preserve some of the flavor of the Chinese.

One area in which this translation departs from the original Chinese is in the handling of Sanskrit terminology. In the interests of clarity I have translated most of the technical terms that are merely transliterated in the Chinese. (The one exception is the term *śramaṇa*—used throughout the text to refer to ascetics and ordained followers of the Buddha—where I have retained the Sanskrit.) While some of the terms, such as *śramaṇa, arhat,* and *śrotāpanna,* are briefly explained in the opening paragraphs of the text, others, including *upāsaka* and *pratyekabuddha,* are not explained at all. It must be kept in mind that the transliteration of foreign terms is an awkward process in Chinese that often yields unwieldy and bizarre-looking polysyllabic compounds. The copious use of such transliterations, many of which go unexplained, would have lent the text a decidedly exotic character.

This translation of the *Sishi'er zhang jing* is based on the edition found in the Korean Tripiṭaka (K 778:19.865–67). The Korean text, which is reproduced with little alteration in the *Taishō daizōkyō* (T 784:17.722a–24a), is in turn based on the Shu Tripiṭaka published under the Northern Song. While the Korean version of the *Scripture in Forty-two Sections* represents an earlier recension than either the "Shousui" text compiled in the Song (the most popular version of the scripture, although it is also the most "corrupt") or the "Zhenzong" edition (the edition reproduced in the *Nanzang* Tripiṭika of the Ming and all subsequent Chinese collections), even the Korean text shows traces of later redaction when compared with early citations found in pre-Tang works. I have also consulted the commentary by Emperor Zhen Zong of the Song dynasty (r. 998–1022), the *Zhu sishi'er zhang jing* (T 1794:517a–522c), as well as the Japanese translation by Fukaura Masafumi in the *Kokuyaku issaikyō, kyōjūbu* 3, pp. 169–73. The excerpt in the introduction taken from Xiang Kai's memorial is found in fascicle 60b of the *Houhan shu.*

Further Reading

Discussions in English of the dating and significance of the *Scripture in Forty-two Sections* can be found in T'ang Yung-t'ung, "The Editions of the Ssu-shih-erh-chang-ching," *Harvard Journal of Asiatic Studies* 1 (1936): 147–55; E. Zürcher, *The Buddhist Conquest of China: The Spread and Adaptation of Buddhism in Early Medieval China* (Leiden: E. J. Brill, 1959), pp. 29–30; Kenneth Ch'en, *Buddhism in China: A Historical Survey* (Princeton: University of Princeton Press, 1964), pp. 29–36; Henri Maspero, *Taoism and Chinese Religion,* translated by Frank A. Kierman, Jr. (Amherst: University of Massachusetts Press, 1981), pp. 400–404; and Tsukamoto Zenryū, *A History of Early Chinese Buddhism from Its Introduction to the Death of Hui-yūan,* translated by Leon Hurvitz (Tokyo: Kodansha, 1985), vol. 1, pp. 41–50. For English translations of later editions of this scripture, see Samuel Beal, *A Catena of Buddhist Scriptures from the Chinese* (London: Trūbner, 1871), pp. 188–203; D. T. Suzuki, *Sermons of a Buddhist Abbot* (New York: Samuel Weiser, 1906), pp. 3–21; and John Blofeld, *The Sutra of 42 Sections and Two Other Scriptures of the Mahayana School* (London: Buddhist Society, 1947), pp. 10–22.

The Scripture in Forty-two Sections

Translated in the Later Han dynasty by the *śramaṇas* Kāśyapa Mātaṅga and Dharmaratna of the Western Regions.

1. The Buddha said: "Those who leave their families and go forth from their homes to practice the Way are called *śramaṇas* (ascetics). Those who constantly

follow the 250 precepts in order to [realize] the four noble truths and progressively purify their intentions will become saints (*arhat*). A saint is able to fly and assume different forms; he lives a long life and can move Heaven and Earth. Next is the nonreturner (*anāgāmin*): at the end of his life the spirit of a nonreturner ascends the nineteen heavens and there attains sainthood. Next is the once-returner (*sakṛdāgāmin*): the once-returner ascends [to Heaven] once and returns once and then attains sainthood. Next is the stream-winner (*śrotāpanna*): the stream-winner dies and is reborn seven times and then attains sainthood. The severance of passion and desire is like the four limbs severed, they will never be used again."

2. The Buddha said: "Those who shave their heads and faces are *śramaṇas*. They receive the teaching, abandon worldly wealth and possessions, and beg, seeking only what is necessary. Taking a single meal at midday, and lodging a single night under a tree, they take care not to repeat either. That which makes men ignorant and derelict is passion and desire."

3. The Buddha said: "All beings consider ten things as good and ten things as evil. Three concern the body, four the mouth, and three the mind. The three [evil things] of the body are killing, stealing, and adultery. The four of the mouth are duplicity, slander, lying, and lewd speech. The three of the mind are envy, hatred, and delusion. He who lacks faith in the three honored ones [the Buddha, the teaching, and the community of monks], will mistake falsehood for truth. A lay disciple (*upāsaka*) who practices the five precepts [not to kill, to steal, to commit adultery, to speak falsely, or to drink alcohol], without becoming lax and backsliding, will arrive at the ten [good] things [i.e., the antitheses of the ten evil things] and will certainly attain the Way."

4. The Buddha said: "If a man commits multiple transgressions, yet does not repent and quickly quell the [evil] in his heart, his crimes will return to him as water returns to the sea, becoming ever deeper and wider. But should a man come to realize the error of his ways, correct his transgressions, and attain goodness, his days of wrongdoing will come to an end and in time he will attain the Way."

5. The Buddha said: "Should a man malign me and seek to do me harm, I counter with the four virtues of benevolence, [compassion, joy, and equanimity]. The more he approaches me with malice, the more I reach out with kindness. The forces (*qi*) of beneficent virtue lie always in this, while harmful forces and repeated misfortune will revert to the other."

6. Once a man heard that the Buddha's Way lies in persevering in benevolence and compassion, and meeting evil with goodness. He then came and cursed the Buddha. The Buddha, remaining silent, did not respond, but rather had pity for one whose ignorance and rage led to such an act. When his cursing abated the Buddha asked him: "If you offer a gift to someone who does not

accept it, what happens to the gift?" The man replied: "I would have to take it back." The Buddha said: "Now you have offered me curses but I do not accept them. They return to you, bringing harm to your own person. Like an echo responding to sound, or a shadow following an object, in the end there is no escaping it. Take heed of your evil ways."

7. The Buddha said: "An evil man trying to harm a worthy man is like looking toward Heaven and spitting; the spittle will not befoul Heaven but will return and befoul the one spitting. It is like throwing filth at someone while facing into the wind; the filth will not befoul anyone else but will return and befoul the one throwing. A worthy man cannot be harmed; a man's transgressions will surely destroy only himself."

8. The Buddha said: "The virtue of one who practices universal love, compassion, and generosity for the sake of the Way is not that of great generosity. But if he [further] guards his intentions and honors the Way, his merit is truly great. If you see someone practicing generosity and you joyfully assist him, you too will gain merit in return." Someone asked: "Would not the other person's merit be diminished thereby?" The Buddha said: "It is like the flame of a single torch that is approached by several hundred thousand men each bearing torches. Each lights his torch from the flame and departs, using it to cook food and dispel darkness, yet the original flame is ever the same. Merit is also like this."

9. The Buddha said: "Feeding one hundred common men is not as good as feeding one good man. Feeding one thousand good men is not as good as feeding one who observes the five precepts. Feeding ten thousand men who observe the five precepts is not as good as feeding one stream-winner. Feeding one million stream-winners is not as good as feeding one once-returner. Feeding ten million once-returners is not as good as feeding one nonreturner. Feeding one hundred million nonreturners is not as good as feeding one saint. Feeding one billion saints is not as good as feeding one solitary buddha (*pratyekabuddha*). Feeding ten billion solitary buddhas is not as good as liberating one's parents in this life by means of the teaching of the three honored ones. To teach one hundred billion parents is not as good as feeding one buddha, studying with the desire to attain buddhahood, and aspiring to liberate all beings. But the merit of feeding a good man is [still] very great. It is better for a common man to be filial to his parents than for him to serve the spirits of Heaven and Earth, for one's parents are the supreme spirits."

10. The Buddha said: "There are five difficult things under Heaven. It is difficult for the poor to give alms, it is difficult for the powerful and privileged to cultivate the Way, it is difficult to control fate and avoid death, it is difficult to attain a glimpse of the Buddha's scriptures, and it is difficult to be born at the time of a buddha."

11. There was a *śramaṇa* who asked the Buddha: "Through what causal factors does one attain the Way, and how does one come to know of one's previous lives?" The Buddha replied: "The Way is without form, and thus to know these things is of no benefit. What is important is to guard your intentions and actions. It is like polishing a mirror: as the dust is removed the underlying luminosity is revealed and you are able to see your own image. Eliminate desire and hold to emptiness and you will come to see the truth of the Way and know your past lives."

12. The Buddha said: "What is goodness? Goodness is the practice of the Way. What is supreme? A mind in accord with the Way is supreme. What has great power? Patience in the face of insult is strongest, for patience and the absence of anger is honored by all. What is supreme enlightenment? When mental impurities are uprooted, when evil conduct has ceased, when one is pure and free of blemish within, when there is nothing that is not known, seen, or heard—from the time when there was yet no Heaven and Earth down to the present day, including everything extant in the ten quarters as well as that which has yet to appear—when omniscience has been attained, this can indeed be called enlightenment."

13. The Buddha said: "A man who holds to passion and desire will not see the Way. It is as if one muddied water by throwing in five colored pigments and vigorously mixed them together. Many might approach the edge of the water, but they would be unable to see their own reflections on the surface. Passion and desire pollute the mind, leaving it murky, and thus the Way goes unseen. If the water is filtered and the filth removed, leaving it pure and free of dirt, one's own reflection will be seen. But if a kettle is placed over a hot flame bringing water to a rapid boil, or if water is covered with a cloth, then those who approach it will similarly not see their own reflections. The three fundamental poisons [of greed, hatred, and delusion] boil and bubble in the mind, while one is cloaked without by the five hindrances [of desire, hatred, sloth, agitation, and doubt]. In the end the Way goes unseen. When mental impurities are exhausted one knows whence the spirit comes and whither life and death go. The Way and its virtue are present in all buddha lands."

14. The Buddha said: "The practice of the Way is like holding a burning torch and entering a dark room: the darkness immediately vanishes and everything is illumined. Cultivate the Way and perceive the truth and evil and ignorance will both vanish, leaving nothing unseen."

15. The Buddha said: "What do I contemplate? I contemplate the Way. What do I practice? I practice the Way. Of what do I speak? I speak of the Way. I contemplate the true Way, never neglecting it for even an instant."

16. The Buddha said: "When gazing at Heaven and Earth contemplate their impermanence. When gazing at mountains and rivers contemplate their im-

permanence. When gazing at the tremendous variety of shapes and forms of the myriad things in the world contemplate their impermanence. If you keep your mind thus you will attain the Way in no time."

17. The Buddha said: "If for but a single day you continually contemplate and practice the Way you will attain the foundations of faith. Its blessings are incalculable."

18. The Buddha said: "Ardently contemplate the four primary elements that comprise the body. While each has a name, they are all devoid of self. The [sense of an] 'I' emerges from the aggregate, but it is not long lived and is really but an illusion."

19. The Buddha said: "For a person to follow his desires in search of fame is like putting fire to incense. Many may savor the smell of the incense, but the incense is all the while being consumed by the fire. The foolish, coveting worldly fame, hold not to the truth of the Way. Fame brings misfortune and harm, and one is sure to regret it later.

20. The Buddha said: "Riches and sex are to men what sweet honey on the blade of a knife is to a young child: before he has fully enjoyed a single bite he must suffer the pain of a cut tongue."

21. The Buddha said: "The misery of being shackled to wife, children, wealth, and home is greater than that of being shackled in chains and fetters and thrown in prison. In prison there is the possibility of pardon, but even though the desire for wife and children is as perilous as the mouth of a tiger, men throw themselves into it willingly. For this crime there is no pardon."

22. The Buddha said: "There is no desire more powerful than sex. Sexual desire looms so large that nothing stands outside of it. But luckily there is only one such desire, for were there yet another there would not be a single person in all the world capable of the Way."

23. The Buddha said: "Passion and desire are to man what a flaming torch is to one walking against the wind. Foolish ones who do not let go of the torch are sure to burn their hands. The poisons of craving and lust, anger and hatred, ignorance and delusion all reside in the body. He who does not quickly relinquish these perils by means of the Way will surely meet disaster, just as the foolish one who clings to his torch is sure to burn his hands."

24. A deity presented a woman of pleasure to the Buddha, wanting to test the Buddha's will and examine the Buddha's Way. The Buddha said: "Why have you come here bearing this leather sack of filth? Do you think to deceive me? It is difficult to stir [one possessed of] the six supernatural powers. Begone! I have no use for her." The deity, with increased respect for the Buddha, asked about the Way. The Buddha instructed him, whereupon he attained the stage of a stream-winner.

25. The Buddha said: "A man practicing the Way is like a piece of wood floating downstream with the current. As long as it avoids catching either the left or the right banks, as long as it is not picked up by someone or obstructed by some spirit, as long as it does not get stuck in a whirlpool or rot away, then I assure you it will eventually reach the sea. As long as a man practicing the Way is not deluded by passion or deceived by falsehood, as long as he energetically advances without doubt, then I assure you he will eventually attain the Way."

26. The Buddha told a *śramaṇa:* "Take care not to place faith in your own intentions. Ultimately intentions cannot be trusted. Take care not to wallow in sensuality, for wallowing in sensuality gives birth to misfortune. Only when you attain sainthood can you place faith in your own intentions."

27. The Buddha told a *śramaṇa:* "Take care not to look at women. If you meet one, look not, and take care not to converse with her. If you must converse, admonish the mind to right conduct by saying to yourself: 'As a *śramaṇa* I must live in this befouled world like a lotus, unsullied by mud.' Treat an old lady as if she were your mother, an elder woman as your elder sister, a younger woman as your younger sister, and a young girl as your own daughter. Show respect for them through your propriety. Remember that you see only the outside, but if you could peer into the body—from head to foot—what then? It is brimming with foulness. By exposing the impure aggregates [that comprise the body] one can free oneself from [impure] thoughts."

28. The Buddha said: "A man practicing the Way must eliminate sentiment and desire. It must be like grass encountering fire; by the time the fire arrives the grass is already gone. In encountering passion and desire the man of the Way must immediately distance himself."

29. The Buddha said: "Once a man was tormented by feelings of lust that would not cease, so he squatted down on the blade of an ax in order to castrate himself. The Buddha said to him: 'Severing the genitals is not as good as severing the mind, for the mind is chief. Put a stop to the chief and all his followers will cease. But if you do not put a stop to your depraved mind, what good will castration do? It will surely result in death.'" The Buddha said: "The vulgar and topsy-turvy views of the world are like those of this foolish man."

30. There was an adulterous young lady who made a pact with another man, but when the scheduled time arrived she did not come. The man repented and said to himself: "Desire, I know you! The initial intent is born with thought. If I did not think of you, you would not come into being." The Buddha was passing by and heard him. He said to the *śramaṇa:* "I recognize those words! It is a verse once uttered by Kāśyapa Buddha as he passed through this profane world."

31. The Buddha said: "From passion and desire arises sorrow. From sorrow arises dread. Without passion there is no sorrow, and without sorrow there is no dread."

32. The Buddha said: "A man practicing the Way is like a lone man in combat against ten thousand. Bearing armor and brandishing weapons, he charges through the gate eager to do battle, but if he is weakhearted and cowardly he will withdraw and flee. Some get halfway down the road before they retreat; some reach the battle and die; some are victorious and return to their kingdoms triumphantly. If a man is able to keep a firm grip on his wits and advance resolutely, without becoming deluded by worldly or deranged talk, then desire will disappear and evil will vanish, and he is certain to attain the Way."

33. There was a *śramaṇa* who mournfully chanted the scriptures at night, his spirit full of remorse as if wanting to return [to lay life]. The Buddha summoned the *śramaṇa* and asked him: "When you were a householder what did you do?" He answered, "I regularly played the lute." The Buddha asked: "What happened when the strings were too loose?" He replied: "It did not sound." "And when the strings were too taut, what then?" [The *śramaṇa*] replied: "The sound was cut short." "And when it was neither too loose nor too taught, what then?" "Then the tones all came into sympathetic accord." The Buddha told the *śramaṇa:* "The cultivation of the Way is just like that; keep the mind in tune and you can attain the Way."

34. The Buddha said: "Practicing the Way is like forging iron: if you gradually but thoroughly cast out impurities, the vessel is sure to come out well. If you cultivate the Way by gradually but thoroughly removing the impurities of mind, your advance will be steady. But when you are too harsh with yourself, the body becomes fatigued, and when the body is fatigued, the mind becomes frustrated. If the mind is frustrated, one's practice will lapse, and when practice lapses, one falls into wrongdoing."

35. The Buddha said: "Whether or not you practice the way you will certainly suffer. From birth to old age, from old age to sickness, from sickness to death, the misery of man is immeasurable. The distressed mind accumulates misdeeds, and life and death know no surcease. Such misery is beyond description."

36. The Buddha said: "It is difficult to free oneself from the three evil realms [the hells, the realm of hungry ghosts, and the realm of animals], and attain human birth. Even if one attains human birth it is difficult to be born a man rather than a woman. Even if one is born a man it is difficult to be born perfect in all six sense faculties. Even if the six faculties are perfect it is difficult to be born in the Middle Kingdom. Even if one lives in the Middle Kingdom it is difficult to be born at a time when the Buddha's Way is honored. Even if born when the Buddha's Way is honored it is difficult to encounter a noble man of the Way. [Moreover,] it is difficult to be born in the family of bodhisattvas.

Even if born in the family of bodhisattvas it is difficult to encounter the Buddha's presence in the world with a mind of faith in the three honored ones."

37. The Buddha asked a group of *śramaṇas:* "How should one measure the span of a man's life?" [One] replied: "By the span of a few days." The Buddha said: "You are not yet able to practice the Way." He asked another *śramaṇa:* "How should one measure the span of a man's life?" [The *śramaṇa*] replied: "By the space of a single meal." The Buddha said: "You are not yet able to practice the Way." He asked another *śramaṇa:* "How should one measure the span of a man's life?" [The *śramaṇa*] replied: "By the space of a single breath." The Buddha said: "Excellent! You can be called one who practices the Way."

38. The Buddha said: "Should one of my disciples venture several thousand miles from me yet remain mindful of my precepts, he is certain to attain the Way. However, should he stand immediately to my left yet harbor depraved thoughts, in the end he will not attain the Way. The gist lies in one's practice. If one is close to me but does not practice, of what benefit are the myriad divisions [of the path]?"

39. The Buddha said: "Practicing the Way is like eating honey, which is sweet all the way through. My scriptures are also like this: they are all about happiness, and those who practice [in accord with them] will attain the Way."

40. The Buddha said: "A man practicing the Way must be able to pluck up the roots of passion and desire, just as one would pluck a bead from a necklace. One by one they are removed until they are no more. When evil is no more the Way is attained."

41. The Buddha said: "A *śramaṇa* following the Way must be like an ox bearing a heavy burden treading through deep mud, so exhausted that he dares not glance left or right, yearning only to get out of the mud quickly so as to catch his breath. The *śramaṇa* regards his emotions and passions as more formidable than that mud. Mindful of the Way with a one-pointed mind, one is able to escape from myriad sufferings."

42. The Buddha said: "I regard the status of lords as a passing stranger. I regard treasures of gold and jade as gravel. I regard the beauty of fine silks as worn rags."

—28—

The Scripture on Perfect Wisdom for Humane Kings Who Wish to Protect Their States

Charles Orzech

One of the most important dimensions of Buddhism in China, Korea, and Japan was its forging common cause with the state and its promotion of itself as the best religion for the protection of the state. State protection or, more prosaically, the promotion and use of Buddhism for the acumen of its prognosticators, the power of its thaumaturges to produce seasonable rains, or for its power to legitimate a rule by appeal to a grand cosmic vision and the ruler's place in it, has been more the norm than the exception in East Asia. The Chinese apocryphon *The Scripture on Perfect Wisdom for Humane Kings Who Wish to Protect Their States* (*Renwang hu guo banrou boluomiduo jing*, hereafter the *Scripture for Humane Kings*) was, for more than 1,500 years, the scriptural underpinning of what we might call "National Protection Buddhism." Indeed, the scripture was used to repulse invaders, both spiritual and military, from the eighth-century Tibetan invasion of the Chinese heartland to the twentieth-century American invasion of Japan.

The *Scripture for Humane Kings* was purportedly given by the Buddha to the Indian king Prasenajit for use in the future time of the decline of the teaching (*mofa*) and the disappearance of saints. Probably composed in Chinese in Central Asia or North China between 450 and 480, the scripture was based on ideas that flourished in Northwest India in Mahāyāna and proto-tantric circles. Two versions are extant, one from the fifth and one from the eighth century. Although the earliest catalogue notice of the *Scripture for Humane Kings* in *A Compilation of Notices on the Translation of the Tripiṭaka* (*Chu sangzan jiji*) of 515 lists it among texts for which the names of the "translator has been lost," the next catalogues, the *Catalogue of Scriptures* (*Chongjing mulu*) of 594 and the *Record of the Three Treasures throughout Successive Generations* (*Lidai sanbao ji*) of 597, mistakenly attribute it as the work of the famous translator Kumārajīva and list two other proported translations by Dharmarakṣa and Paramārtha.

The first recorded instance of the scripture's use in China was under Emperor

Chen Wudi in the year 559 C.E. when a great vegetarian banquet was ordered and, in accordance with the scripture, an altar with one hundred buddha images was constructed and one hundred teachers were called upon to expound its teachings. Probably composed in the aftermath of the persecution of Buddhism under the Northern Wei between 446 and 452, it apparently circulated anonymously until the last part of the century.

The shift from anonymous circulation to circulation under the names of Kumārajīva Dharmarakṣa, and Paramārtha is linked to the fortunes of the Sui imperial house and the Tiantai founder Zhiyi. In 585 Zhiyi was coaxed down from his mountain retreat by the Chen emperor, and soon thereafter he was instructed to preach on the *Scripture for Humane Kings*. If his later "unofficial biography" (*bie zhuan*) is to be given credence, the lectures were attended by the emperor himself, and though two important clerics raised strenuous objections he overcame them. It is indeed significant that commentaries on the *Scripture for Humane Kings* are listed among the works of Guanding, Zhiyi's chief disciple and proponent. Correspondence between Guanding and the Sui rulers indicate a close link between the Tiantai school and the late Sui aristocracy.

The *Scripture for Humane Kings* quickly spread beyond China. The earliest notice of Japanese use of the *Scripture for Humane Kings* appears about a century after its first circulation in China, in the year 660, and the Korean *History of the Koryŏ (Koryŏ sa)* abounds in references to the scripture and its rites.

A second version, a new "translation" (765–766), was prepared by the monk Bukong jingang (Amoghavajra) at the request of Tang Emperor Daizong, and it became a key text in the propagation of the Zhenyan school (*mi jiao* or esoteric Buddhism) in eighth- and ninth-century China and of its descendant, Japanese Shingon Buddhism. Bukong had his first opportunity to celebrate the rite according to his new version in 765 during the Tibetan invasion of that year. The *Old Tang History* (*Jiu Tang shu*) notes that the rite was expressly ordered by Bukong's patron, Emperor Daizong, and it was carried out at the Shiming and Zesheng temples in the capital both for the repulsion of enemies and for the promotion of rain. In 767 Bukong requested an imperial edict to provide for the ordination of monks for the performance of the rite, which was to be used repeatedly as a centerpiece of Bukong's state cult. Thirty-seven monks (the number of the deities of the Vajradhātu maṇḍala) were ordained by imperial edict to chant the *Scripture for Humane Kings* and perform the rites on Mount Wutai,"to establish the state as a field of merit."

The *Scripture for Humane Kings* is a Perfect Wisdom scripture (*prajñāpāramitā*) extolling the path and salvific action of the bodhisattvas of Mahāyāna Buddhism. Large parts of the scripture are indistinguishable from Perfect Wisdom scriptures composed in Sanskrit, and it has strong affinities with the *Scripture of the Flower Garland* (*Avataṃsaka*, T 278), the *Scripture of the Ten Stages* (*Daśabhūmikasūtra*, T 286) and the *Nirvāṇa Scripture* (T 374–376). Scholars have linked the composition of the *Scripture for Humane Kings* with two other fifth-century Chinese scriptures, the *Scripture of Brahmā's Net* (*Brahmajālasūtra*, T 1484), which quotes the *Scripture for Humane Kings*, and the *Scripture of the Original Acts that Serve as Necklaces of the Bodhisattvas* (*Pusa yingluo benye jing*, T 1485), which is like it both in style and in the content of its bodhisattva path. Yet, unlike other Perfect Wisdom texts, the *Scripture for Humane Kings* is overtly addressed to rulers who, in this age of the decline of the teaching, have assumed roles indispensable for the pursuit of salvation.

The *Scripture for Humane Kings* reflected a broad range of concerns, from achieving enlightenment to attaining material wealth and security. In the *Scripture for Humane Kings* the Buddha, a renunciant, promised to help those who conquer or who wish to avoid conquest. Whether drought or pestilence, enemy armies or spiritual malaise threatened, the rituals prescribed in the text offered relief. If sufficient offerings and recitations were performed, then "the calamities shall be extinguished."

The two versions of the text that are extant are divided into an introduction and eight chapters. The introduction sets the scene of the preaching of the scripture as the Buddha's response to King Prasenajit's request for a teaching that "protects both the Buddha-fruit and the state." Chapters 2, 3, and 4 are in the classical mold of Perfect Wisdom scriptures: they present discourses on the three "gates" to liberation, (the empty, the signless, and the wishless), on the "perfections" of the bodhisattva path (rearranged into Fourteen Forbearances or *ren*, Sanskrit *kṣāntipāramitā*), and on the Two Truths. Chapter 5 directly addresses the problem of the protection of states, prescribing the following in response to a wide variety of disasters: In a gloriously adorned ritual arena, set up one hundred Buddha images, one hundred bodhisattva images, and one hundred lion thrones. Invite one hundred masters of the teaching to explicate this scripture, and before all of the thrones light different kinds of lamps, burn various incenses, scatter various flowers, and make vast and abundant offerings of clothing and utensils, drink and food, medicinal draughts, places of shelter and repose; all of the [appropriate] matters of offering. Twice each day [the masters] should expound and recite this scripture. Chapters 6, 7, and 8 reiterate and reinforce the relationship among the theological doctrine of Perfect Wisdom, the decline of the teaching, the bodhisattva path, and the role of kings.

Both versions of the scripture link the Perfect Wisdom teachings to the decline of the teaching, and the two versions are, in large part, identical word-for-word. Yet there are certain differences that bear noting. The fifth-century version of the text contains references to a favorite Six Dynasties (420–581) Chinese Buddhist apocalyptic figure, Prince Moonlight (Yueguang wang, Candraprabha). All references to him have been expunged from Bukong's version. In a more theological vein, the list of fourteen emptinesses in the fifth-century version owes more to a similar list in the *Nirvāṇa Scripture* than to any list in the Perfect Wisdom corpus. The inconsistency was cleaned up by Bukong. Both versions invoke Buddhist guardians to protect the state, but the eighth-century version supplements the earlier rite of setting up one hundred buddha images and so forth with an esoteric ritual (in chapter 7) to employ the kings of illumination (*mingwang,* Sanskrit *vidyārāja*) to assist in this task and appends there a long spell (*tuo-luo-ni,* Sanskrit *dhāraṇī*). These innovations were the subject of several ritual commentaries produced in the esoteric school in the late T'ang. Perhaps the most striking form of revisionism in Bukong's text is his substitution of the more common five hundred- and one thousand-based calculations of the decline in place of the *Scripture for Humane Kings* peculiar sequence of "eighty, eight hundred, and eight thousand" years.

Key to understanding the ideological and hermeneutic implications of the scripture is the linguistic and cosmological framework of the decline of the teaching and its relationship to the Perfect Wisdom teachings, a combination that brought together the two most widespread and influential Buddhist ideologies, one popular, the other theological. Both ideologies invoke ideas of emptiness and the unreliability of signs and referents. This combination of ideologies provided a compelling interpretive framework applicable to almost any situation.

The *Scripture for Humane Kings* is structured on an analogy between exterior rulers and interior rulers, between the conquerors of states and the conquerors of the self. Both sorts of conquerors must protect and nurture what they have attained. The deeper meaning of the analogy is grounded in the critique of language propounded by Nāgārjuna, the Indian author of the *Mādhyamikakārikàs,* and embodied in the formula of the Two Truths. Just as worldly rulers are related to rulers of the self, so too conventional, everyday truth is related to absolute truth. Further, just as conventional truth is, finally, inseparable from absolute truth, so too are conventional rulers inseparable from rulers of the self. In the *Scripture for Humane Kings* these relationships are the object of a series of word plays, particularly the homophone *ren,* which means both "humane" (the virtue of the Confucian king) and "forbearing" (Sanskrit *kṣānti,* the virtue of the bodhisattva). According to reconstructions of ancient Chinese by Karlgren and others, these words were pronounced *nzien* and *'nzien,* differing only in tone. The relationship between these words has been the starting point of nearly every traditional commentary, from those attributed to Zhiyi and Guiji to the modern Taiwanese productions. We find, for example, the following passage in the commentary attributed to Zhiyi:

> Because the humane king is he who explicates the dharma and disseminates virtue here below, he is called "humane" (*ren*). Because he has transformed himself he is called "king." The humane king's ability is to protect. What is protected is the state. This is possible because the humane king uses the dharma to order the state. Now if we consider the prajñā [pāramitā], its ability is to protect. The humane king is he who is protected. Because he uses the prajñā [pāramitā], the humane king is tranquil and hidden. Thus, if he uses his ability to propagate the dharma, the king is able to protect [the state], and it is the prajñā [pāramitā] that is the [method of] protection. Moreover, one who is humane (*ren*) is forbearing (*ren*). Hearing of good he is not

overjoyed, hearing of bad he is not angry. Because he is able to hold to forebearance in good and bad, therefore he is called forbearing (T 1705 253b28–253c4).

The *Scripture for Humane Kings* builds on this wordplay, as both "humane kings" and "kings of forbearance" are said to "transform" (*hua*) the people. Both "cultivate," "nurture," or "protect" (*hu*) their "states" (*guo, di,* Skt. *bhūmi*). Yet it is clear from the text that this linguistic play reflects a deep structural bond that is normally hidden or disguised. Thus, the *Scripture for Humane Kings* describes the hierarchy of cosmic authority as founded on a single underlying continuity and expressed in "geographic" terms, ranging up to lords of the highest trance-heavens:

> If a bodhisattva-mahāsattva dwells in one hundred buddha-fields he becomes a Wheel-turning King of Jambudvīpa. He cultivates one hundred brilliant gates of the teaching and uses the perfection of giving to abide in equinamity, and he transforms the beings of the four quarters of the world. If a bodhisattva-mahāsattva dwells in one thousand buddha-fields he becomes the celestial king of the Heaven of the Thirty-three. He cultivates one thousand brilliant gates of the teaching, and he discourses on the ten good paths [of virtue], transforming all living beings. . . . (T 246 8378a8–12)

The puns and analogies between conventional and absolute truth, conventional and interior rulers, are crucial to the *Scripture*'s popularity in China and Japan. They allow the text itself to inscribe and reproduce a crisis of referentiality that characterizes the onset of apocalyptic times. In these latter days the outward signs of authority (monastic robes, earlier canonical texts, etc.) no longer refer to inward realities. Indeed, in a key passage the decay of the teaching is signaled by the fact that "White-robed [commoners will occupy] high-seated 'bhikṣu' (monk) positions," a reference to lay officials in positions of power over monastic affairs and to the common topos that in the last age of the teaching monastic robes would of themselves turn white. In such a decayed world, surprising reversals and unusual connections are hidden amid the confusion of images. Rulers are, contrary to common understanding, bodhisattvas, and they are traversing the bodhisattva path.

The hermeneutic structure of the decline of the teaching was used not only by rulers to legitimate their reigns, but also by monks in a ritual triple entendre. For while the "humane kings" could point to the *Scripture for Humane Kings* to undergird their status, esoteric rites performed by monks—the "kings of forbearance"—upheld the "humane kings." Thus, the crisis of referentiality embodied in the decline of the teaching makes possible the puns of the *Scripture for Humane Kings* and the many uses to which the scripture was put.

The translation below includes the most distinctive part of chapter 5 and all of chapter 8 from the eighth-century version by Bukong, *Renwang huguo banruo boluomiduo jing,* T246, 8.840a–45a.

Further Reading

The best treatment of the theme of the "decline of the teaching" is Jan Nattier's *Once upon a Future Time* (San Francisco: Asian Humanities Press, 1991). Charles Orzech's "Puns on the Humane King: Analogy and Application in an East Asian Apocryphon," *Journal of the American Oriental Society* 109.1 (1989) explores some of the implications of the words "humane" and "forbearing." The role of the *Scripture of Brahmā's Net* and other apocrypha related to the *Scripture for Humane Kings* is covered in essays collected by Robert E. Buswell, Jr., in *Chinese Buddhist Apocrypha* (Honolulu: University of Hawaii Press, 1990). On the bodhisattva Moonlight (Candraprabha), see E. Zürcher, "Prince Moonlight: Messianism and Eschatology in Early Medieval Chinese Buddhism," *T'oung Pao* 68 (1982): 1–59. M. W. de Visser's *Ancient Buddhism in Japan: Sūtras and Ceremonies in Use in the Seventh and Eighth Centuries A.D. and Their History in Later Times* (Leiden: E. J. Brill, 1935), vol. 1, pp. 116–242 provides a summary translation of approximately one-third of the *Scripture for Humane Kings* as well as summaries of the important esoteric ritual commentaries. A complete study and translation is found in Charles Orzech, *Politics and Transcendent Wisdom: The Scripture for Humane Kings in the Creation of Chinese Buddhism* (University Park: Pennsylvania State University Press, 1998).

The Perfect Wisdom (Prajñāpāramitā) Scripture for Humane Kings Who Wish to Protect Their States

CHAPTER 5: PROTECTING THE STATE (T 246, 8.840a9–29)

At that time the World-Honored One told King Prasenajit and all of the other kings of great states, "Listen carefully, listen carefully, and on your behalf I will explain the method for protecting states. In all states at times when [things are on] the point of disorder, and all of the disasters, difficulties, and bandits come to wreak havoc, you and all of the kings should receive and keep, read and recite this Perfect Wisdom [scripture]. In a gloriously adorned ritual arena set up one hundred buddha images, one hundred bodhisattva images, and one hundred lion thrones. Invite one hundred masters of the teaching (*fashi*) to explicate this scripture and before all of the thrones light different kinds of lamps, burn various incenses, scatter various flowers, and make vast and abundant offerings of clothing and utensils, drink and food, medicinal draughts, places of shelter and repose; all of the [appropriate] matters of offering. Twice each day [the masters] should expound and recite this scripture. If the king, the great officers, monks, nuns, and male and female lay devotees hear, receive, read, and recite and, according to [the prescribed] method, cultivate and practice it, the disorders and difficulties will then be eradicated.

"Great king! In every territory there are numberless spectres and spirits each of whom has countless minions. If they hear this scripture they will protect your territory. When a state is on the verge of disorder the spectres and spirits are first disorderly. Because of the chaos of the spectres and spirits the myriad people become disorderly, and in due course there are bandit uprisings and the one hundred surnames perish. The king, the heir apparent, the princes, and the one hundred officers engage in mutual recrimination.

"In Heaven and on Earth there are transformations and monstrosities, and the sun, the moon, and all the stars lose their proper times and appearances. There are holocausts, great floods, typhoons, and the like. When these difficulties arise everyone should receive and keep, read and recite this Perfect Wisdom [scripture]. If, as [stipulated] in the scripture, people receive and keep, read and recite, everything they seek—official position, abundant wealth, sons and daughters, wisdom and understanding—will come according to their wishes. Human and celestial rewards will all be attained and fulfilled. Illness and difficulty will be totally eradicated. [Those with] bonds and fetters, cangues and locks encumbering their bodies will all be liberated. [Those who have] broken the four most serious prohibitions, committed the five heinous crimes, or even violated all the prohibitions [will see their] limitless transgressions all be completely wiped out."

CHAPTER 8: THE CHARGE ("ENTRUSTING" THE SCRIPTURE) (T246, 8.844b6–845a1)

The Buddha told King Prasenajit, "Now let me caution you and the others. After my extinction the correct teaching (*zheng fa*, Sanskrit *saddharma*) will be on the point of extinction. After fifty, after five hundred, or after five thousand years there will be no buddha, teaching, or community, and this scripture and the three jewels will be committed to all the kings of states for establishment and protection. [I want to] tell all my disciples of the four categories and so on to receive and keep it, to read and recite it, to understand its meaning and principles, and to broadly expound the essentials of its teaching on behalf of beings and have [them] practice and cultivate it and [thereby] depart from birth and death (*sheng si*, Sanskrit *saṃsāra*).

"Great King, in the latter [part] of the five impure epochs (*wu du shi*, Sanskrit *kasyaya*) all the kings of states, the princes, and great officers will be haughty and hold themselves in great esteem and destroy my teaching. [They] will institute laws to restrain my disciples—the monks and nuns—and [they] will not permit people to leave the family to cultivate and practice the correct way (*zheng dao*), nor will they allow people to make Buddhist stūpas and images. White-robed [lay persons] will assume high seats [hitherto reserved for monks], while monks will stand on the ground. [Their position] will be no different from that [stipulated] in the regulations for soldiers and slaves. [You] should know that at that time the extinction of the teaching will not be long [off].

"Great king, the causes of the destruction of states all are of your own making: Trusting in your awesome power you regulate the fourfold assembly and will not permit the cultivation of blessings. All the evil monks receive preferential treatment (*shou bieqing,* contrary to the vinaya), while [in contrast] monks wise and learned in the teaching come together in a single-minded pursuit of fellowship, vegetarian feasts, and the quest for religious merit. (The passage seems to imply that learned monks are engaged in a selfish pursuit of merit rather than a selfless service to the ruler.) These heterodox rules are completely contrary to my teaching. [Thus,] the one hundred surnames sicken [and face] limitless sufferings and difficulties. [You] should know that at that time the state will be destroyed. Great king, during the teaching's final era (*famo shi*), kings of states, the great officers, and the four classes of disciples all will act contrary to the teaching and in contravention of Buddhist teaching. [They] will commit every transgression and, contrary to the teaching and to the discipline, bind monks and imprison them. [By this you] will know that the extinction of the teaching is not long [off].

"Great king! After my extinction the four classes of disciples, all the kings of states, the princes, and the one hundred officers and all those appointed to hold and protect the three jewels will themselves destroy [the teaching] like worms in a lion's body that consume his own flesh. [And these] are not the heterodox [teachers]! Those who ruin my teaching [are guilty of] a great transgression. When the correct teaching decays and weakens, the people are bereft of proper conduct. Every evil will gradually increase, and their fortunes will daily be diminished. There will no longer be filial sons, and the six relationships will be discordant. The heavenly dragons will not defend [them], and evil demons and evil dragons will daily become more injurious. Calamities and monstrosities will intertwine, causing misfortunes to multiply (lit., vertical and horizontal, criss-cross). As is fitting [they] will be suspended in hell and reborn as animals or hungry ghosts, and [even] if they should attain human birth they will be poor and destitute, and lowborn with faculties impaired or incomplete. Just as shadow follows form, as an echo follows a sound, as a person writes at night when the light has gone out yet the words remain [the next day], the fruit of the destruction of the teaching is just like this.

"Great king! In generations to come, all the kings of states, the princes, the great officers, together with my disciples will perversely establish registration [of monks] and institute overseers and great and small monk directors (*da xiao sengtong*), contravening the principle [forbidding] employment [of monks] as lackeys (lit., as servants). Then you should know that at that time the Buddhist teaching is not long [to survive].

"Great king! In generations to come all the kings of states and the four classes of disciples [will] correctly rely upon all the buddhas of the ten directions, and constantly [these will] practice the Way, establish and disseminate it. Nevertheless, evil monks seeking fame and profit will not rely on my teaching, and they will go before the kings of states and will themselves utter transgressions and evil, becoming the cause of the destruction of the teaching. These kings will not distinguish [between the good and evil monks], and believing and accepting these sayings will perversely establish regulation [of monastic communities] and not rely on the Buddhist prohibitions (vinaya). You should know that at that time the extinction of the teaching is not long [off].

"Great king! In generations to come all the kings of states and the four classes of disciples will themselves be the cause of the destruction of the teaching and the destruction of the state. They themselves will suffer from this, and it is not the Buddhist teaching that is to blame. The heavenly dragons will depart, the five turbidities will in turn increase. A full discussion of this would exhaust an aeon and would still be unfinished."

At that time, [when] the kings of the sixteen great states heard the exposition concerning what was yet to come and all such warnings, the sound of their wailing and crying shook the three thousand [worlds]. Heaven and Earth were darkened and no light shone. Then, all the kings and the others, each and every one, resolved to receive and keep the Buddha's words and [to forgo] regulation of the four classes [of disciples who] leave the family to study the way; [this] is in accordance with the Buddha's teaching.

At that time, these assemblies—numberless as the sands of the Ganges—sighed together, saying: "It would be fitting that at such a time the world would be empty; a world bereft of buddhas."

Then King Prasenajit said to the Buddha: "World-Honored One, what should we call this scripture? How am I and the others to receive and keep it?" The Buddha said: "Great king! This scripture is called *The Perfect Wisdom for Humane Kings Who Wish to Protect Their States.* It may also be called *The Sweet Dew Teaching Medicine* [because] it is like a remedy whose action is able to reduce all illness.

"Great king! The merit and virtue of this perfect wisdom, like [that of] the void, cannot be fathomed. If one receives and keeps it, reads and recites it, the merit and virtue obtained will be able to protect humane kings and even all beings, like walls, yea, like a city's walls. This is why you and the others should receive and keep it."

When the Buddha had finished expounding this scripture, Maitreya the lion-roarer and all the countless bodhisattva-mahāsattvas, Śāriputra, Subhūti, and so forth, the limitless auditors, and the numberless gods and men of the desire realm, the form realm, and the formless realm, the monks and nuns, the male and female lay devotees, the asuras ("demons" or "titans")—all of the great assemblies—heard what the Buddha had said and with great joy trusted [in it], accepted and received [it, and put it into] practice.

—29—

Stories from an Illustrated Explanation of the *Tract of the Most Exalted on Action and Response*

Catherine Bell

Late imperial China (1550–1911) saw a remarkable proliferation of religious books written for nonelite social classes, which were growing in strength and status in conjunction with the economic expansion of the period. The availability of inexpensive mass printing at this time also promoted both widespread literacy or near-literacy and the broad marketing of books. In many of these popular religious works, Daoist, Buddhist, and neo-Confucian ideas were woven into a type of nonsectarian, heavily moralistic message concerning virtue, universal laws of cause and effect, and systems for calculating merit and demerit. Such works are generally known as "morality books."

The oldest and most famous morality book is the twelfth-century *Tract of the Most Exalted on Action and Response* (*Taishang ganying pian*). It is a relatively short work of about 1,200 characters that presents itself as the words of the Most Exalted, usually understood to be the Daoist deity, Laozi. His message is that good and bad fortune do not come into one's life without reason; rather, they follow as natural consequences of what people do, just as a shadow follows a form. Alluding to a complex cosmology in which a variety of deities oversee human behavior, the *Tract* teaches how the merit earned from good deeds will bring long life, wealth, and successful descendants, while the retribution that attends evil deeds ensures the eventual suffering of the wicked.

Within a century of its first published appearance in 1164, a Song dynasty emperor printed and distributed thousands of copies of the *Tract* in order to convey this message to his subjects, launching a long history of reprintings for didactic and meritorious purposes. The brief tract was republished with prefaces, commentaries, and stories to help illustrate its principles. Later editions added miracle tales, woodblock illustrations, proverbs, ledgers with which to calculate one's balance of merit and demerit, as well as lists of those who had donated to the printing of the text. In contrast to the direct message of the Most Exalted, which comprises the original short tract, many of these expanded editions began to call attention to the physical text itself, urging the reader to venerate the book and disseminate it in every way possible. Such piety and enthusiasm gave rise to innumerable large- and small-scale devotional projects to reprint the text. When D. T. Suzuki and Paul Carus published one of several English translations in 1906, they suggested that more copies of the *Tract* had been published in China than any other book in all history.

An "Illustrated Explanation" of the *Tract* compiled by Xu Zuanzeng in 1657 was the basis for an expanded edition published by Huang Zhengyuan (fl. 1713–1755) in 1755. Huang's edition stresses two themes. First, he argues that the *Tract* contains the eternal wisdom of the Confucian sages, but in a form that even the most simple-minded can understand. With the easy commentaries and the selection of appealing stories that he has provided, he goes on, everyone can now read, appreciate, and profit from the message of the *Tract*. Second, Huang repeatedly declares that the most meritorious deeds of all are those activities that help to make the *Tract* available to others. Doing one good deed, such as setting free a caged animal, is certainly laudable, but how can it compare to making others aware of the consequences of their own actions? Hence, in the stories and segment from one of Huang's prefaces that follow, distributing the *Tract* is the height of virtue and sure to bring to anyone the formulaic rewards of prosperity, official position, and filial children.

The ideas of virtue and retribution expressed in these excerpts reflect the neo-Confucian idea that anyone, not just the educated elite, could become a virtuous sage. However, scholars have noted that this idea appears to be highly nuanced by a somewhat mercantile perspective: actions count over intentions; good and bad deeds not only add up or cancel each other out, they are also investments that bear fruit and testify to one's true character; and a practical, this-worldly orientation locates the causes and effects of morality and immorality in the here and now. At the same time, the goals of moral action include not only material prosperity, but also the time-honored goals of social prestige through official recognition by the emperor and a position in the government. It has been suggested that this particular vision of moral action flowered in an era marked by heightened social mobility and the social restructuring that attended urbanization and the expansion of commercial activity. Certainly, morality books like the *Tract* appear to have worked out a simplified and generalized Confucian moral ethos readily appropriated by major segments of the population. This achievement has been linked to the unity and traditionalism of Chinese culture in the late imperial period, on the one hand, and to the emergence of a modern style of moral individualism, on the other.

Huang Zhengyuan, *Taishang ganying pian tushuo* (*Illustrated Explanation of the Tract of the Most Exalted on Action and Response*), also called *Taishang baofa tushuo* (*Illustrated Explanation of the Precious Raft of the Most Exalted*), 8 juan.

Further Reading

Catherine Bell, "Printing and Religion in China: Some Evidence from the *Taishang Ganying Pian*," *Journal of Chinese Religions* 20 (Fall 1992): 173–86; Judith A. Berling, "Religion and Popular Culture: The Management of Moral Capital in *The Romance of the Three Teachings*," in *Popular Culture in Late Imperial China*, edited by David Johnson, Andrew J. Nathan, and Evelyn S. Rawski (Berkeley: University of California Press, 1985), pp. 188–218; Cynthia J. Brokaw, *The Ledgers of Merit and Demerit: Social Change and Moral Order in Late Imperial China* (Princeton: Princeton University Press, 1991); Evelyn S. Rawski, *Education and Popular Literacy in Ch'ing China* (Ann Arbor: Center for Chinese Studies of the University of Michigan, 1979); Sakai Tadao, "Confucianism and Popular Educational Works," in Wm. Theodore de Bary, ed., *Self and Society in Ming Thought*. (New York: Columbia University Press, 1970); D. T. Suzuki and Paul Carus, trans., *Treatise on Response and Retribution by Lao Tze* (La Salle: Open Court, 1973).

"On Distributing Morality Books" by Huang Zhengyuan

It is said that those who do good deeds will obtain good fortune, while those who are not virtuous will experience misfortune. This is the reason for the blessings or calamities that befall the moral and the immoral. How clear it is! There is more than one road to virtue, but none can compare to distributing morality books. By transforming one person, a morality book can go on to transform ten million people. Spreading its teachings through one city, it can spread them through ten million cities. By exhorting one generation to virtue, it can effectively exhort ten million generations. This is different from all other means of virtue, which do things one at a time in only one direction.

If people can make use of this book, they will develop a virtuous heart; then they can be taught how to calculate their merits and demerits, thereby gradually extending their moral character until their virtue is complete. They will come from the towns and villages to advance the nation. The intellectuals will teach the ignorant. Preserving "the way" in this world, they will reverse the degenerate customs of our day. All depends on this book!

Although the book has a philosophy that divides things up into cause and effect, this is the only way to teach people to act virtuously. There is an old saying, "With upper-class people, one talks philosophy; with lower-class people, one talks of cause and effect." Now, it is difficult to exchange talk about philosophy, but there are many who can talk about auspicious or calamitous retribution. And such talk is enough to influence people's hearts. Therefore, while it is appropriate to have books on philosophy, there should be at least as many books on cause and effect.

Those who have composed, compiled, published, or donated to the printing of morality books and were subsequently saved from calamity and danger, amassing blessings and years of long life, both in the past and the present—well, they are too numerous to count! . . . These forebears attained high positions, prosperity, prestige, and longevity because they distributed morality books. These are just some of the good effects that distributing morality books has on the world and on people's hearts. It is not a small thing and yet it does not burden people. Why then are there so few believers and so many unbelievers? People just do not know the truth within morality books. But if you want people to know the truth of morality books, you must first encourage them to be distributed. After they are disseminated, then one can hope that many will actually see the books. The greater the number of people who see it, then naturally the number who come to know its truth will also increase. Those who can sincerely grasp the truth in morality books will grow in virtue.

STORIES

A. Zhu Jiayou of the Qiantang District in Zhejiang Province was employed in the salt business and fond of doing good deeds. When Mr. Lin Shaomu was the General Surveillance Commissioner for Zhejiang, Zhu begged him to write out the two morality books, *Tract on Action and Response* and *Essay on Secret Merit* (*Yinzhi wen*), in handsome script in order to engrave the texts in stone. He also asked him to contribute more than ten thousand sheets of paper to make copies. All those who obtained a copy treasured the fine calligraphy. Night and day Zhu made copies. After a while, he gradually became able to understand the full meaning of the text, fortifying his body and soul. Both the one who wrote out the texts and the one who gave copies of them away received blessings in return. Zhu's son was given an eminent position in Anhui Province, while Lin was later appointed to an office with jurisdiction over the provinces of Hubei and Hunan. (Huang, 1:20b)

B. Once there was a man from the Wu Xi District in Jiangsu, named Zou Yigui, also called Xiaoshan (Little Mountain). At the time of the provincial examinations people were contributing to the printing of morality books and wanted him to donate also. Zou declined, saying, "It is not because I am unwilling to give money. Rather I fear that people will be disrespectful to the text and that would put me at fault." That night he dreamed that the god Guandi appeared to scold him, saying, "You study books and illuminate their basic principles, yet you also speak like this! If all people followed your example, virtue would practically disappear." Zou prostrated himself and begged forgiveness. He printed and circulated one thousand copies in order to atone for his fault. Moreover, by himself he painted a religious image on a board and devoutly chanted in front of it morning and night. Later, in the year 1727, he placed first in special examinations and entered the prestigious Hanlin Academy, where he held a series of official positions, culminating in an appointment as Vice Minister in the Ministry of Rites. Zou always said to people, "One word is enough to incur fault. And among evil doers, no one is worse than the person who hinders the virtue of others." This story demonstrates that anyone who impedes contributions to morality books is guilty of the greatest fault and will be punished by Heaven. (Huang, Zushi shanshu bian section, 1:20a–b)

C. Shan Yangzhu lived at a small Buddhist temple. When he was born, he was weak and often ill. His mother prayed for him, vowing that if her son were cured, he would be a vegetarian for his whole life. In addition, she nursed him at her breast for six full years until he began to eat rice at the age of seven. When his mother died, he continued to live at the temple for forty-one years, yet he was in constant pain and suffering for half his life. One day he read the *Tract on Action and Response* and, thinking about his parents, suddenly repented of all his bad deeds. Thereafter, he collected different editions of the *Tract* and amended them with his own understanding of its meaning—revising, distinguishing and analyzing point by point. Altogether his study came to 330,000 words, divided into eight volumes and entitled *An Exposition of the Tract of the Most Exalted on Action and Response.* He did this in order to made amends for all his misdeeds, but also as an attempt to repay some small part of the boundless loving kindness of his parents. In 1655 he organized people to donate the money for publishing it. Because of these activities, everything that was painful and unhappy in his life gradually improved. (Huang, 1:28b)

D. At the end of the Yuan dynasty (1280–1368) there was a man named Chu Shaoyi, who not only diligently practiced the teachings of the *Tract on Action and Response,* but also printed and distributed it. He set each phrase to music so that his wife and the women in their quarters could understand it and be enlightened.

At that time the country fell into strife caused by rival warlords. One of them was Chen Youliang. When Chen was young and very poor, Chu had once helped him. Many years later, after Youliang and his army had occupied the provinces of Hubei and Guangdong, Youliang falsely proclaimed himself emperor of the country. He summoned Chu to come work for him and frequently gave him gifts of gold and silk. Chu did not dare refuse the gifts, but stored them in a bamboo chest and used them only to aid hungry families. Although he himself needed firewood and rice, he was not willing to use any of the gifts.

After the Ming emperor Taizu quelled the chaos and ascended the throne (1368), he sought out retired scholars of virtue throughout the empire. Civil authorities communicated the proclamation and recommended Chu, who was summoned to the capital. The emperor asked him: "Dear sir, what would give you the most pleasure?" Chu replied: "As for me, I am just an ordinary man who is pleased to live now in an age of great peace and prosperity. I only want the strength and diligence to plow and plant my fields. Virtue comes naturally that way. In addition, I want to instruct my children in virtue and teach my grandchildren. Nothing can give me more pleasure than these things."

Taizu then said: "The day that Chen Youliang usurped the throne, you sir did not join his side. Youliang honored and respected you, so we can see that even though he was an evil man, he was capable of rewarding virtue and righteousness. Virtue can influence anyone—you can trust that. The *Book of Chu* says that only virtue should be treasured. You sir will be called 'the treasure of the nation.'" Then the emperor himself wrote out those four characters, "regard as the treasure of the nation," and bestowed it on him. In addition, the emperor gave him elegantly spun silk and a special one-horse chariot to take him back home. By imperial order, each month the civil authorities were to provide Chu with grain and meat for the rest of his life. His son was appointed a provincial governor in Yunnan and his grandson entered the national university to study. As soon as the grandson's studies were completed, he received an official post in accord with his abilities. (Huang 3:6a)

E. Zhou Guangpu developed an upset stomach and became so ill that for more than twenty days he could not eat or drink. He was so sick that two deputies from the underworld arrived, put him in chains, and led him out the door. When they had traveled approximately ten miles, he saw a man off in the woods calling his name. He quickly went over to him and saw that it was none other than his dear old friend Ji Yunhe. The two men clasped hands and wept, greatly moved to talk with each other again after such a long separation. Then Ji drew close to Zhou's ear and whispered: "While I was alive, I was without fault because of all my education. I am trusted by the chief officers and judge of the underworld beneath Mount Tai. The fates of all the living and dead pass through my hands, so I can help you in the other world. The most important thing is the *Tract on Action and Response*. In a little while, when you come before the court, just say that you once made a vow to recite it ten thousand times. Beg to be released and returned to life in order to complete the vow. If the judge has any questions, I will plead for you myself." When he finished speaking, he left.

The two deputies escorted Zhou to a huge government office where he saw lots of people coming and going. Some were welcomed or sent off with drum rolls in their honor. Some wandered about freely, while others, manacled with chains, were led to and from the hells. Suddenly he heard his name called out as his case was summoned before the court. Zhou went up to the desk and kneeled. The judge spoke: "You are said to have been well-behaved and devout, but you were fond of eating animals and birds—even catching insects for food. If you please, are they not living things too? It is appropriate for you to be sentenced to the hell of the hungry ghosts for punishment."

Weeping and pleading, Zhou repeated what Ji had told him. The judge asked his officers if the story was true or not. Ji, who had been waiting on the side, cried out "It is true!" and presented his record book to the judge. When he had examined it, the judge smiled and said: "Because of this virtuous vow, it is proper to return him." Ji then spoke up again, saying, "This person was very sick. You should order a heavenly doctor to cure him." So the judge issued a command that Zhou be attended by a heavenly physician. The same two deputies escorted Zhou back home where he saw his body lying on the bed. The deputies pushed his soul back into its place and Zhou immediately regained consciousness.

Thinking that the heavenly doctor would be one of the Daoist immortals, Tao [Hongjing] (456–536 C.E.) and Xu [Mi] (303–373 C.E.), Zhou made a great effort to get up and with a cane started off for the Tao and Xu Temple across the river to pray. By the time he got to the middle of the bridge, he was doubled over and stumbling. A traveler from Shanxi stopped to help him. "I can see from your fatigue and the look on your face that you are troubled by a sick stomach. If it is not cured, you will surely die. I have some small skill and can cure you immediately. Why not follow me?"

They went together to a small house where they found a stove. The traveler started a fire to boil water for tea. From his side he pulled out a silver needle. He inserted it approximately an inch into the right side of Zhou's heart, and then twice lit some herbs on the end of it. Zhou cried out with pain. The traveler immediately stopped the burning, pulled out the needle, and applied a medicated bandage.

By this time the tea was ready. The traveler filled a small cup and asked Zhou to drink. Zhou declined, saying, "For many days I have not been able to consume even small amounts." The traveler replied, "This tea is not the same. Please try it." Zhou then drank two cups without any trouble. He felt his energy suddenly renewed. The traveler advised him, saying: "When you return home, it is best to drink rice soup at first, then eat only diluted rice gruel. After seven days you can eat and drink normally."

Zhou did as he had been told, and as a result he recovered in several days. He went to find the traveler in order to thank him, but there was no trace of him—even the house was gone. Only then did he realize that the stranger must have been the heavenly physician sent to cure him. Throughout his life Zhou faithfully recited the *Tract on Action and Response*, acquiring success, blessings, and long life. (Huang, Lingyan section, 10a)

F. Li Dezhang was a middle-aged man whose wife had died. He had only one child, a fourteen-year-old son named Shouguan. Dezhang acquired some merchandise, one thousand carrying poles, and proceeded to the provinces of Hunan and Guangdong in order to sell them. Liyong, a man-servant with the household, accompanied the merchandise to keep an eye on it, while Li himself and Shouguan looked for a fast boat in order to take a trip on the Wujiang River. Father and son leisurely went ashore to visit the great royal temple there. Inside there was a Daoist priest with a book, who inquired of them, saying: "This temple prints the *Tract on Action and Response*. Would you be so kind as to make a contribution?" Dezhang hesitated without answering. Just then the boatman arrived to say that the wind was favorable and he wanted to set sail. So Li Dezhang put down the book and they hurried away to the depart in the boat.

When they came to the middle of the river, they suddenly encountered a storm that overturned the boat. Father and son both fell into the water, but the two were not able to find each other. Dezhang was rescued by a fishing boat, which let him off where he could meet his own cargo ship. He thanked and generously rewarded the fishermen. Then the master and his servant, Liyong, returned to the temple where they prayed for an explanation. The response was: "The *Tract on Action and Response* is a sacred text to save the world. Earlier you were not willing to make a contribution to it. Hence, you have come to this end." Dezhang replied: "If the Most Exalted has the divine power to enable my son and me to meet again, I will put up the whole cost of the project, and you will not have to use a cent that has been contributed." He ordered Liyong to fetch two hundred ounces of silver from the bank and hand it over to the temple as an offering.

Master and servant supervised the loading of the cargo on the ship and traveled to the city of Wuchang. On route they met an old traveling merchant named Fu Youcai who had lost money and was having trouble making his return trip home. This man was an engaging talker who could flatter people with his charm. Dezhang developed a close friendship with him. While they were traveling, the merchandise was greatly delayed, so Dezhang left half of it in Wuchang and half with Youcai. Liyong left them to go to Jingxiang. Less than a month later he received a letter from his master telling him that the merchandise had already been sold for two thousand ounces of silver. Since Liyong was in Jingxiang taking care of things and unable to get away, he arranged for the receipts to be given to Youcai, who would go to Wuchang and collect the money. When Youcai had the silver in his hands, however, he immediately rolled up his conscience and fled with the money. When Dezhang learned that Youcai had taken the money, he was grieved and depressed, losing all interest in returning home. He drifted for two years before he made any plans to go back. But Heaven helps virtuous people, and Dezhang had already contributed to the *Tract on Action and Response*. When there is virtue, there will be recompense.

When his son Shouguan fell into the water, he grabbed hold of a large piece of wood and floated to a village. There a widow took care of him as if he were her own son. He studied and entered school. Unexpectedly one day at the bank of a stream he saw a young woman throw herself into the water. He immediately dove in to rescue her. When he asked her why she had done it, she answered: "My father's name is Fu Youcai. Years ago he left on business and arranged for me to stay with the family of my maternal uncle, who has no scruples at all. He wanted to sell me into a house of prostitution, so I tried to commit suicide." Suddenly there were lots of people all around. One of them was an old man who asked the young woman in surprise, "You, why are you here?" The woman looked at him and saw that it was her father. Father and daughter were reunited; you can imagine their happiness. Youcai was moved to gratitude by Shouguan's righteousness, so he gave his daughter to the young man as a wife and also arranged that the thousand ounces of swindled silver be entirely turned over to him as well.

Shouguan missed his father, and his heart pressed him to try to find him. So with his father-in-law he bought a boat and went to the Wujiang River to search for clues to his father's whereabouts. Not far from the royal temple, he saw the back of a boat with its sails set in readiness to depart. At the prow stood a man who looked just like his father. When they came up to each other, both father and son rejoiced in wild excitement, stopping only to question the other about what had happened since they had been parted. Shouguan told how he had taken a wife and obtained so much silver, recounting his story detail by detail. Dezhang asked to meet his new in-laws and entered the other ship's hold. He noticed that his son's father-in-law lay in bed with his face covered, not rising to get up. Dezhang lifted the cover and saw that it was Youcai. He laughed and said: "Once we were good friends. Now we are relatives by marriage and the thousand ounces of silver you have given to my son. What harm has there been? Let us be friends as we were before."

Together they went to the royal temple to fulfill Dezhang's vow. The carving of the blocks was completed, so they contributed another three hundred pieces of silver to print one thousand copies and have them distributed widely to exhort people to virtue. Families that were separated are brought back together again—is this not a reward for printing the *Tract on Action and Response?* (Huang, Lingyan section, 14a)

Religions of Tibet in Practice

INTRODUCTION

Tibet

Donald S. Lopez, Jr.

The religions of Tibet have long been objects of Western fascination and fantasy. From the time that Venetian travelers and Catholic missionaries encountered Tibetan monks at the Mongol court, tales of the mysteries of their mountain homeland and the magic of their strange religions have held a peculiar hold over the European and American imagination. Over the past two centuries, the valuation of Tibetan society and, particularly, its religion has fluctuated wildly. Tibetan Buddhism has been portrayed sometimes as the most corrupt deviation from the Buddha's true dharma, sometimes as its most direct descendant. These fluctuations have occurred over the course of this century, as Tibet resisted the colonial ambitions of a European power at its beginning and succumbed to the colonial ambitions of an Asian power at its end.

Until some thirty years ago, knowledge of the religions of Tibet in the West had largely been derived from the reports of travelers and adventurers, who often found the religions both strange and strangely familiar, noting similarities between Tibetan Buddhism and Roman Catholicism, calling the Dalai Lama the Tibetan pope, for example. It is only since the Tibetan diaspora that took place beginning in 1959, after the Chinese invasion and occupation of Tibet, that the texts of the religions of Tibet have begun to be widely translated.

The history of Tibet prior to the seventh century C.E. is difficult to determine. According to a number of chronicles discovered at Dunhuang dating from the seventh through the tenth centuries, Tibet was ruled by a lineage of kings, the first seven of whom descended from the heavens by means of a cord or ladder. Each king ruled until his first son was old enough to ride a horse, at which point the king returned to heaven via the rope. (Buddhist historians say that the first king in the lineage was an Indian prince who arrived by crossing the Himalayas; when the Tibetans asked where he had come from he pointed up, and the credulous Tibetans assumed he had descended from the sky.) These kings founded a system of law that reflected the cosmic order of heaven. As a literal descendant of heaven, the king was the embodiment and protector of the cosmic order and the welfare of the state. The king's stable presence on the throne thus ensured harmony in the realm.

It was only when the eighth king lost his protective warrior god in battle that the sky rope was severed and the king was slain, leaving his corpse behind. To deal with this crisis, according to later sources, priests were invited from an area called Shangshung (Zhang zhung, the precise location and extent of which is unknown but is assumed to include much of western Tibet) to perform death rituals and bury the king. The story reflects the popular notion of Tibet as an untamed and uncivilized realm, with civilization arriving only from the outside. Recent scholarship thus does not assume from this account that foreign priests were actually summoned, seeing it instead as a creation myth meant to explain the origin of the elaborate royal mortuary cult. A class of priests called "reciters" (*bon*) performed a range of sacerdotal functions in service of the divine king, such as officiating at coronation ceremonies and in rites of allegiance to the king. There was also another class of priests, called *shen* (*gshen*), who seem to have performed divinations.

The cult of the divine king included the belief that he was endowed with both magical power and a special magnificence. There was a trinity of the king, the head priest, and the chief minister, with the active power of government in the hands of the head priest and the minister who represented the priestly hierarchy and the clan nobility. The king represented the continually reborn essence of the divine ancestor, who was reincarnated in each king at the age of maturity and remained incarnated in him until his son reached the same age of maturity and ascended the throne as the consecutive link of the ancestral reincarnation. This procedure applied also to both the priest and the minister, so a new trinity was instituted at the accession of each king. The king also had a special guardian called the "body spirit" (*sku bla*) who protected the king's power, encompassing everything from his body to his political authority to the order of the universe. One of the primary responsibilities of the royal priests and ministers, then, seems to have been the maintenance of the king's health, for if the king became ill or if the body spirit was determined otherwise to be displeased, the safety of the kingdom and even of the universe was in jeopardy. Epidemics and droughts were interpreted as signs of this displeasure.

The notion of *la* (*bla*), generally translated as "soul," "spirit," or "life," dates from the ancient period and remains an important component in the religions of Tibet. The *la* is an individual's life force, often associated with the breath. It is seen as the essential support of the physical and mental constitution of the person but is mobile and can leave the body and wander, going into trees, rocks, or animals, to the detriment of the person it animates, who will become either ill or mentally unbalanced. The *la* is especially susceptible during dreams and can be carried off by demons, who particularly covet the life forces of children. There are thus rites designed to bring the *la* back into the body, known as "calling the *la*" (*bla 'bod*).

Even when the *la* is properly restored to its place in the body, it may simultaneously reside in certain external abodes, most often in a particular lake, tree, mountain, or animal. The person in whom the *la* resides stands in a sympathetic relationship with these phenomena, such that if the *la* mountain is dug into, the person will fall sick. The Tibetan epic hero Gesar in his attempt to conquer a certain demoness cuts down her *la* tree and empties her *la* lake; he fails because he does not kill her *la* sheep. The identity of these external *la* are thus often kept secret, and portable abodes of the *la*, usually a precious object of some kind (often a turquoise), are kept in special receptacles and hidden by the person who shares the *la*.

There were thus regular offerings made to the king's body spirit at the site of the king's sacred mountain, the physical locus of his power. Of particular importance to the royal cult, however, were the funeral ceremonies. A king was still expected to abdicate upon the majority of his son and retire to his tomb with a large company of retainers, although whether this entailed the execution of the king and his retinue or simply their exile into a tomb complex remains unknown. The royal funerals were apparently elaborate affairs, with food and other necessities provided for the perilous journey to the next world, a bucolic heaven called the "land of joy" (*bde ba can*). Animals, especially yaks, sheep, and horses, were also offered in sacrifice. Chinese sources suggest that humans were also sacrificed, perhaps to serve as servants to the departed king, perhaps to be offered as gifts or "ransoms" (*glud*) to various spirits who otherwise would block the king's route. This concern with death and the fate of the dead has continued throughout the history of Tibetan religions.

Although Buddhism was flourishing all around Tibet in the first centuries of the common era, there is no mention of Buddhist elements in the chronicles apart from the account of a small stūpa and an illegible Buddhist sūtra falling from the sky into the palace of one of the prehistoric kings. The formal introduction of Buddhism to the Tibetan court seems to have occurred during the reign of King Songtsen Gampo (Srong btsan sgam po, ruled c. 614–650), at a time when Tibet was the dominant military power of Inner Asia. According to later chronicles, as a result of treaties with the courts of China and Nepal, the king received two princesses as wives. Each was a Buddhist, and each brought a precious statue of the Buddha with her to Lhasa, the capital. They are credited with converting their new husband to the dharma, although what this meant in practice is difficult to say. The king dispatched an emissary to India to learn Sanskrit and then return to design a written language for Tibet. Among the many purposes to which such a script could be put, it is said that the king's pious motivation was the translation of Buddhist texts from Sanskrit into Tibetan.

The script invented was modeled on one current in northern India at the time. Tibetan is an agglutinative language, with case endings used to mark grammatical functions. Words are made up of combinations of independent syllables, each of which is constructed by grouping letters in various combinations. The simplest syllable can be made up of a single letter while the most complex can have as many as six, with a prefix, a superscription, a root letter, a subscription, a suffix, and an additional suffix, not to mention a vowel marker. Historical linguists speculate that originally all of these letters were pronounced, but over the centuries the auxiliary letters became silent, such that there is a vast difference today between the way a word is written and the way it is pronounced. To render the spelling of a Tibetan word in English requires that all of the letters be represented. The result, however, appears to be utterly unpronounceable to someone who does not already know Tibetan. For that reason, phonetic renderings (for which there is no widely accepted convention) must be provided. For example, the name of the current Dalai Lama in transliteration is Bstan 'dzin rgya mtsho, but it is commonly written in English as Tenzin Gyatso. Although the same script is employed throughout the Tibetan cultural domain, dozens of regional dialects have developed, many of which are mutually incomprehensible.

The conversion of Tibet to Buddhism is traditionally presented as a process of forceful but ultimately compassionate subjugation (rather than destruction) of native Tibetan deities by the more powerful imported deities of Buddhism, often invoked by Indian yogins. The profoundly chthonic nature of Tibetan religion is evident even from the traditional chronicles, which represent the conversion of Tibet to the true dharma not so much as a matter of bringing new teachings to the populace but of transforming the landscape by bringing the myriad deities of place—of valleys, mountains, hills, passes, rivers, lakes, and plains—under control. Thus Songtsen Gampo was said to have ordered the construction of Buddhist temples at key points throughout his realm, each temple functioning as a great nail impaling a giant demoness (*srin mo*) lying supine over the expanse of Tibet, immobilizing her from impeding the progress of the dharma, the symmetry of a Buddhist maṇḍala superimposed over the unruly landscape of Tibet.

But all this derives from chronicles composed centuries after the fact by authors concerned to promote Buddhism and link the introduction of the dharma to Tibet's greatest king, the king who unified Tibet and led its armies in victory against Chinese, Indians, Nepalese, Turks, and Arabs. The few records surviving from the period make no mention of Buddhism, nor even of the Nepalese princess. The historicity of the emissary to India is questionable. Songtsen Gampo seems to have remained committed to and even to have developed further the cult of divine kingship, a cult that involved both animal and human sacrifice (an anathema to Buddhists), while continuing to worship local deities and supporting his own ministers and priests of the royal mortuary cult. At the same time, it seems unlikely that the Tibetan kingdom, surrounded as it was for centuries by Buddhist societies, should have remained untouched by Buddhist influence until the seventh century, as the traditional histories claim.

The first king to make a choice between Buddhism and the native religion of the Tibetan court was Tri Songdetsen (Khri srong lde btsan, ruled 754–797). Both later Buddhist and Bönpo chronicles report that he promoted Buddhism and suppressed the practices of priests of the native cult; his support of Buddhism may have been motivated by the desire to escape the restricting bonds of the feudal clan nobility who supported the priests. Contemporary inscriptions, however, also indicate that he continued to have rituals performed that involved animal sacrifice. During these ceremonies, the old oaths of loyalty between king and servant were sworn. Before taking the oath, it was the custom for the participants to smear their lips with the blood of the sacrificial animal, a practice from which the Buddhist monks who were present apparently demurred.

Tri Songdetsen invited to Tibet the prominent Indian Buddhist abbot Śāntarakṣita, whose presence angered the local spirits sufficiently for the Indian abbot to request the king to invite a tantric master to aid in the further subjugation of the local spirits. The great master Padmasambhava was invited and proved equal to the task, after which it was possible to establish the first Buddhist monastery at Samye (Bsam yas) circa 779. The further activities of Padmasambhava and the duration of his stay are unknown, but he remains a figure of mythic significance in the history of Tibet, often referred to simply as Guru Rimpoche, the precious guru. The stories of Padmasambhava's defeat and conversion of the local spirits and demons of Tibet are pervasive and popular, and they figure prominently in the descriptions of specific sites found in pilgrimage narratives.

Buddhism is famous for its ability to accommodate local deities into its pantheon. In the case of Tibet, most of the local deities became regarded as "mundane gods" (*'jig rten pa'i lha*), that is, deities who are subject to the law of karma and cycle of rebirth, who, after a lifetime as a particular god, will take rebirth in some other form. The vast pantheon of deities imported from India included such gods, as well as "supramundane gods" (*'jig rten las 'das pa'i lha*), that is, deities who—although they appear in horrifying forms, such as the protector of the Dalai Lama, the goddess Belden Lhamo (Dpal ldan lha mo, the "Glorious Goddess")—are in fact enlightened beings already liberated from the cycle of birth and death. Still, the process of the Buddhist conversion of Tibet should not be understood to mean that Buddhism was not also converted in that process; indeed, many deities cannot be identified as simply Indian or Tibetan.

The deities that Padmasambhava subdued and converted were often identified with mountains, rock formations, and other prominent elements of the topography of Tibet. The Tibetan plateau stands at 12,000 feet, with the surrounding mountains rising yet another mile above the plateau. The northern region is a vast uninhabited plane, but there are also dense forests and fertile valleys that are cultivated to produce barley, the staple crop. It is thus misleading to characterize Tibet as a desolate place, or to suggest (as Western travelers have) that the bleak landscape and vast sky (with its thin air) have turned men's minds toward the contemplation of a rarefied world of gods and demons, their unconscious releasing vivid hallucinations that appear in sharp relief against the distant horizon.

Yet it is difficult to overestimate the importance of the land in Tibetan religion. From early times Tibetans have held a belief in numerous local spirits, demons, and gods, who lived in lakes, rivers, creeks, wells, trees, fields, rocks, and mountains. Deities inhabited unusually shaped mounds; rocks shaped like animals; hills shaped liked sleeping oxen; burial mounds; juniper, birch, and spruce trees; and any anomalous geologic formation. Various types of demons roamed mountains and valleys and chose abodes in rocks, forests, ditches, and overhanging rocks, all places that could be disturbed by humans, to whom they sent both physical affliction (such as leprosy and smallpox) and social affliction (such as gossip). The atmosphere was the domain of another class of spirits, demons who appeared in the form of warriors who would attack travelers. Beneath the surface of the earth and in rivers and lakes lived a class of demons named *lu* (*klu*), who would become enraged if the earth was disturbed by digging, plowing, or laying the foundation for a house. Unless they were properly appeased, they also would inflict disease on humans and livestock. There are also *tsen (btsan)*, "rock spirits"; *sa dak* (*sa bdag*), "lords of the earth"; *ma mo*, "demonesses"; and *dre* (*'dre*), *drip* (*sgrib*), *dön* (*gdon*), and *gek* (*bgegs*). The Tibetan pantheon (although the term pantheon suggests a clearer system than in fact exists) of both benevolent and, especially, malevolent spirits is large and complex, and English lacks sufficient terms to render their names, beyond things like "demon" and "ogress." Even the terms "benevolent" and "malevolent" can be misleading, since many horrifying deities, despite an awful demeanor and testy disposition, can provide protection and aid if they are not offended or disturbed, but properly propitiated.

As mentioned above, Buddhist chronicles describe the Tibetan landscape as itself a giant demoness who must be subdued. There are gods of the plain and gods of the mountains; an entire mountain range is a god. This animated topography is itself further populated by all manner of spirits who must be honored to avoid their wrath. But the landscape is not only a domain of danger, it is also an abode of opportunity, blessing, and power. (There is a legend in which one of these spirits mates with a human, and the two serve as progenitors of a fierce Tibetan tribe.) Thus, pilgrimage is an essential element of Tibetan religious life, with pilgrims seeking to derive power and purification by visiting those places believed to embody a particular potency, either naturally—as when the place is the abode of a god or the god itself—or historically—as when the place is the site of the inspired deeds of a great yogin such as Padmasambhava or Milarepa. The topography even contains hidden countries (*sbas yul*), ideal sites for the practice of tantra, the most famous being the kingdom of Shambala; there are guidebooks with directions to such destinations. It is also the land that yields the treasures (*gter ma*), the texts left behind, hidden in rocks, caves, and pillars by Padmasambhava himself, left safely within the earth until the time is right for them to be discovered and their contents made known to the world. Thus, the landscape is not simply an animated realm of fearful demons and ogresses, but above all the abode of power for those who know where to seek what lies within.

During the reign of Tri Songdetsen, not long after the founding of the Samye monastery, a politically charged doctrinal controversy erupted in Tibet. In addition to the Indian party of Śāntarakṣita, there was also an influential Chinese Buddhist contingent who found favor with the Tibetan nobility. These were monks of the Chan (Zen) school, led by one Mohoyen. According to traditional accounts, Śāntarakṣita foretold of dangers from the Chinese position and left instructions in his will that his student Kamalaśīla be called from India to counter the Chinese view. A conflict seems to have developed between the Indian and Chinese partisans (and their allies in the Tibetan court) over the question of the nature of enlightenment, with the Indians holding that enlightenment takes place as the culmination of a gradual process of purification, the result of combining virtuous action, meditative serenity, and philosophical insight. The Chinese spoke against this view, holding that enlightenment was the intrinsic nature of the mind rather than the goal of a protracted path, such that one need simply to recognize the presence of this innate nature of enlightenment by entering a state of awareness beyond distinctions; all other practices were superfluous. According to both Chinese and Tibetan records, a debate was held between Kamalaśīla and Mohoyen at Samye circa 797, with King Tri Songdetsen himself serving as judge. According to Tibetan accounts (contradicted by the Chinese accounts), Kamalaśīla was declared the winner and Mohoyen and his party were banished from Tibet, with the king proclaiming that thereafter the Middle Way (Madhyamaka) school of Indian Buddhist philosophy (to which Śāntarakṣita and Kamalaśīla belonged) would be followed in Tibet. Recent scholarship has suggested that although a controversy between the Indian and Chinese Buddhists (and their Tibetan partisans) occurred, it is unlikely that a face-to-face debate took place or that the outcome of the controversy was so unequivocal. Furthermore, it is probably important to recall that, regardless of the merits of the Indian and Chinese philosophical positions, China was Tibet's chief military rival at the time, whereas India posed no such threat. Nonetheless, it is significant that from this point Tibet largely sought its Buddhism from India; no school of Chinese Buddhism had any further influence in Tibet. Mohoyen himself was transformed into something of a trickster figure, popular in Tibetan art and drama.

The king Ralpajen (Ral pa can, ruled c. 815–835) seems to have been an even more enthusiastic patron of Buddhism, supporting numerous Indian-Tibetan translation teams who continued the formidable task of rendering a vast corpus of Sanskrit literature into Tibetan. Translation academies were established and standard glossaries of technical terms were developed during the ninth century. The relatively late date of the introduction of Buddhism to Tibet compared with China (first century C.E.) and Japan (fifth century) had important ramifications for the development of the Tibetan Buddhist tradition, the foremost being that the Tibetans had access to large bodies of Indian Buddhist literature that either never were translated into Chinese (and thus never transmitted to Japan) or had little influence in East Asia. This literature fell into two categories: tantras and śāstras.

The origins of tantric Buddhism in India remain nebulous, with some scholars dating the early texts from the fourth century C.E. Its literature, including all manner of ritual texts and meditation manuals, continued to be composed in India for the next six centuries. This literature offered a speedy path to enlightenment, radically truncating the eons-long path set forth in the earlier discourses attributed to the Buddha, called sūtras. To this end, the tantric literature set forth a wide range of techniques for the attainment of goals both mundane and supramundane, techniques for bringing the fantastic worlds described in the sūtras into actuality. Tantric practices were considered so potent that they were often conducted in secret, and aspirants required initiation. The practices themselves involved elaborate and meticulous visualizations, in which the practitioner mentally transformed himself or herself into a fully enlightened buddha, with a resplendent body seated on a throne in the center of a marvelous palace (called a maṇḍala), with speech that intoned sacred syllables (called mantras), and with a mind that saw the ultimate reality directly.

A second body of literature, more important for Buddhist philosophy per se, were the śāstras (treatises). Buddhist literature is sometimes divided into sūtras—those texts traditionally held to be either the word of the Buddha or spoken with his sanction—and śāstras—treatises composed by Indian commentators. In the case of Mahāyāna literature, sūtras often contain fantastic visions of worlds populated by enlightened beings, with entrance to such a world gained through devotion to the sūtra itself. When points of doctrine are presented, it is often in the form of narrative, allegory, or the repetition of stock phrases. The śāstras are closer to what might be called systematic philosophy or theology, with positions presented with reasoned argumentation supported by relevant passages from the sūtras and tantras. East Asian Buddhism was predominantly a sūtra-based tradition, with schools forming around single texts, such as the *Lotus Sūtra* and the *Avataṃsaka Sūtra*. Although many important śāstras were translated into Chinese, the major project of translating Indian texts into Chinese virtually ended with the work of Xuanzang (596–664), by whose time the major East Asian schools were well formed. Consequently, works by such figures as the Middle Way philosophers Candrakīrti (c. 600–650) and Śāntideva (early eighth century) and the logician Dharmakīrti (seventh century), who flourished when the Chinese Buddhist schools had already developed, never gained wide currency in East Asia but were highly influential in Tibet. The works by these and other authors became the basis of the scholastic tradition in Tibet, which from the early period was a śāstra-based Buddhism. Sūtras were venerated but rarely read independently; the śāstras were studied and commented upon at great length.

To undertake the task of translation of the sūtras, tantras, and śāstras, a whole new vocabulary had to be created. To render an often technical Sanskrit vocabulary, hundreds of neologisms were invented. In some cases, these were relatively straightforward translations of folk etymologies; in other cases, rather unwieldy terms were fabricated to capture multiple denotations of a Sanskrit term. When these eighth-century exegetes came to decide upon a Tibetan equivalent for the Sanskrit term for teacher, *guru*, a term classically etymologized in India as "one who is heavy (with virtue)," the translators departed from their storied penchant for approximating the meaning of the Sanskrit and opted instead for the word lama (*bla ma*). Here they combined the term *la* ("soul") with *ma*, which has as least three meanings: as a negative particle, as a substantive indicator, and as the word for "mother." Subsequent Buddhist etymologies, drawing on the meaning of *la* as "high" rather than its pre-Buddhist usage as "soul," were then construed, which explained *la ma* as meaning either "highest" (literally, "above-not," that is, "none above") or as "exalted mother." Although the original intention of the translators remains obscure, lama came to be the standard term for one's religious teacher, a person of such significance as to be appended to the threefold refuge formula: Tibetans say, "I go for refuge to the lama, I go for refuge to the Buddha, I go for refuge to the dharma, I go for refuge to the saṅgha."

It would be impossible to summarize the contents of the myriad sūtras, tantras, and śāstras translated into Tibetan, but it might be appropriate at this juncture to review some of the basic elements of Indian Buddhism that were important in Tibet. Tibetans, both Bönpo and Buddhist, conceive of a beginningless cycle of birth and death, called *korwa* (*'khor ba*, a translation of the Sanskrit *saṃsāra*, "wandering"), in six realms of rebirth: gods, demigods, humans, animals, ghosts, and hell beings. The realms of animals, ghosts, and hell beings are regarded as places of great suffering, whereas the godly realms are abodes of great bliss. Human rebirth falls in between, bringing as it does both pleasure and pain. The engine of saṃsāra is driven by karma, the cause and effect of actions. Like other Buddhists, Tibetans believe that every intentional act, whether it be physical, verbal, or mental, leaves a residue in its agent. That residue, like a seed, will eventually produce an effect at some future point in this life or another life, an effect in the form of pleasure or pain for the person who performed the act. Thus Tibetans imagine a moral universe in which virtuous deeds create experiences of pleasure and nonvirtuous deeds create experiences of pain. These latter are often delineated in a list of ten nonvirtuous deeds: killing, stealing, sexual misconduct, lying, divisive speech, harsh speech, senseless speech, covetousness, harmful intent, and wrong view (notably belief that actions do not have effects). The ten virtues are the opposites of this list: sustaining life, giving gifts, maintaining sexual decorum, and so on. Much of Tibetan religious practice is concerned with accumulating virtuous deeds and preventing, through a variety of ritual means, the fruition of negative deeds already committed. These deeds determine not only the quality of a given life but also the place of the rebirth after death. Depending on the gravity of a negative deed (killing being more serious than senseless speech, and killing a human more serious than killing an insect, for example), one may be reborn as an animal, as a ghost, or in one of the hot or cold hells, where the life span is particularly lengthy.

As in India, karma is not concerned simply with what might be termed in the West moral and immoral deeds. There is, in conjunction with the belief that virtue brings happiness and nonvirtue sorrow, a powerful system of purity and pollution, generally concerned with one's behavior not toward humans but nonhumans, the various gods and spirits that inhabit the world. In determining the cause of some affliction, there is often an attempt by the afflicted or his or her ritual agent to determine both the karmic cause (some nonvirtuous deed in the past) and polluting acts (such as associating with a blacksmith, building a fire on a mountain, or accepting food from a widow) that contributed to that past evil deed coming to fruition in the form of a particular misfortune.

Rebirth as a god or human in the realm of desire is the result of a virtuous deed and is considered very rare. Rarer still is rebirth as a human who has access to the teachings of the Buddha. In a famous analogy, a single blind tortoise is said to swim in a vast ocean, surfacing for air only once every century. On the surface of the ocean floats a single golden yoke. It is rarer, said the Buddha, to be reborn as a human with the opportunity to practice the dharma than it is for the tortoise to surface for its centennial breath with its head through the hole in the golden yoke. One is said to be reborn as a god in the realm of desire as a result of an act of charity: giving gifts results in future wealth. Rebirth as a human is said to result from consciously refraining from a nonvirtuous deed, as when one takes a vow not to kill humans.

Although the various sects of Tibetan Buddhism derive their monastic regulations from the Indian schools known pejoratively as the Hīnayāna ("low vehicle"), all sects of Tibetan Buddhism identify themselves as proponents of the Mahāyāna, both in their practice and in their philosophy. Mahāyāna, a Sanskrit word that means "great vehicle," is the term used to distinguish a rather disparate group of cults of the book that arose in India some four hundred years after the death of the Buddha and continued in India into the twelfth century. During these centuries, the followers of the Mahāyāna produced a vast literature of sūtras that purport to be the word of the historical Buddha, as well as commentaries upon them. Among the factors characteristic of the Mahāyāna are the view of the Buddha as an eternal presence, associated physically with reliquaries (stūpas) and with texts that embody his words, a belief in the existence of myriad buddhas working in multiple universes for the benefit of all beings, and an attendant emphasis on the universal possibility of enlightenment for all, monks and laypeople alike. It is from this last tenet that the term "Great Vehicle" is derived: the proponents of the Mahāyāna believed that their path was capable of bringing all beings in the universe to buddhahood, whereas the earlier teachings were capable only of delivering the individual disciple to a state of solitary peace.

Perhaps the most famous feature of the Mahāyāna is its emphasis on the bodhisattva, a person who makes the compassionate vow to become a buddha in order to lead all beings in the universe out of suffering and to the bliss of enlightenment. The Sanskrit term *bodhisattva* was rendered into Tibetan as *jang chup sem ba (byang chub sems dpa')*, "one who is heroic in his or her aspiration to enlightenment." The path of the bodhisattva is portrayed as one of extraordinary length, encompassing billions of lifetimes devoted to cultivating such virtues as generosity, ethics, patience, effort, concentration, and wisdom, the so-called six perfections, all of these deeds motivated by the wish to liberate all beings from the beginningless cycle of rebirth.

A common tenet of Buddhism is that all suffering is ultimately the result of ignorance. This ignorance is defined as a belief in self. Mahāyāna philosophy expands upon earlier teachings to see ignorance not simply as a misconception concerning the nature of the person, but as a misunderstanding of all things. According to the Middle Way school, the fundamental error is to conceive of things as existing in and of themselves—independently, autonomously, possessed of some intrinsic nature, some inherent existence. Wisdom, the sixth of the perfections to be cultivated by the bodhisattva, is the understanding that all things, including persons, are utterly devoid of such a nature and are, in fact, empty of an independent status, although they exist conventionally. To say that things exist conventionally means, for example, that cause and effect remain viable and that things perform functions; one can sit on a chair and drink tea from a cup. Emptiness, then, does not mean that things do not exist at all, but rather that they do not exist as they appear to the unenlightened.

To become enlightened, then, the bodhisattva must develop not only this wisdom but infinite compassion as well, that is, must dedicate himself or herself to work forever for the welfare of others while simultaneously understanding that all beings, including oneself, do not exist ultimately, that they do not exist as they appear.

The practice of the Mahāyāna generally may be said to take two forms, both focused on the bodhisattva. The most influential of the Mahāyāna sūtras, such as the *Lotus Sūtra*, proclaim that all beings will eventually become buddhas, and that, consequently, all beings will traverse the bodhisattva path. Thus, one form of Mahāyāna belief emphasizes practices for becoming a bodhisattva and performing the bodhisattva's deeds. As bodhisattvas advance along the path, they become increasingly adept at allaying the sufferings of sentient beings who call upon them for aid, often through miraculous intercession. Consequently, the other major form of Mahāyāna practice is concerned with devotions intended to procure the aid of these compassionate beings. The bodhisattva who is said to be the physical manifestation of all the compassion of all the buddhas in the universe, Avalokiteśvara, is the particular object of such reverence in Tibet, as discussed below. Avalokiteśvara is invoked by the famous mantra *oṃ maṇi padme hūṃ*, which might be rendered as, "O you who hold the jeweled [rosary] and the lotus [have mercy on us]." (It certainly does not mean "the jewel in the lotus.") Avalokiteśvara is depicted in a wide variety of forms in Tibetan art, two of the most frequent being with one head and four arms (two of which hold a rosary and a lotus evoked in the mantra) or with eleven heads and a thousand arms. The multiple arms are said to represent the bodhisattva's extraordinary ability to come to the aid of suffering sentient beings. Paintings of the thousand-armed Avalokiteśvara often show an eye in the palm of each of the hands. The bodhisattva thus serves as both role model and object of devotion in Mahāyāna Buddhism, functions that are by no means deemed mutually exclusive; it is quite common for persons who consider themselves to have embarked on the bodhisattva path to seek the assistance of more advanced bodhisattvas in their long quest for enlightenment.

In the realm of Buddhist practice, the Tibetans were able to witness and assimilate the most important development of late Indian Buddhism, Buddhist tantra. Tantra, known also as the *vajrayāna*, the "Diamond Vehicle," and the *mantrayāna*, the "Mantra Vehicle," was considered an esoteric approach to the Mahāyāna path whereby the length of time required to achieve buddhahood could be abbreviated from the standard length of three periods of countless aeons (reckoned by some as 384×10^{58} years) to as little as three years and three months. One of the chief techniques for effecting such an extraordinary reduction in the length of the path was an elaborate system of ritual, visualization, and meditation, sometimes called deity yoga, in which the practitioner imagined himself or herself to be already fully enlightened with the marvelous body, speech, mind, and abode of a buddha. In addition to the ultimate attainment of buddhahood, tantric practice was said to bestow a wide range of lesser magical powers, such as the power to increase wealth and life span, to pacify the inauspicious, and to destroy enemies, both human and nonhuman. Yogins who developed these powers were known as *mahāsiddhas*, "great adepts"; they are popular subjects of Tibetan Buddhist literature.

Among the elements of tantric Buddhism most commonly identified in the West are its erotic and wrathful motifs, where male and female are depicted in sexual union and bull-headed deities, adorned with garlands of human heads, brandish cleavers and skullcups. In Mahāyāna Buddhism, as already mentioned, wisdom and compassion (also referred to as method, that is, the compassionate means whereby bodhisattvas become buddhas) are the essential components of the bodhisattva's path to buddhahood. Wisdom, especially the perfection of wisdom, is identified with the female. In tantra, the symbolism is rendered in more explicitly sexual terms, with wisdom as female and method male, their union being essential to the achievement of enlightenment. Buddhist tantra is said to be the "Diamond Vehicle" because wisdom and method are joined in an adamantine and indivisible union, bestowing buddhahood quickly. This is the chief symbolic meaning of depiction of sexual union. However, part of the unique nature of the tantric path is its capacity to employ deeds that are ordinarily prohibited in practices that speed progress on the path to enlightenment, hence the great emphasis on antinomian behavior, such as the consumption of meat and alcohol, in the hagiographies of the *mahāsiddhas*. One such deed is sexual intercourse, and many tantric texts, especially of the Unexcelled Yoga (*anuttarayoga*) variety, prescribe ritual union as a means of unifying the mind of the clear light and the immutable bliss. Whether this intercourse is to be performed only in imagination or in fact, and at what point on the path it is to take place, has been a point of considerable discussion in Tibetan tantric exegesis.

Wrathful deities also populate the tantric pantheon. Despite claims by nineteenth-century scholars that continue to be repeated, the most important of these deities are not of Tibetan shamanic origin, added to Indian Buddhism after its arrival in Tibet. It is clear from Indian tantric texts that these deities derive directly from India. Some are buddhas and bodhisattvas in their wrathful aspects, the most famous of these being Yamantaka, the wrathful manifestation of the bodhisattva of wisdom, Mañjuśrī. His terrifying form is said to be intended to frighten away the egotism and selfishness that are the cause of all suffering. Other wrathful deities have the task of protecting the dharma; others are worldly deities with specific powers that may be propitiated. Despite such explanations, Western scholars of Tibet have yet to engage adequately the issue of the apparent presence of the demonic in the divine that confronts the observer so richly in Tibetan religious iconography.

Tantric Buddhism places especial emphasis on the role of the teacher. The teacher-student relationship was always of great importance in Buddhism, providing the means by which the dharma was passed from one generation to the next. In tantra, however, the teacher or guru took on an even more important role. The practice of the Vajrayāna, the rapid path to enlightenment, was regarded as a secret teaching, not suitable for everyone. For that reason, the teacher was both the repository of secret knowledge and the person who was to judge the qualifications of the student as a receptacle for that knowledge. Once the student was deemed ready, the teacher provided the student with an initiation, serving as the surrogate of the Buddha, and one of the basic practices of Buddhist tantra is thus to regard one's own teacher as the Buddha. In fact, Tibetans are fond of saying that the teacher is actually kinder than the Buddha, because the Buddha did not remain in the world to teach us benighted beings of this degenerate age. This great emphasis on the importance of the teacher was inherited from India, as the accounts of Tibetans' sojourns to India make clear. Because of this importance of the teacher, or lama, during the nineteenth century Tibetan Buddhism was dubbed "Lamaism," a term that continues to appear today. Tibetan Buddhists regard this as a pejorative term, because it suggests that whereas there is Chinese Buddhism, Japanese Buddhism, Thai Buddhism, and so forth, the Buddhism of Tibet is so different that it does not warrant the name "Tibetan Buddhism" but should be called "Lamaism."

In the Vajrayāna, rituals called *sādhanas* (literally, "means of achievement") are set forth in which the practitioner, through a practice of visualization, petitions a buddha or bodhisattva to come into his or her presence. Much of the practice described in tantric sādhanas involves the enactment of a world—the fantastic jewel-encrusted world of the Mahāyāna sūtras or the horrific world of the charnel ground. In the tantric sādhana, the practitioner manifests that world through visualization, through a process of invitation, descent, and identification. Tantric sādhanas generally take one of two forms. In the first, the buddha or bodhisattva is requested to appear before the meditator and is then worshipped in the expectation of receiving blessings. In the other type of tantric sādhana, the meditator imagines himself or herself to be a fully enlightened buddha or bodhisattva now, to have the exalted body, speech, and mind of an enlightened being. In either case, the central deity in the visualization is called a *yi dam*, a word difficult to translate into English. It is sometimes rendered as "tutelary deity," but the *yi dam* offers much more than protection. The *yi dam* is the tantric buddha with which the meditator identifies in daily meditation and whom he or she propitiates in daily rituals. Some *yi dams* take peaceful forms, adorned with the silks and jewels of an Indian monarch. Others appear in wrathful forms, brandishing weapons and wreathed in flames.

Tantric sādhanas tend to follow a fairly set sequence, whether they are simple and brief or more detailed and prolix. More elaborate sādhanas may include the recitation of a lineage of gurus; the creation of a protection wheel guarded by wrathful deities to subjugate enemies; the creation of a body maṇḍala, in which a pantheon of deities take residence at various parts of the meditator's body; etc.

In many sādhanas, the meditator is instructed to imagine light radiating from the body, inviting buddhas and bodhisattvas from throughout the universe. Visualizing them arrayed in the space before him or her, the meditator then performs a series of standard preliminary practices called the sevenfold service, a standard component of sādhanas and prayers that developed from an Indian Mahāyāna three-part liturgy (the *triskandhaka*). Prior to the actual sevenfold service, the assembled deities are offered (again, in visualization) a bath and new clothing and are treated just as an honored guest would be in India. The sevenfold service is then performed. The first of the seven elements is obeisance, an expression of homage to the assembled deities. Next comes offering, usually the longest section of the seven parts. Here fantastic gifts are imagined to be arrayed before the buddhas and bodhisattvas to please each of their five senses: beautiful forms for the eye, music for the ears, fragrances for the nose, delicacies for the tongue, and sensuous silks for the body. The offering often concludes with a gift of the entire physical universe with all its marvels. The third step is confession of misdeeds. Despite the apparent inexorability of the law of karma, it is nonetheless believed that by sincerely confessing a sin to the buddhas and bodhisattvas, promising not to commit it again in the future, and performing some kind of purificatory penance (usually the recitation of mantra) as an antidote to the sin, the eventual negative effect of the negative deed can be avoided. The fourth step, admiration, also relates to the law of karma. It is believed that acknowledging, praising, and otherwise taking pleasure in the virtuous deeds of others causes the taker of such pleasure to accumulate the same merit as that accrued by the person who actually performed the good deed.

The fifth step is an entreaty to the buddhas not to pass into nirvāṇa. A buddha is said to have the ability to live for aeons but will do so only if he is asked; otherwise, he will disappear from the world, pretending to die and pass into nirvāṇa. Indian sūtras recount the Buddha scolding his attendant for not making such a request. In Tibet this entreaty to the buddhas to remain in the world developed from a standard component of daily prayers to a separate genre of literature, called *shap den* (*zhabs brtan*); the term literally means "steadfast feet," suggesting that the buddhas remain with their feet firmly planted in this world. However, in Tibet these prayers were composed and recited for the surrogate of the absent Buddha, the lama. Prayers for "steadfast feet" or long-life prayers are hence composed for one's teacher. The sixth of the seven branches follows naturally from the entreaty to remain in the world; it is a supplication of the buddhas and bodhisattvas to teach the dharma. The final step is the dedication of the merit of performing the preceding toward the enlightenment of all beings.

The meditator then goes for refuge to the three jewels, creates the aspiration to enlightenment, the promise to achieve buddhahood in order to liberate all beings in the universe from suffering, and dedicates the merit from the foregoing and subsequent practices toward that end. The meditator next cultivates the four attitudes of love, compassion, joy, and equanimity, before meditating on emptiness and reciting the purificatory mantra, *oṃ svabhāvaśuddhāḥ sarvadharmāḥ svabhāvaśuddho 'haṃ*, "Oṃ, naturally pure are all phenomena, naturally pure am I," understanding that emptiness is the primordial nature of everything, the unmoving world and the beings who move upon it. Out of this emptiness, the meditator next creates the maṇḍala.

The meditator here creates an imaginary universe out of emptiness. The foundation is provided by the four elements wind, fire, water, and earth (represented by Sanskrit syllables). On top of these, the meditator visualizes the maṇḍala. The Sanskrit term *maṇḍala* simply means circle, but in this context within a tantric sādhana, a maṇḍala is the residence of a buddha, an extraordinary palace inhabited by buddhas and their consorts, by bodhisattvas, and protectors. A maṇḍala may be quite spare, an undescribed palace with only five deities, one deity in the center and one in each of the cardinal directions. But usually maṇḍalas are much more elaborate. The Guhyasamāja maṇḍala, for example, is articulated in great detail, with five layers of walls of white, yellow, red, green, and blue. It has a jeweled molding, archways, and a quadruple colonnade. It is festooned with jewels and pendants and is populated by thirty-two deities, each on its own throne, arrayed on two levels. The maṇḍala is the perfected world that the meditator seeks to manifest and then inhabit, either by identifying with the central deity or by making offerings to him or her. It was said to be essential that the visualization be carried out in precise detail, with each item of silk clothing and gold ornament appearing clearly. It was also necessary for the meditator to imagine the fantastic palace of the buddha, the maṇḍala, which he or she inhabited, noting the particular bodhisattvas, protectors, gods, and goddesses located throughout the multistoried dwelling. Part of this visualization was accomplished through the description of the details in the tantric text itself. However, meditators were typically advised to study a visual image of the particular buddha and maṇḍala, and this was one of the uses to which paintings and statues were put by those involved in meditation practice. Paintings and statues were not considered to be functional in any context, even as the object of simple devotion, until they were consecrated in a special ceremony in which the dharmakāya was caused to descend into and animate the icon.

The next step in the sādhana is for the meditator to animate the residents of the maṇḍala by causing the actual buddhas and bodhisattvas, referred to as "wisdom beings" (*ye shes sems dpa', jñānasattva*), to descend and merge with their imagined doubles, the "pledge beings" (*dam tshig sems dpa', samayasattva*). Light radiates from meditator's heart, drawing the wisdom beings to the maṇḍala where, through offerings and the recitation of the mantra *jaḥ hūṃ baṃ hoḥ* ("Be summoned, enter, become fused with, be pleased"), they are caused to enter the residents of the maṇḍala. The residents are then often blessed with three syllables: a white *oṃ* at the crown of the head, a red *āḥ* at the throat, and a blue *hūṃ* at the heart.

With the preliminary visualization now complete, the stage is set for the central meditation of the sādhana, and this varies depending upon the purpose of the sādhana. Generally, offerings and prayers are made to a sequence of deities and boons are requested from them, each time accompanied by the recitation of appropriate mantra. At the end of the session, the meditator makes mental offerings to the assembly before inviting them to leave, at which point the entire visualization, the palace and its residents, dissolves into emptiness. The sādhana ends with a dedication of the merit accrued from the session to the welfare of all beings.

From this brief survey of Buddhist doctrine and practice, several distinctive elements of Tibetan Buddhism become apparent. First, Tibetan Buddhism is the last of the major national Buddhisms to develop, having access to a larger corpus of Indian Buddhist literature than reached China or Japan, for example. As discussed above, this literature included the śāstras and the tantras, such that Tibetan Buddhism can generally be characterized as śāstra-based in its doctrine and tantra-based in its practice. It is important to note, however, that certain central elements of practice, such as monastic regulations and the techniques for creating the bodhisattva's compassionate aspiration to buddhahood, are delineated in śāstras. Furthermore, all sects of Tibetan Buddhism developed sophisticated scholastic traditions of tantric exegesis.

Second, the Tibetans had sustained contact with major figures of the late Indian Buddhist tradition for over a century, and the legacies of these figures, such as Atiśa and Niguma, remain powerful elements of the tradition. Third, Tibet was perhaps the least culturally evolved of the major Buddhist nations at the time of the introduction of Buddhism, when culture is measured in terms of written language, literature, and structures of state. The introduction of Buddhism encountered resistance, as noted above, but with the demise of the royal line in 842, the way was left open for Buddhism to provide the dominant ideology for the entire Inner Asian cultural area. Finally, Tibetan Buddhism is the only major form of Buddhism to continue in a fairly traditional form into the second half of this century.

The evidence of the early records indicates that, despite their patronage of Buddhism, Ralpajen and his two predecessor kings gave numerous public testimonies to their attachment to principles irreconcilable with Buddhism, principles pertaining to the highly structured politico-religious system of divine kingship (called *gtsug lag*), while at the same time propagating the new religion. The translation of Indian Buddhist literature, the sūtras, tantras, and śāstras, from Sanskrit into Tibetan was interrupted by the suppression of Buddhist monastic institutions in 838 by the king Langdarma (Glang dar ma, ruled c. 836–842). Although Langdarma is represented as the embodiment of evil in Buddhist accounts, persecuting monks and nuns and closing monasteries, recent scholarship indicates that his persecution, if it took place at all, amounted to a withdrawal of state patronage to the growing monastic institutions.

Nevertheless, his reign, which according to later Buddhist accounts ended with his assassination in 842 by a Buddhist monk (an event some scholars question), is traditionally seen as the end of what is called the early dissemination of Buddhism in Tibet and the beginning of a dark period of disorder, at least in central Tibet. It marked the beginning of the end of the royal line and the eventual disintegration of the Tibetan empire. Although it is the case that the status of

Buddhist thought and practice during the next century and a half remains only vaguely understood by modern scholars, its representation in traditional Buddhist histories as a time of degradation and chaos may be something of an exaggeration, motivated to provide a striking contrast with the glorious renaissance that was to follow. Nevertheless, little of "pre-Buddhist" religion of Tibet survived intact after this period. This religion, which Tibetans call "the religion of humans" (*mi chos*), as opposed to the "religion of the gods" (*lha chos*, identified with Buddhism and Bön) is all but impossible to identify, with much of its content assimilated by Buddhism and Bön after the eleventh century, leaving only a few legends, aphorisms, and folk songs.

After the so-called dark period a Buddhist revival began in western Tibet in the eleventh century, a period of active translation of numerous philosophical texts and the retranslation of texts, especially tantras, first translated during the period of the earlier dissemination. The eleventh century was also a time of active travel of Tibetan translators to India, where they studied with Indian Buddhist masters in Bihar, Bengal, and Kashmir. Many of the sects of Tibetan Buddhism trace their lineages back to these encounters.

The most famous Indian scholar to visit Tibet during what came to be called the second dissemination was the Bengali master Atiśa (982–1054). A Tibetan named Dromdön ('Brom ston pa) was Atiśa's first and closest Tibetan disciple. He urged Atiśa to visit central Tibet and organized his tour of the area, where Atiśa taught and translated until his death in 1054. Dromdön devoted the rest of his life to preserving Atiśa's teachings, establishing the monastery of Rva sgreng in 1056 and founding the first Tibetan Buddhist monastic order, the Kadampa (Bka' gdams pa, which is traditionally etymologized as "those who take all of the Buddha's words as instructions"). Although Drom was a respected scholar and translator, he is best remembered for the rigor and austerity of his Buddhist practice. He seems to have been wary of the potential for abuse in tantrism and imposed on his followers a strict discipline and devotion to practice for which they became famous. They abstained from marriage, intoxicants, travel, and the possession of money. Although later Tibetan orders were not as strict, the Kadampa provided the model for all later Tibetan monasticism.

The monastery was an institution of fundamental importance for all sects of Tibetan Buddhism. The first monastery was constructed around 779 under the direction of the Indian paṇḍita Śāntarakṣita and the tantric master Padmasambhava. From the outset, Tibetan monasteries were modeled on the great monastic centers of late Indian Buddhism, where the monastic code was maintained in conjunction with scholastic education and tantric practice. With the growth in lay and state patronage, some monasteries grew from small retreat centers to vast monastic complexes. The largest of these, such as Drepung (which, with some 13,000 monks in 1959, was the largest Buddhist monastery in the world), functioned as self-sufficient cities, with their own economy (with farms worked by sharecroppers), government, and police force. Tibetan monks were not fully supported by the monasteries, receiving only a small ration of tea and roasted barley for their subsistence; they had to rely on their families or their own earnings (from trade or performing rituals) for anything more. Monks did not go on begging rounds, like their counterparts in Southeast Asia, but engaged in a wide range of occupations. It is therefore inaccurate to imagine that all Tibetan monks spent their days in meditation or in debating sophisticated points of doctrine; only a small percentage were thus occupied. Furthermore, the majority of the occupants of Tibetan monasteries remained as novices throughout their lives, not going on to take the vows of a fully ordained monk (*dge slong*, *bhikṣu*).

To be a monk was to hold a respected social status in the Tibetan world, and monkhood provided one of the few routes to social advancement. Monks who distinguished themselves as scholars, teachers, or meditators commanded great respect and attracted substantial patronage, especially those considered to be effective in performance of rituals and divinations. Such monks could rise through the monastic ranks to positions of great authority as abbots or (among the Geluk) as government officials.

Each of the sects, both Buddhist and Bönpo, had large monasteries that drew monks from all over the Tibetan cultural sphere, which extended from as far west as the Kalmyk region between the Caspian Sea and the Black Sea, from as far east as Sichuan, from as far north as the Buryiat region near Lake Baikal, and from as far south as Nepal. Some came for an education and then returned to their home regions, while others remained for life. However, the majority of monasteries in Tibet were isolated places (as the Tibetan term for monastery, *dgon pa*, suggests), populated by a few dozen local monks who performed rituals for the local community and were supported by their families. Monastic life, whether in a major center or a remote hermitage, was not so much a matter of doctrine or belief, but of behavior, a behavior that creates the identity of the monk. That behavior was governed by a monastic code inherited from India but adapted for each monastery in its constitution called a *ja yik* (*bca' yig*).

Although a substantial segment of the male population of Tibetan was monks (estimated between 10 and 15 percent), the community of nuns (*a ni*) was much smaller (perhaps 3 percent). They lived in some six hundred nunneries, the largest of which, a Kagyu institution called Gechak Thekchen Ling (Dge chag theg chen gling), housed approximately one thousand nuns. Whereas Tibetan monks could eventually receive the full ordination of the gelong (*dge slong*), the order of full nuns was never established in Tibet, such that nuns could advance no higher than the rank of novice. (There have been efforts in recent years, led largely by Western women who have become Tibetan nuns, to receive full ordination from Chinese nuns in Taiwan and Singapore). Being a nun carried little of the status held by a monk; there is a Tibetan proverb that if you want to be a servant, make your son a monk; if you want a servant, make your daughter a nun. Unmarried daughters often became nuns (sometimes remaining at home). Other women became nuns to escape a bad marriage, to avoid pregnancy, or after the death of a spouse. The educational opportunities and chances for social advancement open to monks were generally absent for nuns, whose chief activities involved the memorization and recitation of prayer and the performance of ritual.

The role of women in Tibetan religions was not, however, limited simply to the order of nuns. There are many important females divinities, both peaceful and wrathful, benevolent and malevolent. The goddess Tārā stands with Avalokiteśvara as the most commonly invoked of Buddhist deities. The wrathful tantric goddess Belden Lhamo is the special protectoress of the Tibetan state. Among the many malevolent female forms, one finds the "gossip girl" who sows discord in the community. Women have also played significant roles in various meditation and ritual lineages, such as the Indian yoginī Niguma, the wife of king Tri Songdetsen and consort of Padmasambhava, Yeshe Tsogyal (Ye shes mtsho rgyal), and the tantric master Majik Lapdön (Ma gcig lab sgron). There are lines of female incarnations, the most famous of whom is Dorje Pamo (Rdo rje phag mo, the "Diamond Sow"). Beyond these famous figures, Tibetan women have played important roles as mediums for deities or as messengers for bodhisattvas. The majority of those who return from the dead to bring messages from the deceased and exhortations to observe the laws of karma are women. Despite the disproportionate investment of religious power and authority in the males of Tibetan society, women enjoyed a greater economic and sexual autonomy in Tibet than generally was the case elsewhere in Asia. Many of the rituals and practices described in this volume would have been practiced by women as well as men.

With the decline of the monarchy, both political and religious authority (although the strict distinction between the two should not be immediately assumed in the case of Tibet) shifted gradually to Buddhist teachers. Since many of these were Buddhist monks who had taken vows of celibacy, the problem of succession eventually arose. In some cases, authority was passed from a monk to his nephew. However, by the fourteenth century (and perhaps even earlier) a form of succession developed in Tibet that, although supported by standard Buddhist doctrine, seems unique in the Buddhist world. This was the institution of the incarnate lama or *tulku* (*sprul sku*).

In Mahāyāna literature there is a doctrine of the three bodies of the Buddha. The first is the *dharmakāya*. Prior to the rise of the Mahāyāna, this term meant the "body of [uncontaminated] qualities," those qualities of the Buddha, such as his wisdom, patience, and fearlessness, that were not subject to suffering and decay. It was this body that was deemed the true object of the practice of refuge. Thus, the term "body" came to shift its meaning from the physical form of the Buddha to a collection of timeless abstract virtues. In Mahāyāna literature, the dharmakāya is often represented as almost a cosmic principle, an ultimate reality in which all buddhas partake through their omniscient minds. For this reason, some scholars translate dharmakāya as "Truth Body." After the dharmakāya comes the enjoyment body (*saṃbhogakāya*), a fantastic form of a buddha that resides only in the highest pure land, adorned with thirty-two major and eighty minor physical marks, eternally teaching the Mahāyāna to highly advanced bodhisattvas; the enjoyment body does not appear to ordinary beings. Many tantric deities are depicted in the enjoyment body form. The third body is the emanation body (*nirmāṇakāya*). It is this body that appears in the world to teach the dharma. The emanation bodies are not limited to the form of the Buddha with which we are familiar; a buddha is able to appear in whatever form, animate or inanimate, that is appropriate to benefit suffering sentient beings.

Tibetans chose the term for the third body of a buddha to name their notion of incarnation. That is, the next incarnation of a former great teacher is called a tulku (*sprul sku*), the Tibetan translation of nirmāṇakāya, "emanation body." The implication is that there is a profound difference in the processes whereby ordinary beings and incarnate lamas take birth in the world. For the former, rebirth is harrowing process, a frightful journey into the unknown, a process over which one has no control. One is blown by the winds of karma into an intermediate state (*bar do*) and then into a new lifetime. There is a strong possibility that new life will be in the lower realms as an animal, hungry ghost, or hell being; Tibetans say that the number of beings in these three lower realms is as large as the number of stars seen on a clear night and the number of beings in the realms of gods and humans is as large as the number stars seen on a clear day. The fate of the denizens of hell is particularly horrific, and Tibetans recount the journeys of those who are able to visit the lower realms of rebirth and return to tell the tale. The process of powerless rebirth is a beginningless cycle and can only be brought to an end by the individual achievement of liberation and enlightenment through the practice of the path.

The rebirth of an incarnate lama is a very different matter. As "emanation bodies," incarnate lamas are technically buddhas, free from the bonds of karma. Their rebirth is thus entirely voluntary. They need not be reborn at all, yet they decide to return to the world out of their compassion for others. Furthermore, they exercise full control over their rebirth. For ordinary beings, rebirth must take place within forty-nine days from the time of death. Incarnate lamas are under no such constraints. For ordinary beings, the circumstances of the rebirth—the place, the parents, the form of the body, and the capacity of the mind—are all determined by karma. For the incarnate lama, all of these are a matter of choice and are said to have been decided in advance, so that a dying incarnation will often leave instructions for his disciples as to where to find his next rebirth.

Since the fourteenth century, all sects of Tibetan Buddhism have adopted the practice of identifying the successive rebirths of a great teacher, the most famous instance of which being of course the Dalai Lamas. But there some three thousand other lines of incarnation in Tibet (only several of whom are female). The institution of the incarnate lama has proved to be a central component of Tibetan society, providing the means by which authority and charisma, in all of their symbolic and material forms, are passed from one generation to another. Indeed, the spread of Tibetan Buddhism can usefully be traced by the increasingly large geographical areas in which incarnate lamas are discovered, extending today to Europe and North America.

A common use of the term "lama" is as the designation of incarnations. In ordinary Tibetan parlance, such persons are called "lamas" whether or not they have distinguished themselves as scholars, adepts, or teachers in their present lives. The ambiguity in usage between "lama" as a religious preceptor and "lama" as an incarnation has led the current Dalai Lama in his sermons to admonish his followers that a lama (as one's religious teacher) need not be an incarnation and that an incarnation is not necessarily a lama (in the sense of a fully qualified religious teacher).

The period of the thirteenth through fifteenth centuries was among the most consequential for the history of Tibetan Buddhism, with the development of distinct sects that evolved from the various lineages of teaching that had been initiated during the previous periods. These sects are traditionally divided under two major headings: those who base their tantric practice on texts translated during the period of the first dissemination and those who base their tantric practice on texts translated or retranslated during the period of the second dissemination. These two groups are referred to simply as the old (*rnying ma*) and the new (*gsar ma*), with the old obviously including the Nyingmapa (Rnying ma pa) sect and the new including the Kagyu, Sakya, and Geluk. The Nyingmapa sect traces its origins back to the first dissemination and the teachings of Padmasambhava, who visited Tibet during the eighth century. "Treasures," called *terma* (*gter ma*), believed to have been hidden by him, began to be discovered in the eleventh century and continue to be discovered even into the twentieth century; the fourteenth century was an especially active period for text discoverers (*gter ston*). According to their claim, these texts were sometimes discovered in physical form, often within stone, or mentally, within the mind of the discoverer. Often ignored in the old-new categorization are the Bönpos, who seem to have appeared as a self-conscious "sect" in the eleventh century, along with new sects, but who represent themselves as even older than the old (Nyingma), predating the introduction of Buddhism into Tibet.

The various institutional entities of Tibetan Buddhism are referred to in Tibetan as *chos lugs*, literally, "dharma systems." This term is generally rendered into English with one of three terms: order, school, or sect. Each of these translations is misleading. "Order" implies a monastic unit with its own code of conduct, whereas in Tibet all Buddhist monks followed the same Indian monastic code. Furthermore, many adherents of the Tibetan groups are not monks or nuns. "School" implies a group distinguished on the basis of philosophical tenets, and although there are differences among the Tibetan Buddhist groups, there is much more that they share. "Sect" carries the negative connotation of a group dissenting from a majority that perceives it as somehow heretical. If that connotation can be ignored, however, "sect" provides a serviceable translation and is used here. What is perhaps more important than the translation used is to understand that central to each of these groups is the notion of lineage. Like other Buddhist traditions, the Tibetans based claims to authority largely on lineage, and in their case, they claimed that the Buddhism taught in Tibet and by Tibetan lamas abroad could be traced backward in an unbroken line to the eleventh century, when the founders of the major Tibetan sects made the perilous journey to India to receive the dharma from the great masters of Bengal, Bihar, and Kashmir, who were themselves direct recipients of teachings that could be traced back to the Buddha himself. Moreover, this lineage was represented as essentially oral, with instructions being passed down from master to disciple as an unwritten commentary on a sacred text. Even those sects that could not so easily list a successive line of teachers stretching back through the past, such as the Nyingmapas and Bönpos, were able to maintain the power of their lineage through the device of the hidden and rediscovered text, the *terma*, designed to leapfrog over centuries, bringing the authentic teaching directly into the present. These texts thus provided the present with the sanction of the past by ascribing to their ancient and absent author (usually Padmasambhava) the gift of prophecy.

Nyingma (Rnying ma)

The Nyingma sect traces its origins back to the teachings of the mysterious figure Padmasambhava, who visited Tibet during the eight century. The Nyingmapas include in their canonical corpus a collection of tantras (the *Rnying ma rgyud 'bum*) as well as these discovered texts, all works that the other sects generally regard as apocryphal, that is, not of Indian origin.

The Nyingma sect produced many famous scholars and visionaries, such as Longchenpa (Klong chen rab 'byams, 1308–1363), Jigme Lingpa ('Jigs med gling pa, 1729–1798), and Mipham ('Ju Mi pham rnam rgyal, 1846–1912). Nyingma identifies nine vehicles among the corpus of Buddhist teachings, the highest of which is known as Atiyoga or, more commonly, the Great Perfection (*rdzogs chen*). These teachings, found also in Bön, describe the mind as the primordial basis, characterized by qualities such as presence, spontaneity, luminosity, original purity, unobstructed freedom, expanse, clarity, self-liberation, openness, effortlessness, and intrinsic awareness. It is not accessible through conceptual elaboration or logical analysis. Rather, the primordial basis is an eternally pure state free from dualism of subject and object, infinite and perfect from the beginning, ever complete. The Great Perfection tradition shares with certain Indian Buddhist schools the view that the mind creates the appearances of the world, the arena of human suffering. All of these appearances are said to be illusory, however. The ignorant mind believes that its own creations are real, forgetting its true nature of original purity. For the mind willfully to seek to liberate itself is both inappropriate and futile because it is already self-liberated. The technique for the discovery of the ubiquitous original purity and self-liberation is to engage in a variety of practices designed to eliminate karmic obstacles, at which point the mind eliminates all thought and experiences itself, thereby recognizing its true nature. The Great Perfection doctrine does not seem to be directly derived from any of the Indian philosophical schools; its precise connections to the Indian Buddhist tradition have yet to be established. Some scholars have claimed a historical link and doctrinal affinity between the Great Perfection and the Chan tradition of Chinese Buddhism, but the precise relationship between the two remains to be fully investigated. It is noteworthy that certain of the earliest extant Great Perfection texts specifically contrast their own tradition with that of Chan.

Unlike the Geluks, Kagyu, and Sakya, the Nyingma (along with the Bönpo, with whom they share much in common) remained largely uninvolved in politics, both within Tibet and in foreign relations. They also lacked the kind of hierarchies found in the other sects. Although they developed great monasteries such as Mindroling (Smin grol gling), they also maintained a strong local presence as lay tantric practioners (*sngags pa*) who performed a range of ritual functions for the community.

Kagyu (Bka' brgyud)

The Kagyu sect derives its lineage from the visits by Marpa the Translator (1012–1099) to India, where he studied under several of the famous tantric masters of the day, including Nāropa (the disciple of Tilopa) and Maitrīpa. Marpa's disciple Milarepa (Mi la ras pa, "Cotton-clad Mila") is said to have achieved buddhahood in one lifetime (an achievement usually considered to require aeons of practice) through his diligent meditation practice in the caves of southern Tibet, despite having committed murder as a youth through the practice of black magic. His moving biography and didactic songs are among the most famous works of Tibetan literature. Milarepa's most illustrious disciple was the scholar and physician Gampopa (Sgam po pa, 1079–1153), who gave a strong monastic foundation to the sect. His own disciples, in turn, are regarded as the founders of the four major schools and the eight minor schools of the Kagyu. The most important of these is the Karma Kagyu, led by a succession of incarnate lamas called the Karmapas, headquartered at Tshurpu (Mtshur pu) monastery. Among the prominent philosophers of the Kagyu sect are the eighth Karmapa, Migyö Dorje (Mi bskyod rdo rje, 1507–1554), Pema Garpo (Padma dkar po, 1527–1592), and Kongtrül (Kong sprul yon tan rgya mtsho, 1813–1899).

The defining doctrine of the Kagyu sect is the Great Seal (*phyag rgya chen mo, mahāmudrā*), which Kagyus regard as the crowning experience of Buddhist practice. The Great Seal is a state of enlightened awareness in which phenomenal appearance and noumenal emptiness are unified. Like the Great Perfection of the Nyingmapas, it is considered to be primordially present, that is, not something that is newly created. Rather than emphasizing the attainment of an extraordinary level of consciousness, the Great Seal literature exalts the ordinary state of mind as both the natural and ultimate state, characterized by lucidity and simplicity. In Kagyu literature, this ordinary mind is contrasted with the worldly mind. The former, compared to a mirror, reflects reality exactly as it is, simply and purely, whereas the worldly mind is distorted by its mistaken perception of subject and object as real. Rather than seeking to destroy this worldly mind as other systems do, however, in the Great Seal the worldly mind is valued for its ultimate identity with the ordinary mind; every deluded thought contains within it the lucidity and simplicity of the ordinary mind. This identity merely needs to be recognized to bring about the dawning of wisdom, the realization that a natural purity pervades all existence, including the deluded mind.

Sakya (Sa skya)

The Sakya sect looks back to another translator, Drokmi Shakya Yeshe ('Brog mi Shākya ye shes, 993–1050), who studied in India under disciples of the tantric master Virūpa. Khon Gonchok Gyalpo ('Khon dkon mchog rgyal po), a disciple of Drokmi, founded a monastery at Sakya ("gray earth") in 1073. This monastery became the seat of the sect, hence its name. The most influential scholars of the Sakya sect in the twelfth and thirteenth centuries were members of the 'Khon family, the most notable of whom was Gunga Gyaltsen (Kun dga' rgyal mtshan, 1181–1251), better known as Sakya Paṇḍita. He studied under one of the last generations of Indian Buddhist scholars to visit Tibet, notably Śākyaśrībhadra. Sakya Paṇḍita claims two important achievements in the history of Tibetan philosophy. First, he defeated a Hindu paṇḍita in formal philosophical debate. Second, his master work on logic, the *Treasury of Reasoning* (*Rigs gter*), was so highly regarded that it is said to have been translated from Tibetan into Sanskrit and circulated in northern India. In his other writings, Sakya Paṇḍita insisted on rational consistency and fidelity to Indian sources in all branches of Buddhist theory and practice. This conviction resulted in often polemical evaluations of the doctrines of other sects, particularly the Kagyu.

In 1244 Sakya Paṇḍita was selected to respond to the summons to the court of the Mongol prince Godan, who had sent raiding parties into Tibet 1239. He impressed the Mongols with his magical powers as much as with his learning and offered submission to Godan on behalf of Tibet in return for freedom from military attack and occupation. He remained at Godan's court as regent, sending orders to officials in Tibet. For roughly the next century, the head lamas of the Sakya sect exercised political control over Tibet with Mongol support. Sakya Paṇḍita's nephew, Pakpa ('Phags pa blo gros rgyal mtshan, 1235–1280?), became the religious teacher of Qubilai Khan.

The early Sakya tradition was concerned primarily with tantric practice, especially the "path and fruition" (*lam 'bras*) tradition associated with the *Hevajra Tantra*, but there was very soon a move to balance and harmonize tantric studies with the study of scholastic philosophy (*mtshan nyid*). Sakya scholars wrote extensively on Mādhyamika philosophy but are particularly famous for their work in logic and epistemology (*tshad ma, pramāṇa*). It was the Sakya scholar Budön (Bu ston, 1290–1364) who systematized the various collections of Indian Buddhist texts circulating in Tibet into the well-known Kanjur (*bka' 'gyur*, literally, "translation of the word [of the Buddha]") and the Tanjur (*bstan 'gyur*, literally "translation of the śāstras").

Geluk (Dge lugs)

Unlike the other major sects of Tibetan Buddhism, the Gelukpas do not identify a specific Indian master as the source of their tradition, although they see themselves as inheriting the tradition of Atiśa, the Bengali scholar who arrived in Tibet in 1042. The preeminent figure for the sect (who may only retrospectively be identified as the "founder") is Tsong kha pa (1357–1419). While known in the West primarily as a reformer, apparently because of his commitment to monasticism, Tsong kha pa was also a creative and controversial interpreter of Buddhist philosophy, especially of Mādhyamika. His stature, which seems to have been considerable during his lifetime, was only enhanced by the subsequent political ascendancy of his followers through the institution of the Dalai Lama, the first of whom (identified as such retrospectively) was Tsong kha pa's disciple Gendundrup (Dge 'dun grub, 1391–1474). Tsong kha pa founded the monastery of Ganden (Dga' ldan, named after the Buddhist heaven Tuṣita) outside Lhasa in 1409, and his followers were originally known as the Gandenpas (Dga' ldan pa). This eventually evolved to Gelukpa, the "system of virtue." The Gelukpas established large monastic universities throughout Tibet, one of which, Drepung ('Bras spung), was the largest Buddhist monastery in the world, with over 13,000 monks in 1959. The third of the "three seats" of the Geluk, in addition to Drepung and Ganden, is Sera monastery, just outside Lhasa.

Bön

Some scholars regard Bön as a heterodox sect of Tibetan Buddhism that began (or a least developed a self-conscious identity), like the other sects (with the exception of Nyingma), in the eleventh century. This is a characterization that both Buddhists and Bönpos would reject. There has been a long antagonism between the two, with Buddhists regarding Bönpos as the descendants of benighted performers of animal sacrifice who plagued Tibet prior to the introduction of the true dharma. For Bönpos, Buddhists are adherents of a heretical alien religion whose interference deprived Tibet of its past glory. The Buddhists look back to India as the source of their religion, portraying Tibet prior to the introduction of Buddhism as an amoral and even demonic realm. The Bönpos look back to Tibet and to Shangshung as their source, seeking to establish a link with the religious tradition(s) of Tibet prior to the seventh century, a link that most scholars regard as tenuous. Both Buddhist and Bönpo chronicles suggest that there was strong opposition to Buddhism among certain factions of the Tibetan court during the seventh and eighth centuries, especially among the priests who were called *bon*. But with the eventual triumph of the Buddhism, those priests seem to have completely disappeared. Little more than the name remained, to be taken up in the eleventh century by those who claimed to represent the continuation of that lost tradition. However, the pre-Buddhist practices centered around a royal funerary cult dedicated to assuring the arrival of the king in a pastoral heaven. The practices of post-eleventh-century Bönpos represent a fully elaborated path to enlightenment ending in liberation from rebirth and buddhahood.

Both Buddhists and Bönpos regard a buddha as their founder. For the Buddhists, he is the Indian Śākyamuni; for the Bönpos, he is the great teacher Shenrap

(Ston pa Gshen rab), from the land of Tazig (Stag gzig, identified by some scholars with Persia and Tajikistan) to the west of the kingdom of Shangshung. When Shenrap arrived in Tibet, he subdued the local demons and converted them to the true religion, much like Padmasambhava did. (Indeed, recent scholarship has shown that some of the accounts of Padmasambhava's conquests are based on Bönpo accounts of Shenrap.) Bönpos themselves regard their religion as having been imported by the teacher Shenrap, the true Buddha, long before the arrival of Indian Buddhists. Unlike the Indian Buddha, Śākyamuni, Shenrap was enlightened from birth and lived the life of a layman (eventually becoming a monk late in life). Thus, his extensive biography is not simply a version of the life of the Indian Buddha (although he also is said to have performed twelve major deeds) but tells a very different story. In an attempt at reconciliation and appropriation, later Bönpo texts state that Śākyamuni was actually an emanation of Shenrap.

Buddhists and Bönpos have different names for their traditions; Buddhists call theirs *chö* (*chos*) while Bönpos call their *bon*. The terms are equally untranslatable and multivalent, ranging from "law" to "truth," but their use is perfectly parallel in the two traditions. Each has its own canon, containing similar genres of texts, each believes in karma and rebirth, each has a bodhisattva path, and so forth. Like the Nyingmas, Bonpos have continued to rediscover treasure texts since at least the eleventh century. (However, rather than being texts left by Padmasambhava to be revealed at an appropriate moment in the future, the texts the Bönpos discover are said to be as those hidden to escape destruction during the persecutions of Bön by Tri Songdetsen.) Like Nyingma, the highest teaching is the Great Perfection (and the lines of influence are uncertain). Like the Geluks, Bönpo monks engage in formal debates on points of doctrine.

Because Bönpos do things in an opposite direction to Buddhists (they circumambulate and turn their prayer wheels counter-clockwise, for example), Bön has been long regarded as simply a "backwards Buddhism" that plagiarized everything from Buddhism, only substituting the word *bon* wherever the term *chö* occurred. Recent scholarship has demonstrated that this is inaccurate, that despite the protestations of both parties there has been significant mutual influence between the two, such that it is often very difficult to regard any Tibetan ritual as purely Buddhist or purely Bönpo. It is also not the case, as was once assumed, that all non-Buddhist Tibetan religion is by default Bönpo. Both Buddhists and Bönpos regard their lineages as self-conscious traditions with specific histories. And again, despite their protestations, both partake fully of rituals, beliefs, and pantheons that predate either of them. However, whereas Buddhists insist on the Indian origins of those practices, Bönpos appropriated pre-Buddhist Tibetan cosmologies, deities, and terminology, all of which were employed to establish the historical priority of Bön in Tibet and thus to demarcate their traditions from those of the Buddhists. Thus Bön is not the pre-Buddhist religion of Tibet, not Tibetan "folk religion," and not a primitive animism. It is perhaps best described as a heretical sect of Tibetan Buddhism, with its own creation myths, cosmology, and pantheon (sometimes with obvious Buddhist correlates, sometimes without), which does not accept the teachings of Śākyamuni Buddha and his tradition as the true dharma. It must be noted, however, that such a characterization could be taken to imply both a devaluation of Bönpo innovation and a capitulation to the anti-Bön polemics of Tibetan Buddhists. It may be, as some scholars have postulated, that Bön is a form of Buddhism that entered Tibet from Central Asia rather than from India. Regardless, the Bön tradition that exists today is difficult to trace back beyond the formation of the other sects of Tibetan Buddhism in the eleventh century.

As is clear from the foregoing description of the major sects, Tibetans (usually Buddhist or Bönpo monks or lamas) have produced a large corpus of what might be termed philosophical literature. What is clear from their works is that the Buddhist or Bönpo philosopher was also a Buddhist or Bönpo and thus a participant in rituals and institutions that provided the setting for his writing. Thus, what we might term "philosophy" was but one concern of these authors; a perusal of the titles in the collected works of any of Tibet's most revered scholars reveals that among the commentaries on Indian logical treatises and expositions of emptiness are works devoted to tantric initiations and consecrations, propitiations of deities, biographies of Indian and Tibetan masters, and instructions for drawing maṇḍalas, making rain, stopping smallpox, and manufacturing magical pills.

As mentioned above, during the Mongol Yuan dynasty (1260–1368), Tibetan Buddhism played an important role at the court of Qubilai Khan, where the emperor's Buddhist preceptor was the famous monk Pakpa ('Phags pa, died 1280) of the Sakya sect. When Pakpa's uncle, Sakya Paṇḍita, was summoned to the court of the Mongol prince Godan in 1244, he took his young nephew with him. As a result of Sakya Paṇḍita's influence, the head lamas of the Sakya sect were given political rule over Tibet with Mongol patronage. With the founding of the Yuan dynasty, the new emperor of China, Qubilai Khan, wished to keep an important member of the Sakya hierarchy at his court to ensure Tibet's continued submission to Mongol rule. Pakpa thus went to the Chinese court as a hostage. He soon so impressed the emperor with his learning and magical powers that he was asked to bestow tantric initiation on the emperor and his consort and later converted the members of the court to Tibetan Buddhism. Their interest seems to be have been based less on an appreciation of Buddhist doctrine than on the fact that Tibetan medicine and magic proved more efficacious than that of the court shamans. Qubilai Khan appointed Pakpa as teacher to the emperor (*dishi*) and teacher to the state (*guoshi*), making him in the process the vassal-ruler (in absentia) of Tibet. Their relationship provided the model for the subsequent relationship between Tibet and China, at least as perceived by the Tibetans. In this relationship, known as "patron and priest" (*yon mchod*), the leading lama of Tibet (in subsequent centuries, the Dalai Lama) was seen as spiritual adviser and chief priest to the emperor, who acted as patron and protector of the lama and, by extension, of Tibet.

With the decline of Mongol rule, there occurred a new sense of Tibetan national identity, especially under the rule of Jangchup Gyaltsen (Byang chub rgyal mtshan, 1302–1364). A nostalgia for the ancient Tibetan empire and its military dominance of Inner Asia was manifested in festivals in which officials dressed in the garb of the ancient kings. Native Tibetan deities, even those tamed by Buddhism, such as the *dapla* (*dgra lha*), are depicted as fierce warriors clad in armor and riding battle steeds. During Jangchup Gyaltsen's reign, many terma texts were unearthed that told of the glory of the imperial age.

Jangchup Gyaltsen and his descendants ruled Tibet for over a century. After that, rule came into the hands of the princes of Rinpung (Rin spung) and then the kings of the western province of Tsang (Gtsang), both groups being patrons of the Karmapas. Meanwhile, in China, the Ming (1368–1644) emperors continued to confer gifts and titles on lamas of the Kagyu, Sakya, and Geluk sects. The Gelukpas received important patronage from the Tümed Mongols when the third Dalai Lama, Sonam Gyatso (Bsod nams rgya mtsho), was summoned to the Altan Khan in 1578. It was actually the Altan Khan who bestowed the appellation "Dalai Lama" on the third incarnation of Tsong kha pa's disciple by translating part of his name, Gyatso ("ocean"), into Mongolian; Dalai Lama means "Ocean Lama." The Mongols converted to Tibetan Buddhism and proved powerful patrons of the Geluk, especially when, after Sonam Gyatso's death, a grandson of the Altan Khan was identified as the fourth Dalai Lama. Another Mongol leader, Gushri Khan of the Qoshot, supported the fifth Dalai Lama against his Kagyu rivals, eventually establishing him as the ruler of Tibet in 1642. This consolidation of religious and secular power in a single figure was an important moment in Tibetan history, a consolidation that received strong ideological support through the promotion of the cult of Avalokiteśvara.

In a treasure text discovered in the twelfth century (but with significant additions apparently made in the fourteenth century) called the *Hundred Thousand Words of Maṇi* (*Maṇi bka' 'bum*), Avalokiteśvara, the bodhisattva of compassion, was retrojected into Tibet's past as both Tibet's protector and the central agent in Tibetan history. Thus, in the prehistoric past, the bodhisattva was said to have taken the form of a monkey and mated with a ogress; their offspring were the first Tibetans. The illegible text that fell into the king's palace was none other than the *Kāraṇḍavyūha*, which tells many tales of Avalokiteśvara. And the three great "dharma kings" (*chos rgyal*) who oversaw the introduction of Buddhism into Tibet were none other than incarnations of Avalokiteśvara. The great epic hero Gesar of Ling is an emanation of Avalokiteśvara. Finally, the fifth Dalai Lama identified himself not only as the fifth incarnation of Tsong kha pa's disciple but as the present incarnation of Avalokiteśvara. From that point on, the bodhisattva protector of Tibet was believed to take human form as the Dalai Lama, thus establishing an unbroken link with Tibet's prehistoric past and exalting the religious lineage of one of many lines of incarnation to the level of kingship through identification with Avalokiteśvara; the Dalai Lama was both Tsong kha pa's historical successor and the human embodiment of the transhistorical bodhisattva of compassion. The fifth Dalai Lama also declared his own teacher to be an incarnation of Amitābha, the Buddha of Infinite Light, and Avalokiteśvara's teacher, bestowing upon him the title of Panchen Lama, establishing a new line of incarnation, which was to have its seat at Tashilhunpo (Bkra shis lhun po) monastery in Tsang province, the former center of his opponent's power. The Dalai Lama moved the capital back to Lhasa, the seat of the ancient kings, and built his palace there, a massive edifice called the Potala, taking its name from Potalaka, the name of Avalokiteśvara's palace. Thus, the power and authority that had once descended in the form of the ancient kings, which had then devolved to local incarnate lamas, was now arrogated (at least in part) back to a single divine figure, the Dalai Lama.

During the eighteenth and nineteenth centuries, the Gelukpas maintained their political control over central Tibet, with the occasional aid of the Manchu rulers of China's Qing dynasty. Especially from the time of the Kangxi emperor (ruled 1661–1722), imperial favor was directed especially toward the Gelukpas. Under the Qianlong emperor (ruled 1736–1795), for example, the entire Tibetan Kanjur was translated into Manchu under the direction of the Geluk hierarch Janggya (Lcang skya rol pa'i rdo rje, 1717–1786, see chapter 29).

With the fall of the Qing, Chinese influence in Tibet dwindled through the Second World War (during which Tibet remained neutral). In 1950 Tibet was invaded and occupied by troops of the People's Liberation Army. The situation deteriorated over the next decade. A popular uprising against the Chinese began on March 17, 1959. When it became clear that the Chinese intended to arrest the Dalai Lama, he escaped to India, eventually to be followed by some 250,000 of his people, one-fourth of whom arrived safely in India and Nepal. Today there are over 100,000 Tibetans living in exile, while Tibet, much of its territory divided among Chinese provinces, remains a Chinese colony.

Since 1959 the practice of Tibetan religion has taken place in two very different domains. In Tibet, Tibetan religion has been severely proscribed, as have all forms of traditional Tibetan culture. The violent suppression reached its peak during the Cultural Revolution when all but a handful of the thousands of monasteries and temples that existed in Tibet in 1959 were destroyed. From 1959 to 1979 it has been estimated that one million of the six million ethnic Tibetans died as a result of Chinese policies. Since 1979 there has been some relaxation of the strictest constraints, and a number of monasteries and temples have been rebuilt, although whatever Chinese funds have been provided for this purpose seem directed ultimately toward the promotion of Western tourism. The monastic population has been reduced drastically, as has the program of monastic education.

The other domain of Tibetan religious practice is in exile, with most refugees living in India and Nepal. Of the approximately 70,000 Tibetans who successfully followed the Dalai Lama into exile in 1959 and 1960, an estimated 5,000–7,000 were monks, a tiny fraction of the monastic population of Tibet. But a disproportionate number of the monks who escaped (and remained monks in exile) were from the ranks of incarnate lamas and the scholarly elite, and they worked to reestablish their monastic institutions (of all sects) in exile. Their presence and accessibility has attracted the attention of a large number of Western scholars and enthusiasts, and the last three decades have seen an explosion in interest in Tibetan Buddhism, with a wide variety of translations of Tibetan Buddhist texts.

Indeed, a certain reversal in the perception of Tibetan religion has taken place since 1959. During the Victorian period and lasting well into this century, representations of Tibetan religions generally fell into one of two categories. By some it was portrayed as the most depraved deviation from the Buddha's true teaching, an abomination born from mixing superstition and animism (identified with Bön) with the decrepit remnants of original Buddhism, the remnants named Mahāyāna and tantra. By others, Tibet was seen as the abode of Atlantean masters who held the secrets of the universe; Tibet was a land of "magic and mystery," a Shangri-La.

The Victorian representation of Tibetan Buddhism as the most corrupt and therefore least truly Buddhist of the Asian traditions reached its inevitable antipodes. In the 1960s and 1970s, the earlier Buddhological valuation of Tibetan Buddhism was reversed, as a generation of young scholars came to exalt Tibet, just at the moment of its invasion and annexation by China, as a pristine preserve of authentic Buddhist doctrine and practice. Unlike the Buddhisms of China, Japan, and Southeast Asia, Tibetan Buddhism was perceived as uncorrupted because it had been untainted by Western domination. The value of Tibet to scholars of Buddhism was no longer simply as an archive of the scriptures of Indian Buddhism. The Tibetan diaspora after the Dalai Lama's flight to India in 1959 made widely available to the universities of Europe and North America (largely through the efforts of the Library of Congress office in New Delhi) a great flood of autochthonous Tibetan Buddhism literature, heretofore unstudied. This literature, scorned by scholars at the end of the last century as "contemptible mummery," was now hailed as a repository of ancient wisdom whose lineage could be traced back to the Buddha himself. Much of the scholarship and more popular translations produced since the Tibetan diaspora have, as if, sought to counter the prior negative valuation of Tibetan religion as polluted by representing it as pristine, reflecting largely the normative Buddhism of the scholarly elite, such that the essential ritual practices of Tibetan religions have been ignored to a great degree. In Bönpo studies, Bön has moved from being dismissed as a primitive animism to being hailed as the authentic and original source of Tibetan culture. Works on meditation, compassion, and the stages of the path to enlightenment are certainly famous in Tibet and hold an important place in the histories of the traditions. But without placing such works within their larger ritual context, the religions of Tibet can be misconstrued as merely a sophisticated philosophy divorced from the concerns of the everyday. This attitude is sometimes found among modern Buddhist clerics who see Tibetan Buddhism as entirely of Indian origin, free from any pollution by the pre-Buddhist past. It is important, therefore, to provide the materials for the foundation of a middle ground between these two extreme views of Tibetan religion by presenting a wide range of Tibetan religious literature, derived from many different centuries, regions, and sects, with no attempt to occlude those elements that some might construe as "magical," while attempting to demonstrate how those elements are designed most often to address the most quotidian of human concerns.

Further Reading

For general surveys of Tibetan religion and culture, see David Snellgrove and Hugh Richardson, *A Cultural History of Tibet* (Boston: Shambala, 1968); Giuseppe Tucci, *The Religions of Tibet* (Berkeley: University of California Press, 1980); R. A. Stein, *Tibetan Civilization* (Stanford: Stanford University Press, 1972); Geoffrey Samuel, *Civilized Shamans: Buddhism in Tibetan Societies* (Washington, D.C.: Smithsonian Institution Press, 1993); and the articles "The Religions of Tibet" by Per Kvaerne and "The Schools of Tibetan Buddhism" in *The Encyclopedia of Religion*, edited by Mircea Eliade (New York: Macmillan, 1987). For an encyclopedic survey of Tibetan literature, see José Ignacio Cabezón and Roger R. Jackson, eds., *Tibetan Literature: Studies in Genre* (Ithaca, N.Y.: Snow Lion, 1995).

—30—

The Royal Way of Supreme Compassion

Matthew Kapstein

The reign of King Songtsen Gampo (Srong btsan sgam po, 613/14–649/50) marks the beginning of the age of Tibetan imperial power, when for some two centuries Tibet vied with China's Tang dynasty for the control of what is today northwest China. Relentlessly pursuing the expansionist policies of his father, Namri Songtsen (Gnam ri srong btsan), the lord of the small Yarlung valley, Songtsen Gampo consolidated his rule over most of the Tibetan plateau and then proceeded to move into the surrounding countries in all directions. In tandem with the growth of the empire, Songtsen Gampo concerned himself too with the problems relating to the administration of his vast territories, and so it was under his rule that the Tibetan system of writing was developed and the creation of a legal and administrative code was begun. Following the arrival of the Tang Princess Wencheng, who was certainly accompanied by her own court when she came to wed the Tibetan monarch, elements of Chinese learning began to make inroads in Tibet at this time as well. Scholars at present debate whether Buddhism was in fact adopted in Tibet under King Songtsen, but a considerable body of tradition suggests that some presence of the foreign religion was at least tolerated during his reign.

This, in brief, summarizes our rather scanty historical knowledge of Songtsen Gampo, but Tibet writers have woven around such threads a rich tapestry of legend and tradition. In many respects, Songtsen Gampo, Princess Wencheng, and the other members of the king's family and court figure in Tibetan literature and folklore much as do Arthur, Guinevere, and the Knights of the Round Table in the medieval traditions of England and France. In recent years the Chinese government has even sought to manipulate the popularity of this lore for its own ends, by promoting the notion that Tibet's modern "marriage" with China had its origins in the union of the Tibetan emperor with the Tang princess. For the Tibetans, however, King Songtsen is an enduring emblem of Tibetan sovereignty and power, a conception reinforced both by history and by legend.

Perhaps the most influential of the popular traditions connected with Songtsen

Gampo are those associated with the collection of texts called the *Maṇi Kambum* (*Maṇi Bka' 'bum*). The writings found here originated as *terma* (*gter ma*) or "treasures," texts said to have been concealed by ancient masters and rediscovered during a later age by prophetically designated "treasure-finders." Their discovery is attributed to three such persons who lived during the twelfth and thirteenth centuries, and by the fourteenth century the *Maṇi Kambum* was already in circulation in a form close to that which we have today. According to the tradition contained here, Avalokiteśvara, the bodhisattva of compassion, is the special divine protector of Tibet and in fact is to be identified with the fundamental principle of enlightenment throughout the universe as a whole. This principle, which is also the name preferred by Avalokiteśvara as he appears in the *Maṇi Kambum*, is Supreme Compassion (Skt. *Mahākāruṇika*, Tib. *Thugs rje chen po*). Supreme Compassion is the basis for love, kindness, and nurturing among all living creatures, but it is much more than a positive sentiment alone; for Supreme Compassion is none other than the open and creative power of mind or spirit, whose infinite potentialities for self-actualization constitute the very basis for creation itself. The bodhisattva Avalokiteśvara, therefore, is in effect the concrete embodiment of the abstract and unlimited principle of Supreme Compassion.

In his special relation with Tibet, Avalokiteśvara is said to have taken birth as the monkey who, having united with an ogress, became the progenitor of the Tibetan people. When the Tibetans later mature to the point at which they are receptive to the Buddha's teaching, Avalokiteśvara takes birth among them once more as none other than King Songtsen Gampo. The *Maṇi Kambum*, then, represents the collected teachings of this figure, who is at once the father of the Tibetan people, the highest spiritual principle, the bodhisattva of compassion, and the king of Tibet.

According to the *Maṇi Kambum*, the king marries two foreign princesses, the second being Tritsün (Khri btsun), daughter of the ruler of Nepal. Both princesses are themselves the emanations of goddesses, and both bring with them, as part of their dowries, sacred images of the Buddha Śākyamuni, which are installed in temples specially built to house them. The tale of the king and his brides, as it is told here, is the drama of Buddhism's introduction to Tibet. The image said to have been brought by the princess of Wencheng, and known as the Jowo or "Lord" (*Jo bo*), and the Jokhang temple constructed for it in Lhasa became Tibet's greatest center of pilgrimage, which virtually all Tibetans aspire to visit. The *Maṇi Kambum* played a crucial role in the promotion of the cult of the Jowo, and the pilgrims who flock to it find there Tibet's ancient ruler and his court always present before their eyes in the statuary of the temple itself. Text and monument together engender a uniform vision of Tibet's imperial past and its enduring spiritual presence. This perspective is strengthened in popular belief by strong associations with the living figure of the Dalai Lama, who, as a contemporary emanation of Avalokiteśvara, is also identified with King Songtsen.

The title *Maṇi Kambum* literally means the "Collected Pronouncements [concerning] Maṇi," referring here to the famous six-syllable mantra of Avalokiteśvara, *oṃ Maṇipadme hūṃ*. As early as the seventeenth century, European visitors noted the importance of this formula in Tibetan popular religion—it is often uttered aloud while a "prayer-wheel," containing the mantra written many times on a paper scroll, is turned. The recitation of the "six-syllable mantra" is indeed a ubiquitous devotional act, and even a 1992 popular song in Lhasa used it as a lyric, expressive in this modern context of a Tibetan national prayer, and hence a prayer for the Tibetan nation. The mantra is to all intents and purposes the central teaching of the *Maṇi Kambum*, as indeed its title suggests (see chapters 16 and 32).

Since the nineteenth century Western writers on Buddhism have frequently asserted that the six-syllable mantra may be translated as "Hail to the jewel in the lotus!" This expression has even become, for many, emblematic of Tibetan Buddhism as a whole. It is ironic, therefore, that not only would such a translation require that the mantra be composed in grammatically incorrect Sanskrit, but the popular Western interpretation of it is not supported by any known Indian or Tibetan sources. The Indian interpretation, known also to Tibetan scholars trained in the study of Sanskrit grammar, understands *Maṇipadme* to be a term of address for Avalokiteśvara, meaning "[possessor of] jewel and lotus," for these indeed are the objects most frequently held by the bodhisattva in his iconographic representations. *Oṃ* and *hūṃ* are purely symbolic expressions, not capable of translation, but commonly used in the formation of mantras. They are interpreted in many ways, according to context, but are generally taken as utterances bridging the gap between mundane and sacred planes of experience.

The *Maṇi Kambum*, however, is not at all interested in Sanskrit grammar and treats each of the six syllables as being purely symbolic. It elaborates literally dozens of ways of understanding their symbolism, intending that the devotee should incorporate this rich field of meaning into his or her meditations while reciting the mantra. Thus, for example, the six syllables represent the six states of being (gods, demigods, humans, animals, tormented spirits, and creatures in the hells) that Avalokiteśvara seeks to liberate through compassion; they are the six psychological poisons (pride, envy, lust, stupidity, greed, and anger) that must be pacified in meditation; they are the six basic colors (white, green, red, blue, yellow, and black) of which visual experience is constituted; and so on. The devoted religious practitioner, who will sometimes aspire to recite the six-syllable mantra one hundred million times during the course of a lifetime, by contemplating such associations thus endeavors to find Supreme Compassion permeating all possibilities of experience.

The *Maṇi Kambum* is a large work, occupying two thick volumes in most editions. It has three major sections concerned, respectively, with the legends of Avalokiteśvara and his emanation in Tibet as King Songtsen, with the rituals of Avalokiteśvara according to the "royal tradition" associated with the king, and with the ethical and meditational teachings that the king is said to have delivered. In the selections that follow, the first and third sections are represented.

The first text is drawn from a recent history of the ancient Nyingma school of Tibetan Buddhism by the late head of the school, H. H. Dudjom Rinpoche (1904–

1987). In summarizing the traditional story of Songtsen Gampo, he bases himself primarily on the accounts given at length in the *Maṇi Kambum* and includes a brief discussion of its discovery. The second and third texts are taken from the third section of the *Maṇi Kambum* itself, where they are said to be the king's teachings to his own son and daughter regarding the way of Supreme Compassion. See *Maṇi bka' 'bum: A Collection of Rediscovered Teachings* (New Delhi: Trayang and Jamyang Samten, 1975), vol. 2.

Further Reading

For a more detailed introduction to the *Maṇi Kambum*, refer to my article "Remarks on the *Maṇi bKa'-'bum* and the Cult of Avalokiteśvara in Tibet," in Steven D. Goodman and Ronald M. Davidson, eds., *Tibetan Buddhism: Reason and Revelation* (Albany: State University of New York Press, 1992). On the cult of Avalokiteśvara in the Tibetan Nyingma tradition, see Dudjom Rinpoche, Jikdrel Yeshe Dorje, *The Nyingma School of Tibetan Buddhism: Its Fundamentals and History*, vol. 1, translated by Gyurme Dorje and Matthew Kapstein (Boston: Wisdom Publications, 1991), pp. 510–12. The selection on "The Legend of King Songtsen Gampo" has been made available for the present publication, with minor editorial emendations, by permission of the translators and Wisdom Publications. The story of Songtsen Gampo's construction of temples over the supine ogress is discussed in Janet Gyatso's "Down with the Demoness: Reflections on a Feminine Ground in Tibet," in Janice D. Willis, ed., *Feminine Ground: Essays on Women and Tibet* (Ithaca: Snow Lion Publications, 1987), pp. 33–51.

The Legend of King Songtsen Gampo

There is a prophecy in the *Root Tantra of Mañjuśrī:*

> In the place called the divine land,
> Surrounded by snowy mountains,
> A king called "God among Men" will be born
> Into the Licchavi race.

The fifth hereditary monarch after Lha Totori was the religious king Songtsen Gampo, an emanation of Avalokiteśvara in the form of a mighty lord of men, who began to rule the kingdom at the age of thirteen. When he was fifteen the emanational monk Ā-kar Matiśīla brought him a self-created image of the Sublime One [Avalokiteśvara]. Then, the king commanded the religious minister Gar, an emanation of Vajrapāṇi, to invite the Nepalese princess Tritsün, an emanation of Bhṛkuṭī, and the Chinese princess of Wencheng, an emanation of Tārā, both of whom were agreeable to the people, to be his two consorts.

This he did in order to introduce two images of the Teacher, representative of the Buddha himself, which were, respectively, the size of an eight-year-old and a twelve-year-old. The princesses came to be known as the two "Lotuses of the Lake."

While the Trülnang Temple [i.e., the Jokhang, the "Cathedral of Lhasa"] was being constructed, the building-work was disrupted by nonhuman beings. Therefore, the king and his two consorts went into retreat in the palace known as Maru, at Nyangdren Phawongkha in the valley of the Kyichu. They attained accomplishment by propitiating their meditative deity, on whose advice the king built the temples to tame the borders, frontiers, and districts, which were situated on geomantic sites on the body of the supine ogress [that is, Tibet]; and so it was that he exorcised the malignant earth spirits. He then erected Trülnang and Ramoche temples and the images they housed.

Songtsen Gampo invited the master Kusara and the brahman Śaṅkara from India, the master Śīlamañju from Nepal, and the master Hoshang Mohoyen from China. With others, they translated many sections of the tripiṭaka and of the tantras and thus introduced the teaching to Tibet. Though no actual teaching or study took place, the king himself secretly gave instruction on the peaceful and wrathful forms of Supreme Compassion to many fortunate beings, who then practiced these teachings. No one was ordained [as a monk] prior to the "seven men who were tested," but it is said that there were always about a hundred long-haired yogins engaged in the practices of Supreme Compassion at Nyangdren Phawongkha. At that time the scriptures that formed the king's testament were collected and hidden in separate treasures. Later, these treasures were revealed by the accomplished master Ngödrup, Lord Nyang, and the teacher Śākya-ö. Today they are renowned as the *Collected Works of the King Concerning the Mantra "Oṃ Maṇipadme Hūṃ,"* the first Tibetan doctrinal work.

The king also sent Tönmi Sambhoṭa, an emanation of Mañjughoṣa, to India to study grammar and writing. On the basis of the Indian scripts he created the forms of the Tibetan letters, and he composed eight treatises on Tibetan grammar. Before Songsten Gampo's time there had been no proponents in the Land of Snows of a code of conduct in accord with the doctrine, but thereafter the great door of the true doctrine and of theories in accord with the doctrine was opened for the first time. The king innovated the just spiritual and temporal laws, as illustrated by the ten divine virtues and the sixteen pure human laws. In these ways, King Songtsen Gampo blessed the country of Tibet to become a prosperous and luxurious source of the true doctrine.

TWO SELECTIONS FROM THE MAṆI KAMBUM

Oṃ Maṇipadme hūṃ!
King Songstsen Gampo, who was himself an emanation of Supreme Compassion, gave these precepts to his son Kungsong Kungtsen:

Meditation upon the body of Supreme Compassion may be associated with the six bodies of enlightenment:
His *body*, endowed with the signs and attributes of the fully enlightened Buddha, is like the Sun.
It is the body of perfect spiritual rapture.
His *speech*, a union of sound and emptiness, which arises with incessant variety, is like the Moon, which has many varied reflections.
It is the emanational body.
His *mind*, abiding without change, birthless and empty, is like the sky.
It is the body of all that is real.
The *qualities* of his enlightenment, whereby he acts on behalf of living beings without interruption, are like the planets and stars.
They are the body of essential being.
His *enlightened activity*, which teaches beings throughout the three realms in accord with their particular spiritual needs, is like a panacea.
It is the body of actual awakening.
And *Supreme Compassion* itself, which remains one-pointed, without change or transformation throughout the three times, for the sake of living beings, is the vajra-like body, the body of indestructible reality.

Thus Supreme Compassion is fully endowed with the six bodies.

They are not something that is attained by meditation or practice directed to anything outside of yourself.
When you cultivate the realization that your own mind is Supreme Compassion they arise by themselves.
Thus his body, which is free from birth and death, is like a reflected image: it is free, it appears, but it is devoid of substantial existence.

Speech as Supreme Compassion is like an echo, and is incessant.
Oṃ Maṇipadme Hūṃ, the natural voice of reality, is uninterrupted:
Oṃ stills pride, purifies the heavens of the gods, and cuts off birth among them.
Ma stills jealous rage, purifies the realms of the demigods, and cuts off birth among them.
Ṇi stills lust, purifies the world of human beings, and cuts off birth among them.
Pad stills stupidity, purifies the habitats of animals, and cuts off birth among them.
Me stills greed, purifies the lands of tormented spirits, and cuts off birth among them.
Hūṃ stills hatred, purifies the hells, and cuts off birth within them.

> When the six afflictions are thus stilled, and the realms of the six classes of beings thus are emptied,
> You will realize that saṃsāra arises and subsides by itself.
> And it is something that is not found elsewhere, but occurs when the six-syllable heart-mantra is uttered.
>
> The mind of Supreme Compassion is clear like a mirror, free from the ideas and concepts, and endowed with the five modes of enlightened cognition.
> Hence, it is pure intuitiveness that is free from conceptualization.
> Because mind emerges by itself, arises by itself, it is the enlightened cognition of the foundation of all that is real.
> Because it is clear and incessant, it is the enlightened cognition that is like a mirror.
> Because it abides in equality, without divisions, it is the enlightened cognition of sameness.
> Because it arises and subsides by itself, coming to rest at its point of origination, it is the enlightened cognition that distinguishes particulars as they arise and subside.
> And because it abides as the indivisible union of clarity and emptiness, it is enlightened cognition engaged in action.
> None of that is to be found elsewhere, for it emerges from mind itself and dissolves into the mind itself.
> Therefore, it is enlightened cognition that is coemergent, the enlightened intention that arises and subsides by itself.

These are the precepts the king gave to his son, sixfold precepts introducing Supreme Compassion's body, speech and mind.

Oṃ Maṇipadme hūṃ!
Songtsen Gampo, the dharma-protecting king who was himself an emanation of Supreme Compassion, gave these precepts to his daughter Trompa-gyen ["the ornament of the town"]:

> The *view* of Supreme Compassion is the indivisible union of appearance and emptiness and is like the sky.
> External appearances, the incessant appearing of whatever may be, is nonetheless the appearance of mind, which appears by itself. The essential character of mind is that it is empty.
> And the essential character of appearance is that it is empty in being apparent, but without substantial existence.
>
> The *meditation* of Supreme Compassion is the indivisible union of clarity and emptiness and is like a rainbow appearing in the sky.
> You must cultivate the realization that the essential character of mind,

which is clear and unobscured, and which emerges by itself, arises by itself, is that it is empty.

The *action* of Supreme Compassion is the indivisible union of awareness and emptiness and is like the sun rising in the sky.
Action is freedom from hankering after whatever there is that arises incessantly in mind, whose nature is pure awareness.
Though you act, you act in emptiness, not grasping at entities as real.

The *fruit* of Supreme Compassion is the indivisible union of bliss and emptiness.
Mind itself, without contrivances, is blissful within the expanse that is the foundation of all that is real.
Being empty and free from grasping, it is like the moon reflected in water.
Being free from all superimposed limits, it is without features that serve to define it.
And because it has forever abided within you, it cannot be achieved.

The *spiritual commitment* of Supreme Compassion
Is emptiness of which the core is compassion.
Its characteristic being just that,
You will grasp all living beings in all three realms
With unqualified compassion.
Being equal, you will act without "levels."

The *enlightened activity* of Supreme Compassion
Grasps beings with a snare of compassion in which
Buddhas and sentient beings are no different.
It slaughters their pain with the weapon of emptiness,
And draws sentient beings to the level of bliss supreme.

These are the precepts he gave to his daughter, six precepts introducing Supreme Compassion.

—31—

Guidebook to Lapchi

Toni Huber

The translation that follows comprises the opening three chapters of a Tibetan pilgrimage manual, bearing the abbreviated title *Guidebook to Lapchi* (*La phyi gnas yig*). This example of noncanonical Tibetan literature serves to introduce a paradigmatic feature of Tibetan religious culture: the representation of interplay between the Buddhist belief system and the indigenous Tibetan world view. The opening narratives of the *Guidebook to Lapchi* are complex in terms of both space and time and invoke a host of cultural discourses and icons. These need to be briefly introduced so that the text can be appreciated from points of view that begin to reflect the Tibetan understandings and uses of the guidebook. But first, a few comments are in order concerning the type of document and associated cultural practices we are dealing with here.

The *Guidebook to Lapchi* is a modest text by Tibetan standards. Although guidebooks can vary greatly in style and content, several general features are worthy of particular note. Many are compilations of a range of materials, which might include anything from cosmology and points of formal doctrine to local songs, detailed travel instructions, or personal anecdotes. When reading guidebooks it is important to recognize that they are constructed and styled in particular ways in order to direct and to evoke certain responses from those who use them. They are actively advertising the sanctity of sites and promoting the powers and beliefs that play a significant role in controlling and shaping the lives of individual pilgrims. This is no less true today than it was in traditional times, and it should be noted that editions of the *Guidebook to Lapchi* are still being printed and are used by contemporary Tibetan pilgrims. As a genre, pilgrimage guidebooks have a very significant oral dimension, which sets them apart from many other types of Tibetan religious literature. Their contents are often publicly repeated by clerics, shrine-keepers, and local residents for the benefit of pilgrims, and they are always elaborated upon by oral traditions in different ways. Moreover, they are often composed on the basis of oral texts that their authors collect while on pilgrimage. Thus, in both oral and written forms, guidebooks constitute a popular and widely circulated type of religious literature in Tibetan culture. This reflects the fact that pilgrimage, the raison d'être of such texts, is one of the most widespread ritual ensembles practiced in the Tibetan world.

Textual narrative and ritual journey or action are not separate modes for Tibetan pilgrims. Because oral and written guides present certain scenarios and then anchor them in the landscapes and features of pilgrimage sites, such texts become manuals for explaining and interpreting the very terrain that the pilgrim is negotiating and, indeed, experiencing. By relating the great events of the past that occurred at a site, guides do not simply direct one to ascend to the very same stage on which these dramas occurred in order to reenact retrospectively the roles that various divine and human superheroes once played there. They are also unequivocal in implying that what initially happened in bygone eras at a particular place remains both evident there and active in certain ways. Thus, the very details of topographical form are attributed to the results of battles of magic, struggles for power, or other acts, while the landscape becomes named and recognized on the basis of these events. Furthermore, the physical environment is regarded as being animated in various ways. Places, objects, and their substances are thought of as becoming purified or morally superior through a process of empowerment effected by the presence and actions of deities and saints. Many Tibetans conceive of empowerment in ways that are not too different from the nature and effects of the fields of energy or radiation posited by modern physics. An empowered site or thing is credited with the ability to transform subtly that with which it comes in contact. Aspects of both the natural and the human-made world are also considered as the abodes (*gnas*) of a wide variety of nonhuman beings. The Tibetan word for pilgrimage literally means "circling around an abode" (*gnas skor*), referring to the general practice of circumambulation as a way of relating to such places.

The specific environments, objects, and persons upon which pilgrimages focus, and the pattern of relationships between these and the pilgrims themselves, are what forms the basis of pilgrimage practice for Tibetans. Thus, although most Tibetans identify themselves and their culture as Buddhist, it is often misleading to justify—as outside observers and interpreters often do—aspects of Tibetan life primarily in terms of abstract Buddhist doctrines. This is a tendency shared to a certain extent by highly educated Tibetan Buddhist clerics as well. Explaining Tibetan pilgrimages in terms of a static system of Indic metaphysical imperatives, such as karma, saṃsāra, and nirvāṇa, not only lacks the explanatory power required to account for such complex phenomena, but it also negates the fundamental assumptions and categories Tibetans draw from their own worldview in order to construct and negotiate their social reality.

The fact that Indian Buddhist and indigenous Tibetan views of the world exist in complex relation to one another is well attested in the discourses operating throughout Tibetan cultural history. Our small *Guidebook to Lapchi* provides some specific local examples of this. The text was written by a learned lama named Tenzin Chökyi Lodrö (Bstan 'dzin chos kyi blo gros, 1868–1906), the thirty-fourth hierarch of the Drigungpa ('Bri gung pa) sect, a branch of the important Kagyü (Bka' brgyud) school of Tibetan Buddhism. He compiled his *Guidebook to Lapchi* from a number of sources after a pilgrimage to the area 1901. His text purports to offer a Buddhist account of the process of the introduction of Buddhism into a Tibetan-speaking zone of the high Himalaya. Its central narrative reveals a dramatic ideological struggle between the powers represented by Indian tantric Buddhism, and those identified with other Indian belief systems and the spirit forces that many Tibetans recognize as inhabiting and animating their physical environment. While this contest of powers is played out between divine beings on a cosmic level, it also comes down to Earth and involves human beings and their history, as our text situates the story at a geographical location, the place of Lapchi, in the actual landscape of Tibet.

Lapchi, or more fully in Tibetan, the "Snowy Enclave of Nomadic Lapchi" ('Brog la phyi gangs kyi ra ba), is an area of glaciated mountains and luxuriant alpine valleys located on the present border between Nepal and the Tibetan Autonomous Region of the People's Republic of China. It lies just to the west of the great Himalayan summit of Gaurishankar (7,150 m), or Jomo Tseringma (Jo mo tshe ring ma) as it is known to Tibetans. At present the region is inhabited by pastoralists and seasonally frequented by pilgrims and traders from both sides of the border. While today it is possible for people to locate the place on a map and visit it as a pilgrim or nomad, according to the *Guidebook to Lapchi* this has not always been the case. To explain the ways in which Lapchi became an empowered landscape worthy of performing pilgrimage at, and how human beings "opened the door to the place" (*gnas sgo phye ba*), the author resorts to two important narrative traditions. Both of these, the story of Rudra's subjugation in chapters 1 and 2 and the exploits of Milarepa (1040–1123 C.E.) in chapter 3, require some interpretive commentary.

First, the story of the subjugation of the evil Indian god Rudra by the virtuous buddha Vajradhara. Both main characters are referred to in the text under various names that mark their different manifestations and qualities, with Rudra also being called Mahādeva, Maheśvara, and Bhairava in places, while the buddha Vajradhara is identified as Heruka, Saṃvara, or Cakrasaṃvara as well. Both are also coupled with female consorts and served by their respective demonic or divine retinues. From a Buddhist point of view, Rudra can be seen to represent the powers and teachings of the heterodox Indian school of Śaivism, particularly as it developed in its tantric mode. The Tibetan area of Lapchi itself has a double Indian identity in the text, being equated with the tantric power place of Godāvarī. This is a site found listed in both Buddhist and Śaiva tantric literature and is associated with an area in the southern part of the Indian subcontinent. How, therefore, did Godāvarī come to be located in the high Himalaya by Tibetans, and become the setting for such a divine contest?

The answer to this question is complex and still not fully understood, but a few points seem clear. When Tibetan scholars and their Indian teachers began systematically to transfer late North Indian tantric Buddhism across the Himalaya into Tibet, they carried more than just texts, religious icons, and philosophies with them. They took with them a series of sophisticated narratives and rituals that related conceptions of the inner person to the ordering of the cosmos and the cult geography of the Indian subcontinent. As Tibetans began to engage in tantric meditation and yoga in their own land, many of the set of twenty-four or thirty-two famous tantric cult places of India gradually became identified with accessible locations in the high Himalaya and great plateau lands to the north. Some of the places at which Indian sites became duplicated were already significant to Tibetans as being the dwellings of powerful mountain gods and goddesses, along with a host of other local spirit forces. The Snowy Enclave of Lapchi is one such area.

The initial spatial setting for the story of the subjugation of Rudra at Lapchi is the universe itself, but more specifically our southern cosmic continent (Jambudvīpa), as it is conceived of in Buddhist cosmologies that have long been known in Tibet. The events unfold in the context of cosmic time, over the countless millions of years of the four world-ages (*yuga*). It was at the beginning of the present age of disharmony (*kali yuga*) that a cosmic drama unfolded in which two sets of divine forces competed for hegemonic power, and the control of the world changed hands. The fact that Buddhist gods are vanquishing those that represent other non-Buddhist Indian religious schools in the story in part reflects the themes in the earlier Sanskrit sources upon which Tibetan storytellers later based their own versions, and not necessarily any actual conversion struggle that took place in Tibet itself. As we shall see, there are other interpretations of this conflict to consider. On a grand scale, then, the entire world-system is converted in this drama, although during the process essentially the same scenario is played out locally at each of the twenty-four tantric power places located on Earth, Godāvarī (alias Lapchi) being one of them. The subtle operations by which this conversion takes place are of great importance if we are to appreciate the multiple implications of the story for Tibetans.

In the Buddhist tantras, one of the primary systems of representation is that of the cryptogram or psycho-cosmogram (maṇḍala). Essentially, a maṇḍala is a complex, three-dimensional system of organization or interrelations applied to reality at different levels. It can be conceived of as an elaborate, tiered palace inhabited by buddhas or their emanations, together with a divine host of beings all hierarchically assembled from top to bottom, and from center to periphery. For Tibetan Buddhists the universe is ordered in this way, with the Buddha dwelling upon the central cosmic mountain (Meru) and the world arranged around it in a great circle divided into different planes. The particular maṇḍala found in the *Guidebook to Lapchi*, that of Heruka or Saṃvara as a heroic emanation of the buddha Vajradhara, is organized on three planes: the celestial or "sky" zone, the surface of the Earth, and the subterranean or "underworld" zone. This threefold ordering of space (known as *tribhuvana* in Sanskrit or *sa gsum* in Tibetan) is pervasive in both Indian and Tibetan worldviews. The twenty-four tantric power places are arrayed within this system, with eight existing on each of the three planes. A further eight sites are included, these being a series of charnel grounds located around the circumference of the great circle of the maṇḍala itself, thus yielding a total of thirty-two locations often mentioned in the texts. Godāvarī or Lapchi is counted as existing on the celestial plane of the world-system maṇḍala, hence its designation as one of the "eight sites of celestial action."

For Tibetans, the organization of the maṇḍala is also repeated on various subcosmic levels. Thus, the *Guidebook to Lapchi* 1 goes on to describe the conversion of the spirit powers at the site in terms of the establishment of a maṇḍala right there in the actual mountain environment of Lapchi, and the place becomes animated in a particular way as a result. This is one of the main reasons why Lapchi is regarded as empowered and important to visit by pilgrims, whether they be tantric yogins or lay worshippers. Many oral and written sources make it clear that to the ordinary observer such places appear mundane, as just earth, rock, sky, and water, although features of the landscape are often held to be shaped in certain ways as they reveal the form of another level of reality beneath their surface. To highly qualified meditators and enlightened beings who visit Lapchi, the true reality of the maṇḍala, as a celestial palace with divine inhabitants, is visible and accessible there.

Furthermore, on another, more esoteric level, the same maṇḍala is also repeated within the human body itself, particularly so when it is activated during the specialized meditation and yoga performed by advanced tantric Buddhist practitioners in Tibet. Thus, when the subtle psychic body of the meditator is generated in accord with this, it too has twenty-four related internal power points organized like the cosmic maṇḍala. This yogic network is often referred to as the adamantine-body (*vajrakāya*), and its internal points are homologized with the external tantric cult sites, such that the reality of the microcosm and macrocosm are equated. Thus, within the logic of this system we find that in the text the external power place of Lapchi is equated with, and said to correspond to, the left ear of the adamantine-body. Furthermore, it is to the external cult places like Lapchi, which had become established as natural maṇḍalas, the yogins made actual pilgrimages to develop and perfect their internal adamantine-body.

Bearing all this in mind, it is possible that the story of Rudra's subjugation can also be read as an implicit description of internal psychic transformations that the practitioner of tantric Buddhist yoga undergoes. In later parts of Milarepa's story we find these meditative processes explicitly referred to. Thus, the character of Rudra and his vile horde of demons also represent the negative predispositions that need to be overcome by the tantric yogin. The Buddhist Heruka and his potent and virtuous assembly are also the yogin's own overcoming of tendencies toward defilement. Attempting to understand such esoteric levels of meaning that the *Guidebook to Lapchi* may have is valuable as a key to how Tibetans might relate to the site itself as pilgrims. But it is also essential if we are to grasp the Tibetan significance of the character featured in the final part of the story of Lapchi, that is, the universally popular Tibetan saint and yogin Milarepa.

After its conversion into a Buddhist maṇḍala and subsequent empowerment, the place of Lapchi is finally fully opened to human beings by the bold activities of Milarepa. As his capsule biography in the text indicates, Milarepa wandered to remote tantric power places and through his meditative training became an accomplished yogin who was able to activate the adamantine-body within himself and identify with the powers and qualities of the divinities in residence. It is common knowledge for Tibetans that yogins attain many potent magical abilities, the so-called paranormal powers (*siddhi*), as a partial result of their practice toward enlightenment. From this point of view alone they are very highly regarded figures in Tibetan culture. Furthermore, as embodied representatives of realized divinity and the maṇḍala, they are personally empowered individuals whose psycho-physical body is highly purified and morally superior. Given all these qualities, in our story of Lapchi, Milarepa is able not only to defeat successive waves of demonic attack with his superior tantric magic, but also at times seemingly to play with reality and leave miraculous traces behind, such as footprints in rocks, at the places he passes. For the Tibetan pilgrim at Lapchi these amazing traces of the saint, and the other places where he spent time in his supercharged body, are all empowered sites in their own right. They are important not only to witness as a record of his actions, but also to encounter and experience personally because of the spiritual transformations they are believed to be able to effect.

Finally, we should reflect on the general theme of subjugation and conversion that runs throughout the whole three chapters below. Discerning readers will notice that at no point are the forces of evil and perversity ever completely banished or totally annihilated by Buddhist deities or tantric yogins. Using the full force of Buddhist magical and moral superiority, divine residences are taken over and redecorated, the accessories and symbols of the vanquished are adopted and employed by the vanquishers, and identities and allegiances are changed and fixed with binding oaths. The benefits of Buddhist doctrines, including salvation, are available to those conquered and converted. In the case of Milarepa, the potent human conduit through which this process operates, he becomes the principal teacher or lama (*bla ma*) of the spirit world as well as that of the human one. We should note that while this tantric yogin wages magical warfare to battle male demons into submission, he conquers a feminine environment and its female spirit leader by means of ritual sexual penetration. The idea of the land of Tibet as a feminine ground tamed and converted by an introduced male Buddhist power is a recurrent theme in subjugation narratives surrounding the introduction of Buddhism to the high plateau.

Ultimately, then, there would seem to be no final or complete victory in the story of Lapchi. The indigenous forces of evil and perversity are still present in the world, although now pinned down, bound, or contained; they are neutralized and held in check by Buddhism in a variety of ways. Considering this, there is perhaps an important question that this small pilgrim's guide to Lapchi should provoke in its critical readers: Can we ever afford to assume that the Buddhist conversion of Tibetan culture was a historically or socially complete process? Or is it still an ongoing one; the maintenance of a balance between two sets of forces, which must be replayed or reconstituted continually by way of a welter of narrative and ritual scenarios developed and reproduced for the best part of a millennium? There is much in traditional Tibetan religious culture that is dedicated to this end, and this itself is a fact that has important social ramifications. As the powers of Buddhism must be continually employed to maintain this state of affairs and keep the balance, we find that they are channeled especially via its human representatives, that is, the high-status specialist figures of lamas, yogins, oracles, clerics, and various others, who occupy significant loci of social power in the Tibetan world. Such issues are surely worthy of continuing debate and inquiry in the study of Tibetan religion.

The translation below is based on two editions: Bstan 'dzin chos kyi blo gros, 34th 'Bri gung gdan rabs (1868–1906), *Gsang lam sgrub pa'i gnas chen nyer bzhi'i ya gyal gau dā wa ri 'am / 'brog la phyi gangs kyi ra ba'i sngon byung gi tshul las tsam pa'i gtam gyi rab tu phyed pa nyung ngu rnam gsal*. In *Dpal 'khor lo sdom pa'i sku yi gnas gangs ri ti se dang gsung gi gnas la phyi gangs ra gnyis kyi gnas yig* (Delhi: Damcho Sangpo Jayyed Press, 1983), ff. 261–402 (translation covers ff. 264–92 = 2b–16b); Bstan 'dzin chos kyi blo gros, 34th 'Bri gung gdan rabs (1868–1906), *Gsang lam sgrub pa'i gnas chen nyer bzhi'i ya gyal gau dā wa ri 'am / 'brog la phyi gangs kyi ra ba'i sngon byung gi tshul las brtsams pa'i gtam gyi rab tu byed pa nyung ngu rnam gsal (An account of the place of meditation known as Lachi in western Tibet)* (Gangtok: Sherab Gyaltsen, Palace Monastery, 1983) (translation covers pp. 1–16).

Further Reading

For more on the life and travels of Milarepa, see G.C.C. Chang, *The Hundred Thousand Songs of Milarepa*, 2 vols. (Boulder: Shambhala, 1977); and L. P. Lhalungpa, *The Life of Milarepa* (Boulder: Shambhala, 1984). For more on Indian and Tibetan conversion and subjugation narratives, see Ronald Davidson, "The Bodhisattva Vajrapāṇi's Subjugation of Śiva," in *Religions of India in Practice*, edited by Donald S. Lopez, Jr. (Princeton: Princeton University Press, 1995), pp. 547–55; Janet Gyatso, "Down with the Demoness: Reflections on a Feminine Ground in Tibet," in *Feminine Ground: Essays on Women and Tibet.*, edited by J. D. Willis (Ithaca: Snow Lion, 1989), pp. 33–51. On Tibetan tantric pilgrimage sites and the area of Lapchi, see Toni Huber, "Where Exactly are Cāritra, Devikota and Himavat? A Sacred Geography of Controversy and the Development of Tantric Buddhist Pilgrimage Sites in Tibet," *Kailash, a Journal of Himalayan Studies* 16.3–4 (1990):121–65; Huber, "Guide to the La-phyi Maṇḍala: History, Landscape and Ritual in South-Western Tibet," in *Maṇḍala and Landscapes*, edited by A. W. Macdonald (New Delhi: D. K. Printworld, 1996); A. W. Macdonald, "Hinduisation, Buddha-isation, Then Lama-isation or: What Happened at La-phyi?," in *Indo-Tibetan Studies: Papers in Honour and Appreciation of Professor David L. Snell-*

grove's Contribution to Indo-Tibetan Studies, edited by T. Skorupski (Tring, UK: Institute of Buddhist Studies 1990), pp. 199–208.

An Elucidatory and Concise Analysis of Stories Concerning the History of Godāvarī, alias the Snowy Enclave of Nomadic Lapchi, One of the Twenty-four Power Places for Accomplishing the Secret Path

I
HOW THIS INANIMATE MOUNTAIN ITSELF WAS ORIGINALLY TAKEN OVER BY THE ARROGANT RUDRA

Long, long ago, after the elapse of a very great period of time following the creation of this very world-system, the lord of this world, the great god called Mahādeva alias Maheśvara, ferocious Bhairava [or Rudra], appeared in fierce and violent forms and then took up residence in and ruled over the country of Magadha in India. At the same time, there appeared four serpent deities and four demigods from the underworld, four bestowers of harm and four ogres from the surface of the Earth, and four gods and four gandharvas from the sky. These twenty-four fierce and violent spirits assumed control of their respective dwelling places in those twenty-four countries extending from Pullīramalaya to Kulutā in the southern cosmic continent and then took up residence in them. In particular, at that time the Snowy Enclave of Lapchi was known by the name Godāvarī. A certain fierce and venomous couple who were gods of the demon class, the gandharva Suravairiṇa and his consort Vīramatī, appropriated this place, establishing a palace there.

Thereafter, because of their excessive anger these twenty-four fierce ones consumed the life force of many sentient beings. Because of their excessive lust they made love at all times. Because of their excessive ignorance they accepted heretical views themselves and then imposed them on others. Having also taken Mahādeva as their ultimate refuge, they performed obeisance to him. As a result Maheśvara, after abandoning his own form and having manifested in the form of twenty-four stone phallic symbols (*liṅga*), dwelt thus in each of those places.

II
HOW THE PLACE WAS CONVERTED INTO A FIELD OF CELESTIAL ACTION, AFTER BEING SUBDUED BY AN EMANATION OF SAṂVARA

When the present cosmic age of disharmony issued in, following a passage of incalculable hundreds of thousands of years, after the completion of the cosmic age of perfection and the second and third cosmic ages accordingly, the great buddha Vajradhara saw that the time had come to descend and subdue those fierce ones. Having arisen in the form [of Heruka, a heroic archetype deity] with four faces and twelve arms, expressing highly enraged great wrath, even while his mind was not moved from objectless compassion, and assuming a dancing pose, he trampled ferocious Bhairava and his consort underfoot, as a result of which Bhairava attained great bliss, and gained complete awakening under the earth.

Thus, after conquering ferocious Bhairava, Heruka remained on the summit of the central cosmic mountain, at which time he was presented with a heavenly mansion provided with a throne by the buddha Akṣobhya, with twenty-four male and twenty-four female bodhisattvas by the buddha Ratnasambhava, with twelve goddesses by the buddha Amitābha, with armored gods by the buddha Amoghasiddhi, and with gods representing the magically empowered aggregates, constituents, and sources by the buddha Vairocana. After which, the maṇḍala of the sixty-two emanations of Saṃvara was completed.

At that time, the twenty-four pairs of male and female bodhisattvas, having also arisen in the form of wrathful father-mother unions (*yab yum*), subdued the twenty-four arrogant ones [and their consorts] living in the twenty-four countries of the southern cosmic continent. Eight of the wrathful father-mother unions, having manifested as eight guardians of the cardinal gates and intermediate points, subdued the eight wrathful goddesses of the cemeteries [surrounding the maṇḍala]. In particular, from among the aforementioned twenty-four pairs of bodhisattvas, both the male bodhisattva Vajrapāṇi and the female bodhisattva Vajravetālī, having arisen in the form of a wrathful father-mother union, subdued both of the couple of gandharvas who resided at the Snowy Enclave of Lapchi. The manner of their subjugation was as follows: Having seized the abode of those venomous ones, they transformed it into a palace; having taken away their power and strength, they rendered them powerless; having seized their elephant hides, tiger skins, and other garments, they dressed themselves in them; having seized their knives, skull-cups, ceremonial staffs, and other hand-held accoutrements, they used them as their own instruments; having appropriated their essential cries of rage, and so forth, they reempowered them as their own primary ritual formulas; having seized their meat, beer, and other edibles and drinkables, they performed circular feast offerings with them and then made their minds dissolve in the clear light and brought them to awakening. In particular, they empowered the receptacles of Mahādeva's emanations [i.e., the stone phallic symbols] so that the maṇḍala of the emanations of the sixty-two deities of Cakrasaṃvara was directly manifest there. And in that way, the maṇḍala of the emanations of Cakrasaṃvara as vanquishers was completed without abandoning the form of those to be vanquished. Regarding that, at the time when the twenty-four [external] countries were assigned to the internal adamantine-body, it was said: "The face was Pullīramalaya, the crown of the head was Jālandhara, the right ear was Oḍḍiyāna, and the neck was Arbuta." This place, Lapchi, was known as the left ear, Godāvarī, and nowadays the proof of this is so made as a self-manifest ear on a rock called Left Ear.

In brief, after the subjugation of ferocious Bhairava by glorious Heruka during the cosmic age of disharmony, the district known as Godāvarī, which is one of the eight sites of celestial action, was established as the physical field of Cakrasaṃvara. But it should be understood that before ferocious Bhairava was conquered, it was nothing but a heap of earth and rock, or an ordinary abode of nonhuman beings.

III
HOW THE ENTRANCE TO THE PLACE WAS OPENED BY THE MASTERS REALIZED IN TRUTH

Following glorious Heruka's magical transformation of it into a place of attainment of the powers of secret tantric Buddhism, for a long time after there were just flesh-eating celestial heroes and amazons roaming and playing there at will, and because of this there were no ordinary beings belonging to the human race there. But 336 years after the Buddha's passing beyond suffering and rebirth, in the holy land of India the great realized meditation master glorious Saraha appeared and initiated the vehicle of the Vajrayāna of secret tantric Buddhism, after which he visited all the twenty-four countries and thirty-two places. From that time on there is really no question that many of the great accomplished ones of India came to that place. Now, due to the vicissitudes of time, we can no longer be certain exactly who went there.

However, after the exalted Avalokiteśvara manifested as the king of Tibet, Songtsen Gampo (Srong brtsan sgam po), and acted as the protector of Snowy Tibet [see chapter 2], the flesh-eating celestial amazons became a little milder, whereupon Mangyül (Mang yul) and Nyanang (Gnya' nang) and other locations on the borders of this place began to be habitable by human beings. After that, because the great meditation master Padmasambhava visited the place and bound the flesh-eating celestial amazons by oath, they became even milder than before, and human beings could travel, to a certain extent, to the very center of Lapchi as well. Later on, because the learned and accomplished great Yuthogpa Dreje Badzra (G.yu thog pa 'dre rje badzra) went there, there are also various acknowledged meditation caves of Yuthogpa there nowadays. Finally, concerning the full completion of the entrance to the place, since the mightiest of yoga practitioners, the master Milarepa, is the one who opened it, I shall relate the brief account of that now.

As for the master Milarepa himself, he was born in Mangyül Gungthang (Gung thang) during the water-dragon year (1052) of the first sixty-year calendrical cycle (1027–1087), the time at which the translator Marpa (Mar pa) reached the age of forty. During his youth, he employed the black arts against his paternal relatives who had come forward as his enemies, and he destroyed thirty-five members of the enemy party. Having made it hail, he destroyed the harvest. Out of remorse for that, he came into the presence of Marpa the translator in the valley of Lhodrak Drowo (Lho brag gro wo). He won his favor by single-handedly erecting a nine-storied tower many times, as well as performing other deeds, and requested the teachings that had been handed down from glorious Nāropa. After he mastered them, on the occasion of his going to Latö, his lama prophesied to him the best meditation places at which to perform his practice, in particular:

> Because the Latö Gyelgiri (La stod rgyal gyi ri) is a mountain empowered by the great accomplished ones of India, meditate there. Because Tise (Ti se) snow mountain [Mount Meru] was prophesied by the Buddha to be the "snowy mountain" [in Buddhist scriptures] and is the palace of Cakrasaṃvara, meditate there. Because the Snowy Enclave of Lapchi is Godāvarī, one of the twenty-four countries, meditate there. Because Mount Pelbar (Dpal 'bar) of Mangyül and the Snowy Enclave of Yolmo (Yol mo) in Nepal are the places prophesied in the *Garland Discourse* (*Avataṃsaka Sūtra*), meditate there. Because Chubar (Chu dbar) of Drin (Brin) is the place where the celestial amazons who are field-protectors assemble and reside, meditate there. Furthermore, in any deserted place that is perfectly suitable, meditate and raise the banner of realization in each one.

Thus was his prophecy. After that, the master returned to Mangyül Gungthang and as a consequence of observing the condition of his homeland, his mind was softened by a liberating aversion to this world. Through the perfection of ascetic practices during his twelve years at Drakar Taso (Brag dkar rta so), he acquired special qualities, to the extent of being able to fly through the air. At that time, he resolved to go to open the entrance to the area of the Snowy Enclave of Lapchi and fully realize the instructions of his principal teacher. After he had traversed the Dringi Poze (Brin gyi spo ze) pass, he went to Drakmar Chonglung (Brag dmar mchong lung) and gained realizations there. As a result, at that time the king of the obstacle-making demons known as Vināyaka, who is at present the field-protector of Lapchi, transformed himself into seven iron festival clowns with hollow and sunken eyes and appeared looking for an opportunity to get at the master. Then Milarepa said:

> I, Milarepa, am not afraid of demons.
> If Milarepa was afraid of demons,
> There would be little profit in a knowledge of things as they really are.
> You! Hosts of obstacle-makers, demons, and evil spirits who have come here,
> How wonderful it is that you have arrived.
> Do not hasten to leave, but please stay here.
> Let us discuss this together clearly.
> Though you may be in a hurry, by all means stay here tonight.
> We should vie in skill of body, speech, and mind,
> And see the difference in greatness between the white and the black religions.
> Do not leave without having made a nuisance of yourselves.

> If you leave without having made a nuisance of yourselves,
> How shameful your coming here on this occasion!

Having said that, he raised the pride of his archetype deity and went directly for the festival clowns. The festival clowns, their eyes bulging in panic from their fear, fright, and terror, disappeared rapidly one into the other until the last remaining one, having formed itself into a whirling tornado, disappeared from sight. After, he performed a little meditation in that place. Following the field-protector's failure to get at him with this first magical trick, he resolved to go to the central place of Lapchi. He traversed the Drin Poze pass and the Nyanang Thong (Gnya' nang mthong) pass and went to the entrance of Lapchi, Nyanang Tashigang (Bkra shis sgang). Since the people of Tsarma (Rtsar ma) had already heard of the master's fame, there was a desire to meet him that coincided favorably with the master's arrival in Tsarma on this occasion. Because of that a wealthy resident of Tsarma, Shendormo (Gshen rdor mo), and his wife Leksebum (Legs se 'bum), and also Kyotön Shākya Guṇa (Skyo ston shākya guṇa) and others, were overjoyed when they realized that it was the master.

At that time, Lapchi was the nomadic pastureland of the residents of Nyanang Tsarma. But because it had become a physical field of celestial action, a land roamed by flesh-eating celestial amazons, there was a frequent occurrence of open attacks by goblins and demons against the people who went there. As a result, the name of Drelung Kyomo ('Dre lung skyo mo, "Discontented Demon Valley") was given to the region. They requested that the master go there to subdue the demons and open the entrance to the place. Then the master also went toward the Züleigang (Zul le'i gangs) pass of Lapchi, and from the top of the pass the nonhuman beings produced specters to frighten him. As soon as he reached the summit of the pass there were violent claps of thunder and flashes of lightning, and the mountains on both sides of the valley moved, so that the mountain torrent, diverted from its course and churned up in violent waves, turned into a lake. At this, the master gave a concentrated stare, took his staff and pushed it in, and the lake drained out from the bottom and disappeared. The place is known as Mudzing (Dmu rdzing, "Demon Pond"). From there, he descended a little way, and the nonhuman beings stirred up waves consisting of many boulders, to the point where the mountains on both sides were thrown down. The celestial amazons provided a safe path for him out of a hill running downward like a snake, between the sides of the valley. That "wave-stilling" path is known as the Khandro Ganglam (Mkha' 'gro sgang lam, "Ḍākinī Ridge Path").

Then, the nonhuman beings of lesser powers became calm of their own accord, while those of great powers, even though they did not find a point of attack, once again sought to get at him. The master, at the point where the Khandro Ganglam terminates, gave a concentrated stare causing reversion of their views and subjugation, whereby the magical tricks ceased completely, and after, in the spot where he stood, a footprint appeared on the rock. On a ridge a short distance from there, after the sky had cleared, he dwelt and cultivated the meditation of benevolence, and that spot is called Jamgang (Byams sgang, "Compassion Ridge"). When he went to Chuzang (Chu bzang) from there and stayed a short time, once again the field-protector of Lapchi the lord of obstacle-makers Vināyaka himself, in the guise of a Nepalese demon called Bharo with a demonic army as retinue, which filled the earth and sky of the valley of Chuzang, came and displayed many magical tricks, such as throwing mountains down on the master's head, pouring down fierce deluges of weapons, and so forth. The master said such things as:

Due to the essential instructions of my supreme principal teacher,
By the power of the firmly cultivated production and completion stages of meditation, and
Because of an understanding of the causal nexus of inner being,
In the outer world, I am not afraid of demons.

In my lineage, that of Saraha,
Are many yogins, effulgent as the sky.
Having repeatedly meditated on the significance of primal mind,
Illusory thoughts disappear into space.
I see neither the hindered nor the hinderer.

And then he bound the nonhuman beings by oath. On that occasion they gave him various things, such as provisions for a month, and from then on they became the master's patrons. After that, when he stayed in a cave at Ramding (Ram sdings), many celestial amazons from Lapchi performed prostrations, gave him offerings of every kind of desirable thing, and circumambulated him, and as a consequence there appeared here on a rock the footprints of two celestial amazons. On the way down from there the nonhuman beings created the magical appearance of many enormous vulvas on the path before him. The master, his penis having become erect in anger, advanced on his way brandishing it, and through rubbing his penis on a rock in which was collected the quintessence of the place at a point past nine of the illusory vulvas, and by giving a powerful stare, the magic tricks were all brought to a stop. That place is called Lagu Lungu (La dgu lung dgu, "Nine Crests Nine Valleys").

Then, when he was close to arriving at the central place, again the field-protector, the lord of obstacle-makers himself, went to meet him and present offerings to him. After constructing a religious throne, he requested Buddhist teachings and finally was absorbed into a boulder in front of the throne, which is why nowadays in that place there is a ritual cairn of stones. Then, at the center of the place, which has the appearance of three matrix-triangles stacked one upon the other because the sky outside it is triangular, the ground inside it is triangular, and the rivers in between it are triangular; in the presence of Vajrayoginī, and other celestial heroes and amazons happily amusing themselves like the gathering clouds, he remained in meditation for one month in a cave known as the Dudül Phukmoche (Bdud 'dul phug mo che, "Great Demon Subduing Cave").

After that, he went to the place of his patrons from Nyanang and told them: "I have stayed at your grazing grounds in Drelung Kyomo. Since I have subdued all the demons it has become a place of practice, and I shall be the first to go there and meditate." Because of this they rejoiced and were filled with faith, and also this is said to be the beginning of the human practice of performing prostrations, making offerings, and circumambulating there. Then, many years later, after the master had converted the hunter Khyira Repa (Khyi ra ras pa), when he went into the presence of the ear of the Buddha glorious Cakrasaṃvara, which had arrived self-manifest on the rock known as Lapchi Nyenyön (Snyan g.yon, "Left Ear"), and stayed there, the five field-protecting celestial amazons, the Tsering Chenga (Tshe ring mched lnga), came to snoop and see what the master's meditative understanding was. At the time, the master was enjoying a low-caste girl in the forest of Sengdeng (Seng ldeng), and through looking in a white silver mirror he spotted them and finally disappeared into the sky. A year later, when he was staying in Chonglung, they came to snoop as before. At that time they saw the master riding on a lion, his body smeared with funeral ashes and blood, with a garland of flowers upon his head, wearing the sun and moon as clothing. In his hands he held a parasol and a banner. Finally he went, disappearing into the sky, so that they were unable to get at him.

Later on, in the year of the water-dragon (1112) when the master was age sixty-one, on the occasion of his sojourn in the Khyung gong (Khyung sgong) cave in the center of Menlung Chubar (Sman lung chu dbar) during the first summer month, one night an army of eighteen great demons, which filled the sky, the Earth, and the intermediate realm, came with these five at its head: a woman with a skeleton-like appearance, bearing the central cosmic mountain in her arms; a red jackal-faced woman, whose orifices were all gushing blood, who was disgorging an ocean by the mouthful; a fierce woman with the appearance of the lord of death, who was playing the Sun and Moon like a pair of cymbals; a black, terrifying woman, the color of coal, who was throwing the Sun, Moon, and stars to the ground, laughing out loud, "Strike, kill!"; and a woman as beautiful as a goddess, whose smile was seductive and coquettish. Even though they sought an opportunity, the demons failed to get at him, and once again they became faithful and earnest. As a result of that, they said, "You are a yogin who has attained a state of firmness. In our ignorance, we formerly ridiculed and hindered you, and because of this we are greatly ashamed and remorseful. From now on, we will obey whatever you command. We, the demons, will carry out all those actions and duties, whatever they are, that you command." Having promised this, they returned to their own abodes.

Later, in the water-female-snake year (1113) when the master was aged sixty-two, the queen of medicine deities, the auspicious Tsering Chenga, having come in the guise of five beautiful women, placed in the master's hands a full gemstone ladle, telling him it was wild-ox yogurt. After offering the five types of worldly paranormal powers, which are the powers of immortality, the divining mirror, food and prosperity, a treasury of jewels, and four-footed livestock, they requested to take the vow connected with conceiving the aspiration to highest awakening. Later, the five women made eye-viewed offerings consisting of incense, flowers, food, and drink, and as a result of their request he bestowed on them the teachings of definitive meaning and conferred the initiation of the goddess Tārā and the essence of the cycle of views of the Adamantine Path of Buddhism. He bestowed afterward the initiation of the goddess Kurukullā and advised them of the cycle of vows of the supreme ritual formula, and so forth.

Later, in the wood-horse year (1114), because some cowherds of Drin polluted their campfire with scraps of meat, the auspicious Tseringma became afflicted by a severe illness. When she invited the master himself from Chubar (Chu dbar), he arrived with the speed of flashing lightning on the path of magic light, Sa-manta tsa ri. On the left slope of the snow mountain Thönting Gyelmo (Mthon mthing rgyal mo), there was a tent of white silk, with golden walls, whose ropes were all made of precious stones. Inside, the center pole was a conch, and the tent pegs were of coral. Within this tent, looking gravely ill, was the auspicious lady Tseringma. She made a request, after which, from that evening, the master performed an ablution by means of the hundred syllable ritual, made an invocation to the principal teachers and precious ones, and prolonged her life by means of the Uṣṇīṣavijayā ritual.

She recovered gradually from the illness and gave thanks in gratitude to the master, her principal teacher. After that, the master gave her an explanation of the intermediate state between death and rebirth and the three bodies and led her on to the path of great awakening. The chief of the field-protecting celestial amazons, Tseringma, was accepted as his ritual sexual consort. Thus, as she was the chief and was now under his power, all the celestial heroes and amazons of the region of Lapchi perforce came under his power and were bound by oath. He took the life-force of all the eight types of demons and commanded that from then on they should not harm human beings. The various demons listened obediently. From that time up until the present day, there has never been any harm from the demons for us human beings who went there. This is due solely to the grace of the principal teacher and master Milarepa, his spiritual sons, and those aforementioned accomplished ones. Those narrations concern the manner in which the entrance to the place was opened.

—32—

The Yogin Lorepa's Retreat at Lake Namtso

Nālandā Translation Committee

The story that follows narrates events from the life of Lorepa (Lo ras pa), a thirteenth-century Tibetan tantric master of the Kagyü lineage. This episode from his life is presented in *The Rain of Wisdom*, a collection of devotional songs and religious poetry by Kagyü gurus. The stories about Lorepa's life are meant to be both inspiring and entertaining. Much of the narrative is quite serious in tone, telling of Lorepa's fierce efforts to meditate and practice diligently while living in the most austere conditions in isolated retreat; but aside from this inspirational theme, there are amusing anecdotes of the disciples and various helpers, who attempt to emulate Lorepa's lofty detachment and serene confidence without much initial success.

Lorepa belongs to the Drukpa (*'brug pa*), subsect of the Kagyü lineage and in the first song that he sings, he invokes the protection of the Kagyü gurus. All of the Kagyü lineages trace their origins in Tibet back to the lay practitioner, Marpa the translator, but in his song Lorepa also includes the Indian gurus and the buddhas who are considered the source of the Kagyü tradition. For the modern devotee of the Kagyü tradition, this list of enlightened teachers would include more than forty-five gurus, and Lorepa's abbreviated version shows that we are still at an early stage in the lineage's development.

First he invokes the primordial buddhas Samantabhadra and Vajradhara, the mystical sources of the tantras, and symbols for absolute awakened mind in itself. Then we have in succession the Bengali mahāsiddha Tilopa, his Indian disciple Nāropa, who in turn taught the first Tibetan, Marpa the translator. Next in the lineage is Marpa's disciple Milarepa, the famous bard and wild yogin ascetic, who mastered the tantric meditation practice of generating inner heat (*gtum mo*) and wore only thin cotton robes (*ras pa*) while dwelling in the mountain caves of Tibet and Nepal. Next in the lineage mentioned by Lorepa is Milarepa's disciple, the doctor Gampopa (Sgam po pa), followed by the two founders of the Drukpa Kagyü sublineage: Lingchen Repa (Gling chen ras pa) and his student Tsangpa Gyare (Gtsang pa rgya ras), who was Lorepa's teacher. The other Kagyü lineage chants are written by another subsect, the Karma Kagyü. They are exactly like this list of gurus except that they branch after Gampopa to form a different series of teachers and disciples, apart from the line begun by Tsangpa Gyare.

Lorepa continued the practices of his teachers, and his life-style as a wandering yogin and a religious poet reminds one especially of Milarepa. Lorepa first met his guru Tsangpa Gyare when he was sixteen years old, and two years later he abandoned his family and all worldly activities to devote himself exclusively to his teacher. He studied intensively with the aging Tsangpa Gyare until he died, when Lorepa was twenty-six. Following the death of his beloved teacher, Lorepa practiced for numerous years under extremely harsh conditions, dealing constantly with overwhelming physical and psychological obstacles, but ultimately gaining great realization. The biographies of Lorepa emphasize several points in his life story: his generosity in providing material and spiritual support for other practitioners, the abundant ritual offerings he would regularly make, even to the point of personal impoverishment, and the important monasteries he founded in the later part of his life.

The story of Lorepa's retreat translated here takes place at Lake Namtso (Gnam mtsho), one of the three famous sites associated with Lorepa's life as a yogin. It is one of the largest bodies of water in Tibet, a sort of inland sea, with rocky hermitages situated on its banks and on its islands, which provide an ideal setting for a yogin's solitary retreat. The opening scene describing Lorepa's passage across the lake contains several interesting points. We see a medieval description of a Tibetan coracle boat, fashioned from leather pontoons by the fisherman who promises to help Lorepa. Such vessels are still used today in Tibet as ferries, often manufactured on the spot for the purpose of single crossings of rivers and lakes. Their voyage across the lake on this flimsy raft is a perilous journey, for despite their precaution of setting out on an auspicious day, they encounter rough, stormy weather, enormous waves, and monstrous frogs, all of which terrify the poor fisherman. The fisherman begs Lorepa to protect them from these perils by calling upon the divine assistance of the gods or of his gurus, and Lorepa responds with his invocation to the Kagyü lineage.

After his prayer, Lorepa's teacher Tsangpa Gyare himself appears in the sky, demonstrating the principle of the universality of the guru, the tantric precept that the spiritual teacher is the source of all protection and the truly effective refuge in the world. This visionary appearance is meant to illustrate the proper attitude of a disciple toward his guru for those who practice tantra. That is, the guru is taken to be the all-powerful spokesperson of the phenomenal world: ever present, ever active, the true cause of everything that happens to the disciple on his or her path. In the song Lorepa sings to the vision of his guru, he uses the crossing of the stormy lake as a metaphor for navigating the ocean of saṃsāra, and in evocative poetic imagery he lists six other similes for the unsatisfactoriness of cyclic existence. Saṃsāra is like a flaming fire, into which sentient beings are attracted like naive moths; saṃsāra is like a deep, dark abyss, a pitfall for blind and lost beings; it is like a futile mirage seen in a desert by hot and thirsty beings; and so on. Lorepa's supplication to Tsangpa Gyare as a guide who will protect and deliver them to safety on the "other shore" is heard, resulting in the immediate pacification of the storm; when they reach dry land the fisherman realizes that he was in the presence of a master all along, and he prostrates to Lorepa and asks for his blessing.

Upon arriving at the island in Lake Namtso, Lorepa finds a place that is perfectly conducive to meditation practice. It is unpopulated, except for the presence of the native deities. In the Tibetan worldview these gods and demons are the true proprietors of the land. Specifically this is the palace or earthly headquarters, if you will, of Dorje Küntragma (Lady Vajra All-Renowned, Rdo rje kun grags ma), the goddess of Lake Namtso. She is one of the twelve Tenma (*bstan ma*), native deities who are guardians of Tibet. Originally the Tenma opposed the importation of Buddhism, but through the wrathful magical power of the tantric master Padmasambhava and of the yogin Milarepa, they have been tamed and made protectors of the dharma. So we see Dorje Küntragma peacefully attending Lorepa's lectures, along with the important mountain god Nyenchen Thanglha and a host of local deities. This scene evokes the romance of being a solitary yogin. The practitioner on retreat may suffer intense loneliness, but he or she is never altogether alone, for there is a compensatory relationship that develops with the deities of land and water. These subtle beings become the yogin's true society.

In addition to teaching the local deities about the dharma, Lorepa also makes ritual cake or torma offerings to them religiously, even though his meager provisions require that they be much smaller than usual. The size of the torma offering cakes Lorepa makes is supposed to be quite cute and humorous, the size of a small rodent's ear and pellets. Lorepa was famous for taking vows to make particularly elaborate ceremonial offerings to the deities of the maṇḍala and for the benefit of beings. The twenty-fifth day is the time when a religious feast in honor of the tantric deities must be performed. Usually this involves consecrating a full meal and eating it with meditative enjoyment. But so poor and ascetic is Lorepa that his main feast offering, usually a foot-high cake, is merely a bowl of sugar water.

Yet it is clear that both he and the deities were very satisfied by the offerings, and it is no wonder that he has befriended so many. When he decides to leave Semo Island for another island, he encounters an angry scorpion deity who blocks his way with her stingers. In the full version of this story, the argument with the scorpion deity must have been a longer exchange, including an enlightening song. Here, after singing his song about overcoming the obstacles of conceptual mind, Lorepa naturally tames the impulsiveness of the local goddess, who promises to serve him at his new island retreat. This incident reenacts a familiar motif in Tibetan literature, in which the local spirits and earth guardians are tamed, civilized, and converted into protectors of the dharma. We see that Lorepa deserves indeed the honorific title given to Buddhist preachers: "a teacher of gods and men."

The narrative shifts abruptly then to the story of Lorepa's parents going on their pilgrimage to find their son, bringing Gendündar (Dge 'dun dar) with them as their guide. When parents and son are joyfully reunited, Lorepa teaches them some dharma, performs some songs and a few miracles, and then sends them off; but he keeps Gendündar, who becomes his faithful servant during his retreat. For this solitary retreat Lorepa moves into a cave, whose entrance is sealed by Gendündar, and he remains there meditating for years on end. Ordinarily Lorepa and Gendündar would be able to reprovision themselves each year by walking across the ice of the lake. But this is not to be. Quite mysteriously, the lake refuses to freeze over, winter after winter. Trapped on the island, with an ever-decreasing supply of food, Gendündar grows increasingly concerned that they will starve to death. Lorepa seems willing to sacrifice anything to continue his ascetic retreat, and they are reduced to boiling their own shoes for sustenance. In the end it is the universality of the guru in the form of a vision of Tsangpa Gyare that saves them both.

The five wisdom ḍākinīs who assist Lorepa at this point are female principles of enlightenment who bring messages and secret teachings to great yogins. Here the local deities serve the dharma and are ready to help Lorepa at the command of his all-powerful guru. They lay down a scarf, which appears as a path of frozen ice across the lake. Gendündar, accidentally beholding them, is harmed. It is not unusual for the sight of these goddesses to be dangerous. Many local deities were originally demons or gods of particular diseases. Some kill by being seen, some through their noxious breath, some through their penetrating gaze. Others, particularly the ḍākinīs, are messengers of tantric secrets, and the uninitiated may not see them.

When Lorepa and Gendündar reach the shores of Lake Namtso, they are met by three nomad herdboys. It is interesting that when these three boys see Lorepa, each sees him in a different way. This is because the true image of the realized guru is beyond conception, and each disciple sees him according to his propensities and abilities. Amazed at their apparent ability to walk on water, the boys prostrate and request Lorepa to teach them some dharma. The "Song of Five Buddha Fields" sung at this point sounds as if it would be quite interesting, but it has been deleted from this abbreviated account. In fact, throughout this version of Lorepa's retreat we can see places in the text where the tales have been abbreviated or songs have been left out for the *Rain of Wisdom* edition. We do, however, enjoy one last *dohā* or tantric song of experience by Lorepa, the lovely "Song of the Six Encouragements." These songs urge people to practice religion diligently, since everything (one's mind, body, property, wealth, relatives, and children) is impermanent, and only the dharma will bring ultimate satisfaction.

The disciples Lorepa gains on the shore of Lake Namtso follow him north to Uri, where he remains for six years and develops a sizable monastic community. The last paragraph actually is very specific about what kind of practices they are given. They become accomplished in the formless meditation known as *mahāmudrā*, or the "great symbol" or "great seal." This is a meditation practice in which one looks at one's mind directly, without supports or complicated techniques. The outcome of it is that one sees the entire world as being of the nature of mind itself. At that point, things that once seemed solid appear so no longer, but rather seem to carry their own symbolic message. And since the entire world is seen as mind, it is as if the "seal of mind" has been stamped on all of reality. This practice is based on penetrating down to the subconscious mind, the "basis" (Skt.: *ālaya*). It is by observing the basis of mind, its own subconscious, that one can see the phenomenal world being projected by mind. And so the text concludes that his disciples "became realized, establishing confidence in the wisdom of the basis."

The translation below (with some corrections here) appears in *The Rain of Wisdom*, translated by the Nālandā Translation Committee under the direction of Chögyam Trungpa (Boulder: Shambhala, 1980), pp. 246–55. It is based upon a text compiled by Mikyö Dorje in 1542, the abbreviated title of which is *Bka' brgyud mgur mtsho* (*The Ocean of the Songs of the Kagyüs*).

Further Reading

The Rain of Wisdom, translated by the Nālandā Translation Committee (Boulder: Shambhala, 1980).

Jetsün Lorepa's Retreat at Lake Namtso

Carrying a pair of shoulder bags full of roasted barley flour, Jetsün Lorepa journeyed to the great lake of Namtso in the north, which surrounds the island of Semo. The ice on the lake had melted, and so he had to stay on the shore where many fishermen were living nearby. Although he had made a strong resolution to practice on the island, since the ice had melted, there was no way to get to the island. So he supplicated the guru and wept.

One of the fisherboys said, "Young monk, why are you weeping?"

Lorepa replied, "I made a vow to meditate on that island, but since the ice has melted, my practice is hindered; therefore, I am sad."

The fisherboy exclaimed, "How wonderful that you have such faith! I will ferry you to the island."

But the boy's father said, "This lake is brackish. There is no water to sustain you during your ascetic practices, and if the lake does not freeze, your two years of provisions will not be enough. There is no history of anyone living there except glorious Galo and the Master Padmākara. This boy is my only son and I dare not send him. I know this lake better and I am stronger than my son. Since you have such great faith, I will take you now, but we both might die. Even so, I have committed evil by killing many fish, and you might liberate me."

They tied three pieces of wood together as a base, and underneath they attached three inflated leather bags. On top of that, they made a latticework of rope and sticks. Then they put the two full bags of roasted barley flour on the raft. The fisherman sat on one side, and the lord of dharma [Lorepa] sat on the other. On the eleventh day, as the stars came out, they launched their raft. At midnight the lake roared and crashed about, making a great tumult. The waves of the lake rose to the height of a man. Lightning flashed in the sky, and a great hailstorm came down. Frogs as big as goat-kids leapt onto the raft.

The boatman became extremely frightened and said, "It is unfortunate that you want to meditate on the island; both of us are going to die. Don't you have someone like the Kagyü gurus to supplicate? Can't you give a command to the local deities?"

With intense yearning and longing, Lorepa made a supplication to the Kagyü gurus, asking for help. He sang this secret song:

> Dharma body Samantabhadra and consort, inseparable from guru Vajradhara,
> Your emanation, guru Tilo, protector of beings,
> Guru Nāropa, free of faults and perfected in virtue,
> From the dharma realm of great bliss, please protect sentient beings.
>
> Teacher Marpa Dharma Intellect (Chos kyi blo gros), kind guru,
> Great lord of yogins, guru Milarepa,
> Guru Physician [Gampopa], who realized compassion-emptiness,
> From the realm of unconditioned luminosity-emptiness, please protect sentient beings.
>
> Omniscient protector of beings, guru vajra-king,
> Supreme heruka, glorious guru Lingchen Repa,
> Lord of the four bodies of the buddha, lord of dharma, protector of beings, honorable Drukpa,
> Please protect sentient beings with your compassion free of concepts.
>
> Authentic lord of dharma who accomplishes benefit for himself and others,
> Kind precious one who mercifully accomplishes benefit for beings,
> Merciful guru, wise in the ways of kindness,
> Please protect sentient beings of this dark age.

Thus, Lorepa supplicated.

From the direction of Semo Island they saw a mass of rainbow light shaped like a pitched tent. In the middle of this, they saw a vision of Tsangpa Gyare in enjoyment body aspect (*sambhogakāya*) holding a vase of eternal life in his hand. Again Lorepa supplicated:

O gurus, victorious ones of the three times and your descendents,
Please hear the lamentations from my heart.

Gurus and hosts of vajra brothers and sisters,
Learned and disciplined meditators who have attained unsurpassable enlightenment,
Decent dharma practitioners who have entered the gate of the teachings,
Please join your minds together and protect sentient beings.

In this terrifying fire pit of saṃsāra,
Please protect sentient beings who are as naive as moths.

In this fathomless and boundless ocean of saṃsāra,
Please protect sentient beings who are fragile as a cobweb.

In this pitch-black abyss of saṃsāra,
Please protect sentient beings who are blind and have lost their way.

In this great prison of saṃsāra without escape,
Please protect sentient beings who are defenseless captives.

In this poisonous pit of great suffering, saṃsāra,
Please protect sentient beings who are blind and mad.

In this futile mirage of great suffering, saṃsāra,
Please protect sentient beings who are hot and thirsty wild animals.

In this deceptive dream and illusion of saṃsāra,
Please protect sentient beings, long tormented through lack of realization.

O protector, lord of dharma, be a refuge for all, both high and low.
Please protect sentient beings with your great kindness and supreme consideration.

Gurus, victorious ones and your descendents, peaceful and wrathful deities throughout the universe,
Oath-bound protectors who delight in the side of the white,
Quell obstacles and the hosts of demons and establish sentient beings in happiness.

You gurus who do not discriminate
Between sentient beings and buddhas,
Please protect sentient beings who suffer!
Pacify obstacles and perfect virtues!
Cause the teachings to flourish and purify the realms!

Through the blessings of this supplication, the chaos was pacified instantly, and they easily arrived at dry land. The fisherman saw that the lord of dharma was the Buddha in person and he prostrated, circumambulated, and requested his blessings.

Before the fisherman returned, the lord of dharma said, "Surrender your mind, heart, and chest to the three jewels, and they will certainly not deceive you. You will meet your son easily without obstacles." The fisherman then easily returned to the other shore.

The lord of dharma inspected the qualities of that place. He saw that the lake was naturally clear and the color of vaiḍūrya gems. As the Sun rose and set, it seemed to rise and set from the depths of the lake. It was the palace of Dorje Küntragma (Rdo rje kun grags ma). In the middle of the island there was a field that was not very large, but flat like the palm of a hand. In the middle of this field, rock formations were piled up like jewels. To the right and left of the field there were hills that looked like the outstretched wings of a vulture. At the south end of the field there was a nāga cave and a maṇḍala cave, clean and clear, naturally pleasant, and giving rise to meditative concentration (*samādhi*). He saw that this was a place for practice, free from bustle and distraction, where experience and realization would increase like the waxing moon. He was very pleased.

Lorepa set aside one-half of a full bag of roasted barley flour for the next year and the other half of the first year's provisions. He made the deity offerings and sacrificial cakes (*gtor ma*) regularly. He made the deity offerings the size of a small rodent's ear, the middle sacrificial cakes the size of sheep pellets, and the one hundred cakes the size of small rodents' pellets. He made the stock of his gruel from the cake water of these. He said that he had never experienced more joy than in that year. For the offering of the twenty-fifth day [of the lunar calendar] the lord of dharma would dissolve a piece of rock-crystal sugar in a small offering bowl and then perform the long Cakrasaṃvara sādhana. He said it was very satisfying.

At that time, both the great Nyenchen Thanglha, in the garb of a young sorceror, and Dorje Küntragma, in the garb of a nobleman's daughter, surrounded by a great assembly of lake goddesses and local deities, came from time to time to listen to the lord of dharma's teachings and songs. Because all the gods and demons enjoyed his songs, they assembled in turns and said, "Yogin, please either sing or expound the dharma." So Lorepa expounded the dharma and sang many songs.

One day he went to view the scenery. He saw that on the far shore the fishermen had placed some fish in heaps and had spread out others. He sang the song of seven compassions.

In the following year, the Dritak nomads who lived on the shore said, "Last year a young Drukpa monk went to Semo Island without many provisions. We should see if he is still alive." Two of them went to see. They heard the voice of the lord of dharma making supplications in his practice cave, and they said, "He has gone mad!"

But as they approached, they saw that, although the lord of dharma had not used more than half of that full bag of roasted barley flour, he looked extremely healthy and his practice was prospering. They were amazed and their faith was aroused. They requested him to leave the island at that time, but he said, "I still have half a bag of barley flour and I will stay here."

Lorepa stayed for a whole year. Then he thought that in the winter, when the ice had formed on the lake, he would go to Shamo Island. However, the local deity manifested as a scorpion. At the entrance to the cave she placed one stinger on the floor and one stinger on the roof and blocked his way. So he sang the song of nine resolutions, ways of transcending conceptual mind.

The local deity then transformed herself into a twenty-year-old maiden, prostrated, and said, "I was not really trying to harm you, but I do not like your leaving! Now that I see that you are not to be diverted, I will serve you during your stay at Shamo Island." Then she vanished, and the lord of dharma went to Shamo Island and stayed there.

Then Lorepa's father and mother went to the refuge of beings, Tsangpa Gyare, who gave them his own attendant, Gendündar, as a guide. Joining together, they all traveled to the north. As there was ice on the lake, they were able to meet with the lord of dharma on Shamo Island. Both mother and father embraced the lord of dharma and cried. As it is said, "Where there is great joy, there are many tears." For several days, he made his parents content by teaching the dharma, singing songs, and performing miracles. He then sent them back to Central Tibet.

Lorepa told Gendündar [to prepare for a solitary retreat, saying], "Live in the eastern rock cave, cook the food, and practice. Now wall up the entrance to my rock cave." The lord of dharma stayed sealed up inside. Each time Gendündar would offer him food, he would eat just a portion of it and leave the rest to dry.

After seven years passed, Gendündar said to the lord of dharma, "The barley flour is completely consumed and ice has not formed on the lake." The lord of dharma gave him the dry food and said, "Make this into a soup; bring it here to me and drink some yourself." He saved the dregs of the soup and left them to dry.

Again Gendündar said, "The dry food is consumed."

The lord of dharma said, "Cook this." He gave him the soup dregs and said, "Make this into soup; bring it to me and drink some yourself."

Later on, Gendündar said, "Again the food is consumed and ice has not formed."

The lord of dharma said, "Shake out the bags and roll it into dough." When it was rolled, there was only as much as the size of a thumb. The lord of dharma performed a feast offering (*gaṇacakra*) and a visualization. He then realized that a local deity had brought the corpse of a deer to the beach, and he told Gendündar that there was something wonderous on the beach. Gendündar went to the beach and cut up the corpse that he found there. He offered some to the lord of dharma and ate a little himself. In this way, they were able to pass the eighth year.

Later on, Gendündar said, "The meat is now consumed."

The lord of dharma said, "Boil my shoes and meditation belt, your shoes and meditation belt, and the flour bags!" and he threw his shoes and meditation belt out to his attendant. Immeasurable suffering arose in Gendündar. He boiled them well and offered them to the lord of dharma.

Later on, Gendündar thought, "These too are finished. If I were to die, that would be sustenance for the guru." He said, "Guru sir, there is a human corpse down on the beach. Is it all right to eat it or not?"

The lord of dharma said, "It is all right."

Then the attendant tied one end of his sash to a bush and the other end around his neck. However, the lord of dharma knew that Gendündar was preparing to drown himself, and he quickly went out to him. The lord of dharma took him by the hand and brought him back up, saying, "Son, it is not necessary to make such a mistake! Although I may die, I have no regrets. For the sake of the dharma, I have practiced asceticism." He then sang the song of the four nonregrets.

That night the lord of dharma dreamt that the refuge of beings, Tsangpa Gyare, was on the beach in a white pitched tent, surrounded by a retinue of many local deities. At dawn the sound of a ritual hand drum (*ḍamaru*) was heard in the sky. The lord of dharma thought, "What is that?" He looked and he had a vision of the five wisdom ḍākinīs.

The ḍākinīs said, "Brother, you have been overburdened for a long time. Now you may go to Central Tibet. We request that you walk on the surface of the ice." Then they vanished like a rainbow.

The lord of dharma said, "Gendündar, get up and see if it is possible that ice has formed on the lake in accordance with the omen in my dream."

Gendündar thought, "Are we going to Central Tibet? It has been nine years since the lake has frozen. Since ice has not formed in the winter months, it is impossible for it to form during the summer!" Nevertheless, since it was the command of his guru, he went and looked. On the lake there was ice, an arrow's flight in width and a cubit in depth. On its surface there was a moderate snowfall, in which lay the footprints of a fox. Intense joy and immeasurable faith and devotion for the lord of dharma arose in him and he said, "Since the ice has formed, please let us be off."

The lord of dharma said, "Go and put the books and personal belongings in the bag and bring them along." They then departed.

The lord of dharma said, "Gendündar, you go first." Just as he reached the shore, Gendündar wondered if the lord of dharma was coming behind him, and he turned around to look. The ḍākinīs quickly gathered up the silk scarf on which they both walked, but since the lord of dharma had not reached the shore, the lower part of his body was immersed in the water.

The lord of dharma said, "If you had not looked back, it would have been better. The sight of the local deities is poisonous; therefore, your life will be short. If I bless you, you will have a long life, but you will not meet with me in the next life. Son, would you like a long life, or would you like to be with me in the next life?"

Gendündar said, "What joy is there in this life? I would prefer the joy of being with the guru in the next life." Therefore, his life was short, but in his next life, he was born as the son of a potter and met with his guru.

The lord of dharma and his disciple were seen coming from the middle of the lake by three herdboys. Each one saw them in a different form, and the herdboys were amazed. When the lord and his disciple arrived on the shore, the herdboys prostrated, offered them their barley flour and leeks, and said, "Both of you, master and disciple, must be accomplished ones (*siddhas*)! What a great wonder that you have now come across the water in this season! We request you to teach the dharma." The lord of dharma then sang a song called "The Five Buddha Fields" for the boys.

The boys said, "If you cross this hill, you will find our camp. Please go there! We will round up our sheep and cattle earlier than usual and come there."

So the master and disciple went toward the large encampment called Kyangpa, but they stayed in a field at a distance from the tents. The attendant asked if he could go into the encampment.

The lord of dharma said, "If you are hungry, eat the flour and leeks. Practice!"

Gendündar replied, "Lord of dharma, even if you will not go, I must go."

"If you must go, do not say that we came from Shamo Island."

When the attendant arrived at the encampment, he found many dogs. There was also a group of young toughs who demanded, "Where do you come from?" Nervously, Gendündar blurted out that he was from Shamo Island. They said, "The lake has not frozen for many years. You must be a bandit chief!" and they beat him.

When Gendündar returned, the lord of dharma asked him if he had gotten any alms. He said, "I did not get any alms—I got a beating!"

The lord of dharma said, "I told you before to stay and practice. Now practice!"

The three boys arrived at the camp at sunset and told their parents about the lord of dharma, and the parents went over and invited them both back to their camp. "Come to our camp, and we will serve you," they said. "Earlier on, we did not realize that you were the attendant of the lord of dharma—please forgive us!"

The lord of dharma and his attendant stayed there about seven or eight days. Then, their patrons again requested the dharma, saying, "For the past few days, you have constantly and naturally taught the dharma to us. But since we are highlanders, we have not understood very much. Therefore, please put the holy dharma into a melodious song."

Then, the lord of dharma sang this song of the six encouragements to practice, which bring impermanence to mind:

> This workable mind
> Is like mist on white glacier mountains.
> One never knows when the mist will disappear, so resort to practice!
> It is certain that it will disappear, so resort to the holy dharma!
>
> This illusory body composed of the four elements
> Is like a tree root rotting.
> One never knows when the tree will fall, so resort to practice!
> It is certain that it will fall, so resort to the holy dharma!
>
> This property built up by competitive ancestors
> Is like the illusion of a magician.
> One never knows when the illusion will be destroyed, so resort to practice!
> It is certain that it will be destroyed, so resort to the holy dharma!
>
> These objects of wealth collected through avarice
> Are like honey collected by bees.
> One never knows who will enjoy the honey, so resort to practice!
> It is certain that others will enjoy it, so resort to the holy dharma!
>
> Agreeable and loving relatives
> Are like travelers gathered in a marketplace.
> One never knows when the travelers will disperse, so resort to practice!
> It is certain that they will disperse, so resort to the holy dharma!
>
> These sons of your own flesh
> Are like hundred-year-old dotards.
> One never knows if they will help you, so resort to practice!
> It is certain they will not help you, so resort to the holy dharma!

Thus, the lord of dharma sang. Great faith arose in their patrons. They said, "Let us find out where the precious lord of dharma lives, so that we may practice the dharma."

Later, when the lord of dharma was living at Uri in the north, the patroness known as Karlek, the three herdboys, and a few others came there, cut their hair, changed their names, and became monks and nuns. They requested teaching and received transmission. In particular, they were given the view of the holy dharma of mahāmudrā, and the meditation of emptiness and stainless luminosity. Thus, the play of unobstructed experience arose in them. By doing just this practice, some of them, both male and female, wandered carefree from retreat to retreat and became realized, establishing confidence in the wisdom of the basis (*ālaya*).

—33—

A Fasting Ritual

Roger Jackson

Fasting rituals have been an important element of religious life in Tibetan culture areas for centuries. The collected writings of many of Tibet's greatest lamas include the texts of fasting rituals, and, in more recent times, anthropologists have explored the social and performative dimensions of the rite. In most places, the fasting ritual or *nyungne* (*smyung gnas*) is held annually and draws members of the laity to the local monastery or temple for three days of prayer, prostration, and ascetic practices focused on the great compassionate bodhisattva, Avalokiteśvara or Chenrezi (Spyan ras gzigs). Though there is no solid historical evidence that the type of fasting ritual practiced in Tibetan culture areas originated in India, Tibetans writers do trace the lineage of its practice back to India, and the Tibetan rite clearly combines in it a number of elements that are crucial to Buddhism in India, and elsewhere in Asia.

Socially, the fasting ritual is an instance of a common Buddhist phenomenon: occasions on which laypeople are permitted for a time to participate in the life of their society's most valued religious institution, the monastery or temple. The hallmark of such occasions, whatever their locale or duration, is the assumption by laypeople of some of the vows incumbent upon monastics. In lands throughout Buddhist Asia, laypeople will gather on new- and/or full-moon days (in Tibetan areas, more often the lunar tenth or twenty-fifth days) at their local monastery or temple, observe eight vows (against killing, stealing, lying, sexual activity, using intoxicants, eating after noon, entertainment and ornamentation, and taking an exalted seat), and spend the day praying, making offerings, and listening to religious discourses. The eight vows also may be taken for life by men or women who wish to renounce the world outside the monastic context, or women who wish to live a monastic life but are barred from doing so by the loss of the lineage of ordination. Women also may take for life the same ten vows as a novice monk (the eight listed, with the seventh divided into two and the promise not to handle money added as the tenth). The Tibetan fasting ritual is most closely modeled on the traditions involving lay attendance at monasteries and temples on lunar cycle days; however, it is scheduled less frequently, lasts longer, and is more demanding.

The fasting ritual is also an instance of a phenomenon that is not only Buddhist, but universal: asceticism. Such practices as fasting, silence, and celibacy have found a place in most of the world's religious traditions. Like all ascetic practices, they are aimed at reducing the individual's concern with outer, physical matters and increasing their concern with the inner and spiritual dimension of life. Most traditions believe that by undergoing the hardships involved in ascetic practices, individuals are "purified" and thereby made more capable of the sort of transformation that is held out as the ideal of human life—whether it is described as salvation, nirvāṇa, or living as God or the ancestors may prescribe. Buddhism often has been seen as a tradition that eschews asceticism. The Buddha, after all, tried and rejected the life of extreme austerity, and prescribed for his followers a "middle way" between asceticism and hedonism. It must be remembered, however, that the life of a Buddhist monk or nun was, by the standards of lay life in any culture or era, an austere one: celibacy was required, and while neither fasting nor silence was considered essential to spiritual progress, such practices often were adopted by the great meditators and adepts who have been the tradition's most charismatic and influential figures.

Cultically, the fasting ritual is an instance of the worship of Avalokiteśvara, the compassionate "Down-Looking Lord" who is perhaps the most popular deity of Mahāyāna Buddhism. Avalokiteśvara first assumes textual prominence in the Pure Land sūtras, where he is an attendant of the savior-buddha Amitābha ("Infinite Light"). In the *Lotus Sūtra*, he is described as a great being who hears the appeals of all those in distress and comes to their aid. In a sūtra devoted entirely to him, the *Karaṇḍavyūha*, he possesses his own pure land, on Mount Potala, to which he will bring all those who pray to him or recite his six-syllable mantra, *oṃ maṇi padme hūṃ*. In the tantric tradition, he takes on a variety of forms (often numbered at 108), any one of which a practitioner may ritually serve and contemplatively identify with. Wherever Mahāyāna spread in Asia, Avalokiteśvara followed: he was worshipped in Southeast Asia as Lokanātha, the "Lord of the World," in China, in a feminine guise, as the graceful savioress, Kuan Yin (Guanyin), and in Japan as the multifaceted, powerful Kannon. So important was he in Tibet that he came to be considered the father and protector of the nation, incarnate in the great early kings who promoted Buddhism and in the Dalai Lamas (see chapter 30). Avalokiteśvara also protects individual devotees from rebirth into the various realms of cyclic existence: the six-syllable mantra is often on the lips of the faithful, especially elderly laypeople. The particular form of Avalokiteśvara to which the fasting ritual is devoted is his most elaborate, that with eleven heads and a thousand arms. According to tradition, frustrated by the seeming infinity of beings to save, Avalokiteśvara felt his body and head split apart; his guiding buddha, Amitābha, restored him, giving him a thousand arms and eleven heads, Amitābha's own being topmost. The eleven heads express all moods and see in all directions; each of the thousand hands has in its palm an eye of wisdom, symbolic of Avalokiteśvara's perfect fusion of compassion, discernment, and skill in assisting suffering beings.

The actual historical origins of the fasting ritual itself are obscure. The most common legend of its foundation traces it back to India and tells of a poor, detested Indian woman afflicted with leprosy, who in desperation worshipped Avalokiteśvara in something like a prototype of the fasting ritual. He cured her, and out of gratitude, she took full ordination as a Buddhist nun. It is in remembrance of her that participants in the fasting ritual imagine that the Long Request Prayer at the heart of the rite (section III.E.1) actually is recited by this nun, Lakṣmī. A second legend, related among the Sherpas of Nepal, tells of a group of seven demons who enjoyed feasting daily on humans. One female demon, Adakpalum, had five hundred children, and each of them captured and ate a human being each day. A great lama, Dzichen Rinpoche, managed to capture one of Adakpalum's sons and returned him to her only on the condition that she and her brood desist from cannibalism. They did so, and Adakpalum, having experienced the temporary loss of her son, came to understand how the families of her victims must feel. She repented and convinced her fellow demons to do likewise. Dzichen Rinpoche then prescribed for all of them as a penance three years of continuous practice of the fasting ritual. As a result of observing it purely, the former demons were reborn in Amitābha's paradise, Sukhāvatī, and because the fasting ritual proved so efficacious, it was institutionalized and prescribed for ordinary laypeople who wished to purify negative karma and accumulate merit.

As noted above, the fasting ritual is practiced throughout the Inner Asian area influenced by Tibetan forms of Buddhism, including Nepal, Bhutan, Sikkim, Ladakh, Mongolia, Tibet itself, and, since 1959, in the Tibetan diaspora. The ritual is most often undertaken on an annual basis, in the period preceding the celebration of Wesak, the anniversary of the Buddha's birth, enlightenment, and final nirvāṇa (May–June). Though the rite occasionally was performed by monks in the great Tibetan monasteries, it really is a layperson's practice and so has most often been practiced in smaller monasteries or temples that play a central role in the life of a lay community. Usually, the ritual will be conducted by the local lama or lamas, who often are monks but also (as in the Nyingma tradition) may be laymen; the vast majority of participants are laypeople, and the majority of those middle-aged or older.

The ritual itself formally takes two and a half days, though a day of preparations and a celebratory conclusion may draw the process out for four full days. On the day of preparation, the presiding lama or lamas generally will conduct a ceremony of propitiation to the earth-deities, who are urged to purify the place where the fasting ritual will occur. The lamas also will prepare the ritual altar, replete with water bowls, various offering substances (including specially molded dough offerings called *torma*), and images of the ritual's presiding deity, Avalokiteśvara. If necessary, the lamas may conduct a permission ceremony or empowerment, which will permit those participating in the ritual to visualize themselves as Avalokiteśvara—a quintessentially tantric procedure that requires formal initiation.

The actual fasting ritual begins the next day at dawn with the taking of eight vows. On this day, just one meal (almost always vegetarian) is taken, at noon. Most of the day is spent in three separate performances of the actual fasting ritual (section III), from going for refuge right through to the final dedication of merit. The centerpiece of each ritual session is the chanting of a long "vow prayer" directed to Avalokiteśvara (section III.E.1). As the practitioners recite it (seeing themselves as Avalokiteśvara), they prostrate their bodies fully toward the image of Avalokiteśvara on the altar, as well as toward a visualized Avalokiteśvara they picture constantly before them. The chanting of this prayer while one simultaneously prostrates and visualizes is believed to be especially efficacious in purifying negative imprints and generating merit.

On the second day of the actual ritual, precepts again are taken at dawn, but the strictures on participants on this day will be far more severe: no food at all is to be ingested, and not a drop of liquid is to be drunk—not even, it is said, one's own saliva! Also, apart from the chanting that is done during the three ritual sessions, silence is strictly observed: there is to be no conversation whatsoever. This second day of the ritual is the most grueling, for to chant and perform hundreds of prostrations on an empty stomach is no easy task; also, the elimination of speaking as an outlet adds psychological pressure to the physical duress. It is not unusual for participants to feel weak and highly emotional during the second day. Yet the hardship they are enduring is believed to serve as a powerful purifier, and it is borne stoically, if not always enthusiastically.

Silence and the fast are maintained until the morning of the third day. No precepts are taken, and after a final session of the ritual (in which the obligatory chants and prostrations are lessened), the participants are given a great meal to mark the formal conclusion of the retreat. The celebration often will continue through the day, culminating in an evening offering ceremony accompanied by a ritual feast, at the conclusion of which volunteers and donors will come forward to begin planning for the next year's fasting ritual. It might be noted that although the schedule just described is most typical, on occasion the ritual may cover the entire two weeks prior to Wesak, with pairs of one-meal and fast days following one another again and again. This makes for a retreat whose intensity and difficulty is comparable to that of the austere retreats in Zen monasteries (*rohatsu sesshin*).

In the context of the normative spiritual vision of the Tibetan Buddhist world, the major purposes of the fasting ritual are those already suggested: the purification of negative karma and the accumulation of merit. Given Buddhist assumptions about the infinity of previous rebirths we all have had and the deluded way in which we have conducted ourselves through most of those rebirths, it is axiomatic that we all bear with us in our mindstreams the seeds sown by countless actions motivated by greed, anger, and ignorance. According to karmic theory, each of these seeds must bear fruit and will do so when the appropriate conditions arise. In most Buddhist traditions, however, this rather gloomy prospect is mitigated by the assurance that—short of attaining a full enlightenment that will destroy all previous negative karma—one may delay such fruition through cultivating positive actions and reduce or even eliminate some negative results through sincere repentance and purification. Generally, it is assumed that the more zealous the pursuit of purification, the greater the number of negative seeds that will be destroyed or damaged. Thus, an ascetic discipline like that imposed in the fasting ritual, in which repentance is expressed and penance performed in the presence of a loving and potent deity, is held to be especially efficacious. At the same time, the generation, during the ritual, of positive states of mind (devotion, compassion, some insight into the nature of reality) sows positive seeds in the mindstream, which will bear fruit in this and future lives, delaying the fruition of unpurified negativity, and increasing one's potential to attain the ultimate positive condition, enlightenment itself.

Typically, the normative view of the benefits of the fasting ritual is expressed in terms of its effects on the individual. Clearly, however, there is also a social dimension to the practice, unstated but highly important. On the broadest level, as a collective experience, the fasting ritual provides for the participants a natural sense of community, which ideally will extend beyond the ritual period and find expression in people's ordinary lives. The greater the proportion of a community that participates in the fasting ritual, the greater the ritual's effect on social cohesion will be. The fact that the ritual centers on the worship of the great merciful bodhisattva, Avalokiteśvara, and that one attempts both to receive and to identify with his boundless compassion, only reinforces the potential for its effecting social cohesion: compassion and forgiveness are, obviously, of considerable social value, whatever their "karmic" effects on the individual. A further social function of the fasting ritual is to bring the lay and monastic communities together. Laypeople are permitted for a time to share in something resembling a monastic life-style, and thereby to gain access to the sort of religious power usually reserved for the clergy. Still, the ritual is overseen by lamas, and the attitude laypeople are likely to develop from the experience is perhaps less often one of spiritual self-sufficiency than of gratitude to and a renewed sense of dependence upon the clergy. A further social function that may be performed by the fasting ritual is that of easing the transition to a less active life for that considerable proportion of the participants who are older people. In Buddhist cultures, one form of "retirement"—especially for widows and widowers—is to join a monastery, and the fasting ritual clearly paves the way for this.

Both Tibetans themselves and Western scholars have tended to view Tibetan Buddhism as a "complete" Buddhism, one that weaves together into a single tradition virtually every strand of thought and practice that developed in the Indian Buddhism from which the Tibetans drew their inspiration. Such a characterization may be a bit simplistic, but there is an element of truth to it. From the eighth to the fourteenth century, Tibetans self-consciously appropriated as much of North Indian Buddhism as they could, and they attempted to organize a vast body of material into a coherent, integrated system. The fasting ritual exemplifies this, and we can see in it a subtle integration of the three major "vehicles" of Indian Buddhism: Hīnayāna, Mahāyāna, and the tantric tradition, the Mantrayāna or Vajrayāna, which is itself a subset of Mahāyāna. Also, the ritual reflects a remarkable combination of three approaches to religiousness identified in India, and often seen as equally valuable but incompatible: ritual, knowledge, and devotion.

From the Tibetan perspective, the most important feature of Hīnayāna Buddhism is its promulgation of standards of morality. In particular, the Hīnayāna tradition has contributed to Buddhism as a whole the basic sets of vows to be observed by laypeople and monastics. Lay practitioners generally will observe a set of five vows, against killing, stealing, lying, sexual misconduct, and taking intoxicants; fully ordained monks will observe well over two hundred vows, and fully ordained nuns (who are rare outside China nowadays) will observe well over three hundred. The set of eight vows, which are taken by participants on the two full days of the fasting ritual, clearly fall somewhere in between lay and full monastic vows: they extend lay vows by forbidding all sexual activity rather than just sexual misconduct, as well as by severely restricting usual modes of eating and entertainment; at the same time, they fall well short of full monasticism by their failure to regulate behavior in anywhere near the detail that full vows do (see chapter 20). Though the eight vows taken by fasting ritual participants are regarded as "Mahāyāna" precepts, and the prayer that precedes them (section II) does employ distinctively Mahāyāna terminology, the vows themselves are identical to those taken by "Hīnayānists"; there is nothing specifically Mahāyānist about them, and they remain the most clearly Hīnayāna aspect of the rite.

Tibetan Buddhists are self-consciously Mahāyānist, so it is not surprising that the fasting ritual contains many elements typical of the Great Vehicle. We already have noted that one way of locating the rite in the history of Buddhism is by considering it as a manifestation of the cult of Avalokiteśvara. As noted above, only in Mahāyāna texts and cultures is Avalokiteśvara so important a deity, and only there does compassion receive so central an emphasis in religious rhetoric. Similarly, while the purification of negative karma and accumulation of merit that are immediate goals of the fasting ritual are common to Hīnayāna and Mahāyāna practices, the achievement of complete buddhahood that is the ultimate purpose of the fasting ritual is a uniquely Mahāyānist ideal: in the prayer preceding the taking of precepts (section II), one expresses the hope of achieving "the stage of fully completed buddhahood," and at the conclusion of each ritual session (section III.M), one prays that one may oneself someday "become a greatly compassionate one," equal in knowledge, compassion, and power to the Buddha himself. This sort of aspiration is encountered only infrequently outside the Mahāyāna.

Also, the ritual is framed in a distinctly Mahāyāna way. Though it begins like almost any Buddhist practice with an invocation of the three jewels of refuge, the Buddha, dharma, and saṅgha, the text immediately adds a uniquely Mahāyāna touch by insisting that the practitioner generate the thought of enlightenment, *bodhicitta*, the aspiration to attain the full enlightenment of buddhahood so that one may assist all sentient beings in their temporal and spiritual undertakings (section II). This spirit is supposed to inform every action that one performs, within the ritual or outside it. As the ritual in general and (though it is not stated) each session begins with a distinctly Mahāyānist aspiration, so it concludes with one: the wish that any merit one may have accrued not be selfishly hoarded but, rather, be "dedicated" to the enlightenment of others (sections III.I, III.M, IV). In between the initial aspiration and final dedication, there is much else that is typically Mahāyāna: reference to the nature of the reality as emptiness (*śūnyatā*); active visualization of the deity one worships, Avalokiteśvara; praise of him in the most elaborate terms; and the performance for him of the seven-branch liturgy and various ablutions—all elements of proper ritual (*pūjā*) that Mahāyānists freely adapted from Hindu models.

The tantric tradition of Mahāyāna—known as the Mantrayāna or Vajrayāna—was the dominant style of Buddhism during the period when Tibetans absorbed the religion from India, and the fasting ritual, like virtually any Tibetan practice-tradition, is deeply influenced by tantric conceptions. Perhaps the most crucial of these is the idea that the practitioner must identify with the deity to whom the ritual is directed, in this case by visualizing himself or herself as possessing the body, speech, and mind of Avalokiteśvara. This "preenactment" of the wisdom, form, and functions one will attain at the time of enlightenment is known as "taking the goal as path" and is unique to tantric traditions of meditation. It cannot be practiced without a formal initiation from a lama, whether the initiation be a full empowerment imposing long-term vows and responsibilities upon the disciple or a permission ceremony of more limited scope. The fasting ritual is not only a rite of worship, purification, and merit-making, but a tantric sādhana, or meditative scenario, which involves first reducing oneself and one's environment to a natural state of emptiness; then from that state of emptiness generating the deity both in front of and as oneself; next drawing into the visualized deity, or "pledge being," the actual deity, or "wisdom being," and receiving blessings in the form of light from the actual deity; reciting various mantras of the deity's and performing various ritual movements, including prostrations and hand-gestures (*mudrā*); making offerings of dough-cakes, *tormas*, to transmundane and worldly divinities; and, finally, dismissing/dissolving the visualized deity—though afterward, one is to resume not one's ordinary form, but a simplified version of Avalokiteśvara, with whom one continues to identify.

As the fasting ritual reflects an integration of the three vehicles of Indo-Tibetan Buddhism, so, too, does it integrate in a remarkable fashion the three "yogas," or approaches to the divine that have been singled out—and often considered quite separately—in Indian traditions: devotion, knowledge, and ritual. That devotion is central to the ritual is fairly obvious: verse after verse refers to the salvific, purifying powers of Avalokiteśvara, whose intervention is requested repeatedly in the most heartfelt manner. The verses of praise and request, in particular (sections III.E–F), stand as beautiful examples of what might be called Buddhist devotionalism (*bhakti*). Knowledge, on the other hand, is not so obviously a part of the text—certainly, there is little in it that is overtly philosophical. However, the tantric element of the ritual is predicated on the practitioners' ability to reduce themselves to emptiness, then to visualize themselves as Avalokiteśvara while simultaneously being aware of the visualization's empty nature. Also, by seeing themselves as Avalokiteśvara, practitioners imitate his omniscient mind, which has direct knowledge of all conventional and ultimate truths. All this, in turn, requires that one have at least an "imaginative" understanding of the nature of reality, which requires at least a general philosophical appreciation for ultimate truth—hence a certain type of knowledge. Indeed, it is important to remember that normative Buddhism in Tibet is essentially a gnostic enterprise, and that the most passionate devotee or obsessive ritualist must have knowledge of the true nature of things in order to attain the prescribed goal of full buddhahood.

The fasting ritual is, of course, above all a ritual—it is identified by the Tibetan word for rite or ritual, *cho ga*. What does this mean, though? In the most general sense, religious ritual involves the repeated performance of certain prescribed actions, which are believed to narrow the gulf between the human and the divine. In the fasting ritual, the divine that one hopes to effectuate is Avalokiteśvara, and the actions one performs are hallowed by tradition and intensified by repetition. What is more, tantric ritual is repeated, prescribed action that is deliberately integrative of the whole human person. Here, the practitioner's body (through prostration and hand-gestures), speech (through mantra and prayer), and mind (through visualization and contemplation) are all involved in the ritual process.

The fasting ritual, like so many Tibetan ritual practices, is like a fabric in which many diverse strands have been woven together: Hīnayāna discipline, Mahāyāna worship and aspiration, and tantric meditative procedures; passionate devotion, detached understanding of reality, and detailed ritual performance; and, finally, activity by all elements of the participant's person: body, speech, and mind. Tibetan Buddhism may or may not really be "complete" Buddhism, but the fasting ritual provides compelling evidence that, at the very least, it is a complex and many-layered tradition.

The fasting ritual text translated below is entitled the "Nectar-Drop: The Extremely Condensed Fasting Ritual of Eleven-Headed Avalokiteśvara." It was composed by Tuken Chökyi Nyima (Thu'u bkwan chos kyi nyi ma, 1737–1802), a great scholiast of the Gelukpa sect of Tibetan Buddhism. As with many ritual texts, Tuken's involves more than appears on paper. It is, after all, meant to be performed, and while in Tibetan traditions ritual performance is usually keyed to texts, it is by no means enslaved to them. Thus, depending on the circumstances of a ritual performance (the nature and capacity of the participants, the inclinations of the presiding lama), sections may be added or subtracted from the text, without the performance thereby ceasing to be "of" that text. Performances of Tuken's text often will involve changes of ordering (for example, the abbreviated sevenfold liturgy sometimes is recited much later) or the addition of other prayers and practices, most notably: refuge and thought of enlightenment prayers, which will be recited at the outset of every ritual session, prior to consecrating the offerings; the maṇḍala offering of Mount Meru, the continents and various precious substances, which may be added after the seven-branch liturgy; and a four-line version of the vow prayer, which may be recited in lieu of the long one as one prostrates. In addition, Tuken occasionally gives instructions in so sketchy a manner that interpolation is required to follow them; for instance, he specifies toward the beginning of the ritual session that one should "take refuge, generate the thought of enlightenment, and contemplate the four immeasurables." Each of these entails a specific prayer that must be recited, usually three times. Similarly, when Tuken incorporates into his text much material that he has drawn from earlier texts, he will give only the first line; the rest is to be supplied by the practitioner, who is presumed to know it.

In the translation below, prayers given by Tuken in abbreviated form have been spelled out fully; the only other addition made to the printed text is to supply section titles, so that the text's structure may be clearer. Sections that communicate instructions are set apart here in smaller type. Sections that are metrical in the original are broken into poetic lines here, though no attempt has been made to duplicate the original meter. Finally, mantras have been translated to the degree that their syllables have a discernible meaning; untranslatable syllables, such as *oṃ, hūṃ*, and *phaṭ*, have been left as they are. The mantras have been translated simply so the reader may get a sense of the mixture of semantic and lexical items of which they are composed; it must be recalled, however, that the power of a mantra resides not in its semantic sense but in the sounds themselves, each of which, and in various combinations, has particular divine associations. That is why Tibetans invariably write and recite mantras in the original Sanskrit, and in most cases have no idea what a mantra's "translation" (or, on occasion, original pronunciation) may be.

The translation is from *Spyan ras gzigs zhal bcu gcig pa'i smyung gnas kyi cho ga shin tu bsdus pa bdud rtsi thigs pa zhes bya ba,* from *The Collected Works (gsung 'bum) of Thu'u bkvan Chos kyi nyi ma* (New Delhi: Ngawang Gelek Demo, 1969), vol. 5, folios 233–46.

Further Reading

An earlier translation appears in *Eleven-Headed Avalokiteśvara's Fasting Ritual Condensed into a Nectar Drop*, translated by Roger Jackson, with additional translation by John Makransky (Oregon, WI: Deer Park Books, 1989). See also the Seventh Dalai Lama, *Nyung Nä: The Means of Achievement of the Eleven-Faced Great Compassionate One, Avalakiteśhvara*, translated by Lama Thubten Zopa Rinpoche and George Churinoff (Boston: Wisdom Publications, 1995). For anthropological studies of this ritual in the Nepali context, see Christoph von Fürer-Haimendorf, *The Sherpas of Nepal: Buddhist Highlanders* (Berkeley and Los Angeles: University of California Press, 1964), pp. 180–85; and Sherry B. Ortner, *Sherpas through Their Rituals* (Cambridge: Cambridge University Press, 1978), pp. 33–60.

Nectar-Drop: The Extremely Condensed Fasting Ritual of Eleven-Headed Avalokiteśvara

I. AUTHOR'S PREFACE

Having prostrated with my body, speech, and mind to the lotus feet of the kindly guru,
Who is the compassion of all the conquerers gathered into one,
The one with a white lotus who performs as a saffron-clad monk,
I will set down the practice of this fasting ritual.

II. ONE-DAY MAHĀYĀNA PRECEPTS [DAYS 1 AND 2, AT DAWN]

Wishing to perform the fasting ritual of the eleven-faced noble Avalokiteśvara, you should arrange a drawing or actual statue of the body, etc., of the Greatly Compassionate One. Or, if they are unavailable, you should put white points in the center of a mirror, and in front of that put a vase two-thirds filled with pure water. Then, put into the vase the various Action Tantra substances. In front [of the vase] place three rounded tormas and arrange whatever offering is to be received. Then, at daybreak, when the lines of the hand can just be seen, after you have washed well, you should take the one-day Mahāyāna precepts. You should prostrate to the altar, conceiving it as the actual Greatly Compassionate One. First, take refuge [in the Buddha, dharma, and saṅgha], generate the enlightened thought, and contemplate the four immeasurables [love, compassion, joy, and equanimity].

All buddhas and bodhisattvas of the ten directions, with your divine wisdom please pay attention to me. As the previous tathāgatas, the arhats, the fully enlightened buddhas like a divine skillful wise horse, a great elephant, did what had to be done, accomplished all tasks, overcame all the burdens of the five aggregates controlled by delusion and karma, fulfilled all their aspirations by relinquishing their attachments, by speaking immaculately divine words and liberating the minds of all from the bondage of subtle delusions' impression, and who possess great liberated transcendental wisdom, for the sake of all that lives, in order to benefit all, in order to prevent famine, in order to prevent mental and physical sicknesses, in order for living beings to complete a buddha's thirty-seven realizations, and to receive the stage of fully completed buddhahood, I, who am named ____, from now until sunrise tomorrow shall take the eight Mahāyāna precepts just as you have done.

Three times.

From now on I shall not kill, nor steal others' possessions, nor engage in sexual conduct, nor lie. I shall avoid intoxicants from which many mistakes arise. I shall not sit on large, high, expensive beds. I shall not eat food at the wrong time. I shall avoid singing, dancing, and playing music, and I shall not wear perfumes, rosaries or ornaments. As arhats have avoided wrong actions such as taking the lives of others, I shall also avoid actions such as taking the lives of others. May I quickly receive enlightenment and may the living beings who are experiencing various sufferings be released from the ocean of cyclic existence.

To keep morality purely, say twenty-one times:

Oṃ maintain effective morality, maintain, maintain. Being of great purity, lotus-bearing, hold, hold with your hand. Look down continuously *hūṃ phaṭ svāhā.*

III. THE RITUAL SESSION [3 TIMES ON DAYS 1 AND 2, 1 TIME ON DAY 3]

A. Consecrating the Offerings

Instantly I assume the form of the Greatly Compassionate One.

> *Oṃ padmanta kṛta hūṃ phaṭ*
> *Oṃ* naturally pure are all dharmas, naturally pure am I.

I become emptiness. From the state of emptiness comes the syllable *bhrūṃ*. From *bhrūṃ* comes a vast and delicate precious vessel. In it is an *oṃ*. The *oṃ* melts into light. From the light arises drinking water, foot-washing water, flowers, incense, lamps, perfume, food, and music. They are inherently empty. In appearance, they are themselves, but their function is to confer extraordinary undefiled bliss.

> *Oṃ* mouth-water *āḥ hūṃ*.
> *Oṃ* foot-water *āḥ hūṃ*.
> *Oṃ* flowers *āḥ hūṃ*.
> *Oṃ* incense *āḥ hūṃ*.
> *Oṃ* light *āḥ hūṃ*.
> *Oṃ* perfume *āḥ hūṃ*.
> *Oṃ* cakes *āḥ hūṃ*.
> *Oṃ* sound *āḥ hūṃ*.

B. Visualization

> *Oṃ* naturally pure are all dharmas, naturally pure am I.

> I am in the state of natural emptiness that is the inseparability of the dharma-sphere and knowledge.
> In my place and in the space in front of me is a lotus. On it is a moon-seat.
> On the moon is a white *hrīḥ*. From it comes Avalokiteśvara.
> His central face is white, the right is green, the left is red.
> Above those, the central face is green, the right is red, the left is white.

Above those, the central face is red, the right is white, the left is green.
Above those is a dark blue wrathful face. Above that
Is the beautiful face of Amitābha. The two main hands
Are pressed together at the heart. The upper right holds a crystal rosary,
The upper left a lotus. The lower right is in the gesture of supreme giving, the lower left holds a nectar-vase.
The middle right holds a wheel, the middle left a bow and arrow.
The other nine hundred and ninety-two hands
Are in the gesture of supreme giving. In the palm of each
Is a mighty eye that gazes on sentient beings.
Avalokiteśvara is beautifully adorned with jewels,
And is clothed in flowing silk.
His body is a perfect enjoyment body, gloriously blazing with all major and minor marks.
His two feet are placed together. The main gurus of the lineage
And a vast assembly of peaceful and wrathful deities surround him. They are marked at their forehead, throat, and heart
By [*oṃ*, *āḥ*, and *hūṃ*]. From the *hrīḥ* [at my heart and that of the front visualization], light rays
Invite Guru Avalokiteśvara and his retinue from their true abode,
And they melt into nonduality with me and the front visualization. We are empowered [by initiatory goddesses], then adorned by Amitābha.

C. The Seven-branch Liturgy

1. Prostration

I prostrate to the gurus,
Who are the sum of all the buddhas' bodies,
Whose essence is Vajradhara,
Who are the root of the three jewels.
I prostrate to Avalokiteśvara,
Whose white form is clothed with no fault,
Whose head is adorned by a perfect buddha,
Who looks down on beings with compassionate eyes.
I prostrate with supreme faith,
With as many bodies
As the number of atoms,
To all those worthy of prostration.

Wherever in the world's ten directions
Reside all those lions among humans who come in the three times,
To them all, none excepted,
I prostrate with my body, speech, and mind.
With all the conquerors directly before my mind,

By the force of my prayer to practice the good,
I prostrate to all those conquerors
By bowing as many bodies as there are atoms in the world.
Seated on each atom are buddhas numerous as the atoms,
Each encircled by bodhisattvas;
Thus I visualize each and every dharma-realm filled up with
  conquerors.
With oceans of unending praises of them,
With every sound in an ocean of songs,
I recite the virtues of all the conquerors
And utter the praises of every tathāgata.

2. Offering

From the *hrīḥ* at my heart come offering goddesses with offerings for me and the front visualization.

a. Short Offering Mantra

Oṃ noble lord of the world and your retinue: accept mouth-water
  svāhā.
Oṃ noble lord of the world and your retinue: accept foot-water *svāhā*.
Oṃ noble lord of the world and your retinue: accept flowers *svāhā*.
Oṃ noble lord of the world and your retinue: accept incense *svāhā*.
Oṃ noble lord of the world and your retinue: accept light *svāhā*.
Oṃ noble lord of the world and your retinue: accept perfume *svāhā*.
Oṃ noble lord of the world and your retinue: accept cakes *svāhā*.
Oṃ noble lord of the world and your retinue: accept sound *svāḥā*.

To those conquerors I make offerings
Of holy flowers and garlands,
Cymbals, balms, and superior umbrellas,
Superior lamps and holy incense.
To those conquerors I make offerings
Of holy garments and superior perfumes,
Incense and powders equal to Mount Meru,
All superior things specially arrayed.
I visualize for all the conquerors
Whatever offerings are excellent and vast.
By the strength of my faith in practicing the good,
I prostrate and make offerings to all the conquerors.

3. Confession

Whatever sins I have committed
With body, speech, and mind,
By force of attachment, anger, and delusion,

All those I confess.
If you have time, recite the general confession [to the 35 Buddhas].

4. Rejoicing

Whatever merit all the conquerors
In the ten directions, the bodhisattvas, solitary buddhas
And those training and beyond training may have,
In all that I rejoice.

5. Requesting

Those who are the lamps of the world of ten directions,
Who have awakened to the stage of enlightenment and attained nonattachment,
I ask all those, my protectors,
To turn the unexcelled wheel of dharma.

6. Entreating

To those who wish to show nirvāṇa,
I make this entreaty with folded palms:
For the benefit and happiness of all beings,
Remain for as many aeons as there are atoms in a field.

7. Dedication

Whatever little merit I may have accrued
By prostration, offerings, confession,
Rejoicing, requesting, and entreating,
I dedicate for the sake of the enlightenment of all.

8. Abbreviated Seven-branch Liturgy

I prostrate respectfully with my body, speech, and mind to the lotus feet
Of Guru Avalokiteśvara and his retinue.
I present all real and imagined offerings.
I confess all sins accumulated from beginningless time.
I rejoice at the virtues of ordinary and holy beings.
[I entreat you to] remain until cyclic existence is emptied.
I request you to turn every dharma-wheel for the sake of beings.
I dedicate all my and others' virtues to the great enlightenment.

D. Recitation

On a moon-seat at my heart and the heart of the front visualization,
There is a *hrīḥ*. There is a mantra rosary spinning around the *hrīḥ*.
From the rosary emanate divine bodies and infinite light rays,

Which purify the sins, obscurations, and sufferings of the six classes of beings,
Who attain the rank of noble. The conquerors
Are delighted by a cloud of vast offerings.
All their blessings and attainments are gathered into the form
Of light rays and melt into me.
From the fingers of the two visualized deities, myself and that before me,
A stream of nectar falls, filling the vase [visualized earlier].

1. Long Mantra

Homage to the three jewels. Homage to the holy gnosis-ocean, to royally arrayed Vairocana, to the Tathāgata. Homage to all the tathāgatas, the arhats, the perfect buddhas. Homage to noble Avalokiteśvara, the bodhisattva, the great being, the greatly compassionate one. It is thus: *Oṃ* hold, hold, be firm, be firm, support, support, make haste, find me, proceed, proceed, go forward, go forward, O blossom, O precious blossom, come, join, remove my mental obstructions *svāhā*.

Twenty-one times or more.

2. Short Mantra

Oṃ jewel-lotus *hūṃ*.

As many times as possible.

3. Hundred-Syllable Mantra

Oṃ lotus being, guard my vows; lotus being, let them be firm. Be steadfast for me, be satisfied, be nourished; be favorable for me. Grant me all accomplishments. Indicator of all karma, make glorious my mind *hūṃ*. *Ha ha ha ha hoḥ*. Blessed one, lotus of all the tathāgatas, do not forsake me, lotus being, great vow being *āḥ hūṃ phaṭ*.

Three times

E. Praises

The wisdom-being of my self-visualization melts into the front visualization. On top of my head appears the nun Lakṣmī, dressed as a renunciate. With her two hands pressed together at her heart, she asks for intercession.

1. Long Vow Prayer

Oṃ I prostrate to the protector of the world.
The one praised by the supramundane world.
The one praised by the chief gods, Māra and Brahmā.

The one who is accomplished by the praises of the supreme royal master.
I prostrate to the supreme protector of the three worlds.
The one with the form of infinite tathāgatas, with a virtuous form.
The one with the crest-ornament of the infinite brilliance of the tathāgatas.
The one who clears up the ghosts' hunger and thirst by the supremely generous gesture of his right hand.
The one adorned by a golden lotus in his left hand.
The one shining with a red-yellow garland in his fragrant locks.
The one whose face is beautiful like the brilliant moon.
The one whose lotus-eyes are extremely noble and bright.
The one whose scent is perfect, like that of a snow-white shell.
The one marked by pearls of stainless light.
The one adorned with the beautiful rays of reddish dawn.
The one whose hands are like an ocean of sweetened lotuses.
The one with a youthful face the color of an autumn cloud.
The one whose shoulders are adorned by many jewels.
The one whose palms are young and smooth like the highest leaves.
The one whose left breast is covered with an antelope hide.
The one who is gracefully adorned with earrings and anklets.
The one whose abode is a supreme stainless lotus.
The one whose abdomen is smooth as a lotus petal.
The one bedecked with jewels in a magnificent belt of gold.
The one with a fine cotton garment around his hips.
The one who has crossed the great ocean of the master's supreme knowledge.
The one who has accumulated many wonderful merits.
The one who is the source of all happiness, who clears up aging and disease.
The one who has put the three realms behind him and shows the practice [for attaining the pure land] of Vajrayoginī.
The one who is the supreme living being, who conquers the trembling host of demons.
The one with lovely feet adorned by golden rings.
The one who liberates beings by practicing [love, compassion, joy and equanimity].
The one who strides like a proud elephant moving among geese.
The one who has completed the accumulations [of merit] and obtained the teaching.
The one who rescues beings from oceans of milk and water.

Those who habitually rise at dawn should respectfully
Think of the power of Avalokiteśvara.

If one celebrates him with these supreme epithets,
Then whether one must be born a man or a woman, in that and all future births
One will accomplish what is necessary for transcending the world.

This is to be recited twenty-one times, while prostrating.

F. Requests

O noble Avalokiteśvara, treasury of compassion,
You and your retinue please heed me.
Please quickly free me and mother and father
Sentient beings of the six realms from cyclic existence.
May I quickly arouse in my mindstream
The deep and vast supreme enlightened thought.
With your power, please quickly purify
My karma and defilements, accumulated from beginningless time,
And with your compassionate hands
Lead me and all beings into the pure land of Sukhāvatī.
O Amitābha and Avalokiteśvara,
Please be my spiritual friends in all my lives,
Teach me well the precious good path,
And place me quickly on the level of a buddha.

This should be requested with intense longing.

G. Torma Offering

Oṃ padmanta kṛta hūṃ phaṭ
Oṃ naturally pure are all dharmas, naturally pure am I.

The tormas become empty. From the state of emptiness comes a *bhrūṃ*. From the *bhrūṃ* comes a wide and delicate precious vessel. Inside of it is an *oṃ*. The *oṃ* melts into light. From the light arise tormas. They turn into a great ocean of undefiled wisdom-nectar.

Oṃ āḥ hūṃ

Three times

1. First Torma

Offer the torma to the chief deity—the Greatly Compassionate One—and his retinue, by saying three times:

Oṃ noble Avalokiteśvara and your retinue, please take this torma; take it and eat it, eat it.

Then offer:

Oṃ noble lord of the world and your retinue, please accept mouth-water *svāhā*.
Oṃ noble lord of the world and your retinue, please accept foot-water *svāhā*.
Oṃ noble lord of the world and your retinue, please accept flowers *svāhā*.
Oṃ noble lord of the world and your retinue, please accept incense *svāhā*.
Oṃ noble lord of the world and your retinue, please accept light *svāhā*.
Oṃ noble lord of the world and your retinue, please accept perfume *svāhā*.
Oṃ noble lord of the world and your retinue, please accept cakes *svāhā*.
Oṃ noble lord of the world and your retinue, please accept sound *svāhā*.

I offer this torma of a nectar-ocean
To noble Avalokiteśvara.
Accept it and grant me and all other beings
Superior and ordinary attainments.

2. Second Torma

Oṃ the syllable *a* is first because of the primordial nonarising of all dharmas *oṃ āḥ hūṃ phaṭ svāhā*.

Three times. Then:

Oṃ ḍākinīs and dharma-protectors and your retinue please accept mouth-water *svāhā*.
Oṃ ḍākinīs and dharma-protectors and your retinue please accept foot-water *svāhā*.
Oṃ ḍākinīs and dharma-protectors and your retinue please accept flowers *svāhā*.
Oṃ ḍākinīs and dharma-protectors and your retinue please accept incense *svāhā*.
Oṃ ḍākinīs and dharma-protectors and your retinue please accept light *svāhā*.
Oṃ ḍākinīs and dharma-protectors and your retinue please accept perfume *svāhā*.
Oṃ ḍākinīs and dharma-protectors and your retinue please accept cakes *svāhā*.
Oṃ ḍākinīs and dharma-protectors and your retinue please accept sound *svāhā*.

I offer this torma of a nectar-ocean
To the assembly of dharma-protectors and ḍākinīs.
Please accept it and help me accomplish enlightened deeds,

Those that pacify, increase, empower, and compel.

3. Third Torma

Say three times either "*Oṃ* the syllable *a* . . ." or:

Homage! Seen by all the tathāgatas. *Oṃ* maintenance, maintenance *hūṃ*.

I prostrate to the tathāgata Many-Jewels.
I prostrate to the tathāgata Holy Beauty.
I prostrate to the tathāgata Soft-and-Peaceful-Body.
I prostrate to the tathāgata Free-from-all-Fear.

I offer this torma of a nectar-ocean
To the lords of place and soil.
Please accept it, and without malice
Be my good and steadfast friends.

H. Ablution

Next, pour the water from the physical vase onto the divine image appearing in the mirror:

With a stream of saffron-water nectar I bathe
The lamp of beings, the protector Avalokiteśvara.
May all the stains of beings' two obscurations be cleansed,
And may they have the fortune to obtain the three stainless bodies.

Oṃ the glorious vows from empowerment by all the tathāgatas and the noble lord of the world and his retinue *hūṃ*.

I dry all those bodies by applying
A matchless cloth, clean and fragrant.

Oṃ hūṃ traṃ hrīḥ aḥ purified body *svāhā*.

For the sake of training my mind, I offer jeweled clothes
Exquisite as a rainbow
And the cause of joy to anyone who touches them.
By this may I and others be adorned by the clothing of holy patience.
Because the conquerors are naturally adorned with the major and minor marks,
There is no need to adorn them with further ornaments.
By my offering superior jewel-ornaments,
May I and all beings attain the body adorned with the major and minor marks.

I. Dedication

Through these virtuous actions of mine,
May a buddha quickly arise in this world.

May this buddha show dharmas for the sake of beings
And quickly liberate sentient beings from their manifold sufferings and torments.
In this and all my lives,
May I attain a good [rebirth] realm, a clear mind, and humility.
Respecting great compassion and my guru,
May I remain steadfast in Avalokiteśvara's vow.
O Avalokiteśvara, whatever your form is like,
Whatever your retinue, longevity and world-sphere,
Whatever your superior good signs are like,
May I and all others be only like that.
By the power of offering and praying to you,
Please pacify sickness and poverty
In the world where I and others abide,
And increase dharma and good fortune.

May the supreme enlightened thought
That has not arisen arise;
May that which has arisen not decline,
But only increase more and more.

J. Hundred-Syllable Mantra

Oṃ lotus being, guard my vows; lotus being, let them be firm. Be steadfast for me, be satisfied, be nourished; be favorable for me. Grant me all accomplishments. Indicator of all karma, make glorious my mind *hūṃ. Ha ha ha ha hoḥ.* Blessed one, lotus of all the tathāgatas, do not forsake me, lotus being, great vow being *āḥ hūṃ phaṭ*.

Three times

K. Entreating Forbearance

O blessed one, greatly compassionate, pay heed to me.
When we are beginners, our concentration is dimmed
By the forces of sinking and scattering;
Our recitations are impure and our rituals either excessive
Or deficient. Please, O noble, greatly compassionate one, accept patiently our limited purity;
May we not encounter obstacles.

Om jewel-lotus hūṃ.

Several times.

L. Final Purification

The noble, the Greatly Compassionate One, is a little closer in the space before me, at the head of his retinue. A stream of nectar falls from his body parts. It bathes the outside, inside, and middle of my body and purifies without exception all the illnesses, demons, sins, and obscurations of my three doors, together with the propensities thereto.

Then pour and drink a little of the water used for washing and bathing.

M. Final Dedication ***Through this virtue may I quickly become***
A greatly compassionate one
And lead each and every being,
None excepted, to his pure land.

N. General Instructions

There are three sessions on both the preparatory and the actual day. Take the one-day Mahāyāna precepts each day at dawn. The rest of the ritual is the same in all sessions. On the preparatory day, make a gold throne that supports the three white substances (curds, milk, butter). Do not eat from bronze vessels, leaves, or the palm of your hand. In the afternoon, take tea without sugar or honey. Apart from that, do not eat suitable (foods for the morning, such as) curds, milk, or fruit. At dawn on the day of the actual fast, you begin to observe silence. Do not eat even a single grain of barley or drink a single drop of water. Except for the precepts, (the ritual) on the third day is as on the day before, but the required recitations are fewer: it is suitable to say the praises merely five or seven times.

O. Special Offering Prayer

On the third day, after ablution, say:

Oṃ vajra muḥ.

The wisdom-being of the front visualization returns to his natural abode. The pledge being melts into me. I become the one-faced, two-armed greatly compassionate one. Atop my head is a white *oṃ*. At my throat is a red *āḥ*. At my heart is a blue *hūṃ*. I am marked by these.

By saying this auspicious prayer, I am adorned.

IV. EPILOGUE

I have arranged this ritual with the intention of benefiting some householders and others of feeble intellect and energy. It is very important for those of forceful intellect, without believing these few words to be the essence, to practice the extensive rituals written by the earlier and later conquerors (Dalai Lamas) and by Panchen Chökyi Gyelpo. Even this abridged ritual should be known in detail from the great texts.

The sādhana of the noble, supreme lotus-bearer,
The treasury of compassion who looks down

Perpetually with a thousand compassionate eyes
On the countless tormented and protectorless beings:
Rightly explained by my holy predecessors, it was a beautiful
Jeweled garland, a brilliant blessing, a mass of blazing light
Set in array. Why, then should one such as I
Add to the rosary his half-baked foolishness?
Nevertheless, in this case, with a respectful heart,
I have composed this brief collection of words
For the benefit of some present-day people
Who are trapped by low intelligence and wavering mind.
Through this virtue, may I and all other beings
Be held at all times by Avalokiteśvara.
May he quickly save us from the worldly ocean agitated by waves of suffering,
And place us in a the bliss of a liberated state.

V. COLOPHON

This is the extremely condensed fasting ritual, called "Nectar Drop." Here in lower Amdo, the rituals found in the collected works of the great paṇḍitas are quite widespread. Still, some people of low intelligence need their mouths to be filled, so—entreated again and again by many great and ordinary monks and laymen, I have sent forth as a stream of water this ritual to be read by the ignorant.

—34—

The Regulations of a Monastery

José Ignacio Cabezón

According to tradition, Tsong kha pa (1357–1419), founder of the Gelukpa sect of Tibetan Buddhism, composed his commentary on Nāgārjuna's *Mūlamadhyamakakārikās*, the *Ocean of Reasoning*, while he was in residence in a small hermitage outside of Lhasa called Sera Chöding around the year 1409. In the midst of writing this work, one of the pages of the text is said to have flown into the air in a gust of wind. It began to emit "*a*" letters (the symbol of the Perfection of Wisdom) in the color of molten gold. Some of these melted into a stone at the base of the hill and became permanently imprinted on it. Witnessing this, Tsong kha pa prophesied that this place would be the future site of a great center of Buddhist learning, an institution of particular importance for the study and practice of the Madhyamaka doctrine of emptiness. This was in fact the very place where Tsong kha pa's disciple Jamchen Chöje (Byams chen chos rje shākya ye shes, 1354–1435), would found Sera monastery in the year 1419.

The three great monasteries of the Gelukpa sect, Drepung, Ganden, and Sera, are religious universities, centers for the study and practice of Buddhist doctrine. There, some of the monks engage in a twenty-year program of study and prayer that culminates in the degree of geshe. Based on the classical texts of Indian Buddhism and their Tibetan Gelukpa commentaries, the full curriculum included the study of Collected Topics (introductory metaphysics, logic, psychology, and epistemology), Perfection of Wisdom (the fundamentals of the Mahāyāna Buddhist path), Pramāṇa (advanced logic, studied during special winter interterm sessions at a retreat outside of Lhasa, with monks of all three monasteries in attendance), Madhyamaka (the theory of emptiness), Vinaya (the monastic precepts), and Abhidharma (advanced metaphysics). With these subjects and texts as the basis of their curriculum, monks engage in memorization, oral explanation, and study, and especially debate as the chief methods of transmitting Buddhist doctrine from one generation to the next. The text translated below deals with the traditions and customs of one of Tibet's great monastic institutions, the Je (Byes) College of Sera.

The fifth holder of the Sera throne is a particularly important figure because he is credited with having founded the Je College of that institution. This is Günkhyenpa Rinchen Lodrö Senge (Kun mkhyen pa Rin chen blo gros seng ge), a disciple of Tsong kha pa and Jamchen Chöje. Many interesting stories surround the life of Günkhyenpa. According to oral tradition, after he received a hand-blessing from Tsong kha pa, Günkhyenpa had permanently imprinted on his head the palmprint of his hand. According to another well-known tradition, when he first arrived at Sera and visited the main temple, one of the sixteen arhat statues came to life. Moving forward to greet him, it said, "It is good that the great Günkhyenpa has come. How appropriate that you are raising the banner of the teachings here." This legend is perhaps meant to explain why Günkhyenpa, along with a hundred or so followers, abandoned his original monastery at Drepung to establish the Je College at Sera.

Günkhyenpa is one of the most interesting and controversial figures of his day, partly because of his multiple sectarian and monastic affiliations. Born as the son of a Nyingma lama, he is said to have made an oath to him never to abandon the practice of the deity Hayagrīva, a deity with strong historical roots in the Nyingma sect (see chapter 35). Keeping to his word, he eventually made Hayagrīva the tantric meditational deity (*yi dam*) of Sera Je. Although Günkhyenpa wrote several monastic textbooks (*yig cha*) that were used at the Je College in the early days of that institution, these were apparently confiscated in later times by the Tibetan government because they were perceived as not being in complete accord with what had come to be considered Tsong kha pa's ultimate stance concerning the profound view of emptiness.

The early history of Sera is obscure. It seems that initially this monastery contained four separate colleges, which underwent numerous transformations until only two colleges remained, known as Je and Me (Smad). A third Tantric College (Sngags pa) was founded at Sera much later under the patronage of the Mongolian ruler Lhazang Khan, who controlled Lhasa during the early part of the eighteenth century (1706–1717). Hence, from that time until the final occupation of Lhasa by the Chinese in 1959, Sera monastery had three colleges and could boast a monastic population of somewhere between 8,000 and 10,000 monks, making it the second largest monastery in the world (after Drepung). During the final take-over of Lhasa by Chinese forces in 1959, Sera was bombed and many of its temples, libraries, and monastic living quarters were completely destroyed. Most of what remained was either neglected or pillaged during the Cultural Revolution. Today Sera monastery in Lhasa, partially rebuilt, primarily with private Tibetan donations, has a resident population of close to 500 monks (the limit set by Chinese authorities). A "new" Sera monastery in the Tibetan settlement camp of Bylakuppe in South India was founded by monks of the original Sera, who went into exile in India after the overthrow of the Tibetan government by the Chinese. This latter institution, thriving to this day as a center of Buddhist learning, has a resident monastic population of approximately 2,000 monks.

The translation that follows is an excerpt from a work that deals with the traditions of the Je College. The *Great Exhortation* (*Tshogs gtam chen mo*), as the work is known colloquially, is an oral text that was published in written form for the first time only in 1991. Surviving in oral form for hundreds of years, it has been passed on from one generation of monks to the next simply by being recited several times a year in assembly. In the Je College, the oral nature of the transmission of the *Great Exhortation* is expressed by the saying, "a lineage from mouth to mouth, a lineage from ear to ear." The monks of the college consider the work to be of great profundity. Hearing it is said to be equivalent to hearing the complete teaching of Tsong kha pa's magnum opus, the *Great Exposition of the Stages of the Path to Enlightenment* (*Lam rim chen mo*).

As regards content, the *Great Exhortation* is a conglomeration of historical anecdotes, spiritual advice, and the rules and customs particular to the Je College. It belongs to a genre of Tibetan literature known as *cha-yik* (*bca' yig*), documents that deal with the rules and regulations of particular monastic institutions. Although all Buddhist monks and nuns in Tibet follow as their principle discipline the monastic vows as set forth in the Indian Buddhist vinaya tradition of the Mūlasarvāstivādin sect, Tibetan monasteries felt a need to supplement this general discipline with more specific documents that focused on the practical aspects of daily life: the *cha-yik*. The Je College's *cha-yik*, the *Great Exhortation*, is unique in that it is the only one, to my knowledge, that has been preserved orally. The work is composed in a highly honorific and formal style and, typical of oral texts, is quite repetitive. As one would expect of a living oral tradition, the work has become a hodgepodge of information by virtue of having been added to throughout the generations. It gives "the listener" information on such practical matters as the process that novices must follow to enter the monastery, the types and quality of robes and shoes that may be worn and their symbolism, the kinds of rosaries that may be used, and even where monks may urinate. The several discussions that preface the actual *Exhortation* (the last of the six divisions) provide us with interesting historical clues concerning life in the Je College. For example, the clear limitations concerning place, time, and the individual expounding the *Exhortation* are reflective of a historical period in which "advice" must have been plentiful and gratuitous, to the point where those in positions of power must have felt a need to limit and standardize it. Clues such as these make the present work one that is an important source not only for the study of monastic life, but for the study of Tibetan religious history as well. Its eclectic and synthetic character, combining themes and styles from both high and popular cultures, makes it unique in Tibetan "literary" history, and very enjoyable reading.

The present translation is based on a manuscript that would become the first printed edition of the text, published by the Je College in India. Fearing that the work would be lost unless it was preserved in written form, several of the older monks of the monastery compiled a working manuscript. This preliminary version was then circulated more widely until consensus was achieved. Although now existing in a written version, the text continues to be recited by heart at regular intervals in the assembly of the Je College in India, either by the disciplinarian (*dge skyos*) or by the abbot (*mkhen po*).

The passage that follows is a translation of the first third of the text *Byang chub lam rim chen mo dang 'brel ba'i ser byes mkhas snyan grwa tshang gi bca' khrims che mo* (Bylakuppe: Ser jhe Printing Press, 1991). The full title reads "The Great Regulations of the Sera Je College of Learned Scholars, [Composed] in Relation to [Tsong kha pa's] *Great [Exposition] of the Stages of the Path to Enlightenment.*" According to the Mongolian Geshe Senge, the recently deceased abbot of the Je College of Sera in Tibet, the *Great Exhortation* was written down by the Mongolian scholar Janglung Paṇḍita (Lcang lung paṇḍita). Upon searching the indices to the seven volumes of his collected works, however, I was able to find nothing under the title "Great Exhortation." The seventh text in the *ca* volume entitled *Dge' ldan theg chen bshad sgrub gling gi bca' yig chen mo'i zur 'debs dren gso'i brjed byang*, which was missing from Geshe Senge's edition of the collected works, might very well be the work in question. It is possible that Janglung Paṇḍita, who studied at Sera Je, adopted the *Great Exhortation* as the disciplinary text (*bca' yig*) for his own monastery, Ganden Thekchen Shedrupling (Dka' ldan theg chen shes sgrub gling). The present disciplinarian of the Je College in Tibet, who has seen the Janglung Paṇḍita version, claims that it varied considerably from the one used at present. For example, the former is said to have only five major divisions, as opposed to the six major and three minor divisions of the version now recited at the Je College. Until Janglung's work is found, however, we must be content with the Indian edition as the only available one.

The *Great Exhortation*, being the transcription of an oral text, is not an easy work to translate. The text is full of archaisms, honorifics, and formal expressions, and the phrasing is often difficult to render into English. At times one has the feeling that a sentence will never end. When it does the point is often lost in the ceremonial and poetical nature of the language. In my translation I have tried to strike a balance between, on the one hand, capturing the oral flavor of the text and, on the other, creating an intelligible translation. In the interests of the latter, some explanations have been inserted in square brackets. The numerous repetitions, the set phrasings, and the clear evidence of textual layering are of course vestiges of the *Great Exhortation*'s very recent past as an exclusively oral text. This is an aspect of the text I wanted to preserve in translation because it is innate to the text's self-identity.

Further Reading

The most detailed discussion of the *Bca' yig* literature in a Western language is Ter Ellingson's "Tibetan Monastic Constitutions: The Bca' Yig," in *Reflections on Tibetan Culture: Essays in Memory of Turrell V. Wylie*, edited by L. Epstein and R. F. Sherburne, Studies in Asian Thought and Religion, vol. 12 (Lewiston: Edwin Mellen Press, 1990), pp. 205–30. An excellent general overview of the curriculum of the Gelukpa colleges is Guy Newland's "Debate Manuals (*yig cha*) in dGe lugs pa Monastic Colleges," in *Tibetan Literature: Essays in Honor of Geshe Lhundub Sopa*, edited by J. I. Cabezon and R. R. Jackson (Ithaca: Snow Lion, 1995). On the tradition of Indo-Tibetan scholasticism pursued in Tibetan monasteries, see my *Buddhism and Language: A Study of Indo-Tibetan Scholasticism* (Albany: State University of New York Press, 1994).

The Great Exhortation

It has been said, from the supremely vast and beautiful vase that is the mouth of the glorious Gendün Gyatso (Dge 'dun rgya mtsho, the second Dalai Lama), who [in his eloquence] brings a smile to the lips of Sarasvatī [the goddess of scholarship]:

> The Je College is the place for the systematic study of the scriptures
> Of the two trailblazers [Asaṅga and Nāgārjuna], of Vasubandhu,
> Guṇaprabha, and Śākyaprabha, [Indian scholar-saints whose works, in Tibetan translation, form the basis for the monastic curriculum.]
> May this assembly increase like a lake in summer,
> And may the three aspects of scholarly activity flourish.

As he has said, [our college] is completely without an equal in elucidating, like the sun, the precious teachings of the Conqueror through the three activities of exegesis, dialectics, and composition and through the three actions of hearing, contemplating, and meditating upon the oceanlike scriptural tradition of the scholars and sages of India and Tibet, like those of the trailblazers Nāgārjuna and Asaṅga.

Lord refuge, great abbot, great Vajradhara, and those who sit before you, the supreme congregation, a disciplined assembly of āryans, a congregation of a multitude of scholars, a precious oceanlike assembly, and also the general assembly of the deities of the maṇḍala that are the play of the blessed one, the great glory, the Supreme Stallion [Hayagrīva], the merest remembrance of whom allows one easily to obtain every accomplishment, both supreme and ordinary, as well as those who have been sworn into allegiance, Ging-nga (Ging lnga), Za (Bza'), Dong (Gdong mo bzhi), Begdze Chamsing (Beg rtse lcam sring), lend me your precious ears.

What is it that I have to say? The white banner, which is renowned under the name of our own "Sera Je College of Renowned Scholars," flies forcefully from Tö, where the air is filled with the sweet aroma of the Dzāti, to Me, where the silk is manufactured. As you are all aware, from today we begin our famous great Summer Doctrinal Session [one of the major periods of study and debate in the monastery's academic year]. So be it. As the first of the series of rules and regulations for this period of time, the disciplinarian must make the assignments for the begging of wood. [It must have been the case in the early days of the college that the monks depended on the wood they received through begging for cooking fuel. This they used especially for making tea that would be drunk during special debate sessions. In the later days, once the college achieved a greater level of economic stability, the practice of begging for wood became a ceremonial one, though these debate sessions never lost the name of the "Begged Wood Debates" (*shing slong dam bca'*).] After that the lord refuge, the great abbot, the great Vajradhara, will give a detailed and extensive exhortation based upon the *Great Exposition of the Stages of the Path to Enlightenment*. If there arises no other urgent business, such as a religious festival, the debate session is then held after the third day, and then I, just as water is poured from one vase to another and a stone is passed from one hand to another, must offer the *Great Exhortation*. This is a fine and old custom. May it never deteriorate but only flourish. So be it.

O field of merit for beings, and even for the gods, unsurpassed earth, source of refuge, O disciplined assembly of āryans, congregation of a multitude of scholars, precious oceanlike assembly, O general assembly of the deities of the maṇḍala that are the play of the blessed one, the great glory, the Supreme Stallion, the merest remembrance of whom allows one easily to obtain every accomplishment, both supreme and ordinary, as well as those who have been sworn into allegiance, Ging nga, Za, Dong (mozhi), Begdze Chamsing, whose power, like the blazing of the flames of lightning, overcomes an entire stone mountain's worth of the demonic hordes of the dark side, lend me your ears for this profound message.

What is it that I have to say? As you are all aware, the time has come for the famous great Summer Doctrinal Session of this white banner that flies forcefully over the three worlds, renowned under the name of our own "Sera Je College of Renowned Scholars." So be it.

The disciplinarian must now offer you a rough outline of the series of rules and regulations to be followed during this period based upon the *Great Exhortation*. These six fundamental divisions are (1) the object to whom the *Great Exhortation* is to be offered, (2) the time during which it is to be offered, (3) the individuals who should offer it, (4) how it should be offered, (5) the stages of listening, and (6) the actual *Great Exhortation*, which is what is to be listened to.

(1) The place where the *Great Exhortation* is to be offered is, for example, as follows. It should be offered only before this kind assembly of masters of the three baskets [of the teachings: discourses (*sūtra*), monastic discipline (*vinaya*), and metaphysics (*abhidharma*)]. If from ancient times there is no example of houses or dormitories bringing [this advice] to each other's doorsteps, how is it possible to do so now? The Great Debate Session, the Great Festival, the *Great Exhortation*, and so forth are all times during which permission to be absent is revoked. This being the case, I am assuming that all of you, the elderly, the young, and the middle-aged, have all come and are present at the assembly.

(2) The time when it is to be offered is, for example, as follows. An exhortation connected to a doctrinal period should be offered in the middle of the doctrinal period and an exhortation associated with a doctrinal off-period

should be offered at the end of the [preceding] doctrinal period. [A "doctrinal period" is the time when the debate sessions are meeting and the full curriculum is in effect. During "doctrinal off-periods" the debate sessions are suspended, and this gives monks the opportunity to devote more time to the intensive memorization of texts.] The exhortations connected with the Great Debate Session, the Great Festival, and Wood Begging are to be given only sporadically. It is not permissible to offer a speech during every assembly, for it will act as an impediment to the study of the doctrine.

(3) The individuals who should offer it are as follows. Only the master [the abbot] and the disciplinarian count. No more than these [two] are necessary. No fewer than these [two] can encompass it.

As for the fact that no more than these [two] are necessary, it is as follows. Even though this college has a faculty of administrators and scholars comparable to the collection of the stars in space, if all of them offer the *Great Exhortation*, some would disclaim what others said, while some would affirm positions that others disclaimed. This being an obstacle to discipline, we say "too many are not necessary." Regarding "too few cannot encompass it," the series of rules and regulations of this college is greater than Mount Meru, deeper than the ocean, more subtle than a mustard seed, finer than a horse's tail hair. Hence, it is difficult for a single person to recite the *Great Exhortation*. What the disciplinarian does not recite, the master must offer with added emphasis, and what the master misses, the disciplinarian must offer with added emphasis. This is what is meant by "too few cannot encompass it." So be it.

(4) Regarding how it should be offered, there are two points to mention: the fact that it should be offered using honorific terms and metaphors, and the fact that it is to be offered just as water is poured from one vase to another and a stone is passed from one hand to another.

(4.1.1) The first point, that it should be offered using honorific terms and poetical expressions, is as follows. "Honorific terms" refers to the fact that it is necessary to offer it using words that express the good qualities of the body, speech, and mind of the saṅgha. This means not only expressing their qualities by using "top hat" (*dbu zhwa*) for "hat" (*zhwa mo*) and using "venerable shoes" (*zhabs lcag*) for "shoes" (*lham gog*), but also that one is not allowed to offer it using ordinary words, that is, saying "you" and "me," or "horse" and "shit," and so forth.

(4.1.2) That it should be offered using metaphors does not refer to [using] the metaphors explained in the Vedic scriptures, but instead to being subtle while offering it. When someone creates a small infraction of the rules of this great and precious college, if such a person is sitting at the head of the row one should look toward the back of it, and if he is sitting toward the east then one should look toward the west. In other words, one should offer [the exhortation] so that others are not aware [of the identity of the perpetrator of the offense], even though one is oneself aware. If that individual does not recognize that [the advice] is being directed at *him*, then during the second exhortation it is necessary to make others slightly aware [of the identity of the person] by referring oneself to those who sit near him in the row and to his housemates. If the individual still does not recognize that it is being directed at him, then on the third occasion one must direct oneself at that very person and say, "*You* have broken such and such a rule," offering [the exhortation] by pointing the finger at him. The reason for offering the exhortation twice [before actually identifying the individual] is that this college is an honorable and compassionate college. Hence, one is not allowed to point the finger from the very beginning. Given that it could harm the reputation of a particular person, it is necessary to offer the first and second exhortations. It is permissible to skip the first two exhortations in the case that one sees, hears, or suspects that one of the four root monastic infractions or the drinking of alcohol has taken place, in which case it is necessary to point the finger from the outset.

(4.2) The fact that it is offered just as water is poured from one vase to another and a stone is passed from one hand to another refers to this. For example, whether it be water or nectar, if one pours it from a gold pot into a copper pot and from a copper pot into a clay pot, what one is pouring is the same in essence. It does not change [according to the receptacle]. Likewise, whether it be the *Great Exhortation* of this college or all of its great rules and regulations, insofar as these rules, which have been passed down in a lineage from mouth to mouth and from ear to ear, have not changed in essence from the time of the great Günkhyen Lodrö Rinchen Sengewa (Kun mkhyen Blo gros rin chen seng ge ba) to the present time, this situation resembles that of the example. And just as the vessels into which it is poured can have different shapes, colors, and prices, etc., the one who is giving the *Exhortation* can have one of three types of mental faculties, sharp, middling, or dull. This is how it is similar to the example. How it is offered like a stone passed from one hand to another refers to this. Whether it is a round stone or a square stone and whether one passes it from the front of the line to the rear or from the rear of the line to the front, there is no change in the shape and nature of the stone. Likewise, the lack of change in the nature of the rules of this precious college is what makes it similar to the example. [This is a claim as to the accuracy of the oral lineage, the point being that the text can and does remain intact regardless of the nature of the individuals who pass it from one generation to the next.] Just as the man who holds the stone in his hand can be good, bad, or middling, likewise, the person who gives the *Exhortation* might be the likes of even Maitreya or Mañjuśrī, or he might simply be like myself, someone who has no innate knowledge of spiritual or worldly affairs, nor any of the good qualities attained through training. This is how it is similar to the example.

(5) The stages of listening have four subdivisions: (5.1) how one should listen to it from the viewpoint of body, speech, and mind, (5.2) how one should listen to it from the point of view of seniority, (5.3) how one should listen to it from the point of view of position, and (5.4) how one should listen to it from the viewpoint of abandoning the three faults of the vessel, which act as

negative conditions, and of relying on the six recognitions that serve as positive conditions.

(5.1) As for how one should listen to it from the viewpoint of body, speech and mind, it is as follows. Body: One should not rest one's back against pillars or walls and so forth. Speech: No matter what kind of profound tantric recitations one may be applying oneself to, one must cease those recitations and listen. As regards how one should listen from the viewpoint of the mind: even if one's mind is equipoised in the nonconceptual samādhi of bliss and clear [light], one must arise from that samādhi and listen. This is not because profound tantric recitations and the nonconceptual samādhi of bliss and clear light are not important, but because these very rules of the monastery and college are even more important; [it is for this reason] that one must cease those practices and listen.

(5.2) As for "how one should listen to it from the viewpoint of seniority," it is as follows. The elders must listen to it as if they were judges. The middle-aged should listen to it to refresh their memories. Novices should listen to it for the sake of learning something they did not know before.

How is it that the elders should listen to it as if they were judges? It should not be the case that, influenced by their like or dislike of an administrator, they say that something is not one of the rules of the college when it is, or that something is one of the rules of the college when it is not. Instead, they should listen as impartial spectators to the law of karma. For example, they should listen as spectators to the law of karma, just as in the realm of embodied beings, the two chief disciples of our teacher [the Buddha] did; and, just as in the realm of the disembodied, the wrathful protector of the doctrine, Chamsing, does. [Tradition has it that some of the Buddha's chief disciples had the ability to discern the karmic actions in the past lives of beings that had led them to their present predicament. This allowed them to perceive a particular situation simply in terms of karmic causes and effects and presumably vitiated the tendency on their part to make judgments concerning the agents involved.]

How is it that the middle-aged should listen to it to refresh their memories? Even if one has previously fathomed all of the rules of this college, and even if one has ascertained them in one's mind, in the meantime one might have gone on a short or long pilgrimage, or one might have gone to visit one's parents in one's native place, in the process slightly forgetting the rules. If this has been the case, then one should listen so as to refresh one's memory of them.

How is it that novices should listen to it so as to learn something they did not know before? Realizing that they have never before heard the *Great Exhortation* of this college, they should listen to it for the sake of learning something they did not know before.

As regards the term "elder," there are two types: those who are elders from the viewpoint of provisional meaning and those who are elders from the viewpoint of definitive meaning. The first refers to those [elder monks] who do not know how to follow the rules of the monastery and college and who do not know how to explain them to others. Even if these individuals have spent one hundred years in the college, they are nonetheless provisional elders and definitive novices. Those who *do* know how to follow the rules and who know how to explain them to others, even if such individuals are only in the lowest Collected Topics class [for monks in their teens and preteens], are nonetheless definitive elders and provisional novices.

Now someone may be an elder from the viewpoint of class or from the viewpoint of years. From the viewpoint of class, someone is an elder if they have reached the Vinaya class or above. From the viewpoint of age, someone is an elder if they have been at the college for more than fifteen years. Someone who is middle-aged can be middle-aged from the viewpoint of class or from the viewpoint of years. From the viewpoint of class, someone is middle-aged if they are in a class between Beginning Scripture [the first subclass in the Perfection of Wisdom class] and Advanced Madhyamaka. From the viewpoint of years, someone is middle-aged if they have been at the college between four and fifteen years. Someone can also be a novice from the viewpoint of class or from the viewpoint of years. From the viewpoint of class, someone is a novice if they are in one of the three Collected Topics classes. From the viewpoint of years, someone is a novice if it has been three years or less since they have arrived at the college.

(5.3) As for "how one should listen from the viewpoint of position," it is as follows. From on high, the lord refuge, the precious abbot, even if he has been residing in the western suite during the doctrinal off-period, during the doctrinal period must listen to the *Great Exhortation* by moving into the eastern suite [which is just above the debate courtyard where the exhortation is given]. From the intermediate level, the abbot's private secretary, the two managers, and so forth must listen to the exhortation from the various windows of the print shop [located just inside from the debate courtyard]. From below, the cook, water bearers, temple manager, teachers, students, and so forth must listen from the two side doors that face each other on both sides of the debate courtyard.

As for "how one should listen to it from the viewpoint of abandoning the three faults of the vessel, and of relying on the six recognitions," it is as follows. One must listen devoid of the three faults: that of a vessel turned upside down, that of the leaking vessel, and that of the filthy vessel. For example, no matter how excellent the food or beverage one attempts to put inside the vessel, if it is turned upside down, nothing at all will enter it. Likewise, it is as if, having come to listen to the exhortation, under the influence of a lack of discipline and of distraction one shows not the slightest interest in listening when the master or administrator offers the exhortation. This is how it is similar to the example.

As for how to listen to it devoid of the fault of the leaking vessel, it is as follows. Even if one puts food or beverage into a leaking vessel, it will not remain there for long. Likewise, it is as if, having come to listen to the exhortation, one does not retain in memory the little that one has managed to ascertain, so that when one arrives at one's quarters and one's teacher asks how the exhortation went today, one has nothing to say in response. This is how it is similar to the example.

As for how to listen to it devoid of the fault of the filthy vessel, it is as follows. No matter how excellent the food or beverage one puts inside a filthy vessel, even if it is divine ambrosia, it cannot be used due to the filth. Likewise, it is as if, no matter how excellent a job the master or disciplinarian does in giving the exhortation, even to the point of giving extensive scriptural citations and reasoning, if one is oneself influenced by an evil motivation, instead of taking it as a method for disciplining oneself, one claims that what is part of the exhortation is not part of it, and so forth. This is how it is similar to the example of the filthy vessel. In brief, just as the Blessed Lord has said, "Dedicate yourself to listening well." It is necessary to listen with a proper motivation.

As for how one should listen from the viewpoint of relying on the six recognitions, it is as follows. The six recognitions are:

1. One should recognize the one who gives the exhortation to be like a doctor.
2. One should recognize oneself as the patient.
3. One should recognize the exhortation to be like the medicine.
4. One should recognize its sustained practice to be like the cure of the disease.
5. One should recognize the Tathāgata to be a holy being.
6. One should have the recognition, "may the doctrinal methods remain for a long period of time."

Alternatively, one can recognize the one who is giving the exhortation as one's master, one can recognize oneself as the disciple, and one can recognize the exhortation itself as the stages of the path to enlightenment. On top of these three recognitions, one can add the last three recognitions [of the previous grouping of six]. But whichever of these two systems of enumeration one adopts, it is important to realize that individuals who are afflicted with a serious illness will liberate themselves of the disease in dependence upon the assiduous application of medicinal treatment that is consistent with the advice of an expert doctor. In this same way, one should have a recognition of oneself as the disciple. One should have a recognition of the person giving the exhortation as one's master, and one should have a recognition of the *Great Exhortation* as the doctrine, the stages of the path to enlightenment. It is also necessary to listen with the thought, "How wonderful it would be if by my assiduous practice of these series of rules and regulations, the precious teachings of the Conqueror, would remain in the world for a long period of time." As the *Bodhicaryāvatāra* says:

> If, being frightened by the possibility of ordinary illness,
> One follows the advice of a doctor,

What need is there to speak of the need to constantly apply oneself
When one is afflicted with the illness of the manifold faults such as attachment, etc.?

Hence, it is necessary to listen with a good basis in these nonmistaken recognitions.

(6) As for the actual *Great Exhortation*, which is what is to be listened to, it is as follows: (6.1) the series concerned with the entrance of a postulant, (6.2) the series concerned with the practice of the rules once one has entered, (6.3) the series concerned with taking up the banner of the accomplishments at the end, that is, after having practiced, and (6.4) as an aside, a discussion on asking permission to be absent.

(6.1) As for the series concerned with the entrance of postulants, it is as follows. Postulants are of two types, laymen, who wear white clothing, and branch monks, who come from afar. Let us consider the case of laymen, who wear white clothing. [The layman] must be the kind of person [who is malleable], like a stainless white piece of wool that can take up whatever color one applies to it, be it yellow or red. He must be seven years of age or older, and even if he is seven years of age, he must be able to scare away a crow. [These are the criteria that the Vinaya gives for the time at which a young boy is allowed to take novice vows.] In short, he must be someone who is devoid of the four impediments that act as conditions obstructing ordination [the obstacles to the arising of the vows (e.g., not being human or being a hermaphrodite), the obstacles to the maintenance of the vows (e.g., not having the permission of one's parents), the obstacle to the betterment of the vows (e.g., illness), and the obstacle to the beautification of the one who possesses the vows (e.g., having a crippled or mutilated hand)], and they must possess the five concordant conditions. [It is not clear what these five conditions refer to, although the *'Dul ba'i sdoms* suggests that a series of four concordant conditions refer to the three requisite robes of a monk together with the begging bowl.]

Let us consider the case of branch monks who come from afar. They must be men who have not come after having embezzled funds or offerings from their own outlying monasteries, and who have never had to be even slightly reprimanded by qualified masters and administrators in their outlying monastery. In short, they must not be monks who make the rounds of all the great monasteries as if they were a circular earring [causing havoc in one and moving on to the next], they must not be the type of monk who makes the rounds of the outlying monasteries as if he were shifting through the string of his beads.

Such a person should then be properly examined so as to determine to which house or regional house he belongs. [Sera Je monastery had ten houses and six regional houses. All of the latter were, at least in theory and perhaps in the very distant past, associated with one house, but in recent history all have acted as essentially independent entities with almost the same authority as the houses themselves.] He should then be taken care of well. He should not immediately be pounced upon [by monks of a certain house] like dogs attacking a piece of lung. If someone is a branch monk who belongs to one's own [house], whether he is a king who comes on a throne of gold or a beggar who comes with a stick and an empty satchel, the house or regional house to which he belongs must take care of him well. If I hear that there is a difference in the attention given to a monk based on his economic position, I will not leave it at that, but, calling in the offending parties, I will mete out punishment that will not be light. On the other hand, if a monk does not belong to one's own house or regional house, even if it be a king on a golden throne who should arrive, one is not allowed to take care of him. It is necessary to take care of those who belong to one's own [house], whatever their position, because one never knows how a particular person will in the future be able to benefit the teachings of the Buddha or, in particular, the religious and political status of this college. It is necessary to practice as it is stated in the *Vinaya*: "Caste and family line are not the chief thing; spiritual attainment is the chief thing."

It is necessary for the teacher of that postulant first to present to him a complete set of robes, from the hat to the boots. Let us take the case of the hat. It should be as yellow as possible—black, the color of crows, is not allowed. Moreover, the main portion of hat [called the "lawn"] symbolizes a Buddha field; the threads that stick up from the top symbolize the thousand buddhas [of this aeon]; the lining of the lawn should be white, the lining of the trailer must be blue, and its outer covering should be red—this symbolizes the threefold protectors [Avalokiteśvara, Mañjuśrī, and Vajrapāṇi, respectively]; the twelve lines of stitching to be found in the front part of the trailer represent the twelve branches of scripture; the three blue strings that hang from the trailer represent the three baskets of teachings. Even if one is an ordinary run-of-the-mill monk who possesses no other religious objects, it is sufficient if one makes one's hat an icon and makes offerings to it. No other [icon] is necessary.

Let us now turn to the overcoat. It must have a lotus collar, and it must have been cut [and restitched] at the waist. The lotus collar is necessary because it is an auspicious symbol for one's taking future birth within a lotus in the pure land, with a body that is of the nature of mind. The upper part of the overcoat must be turned inside out and stitched to the lower part of the overcoat, and the symbolism is this. This serves as an auspicious symbol of [the continuity of the teachings, that is, of] the fact that immediately after the teachings of our incomparable teacher, the Lion of the Śākyas, there will arise the teachings of the conqueror, the protector Ajita [Maitreya]. It is necessary to line the inside border of the overcoat with yellow cloth, and this serves as an auspicious symbol for the spread, in all directions, of the teachings of the great master Tsong kha pa, the bearer of the yellow hat, the protector Mañjuśrī himself.

Let us now turn to the vest. It must have "lion shoulders" [symbols of fearlessness]; it must have "elephant tusks" [on the back, symbols of constantly being in the jaws of death]; and it must have the blue thread [lining the arm openings]. It is necessary to have the blue thread so as to remember the kindness of the Chinese monks [who wore blue robes and who helped to reestablish the monastic lineage in Tibet after a period of persecution]. The master, the recognized incarnations, the college's *chos mdzad* [a class of men from aristocratic or wealthy families who enter the monastery as monks and, due to their families' benefaction, are given special status], and so forth are allowed to wear fine wool on the backs of their vests. Everyone else must either wear a vest made of rough wool or else a vest like those worn at the Lower Tantric College.

Let us now turn to the shawl. It is not permissible to wear a fine woolen shawl with full hemming in the summer time, nor is it permissible to wear a finely woven hundred-stitches-to-the-thumb woolen shawl in the winter time.

Let us now turn to the skirt. If one is a fully ordained monk, one must wear a real lower garment [with patches]; if one is a novice, one must wear an "imitation" lower garment [without patches]. Both must have an upper border and a lower border. In short, it is necessary that one's robes be such that they are capable of acquiring the blessing as explained in the *Vinaya*. [Robes that meet the criteria set forth in the *Vinaya* can and must be blessed. Fully ordained monks must keep their robes with them and never sleep apart from them. If they do so, the blessing is lost and the garments must be reblessed.]

Let us now turn to the underskirt. From among the one that is open in the front and the one that loops in a closed circle, the former, which is open in the front, is not allowed. Let us now turn to the shoes. One is allowed to wear only Sangpu (Gsang phu)-like shoes. One is not allowed to wear any of other brands that are in fashion, such as white shoes. What is more, the Sangpu-like shoes symbolize the three poisons of the afflictions. It is necessary to wear only these because they serve as a special auspicious symbol of the fact that our own minds are under the power of the three poisons of the afflictions. One is allowed to fix [broken] soles only with a piece that is spliced at the middle and not with an entire new sole.

Let us now turn to the water receptacle. Gold or silver, etc., are not allowed. It is necessary that the water pot should be made either of copper or of bronze, and for the pot cover to have all of the proper characteristics, such as having an exterior of red wool and a lining that is blue.

Let us now turn to the rosary. One is allowed to carry only those made of the seeds of the bodhi tree or of six-faced bodhi seeds. As an exception, the monks who are engaged in the Hayagrīva propitiation rituals are allowed to carry, discreetly, rosaries made from the likes of 'Bo ti rtse and Rakṣa. One is not allowed to carry anything apart from these, to wit the different rosaries that are in fashion. When one reaches Introductory Vinaya class one is allowed to add one counter [to one's rosary], and when one reaches Abhidharma one is allowed another counter [to help one keep track of all the divisions, subdivisions, and other enumerations that are covered in these two classes]. One is allowed no more than a pair of counters. Also, one must not separate the two counters on one's rosary but must put one beside the other. It is completely forbidden to put turquoise, coral, or other ornamental stones among the beads of the rosary.

Let us now turn to the bowl and flour bag. One must carry a bowl of the Ganden indentation style, and that too must not be of a random size. It should be a bowl the size of that of the general saṅgha, and should be the same size as the bowl of the great chanting leader. The bowl of the chanting leader should also not be of a random size but should be such that it can fit within his five fingers. Let us now turn to the flour bag. It should have the rainbow red and yellow strips. The outer covering should be blue and the inner lining white. This symbolizes the objects focused upon within *kṛtsna-samādhi*. The flour bag should be just large enough to carry one meal's worth of barley flour. The strings for closing the flour bag, for the rosary, and for the hat handle should be made only of stretched musk-deer leather. Cotton strings and so forth are not allowed. The mat should be such that [when placed on the cushions in the assembly] it can protect the property of the saṅgha. In short, the required dress should not be so good that it rivals that of the master and administrators, etc., nor so poor that it is just a series of patches with none of the original material left. One should avoid falling into either of these two extremes.

All of the administrators of this college, the general manager [of the monastery], the main enforcer [of the monastery], the abbot's private secretary, the [college] managers, the housing manager, the treasurers, secretary, and so forth, all have attire that is proper to their station. Some are allowed to wear vests with brocade, some are not. Some are allowed to wear *re zon* shoes, some are allowed *re zon* shoes with brocade on the calves. It is completely forbidden to have shoes with layered leather soles.

After the teacher has made the proper arrangements for the required dress of the student, it is necessary for the house warden first to inform the abbot's household. He must therefore come before either the steward of the abbot's household or the chef and partially unravel his shawl [as a sign of respect]. If they are sitting, he must kneel properly before them and state that there is such and such a postulant who belongs to his house and who is either a branch monk from afar or, if he is not a branch monk, a layman, who wears white clothing, who is a postulant for admission into the college. He must then ask when they can have an audience with the lord refuge, the precious abbot. If [the members of the abbot's household] are standing, then he must partially unravel his shawl and ask hunched over. Moreover, he is not allowed to make a suggestion as to the time, saying, "Can I bring him tomorrow morning?" or "Can I bring him now?" He must be ready to bring him whenever he is told to do so. After the individual teacher has made the proper arrangement for the robes of the postulant, since it is considered the first auspicious symbol for the postulant's entering the doctrinal door of the college and monastery, he [must offer to the abbot] a pitcher full of tea and a ceremonial scarf that is as clean as possible. The butter to be used in the tea should be as delicious as possible and the tea itself as fine as possible so as to insure that the lord refuge, the precious abbot, finds it to his liking. There is a saying that in olden days a ceremonial scarf worth five *kar ma* was to be offered. Be that as it may, since this is the first auspicious act [the student will engage in], he should have a ceremonial scarf that is as white as possible, and if [the postulant] is a layman, who wears white clothing, he should also offer one *tam kar* as a fee for the ritual cutting of the hair. In brief, one should offer the master at least a needle and some thread and [if one is well off] a horse or even an elephant.

Then, an elder monk who has at last arrived at the Vinaya class must bring the postulant and open the entry curtain of the steward of the abbot's household. When they go in for the audience, the postulant must do three full prostrations [extending his body full length], while for the teacher it is permissible to do three abbreviated prostrations. Moreover, it is not permissible for the elder monk to prostrate placing himself in front and the postulant behind. The postulant must do full prostrations so that it can be determined whether or not he has any defects in his limbs.

As soon as the audience is over [the abbot] will offer one cup of tea. Squatting, the postulant should take the cup respectfully with both hands and drink immediately. One is not allowed to set it down. Then, so as to examine whether or not the postulant has any faults in his speech, the lord refuge, the precious abbot, will ask the elder monk, "What is his native place? Where is his home monastery?" and the elder monk must answer. Then he asks the postulant, "What is your home monastery? What is your name?" in response to which the postulant must answer. When the question is being asked of the postulant, if the elder monk answers, this is an indication that the postulant has something wrong with his speech. When the question is being asked of the elder monk, if the postulant answers, it is an indication that he has a disrespectful or slanderous nature. As soon as the tea is finished [the elder monk] must partially remove his shawl, kneel on the floor, and ask permission [for the student to attend assembly], prefaced by a reason. If [the student] is a branch monk from afar [the elder monk] must ask, "Please be so kind as to allow this postulant to attend the tea-assemblies of the college and the tea-assemblies of the monastery discreetly for three doctrinal sessions [approximately three months], until he has prepared [that is, memorized] the threefold special recitations and the ninefold ritual cake offering of this precious college." [These are the ritual recitations special to the Je College that all monks must know by heart before they enter the monastery officially. Until that time, the postulant is allowed to attend communal tea-assemblies "discreetly," which is to say unofficially. It is assumed that the monastic postulant who comes from a branch monastery has already memorized other essential and common texts and prayers. A newly ordained layman is given a more lengthy period of time in which to prepare all of the required texts, as we see in the lines that follow.] If he is a layman, who wears white clothing, [the elder monk] must ask, "Please be so kind as to allow this postulant to attend the tea-assemblies of the college and the tea-assemblies of the monastery discreetly for three years until he has prepared the one-volume *Special Recitations Called 'The Extremely Clear'* that begins with 'Refuge' and ends with the 'Prayer for the Long Life of the Doctrine,' the *Abhisamayālaṃkāra*, the *Madhyamakāvatāra*, the threefold special recitations, and the ninefold ritual cake offering of this precious college."

After the audience with the lord refuge, the precious abbot, is finished they must go, in order, to the disciplinarian of the Great Assembly [the common assembly hall of all of Sera's colleges], to the disciplinarian of the college, and to the house master, tell them that the audience with the lord refuge, the precious abbot, has now been completed, and request, as above, that the postulant [be allowed to attend assembly, etc.]. If the postulant finishes memorizing the *Special Recitations Called "The Extremely Clear"* in one month, then it is not necessary for him to wait three months or three years. He is allowed to attend the debate sessions [immediately].

—35—

A Prayer for Deliverance from Rebirth

Donald S. Lopez, Jr.

Tibetans compose prayers for myriad purposes, but one of the most common is for a favorable rebirth. Death is seen as a harrowing experience, one over which the dying person often exercises little control, overcome as he or she may be by sickness and fear. The time of death is regarded as of supreme importance because it is then that the next lifetime will be determined. According to karmic theory, each person carries a vast store of seeds for future rebirth, any one of which can fructify as an entire lifetime. There are seeds for favorable rebirths as humans or gods, and there are seeds for horrific rebirths as ghosts or hell beings. It is said that one's mental state at the moment of death determines which of these seeds will create the next lifetime. That final mental state in turn is said to depend on one's prior practice. One's habitual attitudes, developed over the course of a lifetime, tend to come to the fore at death; it is difficult for a perennially angry person to become beneficent in a moment as overwhelming as death.

Tibetans therefore go to great lengths to affect favorably the state of mind of the dying person, placing statues of buddhas and bodhisattvas in the room and reading sūtras and prayers. But the preparation for death should begin long before the terminal moments, and there are many prayers that are recited daily whose purpose is to review the stages of death so that they will be familiar when they ultimately arrive. One such work is translated below, with a commentary. The prayer was written by the first Panchen Lama, Losang Chögyi Gyaltsen (Blo bzang chos kyi rgyal mtshan, 1567–1662. It was quite common for famous poems to receive prose commentaries from later scholars. The first Panchen Lama's poem is commented upon here by Janggya (Lcang skya rol pa'i rdo rje, 1717–1786), a great scholar who served as the teacher of the Qianlong emperor of China.

The poem begins by summarizing some of the instructions on the mindfulness of death. One of the chief concerns of the prayer, however, is that one die a good death, a death that is not unexpected or sudden and in which one is not so overcome by pain or regret that one is unable to make use of the opportunity that death provides. According to the systems of Unexcelled Yoga Tantra, death is a potent moment in which the most subtle form of consciousness, called the mind of clear light, becomes accessible. For the Gelukpas, this mind of clear light is not present in ordinary consciousness but remains locked in the center of the chest in something called the "indestructible drop" (*thig le, bindhu*). Hence, not only is death important because one can try to avoid an unfavorable rebirth, but for the person with the proper training, death can be "brought to the path" and used for the immediate achievement of buddhahood. By proper use of the stages of death, the ordinary states of death, the intermediate state (*bar do*), and rebirth can be transformed into the three bodies of a buddha.

The stages of death described here derive from the system of the *Secret Gathering Tantra* (*Guhyasamāja*). In these texts, the process of death is described in terms of eight dissolutions, as consciousness gradually retreats from the senses toward the heart and the physical elements of earth, water, fire, and wind lose the capacity to serve as the physical basis for consciousness. In the first dissolution, the earth constituent dissolves and the dying person loses the capacity to perceive forms clearly. With each stage, there is a sign that appears to the dying person. Thus, with the first dissolution, there is the appearance of a mirage, like that of water in a desert.

In the second dissolution, the water constituent dissolves and the dying person is no longer able to hear sounds. The sign is the appearance of smoke. With the third dissolution, that of the fire constituent, the dying person loses the ability to smell and perceives a sign called "like fireflies," red sparks of light in darkness. The last of the four elements, the wind constituent, dissolves at the fourth stage. The dying person can no longer taste, experience physical sensation, or move about. At this point, the person stops breathing. The sign that appears to the dying person is called "like a burning butterlamp," that is, a sputtering flame.

According to this tantric physiology, during the process of death, the winds (*rlung, prāṇa*) or subtle energies that serve as the vehicles for consciousness withdraw from the network of 72,000 channels (*rtsa, nāḍi*) that course throughout the body. Among all these channels, the most important is the central channel (*rtsa dbu ma, avadhūtī*), which runs from the genitals upward to the crown of the head, then curves down to end in the space between the eyes. Parallel to the central channel are the right and left channel, which wrap around it at several points, creating constrictions that prevent wind from moving through the central channel. At these points of constriction, there are also networks of smaller channels that radiate throughout the body. These points are called wheels (*'khor lo, cakra*). These are often enumerated as seven: at the forehead, the crown of the head, the throat, the heart, the navel, the base of the spine, and the opening of the sexual organ.

By the time of the fifth dissolution, the sense consciousnesses have ceased to operate. At this point, conceptual consciousnesses, known as the eighty conceptions, dissolve. The winds from the channels that course through the upper part of the body have further withdrawn from the right and left channels and have gathered at the crown of the head at the top of the central channel. When these winds descend the central channel to the heart wheel, what appears to the mind of the dying persons changes from a burning butter lamp to a radiant whiteness, described as being like a pure autumn night sky before dawn, pervaded by moonlight. In the sixth cycle the winds from the lower part of the body enter the center channel at the base of the spine and ascend to the heart. This produces an appearance of a bright red color, like a clear autumn sky pervaded by sunlight. Next, at the seventh stage, the winds that have gathered above and below enter the heart center, bringing about an appearance of radiant blackness, like a clear autumn sky in the evening after the sun has set and before the moon has risen, pervaded by thick darkness. Here, it is said that the dying person loses mindfulness, swooning in the darkness into unconsciousness. Finally, in the last stage, the mind of clear light dawns, with the appearance of the natural color of the sky at dawn, free from sunlight, moonlight, and darkness. This is death. The mind of clear light then passes into the intermediate state (*bar do*), which can last up to forty-nine days, and then, impelled by previous actions, finds a place of rebirth. The process of birth into the next lifetime follows a reverse process of the eight dissolutions, with the appearance of clear light changing to blackness, to radiant red, to radiant white, and so forth.

The tantric yogin is able to make use of these stages of death on the quick path to buddhahood. The mind of clear light provides an extremely subtle, clear, and nonconceptual consciousness, which can be employed, indeed, which eventually must be employed, to perceive emptiness and destroy the most subtle obstructions to the attainment of perfect enlightenment. He or she is said to "bring death to the path" by either using the mind of clear light at the time of death or by inducing the process of death on the stage of completion through various practices (such as sexual yoga) that cause the eight signs to appear in sequence. Through growing accustomed to the process of death and by causing the winds to enter and abide in the central channel again and again, the yogin eventually enters the dawn of the clear light eternally with the attainment of buddhahood.

At the successful conclusion of this practice the yogin creates an illusory body (*mehakāya, sgyu lus*), an immortal body made of the most subtle wind and mind, which, upon enlightenment, becomes the form body (*rūpakāya, gsugs sku*) of a buddha, adorned with the major and minor marks. The yogin must still go through the process of death one last time, a final death in which the gross physical body is left behind, the illusory body is left behind, and buddhahood with its truth body (*dharmakāya*) and form body is attained. After making oneself aware of the fact of death over the course of the path and after simulating death on the tantric path, one must die once again, passing through the radiant night of near-attainment to be born as a buddha in the clear light of dawn. If the dying person is unable to make use of death to achieve buddhahood, one may at least be reborn in a pure land where the path to enlightenment may be completed.

This is the background to the Panchen Lama's eloquent poem, with the allusions articulated and amplified in the commentary by Janggya. Following the convention of the Tibetan text, the poem is presented in its entirety first and is then repeated, interspersed with Janggya's comments.

The following is translated from Blo bzang chos kyi rgyal mtshan, *Bar do 'phrang sgrol gyi gsol 'debs 'jigs sgrol gyi dba' bo zhes bya ba dang de'i 'grel pa gten bde'i bsil ba ster byed zla zer zhes bya ba bcas bzhugs so paṇ chen blo bzang chos kyi rgyal mtshan gyis mdzad pa'i don rnams bshad pa lcang skya rol pa'i rdo rjes sbyar ba* (Gangtok, 1969).

Further Reading

On the stages of death, see Jeffrey Hopkins and Lati Rinbochay, *Death, Intermediate State, and Rebirth in Tibetan Buddhism* (Ithaca: Snow Lion, 1980). On the tantric practices described here, see Daniel Cozort, *Highest Yoga Tantra* (Ithaca: Snow Lion, 1986).

PRAYERS FOR DELIVERANCE FROM THE STRAITS OF THE BARDO, A HERO THAT FREES FROM FEAR

by the first Panchen Lama

Homage to the Guru Mañjughoṣa

I and all transmigrators, equal to space
Go for refuge until the essence of enlightenment
To the sugatas of the three times, together with the doctrine and the assembly.
We pray to be delivered from the frights of this [lifetime], future [lifetimes], and the bardo.

This auspicious base [the human body], difficult to find and easy to destroy,
Is the opportunity to chose profit or loss, joy or sorrow.
Thus, empower us to take the essence, great in meaning,
Without being distracted by the meaningless affairs of this life.

What was joined is parted, all that was accumulated is consumed,
The end of height is sinking, the end of life is death.
Empower us to understand that there is no time;
Not only will we die, but the time of death is uncertain.

Empower us to pacify the suffering in which the body is destroyed
By various causes of death when consciousness is about to leave
The four impure elements and the illusory aggregates
In the city of the mistaken conception of subject and object.

Empower us to pacify the mistaken appearances of nonvirtue
When we are deceived at a time of need by this body lovingly protected,
When the enemies, the frightful lords of death appear,
When we kill ourselves with the weapons of the three poisons.

Empower us to remember the instructions of the lama
When the doctors give up and rites cannot reverse it
And friends have lost the hope that we will live
And we do not know what to do.

Empower us to have joy and confidence
When the food and wealth greedily amassed remain behind,
We leave forever friends loved and longed for,
And go alone to a dangerous place.

Empower us to have the strength of a virtuous mind
When the elements of earth, water, fire, and wind gradually dissolve,
The strength of the body is lost, the mouth and nose dry and contract,
The warmth gathers, we gasp for breath, and a wheezing sound occurs.

Empower us to realize the deathless mode of being
When the various mistaken appearances, frightful and horrific,
Occur, specifically mirage, smoke, and fireflies,
And the mounts of the eighty conceptions cease.

Empower us to produce strong mindfulness
When the wind constituent begins to dissolve into consciousness,
The outer breath ceases and coarse dualistic appearance disappears
And there dawns an appearance like a blazing butterlamp.

Empower us to know our own nature
Through the yoga that realizes that saṃsāra and nirvāṇa are empty
When appearance, increase, and attainment dissolve, the former into the latter
And the experiences like being pervaded by sunlight, moonlight, and darkness dawn.

Empower the mother and son clear lights to meet
Upon the dissolution of near-attainment into the all empty,
When all conceptual elaborations are completely pacified
And an experience dawns like an autumn sky free from taint.

Empower us to be placed in one-pointed equipose
On the wisdom of the union of innate bliss and emptiness
As the moon is melted by the lightning-like fire of Brahmā
At the time of the four empties.

Empower us to complete the meditative state of illusion
When, rising from that, we ascend to an enjoyment body of the bardo
Blazing with the glorious major and minor marks
[Made] just from the wind and mind of the clear light of death.

If the bardo becomes established due to actions
Empower us so that erroneous appearances appear purely,
Realizing, with immediate analysis, how the sufferings
Of birth, death, and the bardo do not truly exist.

Empower us to be reborn in a pure land
Through the yoga of the transformation of the outer, inner, and secret
When the varieties of the four sounds of the reversal of the elements,
The three frightening appearances, the uncertainties, and the signs
appear.

Empower us to attain quickly the three bodies
Upon assuming a supreme base of a knowledge bearer of the sky
Or the body of one with pure behavior, endowed with the three
trainings
Completing the realizations of the two-staged path.

A COMMENTARY ON THIS PRAYER, CALLED "A MOON BESTOWING THE COOLNESS OF COMPLETE BLISS"

by Janggya

I bow down to the pervasive lord, the lama Vajrasattva
Through relying on whom the great bliss of union
Is bestowed in this very lifetime.
I will comment upon the profound instructions.

Here, I will discuss, for the sake of easy understanding, the stages of practice of this text, *Prayers for Deliverance from the Straits of the Bardo, A Hero That Frees from Fear*, composed by the Panchen, the all-knowing Losang Chögyi Gyaltsen Bel Zangpo (Blo bzang chos kyi rgyal mtshan dbal bzang po), the lord of the complete teaching who has gone to the highest state of attainment, the keeper of the treasury of all the secret instructions of the foremost great being, [Tsong kha pa]. Initially, one should build one's motivation and purify one's continuum by going for refuge and engendering the aspiration to enlightenment. Perform as before the guru yoga that is connected with the *yi dam* of

Unexcelled Yoga Tantra, such as Bhairava, Cakrasaṃvara, or Guhyasamāja, together with the seven-limbed service and the offering of maṇḍala. The prayers are to be [recited] as it appears below with mindfulness of the meaning through strong conviction regarding the inseparability of one's teacher and *yi dam*. In other contexts, when this is connected with meditation in the circle of a maṇḍala, one may conclude with torma offering of self-generation or may conclude with offering and praise of the [deity] generated in front; since either is suitable, it depends on the context.

The actual prayers are of four [types], the preliminaries, connected with the common path; those connected with the instructions for someone about to die; those connected with instructions for the intermediate state, and those connected with instructions for taking rebirth. The first, [those connected with the common path] comprise the first three stanzas.

Homage to the Guru Mañjughoṣa

This is an obeisance and an expression of worship to the lama and supreme of deities, Mañjughoṣa.

> I and all transmigrators, equal to space
> Go for refuge until the essence of enlightenment
> To the sugatas of the three times, together with the doctrine and the assembly.
> We pray to be delivered from the frights of this [life], future [lives], and the bardo.

[The first stanza] concerns going for refuge. [Going for refuge] is the heartfelt promise that is not broken from now until enlightenment, unwaveringly seeking protection in the place of protection—the tathāgatas of the three times, that is, the buddhas, the dharma, and the saṅgha—for oneself and all transmigrators equal to space from the fears of this life, the next life, and the intermediate state. [Refuge is sought from two perspectives]: a strong awareness fearful of the general and specific sufferings of saṃsāra of myself and all the kind transmigrators, equal to space, and with an authentic awareness that the lama and the three jewels have the capacity to protect us from that [suffering].

> This auspicious base, difficult to find and easy to destroy,
> Is the opportunity to chose profit or loss, joy or sorrow.
> Thus, empower us to take the essence, great in meaning,
> Without being distracted by the meaningless affairs of this life.

The second stanza is concerned with the great meaning of leisure and opportunity and the difficulty of finding them. An auspicious basis endowed with the eighteen qualities of leisure and opportunity, [see chapter 28] whether [considered] from the viewpoint of cause, entity, or example, is difficult to find and the conditions for its destruction are numerous. Hence, it is easy for it to be destroyed, like the flame of a butterlamp in a strong wind. This [basis], attained merely fortuitously this time, is an opportunity to have the independence to choose joy or sorrow; to acquire the profit of high status [i.e., a good rebirth] and liberation for oneself from now on, or to bring about a loss, such as the sufferings of the bad realms. We pray for empowerment to extract the pure essence through practicing the excellent doctrine of the Mahāyāna, having the great meaning, practicing daily with determination, never being distracted by the meaningless affairs of this lifetime, such as praise, fame, and resources, which are insignificant because they are not rare; they are even acquired by animals.

> What was joined is parted, all that was accumulated is consumed,
> The end of height is sinking, the end of life is death.
> Empower us to understand that there is no time;
> Not only will we die, but the time of death is uncertain.

The third stanza teaches about impermanence. Like traders at a festival, the happy gatherings of relatives and dear friends in the end powerlessly disperse. Like the honey of a bee, not only is all accumulated wealth consumed in the end; there is no certainty that one will be able to use it oneself. Like an arrow shot into the sky by a child, one achieves a high rank of glory in the world and in the end one does not escape sinking. This very body that is born complete and is lovingly protected is finally destroyed by the Lord of Death. At that time, being cast as if into an empty wilderness, consciousness must always go on alone. Thus, not only will one die, but the time when one will die—the year, the month, the week—is uncertain. Therefore, there can be no confidence that one will not die even today. Empower us to practice only the excellent doctrine quickly, having understood that there is no time for the limitless affairs which are to be put aside—the appearances of this life—[such as] accumulating and maintaining possessions, subduing enemies and protecting friends.

The preceding has taught the way to train the mind in the prerequisites to the instructions on death. The second group of prayers applies to the instructions for those who are about to die. This has two parts, removing obstacles to the cultivation of the path, that is, engendering the kind of awareness that is concordant with the doctrine, and the actual mode of cultivating the instructions for one about to die. The first is dealt with in four stanzas.

> Empower us to pacify the suffering in which the body is destroyed
> By various causes of death when consciousness is about to leave
> The four impure elements and the illusory aggregates
> In the city of the mistaken conception of subject and object.

If there is a great suffering that destroys the essential [parts of the body] at the time of death, one is prevented from putting the instructions into practice.

Therefore, the first stanza is a prayer for empowerment in order that that [suffering] be pacified. This city of the gandhārvas, the mundane existence of the mistaken appearances of this life, is produced by dualistic conceptions that perceive the apprehended [objects] and the apprehender [i.e., consciousnesses] to be true. Here, the illusory aggregates are composed of the four elements of earth, water, fire, and wind, which are established from the impure factors of blood and semen from one's parents. These aggregates and one's own consciousness are divided and separated through the divisiveness of the pernicious Lord of Death. As that time draws near, empower us to pacify suffering such that it does not happen that the elements are disturbed by the power of various harmful external and internal causes of death, such as sickness, weapons, and poison, and that a fierce disease ceases and destroys the essential [parts of the] body—the winds, constituents, and the channels that are the basis of the life force.

> Empower us to pacify the mistaken appearances of nonvirtue
> When we are deceived at a time of need by this body lovingly
> protected,
> When the enemies, the frightful lords of death appear,
> When we kill ourselves with the weapons of the three poisons.

If one conceives the mistaken appearances at the time of death to be true and comes under the power of fear and dread, one is prevented from meditating on the instructions. Therefore, the second stanza is a prayer for empowerment in order to pacify that. Arriving at an inescapable passage, one is deceived at [this] time of need by the body that is cherished and protected with food, clothing, and wealth, without shunning sin, suffering, or ill-repute, and [mind and body] separate. The enemies, the difficult to withstand and frightening lords of death, that is, the various forms of the lords of death such as the fear of the separation of life from the body and the fear of fear itself appear. At that time, one murders oneself with the weapons of the three poisons—attachment to this body, unbearable hatred of fear and suffering, and the obscuration that conceives whatever appears to be true. We pray that, when we arrive at that point, we be empowered to pacify all the appearances of unpleasant objects created by nonvirtuous misconception and all the mistaken perceptions of subjects that conceive these to be true.

> Empower us to remember the instructions of the lama
> When the doctors give up and rites cannot reverse it
> And friends have lost the hope that we will live
> And we do not know what to do.

Regarding the third, one prays for empowerment in order to have the ability to meditate on the instructions, without being impeded by fear or forgetfulness at that time. The doctors who hope to cure sicknesses give up and various rites do not overcome the fear of death. Relatives, such as one's father and mother, lose hope that one will live; with eyes filled with tears they make arrangements for the funeral ceremonies. One oneself does not know what to do, like someone abandoned by a guide in a frightful place. At that time, abandoning anguish and panic, we pray for empowerment to remember the instructions of the lama, having the confidence to use death on the path.

Empower us to have joy and confidence
When the food and wealth greedily amassed remain behind,
We leave forever friends loved and longed for,
And go alone to a dangerous place.

Regarding the fourth, all the wealth and possessions, the home and power that one has greedily accumulated and toiled and worried to protect is left as inheritance. Without ever meeting them again, one leaves forever friends loved and longed for, one's father and mother, one's retinue, and students, from whom one cannot bear to be apart from even for a short time. One will be carried powerlessly, alone and without a companion, by the winds of karma to the dangerous place of the bardo where one has never been before and which is unfamiliar, not knowing what frights and sufferings are there. At that time, we pray for empowerment to have a joy and confidence that are agreeable and cheerful, without the slightest panic or anguish, like a child going home, placing confidence in the lama, *yi dam*, and three jewels. That is, one prays for empowerment in order to increase the happiness of the mind, understanding that all of these appearances of the circumstances of death are to be visualized in meditation prior [to death] and are exhortations to the practice of virtue at the time of death.

The second, the actual mode of meditating on the instructions for one about to die, is [dealt with in the next] six stanzas.

Empower us to have the strength of a virtuous mind
When the elements of earth, water, fire, and wind gradually dissolve,
The strength of the body is lost, the mouth and nose dry and contract,
The warmth gathers, we gasp for breath, and a wheezing sound occurs.

Regarding the first, when the power of the wind that serves as the basis of the physical earth constituent declines and it dissolves into the water constituent, the external sign is that the strength of the body is lost, that is, one says, "I am being pulled down," thinking that one is sinking into the earth. Similarly, when the water constituent dissolves into the fire constituent, the external sign is that the moisture of the mouth and nose dry up and the lips become puckered and so forth. When the fire constituent dissolves into the wind constituent, the external sign is that warmth of the body gathers from the extremities at the heart and one's luster deteriorates. The external sign of the wind constituent dissolving into consciousness is a gasping for breath, and one makes a wheezing sound from [the breath] collecting uneveningly within. Therefore, when those occur, we pray for empowerment not to be moved by nonvirtuous thoughts, but to have the strength of virtuous minds, in general, virtuous minds such as going for refuge and training in the aspiration to enlightenment through giving and taking and, in particular, meditating on one's lama as being inseparable from one's *yi dam* and visualizing oneself and one's environment as the supported and supporting maṇḍala.

> Empower us to realize the deathless mode of being
> When the various mistaken appearances, frightful and horrific,
> Occur, specifically mirage, smoke, and fireflies,
> And the mounts of the eighty conceptions cease.

As the potencies of the physical body begin to disintegrate, appearances occur. There are many frightful and horrific things, such as unpleasant forms and sounds appearing to those who have been nonvirtuous. Various mistaken appearances, such as pleasant forms and sounds, appear to those who have been virtuous. Yogins who have made progress on the path are welcomed by the lama, the *yi dam*, and ḍākinīs, together with amazing visions. Specifically, an appearance like a mirage arises as the internal sign of the dissolution of earth into water, an appearance like smoke as the internal sign of the dissolution of water into fire, and an appearance like fireflies as the internal sign of the dissolution of fire into wind. After that the movements of the karmic winds that serve as the mounts of the eighty thorough conceptions—the forty natural conceptions of appearance, the thirty-three natural conceptions of increase, and the seven natural conceptions of near attainment—grow weaker and weaker and gradually cease. At that time, we pray for empowerment for the ability to sustain the understanding of the profound mode of being, deciding that birth, death, and all of saṃsāra and, specifically, all of these appearance and the mind are mere projections by mistaken conceptions and that ultimately that which is called "death" does not exist even in name.

> Empower us to produce strong mindfulness
> When the wind constituent begins to dissolve into consciousness,
> The outer breath ceases and coarse dualistic appearance disappears
> And there dawns an appearance like a blazing butterlamp.

Regarding the third, then the constituent of the movement of wind becomes very weak and begins to dissolve into the subtle constituent of consciousness. An external sign of this is that movement of the breath ceases and there is no inhalation. As an internal sign, all coarse dualistic appearances such as the aspect of the external object being distant and cut off from the internal apprehending consciousness disappear and an appearance dawns like a blazing butterlamp unmoved by the wind. At that time, empower us so that the aspect of clarity and knowledge, the conventional entity of the mind, will appear nakedly and so that we will produce a mindfulness that thinks, "I know this sign and that sign," when all of those internal and external signs explained above appear and so that earlier [before death] we will produce an introspection that knows whether or not we are performing the meditation that brings [death] to the path of the two stages.

> Empower us to know our own nature
> Through the yoga that realizes that saṃsāra and nirvāṇa are empty
> When appearance, increase, and attainment dissolve, the former into the latter
> And the experiences like being pervaded by sunlight, moonlight, and darkness dawn.

Regarding the fourth, then, at the time of appearance itself the winds dissolve into the appearance of subtle consciousness and there is the appearance of radiant whiteness in utter vacuity, like a clear autumn sky pervaded by moonlight. At the time of increase itself appearance dissolves into increase and there is the appearance of radiant redness, like a clear autumn sky pervaded by sunlight. At the time of near attainment itself, when increase dissolves into near attainment, there arises the appearance of radiant blackness, like a clear autumn sky pervaded by the thick darkness of evening. When the three appearances, the signs of the gradual dissolution of the former into the latter, appear in that way, empower us to have the ability to understand experientially the entity or mode of being of our own mind exactly as it is through the yoga of the special realization that inseparably joins the entities of the object emptiness—the nonexistence of even a particle of that which is established from its own side among all the phenomena included in cycle of mundane existence and the peace of nirvāṇa—and the subject, the spontaneous great bliss that arises through the method of focusing on important points in the body.

> Empower the mother and son clear lights to meet
> Upon the dissolution of near-attainment into the all empty,
> When all conceptual elaborations are completely pacified
> And an experience dawns like an autumn sky free from taint.

Regarding the fifth, then, upon the dissolution of the subtle mind of near attainment itself into the clear light of the all empty, all the elaborations of thought that conceive various objects such as unity and plurality cease and become pacified and an experience dawns like the utter vacuity of a pure autumn sky free from moonlight, sunlight, and thick darkness, the three tainting conditions that prevent the natural color of the sky from coming out just as it is. The manifestation, just as it is, of the entity of the basic clear light, fundamental and spontaneous, is the mother clear light. That same mind, the path clear light, which, through meditating on the instructions of the lama, is generated into exalted wisdom that realizes the subtle emptiness with spontaneous great bliss is the son clear light. The union of those in one entity is the meeting of mother and son clear lights. We pray for empowerment to be able to [have them meet when the clear light of death dawns].

Empower us to be placed in one-pointed equipose
On the wisdom of the union of innate bliss and emptiness
As the moon is melted by the lightning-like fire of Brahmā
At the time of the four empties.

Regarding the sixth, at the time of all four empties and specifically of the all empty, the clear light, the fire of Brahmā that abides at the triangular junction, that is, the fire of the fierce woman, blazes up like lightning, with the speed of lightning by the yogic power of the basic path. By moving up the central channel it melts the moon, the white mind of enlightenment, at the crown of the head which descends through the *dhūti*, thereby engendering the spontaneous great bliss. We pray for empowerment to be placed in one-pointed equipoise without distraction on the exalted wisdom that inseparably joins in entity that [bliss] and the subtle emptiness.

The foremost great being Tsong kha pa said that the king of instructions for the benefit of those who are about to die is the uninterrupted daily practice that combines three things: mixing in the mind again and again, beginning today, the instructions for one about to die, as they were explained above; forcing oneself to think repeatedly, "At death I should meditate in this way"; and strongly beseeching the lamas and gods for the purpose of that. It is similar with regard to the instruction on the bardo below.

The third group applies to instruction on the bardo and is set forth in three stanzas.

Empower us to complete the meditative state of illusion
When, rising from that, we ascend to an enjoyment body of the bardo
Blazing with the glorious major and minor marks
[Made] just from the wind and mind of the clear light of death.

Regarding the first, thus, when the wind and mind of the clear light of death are themselves moved by the wind, that is, when one rises from that meditative equipoise, the wind that serves as the mount of the clear light of death acts as the substantial cause of and the mind of clear light acts as the cooperative condition of a body that blazes with the glory of the thirty-two major marks and the eighty minor marks. It is a clear and unobstructed rainbow body, having a nature of mere wind and mind and not a coarse body of physical flesh and bone. The bardo of ordinary sentient beings comes about in the same way, but this yogin who is able to generate the clear light of death, the basis, into the entity of the example clear light on the path rises in an enjoyment body, that is, an impure illusory body. We pray for empowerment to complete the illusion-like meditative stabilization of such an Unexcelled Mantra path. This [discussion] applies to a single yogin who, in this lifetime, has achieved realization of isolated speech, or below, of the stage of completion.

If the bardo becomes established due to actions
Empower us so that erroneous appearances appear purely,

Realizing, with immediate analysis, how the sufferings
Of birth, death, and the bardo do not truly exist.

Regarding the second, if an ordinary body of the mundane bardo becomes established due to actions that did not [permit] the attainment in this lifetime of the realization of the stage of completion such as that [described] above, analyze well immediately and understand that one has established the bardo and then realize that all the appearances of birth, death, and the intermediate state are appearances of a mistaken mind and realize the way in which all of those sufferings are not true, that is, they are not established from their own side even slightly. Empower us so that all of the mistaken appearances that arise will appear purely, as the sport of bliss and emptiness.

Empower us to be reborn in a pure land
Through the yoga of the transformation of the outer, inner, and secret
When the varieties of the four sounds of the reversal of the elements,
The three frightening appearances, the uncertainties, and the signs appear.

Regarding the third, thus, at the time of the bardo, the signs of the reversal of the elements come. With the reversal of the earth wind there is the sound of an avalanche; with the reversal of the water wind, the sound of a stormy sea; with the reversal of the fire wind, the sound of a forest fire; with the reversal of the wind wind, the sound of the wind storm [at the end of an] aeon. There are four such sounds. The three frightful appearances are the appearance of hell beings, hungry ghosts, and animals or [they are] the form of lords of death carrying weapons, the sound of their saying "I'm going to kill you!" and one becoming sorrowful and terrified because of that. The uncertainties are such things as the uncertainty of abode, because of not abiding in one place and the uncertainty of companions because one is accompanied by a variety of companions. Various signs appear such as being endowed with the power of magical activity and [passing] without obstruction through mountains, walls, buildings, and so forth. At that time, empower us to be born in a pure buddha land, a special place for cultivating the path of Unexcelled Secret Mantra, having closed the door of birth in impure saṃsāra through the force of the three yogas: the transformation of all the appearances of the environment—the outer—into pure divine mansions, the transformation of all the inhabiting sentient beings—the inner—into *yi dams* in the aspect of father and mother, and the transformation of all the movements of mindfulness and thought—the secret—into the meditative state of bliss and emptiness.

The fourth section applies to taking rebirth and is set forth in one stanza.

Empower us to attain quickly the three bodies
Upon assuming a supreme base of a knowledge bearer of the sky

Or the body of one with pure behavior, endowed with the three trainings
Completing the realizations of the two-staged path.

In dependence upon the instructions of taking the bardo as the path in this way, one takes birth as a supreme knowledge bearer in a special abode caused and assembled by the very forms of outer flying heroes and ḍākinīs. One then completes the remainder of the path and achieves the supreme state. Otherwise, if one takes birth like those endowed with six constituents who are born from a human womb in Jambudvīpa, one should stop the mind of desire and hatred for one's father and mother and view them as *yi dams* in the aspect of father and mother. One enters the mother's womb and, upon being born outside, one takes the body of a monk endowed with three trainings of those with pure behavior and enters into the teaching of the Conqueror in accordance with its stages. Then, one's continuum is ripened by the four pure initiations, the doors of entry into Unexcelled Secret Mantra Mahāyāna. Having kept the pledges and vows correctly, one brings to fulfillment the progression on the paths of the stage of generation and the stage of completion. Having thereby transformed the basic three bodies into the three bodies of the path, one quickly attains, in this very lifetime, the three bodies of a buddha, the effect: the wisdom truth body, the enjoyment body, and the emanation body. Having done that, we pray for empowerment to establish all sentient beings throughout space on the path to ripening and liberation.

Because the meaning of colophon is easy to understand, I will not elaborate. It is said that these instructions should be kept secret from those who are not vessels, such as those without faith, and from those who have not received initiation into Unexcelled Mantra. The explanations above of the instructions on death and the bardo appear to be intended for the profound instructions on the stage of completion. Therefore, regarding the mode of transforming [these instructions] into the king of instructions on death, the practice is to be done daily, as already explained, through causing the meanings of the instructions to appear in meditation, not through merely reciting the words of the prayers but by being mindful of the meaning. If it is practiced in that way, it becomes the supreme method for taking advantage of the basis of leisure and opportunity. I say:

How wonderful it is to explain clearly with few words
The essences of the path of the highest vehicle,
The essentials of the profound thought of Vajradhara,
The basic promise of the kings of adepts.

By the virtue of striving at this,
May I and all transmigrators
Peerlessly uphold and increase

The path of the highest vehicle in birth after birth
And become equal to the vajra-bearing Nāgārjuna.

The elder lama and monk, Chöje Losang Sangye (Chos rje blo bzang sangs rgyas), asked on behalf of one from Mongolia with a youthful mind who is beginning the complete and profound practice that there be made an explanation, condensed and easy to understand, of the meanings of *Prayers for Deliverance from the Straits of the Bardo, A Hero That Frees from Fear* by the crown of millions of scholars and adepts, the omniscient Panchen Losang Chögyi Gyaltsen. The scribe of the learned Janggya (Lcang skya rol pa'i rdo rje) was the lama and geshe Tshultrim Dargye (Tshul khrims dar rgyas), for whom billions of texts have been spoken. By [the merit] of having done this, may the teaching of the conqueror Losang [Tsong kha pa] spread and increase in all directions.

—36—

Turning Back Gossip

Matthew Kapstein

The religious life of Tibet embraces a wide range of ritual practices whose origins are clearly indigenous. Among them are important rituals of the Tibetan state, such as those concerned with the state oracles and protective deities, that have developed over the course of centuries as solemn rites of national significance. On a more humble scale, daily observances such as the offering of the fragrant smoke of burnt juniper to the gods and spirits of the local environment are performed in virtually every Tibetan household. Rituals of these types have long been incorporated within the Buddhist religion in Tibet and have been reformulated over the centuries to accord, more or less, with Buddhist doctrinal norms.

A particularly important and broad category of ritual practice is devoted to the expulsion of various types of evil forces. The manner in which such rituals have been adopted for Buddhist use has been extremely uneven, varying according to both geographical region and sectarian difference. Throughout the country, however, monks or lay priests associated with village temples had to be proficient in these practices in order to minister to the common troubles, fears, and complaints of the populace. Because this grass-roots priesthood frequently adhered, at least nominally, to the Nyingmapa sect, or sometimes to the Bön religion, a veneer of conformity with the normative teachings of these traditions was often given to the exorcistic rituals intended for village use. Often, for instance, the Nyingmapa versions of the rituals in question are presented as the instructions of Padmasambhava.

The ritual that is presented here concerns the exorcism of "malicious gossip" (*mi kha*). In small and isolated communities it is clearly of great importance that cooperative and harmonious relationships be maintained to the extent possible. Even under relatively favorable circumstances, however, this proves to be a difficult thing to accomplish. Discrepancies of wealth and worldly success, disputes over privileges or prior agreements, and a thousand and one other circumstances may lead neighbors, friends, and even siblings to begin to cast aspersions upon one another, and eventually to fall out. Consider what might take place if the crops of all but a few farmers in a given community be afflicted with blight. Some may suggest that a special twist of fate, or a supernatural power, brought about the unusual success of the lucky households. Perhaps some magical ability was involved. Perhaps a curse was brought down on the less fortunate neighbors. It is not difficult to imagine that the amplification through gossip of what were at first relatively innocent innuendos might soon endanger the social fabric of the community. The exorcism of gossip therefore addressed an important communal and psychological need. It attempted to promote mutual healing and forgiveness by attributing gossip and its pernicious effects to a demonic agent, the "gossip girl" (*mi kha bu mo*), who was not a member of the community at all, but rather an alien and unwanted presence within it. By identifying her origins as lying far outside of the community, demonstrating that her evil influence worked on human and animal alike, and creating an effigy whereby she could be visibly expelled, this ritual, in effect, served as a public disavowal of gossip and all of the terrible effects it was thought to have had on the household or village that sponsored the rite.

Presented as the work of the great eighth-century culture hero Padmasambhava, the ritual as we have it here attributes a Chinese origin to the "gossip girl," a feature that is shared with certain other Tibetan accounts of social ills. For instance, the condemnations of tobacco use that were widely circulated after the mid-nineteenth century attribute the origins of the tobacco plant to a cursed daughter of Chinese demons. The attribution of gossiping, smoking, and other negatively valued behavior to China reflects, to some extent, the degree to which the Tibetans felt themselves to be threatened by the powerful neighbor that often sought to dominate Tibetan affairs. After gossip spread to Tibet, the text goes on to say, its pernicious influence affected even the animal world: by praising and thus calling attention to the positive attributes of various species (the lion's mane, the vulture's quills, etc.), just as human gossip often focuses on achievements that arouse some element of envy ("how did *she* get so popular?"), the gossip girl ultimately destroys all those she commends.

The text begins with the mantra of Guru Padmasambhava and here serves to invoke his presence in connection with the performance of this ritual, and also to authenticate the ritual as an aspect of his teaching. The formula *Hūṃ hūṃ! Bhyo bhyo!* in the second line is specifically connected with exorcistic ritual and is used to dispel evil or polluting influences from the surroundings. Because gossip may attach to any of our possessions, the ritual goes through the main features of the household, expelling gossip from each in turn. Indeed, the entire historical fate of Tibet is related here to gossip's influence. Its final expulsion, however, falters on an apparent paradox: how can one get rid of something disembodied, and hence, presumably, ubiquitous? Padmasambhava, the master exorcist, resolves this difficulty by providing the gossip girl with an effigy and commanding her to identify herself with it. In village ritual performance, the effigy is actually to be removed from the village and destroyed at a safe distance, the spiritual equivalent, perhaps, of the removal of the dangerously polluted waste we at present find so difficult to discard.

The version of the ritual given here, called *Turning Back Malicious Gossip*, was collected by Nancy E. Levine of the University of California, Los Angeles, and Tshewang Lama of Khor Gompa in Humla District, northwestern Nepal, during the course of anthropological fieldwork in ethnically Tibetan communities of Humla. The manuscript is often very irregular in spelling and grammar, so that its interpretation is sometimes uncertain. In editing this translation for the present publication, I have aimed to facilitate the reader's understanding and so have avoided lengthy discussion of many of the difficulties that would be of interest to specialists alone. Explanatory notes are provided in the body of the translation in square brackets.

Further Reading

For a detailed study of the Nyinba community of Humla, readers are referred to Nancy E. Levine's study, *The Dynamics of Polyandry: Kinship, Domesticity and Population on the Tibetan Border* (Chicago: University of Chicago Press, 1988). For a useful overview of Tibetan folk religious practices, see Giuseppe Tucci, *The Religions of Tibet*, translated by Geoffrey Samuel (Berkeley: University of California Press, 1980), pp. 163–212.

HERE IS CONTAINED *THE TURNING BACK OF MALICIOUS GOSSIP* COMPOSED BY MASTER PADMASAMBHAVA.

Oṃ āḥ hūṃ badzra guru padma siddhi hūṃ!
Hūṃ hūṃ! Bhyo bhyo! Turn back! Turn back!
Carnivorous daughter of malicious gossip!
Blood-drinking daughter of malicious gossip!
Red-mouthed daughter of malicious gossip!
Red-eyed daughter of malicious gossip!
Red-nosed daughter of malicious gossip!
You know all the news like a jack of all trades.
You do all sorts of things that ought not to be done.
You make the healthy sick in all sorts of ways.
You cause everything unspeakable to be said.
Daughter of malicious gossip, listen to me!

Girl with black, grimy, tangled hair,
When you first arrived, where did you come from?
You came from the borders of Tibet and China,

Where malicious gossip afflicted the Chinese,
So that the Chinese king sent you to Tibet.
Many Chinese demons then afflicted our tribes.
In the country called Yarlung [south of Lhasa, the seat of the ancient Tibetan empire],
Auguring evil, malicious gossip struck;
The horses got all the horse-ailments there are,
The people got all the human-ailments there are,
And the boys and girls were gradually made sick.
That was retribution for their meeting with you, malicious gossip!
May they now run to my enemy,
O evil-auguring, malicious gossip,
And overturn your scandalous accusations!

Malicious gossip, on the path on which you approached,
You met with the [snow] lion of the upper glaciers,
To whom, malicious gossip, you said,
"For the happiness of the lioness and her cubs,
The turquoise mane suffices, just to roam in the upper glaciers!"
[The so-called "snow lion", an auspicious national symbol of Tibet, is always depicted in Tibetan art with a bright blue-green mane.]
Three days passed after that,
And the lioness and her cubs were buried in an avalanche.
That was retribution for their meeting with you, malicious gossip!
May they run now to my enemy,
O evil-auguring, malicious gossip,
And overturn your scandalous accusations!

Malicious gossip! on the path on which you approached,
You met with the deer of the upper meadows,
To whom, malicious gossip, you said,
"For the happiness of the doe and her fawns,
The pointed horn suffices, just to roam in the upper meadows."
Three days passed after that,
And the doe and her fawns were slain by a predator.
That, too, was retribution for their meeting with you, malicious gossip!
May they run now to my enemy,
O evil-auguring, malicious gossip,
And overturn your scandalous accusations!

Malicious gossip! on the path on which you approached,
You met with the vulture of the upper cliffs,
To whom, malicious gossip, you said,
"For the happiness of the white-tailed vulture,

Sharp feathers suffice, just to roam about the upper cliffs."
Three days passed after that,
And the white-tailed vulture fell into an abyss!
That, too, was retribution for his meeting with you, malicious gossip!
May he run now to my enemy,
O evil-auguring, malicious gossip,
And overturn your scandalous accusations!

Malicious gossip! on the path on which you approached,
You met with the willow-grove's quail,
To whom, malicious gossip, you said,
"For the happiness of the quail and her chicks,
A sweet voice suffices, just to circle amongst the willows."
Three days passed after that,
And the pale, speckled quail were slain by a Hor-pa tribesman [from the north of Tibet].
That, too, was retribution for their meeting with you, malicious gossip!
May they run now to my enemy,
O evil-auguring, malicious gossip,
And overturn your scandalous accusations!

Malicious gossip! on the path on which you approached,
You met with the fish of the upper lake,
To whom, O daughter of malicious gossip, you said,
"For the happiness of the fish and her spawn,
A bright eye suffices, just to swim in the confines of the lake."
Three days passed after that,
And an outcaste hooked the fish.
That, too, was retribution for their meeting with you, malicious gossip!
May they run now to my enemy,
O evil-auguring, malicious gossip,
And overturn your scandalous accusations!

That describes how malicious gossip behaves;
Now, this is how malicious gossip emanates:
Sometimes she dwells on a mountain-top.
"I am Mount Meru," she says.
Sometimes she dwells on the ocean's shore.
"I am the lake's medicine queen," she says.
Sometimes she dwells in the midst of the sky.
"I am the eightfold group of gods and demons," she says.
[Tibetan deities and demons are often listed in groups of eight; in this context, the expression implies "all the worldly gods and demons."]

Sometimes she dwells beneath the red rock.
"I am the *tsen* [*btsan*, malevolent local spirit] who lives beneath the red rock," she says.

Sometimes she dwells at the top of the mansion.
"I am the superior paternal deity!" she says.
Sometimes she dwells in the home's inner recesses.
[In Tibetan belief the house is a sacred realm,
the abode of ancestral and protective divinities.]
"I am the god of the treasury!" she says.
Three brother-gods of the treasury, arise!
May you run now to my enemy,
Evil-auguring, malicious gossip,
And overturn her scandalous accusations!

Sometimes she dwells by the hearth.
"I am the god of the hearth!" she says.
Three brother-gods of the hearth, arise!
May you run now to my enemy,
Evil-auguring, malicious gossip,
And overturn her scandalous accusations!

Sometimes she dwells at the head of the stairs
"I am the stair-god!" she says.
God of the stair, great rafter, arise!
May you run now to my enemy,
Evil-auguring, malicious gossip,
And overturn her scandalous accusations!

Sometimes she dwells in the interior court.
"I am the god of the courtyard!" she says.
Three brother-gods of the interior, arise!
May you run now to my enemy,
Evil-auguring, malicious gossip,
And overturn her scandalous accusations!

Sometimes she dwells behind the door.
"I am the god of the portal!" she says.
Four Great Kings, please arise!
[These four kings of Indian Buddhist mythology rule the four cardinal directions and are regarded in Tibet as the guardians of doorways.]
May you run now to my enemy,
Evil-auguring, malicious gossip,
And overturn her scandalous accusations!

Now concerning malicious gossip's past emanations [earlier in Tibetan history]:
At first, in glorious Samye,
In the king's fortress, the uppermost shrine,
The king, Tri Songdetsen (Khri srong lde btsan),
Was afflicted with the malicious gossip of all the black-headed Tibetans.
The prince, Mutri Tsenpo (Mu khri Btsan po),
Was afflicted with the malicious gossip of all the youths.
The master Padmasambhava
Was afflicted with the malicious gossip of all the gods and demons.
The preceptor Bodhisattva [i.e., Śāntarakṣita]
Was afflicted with the malicious gossip of all the monks.
The great translator Vairocana
Was afflicted with the malicious gossip of all the translators.
The monk Namkhai Nyingpo (Nam mkha'i snying po)
Was afflicted with the malicious gossip of the whole religious community.
Nanam Dorje Düjom (Sna nam Rdo rje bdud 'joms)
Was afflicted with the malicious gossip of all the masters of mantras.
The royal queen Margyen (Dmar brgyan)
Was afflicted with the malicious gossip of all the women.
The wealthy patrons
Were afflicted with the malicious gossip of the whole populace.
All gods and men subject to Tibet
Were afflicted with the malicious gossip of all nations,
With the malicious gossip of corporeal men,
With the malicious gossip of incorporeal gods and demons,
With the malicious gossip of whatever exists,
With the malicious gossip of whatever doesn't exist.

Daughter of malicious gossip, listen here!
First you became nine demon-sisters in China.
[Nine is a prominent magical number in indigenous Tibetan cosmology and is here associated with malignant powers or practices.]
Second you became the nine demonesses.
At last you became the nine gossip sisters.
But whatever you become, now you are turned back!
You have no place at all to stay here.
Malicious gossip, do not stay! Malicious gossip, go away!

Go away to the east, malicious gossip, where your path is revealed!
As soon as you go there from here,
There is a plain gathering beings from all about.
It is the maṇḍala of three plains gathered together.

It is the assembly of a million *the'u rang* spirits.
[The *the'u rang* are minor harmful spirits,
associated primarily with disease and misfortune during childhood.]
Do not stay there! Go even farther away!

As soon as you go farther that way,
There is a mountain gathering beings from all about.
It is the maṇḍala of three mountains gathered together.
It is the assembly of the male and female vampire spirits.
Do not stay there! Go even farther away!

As soon as you go farther that way,
There is a river gatherings beings from all about.
It is the maṇḍala of three rivers gathered together.
It is the assembly of the male and female water-spirits.
Do not stay there! Go farther away upland!

As one goes upland from there,
In the place called Kongyül to the east [an "upside down land" thought to be a center of sorcery],
Malicious gossip appears as a god.
Malicious gossip appears as a nāga.
So that which augurs ill here is trapped for good luck there.
Malicious gossip, you have no place to dwell here.
Malicious gossip, do not stay! Malicious gossip go away!
Go where you appear as a god.
Go where you appear as a nāga.
Go where you will be trapped for good luck!
Malicious gossip, do not stay! Malicious gossip, go away!

The daughter of malicious gossip said,
"Great Master, listen to me!
Padmasambhava, listen to me!
For me to go and not to stay here,
I, malicious gossip, need a body in order to go!"

To this the great master said:
"Daughter of malicious gossip! listen up!
If you, malicious gossip, have no body in order to go,
Let this hollow straw be malicious gossip's body.
Malicious gossip, associate yourself with this body and go away!
If malicious gossip's body needs a head,
Let this red clay pot be malicious gossip's head!
Malicious gossip, associate yourself with this head and go away!
If malicious gossip's head has no brain,
Let this watery mash be malicious gossip's brain!

Malicious gossip, associate yourself with this brain and go away!
If malicious gossip's head has no hair,
Let this black pig-hair brush be malicious gossip's hair!
Malicious gossip, associate yourself with this hair and go away!
If malicious gossip has no ears with which to hear,
Let these radish and turnip slices be malicious gossip's ears!
Malicious gossip, associate yourself with these ears and go away!
If malicious gossip has no eyes with which to see,
Let these little black peas be malicious gossip's eyes!
Malicious gossip, associate yourself with these eyes and go away!
If malicious gossip has no nose with which to smell,
Let this red pot-handle be malicious gossip's nose!
Malicious gossip, associate yourself with this nose and go away!
If malicious gossip has no blabbering mouth,
Let this hot red pepper be malicious gossip's mouth!
Malicious gossip, associate yourself with this mouth and go away!
If malicious gossip has no teeth with which to chew,
Let these hollow cowrie shells be malicious gossip's teeth!
Malicious gossip, associate yourself with these teeth and go away!
If malicious gossip has no tongue with which to speak,
Let a small red smear be malicious gossip's tongue!
Malicious gossip, associate yourself with this tongue and go away!
If malicious gossip has no heart with which to think,
Let this triangular buckwheat grain be malicious gossip's heart!
Malicious gossip, associate yourself with this heart and go away!
If malicious gossip has no hand to stretch out,
Let this ginseng root be malicious gossip's hand!
Malicious gossip, associate yourself with this hand and go away!
If malicious gossip has no clothes to wear,
Let these black shreds of cloth be malicious gossip's clothes!
Malicious gossip, associate yourself with these clothes and go away!
If malicious gossip has no belt with which to bind,
Let this twined mule-tether be malicious gossip's belt!
Malicious gossip, associate yourself with this belt and go away!
If malicious gossip has no feet to stand on,
Let these goat-bones and sheep-bones be malicious gossip's feet!
Malicious gossip, associate yourself with these feet and go away!
If malicious gossip has no boots to wear,
Let these cloven hoofs be malicious gossip's boots!
Malicious gossip, associate yourself with these boots and go away!
If malicious gossip has no hat for the head,
Let these tatters and shreds be malicious gossip's hat.
Malicious gossip, associate yourself with this hat and go away!
If malicious gossip has no horse to ride,

Let this black and white rodent be malicious gossip's horse!
Malicious gossip, associate yourself with this horse and go away!
If malicious gossip has no knife to carry,
Let this tempered iron blade be malicious gossip's knife!
Let this red copper blade be malicious gossip's knife!
Let this dull wooden blade be malicious gossip's knife!
Malicious gossip, associate yourself with this knife and go away!
If malicious gossip has no arrow and bow,
Let this briarwood arrow and bow be malicious gossip's bow and arrow!
Let this bamboo arrow and bow be malicious gossip's bow and arrow!
Malicious gossip, associate yourself with this arrow and bow and go away!
If malicious gossip has no food to eat,
Let these raw vegetables be malicious gossip's food!
Let these garlic-bulbs, onions and turnips be malicious gossip's food!
Let these radish slices and turnip slices be malicious gossip's food!
Let these left-over meat-bones be malicious gossip's food!
Let these leftover grains from the ale-mash be malicious gossip's food!
Let these discarded tea-leaves be malicious gossip's food!
Let this salt, soda, and butter be malicious gossip's food!
Let the leftover food and drink be malicious gossip's food!
Let the dregs of what has been drunk be malicious gossip's food!
Malicious gossip, associate yourself with this food and go away!
If malicious gossip has no wealth to hoard,
Let broken goods and cracked wooden bowls be malicious gossip's wealth!
Let scraps of gold, silver, copper, and iron be malicious gossip's wealth!
Let clippings of silk and clippings of cloth be malicious gossip's wealth!
Let all sorts of grains be malicious gossip's wealth!
Let white and red woolen yarns be malicious gossip's wealth!
Malicious gossip, associate yourself with this wealth and go away!
If malicious gossip has no palace to stay,
Let this gnarled yak-horn be malicious gossip's palace!
Let thread-crosses (*nam mkha'*) and spirit-traps (*rgyang bu*) be malicious gossip's palace!
Malicious gossip, associate yourself with this palace and go away!
If malicious gossip has no paths on which to depart,
Let the path of dung, the path of *chang* be malicious gossip's path!
Let the way of ashes that have vanished be malicious gossip's path!
Let the twisted path of demons be malicious gossip's path!
Let the black demoness reveal malicious gossip's path!
Malicious gossip, associate yourself with this path and go away!

Go away having taken the ritual substitutes and talismans,
[which are offered to the evil being that is exorcized
as symbolic substitutes for the victims of gossip],
Representing the patron along with his household, wealth, and servants.
Daughter of malicious gossip, do not stay! go away!
Carry off the bodily ailments of these patrons
From the roofs of their mansions and down to the plain below,
For the 360 days there are in the twelve months of a [lunar] year.
Carry off their mental distress!
Carry the scandal from their mouths!
Carry off evil-conditions and accidents!
Carry off the lord's Gongpo spirits! [Gongpo (*'gong po*) spirits are thought to afflict adult men and are associated with arrogance and hubris.]
Carry off the curse-bearing talismans!
Carry off the malicious gossip from the four continents!
Malicious gossip, do not stay! malicious gossip, go away!"

Do not stick around the walls of our mansion!
Do not stick around the people above [who live in upper story]!
Do not stick around the cattle below [who live in the lower story]!
Do not stick around our watchdog!
Do not stick around the men of the house!
Do not stick around the household's women!
Do not stick around our little children!
Do not stick around the fields that we sow!
Do not stick around our dairy's yogurt!
Do not stick around our fermented chang!
Do not stick around our gold and silver!
Malicious gossip, do not stay! malicious gossip, go away!

—37—

A Prayer Flag for Tārā

Donald S. Lopez, Jr.

Prayer flags are a ubiquitous feature of the Tibetan landscape, designed to promote good fortune and dispel danger. They are colored squares of cloth, usually about a foot square, imprinted with a prayer or mantra. These flags are then attached to poles or to the rooftops of temples and dwellings, or are strung from the cairns found at the summits of mountain passes. The wind is said to carry the benefits beseeched by the prayer imprinted on the fluttering flag, both to the person who flies the flag and to all beings in the region.

The prayer translated below was printed on a yellow piece of cotton cloth, 11 by 14 inches in size. The prayer on the flag is one of the most widely recited in Tibetan Buddhism, the prayer to the twenty-one Tārās.

Tārā was born from a lotus blossom that sprang from a tear shed by Avalokiteśvara, the bodhisattva of compassion, as he surveyed the suffering universe. She is thus said to be the physical manifestation of the compassion of Avalokiteśvara, himself said to be the quintessence of all the compassion of all the buddhas. Because buddhas are produced from wisdom and compassion, Tārā, like the goddess Prajñāpāramitā ("Perfection of Wisdom"), is hailed as "the mother of all buddhas" despite the fact that she is most commonly represented as a beautiful sixteen-year-old maiden.

She is often depicted as one of two female bodhisattvas flanking Avalokiteśvara: Tārā, the personification of his compassion, and Bhṛkutī, the personification of his wisdom. But Tārā is the subject of much devotion in her own right, serving as the subject of many stories, prayers, and tantric sādhanas. Like Avalokiteśvara, she has played a crucial role in Tibet's history, in both divine and human forms. She was the protective deity of Atiśa, appearing to him at crucial points in his life, advising him to make his fateful journey to Tibet, despite the fact that his lifespan would be shortened as a result. She took human form as the Chinese princess who married King Songtsen Gampo, bringing with her the buddha image that would become the most revered in Tibet. In the next generation, she appeared as the wife of King Tri Songdetsen and consort of Padmasambhava, Yeshe Tsogyal

(Ye she mtsho rgyal), who, in addition to becoming a great tantric master herself, served as scribe as Padmasambhava dictated the treasure texts (*gter ma*). Later Tārā is said to have appeared as the great practitioner of the *chö* (*gcod*) tradition, Majik Lapdön (Ma gcig lap sgron, 1062–1149). Indeed, Tārā has promised aeons ago, when she first vowed to achieve buddhahood in order to free all beings from saṃsāra, always to appear in the female form.

She has many iconographic forms, the most common being as Green Tārā and as White Tārā, propitiated especially to bestow long life. She has numerous wrathful forms; especially famous is Kurukullā, a dancing naked yoginī, red in color, brandishing bow and arrow in her four arms. In tantric maṇḍalas, she appears as the consort of Amoghasiddhi, the buddha of the northern quarter; together they are lord and lady of the action (*karma*) lineage. But she is herself also the sole deity in many tantric sādhanas (see chapter 27 in *Buddhism in Practice*), in which the meditator, whether male or female, visualizes himself or herself in Tārā's feminine form.

But Tārā is best known for her salvific powers, appearing in the instant her devotee recites her mantra, *oṃ tāre tuttāre ture svāhā*. She is especially renowned for her ability to deliver those who call upon her from eight fears: lions, elephants, fire, snakes, bandits, prison, water, and demons, and many tales are told recounting her miraculous interventions. She can appear in peaceful or wrathful forms, depending on the circumstances, her powers extending beyond the subjugation of these worldly frights, into the heavens and into the hells.

Apart from the recitation of her mantra, the prayer below is the most common medium of invoking Tārā in Tibet. It is a prayer to twenty-one Tārās, derived from an Indian tantra devoted to Tārā, the *Source of All Rites to Tārā, the Mother of All Tathāgatas* (*Sarvatathāgatamatṛtāra-viśvakarmabhavatantra*). According to some traditions of commentary on the prayer, each verse refers to a different form of Tārā, totaling twenty-one. According to others, the forms of Tārā are iconographically almost indistinguishable. The famous Tārā chapel at Atiśa's temple at Nyethang (Snye thang) contains nearly identical statues of the twenty-one Tārās. (For a beautiful eleventh-century stele depicting the twenty-one Tārās, see Rhie and Thurman, p. 124.) The prayer is known by heart throughout the Tibetan cultural region, recited especially by travelers to protect them in their long journeys on foot and horseback across mountains and plains. The final stanzas of the prayer (generally not recited by Tibetans) promise that one who recites the prayer with faith in Tārā will be free from fear, the sins that cause rebirth as animal, ghost, or hell being destroyed. The person who calls the prayer to mind will be immune to all poisons and fevers. If one wants a child one will have one; indeed, all desires will be granted, no hindrances will stand in the way, and buddhahood will be achieved.

The prayer is filled with allusions to the Indian cosmology and pantheon, demonstrating that Tārā's powers extend throughout the universe, from the heavens to the underworld, that she has dominion over all worldly gods and demons. There is insufficient space to identify all the allusions here; they are treated in some detail in Wilson (1986). Indeed, it might be argued that it is superfluous even to translate the words on a prayer flag. Those who raise them often cannot read them, the very shapes of the letters bearing sufficient symbolic power.

The prayer flag has in its center an image of Tārā approximately two inches square, set within a single-line frame. The prayer itself appears on the flag as if on a sheet of paper, with lines breaking in the middle of the flag to accommodate the picture of the goddess. Like all prayer flags, this one was made from a wooden blockprint, in which a craftsman would have carved the prayers and the picture of Tārā, in relief and backward, after which the block would have been inked and the piece of cloth laid across it. A roller would have then been applied to transfer the words and picture onto the cloth. As with other prayer flags, the names of four protective animals of the four directions appear in the corners of the flag: in the upper right-hand corner "lion," in the upper left-hand corner "tiger," in the lower left-hand corner "*khyung*" (the mythical Tibetan eagle), and in the lower right-hand corner "dragon." As with many prayer flags, after the prayer, there is a brief statement of the benefits that will accrue from its flying. In this case, it gives a hint as to the purpose for which this flag was made: "May the lifespan, merit, power, energy, glory, and fame of the person born in ____ year increase!" The person who flies the flag is to write in the name of the year in which he or she was born.

The translation is from a prayer flag acquired by the translator at Tashilhunpo (Bkra shis lhun po) monastery in Tibet in 1985.

Further Reading

On Tārā, see Stephan Beyer, *The Cult of Tārā* (Berkeley: University of California Press, 1973), and Martin Wilson, *In Praise of Tārā: Songs to the Saviouress* (London: Wisdom Publications, 1986). The latter contains an extensive commentary on the prayer. For several color plates depicting various form of Tārā, see Marilyn Rhie and Robert A. F. Thurman, eds., *Wisdom and Compassion: The Sacred Art of Tibet* (New York: Harry N. Abrams, 1991).

Namo Ārya Tāraye
Homage to the Treasury of Compassion, the Noble Avalokiteśvara
Oṃ. Homage to the Exalted Noble Tārā

Homage. Tārā, swift heroine, her eyes like a flash of lightening. Born from the blossoming from the tear on the Protector of the Three Worlds' face. (1)

Homage. Her face a hundred full autumn moons amassed, blazing with the light of a thousand gathered stars. (2)

Homage. Her hand adorned with a water-born lotus, blue and gold. Her sphere is giving, effort, austerity, peace, patience, and concentration. (3)

Homage. Crown of the Tathāgata, her deeds conquer without end, much accompanied by the children of the Conqueror who have attained perfection. (4)

Homage. She fills desire, direction, and space with the letters *tuttāra hūṃ*, pressing down the seven worlds with her feet, able to summon all [beings]. (5)

Homage. She is worshipped by various lords: Indra, Agni, Brahmā, Marut; she is praised by hosts of ghosts, risen corpses, gandharvas, and yakṣas. (6)

Homage. With *traṭ* and *phaṭ* she destroys the strategems of opponents, pressing down with her right foot drawn in and her left foot stretched out, blazing with raging fire. (7)

Homage. *Ture* most horrific, she destroys Māra's hero, with the frown of her lotus face she slays all foes. (8)

Homage. She is adorned at her heart with her fingers in the mudrā symbolizing the three jewels, adorned with wheels of all directions, raging with her gathered light. (9)

Homage. She is joyous, her shining crown emits garlands of light, laughing the laugh of *tuttāra,* she subdues Māra and the world. (10)

Homage. She is able to summon all the hosts of guardians of the earth; with the letter *hūṃ,* frowning, trembling, she frees the destitute. (11)

Homage. Crowned with a crescent moon, all ornaments blazing; from Amitābha in her piled tresses, light is always created. (12)

Homage. Standing amid a blazing circle, like the aeon-ending fire; surrounded by joy, right leg stretched out, left drawn in, destroying the enemy troops. (13)

Homage. She strikes the surface of the earth with the palm of her hand and beats it with her foot; frowning, with the letter *hūṃ*, she subdues the seven underworlds. (14)

Homage. Blissful, virtuous, peaceful, her sphere is the peace of nirvāṇa; perfectly endowed with *svāhā* and *oṃ*, she destroys all sin. (15)

Homage. Surrounded by joy, she vanquishes the body of the enemy; she liberates with the knowledge [mantra] *hūṃ*, arrayed with the ten-syllabled speech [of her mantra]. (16)

Homage. *Ture*, by stamping her foot, her seed is the letter *hūṃ*'s form; trembler of Meru, Mandara, Vindhya, and the three worlds. (17)

Homage. Holding in her hand the deer marked [moon] in the form of the lake of the gods; by saying *tārā* twice with the syllable *phaṭ*, she dispels all poison. (18)

Homage. She is attended by the king of the hosts of gods, by gods and kinnaras; her joyous splendor dispels the disputes and nightmare of armored ones. (19)

Homage. Her two eyes shine with light of the sun and full moon. By saying *hara* twice with *tuttāre,* she dispels the most terrible fever. (20)

Homage. Endowed with pacifying power arrayed with the three realities, she is the supreme *Ture*, destroyer of the hosts of demons, risen corpses, and yakṣas. (21)

This praise of the root mantra and the twenty-one homages.

Oṃ tāre tuttāre ture svāhā. May the lifespan, merit, power, energy, glory, and fame of the person born in ____ year increase!

Religions of Japan in Practice

INTRODUCTION

Japan

George J. Tanabe, Jr.

Ninomiya Sontoku (1787–1856), affectionately called the Peasant Sage of Japan, likened his teaching to a pill consisting of "one spoon of Shintō, and a half-spoon each of Confucianism and Buddhism." When someone drew a circle, marking one half of it Shintō and the remaining two-quarters Confucianism and Buddhism, Ninomiya rejected this schematic diagram of his teaching and said, "You won't find medicine like that anywhere. In a real pill all the ingredients are thoroughly blended so as to be indistinguishable. Otherwise it would taste bad in the mouth and feel bad in the stomach."[1] Like Ninomiya, some scholars find the usual scheme of dividing Japanese religions into Shintō, Buddhist, Confucian, and other segments bad tasting for not being an accurate reflection of religious realities in Japan, and have pointed out the ways in which the different parts blend into each other.[2] This syncretic view is particularly valuable in the attempt to understand the practice of Japanese religions in their complex interrelationships rather than as neatly ordered, discrete systems of thought. For many Japanese there is little, if any, difference to be experienced in praying to a Shintō god (*kami*) or to a Buddhist deity.

This appreciation of the interwoven character of Japanese religions is also a reflection of recent methodological approaches that call into question essentialist readings of texts and highlight the manner in which their meanings are not only influenced by how they are placed in context but also by how researchers, according to their predilections, read them. Our knowledge has been enriched by recent studies that look into these complex relationships and offer insights about the invention of traditions, the history of changing interpretations, the uses of religious ideas and practices to legitimate power, and the impact of ideology on scholarship itself.[3]

This introduction was inspired and produced with an awareness of the inadequacies of the old categories of chronology (Nara, Heian, Kamakura, etc.), religious traditions (Shintō, Buddhism, Confucianism, etc.), and sects (Tendai, Shingon, Zen, etc.) as organizing principles for a reader about Japanese religions. Yet a solution is not to be found in the destabilization of an old order faulted for its assumption that distinctions exist in time, traditions, and sects. Neither is a solution to be found by making light of written texts, all of which are fixed in specific historical contexts, often with clearly discernible sectarian identities or agendas. While it is true that texts are malleable and can be elusive in meaning, they still bend only within a certain range, the boundaries of which define an integrity that can be discerned. Time periods and religious traditions are significant; unlike Ninomiya's pill, which would blend religions so perfectly as to be indistinguishable, texts, in the broadest sense of the term, can be discerned clearly in their historical contexts and with their sectarian identities, even when, for example, Shintō and Buddhist practices are combined together.

Taken as a whole, religious practices can be thought of as the holdings within a vast storehouse of diverse traditions, dozens of sects, large and small institutions, and a host of creative individuals. There is much more in the storehouse than can ever be treated in a single book. Only a portion of this storehouse can be aired, and some practices will lie forever in dusty storage bins. Etymologically related, the words practice and practicality overlap in meaning, but practicality, in the sense of usefulness, allows us to select those practices that are significant for their utilitarian value. Not all practices are useful, not all are practical, but all of the practices contained in the storeroom of this essay have been selected for the practical value they have in helping people make moral decisions, deal with death, realize meanings, ask for divine blessings, and give life to institutions.

In choosing to emphasize practice and practicality, I do not assume that they are always antagonistic to or can be freed from abstract theory. While theory can be distinguished from practice and sometimes has nothing to do with it, a strict dichotomy between the two is mostly false. Thinking, after all, is a practical activity, and, as the Buddhist cleric Eison (1201–1290) notes, scholarship and study are forms of practice for rectifying the mind and prescribing behavior. What I hope to gain in this focus on practice is not liberation from theory but a greater understanding of the different ways in which theory and practice work on each other toward practical ends. I wish to call attention to interrelationships: as the meaning of a text can be shaped by readers, so too can readers be shaped by texts, or at least that is the hope of writers.

The mutual relationship between writers and readers, texts and contexts, and theory and practice can be described as an association between hard rocks and shifting tides. The rocks—writers, texts, and theory—are fairly fixed as definite persons, set documents, and (for the most part) clear ideas. The shifting tides—the flow of different readers, changing contexts, and diverse practices—wash over the rocks and even change their shape, though they remain recognizable for a long time. This interaction of rocks and tides takes place in discernible patterns that are not entirely chaotic because the rocks are fixed points, and even the tides have rhythms of ebb and flow. The unique circumstances of each writer and reader, text and context, and theory and practice are important to this discernment within a structure of thematic patterns.

In organizing this essay under the categories of Ethical Practices, Ritual Practices, and Institutional Practices, I propose a typology that approximates as best we can the actual orientation of real people who engage in religious practices without giving much thought to whether or not they are Shintoists or Buddhists or Confucians, and certainly without having much of an awareness of their being of the Nara or Heian or Kamakura periods. It does not matter to the pilgrims visiting Kannon that they recite the "wrong" chant, the *nembutsu,* which is dedicated to Amida rather than Kannon, or that non-Shingon members go on a pilgrimage to worship Kōbō Daishi, the founder of Shingon. While some texts express an uncompromising sectarianism, others speak of a willingness and desirability to cross sectarian and religious boundaries, and the categories I have chosen fortunately allow for both exclusive and inclusive viewpoints to be expressed with a coherence that would be difficult to maintain in a structure organized according to religious or sectarian traditions.

Ethical Practices

The theme of ethical practices is very broad, covering matters ranging from individual behavior to national values. By further dividing this broad theme into subsections on social values, clerical precepts, and lay precepts, we see the levels at which formal rules and informal advice define preferred or mandatory action for different groups and communities. At the broadest level, ethical advice is given to society as a whole with the expectation that such values apply to all, or at least to all lay citizens. Being mostly without a professional clergy in Japan, Confucian writers did not have to concern themselves with defining clerical as opposed to lay behavior, and therefore could address social values as a whole. This is not to say that the other religions had little to contribute to the discussion, and indeed there are texts such as the *Selected Anecdotes to Illustrate Ten Maxims* (Jikkinshō), which mixes Confucian, Shintō, Buddhist, and even Daoist elements to retell and create short anecdotes illustrating maxims to aid in the formation of moral character in young people. An easy connection is made between the Buddhist idea of karma, in which one reaps what one sows, and Confucian imperatives for right action, such as being filial to parents and showing mercy to people. One of the highest values promoted in these stories is the display of good literary skills, and here too there is no clash between Buddhism and Confucianism. While Confucianism clearly lends itself more readily to maxims of good social behavior, it is interesting to note how Buddhism is presented less as a means towards enlightenment and more as a moral teaching. The moral quality of Buddhism is encountered in many Buddhist writings, which allow us to see how in practical terms Buddhism was widely used for its ethical teachings on how to live in the world and not just for taking leave from it.

In Kaibara Ekken (1630–1714) there is a more exclusively Confucian teaching on family values based on self-discipline, etiquette, mutual respect, "hidden virtue" (whereby acts of kindness need not be publicly recognized), and, most importantly, the joy of doing good. While Ekken's concern is clearly on the individual and family level rather than the political or ideological plane, his moral advice is given with a cosmic framework in which all things and beings of the universe are animated with a life force (*ch'i*) and therefore deserve respectful treatment. In speaking explicitly of the natural world and the moral responsibility to take life from it only as needed, Ekken developed an ecological ethic that demands individual care of the world. Each person is thus woven into the moral fabric that binds the individual with family, society, and the natural world.

Like the anecdotes about the maxims of good behavior, the Shingaku ("learning of the mind") teaching as interpreted by Nakazawa Dōni (1725–1803) is comfortably liberal in its conviction that no single tradition has a monopoly on truth. Since the true mind is universal, Confucianism, Shintō, and Buddhism all have wise teachings that uphold, among other things, the importance of a naturalness that does not interfere with nature. Buddhism, it has already been noted, embraces the world as much as it rejects it, and here we see how Confucianism has its own inward gaze on the true mind and naturalness. What this suggests is that both Buddhism and Confucianism have social and private orientations, and that it is misleading to characterize each just in terms of the individual or society.

So much of what has been written about Buddhism emphasizes the inward search for true self, the realization of emptiness, the attainment of ultimate enlightenment, and the outward journey to metaphysical heavens and hells beyond this life. It is true that Buddhism has a great obsession with such extra-social and metaphysical matters, but it is equally true that the teachings of karma and causality have very real lessons and consequences for ordinary people in all phases of their lives. Indeed, Buddhism should be understood for its strict sense of personal and social responsibility, as well as for its otherworldly interests.

The Buddhist insistence on personal accountability is unrelenting: no one but the individual is to be blamed for anything that goes wrong or is to be credited for what goes right. With good deeds and fortunate happenings, the buddhas and bodhisattvas may also share the credit, but the individual is seldom removed as a responsible agent for everything and anything that takes place. The heavy moral burden for all things that go wrong easily produces guilt and a deep sense of sin, and it is therefore not surprising that so many Buddhist rituals are designed for *metsuzai,* breaking the bonds and canceling the effects of bad karma. The moral burden is not limited to the happenings of this life alone, but is comprised of the cumulative total of karmic consequences of all previous lives. Illness, for example, can be attributed not only to any number of misdeeds in one's lifetime but to some moral failure from a past life now forgotten. Understood as the condemnation by others, shame is a powerful dynamic in Japanese society, but so is guilt, which is self-condemnation. The Buddhist teaching of karma is not as concerned about the shame resulting from what others think of us as it is about our own awareness of our failures and successes. There is no will of God or Providence to blame for what happens; the Buddhist finger can only be pointed at oneself.

The heaviest moral burden is borne by the Buddhist clergy, who dedicate themselves to nothing less than moral and spiritual perfection, and whose conduct must therefore be rigidly and specifically regimented. The clerical precepts define a monastic life of constant effort to combat the natural temptations that tarnish and even destroy the moral purity required for spiritual progress. Dedication to perfection requires total commitment, and seclusion from society and all of its temptations greatly enhances the possibility of achieving the goal. But even those who succeeded in living a pure life could not keep the world from barging into the quiet of their existences, and a serious practitioner, for instance, such as Myōe (1173–1232), known as the Pure Monk, constantly found himself embroiled in the affairs of his relatives and warring soldiers. The world is inescapable, even for those who escape from it, but if the persistence of its troubling presence was lamented as an obstacle to the pure life, the opposite was also held to be true: the virtues of a pure life can be cast onto the troubled world to pacify it. Just as Ekken saw the relationship between individual morality and the welfare of society and the natural world, and just as Nakazawa Dōni called for a balance between the inward cultivation of the pure mind and its outward manifestation in society, so too did the Zen master Eisai (1141–1215) explain the inescapable connection between a monk's moral purity and the condition of the world. It is the monk, but only the monk whose moral and spiritual attainments provide him with access to the truths of Buddhism, who can bring the power of the dharma and the deities to protect the nation. The welfare of society thus being at stake, Eisai argued that the ruler should support Buddhism, in particular Zen Buddhism. For their part in this mutual relationship, monks have a critical role to play in the upholding of society: they must maintain a strict monasticism, for the power of Zen is dependent on the purity of its monks, and any lapse in discipline damages the character of Zen and the health of the nation is put at risk. There is a paradox at work in the assertion that world rejection, which is essential for the monastic pursuit of purity, also protects the world and thereby affirms it. This assertion must be understood within the general framework of a morality that promises definite gains in return for self-denial. Eisai's call for monastic purity was also in response to the deterioration of discipline in the monasteries, a condition that pure monks in every age had occasion to decry.

In the mid-18th century, the Shingon monk Jiun (1718–1804), similarly concerned about the fallen state of clerical discipline, worked diligently to revive the monastic precepts, arguing that to follow those strict rules was to emulate the lifestyle of Śākyamuni himself; failure to do so spelled the death of Buddhism. As a young man, Jiun had received a good Confucian education, which emphasized morality as a matter of inner character, and he accordingly regarded the Buddhist precepts as prescriptions to be internalized into one's mind and body, and not just left as external rules. As a Buddhist monk, Jiun also advocated meditation and sutra study, but far from being merely rules of conduct, the precepts defined for him, no less than meditation and the scriptural teachings, attitudes and actions essential for becoming a buddha. Like Eisai, Jiun was convinced of the mutually beneficial relationship between monastic discipline and society, but his proposal called for taking the precepts out of the monastery and into the streets by placing them squarely on the shoulders of lay persons. Modified to suit the lifestyles of householders, the essence of the clerical precepts was applied to all: do not kill, steal, lie, and so forth. Even in our own time, Buddhist leaders, alarmed by teenage stabbings, school bullying, financial corruption, and all of the other human failings in modern Japanese society, call for the reapplication of the Buddhist rules for moral living.

Jiun was not the first to apply the precepts for the benefit of the world. Aware of the perennial problem of maintaining strict monastic discipline, Eison (1201–1290) vigorously reaffirmed the monastic code, but putting it into practice necessarily meant service to others. Renouncing the world meant working for it, and Eison provided relief for outcastes and prisoners, arranged public works projects like repairing bridges, counseled forbearance and forgiveness, and constantly taught that one must shift one's focus from self-interest to the welfare of others. His disciple Ninshō was even more active in his social work, which was extended to the sick, to orphans, and even to animals.

Though a monk of the Shingon Ritsu (Precepts) school, Eison drew widely from all forms of Buddhist teachings. In a similar fashion, Kokan Shiren (1278–1346), a Rinzai Zen monk, placed Zen within the matrix of other types of Japanese Buddhism. At the same time, Shiren had a very narrow view by which he regarded the bodhisattva Zen precepts to be superior to the Hīnayāna rules. One must, furthermore, believe in the efficacy of ordination, and by extension have faith in the Zen line of masters leading back to Śākyamuni himself. Yet this sectarian view contained a broad understanding that the significance of the precepts exceeds Zen itself since those rules were means for knowing the human heart and what distinguishes human beings from beasts. For those who fail to live up to its demands of being truly human, there is a remedy in the form of repentance. Since the final standard was that of being human, the precepts applied to lay persons as well as to monks and nuns. Breaking the precepts, after all, did not require a prior formal commitment to them, but did demand atonement. Anyone could break the rules, and everyone had recourse through repentance to the expiation of sin and guilt.

For monks and nuns, the moral requirement remained extraordinarily demanding. There were many exemplary monks and nuns who held true to the discipline, but there were also those who broke the rules. The enemy of moral perfection was not just out there in the world beyond the walls of the monastery but dwelt more seriously within the heart, mind, and body. Like Martin Luther, who so desperately felt the hypocrisy of a life governed by external rules that promised to but could not tame unruly passions, Shinran (1173–1262), the founder of the Jōdoshin (True Pure Land) school, declared that his attempt to live the monastic life was but a sham. Suffering from guilt of a failure resulting not from censure of anyone in his monastic community but from his own self-condemnation, he found his salvation in the grace of Amida Buddha rather than in the good works of personal effort. Having made the clerical code his personal standard by which he could judge his failings, he now abandoned it in favor of a new ethic that allowed meat eating and marriage, two of the more important infractions of the monastic rules. Criticized for excessive reliance on divine power at the expense of human action, Shinran defended his insights by insisting that while salvation was not dependent on human effort, morality was. While antinomianism and licentiousness would not make Amida deny salvation to sinners, such behavior was simply not acceptable for the moral life. Salvation and morality worked in different ways.

Other schools of Buddhism did not join in with the Jōdoshin sect in allowing meat eating and marriage, and in the early Edo period (1603–1867), the government enforced this clerical rule by state law. In the Meiji period (1868–1911), however, the government rescinded this law as part of its new emphasis on freedom of religion, and declared that Buddhist clerics were free to eat meat and marry without penalty. They were also free to continue their adherence to the traditional precepts, but, in time and despite some internal protests against liberalization, all of the Buddhist sectarian institutions changed their rules to allow monks—but not nuns—to eat meat and marry, effectively transforming them from monastics into ministers living a householder's life. The relationship between the monastery and the world was thus defined by an interesting, somewhat surprising, range of different proponents: the government removed itself from this aspect of monastic life; individual clergy protested the availability of voluntary laicization and demanded that the government maintain its regulatory intrusion into monastic life; and the sectarian institutions willingly allowed the clergy to embrace the world without breaking the precepts by getting rid of those rules that were offensive. In the context of actual practice, Buddhism in Japan, even as lived by priests, resolutely affirms the world and some of its best pleasures.

Buddhism, Shintō, and Confucianism, despite their many differences, share a common moral vision that takes the world seriously. The forms and specific prescriptions vary, but there is no major disagreement over the value of good human relationships, caring for the natural world, and finding religious meaning in terms of moral behavior. Even withdrawal from society produces benefits for it. This broad understanding of the interrelationship between religion and the world as well as the individual and society can also be seen in ritual practices dedicated to the land, gods, spirits, and self-realization.

Ritual Practices

As diverse as ethical practices, religious rituals cover an immense range of objectives, from benefits in this world to spiritual rewards in the next life. In all cases, however, rituals function generally as the means for establishing a relationship or making contact with normally unseen worlds, powers, gods, and spirits. These unseen worlds can become visible through ritual performance, can be described with a mythic imagination, or can be assumed to exist as places with familiar characteristics long accepted from the past. The objective of making the unseen world seen is an ambitious one, as is the hope of the rituals dedicated to creating the realization that one is a buddha or is already enlightened. The pursuit of this goal, which is also referred to by the term original enlightenment (*hongaku*), is so pervasive that it cuts across many Buddhist sectarian lines and crosses over into areas of Shintō and Shugendō practice as well.

The pursuit of such lofty goals is not likely to turn out successfully for all of those attempting to reach a state of utter perfection. Like the history of moral effort, the record of spiritual endeavor is filled with failure, and some practitioners, after years of effort, lost confidence in the power of certain rituals to produce insight and realization. Some therefore turned to different rituals, often reducing them to radically bare minimums. The founders of the new Buddhisms of the Kamakura period (1185–1333) were famous for their reductionist proposals limiting ritual to single acts: sitting in meditation for Dōgen (1200–1253), reciting the *nembutsu* for Hōnen (1133–1212), and chanting the title of the *Lotus Sutra* for Nichiren (1222–1282). Others, such as Shinran, gave them up altogether, preferring to relegate their salvation to the graces of divine powers instead of taking such weighty matters into their own helpless hands. Shinran's bare minimum, which was also a sufficient maximum, was faith, total trust in nothing other than the power of Amida to accomplish what neither moral acts nor ritual performances could achieve. While faith alone is an attitude or state of mind rather than a performance, it still is a means toward a spiritual goal, and as such can be thought of as a method. Jōdoshin philosophers would deny that faith is a method since they count faith itself as the receivable but unearned gift of Amida, but ordinary believers, feeling the need to be able to do something about their salvation, exert their faith in many ways, including the ritual of reciting the *nembutsu:* "All praise to Amida Buddha."

In stretching the definition of ritual beyond the limits of formal performance, we pass into the broader area of customs and cultural habits, the forms in which so much of Japanese religiosity is clothed. Contemporary surveys show that the vast majority of Japanese still visit family graves, and yet these same respondents at roughly the same percentage levels also say that they are not religious. The explanation of this seeming conundrum lies in the distinction made between formal expressions of religion—creeds, institutional memberships, and explicit beliefs—and cultural habit. Customs such as grave visitations or trips to shrines and temples are seldom placed in the formal and relatively new category of religion (*shūkyō*), the Japanese word for which was invented in the late nineteenth century. Yet customs bear the marks of ritual insofar as they are acts regulated, sometimes rigidly so, by clearly articulated prescriptions aimed at securing secular and spiritual blessings.

This is certainly the case with *Records of the Customs and Land of Izumo* (Izumo fudoki, 733), an early text regarded as one of the scriptures for the Izumo Taisha sect of Shintō. It does not describe a specific ritual but tells of the intimate relationship between the gods (*kami*), the land, and its inhabitants. Neither is an entirely separate mythic world described as the abode of the gods, but the ordinary world is explained as an arena of divine activity. The signs of the link between the land and the gods are the words used to name places, and in the prayers (*norito*) that were ritually offered to the gods, we see the use of words as a magical, potent medium linking people to the gods. As much as the gods, what is celebrated in *norito* is language itself, a verbal feast presented with sonorous richness, for it is primarily through a banquet of words that the gods can be induced to grant blessings, protection, and even the purification of sins. As it is with the Buddhist precepts, there is an element of repentance that depends on words, for it is in the *saying* of one's sins that their existence is recognized and laid open to expiation.

The Buddhist deities are also sources of blessings and sometimes curses. There is an entire genre of Buddhist literature that tells stories about the marvelous workings of the buddhas and bodhisattvas, and in *The Miraculous Tales of the Hasedera Kannon* we read about the miracles granted by Kannon, the bodhisattva of mercy. Here too the catalyst is prayer, supplication made to Kannon, who otherwise does not act. Certainly the extraordinary power of Kannon is lauded in these tales, but the underlying moral is the need for piety and its verbal expression, prayer. Morality is an important element in a nineteenth-century puppet play, also about Kannon, but the virtue of a blind man and his wife must be augmented by prayer and pilgrimage before Kannon restores sight to the blind man. Morality and magic take center stage in this puppet play about the Kannon at Tsubosaka Temple, which presents the old lesson of the Buddhist miracle tales in which good is rewarded and evil punished by divine powers.

The deities can also be petitioned for future blessings, especially when a new venture such as marriage is undertaken. The liturgical core of the wedding ceremony consists of sumptuous words inviting the bestowal of divine blessings on the couple. Though the modern Shintō wedding ritual dates back only to the beginning of the twentieth century, the ancient form of *norito* is still used to invoke nostalgic images of the venerable power of the *kami*. The ceremony is one of binding man and wife with each other along with the ancestors of the past and future progeny. The union is sealed with *sake,* rice wine sipped in an exchange of cups, and a pledge to extend the family from the past to an eternity of an ever increasing line of descendants.

The world of the gods is also the realm of the spirits of the dead, the existence of which is affirmed by all religious traditions in Japan. Along with morality and magic, the beliefs and practices associated with the spirits or souls of the departed form an enduring theme cutting across boundaries of time and sect. The *Man'yōshū,* the earliest of the poetry anthologies, presents details of *tama* (spirit) belief, and how words, again, in poetic form rather than prayer, are deployed to try to recall, bind, or pacify the spirits of the dead. While prayer is addressed to the gods, poetry speaks to people who, when they are gone, elicit strong feelings of love, longing, and loss. There is more to poetic function, however, than just the evocation of human sentiment and personal attachment; politics, too, is sometimes part of the poetry. The public elegy (*banka*) on the occasion of Prince

Takechi's temporary enshrinement was used to legitimate Emperor Temmu's violent assumption of power in the Jinshin War in 672 by rhetorically transforming the events surrounding it into what Gary Ebersole calls a "mythistory."[4]

That the votive document (*gammon*) by Kūkai (774–835) was dedicated to the deceased mother of a government official is an indication that politics may also have played an ancillary role in this ritual text. Kūkai wrote several votive documents for well-placed individuals and their families, and serving their ritual needs with new ceremonies featuring elaborate colors, smells, sounds, and resounding words aided his work in establishing the new form of Shingon Buddhism in Japan. The votive text presents an alternative to recalling or binding the spirit of a loved one and suggests a letting go, a release that is nevertheless comforting since the departed soul is to be received by the compassionate Buddha.

Life after death is not to be feared, ideally at least, especially when the spirit is placed in the care of a priest who has the sacerdotal knowledge for managing its fate through ritual. Even if something goes wrong in the afterlife, usually through ritual negligence on the part of surviving relatives, and the spirit turns out to be agitated and hungry rather than satisfied, the priest can perform a ritual to remedy the problem. The ritual for feeding the hungry ghosts (*segaki*) is one example of this kind of spiritual technology for resolving such crises, but it does require a trained specialist who knows how to form the hand gestures (*mudrā*) and recite the mantras in a greatly Japanized form of Sanskrit. In these mantras, we see again the magical power of words, the basic tool of the spiritual technician.

Related to the idea that words have power to manipulate matters of the spirit is the intriguing notion that one's final thoughts at the moment of death condition one's rebirth. Genshin's (942–1017) deathbed rituals prescribe the details for right consciousness at the critical moment of death, and while one's lifetime of actions and their karmic consequences cannot be totally ignored, negative karma can be offset by holding in mind images of Amida Buddha and chanting the *nembutsu,* "Namu Amida Butsu." Perhaps no other phrase has been uttered by so many people with the belief in the power of those words to guarantee rebirth in the pure land than the *nembutsu*. Mind and voice, thought and word work together toward the end of having Amida come to greet the dying person and provide escort to the pure land. Even women, whose nature and abilities for gaining salvation have been seriously questioned in Buddhism, can gain rebirth through *nembutsu* piety, as can warriors who, in taking human life, commit the deadliest sin of all. Priests belonging to the Jishū, the Time Sect founded by Ippen (1239–1289), typically borrowed ideas and practices from other forms of Buddhism, but basically promoted the *nembutsu* practice, especially among warriors and commoners. In *The Tale [of the Battle] of Ōtō,* which describes a war waged in 1400, the horrors of clashing armies shock the participants into a religious awakening centered on the *nembutsu,* the recitation of which is the simplest of rituals for dealing with the terrors of this world and for insuring peace in the next life. The battle scenes of chopped limbs, severed heads, and gushing blood make the realities of war comparable to the tortures of hell described in texts such as Genshin's *Ōjōyōshū* (The Essentials of Rebirth). The only difference is that they are inflicted by ordinary soldiers instead of demons and devils.

The taking of life assumes many forms, and in modern Japan abortions are carried out in significant numbers. Out of fear that the spirits of the aborted fetuses will curse their parents, or out of a deep sense of guilt, or out of a concern for the well-being of the fetus now in the spirit world, rites (*kuyō*) for a "child of the waters" (*mizuko*) have been performed in recent times. The abortion rituals also tell us much about the role that religious institutions play in promoting and even creating the need for these services, and temple literature brazenly promotes abortion rituals by playing on fear, guilt, and a concern for well-being. Herein lies a lesson in the realities of institutional religion, and while advertising is a powerful creator of need, or at least of felt needs, the promotion of services for the aborted fetuses would not have much effect if it did not resonate with preexisting beliefs about ritual and its capacity for handling the spirits of the dead.

Death carries an intimate association with enlightenment, and indeed the word *hotoke* is used to describe a corpse as well as a buddha. The state of nirvana is likened unto the quiescence of death, which is also the necessary precondition for rebirth in the pure land. But enlightenment is also a possibility in life, and the assertion that ordinary persons are already buddhas presents a paradox or contradiction that has invited many to resolve it. The idea is found in a constellation of other notions variously identified as nonduality, buddha nature, the womb matrix, original enlightenment, inherent enlightenment, enlightenment in this very body, the equality of passion with enlightenment, the identity of the ordinary world with nirvana, and any number of other related claims, including the Jōdoshin equivalent that rebirth takes place at the moment of faith or that everyone, saint and sinner alike, is already saved by Amida. The truth of these claims are not immediately apparent since human experience still seems to lie at a great distance from this ideal state that purports nevertheless to be immediately close by. If these claims are true and one is already a buddha, then the obvious question arises: why practice? The answer, equally obvious, is that one has to practice in order to realize the truth that obviates practice.

Suchness is another term for the identity of the imperfect with the perfect, and in the twelfth-century composition, *Contemplation of Suchness,* the paradoxical claim is put forth with startling simplicity. The text addresses lay persons primarily, and the level of clarity required for such an audience is achieved through a literalism that valorizes the world: even pigs and dogs are suchness, and to feed them is to make offerings to the buddhas. Pigs are buddhas, but in the light of ordinary perception, they falsely appear as smelly beasts. To see animals as enlightened beings requires new sight made possible by the contemplation of suchness, a ritual of realization.

In adopting yin-yang rituals, and especially the idea of inherent enlightenment from Shingon Esoteric Buddhism, the Shintō purification rite radically transformed the practice of ritual purity. According to the idea of inherent enlightenment, all beings are naturally endowed from birth with the qualities of enlightenment, which includes perfect purity, and the purification ritual, no longer needed to purge nonexistent impurity, was therefore placed in the service of realizing one's inherent enlightenment. The rituals of realization are more familiar to us in the context of Zen than in Shintō, and in Dōgen's treatment, the practice of *zazen* (seated meditation) itself becomes the actualization of ultimate truth, and the practitioner, just as he or she is, becomes the incarnation of perfect enlightenment. The Zen master Chidō (13th c.) adopted the less paradoxical view in which a distinction is made between ordinary reality, which is like a dream, and the ultimate reality of Buddhist insight, which results from being awakened from the dream. Aimed at lay persons, Chidō's work is an exhortation about how expansive the mind can be, how grand one's vision can be, if only people were to wake up from their dreams. While Chidō does not engage in the literalism of asserting pigs to be suchness, he does hold up a very ordinary experience, that of being awake rather than sleeping and dreaming, as the closest approximation of Buddhist enlightenment. It is a simile, but it evokes the language that valorizes the mundane. While he is critical of the Pure Land rejection of disciplined practice, Chidō does express a point that is often mistakenly credited only to Pure Land innovations, namely, that the power of faith can overcome the karmic effects of sin.

The idea that one is already a buddha invites everyone to be his or her own authority. Such an authority is assumed when a writer composes a sutra purporting to be a record of the Buddha's preaching. All of the Mahāyāna sutras were written long after Śākyamuni's time, but the fiction of authenticity is maintained in the distinction made between apocryphal and genuine scriptures. All Buddhist sutras begin with the standard phrase, "thus have I heard," which suggests that the writer was nothing other than a scribe dutifully recording the words of Śākyamuni, but the literary evidence in the texts themselves indicates that the sermons were composed by any number of mostly anonymous writers. A few sutras were clearly composed in Japan and could not have come from India by way of China and Korea, the route of so-called authentic sutras. Written in the early nineteenth century within the Shugendō tradition of mountain asceticism, the *Sutra on the Unlimited Life of the Threefold Body* argues that authority and meaning rest in one's own experience and not on some teaching transmitted through an institution. This is a convenient claim made by one who is passing off his experience as the preaching of Śākyamuni, and yet it cannot rest easy with the prospect that the truth it proposes is individually or personally derived, for that would reduce truth to opinion. There must be an external authority, but since it cannot be an institution in this case, it is located in the original buddha of no mind and no thought, the highest buddha. No mind and no thought are terms from the language of original enlightenment and its logic: the reason why we can claim authority in ourselves is because it is the authority of the original buddha. Hence, we can write our own sutras.

Writing a sutra in the name of Śākyamuni is easily seen as arrogant and presumptuous in the extreme, and therefore it is necessary to disguise such self-righteousness in the cloak of a scriptural diction that makes it sound as if it were merely recorded by a faithful disciple standing on Vulture Peak in the presence of the original master. Equally bold but less obvious is the interesting and complex act of interpreting a sutra whose apocryphal origins have been conveniently forgotten in favor of an attribution of authenticity. Interpretation allows for new insights to be derived from or invested in an existing sutra, and thus avoids the offense of writing a new one. This is the most common technique for developing new teachings in a tradition that prides itself on faithfully transmitting an original teaching without the distortions and heresies of innovation. Without interpretation, new schools cannot arise and take issue with received tradition.

In its criticism of traditional ritual practices, Pure Land Buddhism can be seen as a contrast to the other forms of Buddhism that place discipline and practice at their core. In another sense, however, the Pure Land conviction that salvation is not secured by the self-power of practice but only by reliance through faith on the other power of Amida leads to an immediate fulfillment that resonates with the rituals of realizing one is already a buddha. The rhetoric is different—being a buddha in this life versus being identified with Amida through the *nembutsu* in this life—but what is the difference between being a buddha and being Amida? The nonduality between the believer and Amida is the contention of the thirteenth-century work *Attaining the Settled Mind;* it claims that birth in the pure land has already been accomplished through the compassionate vow of Amida, and hence one can have a settled mind. To the question raised earlier as to why practice is necessary if one is already a buddha, the Pure Land answer, at least in this text, is that practices are not necessary as long as one trusts in Amida. The fifteenth-century collection of anecdotes in *Plain Words on the Pure Land Way* depicts monks who have thrown off concerns for status, fame, doctrinal learning, and intellectual calculation in favor of the simplicity of the *nembutsu,* the sole ritual that makes all other rituals unnecessary.

The letters of Shinran suggest that even true faith (*shinjin*) is a gift of Amida and not the result of human volition. There is nothing to do—no ritual, no practice, no contrivance. Faith puts an end to contrivance, and becomes the moment of birth into the pure land. Without removing evil, faith bypasses it and allows sinners (as well as saints) to be reborn in the pure land. This does not mean that people can justifiably commit evil, for compassion requires people to be good even though goodness is not a means to rebirth. Shinran, whose faith allowed him to ignore the clerical precepts and openly marry, occupied a position diametrically opposite to that of the traditional practitioners, but the line separating both can also be bent into a full circle such that his sense of immediate fulfillment meets the end point at which we find the rituals of realizing one is a buddha, perhaps Amida.

Institutional Practices

The rejection of ritual structure on the grounds of the immediacy of faith does not entail a repudiation of institutional structure. Indeed the Jōdoshin sect of True Pure Land Buddhism, which developed in the wake of Shinran's teachings, became one of the most formidable of institutions and could defend itself by force of arms when necessary. Religion and politics often clashed, but they also met on the common ground in which religious truth claims could be used to legitimize or enhance political institutions. The making of institutions requires founders, most of whom have been sanctified as great men, wizards, and even gods. Great efforts were also expended in defining the identity of sectarian institutions in terms of right practice or orthopraxis, and right thought or orthodoxy. In the arena of institutional life we see clearly what is appropriately called sectarianism, that is, the strict definition of exclusive zones of thought and practice. This does not controvert the repeated cases of syncretism across sectarian lines, but neither should such assimilative fluidity obscure the instances of rigid separation. Balancing the ideological tensions of sectarianism is the ordinary administration of buildings and furnishings, and the special social functions that some religious institutions play. Another lesson of the realities of organization is found in the gap between actual practices and stated ideals, and a view of these discrepancies is essential if we are to avoid the mistake of thinking that principles are always put into practice.

While we normally think that practice follows theory, there were times when actual practice preceded and then required the subsequent creation and support of principles. When one clan emerged in ancient Japan as more powerful than others, it could have ruled by brute force alone without concern for whether their rule was justified. The idea of legitimacy, however, made its appearance with some of the earliest writings in Japan, and the *Kojiki* (Record of Ancient Matters, 712) is a definitive text in establishing the principles that justified the practice of supremacy by the imperial clan. Departing from the Chinese principle that the ruler governed by divine right in the form of the mandate of heaven, which could be lost through excessive vice and claimed by another person of greater virtue, the imperial clan in Japan established the principle of divine birth as the basis of legitimate rulership. The *Kojiki* asserts that the imperial house descends from the deity Amaterasu, and the emperor rules by virtue of having been born divine.

Despite their divine origins, the imperial family functioned in a bureaucratic organization that was eminently human. The *Continued Chronicles of Japan* (Nihon shoki, 797) provides a glimpse into the everyday workings of the court, some of which sounds remarkably familiar: new bureaucratic rules devised to correct certain abuses, sanctioning a Crown Prince for his debauchery, and the difficulty of finding suitable princes of acceptable moral behavior. While the dominant values are identifiable as Confucian, it is also clear that there was an easy coexistence with and mutual use of Buddhism and (what we now call) Shintō. There was no need for a theory of syncretism since the assimilation of ideas and practices did not always follow deliberate design but was carried out for practical purposes. Though we can identify Shintō, Buddhist, and Confucian elements in the *Continued Chronicles of Japan,* it is clear that they melded into a single worldview, not three, in which spiritual forces, however they might be identified, were integrated parts of the temporal order.

This is not to say that there were no other circumstances in which religious traditions did appear differently and clash. The *Circumstances Leading to the Founding of the Monastery Complex of Gangōji* (Gangōji engi, 747) is an important document, not only for the founding of the temple but for the official introduction of Buddhism itself. The account is one of contention, strife, and even violence, as two political factions include in their opposing stances different religious understandings of the spiritual forces that affect worldly events. The deities are identified in opposition to each other, the one "Buddhist" and the other, for lack of a better term, "Shintō." Since the temporal world is directly affected by powerful unseen forces identified as deities, the violent struggle between the two factions was also a battle of the gods, and the Buddhist deities proved themselves to be the greater masters of war.

Emerging victorious, Prince Shōtoku (574–622), grateful for the support of the buddhas and bodhisattvas, became an influential supporter of Buddhism. The biographies of Prince Shōtoku are even more explicit about the relationship between Buddhism and power, and we read once again of how the war was won with the backing of the Buddhist deities. In his political uses of Buddhism, Prince Shōtoku is portrayed not just as a pragmatic warrior-politician petitioning the deities to be on his side, but also as a pious believer. Both stances go together, sincerity being an important element in the process of asking the buddhas to answer one's prayers for victory. Prince Shōtoku is reputed to have studied the philosophical teachings of Buddhism and to have gained an admirable mastery of them, but in the account of his struggles with his opponents, little is said about those teachings, although much is reported about the divine powers of the buddhas to help determine the course of history.

Spiritual beings can affect the outcome of wars and, in turn, those who lose their lives fighting a war can become special spiritual beings. The Yasukuni Shrine in modern Tokyo is a burial place for all those who died in service to the country, including the school children on Okinawa and the women telephone operators on Sakhalin who lost their lives in the Great Pacific War. Popular booklets and pamphlets written in an easy-to-understand style relate important lessons about how the war dead become spirits of the nation, a nation that is still symbolized by the emperor. All of Japan's wars, civil and foreign, were unfortunate but were fought for the sake of the nation and the emperor, contributing to the important mission, as a brochure puts it, of creating a marvelous Japan with the Emperor at its center. While this language evokes the diction of wartime Japan, the recently published pamphlets are good reminders of the continuing importance given in some quarters to the intimate connection between citizens, spirits, the nation, and the Emperor in modern Japan.

In turning from the imperial institution to those that are sectarian, we find, as we might expect, intimate connections between divinity and humanity, especially in the founders of sects. Shrouded in so much legend that it is difficult to discern the real man, En the Ascetic (late 7th c.) has become a paradigmatic holy man and wizard of supernatural powers revered widely even outside of the Shugendō sect of which he is the reputed founder. The account of him tells of the importance of mountains as places to acquire spiritual powers through strict discipline, but even this supernatural wizard is also described in very human and moral terms as being filial to his parents. Mountains are also the setting for the story about how Kūkai, the founder of the Shingon sect, established a monastery on Mt. Kōya and eventually died there. His death, however, was only a seeming one, for he remains alive, sitting in eternal meditation in his mausoleum. Even today thousands of pilgrims flock to Mt. Kōya to visit and pray to Kūkai, posthumously and popularly known as Kōbō Daishi, their living savior. The divinization of Kūkai was not the product of popular piety, but the construction by high-ranking monks developing the Shingon institution. They created the living savior, and wandering holy men dispatched from the monastery disseminated the story throughout the countryside.

The telling of tales is an important part of the process of instilling faith in the buddhas and bodhisattvas, as we have already seen with the tales and puppet play about Kannon, and it continued to be instrumental in the later development of Kōbō Daishi as living savior. While the story about Kōbō Daishi's eternal meditation was a creation by a monk at the top of the institution and was then disseminated to believers below, the stories about the encounters with Kōbō Daishi on the Shikoku pilgrimage were told by ordinary pilgrims making the journey. Stories were first collected from pilgrims in the seventeenth century by a monk who had lies with the Shingon headquarters. They tell of pilgrimage as a means of having direct encounters with the holy, and praise the virtue of doing the pilgrimage and offering alms to the pilgrims. Taken together, the stories of Kōbō Daishi's eternal meditation and the Shikoku pilgrimage show that in the making of belief through the telling of tales, stories can be told from the top down as well as the bottom up.

If, as scholars surmise, the *Personal Account of the Life of the Venerable Genkū* was written by Shinkū (1145–1228), then it is another example of a founder having been divinized by those at the top of the sect. Genkū, who is more popularly known as Hōnen, was the founder of the Pure Land sect (Jōdoshū), and Shinkū was one of his earliest disciples. The account transforms Hōnen into a divine savior, like Kūkai, and identifies him as a manifestation of the bodhisattva Seishi, who is often depicted along with Kannon as an attendant of Amida. Responding to criticisms that his master was a heretic for rejecting traditional practices in favor of the exclusive recitation of the *nembutsu,* Shinkū defends Hōnen as a scholar as well as a saint. History and myth depict Hōnen as both human and divine, and the text, like the *Kojiki,* is another example of "mythistory" designed to make something human more divine.

The Nichiren priest Nisshin (1407–1488) was not the founder of his sect, but he became a hero within his organization and the center of a personality cult. What is interesting about his story is that he is not portrayed as a supernatural or divine figure, but as a resolute man, a martyr at most, who withstood government censure and torture for the sake of his sect and belief in the *Lotus Sutra.* A similar case of intense faith can be seen in Teshima Ikurō (1910–1973), who had an intense Christian conversion experience in the midst of his own personal suffering. The founder of a small Christian organization, Kirisuto no Makuya (Tabernacle of Christ), Teshima emphasized individual faith and developed close relations with his followers, some of whom wrote testimonies about his extraordinary character, insight, and power. While his followers report cases of healing (in one instance by Teshima's wife) and revere him tremendously, they still do not regard him as anything other than a remarkable teacher whom they came to love and respect dearly. Personal commitment to each other as well as the gospel of Jesus Christ is the story told of a man remarkable for his humanity and faith.

Nisshin and Teshima were heroes to their causes because of their exclusive commitment to the truths they found respectively in the *Lotus Sutra* and the Bible. They were fundamentalists, unable to recognize other forms of truth. In contrast to this restrictive view, Mujū Ichien (1226–1312), ostensibly a Rinzai Zen priest, held that the Buddhist truth takes on various forms, and that no single way can be upheld over others. While Mujū also presents the idea of how Buddhism is compatible with the other religious traditions, it is important to note that the non-Buddhist teachings "softened people's hearts," as he states it, to make them more amenable to accepting Buddhism. Buddhism therefore enjoys a privileged position over the rest, and it is primarily within the Buddhist fold that pluralism and diversity are celebrated. The Buddha taught different teachings to suit different people, and in making such accommodations expressed his compassion. There is, in short, no single meaning to Buddhism, no orthodoxy.

It was not always the case that when institutions found themselves at odds with each other, the issues were free of concerns about the right articulation of truth. For Nisshin, the conflicts he experienced were directly related to his strict orthodoxy. The connection between conflicting orthodoxies and competing institutional (and personal) interests is not difficult to find even within single traditions. Intrasectarian tension, for example, is easily seen within the world of Zen, and again it is a story of the interrelationship between doctrinal understandings and institutional well-being. The competition between Shūhō Myōchō (National Teacher Daitō, 1282–1337) and the monk Musō Soseki (1275–1351) was not just a debate over the philosophical truth of Zen but about political correctness as well. The definition of doctrinal correctness or orthodoxy in this situation was a pressing issue even in a time of political stability; it is not just a change of rulers or the conduct of war that require religious support and justification. Cultural and even aesthetic realignments also affect the articulation of right religion, and a judgment of heterodoxy in one situation may be beneficial to the gaining of orthodoxy in another circumstance.

The influence of social pressures on the determination of truth can also be seen in the argument between the Inner and Outer Shrines at Ise, which waged their theological debate mindful of the economic consequences of their theoretical formulations. The Outer Shrine claimed that their deity, Toyouke, was equal to and identical with Amaterasu, the *kami* of the Inner Shrine. But the Inner Shrine priests rejected this formulation, saying that Amaterasu was superior. The theological arguments were in form about the *kami* but in function concerned donations from pilgrims who flocked to Ise, pilgrims who would, if Toyouke were inferior, bypass the Outer Shrine and go directly to the Inner Shrine and pray to the superior Amaterasu. The debate spilled into the streets as Outer Shrine priests set up barricades to block entry to the Inner Shrine. The issue was highly volatile at the institutional level, and difficult to resolve theologically. The great scholar Motoori Norinaga (1730–1801) addressed the matter with an aim toward resolving the conflict, but he seemed to have a split mind on the issue and managed not to provide any clear resolution.

Motoori referred to the controversy with the image of split bamboo, but the fracturing of relations between the Inner and Outer Shrines did not elicit cries of dismay about the loss of harmony within Shintō. When Buddhists denounced each other, they sometimes lamented the loss of the "single flavor of the dharma" or the breakup of the harmony of the sangha, the fault for which, of course, could be laid on their opponents. But little is said about the single flavor of Shintō: what, after all, is Shintō? A scholar of our own time, the late Kuroda Toshio (1926–1993) has been influential with his analysis of the nature and function of religion in Japanese history, and in a widely acclaimed essay on the subject, he criticizes the usual characterization of Shintō as an independent indigenous religion. Arguing that an autonomous Shintō is a modern construction, Kuroda sees that the beliefs and practices surrounding the *kami* are so integrated into Buddhist, Daoist, and secular affairs that they cannot be separated out to form an independent "Shintō."

The inextricable integration of Shintō beliefs and practices into the religious views of Buddhists has caused enormous problems for the True Pure Land (Jōdoshin) sect, which officially rejects all magical rituals aimed at acquiring this-worldly benefits such as health, wealth, safety, and happiness.[5] These rituals and beliefs are centered on the use of amulets, talismans, and other paraphernalia sold at most Shintō shrines and Buddhist temples. Concerned about field studies that show Jōdoshin members patronizing temples and shrines offering this-worldly benefits, Sasaki Shōten, a contemporary Jōdoshin priest and scholar, calls for a reconsideration of the official teaching banning such practices. Sasaki recognizes that this primitive magical mentality with Shintōism as its core, as he puts it, is an undeniable part of the Japanese religious view, including that of Buddhists, and it is useless to deny by doctrine what exists in fact. While sounding at times as if he is willing to accept those practices fully, Sasaki fundamentally cannot do so. His proposal is not to accept but to tolerate such folk practices so that people can be drawn in, or more importantly so that members do not have to be expelled. The final goal, however, is to transform such primitive practices into true Jōdoshin faith, which, even in Sasaki's version, cannot tolerate magic as true religion. His willingness to accept the primitive mentality in order to transform it is reminiscent of Mujū's attitude toward the non-Buddhist religions that function to soften people's hearts so that they can embrace the Buddhist dharma. Though they espouse pluralism and toleration, there is ultimately only a single truth defined according to their respective orientations.

Sasaki's argument takes us well into the area in which we see the discrepancies between official doctrine and actual practice. A good example of this can be seen in Sōtō Zen pamphlets written for temple members in which Zen as a religion for peace of mind and general well-being is emphasized to the exclusion of the practice of meditation. This is a striking position to be taken officially by an institution whose very name refers to the centrality of meditation. What is Zen, if not meditation? An overt clash between the original ideal and current practice is avoided simply by not mentioning the doctrines for which Zen is philosophically famous. The dilemma also arises in the matter of funerals. Sōtō Zen and Jōdoshin purists often point out that funeral rites and ancestor veneration are not Buddhist teachings, and yet we find in official Zen pamphlets positive, nostalgic affirmations of rites for commemorating the dead and memorializing the ancestors. This pamphlet Zen bears little resemblance to Dōgen Zen, though both are identified as Sōtō. It is quite significant that this sentimental Zen of general well-being is promoted by the sect itself without any mention of Dōgen's famous advocacy of seated meditation as the means to dropping off mind and body to reveal an originally existing buddha; a conflict between doctrine and practice is avoided by dropping off classical doctrine in favor of popular practice. Or, to put it in other terms, practice prescribes precept.

The priority of practice over doctrine is not limited to modern developments but is also seen in the writings of Keizan (1264–1325), who stands second in importance to Dōgen himself in the line of Sōtō Zen patriarchs in Japan. Keizan, displaying a pragmatism for what works rather than what is doctrinally prescribed, easily adopted ritual practices that Dōgen would not have condoned. The institutional development of Sōtō Zen would have been significantly retarded if Dōgen's successors had confined themselves to the limits of his demanding teachings and not adopted, for instance, mortuary rites and rituals for this-worldly benefits.[6] In his own writings Keizan is not as concerned with sitting in meditation as he is with rituals for warding off evil and inviting blessings, and with the more mundane matters of institutional administration. Women play an important role, as they do today, in the back room life of his temple, and Keizan has much to say about his grandmother, mother, and Sonin, the woman who donated the land for his temple Yōkōji.

Keizan built Yōkōji in a valley he named Tōkoku. Both names were chosen for their associations with Chinese Zen masters in whose lineage he was a dharma descendant. In his sermons, Keizan uses the language of original enlightenment to speak generically about every place being one's own self, one's radiant wisdom, the site of practice, and the practice of buddha activity; when he speaks specifically of Tōkoku Yōkōji, however—its buildings, its activities, its people, his relatives, and how he selected the site in a dream—it becomes apparent that the place is one of belonging, his home, the locus of his everyday spiritual life. Like the *Records of the Customs and Land of Izumo* (Izumo fudoki) and its naming of places in association with the actions of the *kami,* Keizan's *Records of Tōkoku* explains the naming of that place in association with his spiritual tradition and describes it as the venue of buddha activity as well as his everyday routine. Yōkōji is at once an ordinary and a special place.

Tōkeiji in Kamakura is a special place for women, specifically women who seek divorce from their husbands. The temple was founded as a convent in 1285 by Kakusan Shidō (1252–1305), widow of Hōjō Tokimune (1251–1284), the Kamakura military ruler who repelled the Mongol invasions in 1274 and 1281. Its name, Eastern Temple for Rejoicing (Tōkeiji), was an appropriate choice for a woman who seems to have enjoyed a happily married life. By the Tokugawa period, the temple had acquired other names: Enkiridera, Divorce Temple; and Kakekomidera, Temple into Which One Runs for Refuge. The popular verse known as *senryū* speaks poignantly about the unhappy experiences of women seeking refuge from their husbands. In a time when divorce was uncommon and difficult to obtain since it could only be granted by the husband, Tōkeiji was a very special place, but its unique function was possible because of the theoretically normal role any temple plays as a place for the renunciation of the householder's life. Monasticism had its secular use, and though it was not easy being a nun ("how difficult/breaking the relationship/with vegetarian food"), it was a temporary status to be endured until the husband could be convinced of sending a letter of divorce.

Monasticism and divorce are not usually associated in texts on Japanese religion, but the case of Tōkeiji illustrates how natural and practical an alliance it was. Dealing with the world by withdrawing from it was also practiced by Eison, whose monastic vows made it imperative that he work with outcastes and prisoners. On a more ambitious scale, Eisai argued that monasticism was necessary for the welfare and protection of the nation itself. There is a pattern of this association between monasticism and society, and to that degree we can state a generalization, a small one to be sure, but a generalization nevertheless: monasticism can perform social services. The more usual pattern is of monasticism performing services only for monastics; the monks who called for a continued ban against clerical marriage were not addressing the interests of society at large, though they tried to demonstrate that celibacy was not inimical to society. Herein lies another pattern: monasticism is self-serving. The patterns vary: monasticism is a hard rock, but it is used in shifting tides.

The traditions of Japan are filled with double-edged interrelationships that cut both ways. Religion, for instance, legitimates rulership, but the ruler, in turn, legitimates religion by legislating it. Sometimes the government intervenes in religious matters to the dismay of religious communities, and at other times the community complains that the government does not intervene enough. There are patterns of tolerant pluralism that stand in contrast with clear instances of sectarianism and censure, and then there is the kind of sectarian triumphalism that presents itself in the mask of pluralistic tolerance. Morality is a prevalent theme about reaping what we sow, but so is magic equally present with its promises of reaping even if we do not sow. Repeatedly we encounter the conundrum of being a buddha but having to become one nevertheless. This is attended by voices calling for strict practice in order to realize that there is no need to practice—voices that find counterpoints in those who said that there is no need to practice at all. At times the world is a defiled place worthy only of being left behind for the perfect pure land, and at other times it is the very abode of the gods where pigs are buddhas. Rules are external and need to be internalized, but internal realization makes external rules unnecessary. There are living spirits of the dead to be bound, recalled, pacified, or conversely let go; there are also dead masters whose spirits never leave but stay to bless and protect. Divinized humans and anthropomorphic gods grant miracles, induced from them through people performing rituals, reciting chants, uttering prayers, going on pilgrimage, being good, or just having faith. Myth is not to be confused with fact, but it can be blended with history to produce "mythistory," or with biography to create hagiography. For some, human institutions can never be sources of authority, especially when one is a buddha unto oneself, but institutions can also be the only source for defining what is true. Doctrine defines rituals and right conduct, but so can practice determine theory. There are also times when neither is the cause of the other, when one side, usually theory, is simply ignored. Shintō is a recognizable religion, but sometimes becomes invisible in its integration into Buddhist practice. Buddhism also has its own character, but it too can be hidden in a Shintō purification rite. Both Buddhism and Shintō can join together with Confucianism and other systems to form a single worldview, or they can clash to the point of violence. Buddhism is for peace, but also helps to win wars. Orthodoxies have definite consequences in society, and social conditions can help determine orthodoxies. The list of these double- or multiple-edged relationships can continue on and on.

All of the above are patterns that can be seen in repeated instances and therefore can be stated as generalizations, the making of which is essential to teaching and understanding; however, by showing that patterns have opposing counterparts, we see the limits of any generalization, and we see that counter-generalizations, equally valid, also need to be made. The resulting mosaic, seemingly on the verge of conceptual chaos, is what we are after, a kind of ordered disorder, a pattern of the uniformities and disarray that constitute the religions of Japan in practice.

Notes

1. Cited in Ryusaku Tsunoda et al., eds., *Sources of Japanese Tradition* (New York: Columbia University Press, 1961), p. 585.

2. See, for example, Ian Reader, *Religion in Contemporary Japan* (Honolulu: University of Hawaii Press, 1991).

3. See, for example, Stephen Vlastos, ed., *Mirror of Modernity: Invented Traditions of Modern Japan* (Berkeley: University of California Press, 1998); Robert H. Scharf, "The Zen of Japanese Nationalism," in *Curators of the Buddha,* edited by Donald S. Lopez, Jr. (Chicago: University of Chicago Press, 1995), pp. 107–60; Helen Hardacre, *Shintō and the State, 1868–1988* (Princeton: Princeton University Press, 1989); Neil McMullin, *Buddhism and the State in Sixteenth-Century Japan* (Princeton: Princeton University Press, 1984).

4. Gary L. Ebersole, *Ritual Poetry and the Politics of Death in Early Japan* (Princeton: Princeton University Press, 1989).

5. For a full treatment of the religion of this-worldly benefits in Japan, see Ian Reader and George J. Tanabe, Jr., *Practically Religious: Worldly Benefits and the Common Religion of Japan* (Honolulu: University of Hawaii Press, 1998).

6. For the institutional practices of Sōtō Zen, see William M. Bodiford, *Sōtō Zen in Medieval Japan* (Honolulu: University of Hawaii Press, 1993); and Bernard Faure, *The Rhetoric of Immediacy: A Cultural Critique of Ch'an/Zen Buddhism* (Princeton: Princeton University Press, 1991).

—38—

Kaibara Ekken's Precepts on the Family

Mary Evelyn Tucker

The Tokugawa period in Japanese history (1603–1868) is a significant era in the development of Confucian thought in East Asia. It was during this period that various schools and scholars of Confucianism flourished. As the Tokugawa Bakufu began to establish peace and to unify the country after several decades of civil war, new philosophies were encouraged to assist in the political, educational, and social realms. Confucianism in particular seemed suited to the new situation of internal peace presided over by the shogun in Edo (Tokyo). While it is now clear that the shogunate did not simply appropriate Confucian ideas as a means of establishing ideological control, it is true that Confucianism, often in collaboration with Shintoism and Buddhism, became the leading discourse of the period. How this discourse was used and by whom is a matter of some interpretation.

In a figure such as Kaibara Ekken (1630–1714) we have a fascinating example of a Confucian scholar who was interested in far more than political or ideological control. One of the leading intellectuals of his day, he was committed to making Confucian ideas more widely understood and appreciated. He saw that a philosophy with a vitalist metaphysics, a practical learning, and a comprehensive ethics was urgently needed to maintain a peaceful civil society in Tokugawa Japan. For Ekken this philosophy was most fully developed by Chu Hsi (1130–1200), who was the great twelfth-century synthesizer of Chinese neo-Confucianism. After studying Buddhism and Wang Yang-ming neo-Confucianism, Ekken decided that it was Chu Hsi who had articulated a comprehensive yet practical philosophy with definite educational implications.

Ekken set out in his studies, writing, and teaching to spread Chu Hsi neo-Confucianism in Japan. As an adviser and tutor of the ruling lord (*daimyō*) of Kuroda Province (*han*) in Kyūshū, he was well placed to have influence within the han and beyond. For nearly half a century he assisted the understanding of Chu Hsi's writings in Japan by punctuating the texts and writing commentaries on them. He also contributed to the practical learning of his day and wrote popular moral treatises for educational purposes.

In Ekken's life work he strove to articulate his own form of Chu Hsi neo-Confucianism. This might be described as an anthropocosmic philosophy of a vitalistic naturalism. By anthropocosmic I am suggesting that Ekken drew on the Confucian framework of Heaven, Earth, and Human to suggest that humans are a special and indispensable part of the universe. Humans are part of this framework because of the vital material force (*ch'i*) that flows through everything. Human ethical actions affect the universe; as we cultivate ourselves morally and spiritually we are able to form one body with all things.

In all of these discussions we are suggesting that Ekken's philosophy and his ethics have very real implications in the contemporary search for a more viable ecological philosophy and a more functional environmental ethics. Ekken's anthropocosmic worldview may be helpful in our own search for a new cosmological understanding of human-earth relations. His naturalistic ethics may, likewise, be significant in our own contemporary efforts to include nature in our sphere of moral concern, compassion, and protection.

The Creative Principles of Filiality and Humaneness

Ekken's anthropocosmic worldview and his interest in practical learning were inspired by his doctrine of filial piety and humaneness as extended to the natural world. From Chang Tsai's (1020–1077) doctrine in the *Western Inscription* of forming one body with all things, Ekken elaborated his unique understanding of assisting in the transforming and nourishing powers of heaven and earth. While his contemporary Nakae Tōju (1608–1648) saw filiality as having a counterpart in the human and natural worlds, Ekken took this understanding a step further by stressing the need for humans to activate a filial reverence for the whole natural world.

A primary motive in this activation of filiality was a sense of the debt (*on*) to heaven and earth as the parents of things. Ekken recognized the importance of loyalty and reverence to one's parents as the source of life, and he carried this feeling of respect to the cosmic order. He maintained that since nature is the source and sustainer of life, one should respond to it as to one's parents, with care, reverence, and consideration. Indeed, people must serve nature as they would their parents in order to repay their debt for the gift of life.

In this regard, Ekken urged people to cherish living things and to avoid carelessly killing plants or animals. He wrote: "No living creatures such as birds, beasts, insects, and fish should be killed wantonly. Not even grass and trees should be cut down out of season" (de Bary et al. 1958, p. 367). The reason for this care, he maintained, was that "All of these are objects of nature's love, having been brought forth by her and nurtured by her. To cherish them and keep them is therefore the way to serve nature in accordance with the great heart of nature" (ibid.). This care for nature was a key motivating force behind Ekken's own studies of the natural world, for he saw it as connected with filiality.

Central to his anthropocosmic worldview based on filial relationships was an all-embracing humaneness, which he defined as "having a sense of sympathy within and bringing blessings to man and things" (ibid.). His spiritual pursuits and his studies of nature are further linked by his understanding of a direct correspondence between humaneness in persons (C. *jen;* J. *jin*) and the origination principle (C. *yuan*; J. *moto*) in nature.

Indeed, Ekken recognized that the operation of principle in the Supreme Ultimate (C. *t'ai chi,* J. *daikyoku*) had the unique purpose of creating the myriad things and thus can be termed "the heart of nature" (*tenchi no kokoro*). Just as birth or origination are the supreme attributes of the natural world, so is humaneness the supreme attribute of the human. Thus origination is the counterpart in nature of humaneness in persons. In other words, what gives rise to life in the natural and human worlds is analogous.

In this way the creative dynamics of the universe find their richest expression in the creative reciprocity of human beings. The fecundity of nature and the well springs of the human heart are seen as two aspects of the all-embracing process of change and transformation in the universe. Ekken asserted that humans have a harmonious energy granted by nature, and this principle governs their lives. Extending to others is the creative virtue of humaneness.

For Ekken, then, the human was the "soul of the universe" and thus had both great privileges and awesome responsibilities in the hierarchy of the natural world. He wrote, "It is a great fortune to be born a human; let us not fritter away our lives meaninglessly." One can do this through studying the classics, investigating principle, developing practical learning, and activating humaneness. He also added the significant directive to "follow the example of nature" in achieving inner wisdom and contentment. With great detail he described the seasonal changes with which one should harmonize one's own moods and activities. He saw this as participating in the process of transformation, which for the human is the key to both knowledge and practice.

As part of his understanding of the human as the soul of the universe, Ekken adopted Chu Hsi's doctrine of total substance and great functioning (C. *ti-yung*; J. *taiyō*). To achieve this unique balance of theory and practice meant both an exploration of principle and an activation of humaneness.

Briefly stated, then, these are some of the central ideas in Ekken's anthropocosmic worldview, namely, that filial piety should be extended to the whole cosmic order, humaneness is the principle of creativity corresponding to origination in nature, and humans are the soul of the universe and participate through great substance and total functioning in the transformation of heaven and earth. This becomes a driving motivation for the pursuit of practical learning and the investigation of things.

With Ekken the understanding of the cosmic dimensions of reverence that were hinted at in earlier Japanese neo-Confucian thinkers was now transformed into a reverent investigation of nature. Similarly, the cosmic filiality of Nakae Tōju and other earlier neo-Confucians was seen as a reason for both protecting and studying nature through practical learning. All of this was underscored by Ekken's emphasis on *ch'i* as the dynamic unifying element of the universe.

Practical Learning: Content and Methods

Ekken's practical learning was of a broad and comprehensive nature, spanning both the humanities and natural sciences with an end toward personal moral cultivation and alleviation of larger social ills. Ekken's motivation in undertaking practical learning was to participate in the great transforming and nourishing processes of nature by carrying out Chu Hsi's injunction to investigate things and examine their principles. To facilitate this process he advocated a method of investigation that was adapted from Chu Hsi's directives to his students at the White Deer Grotto. He suggested that a correct methodology should be marked by characteristics that may be seen as elaborations of Chu Hsi's instructions, namely, study widely, question thoroughly, think carefully, judge clearly, and act seriously.

With regard to the first principle of the need for broad knowledge, Ekken felt that one must not eliminate either traditional learning or practical contemporary concerns. What is particularly striking about Ekken's breadth is his conscious effort to include knowledge pertinent to the ordinary Japanese of his day. Indeed, he felt it was his mission to study useful popular customs and agricultural techniques as well as to transmit Confucian moral values to the ordinary person.

Yet Ekken was aware of the need to maintain objectivity and rationality in the analysis of principles. He was not interested in simply collecting data or in becoming a specialist or a technician of knowledge. He wanted to be able to bring together specialized research and popular education and to see empirical investigation and ethical practice as part of a single continuum.

Like many Confucians before him, Ekken warned against the limitations of methods used by both the humanist scholar and the scientific researcher. For him, Confucian learning as an essentially ethical path must be distinguished from textual studies or technical skills, which may become ends in themselves. He urged scholars to maintain a reflective and contemplative posture when reading the classics so as not to fall into the traps of linguistic analysis and empty exegesis. Similarly, he rebuked the scholarly specialists who were interested only in personal recognition and the technicians who were obsessed with manipulative processes.

Yet in terms of the content of education he sought to bring together the study of both classical texts and the natural world. He advocated a practical learning that would foster self-cultivation while also assisting others. He urged that learning should be "preserved in the heart and carried out in action" (*juyo no gaku*). Traditional humanistic values and specific technical skills should be used for the benefit of both self and society. In this way the scholar would be assisting in the Confucian aspiration to participate in the transformation of Heaven and Earth.

Kaibara Ekken wrote numerous moral treatises (*kunmono*) for instructing various groups and individuals in Japanese society. In his eagerness to make Confucian moral teachings understood by a large number of people, he wrote these treatises in a simplified Japanese rather than in classical Chinese. This use of the vernacular meant the teachings could become more widespread and better understood. This popularization of Confucian ideas was an important element of Ekken's work as well as a dominant feature of Tokugawa thought. During this era Confucianism was gradually moving from the medieval period confines of the Buddhist monasteries and the province of elite families. Numerous samurai who were attracted to Confucianism for a variety of reasons helped in this spread of Confucian ethics. This occurred through their writings, through their acting as advisers to local lords (*daimyō*), and through the establishment of schools both public and private throughout Japan.

Clearly the samurai class, in particular, was attracted to Confucianism for its humane teachings, embracing a philosophy of education, a means of social ordering, and a pragmatic political program. It is also evident that many of the merchants found Confucianism to be a sound economic philosophy encouraging frugality, hard work, loyalty, and good business practices. All of this meant that during the Tokugawa period there was a significant growth in Confucian texts, schools, and ethical teachings. A major part of this growth was due to the writings of samurai-scholars such as Ekken.

Indeed, it has been suggested that Ekken was "responsible for one of the most systematic accounts" of the rationale of moral education in the Tokugawa period (Dore 1965, 35). This is especially due to his attempts to codify Confucian ethics in more than a dozen moral treatises. These were addressed to a broad spectrum of Tokugawa society, including the samurai, the family, women, and children. They covered topics as wide ranging as ethical practices for individuals and for families, educational curriculum and methods of study, advice on a successful business, caring for one's health, and attaining contentment. An underlying theme of these treatises was self-cultivation to benefit the family and the larger society. This key teaching from the *Great Learning* on the importance of self-cultivation was channeled into the techniques of the learning of the mind-and-heart (*shingaku*). Essentially a means of moral and spiritual discipline, this learning of the mind-and-heart became a vehicle for the transmission and spread of Confucianism across various classes and groups in Japan. Ekken's moral treatises were instrumental in this process.

Ekken's *Precepts on the Way of the Family* (*Kadōkun*) is part of a larger genre of house codes or family precepts (*kakun*). The custom of writing instructions for the family came to Japan from China during the Nara period and continued to be written by court families during the Heian period. In the Kamakura era the samurai wrote *kakun*, and in the Tokugawa period this custom was adopted by merchants as well as samurai. In his *Precepts on the Way of the Family*, Ekken expanded the theme of the *Great Learning* that order in the family will influence the larger society. This can be achieved through self-discipline and the practice of mutual reciprocity with others. The striking feature of Ekken's *Precepts on the Way of the Family* is his integration of instructions for moral cultivation with practical business advice. He stressed the need for ritual and reciprocity in family relations along with effort and diligence in the family business. He continually emphasized the need for restraint and frugality within the household as well as in running a business. He urged careful education of the children, servants, and employees.

Ekken outlined five stages in a person's life that relate to obligations to the family: attending to one's parental education until age twenty, studying the classics and arts from twenty to thirty, supporting one's family and managing its financial affairs between thirty and forty, planning for one's descendants until age fifty, and finally preparing things for after one's death.

For Ekken the external ordering of a person's life should reflect an internal ordering through self-cultivation. He suggested that people should try and harmonize with nature to encourage this cultivation. Specifically he noted that gardening may be most helpful in establishing this reciprocity with nature. Ultimately, for Ekken, self-cultivation reflected the larger patterns of heaven and earth in its ceaseless transformations. For him, the cultivation of oneself and the extension outward to one's family, the society, and the cosmos as a whole are part of one continual process of harmonization.

Thus in typical Confucian tradition, Ekken suggested that the natural biological bonds of the family are the model for other forms of reciprocal morality in the society at large. The patterns of mutual affection and obligations are extended outward from the family and relatives to friends and acquaintances, to all those in need. In several striking passages Ekken urged people to care for the hungry, the sick, the orphaned, and the widowed. In the spirit of Chang Tsai's *Western Inscription*, he suggested that the sense of obligation should move from a primary concern for one's family ever outward toward others.

The following is a translation of one chapter and the beginning of the second from Kaibara Ekken's *Kadōkun*. The entire text of six chapters appears in *Ekken zenshū* (The collected works of Kaibara Ekken) 3 (Tokyo: Ekken Zenshū Kankōbu, 1910–1911), pp. 421–75. Ekken also wrote a shorter *Kakun*, which is less concerned with economic matters than is his *Kadōkun*.

Further Reading

Irene Bloom, *Knowledge Painfully Acquired* (New York: Columbia University Press, 1987); Wm. Theodore de Bary et al., eds., *Sources of Japanese Tradition* (New York: Columbia University Press, 1958); Wm. Theodore de Bary and Irene Bloom, eds., *Principle and Practicality* (New York: Columbia University Press, 1979); Ronald Dore, *Education in Tokugawa Japan* (Berkeley: University of California Press, 1965); Tetsuo Najita, *Visions of Virtue in Tokugawa Japan: The Kaitokudo Merchant*

Academy of Osaka (Chicago: University of Chicago Press, 1987); Peter Nosco, ed., *Confucianism and Tokugawa Culture* (Princeton: Princeton University Press, 1984); Okada Takehiko, "Practical Learning in the Chu Hsi School: Yamazaki Ansai and Kaibara Ekken," in de Bary and Bloom 1979; Herman Ooms, *Tokugawa Ideology: Early Constructs, 1570–1680* (Princeton: Princeton University Press, 1985); Janine Anderson Sawada, *Confucian Values and Popular Zen: Sekimon Shingaku in Eighteenth-Century Japan* (Honolulu: University of Hawaii Press, 1993); Tu Wei-ming, *Centrality and Commonality* (Albany: State University of New York Press, 1989); Tu Wei-ming, *Confucian Thought: Selfhood as Creative Transformation* (Albany: State University of New York Press, 1985); Mary Evelyn Tucker, *Moral and Spiritual Cultivation in Japanese Neo-Confucianism: The Life and Thought of Kaibara Ekken (1630–1714)* (Albany: State University of New York Press, 1989).

CHAPTER 1

REGULATING THE FAMILY BY DISCIPLINING ONESELF

Our duty in living in this world, whether we are of high or low rank, is to regulate the family by disciplining oneself. The root of [order in] the family lies in oneself. Therefore, the master who regulates the family must first discipline himself. Without disciplining oneself, regulating the family will be difficult. When one does not regulate the family, it will be difficult to have harmony. The noble person is always mindful of himself and worries about [the consequences of] future deeds. Thus he is at peace with himself and preserves the family. When the head of the house is honest, he can teach and lead the other family members. When the head is not honest, he cannot be a model for the family. To foster the good it will be difficult to eradicate evil. He cannot practice the family code. Thus, the deeds of the head of the house should be a model for the family's learning. He should behave carefully.

PRACTICING RITUAL

To regulate oneself and discipline the family requires ritual. Ritual means propriety in human relations [namely, ethics]. Ritual is being mindful in one's heart and having a model for oneself. Without mindfulness and without a model, the human heart may be lost and one's actions may degenerate; when such people interact with others, the Way of human relations disappears. Because of ritual people are different from birds and animals; without ritual we are the same as birds and animals. Practicing ritual is not difficult or painful. When many deeds are done according to the code we ought to follow, our heart will be tranquil and our actions will be temperate. Practicing ritual is like following a straight and level road. Consequently, when people have ritual they are peaceful, but without ritual they are anxious. Therefore, we should practice ritual.

We should constantly preserve ritual and be correct within [the household]. When we are not correct within, although we practice the good externally, all will become false. This is the beginning of preserving ritual. Being correct within means being affectionate and encouraging mutual respect between fathers and sons, brothers and sisters, and husbands and wives; taking care of things used in the house; managing employees without haste or negligence; using money without extravagance or waste; controlling lust and desires, knowing shame, and not acting foolishly.

SERVING PARENTS

In serving parents you should devote yourself, always asking about their health and tending to their needs with diligence. You should act according to an ancient saying: "Deliberate in the evening and reflect on it the next morning." Even if you have very little free time, make an effort to visit and serve your parents sometime during the day. Pay close attention to the conditions of their household, making the taste of food and drink good, checking the temperature yourself and then serving it, and making parents warm in the winter and cool in the summer. When you go out of the house you should first take leave of your parents, and when you return to the house you should again greet your parents. In interacting with your parents, you should be gentle in expression and not rude in speech. We must not lose these two practices, namely, seeing to one's parents' happiness and caring for their health. These are practices that are appropriate for all people's children, and we should not undermine these practices. Filiality means always thinking of one's parents and never forgetting them.

FAMILY RELATIONS

There is love between brother and sister and harmony between husband and wife, but in these relations there are also distinctions. A husband treats his wife with propriety. Teach and discipline your children and do not indulge them. Love them and do not despise them. Do not be negligent in guiding children, in practicing propriety, in having them read books, and in making them learn the arts. Their education should definitely be strict.

A person who rules the family as the master of the house tries first to serve his parents well. Next, guiding his wife and educating his children are essential. Finally, he should be considerate in his treatment of servants and have a correct display of propriety. He should not harm nor ridicule nor tyrannize them.

RAISING CHILDREN

In raising children, from an early age we must restrain any excesses and indulgences. The clothes, the belongings, and the way you raise your children should be appropriate to your income and not extravagant. Being too affectionate and being extravagant with things are not good for they teach extravagance to the child. Experiencing luxuries in childhood results in nothing but harm in later life. It is unwise to let children enjoy luxuries and then later try to control them. By being strict in the beginning, gradually one can become more indulgent. From childhood one must be taught the importance of being truthful and sincere. We should encourage frugality in many ways. From early childhood we should admonish children to avoid laziness and selfishness as well as to be humble and conciliatory.

A Chinese minister of the former Han dynasty, Jiayi, had a wise saying regarding raising children: "Teach them from an early age and choose their associates." We should pay attention to these two things. When we do not teach them from an early age, they will easily be steeped in vice. When people near us are evil, by looking at and hearing evil things, evil can become our own bad habit. From childhood if we see and hear evil things, the words that enter become contaminated, and later, although we hear and see good things, we cannot change. When bad habits stick, they become ingrained and we cannot change them.

We should respect ancestors and not neglect seasonal ceremonies. We should be close to our relatives. Being distant from relatives and close to strangers is unnatural. Revering and preserving national law, we must not speak ill of the government or the actions of officials above us.

Slandering those above us, speaking evil of the national government, is the greatest disloyalty and disrespect. We should be careful. Although there are people who slander others, we should not blindly follow the crowd. We should not be careless or garrulous in speaking. Always examining and disciplining ourselves, we should criticize our own faults. We must not blame others and point to their shortcomings.

PEACE IN THE THREE RELATIONS

In ruling the family it is essential not to have abrasiveness with the three relations: namely, between father and son, between brothers and sisters, and between husband and wife. An ancient saying tells us: "Intimacy between father and son; harmony between brothers and sisters; and correctness between husband and wife will enrich the home." When the relations between these three are bad, even though the family has wealth, they are impoverished.

PRACTICING GOODNESS BASED ON LOVE AND RESPECT

In associating with other members of the family, we must warn against evil and practice good. When we do not practice good, the Way of humans is not correct. In practicing good we must take love and respect as the basis. Love is having sympathy for people and avoiding cruelty. Respect is honoring people and not ridiculing them. These two are the method of the heart for practicing the good in human relations. In doing good there is nothing other than respect and love. With respect and love for one's parents as the basis, we must not slander brothers and sisters, husbands and wives, relatives or servants. We must love and respect people according to their rank. Even though we are not close, we must not be negligent. This is love. Even if a person is poor, we must not despise them. This is respect.

THINGS TO DO IN THE MORNING

Every day we should get up early, wash our hands and face, and first inquire about the health of our parents. We should ask what food and drink they would like, and we should prepare these things. If one's parents request a certain thing, we should seek it diligently and try to please them. We should instruct the children carefully in the tasks they should perform that day and order clearly and diligently what the servants should do that day. If there are duties to be done outside the house, have the servants do them. If there are requests from people, we should respond punctually and in an orderly manner. We should have the servants rise early and open the gate. We should make everything clean by sweeping within the house, in the garden, and inside and outside the gate. Rising late in the morning signals the decline of the family and it should be avoided. There is an ancient saying: "The status of a family can be seen according to the hour of their rising."

HOUSEHOLD MATTERS

The usual care with respect to household matters should be done expeditiously: first, taking care of the food and rice supply to have enough for the following autumn; next, storing up salt and soy sauce, making dried fish and salted fish, and gathering and stacking firewood, charcoal, and oil. When we do not have these supplies, we cannot meet our household needs. We should be kind to servants and look after their clothes, their food, and the condition of their rooms. We need to make them feel content and free from hunger or severe cold.

Correct distinctions should be made between men and women and between those who are within the household and those who are without. The samurai should always place instruments (such as spears, long swords, bows and arrows, cannons, staffs, and clubs) in appropriate places. One should always keep the necessary utensils in good shape, fix broken things, and promptly repair things that are damaged, such as houses, storerooms, walls, and fences. One should seek and store wood, bamboo, soil, and stones, feed the horses well, care for the domestic animals, and carefully nurture the plants and vegetables according to the season.

We should pay attention to the opening and closing of the storehouse when we put things in and take them out. We should be careful of thieves and watchful for fires. We should not be negligent. We should have fire prevention tools ready. In this way we should always be mindful and not careless in domestic things.

Each of [the four classes of] samurai, farmers, artisans, and merchants should constantly be diligent and not neglect the family business. In addition, we should be frugal and modest in various things and not act carelessly in domestic matters. Being diligent and frugal are two necessary elements in ruling the family. We should always practice these two things: diligence and frugality.

PRACTICING HIDDEN VIRTUE

Within the household we must practice hidden virtue. Preserving humaneness in the heart, practicing goodness in oneself, and not letting others know is hidden virtue. Even those who are less fortunate can practice goodness within their means. It is good to practice hidden virtue by giving food to those who are hungry, providing warmth for those who are cold, giving water to those who are thirsty, caring for the elderly, loving children, consoling the sick, exhorting younger people to have filiality and faithful service toward others, praising the talent and goodness of others, not blaming others' mistakes, concealing other people's evils yet admonishing the faults and mistakes of others [when appropriate], picking up things that may harm people such as posts, oranges with thorns, or stakes that fall on the road, returning to the owner things found on the road, and not killing living things recklessly just because they are small.

When we practice this for a long time the good will grow and we will be content. Even poor people can do this; how much more so should rich people! People who have wealth to spare should follow the principle that says the heavenly Way blesses those who give away excess. If one does not give alms to people and simply accumulates lots of material goods for oneself, later evil will surely arise, material goods will be lost, and little will remain for their children. People who have material wealth should practice goodness by first caring for their parents, then financially assisting relatives and friends, helping the poor, providing for those who are hungry and cold, and thus loving people broadly. Heaven will be deeply pleased with those who help others. Because of the principle that the heavenly Way rewards goodness with happiness, if we continue for a long time to love people broadly, Heaven will be deeply pleased and there is no doubt that we will receive happiness. There is a saying that "The heavenly Way likes the idea of reciprocity." If we practice goodness we will receive happiness from heaven; if we practice evil we will receive misfortune from heaven. The saying concerning "liking reciprocity" means that there is retribution for evil deeds and reward for good deeds. This principle is certain. This is the sincerity of the heavenly Way. When we practice goodness for a long time, it is worth a hundred times more than the prayers of those who do not practice the human Way and just pray and flatter the gods and buddhas to avoid misfortune.

Foolish people lack respect for the heavenly Way and question it because they do not know the principle that the heavenly Way rewards goodness with happiness. In both China and Japan there have been many such examples throughout the ages of the principle that the heavenly Way rewards goodness with happiness and rewards evil with misfortune. This principle is clear. At first there are no signs [of recompense], but later definitely there will be recompense. There is no doubt. When people practice evil and do not help by giving to others so that they too can have material wealth, they will be despised by heaven. This principle is inescapable. We should respect the heavenly Way.

THE MIND-AND-HEART OF THE SAMURAI

Those who are samurai should put their mind carefully toward military preparations. They should arrange soldiers' equipment, repair anything broken, and from time to time should wipe and polish the large and small swords they usually wear in their belts as well as other swords, bows, arrows, spears, and long swords. They should wipe away the dirt and make them shine. They should store up gold, silver, rice, and money for military armaments. When there is insufficient gold to meet all demands, they should not take out and use what they have stored for military use. Soldiers' armaments, even more than other equipment, should be clean for emergencies. If supplies are low they must stock up in times of peace. They should not be negligent. By this preparation of military equipment they will avoid confusion, and even though war breaks out, they will be able to enter the battle calmly. Furthermore, soldiers' armaments should not be unnecessarily decorative.

MAKING THE PRACTICE OF GOODNESS PLEASURABLE

The master of the house should always show love and make the practice of goodness enjoyable. If he has extra goods, he should give them to family members or poor relatives, help friends who are without money, alleviate the hunger and cold of the farmers of his own fief, assist poor and troubled people who come to his house, and help destitute people in appropriate ways. Among beggars there are old people, sick people, deformed people (especially blind, disabled, and deaf people), old people without children, orphans, and those who cannot obtain food because they have no relatives to care for them and thus have no choice but to become beggars. These are destitute people, and when we see these troubled people we should extend our assistance and compassion as much as possible. It is easy to care for the hungry. Doing good by helping others is the most enjoyable thing in the world. We need to think seriously about this. The Chinese Ming emperor asked his brother, Dong Ping Wang, when he came to see him in the capital, "What is pleasure in your country?" His brother answered, "In my country my highest pleasure is doing good." Both rich and poor should do good according to their rank. If they really mean it, even though they are poor, every day they can practice the good. There is nothing more enjoyable than doing good. If they make an effort to practice the good, they should know this pleasure well. An ancient saying notes: "It is hard to do good if you are unwilling to give." It is foolish to spend money on trifling matters. Such spenders do not intend to practice goodness or to help people.

ENDURANCE IN RULING THE FAMILY

We should use endurance in ruling the family. This means persevering and bearing with certain things. Perservering means avoiding extravagance and suppressing selfish desires. Moreover, it is bearing [the burden of] being poor and not desiring other people's things recklessly. Since most people are not sages, there are many things not suitable for our well-being. If we do not have endurance, relationships with people will not go smoothly. Thus, parents and older siblings rebuke children when the child's behavior toward them is inadequate and they are dissatisfied. When the love of parents or older siblings is inadequate, the children resent them. Moreover, the same problem arises between husbands and wives and between relatives. When people are not mutually patient and when they show anger and resentment, human relations worsen. If we are mutually patient with regard to the unsatisfactory deeds of others, if we are not angry and resentful, we will maintain harmony within the family. This is the Way of regulating the family. Moreover, we should exhaust the human Way in enduring and forgiving the misdeeds of others. We should not do anything that needs to be forgiven by others.

When we employ people in the house we must be empathetic toward them, sympathetic toward their hardships, and we should not cause them suffering. Servants are those who live by relying on their masters. We should sympathize with them and not cause them suffering by cruelty or lack of compassion. Those who employ people should reflect deeply on the hardships of servants.

There are four things necessary to govern a household:

1. Managing a livelihood by diligence in the family business
2. Being thrifty in order not to deplete family funds
3. Preserving oneself by self-restraint
4. Having tolerance, namely, love for people

This was said by Wang Ning, a Chinese historian in the Sui dynasty. Tolerance means understanding the heart of others by means of our own heart, giving people what they like and not giving them what they dislike. In order to rule the family, we must observe these four things.

It is important to choose a good teacher for children from an early age and make them read the books of the sages. Teaching them goodness and warning against evil, they should know and practice the way of filiality, loyalty, propriety, and honor. They should not be allowed to associate with evil people. We should warn against this most of all. They should not be allowed to listen to or hear bad things. In childhood it is especially easy to be infected with evil things. What is first learned as good and evil soon becomes ingrained. Children should be made to seek and mingle with good friends and to learn what is good. Because good and evil can become a habit, we must be mindful of our habits.

To preserve the household by self-discipline we must encourage frugality. Frugality means being thrifty and not being greedy or extravagant. Guarding one's desires and being moderate in family expenses is the way to preserve the family by disciplining oneself. In the *Analects* it says, "Little is lost by frugality." When we have frugality our mistakes are few.

If we become the lord of a house, we should have good relations with three families, namely, the father's family, the mother's family, and the wife's family. The father's family is the principal family. The blood that is passed from the ancestors is the same. There are differences of closeness and distance, but since they have the same material force *(ch'i)* as us, we should be on good terms. Being on good terms with the father's family is the way to serve ancestors. After the father's family, we should be on good terms with the mother's family. The wife's family comes next after the mother's family. Such is the order and importance of having good relations with these three families. This is an ancient custom. Nowadays people are only intimate with the wife's family, and they are distant from the father's and the mother's family. This is not knowing the importance [of relationships]. It is unfilial to parents and it is foolish. This is not to say one should not have good relations with one's wife's family. However, it is good to observe relationships in an appropriate manner.

EXERCISING THE BODY

Make both the cost and intake of daily food and drink moderate and exercise the body. Indulging in good food and drink and being idle is deleterious to the body. We should not be extravagant and lazy. If we follow this teaching we will receive three benefits: first you nurture virtue, then you strengthen the body, and finally you increase your wealth. When we eat and drink simply and exercise the body, we can enjoy good health since there will be no food stagnation. The blood will circulate well and the stomach stays healthy. If you exercise the body you can endure suffering and hard work and can practice loyalty and filiality, and thus it will be beneficial for teaming and for the arts.

If one does not exercise, then idleness becomes a habit; one cannot endure hardship nor make continual efforts of loyalty and filiality, and one neglects scholarship and the arts. Samurai especially will lose their disciplined training; they cannot endure the hardships of the army; they will become sick and their body will deteriorate and become useless, and as a result they cannot exercise their duty. We must make the heart peaceful and the body active.

CHAPTER 2

When we put forth effort in the family business we can earn profit even if we do not seek it. The samurai should make an effort for his lord without flattery. The farrmer should apply himself in the fields; he should revere authority, work hard as a public duty. The artisan should make good things and should not deceive people by making inferior things. The merchant should avoid fraud and usury in his trade. If the four classes act together like this without forcing themselves to be greedy for profit, they will enjoy happiness and fortune naturally. Those who fail to do their duty correctly and are greedy for profit and do evil things may be happy for a while; however, because it is a principle that heaven will despise them, later they will surely suffer misfortune. Foolish people try to make profits quickly and never anticipate later misfortune. The four classes must not be deceptive in performing their family work correctly and revering the Way of heaven. This is the way to escape misfortune and ensure happiness.

NOT BEING GREEDY FOR PROFIT

The family's misfortune arises, in most cases, from seeking profit. When we are greedy for profit, it often happens that instead misfortune comes and we lose assets. Rather than seeking profit, if you make an effort not to neglect the family business and not use family funds carelessly and not seek profit more than is suitable, there will be no misfortune and you will not lose property. Generally speaking, greed for profit is the origin of misfortune. We should avoid that.

EFFORT AND MINDFULNESS ARE THE WAY OF HEAVEN AND EARTH

It is an ancient saying that "If we make an effort we will overcome poverty; if we are mindful we will overcome misfortune." These words are very beneficial. People who diligently make an effort in the family business inevitably become rich. If we are mindful of ourselves there will be no misfortune. These two words [effort and mindfulness] we should always protect and practice. By actualizing these ourselves, our family members will do likewise. Making an effort is the Way of heaven; heaven revolves without ceasing. Being mindful is the way of Earth; earth is quiet and does not move. Making an effort and being mindful is basing our model on the Way of heaven and earth. This is the Way that humans ought to practice, for these are profound principles.

—39—

A Refutation of Clerical Marriage

Richard Jaffe

One of the most remarkable changes in Japanese Buddhism in the Meiji period (1868–1912) was the spread of open clerical marriage among the Buddhist clergy. Since the early Edo period (1603–1867), clerical marriage had been banned by state law for all Buddhist clerics except for those affiliated with denominations that traditionally had allowed marriage—Shugendō and Jōdo Shinshū. Although the prohibition against marriage had been frequently and flagrantly violated by many clerics, the regulation was also sporadically enforced with a vengeance by the Tokugawa authorities. At least superficially the leaders of the "celibate" denominations and the state demanded that their clerics adhere to the stricture against sexual relations and marriage.

In the wake of the violence triggered by the harsh anti-Buddhist measures enacted by the officials of the new Meiji regime from 1868 to 1872, bureaucrats at the Kyōbushō (Ministry of Religious Doctrine), the Ōkurashō (Ministry of Finance), and the Shihōshō (Ministry of Justice) worked toward the complete disestablishment of Buddhism. As part of their efforts, the officials at these ministries steadily dismantled the remaining Edo period regulations governing clerical life and eliminated any perquisites that had previously been granted the clergy by virtue of their status as "home-leavers" (*shukke*). Despite opposition from the Buddhist leadership, in short order the clerics were ordered to assume surnames, to register in the ordinary household registration system (*koseki*), and to serve in the military. These changes reduced the Buddhist clergy to subjects like all other Japanese and rendered the clerical estate an occupation that was no different from any other career in the eyes of the state .

Without doubt the decriminalization of clerical marriage was the most contested of all the changes in clerical regulations. With the support of such Buddhists as Ōtori Sessō (1804–1904), an ex-Sōtō cleric who had been appointed to the Kyōbushō, and the Tendai cleric Ugawa Shōchō, on Meiji 5/4/25 the officials at the Kyōbushō issued a regulation that stated, "From now on Buddhist clerics shall be free to eat meat, marry, grow their hair, and so on. Furthermore, there will be no penalty if they wear ordinary clothing when not engaged in religious activities." Although all aspects of the new regulation, referred to as the *nikujiki saitai* law because it decriminalized meat eating and clerical marriage, were resisted by the leaders of the Buddhist denominations, the most prominent and vexatious feature of the regulation for the Buddhist leadership was the end to state penalties for clerical marriage.

Protest against the new measure came swiftly and strongly. A petition by the Jōdo cleric Fukuda Gyōkai (1809–1888) that strongly denounced the government's efforts to end state enforcement of clerical regulations was signed by the chief abbots (Kanchō) of every Buddhist denomination except the Jōdo Shinshū and was submitted to the government just months after the new law was promulgated. The petition complained that the decriminalization of clerical marriage would lead to enormous confusion of the lay-clerical distinction in Buddhism and, by weakening the clergy, would result in further moral chaos for the Japanese nation. When government officials adamantly refused to reconsider the decriminalization measure, the leadership of the Buddhist clergy continued to meet with government officials and to submit a series of petitions calling for revocation of the new law. In addition, the leaders of almost every Buddhist denomination issued internal directives aimed at the clergy calling for continued adherence to the Buddhist precepts, despite the decriminalization.

The steady resistance of the Buddhist clerical leadership and a gradual moderation of the government's policy toward religious organizations led to a softening of the position with regard to clerical marriage. In 1878 the Naimushō (Ministry of Home Affairs), which now had jurisdiction over Buddhist affairs, issued a terse addendum to the 1872 *nikujiki saitai* law. The modification of the decriminalization measure stated, "Edict 133 [*nikujiki saitai* law], which states that the clergy are free to eat meat and marry, only serves to abolish the state law that had prohibited such activities. In no way does the law have anything to do with sectarian regulations." With that ruling the Naimushō officials turned over all responsibility for the maintenance of clerical discipline to the leadership of each Buddhist denomination, thus differentiating state laws from private religious and moral concerns.

The reaction of the clerical leadership to the modification of the government's position regarding clerical marriage was unified. Although clerical marriage was popular with most lower-ranking members of the Buddhist clergy, over the next several months the leadership of most denominations, including Sōtō, Nichiren, Jōdo, and Shingon, issued new sect laws and directives condemning or even banning clerical marriage. It was in the context of increased independence for the clerical leaders to regulate the behavior of the Buddhist clergy that *Dan sōryo saitai ron* was published in 1879.

Little is known about the identity of the author of *Dan sōryo saitai ron*, Uan Dōnin, but there is a strong possibility that the name Uan Dōnin was a pen name for the Sōtō cleric Nishiari Bokusan (a k a Nishiari Kin'ei, 1821–1910). A prominent scholar of Dōgen's *Shōbōgenzō*, Nishiari served as the abbot of several Sōtō temples before becoming the chief abbot of the Sōtō denomination in 1902. Nishiari is known to have used the very similar pseudonym Uan Rōnin in some of his writings. Nishiari also was a vocal opponent of clerical marriage and expressed his views on the matter frequently. In 1875 he submitted two letters to the Sōtō leadership calling for them to observe traditional monastic strictures against the eating of meat, marriage, abandoning the tonsure, and wearing nonclerical garb. In his letters Nishiari warned his fellow clerics that they must be careful in both words and actions and that, despite changes in state law, they must continue to follow the Buddhist precepts.

Dan sōryo saitai ron is a prime example of the anticlerical marriage tracts that were published by private individuals and officially by the administrations of the various Buddhist denominations during the 1870s and 1880s. Written in question-answer dialogue format, the document presents the main justifications made by proponents of clerical marriage and the author's criticism of those positions. In this brief diatribe, the author refutes the main Confucian, Nativist, and government attacks on the Buddhist practices of *shukke* (home-leaving) and celibacy. Reiterating arguments frequently used by such Buddhist apologists as the Chinese layman Sun Ch'o (ca. 300–380), the Chinese Chan cleric Ch'i-sung (1007–1072, posthumously Ming-chiao Ta-shih; J., Myōk[illegible] Daishi), and the Japanese Ōbaku cleric Chōon Dōkai (1628–1695), Uan Dōnin challenges the common Buddhist dispensationalist argument that because in the Last Age of the Teaching (*mappō*) true practice is impossible, it is permissible for the Buddhist clergy to abandon the precept that proscribes sexual relations. Echoing the traditional Buddhist refutation of charges of unfiliality, the author asserts that "home-leaving" is the highest form of filial piety because, unlike laypeople, who are primarily concerned with the welfare of their immediate family in this life, Buddhist clerics work for the ultimate salvation of all beings.

In addition to responding to Confucian attacks on Buddhist celibacy, Uan Dōnin also attempts to neutralize Shintoist and Nativist critiques of monastic practice. To accomplish that end, the author ties the Buddhist abhorrence of sexual relations and marriage to the ultimate purity of the cosmos that is described in the foundational Shintō creation myths of the *Record of Ancient Matters* (*Kojiki*) and the *Chronicles of Japan* (*Nihon shoki*). Just as ritual purity and celibacy is demanded by the *kami* because of the original purity of the cosmos, Uan argues, so do the Buddhas demand the celibacy of those who enter the Buddhist order.

One of the primary rationales put forward to justify the state's liberalization of laws governing clerical behavior was that state-enforced celibacy was an unnatural and outmoded practice that rendered the Buddhist clergy useless in the efforts to build a "rich country and a strong army." Unlike such proponents of Buddhist modernization as Ōtori Sessō or Ugawa Shōchō, who were concerned with the pragmatic utilization of clerical manpower to strengthen the state, Uan Dōnin claimed that the true value of the clergy depends on their ability to insure the fortunes of the nation by serving the kami and the Buddhas, not on their utility as potential draftees and state proselytizers. The author even problematizes the very notions of progress and enlightenment as they were defined in the early Meiji period. Questioning the dominant emphasis on material progress as the hallmark of civilization, Uan Dōnin concludes that true "civilization and enlightenment" is impossible without the presence of pure, celibate clerics.

This is a translation of Uan Dōnin, "Dan sōryo saitai ron," in Meiji Bukkyō Shisō Shiryō Shūseihen Iinkai, ed., *Meiji Bukkyō shisō shiryō shūsei*, vol. 6 (Kyoto: Dōbōsha Shuppan, 1982), pp. 171–75.

Further Reading

Winston Davis, "Buddhism and the Modernization of Japan," *History of Religions* 28, 4 (1989): 304–39; Richard Jaffe, "Neither Monk nor Layman: The Debate over Clerical Marriage in Japanese Buddhism, 1868–1937," Ph.D. dissertation, Yale University, 1995; Richard Jaffe, "The Buddhist Cleric as Japanese Subject: Buddhism and the Household Registration System," in *New Directions in the Study of Meiji Japan*, edited by Helen Hardacre and Adam L. Kern (Leiden: E. J. Brill, 1997), pp. 670–702; Kawahashi Noriko, "Jizoku (Priest's Wives) in Sōtō Zen Buddhism: An Ambiguous Category," *Japanese Journal of Religious Studies* 22.1–2 (1995): 161–83; James Edward Ketelaar, *Of Heretics and Martyrs in Meiji Japan* (Princeton: Princeton University Press, 1990); Uchino Kumiko, "The Status Elevation Process of Sōtō Sect Nuns in Modern Japan," *Japanese Journal of Religious Studies* 10.1–2 (1983): 177–94.

A Treatise Refuting Clerical Marriage

The marriage of priests is a sign of the extinction of the dharma. The increase of licentiousness is an omen of the end of a nation. Therefore, I often admonish people about this. Although occasionally there are those who believe this, those who uphold [the prohibition against marriage] are quite rare. On occasion in response to this lament it is asked:

Question: In Heaven and Earth there are yin and yang. Accordingly, humans are male and female, husband and wife. Why do the Buddhists proscribe that which follows natural law? Those who disobey the law of nature will become obsolete, but those who accord with the law of nature prosper. Is that not why the celibate schools grow weaker daily and the schools that allow marriage grow more prosperous monthly?

Answer: You understand superficial worldly principles, but you do not understand the profound principles of heaven and earth. Excessive sexual desire harms the body, wrecks the family, and destroys the nation. Licentiousness originally arises from covetousness. When covetousness arises, inevitably greed, hate, delusion, and all the defilements also arise. When due to the three poisons and the defilements karmic causes are produced, retribution will inevitably follow.

Question: If people believe all the Buddha's teaching and, fearing karmic cause and effect, do not marry, then what will become of posterity? Mencius said, "Having no successor is the greatest act of unfilial behavior" [*Meng-tzu*, IV.A.26]. How do you resolve this problem?

Answer: The prohibition against marriage is aimed solely at "home-leavers." It is not an exhortation for all sentient beings to leave home. In Buddhism there are four groups of disciples and precepts appropriate for each of the seven assemblies: monks, nuns, male novices, female novices who receive the six precepts, female novices, laymen, and laywomen. You should understand this fact.

Mencius's words are specific for one situation; how can you take them to be unchanging for all time? This is clear because when Mencius explained the five types of unfilial behavior, he did not include not having an heir as part of the list [*Meng-tzu*, IV.B.30]. It also is said that Mencius wished to explain how Shun did not inform his parents of his marriage because Shun feared his parents would stop his marriage, thus preventing him from having an heir.

Even if it that was not the reason for Mencius making the statement about having an heir, his words still must be viewed as conditional, because having a child is dependent upon causes and conditions. It is not subject to human control. Even if one's family is prosperous and noble and one has both a wife and a concubine, one may not have even one child. By contrast, a poor husband and wife, barely able to eke out a living, may have many children even if they do not want them. How can we judge filial and unfilial behavior on the basis of that which is determined by causes and conditions?

Furthermore, Mencius had no children. The cause for this was Mencius's wife, who did not conduct herself with propriety, so he wished to be rid of her. Mencius's mother took pity on Mencius's wife; therefore his getting rid of his wife would have been unfilial. If he were to love his wife, [a woman who did not act with propriety,] that would compound the impropriety. Therefore he could neither get rid of his wife nor could he love her. Thus what can we tell from the fact that Mencius was without children? Mencius revered propriety; he did not lament that he was without an heir. If people flourish in numbers but are lacking in propriety, then they are animals, not humans. Mencius was successor to Confucius. This is an example of how he valued propriety and lightly regarded the matter of having descendants.

Furthermore, Confucius said, "If one hears of the Way in the morning, it is all right to die in the evening." That is how much Confucius valued propriety. He did not say, "If one has a child in the morning, it is all right to die in the evening." If one has descendants but does not follow the Way and lacks propriety, how could having descendants allow one to be at peace?

Such expressions as "not having children is unfilial," or "it is the natural law of yin and yang,"and so forth, are excuses used by hedonists. In fact, insuring posterity is rarely the aim of licentious behavior. Married men who visit prostitutes contract syphilis and transmit the disease to their wife and children. Does one visit prostitutes in order to have children or because of the principle of yin and yang? Sometimes one who is overwhelmed by sexual desire will even desert his wife who has borne his children. Or a wife and concubine will become jealous of each other, resulting in murder by poisoning or a knifing. Or a double love suicide occurs. Can we say that these occurrences are due to the heavenly principle or that these actions arise out of filial concern for having descendants?

If not having an heir makes one unfilial, then why is only the man unfilial? The same should hold true for the woman as well as the man. If that is so, then if a woman is childless with one husband, she should remarry. One hears that it is admirable if "a virtuous woman does not take a second husband." One does not hear that following the injunction "a virtuous woman should take a second husband in order to have descendants" is the basis for praise. You should think carefully about these things.

Question: Why do "home-leavers" abandon their parents and travel far away, thus not providing filial care for their father and mother?

Answer: The Buddha stated, "All sentient beings are my children." Thus the people of the world should all be considered our siblings. If one's siblings have difficulty, how can one not help them? For example, suppose one's sister marries into another family. If there is a fire or flood, even if one's parents are on their sickbed, one should do what is necessary to go to help her. Not only will one's father and mother not reprimand one for this, but their illnesses will be soothed by such action. If the flood or fire is said to be severe and one does not help because one's parents are ill, then parents' illness will only worsen. Is this not human nature?

In the defiled world the difficulties posed by the three poisons and the four devils [of evil passions, the five human constituents, death, and attachment] are even graver than those from flood or fire. The difficulties arising from a fire or flood are temporary and do not affect negatively one's future rebirths, but the three poisons and the four devils will eternally affect this and future lives. If that is not frightening then what is? If one is always diligent and leaves one's home and parents in order to devote oneself to the amelioration of difficulties caused by the three poisons and the four devils, ultimately there will be no time to worry about not having descendants. Therefore although people who engage in such activities are called "home-leavers," in fact they are "debt-repayers."

If a loyal retainer sacrifices his life for the sake of his lord, how can we say that he has been unfilial? If that is deemed a transgression and is construed as unfilial, then it will not do to laud [the imperial loyalist] Kusunoki Masashige or the retainers of Akō [the forty-seven *rōnin* warriors]. Home-leaving is undertaken for the sake of the Way. The Way saves sentient beings from their delusions and thereby enables them to escape future eternal suffering. Is that not Great Mind? Do you suppose that one who has manifested Great Mind has time to worry about having descendants?

Did not Confucius say, "Serving one's father and mother is taken to be the beginning of filial piety; achieving fame is the ultimate filial piety"? With respect to the filiality of home-leaving, although it is not undertaken for the sake of fame, those individuals whose pure name and world-saving skill are transmitted to all future generations are the most filial people of all. One cannot argue that the petty filiality of those who merely raised children pales by comparison. For more about the superiority of the filial piety of the home-leaver, you should carefully study the *Treatise on Filial Piety* [*Hsiao lun*] by Myōkyō Daishi [Ch'i-sung]. I will not go into detail here.

Question: If this is the case, then do all of the home-leavers today possess Great Mind of this sort?

Answer: We cannot guarantee that all put forth the Great Mind in this manner even in the past. Would this not be even more difficult to guarantee today? Have you not read that when Confucius expounded about humanity (*jen*), he was unable to make all benevolent? Or that when Lao-tzu expounded on spontaneity (*tzu jan*), he was unable to make everyone act with spontaneity? When Jesus expounded on faith and love, how could he make all people faithful and loving? Is it not even more so the case with the Buddha's exposition of putting forth the mind of the bodhisattva who strives to enlighten others before himself and the boundless great nirvana that extends through the three times and escapes the Triple World? If, due to the fact that one cannot make all people realize benevolence, nature, faith, and love, or the mind of the bodhisattva, one says those paths should be destroyed, then since ancient times no teaching should have been founded and no path should have been expounded in this ignorant world. If the sage's leaving the world ultimately is without benefit, we can only say that they are leading astray those in the world. How could it do to revere them? So long as the path that is difficult to enact and difficult to practice exists, no matter how unpopular it is there will be some in the world who follow it. Even if it is the Last Age of the Teaching, it is impossible that there is no one.

One who follows the paths is called a person in possession of the Way. A person who possesses the Way tours the four directions and diligently preaches the Way, just as King Yu helped subdue the flood. It is impossible to predict how many people will be turned away from evil and toward the good by even one such person. It goes without saying that those who preach the Way aid the government.

Question: If people are made to uphold all the Buddhist precepts, won't this mean the extinction of humanity?

Answer: You should not worry too much about this. Even if one thousand buddhas were to appear in the world and preach the Buddhist precepts, is it possible that they would make all sentient beings adhere to all the precepts, thereby causing the extinction of humanity? If due to the precepts the extinction of humanity were to result, then would not this filthy land become a Pure Land, and a race of humans who do not engage in impure relations between men and women be born?

Question: Why is it that those who serve the Buddha emphasize celibacy?

Answer: Why do you think that only those who serve the Buddha emphasize celibacy? Those who serve the kami are supposed to devote themselves to celibacy as well. At the very beginning, Heaven and Earth were truly pure essences. Thus the age of the kami began from one single kami. Even when there were male and female kami it is said there were no sexual relations. It is clear that the interaction of yin and yang resulted in the pollution of Heaven and Earth as well as the birth of the myriad things and human beings. Surely this is why the character *jin* (deity; *kami*) has the Japanese reading *kabi* (mysterious power).

Because human beings were born from the impurity of sexual relations, they only understand the impurity of sexual relations; they do not understand the pure essence [of all things]. They consider impurity to be the fundamental nature of Heaven and Earth and do not know that sexual relations are impure. They resemble insects who, because they are born in stagnant water, think that the original essence of water is stagnancy. The insects have not the slightest inkling of the essential purity of water.

The heavenly kami (*amatsu kami*) appeared at the beginning of Heaven and Earth so their love of purity is a necessity. Has not the Buddha taught that in the heavenly realms, the gods experience pleasure by different means—through intercourse, an embrace, the touch of hands, a smile, or a look? As one ascends, lust correspondingly weakens. Seeing the polluted acts of humankind, how could the heavenly kami not despise them? How much more so this must be true for a buddha who has transcended the Triple World!

When those who serve the kami are pure,. the kami are delighted; when those who serve the buddhas are pure the buddhas are delighted. We know this is so because when the kami and the buddhas are delighted, they obey our prayers and always respond to our appeals. Since ancient times pure priests have moved the virtuous spirits and kami of Heaven and Earth; we know this by the extraordinary fashion in which their prayers were realized. Therefore those who have respect and faith for the buddhas and the kami should love pure priests. The kami and the buddhas take pleasure in an abundance of pure priests. When the kami and the buddhas rejoice, then their protection grows stronger. Thus we can say when pure priests are numerous, those who protect the nation are numerous.

The fate of the Tokugawa family is a recent example of this. At the beginning of the Tokugawa reign the clergy's rules were upheld, in the middle the rules gradually slackened, and by the end the rules were in great disorder. This gave rise to the "abolish the buddhas" movement of Lord Mito. Is it not the case that the vigor and weakness of the pure priests corresponded with the prosperity and decline of the Tokugawa family?

If you love your nation you should support the celibate schools, and you should pray that those who uphold the precepts will increase daily. You should not favor those who break the precepts.

Question: It is said that the decline of Roman Catholicism is due to their clinging to the outmoded custom of celibacy in service to God. Today, Buddhism in Japan is also like this. Is it not the case that the schools that allow marriage increase in strength daily, while the celibate schools decline daily?

Answer: The reasons for this are subtle and hidden and are difficult to explain. It is very difficult to say whether the prosperity of the schools that allow marriage is true prosperity or whether the weakness of the celibate schools is true weakness.

The decline of Tibet is most certainly the source of the decline of Lamaism. Although I don't know yet the source of Tibet's weakness, could it not be due to the oppressiveness of extravagant luxury and the topsy-turviness of too much "civilization"?

I am old-fashioned and there are things I do not understand about "civilization and enlightenment" (*bunmei kaika*). Should what is happening in Japan today be seen as progress or decline? The most striking things about the so-called "progress of civilization" are such external manifestations as machinery, tiled roofs, Western clothes, Western letters, and Western language. However, when we examine the disposition of those who are adolescents or younger, we find that those with flippant, servile, and resentful voices are numerous, but those with a sense of integrity are extremely few.

Precept violation by the clergy, the business enterprises of the nobles (*kazoku*), and ex-samurai (*shizoku*) pulling rickshaws are not considered contemptuous. A woman is not embarrassed about being a consort or a geisha, and it is considered foolish to be a "virtuous woman and a good wife" (*teijo seppu*). Deceit is a natural occurrence. It is difficult to loan and borrow money without collateral, even among fathers and sons or brothers. If this trend continues for a few more years, what will become of the nation, let alone the Buddha Dharma? When compared to the generations in which celibate priests were valued and virtuous women were admired, is the current state of affairs beautiful or ugly, progress or decline? Ultimately my grieving over the decline of the Buddha Dharma results in my grieving for the nation. With deep regret I forget about food and sleep and I, in isolation, can only let out a futile, heavy sigh. Some people remain silent and have withdrawn, but I have something more that attracts my eye. How splendid! I have had a dream. To explain the dream will require another work, so I lay down my writing brush for now.

Meiji 12/3/5 [1879]

—40—

The Contemplation of Suchness

Jacqueline I. Stone

The Contemplation of Suchness (*Shinnyo kan*) is attributed to the great scholar and teacher of the Tendai school of Buddhism, the prelate Genshin (942–1017). However, it actually dates from around the twelfth century. Tendai writings of medieval times were often compiled by unidentified authors who attributed them to earlier Tendai masters. By the early medieval period, a few Buddhist thinkers had begun to write in vernacular Japanese rather than the literary Chinese that formed the accepted scholarly medium for works on Buddhist doctrine. *The Contemplation of Suchness* is an example of this new development. It may have been written for an educated lay person, rather than a monastic reader, and reflects a number of significant developments within early medieval Japanese Buddhist thought.

One important intellectual trend to develop within Tendai Buddhism of the medieval period is known as original enlightenment thought (*hongaku shisō*). This doctrine denies that enlightenment is achieved as the result of a long process of religious cultivation; rather, it holds that all beings are, from the outset, enlightened by their very nature, that is, "originally." From this perspective, Buddhist practice is to be approached, not as a means to "attain" a future result, but to realize that oneself is a buddha already. The present writing describes this in terms of knowing, or believing, that "oneself is precisely suchness." "Suchness" or "thusness" (Skt., *tathatā*; J., *shinnyo*) is a Buddhist term for the true nature of reality, or what an enlightened person is said to realize. Like many such terms, it is intended to designate without describing, for the buddha wisdom can be neither described nor grasped conceptually but only indicated as being "such."

In this text, the idea of original enlightenment is explained in terms of traditional Tendai (C. T'ien-t'ai) forms of doctrinal classification and meditative practice, as well as the Tendai school's particular reverence for the *Lotus Sūtra*. The historical Buddha, Śākyamuni, was said to have preached for fifty years. According to the Tendai systematization of doctrine, for the first forty-two years the Buddha taught provisional teachings that were accommodated to his listeners' understanding, while in the final eight years of his life he taught the true teaching, the *Lotus*

Sūtra, said to be the direct expression of his own enlightenment. *The Contemplation of Suchness* assimilates this distinction between true and provisional teachings to two different views of enlightenment. The provisional teachings preached before the *Lotus Sūtra*, it says, teach that one can attain Buddhahood only after many kalpas (aeons) of austere practices, while the *Lotus Sūtra* uniquely reveals that all beings are enlightened inherently.

In terms of meditative practice, the "contemplation of suchness" discussed in this text is equated with the "contemplation of the Middle Way" or the "threefold contemplation in a single thought" set forth in the *Great Calming and Contemplation* (*Mo-ho chih-kuan*), the influential treatise recording the teachings on meditation of Chih-i (538–597), founder of the T'ien-t'ai school, the Chinese precursor of Japanese Tendai. T'ien-t'ai meditation aims at perceiving all things from the threefold perspective of emptiness, provisional existence, and the Middle, known as the threefold truth. By contemplating all phenomena as empty—that is, as dependent upon conditions and without permanence or underlying essence—one is freed from delusive attachments. This is said to correspond to the practice and insight of persons of the two vehicles (the Hīnayāna teachings) and bodhisattvas of elementary Mahāyāna. However, merely to be freed from attachment is not enough. Therefore, while knowing all things to be empty, one also contemplates them as provisionally existing. In this way, one is able to understand them correctly as conditioned aspects of conventional reality, without imputing to them false notions of essence, and so act wisely and compassionately in the world. This is said to correspond to the insight and practice of bodhisattvas of the higher Mahāyāna teachings. Finally, by contemplating all things as both empty and provisionally existing, one maintains both views simultaneously, the two perspectives holding one another in perfect balance and preventing one-sided adherence to either. This is said to correspond to the practice and insight of buddhas. In explaining the threefold truth, one must unavoidably explain its three aspects sequentially, and novice practitioners were also taught to contemplate the three truths of emptiness, provisional existence, and the middle as a progressive sequence. However, this sequential meditation was regarded as a lesser form of the threefold contemplation. Its ultimate form is to cognize all three truths simultaneously, "in a single thought."

Within the traditional T'ien-t'ai/Tendai structure of meditative discipline, the threefold contemplation, or the contemplation of the Middle Way, required formal meditative practice, usually performed in a monastic context and often carried out in seclusion for a specified number of days, weeks, or months. The "contemplation of suchness" discussed in this writing, however, is not a formally structured meditation but rather the cultivation, in the midst of daily activities, of a particular mental attitude—namely, of seeing oneself and all others as identical to suchness. As the text says,

> Clergy or laity, male or female—all should contemplate in this way. When you provide for your wife, children, and retainers, or even feed oxen, horses, and the

> others of the six kinds of domestic animals, because the myriad things are all suchness, if you think that these others are precisely suchness, you have in effect made offerings to all Buddhas and bodhisattvas of the ten directions and to all living beings, without a single exception.

Because suchness is the real aspect of all things, to think of both oneself and others in this way is to open a perspective from which individuals are not separate, unrelated, or conflicting existences but nondual—each identical with the totality of all that is and encompassing all others within itself. In other words, it is to see all beings manifesting original enlightenment just as they are.

Some evidence suggests that the "contemplation of suchness" described in this text may actually have been conducted as a form of lay practice during the early Kamakura period (1185–1333). A late twelfth- or early thirteenth-century anthology of tales called *A Collection of Treasures* (*Hōbutsu shū*), attributed to Taira Yasuyori (fl. 1190–1200), refers to the above passage from *The Contemplation of Suchness* and says:

> When you eat, visualize [this act] as making offerings to the thirty-seven honored ones [i.e., the buddhas and bodhisattvas depicted on the Diamond-Realm mandala of Esoteric Buddhism], and when you feed others, form the thought that you are, upwardly, making offerings to the buddhas of the ten directions and three periods of time, and downwardly, giving alms to hell-dwellers, hungry ghosts and those in the animal realm. And you should likewise form this thought when you feed your servants and retainers, or give food to horses and cattle, birds and beasts. For lay people, men and women engaged in public and private affairs, what practice could possibly be superior?
>
> [*DNBZ* 147:426]

By cultivating the attitude that "all things are precisely suchness," the simplest acts of daily life in effect become Buddhist practice.

The Contemplation of Suchness links notions of original enlightenment to several other trends that characterized much of Japanese Buddhism in the medieval period. One is a growing emphasis on simple practices, which developed within both older, established schools of Buddhism—Tendai, Shingon, and the Nara schools—and the new Buddhist movements of the Kamakura period. Practices such as the repeated chanting of the nembutsu, the Buddha Amida's name (*Namu-Amida-butsu*), or of the *daimoku*, the title of the *Lotus Sūtra* (*Namu-myōhō-renge-kyō*), gained popularity during this time. Such practices were of course accessible to a great range of persons, including lay people unable to undertake demanding religious disciplines or to read difficult Buddhist texts. Beyond the issue of accessibility, however, the emphasis on simple practices was connected with the idea that the world had entered a period known as the Final Dharma age (*mappō*), regarded as a time of decline when traditional Buddhist disciplines would be beyond the capacity of most persons. The "contemplation of suchness" described here, which can be undertaken by anyone even in the midst of daily activities, appears to have been one of the simple practices regarded as particularly suited to those people born in the Final Dharma age.

While the simple practices were on the one hand touted as appropriate to people of limited capacity unable to undertake traditional Buddhist disciplines, they were at the same time extolled as being superior to those disciplines, in that they were said to encompass all merit in a single religious act and thus offer direct access to the Buddha's enlightenment without lifetimes of austere practice. For example, Hōnen (1133–1212), founder of the Japanese Jōdo or Pure Land sect, praised the nembutsu as encompassing the three bodies, ten powers, and four fearlessnesses—in short, all the virtues of the Buddha Amida. Nichiren (1222–1282), who preached a doctrine of exclusive devotion to the *Lotus Sūtra*, similarly taught that the *daimoku* contains the merit of all the virtuous practices carried out by Śākyamuni Buddha in his quest, over countless lifetimes, for supreme enlightenment; by chanting the *daimoku* of the *Lotus Sūtra*, Nichiren said, one can immediately access the Buddha's merits. Here, at a slightly earlier date, we find similar claims made for the "contemplation of suchness," which is said to encompass all merit within itself.

Related to the notion of simple practices was the idea that sincere devotion to the particular religious act in question was more important to one's salvation than the cultivation of moral conduct. In the present writing, even those who "violate the precepts without shame" are nonetheless said to be able to realize enlightenment and achieve birth in the Pure Land by diligently contemplating suchness. Such passages link this text to broader medieval concerns about the possibility of the salvation of evil persons. For many, the Final Dharma age was a time when proper observance of the Buddhist precepts was thought to be impossible. These concerns also reflected the rise to power of the warrior class, people whose hereditary profession required them to violate the traditional Buddhist precept against killing.

When Saichō (767–822), who established Tendai Buddhism in Japan, studied in China, he received instruction not only in the T'ien-t'ai *Lotus* teachings but also in Esoteric Buddhism, Ch'an (Zen), and the bodhisattva precepts. Building upon this foundation, his successors sought to develop a comprehensive religious system that would encompass all practices within the "one vehicle" of the *Lotus Sūtra*. This all-encompassing approach would become characteristic of Japanese Tendai, and strands of Buddhist thought other than the original Tendai/Lotus teachings are accordingly evident in *The Contemplation of Suchness*. The most obvious of these is Pure Land Buddhism, centering on contemplation of and devotion to the Buddha Amida (Skt. Amitābha), said to live in a pure land called Utmost Bliss (Sukhāvatī, Gokuraku) in the western quarter of the universe. Birth after death in Amida's Pure Land, the goal of many Pure Land practitioners, was seen as liberation from the sufferings of the round of rebirth and equated with the stage of nonretrogression on the path of achieving Buddhahood. Pure Land practices in premodern Japan were extremely widespread, transcending sectarian divisions, and assumed a number of forms. These ranged from various Pure Land meditations that developed within the Tendai school; to the chanting of Amida's name, interpreted as both contemplation and devotion; to popular uses of the nembutsu, for example, as a deathbed practice, to transfer merit to the deceased, and to placate unhappy spirits. The medieval period also witnessed the rise of independent Pure Land traditions, such as the Jōdo (Pure Land) sect of Hōnen, the Jōdo Shin (True Pure Land) sect of Shinran (1173–1262), and the Ji sect of Ippen (1239–1289). *The Contemplation of Suchness* reflects the Pure Land tradition that developed within Tendai Buddhism. Genshin, to whom it is attributed, was a key figure in the development of this tradition and the author of an extremely popular work on Pure Land faith and practice, the *Essentials of Birth in the Pure Land* (*Ōjōyōshū*). It will be noted that *The Contemplation of Suchness* on one hand speaks of birth after death in Amida's pure land as a real event and yet, on the other, urges the necessity of realizing that oneself and the Buddha are nondual in essence. This dual perspective is not altogether uncommon in the Tendai Pure Land writings of this period, which may describe the pure land as both a real place in the western part of the universe and immanent in this world, and Amida, as both a transcendent buddha and identical to one's own mind. For example, *Questions and Answers on the Nembutsu as Self-Cultivation* (*Jigyō nembutsu mondō*), another medieval Tendai text retrospectively attributed to Genshin, says: "Even though one knows Amida to be one's own mind, one forms a relationship with Amida Buddha of the west and in this way manifests the Amida who is one's own mind" (*DNBZ* 31: 212).

Although less prominent than the Pure Land references, elements of the Esoteric strand within Tendai buddhism also occur in this text. The buddha revered in the Esoteric teachings is Dainichi (Skt. Mahāvairocana), the cosmic buddha said to pervade and be embodied by the entire universe: all forms are his body, all sounds are his voice, and all thoughts are his mind, although the unenlightened do not realize this. In Esoteric practice, the practitioner is said to realize the identity of one's own body, speech, and mind with those of Dainichi through performance of the "three mysteries": the forming of ritual gestures (*mūdras*) with the hands and body, the chanting of mantras or secret ritual formulas with the mouth, and the mental contemplation of mandalas or iconographic representations of the cosmos as the expression of Dainichi. Portions of *The Contemplation of Suchness* not included here suggest that contemplating suchness is identical to the adept realizing one's identity with Dainichi in the act of Esoteric practice.

The Contemplation of Suchness makes clear that, although all beings are said to be enlightened inherently, this does not amount to a denial of the need for Buddhist practice: Original enlightenment, according to this text, must be manifested by cultivating the attitude that oneself and all others are inseparable from the Buddha. Its concluding passage admonishes the reader to "think that we are precisely suchness, night and day, whether walking, standing, sitting, or lying down, without forgetting." Moreover, while all creatures, even insects, are deemed to be enlightened innately, there is an implicit privileging of the human state, in that only humans can realize their identity with suchness and so free themselves from the suffering of transmigration. It is also recognized that, due to individual differences in human capacity, not everyone will be able to achieve and sustain this insight with equal speed. Some will require "a day, two days, a month, two months, a year, or even a lifetime," though the implication is that everyone can do so within this present existence.

The translated excerpts are from *Shinnyo kan*, in Tada Kōryū et al., eds., *Tendai hongaku ron*, in Nihon shisō taikei 9 (Tokyo: Iwanami Shoten, 1973), pp. 120–49.

Further Reading

Allan A. Andrews, *The Teachings Essential for Rebirth: A Study of Genshin's Ōjōyōshū* (Tokyo: Sophia University, 1973); Neal Donner and Daniel B. Stevenson, *The Great Calming and Contemplation: A Study and Annotated Translation of the First Chapter of Chih-i's Mo-ho chih-kuan* (Honolulu: Kuroda Institute/University of Hawaii Press, 1993); Paul Groner, "Shortening the Path: Early Tendai Interpretations of the Realization of Buddhahood with This Very Body (*Sokushin Jōbutsu*)," in *Paths to Liberation: The Mārga and Its Transformations in Buddhist Thought*, edited by Robert E. Buswell, Jr., and Robert M. Gimello (Honolulu: Kuroda Institute/University of Hawaii Press, 1992), pp. 439–73; Paul Groner, "The Lotus Sutra and Saichō's Interpretation of the Realization of Buddhahood with This Very Body," in *The Lotus Sutra in Japanese Culture*, edited by George J. Tanabe, Jr., and Willa Jane Tanabe (Honolulu: University of Hawaii Press, 1989), pp. 53–74; Ruben L. F. Habito, *Originary Enlightenment: Tendai Hongaku Doctrine and Japanese Buddhism* (Tokyo: International Institute for Buddhist Studies, 1996); Leon Hurvitz, tr., *Scripture of the Lotus Blossom of the Fine Dharma* (New York: Columbia University Press, 1976); A. K. Reischauer, tr., "Genshin's *Ōjōyōshū*: Collected Essays on Birth into Paradise," *Transactions of the Asiatic Society of Japan*, second series, 7 (1930): 16–97; Daniel B. Stevenson, "The Four Kinds of Samādhi in Early T'ien-t'ai Buddhism," in *Traditions of Meditation in Chinese Buddhism*, edited by Peter N. Gregory (Honolulu: Kuroda Institute/University of Hawaii Press, 1986), pp. 45–97.

The Contemplation of Suchness

Volume 1 of the *[Great] Calming and Contemplation* states: "Of every form and fragrance, there is none that is not the Middle Way. So it is with the realm of the self, as well as the realms of the Buddha and of the beings" [*Mo-ho chih-kuan*, J. *Maka shikan*, *T* 46:1c]. The "realm of the self" is the practitioner's own mind. The "buddha realm" indicates the buddhas of the ten directions. "The beings" means all sentient beings. "Every form and fragrance" means all classes of insentient beings, including grasses and trees, tiles and pebbles, mountains and rivers, the great earth, the vast sea, and empty space. Of all these myriad existents, there is none that is not the Middle Way. The different terms for [this identity] are many. It is called suchness, the real aspect, the universe [Skt. *dharma-dhātu*, J. *hōkai*] the dharma body, the dharma nature, the Thus Come One, and the cardinal meaning. Among these many designations, I will for present purposes employ "suchness" and thus clarify the meaning of the contemplation of the Middle Way that is explained in many places in the sutras and treatises.

If you wish to attain buddhahood quickly or be born without fail in [the pure land] of Utmost Bliss, you must think: "My own mind is precisely the principle of suchness." If you think that suchness, which pervades the universe, is your own essence, you are at once the universe; do not think that there is anything apart from this. When one is awakened, the buddhas in the worlds of the ten directions of the universe and also all bodhisattvas each dwell within oneself. To seek a separate buddha apart from oneself is [the action of] a time when one does not know that oneself is precisely suchness. When one knows that suchness and oneself are the same thing, then, of Shaka (Śākyamuni), [A]mida (Amitābha), Yakushi (Bhaiṣajya-guru) and the other buddhas of the ten directions, as well as Fugen (Samantabhadra), Monju (Mañjuśrī), Kannon (Avalokiteśvara), Miroku (Maitreya), and the other bodhisattvas, there is none that is separate from oneself. Moreover, the *Lotus Sūtra* and the others of eighty thousand repositories of teachings and the twelve kinds of scriptures, as well as the myriad practices of all buddhas and bodhisattvas undertaken as the cause for their enlightenment, the myriad virtues they achieved as a result, and the boundless merit they gained through self-cultivation and through teaching others—of all this, what is there that is not within oneself?

When one forms this thought, because all things are the functions of the mind, all practices are encompassed within one mind, and in a single moment of thought, one comprehends all things: This is called "sitting in the place of practice" (*zadōjō*). It is called "achieving right awakening" (*jōshōgaku*). Because one [thus] realizes buddhahood without abandoning this [present body], it is also called realizing buddhahood with this very body. This is like the case of the eight-year-old dragon girl who, on hearing the principle of the *Lotus Sūtra* that all things are a single suchness, immediately aroused the aspiration for enlightenment and, in the space of a moment, achieved right awakening [Hurvitz, 199–201]. Moreover, for one who contemplates suchness and aspires to be born [in the pure land] of Utmost Bliss, there is no doubt that one shall surely be born there in accordance with one's wish. The reason is: Attaining buddhahood is extremely difficult, because one becomes a buddha by self-cultivation and by teaching others and thus accumulating unfathomable merit, enough to fill the universe. But achieving birth in [the land of] Perfect Bliss is very easy. Even those who commit evil deeds, if, at life's end, they wholeheartedly chant *Namu Amida-butsu* ten times, are certain to be born there.

Thus, when one contemplates suchness, one can quickly realize even buddhahood, which is difficult to attain. How much more is one certain beyond doubt to achieve birth in [the pure land of] Utmost Bliss, which is easy! This being the case, those who wish by all means to be born in the Pure Land should simply contemplate suchness. A hundred people out of a hundred are certain to be born there, surely and without doubt. But if one does not believe [that oneself is suchness], that person slanders all Buddhas of the ten directions in the past, present, and future periods of time. This is because the buddhas of the ten directions, as well as the *Lotus Sūtra*, all take suchness as their essence. One who has slandered the buddhas of the ten directions or the *Lotus Sūtra* falls into the Hell without Respite (*muken jigoku*, *avīci*) and will not [readily] emerge. The "Parable" chapter expounds the karmic retribution for the sin of slandering the *Lotus Sūtra*, saying: "Such a person, at life's end, shall enter the Avīci hell, where he shall fulfill one kalpa. When the kalpa is exhausted, he shall be reborn there, transmigrating in this way for kalpas without number" [*Miao-fa lien-hua ching*, T 9:15b–c].

How awesome! Whether we fall into the Hell without Respite or are born in the land of Utmost Bliss depends solely on our [attitude of] mind in this lifetime. We ourselves are precisely suchness. One who does not believe this will surely fall into hell. But one who believes it deeply without doubting will be born in the Pure Land. Whether we are born in [the land of] Perfect Bliss or fall into hell depends on whether or not we believe in [our identity with] suchness. How pointless that by not believing that one can be born in [the land of] Perfect Bliss by the power of the contemplation of suchness, one falls into the Hell without Respite and suffers for countless kalpas, when, simply by believing deeply, one may be born in [the pure land] of Perfect Bliss and experience happiness that shall not be exhausted in kalpas without number! Therefore we must each firmly believe in the contemplation of suchness. In lifetime after lifetime and age after age, what greater joy could there be than to learn in this life of this way by which one may so easily become a buddha and be born in [the pure land of] Utmost Bliss? Even if one should break the precepts without shame, one should simply—without the slightest negligence, even while lying down with one's sash unloosed, even for a moment—think, "I am suchness." How extremely easy and reliable [a mode of practice]!

Bodhisattvas of the provisional teachings, who did not know this contemplation of suchness, for countless kalpas broke their bones and discarded bodily life; without even a moment's neglect, they engaged in difficult and painful practices (*nangyō kugyō*), undertaking them because they valued the path of attaining buddhahood. And in the case of our great teacher, the Thus Come One Śākyamuni, there is no place even the size of a mustard seed where, throughout countless kalpas in the past, he did not throw away his life [for the beings' sake]. Precisely by cultivating such difficult and painful practices, he was able to become a Buddha. But in our case, we have learned of the way of realizing buddhahood and achieving birth in [the pure land] of Utmost Bliss in a very short time, without cultivating such difficult and painful practices for countless kalpas and without practicing the six perfections [the *pāramitās* of giving, keeping the precepts, forbearance, assiduousness, meditation, and wisdom], simply by a single thought with which we think, "I am suchness." In all the world, [encountering this teaching] is the thing most rare and to be appreciated.

During the time when we did not know that our own mind is precisely the principle of suchness, we thought that the Buddha and ourselves differed greatly and were widely separated. We thought so because we are ordinary worldlings who have not yet extirpated delusions, while the Buddha, throughout countless kalpas, carried out difficult and painful practices, both for his own self-cultivation and to teach others, and is fully endowed with unfathomable merits. Of the Buddha's six perfections and myriad practices, what merit do we possess? Not even in this lifetime have we broken our bones and thrown away our lives [for enlightenment's sake], let alone for countless kalpas! Rather, since it has been our habit since the beginningless past, we value only worldly fame and profit, aspiring to this estate or that temple or shrine; hastening in pursuit of the world's pleasures and prosperity, we have not sustained our aspiration for birth in [the land of] Utmost Bliss, or for buddhahood and enlightened wisdom (bodhi), which are the important things. Having spent this life in vain, in our next life we are certain to sink into the depths of the three evil paths [of the hells, hungry ghosts, and animals]—so we have thought, but this was merely the deluded mind at a time when we did not yet know the contemplation of suchness.

From today on, knowing that your own mind is itself suchness, evil karma and defilements will not be hindrances; fame and profit will instead become nourishment for the fruition of buddha[hood] and enlightened wisdom. Even if you should violate the precepts without shame or be negligent and idle [in religious observances], so long as you always contemplate suchness and never forget to do so, you should never think that evil karma or defilements will obstruct your birth in [the pure land of] Utmost Bliss.

Someone asks: I do not understand this about all beings being buddhas originally. If all beings were buddhas originally, people would not resolve to become buddhas through difficult and painful practices. Nor would there be the divisions among the six paths [of transmigration], that is, hell dwellers, hungry ghosts, animals, asuras, humans, and heavenly beings. Thus the Buddha himself taught that the beings of the six paths always exist. In the *Lotus Sūtra* itself, it states, "[I, with the eye of a buddha,] see the beings on the six courses, reduced to poverty's extreme, having neither merit nor wisdom" [Hurvitz, 42]. Moreover, phenomena do not exceed what they actually appear to be. In reality there are humans and horses, cows, dogs and crows, to say nothing of ants and mole crickets. How can one say that all [such] beings are originally buddhas? And, as people in the world are accustomed to thinking, "buddha" is one endowed with the thirty-two major and eighty minor marks of physical excellence, an unrestricted being whose supernatural powers and wisdom surpass those of all others. That is precisely why he is worthy of respect. How can such creatures as ants and mole crickets, dogs and crows, be deemed respectworthy and revered as Buddhas?

Now in reply it may be said: Oneself and others are from the outset a single reality that is the principle of suchness, without the distinctions of hell-dwellers, animals [, etc.]. Nevertheless, once ignorance has arisen, within the principle that is without discrimination, we give rise to various discriminations. Thinking of suchness or the universe merely in terms of our individual self, we draw the distinctions of self and other, this and that, arousing the passions of the five aggregates [the physical and mental constituents of existence: forms, perceptions, conceptions, mental volitions, and consciousness] and six dusts [the objects of the senses of sight, sound, smell, taste, touch, and thought]. [Toward objects that accord with our wishes, we arouse the defilement that is greed;] toward objects that do not accord with our wishes, we arouse the defilement that is anger; and toward objects that we neither like nor dislike, we arouse the defilement that is folly. On the basis of the three poisons—greed, anger, and folly—we arouse the eighty-four thousand defilements. At the prompting of these various defilements, we perform a variety of actions. As a result of good actions, we experience the recompense of [birth in] the three good realms of heavenly beings, humans, and asuras. And as a result of evil actions, we invite the retribution of [birth] in the three evil realms of the hells, hungry ghosts, and animals.

In this way, [living] beings and [their insentient] environments of the six paths emerge. While transmigrating through these six realms, we arbitrarily regard as self what is not really the self. Therefore, toward those who go against us, we arouse anger and we abuse and strike or even kill them; thus we cannot put an end to the round of birth and death. Or toward those who accord with us, we arouse a possessive love, forming mutual bonds of obligation and affection thoughout lifetime after lifetime and age after age. In this case as well, there is no stopping of transmigration. In other words, transmigrating through the realm of birth and death is simply the result of not knowing that suchness is oneself, and thus of arbitrarily drawing distinctions between self and other, this and that. When one thinks, "Suchness is my own essence," then there is nothing that is not oneself. How could oneself and others not be the same? And if [one realized that] self and others are not different, who would give rise to defilements and evil actions and continue the round of rebirth?

Thus, if while walking, standing, sitting, or lying down, or while performing any kind of action, you think, "I am suchness," then that is realizing buddhahood. What could be an obstruction [to such contemplation]? You should know that suchness is to be contemplated with respect to all things. Clergy or laity, male or female—all should contemplate in this way. When you provide for your wife, children, and retainers, or even feed oxen, horses, and the others of the six kinds of domestic animals [that is, horses, oxen, sheep, dogs, pigs, and chickens], because the myriad things are all suchness, if you think that these others are precisely suchness, you have in effect made offerings to all Buddhas and bodhisattvas of the ten directions and three periods of time, as well as to all living beings, without a single exception. This is because nothing is outside the single principle of suchness. Because the myriad creatures such as ants and mole crickets are all suchness, even giving food to a single ant is praised as [encompassing] the merit of making offerings to all buddhas of the ten directions.

Not only is this true of offerings made to others. Because we ourselves are also suchness [with each thought-moment being mutually identified with and inseparable from all phenomena], one's own person includes all buddhas and bodhisattvas of the ten directions and three time periods and is endowed with the hundred realms, thousand suchnesses, and three thousand realms, lacking none. Thus, when you yourself eat, if you carry out this contemplation, the merit of the perfection of giving at once fills the universe, and because one practice is equivalent to all practices, the single practice of the perfection of giving contains the other perfections. And because cause and effect are nondual, all practices, which represent the causal stage, are simultanously the myriad virtues of the stage of realization. Thus you are a bodhisattva of the highest stage, a Thus Come One of perfect enlightenment.

And not only are living beings suchness. Insentient beings such as grasses and trees are also suchness. Therefore, when one offers a single flower or lights one stick of incense to a single buddha—because, "of every form and fragrance, there is none that is not the Middle Way"—that single flower or single stick of incense is precisely suchness and therefore pervades the universe. And because the single buddha [to whom it is offered] is precisely suchness, that one buddha is all buddhas, and the countless buddhas of the ten directions without exception all at once receive that offering.... When one contemplates suchness with even a small offering, such as a single flower or stick of incense, one's merit shall be thus great. How much more so, if one chants the Buddha's name even once, or reads or copies a single phrase or verse of the sutra! [In so doing], the merit gained by thinking that each character is the principle of suchness [is so vast that it] cannot be explained in full.

In this way, because all living beings, both self and others, are suchness, they are precisely buddhas. Because grasses and trees, tiles and pebbles, mountains and rivers, the great earth, the vast sea, and the empty sky are all suchness, there is none that is not buddha. Looking up at the sky, the sky is buddha. Looking down at the earth, the earth is buddha. Turning toward the eastern quarter, the east is buddha. And the same is true with the south, west, north, the four intermediate directions, up and down.

—41—

Chidō's *Dreams of Buddhism*

William M. Bodiford

Dreams of Buddhism (*Buppō yume monogatari*) was written by a Japanese Buddhist monk known as Chidō sometime during the latter half of the thirteenth century. Little is known about Chidō other than his name and the contents of several short treatises attributed to him. He seems to have enjoyed renown as a master of Shingon Esoteric practices. Only one of his works, *Ten Causes of Favorable Dreams* (*Kōmu jūin*), was dated, and this only with the vague notation: "During the Kōan Era" (i.e., 1278–1287). Other works attributed to him include *Proper Mental Attitude during Illness* (*Byōchū yōjinshō*), *The Uncreated* (*Fushōshō*), and *Procedures for Performing the Mantra of Radiant Light* (*Kōmyō shingon shiki*).

The usual Japanese titles for this text are *Buppō yume monogatari* (Tale of the Buddhist Doctrine of Dreams) or *Yume chishiki monogatari* (Tale of the Dream Teacher). The English title is intended to suggest the ambiguous role of dreams in Chidō's treatise. The text attempts to reveal both what Buddhism teaches about dreams and what dreams can teach us about the true nature of reality, or how Buddhists view reality. The text assumes that the reader already accepts the Buddhist critique of our commonsense world of individual existence as being dreamlike and lacking ultimate validity. It further assumes that the reader already seeks the goal of liberation from such false reality. Its real emphasis, therefore, is not dreaming itself, but the experience of waking up afterward. Chidō insists that our familiar habit of awaking each day should convince us of the possibility of experiencing a similar process of religious awakening. His ultimate goal is to convince us to believe in the efficacy of Buddhist practice. If we are able on our own to awake from sleep-induced dreams, he argues, we must be equally capable of pursuing Buddhist awakening. Thus, Chidō stands in opposition to Pure Land Buddhist leaders who taught that people no longer possessed the ability to attain awakening through individual effort.

The format of *Dreams of Buddhism* is quite simple. It presents a dialogue between a host and a guest on a quiet night in a humble hermitage. As in other Japanese didactic treatises, the guest serves only as a convenient prompt for the host's lengthy instructions. Speaking through the host, Chidō attempts to explain how people can attain liberation from the endless cycle of birth and death, or transmigration, that all sentient beings endure. Chidō's solution consists of merely eliminating the false belief in individual existence that serves to sustain our illusion of transmigration. We should view existence as we already view dreams and should awake from our mistaken belief in existence just as we wake from our dreams each day. In explaining this remedy, Chidō discusses the proper mental attitude toward life and death, ignorance as the source of mistaken beliefs, the equivalence of Buddha and living beings, the principle of moral consequences (i.e., karmic retribution), and meditation on the syllable *A* (*A-ji kan*). He concludes by arguing against Pure Land doctrines that would deny people's aptitude for Esoteric Shingon Buddhist practices during the present degenerate age of Buddhist decline (*mappō*). Section headings have been inserted in the text to identify these themes.

The text also mentions several well-known individuals, the Indian prince Ajātaśatru (Pali, Ajātasattu; J., Ajase), the Chinese Taoist sages Lieh-tzu (Resshi) and Chuang-tzu (Sōshi, 4th century B.C.E.), and the Korean Buddhist master Wŏnhyo (Gangyō, 617–686), as well as one obscure Japanese monk, Rishō-bō of Sennyū Temple. Ajātaśatru is infamous as the evil prince who murdered his father, Bimbisāra the king of Magadha, to usurp the throne. Ajātaśatru's subsequent remorse and concern with the workings of karmic retribution are discussed in a number of Buddhist texts, most notably the *Sutra of the Great Cessation* (*Daihatsu nehangyō, T* 374) and the *Limitless Life Buddha Sutra* (*Muryōjukyō, T* 360). The writings attributed to the Taoist sages Lieh-tzu and Chuang-tzu both emphasize the illusionary nature of our commonsense categories of reality. Their discussions of the transformations of dreams into reality and reality into dreams are well known to all students of Chinese literature and thought. Wŏnhyo is famous both for his prodigious commentaries on Buddhist scriptures (he wrote more than one hundred treatises) and his sometimes bizarre behavior. In Japan, he was regarded as an important patriarch of the Kegon school, the doctrines of which constitute the metaphysical foundation for the Shingon Esoteric practices advocated by Chidō. Wŏnhyo's awakening in a cemetery midway during his aborted journey to China is reported in *Biographies of Eminent Monks of the Sung Dynasty* (*Sung Kao-seng chuan, T* 2061).

The translation is of the text found in Miyasaka Yūshō, ed., *Kana hōgoshū*, in Nihon koten bungaku taikei 83 (Tokyo: Iwanami Shoten, 1964).

Further Reading

Robert E. Morrell, tr., *Early Kamakura Buddhism: A Minority Report* (Berkeley: Asian Humanities Press, 1987); Robert E. Morrell, tr., *Sand and Pebbles (Shasekishū): The Tales of Mujū Ichien, a Voice for Pluralism in Kamakura Buddhism* (Albany:

State University of New York Press, 1985); George J. Tanabe, Jr., *Myōe the Dreamkeeper: Fantasy and Knowledge in Early Kamakura Buddhism* (Cambridge: Harvard University Press, 1993); Taikō Yamasaki, *Shingon: Japanese Esoteric Buddhism*, translated by Richard and Cynthia Peterson (Boston: Shambhala, 1988).

Dreams of Buddhism

BIRTH AND DEATH

One calm night a guest asked for lodging at a monk's rustic hermitage. In the course of discussing affairs ancient and modern, the guest said, "I have encountered the difficult-to-encounter teachings of the Buddha. Although I have not completely lacked a sincere fear of birth and death (*saṃsāra*, *shōji*), I've been habitually involved in worldly filth. Because I wasted my days hither and thither, only now have I noticed that my limited life span has grown short. I have crossed distant mountains and rivers to come and inquire of you concerning just one issue. What attitude can I adopt so as to attain liberation from birth and death during this life?"

The host replied, "You say that you have spent many years nominally in Buddhist training, yet you have never before given consideration to the single great affair of birth and death? Just regard the dreams you see night after night as your teacher. Then at least you will not deepen your attachments to the world. When people lie down and dream, the things they see do not actually exist. Yet under the conditions of sleep they see all kinds of affairs: different places, living creatures, oneself, and others. Because one's own self is involved, if things go contrary one becomes angry. If things go well one rejoices. It is no different from one's waking reality.

"Lieh-tzu dreamed for sixty years. Chuang-tzu dreamed that he spent one hundred years as a butterfly. In just one night they saw many months and years come and go. Just imagine how many karmic acts they performed during that time! How many thoughts of good and evil! While dreaming one never thinks that one's imaginary experience is false. Yet if one considers it after awakening, it is obvious that not one of the imaginary objects seen while lying down in bed actually existed. Each living being's entire experience of transmigration through birth and death is no different from such dreams. Therefore, again and again the Buddha preached in response to various types of ignorance that we should regard the six courses and four modes of rebirth as dreams."

IGNORANCE

"'Ignorance' means not knowing that one's own mind is buddha. Within a single mental instant of this delusion, one leaves the palace of Dharma Nature [i.e., reality as it actually is,] and wanders among the impoverished villages of false thoughts [i.e., our commonsense world of existence]. One might think that the experience of transmigration is real. But if upon encountering the Buddha's teaching that life and death is a dream, one listens with faith, then suddenly one leaves the mistaken beliefs of dreams and awakens on the bed of inherent enlightenment. The fact that one has not yet awakened from dreams is simply because one thinks of them as actually existing. The Buddha appeared in the world to make us become aware of our long night of dreams.

"For those of shallow aptitude, Buddhists first explain the principle of the emptiness of self. This approach is known as the Lesser Vehicle (Hīnayāna, Shōjō). Thoughts of self-existence are what habitually cause infinite sins to arise. If one understands that the self is empty, then the power generated by this understanding transports one out of the three realms of desire, form, and no-form to a land outside of our world system. This approach, however, has the defect of emphasizing the existence of the elements of experience (*dharma*, *hō*). Therefore, for those of deeper aptitude, Buddhists explain the emptiness of both self and these elements. This approach is known as the Great Vehicle (Mahāyāna, Daijō). The emptiness of dharmas teaches that everything seen in dreams, every type of element, are all emptiness: because everything arises from mind, none has reality. Therefore, the knowledge that every type of dharma consists completely of dreams is the doctrine of the Great Vehicle.

"For these reasons, over the course of years in this humble hermitage, during night after night of dreams, I have seen all kinds of things. Sometimes I became upset. Sometimes I became happy. Sometimes I entered the marvelous realm of the immortal sages and became friends with buddhas and bodhisattvas. Sometimes I tormented myself with the afflictions of demons and poisonous serpents. While viewing these events one thinks they exist. But after awakening they leave no trace. From this experience one should realize that birth and death fundamentally are nonexistent.

"Due to various kinds of causes and conditions, within one's tiny brain one can see ten thousand miles of mountains and rivers. Within the span of a short nap one can experience the passing of many months and years. One should realize, based on this same principle, that a single instant of thought can pervade the Dharma Realm, the entire cosmos. The elements that one sees do not come into existence from the future when one dreams. They do not go out of existence into the past when one awakes. Even while one sees them they do not abide, do not persist in the present anywhere. Based on this experience, one can understand the meaning of the saying that the three periods of past, present, and future cannot be grasped. This being so, any sentient being who awakens to this realization can be called a buddha or a patriarch.

"The reason I believe there is no teacher better than dreams is that the process of sleeping in bed, resting my head on the pillow of inherent enlightenment, allows me to see how the production of delusions causes birth and death within dreams. My awaking at dawn reveals the similar process of realizing the wisdom of spiritual awakening in all its clarity. Thus living in clear realization of the fundamental nonbeing of birth and death, I know that the sense objects experienced while awake are not different from those experienced in dreams. Joys and sorrows are both forgotten, and my mind is ready to encounter the infinite teachings of the Buddha.

"So long as you do not know that your self exists only as a dream, then no matter how much good karma you cultivate, the best benefit you can attain is rebirth in a human or heavenly realm. You will not realize the salvation of liberation from the cycle of birth and death. But if you know that your self exists only as a dream and that all sights, sounds, sensations, and thoughts exist only as a dream, then even a simple act of good karma, such as reciting one line of scripture or chanting the Buddha's name once, is a powerful enough act to produce Buddhahood.

"You must thoroughly investigate this thing known as our mind of thought (*ichinen no shin*). When the interaction of sense organs and sense objects produces an instant of awareness, it does not come from somewhere in the future. When the awareness stops, it does not go to someplace in the past. If one investigates where this mind abides in the present, it is not inside the body nor outside the body. It cannot be found between the inside and the outside. Yet it is not something nonexistent. Because it is this mind that projects the visions of dreams and waking reality, both consist of elements that are fundamentally nonexistent."

THE EQUIVALENCE OF BUDDHA AND LIVING BEINGS

"You must thoroughly investigate what are called 'buddha' and 'sentient beings.' The scripture says: 'Because of false thoughts, therefore sinking in birth and death; because of knowing reality, therefore realizing *bodhi* [i.e., wisdom].' This means that Buddhas and sentient beings, because both are pure in their fundamental nature, lack the slightest bit of difference. Yet if false thoughts arise, one becomes a sentient being drowning in birth and death. If one knows reality as it is, then one becomes a Buddha who realizes *bodhi*.

"What does the scripture mean by 'false thoughts'? Merely a confused mind. It is like pointing to the east and thinking it is the west. There is a story told about a man, Rishō-bō of Sennyū Temple. Once as Rishō-bō absentmindedly returned to his temple from Kyoto, he walked across the Fifth Avenue Bridge all the while thinking only that he was traveling west. Then he thought to himself: 'If I am returning from the capital to my temple, then I must be facing east. Why am I thinking that I'm going west?' Although it felt odd, he could not get rid of this thought until he had finished crossing the bridge.

"Your false thoughts of birth and death resemble Rishō-bō's confusion. Sentient beings will, because of a single thought of confused discrimination, cling to no-self as a self and construct dreams of birth and death. Just like when Rishō-bō later thought to himself, 'Since I must be facing east, why do I think that I am facing west?' the realization that our mind plays tricks on us resembles encountering Buddhism, awakening to the mental origin of reality, and knowing the principle of no-self. His knowing how to distinguish east and west, but not changing his mind while crossing the bridge, resembles the persistence of false thoughts—due to habitual karmic tendencies formed during many previous lives—even though one trusts in the teachings of the Buddha. His regaining his senses after crossing the bridge resembles putting an end to false thoughts by believing in and practicing the teachings of the Buddha.

"Rishō-bō realized his mistake in thinking that east is west. Thus he did not stop on the bridge but continued on his way home. If he had been taken in by the false opinion of thinking that east is west, then he would have stopped in midjourney and would not have continued on his way home. Because we know that our false mind is fundamentally empty, we should not be stopped by it. Therefore, [Vasubandhu's] *Treatise on Arousing the Bodhi Mind* (*Hotsu bodaishin gyōron, T* 1659) states: 'If the false mind should arise, recognize it and do not follow it.'

"Once a person known as Wŏnhyo journeyed from the Korean kingdom of Silla to the T'ang empire of China in search of the Buddhist teaching. Encountering rain, he took shelter in a cave. Feeling thirsty, he drank water from a pool in the cavern. The taste of the water resembled sweet nectar. He drank and drank. At dawn he saw a corpse lying in the water. Remembering the water he had drunk, he vomited it up. At that moment he awakened to the fact that all elements of existence (*dharma*) in themselves are neither pure nor impure, but merely coincide to the artifice of the One Mind. Thinking, 'Now there is no further Teaching to seek,' he returned to Silla.

"Not knowing that body and mind are empty with respect to purity and impurity, one performs infinite karmic acts for the sake of the body and thereby randomly engenders suffering. Suppose, for example, there was a crazy person who took a corpse, set it on the side of the road, and decorated it in various ways. Suppose he built a house for it and traveled about getting food and clothing for it. Suppose he became happy when a passerby admired the corpse and became angry when one criticized it. Just for this one corpse he suffered mental and physical exertion. Anyone who saw this would probably say, 'Well, he's crazy!' But our manner of transmigration through birth and death differs not in the slightest. We receive bleached bones from our fathers and obtain red flesh from our mothers. None of this is our own. Yet, what we do every day for ourselves is all just for our corpses, is it not?

"Chinese poets described man's worldly striving as:

> Working late until the stars appear overhead;
> starting early so as to brush off the morning frost:
> Such is one who seeks fame and covets profit.
>
> Polishing jeweled floors, decorating with embroidered banners, sewing fancy clothes:
> Such is one who is concerned only with outlandish beauty.

"If one considers these activities thoroughly, it is clear that we are just slaves to our corpses. Our mental and physical toil infects not just this life, but also engenders pleasures and pains for eons to come. How could our craziness be less than that of the crazy person above? Thus, because we cling to no-self as a self and cling to the false and nonexistent as truly real, we have become ordinary unawakened beings (*bonpu*) caught in birth and death. Therefore, realizing that mind and body absolutely lack any self-sustaining permanent essence and believing that they are just like phantoms and dreams is the event to which the scripture quotation above refers when it says: 'because of knowing reality, therefore realizing wisdom (*bodhi*).'"

THE PRINCIPLE OF MORAL CONSEQUENCES

The guest asked, "You say good and evil in reality do not exist. If that is so, then couldn't one perform evil without incurring karmic sins, and couldn't one cultivate good without obtaining karmic benefits?"

The host replied, "If you understand in such a manner, then you would be denying the law of cause and effect, a horrific false view. In fact, it is because of the lack of permanent essence that the performance of evil leads to baleful retributions and that the cultivation of good engenders pleasant benefits. You should understand that the principle of things lacking any fixed nature implies that the karmic connections between good and evil causes and effects are not random.

"Suppose, for example, that in a dream you see someone killed and see a king investigate and judge the crime. While dreaming, the principle of cause and effect cannot be disrupted. Thinking upon this after awaking, however, it is clear that the murderer, the murder victim, the performance of the crime, and the king actually did not exist. Therefore, if one truly believes that both good and evil are dreams, one will transcend cause and effect and realize highest awakening. Because at that time both karmic sin and karmic benefit are totally nonexistent, it is possible even for one who performed the five heinous crimes to attain Buddhahood.

"But as long as one has not attained buddhahood, the law of cause and effect is completely inviolable. While one is at the level of ordinary unawakened beings, how could the burden of karmic sin not exist? Nonetheless, if one believes that one's sinful heart from its very bottom is fundamentally nonexistent, then there is no doubt that the burden of karmic sin will disappear. Therefore, one should contemplate evil acts before doing them, asking oneself, 'Since these are dreams, how can I do them?' and thereby carefully control body and mind. Because the evil acts that one is about to commit exist only within dreams, they too completely lack any ultimate reality. Even if one seeks throughout the ten directions and three periods for the mind that commits sins, in the end it cannot be grasped. One should reflect well, thinking: 'Since this mind that commits sins actually does not exist, how can it engender any karmic retribution?' This form of mental reflection is known as repentance of the uncreated (*mushō no sange*).

"King Ajātaśatru murdered his father. When he visited the Buddha to repent of his sins, the Buddha told him that all elements of existence are completely without fixed forms. What is that thing called 'father'? What is that thing called 'son'? The Buddha explained that the idea of father and son result at random from temporary relations between a pair of the five groups ('heaps,' *skandha*, of dharma elements) that constitute sentient beings. By means of the power of this wisdom, in no time at all, Ajātaśatru's karmic sins dissolved into the state of fundamental nonbeing. This process is known as the elimination of sins (*metsuzai*).

"Your attempt to rationalize your desire to commit sins by saying, 'Since they are just dreams, how could I suffer consequences?' is a big mistake. You must analyze this distinction well. Just always focus your attention on the situations in which such thoughts arise. Suppose, for example, just when an unexpected thought of dislike toward a person has arisen, you maintain that train of thought in your mind and carefully analyze this occasion of resentment. In the end, you would realize that estrangement characterizes what is called the unawakened being trapped in the currents of life and death. If just when an evil thought is about to arise one asks: 'From where does this thought arise? Who is its subject? Who is its object?' then that train of thought, which initially was hateful, suddenly would disappear without a trace. Suppose, for example, at night one mistakes a post for a demon and runs away in fear. If one asks what kind of demon could be there and goes back to look more carefully, then one would see that the demon fundamentally is a post. All thoughts of fear would vanish. Whenever an instant of false thought is about to arise, carefully return to that instant of arising and ask what is the basis of that instant of thought. Because the fundamental nature of mind is emptiness, ultimately one reaches that state of fundamental nonbeing.

"This attainment is liberation from birth and death. While the mind of an instant of thought has no basis from which to arise, the thought that things actually exist maintains a continuous train of thought that results ultimately in the sea of life and death. Yet if one traces back this thought and analyzes what kind of thing it is, then one realizes that fundamentally it is nothing. Therefore, after reflecting back for awhile, one knows that one is uncreated. Thus, the process of birth and death—heretofore maintained by previous lifetimes of thought—is eliminated."

MEDITATION ON THE SYLLABLE "A" (A-JI KAN)

"The Buddha placed all of the Great Vehicle's doctrines of the uncreated into the one syllable 'A.' Thus, if one unpacks the syllable 'A' it becomes many different doctrines, and if one compresses these, they become the single syllable

'A.' *The Great Sun Sutra* (*Dainichikyō, T* 848) states: 'The syllable "A" is itself uncreated, ungraspable, fundamental emptiness. It universally encompasses all Buddhist teachings. By means of mutual empowerment through this emptiness, one is able to embrace all Buddhist teachings and thereby attain buddhahood.'

"This syllable 'A' consists of color, shape, sound, and meaning. Sometimes one can practice by focusing one's mind on its color and shape. Sometimes one can practice by vocalizing its sound. When one wishes quietude, one can practice by continuous contemplation of its meaning. Because it offers several forms of practice, one's mastery of the highest principle occurs in no time.

"The Pure Land practice of chanting *Namu Amida Butsu*, by contrast, involves many words and is prone to distraction. Because the breath that comes out when one simply opens one's mouth always is the sound 'A' even when one is distracted, no other practice is as easy as this one. Because all the doctrines preached in the hundreds and thousands of scriptures and treatises in their entirety are encompassed by this one syllable, reciting this one syllable produces the same amount of merit as reading the entire Buddhist canon. Moreover, the doctrines I mentioned above [i.e., no-self, uncreated, and elimination of sins], in their entirety constitute the meaning of this syllable. Therefore, even the merit produced by reciting without any knowledge is no trivial amount. The amount of merit produced by adding to one's recitation of this syllable even one instant of belief in the principle of the uncreated, therefore, could not be explained completely even after infinite eons.

"Thus, at the very last when facing the end in death, one should merely open one's mouth, place one's attention on the 'A' breath, and experience the end. At that moment, because all affairs also come to an end, no matter what one ponders over, it is beyond one's ability to imagine something better. If one tries to contemplate the meaning of 'A' too intently, it will become a hindrance. Merely ending one's life on the single 'A' syllable without any intense contemplation is attainment of self-realization beyond thought [i.e., perfect awakening without delusion or mental effort]."

APTITUDE FOR BUDDHIST PRACTICE

The guest asked, "The principles of no-self and noncreation probably are, as you say, the foundation of Buddhism. Yet when I reflect on my own mind, there is not even half a moment when I forget about clinging to a self. Never have I been attentive enough to notice the instant when feelings of happiness or joy come over me. Thus, doctrines and practices like these that you've described must be for wise, flawless people only. Some people [e.g., Pure Land leaders] say that during this evil and declining age ordinary unawakened men should not consider such matters. When I evaluate this in my own mind, I think truly there must be reason in their position. Right?"

The host replied, "Because people's aptitudes for Buddhist practice diverge, the Buddha preached the dharma of a single taste in various ways. One must not necessarily use one version to block all other ways of practice. Because this doctrine of no-self and noncreation is profound, one who lacks affinities from previous lives will not believe it for an instant. But someone who has established many such affinities will, without being able to say why, feel the value of this doctrine upon hearing it. If one arouses even a single instant of faith, then the power of that faith will eliminate the heaviest sins from the beginningless past. One should see that this will plant the seed of buddhahood in the storehouse consciousness (*ālaya vijñāna*).

"Thus, the class of beings who have aptitude for the Great Vehicle does not even exclude those who violate the precepts and freely perform evil. Merely one instant of faith and understanding qualifies one for inclusion. The reason for this is that even before one thinks that 'the permanent self must be something that really exists,' the Great Vehicle already extends to whatever good or evil karmic nature exists within one's heart. Once one believes that birth and death [i.e., *saṃsāra*] and Nirvana are the same as yesterday's dreams, then the power of this faith transports one beyond the distinctions of good and evil. Therefore it matters not in the least if there has been a good or evil determination prior to one's unawakened cognition [i.e., the power of an unawakened person's faith is not limited by his or her moral nature, which has been determined by prior karmic acts]. In this regard, it is because the beginningless cycle of false thoughts and karmic influences has made such a deep impact that people believe only in themselves and distrust the words of the Buddha that promise salvation through the syllable 'A' and think thoughts such as: 'Since I am evil, how could I have the proper aptitude for Buddhism?'

"Examine your lowly self! You are a person within a dream, wherein both good and evil are fundamentally empty. Because everything is fundamentally empty, you are not the slightest bit different from the Buddha. What basis is there for thinking that your aptitude has been fixed at an inferior grade?

"None of the doctrines or practices mentioned above state that one must discard all evil thoughts. Rather they merely encourage one to have faith in the fundamental nonexistence of whatever good or evil thoughts arise. Buddhist tradition has provided the three practices of morality, meditation, and wisdom so that we will attain inner and outer purity, that is, mental insight and physical decorum. Yet even if I were to beg people to practice these, in this latter age they have become too weak to do so. Even if one is unable to manage any kind of multiple practices, I believe that faith in the doctrines of the Great Vehicle for just one instant of thought right now will plant the proper seed of Buddhahood.

"Confused thoughts are characteristic of ordinary unawakened people. Therefore, as long as one is an ordinary person it is impossible for false thoughts not to arise. From this, it is clear that not a single ordinary person who lacks aptitude for the Great Vehicle exists. It is precisely for ordinary unawakened people who lack any foundation in the Buddhist Way that one explains knowledge of the Tathāgata's secret treasure of esoteric contemplation of the syllable 'A.'

"I observe that people of this world, in terms of their attitude toward Buddhism, would rather think only of relying on the merit produced by acts such as chanting Amida Buddha's name (*nembutsu*) or chanting scripture to attain transport to Pure Land in their next life. Hardly anyone exists who expends even a single instant of trust in the Buddhist doctrine. Here is what I know. The Buddhist doctrine is difficult to encounter and difficult to believe. Knowing that it is difficult to believe, upon believing it one obtains inconceivable benefits. The saying that the chanting of one line of verse from the Buddhist scripture will destroy infinite eons worth of sins, being the words of the Buddha, could not possibly be a lie. Yet if these sins were really existing things, then their disappearance would take some amount of time. Because these sins are fundamentally empty, upon chanting the name of the Buddha who awakened to this truth, even without understanding anything, they are eliminated. By adding even an instant of faith in this truth to one's chanting, just think how much more merit would be produced! One should reverently arouse one's mind of faith. My speaking like this also is nothing more than words in a dream. . . ."

As these words were spoken the guest disappeared as if erased. Then the host also disappeared. There was just the humble hermitage and the sound of the wind in the pine trees.

Chidō, who harms the nation, wrote this.

—42—

The Confucian Monarchy of Nara Japan

Charles Holcombe

The *Continued Chronicles of Japan* (*Shoku Nihongi*) follows immediately after the more famous *Chronicles of Japan* (*Nihon shoki*, 720) as the second of six official, Chinese-style, histories of ancient Japan. The text was completed in 797 and provides in forty *maki* (thin volumes) a year-by-year—sometimes even day-by-day—account of important events at the court (which was located in Nara during most of this time) from 697 to 791. Except for a number of especially august imperial proclamations (*semmyō*), which were transcribed phonetically in the Japanese language, the text is written entirely in a rather austere classical Chinese. Despite, or because of, the *Continued Chronicles'* dry, annalistic flavor, however, it is regarded by some modern scholars as being a relatively reliable source for the study of Nara Japan.

The selection translated here, covering the first few months of 757, is intended to highlight typically Confucian court concerns, especially the ideal of rule by imperial grace and ethical example, and the emphasis on filial piety (*kō*) as the fundamental moral principle linking state to family. The court's obvious fascination with omens is also a reflection of early Chinese Confucian practice, although one that had already come under imperial criticism in China itself. Noteworthy, too, is the apparently smooth integration of Confucianism, Buddhism, and Shintō portrayed in this passage. The issue of Korean immigration and assimilation is also addressed with the granting of Japanese surnames to those who so desired and qualified for them. It is estimated that by 761 C.E. about two thousand immigrants had changed their names according to this provision.

This translation is based on the superb new annotated *Shoku Nihongi* (compiled originally by Sugano no Mamichi and Fujiwara no Tsugutada et al. in 797 C.E.) in *Shin Nihon koten bungaku taikei*, vol. 3 (Tokyo: Iwanami Shoten, 1992): 20.174–85.

Further Reading

James Legge, tr., *The Sacred Books of China*, pt.1: *The Texts of Confucianism*, in *The Sacred Books of the East*, vol. 3, edited by F. Max Müller (1879; New Delhi: Motilal Banarsidass, 1966), esp. pp. 447–88 (*The Classic of Filial Piety*); Sakamoto Tarō, *The Six National Histories of Japan*, translated by John S. Brownlee (Tokyo: University of Tokyo Press, 1991); Aat Vervoorn, *Men of the Cliffs and Caves: The Development of the Chinese Eremitic Tradition to the End of the Han Dynasty* (Hong Kong: Chinese University Press, 1990).

Continued Chronicles of Japan

In the first month of spring of the initial year of the Tempyō-hōji (Precious Ideograph of Heavenly Peace) reign period (757), on the New Year of Keng-hsü according to the Chinese cyclical calendar, court was dismissed for reasons of imperial mourning [for Retired Emperor Shōmu, who had died the previous year]. By imperial command, eight hundred persons were ordained as monks.

The fifth day. It was commanded that since [in compliance with an earlier edict] the *Net of Brahma Sutra* (*Bonmōkyō, T* 1484) is to be expounded in every province from the fifteenth day of the next fourth month until the second day of the fifth month [to commemorate the first death anniversary of the late emperor], this year's "Quiet Dwelling" [Summer Seminar, which normally began on the fifteenth day of the fourth month] shall begin immediately afterward on the third day of the fifth month. It was also decreed:

> Recently, commoners have been employed as district heads [*gunryō*] and colonels [*gunki*]. For this reason, people become accustomed to seeking office from their homes and are unaware that their salaries come from serving the ruler. The loyalty that is a transference from filial piety [which also extends to the emperor] therefore gradually declines, and the Tao of encouraging others becomes truly difficult. From now on, we should order the bureau director of the Ministry of Ceremonial not to allow any unranked persons to be considered for appointment. Colonels should be selected by the Ministry of War from those among the Six Guards whose capacities have been distinguished, employing those who are talented, courageous, and strong. Other kinds of fellows are not to be permitted indiscriminate appeal. All other matters remain as in the statutes and codes.

The sixth day. The former Senior First Rank Minister of the Left Tachibana Moroe (684–757) died. Ki Iimaro, of the Junior Fourth Rank, upper grade, and Ishikawa Toyohito, of the Junior Fifth Rank, lower grade, were dispatched to superintend the funeral. The obligatory funerary objects were officially provided. The Minister [Tachibana] was the grandson of Prince Kurikuma of the Posthumous Junior Second Rank, and the son of Prince Mino of the Junior Fourth Rank, lower grade.

The ninth day. The Fujiwara surname was bestowed upon Prince Iwatsu, of the Junior Fifth Rank, lower grade, and he became the son of Major Counselor [Fujiwara] Nakamaro of the Junior Second Rank [who was then ascendant at court, and a longstanding rival of the recently deceased Tachibana Moroe].

The twentieth day of the third month. In the ceiling of the Imperial Residence, the four ideographs "Great Peace Under Heaven" materialized spontaneously.

The twenty-second day. The imperial princes and all of the ministers were summoned and commanded to witness these auspicious ideographs.

The twenty-seventh day. [To avoid taboos on the names Fujiwara and Kimi (Lord),] it was proclaimed that from now on the surname Fujiwarabe would be changed to Kuzuwarabe, and Kimikobe to Kimikobe [written with different ideographs].

The twenty-ninth day. Crown Prince Funato was in imperial mourning, but his mind was set on debauchery. Although he was given imperial instruction, he never repented. Therefore, all of the ministers were summoned, shown the late emperor's last will, and then consulted as to the matter of whether to depose him or not. Everyone from the minister of the right on down memorialized together: "We dare not disobey the final imperial command." On this day, the crown prince was deposed, and he was returned to his brothers as an ordinary prince.

Summer, the fourth day of the fourth month. The empress summoned all of her ministers, asking: "Which prince should we establish as imperial heir"? The Minister of the Right Fujiwara Toyonari (704–765) and the Minister of Central Affairs Fujiwara Nagate (714–771) said: "Prince Funato's elder brother Prince Shioyaki could be established." The High Steward of Settsu Fumiya Chino and the Great Controller of the Left Ōtomo Komaro said: "Prince Ikeda could be established." Major Counselor Fujiwara Nakamaro said: "No one knows his ministers like their lord. No one knows his sons like their father. We will merely serve whoever it is Heaven's inclination to select." It was decreed: Within the imperial house, the two princes [sons of the late prince] of the Imperial Guards Niitabe are most senior. Therefore, having formerly established Prince Funato only to have him disobey the imperial teachings and give in to his debauched intentions, we may now select from among the sons of the Prince of the Imperial Guards. But Prince Fune is unreformed in the women's apartments. Prince Ikeda's filial conduct is deficient. Prince Shioyaki was upbraided by the late Emperor [Shōmu] for lacking propriety. Only Prince Ōi, although he is not yet mature, has never been known for doing wrong. We wish to establish this prince. What do all the ministers think about this?

Thereupon, from the minister of the right on down, they all memorialized, "Whatever is the Imperial Command will be complied with." Before this, Major

Counselor [Fujiwara] Nakamaro invited Prince Ōi to live in his residence at Tamura. Today he dispatched his son Inner Imperial Guard Fujiwara Satsuo with twenty of the Central Guards to meet Prince Ōi and establish him as crown prince. It was decreed:

> The state takes its lord as master. The lord takes his heir apparent as his assurance. Therefore, the late emperor in his last will established Prince Funato as crown prince. But before the imperial mourning was over, and while the grass on the imperial tomb was not yet dry, the prince had illicit intercourse with a young attendant, without respect for the late emperor. In the ritual of mourning, he did not grieve suitably. This confidential matter was moreover entirely disclosed to the people. Despite repeated imperial instructions, he is still without feelings of remorse. He is fond of using women's language, and rather often disobedient. He suddenly departs his official residence in the Spring Palace, and at night he returns home alone. It is said that if a minister is clumsy and simple as a person, he is not fit to undertake weighty responsibilities. Therefore We secretly planned to depose this prince and establish Prince Ōi. We personally beseeched the Three Treasures of Buddhism and prayed to the [Shintō] deities, hoping for a sign that Our rule was either good or bad. Then, on the twentieth day of the third month, in the screen on the ceiling of Our residence, the ideographs "Great Peace Under Heaven" appeared clearly and brightly. This, then, is help from Heaven above, and a sign from the deities. Looking far back into high antiquity, and examining past events in succession, this is something that has never been recorded in books and was unheard of in former ages. Then We knew that the [Three] Treasures of the Buddha, the Dharma, and the Priesthood have prescribed great peace for the nation, and the various deities of Heaven and Earth foretell permanence for Our ancestral altars. Bearing this token of good fortune, we are truly delighted. Even a compassionate father finds it hard to sympathize with his unfilial son; the sage ruler still identifies ministers who are lacking in propriety. We should follow Heaven's instructions and return him [Prince Funato] to his original position.
>
> It is also thanks to the utterly loyal and proper assistance of the aristocracy that we owe this noble omen. How could it have been sent in response to Our single person? We should receive Heaven's bequest together with the princes, nobles, gentlemen, and commoners, and in response to Heaven wash away our old flaws and universally receive the new blessings. We can proclaim a general amnesty throughout the empire. All crimes are forgiven, from capital offenses on down, committed before dawn on the fourth day of the fourth month of 757, whether they are minor or serious, discovered or undiscovered, atoned or un-atoned, or resulted in imprisonment or exile. Only those who commit the [unpardonable] Eight Atrocities [such as treason or depravity], intentionally kill people, privately mint coins, violently rob, or secretly steal are excluded from this provision.

The common people of the empire are registered for light compulsory labor in the year they become youths [at age seventeen, according to the East Asian mode of reckoning], and in the year when they are capped [at age twenty-one] they become eligible for full labor service. Sympathizing with their labor, We are distressed at heart. Formerly, the late Emperor [Shōmu] also had this inclination, but he did not act on it. From now on, we should take eighteen as the age of youth for males, and twenty-two and up as the age for fully adult males.

The ancients, in governing the people and pacifying the country, had to use the principle of filial piety. As a source of all action, nothing takes priority over this. We should command each family in the empire to possess and diligently memorize a copy of the [Confucian] *Classic of Filial Piety*, and redouble their instruction. Among the common people, if there is someone who surpasses other persons in filial conduct and is looked up to in the village, we should order the senior officials in their native places to recommend them all by name. If there are those who are unfilial, disrespectful, unfriendly, or disobedient, they should be banished to Momunofu District of Michinoku Province [Mutsu] or the Okachi District of Dewa Province [on the far Northern front, in confrontation with the supposedly "savage" Emishi] to purify their practices, and to defend the frontier. If there are others who sleep loftily in retirement at Ying River and hide their traces under Mount Chi [as the admirable hermit Hsü Yu did after supposedly refusing an offer of the throne in mythical Chinese antiquity], who are fit to be [paragons like the legendary] Ch'ao or Hsü for Our age, they should be visited with propriety and released from legal requirements to nourish their spirits.

As for the priests and nuns of the Office of Monastic Affairs, and in the vicinity of the capital, from the [minor clerical office of] Fukui on up, We bestow goods in proportion to their status. The servants on inner attendance, the attendants conferred with swords, and all of the men and women responsible for preparing the various materials for the imperial fast commemorating the anniversary of Emperor [Shōmu's] death [5/2], who have labored from morning until night without neglect, each absolute in their sincerity, We should command to be promoted two ranks, and bestow silk on them. Officials who have been remiss will also be reduced one rank. The remaining inner and outer officials, from the master of ceremonies on up, and aged persons above eighty throughout the empire, the Central Guards, the Military Guards, the Palace Gate Guards, commanders, miscellaneous artisans, and soldiers on duty and commoners on government service who have continuously served more than thirty years will be promoted one rank. Only those of senior sixth rank, upper grade, and above, and those who are not serving, are excluded from this provision. To those civil and military officials on official duty in the capital, of the senior sixth rank, upper grade, and above, and those shrines celebrating the monthly fast, we confer goods in

> proportion to their rank. Widowers, widows, orphans, and childless persons throughout the empire, those who are seriously ill or disabled, and those who are unable to sustain themselves will be given a measure of relief. For those persons [who are descendants of immigrants] from Koguryō, Paekche, and Silla [the three Korean states that were united under Sillan rule in 668] who have long desired to be transformed by the presence of a sage [i.e., civilized by contact with imperial Confucian virtue], and who have attached themselves to our customs, hoping to be bestowed with a surname, they are all to be permitted one. Recording their household registers without ideographs for their surnames and families is untenable in principle and ought to be corrected. Also, the workmen at Tōdaiji, the laborers who built the imperial tomb, and the soldiers of the left and right sections of the capital, the four home provinces, Iga, Owari, Chikatsuafumi [Ōmi], Taniwa, Taniwa no michi no shiri [Tango], Tajima, Harima, Mimasaka, Kibi no michi no kuchi [Bizen], and Kii provinces, the defenders, garrisons, imperial guards, supervisors of cooks, commoners on government service, the households attached to the advocate at the Ministry of War, and the head of the household that provided conveyance [at Emperor Shōmu's funeral] are all exempt from this year's rice-field tax.

The numerous officials proceeded to the audience chamber and submitted a memorial congratulating the empress on the appearance of the auspicious ideographs.

The second day of the fifth month, the anniversary of the late emperor's death. Over fifteen hundred monks were invited to Tōdaiji to hold a fast.

The fourth day . . .

—43—

Nationalistic Shintō: A Child's Guide to Yasukuni Shrine

Richard Gardner

The following text is excerpted from a pamphlet, intended for children, explaining the history of Yasukuni Shrine, one of the more controversial religious and political sites in Japan. The shrine was established in 1869 at its present location, the top of Kudan slope in Tokyo's Chiyoda-ku, at the request of Emperor Meiji. It served to enshrine and pacify the spirits of those who had died on both sides of the fighting in the Boshin War (1868–1869), which resulted in the overthrow of the shogunate and restoration of the emperor to power. The shrine came to be understood as the place for enshrining all of those who lost their lives in battle for the sake of the nation in both civil and foreign wars. From early on, Yasukuni had a close connection with the imperial family, came under military jurisdiction, and served as a center for nationalistic propaganda.

Following the Japanese defeat in the Second World War, State Shintō was banned by the occupation authorities and the new Japanese constitution included a provision formally separating church and state. Yasukuni Shrine thus became an independent religious organization. While many younger Japanese rarely if ever think of the shrine, it has remained, nevertheless, a site of contention and dispute. Traditionalists, conservatives, and the Association of Bereaved Families (Izokukai) have, since the mid-1950s, waged a campaign to reestablish the connection between Yasukuni Shrine and the state. Liberals, leftists, Christians, and others have fought to oppose any effort to reforge such a link. The shrine is also a point of contention throughout Asia. For many Asian countries, Yasukuni Shrine is a symbol of Japan's aggression during the war years. The last major "event" in the history of the shrine—Prime Minister Nakasone's official visit to the shrine in 1985—sparked a vehement protest by China and other nations in the region.

The controversy surrounding the shrine today is inevitably bound up with living memories of the period of Japan's militarism in the 1930s and 1940s.

Soldiers departing for the battlefield were told not to worry because they would be taken care of at Yasukuni Shrine. Heading into battle, soldiers would often say to one another, with either seriousness or irony, "See you at Yasukuni!" While some former warriors make their annual pilgrimage to the shrine fully embracing the shrine's views of history, others repudiate what the shrine officially stands for but see their visit as a means of fulfilling promises to or communing with the friends and comrades they lost in the war. Japanese religion provides many occasions for honoring and communing with the dead. The power of Yasukuni for some lies in its claim to provide the most appropriate, the most intimate space for communing with the dead.

Not all of the Japanese war dead are enshrined at Yasukuni. The criteria for enshrinement has shifted over the course of history. Most civilian Japanese war dead, such as the victims of the fire bombing of Tokyo in 1945, are not enshrined here. Within the shrine compound, there is, however, a very small, hidden-away shrine, usually unnoticed by visitors, that enshrines all the war dead of all countries not enshrined in the main shrine.

Much of the support for the shrine comes from those with living memories of family and friends who lost their lives in Second World War and are enshrined at Yasukuni. As the numbers of those with living memories of the dead pass on, it has become necessary for the shrine to attempt to awaken in the young a sense of the meaning and significance of the shrine.

The text translated here is *Yasukuni daihyakka: Watashitachi no Yasukuni Jinja* (Tokyo: Office of Yasukuni Shrine, 1992).

Further Reading

Haruko Taya and Theodore F. Cook, *Japan at War: An Oral History* (New York: New Press, 1992); Wilhelmus H. M. Creemers, *Shrine Shintō after World War II* (Leiden: E. J. Brill, 1968); Helen Hardacre, *Shintō and the State, 1868–1988* (Princeton: Princeton University Press, 1989); Mark R. Mullins, Susumu Shimazono, and Paul L. Swanson, eds., *Religion and Society in Modern Japan* (Berkeley: Asian Humanities Press, 1993); David M. O'Brien with Yasuo Ohkoshi, *To Dream of Dreams: Religious Freedom and Constitutional Politics in Postwar Japan* (Honolulu: University of Hawaii Press, 1996).

A [Child's] Guide to Yasukuni Shrine: Our Yasukuni Shrine

Dear Fathers and Mothers:

The whole family can have an intimate visit with the gods by worshipping at the inner sanctuary of the Main Sanctuary. Please feel free to make an application at the reception office. We also look forward to welcoming your visit on days of celebration such as Coming of Age Day, the Children's Festival, and the First Visit of Newborns to the Shrine.

THE CHERRY TREES OF YASUKINI

At the time of the construction of the Main Sanctuary of Yasukuni Shrine in Meiji 3 (1870), Someiyoshino cherry trees were planted within the shrine grounds. This was the beginning of the cherry trees of Yasukuni. The graceful, beautiful cherry trees of Kudan, which all the gods are very proud of, are a symbol of Yasukuni Shrine. At present there are about a thousand cherry trees—including Someiyoshino, mountain cherry, and others—within the shrine gardens. As spring approaches every year, the Meteorological Agency examines the Someiyoshino at Yasukuni in order to predict when the cherry trees will bloom in Tokyo.

THE WHITE PIGEONS OF YASUKUNI

There are about six hundred of Poppo the Pigeon's friends here. They are all pure white carrier pigeons [*hato*, which also means dove, the symbol of peace], a type born only once every ten thousand births. Twice every day Leopold Mozart's "Toy Symphony" wafts throughout the grounds to tell Poppo and his friends that it is time to dine.

POPPO THE WISE PIGEON'S "ANSWERS TO ANY AND ALL QUESTIONS ABOUT YASUKUNI"

POPPO: Good day everyone! I'm Poppo the White Pigeon. There are about six hundred of my friends living together peacefully here at Yasukuni. We've come to be great friends with everyone looking after and visiting the shrine and are always having fun playing about the shrine grounds. So if it is something to do with Yasukuni, we know every nook and cranny of the place. Let's talk a bit about the history and festivals of Yasukuni Shrine, which everyone is always asking about.

Q: Who built Yasukuni Shrine and when?

A: Yasukuni Shrine is a shrine with a long tradition and was built over 120 years ago in 1869. Throughout the time of national seclusion before the Meiji period, Japan did not have relations with the other countries of the world. But the people of foreign countries gradually took a critical attitude toward Japan and pressured Japan to open itself to the outside world.

Wondering "what in the world should we do," the whole country was in an uproar and public opinion was widely split between those wanting to open the country and those wanting to keep it closed. In this situation, the Tokugawa Bakufu, which had been entrusted with the governing of Japan for over three hundred years, lost the power to quell this disturbance and so returned the authority to govern to the emperor.

At this point was born the idea of everyone in Japan becoming of one heart and mind under the emperor in order to restore the beautiful traditions of Japan, create a splendid modern nation, and become good friends with all the people of the world.

Then in the midst of trying to achieve this great rebirth, the Boshin War—an unfortunate, internal dispute—occurred, and many people came forth to offer their lives for the country. In order to transmit to future ages the story of the people who died in the Meiji Restoration, which aimed at creating a new age, the Emperor Meiji built this shrine, then named Tokyo Shokonsha (Shrine for Summoning the Spirits), here at Kudan in Tokyo in the sixth month of 1869. In 1879 the name was changed to Yasukuni Shrine.

Q: What does "Yasukuni" mean?

A: The Honorable Shrine Name "Yasukuni Shrine" was bestowed on the shrine by Emperor Meiji. The "Yasukuni" in the name means "Let's make our country a place of tranquility and gentle peace, an always peaceful country" and reflects the great and noble feelings of the Emperor Meiji. All the gods who are worshipped at the Yasukuni Shrine gave their noble lives in order to protect Japan while praying for eternal peace, like the Emperor Meiji, from the depths of their heart.

Q: What gods are worshipped at Yasukuni Shrine?

A: I explained a bit about the Boshin War earlier. The over 3,500 pillars (when counting gods, we count not "one, two" but "one pillar, two pillars") who died at that time were the first gods worshipped here. Later, all of those who died devoting themselves to the country, from 1853 (the year the American Admiral Perry led four warships to Uragaoki in Kanagawa Prefecture and everyone was saying with shock, "Black ships have come!") to the end of the Bakufu fifteen years later, were also enshrined and worshipped here.

After that there were also numerous battles within the country—such as those of the Saga Disturbance and the Seinan War [both of which were revolts against the newly established Meiji government]—until the new Japan was firmly established. All those who died for their country in those battles are also worshipped here. Everyone's ancestors helped carry out the important mission of creating a marvelous Japan with the emperor at its center.

However, to protect the independence of Japan and the peace of Asia surrounding Japan, there were also—though it is a very sad thing—several wars with foreign countries. In the Meiji period there were the Sino-Japanese War and the Russian-Japanese War; in the Taishō period, the First World War; and in the Shōwa period, the Manchurian Incident, the China Incident, and then the Great Pacific War (the Second World War).

At the start of the Russian-Japanese War, Emperor Meiji expressed his deep sorrow by composing and reciting an August Poem: "Though all are linked like the waters of the four seas, why do storms arise in the world?" (Why does peace give way to the storms of war when all the countries of the world should be like brothers?)

War is truly a sorrowful thing. But it was necessary to fight to firmly protect the independence of Japan and to exist as a peaceful nation prospering together with the surrounding countries of Asia. All those who offered up their noble lives in such disturbances and wars are worshipped at Yasukuni Shrine as gods.

Q: Could you please teach us some more about the gods?

A: Do you all know how many gods there are at Yasukuni Shrine? The answer is over 2,467,000! There are this many gods in front of all of you who have come to worship here! Let me tell you a little about the gods.

Among the gods at Yasukuni Shrine, there are gods such as Hashimoto Sanai [1834–1859], Yoshida Shōin [1830–1859], Sakamoto Ryōma [1836–1867], and Takasugi Shinsaku [1839–1867], who you all know well from history books and television dramas and who worked hard for the country from the end of the Edo period to the beginning of the Meiji period [by opposing the shogunate and supporting the emperor]. Also worshipped here are the many soldiers who died in battle during the wars of the Meiji, Taishō, and Shōwa periods.

But there are not just soldiers here; there are also over fifty-seven thousand female gods here. There are also children like you, and even younger, who are worshipped here as gods.

Let me tell you a little about the Great Pacific War, which took place over fifty years ago. When the American Army attacked Okinawa, there were junior high school students who stood up and resisted with the soldiers. To defend Okinawa and their hometowns, over sixteen hundred boys of nine schools—Okinawa Shihan School, the Number One and Number Two Prefectural Junior High Schools, etc.—formed groups such as the Blood and Iron Imperial Brigade and fought just like soldiers. Also, over four hundred students of girls schools, such as Number One Prefectural Girl's High School, Number Two Prefectural Girls High School, and Shuri Girls High School, served as nurses on the battlefield or made their way through the battlefield carrying food and ammunition. Most of those boy and girl students fell in battle. Now they are enshrined in Yasukuni Shrine and are sleeping here peacefully.

There are also fifteen hundred who met their sad end when the *Tsushima Maru* transport ship, which was evacuating them from Okinawa to Kagoshima to escape the bombing, was hit by torpedoes from enemy submarines. Among them were seven hundred grade school children.

There are also many, just like your older brothers and older sisters, who died in bombing attacks when they gave up their studies because of the war and worked hard producing goods in factories.

The next story is something that happened on August 20, 1945. Though the war was already over, the Soviet Army suddenly attacked Karafuto (now Sakharin). The girl telephone operators of Maoka in Karafuto continued reporting the movements of the Soviet Army to the mainland as the enemy approached. Their last message before losing their lives was, "Farewell everybody, this is the end, sayonara." All of them are here.

Also among the gods here are many who fell leading the fight to put out the fires caused by enemy bombing attacks on Japan. Nurses attached to the army on the battlefield who bore the noble insignia of the Red Cross and were adored like a mother or older sister. The crews of military transport ships who one and all sank to the bottom of the sea while heading to the southern battlefront. Cameramen and newspaper reporters attached to the army who fell from enemy bullets while gathering stories on the battlefield. Many people like this are worshipped here with great devotion as noble, godly spirits who gave their lives for their homeland Japan.

There are also those here who took the responsibility for the war upon themselves and ended their own lives when the Great Pacific War ended. There are also 1,068 who had their lives cruelly taken after the war when they were falsely and one-sidely branded as "war criminals" by the kangaroo court of the Allies who had fought Japan. At Yasukuni Shrine we call these the "Shōwa Martyrs" [including General Tōjō Hideki], and they are all worshipped as gods.

YASUKUNI SHRINE IS THE SHRINE WHERE ALL JAPANESE GO TO WORSHIP

So now you know what gods are worshipped at Yasukuni Shrine. The gods of Yasukuni Shrine gave their noble lives on the battlefield with the hope that Japan might continue forever in peace and independence and that the marvelous history and traditions of Japan bequeathed by our ancestors might continue on and on forever. That Japan is peaceful and prosperous is thanks to all of those who have become gods at Yasukuni Shrine. From now on you must treasure "Our Japan," which these people protected by giving their lives in times of war. So let's all come to worship at Yasukuni Shrine, offer up our feelings of thanks to the gods, and promise to become splendid people. Flying above the shrine grounds, all us pigeons will be looking forward to your coming to worship.

— 44 —

The Founding of Mount Kōya and Kūkai's Eternal Meditation

George J. Tanabe, Jr.

Mount Kōya, the headquarters of the Shingon sect, is one of the most beautiful of the monastic complexes in Japan. Situated high in the mountains of Wakayama Prefecture south of Nara, Mount Kōya can be reached by train and cable car or by a long, winding road through exceptionally verdant mountains. The monastery consists of dozens of temples scattered in a heavily forested, flat-bottomed bowl several miles across. Ancient cryptomeria trees as straight and majestic as redwoods surround the ornate temples and give to the artifice of sacred architecture the natural sanctity of the mountain. Splendid in isolation from the distant valleys of farms and factories, Mount Kōya is nevertheless crawling with people.

The visitors, mostly pilgrims, come from all over Japan. In this time of modern "tourist Buddhism," most of the temples, in fact, function as inns providing food and lodging for the faithful. They come to sightsee, but they do so as people of faith, filled with unquestioning belief in the sacred virtues of the mountain and its monasteries. Specifically, they believe in the holiness and power of Kūkai (774–835), the founder of the Shingon sect, who is more popularly known as Daishi-sama, a contraction of his posthumous title Kōbō Daishi, the Great Master and Propagator of the Teaching. Whereas believers of other sects chant praises to certain buddhas or scriptures, the Shingon faithful chant the name of their savior, Kōbō Daishi. He is their god.

The apotheosis of Kūkai began shortly after his death when admiring disciples expressed their adoration by writing legends of the virtues and miraculous feats of their master. Unlike fairy tales, which are totally fictional about make-believe people and places, legends center around real personalities and locations. There is a certain veracity to legends, at least to the degree to which they deal with real facts. These facts, of course, are then surrounded with a great deal of fabrication. The stories, however, do more than merely entertain by exaggeration; they make serious arguments as well.

It is these legends that define a good part of what people understand to be the content of their religion. The sublime doctrines studied by scholars and monks seldom reach the popular understanding, and the ordinary believers, if asked about the teachings of their sect, will often reply with reference to legends rather than philosophies. The stream of the philosophical teachings does not always converge with the rivers of popular belief, but it would be a mistake to think that their divergence is due to their having different sources. It is not the case that the popular legends, so filled with miracle and magic, originate from the unsophisticated minds of peasants and farmers and then are only tolerated by educated scholar/priests who know better than to accept those amazing fictions as facts. The origins of the legends can be traced, and the trail leads back to the scholar/priests themselves. They concocted the legends and propagated them to the people, who were the recipients, not the originators. The propagation of these legends was immensely effective: the same stories are still being told and are still attracting the faithful in large numbers.

The temples and shops at Mount Kōya sell a huge number of comic books, banners, plaques, and other paraphernalia that depict three legends in particular. The first of these enduring stories speaks of how Kūkai was led to Mount Kōya by two dogs loaned to him by a hunter. The second legend tells of how Kūkai, led by the dogs, arrived at Mount Kōya only to find hanging from a pine tree (a scion of which still grows at the main compound) a three-pronged ritual implement he had thrown from China. The third is perhaps the most important and claims that Kūkai did not really die but is still alive in his mausoleum (Oku no In), sitting in eternal meditation. The stories of the dogs and the pine tree were first written by a scholar/monk in *A Record of the Practices and the Establishment of the Temple of the Diamond Peak* (*Kongōbuji konryū shugyō engi*, 968). This text, from which the following translation is made, tells of the founding of the Temple of the Diamond Peak, the main compound at Mount Kōya, and weaves all three legends along with a variety of other stories into a more or less coherent account.

The stories are entertaining, but all have serious points to make. While Kūkai was granted the land on Mount Kōya by an imperial decree, the exact boundaries were not fixed. By the eleventh century, when this text was written, the monastic complex had grown, and neighboring landlords complained of encroachments into their properties. The story of the hunter's dogs makes it clear that Kūkai did not wander into the place by accident, and, furthermore, the king of the mountain as well as the resident Shintō deities gave the property to Kūkai. The temple's claim to the lands it occupied was therefore legitimate, and even preordained, as the story of the ritual implement in the pine tree attempts to argue. The land, which only ostensibly belonged to a Shintō deity, was originally the "ancient place of an old buddha." In the hands of Buddhist monks, the land is now possessed by its rightful owners and is vitalized by the power and sanctity of Kūkai, who still reigns over Mount Kōya. The conclusion of the arguments is clear: Mount Kōya was chosen in a divinely special way to be Kūkai's monastery and continues to exude its power and virtue through the majesty of its trees, the loftiness of its mountains, the sanctity of its temples, the purifying practices of its priests, and the living presence of its saint.

The stories are engaging, and their arguments are persuasive to scores of people who take them seriously and go to Kōyasan to worship and make offerings. Take away the philosophy and Mount Kōya will still thrive, but remove its legends and the monastery will lose its call to the people.

The text for this translation of *Kongōbuji konryū shugyō engi* is from Hase Hōshū, ed., *Kōbō Daishi den zenshū* 1 (Tokyo: Pitaka, 1977), pp. 53–55. Authorship of the text is traditionally atributed to the scholar/monk Ninkai (951–1046), but since the work is clearly dated for the year 968, when Ninkai was only seventeen years old, scholars doubt the authenticity of this attribution. Kongōbuji is the name of the main temple that still serves as the headquarters of the Shingon sect at Mount Kōya.

Further Reading

Yoshito S. Hakeda, *Kūkai: Major Works* (New York: Columbia University Press, 1972); Edward Kamens, tr., *The Three Jewels: A Study and Translation of Minamoto Tamenori's* Sanbōe (Ann Arbor: Center for Japanese Studies, University of Michigan, 1988); Robert E. Morrell, tr., *Sand and Pebbles: The Tales of Mujū Ichien, a Voice for Pluralism in Kamakura Buddhism* (Albany: State University of New York Press, 1985); Kyoko M. Nakamura, tr., *Miraculous Tales from the Japanese Buddhist Tradition*: The Nihon Ryōiki *of the Monk Kyōkai* (Cambridge: Harvard University Press, 1973); Marian Ury, tr., *Tales of Times Now Past: Sixty-two Stories from a Medieval Japanese Collection* (Berkeley: University of California Press, 1979).

A Record of the Practices and the Establishment of the Temple of the Diamond Peak

In midsummer of the year 816, Kūkai left the capital to travel beyond it. In Uchi County in the province of Yamato, he met a hunter, who was deep red in appearance and stood about eight feet in height. He wore a short-sleeved blue coat and had long bones and thick muscles. He carried a bow and arrows strapped to his body, and he was accompanied by dogs, one large and one small. He saw Kūkai pass by and asked some questions. Kūkai stopped and also inquired about certain details.

The hunter said, "I am a dog keeper from the southern mountains. I know of a mountain area of about ten thousand square measures, and in that area there is a marvelous flat plain. The place is full of mysterious signs. You should take up residence there; I will help you accomplish this. I will release my dogs and have them run ahead or you will get lost."

Kūkai thought silently about this and proceeded. They stopped for a rest when they came to a large river on the boundaries of Kii Province. Here they met a man who lived in the mountains. Upon being told the details of the place, he said, "South of here there is a flat, swampy plain. The mountains range on three sides and the entry way from the southwest is open. Myriad rivers flow to the east and terminate by converging into one. During the day there are strange clouds, and at night there are always mysterious lights." Upon further investigation, it turned out to be directly south of Ito-no-kōri in Kii Province.

The next day, he followed this mountain man, and they arrived at the swampy plain a short distance away. As he examined the place, he thought that this certainly was the spot where he should build a monastery.

The mountain man secretly said to Kūkai, "I am the king of this mountain, and I donate the land under my control to you in order to increase my power and blessings. I am accustomed to mountains and rivers and remain distant from the activities of men. Fortunately I have met a saint, much to my merit."

The next day they went to Ito-no-kōri and Kūkai thought, "When the Sacred King Who Turns the Wheel of the Buddhist Teaching (*tenrinjōō*; *cakravartin*) ascends the throne, he takes a river willow and offers it to the holy men. If, however, they do not grant him a single iron needle or a single blade of grass, then he is in error."

Therefore, in the middle of the sixth month, Kūkai submitted his request to the emperor for a place for meditation. He built one or two thatched huts. He had myriad things to do and did not have much time, but he managed to go up once a year. On one side of the path in the mountains there was a swamp of about ten square measures. It was the shrine of the mountain king, the Great August Deity Niu. Today it is called the palace of Amano.

The first time Kūkai ascended the mountain, he spent a night in the area of the shrine. He received an oracle saying, "I have been a follower of the way of the Shintō deities, and I have hoped for power and blessings for a long time. Now you have come to this place, much to my great fortune. In the past when I was a human being, the deity Kekunisuera-no-mikoto gave me about ten thousand square measures of land for houses. The boundaries are south to Nankai, north to Yamato River, east to Yamato Province, and west to the valley of Mount Ōjin. I wish to donate this to you for all eternity as an expression of my belief."

In addition, Kūkai was granted an official decree.

While they were clearing the trees in order to build a monastery, they found the three-pronged ritual implement that he had thrown from China hanging majestically from a tree. Kūkai was filled with joy. Then he realized that this was a place suitable for the Esoteric teaching, just as the mountain king, the owner of the land, had said.

At the spot where they were digging in the ground, they uncovered a jewelled sword from beneath the earth. An imperial decree ordered that it be examined, but there was a curse. Diviners did a reading of the curse and found out that the sword should be put into a copper tube and returned to its place. The interpretation of this was that the non-Buddhist protector, the Great August Deity, regretted its loss.

Kūkai said to all of his disciples, "I think I will be leaving this world sometime during the third month of next year. To the great worthy Shinnen (804–891), I bequeath the Temple of the Diamond Peak, the construction of which is still not complete. Since, however, the efforts of this great worthy alone will not suffice, the great worthy Jitsue (785–847) should help him.

"Initially I thought that I might be able to live in this world for a hundred years, propagating the Esoteric Buddhist teachings and attracting ordinary people. Meditation masters are particularly possessed about this, but my own vow is sufficient. You should know that I gave no regard for my own life as I crossed ten thousand waves of the ocean and traveled over a thousand miles to seek the Buddha's teaching. The teaching of the way I have transmitted to you will protect and uphold this place. It will bring peace to the country and nourish the people."

On the fifteenth day of the third month of the year 835, Kūkai said, "I expect to enter the state of eternal meditation in the early morning of the twenty-first day. From now on I will not resort to human food. You should not shed tears of sadness, and do not wear mourning clothes. While I am in eternal meditation, I will be in the heaven of the future Buddha Maitreya, the compassionate one, in whose presence I shall serve. After more than five billion six hundred million years have passed, the compassionate one will descend to earth. At that time I will surely accompany Maitreya, and I will be able to see my old places. Do not let this Diamond Peak fall into neglect. Outwardly it appears that this place is the property of the mountain king Niu, but I have requested this imperial deity to entrust it to me. What no one knows, however, is that this is the ancient place of an old buddha. All the deities of the Diamond and the Matrix mandalas were assembled and enshrined here. To look at a site on this mountain is to know the majesty of its appearance. To hear its sounds is to hear explanations of the compassionate wrath of the deities. My future worth will be a million. Although people will not know my face in person, those who see an elder from one of these temples or who spend some time on this mountain will surely be able to surmise my intentions. When I see that my teaching is not doing well, I will mingle with the black-robed monks to promote my teaching. This is not a matter of my own attachments but is simply to propagate the teachings and that is all."

In the early morning hours of the twenty-first day of the third month of the year 835, Kūkai sat in the lotus position, formed the ritual hand gesture of the Great Sun Buddha (Mahāvairocana), and peacefully entered the state of eternal meditation.

For ten consecutive days services were held four times a day during which his disciples chanted the name of Maitreya. His entry into meditation simply meant that he had closed his eyes and did not speak. In all other respects he was like a living person. He was sixty-two years old at the time. Since he was [still living] like an ordinary person, no funeral was performed and he was positioned in a dignified manner. According to ordinary custom, memorial services were carried out every week for seven weeks. When his disciples looked upon him, they saw that the color of his face had not faded, and that his hair and beard had grown long. Therefore they shaved him and took care of his clothing. They closed off the stone structure and people had to get permission to enter it. They asked a stone mason to build a tombstone on top of it to represent the five elements, and they placed a book of Sanskrit mantras in it. They also built a jewelled pagoda on top of the structure and enshrined some relics of the Buddha in it. These matters were all arranged by Abbot Shinnen.

Sometime around 852 during the reign of Emperor Montoku, Abbot Shinzei (800–860) petitioned the court to grant Kūkai the rank of high abbot. In 921, during the reign of Emperor Daigo, the court granted Kūkai the title Great Master and Propagator of the Teaching (Kōbō Daishi) in response to a request submitted by Abbot Kangen (853–915).

—45—

Motoori Norinaga on the Two Shrines at Ise

Mark Teeuwen

Motoori Norinaga (1730–1801) wrote *The Two Shrines of Ise: An Essay of Split Bamboo* (*Ise nikū sakitake no ben*) in early 1798. At this time he was a leading scholar with more than four hundred students and a position as an adviser to the Tokugawa Lord of Kii. He had all but finished his life work and main claim to fame, the *Tradition of the Record of Ancient Matters* (*Kojiki-den*), which he had begun in 1764 and finally completed in the sixth month of 1798. He had in fact already published the first seventeen chapters of this work, in three portions appearing in 1790, 1792, and 1797. During the last period in his life, in which our text was written, Norinaga concentrated on spreading his ideas, rather than new research. *The Two Shrines of Ise* was one outcome of this. As indicated by its title, the text discusses theological matters pertaining to the Inner Shrine (*Naikū*) and the Outer Shrine (*Gekū*) of Ise, concentrating on the identities and characteristics of their deities—Amaterasu at the Inner, and Toyouke (or Toyuke) at the Outer Shrine. Most of the points argued in the text draw on Norinaga's polemic works (such as *Arrowroot Flowers*, Kuzubana, 1780, and *Scolding [Ueda Akinari] from Osaka*, Kagaika, c. 1787–1790) for the discussion of Amaterasu, and on chapter 15 of the *Tradition of the Record of Ancient Matters* on the subject of Toyouke.

Many of the themes that pervade Norinaga's oeuvre also make their appearance in the first part of *The Two Shrines of Ise*. The text stresses that the Japanese of "high antiquity" had had a sincere faith in the ancient tradition, and that this faith was lost when the "Chinese way of thinking" gained a foothold in Japan. Much emphasis is further given to the notion that Japan is the "land of origin," the land in which the gods were born, and from which they spread their beneficence throughout the world. As prime examples of this beneficence, the text mentions the light of the sun and the growth of grains. Both of these prerequisites to life, Norinaga argues, are gifts from Japanese deities—namely, Amaterasu and Toyouke, who reside in the Two Shrines of Ise. Therefore, Norinaga concludes, these deities should be revered at these shrines by all human beings throughout the world.

The text further demonstrates some of the sophisticated philological methods Norinaga had at his disposal. He employs two important analytical "tools" in this particular piece. First, he distinguishes between "ordinary logic" (*jōri*), which is within the grasp of human intelligence, and a higher "mysterious logic" (*myōri*). If the world were ruled by "ordinary logic" alone, it would be impossible for Amaterasu to be at the same time the sun that illuminates the world, and an imperial ancestor with a female human body, as the tradition in the *Record of Ancient Matters* seems to imply. Therefore, Norinaga argues, we can only surmise the existence of an unfathomable "mysterious logic," and he urges us to be sincere and have faith in the ancient tradition as it has been handed down to us. Secondly, there is the distinction between deities who are "physical bodies" (*utsushimimi*) and deities who are "spirits" (*mitama*). This distinction makes it possible to introduce yet another Amaterasu: the spirit that resides in the Inner Shrine.

Both these distinctions were essential to Norinaga's effort to come to terms with an ancient tradition that describes Amaterasu alternatively as the sun, a being with a human body, and a spirit. The fact that Norinaga developed such interpretative tools is revealing in itself: it shows his determination to treat the National Histories, including the chapters recounting the Age of the Gods, as factual history. It is this aspect of his thought that gives it its "fundamentalist" character. For Norinaga, there was only one truth, and that was the historical truth handed down by the ancient Japanese tradition. This approach was not entirely novel, but it was certainly against the mainstream of Japanese religious thought, which tended to recognize different levels of truth, and which disregarded the factual and the historical as "exoteric" and "shallow," and always probed for a metaphorical, "deeper" layer of "esoteric" meaning.

As mentioned above, the ideas expressed in *The Two Shrines of Ise* were not new. The text is a restatement of conclusions reached in Norinaga's research on the *Record of Ancient Matters*, and it contains very little that had not already been published when Norinaga wrote the work. Why then did he write it? This question becomes all the more pressing when we learn that Norinaga went to considerable trouble to have the work published. Fearing problems with the authorities, he went to great lengths to gain some insight into the probable reaction of the Outer Shrine, and the work was not published until the eighth month of 1801, a mere month before Norinaga's death.

The Two Shrines of Ise differs from any other work by Norinaga in that it constitutes his first and last attempt to translate his ideas about Shintō into concrete innovations in the political and juridical reality of the Shintō world. The work was an attempt at diplomacy. Its aim was to persuade the Outer Shrine priesthood to abandon its "medieval" theory about Toyouke and accept the "ancient truth" about this deity, as unearthed from the *Record of Ancient Matters* and other sources by Norinaga.

Norinaga's original intention was to ask the Outer Shrine's first priest to write a preface for *The Two Shrines of Ise*, adopting it as the shrine's official position. However, it soon became clear that official acceptance by the Outer Shrine was out of the question, and the shrine refused to assent even to publication of the work. The Outer Shrine did not take legal action when the work was eventually published, but it did file complaints with the *Yamada bugyō* against two of Norinaga's students at the Inner Shrine (in 1798 and 1803). These students had distributed printed pamphlets in the provinces, propagating their views on the relation between the gods of the Inner and the Outer Shrine. The first complaint resulted in a strict censorship imposed on all publications in Ise, and the second in the conviction of the accused, Masuya Suehogi (1764–1828), who was punished with a prohibition against his leaving the district of Uji (the town that served the Inner Shrine)—a kind of extended house arrest. The views of these two students were not necessarily the same as Norinaga's; in fact, they ranked Toyouke as a "servant" of Amaterasu, and as inferior, while Norinaga insisted that these two deities simply "cannot be compared." But the fact that the first of these complaints was being considered by the *Yamada bugyō* when Norinaga sent *The Two Shrines of Ise* to the Outer Shrine did not help his attempt at diplomacy.

What, then, were the theories of the Inner and the Outer Shrine on the subject of the deities of these shrines and the relation between them? The Inner Shrine argued that Amaterasu alone is the highest deity in the realm, and that Toyouke is a servant of Amaterasu with the task of preparing the food offered to her. This theory was put forward among others by the Inner Shrine priest Inomo Morikazu (1705–1773) in his *Record of Mount Kamiji* (Kamijiki, 1730), and it was adopted by Yoshimi Yukikazu (1673–1761), for example, in his *Essays on the Theories of the Five Books* (*Gobusho setsuben,* 1736). The Outer Shrine, however, propagated the radically different theory that Toyouke is another name for Ame no Minakanushi or Kuni no Tokotachi, the first deity to come into existence at the time of the beginning of the universe (according to different versions of the cosmogony, as recorded in the National Histories). According to the Outer Shrine, this deity was Ninigi's maternal great-grandfather, and thus an imperial ancestor on a par with Amaterasu. What is more, he was in fact "ultimately one" with Amaterasu. In the version of Outer Shrine theology that was current in the Edo period, Ame no Minakanushi/Kuni no Tokotachi was identified with the Confucian concept of *li*, the "principle" underlying the existence of the universe, and the Outer Shrine stated that this deity was the "essence" (*tai*), and Amaterasu the "working" (*yō*) of the primeval unity of the "Great Ultimate" (which Chu Hsi identified as *li*) that lies at the root of all existence. In other words, the gods of the Inner and the Outer Shrine are merely two aspects of the same entity. This theory was propagated by Deguchi Nobuyoshi (1615–1690) and many others at the Outer Shrine. Moreover, it was adopted by many scholars of Yamazaki Ansai's school of Suika Shintō, which dominated Shintō scholarship until the 1760s.

These conflicting views on the nature of the relationship between the Two Ise Shrines had a long history, extending back to the Kamakura period when (a less

Confucian version of) the Outer Shrine's theory was first formulated in a series of so-called Secret Books (*hisho*). These books were attributed to ancient ancestors of the Outer Shrine priests, and it was claimed that they predated even the *Record of Ancient Matters* and the *Chronicles of Japan*. In the Edo period Deguchi Nobuyoshi established a sacred corpus of texts, selected from these books, which he called the "Five Books of Shintō" (*Shintō gobusho*), and defined them as Shintō Classics on a par with the National Histories. The theories about Toyouke expounded in these books were of crucial importance to priests of the Outer Shrine in their competition with the Inner Shrine for the favors of both the various shogunates and private benefactors. One can imagine that if the public were to view the god of the Outer Shrine as a mere servant of Amaterasu, donations would decrease dramatically. This kind of competition did not arise before the early Kamakura period, since until that time the shrines had been able to depend on funding from the imperial court.

If anything, the competition between the Outer and the Inner Shrine was even more severe in the Edo period than in preceding centuries. By the early seventeenth century, a considerable proportion of the inhabitants of Yamada and Uji (the towns that served the Outer and the Inner Shrine, respectively) were so-called pilgrim masters (*onshi*), self-professed "priests" who made a living selling services to pilgrims. By this time, nearly every locality in Japan had its contract with a pilgrim master in Ise, granting him the monopoly over all services to pilgrims from that particular "parish" (*dansho*). Pilgrims were sold deity tablets (*oharai* or *taima*), amulets, and other souvenirs of Ise, and they were required to stay at the mansion of their pilgrim master when they went on a pilgrimage. Even official priests of the Two Shrines doubled as pilgrim masters, and it is no exaggeration to state that the "pilgrimage business" was of fundamental importance both in the economic and the political life of Ise.

The theological question of Toyouke's identity was of great importance to those who depended on this "pilgrimage business." As noted above, the Outer Shrine argued that the Two Shrines represent two aspects of a single sacred entity. From this argument, priests drew the conclusion that the pilgrim masters of the Outer Shrine communicated pilgrims' prayers to the gods of both shrines, rather than to the god of the Outer Shrine alone. The Inner Shrine, however, insisted that the Two Shrines are two separate religious institutions and stated that the prayers handled by the pilgrim masters of the Outer Shrine were prayers to Toyouke only and did not reach the ears of the famous Amaterasu. The Inner Shrine claimed that therefore all pilgrims should have two prayer masters, one at each of the Two Shrines. Needless to say, the Outer Shrine regarded the signing of contracts with two pilgrim masters as completely illegal and said that this argument was simply an excuse for stealing *dansho* from pilgrim masters of the Outer Shrine.

There was no unambiguous legislation on the subject of the relation between the prayer masters of the Two Shrines. Until the early seventeenth century, the Outer Shrine had the upper hand in the numerous conflicts between pilgrim masters that were the inevitable result of this legal ambiguity. On a number of occasions, the road to the Inner Shrine was simply blockaded, and pilgrims with Inner Shrine contracts were denied access. This practice was forbidden by the bakufu only in 1635. This proved to be a turning point, and the Inner Shrine's viewpoint carried the day in two conflicts that were brought before the Edo Supreme Court (Hyōjōsho) in 1668 and 1671. However, even after this, the question of whether the Two Shrines are separate or "one" was not settled until 1826, when a *Yamada bugyō* solved yet another conflict between two pilgrim masters over this matter (that had been going on since 1814!) by announcing that the 1671 verdict "implied" that the shrines are separate.

Although Norinaga had many students at the Inner Shrine, and some (though very few) at the Outer Shrine, he seems to have been unaware of the juridical implications of the various theories about the deities of these shrines. His own theory includes some elements from the theory of the Outer Shrine, such as the idea that Toyouke and Amaterasu are like "a god and an emperor," and the notion that Amaterasu reveres Toyouke. Other ideas can be traced back to the Inner Shrine's views, for example, the identification of Toyouke as Toyouke-bime. However, the crux of the matter, the question whether the Two Shrines are separate or not, is not addressed by Norinaga. *The Two Shrines of Ise* would seem to imply that they are. This fact alone made a positive reaction from the Outer Shrine unlikely. When we moreover find that Norinaga's Inner Shrine students were highly indignant at the few "compromises" Norinaga had made to Outer Shrine theology, it becomes clear that Norinaga's attempt to put his ideas into practice at Ise was a complete failure. *The Two Shrines of Ise* stands as a monument to his naivete and serves as a stark reminder of the fact that theological arguments are reflections not only of the intellectual and religious trends of their age, but also of social and economic circumstances that may either inspire or inhibit theological innovation.

The following extracts were taken from my complete, annotated translation, *Motoori Norinaga's The Two Shrines of Ise, an Essay of Split Bamboo*, Izumi series 3 (Wiesbaden: Harrassowitz Verlag, 1995).

Further Reading

H. D. Harootunian, "The Consciousness of Archaic Form from the New Realism of Kokugaku," in *Japanese Thought in the Tokugawa Period 1600–1868: Methods and Metaphors*, edited by T. Najita and I. Scheiner (Chicago: University of Chicago Press, 1978); Sey Nishimura, tr., "First Steps in the Mountains: Motoori Norinaga's *Uiyamabumi*," *Monumenta Nipponica* 42.4 (Winter 1987); Sey Nishimura, tr., "The Way of the Gods: Motoori Norinaga's *Naobi no mitama*," *Monumenta Nipponica* 46.1 (Spring 1991); Peter Nosco, *Remembering Paradise: Nativism and Nostalgia in Eighteenth Century Japan* (Cambridge: Harvard University Press, 1990); Mark Teeuwen, *Watarai Shintō, An Intellectual History of the Outer Shrine in Ise*

(Leiden: CNWS Publications, 1996); B. M. Young, *Ueda Akinari* (New York: Columbia University Press, 1982).

The Two Shrines of Ise: An Essay of Split Bamboo

Of the Two Shrines of Ise, the Inner Shrine is the shrine of Amaterasu Ōmikami, the very august divine ancestress of the emperors, the Great Sun God of the Heavens, who rules the Plain of High Heaven and who for all eternity, as at this very moment, illuminates the world; and the Outer Shrine is the shrine of Toyuke no Ōkami, the originating spirit of grains and food, who bears the name of Toyouke-bime no Mikoto; she is the great god of the divine food (*miketsu-Ōkami*), whom Amaterasu Ōmikami deeply reveres on the Plain of High Heaven. That Amaterasu Ōmikami resides in the Inner Shrine is well known to the people, and of old there were no aberrant arguments about this fact, but lately there have been aberrant theories concerning Amaterasu Ōmikami herself, and one must beware not to fall into error. These aberrant theories say that, since Amaterasu Ōmikami is the great ancestress of the emperors, it is impossible that she should be the sun in the heavens, and they maintain that she is a god who has lived in this country in the form of an ordinary person, who in the Age of the Gods lived in the country of Yamato, and who has since died. This is the purport of these theories, and it is a most shocking, sacrilegious heresy. If you ask how it is possible that people in such a manner misconstrue the fact that [Amaterasu] Ōmikami is the sun in the heavens that to this day illuminates the world we see around us—a fact concerning which there were of old no aberrant theories because the purport of the holy classics is very clear and not in the least misleading—the reason is that the savants who nowadays expound the holy classics, being conceited and full of Confucian cleverness, cling only to the Chinese texts and are unable to believe the old traditions. Because they attempt to evaluate even the facts of the Age of the Gods through logical principles of the Chinese sort, they assume, for example, that the Plain of High Heaven stands for the imperial capital, or decide that Amaterasu Ōmikami is called "the god of the sun" because her virtue is being compared to the brightness of the sun. To measure everything in this way by Chinese logical principles, and to think that there is nothing beyond these principles, is the narrow-minded way of thinking of those who cannot understand that beyond ordinary logic there is also a mysterious logic. This is a serious error. How can one doubt that Amaterasu Ōmikami is the great ancestress of the emperors, as well as the sun in the heavens that illuminates this world? This principle is one that knows no bounds, that is difficult to fathom and mysterious.

Now then, the Plain of High Heaven, as can be seen in the holy classics, is the sky; and since the sky, over our empire as well as over China and India and other lands, forms but one whole and is not divided, Amaterasu Ōmikami is not only the sun god of our empire, but the all-embracing sun god that illuminates China, India, and all other lands as well. In the theories of Shintō scholars nowadays, however, she seems to be a sun god that is limited to our empire only. They greatly belittle her immeasurable blessings and beneficence, they speak about them as if they were something small and futile, and this is most lamentable. Even worse, they take Amaterasu Ōmikami to be a god who has long since died in the Age of the Gods—a gross sacrilege and the extreme of horror. Can the four seas and the myriad lands of the world continue to exist for even one day without the clear beneficence of this great god? In the Age of the Gods, when the Imperial Grandson Ninigi no Mikoto was about to descend from the Plain of High Heaven to our country, Amaterasu Ōmikami from her own hands gave him a holy mirror with the command: "Regard this mirror as my spirit, and revere it as you revere me!" What is revered as the Divine Object in the Inner Shrine is this mirror, the very one to which Amaterasu Ōmikami, who illuminates this world, has committed her spirit. Therefore the god of this Inner Shrine of Ise is a god whom not only the people of our empire, but also the people of China, India, and other lands, all the people in the countless lands of the world, in all the lands upon which the sun confers her beneficence—she is a god whom all kings and vassals and common people alike must revere and worship for her blessings and beneficence. It is pitiful indeed that in other lands the true traditions of the Age of the Gods have all these years gone unknown, and that to this day naught is known of them; but who in the empire, where this knowledge has been passed down correctly in the holy classics and is clear, will not feel respect for these blessings and this beneficence? Here and now I need not discuss further how august is the fact that she is the divine ancestress of the emperors; however, to think only of this august fact, forgetting that now, at this very moment, all the people in the myriad lands of the world enjoy her beneficence, is lamentable indeed. Do not let this misconception delude you, scorn not this beneficence! How frightful, alas, how frightful!

As I mentioned above, in the Outer Shrine resides Mike-tsu-Ōmikami, a god whom Amaterasu Ōmikami deeply reveres on the Plain of High Heaven. Let me elaborate a bit upon the fact that this Mike-tsu-Ōmikami is a very, very august god, and that Amaterasu Ōmikami reveres her so deeply.

In the world there are countless treasures, but the highest, the ultimate treasure, without which we cannot do even for a day, is food. For all things in this world that pertain to humans presuppose life. Confucianists and Buddhists expound all manner of exalted arguments, but they can neither perform humanity or fidelity, nor practice austerities or study if they do not have life. However extraordinary, however great a matter it may be, one can only accomplish it if one has life. Without life all is futile. And if in the human world life is of such overriding importance, what then is it that allows humans to maintain life? It is food. Money is indeed august, but it cannot help to maintain life even for one day, and that is why I say that the highest and ultimate treasure in the world is food. This principle is well known to everyone; but why then do people regard it only superficially; why does no one take it carefully to heart; why has no one a deep regard for its truth? Moreover the gratitude that we owe our superiors and our parents is extraordinarily vast and great indeed, but, since this gratitude cannot exist if we do not have life, is not the gratitude we owe our food vast and great as well? It is well that we reflect seriously upon this matter.

Thus it is that in the beginning of the world this food that is so august arose from the spirit of Toyouke no Ōkami, and that this food will eternally, as long as heaven and earth exist, continue to grow year after year—all of this we owe to the blessings and the beneficence of this great god. Since there is not one among the people of the world, whether high or low, who does not depend upon food for the continuation of life, we should not forget even for one moment how extraordinary our indebtedness to this great god is; but, as with everything that we grow accustomed to and that comes to seem ordinary, we hardly notice it anymore; we forget how august her beneficence is and fail to appreciate it, and that is most frightful! When every once in a while there is a crop failure and there is little rice and grain, the poor suffer terribly and many die of starvation, and even if it does not go that far, is it not poignant how they can think of nothing but eating when mealtime passes by and their bellies grow empty? Reflecting well upon this, one must always be aware of how important and august is food, and how august is the blessing of this great god, and not forget it.

Now then, since the fact that humans maintain life with the help of food holds not only for the people of our empire but is the same for all people in the myriad lands, there are no people in these lands who do not share in the blessings of this great god. The empire is the land of origin, the ancestral land of the myriad lands, and all the countless things that have appeared and become known all have their origin in our empire; just as the sun and the moon in the Age of the Gods were born in the empire and thereafter spread their beneficence over the four seas and the myriad lands, so it is with the beneficence of Toyouke no Ōkami; the food in the myriad lands with which the people there maintain their lives originates from the spirit of this great god as well. The source of all those stories, that in China a king Shen Nung, and someone called Hou Chi, ancestor of the Chou, taught agriculture to the people and thus were meritorious rulers, lies in the spirit of Toyouke no Ōkami; but because this is a foreign country, people there have not the slightest notion of this truth, and so they just produce any explanation that has an impressive ring to it. Since there is no correct tradition in any of the foreign lands, it is inevitable that people there know nothing of such matters, but in the empire, to our great good fortune, the tradition is clear, and thus one should not take it lightly.

Moreover, the empire is a happy and abundant land where the rice and the grain are better than in any of the myriad lands, and the name by which it is called, the "Land of Fresh Ears," shows that the rice-ears in our country are especially abundant and auspicious. Because people since the Age of the Gods have treated the rice-ears with special reverence, the matter of the "god of the divine food" or *mike-tsu-kami* is of extraordinary importance. Also, as I mentioned above, there are at the court many great ceremonies relating to food. There are, thus, many deep reasons for the fact that Amaterasu Ōmikami particularly reveres Toyouke no Ōkami.

Well then, since this god is a god whom Amaterasu Ōmikami reveres so deeply, it is self-evident that she is boundlessly high and prominent. Yet although in High Antiquity everyone believed everything pertaining to the old traditions, never doubting it, and there were no aberrant theories, in the course of time all manner of theories from other countries intermingled with our own, and there came to be people who thought that this was good and who believed them; this habit spread as the generations succeeded each other, until finally everyone believed only those foreign theories, so that the significance of the correct tradition from the Age of the Gods was lost altogether, and there was no one left who knew it, and the hearts of all the people grew insincere, clever, and distorted. In all things people relied upon Chinese ways of thinking, so that they started to doubt even the tradition from the Age of the Gods. Aberrant theories arose, and they even began to practice deceit in these matters as well. Since Middle Antiquity aberrant theories started to arise about the god of the Outer Shrine, too, and because since that time there have been many aberrant arguments, matters have gone so far that the people can no longer discern what is correct and what is incorrect, and they have become confused as to what kind of a god she is.

It must have been five or six hundred years ago that in Middle Antiquity aberrant theories began to arise about the god of the Outer Shrine. The Five Books, named the "Five Secret Records," came into being, and in these books the name *mike-tsu-kami* is explained as a virtue of the element water. They say: "The element water transforms itself and becomes heaven and earth. . . , the name of this is Ame no Minakanushi no Kami; thus a thousand changes and ten thousand transformations respond to the virtue of the element water and give rise to the skill of the continuation of life; therefore it is also called *mike-tsu-kami*." They state that the *mike-tsu-kami* is Ame no Minakanushi no Mikoto, or they say: "Yorozuhatatoyoakizu-hime no Mikoto is the daughter of Takamimusubi no Kami, who is the crown prince of Toyuke Sumeōkami, she is the mother of Sumemima no Mikoto, therefore the two great gods Amaterasu Sumeōkami and Toyuke Sumeōkami are called the Great Parents of Ninigi no Mikoto." There are many matters about which they expound similar arguments, and if you open these books and read them you will see. They put Amaterasu Ōmikami and Toyuke no Ōkami on a par by saying: "They are equal in brightness and virtue," or "They are the sun and the moon." They regard both the Inner and the Outer Shrine as Great Parents, and they describe them as gods equal in rank and prominence; such is the essence of these books. Moreover, a theory arose recently that would place the Outer Shrine in a higher position than the Inner Shrine. Those people say that the god of the Outer Shrine is Kuni no Tokotachi no Mikoto. Furthermore, there are those who try to degrade the Outer Shrine and make of it an insignificant god. Their theory is that the god of the Outer Shrine, because she is called a "god of the divine food," is a god who prepares meals. In the course of these disputes over the rank and prominence of the Two Shrines, all manner of mistakes and lies have arisen; and as these theories proliferate, everyone becomes more and more confused and no one can determine what sort of a god the god of the Outer Shrine is.

It is a very, very sad and lamentable affair that the true august beneficence of Toyuke no Ōkami has become hidden and difficult to discern. Therefore I, Norinaga, will now try to distinguish and correct these aberrant theories and arguments, awesome though the task is, and to make manifest the august, true beneficence of this great god. The reason I name this work an "essay of split bamboo" is that, in the spirit of the common expression "as straight as split bamboo," I wish to indicate that I state the case correctly and sincerely without evasion or distortion.

The claim that these Five Books are much older than the *Record of Ancient Matters* (*Kojiki,* 712) and the *Chronicles of Japan* (*Nihon shoki,* 720), and the fact that they have given names to all of the authors that make them seem to be people of ancient times—all of this is the deceit of people of later ages, the purpose of which was only to claim that the Inner and the Outer Shrine are both great ancestors of the imperial line, and that they are gods of equal rank and prominence. These theories are exactly as described, point for point, in the books *Record of Mount Kamiji* (*Kamijiki,* 1730) and *Essays on the Theories of the Five Books* (*Gobusho setsuben,* 1736), to which I shall return later and thus shall not now discuss further. There is, however, something that must be said about them. First of all, of these Five Books, all of them forgeries, only the *Record of Yamato-hime no Mikoto* (*Yamato-hime no mikoto seiki*) does contain some passages that could never have been written by anyone of later ages and thus cannot be dismissed. One must, here and there, distinguish the true from the false. The other four books are vulgar, inferior works that are not worth looking at.

To begin with, [the writers of the Five Books] have, among all the many gods, decided upon Ame no Minakanushi no Kami [as the god of the Outer Shrine], because they thought that this god, being the first born in the beginning of heaven and earth, is a Great Parent who comes before Amaterasu Ōmikami, and that there is no god more prominent than he. This, however, is a most foolish, vulgar notion of later ages. It is not at all true that a god of later birth is less significant. If one decides the prominence of gods on the basis of the order of their birth, does that then mean that one regards all the gods that were born before Amaterasu Ōmikami as more prominent than she?

The god that among all the gods must be called the Great Ancestor of the emperors is Amaterasu Ōmikami. As for relations between lord and servant, this distinction exists only since Amaterasu Ōmikami has reigned in the Plain of High Heaven as its lord; before that there was no such thing as lords and servants. The relations of husband and wife and father and son, too, came into being only when Izanagi and Izanami no Ōkami had sexual intercourse and gave birth to the land and many gods; before that neither the relation of husband and wife nor the relation of father and son existed, so how could Kuni no Tokotachi no Mikoto be a Great Parent of the imperial line?

If one reflects upon the meaning of the aforementioned facts, one will surely realize that Kuni no Tokotachi no Mikoto is neither the first god in the beginning of heaven and earth, nor a heavenly god, nor a Great Parent of the emperors. The reason I elaborate upon this matter so extensively is that I, from the bottom of my heart, long to make the people who think that there is no god more prominent than Kuni no Tokotachi no Mikoto recognize their error, to correct immediately the old theory that this god resides in the Outer Shrine, and to make apparent the true, most august beneficence of Toyouke no Ōkami. Not to recognize the truth even now that I have explained it so extensively would indeed be the extreme of stupidity. There are also those who, even though in their hearts they do recognize the truth, find it hard to change their opinion now, and who continue to add ever more perversions and distortions in order to rescue this old theory; but this, with every word they speak, brings only the more shame of stupidity and deceitfulness upon them and will make them the laughingstock of later generations throughout the world. Since nowadays the Way of learning has been greatly developed, and especially since the advent of the school of Ancient Learning, [that is, National Learning, as developed by Keichū and Kamo no Mabuchi,] matters of the past are very clear; there is hardly anyone left who accepts the old theory on Kuni no Tokotachi no Mikoto. To persist in advocating that theory is like gluing together, again and again, an already shattered teacup that is quite useless, trying to continue using it as a teacup. Is not that the extreme of absurdity?

Further, one may object that these theories on Ame no Minakanushi no Kami and Kuni no Tokotachi no Mikoto are theories of our predecessors, and that one should avoid rejecting them now because they are of long standing and everyone, high and low, knows them well. Even though this at first sight seems entirely reasonable and correct, one must give the matter further thought. If we fail to correct such foolish, blind theories at the right time and continue to expound them, so that we are laughed at by later generations throughout the world, we perpetuate the shame of our predecessors endlessly; and is not that even more to the detriment of our predecessors? Moreover, we should have no little fear for this great god, should we allege that this most august god is some other god to whom she has no relation whatsoever, and should we obscure for long the great beneficence of the most important divine food and fail to make it known.

For all these reasons I want to correct and purify this old theory quickly. It is a fundamental law from High Antiquity that everytime one commits a blunder, one must reveal and purify it, and if one executes such a purification, all will be corrected and washed clean. In foreign countries, too, one finds in the Way of the Confucianists that one must quickly correct one's mistakes, and in the Buddhist teachings there is confession; therefore, whatever Way one follows, it will be in accordance with the intentions of [Amaterasu] Ōmikami, and likewise an act of loyalty and filial piety toward our predecessors, quickly to revise this unfounded old theory and to accept the correct theory, in which the truth is clear.

In the *Record of Ancient Matters*, in the passage where Sumemima no Mikoto descends from heaven to this country, it says:

> Then [Amaterasu Ōmikami] added [to the entourage of Sumemima no Mikoto] Ame no Koyane no Mikoto, Futodama no Mikoto, Ame no Uzume no Mikoto, Ishikoridome no Mikoto, and Tama no Ya no Mikoto, in all five chiefs of workers' groups, and they descended together with him.

The passage continues:

> Thereupon she added to this entourage the eight-foot-long curved jewels and the mirror that had lured her [from the Rock Cave of Heaven], the Herb Quelling sword, and the gods Tokoyo no Omoikane no Kami, Tajikara-wo no Kami, and Ame no Iwatowake no Kami, and she said: "Regard this mirror as my spirit, and revere it as you revere me!" and next she said: "Let Omoikane no Kami take charge of my affairs, and execute my worship." These two gods are worshipped in the shrine at Isuzu. Further, Toyouke no Kami, this is the god who resides in Watarai of the Outer Shrine. Further, Ame no Iwatowake no Kami, who is also called Kushi-iwamato no Kami or Toyo-iwamato no Kami, this god is the god of the gates. Further, Tajikara-wo no Kami, resides in Sanagata.

Then it says:

> Ame no Koyane no Mikoto is the ancestor of the *muraji* of the Nakatomi, Futodama no Mikoto is the ancestor of the *obito* of the Inbe, Ame no Uzume no Mikoto is the ancestor of the *kimi* of the Sarume, Ishikoridome no Mikoto is the ancestor of the *muraji* of the Kagamitsukuri, and Tama no Ya no Mikoto is the ancestor of the *muraji* of the Tamanoya.

On this passage we must reflect well. The five gods who are chiefs of workers' groups, Ame no Koyane no Mikoto and the others, who are mentioned at the beginning, are physical bodies serving Sumemima no Mikoto. The four gods Omoikane no Kami, Tajikara-wo no Kami, Ame no Iwatowake no Kami, and Toyouke no Kami mentioned next to these are not gods who are physical bodies, they are the *mitamashiro*, "spirit containers" of these gods, and [Amaterasu Ōmikami] added them to the mirror and the other objects and then handed them over [to Sumemima no Mikoto]. Everytime the words "(. . .) no Kami" appear in the ancient texts, we must distinguish between physical bodies and spirits. "Physical body" means the actual body of the god; "spirit" means his divine spirit. A *mitamashiro* is a mirror or some other object to which this spirit is committed; in everyday language, a Divine Object. Both physical bodies and *mitamashiro* are referred to as "(. . .) no Kami." In the *Chronicles of Japan*, in the section on Emperor Sujin, it says: "The emperor handed Amaterasu Ōmikami over to Toyosuki Iri-bime no Mikoto, and Yamato no Ōkunimitama no Kami to Nunaki Iri-bime no Mikoto." Since the physical bodies of these two gods were not in the palace at this time, it is beyond doubt that this refers to their *mitamashiro*, and from this we can learn that these, just like their physical bodies, were called "Amaterasu Ōmikami" and "Yamato no Ōkunimitama no Kami" as well. Further, this same section says: "The emperor hereupon proceeded to the plain of Kami-asachi, where he assembled the eighty myriads of gods and inquired of them by means of divination." Since these eighty myriads of gods could not, as in the Age of the Gods on the Plain of High Heaven, be assembled as physical bodies, it is clear that the meaning is that the emperor called up the spirits of these gods. On the basis of these facts we know that, when we find the words "(. . .) no Kami," we must distinguish between physical bodies and spirits.

This distinction exists as well for the gods in the passage from the *Record of Ancient Matters* just quoted; and if one asks how this distinction can be recognized, it is that the gods who are serving physical bodies and the gods who are *mitamashiro* are each mentioned separately, and that, because the five chiefs of workers' groups, Ama no Koyane no Mikoto and the others, mentioned in the beginning, are serving physical bodies, the houses that descend from them are given in the latter part of the above quotation. Also Ame no Oshihi no Mikoto, Ama-tsu-kume no Mikoto, and the other gods who figure in the passage following the one quoted are all physical bodies and have descendants because they came down from heaven to this country. Further, Omoikane no Kami and the other three gods have been recorded separately from those five chiefs of workers' groups, starting anew with the word "Thereupon," and grouping them with the curved jewels, the mirror and the sword. The words "These two gods," refer to the mirror, the *mitamashiro* of Amaterasu Ōmikami, and Omoikane no Kami. From the fact that one of these two gods is a mirror, we know that the other god, Omoikane no Kami, is a *mitamashiro* as well. Accordingly, this means that also Toyouke no Kami, who is mentioned next, is a *mitamashiro*, and that this *mitamashiro* resides in the Outer Shrine. And it also says that Omoikane no Kami is worshipped in the shrine of Isuzu, and that Tajikara-wo no Kami resides in Sanagata; that is what is recorded in the List of Deities [in the *Institutes of the Engi Period*] as "Province of Ise, district Taki, shrine of Sana." That Ame no Iwatowake no Kami is "the god of the gates" is recorded in the List of Deities as "Gods worshipped by the Sacred Maidens of the Gates in the Ministry of Worship, Kushi-iwamato no Kami and Toyo-iwamato no Kami (both major, Tsukinami and Niiname)," and as "Province of Tanba, district Taki, shrine of Kushi-iwamato, two gods (both principal deities, major)." Thus, for these gods only the place of residence is recorded, and nowhere is it mentioned that they are the ancestors of a house. Of the five chiefs of workers' groups, Ame no Koyane no Mikoto and the others, the houses that have descended from them are given, and not their places of residence, and so we can determine that there is indeed a distinction between gods who are physical bodies and gods who are *mitamashiro*.

Now then, the reason that in the passage in the *Chronicles of Japan* relating this descent from heaven these four gods, Toyouke no Kami, Omoikane no Kami, and the others, are not mentioned is likewise that they are not physical bodies. This work lists only the gods who are serving physical bodies and describes the mirror, the curved jewels, and the sword as the regalia of Sumemima no Mikoto, omitting altogether the other gods who are *mitamashiro*. Thus it at last becomes clear that Toyouke no Kami is not a serving physical body, and for the very reason that she is not mentioned in the *Chronicles of Japan*! That Mr. Yoshimi [Yukikazu, the author of *Essays on the Theories of the Five Books*] did not understand this, and, ignorant of the distinction between physical bodies and *mitamashiro*, wrote that this god is a servant from the entourage, is again to be attributed to the well-known thoughtlessness of the Chinese way of thinking. How is it possible that all the Shintō scholars in the world expatiate on useless Sinifications like "heart transformations" and "matter transformations" but do not know that there is a distinction between physical bodies and spirits? Also his idea that Toyouke no Ōkami is an insignificant god because she does not figure in the section on the Age of the Gods in the *Chronicles of Japan* originates in his ignorance of this distinction. To state that she is not a prominent god because the fact that she resides in the Outer Shrine is not to be found in the National Histories is a gross distortion. The fact that Sumemima no Mikoto is worshipped in the Shared Hall at the Outer Shrine cannot be found in the National Histories either, and although Emperor Ōjin is worshipped in Usa in Tsukushi, the fact that this is his place of residence is not to be seen in the National Histories. Moreover we are not told that Emperor Jimmu's spirit is worshipped at all, nor even the shrine where he resides. Are these all to be disposed of as "insignificant"? In the *Chronicles of Japan* and in all the other National Histories, one finds that important matters that definitely should have been recorded are omitted, and also that rather insignificant matters are recorded. One cannot determine the importance of a matter by looking to see whether it is found in the National Histories!

Someone asks: If Toyouke no Ōkami is a god whom Amaterasu Ōmikami reveres, is then the Outer Shrine even more prominent than the Inner Shrine?

I answer: In all the universe there is no god as prominent as Amaterasu Ōmikami. That there are gods whom she reveres may, for example, be compared to the fact that in this country the emperor reveres the countless gods. On the Plain of High Heaven Amaterasu Ōmikami is an emperor with a physical body. Toyouke no Ōkami, whom she reveres, is a god who is a spirit; she has no physical body. Although in this country no one is more prominent than the emperor, he in turn reveres the gods; thus it will not do to say that these gods, for the reason that they are gods whom the emperor reveres, are all more prominent than the emperor. But neither can we say that these gods, for the reason that they are gods whom the emperor reveres, are all less prominent than the emperor; and likewise is it not right to say that the god of the Outer Shrine is less prominent than the god of the Inner Shrine. In the ceremonies of both shrines we worship a god who is a spirit, in the Inner as well as in the Outer Shrine, and in that respect there is no difference between the Two Shrines. As things stand at present, the gods of both shrines appear to be on a par with each other and equal; but they differ from each other as emperor and god differ and are not equal. It is a frightful, vulgar notion that, even though they cannot be compared and designated more and less prominent, people still continue to dispute their prominence.

Again someone asks: Concerning the ceremonial homage they are paid by the court, and a myriad other matters besides, the Two Shrines of Ise differ in prominence and are not equal. In most matters the Inner Shrine is superior and the Outer Shrine inferior. Why then may we not say that [the god of the Outer Shrine] is less prominent than the god of the Inner Shrine, even though the Outer Shrine, in view of these differences, does appear less prominent than the Inner Shrine?

I answer: Because the Inner Shrine is the shrine where we worship the divine ancestress of the emperors, and in particular the mirror of her spirit, which is a most extraordinary imperial mandate, the ceremonies and myriad other matters concerning this shrine naturally are unequaled under heaven, and therefore the shrine of Toyouke no Ōkami, however prominent she herself may be, can never be its equal. That the Outer Shrine must be surpassed by the Inner Shrine is a matter of course. We should, however, not without reason determine the prominence of shrines on the basis of their ceremonies and the like. Therein lies the significance of the comparison of emperor and god that I made above. Now let me make another comparison. We have the Palace of the Emperor (*ōmiya*) and the shrine of a god (*kami no miya*): the shrine of this god is called the Great Shrine (*ōkamumiya* or *daijingū*) of Ise, but the construction of its buildings, for one thing, is not as spacious and magnificent as that of the palace of the emperors, and the deity is far less well off than the imperial court as far as officials, the myriad ceremonies, or the goods she is served are concerned. Would one for that reason say that Amaterasu Ōmikami is less prominent than the emperor? The reason for this difference is that one is an emperor with a physical body, and the other a god who is a spirit. You must realize that this same distinction exists between the gods of the Two Shrines.

In the matter of the great gods of these Two Shrines, proponents of the Outer Shrine dwell only upon the prominence of the Outer Shrine, concealing the fact that it is surpassed by the Inner Shrine, while people who want to denigrate the Outer Shrine dwell only upon its inferiority to the Inner Shrine, concealing the prominence of the Outer Shrine. Determined as they are to combat each other, their discourses are neither upright nor balanced; they are invariably one-sided. In general it is a law of nature in the world, that whenever something is divided into two parts, and these are placed in alignment, there arise automatically feelings of mutual envy and malice, and people begin to fight over which is superior and which inferior, which is higher and which lower. This is a practice that would be difficult indeed to prevent; but, as in the case of the Two Shrines of Ise, where there can be no disputing which is "more prominent" or "less prominent," it is not merely downright common but positively frightful. Though the god of the Outer Shrine is a god whom Amaterasu Ōmikami reveres so deeply, they try to denigrate her with no scruples, and they insist that she is an insignificant god. Would that really make Amaterasu Ōmikami happy? They deliberately conceal the beneficence of the *mike-tsu-kami*, the peerlessly prominent spirit of the divine food, and equate her with gods entirely unrelated to her, arguing that she is Ame no Minakanushi no Mikoto or Kuni no Tokotachi no Mikoto. Would this sort of slander really make Toyouke no Ōkami happy? In the august presence of the physical bodies of these two great gods they would never dare to utter such idle, foolish lies; they do so only because they think superficially and do not fear the divine will of the gods; this because they do not show themselves before our eyes and speak to us. How frightful, alas, how frightful!

—46—

Sasaki Shōten: Toward a Postmodern Shinshū Theology

Jan Van Bragt

Sasaki Shōten, born in 1939, is a priest of the Nishi Hongan-ji branch of Shinshū. After graduating from Ryūkoku University (Kyoto) and being ordained as a priest, he continued his studies in religion at the State University of Kyoto. Soon after, he became a member of the Dendō-in (Pastoral Institute) of Nishi Hongan-ji, where he is still active today. It was in the 1984 issue of the *Bulletin* of this Dendō-in that Sasaki broached for the first time the problematics of the present article, in the form of a report of the results of a research program on the practices of Shinshū believers, which he had jointly undertaken with two sociologists, Omura Eishō and Kaneko Satoru. The strong reaction among the scholars of the sect to this report prompted the three scholars to enlarge on their findings in a jointly authored book, *Posuto-modan no Shinran* (The Postmodern Shinran) (Kyoto: Dōbōsha, 1990).

The term "Shinshū" refers to the adherents of the school of Pure Land Buddhism or Amidism founded by Shinran (1173–1262). By the sixteenth century the Honganji branch of this school, which was organized after Shinran's death around his direct descendants and his tomb in Kyoto, had succeeded in bringing most of Shinran's disciples into its fold. In the beginning of the seventeenth century, however, a succession dispute led to the split of the Honganji into two "sects," commonly known as the Nishi (West or Honganji) branch and the Higashi (East or Ōtani) branch. As part of their official teachings, both branches reject the use of amulets, talismans, votive tablets and other devices and rituals for securing this-worldly benefits (*genze riyaku*) such as health, wealth, and longevity. While these beliefs are officially condemned as magical folk superstitions, what Sasaki and his colleagues confirmed through their field studies is that large numbers of Shinshū adherents engaged in these practices. In proposing a "postmodern Shinshū theology," Sasaki criticizes the "modern" rationalist stance that rejects such superstitions, and the attempts to account for and even embrace folk practices without violating official teaching.

The present article, based on a special lecture delivered at the Center for Religious Education of the Sōtō branch of Zen Buddhism, October 1986, was originally published in the February 12, 15, and 17, 1988, issues of the religious newspaper *Chūgai nippō*. The following considerably abridged translation of that text first appeared in *Nanzan Bulletin* 12 (1988): 13–35.

Further Reading

James C. Dobbins, *Jōdo Shinshū: Shin Buddhism in Medieval Japan* (Bloomington: Indianapolis: Indiana University Press, 1989); James Ketelaar, *Of Heretics and Martyrs in Meiji Japan: Buddhism and Its Persecution* (Princeton: Princeton University Press, 1990); Suzuki Daisetz, tr., *The Kyōgyōshinshō: The Collection of Passages Expounding the True Teaching, Living, Faith, and Realizing of the Pure Land* (Kyoto: Shinshū Ōtaniha, 1973).

Toward a Postmodern Shinshū Theology

We no longer belong to the "modern world." In many areas of culture and in popular religiosity, fundamentally new trends have come to the fore, leading us to conclude that we have entered a "postmodern" period, which naturally requires a postmodern "theology."

It is my contention here that tragedy awaits our sect in the future if we continue to absolutize a modernistic theology and refuse to face the many inadequacies of that theology attested by recent events. In this fin de siècle we must build a postmodern theology able to correct the aberrations of our modernistic theology.

THE DOCTRINE OF THE NISHI HONGANJI

During the three hundred years of the Edo period, the doctrine of our sect had been built up to such a degree of scholastic minuteness that it is no exaggeration to say that our theologians since the Meiji Restoration have had their hands full just with systematizing and cataloging the Edo legacy. That Edo doctrine may seem to be purely theological, but in fact it is intimately tied up with the political situation under the bakufu regime and bears the traces of many clashes with the other branches of the Pure Land School and with various other Buddhist sects. In sum, it shows a history of polemics against the "Path of the Sages" (*shōdō*) and the Pure Land school (Jōdoshū) [founded by Hōnen].

Another legacy of the Edo period are the aftereffects of the great doctrinal dispute that split our sect into two theological camps: the so-called Confusion about the Three Acts (*sangō wakuran*), the eighteenth-century dispute concerning the conditions for assurance in faith (*anjin*). The theologians of the "Forest of Learning" (*gakurin*), who came to be known as the "Progressives" (*shingiha*), demanded that trust in Amida be expressed in the "three kinds of acts" (*sangō*), namely, thought, word, and deed. There was a strong reaction against this from scholars in the field—the so-called Traditionalists (*kogiha*)—and the ensuing polemics were so disruptive and sometimes even violent that the feudal government had to intervene in 1804 and declare orthodoxy to be on the side of the Traditonalists. As a result of this dispute over "assurance in faith," our theology up to the present has been oversensitive to the point of being centered on a nitpicking definition of *anjin* that does not leave room for the slightest jot or tittle of deviation.

Against the background of that theological history, our theology considers the question of folk religious practices to have been solved once and for all; there is no room for further questioning. The whole question is caught in the net of the critical classification of teachings (*kyōhan*) or the "discrimination of true-provisional-false" (*shikegi han*). Jōdo Shinshū is, of course, true; all other Buddhist schools are provisional; and all doctrines outside of Buddhism are false. It is clear that folk beliefs belong to the third category and must be rejected together with everything provisional and false.

In the troubled period of the Meiji Restoration, our Nishi Hongan-ji had the good fortune of clearly siding with the emperor against the feudal lords but was of course caught together with all other Buddhist sects in the movement to "abolish Buddhism and demolish Shakyamuni" (*haibutsu kishaku*), the anti-Buddhist campaign of the beginning of the Meiji era [see Ketelaar 1990], and later in the policy of the Meiji government to make Shintō the state religion. For a time our theologians had their hands full with these things. During the Second World War our sect put up a "headquarters for wartime doctrine," where indeed a wartime theology was developed. It was only with the establishment of the Pastoral Institute (Dendō-in) that a beginning was made with the liquidation of that wartime doctrine. However, in November 1985, this Pastoral Institute was abolished by the senate of the sect and in its stead a "doctrinal headquarters" (*kyōgaku honbu*) established anew.

As for the postwar course of Shinshū doctrine, wherein Ryūkoku University plays a central role, I can say in summary that the influence of the democratization of Japan is certainly felt there, at least to the degree that a Conference of Indian Philosophy and Buddhist Studies was established, and that a modern kind of Shinran and Shinshū studies developed, not only within the sect this time but also among thinkers, literati, and historians at large. All this, of course, caused our theologians their share of headaches. There is at present some *Auseinandersetzung* of our theologians with scientific Buddhist studies, social sciences, humanism, Marxism, existentialism, and Christian theology. But since Meiji, folk beliefs and practices do not appear on the theological agenda; they have been barred from the theological precincts.

THE SHINSHŪ TRADITION AS A RELIGIOUS ORGANIZATION THAT FREED ITSELF OF MAGIC

There is one more important reason why folk belief has not become a topic in Shinshū doctrine. I refer here to the original life-style of Shinshū people: their particular way of relating to folk practices, which has been ridiculed by people of other sects in the saying, "Shinshū believers are ignoramuses" (*Monto mono shirazu*)—meaning that they ignore taboos, unlucky days, and so forth. Folklorists have been saying that "Shinshū destroys local usages and beliefs, so that regions with a strong Shinshū influence are barren ground for folklorists." Max Weber declared that while Buddhism, Taoism, and Confucianism have by and large played the role of fixing people in a "magical garden," only Shinshū has greatly contributed to the breaking of the magical circle (*Entzauberung*), and he gives Shinshū high marks for it. Already in the Edo period there were authors, like Dazai Shundai (1680–1747) and Buyō Inshi (fl. ca. 1816), who expressed their amazement about the fact that there was this tradition of radical adherence to a single Buddha, Amida, without indulging in incantations, magical spells, the use of magical water, and so forth. Professor Kojima of Maritime University observes that even today, on an island off Yamaguchi Prefecture, Shinshū is still called "the does-not-care sect" (Kannanshū). This points, for example, to the fact that even in the postwar period the Shinshū people there, at the cremation of their deceased, simply left the remaining bones in the crematorium (except for a small part that was consigned to the local temple) without minding the taboos surrounding people's bones; and also the fact that they had no memorial tablets, death registers, or god shelves, did not put up any Jizō images, and even had no graves. In other words, in that region the original shape of a Shinshū community, which had done away with all these popular usages, had been preserved. Seen from this kind of tradition, it is perhaps natural that folk practices appeared in theology only as things to be rejected.

And so, when we took up this problem again in *Bulletin 29* of the Pastoral Institute, as a sect for whom the question of folk practices had long since been solved, we were roundly criticized by many learned people for being faithless, for taking the easy path of giving in to actual conditions without regard for Shinran's position, for being promoters of non-Shinshū ways, and for being insolent people throwing sand on the fire of the modernization movement of the sect. But the collective and interdisciplinary study of folk practices within our sect had not simply been undertaken from the standpoint of Shinshū doctrine. It has its origins in a scientific study of the religious consciousness of people in the field and in a resolve of taking the actual situation fully into consideration.

THE ACTUAL RELIGIOUS CONSCIOUSNESS OF SHINSHŪ BELIEVERS

In 1961, on the occasion of the 700th anniversary of Shinran Shōnin's death, our sect launched the "Believers Movement" (*monshinto undō*), a movement aiming at the transformation of the sect from a religion of the household (*ie*) into a religion of the individual. In 1971 the "Assimilation Movement" (*dōbō undō*) was started, attempting to promote among members of our sect, which serves more than half of the discriminated villages (*buraku*) but did not work for their emancipation, a better attitude toward these victims of discrimination. Both movements continue today.

In the meantime, roundtable discussions (*hōza*) were organized to listen to the voice of the lay believers. There were also meetings of the believers on the occasion of the pastoral visitation of the Monshu (head of the sect) to all the districts. On these and similar occasions it became clear that our sect is on the point of losing its character of—in Weberian terms—a community of people freed from magic. These findings were confirmed by scientific research, and we came to the conviction that we are facing here an important and urgent problem.

The data on which our present position is based are mainly those assembled by a psychology professor of Osaka Municipal University, Kaneko Satoru (a Shinshū believer and member of our team), through surveys conducted among temple priests and faithful over more than ten years. It became clear from these data that the religiosity of our people, far from being of the "does-not-care" type, exhibits a primitive mentality with Shintōism as its core. This religiosity is intimately bound up with ancestor worship—which Kaneko calls a factor of animism—and also shows a level of conservative "authority cult," represented by the emperor ideology. One more important outcome of this research is that there exists a great difference in faith structure between the temple priests and the lay people—a real split or polarization of consciousness.

This constitutes, of course, a big problem for our sect, but the situation is further aggravated by demographic differences in the faith of the lay people according to locality, sex, profession, income bracket, education, and so forth. The "faith type" of our faithful can thus be characterized as one colored by a multilayered and this-worldly-benefit-oriented folk religiosity, and tied up with not necessarily desirable strands of social consciousness such as conservatism, blind faith in authority, and social (especially political) indifferentism. Among the male believers, who in general appear to be rather weak in their faith (and are, for example, rather passive when it comes to attending religious services), the data point to a desire to see our sect become more of a "character building organization" (more directed at moral and spiritual training).

These data shook us terribly. But however much we might wish to flee the facts, the reality is there and we cannot ultimately afford to ignore it. We are thus driven to the conclusion that unless we shoulder this situation as a pastoral and doctrinal challenge and come to a critical appraisal of these facts, there is no hope of a concrete revival of our religion. For some reason, however, this judgment of our team appears to win very little understanding within our sect.

A FLEXIBLE, TWO-PRONGED POSTMODERN THEOLOGY

First of all, why do we speak, in this context, of a "postmodern" theology? We certainly do not want to deny that many premodern elements survive in the makeup of our sect, and even in its theology. But when it comes to the attitude toward folk beliefs, the thinking in our sect has fallen in step with a theology that aims at a kind of *Aufklärung* or "modernism." Our call for a postmodern theology is being criticized as if it were a call for an affirmation of the status quo or for a return to premodern times. The reason for its being judged that way must lie in the fact that we have deliberately chosen antimodern terminology, because we felt that, in the question of folk practices, the current theology shows an all too strong modernistic trend. I thought I made my meaning clear enough in my report in the *Bulletin*, but few people seem to have read it carefully. In fact we do not claim at all that premodern things are good and modern things bad. Nor do we say that all postmodern things are ipso facto good. All we said was that, because we recognized serious problems in both the premodern and the modern, we wanted to look for a flexible, two-pronged postmodern theology. We also expressed the hope that, in the present intellectual and religious situation of Japan, a postmodern approach might provide a road for the different Buddhist schools to the spirit of their respective founders.

A THEOLOGY WITHOUT GRASS ROOTS ("THE FIELD")

To characterize the present situation of our theology we have used the expression "a theology without grass roots" (*genba naki kyōgaku*). This expression was eagerly taken up by journalists and has become a kind of fashion word. We meant by it that there is an all too big gap between what the priests are doing in the "field" of our religion and what theologians are talking about in their discourses. We then claimed that the filling up of this gap between actual field conditions and theology is a primary requirement for the revival of our religion and called for a move from a "theology without field" and a "field without theology" to a "theology rooted in the field" and a "theologizing field."

The problem lies not so much on the side of the field, since the priests there all had some kind of training in theology, but rather on the side of the theological establishment, where practically no theological reflection is done on what actually happens in the field. The widespread idea, however, that only the theologians would be faithful followers of Dōgen or Shinran, and the priests in the field simply religious figures serving a religious system of funeral services and folk practices, is little more than the self-conceited prejudice of an elite without an understanding of what religion is all about. One of our lay people, an assistant professor at the Osaka National Ethnological Museum and a participant in our research, had the following to say: "There is no other solution but that the religious establishment and each priest in the field shoulder both the respectable and the 'dirty' elements in a balanced way. Hōnen, Shinran, and all the eminent religious figures have, after all, done exactly that."

Our local temples and the religious life therein are not merely "localities." We have chosen to call them "fields" because we do not consider these local forms of our religion, shaped by historical processes, to be places without theological relevance or sites where Shinran would be absent. On the contrary, we see them as fields of theological sublimation of local folk beliefs and rites, where the question of how to make our Founder present to the present age is at stake. In a word, we see them as fields of bodhisattva activity by Shinran and the temple priests. It is this sense we wanted to restore to them by using the term "field." We have thus proposed to consider the local temple not merely as an administrative unit or as a place where the Buddha Dharma is for sale, but rather as a place for a concrete and realizable revitalization of our sect and a field of return to Shinran Shōnin.

We have, therefore, criticized the traditional theology that ignores or looks down on folk practices, ritual, religious community, and we have advocated instead a "field theology" (*genba no kyōgaku*), which, within its system, would embrace these three elements. Postwar theology has done well in the question of its compatibility with science, but it accords no place to a theology of folk practice, a theology of ritual, and a theology of religious community (ecclesiology). The position of these theologians appears to be that these things are not essential to our doctrine, and every temple priest can freely decide for himself about them. Modernistic theology even tends to say that these elements are alien or adverse to Shinran and should therefore be suppressed. Opposition to folk practice, to ritual, and to community are then treated as if they were self-evident characteristics of Shinran's religion. Folk practice, ritual, and community then are called alien to the spirit of Shinran, products of compromise with folk religion and secularized society, disreputable elements that it is better not to have. In that line one comes finally to advocating the dissolution of the head temple of the sect (*honzan*) as if this were the height of the Shinranesque.

In this view, the only thing that counts is for every individual to possess his faith as an autonomous subject. Therein would then lie the only path for a return to Shinran. That is truly a modern existentialist theology of unassailable respectability! It is the kind of theology which, during the forty years since the war the temple priests, this silent majority carrying the weight of temples and faithful, have been made to listen to. And since they were scolded by the professors with the words "All your doings go against the spirit of Shinran," they have been listening with a feeling of guilt and loss of self-confidence. It is this trend we have challenged by calling for a postmodern theology. Indeed, there is something in what the professors are saying, but would their view really be the only concrete means for a revival of our sect? Would it not be good to have a theology that takes the actual situation of our religion, with all its accretions, really into account?

To say it somewhat differently, with the anthropologists, we wanted to stress that each culture has a system of thought and behavior with regard to the world and the human, and that this system comprises, besides the two complementary elements, science and religion, a third domain, which usually carries the labels of "folk belief," "superstition," "magic." Modern theology has had eyes only for the area where science and religion overlap and has constantly ignored that third domain. We, on the other hand, wish to stress that the factual situation of our sect imposes on us the task of investigating the composite realm where religion and this third domain overlap. The profile not of pure theology but of the concrete faith of our believers in the field can only be drawn against the backdrop of this third domain, and precisely in the overlap of religion and this third domain lies the key to interpret the practices, rituals, and forms of community life of our sect.

Current theology considers that third domain as a kind of "low life" far beneath the level of religion and bound to disappear once people have real faith. Feeling themselves to be the real nembutsu practitioners, they have despised and ridiculed people involved in that domain. Considering themselves to be graduates from that realm of human frailty, they are unable, from that Buddha seat, to see the people as anything but recipients of their enlightening activity. Still, this third domain forms the basic religiosity of the Japanese people and is not likely to disappear merely because scholars in their theories condemn and reject it. It must be given due consideration when thinking of Japanese religion in the future.

We have then tried to catch this basic belief of the Japanese people under the categories of "by your grace" (*okagesama*) and "curse" (*tatari*). The first one being an animistic trend and the second a shamanistic one, the religious mentality of the Japanese can then be characterized as an "animist-shamanist complex." The element of "by your grace" suits very well the requirements of the field and has been adopted there as "by the grace of Amida" and "thanks to Shinran." The element of "curse," however, is something of an embarrassment. One does then, as if one does not see it, say that such things do not exist in Buddhism. That, however, is a little too arbitrary. We have therefore claimed that it is extremely important and urgent to give full attention to the whole "animist-shamanist complex," and we have proposed this as a key for the interpretation of the folk practices, rituals, and forms of community in our sect. For there certainly exist in the field typical Shinshū folk practices, for example, in the way of preaching, in all kinds of ritual, in the organizational patterns, and so forth. And, as appears in the research of the above-mentioned professor Kaneko, one can certainly discern in the collective psychology of our faithful the spirit of *okagesama*, the fear of curses and, moreover, the consciousness of "living together with the dead" (or the belief that communication with the dead is possible).

Next we must refer to the fact that in the actual faith of our believers "Amida belief," "founder belief" (in Shinran), and "ancestor worship" form a trinity. The problems concerning this triune structure of the faith of the Shinshū adherents will surely emerge as extremely important themes—if not as the problem of problems—for the policy-making bodies of our sect. For that, we absolutely need a theology that does not run away from the actual mentality of our people. If our theology remains a solo flight of theory only, it is to be feared that in the future the Buddha Dharma will be found only in the study rooms of our universities—these "Naga palaces." Religious practices, rituals, and community must become the tripod supporting the theories of our theology. A solo flight of theory without this threefold support can possibly be interesting for a part of the elite as a kind of religious construct or philosophy of religion, but history sufficiently proves that it cannot be the religion of the people.

The meeting with the transcendent beyond the secular and the dialogue with the infinite cannot be expressed by the sole one-track logic of theory or, buddcally speaking, "discriminatory knowledge," and it is very well possible that they are more accessible to our people via the above tripod. The idea that everything can be solved by a merely theoretical doctrine, and that through it we could have direct access to our Founder, is certainly not very Buddhist. For, when it comes to looking through the illusions of the subject and the barrenness of logic only, Buddhism may have no rival.

In sum, our theology from now on must develop a doctrine of folk practice, a doctrine of ritual, and a doctrine of community; and clarify the realm where these three interpenetrate. I am convinced that, in so doing, a sketch-map can be drawn for the overcoming of the gap between our theology and the field, and for bringing our sect to a new life wherein our Founder is present.

A PLEA FOR SHINSHŪ CATHOLICISM ("SHINSHŪ C")

It is time now to come to our central theme. The proposal that our collective research on Shinshū doctrine and folk practices popular beliefs has come up with was baptized by us as "Shinshū Catholicism." The history of the religions of the world tells us that all world religions face the problem of the relationship of their doctrine with folk practices and thus of a theological interpretation of these practices. The case of Christianity with its two poles of Puritanism and Catholicism has struck us as typical, and so we have come to speak of Shinshū Puritanism (Shinshū P) over against Shinshū Catholicism (Shinshū C). Since this P-C polarity can be found in all religions, we have even thought of the possibility of this becoming a theme of common research for the theologies of different religions and sects.

In *Bulletin 30* of the Pastoral Institute, Ōmura Eishō, a professor of sociology at Osaka University, clarifies what we mean when we advocate a Shinshū Catholicism:

> In Christian circles it has become common sense to regard Puritanism and Catholicism both as ambivalent, each having positive and negative aspects. Puritanism has the positive aspect of maintaining the purity of the doctrine

with rejection of all compromise, but the negative aspect of falling into a hardened and exclusivistic sectarianism. Catholicism, on the other hand, tends to nestle uncritically in the given situation, disguising its compromise under the label of the "universally human." But when we propose that we should learn from the Catholic Church, we are thinking of its flexible, two-pronged attitude which, on the one hand, promotes puritanism in its monastic orders and, on the other, tries to adopt even the Japanese ancestor cult. In other words, the Roman Catholics appear to be aiming at a meta-Catholicism wherein both Puritanism and Catholicism are *aufgehoben*. For that reason we think that there is much to be learned from them.

When we advocate a Shinshū Catholicism, it is certainly not in the sense of promoting more compromises with folk religion. On the contrary, we maintain that Shinshū has become infected with folk religion precisely because in our theology Shinshū Catholicism has not been thematized. We also have the expectation that a way back to our Founder can be opened by such a thematization.

FUNERAL SERVICES AND THEOLOGY

I have been asked to give special attention to funeral and memorial services, which play such a big role in Japanese religion. And indeed, it is in connection with them that we find in our sect, right from the beginning, the problematics of folk practices and the two trends of Shinshū P and Shinshū C. On the side of Shinshū P we find Kakunyo (1270–1325), the great-grandson of Shinran, and on the side of Shinshū C there is Zonkaku (1290–1373). Although father and son, these two were at loggerheads all their lives precisely on account of their difference in opinion on folk practices. Kakunyo even called Zonkaku a heretic and twice excommunicated him. We can thus say that our Shinshū theology comprises this tension right from its beginning and that our present problem must be seen against this background.

To begin then with Shinshū P, in his *Notes Rectifying Heresy* (*Gaijashō*), Kakunyo writes:

> Shinran has said: "When I shut my eyes for good, you must throw my body into the Kamo River as food for the fish." What he meant was that we must despise our bodies and see faith in the Buddha Dharma as the only thing that counts. On reflection, it follows that we should not consider services for the dead as all-important but rather put an end to them.

Kakunyo thus appears as an abolitionist with regard to folk practices and an advocate of a "no-funeral-ism." His theology is ideological and rigoristic; he is typical of a Shinshū P for which faith is so supreme as to exclude everything else.

On the side of Shinshū C, Zonkaku treats the question in three of his treatises, *On Gratitude* (*Hōonki*), *Things Seen and Heard on the Pure Land* (*Jōdo kenmonshū*), and *On the Highest Path* (*Shidōshō*). He provides a theological underpinning for the Shinshū practice of funerals and memorial services, the monthly sūtra readings for the deceased, the memorial day in the month of death, and the yearly anniversary service. He writes, for example:

> Since the Buddha is uniquely worthy of reverence among all beings past, present, and future, and the guide of the four classes of living beings, there is nobody above him in rank. Still, to show his piety to his father, and his reverence for the king, he raised his body into the air and, attending the funeral of his father, helped carry the coffin. He did that as an example to be followed by the sentient beings of the future.

(The reference is to the early *Sutra of Grouped Records* [*Zōichiagongyō, T* 125]). And again:

> In life, one must admonish to zeal in self-cultivation, giving priority to filial piety; after somebody's death, one must fulfill one's duty of gratitude, giving priority to working good deeds for the deceased. . . . One must not neglect the monthly services for the deceased, and certainly not the yearly observances on the anniversary of the death. Even after many years have passed, on these anniversaries one must absolutely lay aside one's worldly affairs to pray for the peace of these souls.

There is certainly something here that not only Kakunyo but also present-day theologians cannot but see as folk religion, which is un-Shinshū, un-Shinran, and even un-Buddhist. Thus, since the Meiji era these folk religious texts by Zonkaku have been taboo in our sect and have received no attention at all from the theology professors. However, when looking at the life in our temples, it is clear enough that the greater half of that life consists of funeral rites, memorial services in the temple and monthly sūtra readings in the houses of the faithful. Therefore, it is precisely Zonkaku's theology that takes these practices seriously as theological topics and is a "theology of the field" totally incomprehensible to people engaged in "pure theology only." It is a theology for the temple priests whose life goes up in keeping our temples going, taking care of our faithful, and performing funeral rites and memorial services; a theology imbued with the sadness of not being understood by people who never toiled in tears to lead people to Shinran in the midst of all this.

How would Kakunyo and Zonkaku, while living by the same Amida-given faith, have come to such diametrically opposed theological positions with regard to funeral practices? Present-day theologians have nothing but praise for the Shinshū P of Kakunyo and consider it to be a faithful expression of Shinran's true intentions. Zonkaku's Shinshū C, on the other hand, is judged negatively as a theology that came to betray true faith through compromise with folk religion, and consider it therefore as inadmissible. But is this the true state of affairs? The crux of the matter might lie in a correct understanding of Zonkaku's texts. For Zonkaku knew very well that Shinshū is not a kind of Confucianism or ancestor cult and is not built on the performance by us of good works whose merits would be transferred to the deceased; he understood better than anyone else the centrality in Shinshū of Other-Power nembutsu. Still he wrote kindly that funerals, memorial services, and so forth are important—while adding sometimes that he did not like writing these things. What is the secret here? We think that we found the key to this mystery in Zonkaku's "give-and-take logic."

Dōgen, Shinran, and still Zonkaku lived in an age that presented an extremely vivid picture of hell (which is all but lost to the modern imagination), permeated with magic, folk beliefs, evil spirits, and wherein the powers of man were absolutely helpless before disease and natural disasters. It is then only natural that people had recourse to superstition and magic in order to ward off the ills that befell them one after the other. Up to a point that is still true today, of course, and we are all inclined to look down on people who run to "new new" religions, magic, fortune-tellers, and what have you, and to see ourselves as the true Buddhists. However, rather than looking at these superstitions themselves, we should pay attention to the fact that the people who have recourse to them have good reasons to do so. And there are plenty of reasons: incurable diseases, anguishes one cannot tell anybody about, the loneliness so typical of our age, and so on and so forth. Scolding people for their foolish superstitious behavior in self-righteous sermons without any appreciation of these woes in the background is an exercise in self-satisfaction unworthy of a religionist. In the face of the one hundred million Japanese who indulge in superstition, we should rather reflect on our lamentable failure as guides of the people, and come to the conviction that it is high time that we make folk practice and popular belief a topic of our theology.

GIVE-AND-TAKE LOGIC AS SHINSHŪ C

A "give-and-take logic" (*yodatsu no ronri*) was the outcome of Zonkaku's serious consideration of the question how the people of his time, beset as they were by all kinds of ills and relying on folk beliefs and magical practices to relieve them, could be set free from magic and brought to lead a life of true nembutsu. It consists in looking hard at the sufferings that induce people to indulge in magical practices, in understanding that psychology, and from there, with great sensitivity for the intricacies of human feelings, in sharply analyzing these superstitions. This then becomes a way to "jump into the inner castle of the enemy and to make what one grasps there into one's own medicine." Contrary to theology P, which cuts down superstition by logic and rejects it forthwith, one does not directly negate it here, but looks for salvation by way of empathy. One spares and embraces the popular practices to turn them into something Shinshū-like; one gives in to them in order to take them back to one's own side. Rather than drawing one's sword against the sword of the enemy, one grasps the other's sword to remold it into the shape of the nembutsu and give it back as a nembutsu sword that cuts through all superstition. This is ultra-C supreme swordsmanship!

In the eyes of the puritanists, this expedient means appears only as heresy, wishy-washiness, an unwarranted detour, or even as a way of suicide, in that the possibility exists of being cut down by the other's sword; or again as un-Shinranlike logic. It has thus drawn the concentrated fire of the purists. I myself, who have gone through a period of existentialist faith, can very well imagine how I would be on the side of that firing squad if I were an armchair theologian without contact with the field of temple life. Indeed, this give-and-take logic is a pitiful logic one cannot really feel for if one is not a temple priest in the true sense, for whom the relationship of Shinshū doctrine and folk belief is a *kōan* that besets one twenty-four hours a day in one's care for temple and believers. When advocating this logic as a characteristic of Shinshū C, we are well aware that nearly all theology of the Edo period and since Meiji as well, and also the studies on Shinshū and the Shinshū community by the modernists, are of the Shinshū P type, and that this theology has made very valuable contributions to our doctrine. But this does not mean as such that this theology is the only viable one. When the P people say that there are principles that cannot be tampered with if one wants to return to Shinran, I am completely with them, but on the point of folk beliefs I beg to disagree with much of what they say.

According to Shinshū P people, faith was everything for Shinran, and religious organizations and priests were superfluous. Nor is there any need for temples, temple ornaments, funerals, memorial services, tombs, rituals, Buddha images, sūtra readings, priestly robes, . . . Even *danka* (people belonging to a temple and supporting it) are not necessary. Those things did not exist in Shinran's time and Shinran would have proscribed them. A truly no-no theology of faith only! In this view, temple priests become parasites in the body of the lion, feasting on a dharma that leads to hell!

However, although funerals and memorial services may be unnecessary according to Shinshū P people, it remains a historical fact that they have been practiced from the beginning in our sect. Shinshū P theology is then obliged to say that these Shinshū practices and rituals are all "praise to the Buddha's virtues," "thanksgiving for Amida's benefits," "savoring the taste of the dharma," or "inducement to faith." Beautiful phrases those, but while we were caught up in that melody, the alienation of the people and the temple priests from official doctrine went on apace.

According to P theology, Shinshū consists only in this: At the moment of attainment of faith one enters the state of nonretrogression, and at the moment of death one enters great nirvana. Birth in the Pure Land is attainment of Buddhahood and enlightenment, identical with that of Amida. One then immediately becomes a bodhisattva of returning transference, that is, one returns to this world to work for the salvation of all sentient beings. In this scheme, of course, the memorial services for the dead, about which Zonkaku had been racking his brains in his essays, do not come into the picture and are absolutely meaningless. But, of course, Zonkaku himself was well aware of that. He also wrote the *Notes on the Essentials of the the Six Fascicles* (Rokuyōshō), a commentary on Shinran's main work, *The True Teaching, Practice, and Realization of the Pure Land Way* (*Kyōgyōshinshō,* 1224; see Suzuki 1973), which is considered by theologians as the most authoritative commentary on the magnum opus of Shinran. This should be sufficient proof of Zonkaku's theological acumen. Our P theologians gladly accept his *Notes on the Essentials* but want nothing to do with his thought on folk practices as expressed in the other works.

Zonkaku used the memorial services in question as means to bring the ordinary people of his day to the practice of the nembutsu. For these people in distress over the parting with their beloved ones, in great fear of curses worked by the spirits of the dead, and irresistibly inclined to offer prayers and good works for the salvation of their deceased, Zonkaku adopted the whole range of memorial services, found in the sūtras and even some not found there, as "usages of our land." This can be compared with the current tendency among Catholics to adopt the ancestor cult as a beautiful usage of the Japanese people. While observing these memorial services and anniversaries, he endeavored to assuage the pain of parting, to allay the fear of curses, and most of all to make people into true nembutsu practitioners, with the help of beautiful funeral rites, which he sought to imbue with the spirit of the nembutsu, according to which the deceased is first of all a bodhisattva who comes to save me, and it is first of all the people who sincerely revere the Buddha who are set free from the defilements and curses of the dead. In that sense, the *Things Seen and Heard* (*Jōdo kenmonshū*) begins indeed with a quotation from the (apocryphal and popular) *Ten Kings Sutra* (*Jūōkyō;* late T'ang, 10th c.) but ends with a quote from Shinran's *Kyōgyōshinshō*.

There are, thus, in our sect, two trends as to the theology of funeral services. On the point of pure doctrine, P theology is clear-cut, but from the viewpoint of the field with its C practice, there must be found a way to realize a community of nembutsu practitioners as envisaged by Shinran, in trying to liberate the people from their animist-shamanist complex and to transform this into true Shinshū belief, by observing the funeral rites with heart and soul. That is certainly what we are looking for and, therefore, our endeavor to establish a theology that articulates Shinshū C must not evoke the fear that we would be going away from Shinran. Would this not also apply to the Sōtō Zen school? I believe that also in Sōtō, where for seven hundred years the temple priests have elaborated Sōtō practices, Sōtō rituals, and Sōtō patterns of community life, the introduction of a theology C, which evaluates these elements, could prove to be a way of returning to Dōgen and could well reveal aspects of Dōgen and of Zen for which the theologians up to now have had no eye.

All of our faithful have the spirit of "love for the sect and defense of the Dharma." Therefore, freedom to express their faith should be guaranteed to them. If not, we cannot really speak of a sangha, a religious community. If we have trust in the Buddha and in our Founder, there is nothing to fear. The Shinshū P people are admirable in their absolutizing of faith. They may be the bodhisattvas of the era of the final law, and our Founder may have been like them. I, however, am not the Founder, and I can live only a Shinshū C.

Over against the simple negation of the existence in our sect of a Founder cult, of this-worldly benefits, and of prayers and good works for the dead, we have advocated a "theology of the Founder cult," a "theology of this-worldly benefits," and a "theology of ancestor cult." This has upset the P people and brought some turmoil in our sect, but the majority of the temple priests to whom we talked showed appreciation for what we are trying to do and start feeling that theology is an important affair of theirs and that the establishment of a "field theology" would be an unhoped for blessing.

PRAYING FOR THE DEAD AND CURSES

As already said above, prayers for the dead and fear of curses worked by the dead certainly belong to the deepest layers of Japanese religiosity. If we simply keep on rejecting these elements, the result will only be that our believers will stray away from our religion. We have therefore opted for a Shinshū C–type theology with a give-and-take logic.

For example, a believer who feels threatened by a curse is not saved if we simply tell him that curses do not exist. He will then most probably start drifting from one religion or folk belief to another in search of salvation. That is not a solution, and it has become clear from the data of field research on new religions, new new religions, Mount Ikoma, and so forth, that among the people frequenting them surprisingly many are Shinshū believers. One of the motivations behind our movement is the conviction that this is not right, that all the sufferings of the believers must be taken up at our temples by the temple priest and his consort, and that we want our sect to become such that the faithful can come to the temple with whatever concerns or ails them, with the certainty that they will be listened to, even if their feelings are not precisely Shinshūlike. If all our people could be helped by Shinshū P there would be no need for a Shinshū C. In fact, however, there are probably more C people than P people among our faithful.

When someone in fear of a curse comes to the temple, we try first of all to empathize with that person's feelings. And once we have grasped the content of the curse and the suffering lying in its background, we do not directly force Shinshū dogma on that person but try to instill Shinshū doctrine within that content and background of the supposed curse. Only when we are sure that the power of that injected nembutsu has done its work can we finally say: for one embraced by Amida's Primal Vow and living the nembutsu, there are no curses; fear no longer. "Let the curse do what it wants, I am protected by Namu Amida Butsu!" The difference between P and C on this point might be that P proclaims that there are no curses, while C assures that curses cannot touch the faithful. Our believers in the field are very sensitive to the grateful feeling that the nembutsu protects them from curses.

As for the transference of the merits of one's prayers and good works to the dead, would it not be good if there were a give-and-take kind of theology here too, which does not directly say that such transference does not exist but rather gradually leads to the awareness that it is the nembutsu transferred to us by the Other-Power of Amida that is the true help for the dead.

THEOLOGY AS FOLK PRACTICES: A PROBLEM FOR ALL BUDDHIST SCHOOLS

Our research and publications are animated by the hope of seeing our sect transformed into a community that does not run away from what is actually happening in the field, but takes it all upon itself and knows how to transform it into something wherein our Founder is present.

In the theology of folk practices, the Shinshū P line, running back from Rennyo to Shinran via Kakunyo, has been the mainstream. We are now advocating a line running back from Rennyo to Shinran via Zonkaku. Our fundamental position is that, in a big sect like ours, which is like a smaller-scale map of the pluriform society, the existence of a pluriform theology is a good thing. We believe then that Shinshū C is one of the concrete and realizable roads of a return to Shinran.

We further believe that the theme of theology and folk beliefs is practical not only for our sect but equally so for all Japanese Buddhist sects, since it appears to be the case everywhere that theology is dominated by a Buddhist Puritanism, and the practices of the faithful are left without theological reflection. It is therefore necessary that, among the theologians of every sect, there emerge people who specialize in the theology of folk beliefs and practices, the theology of rituals, and the theology of community. We are also convinced that the time has come for the different sects as such to establish research institutes to study these problems on a continual basis. It is true that each sect has already institutes for the study of its theology, but research into folk practice, ritual, and community cannot be done by theologians alone. It requires postmodern, avant-garde theory and can be brought to a good end only by an interdisciplinary approach with the collaboration of folklorists, anthropologists, scientists of religion, and so forth.

I have not limited my proposal to folk belief and practice, but also involved ritual and community, for the simple reason that these too are not treated by traditional theology. It will finally be a question, not of theology and folk practices, and so on, but of theology = folk practice, theology = ritual, theology = community. If not, our communities will always appear as betrayals of our founders, necessary evils, or something to be left to the sociologists. The time has come to consider the community as the doctrine of the sect. Funeral rites—this center of our talk today—are not merely folk practice and ritual.

Praise of the Buddha and thanksgiving for his benefits are not enough by themselves. There is Zen and nembutsu in the funeral rites. We intend the identification: funeral rites = Zen = Dōgen Zenji; or again, funeral rites = nembutsu = Shinran Shōnin.

SPIRIT BELIEF AS POSTMODERN RELIGION

Up to now, I have given you a rather free rendering of what was written up as the report of our research in the Pastoral Institute *Bulletins 29* and *30* (1984 and 1985), under the general title of "Shinshū Doctrine and Folk Practices." To round off my talk, I now want to add a few words on some points that transpired since then and use this to put into clearer relief some themes that I have left rather vague.

I consider as very relevant for our problematics, and in a sense epoch-making, a paper delivered by Professor Shimazono Susumu of Tokyo University at the 1986 convention of the Kantō Sociological Conference. In that paper, Shimazono divides Japan's "new religions" into two categories. The first are religious organizations, like Tenrikyō and Konkōkyō, that originated among the rural population around the time of the Meiji Restoration. These represent a belief in a single saving deity and have much in common with the Amida belief of the Pure Land school. It is the "entrusting, relying type." The second category are those new religions that, like Ōmotokyō, Reiyūkai, and Seichō no Ie, originated in urban centers in the Taishō era and the beginning of the Shōwa era. They are of the "spirit belief" type. They stress the existence of spirits, see them as the causes of all the ills of human life, and promote communication with the spirits in magic saving rituals. The so-called new new religions, like Mahikari and Agonshū, which have come into existence since 1970, still belong to this second type.

Shimazono asks himself, then, why this kind of religion flourishes in modern urban society, and comes up with a startling answer. In contrast with belief in a saving deity, wherein one sees the will of the deity behind all events and aims at an I-thou relationship with that deity, this spirit belief perfectly matches the way of thinking and the manipulative attitude of modern technique. Each spirit is one factor in the environment, which can be captured and manipulated by the proper techniques. Spirit belief thus presents itself as experimental and functional and exudes a feeling of certainty and efficacy. We could call this a "manipulative" type of belief. This can be seen as a simple discovery, somewhat like the egg of Columbus, but still comes as quite a shock. We, who had been looking down on the new religions as premodern, even primitive, and have made great efforts to show that our Buddhism can coexist with science, now are confronted with the idea that the true match for a scientific-technical world is spirit belief, the magical, pseudo-scientific, manipulative type of religion.

Our team is of the opinion that we must take this shocking idea into account in our further research but did not come to any clear conclusions yet.

FERVENT SHINSHŪ BELIEVERS AND FOLK PRACTICES

Around the same time, also one of the researchers of our team, the above-mentioned Kaneko, divulged some surprising results of his research. The idea of Shinshū P is that folk belief diminishes where Shinshū belief deepens and, conversely, folk belief grows rampant where Shinshū belief declines. However, from the field research on the belief structure of average lay believers and of lay representatives of our temples, the following picture emerges. First, among the majority of ordinary lay believers, folk belief is strong and, in general, the stronger specific Shinshū belief the stronger also the belief in folk religious elements. However, when it comes to the temple representatives, this syncretistic trend breaks down. With them, indeed, folk belief appears to be swept away by deep Shinshū faith.

But, in fact, things are a bit more complicated. Among these leaders of our communities, shamanistic folk belief (belief in curses) is beautifully overcome but, at the same time, the deeper their Shinshū faith, the deeper also their faith in two other elements of folk belief, namely, ancestor cult and founder belief, become. For example, as to regular visits to the graves of the ancestors, polls among the general Japanese public of the same age group may register 76 percent yes, while among the said representatives 94 percent answer in the affirmative. Similarly, "founder belief," the veneration of our Founder Shinran as a Buddha, tends to become very strong.

It is not easy to say which conclusions should be drawn from this, but one thing seems clear enough. A theology of folk belief cannot simply carry on with the presupposition of Shinshū P that all folk belief is a minus and to be rejected. For the moment it seems as if our Shinshū practice makes a distinction between the animist (*okagesama*) element and the shamanistic (curse) element of the Japanese religious complex. The shamanistic level of Japan's folk belief, which is rejected by our temples, has vicariously been taken care of by the new religions, like Reiyūkai, Mahikari, and so on. These new religions do not ask our believers to reject Shinshū; they rather say that since the temples take care of the services for the bones of the dead, you must respect them, but we shall take care of your ancestor's spirits and of all your anguishes and distresses. In fact, as I pointed out before, the number of our faithful who run to the new religions with their difficulties is very high.

THE LACK OF A "DOCTRINE FOR EMERGENCIES"

It looks thus as if we have built up a theodicy for the happy days by adopting the animistic *okagesama* mentality but have nothing to offer when misfortune visits our believers. We may then have to say that we have no theodicy for unhappy days, no doctrine for the emergencies of life.

I myself have come to know how necessary such a doctrine is through the unutterable anguish I experienced when my second son drowned in the temple pond. For years afterward, my nembutsu was interspersed with the cry: "Why? Why?" Religionists who tend to despise the practices of folk belief would do good to visit one of these places, say, for example, the Kamikiri Jinja on Mount Ikoma, where people go to pray for beloved ones who are incurably sick, and have a good look at the faces of the people there. . . .

THE LACK OF A THEOLOGY OF ANCESTOR VENERATION

Recently, first-class authorities on Japanese religion, like Yanagawa Keiichi and Yamaori Tetsuo, have again highlighted the important place of the ancestor cult in Japanese religiosity. They have also stressed the stability that this vertical dimension imparts on the family system—a stability not assured by the sole horizontal relationships of husband and wife. And we have already said a few words on how deeply this ancestor cult has penetrated the life in the field of our sect.

In view of these facts and the challenge they present for our sect, it is extremely regrettable that we do not have a "theology of ancestor cult." This reminds me again of the fact that our promotion of Shinshū Catholicism was originally triggered by the publication of the *Guidelines Concerning Ancestors and the Deceased for Catholic Believers* (*Sosen to shisha ni tsuite no katorikku shinja no tebiki*). Therein the Japanese usages are boldly admitted into the lives of Catholics, and there is no shade of fear that this would corrupt Catholic faith. It is admirable in its trust in the strength of the faith of one's own religion.

THE LACK OF A THEOLOGY OF THIS-WORLDLY BENEFITS

Would our believers be running to New Religions in times of need, if we truly had a theology of this-worldly benefits (*genze riyaku*)? It is probably true that Shinran speaks much more about this-worldly benefits than Dōgen, and Kaneko Daiei (1881–1976), one of our most famous theologians of the former generation, has expressed the opinion that we have to rethink fundamentally our doctrine on "nonretrogression in this life" and "this-worldly benefits." In a conference he said, for example: "I want you to study carefully what is meant exactly by earthly benefits. We must come to understand why there is no contradiction between, on the one hand, maintaining that there is no true worldly benefit outside of the Jōdo School and, on the other, rejecting all religion that seeks worldly benefits."

Bandō Shōjun, the priest of the famous Hōon-ji Temple in Tokyo, once said: "The nembutsu at times deigns to enter into the midst of folk practice and magic belief, from there to turn people to a true Buddhist life." May I finally express the heartfelt wish that you, who shoulder the future of Sōtō Zen, may elaborate a theology, not merely of folk practice, but of Zen folk practice, a theology of the true folk practice of Sōtō Zen.

—47—

Contemporary Zen Buddhist Tracts for the Laity: Grassroots Buddhism in Japan

Ian Reader

The translations in this section are samples of the popular literature such as leaflets and pamphlets distributed by Buddhist sects in Japan to their followers. All of the items given here have been produced by one major established Buddhist sect, the Sōtō Zen sect, in the 1980s, but their style and the themes they express can be regarded as typical and representative of the contemporary popular literature of Japanese Buddhism in general. All were published by the sect's head office and governing body in Tokyo, and they reflect the messages that the sect leaders wish to impart to people affiliated to temples of the sect, as well as the basic orientations of Buddhist followers at the grass roots in Japan. Visually attractive and often containing bright photographs and colorful illustrations, such pamphlets and other sect literature are sent (as were numerous other pamphlets and booklets) to the sect's fifteen thousand or so temples throughout Japan, where they are, at least in theory, distributed to sect members and to temple visitors. In practice, whether they are widely distributed depends on the temple priest; it is a reasonable supposition to say that only a small number of those produced actually are read by members of the sect.

Although these pamphlets may not be widely read, and although in terms of content they can hardly be said to offer influential new contributions to Japanese religious understanding, they are important documents because they clearly express, in simple and atmospheric language designed to capture the emotional attention of their Japanese readers, the concerns, nature and orientations of established Buddhism in late-twentieth-century Japan, and which have, indeed, been crucial and central to Buddhism's development and the ways in which it has been assimilated by and permeated into the lives of the Japanese populace over the centuries. Written in language that will be readily understood by ordinary Japanese, and eschewing the use of complex Buddhist terms or philosophical speculation, such pamphlets seek to convey messages and impart emotional feelings that create an empathy between the reader and Buddhism, and that will make him or her feel the need and desire to remain loyal to the sect and (a vital element in the economic and social structure of Japanese Buddhism) to continue to hold the memorial services for their ancestors at sect temples. To some extent this use of plain, direct language and of easily understood pamphlets and other forms of popular media to convey messages (among which, in recent years, can also be included the use of videos, glossy magazines, and even music and song) has been assimilated from the new religions that have been extraordinarily successful in Japan, not just in terms of recruitment but in putting their teachings across to large numbers of people through extensive use of the media and popular tracts, and through their use of straightforward language and images.

Though the translations all come from one sect, they reflect many of the basic concerns of Buddhism in general in Japan. As will be discussed further below, these revolve particularly around the salvific powers of the buddhas, the virtue of faith, the need to venerate one's ancestors, and the importance of maintaining the bonds and relationships that have historically developed in Japan among the Japanese people, their ancestors, and the Buddhist temples. As these translations demonstrate, such concerns are as important in Zen Buddhism as in any other Buddhist sect in Japan. Although Zen, in doctrinal terms at least, holds that meditation is at the core of Buddhism and emphasizes "self-power" (*jiriki*) and its importance in the quest for enlightenment (in contrast to the faith-based concepts of salvation through "other-power" (*tariki*) as expressed in the Pure Land sects), such teachings aimed at the ordinary members of the sect make virtually no mention of meditation or enlightenment, instead emphasizing the salvific powers of the Buddha(s) and the ethical duties and practices concerned with venerating the ancestors and maintaining right relations with them through the medium of Buddhism. What these contemporary Zen Buddhist publications show, then, is that, whatever Buddhism might appear to be doctrinally and in terms of goals and spiritual practice, and although Buddhism has developed numerous schools of thought and spiritual practice in Japan, it is as a religion concerned with the concerns, needs, and worries of ordinary people, particularly in the realms of faith, intercession, and the relationship between the living and the spirits of the dead, that it has made its mark upon the lives of the Japanese.

The first translation provided here, *Trust and Dependence* (*Kie*), affirms the importance of faith in the buddhas as a means of enabling one to lead a happy and peaceful life and tells people to "entrust everything to the Buddhas." It was published by the sect as part of its gesture of worship (*gasshō*) campaign in the 1980s: the *gasshō* gesture is a prayerful one in which the two hands are held with palms together, fingers pointing directly upward. It signifies both veneration and greeting, and in Sōtō Zen literature and contemporary teaching the gesture and posture are considered to have immense symbolic meaning, representing purity of heart and mind, correctness of form, and right behavior. These themes are reflected in the pamphlet translated here, whose comment that followers should express their faith by vowing to say that "I shall live from now on as the child of Buddha" reflects a general understanding, shared by priests and laity alike, that

Buddhism and the buddhas venerated in it serve most clearly as a means of emotional support that provides "peace of mind" and happiness. As such, the basic preoccupations of the Japanese with regard to Buddhism are squarely focused in this world and in personal happiness: concepts such as enlightenment are barely mentioned. The pamphlet also emphasizes the importance of causal or karmic relations (*en*), a term that affirms the notion of interdependence. This is especially important in Japanese terms, suggesting among other things the karmic bonds that tie the living and their ancestors together—a bond that, as will be discussed further below, is vital to Buddhist temples and rituals, and to the involvement of the Japanese with Buddhism. Underlying the emphasis on causal or karmic relationships, then, is the implicit affirmation of the relationship that has arisen between the Japanese and Buddhism and which this and the other translations given here seek to maintain and continue.

Besides its focus on faith, grace, and happiness, Buddhism has become most deeply ingrained in the lives of the Japanese through its role in providing a framework of interpretation and practice through which to deal with death and with the spirits of the dead. From the seventh and eighth centuries onward, Buddhism became the medium through which the processes and problems of death were dealt with: Buddhist funerals and memorial services came to be used as the ritual means whereby the spirits of the dead have been transformed into benevolent ancestors guarding over the living members of its household and kin. In taking on this role, Buddhism in Japan thus assimilated basic Japanese concepts about the soul after death, namely, that it continued to exist as an entity that had a potential influence in this world. As a result, Buddhist philosophical concerns about the nonexistence of a fixed soul or permanent self, or about rebirth, have been of little importance in Japan. The Japanese words for dead person and Buddha are the same (*hotoke*), reflecting a commonly accepted gloss between the two states, and it is fair to suggest that, for the large majority of people, concerns about the attainment of buddhahood have largely been transposed from the world of the living to that of the dead, and are closely connected to the Buddhist rites that transform the soul into a peaceful and benevolent ancestor.

One of the most central and pervasive elements in the social, cultural, and religious lives of the Japanese, namely, venerating and paying homage to their ancestors, thus became expressed through the ritual medium, and became the preserve, of Buddhism. This close relationship between the Japanese and Buddhism developed over centuries but was formally established in the Tokugawa era (1600–1868) when laws were enacted to mandate that everyone become Buddhist and be affiliated with a Buddhist temple, which in turn provided them with their sectarian affiliation. Belonging to a sect thus was often more a matter of convenience or circumstance, dependent on the sectarian affiliation of the temple nearest to one's home, than it was to any particular volition on the members' part, and this factor remains much the same today. People are members of a sect not so much because they prefer a particular form of sectarian teaching but because tradition and historical and family circumstances have made them so.

Although the laws enacted by the Tokugawa were subsequently repealed, Buddhism has continued, at least in the eyes of most Japanese, to be closely associated with the extended series of mortuary rites and practices that follow death and with the veneration of ancestors. Calendrical Buddhist festivals, such as the summer Obon Festival, when the living members of the family gather to make offerings to their ancestors and to have memorial services said for them at the family temple, continue to be among the most widely attended of all religious events in Japan. Many households have a family Buddhist altar (*butsudan*) at which the ancestors are enshrined, and large numbers of Japanese grow up accustomed to the practice of making offerings to the ancestors, visiting Buddhist temples and reciting Buddhist prayers for their souls.

This deeply ingrained social relationship has long been a mainstay of Buddhism in Japan. Indeed, many Japanese, even while openly stating that they have no religious faith, despite not knowing much if anything about Buddhism, and despite eschewing any interest in other Buddhist practices, consider that they will "die Buddhist" and that, should a death occur in their family, they would naturally become involved in Buddhist rites and call for the services of a Buddhist priest.

This deep relationship has had profound effects on the shape and nature of Japanese Buddhism and has conditioned the perspectives of the Japanese and of the Buddhist sects active in Japan. Buddhism for most Japanese is a religion of death and the ancestors, and what ritual and spiritual practices it espouses, and moral and ethical teachings it professes, are intimately bound up with these aspects. Neither philosophical concerns nor the desire to undertake meditational or similar spiritual practices have conditioned the reasons why most people belong to their sect, and consequently they are barely touched upon in the popular literature of Buddhist sects. In contrast, the importance of rites concerning the ancestors, and ritual behavior before the family Buddhist altar, are very important and figure prominently in Buddhist publications such as those translated here, and in the religious practice that they advocate.

The second translation, the *Ten Articles of Faith* (*Shinkō jūkun*), a one-page text that has appeared in many Sōtō publications over the years, shows how central such issues are to Sōtō Zen Buddhism. Faith here, as indeed in the first translation, is closely equated with practice and with the performance of actions connected with the ancestors, and with the bonds that tie people to Buddhist temples. Such bonds are strengthened through the ritual calendar, with various festivals marked out as days when the obligation to attend the temple is stressed. Observances of the ritual and festive calendar are a central feature of Japanese religion, and much of the activity at Buddhist temples is linked to this cycle. The Obon Festival and other occasions (such as the spring and autumn equinoxes, when people visit their ancestors' graves) concerned with the memorialization of the dead are probably the most commonly performed religious activities in Japan, in which (according to contemporary statistics) close to 90 percent of the Japanese participate either regularly or occasionally. Indeed, for most people such ritual and festive times are the only occasions when they might visit a temple. Buddhist organizations such as Sōtō are thus acutely aware of the importance of this calendrical cycle of religious events within the life patterns of the people, and their publications dwell very much on encouraging the observance of such events. Indeed, as the third translation also shows, they may well focus almost entirely on the emotional and cultural significance of such calendrical events for the well-being and continued happiness of the people.

The articles of faith do not, save in the final article, mention meditation; even here it is only brought in as something to be done twice a year. What they emphasize are the importance of the correct observance of etiquette (in bowing to the temple, making a gesture of worship before eating, telling the ancestors the family news) and of paying homage to the ancestors. In this there is a basic morality that centers on paying homage and showing gratitude to the ancestors for what the life they have bestowed on the living, and of recognizing that such benevolence creates obligations that have to be repaid through observing the correct rituals for the ancestors—a theme that is emphasized in the last translation. One could say that in this respect the Buddhist notion of "right action" has, in Japanese Buddhism, been well and truly transformed into and interpreted as "the correct ways of memorializing the dead, and of venerating the ancestors."

This concern with form and with the way in which things are done is endemic in much Japanese social behavior, and in the contemporary teachings of the Sōtō sect this concern can be seen most clearly in the constant references made to the gesture of worship (*gasshō*) that occur in these, and numerous other, Sōtō publications. Most of the people who are affiliated, through their parish temple, with the Sōtō Zen sect have never taken part in meditation. Meditation, indeed, is, in the eyes of the laity, regarded as something for religious specialists, while the priesthood and leading lights within the sect recognize that the sect's growth has historically been a result not of its meditational practices but of the rites it has conducted for the ancestors. Instead of emphasizing meditation, then, one finds other physical forms of posture that can be performed easily and in everyday life emphasized, almost, one might suggest, as alternatives. As the first translation affirms, the gesture of worship allows one to become peaceful and to express a simple but strong faith. Faith is thus expressed through form. Though the shorter *Heart Sūtra* (*Hannya shingyō*), widely recited in Japanese Buddhism and highly popular in Sōtō rituals, states that "form is no other than emptiness" (*shiki soku ze kū*), it is clear from the perspective of the religious etiquette and ritual symbolism illustrated in these texts that form has a specific significance of its own, regardless of any philosophical equation with emptiness.

The third translation, *Peace of Mind in Human Life* (*Jinsei no yasuragi*), provides a further insight into the perspectives and needs of contemporary Buddhism. The circumstances that lie behind the nostalgic imagery brought out in such publications are that in the contemporary era numerous encroachments have been made into the grass-roots support structures of established Buddhism. The growth of the new religions has helped to transfer the allegiance of large numbers of individuals and at times whole families away from the established Buddhist sects, while the processes of secularization and urbanization have contributed to weakening the hold of established and traditional religions such as Buddhism on their followers. For sects such as Sōtō, whose traditional base of support has been more in rural and agricultural areas than in urban areas, demographic change has weakened its base further.

All this has caused Buddhist sects such as Sōtō to do what it can, not so much to gather new converts as to retain the loyalties of its current adherents, many of whom have little or no doctrinal involvement in the sect, and whose affiliations are centered on the ancestors. Thus great emphasis is placed on the importance of the traditions that bind families to particular temples, and on the deep connections between the temple and the ancestors. This often is expressed through the use of powerful nostalgic imagery that seeks to play on the emotional feelings of, and to create a sense of empathy in, the reader that will cause him or her to withstand the social pressures of change and the lure of the new religions that offer the individual a path to salvation. Often these are tied into important festive events in the yearly calendar. This pamphlet, for instance, relates to and was issued prior to the summer Obon Festival.

Such literature often, as here, makes use of idealized images of the past, identifying Buddhism with such images while simultaneously criticizing the modern world, which is depicted as materially rich yet spiritually poor. In contrast to the turmoil of the modern world, Buddhism, its temples, and its deep connections with the ancestors represent a "Japanese spiritual homeland" (*kokoro no furusato*), in which the Japanese can feel at home with themselves and make contact with their culture. Within this nostalgic imagery, too, a strong emphasis on morality is maintained through the concepts of gratitude (to the ancestors) and obligation, which requires one to repay their favors by performing memorial services and attending the temple.

These three short translations, then, indicate much about the actual nature of Japanese Buddhism today and about what it means for the Japanese people: the relationship between the living and the dead, the importance of the correct ritual procedures and postures, the importance of performing memorial services for the ancestors, the importance of faith and of the supportive and sustaining power of the Buddhas that enable people to live happily. These, rather than the philosophical constructs or even the monastic practices such as meditation and teachings focused on the nature and attainment of enlightenment, are the things that dominate the relationship between the Japanese and Buddhism, and these are the themes that have driven and sustained Buddhism through the centuries, and that remain at the heart of its action in contemporary Japan.

Further Reading

William M. Bodiford, "Sōtō Zen in a Japanese Town: Notes on a Once-Every-Thirty-Three-Years Kannon Festival," *Japanese Journal of Religious Studies* 21.1 (1994): 3–36; Kawahashi Noriko, "*Jizoku* (Priests' Wives) in Sōtō Zen Buddhism:

An Ambiguous Category," *Japanese Journal of Religious Studies* 22.1–2 (1995): 161–83; Kenneth Marcure, "The Danka System," *Monumenta Nipponica* 40.1 (1985): 39–67; Ian Reader, "Transformations and Changes in the Teachings of the Sōtō Zen Buddhist Sect," *Japanese Religions* 14.1 (1985): 28–48; Ian Reader, "Zazenless Zen?: The Position of Zazen in Institutional Zen Buddhism," *Japanese Religions* 14.3 (1986): 7–27; Ian Reader, *Religion in Contemporary Japan* (Honolulu: University of Hawaii Press, 1991), esp. pp. 77–106; Ian Reader, "Buddhism as a Religion of the Family" in *Religion and Society in Modern Japan*, edited by Mark Mullins, Shimazono Susumu, and Paul Swanson (Berkeley: Asian Humanities Press, 1993), pp. 139–56; Robert J. Smith, *Ancestor Worship in Contemporary Japan* (Stanford: Stanford University Press, 1974).

Trust and Dependence: For the Sake of a Correct Foundation for Your Life

WHY IS THE WORLD FULL OF UNEASE?

The scientific civilization of the current age has in many ways greatly fulfilled our expectations. Our homes are full of electrical appliances, and thanks to air conditioners we can enjoy cool summers and warm winters. Communications have developed so that we can get to distant places quickly and in comfort. The audiovisual world of televisions and videos relays information and entertainment to us, while in our stores and supermarkets, foodstuffs and clothing from all over the world are widely available. The development of medical knowledge and techniques has had an immense effect on our lives, extending life expectancy greatly.

From such perspectives, the present world has satisfied human expectations and appears to be extremely rosy. However, one has to ask the question: have we become really happy?

In fact, it could be said that, to the extent that our material desires have been fulfilled, people's minds in the present world have slid into an extraordinarily famished state. Human desires have no limit. As soon as one desire is fulfilled, the next one rises up in our heads. Thus, however much we progress materially, we are never satisfied but are caught up in a trap of unsatisfied desires.

If, in all of this, we happen to look into the depths of our minds, we are liable to be stricken with an indescribable isolation and unease and become aware of the vacuity of just satiating our material desires.

WHAT ARE THE UNDERLYING PRINCIPLES BY WHICH WE LIVE AT PRESENT?

On a daily basis we uphold our spirits by thinking about various things, such as our position in our company, our academic record, money, our house, or our family and friends. There may also be those who say that having a good healthy body is foundation enough for a satisfied life.

But please think a little about this. All these things are ephemeral. One has to leave one's company when one reaches retirement age. However good one's academic record is, if one does not have a suitable job to go with it, it is of little use. Money, too, can rapidly disappear and lose its value in times of economic crisis and inflation. There is always the fear that the home that one has striven so hard for may disappear in a fire. We cannot even rely on our families. The number of cases of people who want to get divorced from their wives as soon as they retire is growing. Although living a long, healthy life is a good thing, there are many people who end up having to spend the last years of their lives alone and without sufficient support and protection. . . . This is contemporary reality.

You are probably aware of all this. In truth, everything is impermanent. And so you come to the terrible realization that all the things you thought would sustain you in reality have no foundation. What, then, are the things that we ought to have as our correct spiritual foundations?

THE PRAYERFUL GESTURE (GASSHŌ) OF FAITH: A BEAUTIFUL AND PEACEFUL FORM

Trust is something immense that unites body and mind and allows us to live in peace. We usually think we live our lives under our own strength, and everyone lives seeking their own personal happiness. However, if we are asked, "Are you really happy?" why is it that so few people are able to answer, "Yes, I am"? Most people are living in anguish, enveloped in all sorts of problems, forms of unease, and situations that are not what they wished. How, then, can one become happy?

One of the most important teachings of Buddhism is that of karmic relations (*en*). This word expresses the underlying reality that all things, from human beings to animals, minerals, water, and the air we breathe, exist in a state of mutual interconnection and interdependence. One never lives by one's strength alone. Even if you do not recognize this, and think you will be able to act solely on your own, doing just what you want, if the karmic connections (*en*) around you are not properly ordered, you will not be able to achieve any of your wishes. Being aware of this interconnectedness and thinking not just of yourself, but of the happiness of all around you at the same time, and nurturing good relations . . . that is the way to happiness.

Humans are foolish and it is totally impossible for them—even with computers or the advances of science—to control all the infinite and spreading threads of karma. Therefore we, as followers of Buddhism, even while striving with all our might to cooperate and maintain good karmic relations, have to trust in and leave the results up to the buddhas [*omakase suru*, "to leave the results up to, entrust someone with a task," a term that is widely used in Japanese religious contexts (especially by religious practitioners and people praying at religious centers) to indicate acceptance of fate and of human dependence on spiritual beings such as deities and buddhas].

In this life, true peace of mind is attained by receiving and accepting the "fate" that the buddhas give to us. Is this not the true spirit of trust?

THE GESTURE OF WORSHIP (GASSHŌ)

This is the form that manifests one's deep trust [in the buddhas]. Moreover, for human beings it is the most beautiful and indispensable form of action. The gesture of worship is not just a posture to adopt when performing acts of worship and faith before the family Buddhist altar or in front of the Buddha image at a temple. It is also the gesture one uses to pay homage to the Buddha nature that lies within each and every one of us. This includes respecting and acknowledging with this gesture of worship your own Buddha nature, for, as the *Dhammapada* states, "you yourself are your own friend; if you spurn yourself, you are the friend of no one; if you do not regulate and put yourself in order, it is truly difficult to be friends with someone else." Making this gesture of worship is the basic form and way of putting ourselves in order. Therefore, whenever and wherever our minds are seized with unease or suffering, or at any time of crisis or trouble, let us first quietly join our hands together and make the correct form of the gesture of worship.

This is truly marvelous. When your spirit is enveloped in this gesture of worship, don't you feel that all the vexations that have bothered up till this point start to dissolve? As soon as one makes this gesture of worship clearly, a soothing wind can be felt blowing through one's mind.

THE IMPORTANCE OF VENERATING THE THREE JEWELS

There are three elements necessary for the development of Buddhism. One is Áākyamuni, the Buddha, who attained the highest form of human nature and perceived the truth (enlightenment). The second is the law that Buddha taught. The third consists of those people who seek to follow the true path established by that teaching. In Japanese the word used for such people (*sō*) is nowadays considered to refer to priests, but in the original Indian language it signified the *saṅgha*, a word referring to the whole community of Buddhist followers who performed Buddhist practices together. In this saṅgha there were not just people who had become monks, but also lay people as well.

These three basic elements from which Buddhism was formed (Buddha, law, sangha) are known as the "Three Jewels." And for we followers of Buddhism these "Three Jewels" provide the greatest foundation of all. The first step for followers of Buddhism is to have trust in, and pledge oneself, to the Three Jewels; this is not just in Japan, but among all those who have faith in Buddhism, in India, Sri Lanka, Thailand, Tibet, and elsewhere. In these different countries, the words used to recite this item of faith vary, but they all mean the same:

I pledge my trust in the Buddha.
I pledge my trust in the Buddhist law.
I pledge my trust in the sangha.

Zen Master Dōgen [the principal founder of Sōtō Zen in Japan and the sect's main textual authority] exhorted all people to venerate the Three Jewels, and he said the following:

> I place my trust in the Buddha because he is a great teacher. I place my trust in the law because it is good medicine. I place my trust in the saṅgha because it is an unsurpassable friend. You should know the great virtues of the Three Jewels, which are the most unsurpassable, deepest, and wonderful." (From the *Shushōgi* [The Principle of Practice and Enlightenment].) [This text was edited, compiled, and published by the sect in 1890, using sections from many of Dōgen's writings, and has ever since been used in the sect as a cardinal text and basis of faith and sect teachings.]

These are the correct principles to enable each of us to spend this human life, which does not come to us twice, without regret and with a rich spirit.

To express one's trust and dependence in the Three Jewels is none other than to vow that "I shall live from now on as the child of Buddha." That alone is sufficient. Whoever we are, we are all children of Buddha, and if, while expressing our trust in the Three Jewels, and if we mutually respect and greet each other with a gesture of prayer and worship, we shall be able to walk strongly forward along the road to buddhahood together.

The Ten Articles of Faith

1. Let us always clean the family Buddhist altar (*butsudan*) every morning, and, by making a gesture of worship (*gasshō*) and venerating them, let us give thanks to our ancestors.
2. At the dining table, let us make a gesture of worship before eating.
3. At the temple, as we stand before its Main Hall, we should without fail make a gesture of worship and bow.
4. Let us enshrine our household mortuary tablets (*ihai*) at the temple and without fail visit it on the various death anniversaries [of our ancestors]. [These tablets have the posthumous name of the ancestor engraved on them and represent the ancestor's presence. It is normal for one tablet to be placed in the family altar, but a second may also be placed at the Buddhist temple as well. The Buddhist sects exhort their followers to do this as it makes the bond between family members and the temple stronger and encourages them to visit the temple more often.]
5. On the first morning of every month, let us all go to the temple to pray for the safety of the family.

6. When our children are born, let us have them named at the temple, and on the one hundredth day [after the birth] visit the temple and report this news to our ancestors. [While it is most common for parents to take their newborn babies to Shintō shrines to place them under the protection of the Shintō gods, there has also been a tradition of asking the Buddhist priest to bestow a name on the child. This is a practice that still may be found today, and one that Sōtō encourages as it is believed to foster a particularly strong karmic connection among the child, family, and temple.]
7. When our children enter school and come of age, let us without fail visit the temple and report this to our ancestors.
8. Let us celebrate weddings [more commonly celebrated at Shinto shrines or, in recent years, at specialized wedding halls] before our ancestors at the temple. On occasions when this is not possible, let us visit the temple afterward and report the news to our ancestors. [It is customary to report family events to the ancestors at the family Buddhist altar. This injunction, and the injunctions in the previous articles, to report family events to the ancestors also at the temple, thus seeks to further affirm and cement the bonds of loyalty and karmic relationship between the temple and its members.]
9. On Buddha's birthday (*Hanamatsuri*) [in Japan celebrated on April 8, an important date in the Sōtō calendar], let us visit the temple together with our children and commemorate this by drinking sweet sake [*amazake*, which on this occasion is usually a nonalcoholic beverage, or a sweetened tea (*amacha*) given out to those who visit temples].
10. On Enlightenment day [*Jōdō-e*, December 8 in Japan, the most widely celebrated observance in the Zen sects] and on the day of the commemoration of the Buddha's death [*Nehan-e*, February 15 in Japan], let us all gather at the temple and, listening to talks about Buddhism and doing Zen meditation, remember the Buddha.

Peace of Mind in Human Life

Whenever the time of the Obon Festival [which commemorates the ancestors and takes place in most parts of Japan in August] comes around, I think of the way of life of the countryside. I am enlivened by memories of this enjoyable festival, memories of visiting the graves together with one's family and doing the Bon dances and then eating delicious watermelon cooled in the well. When I see melons, eggplants, and deep red tomatoes in the same fields that my ancestors tilled, I instinctively want to offer them to the ancestors. In recent times, one has been able to eat cucumbers and tomatoes at all times of the year, and one can gaze through the windows of flower shops at all sorts of flowers and plants that bloom throughout the four seasons. This is convenient, but, on the other hand, I feel that thoughts of a seasonal nature, in which one felt the texture of things seen by the eye and tasted by the tongue, are gradually becoming less and less. Even for someone who lives in a city, however, seeing the vegetables and fruits arranged outside the greengrocer's shop is a reminder of one's dead ancestors [and the gratitude that is owed to them].

It is often said that forgetting to express gratitude is a normal human trait, but gratitude is an essential part of recognizing where we come from. As you know, the ideogram used to express the term gratitude (*on*) is made up of the ideogram for mind (*shin*) beneath the ideogram for cause (*in*) of origin or source (*gen'in*). If one asks the questions how have I come to be born here and how have I continued to live so far, one will see that this whole process is one that involves one in debts of gratitude. Such debts are not, of course, contractual or materially fixed; rather, they are debts that should lead us to recognize a sense of obligation that one has toward one's parents and ancestors, and that should be recalled whenever one thinks of them. This is I consider a natural human emotion, and Buddhism enables us to reflect on such things by paying homage to and thinking about the dead at the Obon Festival. Not only the dead, however: in the sūtras it is taught that one should also venerate one's living parents. The Obon Festival is a time for respecting one's living parents and one's ancestors. By doing this at the Obon Festival one expresses the wish to be peaceful, to return to one's original self, to think of one's own past and future, and to think of one's ancestors and also one's parents.

This is what in Buddhism we call attaining peace of mind. True peace of mind will never come from worrying or from not being satisfied with anything. When one sees a Buddha statue, one naturally becomes calm, and the turbulence of the mind subsides. At such times we should quietly calm our minds and join our hands together in a gesture of worship (*gasshō*). Without fuss, one should sit quietly and still: this is the mind and form of Zen meditation. The Obon Festival is an important event that occurs once a year to allow us to get such peace of mind.

Peace of mind is one of the greatest blessings of life. For a husband and wife, the real issue is not whether their characters are compatible, or whether they have the same character. Is it not, rather, the question of whether they can be relaxed with each other and can live together in a peaceful state of mind? The problem is that in contemporary society we have lost sight of this peace of mind that enables us to live in true happiness.

This celebration of the Obon Festival has in fact continued for almost 2,500 years according to the teachings of Buddha. Through this festival, which is a vital spiritual home (*kokoro no furusato*) of the Japanese people, we wish to restore our peace of mind and, especially among young people, to cultivate satisfied minds.

INDEX

This index covers the introductions to each section and the introductions to the translations only. It includes the names of selected historical figures, deities, and titles of works. Place names and the names of historical periods are not included.